# Pacific Northwest

## a Lonely Planet travel survival kit

### Bill McRae
### Judy Jewell

**Pacific Northwest USA – a travel survival kit**

**1st edition**

**Published by**
Lonely Planet Publications
Head Office:    PO Box 617, Hawthorn, Vic 3122, Australia
Branches:    155 Filbert St, Suite 251, Oakland, CA 94607, USA
    10 Barley Mow Passage, Chiswick, London W4 4PH, UK
    71 bis rue du Cardinal Lemoine, 75005 Paris, France

**Printed by**
Colorcraft Ltd, Hong Kong

**Photographs by**

| | |
|---|---|
| Wayne Bernhardson (WB) | Bill McRae (BM) |
| Richard Flasher (RF) | Kevin Schafer (KS) |
| Dennis Frates (DF) | Dave Skibinski (DS) |
| Carolyn Hubbard (CH) | Stuart Wasserman (SW) |
| Judy Jewell (JJ) | Tony Wheeler (TW) |

Front cover: The Oregon coast from Cape Perpetua (DF)
Title page: Northwest coast Native American painting (SW)

**This Edition**
October 1995

National Library of Australia Cataloguing in Publication Data

McRae, Bill.
    Pacific Northwest USA.

    1st edition.
    Includes index.
    ISBN 0 86442 240 7.

    1. Northwest, Pacifc – Guidebooks.
    I. Title. (Series: Lonely Planet travel survival kit).

917.950443

text & maps © Lonely Planet 1995
photos © photographers as indicated 1995
Climate charts compiled from information supplied by Patrick J Tyson, © Patrick J Tyson, 1995

## Bill McRae

Bill McRae was born and raised in rural eastern Montana on a cattle and sheep ranch. After a year of university, a rather misguided, late adolescent nostalgia for his grandparents' homeland in Scotland led him back to the Old Country. The trip brought a serious travel bug to the fore. This was the mid-1970s, and much of the world seemed a well-meaning and courteous place to have a party. For the next 10 years he manipulated his academic career to study at as many foreign universities as possible. Five university settings in seven years didn't make for a great scholastic career, but did make for a great education.

Bill has lived in Portland, Oregon, for a dozen years, where he has operated a catering company, written for newspapers, installed ceramic tiles, waited a lot of tables, taught English and managed a bookstore. He has also written for Moon Publications (with Judy Jewell) and Frommer's.

## Judy Jewell

When Judy Jewell was a very young woman, she lit out of Baltimore and made her way to Oregon. She got hooked on spontaneous trips across the western USA after hopping a freight to Seattle, and somehow ending up in Montana.

Since then, she has swum the Columbia River twice, worked as a crayfish-eyestalk plucker and climbed Mt Rainier. There's little that makes her happier than heading out on a road trip with her tent, laptop computer, dictating tape recorder and travel pal, Dusty.

When not on the road, Judy can be found behind the counter of Powell's Travel Store, where she buys and sells travel books. She has also authored books for Moon Publications and the Compass American Guides.

## From the Authors

Many people played a helpful role during the writing of this book. An especially big thank you goes out to Jennifer Snarski, without whose diligence and hard work the material of this book would still be just a pile of paper on our desks. For hospitality and good ideas, thanks go to Kerrie Padgett, Carlotta Troy, Larry Palmer and Lydia Fisher in Seattle; Cindy Burdell, ex of Seattle; and Jackie Haskins and Pierre Dawson in Leavenworth. Thank you Tack Goodell, Michael Powell and Steve McGeady for travel tips and enthusiasm for the project. The folks in Irvington and at the Travel Store have almost gotten used to seeing us under deadline pressure; thanks for the support and understanding. A special thanks to Ken Rhodes, Steve McGeady, Paul Pope and Randy Hinkle for the free computer support. Steve Bardi and Maggie made great travel companions and usually understanding roommates; thank you for enduring the project.

## From the Publisher

This book is the product of many people's efforts and creativity. Scott Summers coordinated the production of the book. Laini Taylor was the project editor. Carolyn Hubbard, Kate Hoffman, Jeff Campbell, Kim Haglund and Liz Sizensky all added some red ink to the text.

Alex Guilbert, Hayden Foell, Cyndy Johnsen, Hugh D'Andrade, Julie Bilski, Patti Keelin, Blake Summers, Scott Noren, Jack Kendrick, Mark Williams and Inbar Berman all drew maps. Hugh D'Andrade, Hayden Foell, Ann Schwartzburg, Mark Butler, and Piper Snow illustrated the book. Robert Arnold created the photo-collage title pages with photos by Bill McRae, Judy Jewell, Wayne Bernhardson and Stuart Wasserman. Hugh, Cyndy Johnsen and Richard Wilson were responsible for layout.

Many thanks to Adrienne Costanzo, Tom Smallman, James Lyon, Sue Mitra and David Russ for their insight and help in production. Thanks also to Carolyn Hubbard for writing up the wilder side of Seattle and to Seattle locals Kari Lerum (who wrote the aside on piercings and tattoos), Tricia Stahl, Kenny Alton and Alexandra Saperstein.

## About the Book

This 1st edition is one of the first books to be produced in Lonely Planet's US office. Bill McRae was the coordinating author. Judy Jewell wrote parts of Washington and Idaho.

## Warning & Request

Things change - prices go up, schedules change, good places go bad and bad places go bankrupt - nothing stays the same. So if you find things better or worse, recently opened or long since closed, please write and tell us and help make the next edition better.

Your letters will be used to help update future editions and, where possible, important changes will also be included as a Stop Press section in reprints.

We greatly appreciate all information that is sent to us by travelers. Back at Lonely Planet we employ a hard-working readers' letters team to sort through the many letters we receive. The best ones will be rewarded with a free copy of the next edition or another Lonely Planet guide if you prefer. We give away lots of books, but, unfortunately, not every letter/postcard receives one.

# Contents

# Map Legend

## BOUNDARIES

- — · — · — International Boundary
- — · · — · · — State Boundary

## AREA FEATURES

| City Park | Park |
| NATIONAL PARK | National Park |
| Indian Reservation | Reservation |

## HYDROGRAPHIC FEATURES

- Water
- Coastline, Beach
- Creek
- River, Waterfall
- Swamp, Spring

## ROUTES

- Freeway
- Major Road
- Minor Road
- Unpaved Road
- (80) Interstate Freeway
- (70) US Highway
- (99) State Highway
- Bicycle Trail
- Foot Trail
- Ferry Route
- Railway, Railway Station
- Metro, Metro Station
- Ski Lift

## SYMBOLS

- ◉ **State Capital**
- • City
- • Town

- ■ Hotel, B&B
- ▲ Campground
- ⛺ Hostel
- ⛺ RV Park
- ▼ Restaurant
- 🍺 Bar (Place to Drink)
- ☕ Cafe

- ✈ Airfield
- ✈ Airport
- ∴ Archaeology Site, Ruins

- ⑤ Bank, ATM
- ⚾ Baseball Diamond
- ✕ Battlefield
- ⚊ Buddhist Temple
- ⦿ Bus Depot, Bus Stop
- 🏰 Castle, Chateau
- ⛪ Cathedral
- ⛰ Cave
- † Church
- ⬗ Dive Site
- 🐟 Fishing, Fish Hatchery
- 🌿 Garden
- ⛽ Gas Station
- ⛳ Golf Course
- ⚎ Hindu Temple

- ✚ Hospital, Clinic
- 🗼 Lighthouse
- ❉ Lookout
- ⛏ Mine
- 🗿 Monument
- ☪ Mosque
- ▲ Mountain
- 🏛 Museum
- ← One-way Street.
- ⛨ Observatory
- Ⓟ Parking
- ♣ Park
- ⋔ Picnic Area
- ★ Police Station
- ⬛ Pool

- ✉ Post Office
- ⛷ Skiing, Nordic
- ⛷ Skiing, Alpine
- ⛩ Shinto Shrine
- ⚓ Shipwreck
- ❖ Shopping Mall
- 🏛 Stately Home
- ✡ Synagogue
- ☎ Telephone
- ☯ Taoist Temple
- ❶ Tourist Information
- ◼ Tomb, Mausoleum
- 🚶 Trailhead
- 🍇 Winery
- 🐾 Zoo

Note: not all symbols displayed above appear in this book.

# Introduction

The three states of the Pacific Northwest – Washington, Oregon and Idaho – contain some of the most diverse and extravagantly scenic landscapes in the USA. To the west, the turbulent Pacific Ocean pounds the cliff-hung Oregon coast and swirls among the islands and fjords of the Puget Sound. Just inland, massive volcanic peaks, including Mt St Helens, Mt Rainier, Mt Hood and the imploded cone that now forms Crater Lake, rise above dense forests. Canyon-cut plateaus and arid mountain ranges stretch for hundreds of desert miles to the east before buckling up to form the foothills of the Rocky Mountains, the spine of the continent. These pristine landscapes aren't just to look at: in the Northwest, you're expected to get outdoors and enjoy yourself. Some of the best skiing in the USA is found here, at Sun Valley, Mt Bachelor and dozens of other ski resorts. Hood River, in the imposing Columbia River Gorge, is one of the most popular and challenging wind-surfing spots in the world. The forests and coastlines are webbed with hiking trails, rafts and kayaks plunge down white-water rivers, and every mountain peak is fair game for rock climbers and mountaineers.

The cities of the Northwest are noted for their high standards of living and vibrant civic and cultural life: in the last decade, Seattle, Portland and Boise have each been named the nation's most 'livable city'. They're also among the fastest growing cities in the country, as the dynamic economies of the region attract a youthful generation that likes the Northwest's progressive politics, its easy-going sophistication and the vast tracts of wilderness right out the back door.

Seattle is the largest city of the Northwest. Long known as a slightly stodgy – if beautifully situated – city, it is now recognized around the world as one of the most vital, trendy hotspots of youth culture and high-tech industry, complete with Boeing and Microsoft headquarters. More reserved, Portland hides its fun-loving and sophisticated spirit behind an outwardly quiet, gracious facade. The national headquarters for Nike make their home in Beaverton, just outside of Portland. Backed up against the foothills of the Rocky Mountains, Boise is a sporty, recreation-minded small city with tons of youthful energy. Increasingly, these urban centers sit at the head table of popular culture.

But there's more to the Pacific Northwest than just hip cosmopolitan cities and rugged landscapes: there's something quirky to life up in the left-hand corner of the USA. Today's Northwest was born of the Oregon Trail, whose pioneers were fueled by resilience and determination. Nowadays, life is a lot easier than 150 years ago, when this region was settled, and people are as likely to be fueled by espresso as by higher purpose. However, this is a culture founded on restless idealism, and there's the strong, slightly uneasy sense that there's still more exploring to do. The Northwest is a long way from the traditional centers of US culture and power, and the locals like it that way.

# Facts about the Pacific Northwest

## HISTORY

Nearly 20,000 years ago, when the accumulated ice of the great polar glaciers of the Pleistocene Epoch lowered sea levels throughout the world, the ancestors of American Indians crossed from Siberia to Alaska via a land bridge over the Bering Strait. Over millennia, subsequent migrations distributed the population southward through North and Central America and down to the southern tip of South America.

## Native Peoples

The first inhabitants of North America were nomadic hunter-gatherers who lived in small bands, and this type of society existed on the continent even into very recent times. In the West, along the Pacific Ocean, the Puget Sound and the major coastal river valleys, natives evolved societies based on fishing and scavenging from the sea. While tribes like the Quinault, Quileute and Makah along the Olympic Peninsula went to sea in pursuit of whales, other groups – notably the Chinook, Coos and Tillamooks – depended on catching salmon, cod and shellfish. Although deer and elk were hunted, it was the hides of the animals, not the flesh, that was treasured.

Summer and fall were dedicated to harvesting the bounty of the sea and forest; food was stored in such quantities that the long winter months could be given over to activities other than those concerned with subsistence. In terms of artistic, religious and cultural forms, the Northwest Coastal Indians reached a pinnacle of sophistication unmatched in most Native American groups.

Ornately carved cedar canoes served as transport and led to extensive trading networks between permanent settlements that stretched up and down the coast and along river valleys. Extended family groups lived in cedar-sided longhouses, which were constructed over a central pit-like living area. The social structure in these self-sustaining villages was quite stratified, with wealth and power held by an aristocratic class of chiefs. Wealth was measured in goods such as blankets, salmon and fish oil; these items were consumed and to some degree redistributed in potlatches, ceremonial feasts in which great honor accrued to the person who gave away valued items.

The aristocrats of these tribes often practiced head-flattening. Infants were strapped to a cradle board, while another board at an angle pressed against the forehead. The result was a sloped forehead and a conical skull, a sign of high birth. Coastal tribes also kept slaves, which they generally received from trade, not from warfare.

Inland, on the arid plateaus between the Cascades and the Rocky Mountains, a culture developed based on seasonal migration between rivers and temperate uplands. These tribes, which included the Nez Perce, Cayuse, Spokane, Yakama and Kootenai, displayed cultural features of both Coastal Indians and Plains Indians east of the Rockies. During salmon runs, the tribes gathered at rapids and falls to net or harpoon fish, which they dried or smoked. At other times, these tribes would move to upland hunting grounds, where they gathered fruit and pursued deer and elk. Tribal groups returned to traditional winter camps at the end of the year, where they maintained semi-permanent pit-type dwellings. Most transportation was overland, with large dogs serving as pack animals before horses arrived on the scene in the 18th century. Authority in tribal units was loosely organized, with responsibility for leading the tribe divided between a number of chiefs, each of whom had specific duties. Great religious importance was attached to vision quests, in which young men sought to recognize the supernatural guardian that guided individual lives.

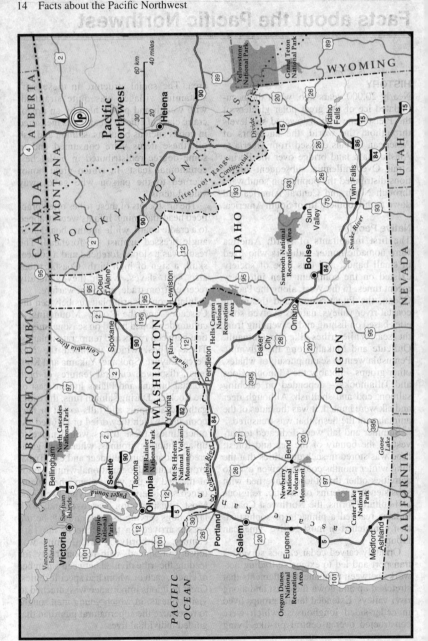

In the harsh landscapes of Oregon and Idaho's southern desert, another culture evolved. Tribes like the Shoshone, Paiute and Bannock were nomadic peoples who hunted and scavenged in the northern reaches of the Great Basin Desert. Berries and roots and small game such as gophers and rabbits constituted their meager diet. Easily transported shelters constructed of woven reeds made up migratory villages. Religious and cultural life focused on shamans, who could intercede with the spirit world to heal sickness or bring success in hunting. The Shoshone and Paiute became fearsome warriors and hunters after the 18th century, when horses – stolen from Spanish California – gave them easy mobility.

These desert tribes were remnants of a larger culture that once lived along the enormous freshwater lakes that formed in the Great Basin after the melting of the last ice age, about 12,000 years ago. An isolated pocket of this culture survived along shallow seasonal lakes and marshes of the Klamath River valley in southern Oregon, where Klamath and Modoc tribe members hunted birds and small game from cedar canoes and lived in domed structures woven from reeds.

The Pacific Northwest's one great center of trade and activity was Celilo Falls, a series of rapids and waterfalls on the Columbia River near today's The Dalles. Here, the river's enormous population of migrating salmon were forced to struggle up through powerful eddies and chutes, making them prey for natives wielding nets and harpoons. During the summer salmon run, tribal rivalries were laid aside and individuals from all over the inland Northwest would journey here to harvest salmon and dry the fish for winter usage; beads, tools, skins and food stuffs were traded, and a great deal of socializing and gambling took place. Coastal Indians would paddle upriver to the falls to trade precious dentalia (tooth shells) and other shells for hides and slaves. A variation of the Chinookan language, called Chinookan Jargon (which included words from many native languages as well as English, French and Russian), evolved to serve as a common language of trade at areas like Celilo Falls.

Based on studies of oral histories and the wealth of rock carvings in the area, anthropologists consider the Celilo Falls site one of the greatest trade centers in prehistoric America. Kettle Falls on the Columbia River in northeastern Washington was another large trading area. Both sites are now flooded by hydroelectric dams.

## Early Exploration

This distant corner of the world map was one of the last to be explored by Europeans. In fact, exactly 300 years passed between the discovery of America and the discovery of the Columbia River, the continent's second-largest river. The Pacific Northwest was therefore one of the last areas up for grabs for European colonialism and economic exploitation.

The rocky and storm-wracked coast of the Pacific Northwest resisted many early seafaring explorers. Probably the first Europeans to see Oregon accompanied the Spanish explorer Juan Rodriguez Cabrillo. In 1543 his ship reached the mouth of the Rogue River, but the coastline was too wild and stormy to attempt landing. By the 18th century, the Spanish had colonized the southern parts of California, and began to explore the northern Pacific coast, in part seeking to discover the Strait of Anian (the Spanish term for the fabled Northwest Passage). The Spanish also sought to explore the land that lay between them and their potential new neighbor to the north, Russia. (The Russians had begun to make claims along the Pacific coast of North America in the late 18th century, after the voyages of Vitus Bering.)

The British also sought to find a northwest passage. Fresh from their victory over the French in the French & Indian War (1756-63), they were eager to explore the western shores of British Canada. In 1778, Captain James Cook explored the coast of present-day Oregon, Washington and British Columbia. Captain George

Vancouver was, in 1792, the first explorer to sail the waters of Puget Sound, laying claim to the area for the British; he was also responsible for the first accurate maps of the region.

The Americans also entered the region in 1792, when Captain Robert Gray discovered the mouth of the Columbia River, obscured by sandbars and hazardous currents. Gray sailed up the great river, traded with the natives, and named his discovery the Columbia, after his ship.

The Lewis and Clark Expedition (1804-1806) was promoted as an exploration of the USA's newly acquired Louisiana Pur-

chase, which extended from the Mississippi River to the northern Continental Divide of the Rocky Mountains. Somewhat circumspectly, the US explorers also crossed over the Rockies into then-Spanish territory, and made their way down the Columbia River to the Pacific. By doing so, they established a further US claim on the territory.

The Corps of Discovery, as the Lewis and Clark party was known, spent a miserable winter on the Oregon coast near Seaside, battling fleas, suffering from venereal disease and eating dog meat. Come spring, they returned up the Columbia, Snake and Clearwater rivers, eventually

## The Lewis & Clark Expedition

When President Thomas Jefferson made the decision in 1801 to explore the western part of North America to find a water way to the Pacific, he enlisted his young protégé and personal secretary, Meriwether Lewis, to lead an expedition. Lewis, then 27, had no expertise in botany, cartography or Indian languages and was known to have bouts of 'hypochondriac affections' – a euphemism for schizophrenia – but couldn't resist the opportunity. He in turn asked his

Meriwether Lewis          William Clark

good friend William Clark, already an experienced frontiersman and army veteran at the age of 33, to join him. In 1803, they left St Louis, MO and headed west with an entourage of 40, including 27 bachelors, a dog and Clark's African American servant, York.

They traveled some 8000 miles in about two years, documenting everything they came across in their journals with such bad spelling that it must have taken historians a few extra years just to sort out what they wrote. In an almost biblical fashion they named some 120 animals and 170 plants, including the grizzly bear and the prairie dog. While Clark's entries are the more scientific, Lewis was known to explore alone and write pensive, almost romantic, accounts of the journey.

Depite hostilities shown to them, the group faired quite well, in part because they were accompanied by Sacajawea, a young Shoshone woman who had been married off to a French trapper. Her presence, along with her child's, and her ability to liaise between the explorers and the Indians eased many a potential conflict. York also eased tensions between the group and the locals – his color and stature of six feet and 200 pounds being both fascinating and intimidating to the Indians.

Meriwether and William returned to a heroes' welcome in St Louis in 1806 and were soon appointed to high offices. In 1808 Lewis was appointed governor of the just-purchased Louisiana Territory, but died a year later, purportedly during a 'fit' in which he either committed suicide or was murdered. Clark dealt with his new fame a bit better, and was appointed superintendent of Indian Affairs in the Louisiana Territory and governor of the Missouri Territory. He died at the age of 68. ∎

arriving in St Louis, where stories of the Northwest caught the fancy of American merchants and frontiersmen.

It is important to note that none of this exploration led directly to a pioneer settlement or even a permanent trading post. However, what the British and Americans did discover was the Northwest's bounty of fur-bearing wildlife and the profits to be made in the peltry trade. While in the Northwest in 1778, Captain Cook's crew traded with natives for sea otter skins. When Cook and his crew later called into Asian ports, they discovered that the Chinese were willing to pay a high price for the pelts.

Thus was born the Chinese trade triangle which would dominate British and US economic interests in the northern Pacific for 30 years. Ships entered the waters of the Pacific Northwest, traded cloth and trinkets with natives for pelts of sea otters, and then set sail for China, where the skins were traded for tea and luxury items. The ships then returned to their port of call – usually London or Boston – where the Asian goods were sold. Vast fortunes were made by profiteers before the sea otters died out and the War of 1812 made such trade expeditions dangerous as ships were often threatened.

## The Fur Trade

The first White settlements in the Pacific Northwest did not arrive from the coast, which had seen dozens of exploratory voyages, but from inland. Trappers from two competing British fur-trading companies (the Hudson's Bay Company and the North West Company) began to expand from their base around Hudson's Bay and the Great Lakes. By 1809, both companies had edged over the Rocky Mountains into today's British Columbia, Montana, Idaho and eastern Washington to establish fur-trading forts. These trading posts were quite successful, even though each was linked to eastern markets by an 1800-mile overland trail. Each fort was given an assortment of trade goods to induce the local Indians to trap beaver, otter, fox, wolf or whatever fur-bearing animals were present. While blankets, beads and cloth were popular with the natives, nothing produced the goods as dependably as whiskey. One historian estimates that 195,000 gallons of alcohol were traded with the natives for fur during the heyday of the Northwest fur trade.

As the fur-trading forts edged closer to the Pacific coast, it became clear that shipment of furs made more and more sense; however, there was as yet no coastal port for the furs to pass through. Even though British fur interests controlled the inland Pacific Northwest, American fur magnate John Jacob Astor was the first to establish a coastal fur-trading post in 1811, at the mouth of the Columbia River. The trading post, called Fort Astoria, was assailed by bad luck from its inception. When British soldiers arrived during the War of 1812 to take possession of the fort, the bedraggled Americans seemed only too glad to sell the operation to British fur-trading companies.

With the Americans out of the way, the Hudson's Bay Company (HBC) moved quickly to establish a network of fur-trading forts and relationships with Indian tribes throughout the region, working their way into the drainages of the Snake River in Idaho, and the Willamette and Umpqua rivers in Oregon. Fort Vancouver was established in 1824 to serve as the headquarters for the entire Columbia region, and was placed under the leadership of the capable Dr John McLoughlin, often called the Father of Oregon. As chief factor of the largest commercial enterprise and administrative organization in the region, McLoughlin played an important role in the economic development of Northwest; he also played both a conscious and an unwitting role in the founding of the Willamette Valley settlements that would become the state of Oregon.

By 1827, significant changes in European and American colonial aspirations in the Northwest had led to treaties and events that served to better define the territory. Spain had withdrawn its claim to the Northwest, establishing the northern border of New Spain at the 47th parallel (the current Oregon/California border); Russian ambitions were limited to the land north of the 54'40" parallel. The USA, through the Louisiana Purchase, owned all the land east of the Rocky Mountains and south of the 49th parallel. Britain controlled what is now Canada. This left a territory unclaimed – then referred to as Oregon – which included all of the present-day states of Oregon, Washington, Idaho and parts of western Montana and Wyoming.

However, the terms of an 1818 codicil to the Treaty of Ghent (which ended the War of 1812) sought to resolve the competing British and US territorial claims in the Northwest by declaring that the region was open to joint occupancy by both nations. Both could continue economic development in the area, but neither could establish an official government.

## The First Settlements

Fort Vancouver was located at the strategically important confluence of the Willamette and Columbia rivers. Unlike most other early trading posts, which were basically repositories for goods, Fort Vancouver became, under the stewardship of the Canadian-born McLoughlin, a thriving, nearly self-sufficient agricultural community complete with mills, a dairy, gardens and fields. Civility and propriety were held in high regard; all evening meals were held in McLoughlin's formal dining room using fine china, and McLoughlin's generosity and consideration extended to all who chanced through this remote area.

McLoughlin also encouraged settlement beyond the precincts of the fort. Contrary to protocol, McLoughlin allowed older trappers who were retiring from the HBC to settle along the Willamette, in an area still called French Prairie. By 1828, these French-Canadians, with their Native American wives, began to clear the land and build cabins: these were the first true settlers in the Northwest. McLoughlin established a mill and incorporated the first town in the Northwest in 1829 at Oregon City.

American trapping and trading parties began to filter into the Northwest in the 1830s. Accompanying one of these groups in 1834 were Daniel and Jason Lee, Methodist missionaries from New England with an interest in converting the local Indians to Christianity. McLoughlin graciously welcomed these groups to Fort Vancouver, traded with them for goods, and then urged the newcomers to move south along the Willamette River. McLoughlin sensed that one day the USA and Britain would probably divide the territory; if US settlement could be limited to the territory south of the Columbia, then Britain would have a stronger claim to the land north of the river.

The Lees founded a mission in 1834 north of present-day Salem, but soon discovered that the local Native Americans weren't particularly susceptible to Christianity. The Methodists did, however, establish the first schools in Oregon, and they succeeded in infusing the young state with rather doctrinal idealism. The Lee's failure didn't deter an increasing number of missionaries from streaming into the Oregon country. Protestant missionaries Marcus and Narcissa Whitman and Henry and Eliza Spalding crossed the continent in 1836 (Narcissa and Eliza were the first women to cross what would become the Oregon Trail), and established missions near Walla Walla, Washington and Lapwai, Idaho. In 1838, a Catholic mission was established at St Paul, on the Willamette River.

The ranks of the Methodists in the Willamette Valley were greatly bolstered in 1837 and 1840, when missionary 'enforcements' arrived from the eastern USA. However, the interests of these Yankee missionaries rather quickly turned from Indian salvation to carving out farmsteads and fomenting anti-British sentiment. The Treaty of Ghent didn't allow either the USA or Britain to establish a government in the territory, but the HBC, with its strict code of procedures and conduct for employees, provided the effective legal background for the nascent settlement, particularly as long as the majority of the settlers were retired trappers. Even though the HBC's influence in matters was largely benign, the Methodists refused to tolerate any degree of British hegemony. To make matters worse, McLoughlin and most of the French-Canadian settler, were Catholic.

This was an era when belief in the USA's 'manifest destiny' ran strong, and sentiment to annex Oregon ran high across the USA. However, despite fulminations from Protestant pulpits and fiery oratory in the US Senate, federal troops were not ordered into a military occupation of the lower Columbia River in order to rid the region of the British and the natives. If the settlers in the Oregon country were to have an independent civil authority, they would have to take steps themselves.

### The Vote at Champoeg

By 1843, most settlers began to feel the need for organized laws and regulations, particularly regarding land ownership, inheritance and community protection. Roughly 700 people lived in the Willamette Valley at that point, a ragtag mixture of French-Canadian trappers and their half-Indian families, Protestant missionaries, and a group of men – both American and British – who are best and most simply described as mountain men, and who were often married to native women.

The Methodists, who were the most

anxious to link the young settlement with the USA, held a series of meetings, and drew up a framework for a provisional government. The French and British settlers initially balked at the plan, which would substitute an independent (but largely American) code of laws for the authority of the HBC. In the end, an up-or-down vote was called at Champoeg, with Americans, Canadians and Britons about equally represented. A bare majority voted to organize a provisional government independent of the HBC, thereby casting the settlement's lot with the USA. Had the vote gone differently, today's maps of the Pacific Northwest might look quite different. Oregon moved toward territorial status, which it gained in 1849.

The USA-Canada boundary dispute became increasingly antagonistic until 1846, when the British and the Americans agreed to the present border along the 49th parallel. The HBC headquarters withdrew to Fort Victoria on Vancouver Island; McLoughlin was forced to retire, in part because of his aid to US settlers. He and his wife moved to Oregon City where he built a home; they later became US citizens.

### The Oregon Trail

American settlers had been straggling into the Willamette Valley since the late 1830s. However, an overland party of

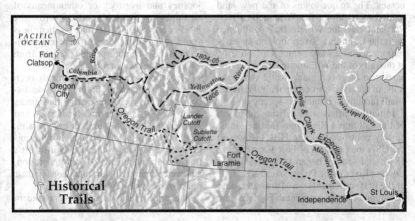

nearly 900 arrived in the Willamette Valley in 1843, more than doubling the region's population. Thus began migration across the 2000-mile-long Oregon Trail, which between the years 1843 and 1860 brought an estimated 53,000 settlers to the Northwest.

The six-month journey across the continent was a time of great adventure, hazard, and hardship. Families embarked with their belongings in canvas-topped wagons, often trailing cattle and livestock. By the time the emigrants reached eastern Oregon, food stores were running low, people and livestock were exhausted, and autumn had arrived in the high mountain passes.

The trail began in Independence, Missouri, followed the North Platte River to South Pass in Wyoming, across the Snake River Plain in Idaho, up and over the Blue Mountains of eastern Oregon to the Columbia River at The Dalles. Here the parties faced one of the most treacherous parts of their journey. Weary travelers had to choose between rafting themselves and all their belongings through the rapids in the Columbia River Gorge, or struggling up the flanks of Mt Hood, and descending into the Willamette Valley via the precipitous Barlow Trail.

· The Oregon Trail ultimately ended at Oregon City, in the Willamette Valley. Here settlers established farms, towns and businesses. The major towns of the new land tended to be along the Willamette River. Portland, near the Willamette's confluence with the Columbia River, took on an early importance as a trade center. Oregon City, at the falls of the Willamette River, was the early seat of government, while above the falls, in the river's broad agricultural basin, small farming communities sprang up.

Initially, settlers avoided moving north of the Columbia River into the area most closely controlled by the HBC. However, the USA took control of Fort Vancouver in 1846, and settlers began to spread up the Cowlitz River to the Puget Sound area. One of the first settlements was Tumwater, near Olympia on the Puget Sound. By 1851, the Denny party set sights on Elliott Bay and founded the port city of Seattle.

The difficult passage of the Columbia River Gorge from The Dalles led a party of pioneers in 1846 to blaze a southern route into the Willamette Valley. This trail, known as the Applegate Trail, cut south through the deserts of northern Nevada and California before turning north and traversing the valleys of southern Oregon. Immigrants along this route were the first to settle the upper Willamette Valley and towns like Eugene; they also scouted the land in the Rogue, Umpqua and Klamath river valleys.

By the late 1850s, the western valleys were filling with settlers, and some emigrants began to move east of the Cascades to begin farms and ranches, particularly in the Walla Walla River valley in Washington, and in the Grande Ronde River valley of Oregon. Settlement of Idaho, and much of eastern Oregon, awaited the discovery of gold during the 1860s.

Latter-day Oregonians have always made much of the assumedly stellar qualities of these early settlers. Indeed, there are some notable traits common to those who chose to settle the Northwest. The Oregon Trail was an arduous and costly adventure. Those who chose to travel it had to be able to afford a wagon or two, sufficient foodstuffs for a six-month journey and livestock or other means of sustaining a living. In other words, the Northwest was not settled by penniless wanderers: early pioneers were economically solid yet enterprising people from established backgrounds.

Also, the Oregon Trail had already been traversed by thousands before gold was discovered in the West: these early immigrants went West to start farms, businesses and communities, not in search of easy wealth. Also important is the fact that early immigrants were quite young: the Northwest's first settlers were mostly of a generation, and were remarkably homogeneous in their philosophy, goals and culture.

The pride that Northwesterners take in

their early settlers is best illustrated by an apocryphal story. At a fork in the Oregon Trail, a sign indicated the terminus of each route. Pointing to California, the sign pictured a sparkling gold nugget. Pointing to the north the sign read: To Oregon. Only those who could read made their way to the Northwest.

## End of the Frontier

By 1860, much of the Pacific Northwest was settled, and most major cities had been established. However, the rapid development of the region had come at some cost. The long domination of the Northwest by fur companies meant that trappers and hunters had decimated the region's wealth in wildlife, especially its populations of beaver and otter.

More deplorable was the toll that contact with Whites brought to the region's Native American population. Alcohol and disease corrupted the natives' culture, replacing it with dependence on the Whites' trade goods. Indian hunters and gatherers, who once followed a seasonal pattern of fishing salmon and stalking deer, now trapped the streams of their homelands free of beaver in return for a steady flow of whiskey. The natives had no natural immunity to diseases brought by the Whites, and the mortality rate, particularly along the coast, was devastating. Contemporary observers estimated that nine-tenths of the population of Chinook tribes along the Columbia River died of a mysterious fever during the summer of 1829.

However lamentable was the impact of the fur traders on the natives, the traders made no conscious attempt to change the general culture of the Indians or to move them from their homelands. This awaited the arrival of the missionaries and agricultural settlers of the 1830s and '40s. Methodist missionaries among the Calapooia Indians in Oregon had little luck converting adult Indians, so they turned their attention to native children, whom they took from their families and placed in Methodist religious schools.

The Whitman mission at Walla Walla also attempted to bring Christianity to the native Cayuse, Umatilla and Walla Walla tribes. Here, misunderstandings between the cultures reached a tragic conclusion. In 1847, after an epidemic of measles raged through the Cayuse villages, resentful natives began to believe that Whitman, a medical doctor, had introduced the disease in order to decimate the Indians. In early winter, a group of Cayuse entered the mission, asking to speak to Whitman. After Whitman welcomed the Indians into his kitchen, they drew their weapons, killing the missionary and his wife. The attack spread throughout the mission grounds. Within minutes, 12 others were dead, and 53 women and children were taken captive.

The Whitman Massacre, as the attack became known, horrified and frightened White settlers throughout the Northwest. Until this event, the natives and the settlers had lived in an uneasy peace. Hereafter, the American settlers felt justified and compelled to remove the Indians from their land and incarcerate them on reservations. That this would also make the territory safer for farmers and miners could not be ignored.

In general, the coastal Indians had been so debilitated by disease that they could mount little resistance to White incursions. These tribes were marched or shipped to reservations in 1855 and 1856, where increased illness, starvation and dislocation led to the complete extinction of many tribal groups.

The Native Americans east of the Cascades resisted manipulation by White settlers and the military more strenuously. A series of fierce battles were fought between the US Army and various Indian tribes from 1855 to 1877. Especially bloody were the Rogue River and the Modoc wars in southern Oregon, the Cayuse War near Walla Walla and the Nez Perce War in Idaho. However, in the end, these Native American groups, too, ended up on reservations, deracinated, alienated from their traditional cultural lives and utterly dependent on the federal government for subsistence.

However, the Northwest was now wide open for US settlement and the states of Oregon, Washington and Idaho quickly grew into economic forces on the national and international stage.

## GEOGRAPHY

The Pacific Northwest is a somewhat imprecisely defined geographical area. While the states of Oregon, Washington and Idaho certainly constitute the bulwark of the region, many people also include the western third of Montana and most of British Columbia in more expansive discussions of the area (never mind that to a Canadian this would be the Pacific Southwest).

The Northwest is made up of a three major geographical regions: the mountains and valleys between the Pacific coastline and the Cascade Range; the plateaus east of the Cascades to the Rocky Mountain foothills; and, in Idaho, the western slopes of the Rocky Mountains to the Continental Divide. Linking all these regions is the mighty Columbia River, which drains a 259,000-sq-mile area, taking in nearly all of Oregon, Washington and Idaho, as well as much of British Columbia, Montana and parts of Utah and Nevada.

### The Columbia River

The Columbia River is an intrinsic part of life throughout the Pacific Northwest. The river rises in British Columbia in Lake Columbia, and flows for 465 miles through western Canada before crossing into the USA. A long series of dams harness the river, the strongest flowing in North America, with the hydroelectric potential to power one-third of the USA. Inexpensive Columbia River electricity was important for the early industrial development of the entire Northwest. Irrigation is another vital element of the river's many reservoirs: in the otherwise arid plateaus between Grand Coulee Dam and The Dalles, many thousands of acres of cropland now flourish beneath center pivot sprinklers.

Two of the Northwest's most significant geological features are due to the Columbia

River. The Grand Coulee in central Washington is an abandoned ice-age channel of the ancient Columbia that cuts through spectacular lava flows. The Columbia River Gorge is the river's canyon incised through the mighty Cascade Range. The Gorge is famous for its many waterfalls, including Multnomah Falls, which at 642 feet is the second-highest year-round falls in North America.

### West of the Cascades

Much of the northern Pacific Coast is quite rugged, lined with cliffs and rocky promontories. Sandy beaches dominate only along the Long Beach Peninsula north of the Columbia River, and along Oregon's central coast at the Oregon Dunes. Rising from the Pacific shore are coastal mountains – in Oregon the Coast Range, in Washington the Olympic Mountains – which are covered with dense forests of Douglas fir, cedar and hemlock. These mighty forests are some of the last remaining virgin woodlands in the USA, and have recently seen a lot of logging, court battles and media attention.

Throughout much of the Northwest, the coastal ranges and the towering volcanic peaks of the Cascades are separated by a low-lying basin officially known as the Willamette-Puget Trough. In Oregon and southern Washington these basins are drained by the Willamette and Cowlitz rivers, respectively, while in northern Washington the ocean has invaded the lowlands to form the Puget Sound and Hood Canal. These valleys are protected to some extent from the extremes of Pacific weather and rainfall, and contain some of the most fertile agricultural land in the USA. Farms, dairies, plant nurseries, orchards and vineyards thrive in the mild climate and rich soil; not coincidentally, these valleys also contain the vast majority of the region's population. The rugged western slopes of the Cascades are heavily forested, and often heavily logged.

In southern Oregon, two major rivers, the Rogue and the Umpqua, drain from the Cascades directly into the Pacific. In northern Washington, several large rivers, notably the Skagit, drain into Puget Sound.

## East of the Cascades

The Cascade Mountains run like a spine along the western third of Washington and Oregon. The famous and eye-catching peaks of this range include Mt Rainier, Mt St Helens, Mt Hood and Crater Lake's Mt Mazama among many others. These geologically very recent peaks sit atop a much older and more massive volcanic province, and it is this wide barrier that serves to halt the moist easterly flow of Pacific air, creating the arid plateaus of central and eastern Oregon and Washington.

This entire region is underlain by enormous flows of lava, some of the largest in the world. These vast steppe-like uplands are now devoted to dry-land farming and ranching. The meager rainfall in this region nonetheless produces some major rivers and has trenched majestic canyons: the Deschutes, John Day, Grande Ronde and Yakima rivers – to say nothing of the massive Columbia – have each furrowed deeply into the underlying basalt.

Isolated mountain ranges also float above the lava prairies, especially in northeastern Washington and in eastern Oregon, where in the Ochoco, Blue and Wallowa ranges peaks reach as high as 10,000 feet. Ponderosa pine forests coat these rambling mountains, and valleys are filled with livestock ranches.

South of the Columbia Basin in southern Oregon and Idaho are the arid fault-block mountain ranges of the Great Basin Desert. Rainfall is so slight in these regions that no stream network exists to carry runoff to the ocean. Instead, what rainfall accumulates in land-locked basins; these lakes are usually saline.

The mighty Snake River rises in the mountains of Yellowstone Park, only to drain through a desert-like volcanic basin in southern Idaho. However, extensive irrigation projects have converted this once-hostile area into one of the nation's leading producers of farm products, especially potatoes. As the Snake River drops out of its high basin on its way to meet the Columbia, it charges through the wild Hells Canyon, the deepest gorge in North America.

## Western Rocky Mountains

The forested foothills and ranges of the Rocky Mountains form the northern and central reaches of Idaho. This is a very wild and contorted landscape, deeply incised by rushing rivers. Central Idaho in particular is an amazingly rugged and isolated province little served by roads; in fact, much of the area is accessible only by white-water raft or on foot.

The historic ski resort of Sun Valley perches in a valley beneath towering peaks. Just to the north, the dramatic Sawtooth Mountains rise to form the headwaters of the Salmon River, which flows northeast through ranch country, collecting the waters of mountain valleys. At North Fork, the river abruptly changes direction and (popularly) changes name to the River of No Return, shooting down an impassable canyon to meet the Snake River.

The many lakes of the Idaho Panhandle sit in bowls gouged out by ice-age glaciers; these lakes, and the dense forests that flank them, are now cherished for their resort communities and water sports.

## GEOLOGY

The Pacific Northwest's geology is a textbook example of plate tectonics, a theory which holds in part that the continents drift around the earth's surface on crustal plates. Nearly all the elements of the region's geology derive from the fact that Washington and Oregon are at the leading edge of North America's westward movement.

## The Rockies Rise

About 200 million years ago, the North American continent wrenched loose from Europe and Africa and began its inexorable westward journey. At that time, the continent's western coastline stretched along a line that roughly follows the present western border of Idaho.

As the continent drifted westward (an inch or two a year, over millions of years), the former coastal plain of ancient Idaho was buckled by the collision with the Pacific sea floor, forming the mountainous ridges that would grow into the Rocky Mountains. As the impact continued, the heavier rocks of the sea floor dove under the lighter rocks of the continent. Eventually, the basaltic sea floor began to melt into the earth's mantle, then rose back up through the earth's crust as magma.

In central Idaho, a lake of molten rock pushed up beneath the surface of the new mountains, but didn't erupt. Instead, this tremendous plug of magma bulged up beneath the bedrock carrying parts of the newly formed Rocky Mountains. As more and more magma filled the chambers beneath the mountains, the Rockies rose higher and higher. Finally, about 65 million years ago, the sedimentary ridges that formed the young Rockies were elevated to heights over 20,000 feet in altitude. The mountainous plates became increasingly unstable, and began to skid off the rising molten dome. Vast blocks of the crust slipped, riding a layer of liquid rock as they bulldozed eastward. Today these ancient segments of sedimentary crust comprise parts of the Bitterroot Mountains between Montana and Idaho.

The vast molten lake of lava – known as the Idaho Batholith – eventually cooled, and erosion cut deep canyons into its granite slopes. Deposits of precious metals in the batholith would eventually draw thousands of prospectors and miners to this rugged and remote area.

## Islands Dock

As North America continued to move westward into the Pacific Ocean, the continental landmass occasionally encountered offshore islands and small continents. Because these pieces of land were too light to be forced beneath the continent, they collided with the moving landmass. Eventually, these independent provinces became imbedded along the coast of North America, adding mountain ranges to eastern and southern Oregon (the Klamaths, Wallowas, Ochocos and Blues) and to northern Wash-

ington (the Okanogans and the Northern Cascades). Between these northern and southern highlands was a large shallow bay.

A snapshot of the Pacific Northwest 60 million years ago would show a vista of jumbled offshore islands, low coastal mountains and marine marshes, all invaded by the shallow Pacific. Slowly, sediment was filling the channels between the island chains that had accreted to the coast. Plant and animal life thrived in the warm tropical climate: fish-like swimming reptiles, flying pteranodons, and tree ferns were abundant. As there was no extensive coastal mountain range, Pacific weather flowed inland unobstructed, resulting in a widespread moist environment.

## Come the Volcanoes

At the beginning of the Cenozoic era, about 60 million years ago, a large chunk of continental crust again docked onto the westward-trending edge of the Northwest. The sea coast shifted from present-day central Oregon and Washington far to the west. The sea floor continued to descend beneath the Northwest, but now along a line parallel to the present coastline. As before, coastal sediments and offshore islands began to be wedged and jumbled together along the new shoreline to form today's Coast Range and Olympic Mountains.

Three intense periods of volcanism soon followed, each of which would utterly change the face of the region. First, a line of volcanoes shot up through the newly-arrived land mass, about 40 million years ago. As the range, called the Old or Western Cascades, grew higher, it isolated the old ocean bay of the interior Northwest, creating an inland sea surrounded by temperate grasslands. Enormous volcanic explosions of ash and mud repeatedly buried the plant and animal life of this area, resulting in the John Day formations, whose fossil beds have become national monuments.

Then, about 20 million years ago, the volcanic scene shifted eastward. Extensive faulting of the southern and eastern Oregon and Idaho bedrock allowed vast amounts of lava to rise to the surface. Rather than create volcanic peaks, the lava simply oozed out of the earth in incredible amounts. From volcanic sources near the Wallowa Mountains, lava leaked out of the earth in sufficient quantities to repeatedly flood the sea of central Oregon and Washington with molten rock. In fact, successive lava flows (there was a major eruption about every 10,000 years for a period of almost 10 million years) eventually left only the highest peaks of Oregon's eastern mountains above the basalt plain, known as the Columbia Plateau. Several eruptions of lava were so huge and so hot that lava from the Grande Ronde valley of eastern Oregon flowed down the Columbia River all the way to the Pacific, nearly 300 miles away. In places in central Washington, the basalt formations are more than a mile deep.

At the end of this period, the Northwest had taken on much its present shape. However, it would be many millions of years before the barren lava fields would erode into soil.

About 17 million years ago in southeastern Oregon and southern Idaho the lava plateau was fractured by massive faulting, producing the scarps and lakes of the Basin and Range provinces. After the bedrock had rifted, geologic pressure forced up one side of the fault, while the other sank. The rising fault block often rose to mountain heights, while the descending basin filled with water. As the climate became increasingly arid, these isolated bodies of water lost their outlet streams and became salt lakes. These mountain ridges and saline lakes became the northernmost extension of the continent's Great Basin Desert.

The region's last great volcanic era began relatively recently. The present peaks of the Cascade range began to rise about four million years ago, but the conical, uneroded peaks of the Northwest skyline indicate much more recent activity. Mt Mazama, better known as the caldera of Crater Lake, erupted 6900 years ago, devastating much of central Oregon with its massive explosion. Mt St Helens drew worldwide attention in 1980 when its erup-

tion killed 55 people and spread ash through five states and three Canadian provinces. Mt Hood, Mt Rainier, Mt Baker and the region around the Three Sisters have each seen eruptions in the last 500 years, and are still considered volcanically active.

## Ice-Age Floods

The climatic chill of the ice ages produced extensive glaciation in the Northwest. The northern third of Washington and Idaho was overlain by continental ice fields, and the mountains throughout the region were clad in glaciers (glaciers remain in the Cascade, Olympic and Wallowa ranges).

The most amazing effect of the ice ages in the Northwest, however, was not the effect of the glaciers themselves, but of the floods they caused indirectly. Lake Missoula in western Montana was formed 15,000 years ago when part of a glacier blocked the drainage of the Clark Fork River, a major Columbia River tributary. This ice dam backed up a lake containing about 500 cubic miles of water, reaching depths of more than 2000 feet. In many ways, ice isn't a very good material for making dams, because after sufficient water mass forms behind an ice dam, the dam floats, releasing the backed up water. However, after the water escapes, the glacier again begins to dam the valley, renewing the flood cycle; geologists believe that as many as 40 different catastrophic floods barreled out of Montana, heading for the Columbia Basin and the Pacific Ocean.

Each time the dam broke, an enormous surge of water thundered across central Washington and down the Columbia drainage. The floods scoured the soil off the Columbia Plateau, furrowing deep channels into the underlying basalt; these still barren and rocky plains are known as the Channeled Scablands. The flood waters dammed behind the narrow defile where the Columbia cuts through the Cascade Range, and served to trench the deep and spectacular canyon that we now know as the Columbia Gorge. Geologists claim that the floods from Glacial Lake Missoula were probably the greatest floods in the world's geological record.

## CLIMATE

Generally speaking, there are two distinct weather patterns in the Pacific Northwest. West of the Cascade Mountains the weather is dominated by the marine air of the Pacific Ocean. Winter temperatures are moderate, with freezing temperatures uncommon except at higher elevations. Winter temperatures in Seattle and Portland range from lows in the 30°F range to highs of 50°F. Summer highs occasionally reach into the 90s, though pleasant 80°F days are more the rule. Summer evenings are usually cool enough for a jacket. Spring and fall are transitional, with warm but rainy days common in spring. Beautiful Indian summers can last well into October.

Rainfall is seasonally abundant, particularly along the coastal areas and the Coast Range and Olympic Mountains, where precipitation in excess of 100 inches falls yearly. In the interior Willamette Valley and Puget Sound area, rainfall is more moderate; both Seattle and Portland receive less than 40 inches of rain a year. However, marine clouds and fog are prevalent year round, particularly in the winter and early spring, when gray and damp weather prevails. Snowfalls are heavy in the Coast Range and the Cascade Mountains. However, little snow falls in the Willamette Valley, Puget Sound or coastal areas.

The Cascade Mountains serve to halt the flow of moist and cloudy Pacific air, allowing a continental weather pattern to prevail in the east. Precipitation is much less abundant, though rainfall patterns vary greatly throughout the region. Some areas of southeastern Oregon and southern Idaho receive as little as four inches of rain a year, while mountainous areas receive as much as 20 inches, much of it as snow. Sunshine is the norm in both winter and summer.

Summer temperatures can be extreme. Highs above 100°F are common, particularly along the Columbia Plateau and the deserts of southern Oregon and Idaho. Even in the mountains of eastern Oregon

and Idaho, expect summer highs in the 90s. Humidity is low, however, and evenings are cool. Snow is common throughout the area, and can make for difficult driving conditions. Winter temperatures vary greatly, and can drop below 0° for short periods. Spring weather doesn't really arrive in the region until May; fall arrives in September, with unpredictable winter weather in tow.

## FLORA & FAUNA

The Cascade Mountains effectively divide Washington and Oregon into two ecosystems. West of the mountains are mossy, heavily forested valleys, while east of the Cascades stretch arid uplands and high deserts. The western slopes of the Rocky Mountains in Idaho comprise a third major ecosystem.

### West of the Cascades

**Flora** Forests on the Pacific side of Washington and Oregon are dense and fast-growing. In established stands, there is a wide mix of trees. The dominant tree throughout the western valleys is the Douglas fir, a statuesque conifer that can grow to nearly 300 feet in height. Also joining the Douglas fir in coastal forests are Sitka spruce, Western hemlock, maples, oaks and, especially along streams, red cedar.

In southern Oregon forests, watch for madrone trees, with distinctive red, peeling bark and broad, though evergreen, leaves, and stands of white oak. In isolated areas near the California border are several redwood groves; you can walk through old-growth redwoods along the Chetco River, near Brookings, at Loeb State Park.

In the understory of old forests grow a number of ferns, rhododendrons and the purple-fruited Oregon grape. Fall brings bright red leaves to vine maple, salmonberries with orange fruit and omnipresent thorny blackberries that grab at clothing but provide welcome sweet snacks.

Find the newest of the Northwest's riches on the forest floor. In many coastal centers, wild mushroom gathering has replaced logging as the forest's contribution to local economies. Chanterelle, morel, porcini and oyster mushrooms are a few of the mountain's fungal varieties. Northwest mushrooms are flown out daily from obscure rural airports to Tokyo and Paris.

**Fauna** Despite the area's logging history, much of western Oregon and Washington, still seems wild and unpopulated. However, its lack of major wildlife reveals the fragility of these ecosystems.

Crested, blue-bodied Steller's jays are noisy and common in forests, as are enormous crows and ravens. Sharp eyes may spot rufous hummingbirds around flowers. Bird watchers may want to concentrate on the region's many varieties of woodpeckers. The large, red-crested pileated woodpecker is especially worthy of pursuit.

Notable streamside birds include blue herons, belted kingfishers and many kinds of ducks; watch for handsome, black-necked loons. Along the coast, gulls are ubiquitous, but to see other seabirds, like puffins, cormorants and pelicans, usually requires more stealth and a pair of binoculars. Tidepools provide a window into the ocean. Look for sea anemones, starfish, mussels and hermit crabs.

Almost all sea-flowing rivers and streams in Oregon produce their own salmon runs; salmon must return to their own birthplace to spawn. This means that each river has essentially engendered its own native species of salmon; the salmon that run the Rogue River are not the same fish, say, that run the Skagit River. Northwestern waters are also trout-rich. Notable is the steelhead trout.

Sea mammals such as seals and sea lions are not uncommon along the coast, especially along quiet, rocky promontories. From these same outcroppings, spring travelers can watch for whales migrating up the coast. Ferry travelers between the San Juan Islands are often treated to views of orcas, or killer whales, as they cross the Puget Sound.

Harder to spot along streams are river otters and mink; a patient stance near a logjam is usually necessary. Beavers, whose abundance was responsible for bringing White settlement to the Northwest in the first place, are still found along mountain streams.

Mule deer and elk are the most easily seen of the forests' large mammals. Black bears inhabit the deep woods of the Cascades and Coast ranges. Although not as dangerous as the grizzly (which isn't found here), black bears deserve respect. If you see a bear, allow it ample time to vacate the area, which it almost certainly will do. The old saw about coming between a bear and its cubs contains a central truth: bears with young offspring are protective, which can translate into aggression. If you come upon a young bear, return the way you came.

## East of the Cascades

**Flora** The dry uplands east of the Cascades receive much less rain than the western valleys, and the shallow soils eroded from the region's vast lava flows don't allow for deep-rooted growth. Forests are dominated by ponderosa and lodgepole pines. The former are tall handsome trees with long, bunched needles, and, when mature, characteristic cinnamon-stick colored trunks. Sporadic, low-growing western juniper trees take over on the region's extensive savannas, along with silver sage. Along prairie rivers and irrigation canals, cottonwood and poplar trees abound.

Eastern Oregon and Washington hillsides are covered in late spring with bunches of vibrant-colored yellow flowers with silvery sword-like leaves. The balsamroot was an important food source for early Indians, who dug the bitter, bulbous root and treated it like a potato. You will often find spectacular displays of deep-blue spikes of lupine sharing a hillside with golden balsamroot and fresh green grass shoots.

In the desert areas of southeastern Oregon and southern Idaho, plant life is found along seasonal lakes and intermittent streams. Tule, a rush-like reed, grows in marshy lake bottoms; it was used by Native Americans to weave house-building mats. Where alkaline soils dominate, light green, spindly greasewood endures. In arid steppes, rabbit-brush, with its brushy yellow flowers, brings the late-summer desert to bloom.

**Fauna** The open landscapes of central and eastern Oregon and Washington make bird life even more easily seen. Western meadowlark, Oregon's state bird, trills its lovely song across the region. Spot the male's tell-tale black 'V' on a yellow breast. Listen at dusk for the swooping whistle of the nighthawk, whose sudden dives to seize insects creates a sound like a sharp, echoing intake of breath. Raptors are common: watch for falcons, hawks and especially along the desert lakes, osprey and bald eagles. One of the best places to see large hunting birds is at the Snake River Birds of Prey Natural Area, south of Boise, and near the Klamath lakes in southern Oregon.

The large rivers of central and eastern Oregon are home to salmon and various kinds of trout, though bass and sturgeon tempt anglers in the Columbia. Salmon runs up the Snake and Salmon rivers into Idaho have all but ceased, because of hydroelectric dams.

Campers in any part of eastern Oregon and Washington are likely to be serenaded by coyotes. Large herds of elk are found in the Blue Mountains of Oregon; mule deer are also abundant throughout the region and, with pronghorn antelope, make the region popular in the autumn with hunters. Bighorn sheep have been reintroduced into the high mountain peaks and river canyons.

The hot, dry conditions in central and eastern Oregon make for snake territory. Rattlesnakes are common in rocky terrain. If you're hiking in the desert, or around boulders, watch where you put your feet. Even more importantly, if you are scrambling or climbing on rock faces, watch out for rattlers sunning themselves on the ledges.

## The Rocky Mountains

**Flora** The forests of central and northern Idaho are dominated by evergreens like ponderosa and lodgepole pines, red cedars, Douglas firs and Engelmann spruce. A deciduous conifer – a cone-producing tree that seasonally drops its needles – called the Western larch (or tamarack) is common throughout; watch for its golden yellow needles in the autumn. Joining the larch in the autumn display aspen trees, the white-trunked beauty that thrives along streams.

**Fauna** Wildlife is much more common in the Rocky Mountains than in the Cascades; miles of unprotected border with Canada and Montana allow Idaho the distinction of preserving several species that are all but extinct in other parts of the USA. Grizzly bears are rare but present in several parts of Idaho, notably in the area just west of Yellowstone Park; they have also been reintroduced into the Selway Bitterroot Wilderness, along the Idaho-Montana border. Unless you head into the outback, it's unlikely that you'll encounter a grizzly; if you do, however, retreat calmly and quickly.

Gray wolves are also present in Idaho. They are most frequently seen in the northern Panhandle, close to sanctuaries in Glacier National Park and Canada. Reintroduction of the wolf into Yellowstone Park has become a flashpoint between ranchers and environmentalists: agriculturists fear that wolves will soon leave the park to prey on sheep and calves on nearby ranches.

Another large denizen of the Rocky Mountain forest is the moose, a wide-racked, 1800-pound member of the deer family that feeds on aquatic plants. Black bears are relatively common in the forests, as are both elk and deer.

Idaho rivers are noted for their runs of sea-going cutthroat trout, as well as rainbow, brook, lake and Dolly Varden trout. Sturgeon live in the depths of the Snake River.

## Parks & Refuges

The Pacific Northwest has four national parks: Olympic, North Cascades and Mt Rainier national parks in Washington, and

Crater Lake National Park in Oregon. The NPS also administers a number of other sites throughout the Northwest, notably the John Day Fossil Beds, Fort Clatsop and Oregon Caves in Oregon; the Whitman Mission and Fort Vancouver in Washington; and the Nez Perce Historical Park in Idaho.

The real riches in the Northwest, however, are the region's many state parks and wildlife refuges, which preserve historic and geologic curiosities, as well as a valuable habitat for plants and animals. Often these less hyped sites provide more intimate contact with nature or history than the major nationally administered parks.

Oregon has, at 224, the greatest number of state parks in the nation. Washington isn't far behind, and between the two states there are over 400 state parks. Eighty of Oregon's state parks are along the coast; at times, it can seem as if the entire shoreline is one long state park. State parks throughout the region feature facilities as diverse as historic hotels, caverns, islands, museums, waterfalls, rock-climbing areas, botanical gardens and an observatory.

Parks designed to be used for picnicking or other daytime recreation are called day-use parks: you can't camp at these. Parks open for camping will have a sign stating 'camping' as well as a tent symbol. The effect of tax revenue shortages is being felt at many state parks. Increasingly, even day use (ie picnicking or hiking) demands the payment of a usage fee, and camping fees are also escalating to the point where there's not a lot of difference between camping and staying at a bottom-end motel. Expect these fees to go up even more, and for more and more facilities formerly paid for by tax dollars to become fee-based.

Wildlife refuges are increasingly a draw for travelers focused on the environment, as well as for bird watchers and plant and animal enthusiasts. Of special note are Malheur Wildlife Refuge and Hart Mountain National Antelope Refuge in southeastern Oregon; near Klamath Falls, where the nation's greatest concentration of bald eagles winter at Bear Valley National Wildlife Refuge; and the South Slough Estuarine Reserve near Coos Bay which is an extensive and fragile preserve of coastal plant and animal life. In Washington, the Willapa Bay National Wildlife Refuge preserves a marine tide flat and bay famous for its oysters. Just north of the otherwise spooky Hanford Atomic Reservation, is the Saddle Mountain National Wildlife Refuge, which preserves the high desert plant and wildlife of the Columbia Plateau. In Idaho, the Birds of Prey Natural Area is a refuge for the many raptors drawn to the cliff-lined Snake River.

Many refuges and wilderness areas have informal campsites on or near the facility.

## GOVERNMENT

The USA has a federal system with a president and a bicameral Congress, consisting of the 100-member Senate and the 435-member House of Representatives. Each of the 50 states has two senators and a number of representatives in proportion to its population. The President, whose term is four years, is chosen by the Electoral College, which consists of a number of individual electors from each state equivalent to its number of senators and representatives, who vote in accordance with the popular vote within their state. To be elected, the President must obtain a majority of 270 of the total 538 electoral votes (the District of Columbia, which has no voting representatives in Congress, nevertheless has three electoral votes). The President can only stand for two terms.

The head of the state government is the governor, who presides over a bicameral legislature consisting of a senate and a house delegation. Smaller administrative districts within the states are counties (parishes in Louisiana) and cities.

Oregon and Washington both share a reputation for progressive, somewhat maverick politics. State government is usually in the hands of the Democrats, while US Senate seats tend to go to moderate or liberal Republicans. Idaho tends to be a more politically conservative state.

**Reservation Self-Government**

Indian reservations are recognized by the federal government as independent political units. Legal jurisdiction can therefore be something of a puzzle on reservations.

Tribes have certain inherent sovereign rights. They can run their own schools, regulate transport and trade and have their own constitutions, legislative councils, and tribal court and police systems. The state cannot tax reservation land or transactions that occur on reservations. While such legal considerations may not seem crucial to the traveler, the Northwest has in effect 50 independent political entities within its borders. Visitors need to be aware that certain state laws do not apply on reservations.

State fuel and cigarette taxes aren't levied on those products sold by tribal members within reservations. State gambling restrictions likewise don't pertain to reservations, and some Northwest tribes are in the process of building casinos on their land. Some local roads on reservation land are maintained by the tribes. Do not automatically assume that there is public access; sometimes use is reserved for tribal members. For instance, much of the Yakama Reservation is off-limits to non-Indians.

Not all areas are open for recreation. The state does not have authority to regulate hunting, fishing and recreation on reservations. Tribes can issue their own licenses for hunting and fishing, and may levy a user fee for hikers and campers. If you are not a tribe member, always check with tribal authorities before crossing reservation land.

**ECONOMY**

Even though the United States has the largest Gross National Product in the world at $6350 billion, the average Belgian, Norwegian or Kuwaiti has a higher per capita income. However, the national debt, bloated by a truly breathtaking spate of overspending that began in the early 1980s, stands at a rough $4350 billion and keeps growing. A trade deficit of $254 billion has also been a point of concern.

US citizens pay taxes on a sliding scale, with the poorest paying around 15% of personal earnings. The richest fifth pays around 40%. The average American can expect to pay out 20% of their earnings.

While TV programs and Hollywood movies may show the flashy, wealthy side of the USA, the country is as diverse in its economic circumstances as it is in its cultures. Whole areas of the USA are wealthier than others and within a city the standard of living can vary considerably from neighborhood to neighborhood. The lowest 20% of the population receives only 4.4% of the national income distribution, while the top 5% receives 17.6%.

Blessed with abundant natural resources, busy international waterways, and a well-educated populace, the Pacific Northwest's economy has out-performed the national average since the 1980s. The traditional engines of the Pacific Northwest economy have been resource-extractive industries. Logging especially has been and still is a very big business – Oregon leads the nation in lumber production. However, high-tech firms and computer hardware and software companies are fast making inroads.

**Logging**

The Northwest's economy has traditionally been tied to lumber and wood products. However, most of the easily cut, easily transportable trees were logged long ago. The federal government's restrictions on logging public land has crippled much of what remained of the established forest-products industry. Also, state laws prohibit exportation of raw lumber from state-owned lands, leaving only private land available to old-fashioned, wide-open logging.

In this debate, the lowly spotted owl, a sensitive denizen of the old-growth forest, has become the symbol of the enormous changes taking place in the Northwest's lumber industry. In addition to the federal protection of ancient forests, many other factors have contributed to the decline of the lumber industry, including outmoded

The endangered spotted owl has become a symbol of the heated controversy between environmentalists and the timber industry.

equipment, high labor costs, raw log exports to mills in East Asia and dwindling stands of adult trees.

## Agriculture

The moist valleys of the Rogue, Umpqua, Willamette and Cowlitz rivers and the temperate grasslands east of the Cascades combine to make the Northwest one of the nation's largest and most varied producers of agricultural products.

Cattle and sheep graze the eastern uplands, and golden wheat fields stretch across volcanic plateaus. Federally-funded irrigation projects have made the desert bloom along a number of rivers, notably the Snake, Yakima and Deschutes. Crops as varied as marigolds, garlic, mint, potatoes, melons, grapes and onions are grown in irrigated fields east of the Cascades. Along the Columbia and Okanogan rivers are vast orchards where apples, cherries, peaches and pears are produced for the national market.

West of the Cascades it's a completely different picture. In the extraordinarily fertile Willamette Valley, crops are as varied as hops, sod, berries, Christmas trees and grass seed. Wine grapes are planted in the northern end of the Willamette, and have achieved great success. Another Northwest specialty is nuts, especially walnuts and filberts. The region's mild climate makes it ideal for plant nurseries and tree farms, which comprise the Northwest's third-largest agricultural commodity.

Along the Pacific coast, the rain-swept valleys are famous for their dairy farms, especially along the Tillamook estuary and the Rogue River. Bulb farms are grown extensively along the Skagit River in Northern Washington. Although not strictly agricultural, mushroom gathering is an increasingly fundamental part of coastal Oregon economies.

## Fishing

The Northwest has long been one of the world's great salmon fisheries, until hydroelectric dams – which serve to halt the migration of the sea-going fish – brought about the near extinction of the species in many rivers. Many small coastal towns have lost most of their sport-fishing industries. Fishing for crab, cod, shark, tuna, shrimp, bottom fish and salmon continues. In contrast, oyster and mussel farming is a growth business along much of the coast.

## International Trade

The ports of Seattle, Tacoma and Portland are among the largest along the US West Coast, and are the closest US ports for imported products from Japan and Korea. Consumer goods like TVs and electronic gadgets pour through the port of Seattle, while Japanese and Korean cars arrive in Tacoma and Portland. Portland, at the terminus of the Columbia River barge system, is also the principal grain shipment point for the West Coast. Even after all the legal restrictions, vast flotillas of logs leave the ports of Longview and Coos Bay for foreign mills.

## Hi-Tech Industries

The Northwest is home to some of the largest high-tech firms in the world. Boeing, the largest aircraft manufacturer in the world, is the main economic engine of western Washington. Also in the Seattle area is the headquarters for Microsoft, the software giant. The suburbs west of Portland are home to software developers Techtronix and to Intel's largest 'campuses' and construction plants. Hewlett-Packard is a cornerstone of the Boise economy.

## POPULATION & PEOPLE

The current population of the Pacific Northwest is about 9.2 million, which amounts to about 4% of the total US population. By far the greatest concentration of people is in Washington's Puget Sound area and Oregon's Willamette Valley. Nearly three-quarters of each state's population live in these metropolitan areas. These areas are also among the fastest growing in the USA: urban planners anticipate that Washington and Oregon will absorb another two million inhabitants in the next 15 years.

Idaho's population center stretches along the irrigated Snake River valley. Idaho can't boast any cities that vie with Portland or Seattle in population; however, Boise holds the title of fastest growing city in the USA, so it is well on its way to metropolitan status.

## Ethnicity

The population of the Northwest is overwhelmingly White. According to the 1990 census, Oregon and Idaho are over 93% White, and Washington is 87% White. Hispanics make up the second-largest ethnic group in the Northwest, closely followed by Asians. African Americans comprise about 1.5% of the population, just slightly more than the number of Native Americans in the region.

## Native Americans

The federal government recognizes 50 tribes in the Pacific Northwest. These are tribes that have reservations or trust lands set aside for them. In addition, there are a number of Native Americans groups in the Northwest without federally recognized status or a land base. Federally recognized status is very important to a tribe. Not only is government assistance important to support tribal schools and cultural centers, but without recognition, it is difficult to maintain cultural identity. The total Native American population of the region is over 130,000 people.

## EDUCATION

The literacy rate is very high in the USA in general, but there is serious concern about the quality of writing skills and critical thinking among US students.

School attendance is usually obligatory to the age of 16, and almost everyone graduates from high school. However, local school districts are funded by property taxes, and consequently there are great disparities in the resources available to affluent suburbs versus the impoverished inner city neighborhoods or depressed rural areas.

The percentage of students who go to colleges or universities is much higher than in most European countries, as secondary instruction is much less rigid. There are several levels of higher education: junior colleges (two-year institutions with advanced career training or introductory university courses); colleges or universities with four-year baccalaureate programs; and research universities with advanced degree programs.

## ARTS

### Literature

Portland and Seattle boast some of the largest independent bookstores in the nation, with author readings and signings among the cities' most popular events. Seattle claims to have the most bookstores per capita in the nation, while Portland boasts the busiest public library system per capita. Book clubs are in vogue and coffeeshops bring readers out of their seclusion. The standard joke is that it rains so much in the Northwest that there's little to do but read.

The Northwest isn't just a consumer of reading material, it is also a major producer. Small publishing houses abound in the Northwest, and small newspapers and tabloids are published to serve just about every interest group. Writers also find the Northwest an accommodating place in which to live and write. Nationally recognized writers like Ken Kesey, Tom Robbins, Ursula LeGuin, Jean Auel, Anne McCaffrey, Barry Lopez, Sallie Tisdale, Robert Fulghum, Ivan Doig, Gary Snyder and J A Jance live in the region. For information on some good literature about the Northwest see Books in the Facts for the Visitor chapter.

## Music

Portland and Seattle offer a full array of classical music venues, including well-respected professional symphony and opera companies. Smaller centers like Spokane, Boise and Eugene also offer community classical music companies.

Summer music festivals take music out of doors, to unlikely places like vineyards, remote islands and mountain lakes. Ask representatives of state tourist boards for a full listing of summer festivals. (see Special Events in the Facts for the Visitor chapter for more information.)

Thanks to the success of several Seattle bands, who gave birth to a post-Punk rock phenomenon called 'grunge', the North-west is known for its modern music scene. Seattle and Portland are filled with dark and smoky music clubs, each with angst-ridden musicians hoping to make the leap to stardom.

Although the grunge scene dominates nightlife in Northwestern cities, jazz and blues clubs – and some Celtic music bars – are also found. Check with local newspapers for listings. Country & western music is popular in smaller towns: many bars will have a local band playing familiar cowboy hits on weekend nights.

## Theater & Film

Seattle has one of the most vibrant professional theater scenes on the West Coast. There are apparently more equity theaters in Seattle than anywhere west of Chicago. Portland is no slouch either: if you simply count theater companies (amateur and equity), Portland has even more venues than Seattle. Ashland, in southern Oregon, is famous for its Shakespeare Festival, with open-air and indoor productions of Elizabethan drama.

The film and TV industry is quite active in the Northwest, largely because production costs are lower here than in California and other major film centers. Portland and Seattle also have well-preserved old downtown areas that can be used to create a period mood. The Seattle skyline and quirky lifestyles have become recognizable internationally from such comedy films as *Sleepless in Seattle* and *Singles*. TV also mines the Northwest's reputation as a hip

### Informal Doesn't Equal Casual

Visitors from other parts of the world are often struck by the informality of Northwesterners: dressing up and putting on airs is not a part of life for very many people, even in situations where formal dressing is usually expected (the opera, dining out). In general, this is good news for travelers, who don't have to worry about dress codes at restaurants, concerts or social functions. However, it would be a mistake to think that this informality is a face put on a classless, totally casual society.

In fact, Northwesterners can be quite reserved socially. People are friendly and polite, but travelers shouldn't expect the kind of rapt affability that strangers can encounter in parts of the US South or Midwest. ■

hotbed for Seattle-based *Frasier* and *Northern Exposure*, shot in Roslyn. A far darker treatment of the Northwest's quirky culture was *Twin Peaks*, David Lynch's odd and disturbing series in 1990. Portland also shows up as a menacing backdrop in the brooding films – like *Mala Noche* and *Drugstore Cowboy* – of Gus Van Sant, a Portland native.

## Visual Arts

The Northwest has a lively and sophisticated art scene, based largely in Portland and Seattle, the Oregon coast and the San Juan Islands.

One of the most noted art forms in the Northwest is art glass from the Pilchuk School, which seeks to create a sculptural yet fluid substantiality out of brightly colored blown glass. Dale Chihuly is the most prominent of many glass artists in the Seattle area.

A number of galleries also feature contemporary and historic Native American art from the Northwest.

## CULTURE

In a broad sense, the Northwest shares the general US culture, but with a few important twists. Parts of eastern Oregon and Washington and most of Idaho are very rural; the culture of the Old West and the cowboy are still very much alive here. Fishing towns along the coast and islands have a distinctive and often gritty sensibility that comes from making a living on the stormy and dangerous Pacific. Urban dwellers get out of town on weekends to ski, hike, climb or windsurf. It's fair to say that the natural environment is an overriding and cherished part of life for most people in the region.

The Northwest still puts a lot of emphasis on 'old family' legitimacy and connections. People who can boast ancestors who came across the Oregon Trail are inordinately proud of their birthright; people will notice if you have a last name like Applegate, or share a surname with a frontier-era county. While not exactly clubby, there are certainly some long-time Northwesterners who differentiate between newcomers (ie anyone who moved to the region after WW II) and members of old families.

## Avoiding Offense

While most Americans are tolerant of individual eccentricities, rural Northwesterners in particular may be skeptical of outsiders and may resent what they perceive as unfair criticism of their country or interference in local matters. Visitors should try to be aware of local political issues – don't broadcast your animal rights convictions in a bar full of hunters or denounce clearcutting in a mill town, for example, without having some idea of your audience. Some locals will take advantage of outsiders or foreigners to declare their own strong opinions which some visitors may find repellent.

## Sports

Sports in the USA developed separately from the rest of the world and, consequently, baseball (with its clone, softball), football and basketball dominate the sports scene, both for spectators and participants. The fact that football and basketball are sponsored by high schools and universities gives them a community foundation that reinforces their primacy. Basketball has the additional advantages of requiring only limited space and equipment, making it a popular pastime among inner-city residents.

Baseball is so imbedded in the American psyche that, despite complex rules and labor-management conflicts at professional levels, it continues to flourish. Many of the most meaningful metaphors in American language and political discourse come from the sport – such as 'getting to first base' or the recently debased 'three strikes and you're out'.

Despite the success of the 1994 World Cup, soccer has made limited inroads, mostly among immigrants, and has not really succeeded as a spectator sport.

## RELIGION

The US Constitution mandates separation of church and state and tolerance is the norm. However, matters like prayer in public schools and abortion have brought theological issues onto the secular stage. Nominal allegiance is more widespread than church attendance, but many church-goers are extremely devout.

The oldest religions in North America are Native American religions, greatly modified since contact with Europeans; some, like the Native American Church, which uses hallucinatory peyote buttons as a sacrament, are in part pan-Indian responses to encroachment by the politically dominant culture.

The dominant religion in the USA is Christianity, with Catholicism and Protestant sects roughly equal in number of adherents. The Mormon church is prevalent throughout the Northwest, and is the majority religion in parts of Idaho. Judaism, Islam and Buddhism are also represented in urban areas. Rural areas, especially in the Willamette Valley and northeastern Washington, are home to Mennonites and Protestant communes (there's a Russian Old Believer community in the Willamette Valley).

The libertarian Northwest also attracts a number of religious sects of dubious derivation. The most famous of these was the cult of the Bhagwan Shree Rajneesh (see the aside in the Northeastern Oregon chapter), who built a religious empire in central Oregon before federal marshals deported him and jailed some of his followers on a variety of charges, including attempted murder. The White supremacist Aryan Nation has several churches in northern Idaho. Forms of Wicca (a pagan nature religion), and a myriad of other nature-based spiritual movements, are found in the woods of western Oregon and Washington.

Oregon has the distinction of having the lowest church-going rate in the nation. Evangelist Billy Graham cited this fact when he brought his crusade to Portland in 1992.

# Facts for the Visitor

## VISAS & EMBASSIES

Canadians must have proper proof of Canadian citizenship, such as a citizenship card with photo ID or a passport. Visitors from other countries must have a valid passport and most visitors also require a US visa.

However, there is a reciprocal visa-waiver program in which citizens of certain countries may enter the USA for stays of 90 days or less without first obtaining a US visa. Currently these countries are the UK, New Zealand, Japan, Italy, Spain, Austria, the Netherlands, Belgium, Switzerland, France, Germany, Norway, Denmark, Sweden, Finland, Iceland, San Marino, Andorra, Luxembourg, Liechtenstein and Monaco. Under this program you must have a roundtrip ticket that is non-refundable in the USA and you will not be allowed to extend your stay beyond 90 days.

Other travelers will need to obtain a visa from a US consulate or embassy. In most countries the process can be done by mail.

Your passport should be valid for at least six months longer than your intended stay in the USA and you'll need to submit a recent photo (37 x 37 mm) with the application. Documents of financial stability and/or guarantees from a US resident are sometimes required, particularly for those from Third World countries.

Visa applicants may be required to 'demonstrate binding obligations' that will insure their return back home. Because of this requirement, those planning to travel through other countries before arriving in the USA are generally better off applying for their US visa while they are still in their home country – rather than while on the road.

The validity period for US visitor visas depends on what country you're from. The length of time you'll be allowed to stay in the USA is ultimately determined by US immigration authorities at the port of entry.

Incidentally, the infamous prohibition against issuing visas to people who 'have been members of communist organizations' has been dropped. An anachronism of the Cold War, it still appears on the visa applications although most consular offices have penned a line through the item.

### US Embassies & Consulates

US diplomatic offices abroad include the following:

Australia
US Embassy: 21 Moonah Place, Yarralumla ACT 2600 (☎ (6) 270 5900)
American Consulate General: Level 59 MLC Center 19-29 Martin Place, Sydney NSW 2000 (☎ (2) 373 9200)
There are also consulates in Melbourne, Perth, and Brisbane.

Austria
Boltzmanngasse 16, A-1091, Vienna (☎ (1) 313-39)

Belgium
Blvd du Régent 27, B-1000, Brussels (☎ (2) 513 38 30)

Canada
US Embassy: 100 Wellington St, Ottawa, Ontario 1P 5T1 (☎ (613) 238-5335)
US Consulate-General: 1095 West Pender St, Vancouver, BC V6E 2M6 (☎ (604) 685-1930)
US Consulate-General: 1155 rue St-Alexandre, Montreal, Quebec (☎ (514) 398-9695)
There are also consulates in Toronto, Calgary and Halifax.

Denmark
Dag Hammarskjolds Allé 24, Copenhagen (☎ 31 42 31 44)

Finland
Itainen Puistotie 14A, Helsinki (☎ (0) 171-931)

France
US Embassy, 2 rue Saint Florentin, 75001 Paris (☎ (1) 42.96.12.02)
There are also consulates in Bordeaux, Lyon, Marseille, Nice, Strasbourg and Toulouse.

Germany
Deichmanns Aue 29, 53179 Bonn (☎ (228) 33 91)

Greece
    91 Vasilissis Sophias Blvd, 10160 Athens
    (☎ (1)721-2951)
India
    Shanti Path, Chanakyapuri 110021, New
    Delhi (☎ (11) 60-0651)
Indonesia
    Medan Merdeka Selatan 5, Jakarta
    (☎ (21) 360-360)
Ireland
    42 Elgin Rd, Ballsbridge, Dublin
    (☎ (1) 687 122)
Israel
    71 Hayarkon St, Tel Aviv (☎ (3) 517-4338)
Italy
    Via Vittorio Veneto 119a-121, Rome
    (☎ (6) 46 741)
Japan
    1-10-5 Akasaka Chome, Minato-ku, Tokyo
    (☎ (3) 224-5000)
Korea
    82 Sejong-Ro, Chongro-ku, Seoul
    (☎ (2) 397-4114)
Malaysia
    376 Jalan Tun Razak, 50400 Kuala Lumpur
    (☎ (3) 248-9011)
Mexico
    Paseo de la Reforma 305, Cuauhtémoc,
    06500 Mexico City (☎ (5) 211-00-42)
Netherlands
    US Embassy: Lange Voorhout 102, 2514 EJ
    The Hague (☎ (70) 310 92 09)
    US Consulate: Museumplein 19, 1071 DJ
    Amsterdam (☎ (20) 310 9209)
New Zealand
    29 Fitzherbert Terrace, Thorndon, Welling-
    ton (☎ (4) 722 068)
Norway
    Drammensvein 18, Oslo (☎ (22) 44 85 50)
Phillipines
    1201 Roxas Blvd, Ermita Manila 1000
    (☎ (2) 521-7116)
Russia
    Novinskiy Bul'var 19/23, Moscow
    (☎ (095) 252-2451)
Singapore
    30 Hill St, Singapore 0617 (☎ 338-0251)
South Africa
    877 Pretorius St, Box 9536, Pretoria 0001
    (☎ (12) 342-1048)
Spain
    Calle Serrano 75, 28006 Madrid,
    (☎ (1) 577 4000)
Sweden
    Strandvagen 101, S-115 89 Stockholm
    (☎ (8) 783 5300)

Switzerland
    Jubilaumsstrasse 93, 3005 Berne
    (☎ (31) 357 70 11)
Thailand
    95 Wireless Rd, Bangkok (☎ (2) 252-5040)
UK
    US Embassy, 5 Upper Grosvenor St, London
    W1 (☎ (71) 499 9000)
    US Consulate-General, 3 Regent Terrace,
    Edinburgh EH7 5BW (☎ (31) 556 8315)
    US Consulate-General, Queens House,
    Belfast BT1 6EQ, (☎ (232) 328 239)

## Visa Extensions

If you want, need or hope to stay in the
USA longer than the date stamped on your
passport, go to the local Immigration &
Naturalization Service (INS) office (look
in the local White Pages telephone directory under 'US Government') *before* the
stamped date to apply for an extension. If
you remain more than a few days past the
expiration date the INS will assume you
want to work illegally. At an interview with
the INS you will need to explain why you
didn't leave by the expiry date and convince the officials you're not looking for
work and that you have enough money to
support yourself until you do leave.

## DOCUMENTS

All foreign visitors (other than Canadians)
must bring their passport. US citizens and
Canadians may want a passport as well, in
the event they're tempted to extend their
travels into Mexico or beyond. All visitors
should bring their driver's license and any
health-insurance or travel-insurance cards.

    You'll need a picture ID to show that you
are over 21 to buy alcohol or gain admission to bars or clubs (make sure your driver's license has a photo on it, or else get
some other form of ID). A good idea is to
make a couple photocopies of all your
travel documents including airline tickets,
your passport and international ID. Keep
one copy separate from the originals and
use the other to carry around instead of the
originals. There's nothing worse than
losing your identity on a trip.

## International Driving Permit

An International Driving Permit is a useful accessory for foreign visitors in the USA. Local traffic police are more likely to accept it as valid identification than an unfamiliar document from another country. Your national automobile association can provide one for a nominal fee. They're usually valid for one year.

## Automobile Association Membership Cards

If you plan on doing a lot of driving in the USA, it would be beneficial to join your national automobile association. Members of the American Automobile Association (AAA) or an affiliated automobile club can get car rental and sightseeing admission discounts with membership cards. More importantly, it gives you access to AAA road service in case of an emergency (eg locking your keys in the car or having major blow-ups).

## Hostelling International Card

Most hostels in the USA are members of Hostelling International/American Youth Hostel (HI/AYH). HI was formerly the International Youth Hostel Federation or IYHF. You can purchase membership on the spot when checking in, although it's probably advisable to purchase it before you leave home.

## Student Identification

If you're a student, get an international student ID or bring along a school or university ID card to take advantage of the discounts available to students.

## CUSTOMS

US customs allows each person over the age of 21 to bring one liter of liquor and 200 cigarettes duty-free into the USA. US citizens are allowed to import, duty-free, $400 worth of gifts from abroad while non-US citizens are allowed to bring in $100 worth. Should you be carrying more than $10,000 in US and foreign cash, traveler's checks, money orders and the like), you need to declare the excess amount. There is no legal restriction on the amount which may be imported, but undeclared sums in excess of $10,000 may be subject to confiscation.

### HIV & Entering Customs

Everyone entering the USA who is not a US citizen is subject to the whim and authority of the Immigration & Naturalization Service (INS), regardless of whether that person has legal immigration documents. The INS can keep someone from entering or staying in the USA by excluding or deporting them. This is especially relevant to travelers with HIV (Human Immunodeficiency Virus). Though being HIV positive is not a ground for deportation, it is a 'ground of exclusion' and the INS can invoke it to refuse to admit visitors to the country.

Although the INS doesn't test people for HIV at customs, they may try to exclude anyone who answers yes to this question on the non-immigrant visa application form: 'Have you ever been afflicted with a communicable disease of public health significance?' INS officials may also stop people if they seem sick, are carrying AIDS/HIV medicine or, sadly, if the officer happens to think the person looks gay, though sexual orientation is not legally a ground of exclusion. Because the INS can refuse or delay admission to anyone they suspect of being HIV positive, your best protection is not to tip them off.

It is imperative that visitors know and assert their rights. Immigrants and visitors should avoid contact with the INS until they discuss their rights and options with a trained immigration advocate. For legal immigration information and referrals to immigration advocates, contact The National Immigration Project of the National Lawyers Guild (☎ (617) 227-9727), 14 Beacon St, Suite 506, Boston, MA 02108, or Immigrant HIV Assistance Project, Bar Association of San Francisco (☎ (415) 267-0795), 685 Market St, Suite 700, San Francisco, CA 94105. ∎

Certain items are either restricted or completely banned from entry into the country. These include liquor-filled candies, fruits and plants, articles made from plants and animals in danger of extinction, firearms and munitions, fireworks, toxic substances, lottery tickets, meat, birds and their derivatives (such as paté), dangerous drugs, domestic animals, pornographic articles, antiquities, switchblade knives, and vehicles not in accordance with US pollution laws.

## MONEY
### Currency
The US dollar is divided into 100 cents (c). Coins come in denominations of 1c (penny), 5c (nickel), 10c (dime), 25c (quarter) and the seldom seen 50c (half dollar). Notes come in $1, $2, $5, $10, $20, $50 and $100 denominations (you'll only occasionally come across $2 bills – they're perfectly legal). There is also a $1 coin that the government has tried unsuccessfully to bring into mass circulation; you may get them as change from ticket and stamp machines. Be aware that they look similar to quarters.

### Exchange Rates
If you plan to carry money in the form of traveler's checks, you will save yourself quite a bit of trouble and expense if you buy them in US dollars. While you may lose out on blips in the foreign exchange rates, the hassle of having to exchange money at banks and other facilities makes up for the savings. Restaurants, hotels and most stores accept US dollar traveler's checks as if they were cash, so if you're carrying traveler's checks in US dollars, odds are you'll never have to use a bank or pay an exchange fee.

All branches of several regional banks will exchange foreign currency or travelers checks at regular teller windows. However, banks in outlying areas aren't asked to exchange money very often. You will probably find it less of a hassle and waste of time if you change your money at larger cities. Nearly all banks will buy and sell

Canadian currency; some businesses near the border will offer to accept Canadian dollars 'at par', meaning that they will accept Canadian dollars at the same rate as US dollars.

At the main branch of banks money can be wired, currency purchased, etc. Additionally, Thomas Cook, American Express and exchange windows in airports offer exchange (although you'll get a better rate at a bank).

At press time, exchange rates were:

| | | |
|---|---|---|
| A$1 | = | $0.74 |
| C$1 | = | $0.74 |
| DM1 | = | $0.75 |
| HK$10 | = | $1.34 |
| NZ$1 | = | $0.69 |
| UK£1 | = | $1.64 |
| ¥100 | = | $1.17 |

### Credit & Debit Cards
Major credit and charge cards are widely accepted by car-rental agencies and most hotels, restaurants, gas stations, shops and larger grocery stores. Many recreational and tourist activities can also be paid for by credit card. The most commonly accepted cards are Visa, MasterCard and American Express. However, Discover and Diners Club cards are also accepted by a fair number of businesses.

You'll find it hard to perform certain transactions without one. Ticket buying services, for instance, won't reserve tickets over the phone unless you offer a credit card number, and it's virtually impossible to rent a car without a credit card. Even if you loathe credit cards and prefer to rely on traveler's checks and ATMs, it's a good idea to carry one (best bets are Visa or MasterCard) for emergencies.

Places that accept Visa and MasterCard are also likely to accept debit cards. Unlike a credit card, a debit card deducts payment directly from the user's savings account. Instead of an interest rate, users are charged a minimal fee for the transaction. Be sure to check with your bank to confirm that your debit card will be accepted in other states – debit cards from large commercial banks can often be used worldwide. For telephone numbers to call in case your card is lost or stolen, see the Emergency section.

## Automatic Teller Machines (ATMs)

ATMs are another plastic alternative. Most banks have these machines which are usually open 24 hours a day. There are various ATM networks and most banks are affiliated with several. Some of the most common are Cirrus, Plus, Star Systems and Interlink. For a nominal service charge, you can withdraw cash from an ATM using a credit card or a charge card. Credit cards usually have a 2% fee with a $2 minimum, but using bank cards linked to your personal checking account is usually far cheaper. Check with your bank or credit card company for exact information.

In addition to traditional bank locations, you can also find ATMs at most airports, large grocery stores, shopping malls and in a growing number of convenience stores.

## Costs

Cost for accommodations vary seasonally, between the cities and the countryside, and between resorts and everywhere else. Generally, rates are higher in summer, between Memorial Day and Labor Day, but winter rates at ski resorts can be astronomical. The cheapest motel rates will usually be in the $20 to $30 range, though a few places have inexpensive hotels. Rustic camping is inexpensive at only about $5 or so per night, but only costlier formal sites have amenities like hot showers.

Food is very reasonable by European standards. The occasional splurge at a first-rate restaurant is expensive, but good restaurant meals can be found for $10 – or even half that for some lunch specials. If you purchase food at markets you may get by even more cheaply.

Intercity public transportation is relatively expensive compared to owning or renting a car, and is much less extensive than in other parts of the world. In some areas a car is the only way of getting around; rentals are fairly inexpensive in large cities, and gasoline costs a fraction of

what it does in Europe and most of the rest of the world. For more information on purchasing and operating a car, see the entry Car & Motorbike in the Getting Around chapter.

## Tipping

Tipping is expected in restaurants and better hotels, as well as by taxi drivers, hairdressers and baggage carriers. In restaurants, wait staff are paid minimal wages and rely upon tips for their livelihoods. Tip 15% unless the service is terrible (in which case a complaint to the manager is warranted) or up to 20% if the service is great. Never tip in fast-food, take-out or buffet-style restaurants where you serve yourself.

Taxi drivers expect 10% and hairdressers get 15% if their service is satisfactory. Baggage carriers (skycaps in airports, bell-boys in hotels) receive $1 for the first bag and 50c for each additional bag carried. In budget hotels (where there aren't bellboys anyway) tips are not expected. In 1st class and luxury hotels, tipping can reach irritating proportions – doormen, bellboys, parking attendants, chambermaids are all tipped at least $1 for each service performed. However, simply saying 'thank you' to an attendant who merely opens the door when you could just as easily have done it yourself is OK.

In hotels, beware of grossly inflated charges for some services, especially telephones and laundry. To avoid unpleasant surprises, ask about these before you incur any expenses. Many expensive hotels have pay phones in their lobbies which are much cheaper than calling from your room, and cheap coin-operated laundries outside the hotel are an alternative to expensive hotel laundry charges.

## Special Deals

The USA is probably the most promotion-oriented society on earth. Everything has an angle and with a little detective work and a lot of gumption, the traveler stands to find some worthwhile bargains.

Off-season hotel prices, for example, are

frequently negotiable. 'You know, I'd love to stay at your fine establishment, but Joe Bob's Hotel down the street is much cheaper . . . ' Be confident, but don't be rude.

One of the newer retail trends is the bulk warehouse store. These are huge buildings that sell everything you could possibly want at a discount. Items tend to come in ungainly institutional-sized units, so you probably need a strong liking for a certain product to insure you don't get sick of it. These are good places for items like batteries and film. Sometimes you can even find bargains on computers.

Sunday newspapers typically have discount coupons for local supermarkets and advertising circulars for sales at department stores.

Supermarkets also run specials on tickets for local attractions, especially 'family' attractions, like amusement parks or professional sporting events (usually baseball). If there is skiing within a two-hour drive, cheap lift tickets are often available at supermarkets as well.

Enterprising local publishers often put together coupon books for local merchants that can be purchased at independent book shops. They're usually on display at the front counter and typically offer discounts at local cafes and restaurants. Tourist offices and chambers of commerce usually have something similar.

If you plan to rent a car, rental agencies sometimes offer discounts in tandem with national motel chains. Since the deregulation of the US airline industry, airlines have been jockeying to provide the most appealing premiums for potential flyers. If you belong to any frequent-flyer programs, be sure to ask what discounts they entitle you to.

The granddaddy of discount programs is something called *Entertainment Publications*. This is a thick tome of coupons used in conjunction with a membership card that allows discounts for everything from restaurants and hotels to baseball games. They're available for specific geographic regions of the USA and Canada and cost $40 for a year's membership. They're ideal if you plan to spend more than a few months in the USA. Call (☎ (800) 285-5525) for information.

## Taxes

While Oregon claims the distinction of having no sales tax, visitors to Washington and Idaho will find that a percentage tax is added to most bills, similar to European VAT (value-added tax). Sales taxes vary from state to state and even county to county, and may be higher for accommodations than for other purchases. Washington State sales tax is around 8.2%; the bed tax, applicable in many of the larger hotels, is a whopping 15%, including (not in addition to) the 8.2%. Idaho's sales tax is a little more reasonable at 5%, with a 6% bed tax. Parts of Oregon also have a bed tax.

When inquiring about hotel or motel rates, be sure to ask whether taxes are included or not.

## WHEN TO GO

When to visit the Northwest depends largely on what you want to do when you get there.

Most travelers choose to visit the region in the summer and fall, when the weather is pleasant and rainfall infrequent. If your trip includes hiking and camping, then it's best to plan to be west of the Cascades after May, when the weather has settled down a bit (this part of the region receives 65% of its precipitation from November to March). September and October are often glorious months, as the Indian summer brings warm days and cool nights. In the bountiful Northwest, there is a palpable sense of harvest in the autumn, with apples, pears, wine grapes, nuts and vegetables all coming ripe at once. The weather deteriorates after October.

Spring comes to eastern Oregon, Washington and Idaho in May; a trip to the high desert and the eastern mountain ranges in May and June will reward the traveler with beautiful weather and wildflower viewing.

If your itinerary brings you to the Northwest in winter, all is not lost. Many cultural events like the symphony, opera and theater are most active during winter months. The Northwest has some incredible skiing in Idaho's Sun Valley, Oregon's Mt Bachelor and Mt Hood, and Snoqualmie Pass and Stevens Pass in Washington.

Winter also brings storms to the Pacific coast, and coastal towns are often busy at such times with 'storm watchers.' These are people who come to watch and be part of the spectacular weather changes, high winds and waves that batter the coast.

## WHAT TO BRING

The Northwest is a very casual place, so pack the clothes that you are comfortable wearing. Even if your trip will include dining out or attending formal events, there's no special need to wear formal clothes. People in the Northwest do dress up; they just don't require it.

Summers are usually warm, but not too humid. Evenings are often cool, so bring a jacket. In all seasons but the height of summer, it's a good idea to bring a rain jacket, or at least an umbrella. Don't bring clothing that can't stand up to a little rain.

Unless you're planning a sustained mountain trip in winter, heavy winter gear isn't usually necessary. Winters in western Oregon and Washington are usually chilly and wet, but not extremely cold. If you're planning to travel in the eastern parts of the state, or in Idaho in winter, take along a wind-proof coat, gloves, hat and scarf.

If you're planning on camping, make sure that your tent is waterproof: Northwestern dews are as heavy as rain showers elsewhere. Nights will be cool, so bring a reasonable weight of sleeping bag. Hiking trails are often muddy; dedicating a pair of shoes (tennis shoes are usually OK unless you're planning strenuous outings) to trail-walking and beach-combing is probably a good idea.

In all seasons, it's a good idea to bring along a pair of binoculars. You'll be glad to have them when you spot your first sea lion or bighorn sheep. Likewise, consider bringing along or buying a good wildlife or wildflower guide. There's a rich diversity of plants and animals in the Northwest, and you'll end up wishing that you knew how to identify them.

## TOURIST INFORMATION

Local chambers of commerce may be good sources of information on local attractions, but they often assume that tourists have unlimited budgets and travel by car; they are unlikely to refer visitors to budget accommodations and restaurants, and may be totally unaware of public transportation options. Oregon, Washington and Idaho have state tourist bureaus that offer glossy guides, maps and scads of other pertinent travel information to travelers. If you have any special interest (ie wineries, B&Bs, ranch vacations, fishing trips, etc), be sure to ask.

### Washington

Washington has several staffed point-of-entry visitors centers stationed around the state, many at rest areas near the state's borders. Except for the Vancouver/Fourth Plain information center off I-5, which is open year round, these centers are open from May to September only. The visitors center at Sea-Tac International Airport (open year round) is at baggage claim No 9.

Order the comprehensive *Washington State Field Guide* from the Washington State Tourism Division (☎ (800) 544-1800, ext 001). Ask them to throw in a copy of the *Washington State Lodging & Travel Guide* and a map, and you should have all the information and special interest contacts you'll ever need. Just in case, the tourist division headquarters (☎ (360) 586-2088) can be reached weekdays from 9 am to 4 pm for questions. For more specific information you may want to contact the following:

Washington State Tourism Office
   101 General Administration Bldg, AX-13, Olympia WA, 98504-1800
   (☎ (206) 586-2088, (800) 544-1800)
Washington State Parks Headquarters
   7150 Clearwater Lane, PO Box 42650, Olympia WA, 98504-2650
   (☎ (360) 902-8563)

Washington State Department of Fisheries
  PO Box 43135, 1111 Washington St SE,
  Olympia, WA 98504 (☎ (360) 902-2200)
Washington State Department of Wildlife
  600 Capitol Way N, Olympia, WA 98501
  (☎ (360) 902-1234)

## Oregon

When you call, write or visit a tourist information office in Oregon, there are a few publications that you should be sure to ask for: *Where To Stay In Oregon*, a listing of accommodations throughout the state, with prices and amenities noted; the official state road map; a state campground map; the *Oregon State Park Guide*; an Oregon events calendar; and, if you're planning on outdoor recreation, *Oregon Outdoors*, the official directory to outfitters and guides.

*Oregon: The Official Travel Guide*, a glossy magazine-sized publication, is a good introduction to the state and its regions; there are also lots of addresses of local tourism bureaus and tourist facilities.

Oregon Tourism Division
  775 Summer St, Salem OR, 97310
  (☎ (800) 547-7842 out of state,
  (800) 543-8838 in state)
Oregon State Parks & Recreation Department
  525 Trade St SE, Salem, OR 97310
  (☎ 378-6305)
Oregon Department of Fish & Game
  PO Box 59, Portland, OR 97207
  (☎ 229-5403)
United States Forest Service
  PO Box 3623, Portland, OR 97208
  (☎ 326-2877)
Bureau of Land Management
  1300 NE 44th Ave, Portland, OR 97208
  (☎ 280-7001)

## Idaho

Idaho has three, clearly signed Welcome Centers stationed on its borders – near Post Falls off I-90, near Payette off I-84, and near Malad City off I-15. Tourist bureaus work together in Idaho so you'll be able to get a lot of information out of these centers. Operators on the receiving end of Idaho's statewide tourism hotline (☎ (800) VISIT-ID) speak on the behalf of several bureaus

and organizations, from the Idaho Travel Council to the Department of Fish & Game. You can also write to obtain information from the Idaho Travel Council, Idaho Department of Commerce, PO Box 83720, Boise, ID 83720-0093.

Pick up or order the *Official Idaho State Travel Guide* and you're set. It's filled with regional travel information including good maps, recreational highlights, festival listings, and enticing photos, and comes complete with a mandatory accommodations guide in back and a glossy road map in the centerfold (be sure to get a regular state highway map as well). You'll also want to request the *Idaho State Park Guide*, and the useful *Idaho RV & Campground Directory*, which details public and private tent and RV campgrounds in Idaho.

For more detailed information on a particular area of interest, contact one of the regional travel bureaus below:

Idaho Travel Council
  700 W State St, Boise ID, 83720
  (☎ (800) 635-7820)
North Idaho Travel Committee
  PO Box 928, Sandpoint, ID 83864
  (☎ (800) 800-2106)
North Central Idaho Travel Committee
  2207 E Main, Suite G, Lewiston, ID 83501
  (☎ (800) 473-3543)
Southwest Idaho Travel Association
  PO Box 2106, Boise, ID 83701
  (☎ (800) 635-5240)
South Central Travel Committee
  858 Blue Lakes Blvd, North Twin Falls, ID
  83301 (☎ (800) 255-8946)
Southeastern Idaho Travel Council
  c/o Lava Hot Springs Foundation, Box 668,
  Lava Hot Springs, ID 83246
  (☎ (800) 423-8597)
Yellowstone/Teton Territory
  Box 50498, Idaho Falls, ID 83402
  (☎ (800) 634-3246)

## Tourist Offices Abroad

US Embassies will often have tourist information (see the preceding entry US Embassies & Consulates Abroad). The United States Travel & Tourism Administration (USTTA) has the following offices abroad:

Australia
Level 59, MLC Centre, King & Castlereagh Sts, Sydney, NSW 2001 (☎ (2) 233-4666)
Canada
480 University Ave, Suite 602, Toronto, Ontario, M5G 1V2 (☎ (416) 595-5082)
1253 McGill College Ave, Suite 328, Montreal, Quebec H3B 2Y5 (☎ (514) 861-5040)
1095 West Pender St, Vancouver, BC VBE 2M6 (☎ (604) 685-1930)
Mexico
Edificio Plaza Comermex, 402, Blvd M Avila Camacho No1, Colonia Polanco Chapultepec,11560 Mexico, DF
(☎ (5) 520-3010)
UK
24 Grosvenor Square, London, England W1A 1AE (☎ (171) 495-4466)
France
2 Ave Gabriel, 75382 Paris Cedex OB
(☎ (1) 42.60.00.66)

## USEFUL ORGANIZATIONS
### American Automobile Association
The AAA, with offices in all major cities and many smaller towns, provides useful information, free maps and routine road services like tire repair and towing (free within a limited radius) to its members. Members of its foreign affiliates, like the Automobile Association in the UK, are entitled to the same services; for others, the basic membership fee is $39 per annum, plus a one-time initiation fee of $17 (still an excellent investment for the maps alone, even for non-motorists). Its nationwide toll-free roadside assistance number is (800) AAA-HELP or (800) 222-4357.

### National Park Service (NPS) & US Forest Service (USFS)
The NPS and USFS administer the use of parks and forests. National forests are less protected than parks, allowing commercial exploitation in some areas (usually logging or privately owned recreational facilities).

National parks most often surround spectacular natural features and cover hundreds of sq miles. A full range of accommodations can be found in and around national parks. Contact individual parks for more specific information. National park campground and reservations information can be

obtained by calling (800) 365-2267 or writing to the National Park Service Public Inquiry, Department of the Interior, 18th and C Sts NW, Washington DC 20013.

Current information about national forests can be obtained from ranger stations which are also listed in the text. National forest campground and reservation information can be obtained by calling (800) 280-2267. General information about federal lands is also available from the Fish & Wildlife Service and the Bureau of Land Management (see below).

### Golden Age Passports
Golden Age Passports are free and allow permanent US residents 62 years and older unlimited entry to all sites in the national park system, with discounts on camping and other fees.

Golden Access passports offer the same to US residents who are medically blind or permanently disabled.

Golden Eagle passports cost $25 annually and offer one-year entry into national parks to the holder and accompanying guests. You can apply in person for any of these at any national park or regional office of the USFS or NPS or call (800) 280-2267 for information and ordering.

### Bureau of Land Management (BLM)
The BLM manages public use of federal lands, including grazing and mining leases. They offer no-frills camping, often in untouched settings. Each state has a regional office in the state capital. Look in the White Pages under 'US Government', or call the Federal Information Directory (☎ (800) 726-4995).

### US Fish & Wildlife Service (USFWS)
Each state has a few regional offices that can provide information about viewing local wildlife. Their phone numbers can be found in the White Pages phone directory under 'US Government' or you can call the Federal Information Directory (☎ (800) 726-4995).

### Nature Conservancy
With a mission to protect the rarest living

things for future generations, the Nature Conservancy organizes field tours for members and can advise on interesting areas for the general public. The Oregon office (☎ (503) 228-9561) is at 1205 NW 25th Ave, Portland, OR 97210. The Washington office (☎ (206) 343-4344) is at 217 Pine St, Suite 1100, Seattle, WA 98101, and the Idaho office (☎ (208) 926-3007) is at PO Box 165, Sun Valley, ID 83353.

## BUSINESS HOURS & HOLIDAYS

Generally speaking, business hours are from 9 am to 5 pm, but there are certainly no hard and fast rules. In any large city, a few supermarkets, restaurants and the lobby of the main post office are open 24 hours a day. Shops are usually open from 9 or 10 am to 5 or 6 pm, but are often open until 9 pm in shopping malls, except on Sundays when hours are noon to 5 pm. Post offices are open from 8 am to 4 or 5:30 pm Monday to Friday, and some are open from 8 am to 3 pm on Saturday. Banks are usually open from either 9 or 10 am to 5 or 6 pm Monday to Friday. A few banks are open from 9 am to 2 or 4 pm on Saturdays. Basically, hours are decided by the individual branch so if you need specifics give the branch you want a call.

National public holidays are celebrated throughout the USA. Banks, schools and government offices (including post offices) are closed and transportation, museums and other services are on a Sunday schedule. Holidays falling on a Sunday are usually observed on the following Monday.

January
  *New Year's Day*, January 1
  *Martin Luther King, Jr Day* – held on the third Monday of the month it celebrates this civil rights leader's birthday (January 15, 1929).
February
  *Presidents' Day* – held on the third Monday of the month, it celebrates the birthdays of Abraham Lincoln (February 12, 1809) and George Washington (February 22, 1732).
March/April
  *Easter* – observed the first Sunday after a full moon in March or April.

May
  *Memorial Day* – held on the last Monday in the month, it honors the war dead (and is also the unofficial first day of the summer tourist season).
July
  *Independence Day* – July 4, celebrates the adoption of the Declaration of Independence on that day in 1776; parades, fireworks displays and a huge variety of other events are held throughout the country.
September
  *Labor Day* – held on the first Monday of the month, it honors working people (and is also the unofficial end of the summer season).
October
  *Columbus Day* – held on the second Monday of the month, it commemorates the landing of Christopher Columbus in the Bahamas on October 12, 1492. Though it is a federal holiday, many Native Americans do not consider this day a cause for celebration.
November
  *Veterans Day* – November 11, honors war veterans.
  *Thanksgiving* – held on the fourth Thursday of the month, it's a day of giving thanks and is traditionally celebrated with a big family dinner, usually turkey, potatoes and other fall harvest vegetables.
December
  *Christmas Day* – December 25

## CULTURAL EVENTS

The USA is always ready to call a day an event. Retailers remind the masses of coming events with huge advertising binges running for months before the actual day. Because of this tacky overexposure some of these events are nicknamed 'Hallmark Holidays' after the greeting card manufacturer. In larger cities with diverse cultures, traditional holidays of other countries are also celebrated with as much, if not more, fanfare. Some of these are also public holidays (see above) and therefore banks, schools and government buildings are closed.

January
  *Chinese New Year* – begins at the end of January or the beginning of February and lasts two weeks. The first day is celebrated with parades, firecrackers, fireworks and food.

## February

*Valentine's Day* – February 14. No one knows why St Valentine is associated with romance in the USA but this is the day of roses, sappy greeting cards and packed restaurants. Some people wear red and give out 'Be My Valentine' candies.

## March

*St Patrick's Day* – March 17. The patron saint of Ireland is honored by all those who feel the Irish in their blood, and by those who want to feel Irish beer in their blood. Everyone wears green (or you can get pinched), stores sell green bread, bars serve green beer and towns and cities put on frolicking parades of marching bands and community groups.

## April

*Easter* Those who observe the holiday may go to church, paint eggs, eat chocolate eggs or any mixture of the above. Travel during this weekend is usually expensive and crowded. Incidentally, Good Friday is not a public holiday and often goes unnoticed.

*Passover* – celebrated either in March or April, depending on the Jewish calendar. Families get together to honor persecuted forebears, partake in the symbolic seder dinner and eat unleavened bread.

## May

*Cinco de Mayo* – the day the Mexicans wiped out the French army in 1862. Now it's the day on which all Americans get to eat lots of Mexican food and drink margaritas.

*Mothers Day* – held on the third Sunday of the month with lots of cards, flowers and busy restaurants.

## June

*Fathers Day* – same Sunday, same idea, different parent.

## July

*Independence Day* – more commonly called 4th of July. Lots of flags are flown, barbecues abound, parades storm the streets of many towns, fireworks litter the air and ground.

## October

*Halloween* – October 31. Kids and adults dress up in costumes, in the safer neighborhoods. Children go 'trick-or-treating' for candy and adults go to parties to act out their alter egos.

## November

*Day of the Dead* – observed in areas with Mexican communities on November 2. This is a day for families to honor dead relatives, and make breads and sweets resembling skeletons, skulls and such.

*Election Day* – held on the second Tuesday of the month. This is the chance for US citizens to perform their patriotic duty and vote. Even more flags are flown than on July 4 and signs with corny photos of candidates decorate the land.

*Thanksgiving* – held on the last Thursday of the month. The most important family gathering is celebrated with a bounty of food and football games on TV. The following day is declared by retailers as the biggest shopping day of the year with everyone burning off pumpkin pie by running shopping relays through the malls.

## December

*Christmas* – The night before the 25th is as much an event as the day itself with church services, caroling in the streets, people cruising neighborhoods looking for the best light displays and stores full of procrastinators.

*Kwanzaa* – held from December 26 to 31. This seven-day African American celebration give thanks to the harvest. Families join together for a feast and practice seven different principles corresponding to the seven days of celebration.

*New Year's Eve* – December 31. People celebrate with little tradition other than dressing up and drinking champagne, or staying home and watching the festivities on TV. The following day people stay at home to nurse their hangovers and watch college football on TV.

# SPECIAL EVENTS
## Washington

### January

*Outhouse Race/Winter Swap Meet*, Conconully, third weekend in January

### February

*Upper Skagit Bald Eagle Festival*, Concrete, Rockport and Marblemount, early February

*Fat Tuesday*, Seattle, day before Ash Wednesday (February or March)

### March

*Cowboy Poetry Jubilee*, Omak, third weekend in March

### April

*Skagit Valley Tulip Festival*, Mount Vernon, first two weeks of April

*Hulda Klager Lilac Festival*, Woodland, late April to early May

### May

*Ilwaco Salmon Barbeque & Blessing of the Fleet*, Ilwaco, first weekend in May

*Bloomsday Run*, Spokane, first weekend in May

*Seattle International Children's Festival*, Seattle, second week of May

*Irrigation Festival*, Sequim, second weekend in May

*Maifest*, Leavenworth, second weekend in May

*Norwegian 17th of May Festival*, Ballard/Seattle, May 17

*Wild Goose Bill Days*, Wilbur, mid-May

*Lilac Festival Torchlight Parade*, Spokane, third Saturday in May

June

*Northwest Folklife Festival*, Seattle, Memorial Day Weekend

*Scottish Highland Games*, Ferndale, first weekend in June

*Annual Tinowit International Powwow*, Yakima, second weekend in June

*Northwest Microbrewery Festival*, Fall City, third weekend in June

July

*Yakama National Cultural Powwow & Rodeo,* Toppenish, Fourth of July weekend

*Colville Tribal Powwow Encampment*, Nespelem, first week of July

*Seafair*, Seattle, third weekend in July

*Walla Walla Sweet Onion Harvest Fest*, Walla Walla, end of July

August

*Omak Stampede*, Omak, second week in August

*Bellingham Festival of Music*, Bellingham, late August to early September

*International Accordian Festival*, Leavenworth, mid-August

*Washington State International Kite Festival*, Long Beach, late August

*Fort Vancouver Founder's Day*, Vancouver, August 25

*Spokane Falls Northwest Indian Encampment and Powwow*, Spokane, late August

*National Lentil Festival*, Pullman, late August

September

*Bumbershoot*, Seattle, Labor Day weekend

*Huckleberry Festival*, Bingen, second weekend in September

*Fall Historic Homes Tour*, Port Townsend, mid September

*Cranberry Festival*, Ilwaco, third or fourth weekend in September

December

*Country Christmas Lighted Farm Implement Parade*, Sunnyside, first Friday in December.

## Oregon

May

*Cinco de Mayo*, Portland, May 5

*Tygh Valley All-Indian Rodeo*, Tygh Valley, mid-May

*Powwow & Rodeo*, Klamath Falls, late May

*Azalea Festival*, Brookings, late May

June

*Portland Rose Festival*, Portland, early to mid-June

*Cascade Festival of Music*, Bend, mid-June

*Sisters Rodeo*, Sisters, mid-June

*Portland Gay Pride Celebration*, late June

*Pi-Ume-Sha Treaty Days*, Warm Springs, late June

*Oregon Folklife Festival*, Corvallis, late June

July

*World Championship Timber Carnival*, Albany, early July

*St Paul Rodeo*, St Paul, July 4

*Oregon Country Fair*, Veneta, first weekend after the 4th of July

*Scottish Highland Games*, Gresham, July

*Obon Festival*, Ontario, mid-July

*Chief Joseph Days*, Joseph, late July

*Sand Castle Building Contest*, Lincoln City, late July

*Oregon Blueberry Festival*, Cornelius, late July

*Mosquito Festival*, Paisley, late July

August

*Mt Hood Festival of Jazz*, Gresham, early August

*Dufur Threshing Bee*, Dufur, early August

*Blackberry Arts Festival*, Coos Bay, late August

*Swan Island Dahlia Show*, Canby, late August

September

*ArtQuake*, Portland, early September

*Pendleton Roundup*, Pendleton, mid-September

*Mt Angel Octoberfest*, Mt Angel, mid-September

*Eugene Celebration*, Eugene, late September

October

*Cranberry Festival*, Bandon, October

## Idaho

January

*Sandpoint Winter Carnival*, Sandpoint, third week of January

June

*National Old Time Fiddlers Contest*, Weiser, third week in June

*Boise River Festival*, Boise, late June

July

> Snake River Stampede, Nampa mid-July
>
> Festival at Sandpoint, Sandpoint, three weeks of late July, early August
>
> San Inazio Basque Festival, Boise, last weekend of July
>
> Idaho International Folk Dance Festival, Rexburg, late July and early August

August

> Coeur d'Alene Indian Pilgrimage, Cataldo, August 15
>
> Shoshone-Bannock Indian Festival, Fort Hall, mid-August

September

> Lewiston Roundup, Lewiston, second week of September
>
> Art in the Park, Boise, second week in September

## POST & TELECOMMUNICATIONS
### Postal Rates

Postage rates increase every few years. The next increase is expected in 1997, when postage rates will probably go up by about 10%. Currently, rates for 1st-class mail within the USA are 32c for letters up to one ounce (23c for each additional ounce) and 20c for postcards.

International airmail rates (except Canada and Mexico) are 60c for a half-ounce letter, 95c for a one-ounce letter and 39c for each additional half ounce. International postcard rates are 40c. Letters to Canada are 46c for a one-ounce letter, 23c for each additional ounce and 30c for a postcard. Letters to Mexico are 35c for a half-ounce letter, 45c for a one-ounce letter and 30c for a postcard. Aerogrammes are 45c.

The cost for parcels airmailed anywhere within the USA is $3 for two pounds or less, increasing by $1 per pound up to $6 for five pounds. For heavier items, rates differ according to the distance mailed. Books, periodicals and computer disks can be sent by a cheaper 4th-class rate but will take longer to reach their destination.

### Sending Mail

If you have the correct postage, you can drop your mail into any blue mail box. These are found at many convenient locations including shopping centers, airports, street corners etc. The times of the next mail pickup are written on the inside of the lid of the mail box. This sign also indicates the location of the nearest mail box with later or more frequent pickup.

If you need to buy stamps or weigh your mail, go to the nearest post office. The addresses of each town's main post office is given in the text. In addition, larger towns have branch post offices and post office centers in some supermarkets and drugstores. For the address of the nearest office, call the main post office listed under 'Postal Service' in the 'US Government' section in the White Pages of the telephone directory.

Usually, post offices in main towns are open from 8:00 am to 5 pm Monday to Friday and 8 am to 3 pm on Saturday, but it all depends on the branch. The major cities have a 24-hour Express Mail service (at a higher cost) in the city's main post office.

### Receiving Mail

You can have mail sent to you care of General Delivery at any US post office that has its own zip (postal) code. Mail is usually held for 10 days before it's returned to the sender; you might request your correspondents to write 'hold for arrival' on their letters. Alternatively, have mail sent to the local representative of American Express or Thomas Cook, which provide mail service for their clients.

### Telephone

All phone numbers within the USA consist of a three-digit area code followed by a seven-digit local number. Oregon's area code is 503 and Idaho's is 208. Washington has three area codes: 206 covers the greater Seattle/Tacoma area, 360 covers the rest of the west side and 509 covers the east side. There's a map in Facts about Washington that outlines the boundaries.

If you are calling locally, just dial the seven-digit number. If you are calling long distance, dial 1 + the three-digit area code + the seven-digit number.

If you're calling from abroad, the international country code for the USA is '1'.

The 800 area code is designated for toll-free numbers within the USA and sometimes from Canada as well. Some can be called from anywhere in the USA, others are only used within the state. Those that are state specific are indicated in the text.

The 900 area code is designated for calls for which the caller pays at a premium rate. They have a reputation of being sleazy operations – a smorgasbord of phone sex at $2.99 a minute is one of many offerings.

Directory assistance can be reached locally by dialing 411. For directory assistance outside your area code, dial 1 + the three-digit area code of the place you want to call + 555-1212. For example, to obtain directory assistance for a toll-free number, dial 1 (800) 555-1212. Area codes for places outside the region are listed in telephone directories.

Many businesses use letters instead of numbers for their telephone numbers in an attempt to make them snappy and memorable. Sometimes it works, but sometimes it's difficult to read the letters on the dial pad. If you can't read the letters, here they are: 1 doesn't get any; 2 – ABC, 3 – DEF, 4 – GHI, 5 – JKL, 6 – MNO, 7 – PRS, 8 – TUV, 9 – WXY. Sorry no Qs or Zs.

**Rates** Local calls usually cost 25c at pay phones, but watch out for occasional private phones which may charge more. Many hotels (especially the more expensive ones) add a service charge of 50c to $1 for each local call made from a room phone and they also have hefty surcharges for long-distance calls. Public pay phones, which can be found in most lobbies, are always cheaper. You can pump in quarters, use a phone card, or make collect calls from pay phones. A new long-distance alternative is phone debit cards, which allow purchasers to pay in advance, with access through a 800 number. In amounts of $5, $10, $20 and $50, these are available in airports and from Western Union and some other sources.

When using phone credit cards, be aware of people watching you, especially in public places like airports. Thieves will memorize numbers and use them to make large numbers of international calls. Shield the telephone with your body when punching in your credit card number.

Long-distance rates vary depending on the destination and which telephone company you use – call the operator (0) for rates information. Don't ask the operator to put your call through, however, because operator-assisted calls are much more expensive than direct-dial calls. Generally, nights (11 pm to 8 am), all day Saturday and from 8 am to 5 pm Sunday are the cheapest times to call (60% discount). A 35% discount applies in the evenings from 5 to 11 pm Sunday to Friday. Daytime calls (8 am to 5 pm Monday to Friday) are full-price calls within the USA.

**International Calls** To make an international call direct, dial 011, then the country code, followed by the area code and the phone number. You may need to wait as long as 45 seconds for the ringing to start. International rates vary depending on the time of day and the destination. For example, the cheapest rates to London are between 6 pm and 7 am, while when calling Melbourne, the cheapest rates are from 3 am to 2 pm. Again, rates vary depending on the telephone company used and the destination. Call the operator (0) for rates. The first minute is always more expensive than the following extra minutes.

**Fax, Telegraph & Email**
Fax machines are easy to find in the USA, at shipping companies like Mail Boxes, Etc, photocopy services and hotel business service centers, but be prepared to pay high prices (over $1 a page). Telegraphs can be sent from Western Union (☎ (800) 325-6000). Email is quickly becoming a preferred method of communication; however, unless you have a laptop and modem that can be plugged into a telephone socket, it's difficult to get on-line. Hotel business service centers may provide connections, and trendy restaurants and cafes sometimes offer internet service as well.

## TIME

All of Washington, most of Oregon and northern Idaho are in the Pacific Time Zone. A small sliver of easternmost Oregon, containing Ontario and the southern half of Idaho are in the Mountain Time Zone. The Pacific Time Zone is eight hours behind Greenwich Mean Time, three hours behind New York City, in Eastern Time, and 17 hours ahead of Tokyo.

All Northwestern states observe the switch to daylight-saving time, which goes into effect from the first Sunday in April to the last Sunday in October.

## ELECTRICITY

In the USA voltage is 110 V and the plugs have two (flat) or three (two flat, one round) pins. Plugs with three pins don't fit into a two-hole socket, but adapters are easy to buy. Two-pin plugs, especially ones with equal dimensions, can easily slip out of the socket. Should this happen a quick remedy is to stretch the prongs apart a bit for a tighter fit.

## LAUNDRY

There are self-service, coin-operated laundry facilities in most towns of any size and in better campgrounds. Washing a load costs about $1 and drying it another $1. Coin-operated vending machines sell single-wash size packages of detergent but it's usually cheaper to pick up a small box at the supermarket. Some laundries have attendants who will wash, dry and fold your clothes for you for an additional charge. To find a laundry, look under 'Laundries' or 'Laundries – Self-Service' in the Yellow Pages of the telephone directory. Dry cleaners are also listed under 'Laundries' or 'Cleaners'.

## RECYCLING

Traveling in a car seems to generate large numbers of cans and bottles. If you'd like to save these for recycling, you'll find recycling centers in the larger towns. Materials accepted are usually plastic and glass bottles, aluminum and tin cans and newspapers. Some campgrounds and a few road-side rest areas also have recycling bins next to the trash bins so look out for those.

Perhaps better than recycling is to reduce your use of these products. Many gas stations and convenience stores sell large plastic insulated cups with lids which are inexpensive and ideal for hot and cold drinks. You can usually save a few cents by using your cup to buy drinks.

Despite the appearance of many large cities, littering is frowned upon by most Americans. Travelers need to respect the places they are visiting even though it may seem that some locals think it's OK to trash their territory. Some states have implemented anti-littering laws (which impose fines for violation) to try to curb the problem. When hiking and camping in the

---

### The Bottle Bill

In 1973, Oregon was the first state in the nation to pass a revolutionary law geared towards eliminating litter and promoting recycling. For every beer or soda purchased at a grocery store, an extra 5c deposit is charged for the container at the register. This 5c deposit is later returned when these plastic or glass bottles and aluminum cans are returned, or "redeemed" at the store. Beverage distributors pick up the cans and bottles from here, and take them to be recycled.

Stores will take back the cans and bottles of beverage brands they sell in their stores, and may refuse brands they don't carry or ones purchased in other states. Wine and liquor bottles are exempt from the bottle bill, as are certain juices and mineral waters. Check the labels to see if containers are redeemable.

Oregonians save and redeem their cans and bottles religiously, but to an out-of-state visitor, five cents may seem too petty to warrant an extra trip to the store. Whatever you do, don't throw redeemable cans and bottles away. Instead, leave empty cans and bottles near, but not in, a garbage can, where they will all but certainly be picked up by someone who needs a nickel. ■

wilderness, take out everything you bring in – this includes *any* kind of garbage you may create.

## WEIGHTS & MEASURES

Despite the evangelical exhortations of metric missionaries and concerted efforts on the part of federal authorities since the 1970s, Americans continue to resist the imposition of the metric system.

Distances are in feet (ft), yards (yds) and miles (m). Three feet equal one yard, which is .914 meters; 1760 yards or 5280 feet equal one mile. Dry weights are in ounces (oz), pounds (lbs) and tons (16 ounces are one pound; 2000 pounds are one ton), but liquid measures differ from dry measures. One pint equals 16 fluid ounces; two pints equal one quart, a common measure for liquids like milk (which is also sold in half gallons (two quarts) and gallons (four quarts). Gasoline is dispensed by the US gallon, which is about 20% less than the imperial gallon. Pints and quarts are also 20% less than imperial ones. The most significant exception to the use of Imperial measures is the wine industry, whose standard size is 700 ml, but the labels of canned and liquid supermarket foods usually list both imperial measures and their international equivalents. There is a conversion chart at the back of the book to make this all easier.

## BOOKS

There's a vast array of books written about the Pacific Northwest. Following are titles of general interest as well as titles specific to each state.

### History, Politics & Culture

Oddly, there isn't one single book currently in print that does a decent job of detailing Northwest history. History buffs are left to individual state histories; or look for *The Great Northwest* by O O Winther (Knopf, New York, 1955 and 1982) in a used book store or library. It's about the best book on the area, and very readable. *The Way to the Western Sea* by David Lavender (Doubleday, New York, 1988) is a compulsively

fascinating narrative recounting of the Lewis and Clark Expedition.

In *Stepping Westward*, Sally Tisdale (Holt, New York, 1991) tells her story of growing up in the Northwest, with insights into its culture. *The Good Rain* by Timothy Egan (Vintage Departures, New York, 1990) is an insightful discussion of the Northwest and its people by the local *New York Times* correspondent.

*Atomic Marbles & Branding Irons* by Harriet Baskas & Adam Woog (Sasquatch Books, Seattle, 1993) is a guide to museums and collections throughout the Northwest. *Festivals of the Pacific Northwest* by Kathy Kincade & Steve Rank (Landau Communications, San Francisco, 1990) lists special events of the region.

**Washington** *Exploring Washington's Past* by Ruth Kirk & Carmela Alexander (University of Washington Press, Seattle, 1990) is the single best traveler's guide to Washington history.

*A Guide to Architecture in Washington State* by Sally B Woodbridge & Roger Montgomery (University of Washington Press, Seattle, 1980) is unfortunately out of print, but anyone interested in architecture or the growth of cities in Washington should look for this in a used book store.

Early writing in Washington tended to be chronicles of pioneer days. In 1888 Arthur Denny, one of the founders of Seattle, wrote *Pioneer Days on Puget Sound* (Harriman, Seattle, 1908); James Swan, a colorful character whose life was later documented by Ivan Doig, wrote *The Northwest Coast* (Harper & Row, New York, 1969) and *Indians of Cape Flattery* (Smithsonian, Philadelphia, 1870) during the 1850s. *The Canoe and the Saddle* by Theodore Winthrop (Tickner & Fields, Boston, 1863) recounts a young man's trip across Washington in 1853.

**Oregon** *Roadside History of Oregon* by Bill Gulick (Mountain Press Publishing Co, Missoula, MT, 1991), is a good history-from-the-highway guide, though it is episodic in its coverage.

*The Balance So Rare: The Story of Oregon* by Terrance O'Donnell (Oregon Historical Society Press, Portland, OR, 1988), is, in an oddly limited field, the most recent catechistic history of the state.

*The Well-Traveled Casket* by Tom Nash & Twilo Scofield (University of Utah Press, Salt Lake City, UT, 1992), is a collection of folktales from Oregon communities, and a good source for regional history as well.

Oregon's Native American oral literary tradition has largely been lost. For a flavor of indigenous myths and stories, read *Coyote Was Going There* by Jarold Ramsey (University of Washington Press, Seattle, 1977).

Oregon's written literary history begins with journal keeping; journals and memoirs remain one of the state's major literary forms. The daily journals of Lewis and Clark, full of equally wild adventures and misspellings, are wonderful in their detail and candor. Bernard DeVoto's carefully edited *Journals of Lewis and Clark* (Houghton Mifflin Co, New York, 1953) makes for fascinating reading. For a narrative retelling of the Corps of Discovery's journey, turn to David Lavender's *The Way to the Western Sea* (Anchor Books, New York, 1988).

Journal-keeping was also part of the long trek made by tens of thousands along the Oregon Trail during the 1840s and 50s. Diaries kept by women along the trail provide an especially revealing look into the day-to-day life of travelers in the American West's greatest migration. *Women's Journals of the Westward Journey* edited by Lillian Schlissel (Schocken Books, New York, 1982) is a good compilation of these writings.

Memoirs of frontier childhood also form an important part of Oregon literature. *Cathlamet on the Columbia* by attorney Thomas Nelson Strong (Metropolitan Press, New York, 1936) is a vivid retelling of his pioneer upbringing, and also provides a picture of early Portland. Contemporary memoirists include Clyde Rice (*Heaven in the Eye* and *Night Freight*), and William Kittredge (*A Hole in the Sky*).

**Idaho** *Idaho: A Guide in Word & Picture* by the WPA Federal Writers' Project (Oxford University Press, New York, 1950), written by iconic Depression-era writer Vardus Fisher, is now hard to find. It manages to convey a sense of rough and tumble Idaho in the not too distant past. *River of No Return* by Johnny Carrey & Cort Conley (Backeddy Books, Cambridge, ID, 1978) is a history of settlement in the Salmon River valley. *Idaho for the Curious* by Cort Conley (Backeddy Books, Cambridge, ID, 1982) is the single best guide to history of Idaho.

## Natural History

In addition to the following books, Audubon Society and Peterson Field Guides are available to many specialized areas of natural history such as butterflies, birds of prey and mushrooms.

*The Sierra Club Guide to the Natural Areas of Oregon & Washington* by John & Jane Greverus Perry (Sierra Club Books, San Francisco, 1983) contains species lists and good natural history for dozens of sites.

The Audubon Society's guide to *Western Forests* (Alfred A Knopf, New York, 1985) and *A Field Guide to the Cascades & Olympics* (The Mountaineers, Seattle, 1983), are both by Stephen R Whitney. The latter is a good one-volume guide to the region's plant and wildlife. *Cascade-Olympic Natural History* by Daniel Matthews (Raven Press, Portland, OR, 1984) is the single best guide to plants and wildlife on the western slopes of Washington and Oregon.

Bird watchers might want to pick up a copy of *Familiar Birds of the Northwest* by Harry B Nehls (Portland Audubon Society, Portland, OR,1981). Flower enthusiasts should check out *Wayside Wildflowers of the Pacific Northwest* by Dr Dee Strickler (The Flower Press, Columbia Falls, MT, 1993) and *Sagebrush Country: A Wildflower Sanctuary* by Ronald J Taylor (Mountain Press Publishing Co, Missoula, MT, 1993).

Also of interest are *A Waterfall Lover's Guide to the Pacific Northwest* by Gregory

A Plumb (The Mountaineers, Seattle, 1989) and *Garden Touring in the Pacific Northwest* by Jan Kowlaczewski Whitner (Alaska Northwest Books, Anchorage, AK, 1993).

**Washington** *Washington Wildlife Viewing Guide* by Joe La Tourrette (Falcon Press, Billings MT 1992) is a guide to the designated wildlife-viewing sites in Washington. *Roadside Geology of Washington* by David D Alt and Donald W Hyndman (Mountain Press Publishing Co, Missoula, MT, 1984) takes the geology of the state road by road.

*Ferry Boat Field Guide to Puget Sound* by Robert Steelquist (American Geologic Publishing, Helena, MT, 1989) is a naturalist's guide to the wildlife and ecology of the Puget Sound, written to accompany various ferry crossings.

**Oregon** *Oregon Wildlife Viewing Guide* (Defenders of Wildlife, Lake Oswego, OR), is a guide to designated wildlife-viewing areas throughout the state. *The Birder's Guide to Oregon* by Joseph E Evanich, Jr (Portland Audubon Society, Portland, OR,1990) contains information for serious birders.

*Geology of Oregon* by Elizabeth L Orr, William N Orr & Ewart M Baldwin (Kendall/Hunt, Dubuque, IA, 1964 and 1992) is the single best book on Oregon's curious geologic story. *Roadside Geology of Oregon* by David D Alt and Donald W Hyndman (Mountain Press Publishing Co, Missoula, MT, 1978) takes you road by road, rock by rock, across Oregon.

**Idaho** *Roadside Geology of Idaho* by David D Alt & Donald W Hyndman (Mountain Press Publishing Co, Missoula, MT, 1989) is a guide to the complex geology of the Gem State.

## Indigenous Peoples

*A Guide to the Indian Tribes of the Pacific Northwest* (University of Oklahoma Press, Norman, OK, 1986) and *Indians of the Pacific Northwest* (University of Oklahoma Press, Norman, OK, 1981) by Robert H Ruby & John A Brown are both superla-

tive. The first is a tribe-by-tribe encyclopedia of the region's Native Americans, the second an overview of Northwest Indian history and culture. Also of interest is *Indian Rock Art of the Columbia Plateau* by James D Keyser (University of Washington Press, Seattle, 1992).

**Oregon** *Coyote Was Going There: Indian Literature of the Oregon Country* edited by Jarold Ramsey (University of Washington Press, Seattle, 1977) is a compilation of tales from Oregon Native American storytellers.

**Idaho** *Idaho Indians: Tribal Histories* by the Native American Committee, Idaho Centennial Commission (Idaho Museum of Natural History, Pocatello, ID,1990) is written for a youthful audience, but is still a good brief source of information on regional Native America.

## Fiction

A good place to start reading about the Northwest is in the contemporary fiction of Tom Robbins and Ken Kesey. Otherwise the list of fiction about the Northwest or by local authors and writers is too massive to include here.Here are a some good ideas to start you off.

*Astoria* by Washington Irving, found in many editions in used book stores and libraries, is a classic of frontier travel to the Northwest, written in 1836. *Honey in the Horn* by H L Davis (Harper & Bros, New York, 1935), again in many editions, tells the gritty story of Oregon pioneer farmers, and won the Pulitzer Prize in 1936. *Northwest Passage* edited by Bruce Barcott (Sasquatch Books, Seattle, 1994) and *Edge Walking on the Western Rim* edited by Sherman Alexie & Tom Spanbauer (Sasquatch Books, Seattle 1994) are both anthologies of modern Northwest writers.

**Washington** One of the most prolific Washington writers of the early 20th century was Archie Binns; of his many novels, *The Land is Bright* (Scribners & Sons, New York, 1939) – the story of an

Oregon Trail family – is still read today. James Stevens, who worked as a journalist, compiled many tales of Paul Bunyan that he had heard in his timber-camp childhood and published them in his book *Paul Bunyan* (Knopf, New York, 1925). Betty McDonald recounted adventures of running a poultry fam in Washington in her successful comic novel *The Egg and I* (Lippincott, Philadelphia, 1946). Critic and novelist Mary McCarthy was born and raised in Seattle, though she conducted her disputatious career from New York and Paris.

In the 1960s and 70s, Washington attracted a number of countercultural writers. The most famous of these is Tom Robbins, whose books *(Another Roadside Attraction* and *Even Cowgirls Get the Blues)* became the scripture for a generation. Poet Theodore Roethke taught for years at the University of Washington, and, with Washington native Richard Hugo, cast a profound influence over Northwest poetry. Raymond Carver, the short story master whose books include *Can You Please Be Quiet Please*, lived on the Olympic Peninsula; his wife Tess Gallagher is also a novelist and poet whose books include *Instructions for the Double*.

Ivan Doig, many of whose books concern his boyhood youth in Montana, also writes of his new Washington home in *The Sea Runners*. In *Winter Brothers* (Harcourt, Brace, Jovanovich, San Diego, CA, 1980), Doig examines the diaries of early Washington writer James Swan, who lived among the Makah on the tip of the Olympic Peninsula. Noted travel writer Jonathan Raban, also a new emigrant to Washington, has written such books as *Coasting* and *Huntin' Mister Heartbreak*. Annie Dillard, essayist and novelist, wrote about the Northwest in *The Living* (Harper Collins, New York, 1992).

Sherman Alexie writes from a Native American perspective. His book *The Lone Ranger and Tonto Fistfight in Heaven* (Atlantic Monthly Press, New York, 1993) is a collection of stories about reservation life. David Gutterson writes about the Puget Sound area and the internment of Japanese Americans during WW II in *Snow Falling on Cedars* (Harcourt, Brace, Jovanovich, San Diego, CA, 1994).

The misty environ of western Washington is a fecund habitat for mystery writers. Dashiell Hammett once lived in the state, while noted writers J A Jance, Earl Emerson and Frederick D Huebner currently also live here. Another peculiar phenomenon is the number of cartoonists who have lived in Washington. Linda Berry *(Ernie Pook's Comeek)* and Matt Groening (creator of *The Simpsons)* were students together at Olympia's Evergreen State College. Gary Larson, whose *Far Side* animal antics have netted international fame and great fortune, lives in Seattle.

**Oregon** Oregon history was a rich vein to mine for early novelists. *Bridge of the Gods*, by Frederic Homer Balch (Binford & Mart, Portland, OR, 1965) was an early bestseller; although its style is dated, this novel of early Indian life along the Columbia was historically accurate. Don Berry's *Trask* (Comstock Editions, Inc, Sausalito, CA, 1960) tells the story of an early Oregon trapper and his life on the land. *Jump Off Creek* by Molly Glass (Houghton Mifflin Co, Boston, 1989) is the novelization of the diaries of a women homesteader in Northeastern Oregon.

Quite a number of noted contemporary writers live in Oregon. Ken Kesey, whose *One Flew Over the Cuckoo's Nest* (Viking, New York, 1962) became a textbook of 1960s nonconformity, is a native Oregonian. His earlier novel, *Sometimes a Great Notion* captures the brio of rural life in a small logging community. Craig Lesley's *Winterkill* (Dell Publishing, New York, 1984) is the story of an eastern Oregon Native American rodeo rider down on his luck and looking to get out. David Duncan *(The River Why* and *The Brothers K)*, Katherine Dunn *(Geek Love)*, and Tom Spanbauer *(The Man Who Fell in Love With the Moon)* are highly acclaimed younger novelists.

Oregon seems to attract novelists whose

bent is toward science fiction and fantasy. Ursula K LeGuin *(The Left Hand of God)*, Jean Auel *(Clan of the Cave Bear)* and Ann McCaffrey *(Dragon Quest)* all live in the state.

## Travel Guides

*The Smithsonian Guide to Historic America: The Pacific States* by William Bryant Logan & Susan Ochshorn (Stewart, Tabori & Chang, New York, 1989) is a good supplement with a focus on architectural history. *Driving the Pacific Coast in Oregon and Washington* by Kenn Oberrecht (The Globe Pequot Press, Old Saybrook, CT, 1990) is a good resource for road-trippers.

*The Traveler's Guide to the Oregon Trail* by Julie Fanselow (Falcon Press, Helena, MT, 1992), follows the Oregon Trail across the Western USA.

*Northwest Best Places* by David Brewster & Stephanie Irving (Sasquatch Books, Seattle) lists the best in eats and lodgings throughout the region, and is updated annually. See also *Where to Stay & Play Along the Pacific Coast* by Wendy Holman & Sheila K Nolan (Northwest Beachcomber, Seattle, 1990), an exhaustive resource for motels along the entire Pacific Coast, including northern California and BC. Other titles to help you find accomodations are *Northwest Cheap Sleeps* by Stephanie Irving (Sasquatch Books, Seattle, 1992), *The Best in Tent Camping: Washington & Oregon* by Jeanne Pyle (Menasha Ridge Press, Birmingham, AL), and *Pacific Northwest Camping* by Tom Stienstra (Foghorn Press, San Francisco, 1992).

**Washington** If you want to carry around another general travel guide, *Washington Discovery Guide* by Don & Betty Martin (Pine Cone Press, Columbia, CA, 1994) is one of the best. *Traveler's Affordable Accommodations: Washington State* by Elaine Ingle (Cottage Computer Publishing, Wenatchee, WA, 1994) is a great reference book on inexpensive lodgings across the state.

*Seattle Best Places* by Stephanie Irving (Sasquatch Books, Seattle, 1993), updated regularly, is the last word on all things Seattle. If you plan to spend any time in Seattle, the small-scale *Insight Guides: Seattle* edited by John Wilcock (APA Publications, Singapore, 1993) is possibly the best guide to the city and its people. *The Pocket Guide to Seattle* by Duse McLean (Thistle Press, Bellevue, WA, 1994) is absolutely packed with just the right information. Find Seattle's meal deals with the in-the-know *Seattle Cheap Eats* edited by Kathryn Robinson & Stephanie Irving (Sasquatch Books, Seattle, 1993).

*The Essential San Juan Islands Guide* by Marge & Tel Mueller (JASI, Medina, WA, 1994) is the authoritative guide to the San Juans.

**Oregon** *Oregon* by Judy Jewell (Compass American Guides, Oakland, CA, 1994) combines wonderful photos and intelligent text for one of Oregon's most revealing portraits. *Oregon Scenic Drives* by Tom Barr (Falcon Press, Helena, MT, 1993) is a motorists' guide to the backroads of a scenic state. *Oregon's Coast: A Guide to the Best Family Attractions from Astoria to Brookings* by David & Carolyn Gabble (Johnston Associates International, Medina, WA, 1992) is a good activity guide for those focused on the coast.

*Oregon's Big Country: A Portrait of Southeastern Oregon* by Raymond R Hatton (Maverick Publications, Bend, OR, 1988), is the best history and rumination on remote and wondrous southeastern Oregon. *Atlas of Oregon Lakes* by Daniel M Johnson, Richard R Petersen, D Richard Lycan, James W Sweet, Mark E Neuhaus & Andrew L Schaedel (Oregon State University Press, Corvallis, OR) tells you everything about the state's many lakes.

**Idaho** For further exploration of Idaho, try *Idaho Off-road* by Tony Huegel (The Post Co, Idaho Falls, ID, 1993), a guide to backroad explorations, with good maps. *Idaho for the Hungry: Home Cookin' Away From Home* by Jenna Gaston (Writers of the

Purple Sage, Boise, 1991), is a guide to homestyle eateries in Idaho.

## Reference
The *Pocket Doctor* by Dr Stephen Bez-ruchka, (Mountaineers, Seattle, 1992) is a good general medical guide for travelers, written by a Seattle doctor. *Medicine for Mountaineering & Other Wilderness Activities* edited by Dr Wilkerson (Mountaineers, Seattle, 1992) is a good resource if you're planning extensive outdoor recreation.

**Washington** The *Washington State Yearbook* edited by Richard & Charity Yates (Public Sector Information, Eugene, OR, 1994), gives tons of information here for the compulsive fact-checker. *Washington State Place Names* by James W Phillips (University of Washington Press, Seattle, 1971) is a good resource on names and pronunciation, including derivations of Washington's many Native American place names.

**Oregon** Why is Murderer's Creek called Murderer's Creek? Find out in *Oregon Geographic Names* by Lewis A McArthur (Oregon Historical Society Press, Portland, 1992), an amazingly hefty guide to place names; it's also a solid guide to regional history. *Oregon Blue Book* compiled and published by the Secretary of State, is the bible of state government and institutions; a great resource for the curious.

**Idaho** *Idaho Blue Book*, compiled by Secretary of State Pete T Cenarrusa (State of Idaho), is the almanac of Idaho State government.

## MAPS
Maps of excellent quality are available throughout the USA. Depending on your interests, and the way in which you intend to travel, there are several different sources.

### Highway Maps
The AAA issues the most comprehensive and dependable highway maps, which are free with AAA membership (see Useful Organizations above). These range from national, regional and state maps to very detailed maps of cities, counties, and even relatively small towns; AAA also prepares suggested travel routes for its members, and issues regional TourBooks and Camp-Books which contain equally useful maps, also free of charge for AAA members.

### Topographic Maps
The US Geological Survey (USGS), an agency of the federal Department of the Interior, publishes very detailed topographic maps of the entire country, at different scales up to 1:250,000. Maps at 1:62,500, or approximately 1 inch=1 mile, are ideal for backcountry hiking and backpacking. The USGS has begun to produce maps on a metric scale of 1:100,000 which, with contour intervals of 50 meters, are very poor at portraying mountainous topography. Fortunately, some private cartographers are producing updated versions of old USGS maps at 1:62,500, whose 80-foot contours give hikers a much clearer notion of mountain terrain.

Many bookstores and outdoor equipment specialists carry a wide selection of topographic maps. The USGS has its nationwide distribution office in Denver, CO (☎ (303) 236-7477); though they can't take orders over the phone, they will send out a free catalogue and a list of stores that sell their maps. Another good resource is Washington's Metsker Maps (☎ (206) 623-8747), with offices in Seattle, Tacoma and Bellevue. They sell USGS maps for Washington, Idaho and most of Oregon, and do mail order.

Washington's Department of Transportation puts out a free map that's available from any visitors center in the state. Pick up several, as the paper quality is poor, and the map falls apart in no time.

The only map you'll need for most uses is the Official Highway Map of Oregon from the Oregon Department of Transportation. This free map is available form any visitors information center or by calling the Oregon Tourism Division (☎ (800) 547-7842). There is also a specialized map of campsites for campers.

Unfortunately, since the midterm Congressional elections of 1994, the Republican leadership has astonishingly proposed abolishing what, for more than a century, has been one of the most efficient and productive of all government agencies. In addition to surveying the countryside and producing maps, the USGS is responsible for primary research into earthquakes and other natural phenomena, and its abolition would be a shortsighted blunder.

### Atlases

Visitors spending a significant amount of time in the region should try to acquire the appropriate state volume of the DeLorme Mapping series of atlases and gazeteers, which contain detailed topographic and highway maps at a scale of 1:250,000 as well as very helpful listings of campgrounds, historic sites, parks, natural features and even scenic drives. Readily available in good bookstores, these are especially useful off the main highways and cost about $20 each.

## MEDIA

The USA is among the most literate countries in the world, supporting a wide spectrum of newspapers, magazines and book publishers, both nationally and regionally.

Radio and TV also support a wide variety of news programs, though most of the reporting tends to center on the USA.

### Newspapers & Magazines

There are over 1500 daily newspapers published in the USA, with a combined circulation of about 60 million. The newspaper with the highest circulation is the *Wall Street Journal* followed by *USA Today*, *New York Times* and *Los Angeles Times*, which are all available in major cities.

### Radio & TV

All rental cars have car radios and travelers can choose from hundreds of stations. Most stations have a range of less than 100 miles, and in and near major cities scores of stations crowd the airwaves with a wide variety of music and entertainment. In rural areas, be prepared for a predominance of country & western music, local news and 'talk radio'.

National Public Radio (NPR) features a more level-headed approach to discussion, music and sophisticated news on the FM band. NPR's *Morning Edition* and its afternoon *All Things Considered* are the most worthwhile news programs, but FM signals, unfortunately, have limited range and the irregular terrain of the Rockies often disrupts their signal.

All the major TV networks have affiliated stations throughout the USA. These include ABC, CBS, NBC, FOX and PBS. Cable News Network (CNN), a cable channel, provides continuous news coverage.

## PHOTOGRAPHY & VIDEO

Print film for amateur photography is widely available at supermarkets and discount drugstores throughout the Pacific Northwest. Color print film tolerates a wide variety of conditions but lacks the resolution of slide film. Like B&W film, the availability of slide film outside of major cities is rare or at inflated prices when found.

Kodachrome slide film, which portrays reds and nearby spectrum colors exceptionally well, is ideal for desert scenery, but Fujichrome is much cheaper and by no means inferior, especially for forest greens. For certain subjects, like Native American petroglyphs, carry high-speed (400 ASA) film to avoid using flash, which is not permitted at these sites.

Film can be affected by excessive heat; don't leave your camera and film in the car on a hot summer's day.

It's worth carrying a spare battery for your camera to avoid disappointment when your camera dies in the middle of nowhere. If you're buying a new camera for your trip do so several weeks before you leave, practice using it and have a few rolls developed.

Drugstores are a good place to get your film cheaply processed. If it's dropped off by noon, you can usually pick it up the next day. A roll of 100 ASA 35 mm color film with 24 exposures will cost about $6 to get processed.

If you want your pictures right away, you can find one-hour processing services in the Yellow Pages under 'Photo Processing'. The prices tend to creep up to the $11 scale, so be prepared to pay dearly. Many one-hour photo finishers operate in the larger cities, and a few can be found near tourist attractions.

### Technique
When the sun is high in the sky, photographs tend to emphasize shadows and wash out highlights. It's best to take photos during the early morning and the late afternoon hours when light is softer. This is especially true of landscape photography. Always protect camera lenses with a haze or ultraviolet (UV) filter. At high altitudes, a UV filmay not adequately prevent washed-out photos; a polarized filter can correct this problem and, incidentally, dramatically emphasizes cloud formations in mountain and plains landscapes.

### Airport Security
All passengers on flights have to pass their luggage through X-ray machines. Technology as it is today doesn't jeopardize lower speed film, but it's best to carry film and cameras with you and ask the X-ray inspector to visually check your camera and film.

### Video Systems
Overseas visitors who are thinking of purchasing videos should remember that the USA uses the National Television System Committee (NTSC) color TV standard, which is not compatible with other standards (Phase Alternative Line or PAL; Système Electronique Couleur avec Mémoire or SECAM) used in Africa, Europe, Asia and Australasia unless converted. It's best to keep those seemingly cheap movie purchases on hold until you get home.

## HEALTH
Generally speaking, the USA is a healthy place to visit. There are no prevalent diseases or risks associated with traveling here, and the country is well served by hospitals. However, because of the high cost of health care, international travelers should take out comprehensive travel insurance before they leave. If you're from a country with socialized medicine, you should find out what you'll need to do in order to be reimbursed for out-of-pocket money you may spend for health care in the USA.

Also, if you should fall ill in the USA, avoid going to emergency rooms. Although these are often the easiest places to go for treatment, they are also incredibly expensive. Many city hospitals have 'urgent care clinics', which are designed to deal with walk-in clients with less than catastrophic injuries and illnesses. You'll pay a lot less for treatment at these clinics. If you know someone in the area, consider asking them to ring their doctor: often private doctors are willing to examine foreign visitors as a courtesy to their regular patients, but a fee, often around $100 may still be applied.

### Travel Health Guides
There are a number of books on travel health, including the following:

*Staying Healthy in Asia, Africa & Latin America*, Dick Schroeder (Chico: Moon Publications, 1994), though not specifically oriented toward North American travel, this is probably the best all-round guide. It's compact but very detailed and well organized.

*Travelers' Health*, Dr Richard Dawood (New York: Random House, 1994), is comprehensive, easy to read, authoritative and highly recommended, but rather large to lug around.

*Where There is No Doctor*, David Werner (Macmillan, 1994), is a very detailed guide, more suited to those working in undeveloped countries than to travelers.

*Travel with Children*, Maureen Wheeler (Lonely Planet Publications, 1995), offers basic advice on travel health for younger children.

## Predeparture Preparations

Make sure you're healthy before you start traveling. If you are embarking on a long trip make sure your teeth are OK; there are lots of places where a visit to the dentist would be the last thing you'd want.

If you wear glasses take a spare pair and your prescription. Losing your glasses can be a real problem, although in many places you can get new spectacles made up quickly, cheaply and competently.If you require a particular medication take an adequate supply, as it may be very expensive or unavailable locally. Take the prescription or, better still, part of the packaging showing the generic rather than the brand name (which may be locally unavailable), as it will make getting replacements easier. It's a wise idea to have a legible prescription with you to show you legally use the medication – many prescriptions sold over the counter in other countries require a prescription in the USA.

## Health Insurance

A travel insurance policy to cover theft, loss and medical problems is a good idea, especially in the USA, where some hospitals will refuse care without evidence of insurance. There are a wide variety of policies and your travel agent will have recommendations. International student travel policies handled by STA Travel or other student travel organizations are usually good value. Some policies offer lower and higher medical expenses options, but the higher one is chiefly for countries like the USA with extremely high medical costs. Check the small print.

- Some policies specifically exclude 'dangerous activities' like scuba diving, motorcycling and even trekking. If these activities are on your agenda avoid this sort of policy.
- You may prefer a policy which pays doctors or hospitals directly, rather than your having to pay first and claim later. If you have to claim later, keep all documentation. Some policies ask you to call back (reverse charges) to a center in your home country for an immediate assessment of your problem.

- Check whether the policy covers ambulance fees or an emergency flight home. If you have to stretch out you will need two seats and somebody has to pay for it!

## Medical Kit

It's useful to carry a small, straightforward medical kit. This should include:

- Aspirin, acetaminophen or panadol, for pain or fever
- Antihistamine (such as Benadryl), which is useful as a decongestant for colds, and to ease the itch from allergies, insect bites or stings or to help prevent motion sickness
- Antibiotics, which are useful for traveling off the beaten track, but they must be prescribed and you should carry the prescription with you
- Kaolin preparation (Pepto-Bismol), Immodium or Lomotil, for stomach upsets
- Rehydration mixture, to treat severe diarrhea, which is particularly important if you're traveling with children
- Antiseptic, mercurochrome and antibiotic powder or similar 'dry' spray, for cuts and grazes
- Calamine lotion, to ease irritation from bites or stings
- Bandages, for minor injuries
- Scissors, tweezers and a thermometer (airlines prohibit mercury thermometers)
- Insect repellent, sun-screen lotion, chapstick and water purification tablets.

## Note

Antibiotics are specific to the infections they can treat. Ideally they should be administered only under medical supervision and never taken indiscriminately. Take only the recommended dose at the prescribed intervals and continue using it for the prescribed period, even if symptoms disappear earlier. Stop immediately if there are any serious reactions and don't use the antibiotic at all if you are unsure if you have the correct one.

## Immunizations

Vaccinations provide protection against diseases you might meet along the way. For some countries no immunizations are necessary, but the further off the beaten track you go the more necessary it is to take precautions.

It is important to understand the distinction between vaccines recommended for travel in certain areas and those required by law. Essentially the number of vaccines subject to international health regulations has been dramatically reduced over the last 10 years. Currently yellow fever is the only vaccine subject to international health regulations. Vaccination as an entry requirement is usually only enforced when coming from an infected area.

On the other hand a number of vaccines are recommended for travel in certain areas. These may not be required by law but are recommended for your own personal protection. All vaccinations should be recorded on an International Health Certificate, which is available from your physician or government health department.

Plan ahead for getting your vaccinations: some of them require an initial shot followed by a booster, while some vaccinations should not be given together. It is recommended you seek medical advice at least six weeks prior to travel.

Most travelers from Western countries will have been immunized against various diseases during childhood but your doctor may still recommend booster shots against measles or polio, diseases still prevalent in many developing countries. The period of protection offered by vaccinations differs widely and some are contraindicated if you are pregnant.

In some countries immunizations are available from airport or government health centres. Travel agents or airline offices will tell you where. Vaccinations include:

*Smallpox* Smallpox has now been wiped out worldwide, so immunization is no longer necessary.

*Tetanus & Diphtheria* Boosters are necessary every 10 years and protection is highly recommended.

*Hepatitis A* The most common travel-acquired illness which can be prevented by vaccination. Protection can be provided in two ways – either with the antibody gamma globulin or with a new vaccine called Havrix, which provides long term immunity (possibly more than 10 years) after an initial course of two injections and a booster at one year. It may be more expensive than gamma globulin but certainly has many advantages, including length of protection and ease of administration. It is important to know that as a vaccine it will take about three weeks to provide satisfactory protection – hence the need for careful planning prior to travel.

Gamma globulin is not a vaccination but a ready-made antibody which has proven very successful in reducing the chances of hepatitis infection. Because it may interfere with the development of immunity, it should not be given until at least 10 days after administration of the last vaccine needed; it should also be given as close as possible to departure because it is at its most effective in the first few weeks after administration and the effectiveness tapers off gradually between three and six months.

## Basic Rules

Care in what you eat and drink is the most important health rule; stomach upsets are the most likely travel health problem (between 30% and 50% of travelers in a two-week stay experience this) but the majority of these upsets will be relatively minor. Don't become paranoid; trying the local food is part of the experience of travel, after all.

**Water** Bottled drinking water, both carbonated and non-carbonated, is now widely available in the USA.

*Water Purification* The simplest way of purifying water is to boil it thoroughly – vigorous boiling for ten minutes should be satisfactory even at a high altitude (where water boils at a lower temperature and germs are less likely to be killed).

Simple filtering will not remove all dangerous organisms, so if you cannot boil water it should be treated chemically. Chlorine tablets (Puritabs, Steritabs or other brand names) will kill many but not all pathogens, including giardia and amebic cysts. Iodine is very effective in purifying water and is available in tablet form (such as Potable Aqua), but follow the directions carefully – too much iodine can be harmful.

If you can't find tablets, tincture of iodine (2%) or iodine crystals can be used. Four drops of tincture of iodine per liter or quart of clear water is the recommended dosage; let the treated water stand for 20 to 30 minutes before drinking. Iodine crystals can also be used to purify water, but this is a more complicated process, as you must first prepare a saturated iodine solution (iodine loses its effectiveness if exposed to air or damp, so keep it in a tightly sealed container). Flavored powder will disguise the taste of treated water and is a good idea if traveling with children.

**Food** If a place looks clean and well run and if the vendor also looks clean and healthy, then the food is probably safe. In general, places that are packed with travellers or locals will be fine, while empty restaurants are questionable.

*Nutrition* If your food is poor or limited in availability, if you're travelling hard and fast and therefore missing meals, or if you simply lose your appetite, you can soon start to lose weight and place your health at risk.

Make sure your diet is well balanced. Eggs, tofu, beans, lentils and nuts are all safe ways to get protein. Fruit you can peel (bananas, oranges or mandarins for example) is always safe and a good source of vitamins. Try to eat plenty of grains and bread. Remember that although food is generally safer if it is cooked well, over-cooked food loses much of its nutritional value. If your diet isn't well balanced or if your food intake is insufficient, it's a good idea to take vitamin and iron pills.

In hot climates make sure you drink enough – don't rely on feeling thirsty to indicate when you should drink. Not needing to urinate or very dark yellow urine is a danger sign. Always carry a water bottle with you on long trips. Excessive sweating can lead to loss of salt and therefore muscle cramping. Salt tablets are not a good idea as a preventative, but in places

where salt is not used much adding salt to food can help.

**Everyday Health**
Normal body temperature is 98.6°F or 37°C; more than 2°C or 4°F higher indicates a 'high' fever. The normal adult pulse rate is 60 to 80 per minute (children 80 to 100, babies 100 to 140). You should know how to take a temperature and a pulse rate.

Respiration (breathing) rate is also an indicator of illness. Count the number of breaths per minute: between 12 and 20 is normal for adults and older children (up to 30 for younger children, 40 for babies). People with a high fever or serious respiratory illness (like pneumonia) breathe more quickly than normal. More than 40 shallow breaths a minute usually means pneumonia.

**Medical Problems & Treatment**
Potential medical problems can be broken down into several areas. Firstly there are the problems caused by extremes of temperature, altitude or motion. Then there are diseases and illnesses caused through poor environmental sanitation, insect bites or stings, and animal or human contact. Simple cuts, bites and scratches can also cause problems.

Self-diagnosis and treatment can be risky, so wherever possible seek qualified help. Although we do give drug dosages in this section, they are for emergency use only. Medical advice should be sought where possible before administering any drugs. An embassy or consulate can usually recommend a good place to go for such advice.

**Climatic & Geographical Ailments**
**Sunburn** In the desert or at high altitude you can get sunburned surprisingly quickly, even through cloud. Use a sunscreen and take extra care to cover areas not normally exposed to sun. A hat provides added protection, and you should also use zinc cream or some other barrier cream for your nose and lips. Calamine lotion is good for mild sunburn.

**Heat Exhaustion** Dehydration or salt deficiency can cause heat exhaustion. Take time to acclimatize to high temperatures and make sure that you get enough liquids. Salt deficiency is characterized by fatigue, lethargy, headaches, giddiness and muscle cramps. Salt tablets may help. Vomiting or diarrhea can also deplete your liquid and salt levels. Anhydrotic heat exhaustion, caused by the inability to sweat, is quite rare. Unlike the other forms of heat exhaustion it is likely to strike people who have been in a hot climate for some time, rather than newcomers.

**Heat Stroke** Long, continuous periods of exposure to high temperatures can leave you vulnerable to this serious, sometimes fatal, condition, which occurs when the body's heat-regulating mechanism breaks down and body temperature rises to dangerous levels. Avoid excessive alcohol intake or strenuous activity when you first arrive in a hot climate.

Symptoms include feeling unwell, lack of perspiration, and a high body temperature of 102°F to 105° F (39°C to 41°C). Hospitalization is essential for extreme cases, but meanwhile get out of the sun, remove clothing, cover with a wet sheet or towel, and fan continually.

**Hypothermia** Changeable weather at high altitudes can leave you vulnerable to exposure: after dark, temperatures in the mountains or desert can drop from balmy to below freezing, while a sudden soaking and high winds can lower your body temperature too rapidly. If possible, avoid traveling alone; partners are more likely to avoid hypothermia successfully. If you must travel alone, especially when hiking, be sure someone knows your route and when you expect to return.

Seek shelter when bad weather is unavoidable. Woolen clothing and synthetics, which retain warmth even when wet, are superior to cottons. A quality sleeping bag is a worthwhile investment, although goose down loses much of its insulating qualities when wet. Carry high-energy,

easily digestible snacks like chocolate or dried fruit.

Get hypothermia victims out of the wind or rain, remove their clothing if it's wet and replace it with dry, warm clothing. Give them hot liquids – not alcohol – and high-calorie, easily digestible food. In advanced stages it may be necessary to place victims in warm sleeping bags and get in with them. Do not rub victims but place them near a fire or, if possible, in a warm (not hot) bath.

**Fungal Infections** Fungal infections, which occur with greater frequency in hot weather, are most likely to occur on the scalp, between the toes or fingers (athlete's foot), in the groin (jock itch or crotch rot) and on the body (ringworm). You get ringworm (which is a fungal infection, not a worm) from infected animals or by walking on damp areas, like shower floors.

To prevent fungal infections wear loose, comfortable clothes, avoid artificial fibres, wash frequently and dry carefully. If you do get an infection, wash the infected area daily with a disinfectant or medicated soap and water, and rinse and dry well. Apply an antifungal powder and try to expose the infected area to air or sunlight as much as possible, and wash all towels and underwear in hot water as well as changing them often.

**Altitude Sickness** Acute Mountain Sickness (AMS) occurs at high altitude and can be fatal. In the thinner atmosphere of the high mountains, lack of oxygen causes many individuals to suffer headaches, nausea, shortness of breath, physical weakness and other symptoms which can lead to very serious consequences, especially if combined with heat exhaustion, sunburn or hypothermia. Most people recover within a few hours or days. If the symptoms persist it is imperative to descend to lower elevations. For mild cases, everyday painkillers such as aspirin will relieve symptoms until the body adapts. Avoid smoking, drinking alcohol, eating heavily or exercising strenuously.

There is no hard and fast rule as to how high is too high: AMS has been fatal at altitudes of 10,000 ft, although it is much more common above 11,500 ft. It is always wise to sleep at a lower altitude than the greatest height reached during the day. A number of other measures can prevent or minimize AMS:

• Ascend slowly – take frequent rest days, spending two to three nights for each climb of 3000 ft (1000 metros). If you reach a high altitude by trekking, acclimatization takes place gradually and you are less likely to be affected than if you fly direct.
• Drink extra fluids. The mountain air is dry and cold and you lose moisture as you breathe.
• Eat light, high-carbohydrate meals for more energy.
• Avoid alcohol, which may increase the risk of dehydration.
• Avoid sedatives.

**Motion Sickness** Eating lightly before and during a trip will reduce the chances of motion sickness. If you are prone to motion sickness, try to find a place that minimizes disturbance, for example, near the wing on aircraft, near the center on buses. Fresh air usually helps, while reading or cigarette smoke doesn't. Commercial anti-motion sickness preparations, which can cause drowsiness, have to be taken before the trip commences; when you're feeling sick it's too late. Ginger, a natural preventative, is available in capsule form.

**Jet Lag** Jet lag is experienced when a person travels by air across more than three time zones (each time zone usually represents a one-hour time difference). It occurs because many of the functions of the human body (such as temperature, pulse rate and emptying of the bladder and bowels) are regulated by internal 24-hour cycles called circadian rhythms. When we travel long distances rapidly, our bodies take time to adjust to the 'new time' of our destination, and we may experience fatigue, disorientation, insomnia, anxiety, impaired concentration and loss of appetite. These effects will usually be gone

within three days of arrival, but there are ways of minimizing the impact of jet lag:

• Rest for a couple of days prior to departure; try to avoid late nights and last-minute dashes for traveler's checks, passport etc.
• Try to select flight schedules that minimize sleep deprivation; arriving late in the day means you can go to sleep soon after you arrive. For very long flights, try to organize a stopover.
• Avoid excessive eating (which bloats the stomach) and alcohol (which causes dehydration) during the flight. Instead, drink plenty of noncarbonated, nonalcoholic drinks such as fruit juice or water.
• Avoid smoking, as this reduces the amount of oxygen in the airplane cabin even further and causes greater fatigue.
• Make yourself comfortable by wearing loose-fitting clothes and perhaps bringing an eye mask and ear plugs to help you sleep.

## Infectious Diseases

**Diarrhea** A change of water, food or climate can all cause the runs; diarrhea caused by contaminated food or water is more serious. Despite all your precautions you may still have a mild bout of travelers' diarrhea but a few rushed toilet trips with no other symptoms is not indicative of a serious problem. Moderate diarrhea, involving half a dozen loose movements in a day, is more of a nuisance.

Dehydration is the main danger with any diarrhea, particularly for children where dehydration can occur quite quickly. Fluid replacement remains the mainstay of management. Weak black tea with a little sugar, soda water, or soft drinks allowed to go flat and diluted 50% with water are all good. With severe diarrhea a rehydrating solution is necessary to replace minerals and salts.

Commercially available ORS (oral rehydration salts) are very useful; add the contents of one sachet to a liter of boiled or bottled water. In an emergency you can make up a solution of eight teaspoons of sugar to a liter of boiled water and provide salted cracker biscuits at the same time. You should stick to a bland diet as you recover.

Lomotil or Imodium can be used to bring relief from the symptoms, although they do not actually cure the problem. Only use these drugs if absolutely necessary – eg if you *must* travel. For children Imodium is preferable, but under all circumstances fluid replacement is the most important thing to remember. Do not use these drugs if the person has a high fever or is severely dehydrated.

In certain situations antibiotics may be indicated:

- Watery diarrhea with blood and mucous. (Gut-paralyzing drugs like Imodium or Lomotil should be avoided in this situation.)
- Watery diarrhea with fever and lethargy.
- Persistent diarrhea for more than five days.
- Severe diarrhea, if it is logistically difficult to stay in one place.

The recommended drugs (adults only) would be either norfloxacin 400 mg twice daily for three days or ciprofloxacin 500 mg twice daily for three days.

The drug bismuth subsalicylate has also been used successfully. It is not available in Australia. The dosage for adults is two tablets or 30 ml and for children it is one tablet or 10ml. This dose can be repeated every 30 minutes to one hour, with no more than eight doses in a 24-hour period.

The drug of choice in children would be co-trimoxazole (Bactrim, Septrin, Resprim) with dosage dependent on weight. A three-day course is also given. Ampicillin has been recommended in the past and may still be an alternative.

**Dysentery** This serious illness is caused by contaminated food or water and is characterised by severe diarrhea, often with blood or mucus in the stool. There are two kinds of dysentery. Bacillary dysentery is characterized by a high fever and rapid onset; headache, vomiting and stomach pains are also symptoms. It generally does not last longer than a week, but it is highly contagious.

Amoebic dysentery is often more gradual in the onset of symptoms, with cramping abdominal pain and vomiting less

likely; fever may not be present. It is not a self-limiting disease: it will persist until treated and can recur and cause long-term health problems.

A stool test is necessary to diagnose which kind of dysentery you have, so you should seek medical help urgently. In case of an emergency the drugs norfloxacin or ciprofloxacin can be used as presumptive treatment for bacillary dysentery, and metronidazole (Flagyl) for amoebic dysentery.

For bacillary dysentery, norfloxacin 400 mg twice daily for seven days or ciprofloxacin 500 mg twice daily for seven days are the recommended dosages.

If you're unable to find either of these drugs then a useful alternative is co-trimoxazole 160/800 mg (Bactrim, Septrin, Resprim) twice daily for seven days. This is a sulpha drug and must not be used by people with a known sulpha allergy.

In the case of children the drug co-trimoxazole is a reasonable first-line treatment. For amoebic dysentery, the recommended adult dosage of metronidazole (Flagyl) is one 750-mg to 800-mg capsule three times daily for five days. Children aged between eight and 12 years should have half the adult dose; the dosage for younger children is one-third the adult dose.

An alternative to Flagyl is Fasigyn, taken as a two gram daily dose for three days. Alcohol must be avoided during treatment and for 48 hours afterwards.

**Giardiasis** Commonly known as Giardia, and sometimes 'Beaver Fever', this intestinal parasite is present in contaminated water. Giardia has even contaminated apparently pristine rushing streams in the backcountry.

Symptoms are stomach cramps, nausea, a bloated stomach, watery, foul-smelling diarrhea and frequent gas. Giardia can appear several weeks after exposure to the parasite; symptoms may disappear for a few days and then return, a pattern which may continue. Tinidazole, known as Fasigyn, or metronidazole (Flagyl) are the recommended drugs for treatment. Either

Totem pole at Occidental Park, Pioneer Square area, Seattle (KS)

Picking flowers on Sauvie Island, Oregon (BM)

Mt Hood, Oregon (KS)

Hiking near Leavenworth, Washington (JJ)

The Skagit Valley in northwestern Washington is known for its tulips. (KS)

Ponderosa pine (BM)

Three Sisters Wilderness, Oregon (BM)

*Darlingtonia californica* is a flesh-eating plant found along the Oregon coast. (BM)

Autumn foliage in the Caribou National Forest near Pocatello, Idaho (BM)

Mt Rainier National Park, Washington (WB)

can be used in a single treatment dose. Antibiotics are useless.

**Hepatitis** Hepatitis is a general term for inflammation of the liver. There are many causes of this condition: drugs, alcohol and infections are but a few. The discovery of new strains has led to a virtual alphabet soup, with hepatitis A, B, C, D, E and a rumored G. These letters identify specific agents that cause viral hepatitis. Viral hepatitis is an infection of the liver, which can lead to jaundice (yellow skin), fever, lethargy and digestive problems. It can have no symptoms at all, with the infected person not knowing that they have the disease. Travelers shouldn't be too paranoid about this apparent proliferation of hepatitis strains; hep C, D, E and G are fairly rare (so far) and following the same precautions as for A and B should be all that's necessary to avoid them.

Viral hepatitis can be divided into two groups on the basis of how it is spread. The first route of transmission is via contaminated food and water, and the second route is via blood and bodily fluids.

**Hepatitis A** This is a very common disease in most countries, especially those with poor standards of sanitation. Most people in developing countries are infected as children; they often don't develop symptoms, but do develop life-long immunity. The disease poses a real threat to the traveler, as people are unlikely to have been exposed to hepatitis A in developed countries.

The symptoms are fever, chills, headache, fatigue, feelings of weakness and aches and pains, followed by loss of appetite, nausea, vomiting, abdominal pain, dark urine, light colored feces and jaundiced skin, and the whites of the eyes may turn yellow. In some cases you may feel unwell, tired, have no appetite, experience aches and pains and be jaundiced. You should seek medical advice, but in general there is not much you can do apart from resting, drinking lots of fluids, eating lightly and avoiding fatty foods. People

who have had hepatitis must forego alcohol for six months after the illness, as hepatitis attacks the liver and it needs that amount of time to recover.

The routes of transmission are via contaminated water, shellfish contaminated by sewerage, or foodstuffs sold by food handlers with poor standards of hygiene. Taking care with what you eat and drink can go a long way towards preventing this disease. But this is a very infectious virus, so if there is any risk of exposure, additional cover is highly recommended. This cover comes in two forms: Gammaglobulin and Havrix. Gammaglobulin is an injection where you are given the antibodies for hepatitis A, which provide immunity for a limited time. Havrix is a vaccine, where you develop your own antibodies, which gives lasting immunity.

**Hepatitis E** This is a very recently discovered virus, of which little is yet known. It appears to be rather common in developing countries, generally causing mild hepatitis, although it can be very serious in pregnant women. Care with water supplies is the only current prevention, as there are no specific vaccines for this type of hepatitis. At present it doesn't appear to be too great a risk for travelers.

**Hepatitis B** Hepatitis B, which used to be called serum hepatitis, is spread through contact with infected blood, blood products or bodily fluids, for example through sexual contact, unsterilized needles and blood transfusions. Other risk situations include having a shave or tattoo in a local shop, or having your ears pierced. The symptoms of type B are much the same as type A except that they are more severe and may lead to irreparable liver damage or even liver cancer. Although there is no treatment for hepatitis B, a cheap and effective vaccine is available; the only problem is that for long-lasting cover you need a six-month course. The immunization schedule requires two injections at least a month apart followed by a third dose five months after the second.

Persons who should receive a hepatitis B vaccination include anyone who anticipates contact with blood or other bodily secretions, either as a health-care worker or through sexual contact, particularly those who intend to stay in the country for a long period of time.

**Hepatitis C** This is another recently defined virus. It is a concern because it seems to lead to liver disease more rapidly than hepatitis B. The virus is spread by contact with blood – usually via contaminated transfusions or shared needles. Avoiding these is the only means of prevention, as there is no available vaccine.

**Hepatitis D** Often referred to as the 'Delta' virus, this infection only occurs in chronic carriers of hepatitis B. It is transmitted by blood and bodily fluids. Again there is no vaccine for this virus, so avoidance is the best prevention. The risk to travelers is certainly limited.

**Rabies** Dogs are noted carriers of rabies. Any bite, scratch or even lick from a warm-blooded, furry animal should be cleaned immediately and thoroughly. Scrub with soap and running water, and then clean with an alcohol solution. If there is any possibility that the animal is infected medical help should be sought immediately. Even if the animal is not rabid, all bites should be treated seriously as they can become infected or can result in tetánus. A rabies vaccination is now available and should be considered if you are in a high-risk category – eg if you intend to explore caves (bat bites can be dangerous) or work with animals.

**Red Tide** Before harvesting wild shellfish from the Pacific Ocean, check with local health officials. A bacterial condition called 'red tide' can affect shellfish, rendering them lethal to humans. When a red tide alert is in effect, most beach access sites are posted with warning signs. The Puget Sound area in Washington is often affected by red tide. Red tide areas have recently begun to spring up increasingly in small bays along the Oregon coast.

**Tetanus** Tetanus is difficult to treat but is preventable with immunization. Tetanus occurs when a wound becomes infected by a germ which lives in the feces of animals or people, so clean all cuts, punctures or animal bites. Tetanus is also known as lockjaw, and the first symptom may be discomfort in swallowing, or stiffening of the jaw and neck; this is followed by painful convulsions of the jaw and whole body.

**Sexually Transmitted Diseases** Sexual contact with an infected sexual partner spreads these diseases. While abstinence is the only 100% preventative, using condoms is also effective. Gonorrhoea and syphilis are the most common of these diseases; sores, blisters or rashes around the genitals, discharges or pain when urinating are common symptoms. Symptoms may be less marked or not observed at all in women. Syphilis symptoms eventually disappear completely but the disease continues and can cause severe problems in later years. The treatment of gonorrhoea and syphilis is by antibiotics.

There are numerous other sexually transmitted diseases, for most of which effective treatment is available. However, there is no cure for herpes and there is also currently no cure for AIDS.

**HIV/AIDS** HIV, the Human Immunodeficiency Virus, may develop into AIDS, Acquired Immune Deficiency Syndrome. HIV is a major problem in many countries. Any exposure to blood, blood products or bodily fluids may put the individual at risk. In many developing countries transmission is predominantly through heterosexual sexual activity. This is quite different from industrialized countries where transmission is mostly through contact between homosexual or bisexual males, or via contaminated needles shared by IV drug users. Apart from abstinence, the most effective preventative is always to practice safe sex using condoms. It is impossible to detect the HIV-positive status of an otherwise healthy-looking person without a blood test.

HIV/AIDS can also be spread through infected blood transfusions; most developing countries cannot afford to screen blood for transfusions. It can also be spread by dirty needles – vaccinations, acupuncture, tattooing and ear or nose piercing can potentially be as dangerous as intravenous drug use if the equipment is not clean. If you do need an injection, ask to see the syringe unwrapped in front of you, or better still, take a needle and syringe pack with you overseas – it is a cheap insurance package against infection with HIV.

Fear of HIV infection should never preclude treatment for serious medical conditions. Although there may be a risk of infection, it is very small indeed. A good resource for help and information is the US Center of Disease Control AIDS hotline (☎ (800) 343-2347).

### Insect-Borne Diseases

**Ticks** Ticks are a parasitic arachnid that may be present in brush, forest and grasslands, where hikers often get them on their legs or in their boots. The adults suck blood from hosts by burying their head into skin, but are often found unattached and can simply be brushed off. However, if one has attached itself to you, pulling it off and leaving the head in the skin increases the likelihood of infection or disease, the most common of which are outlined below.

To avoid the tick, use insect repellent or rub on Vaseline, alcohol or oil to induce ticks to let go. Always check your body for ticks after walking through a tick-infested area.

*Colorado Tick Fever* This is a virus spread by the Rocky Mountain wood tick, which, despite the name of the disease, may be found outside of Colorado. One to 300 cases are reported each year. The sickness has a three to five-day incubation period and lasts five to 10 days on average for those ages eight to 30, and to three weeks for those over 30.

Symptoms include head and body aches, lethargy, nausea and vomiting, sensitivity to light, abdominal pain and a skin rash (rare). There is no vaccine, treatment is by antibiotics and 20% of cases require hospitalization if lasting to three weeks.

*Rocky Mountain Spotted Fever* This disease is rare in Colorado, but may be found in outlying areas and is caused by *Rickettsia rickessii* bacteria carried by the Rocky Mountain wood tick. Only the adult wood tick will bite, and it has to have been feeding six to 10 hours to transmit the disease.

A two to four-day incubation period will result with symptoms like fever, spotted rash on the wrists, ankles or waist that may spread over the entire body, headache, nausea, vomiting and abdominal pain. All symptoms but fever may or may not occur, and muscle cramping is possible.

More severe problems can develop. Treatment consists of doses of antibiotics and 20% of cases left untreated end in death. If after 12 hours of being in the woods symptoms appear, seek medical attention immediately.

*Lyme Disease* This disease is also spread by tick bites. It's extremely rare in the Pacific Northwest, and more common in the Northeastern states.

### Cuts, Bites & Stings

**Cuts & Scratches** Skin punctures can easily become infected in hot climates and may be difficult to heal. Treat any cut with an antiseptic such as Betadine. Where possible avoid bandages and Band-aids, which can keep wounds wet.

**Bites & Stings** Bee and wasp stings are usually painful rather than dangerous. Calamine lotion will give relief and ice packs will reduce the pain and swelling. There are some spiders with dangerous bites but antivenins are usually available. Scorpion stings are notoriously painful. Scorpions often shelter in shoes or clothing.

**Bedbugs & Lice** Bedbugs live in various places, but particularly in dirty mattresses and bedding. Spots of blood on bedclothes or on the wall around the bed can be read as a suggestion to find another hotel. Bedbugs leave itchy bites in neat rows. Calamine lotion may help.

All lice cause itching and discomfort. They make themselves at home in your hair (head lice), your clothing (body lice) or in your pubic hair (crabs). You catch lice through direct contact with infected people or by sharing combs, clothing and the like. Powder or shampoo treatment will kill the lice and infected clothing should then be washed in very hot water.

**Mosquitoes** Mosquitoes breed readily in the damp climate of the Northwest, and can be especially heavily in forest areas from spring to late summer. Although they don't spread any illnesses in the Northwest, they're voracious enough to irritate even the hardiest recreation enthusiast. Pet owners should know that fleas also thrive in the Northwest climate.

**Black Widow Spiders** This glossy black spider is relatively small and sports a characteristic red hourglass mark on it's abdomen. Classified as a ground dwelling spider, black widows prefer dark, quiet nooks and crannies such as brushpiles, sheds and under rocks as their choice habitat. A black widow bite may be barely noticeable, but their venom can be dangerous, and if you're bitten you should seek medical attention immediately.

**Scorpions** Scorpions are members of the arachnid family (along with spiders and ticks) that live in rocks in desert areas. Although not as prevalent a problem here as in other parts of the world, scorpions are able to deliver a nasty and painful sting with their tail.

**Rattlesnakes** Rattlesnakes are common in the desert, the plains and even in some elevated forest areas. To minimize chances of being bitten, always wear boots, socks and long trousers when walking through undergrowth where snakes may be present. Keep

your hands out of holes and crevices, and be cautious when collecting firewood.

Though painful, rattlesnake bites do not cause instantaneous death, rarely kill healthy adults under any circumstances, and antivenin is usually available. Keep the victim calm and still, wrap the bitten limb tightly, as you would for a sprained ankle, and then attach a splint to immobilize it. Seek medical help; tourniquets and sucking out the poison are now completely discredited.

**Poison Oak** Just brushing past this plant while on a hike can cause a blistery and extremely itchy rash on bare skin, which should be washed with a strong soap (Fels Naptha is a recommended brand) immediately after exposure. Cortisone creams can lessen the itching in minor cases. Poison oak, related to poison ivy, is a tall, thin shrub with shiny three-part leaves that grows in shady, moist areas in western USA, including the Pacific Northwest.

## Women's Health

**Gynecological Problems** Poor diet, lowered resistance due to the use of antibiotics for stomach upsets and even contraceptive pills can lead to vaginal infections when traveling in hot climates. Maintaining good hygiene and wearing skirts or loose-fitting trousers and cotton underwear will help to prevent infections.

Yeast infections, characterized by a rash, itch and discharge, can be treated with a vinegar or lemon-juice douche, or with yogurt. Nystatin suppositories are the usual medical prescription. Trichomoniasis is a more serious infection; symptoms are a discharge and a burning sensation when urinating. Male sexual partners must also be treated, and if a vinegar-water douche is not effective medical attention should be sought. Metronidazole (Flagyl) is the prescribed drug.

## WOMEN TRAVELERS

Women often face different situations when traveling than men do. If you are a woman traveler, especially a woman traveling alone, it's not a bad idea to get in the habit of traveling with a little extra awareness of your surroundings.

The USA is such a diverse and varied country that it's impossible to give advice that will fit every place and every situation. People are generally friendly and happy to help travelers, and you will probably have a wonderful time unmarred by dangerous encounters. To ensure that this is the case, consider the following suggestions, which should reduce or eliminate your chances of problems. The best advice is to trust your instincts.

In general, you must exercise more vigilance in large cities than in rural areas. Try to avoid the 'bad' or unsafe neighborhoods or districts; if you must go into or through these areas, it's best to go in a private vehicle (car or taxi). It's more dangerous at night, but in the worst areas crime can occur even in the daytime. If you are unsure which areas are considered unsafe, ask at your hotel or telephone the tourist office for advice. Tourist maps can sometimes be deceiving, compressing areas that are not tourist attractions and making the distances look shorter than they are.

While there is less to watch out for in rural areas, women may still be harassed by men unaccustomed to seeing women traveling solo. Try to avoid hiking or camping alone, especially in unfamiliar places. Hikers all over the world use the 'buddy system,' not only for protection from other humans, but also for aid in case of unexpected falls or other injuries, or encounters with rattlesnakes, bears or other potentially dangerous wildlife.

Women must recognize the extra threat of rape, which is a problem not only in urban but also in rural areas, albeit to a lesser degree. The best way to deal with the threat of rape is to avoid putting yourself in vulnerable situations. Conducting yourself in a common-sense manner will help you to avoid most problems. For example, you're more vulnerable if you've been drinking or using drugs than if you're sober; you're more vulnerable alone than if you're with company; and you're more vulnerable in a high-crime urban area than in a 'better' district.

If despite all precautions you are assaulted, call the police; in any emergency, telephoning '911' will connect you with the emergency operator for police, fire and ambulance services. In some rural areas where 911 is not active, just dial '0' for the operator. The cities and larger towns have rape crisis centers and women's shelters that provide help and support; these are listed in the telephone directory, or if they're not, the police should be able to refer you to them.

Carry your money (and only the money you'll need for that day) somewhere inside your clothing (in a money belt, a bra or your socks) rather than in a handbag or an outside pocket. Stash the money in several places. Most hotels and hostels provide safekeeping, so you can leave your money, passport and other valuables with them. Hide, or don't wear, any valuable jewelry.

Men may interpret a woman drinking alone in a bar as a bid for male company, whether you intended it that way or not. If you don't want the company, most men will respect a firm but polite 'no thank you'.

Don't hitchhike alone, and don't pick up hitchhikers if driving alone. If you get stuck on a road and need help, it's a good idea to have a pre-made sign to signal for help. At night avoid getting out of your car to flag down help; turn on your hazard lights and wait for the police to arrive. Be extra careful at night on public transit, and remember to check the times of the last bus or train before you go out at night.

To deal with potential dangers, many women protect themselves with a whistle, mace, cayenne pepper spray or some self-defense training. If you do decide to purchase a spray, contact a police station to find out about regulations and training classes. Laws regarding sprays vary from state to state, so be informed based on your destination. One law that doesn't vary is carrying sprays on airplanes – because of their combustible design it is a federal felony to carry them on board.

The headquarters for the National Organization for Women (NOW; ☎ (202) 331-0066), 1000 16th St NW, Suite 700, Washington, DC 20036, is a good resource for any woman-related information and can refer you to state and local chapters. Planned Parenthood (☎ (212) 541-7800), 810 7th Ave, New York, NY 10019, can refer you to clinics throughout the country and offer advice on medical issues. Check the Yellow Pages under 'Women's Organizations & Services' for local resources.

## GAY & LESBIAN TRAVELERS

There are gay people throughout the USA, but by far the most established gay communities are in the major cities. In the cities and on both coasts it is easier for gay men and women to live their lives with a certain amount of openness. As you travel into the middle of the country it is much harder to be open about your sexual preferences and many gays are still in the closet. This matches the prevailing attitude of the country, which prefers that gay people are neither seen nor heard. Gay travelers should be careful, *especially* in the predominantly rural Pacific Northwest – holding hands might get you bashed.

San Francisco and New York have the largest gay populations, but larger cities have a gay neighborhood or area. Examples are Hillcrest in San Diego, West Hollywood in LA, Capitol Hill in Seattle and the South End in Boston. Whereas Seattle and Portland, and even some smaller towns like Eugene, are liberal-minded and accepting of alternative lifestyles, much of rural Washington, Oregon and Idaho are extremely conservative - the Oregon Community Alliance (OCA) is known for its attempts to limit gay civil rights.

A couple of good national guidebooks are *The Womens' Traveler*, providing listings for lesbians and *Damron's Address Book* for men, both published by the Damron Company (☎ (800) 462-6654, (415) 255-0404) PO Box 422458, San Francisco, CA 94142-2458. Ferrari's *Places for Women* and *Places for Men* are also useful, as are guides to specific cities (check out *Betty & Pansy's Severe Queer*

*Reviews* to San Francisco, New York City and Washington, DC). These can be found at any good bookstore.

Another good resource is the Gay Yellow Pages (☎ (212) 674-0120), PO Box 533, Village Station, NY 10014-0533, which has a national edition as well as regional editions.

The club scene is ever changing, and most cities have a gay paper or alternative paper that will list what's happening or at least provide phone numbers of local organizations.

For people with online capabilities America Online (AOL) hosts the Gay & Lesbian Community Forum. This is also the on-line home of National Gay/Lesbian Task Force (NGLTF), Gay and Lesbian Alliance Against Defamation (GLAAD), Parents-Friends of Lesbians and Gays (P-FLAG) and other regional, state and national organizations. Michelle Quirk, host of AOL's Gay & Lesbian Community Forum, can be contacted at quirk@aol.com.

National resource numbers include the National AIDS/HIV Hotline (☎ (800) 342-2437), the National Gay/Lesbian Task Force (☎ (202) 332-6483 in Washington, DC) and the Lambda Legal Defense Fund (☎ (212) 995-8585 in New York City, (213) 937-2727 in Los Angeles)

**Washington** In Seattle, there's the Lesbian Resource Center (☎ 322-3953) at 1208 E Pine St, or stop by Beyond the Closet bookstore (☎ 322-4609), 1501 Belmont Ave, to pick up flyers and newspapers and check the bulletin board. Gay Community Social Services (☎ (206) 322-2873) at PO Box 22228, Seattle, WA 98122 is another good contact.

**Oregon** Phoenix Rising (☎ 223-8299) 620 SW 5th Ave, Suite 710, Portland, OR 97204, is a lesbian and gay advocacy group and community resource that specializes in mental health counseling.

**Idaho** *Diversity* (☎/fax 323-0805) is Boise's newspaper for the gay community and has entertainment listings.

## SENIOR TRAVELERS

When retirement leaves the time clock behind and the myriad 'senior' discounts begin to apply, the prospect of rediscovering the USA elicits a magnetic draw for foreigners and the native-born alike. Though the age where the benefits begin varies with the attraction, travelers from 50 years and up can expect to receive cut rates and benefits unknown to (and the envy of) their younger fellows. Be sure to inquire about such rates at hotels, museums and restaurants.

Visitors to national parks and camp-grounds can cut costs greatly by using the Golden Age Passport, a card that allows US citizens aged 62 and over (and those traveling in the same car) free admission nationwide and a 50% reduction on camping fees. You can apply in person for any of these at any national park or regional office of the USFS or NPS or call (800) 280-2267 for information and ordering.

Some national advocacy groups that can help in planning your travels include the following:

American Association of Retired Persons
The AARP (☎ (800) 227-7737), 601 E St NW, Washington, DC 20049, is an advocacy group for Americans 50 years and older and is a good resource for travel bargains. A one-year membership is available to US residents for $8.

Elderhostel
Elderhostel (☎ (617) 426-8056), 75 Federal St, Boston, MA 02110-1941, is a non-profit organization that offers seniors the opportunity to attend academic college courses throughout the USA and Canada. The programs last one to three weeks and include meals and accommodations, and are open to people 55 years and older and their companions.

Grand Circle Travel
This organization offers escorted tours and travel information in a variety of formats and distributes a free useful booklet, *Going Abroad: 101 Tips for Mature Travelers*. Contact them at 347 Congress Street, Boston, MA 02210 (☎ (617) 350-7500, fax 350-6206)

National Council of Senior Citizens
Membership (you do not need to be a US citizen to apply) to this group gives access to added Medicare insurance, a mail-order prescription service and a variety of discount information and travel-related advice. Fees are $13/30/150 for one year/three years/lifetime. The council is based at 1331 F Street NW, Washington DC, 20004 (☎ (202) 347-8800).

## DISABLED TRAVELERS

Travel within USA is becoming easier for people with disabilities. Public buildings (including hotels, restaurants, theaters and museums) are now required by law to be wheelchair accessible and to have available restroom facilities. Public transportation services (buses, trains and taxis) must be made accessible to all, including those in wheelchairs, and telephone companies are required to provide relay operators for the hearing impaired. Many banks now provide ATM instructions in Braille and you will find audible crossing signals as well as dropped curbs at busier roadway intersections.

Larger private and chain hotels (see Accommodations for listings) have suites for disabled guests. Main car rental agencies offer hand-controlled models at no extra charge. All major airlines, Greyhound buses and Amtrak trains will allow service animals to accompany passengers and will frequently sell two-for-one packages when attendants of seriously disabled passengers are required. Airlines will also provide assistance for connecting, boarding and deplaning the flight – just ask for assistance when making your reservation. (Note: airlines must accept wheelchairs as checked baggage and have an onboard chair available, though some advance notice may be required on smaller aircraft.) Of course, the more populous the area, the greater the likelihood of facilities for the disabled, so it's important to call ahead to see what is available.

There are a number of organizations and tour providers that specialize in the needs of disabled travelers:

Access
  The Foundation for Accessibility by the Disabled, PO Box 356, Malverne, NY 11565 (☎ (516) 887-5798)

Information Center for Individuals with Disabilities
  Call or write for their free listings and travel advice. Fort Point Place, 1st Floor, 27-43 Wormwood Street, Boston, MA 02210 (☎ (617) 727-5540, TTY 345-9743 or (800) 248-3737).

Mobility International USA
  Mobility International (☎ (503) 343-1284), PO Box 3551, Eugene, OR 97403, advises disabled travelers on mobility issues. It also runs an exchange program.

Moss Rehabilitation Hospital's Travel Information Service
  1200 W Tabor Road, Philadelphia, PA 19141-3099 (☎ (215) 456-9600, TTY 456-9602)

SATH
  Society for the Advancement of Travel for the Handicapped 347 Fifth Ave No 610, New York, NY 10016 (☎ (212) 447-7284)

Twin Peaks Press
  Publishes several handbooks for disabled travelers and can be contacted at PO Box 129, Vancouver, WA 98666. (☎ (202) 694-2462, (800) 637-2256)

## DANGERS & ANNOYANCES

For a largely sedate and seemingly sensible culture, the Pacific Northwest has a high rate of crime. As most crimes are 'property' crimes (that is, theft), travelers needn't inordinately fear random violence. However, there's no denying that urban US culture can be menacing, and too frequently dangerous. As a rule of thumb, you'll be safer if you don't walk around central Portland or Seattle at night alone.

### Personal Security & Theft

Although street crime is a serious issue in large urban areas visitors need not be obsessed with security.

Always lock cars and put valuables out of sight, whether leaving the car for a few minutes or longer, and whether you are in a town or in the remote backcountry. Rent a car with a lockable trunk. If your car is bumped from behind in a remote area, it's best not to stop but to keep going to a well-lit area or service station.

Be aware of your surroundings and who may be watching you. Avoid walking on dimly lit streets at night, particularly when alone. Walk purposefully. Avoid unnecessary displays of money or jewelry. Divide money and credit cards to avoid losing everything, and aim to use ATM machines in well-trafficked areas.

In hotels, don't leave valuables lying around your room. Use safety-deposit boxes or at least place valuables in a locked bag. Don't open your door to strangers – check the peephole or call the front desk if unexpected guests try to enter.

**Street People** The USA has a lamentable record in dealing with its most unfortunate citizens, who often roam the streets of large cities in the daytime and sleep by storefronts, under freeways or in alleyways and abandoned buildings.

This problem is less acute in the mostly rural states than in urban areas on both coasts, but it is certainly not absent. While most homeless people pose no threat whatsoever to travelers, aggressive panhandling can seem menacing and unpleasant. Usually the best reaction to an assertive panhandler is to ignore him or her; if you are followed, contact a security officer or duck into a shop. Ask a clerk for help if necessary.

**Guns** The USA has a widespread reputation as a dangerous place because of the availability of firearms, and it's true that in parts of the big cities, even youth are packing guns. Residents of more rural states frequently carry guns as well – rifle racks in pickup trucks are almost universal – but they most often use them against animals or against isolated traffic signs. Do be careful in the woods during the fall hunting season, when unsuccessful or drunken hunters may be less selective in their targets than one might hope.

## Wildlife

**Bears** There are two species of bears in the Northwest. Black bears are found in mountainous areas throughout the region, while grizzly bears are found only in the Rocky Mountains in Idaho. While grizzly bears are by far the most dangerous, both bears deserve respect.

Grizzly bears are huge: adults commonly weigh 600 to 800 pounds and stand four feet high at their muscular shoulder humps. A grizzly's dish-shaped profile contrasts with the black bear's straight Roman nose. Smaller size and the lack of a shoulder hump further distinguish the black bear from the grizzly; black bears weigh about 200 pounds and stand about three feet tall. Color is not a reliable distinguishing trait – no shade of brown is unusual for either bear. Black bears can be honey-colored and are commonly cinnamon; grizzlies are not always silver-tipped and grizzled looking. But perhaps the ability to tell bears apart is not the most important thing to know when confronted by any ursine species.

Find out where bears, especially grizzlies, live, and take precautions. In Idaho, grizzlies live in the west of Yellowstone National Park, and in wilderness areas throughout the Rockies. Rangers will usually know if bears have been spotted locally, and trails are sometimes closed due to bear activity.

Try not to surprise a bear. Stay alert and make some noise while hiking--many hikers wear bells. Avoid strong odors by not wearing perfumes or cooking strong-smelling foods (freeze-dried foods are almost odor-free). At night, keep food and smelly clothing inside a car or strung high in a tree. Sleep well away from the cooking area.

If you do see a bear, give it plenty of room. Try to stay upwind of the bear so it can get your scent. If the bear becomes aggressive, drop something that may absorb its attention and climb the nearest tall tree. If this isn't possible, the next best bet is probably to curl up into a ball, clasp your hands behind your neck, and play

### Mushrooms & Marijuana

In the USA, possession, distribution and use of marijuana are all federal felonies. However, persistent demand for cannabis creates a lively, highly profitable market for the producer. Conditions for growing pot – which calls for both the right climate and near total seclusion – are perfect in remote southern Oregon and other parts of the Northwest. There, maverick pot growers often hide plots of marijuana in isolated pockets of national forests. In Douglas County, OR, marijuana is one of the biggest cash crops.

Growers are especially protective of their plots, and have been known to rig the area with traps set to maim or kill trespassers. Hikers venturing off the beaten path should be able to identify this plant. Accidentally wandering into a marijuana field is extremely dangerous, and it is important to leave the area as quickly and quietly as possible.

Some of the same conditions, but not quite the same threat of harm, apply to the harvesting of wild mushrooms. For many unemployed timber workers, and others in rural communities, picking wild mushrooms has become a vital part of making a living, as prices for rare mushrooms right out of the forest can be as high as $40 a pound.

Understandably, knowledge of especially rich mushroom gathering areas has become highly guarded information. There have been instances where territorial disputes over mushroom beds have been settled with guns. The USFS is now trying to regulate mushroom hunting a bit more carefully, though casual mushroom picking by amateurs or hobbyists continues to be perfectly legal within guidelines. However, if while harvesting or hiking, you come upon an armed mushroom baron, simply retreat quietly. It's not worth fighting over fungus. ∎

dead, even if the bear begins to bat you around.

Bears can, and occasionally do, kill people, but most people who enter bear country never have any problem. In fact, it is a special thing to see a grizzly; they are as impressive as they are rare. Precautions and respect for bears will ensure not only your continued survival, but theirs as well.

**Other Wildlife** Mountain lions (also called cougars or pumas) are not as dangerous as bears, but as their territory in the mountains gets whittled away by development, there is more and more contact between humans and mountain lions. Also, mountain lions are increasing in population, which makes sighting one of these big cats more of a possibility than in the past. Adults aren't much at risk of mountain lion attack, but unattended children have been attacked and killed in recent years. Moose, which live in northern Idaho, aren't blood-thirsty, but they are given to anger. If surprised, they can charge. Fleeing an angry, 1800-pound moose is to be avoided. Keep your distance if you come upon one.

The most annoying of all wildlife is actually the quite harmless skunk. This cat-sized, bushy-tailed mammal protects itself by spraying the most foul-smelling musk that permeates everything. Sleeping bags and tents will carry the smell until you get tired of smelling it and throw the stuff out. Taking a nice long bath in tomato juice is the most effective way of removing the musk from the skin. The best way to avoid such creatures is not to entice them – don't leave food out at campsites and store it safely in the car or high above ground. Raccoons, though not smelly, are equally pesky and some carry rabies.

## EMERGENCY
Throughout the Pacific Northwest and most of the USA, dial 911 for emergency service of any sort; in large cities like Seattle or areas with substantial Hispanic populations, Spanish-speaking emergency operators may be available, but other languages are less likely to be spoken. For numbers not listed below, call local directory assistance at 411.

### Washington
| | |
|---|---|
| State Police | ☎ (206) 649-4370 |
| Road Conditions | ☎ (206) 434-7277 |
| Weather Reports | ☎ (206) 526-6087 |

### Oregon
| | |
|---|---|
| State Police | ☎ (503) 731-3020 |
| Road Conditions | ☎ (503) 889-3999 |
| Weather Reports | ☎ (503) 779-5990 |

### Idaho
| | |
|---|---|
| State Police | ☎ (208) 334-2900 |
| Road Conditions | ☎ (208) 336-6600 |
| Weather Reports | ☎ (208) 334-9860 |

### Credit Card Numbers
If you lose your credit cards or they get stolen contact the company immediately. Following are toll-free numbers for the main credit cards. Contact your bank if you lose your ATM card.

| | |
|---|---|
| Visa | ☎ (800) 336-8472 |
| MasterCard | ☎ (800) 826-2181 |
| American Express | ☎ (800) 528-4800 |
| Discover | ☎ (800) 347-2683 |
| Diners Club | ☎ (800) 234-6377 |

## LEGAL MATTERS
If you are stopped by the police for any reason, bear in mind that there is no system of paying fines on the spot. For traffic offenses, the police officer will explain your options to you. Attempting to pay the fine to the officer is frowned upon at best and may lead to a charge of bribery to compound your troubles. Should the officer decide that you should pay up front, he or she can exercise their authority and take you directly to the magistrate instead of allowing you the usual 30-day period to pay the fine.

If you are arrested for more serious offenses, you are allowed to remain silent and are presumed innocent until proven guilty. There is no legal reason to speak to a police officer if you don't wish. All persons who are arrested are legally allowed (and given) the right to make one phone call. If you don't have a lawyer or family member to help you, call your embassy. The police will give you the number upon request.

### Driving & Drinking Laws

Each state has its own laws and what may be legal in one state may be illegal in others.

Some general rules are that you must be at least 16 years of age to drive (older in some states). Speed limits are 65 mph on interstates and freeways unless otherwise posted. You can drive five mph over the limit without much likelihood of being pulled over, but if you're doing 10 mph over the limit, you'll be caught sooner or later. Speed limits on other highways are 55 mph or less, and in cities can vary from 25 to 45 mph. Watch for school zones which can be as low as 15 mph during school hours – these limits are strictly enforced. Seat belts must be worn in most states. Motorcyclists must wear helmets.

The drinking age is 21 and you need a photo ID to prove your age. Stiff fines, jail time and penalties could be incurred when caught driving under the influence of alcohol. During festive holidays and special events, road blocks are sometimes set up to deter drunk drivers.

For more information on car rental, insurance and other car-related concerns, see the Getting Around chapter.

### WORK

Seasonal work is possible in national parks and other tourist sites, especially ski areas; for information, contact park concessionaires or local chambers of commerce.

If you're coming from abroad and want to work in the USA, you'll need to apply for a work visa from the US embassy in your home country before you leave. The type of visa varies depending on how long you're staying and the kind of work you plan to do. Generally, you'll need either a J-1 visa which you can obtain by joining a visitor-exchange program, or a H-2B visa

which you get when being sponsored by a US employer. The latter is not easy to obtain (since the employer has to prove that no US citizen or permanent resident is available to do the job); the former is issued mostly to students for work in summer camps.

## HIGHLIGHTS
### Washington

**Western Washington** The largest and most exciting city in the Northwest, Seattle is located on a large bay of the Pacific Ocean, and is skirted by freshwater lakes and rivers. Rising in all directions are mountains, while the seafront is studded with forested islands. Beautiful and cosmopolitan, Seattle is famous for its youthful music scene, good restaurants and lively street life.

The San Juan Islands, northwest of Seattle toward Vancouver Island, are small rural islands with a sleepy pace and an abundance of cozy resorts and B&Bs. Popular with bicyclists, wildlife watchers and boaters, these islands are linked by ferries to the mainland.

West of Seattle rises the Olympic Peninsula, whose rugged glacier-hung peaks are enclosed in the Olympic National Park. The remote western side of the peninsula is home to dense temperate rainforests, and Native American villages. The Makah Cultural Center at Neah Bay is one of the best museums of traditional Northwest Coast Indian life in the state. Just north of the Columbia River confluence with the Pacific is the Long Beach Peninsula, a long finger of sand stretching for 25 miles between the ocean and Willapa Bay, world famous for its oysterbeds. Some of the region's best restaurants are found in the peninsula's tiny villages.

Also along the Columbia is Fort Vancouver National Monument, a replica of the 1825 fur fort that was in many ways the first important settlement in the Northwest. Costumed docents give tours of the buildings, while artisans work period forges, ovens and mills.

**The Cascades** Washington's wide band of Cascade peaks is a mecca for outdoor recreationalists. Towering Mt Rainier, the region's highest peak at 14,411 feet, is the centerpiece of one of the oldest national parks. Hiking trails lead to gentle alpine meadows, bursting with mid-summer wildflowers, or climb up to the toes of mighty glaciers. The jumbled and serrated peaks of the North Cascades are also protected as a national park. Highway 20 winds through this craggy landscape, offering outstanding views and access to a network of long-distance hiking trails. Mount St Helens is famous for its massive 1980 eruption; today the area is laced with hiking trails. A brand new visitors center looks into the volcano's crater and provides information about the rebirth of life in the charred blast zone.

The resort towns of Leavenworth and Chelan provide year-round recreation, with cross-country skiing by winter, and hiking and water sports by summer. Nearly every mountain pass in the Cascades boast large downhill ski areas.

**Eastern Washington** The eastern part of the state is dominated by the Columbia River and its dams. Immense Grand Coulee Dam is one of the world's largest; water from the dam provides irrigation to vast apple orchards and farms. Dry Falls, once a massive waterfall in an ancient channel of the Columbia River, now looms above a desert chasm. Washington's principal wine-growing area is in the lower Yakima River valley; visit wineries perched on parched hillsides, surrounded by miles of irrigated vineyards.

Spokane is the principal trade center for the wheat farms and cattle ranches that dominate the far eastern part of the state. The far southeastern corner of the state offers richly varied scenery, ranging from the canyons of the Snake River to the attractive, undulating hills of the Palouse. Prim and prosperous Walla Walla, with its well-preserved downtown and handsome Whitman College grounds, is a good hub city for exploring the area.

## Oregon
**Pacific Coast** The southern coast of Oregon is one of the most beautiful parts of the state: spectacular cliffs drop off into the throbbing surf, small towns cling to rocky escarpments, and wild, forested mountains rise into the Pacific mists. The drama of the southern coast is reprised near Cape Perpetua, near Yachats, and at Cape Lookout, along the northern coast. Swaggering, seafaring ways are still apparent in coastal towns like Charleston, Bandon, Newport, Port Orford and Astoria.

**Portland** Portland has the reputation as one of USA's most livable cities. Certainly it's an easy place to like, with ample parks and gardens, a clean and accessible downtown, and an easy-going pace.

**Willamette Valley** Southwest of Portland are the state's most famous vineyards. Any visitor with the remotest interest in wine ought to spend a day in the beautiful rolling hills of Yamhill County, where winegrowers open their tasting rooms to visitors; bring a picnic and enjoy views of fields and distant mountains (many vineyards provide picnic tables).

**The Cascades & Central Oregon** Mount Hood rises like a white incisor above northern Oregon. The state's highest peak (11,235 feet), Mt Hood provides year-round skiing (the US Olympic ski team trains here in the summer), and great summer hiking and camping.

The mile-wide Columbia River carves a majestically deep canyon through the Cascade Mountain lava flows. Spectacular waterfalls, like 640-foot high Multnomah Falls, spill over the edge of the gorge and tumble into the Columbia River.

The Cascade volcanic peaks parade along the length of Oregon. Wilderness areas surround many of the summits, such as Mt Jefferson and the Three Sisters. Oregon's only national park, Crater Lake National Park, contains the continent's deepest lake (1932 feet), a startlingly blue souvenir of an immense volcanic explosion.

The recreation-minded town of Bend is Oregon's fastest-growing community. It has a sunny climate, access to the state's best skiing at Mt Bachelor and outstanding fishing and rafting on the wild Deschutes River. One of Oregon's best museums (the High Desert Museum), the Newberry Crater Volcanic Monument and access to high mountain lakes make Bend a great year-round destination.

**Eastern Oregon** The three units of the John Day Fossil Beds National Monument are among the most overlooked but fascinating sidetrips in the state. Immense formations of volcanic ash trapped and preserved the 40 million-year-old plant and animal life. Interpretive hikes and museums explain the fossil remains. The John Day River cuts a stair-stepped canyon through these colorful formations.

The Hart Mountain National Antelope Refuge is just about as far as you can get from civilization. But the towering fault block mountains which rise off of shallow saline lakes (themselves waterfowl refuges) and the wild lava plateaus that slope away toward the Steens Mountains are ruggedly beautiful.

Steens Mountain in far southeastern Oregon contains some of the most astonishing scenery in the state. From the historic hotel at Frenchglen, Steens Mountain Loop Rd winds up the back of an immense fault block. After the road mounts almost 9000 feet to a plateau of fragile alpine meadows, the mountain drops away in astonishing 5000 feet high cliffs onto a barren desert.

Of Oregon's highest 25 peaks, 17 are in the tightly contorted Wallowa Range. Glacial lakes and trendy art colonies make the Wallowas a much-talked-about, but still remote, destination.

Just past the Wallowas lies the Hells Canyon of the Snake River. Over 6000 feet deep, Hells Canyon is the deepest canyon in North America. This spectacular chasm is almost inaccessible to the visitor except by foot, raft or jet boat. Enterprising and vertigo-free drivers can view the gorge from Hat Point.

## Idaho
**The Panhandle** Densely forested and filled with glacier-gouged lakes, Idaho's Panhandle is filled with resorts and old mining towns. Sandpoint and Coeur d'Alene are major destinations for skiers, anglers and watersport enthusiasts. The old silver-mining town of Wallace preserves the flavor of the Old West with its historic town center. Nearby Kellogg offers gondola rides to the top of 6300-foot-high Silver Mountain.

**Central Idaho** Central Idaho is only marginally served by roads, and lies within two enormous wilderness areas accessible only to hikers and adventurous white-water enthusiasts rafting the wild Salmon River. The incredibly rugged Sawtooth Range shadow over the lakes of the upper Salmon River valley near Stanley. Campers and hikers can take in the backcountry beauty of this remote area.

McCall, Ketchum and Sun Valley, the historic and upscale ski resort, offer more civilized comforts.

**Southern Idaho** The principal attraction in this vast agricultural valley is Boise, Idaho's capital city and 1990s boomtown. Boise is a lovely city, backed up to the foothills of the Rocky Mountains, filled with historic sites, fine restaurants and youthful high spirits. South of the city is the Birds of Prey Natural Area, a large cliff-lined refuge along the Snake River dedicated to preserving native raptors and other desert wildlife.

## ACCOMMODATIONS
A full range of lodging options in all price ranges is available in the Pacific Northwest. Note that in some areas, particularly in resort areas in the Cascade and Rocky mountains, and along the Pacific Coast, there is a vast difference between high and low-season rates, and also between weekend and weekday prices. Prices

included in this guide are generally high-season rates. In the off-season, sometimes motel owners will be willing to dicker over the price of rooms if you give the impression that you're shopping around or if you're staying more than one night. Discounts are available at some motels for senior citizens, commercial travelers (all you usually need to do is show a business card), and for members of AAA.

Lodging can be hard to find at the last minute, especially in high season along the Oregon Coast and in the San Juan Islands. Seattle and Portland host many conventions and trade shows, which can tie up hotel and motel rooms during otherwise sleepy times of the year. Reserve rooms at these locations as soon as you know your itinerary. It's a good idea to have rooms reserved at least a day ahead of your travel schedule in other parts of the region.

Pets are allowed in many older motels, usually with a surcharge of $5 or so, or a refundable deposit. Almost all hotels and motels have smoking and non-smoking rooms; however, be sure to ask for your preference when you reserve the room; last minute requests cannot always be honored. Smoking rooms are frequently also the rooms that dog owners are allowed to stay in. For information on taxes see Taxes earlier in this chapter.

### Camping

The Northwest is a camper's dream. National forests stretch across the region, each with many free and inexpensive campgrounds. Oregon and Washington's state parks systems are two of the nation's largest, with 224 individual parks in Oregon and nearly 200 in Washington; Idaho's is somewhat more modest, but includes some gems. In addition, there are many county, BLM and private parks open to both RV and tent campers.

Twelve Washington and 13 Oregon state parks accept campsite reservations, through an application system. In Washington, application forms can be obtained from the State Parks Headquarters ($\pi$ (360) 902-8563), 7150 Cleanwater Lane, PO Box 42650, Olympia, WA 98504-2650. In Oregon, call the State Parks Department at (503) 378-3605 for forms. You can also call Campsite Information Center ($\pi$ (503) 238-7488, (800) 452-5687) to find out if there is unreserved space at specific campgrounds. Reservations cannot be made by telephone. Send completed forms directly to the park of interest, at least 14 days before the requested camping date, along with the first night's camping fee ($10) and an additional $5 reservation fee. Confirmations will be sent, or you can call to confirm.

### Public Campgrounds
These are on public lands such as in national forests, state and national parks and BLM land.

Free dispersed camping (meaning you can camp almost anywhere) is permitted in many public backcountry areas. Sometimes you can camp right from your car along a dirt road, and sometimes you can backpack your gear in. Information on where camping is permitted and detailed maps are available from many local ranger stations (addresses and telephone numbers are given in the text) and may be posted along the road. Sometimes, a free camping permit is required, particularly in national parks, less so in forest and BLM areas. The less developed sites are often on a first-come, first-served basis, and can fill up on Friday

---

### Camping Etiquette
Camping in an undeveloped area, whether from your car or backpacking, entails basic responsibility. Choose a camp site at least 100 yards from water and wash up at camp, not in the stream. Dig a six-inch-deep hole to use as a latrine and burn your toilet paper (unless fires are prohibited because of high forest-fire danger). Carry out all trash. Use a portable charcoal grill or camping stove instead of building new fires. If there already is a fire ring, use only dead and down wood or wood you have carried in yourself. Make sure to leave the campsite as you found it. ∎

nights. More-developed areas may accept or require reservations; details are given in the text.

Developed areas usually have toilets, drinking water, fire pits (or charcoal grills) and picnic benches. Some don't have drinking water. At any rate, it is always a good idea to have a few gallons of water with you if you are going to be out in the boonies. These basic campgrounds usually cost about $7 to $10 a night. More developed areas may have showers or Recreational Vehicle (RV) hookups. These will cost several dollars more.

Costs given in the text for public campgrounds are per site. A site is normally for up to six people (or two vehicles). If there are more of you, you'll need two sites. Public campgrounds often have seven or 14-night limits.

**Private Campgrounds** These are on private property and are usually close to or in town. Most are designed with recreational vehicles (RVs) in mind; tenters can camp but fees are several dollars higher than in public campgrounds. Also, fees given in the text are for two people per site. There is usually a charge of $1 to $3 per extra person and state and city taxes apply. However, they may offer discounts for week or month stays. Private campgrounds often have many facilities lacking in public ones. These include hot showers, coin laundry, swimming pool, full RV hook-ups, games area, playground and convenience store. Kampgrounds of America (KOA) is a national network of private campgrounds. You can get its annual directory of KOA sites by calling or writing: KOA (☎ (406) 248-7444), PO Box 30558, Billings, MT 59114-0558.

**Hostels**
The US hostel network is less widespread than in Canada, the UK, Europe and Australia, and is predominately in the north and coastal parts of the country. Not all of them are directly affiliated with Hostels International/American Youth Hostels (HI/AYH; HI was formerly the International Youth Hostel Federation or IYHF). Those that are offer discounts to HI/AYH members and usually allow non-members to stay for a few dollars more. Dormitory beds cost about $10 to $12 a night. Rooms are in the $20s for one or two people, sometimes more.

HI/AYH hostels expect you to rent or carry a sheet or sleeping bag to keep the beds clean. Dormitories are segregated by sex and curfews may exist. Kitchen and laundry privileges are usually available in return for light house-keeping duties. There are information and advertising boards, TV rooms and lounge areas. Alcohol may be banned. Reservations are accepted and advised during the high season – there may be a limit of a three-night stay then. You can call HI/AYH's national toll-free number (☎ (800) 444-6111) to make reservations for any HI/AYH hostel.

Hostels aren't exactly everywhere in the Northwest; if you're relying on hostels for your trip, then you will somewhat limit your itinerary. In addition to hostels, some YWCAs and YMCAs offer inexpensive lodging. Bottom-range motels, shared by at least two people, will be as cheap as most hostels. For general information about hostels in the USA, contact HI/AYH (☎ (202) 783-6161), Dept 801, Box 37613, Washington, DC 20013.

For a complete description of all eight HI/AYH hostels throughout Washington, contact Hostelling International, Washington State Council (☎ (206) 281-7306), 419 Queen Anne Ave N No102, Seattle, WA 98109. There are hostels in Bellingham, Blaine, Chinook, Fort Flagler, Port Townsend, Seattle, Spokane and Vashon Island.

Oregon also has eight hostels, in Ashland, Bandon, Bend, Cave Junction, Corvallis, Dexter, Portland and Seaside. The HI/AYH office in Portland (☎ (503) 223-1873, 235-9493) is at 1520 SE 37th Ave.

Idaho has three, in Gooding, Kellogg and Naples.

**B&Bs**
If you've only ever experienced B&Bs in Britain, then you are probably in for a

surprise when you stay at most Northwestern B&Bs. Bed and Breakfasts here are almost totally the province of fancy and large historic homes, which offer opulantly decorated rooms and epicurean breakfasts, with extras like wine tastings and afternoon tea thrown in for effect. Most B&Bs are better thought of as exclusive small inns, usually with prices comparable to mid-range motels and hotels. They aren't inexpensive spare bedrooms at the back of people's homes. That being said, many people like the hospitality extended at these private homes, as well as the chance to stay in stately old houses.

There are exceptions, of course. Particularly in rural areas, homes advertising 'bed and breakfast' are usually more modest, and you'll be dealing with a family whose main business is usually agriculture rather than serving as professional innkeeper. You be the judge if that's something you'd prefer.

The B&Bs listed in this guide are usually well-established and reputable. However, B&Bs come and go quickly (some are only seasonal), so be sure and call ahead to make sure the inn is still in operation; check with the local chamber of commerce to find out what new B&Bs might have opened. Most B&Bs don't take walk-in customers; you're expected to have a reservation. Many B&Bs don't accept children or smokers, and pets are usually verboten; some will have prohibitions like no alcohol or try to enforce a curfew. This may or may not be how you chose to spend your holiday.

**Washington** The Washington State Bed & Breakfast Guild (☎ (800) 647-2918), 2442 NW Market St, Seattle, WA 98107, publishes a yearly directory of member B&Bs. The islands of the Puget Sound, particularly the San Juans, are loaded with B&Bs.

**Oregon** There are a number of Oregon B&B associations. Contact either Oregon B&B Directory, 230 Red Spur Drive, Grants Pass, OR 97527, or Oregon B&B Guild, PO Box 3187, Ashland, OR 97520, for brochures with B&B listings statewide.

Western Oregon, with its multitude of historic homes, offers a great many to choose from. Ashland is Oregon's B&B hotbed with over 60 in this little theater-loving town. Portland offers some spectacular B&Bs in old mansions. Older towns along the coast, like Newport and Astoria, also offer quality B&B lodgings in classic old homes.

## Motels & Hotels

Motel and hotel prices vary tremendously in price from season to season. A hotel charging $40 for a double in the high season may drop to $25 in the low and may raise its rates to $55 for a special event when the town is overflowing. A $200-a-night luxury resort may offer special weekend packages for $79 in the low season. So be aware that prices in this guide can only be an approximate guideline at best. Also, be prepared to add room tax to prices. Children are often allowed to stay free with their parents, but rules for this vary. Some hotels allow children under 18 to stay free with parents, others allow children under 12 and others may charge a few dollars per child. You should call and inquire if traveling with a family.

The prices advertised by hotels are called 'rack rates' and are not written in stone. If you simply ask about any specials that might apply you can often save quite a bit of money. Booking through a travel agent also saves you quite a bit of money as well. Members of the AARP and the AAA can qualify for a 'corporate' rate at several hotel chains.

Making phone calls directly from your hotel room is usually a losing proposition. Hotels charge around 75c for local calls vs 20c or 25c at a pay phone. Long distance rates are inflated up 100% to 200%! The best plan of action is simply to carry a fistful of quarters or a phone card and use a pay phone for all your calls.

Special events and conventions can fill up a town's hotels quickly, so call ahead to find out what will be going on. The chamber of commerce is always a good resource.

**Bottom End** Motels with $20 rooms are found especially in small towns on major highways and the motel strips of larger towns. A quick drive through one of these will yield a selection of neon-lit signs: '$19.95 for Two', etc. Take your pick. A few towns which may currently be experiencing great popularity just won't have rock-bottom budget motels. Therefore what may be a bottom-end motel in one town may pass for a middle hotel in another.

Rooms are usually small, beds may be soft or saggy, but the sheets should be clean. A minimal level of cleanliness is maintained, but expect scuffed walls, atrocious decor, old furniture and strange noises from your shower. Even these places, however, normally have a private shower and toilet and a TV in each room. Most have air-conditioning and heat. Some of even the cheapest motels may advertise kitchenettes. These may cost a few dollars more but give you the chance to cook a simple meal for yourself if you are fed up with restaurants. Kitchenettes vary from a two-ring burner to a spiffy little mini-kitchen and may or may not have utensils. If you plan on doing a lot of kitchenette cooking, carry your own set.

**Motel & Hotel Chains** There are many motel and hotel chains in the USA. These offer a certain level of quality and style which tend to be repeated throughout the chain. People may say 'If you've stayed in one, you've stayed in them all!'. This is partially true, but there are certainly individual variations in both standards and, especially, prices depending on location. Some travelers like a particular chain and stay there repeatedly, expecting and generally receiving the level of comfort they want. These travelers should investigate the chain's frequent-guest program – discounts and guaranteed reservations are offered to faithful guests.

The cheapest national chain is *Motel 6*. Rooms are small and very bland, but the beds are usually OK, every room has a TV and phone (local calls are free) and most properties have a swimming pool. Rooms start in the $20s for a single in smaller towns, in the $30s in larger towns. They usually charge a flat $6 for each extra person. Motel 6 are pretty basic but offer reasonable value for money.

Several motel chains compete with one another at the next price level, with rooms starting in the $30s in the smaller towns or in the $40s in larger or more popular places. The main difference between these and Motel 6 rooms is the size of each room – more space to spread out in. Beds are always reliably firm, decor may be a little more attractive, a 24-hour desk is often available and little extras like free coffee, a table, cable or rental movies, or a bathtub with your shower may be offered. If these sorts of things are worth an extra $10 or $15 a night, then you'll be happy with the *Super 8 Motels*, *Days Inn* or *Econo Lodge*. Not all of these have pools, however – Super 8 Motels especially have a good number of properties lacking a pool.

Stepping up to chains with rooms in the $45 to $80 range (depending on location), you'll find noticeably nicer rooms, cafes, restaurants or bars may be on the premises or adjacent to them, the swimming pool may be indoor with a spa or exercise room also available. The *Best Western* chain consistently has properties in almost every town of any size and offers good rooms in this price range. Often they are the best available in a given town. Less widespread but also good are the *Comfort Inns* and *Sleep Inns*. *Rodeway Inns* fall at the lower end of this category.

**Private** There are, of course, non-chain establishments in these price ranges. Some of them are funky historical hotels, full of turn-of-the-century furniture. Others are privately run establishments which just don't want to be a part of a chain. In smaller towns, complexes of cabins are available – these often come complete with fireplace, kitchen and an outdoor area with trees and maybe a stream a few steps away.

## Lodges & Resorts

The word 'lodge' is used with great latitude in the Northwest. Places like Timberline Lodge and Paradise Lodge are magnificent old log structures with dozens of rooms infused with a sense of the woods and hand-crafted venerability. Most other 'lodges' are more modest. Many lakes in the Cascades boast lodges which offer cabin accommodations, campsites, boat rentals and at least a small store if not a cafe. Some of these lodges are just fine; others are quite funky and unspectacular. If your standards are exacting, make careful inquiries before heading up long mountain roads to marginal accommodations best suited to hardened anglers.

In central Oregon and Washington especially, the last 20 years has seen a proliferation of 'resorts.' Most of these establishments are quite up-scale and include many recreational facilities, including golf courses, tennis courts, swimming pools and guided outdoor activities. The price for resort accommodations can be steep, but if it includes golf fees and access to recreational facilities, then the price tag may not seem prohibitive. Lodging options usually include staying in condominiums, hotel-like lodge rooms, or in privately owned homes rented on a short-term basis.

## Property Management Agents

In many coastal areas, and in central Oregon and Washington, private homeowners keep weekend or vacation homes, but depend on occasional rentals to help pay the mortgage. Most of these homes have at least three bedrooms, and are decorated, kept up, and furnished like a regular home.

To rent a private home, contact a local property management company. Obviously some restrictions apply: the family has first dibs on the home, usually for major holiday and summer weekends. There's usually a minimum stay of two nights and there may be a housekeeping fee. However, for a family, or for a group of friends, these homes represent one of the best lodging values in the area.

A good way to determine the real value of a rental home is to divide the cost of the house per night by the number of bedrooms, and then compare that price to the cost of a local motel. Usually, if you plan on filling at least three bedrooms, you are probably more comfortable and more cheaply lodged in a private home.

Listings for property agents are included for those communities where there is a sufficient number of rental homes. Contact the local chamber of commerce for property management firms in other communities.

## FOOD

With a long seacoast, fertile valleys filled with farms and orchards, and miles and miles of grasslands devoted to livestock, the Northwest offers high quality, locally

**Gas, Food, Lodging**
When coming into a city on the highway you will notice signs that say 'Gas Food Lodging' followed by something like 'Next Three Exits'. Don't assume these exits will lead you directly into the city center – they won't. You'll end up traveling along strips of chain motels, fast-food restaurants and gas stations with small grocery stores. If you have no intention of staying in town, but would rather catch a few hours' sleep and head out early on the road, these establishments do provide a cheap alternative to downtown and a bit of true Americana. ■

grown food products to both enterprising home cooks and restaurant chefs. There's little that's unique to Northwest kitchens, but there are a number of items and dishes that are regional specialties, or that at least are symptomatic of the Northwest's taste in food.

James Beard was a native of Portland, and many Northwest chefs have personal stories to tell of this master chef and food writer. Beard's legacy to Northwest regional food is an appreciation of local or indigenous ingredients, prepared with simple elegance, and an attitude that eating great food ought to be great fun.

## Mealtimes

Usually served between about 6 am and 10 am, standard breakfasts are large and filling, often including eggs or an omelette, bacon or ham, fried potatoes, toast with butter and jam and coffee or tea.

Lunch is available between 11 am and 2 pm. One strategy for enjoying good restaurants on a budget is to frequent them for lunch, when fixed-price specials for as little as $5 or slightly more are common.

Dinners, served anytime between about 5 and 10 pm, are more expensive but often very reasonably priced, and portions are usually large. Specials may also be available, but they will usually be more expensive than lunch specials. Some of the better restaurants will require reservations. Restaurants are often closed on Mondays.

## Fast Food

All the usual run-of-the-mill chains – McDonald's, Burger King, KFC, Taco Bell, etc, are widely dispersed throughout the Pacific Northwest, as are pizza outlets like Pizza Hut. Since these are so abundant and conspicuous, they're only rarely mentioned in the text.

## Self-Catering

Nearly every town of any size has a supermarket with a wide variety of fresh and prepared foods at reasonable prices; these are good places to stock up on supplies for camping trips, rather than outlying convenience stores which may inflate prices considerably.

Some towns have produce or farmers' markets that offer a good selection of fresh fruits and vegetables at very reasonable prices. These are indicated in the text.

## Northwest Cuisine

**From the Sea** Seafood and fish is a corner stone of the Northwest table. Coastal restaurants vie to claim the best clam chowder, which is often thick and starchy. Crab, fresh from the boat, is available almost everywhere along the coast. It's usually served in salad, or else simply with drawn butter.

Oyster farms are springing up along the coast; the chill waters of the Pacific produce sweet-tasting, delicately tangy oysters of the highest quality. In good restaurants, discerning diners can choose what Northwest bay their oysters on the half shell hail from. Stop by an oyster farm and hand pick a dozen tiny komomoto oysters for an impromptu hors-d'oeuvre. Clams, usually steamed in broth or seawater, are a common appetizer; if you have a chance to order razor clams, by all means do. These elongated, delicately flavored clams are the nobility of Northwest shellfish. Mussels, which cover practically every rock along the Pacific coast, are only lately catching favor as a harvestable seafood.

Locally caught fish include red snapper, flounder and sole, halibut and cod. Shrimp is another major catch. Salmon, still a menu staple, are as likely to be from Alaska as from the Northwest. Local trout are also found in fish markets and menus: watch for vibrantly yellow golden trout.

**From the Field & Orchard** The Northwest offers an incredibly rich diversity in fruits and berries. Marionberries, unique to Oregon, are like a cross between raspberries and blackberries, but twice as big and more succulent. Try a slice of marionberry pie or cobbler with a scoop of local ice cream. Blueberries thrive in the acidic soil of the Northwest, and appear in pies, breads, muffins and scones. Mt Hood strawberries are renowned for their spicy, near-wild taste; they're completely unlike the hard red-and-white objects found in most grocery stores.

The thick forests also provides a bounty of fruit. Blackberry brambles snag clothing and grab at the legs of hikers. They're a great annoyance until they produce their heady abundance of purple-black fruit, which makes great jam and pies. More delicate salmonberries are a light orange, and make a good hiker's snack, or, if you can gather enough, a beautiful pastel jelly. Huckleberries are found high up in mountain meadows. A favorite of black bears, these small wild blueberries are fun to pick and make great pies. Look for huckleberry ice cream in out-of-the-way mountain cafes. Another berry that's become an important component of the coastal economy and of cutting-edge cooking is the cranberry. This part of the country is a major producer of this tart, bright red berry.

Another woodland group of plants has garnered a great deal in interest in the last ten years. Wild forest mushrooms are indigenous to Northwest forests, including the most noted and expensive varieties favored in French, Italian and Japanese cuisine. Chantrelle, oyster, morel, porcini and shitake mushrooms from the Northwest are shipped worldwide. Expect forest mushrooms to turn up on your plate indiscriminately as the pedigree of genuine Northwest Cuisine.

Many of the vegetables produced by small specialty farmers in the lower Willamette Valley, Sauvies Island and along the Puget Sound are grown organically. Some eastern Oregon and Washington ranchers have taken to raising organic cattle and sheep.

Along the coast and western valleys, dairies produce abundant milk, which is made into noted cheeses. The center of Oregon's dairy industry is the Tillamook Valley, with its famous Tillamook Cheddar. Other dairies in the Rogue and Umpqua valleys also produce traditional orange cheeses; one Tillamook-area dairy has

begun to fashion French-style brie cheeses. Local Tillamook and Umpqua dairy ice cream is also favored by locals.

No discussion of food from the Northwest would be complete without mentioning nuts; Oregon is one of the few states that has an official state nut. The filbert (or hazelnut) grows profusely here. Look for hazelnut gift packs (some jazzed up in smoke-house or jalepeno-style) or hazelnuts served in baked goods or with meat for that special, Northwest touch.

## DRINKS

Tapwater in the Northwest is safe and perfectly acceptable to drink. In fact, its purity is legendary. Bottled waters, including local brands from storied glaciers or lakes, are readily available in supermarkets. Water from streams should never be drunk without purifying, as giardia is a major problem See the entry on Health earlier in this chapter.

### Alcohol & Drinking Age

In all three states, persons under the age of 21 (minors) are prohibited from consuming alcohol in the USA. Carry a driver's license or passport as proof of age to enter a bar, order alcohol at a restaurant, or buy alcohol. Servers have the right to ask to see your ID and may refuse service without it. Minors are not allowed in bars and pubs, even to order non-alcoholic beverages. Unfortunately, this means that most dance clubs are also off-limits to minors, although a few clubs have solved the under-age problem with a segregated drinking area. Minors are, however, welcome in the dining areas of restaurants where alcohol may be served.

### Wines

Northwestern wines have an excellent international reputation. Especially noted are wines from an area south and west of Portland called Yamhill County. Conditions are very similar to France's Burgundy region, and chardonnay and pinot noir grapes do very well. Further south, in the Rogue River drainage, hot-weather grapes

**Microbreweries**

The Pacific Northwest is a major center of the US boom in small, specialty beer-making operations called microbreweries. Beers from these small independent businesses tend to echo either British or German brewing styles, but generally conform to the sorts of standards and styles known as British 'real ale' beers. While microbrewed beer is available throughout the region either in bottles or on tap at many bars and restaurants, for the real microbrew experience, head to the brewery itself, which often features a pub within sight of the brewing tanks. In addition to standard brews, at the brewpub there are often seasonal or specialty beers and ales available, often cask-conditioned. You can usually arrange a tour of the brewery, if sufficient notice is given.

Portland is a real center for microbrewing; its summer Oregon Brewers Festival brings in microbrewed beers from all over the nation. In the tradition of the frontier era, when every town had its own brewery, many out-of-the-way places now have their own, sometimes *very micro* brewery. Look for the local beer in places as diverse as Hood River, Cave Junction, Newport, Roslyn, Boise, Kalama, Government Camp, Yakima and Bend.

Most brewpubs exist to sell only their own beers and ales, though others are like British 'free-houses' and offer a selection of regional brews. In this guide, brewpubs are found under Entertainment or Places to Eat. ■

---

like Cabernet sauvignon and merlot are more the norm. On the slopes of the Columbia River Gorge, rieslings, pinot gris and Gewürztraminer grapes produce soft, dry white wines.

In Washington, the principal wine-growing region is east of the Cascades, in the arid foothills of the Yakima and Walla Walla rivers. The sturdy, hot-weather grapes of southern France do best out here; Cabernet sauvignon wines from these areas can rival California wines in strength, if not always in subtlety. Merlots and semillons are also popular, often boasting an herbaceous intensity not found in these varieties elsewhere. Enologists can contact the Washington Wine Commission (☎ (206) 728-2252) PO Box 61217, Seattle, WA 98121 and the Oregon Winegrowers Association (☎ (503) 228-8403) 1200 NW Front Ave, Ste 400, Portland, OR 97209 for more information:

**Winery Visits** Most wineries are owner-operated and welcome visitors to their vineyard tasting rooms for small sips of wines gratis or for a nominal fee. There is no obligation to buy wine after a tasting. The wineries recommended in this guide are among the best, though some are included as much for the view or gracious facility as much as for the quality of wine.

*Northwest Wines & Wineries* by Chuck Hill (Speed Graphics, Seattle 1993) is a good resource for traveling wine lovers.

## ENTERTAINMENT

Portland and Seattle are cosmopolitan cities, and offer a wide variety of films, music, theatre, sports and nightlife. Eugene and Bellingham are home to large well-respected universities that draw speakers, concerts, foreign films, art shows and student-oriented happenings like dance clubs and demonstrations.

In Ashland, with its Shakespearean theaters, bars fill up with young actors recently divested of roles like Hamlet, Juliet or Bottom. Boise, Bend, Spokane and Hood River also serve up diversions for the traveler, mostly live music in the back of energetic bars.

### Coffeehouses

In case you haven't heard, the Pacific Northwest is the hub of a coffee craze that seems to be sweeping the USA and Canada. It started out with a few espresso bars that served up European-style coffee drinks like cappuccinos and caffe lattes. Soon, the entire region was buzzing with caffeine, and asking for more. Standards for coffee quality – and strength – keep elevating.

In centers like Portland, Seattle, Bellingham and Eugene, you can expect to have at least one coffee shop on almost every downtown block; every major building will have an espresso cart out front. Even out-of-the-way gas stations and fast-food restaurants offer espresso drinks. It's part of life in the Northwest.

In addition to simple dash-in dash-out coffee bars and on-the-fly espresso carts, there are drive-in espresso bars, coffee delivery services (they'll bring coffee to your motel room) and coffeehouses. Portland and Seattle particularly abound with coffeehouses, which often offer some of the most unique and inexpensive entertainment. Coffeehouses are also just about the only venue where under-age travelers can easily meet their peers. Throughout this guide, coffeehouses of note (whether for entertainment, food, the scene or just for the quality of their coffee) are noted under Entertainment or Places to Eat.

Starbucks, the now-national chain of coffee bars from the Seattle area, is by no means the only coffee emporium in the region. As standards for taste and strength of coffee increase, locals can be fickle about Starbucks, now that they have achieved such notoriety. There's competition too, inluding Seattle's Best Coffee (SBC) in Seattle, Torrefazione Italia in Portland and Seattle, Coffee People in Portland and Allann Bros in Eugene and Corvallis.

### Bars, Taverns & Brewpubs

Oregon and Washington law makes a strict differentiation between bars and taverns. The former can sell hard liquor as well as beer and wine; taverns can sell only beer and wine. Brewpubs sell locally made beers, ales, wine, and are quite trendy. They often serve quite good food too. Taverns are more often than not intensely local pubs with limited tolerance for strangers. Idaho bars usually serve both hard alcohol and beer and wine.

### Spectator Sports

There aren't a lot of professional teams in the Pacific Northwest. Universities offer the most events throughout the year and are very popular with both students and the general community.

Football draws enormous crowds in the fall. The Seattle Seahawks are the most popular team. Games with university teams, most notably the U of W Huskies, the WSU Cougars and the U of O Ducks are always big crowd pleasers. The season runs from the first week in September (when school starts) to the end of January.

The Seattle Mariners are the most known baseball team in the Northwest, but they haven't made any headway in national reputation. The season starts the first week of April and ends in October with the World Series.

The basketball season runs from late October to mid-June. The Seattle Supersonics and Portland Trailblazers always draw a crowd of frenzied fans.

Universities throughout the region offer a great wealth of sporting events. Around the Puget Sound university crew teams and sailing teams compete in regattas in the spring.

Hockey and soccer still aren't very popular but occasionally a good game comes up. More detailed coverage, including sports venues, is given in each city with a team worth seeing.

### THINGS TO BUY

Oregon is a good place to shop, because it doesn't have a sales tax or VAT. Seattle is a shoppers paradise, especially the area around Pike Place Market and the downtown core. Many towns along the Oregon Coast, particularly Cannon Beach, are full of boutiques, as is Friday Harbor in the San Juan Islands.

Probably the most common souvenir of Oregon is something made from myrtlewood. This rare tree grows only in southern Oregon and Lebanon; it's even mentioned in the Bible. If it weren't uncommon no one would be making a fuss about it. But here, it's turned into a dizzying array of carved items, from bowls to statuettes to golf clubs.

Pendleton Woolen Mills has its headquarters in the Northwest, and their trademark plaid shirts make a nice, although pricey, souvenir. Outside of Portland there's a Niketown where just about anything sporting the Nike label can be bought.

Northwest food and wine are good purchases. Oregon grows over 90% of the nation's filberts, so various kinds of hazelnut products are everywhere. Smoked salmon has a long pedigree here, beginning with the Northwest Indian tribes, who smoked the fish to preserve it over long periods. Local cheeses are popular throughout the region. Northwest's wine has been accorded international honors, and is worth a try. Most fish markets can pack fresh fish or seafood for air journeys or overnight delivery. Berry jams and syrups made from wild and local-grown berries are easily found; as are candies and food products made from cranberries.

A number of Northwest cities have 'Saturday Markets' where local artisans and farmers bring products to sell. Portland's Saturday Market is reputed to be the largest open-air crafts fair in the nation; Eugene, Sisters, and other cities have also picked up on the idea. Over half of Pike Place Market in Seattle is devoted to local crafts and gifts.

# Outdoor Activities

This chapter explores the many options available to a recreationalist in the Pacific Northwest, ranging from near universals like hiking and backpacking to more esoteric, specialized pursuits like rock collecting and clamming.

## USEFUL ORGANIZATIONS
### Washington

Washington State Park Headquarters
7150 Cleanwater Lane, PO Box 42650, Olympia WA 98504-2650 (☎ (360) 902-8563) Detailed listings of campgrounds and facilities.

Outdoor Recreation Information Center
915 2nd Ave, Suite 422, Seattle, WA 98174 (☎ (206) 220-7450) A shared USFS headquarters and National Park information center.

Washington State Outfitters & Guides Association
c/o High Country Outfitters, 22845 NE 8th, Suite 331, Redmond, WA 98053 (☎ (206) 753-5700)

Professional River Outfitters of Washington
c/o Cascade Adventures, 1202 E Pike St, No 1142, Seattle, WA 98122 (☎ (206) 323-5485)

Washington Trails Association
1305 4th Ave, No 512, Seattle, WA 98101 (☎ (206) 625-1367)

Cascade Orienteering Club
PO Box 31375, Seattle, WA 98103 (☎ (206) 783-3899)

### Oregon

Oregon Guides & Packers Association
PO Box 10841, Eugene, OR 97440 (☎ (503) 683-9552) State-wide listings for guided fishing, hunting, and river floating trips.

Oregon State Parks & Recreation Department
525 Trade St SE, Salem, OR 97310 (☎ (503) 378-5012)

Oregon Natural Resources Council
3921 SE Salmon St, Portland, OR 97214 (☎ (502 236-9772)

### Idaho

Idaho Department of Parks & Recreation
PO Box 83720, Boise, ID 83720-0065 (☎ (208) 334-4199)

United States Forest Service
1750 Front St, Boise, ID 83702 (☎ (208) 364-4100)

Bureau of Land Management
Idaho State Office, 3380 Americana Terrace, Boise, ID 83706 (☎ (208) 384-3300)

Idaho Department of Fish & Game
600 S Walnut, PO Box 25, Boise, ID 83707 (☎ (800) 635-7820)

Idaho Outfitters & Guides Association
PO Box 95, Boise, ID 83701 (☎ (800) 847-4843)

Idaho Trail Machine Association
Idaho Department of Parks & Recreation, Statehouse Mail, Boise, ID 83720 (☎ (208) 327-7444)

## HIKING & BACKPACKING

Hiking is a major part of the recreational lifeblood of the Northwest. With so many mountain ranges, public forests, wilderness areas, wildlife refuges and coastal regions, the incentive to get out there and walk around is nearly overwhelming.

The Pacific Crest Trail (see below) is one of several National Scenic Trails, and is the perfect way for the outdoorsperson to see the Northwest.

### Treading Lightly

Backcountry areas are composed of fragile environments and cannot support an inundation of human activity, especially insensitive and careless activity. A good suggestion is to treat the backcountry like you would your own backyard.

A new code of backcountry ethics is evolving to deal with the growing numbers of people in the wilderness. Most conservation organizations and hiker's manuals have their own set of backcountry codes, all of which outline the same important principles: minimizing the impact on the land, leaving no trace and taking nothing but photographs and memories. The three important rules to remember are: stay on the main trail, stay on the main trail, and, lastly, even if it means walking through mud or crossing a patch of snow, *stay on the main trail*.

## National Parks

Crater Lake National Park is Oregon's only national park. Washington has three: the Olympic, Mt Rainier and North Cascades national parks. Idaho has none, but its eastern border touches Wyoming's Yellowstone and Grand Teton national parks. Unless you have a few days to get into the backcountry of a national park, or are visiting during non-tourist season (before Memorial Day and after Labor Day), expect hiking in the Northwest's big parks to be crowded.

Travelers with little hiking experience will appreciate well-marked, well-maintained trails, often with restroom facilities at either end and interpretive displays along the way. The trails give access to some parks' most accessible natural features and usually show up on NPS maps as 'nature trails' or 'self-guided interpretive trails' and are usually no longer than two miles.

Hikers seeking a true wilderness trip, away from heavy foot traffic, should avoid national parks and try less-celebrated wilderness areas and mountain ranges. Most national parks require overnight hikers to follow a specific itinerary and carry backcountry permits, available from visitors centers or ranger stations, which must be obtained 24 hours in advance. While this system reduces the chance of people getting lost in the backcountry, and limits the number of people using one area at any given time, it may detract from the sense of space and freedom hiking can give.

## Wilderness Areas

The NPS, USFS and BLM all manage substantial roadless areas in the Pacific Northwest as wilderness, inaccessible to mechanized travel. Most of these designated areas are on USFS land; while the BLM is a relative latecomer to the concept, its wilderness areas can be among the best in terms of sheer solitude.

The 1964 Wilderness Act, the first major act of Congress to set aside large roadless areas as federally administered wilderness, defines wilderness as:

an area where the earth and its community of life are untrammeled by man, where man himself is a visitor who does not remain . . . . It is a region which contains no permanent human inhabitants, no possibility for motorized travel, and is spacious enough so that a traveler crossing it by foot or horse must have the experience of sleeping out of doors.

## Wilderness Camping

Camping in undeveloped areas is rewarding for its peacefulness, but presents special concerns. Take care to insure that the area you choose can comfortably support your presence, and leave the surroundings in better condition than on arrival. The following list of guidelines should help:

• Camp below timberline, since alpine areas are generally more fragile. Good campsites are found, not made. Altering a site shouldn't be necessary.

• Camp at least 200 feet (70 adult steps) away from the nearest lake, river, or stream.

• Bury human waste in holes dug six to eight inches deep at least 200 feet from water, camp or trails. The salt and minerals in urine attract deer; use a tent-bottle (funnel attachments are available for women) if you are prone to middle-of-the-night calls by Mother Nature. Camouflage the hole when finished

• Use soaps and detergents sparingly or not at all, and never allow these things to enter streams or lakes. When washing yourself (a backcountry luxury, not necessity), lather-up (with biodegradable soap) and rinse yourself with cans of water 200 feet away from your water source. Scatter dish water after removing all food particles.

• It's recommended to carry a lightweight stove for cooking, and to use a lantern instead of a fire.

• If a fire is allowed and appropriate, dig out the native topsoil, and build a fire in the hole. Gather sticks no larger than an adult's wrist from the ground. Do not snap branches off live, dead or downed trees. Pour wastewater from meals around the perimeter of the campfire to prevent it from spreading, and thoroughly douse it before leaving or going to bed.

• Establish a cooking area at least 100 yards away from your tent and designate cooking-clothes to leave in the food bag, away from your tent.

• Burn cans to get rid of their odor, then remove the ashes and pack them out with you.

• Pack out what you pack in, including all trash – yours *and* others'.

## Safety

The major forces to be reckoned with while hiking and camping are the weather (which is uncontrollable), and your own frame of mind. Be prepared for the Northwest's unpredictable weather – you may go to bed under a clear sky and wake up to two feet of snow. Carry a rain jacket and light pair of long underwear at all times, even on short afternoon hikes. Backpackers should have a pack-liner (heavy-duty garbage bags work well), full set of rain gear and food which does not require cooking. A positive attitude is helpful in any situation. If a hot shower, comfortable mattress and clean clothes are essential to your well-being, don't head out into the wilderness for five days – stick to day hikes.

Highest safety measures suggest never hiking alone, but solo travelers should not be discouraged, especially if they value solitude. The important thing is to always let someone know where you are going and how long you plan to be gone. Use sign-in boards at trailheads or ranger stations. Travelers looking for hiking companions can inquire or post notices at ranger stations, outdoors stores, campgrounds and youth hostels.

Forging rivers and streams is another potentially dangerous but often necessary part of being on the trail. In national parks and along maintained trails in national forests, bridges usually cross large bodies of water (this is not the case in designated wilderness areas, where bridges are taboo). Upon reaching a river, unclip all of your pack straps – your pack is expendable, you

are not. Avoid crossing barefoot – river cobbles will suck body heat right out of your feet, numbing them and making it impossible to navigate. Bring a pair of lightweight canvas sneakers to avoid sloshing around in wet boots for the rest of your hike. Although cold water will make you want to cross as quickly as possible, don't rush things: take small steps, watch where you are stepping, and keep your balance. Using a staff for balance is helpful, but don't rely on it to support all your weight. Don't enter water higher than mid-thigh; any higher than that and your body gives the current a large mass to work against.

If you should get wet, wring your clothes out immediately, wipe off all the excess water on your body and hair that you can and put on any dry clothes you might have. Synthetic fabrics and wool retain heat when they get wet, but cotton does not.

People with little hiking or backpacking experience should not attempt to do too much, too soon or they might end up being non-hikers for the wrong reasons. Know your limitations, know the route you are going to take, and pace yourself accordingly. Remember, there is absolutely nothing wrong with turning back or not going as far as you originally planned.

### Long-Distance Backpacking

Careful preparations for a long-distance backpack hike (that is, long enough that you will need to resupply along the way) are of the utmost importance. Don't think you can jump from weekend trips into a several-weeks trek; you've got to train yourself and you've got to lay out a resupply plan in advance. Many established hiking trails have organizations which can supply you with a list of area post offices, stores and ranger stations who can receive your re-supply packages in the mail and hold them until you arrive to claim them. If you can't dig up such a list, try calling post offices. Some establishments may charge a holding fee. Preparations for a long-distance trip should include the following:

- Buy the proper equipment; learn first aid suitable to mountaineering situations, back-country protocol, and how to care for the outdoors.
- Practice on weekend trips; be able to cover between 10 and 20 miles per day
- Study guides and maps to the trail or region you plan to cover; plan a daily itinerary taking into account re-supply points.
- Buy supplies; pack resupply packages for mailing to resupply points.

## What to Bring

**Equipment** The following is meant to be a general guideline for backpackers, not an 'if-I-have-everything-here-I'll-be-fine' checklist. Know yourself and what special things you may need on the trail, and consider the area and climactic conditions you will be traveling in. This list is inadequate for snow country or winter.

- Boots – light to medium are recommended for day hikes, while sturdy boots are necessary for extended trips with a heavy pack. Most importantly they should be well broken in and have a good heel.
- Alternative footwear – thongs/sandals/mucklucks/running shoes for wearing around camp (optional), and canvas sneakers for crossing streams.
- Socks – heavy polypropylene or wool will stay warm even if they get wet. Frequent changes during the day reduce the chance of blisters, but are usually impractical.
- Subdued colors are recommended, but if hiking during hunting season, blaze orange is a necessity.
- Shorts, light shirt – for everyday wear; remember that heavy cotton takes a long time to dry and is very cold when wet.
- Long-sleeve shirt – light cotton, wool or polypropylene. A button-down front makes layering easy and can be left open when the weather is hot and your arms need protection from the sun.
- Long pants – heavy denim jeans take forever to dry. Sturdy cotton or canvas pants are good for trekking through brush, and cotton or nylon sweats are comfortable to wear around camp. Long underwear with shorts over them is the perfect combo – warm but not cumbersome – for trail hiking where there is not much brush.

- Wool/polypropylene/polar fleece sweater/pullover – essential in cold weather.
- Rain gear – light, breathable, and waterproof is the ideal combination. If nothing else is available, use heavy duty trashbags to cover you and your packs.
- Hat – wool or polypropylene is best for cold weather, while a cotton hat with a brim is good for sun protection. About 80% of body heat escapes through the top of the head. Keep your head (and neck) warm to reduce the chances of hypothermia.
- Bandana/handkerchief – good for a runny nose, dirty face, unmanageable hair, picnic lunch and flag (especially a red one).
- Small towel – one which is indestructible and will dry quickly.
- First Aid Kit – should include self-adhesive bandages, disinfectant, antibiotic salve or cream, gauze, small scissors and tweezers.
- Knife, fork, spoon and mug – a double-layer plastic mug with a lid is best. A mug acts as eating and drinking receptacle, mixing bowl and wash basin; the handle will prevent you from getting burned. Bring an extra cup if you like to eat and drink simultaneously.
- Pots and pans – aluminum cook sets are best, but any sturdy one-quart pot is sufficient. True gourmands who want more than pasta, soup and freeze-dried food will need a skillet or frying pan. A pot scrubber is helpful for removing stubborn oatmeal, especially using cold water and no soap.
- Stove – lightweight and easy to operate is ideal. Most outdoors stores rent propane or butane stoves; test the stove before you head out, even cook a meal on it, to familiarize yourself with any quirks it may have.
- Water purifier – optional but really nice to have; water can be purified by boiling for at least 10 minutes.
- Matches/lighter – waterproof matches are good, and having several lighters on hand is smart.
- Candle/lantern – candles are easy to operate, but do not stay lit when they are dropped or wet and can be hazardous inside a tent. Outdoors stores rent lanterns; as with a stove, test it before you hit the trail.
- Flashlight – each person should have his/her own, and should be sure its batteries have plenty of life left in them.
- Sleeping bag – goosedown bags are warm and lightweight, but worthless if they get wet; most outdoors stores rent synthetic bags.

- Sleeping pad – this is strictly a personal preference. Use a sweater or sleeping bag sack stuffed with clothes as a pillow.
- Tent – make sure it is waterproof, or has a waterproof cover, and know how to put it up *before* you reach camp. Remember that your packs will be sharing the tent with you.
- Camera/binoculars – don't forget extra film and waterproof film canisters (sealable plastic bags work well).
- Compass and maps – each person should have his/her own.
- Eyeglasses – contact lens wearers should always bring a back-up set.
- Sundries – toilet paper, small sealable plastic bags, insect repellent, sun screen, lip balm, unscented moisturizing creme, moleskin for foot blisters, dental floss (burnable, and good when there is no water for brushing), sunglasses, deck of cards, pen/pencil and paper/notebook/journal, books and nature guides.

**Food** Keeping your energy up is important, but so is keeping your pack light. Backpackers tend to eat a substantial breakfast and dinner, and snack heavily in between. There is no need to be excessive. If you pack loads of food you'll probably use it, but if you have just enough you will probably not miss anything.

Some basic staples are packaged instant oatmeal, bread (the denser the better), rice or pasta, instant soup or ramen noodles, dehydrated meat (jerky), dried fruit, energy bars, chocolate, trail mix, (gorp – raisins and peanuts mixed with various other goodies like sunflower seed, M&Ms or dried fruit) and peanut butter, honey or jam (in plastic jars or squeeze bottles). Don't forget the wet-wipes, but be sure to dispose of them properly or pack them out.

**Books**
If you are interested in outdoor recreation in the Northwest, you might begin your search by contacting The Mountaineers, a Seattle-based publisher that offers the largest selection, and most reliable books on the Northwest. Call (☎ (800) 553-4453) or write for a catalog at 1011 SW Klickitat Way, Seattle, WA 98134.

There are quite a few good 'how-to' and 'where-to' books on the market, usually found in outdoors stores, or bookshops' Sports & Recreation or Outdoors section. Chris Camden's *Backpacker's Handbook* (Ragged Mountain Press, Camden, ME, 1992) is a beefy collection of tips for the trail. More candid is *A Hiker's Companion* (The Mountaineers, Seattle, 1992), by Cindy Ross and Todd Gladfelter, who hiked 12,000 miles before sitting down to write. *How to Shit in the Woods* (Ten Speed Press, Berkeley, CA, 1994) is Kathleen Meyer's explicit, comic and useful manual on toilet training in the wilderness.

**Maps**
A good map is essential for any hiking trip. NPS and USFS ranger stations usually stock topographical maps which cost about $2 to $6. In the absence of a ranger station, try the local stationary or hardware store.

Longer hikes require two types of maps: USGS Quadrangles, and US Department of Agriculture-Forest Service maps. To order a map index and price list, contact the US Geological Survey, PO Box 25286, Denver, CO, 80225. For general information on maps, see that entry in the Facts for the Visitor chapter.

**Washington**
Washington, it is said, is where hikers go when they die. There are gorgeous trails in virtually every corner of the state. Olympic National Park is a particularly rich area, as most of its interior is accessible only by foot. The Hoh River Trail is one of the longest and most popular hikes, passing through the Hoh Rainforest on the way to Mt Olympus, the park's highest peak.

The Wonderland Trail, in Mt Rainier National Park, is a 93-mile loop trail that circles the heavily glaciated mountain; it takes about a week and a half to complete in its entirety. At nearby Mt St Helens National Volcanic Monument, the short Ape Cave trail passes through the longest lava tube in the continental USA.

The northern Cascades are a wonderfully rich region for hikers. Many trails around nearby Mt Baker require fairly strenuous

## The Pacific Crest Trail

A truly amazing thing about the West Coast of the USA is that you can walk from Mexico to Canada, across the entire expanse of California, Oregon and Washington, almost without setting foot off of national park or national forest lands. Simply follow the Pacific Crest Trail (PCT). This 2638-mile trail passes through 24 national forests, seven national parks, 33 designated wilderness areas and six state parks, always following as closely as possible the crest of the Sierra Mountains in California and the Cascade Range in Oregon and Washington, at an average elevation of 5000 feet.

To hike the trail in its entirety, at a good clip of 15 miles a day, would take nearly half a year; the Oregon and Washington portions can each feasibly be hiked in one month. But you don't have to undertake such a dramatic, cross-state trek to take advantage of the PCT. Day or weekend hikers can plan short trips along any stretch of the trail.

Many of the West Coast's most spectacular wilderness sites are traversed by the PCT, including Yosemite and Sequoia national parks in California, Crater Lake National Park, Three Sisters Wilderness and Mt Hood in Oregon, and Mt Rainier and North Cascades national parks in Washington.

The Pacific Crest Trail Association, headquartered in California, can provide detailed information on the trail, as well as addresses for regional USFS and Wilderness Area offices, tips on long and short-distance backpacking trips, weather conditions and which areas require wilderness permits. Call them at (800) 817-2243, or write to 5325 Elkhorn Blvd, Suite 256, Sacramento, CA 95842. ■

climbs up glacier-carved valleys to viewpoints and wildflower meadows.

On Lake Chelan, the village of Stehekin is approachable only by ferry, seaplane or foot, and makes for a good long-distance hike over Cascade Pass from Marblemount. The Alpine Lakes Wilderness Area, near Leavenworth, is another region of countless hikes, encompassing the aptly named Enchantment Lakes.

In the northeastern corner of the state, the Shedroof Divide National Recreation Trail is a 22-mile trail through the Salmo-Priest Wilderness Area, where a few grizzly bears and caribou still dwell.

And don't forget the San Juan Islands. Orcas Island's Moran State Park is well-fixed for hikers and campers.

### Oregon

From coast to river gorge, mountainscape to desert, Oregon offers some of the USA's most diverse hiking. Below is a sampler of the state's spectacular trails.

A good way to see the country around Portland is by following the 40-Mile Loop, which originates in Portland's Washington Park and circles the city, linking 35 state and city parks.

The Oregon Coast Trail is a not-yet-complete trail system that will link the entire 362-mile Oregon coast. Significant portions of the trail are complete, and can be utilized as either a long-distance hike or as a day-hiking trail. A brochure is available from the Oregon State Parks Department (see above).

The Timberline Trail, encircling Mt Hood, is a 40-mile long trail that passes waterfalls and glaciers, wildflower meadows and alpine forests. It is coincident, in segments, with the Pacific Crest Trail. Also in the Mt Hood National Forest, the Eagle Creek Trail is a 13-mile route that follows the cliffs of the Columbia River Gorge past many spectacular waterfalls.

Southwestern Oregon's two primary rivers, the Rogue and the Umpqua, are accompanied by hiking trails. The 40-mile Rogue River Trail and the 77-mile North Umpqua Trail both offer terrific wildlife viewing and recreational opportunities.

The Nee-Me-Poo Trail follows the path of Chief Joseph and the Nez Perce through three states, begins just north of the Imnaha Bridge near Hells Canyon, and in 3.5 miles climbs to a view point over the Snake River.

## Idaho

The Idaho State Centennial Trail is a 1200-mile long trek from Canada to Nevada, passing Priest Lake, Lake Pend Oreille, the Sawtooth National Recreation Area and many national forests and wildernesses.

To the east, Yellowstone and Grand Teton national parks lie just across the Wyoming border and offer up some of the most spectacular and justly famous hiking in the USA.

## BIKING
## Washington

A favorite destination for cyclists, the San Juan Islands are mostly flat, with gently rolling hills and inland lakes and forests just minutes from stunning coastal paths.

### Organized Bicycling Tours

A terrific way to see off-the-beaten-path regions of Oregon and Washington is on an organized bike tour. The Cycle Oregon event and the Washington State Sampler are annual rides for cyclists of all ages and skill levels (but you've got to be in pretty good shape, as some days you can expect to climb thousands of feet in elevation). Trucks carry your gear for you and food is sometimes provided. It's often the most exciting event of the year for the residents of quiet Northwestern towns, who crowd the roadsides when the herd comes wheeling through. For a complete list of these rides in the USA, contact the National Bicycle Tour Directors Assn, c/o Free Wheel, Inc, PO Box 1770, Tulsa, OK 74102.

**Cycle Oregon** A kind of week-long party on wheels, the Cycle Oregon ride traverses 60 to 80 miles a day of Oregon landscape, covering a different route each year. Cyclists from all over the USA vie for one of 2000 spaces in the limited registration, and then take to the road in September in a huge caravan of bikes, supply trucks, portable toilets, mobile snack stands and the like. The $400 fee covers camping (bring your own tent), food, gear transport and emergency bike repair and medical care. Call (800) 292-5367, or write to Cycle Oregon at 8700 Nimbus Ave, Suite B, Beaverton, OR 97005.

Cycle Oregon also organizes the one-day Summer Century Ride in July. This $50 all-day ride includes meals, and is a great diversion for in-shape travelers looking for some serious exercise.

**Washington State Sampler** Much smaller than its Oregon counterpart, the Washington State Sampler is limited to 100 riders and covers 600 miles in nine days in late June. The cost of $250 covers camping, gear transport and snacks. Call (206) 353-4548 or write to 1402 73rd St, Everett, WA 98203, for information.

**Cycle America** Riders who really want to see America can go all out on the Cycle America ride, which crosses the country from coast to coast for the duration of the summer. The ride is broken down into 12 week-long segments; you can do any or all of them, and the cost depends on how long you're on the road. Cycle America (π (800) 245-3263), PO Box 485, Cannon Falls, MN 55009, can provide information. ∎

Bikes can be transported by ferry to the islands for a fee, or rented on the islands.

Other popular cycling areas include the Methow valley, where cross-country skiing trails are taken over by mountain bikers in the summer.

## Oregon

The Oregon Coast Bike Route follows Hwy 101 between Astoria and Brookings, on the California border. A few side loop routes make passes of scenic areas not accessible from the highway. The Cascade Lakes Hwy, in Central Oregon, is also popular with bikers. It passes many small lakes in the mountainous region south of Mt Bachelor and the Three Sisters Wilderness. Not far away, the Newberry Crater Rim Loop, 14 miles long, winds around one of the state's fascinating volcanic features.

Write to Bikeway Program Manager, Oregon Department of Transportation, Room 200, Transportation Building, Salem, OR 97310 (☎ (503) 378-3432), for the free pamphlet *Oregon Bicycling Guide*, and Oregon Coast Bike Route. Send $5.50 for the *Moutain Bike guide to Oregon* to the Parks & Recreation Department, 25 Trade St SE, Salem, OR 97310, (☎ (503) 378-6305).

## Idaho

Idaho's Taft Tunnel Bike Trail follows a converted rail line through mountain tunnels and over high railway trestles, across the state line to Montana. The centerpiece of the trail is the 8771-foot-long Taft Tunnel, constructed in 1909.

## SKIING

In winter, skiing takes over the slopes of the volcanic peaks of the Cascade Range, as well as the snow-glazed back-country byways, riveside trails and non-mountainous wilderness areas.

## Downhill

Noted downhill ski areas in Oregon include the five resorts at Mt Hood – the most famous of which, Timberline Lodge, offers nearly year-round conditions – and Mt Bachelor and Anthony Lakes, both famous for their powder skiing. In Washington, Crystal Mountain, Snoqualmie Pass, Stevens Pass and Mt Baker are the popular resorts. Idaho offers probably the best skiing in the Northwest at Sun Valley in Ketchum, where powder-dry snow and steep descents have been attracting celebrity skiers for decades. Bogus Basin, just north of Boise; Silver Mountain Resort, on the Panhandle; Brundage Mountain, near McCall; Schweitzer Mountain Resort, near Sandpoint; and Grand Targhee, just across the Wyoming border, are other quality Idaho resorts.

## Snowboarding

Snowboarding has recently swept the nation's ski culture and taken on a following of its own. Baggy pants, psychedelic jackets and funky hats have replaced more traditional ski garb. Snowboarders stand sideways, strapped to a board four or five feet long, to cruise down the mountains. The motion is comparable to surfing or skateboarding, rather than skiing, which may explain why many snowboarders look like skate rats. As a rule, snowboarders love powder snow, hate moguls and ice, and need an older sibling's ID to get into bars at night.

Snowboarders find the Cascades' powder perfect for carving.

## Cross-Country

Cross-country skiing is also very popular in the Northwest. A number of downhill resorts also offer groomed cross-country trails; private ski groups sometimes offer groomed trails for a small fee. However, cross-country skiing need not be so regimented. The heavy snowfall in the Northwest converts the vast wilderness areas of Washington, Oregon and Idaho into winter playgrounds. When there's snow enough, any USFS road is a make-shift ski trail; better yet, you'll probably have the road, and the mountainside, to yourself.

Some spectacular regions for off-the-beaten-path skiing in Washington are Mt St Helens, Mt Rainier, the Lake Chelan area and Olympic National Park (Hurricane Ridge, near the park's northern entrance, accesses high mountain meadows). In the Methow valley, a series of ski huts are spaced along the trails for multi-day expeditions; you can even hire outfitters to transport your gear.

In Oregon, the Rim Drive that circles Crater Lake is popular with nordic skiers in the winter. All Mt Hood downhill resorts also offer trails, but a better bet may be the Tea Cup Lake trails maintained by the Oregon Nordic Club, with 18.6 miles of skiing. Mt Hood National Forest offices can provide a list of other trails in the area.

There are miles of groomed cross-country trails around Sun Valley, Idaho's premier ski resort.

## CLIMBING & MOUNTAINEERING

If you're interested in climbing in the Cascades, the local USFS office is a good place to inquire for information about guided hikes. You'll also want to procure the book *Selected Climbs in the Cascades* by Jim Nelson and Peter Potterfield (The Mountaineers). This book also covers rock climbing, particularly in the Northern Cascades area.

Recently, rock climbers have subordinated the idea of reaching summits to testing their skills on varied routes on diffi-

cult terrain, with the achievement of a summit either secondary or unimportant; the technique of climbing is the important matter.

Climbing and mountaineering are demanding activities requiring top physical condition, an understanding of the composition of various rock types and their hazards, other hazards of the high country and familiarity with a variety of equipment, including ropes, chocks, bolts, carabiners and harnesses. Many climbers prefer granite, because of its strength and frequent handholds, but some climbers prefer limestone for a challenge. Some sedimentary rock is suitable for climbing, but crumbling volcanic rock can be very difficult.

Mountaineers and climbers categorize routes on a scale of one to five; Class I is hiking, while Class II involves climbing on unstable materials like talus and may require use of the hands for keeping balance, especially with a heavy pack. Class III places the climber in dangerous situations, involving exposed terrain (the Sierra Club uses the example of a staircase on a high building without handholds – scary but not difficult), with the likely consequences of a fall being a broken limb.

Class IV involves steep rock, smaller holds and great exposure, with obligatory use of ropes and knowledge of knots and techniques like belaying and rappelling; the consequences of falling are death rather than injury. Class V divides into a dozen or more subcategories based on degree of difficulty and requires advanced techniques, including proficiency with rope.

The Access Fund, PO Box 67A25, Los Angeles, CA 90067, is a non-profit organization working to keep climbing areas open to the public by purchasing or negotiating access to key sites.

## Safety

Climbing is potentially a hazardous activity, though serious accidents are more spectacular than frequent; driving to the climbing site can be more dangerous than the climb itself. Nevertheless, climbers

Cattle Point, San Juan Island, Washington (BM)

Halfway, Oregon, and the Wallowa Mountains (BM)

Crown Point Vista House, Columbia River Gorge, Oregon (DF)

should be aware of hazards which can contribute to falls and very serious injury or death.

Weather is an important factor, as rain makes slippery rock and lightning can strike an exposed climber; hypothermia is an additional concern. In dry weather, lack of water can lead to dehydration.

## Minimum Impact

Many climbers are now following guidelines similar to those established for hikers to preserve the resource on which their sport relies. These include concentrating impact in high use areas by using established roads, trails and routes for access; dispersing use in pristine areas and avoiding the creation of new trails; refraining from creating or enhancing handholds; and eschewing the placement of bolts wherever possible. Climbers should also take special caution to respect archaeological and cultural resources, such as rock art, and refrain from climbing in such areas.

## Washington

The highest peak in the Cascades is Mt Rainier at 14,411 feet; it's also the most heavily glaciated peak in the lower 48 states. Emmons Glacier, on the mountain's east side, is a popular and challenging ascent. Mt Adams (12,276 feet), also in the southern Cascades, is one of the state's easiest peak climbs, and the all-too-recently-active volcano, Mt St Helens, is a unique challenge.

The craggy peaks of the northern Cascades offer extremely challenging ascents for experienced climbers. Mt Baker, at 10,778 feet, is another heavily glaciated peak with a number of glacier climbs; Easton Glacier is the easiest ascent and Coleman and Roosevelt are more technically demanding.

To complete the trio of Washington's national parks, Olympic National Park also contains glaciated mountain peaks for climbers. Mt Olympus, at 7965 feet, is the most popular, but is reached only by a 17-mile trail from the nearest road, at the Hoh Rain Forest Visitors Center.

## Oregon

Oregon's Mt Hood claims the distinction of being the world's second most climbed peak over 10,000 feet (after Japan's Mt Fuji). The climb is a sort of Oregonian pilgrimage, a trek that many feel must be made at least once during one's lifetime.

Smith Rock is a world-renowned rock-climbing venue, towering above central Oregon's Crooked River, and the Cascades' South Sister, at 10,358 feet, can be conquered without technical equipment.

## FISHING

The fishing mainstay of the Northwest for thousands of years has been the salmon; today, populations of the sea-going fish are so threatened that sport-fishing seasons on many rivers are offered only sporadically. If you want to go salmon fishing, it's still possible, but be sure to link up with a reputable outfitter, and keep in contact with the local fish & wildlife departments. Regulations and seasons change quickly.

Fish with a less ambitious life-cycle than salmon are still abundant in the Northwest, and make for great fishing. Various kinds of trout, sturgeon and bass are found in most streams and rivers. The great fishing rivers of Oregon include the Deschutes River in central Oregon and the Rogue and Umpqua rivers in the southern part of the state.

The Yakima and Wenatchee rivers in central Washington, the many rivers and lakes in Olympic National Park, the northern Cascades' Methow and Stehekin rivers, Lake Chelan (the USA's third-deepest lake) and Lake Roosevelt are Washington hotspots, and the Salmon, Clearwater and Henry's Fork rivers in Idaho are also well-loved. Many coastal towns offers charter fishing trips into the Pacific; see Coastal Activities, below, for more information.

Anglers are required in all situations to have the appropriate state licenses and to abide by whatever seasonal or territorial restrictions are in place. For instance, the same stream may have several sections that have quite different restrictions on types of hooks, bait, seasons and what size and type of fish can be kept. It can be complicated, so be sure to ask for current regulations at bait or sporting good stores or fish and wildlife offices.

Fishing licenses are issued to in-state and out-of-state anglers; the latter are more expensive. Both licenses can be bought for a year, or for shorter intervals.

## WHITE-WATER RAFTING & KAYAKING

The mighty rivers of the Northwest make this one of the top rafting and kayaking areas in the nation. A large number of outfitters guide trips down the many rivers, ranging from half-day floats to three and four day expeditions through untracked wilderness.

Kayak and raft rentals are also available for those who feel confident enough to take on a river, although be aware that many of these rivers are not for novices. Note that some rivers are closely regulated and have rafting seasons; permits, which are limited in number and issued by a random draw, are necessary on some rivers. Another type of thrill offered on the river is a jet boat tour, particularly popular on the Rogue in Oregon and the Snake, which cuts across Idaho to Hells Canyon on the Idaho/Oregon border. These flat-bottomed boats skim at great speeds over the surface of the water, making for loud, bumpy, exciting entertainment. Grants Pass, OR, is the place to go for excursions on the Rogue; Lewiston, ID is a center for jet boat outfitters on the Snake.

River trips are classified on a scale of I to VI according to difficulty (see below). On any given river, classifications can vary over the course of the year, depending on the water level. Higher water levels, usually associated with spring runoff, can make a river trip either easier or more difficult by covering up hazards or increasing the velocity of the river, while lower water levels can expose hazards like rocks and whirlpools, making the river more exciting. Some, if not most, rivers depend on water releases from upstream dams.

White-water trips take place in either large rafts seating a dozen or more people, or smaller rafts seating half a dozen; the latter are more interesting and exciting because the ride over the rapids can be rougher, and because everyone participates in rowing. While white-water trips are not without danger, and it's not unusual for participants to fall out of the raft in rough water, serious injuries are rare and a huge majority of trips are without incident. All participants must wear US Coast Guard approved life jackets, and even non-swimmers are welcome. All trips have at least one river guide trained in life-saving techniques.

## River Rankings

Class I – easy
The river ranges from flatwater to occasional series of mild rapids.

Class II – medium
The river has frequent stretches of rapids with waves up to three feet high and easy chutes, ledges and falls. The best route is easy to identify and the entire river can be run in open canoes.

Class III – difficult
The rivers feature numerous rapids with high, irregular waves and difficult chutes and falls that often require scouting. They are for experienced paddlers who either use kayaks and rafts or have a spray cover for their canoe.

Class IV – very difficult
Rivers with long stretches of irregular waves, powerful back eddies and even constricted canyons. Scouting is mandatory and rescues can be difficult in many places. Suitable in rafts or white-water kayaks with paddlers equipped with helmets.

Class V – extremely difficult
Rivers with continuous violent rapids, powerful rollers and high, unavoidable waves and haystacks. These rivers are only for white-water kayaks and paddlers who are proficient in the Eskimo roll.

Class VI- highest level of difficulty
These rivers are rarely run except by highly experienced kayakers under ideal conditions.

## Wild & Scenic Rivers

Congressional legislation establishes certain criteria for the preservation of rivers with outstanding natural qualities; these are called Wild & Scenic Rivers. Wild rivers are, simply speaking, free-flowing and remote, while scenic rivers enjoy relatively natural surroundings and are free of impoundments, but have better access by road. Recreational rivers are more developed and usually have roads close by.

## Washington

The Skagit, Yakima and Wenatchee rivers in Washington are the principle kayaking and rafting rivers. Some outfitters on the Skagit offer eagle-watching trips in winter. In the Olympic National Park, outfitters run white-water trips down the Hoh, Elwha and Queets rivers, through some of North America's only rainforests. Along the park's Coastal Strip, the same outfitters run sea kayaking trips.

Sea kayaking in the Puget Sound can be an extraordinary adventure. Whether you're just puttering in the shadow of Seattle's skyline or paddling from island to island in the San Juans, kayaks make for a unique Northwest experience. Outfitters offer rentals or guided tours; this is an exciting way to see the killer whales.

## Oregon

Favorite rafting rivers in Oregon are the Deschutes and the Rogue. On the Deschutes, the trip between Sherar's Falls and the Columbia River is a multi-day trip with class IV rapids and no road access for miles and miles. The 84-mile stretch of the Rogue River within the Wild Rogue Wilderness Area is one of the most legendary white-water runs in the country, with abundant class IV rapids and waterfalls, and rustic fishermen's lodges along the way where you can sleep and eat. The Upper Rogue, where runoff from Crater Lake and the Cascades gives birth to the river, is popular for gentler, more leisurely float trips.

The Snake River through Hells Canyon, on the Oregon/Idaho border, also offers some mean rapids and some of the most striking scenery in the state.

## Idaho

Idaho's Snake and Salmon rivers are legendary for their white water, and there's no shortage of outfitters waiting to guide you down the rapids. For rafting trips on the Snake, the outfitters are concentrated in Lewiston, Riggins and Twin Falls. You can catch trips down the Salmon River from Riggins, Salmon, Stanley and McCall. Central Idaho's Lochsa River is also popular, with a number of Class III and IV rapids.

## WINDSURFING

While activities like fishing and sailing have always been popular on the mighty Columbia River, it's windsurfing that has elevated the town of Hood River from a sleepy orchard town to a sports capital. Reckoned to be one of the world's best windsurfing locales, the Columbia River Gorge is now the gathering place of 'board-heads' from around the world. Certainly nowhere else in Oregon can boast more colorful, polyglot and youthful crowds than Hood River.

Lakes throughout the Northwest are havens for wind-surfing, and rentals are easy to find in most towns. Summer is obviously the best time to be in the water anywhere in the Northwest; besides, that's when the big afternoon winds blow up the Gorge, against the current, creating the kinds of waves that bring board-heads in from around the world.

## BIRD & WILDLIFE WATCHING

The vast number wildlife refuges and public land in the Northwest – ranging from rocky shores of the Pacific to the Rocky Mountains – make this a great place to watch for wildlife. Bird watching is particularly well-rewarded. Local Audubon Society organizations often sponsor hikes and trips to birding areas.

## Washington

The Upper Skagit Bald Eagle Area, in the northern Cascades, is best visited in the winter, when eagles come to feast on the salmon spawning in the Skagit River. The

Turnbull National Wildlife Area near Spokane and the Little Pend Oreille Wildlife Area north, near Colville, are stopovers for migratory waterfowl; you may see some black bear, too.

Potholes Wildlife & Recreation Area, in central Washington, an irrigated wetlands surrounded by sand dunes, is a haven for a variety of waterfowl. Near Ellensburg, to the west, the Department of Wildlife's elk-feeding program brings in hundreds of breakfasting elk each day (when there's snow on the ground).

The Willapa National Wildlife Refuge, composed of five different areas in and around Willapa Bay on Washington's southern coast, is an excellent spot for watching shorebirds. On Long Island – a part of the refuge accessible only by canoe or kayak – black bear, coyote and elk roam undisturbed by man.

Wolves aren't exactly prolific in Washington, but Wolf Haven America, a wolf-rehab center south of Olympia, offers visitors an educational look at these beautiful animals.

### Oregon

The Malheur Wildlife Refuge in southeastern Oregon covers 289 sq miles of protected lands, teeming with coyote, deer and over 200 species of birds. It's the perfect place to study a high-desert ecosystem; seminars are offered at its facilities.

The Klamath Basin Wildlife Refuges in southern Oregon supports over 400 species of wildlife. The Lower Klamath Refuge was established in 1908 as the nation's first wildlife refuge. Bird watchers may be interested in the Klamath Basin Eagle Conference held in February, open to the public.

### Idaho

Raptor-watchers will find lots to look at in the Boise area. Between the World Center for Birds of Prey and the Snake River Birds of Prey National Conservation Area, the region is home to the densest nesting concentration of birds of prey in North America. Falcons, eagles, hawks and owls breed here along the arid cliffs of the Snake River. The Bear Lake National Wildlife Refuge in the southeastern corner of the state is noted for waterfowl watching.

## ROCK COLLECTING

The dusky volcanic mesas of central and eastern Oregon and Washington yield treasures for the rock hound. Sunstones, a pale yellow gemstone, are found north of Plush; to find thundereggs, round agatized geodes, go to commercial locations near Prineville, or Succor Creek State Park in far eastern Oregon. The Priday Agate Beds, north of Madras in central Oregon, is a fun thunderegg-hunting site, with campground and showers on the premises. Agates are also found along the southern Oregon coast, and famous blue agates are found near Ellensburg. Concessionaires in old gold mining areas of eastern Oregon and Idaho offer opportunities to pan for gold.

If gemstones are your thing, the Emerald Creek Public Garnet Mines south of Lake Coeur d'Alene in Idaho is one of the world's only public garnet-digging sites.

If you're interested in collecting rocks, check with the local BLM or USFS offices, who can usually direct you to likely areas. In some cases, you may need a permit to collect specimens. Remember that it is a federal felony to remove Native American artifacts from public land.

## COASTAL ACTIVITIES

While the coast is too cold much of the year for sun-bathing and swimming, its brisk climate is perfect for other activities. The Oregon Coast Trail runs nearly the length of the entire coast, although state parks often have shorter hiking trails to hidden beaches or tide pools. The Coast Range and the Olympic Mountains, damp and heavily wooded (where not lumbered off), also make for good summer hikes. Biking coast roads is also popular, but heavy traffic and narrow roads can make it unpleasant. Kite flying approaches near mania on sandy beaches; exploring rocky

The gray whales' migration takes them up the coast of Oregon and Washington.

tide pools for colorful marine life is a more introspective coastal pursuit. While not the surf capital of the world, the Northwest does nonetheless feature surfing and 'boogie-boarding' along the Pacific coast. Most coastal destinations offer rentals and sales, as well as advice.

### Charter Fishing

For decades, charter fishing for salmon was one of the Northwest coast's biggest industries. However, in recent years declining salmon numbers have led federal agencies to severely limit sport fishing for salmon. Fishing for halibut and other fish is still legal, however.

Charter boats out of Port Townsend, Washington prowl the Strait of Juan de Fuca in search of salmon and bottom fish, and excursions depart from Gray's Harbor and the Long Beach Peninsula on the Pacific coast.

The Columbia's convergence with the Pacific is a noted fishing area; a number of companies in Astoria and Warrenton offer charter trips. Fishing is excellent off Garibaldi, whether in Tillamook Bay or the Pacific. Charter boats fish for whatever is in season or available at the time, including salmon, cod, red snapper or rockfish. Depoe Bay, Newport and Winchester Bay are some of the coast's busiest charter fishing harbors, offering good ocean fishing, and whale watching during the spring whale migration.

### Whale Watching

The high capes and headlands of the Oregon coast are good vantage points to watch for gray whales. There are both spring and fall migrations; the spring migration – peaking in March – brings the whales closer to the shore. Favorite whale-watching spots include Cape Sebastian, Cape Blanco, Cape Perpetua, Neahkahnie Mountain and Cape Arago. On weekends at most of these sites, volunteers from local wildlife groups will answer questions and help locate whales. Although whales can occasionally be seen with the naked eye, it's a good idea to have a good pair of binoculars.

The Washington coastline, too, offers glimpses of the migrating mammals. But whale lovers should not stick to the ocean: the Puget Sound waters around the San Juan Islands are home to the sleek and powerful orca, or killer whale, and expeditions can be organized out of Bellingham or the islands themselves. Guided wildlife-seeking kayaking tours are an adventurous way to cruise the coves and channels of this archipelago. There's even a state park (Lime Kiln State Park on San Juan Island) devoted to whale watching.

Many charter fishing boats also offer whale-watching trips.

### Clamming & Crabbing

Clamming and crabbing are fun alternatives to fishing: rent a boat and crab rings and catch yourself some dinner, or dig a big bucket of clams and have yourself a bake. Most Oregon beaches are open for gathering shellfish; Netarts and the Reedsport are known for great clam digging.

Washington's Willapa Bay is world renowned for its oysters; in fact, one of its towns is named 'Oysterville'. It's on the National Register of Historic Places, and if peace and quiet, oyster digging and elegant dinners sound appealing, this is the place. The Jazz & Oysters festival combines seafood and live music for a slightly quirky event.

A state fishing license is not needed, though you must abide by the bag limits stated in the most recent Fish & Wildlife guidelines (available from most public offices on the coast). Otherwise all you need is a shovel and a bucket. Mussels are found in abundant numbers along intertidal rocks. Clams require a bit of excavation along riverbeds and sandy beaches. Razor clams quickly burrow into the sand and demand a fair amount of spading to unearth. Be sure that the shellfish is free of red tide. (See information on red tide in the Facts for the Visitor chapter.)

Dungeness crab live in quiet bays along the coast and are easily caught. Rowing out into the bay and waiting for the crab rings to fill is a relaxing way to snare a fine meal. Many marinas will rent a boat and crab rings, and will clean and boil the crabs for around $35 for a two-hour rental. The namesake of the scrumptious Dungeness crab is in Washington. Dungeness Spit is a long arm of land north of Sequim, on the Olympic Peninsula.

# Getting There & Away

This chapter focuses on getting to the major transport hubs in the Pacific Northwest from the major US ports of entry and other parts of the world. Because of the proliferation of routes into and out of the USA and the complexity of air travel, much of this information is general.

## TRAVEL INSURANCE

No matter how you're traveling, make sure you take out travel insurance. This not only covers you for medical expenses and luggage theft or losses incurred abroad, but also for cancellation or delays in your travel arrangements (you might fall seriously ill two days before departure, for example), and everyone should be covered for the worst possible case, such as an accident that requires hospital treatment and a flight home.

Coverage depends on your insurance and type of ticket, so ask both your insurer and your ticket-issuing agency to explain the finer points of the policies. STA Travel offers a variety of travel insurance options at reasonable prices.

Ticket loss is also covered by travel insurance. Make sure you have a separate record of all your ticket details – or better still, a photocopy of it. Also make a copy of your policy, in case the original is lost, and store these in a separate piece of luggage.

Buy travel insurance as early as possible. If you buy it the week before you fly, you may find, for instance, that you're not covered for delays to your flight caused by strikes or other industrial action that may have been in force before you took out the insurance.

If you're planning to travel for a long time, the insurance may seem very expensive – but if you can't afford it, you certainly won't be able to afford a medical emergency in the USA, where the exorbitant costs of health care are infamous.

# Within the USA

The *New York Times*, *Los Angeles Times*, *Chicago Tribune*, *San Francisco Examiner* and other major newspapers all produce weekly travel sections with numerous travel agents' ads. Council Travel (☎ (800) 226-8624) and STA Travel have offices in major cities nationwide.

The magazine *Travel Unlimited* (PO Box 1058, Allston, MA 02134) publishes details of the cheapest air fares and courier possibilities.

## AIR

Most air travelers will arrive at Seattle's Sea-Tac, the region's largest airport. It is served by nearly 40 airlines, and has regularly scheduled flights to most points world-wide. Portland's airport, called PDX, has connections to most domestic destinations, as well as direct flights to Asia. These two airports are the principal hubs for commuter flights to outlying Northwest communities. These short flights are usually moderately priced if bought with sufficient advance notice, especially when considering the distance covered and the rather grim overland alternatives.

US domestic air fares vary tremendously depending on the season you travel, the day of the week you fly, the length of your stay and the flexibility the ticket allows for flight changes and refunds. Still, nothing determines fares more than demand, and when things are slow, regardless of the season, airlines will lower their fares to fill empty seats. There's a lot of competition, and at any given time any one of the airlines could have the cheapest fare.

See Buying Tickets in the To/From Abroad section for more air-travel hints.

## Major US Domestic Airlines

| | |
|---|---|
| Alaska Airlines | ☎ (800) 426-0333 |
| America West | ☎ (800) 235-9292 |
| American | ☎ (800) 433-7300 |
| Continental | ☎ (800) 525-0280 |
| Delta | ☎ (800) 221-1212 |
| Hawaiian Airlines | ☎ (800) 367-5320 |
| Northwest | ☎ (800) 225-2525 |
| Southwest | ☎ (800) 531-5601 |
| TWA | ☎ (800) 892-4141 |
| United | ☎ (800) 241-6522 |

## Visit USA Passes

Almost all domestic carriers offer Visit USA passes to non-US citizens. The passes are actually a book of coupons – each coupon equals a flight. The following airlines are representative of the kinds of deals available, but it's a good idea to ask your travel agent about other airlines that offer the service.

Continental Airlines' Visit USA pass can be purchased in conjunction with an international airline ticket anywhere outside the USA except Canada and Mexico. All travel must be completed within 60 days of the first flight into the USA or 81 days after arrival in the USA. You must have your trip planned out in advance. If you decide to change destinations once in the USA, you will be fined $50. High-season prices are $479 for three coupons (minimum purchase) and $769 for eight (maximum purchase).

Northwest offers the same deal, but it gives you the option of flying standby.

American Airlines uses the same coupon structure and also sells the passes outside of the USA, excluding Canada and Mexico, in conjuction with an international ticket. You must reserve flights one day in advance, and if a coupon only takes you halfway to your destination, you will have to buy the remaining ticket at full price.

Delta has two different systems for travelers coming from abroad. Visit USA gives travelers a discount, but you need to have your itinerary mapped out to take advantage of this. The other option is Discover America, in which a traveler buys coupons good for standby travel anywhere in the continental USA. One flight equals one coupon. Only two transcontinental flights are allowed – Delta prefers that your travels follow some sort of circular pattern. Four coupons cost about $550, 10 cost $1250. Children's fares are about $40 less. Coupons can only be purchased in conjunction with an international flight, Canada and Mexico excluded.

When flying standby, call the airline a day or two before the flight and make a 'standby reservation'. This way you get priority over all the others who just appear and hope to get on the flight the same day.

## Getting Bumped

Airlines try to guarantee themselves consistently full planes by overbooking and counting on some passengers not showing up. This usually involves 'bumping' passengers off full flights. Getting bumped can be a nuisance because you have to wait around for the next flight, but if you have a day's leeway, you can really take advantage of the system.

When you check in at the airline counter, ask if they will need volunteers to be bumped, and ask what the compensation will be. Depending on the desirability of the flight, this can range from a $200 voucher toward your next flight to a fully paid roundtrip ticket. Be sure to try and confirm a later flight so you don't get stuck in the airport on standby. If you have to spend the night, airlines frequently foot the hotel bill for their bumpees. All in all, it can be a great deal, and many people plan their trips with a day to spare in order to try for a free ticket that will cover their next trip.

However, be aware that, due to this same system, being just a little late for boarding could get you bumped with none of these benefits.

## LAND

Interstate 5 is the major north-south route of the US West Coast, and stretches from Mexico to Canada. Portland, Eugene, Ashland, Tacoma and Seattle all lie on I-5. Intersecting at Portland is I-84, a major east-west route that continues to Boise, ID, Salt Lake City, UT, and points east. Seattle is the terminus of I-90, which runs east-west to Spokane, Northern Idaho, and to Montana. Eastern Idaho is served by I-15, which runs north-south between Salt Lake City, UT, Pocatello, ID, and points north as far as Calgary.

## Bus

Greyhound, the only nationwide bus company, has reduced local services considerably, but still runs cross-country buses between Seattle and New York ($149 one way, $259 roundtrip). Along the West Coast, you can go from Seattle to Los Angeles ($74 one way, $119 roundtrip) via Portland and San Francisco. Boise, ID, is also accessible from major cities in Washington and Oregon – it's $49 one way from Seattle, $79 roundtrip.

Because buses are so few, schedules are often inconvenient, fares are relatively high and bargain air fares can undercut buses on long-distance routes; in some cases, on shorter routes, it can be cheaper to rent a car than to ride the bus. However, very long distance bus trips are often available at bargain prices by purchasing or reserving tickets three days in advance. For more fare details, see Buses in the Getting Around chapter.

Other interstate bus lines serving the Pacific Northwest include the near mythic Green Tortoise buses which link San Francisco, Portland and Seattle via intervening hot springs and health food restaurants. Green Tortoise buses are cheaper than Greyhound and *a lot* more interesting. Easy chairs replace bus seats, and food, music, drink and a carnival atmosphere prevail. Two buses a week make the trip back and forth between Seattle and San Francisco. One-way fare from the San Francisco Bay Area to Portland is less than $40; just add $15 to continue onto Seattle. Call (800) 227-4766 for information and reservations.

## Train

The Northwest is better served by train service than many places in the west.

Amtrak's *Coast Starlight* links Portland and Seattle to major US West Coast cities, but not to Vancouver, BC; there's an annoying bus/rail link between Seattle and Vancouver. Portland and Seattle are both western termini of the *Empire Builder* line, with links to Spokane, WA, Minneapolis, MN and Chicago, IL. The *Pioneer* line from Chicago ends up in Seattle and Portland, with stops in Denver, CO, Salt Lake City, UT and Boise, ID. There are four trains a day between Portland and Seattle; the fare is about $30 return.

Amtrak tickets may be purchased aboard the train without penalty if the station is not open 30 minutes prior to boarding; otherwise there is a $7 penalty. Rail travel is generally cheaper by purchasing special fares in advance. Roundtrips are the best bargain, but even these are usually as expensive as air fares.

The best value overall is their All Aboard America fare. This costs $278 for adults and enables you to travel anywhere you want. There are limitations, however. Travel must be completed in 45 days, and you are allowed up to three stopovers. Additional stopovers can be arranged at extra cost. Your entire trip must be reserved in advance and the seats are limited, so book as far ahead as possible. Travel between mid-June and late August costs $338. These tickets are for reclining seats; sleeping cars cost extra.

If you want to travel in just the eastern, central or western parts of the country, $178 All Aboard America fares are available.

For further travel assistance, call Amtrak (☎ (800) USA-RAIL, 872-7245) or ask your travel agent. Note that most small train stations don't sell tickets; you have to book them with Amtrak over the phone. Some small stations have no porters or other facilities, and trains may stop there only if you have bought a ticket in advance.

## Car

For information on buying or renting a car, or using a drive-away (driving a car for someone else) see the Getting Around chapter.

## TOURS

Tours of the USA are so numerous that it would be impossible to attempt any kind of comprehensive listing; for overseas visitors, the most reliable sources of information on the constantly changing offerings are major international travel agents like Thomas Cook and American Express. Probably those of most interest to the general traveler are coach tours that visit the national parks and guest ranch excursions; for those with limited time, package tours can be an efficient and relatively inexpensive way to go.

Green Tortoise (☎ (415) 956-7500, (800) 867-8647), 494 Broadway, San Francisco, CA 94133, offers alternative bus transportation with stops at places like hot springs and national parks. Meals are cooperatively cooked and you sleep on bunks on the bus or camp. This is not luxury travel, but it is fun.

Trek America (☎ (908) 362-9198, (800) 221-0596, fax 362-9313), PO Box 470, Blairstown, NJ 07825, offers roundtrip camping tours of different areas of the country. In England, contact Trek House (☎ (869) 38777, fax 338846), The Bullring, Deddington, Banbury, Oxon OX15 0TT. These tours last from one to nine weeks and are designed for small, international groups (13 people maximum) between the ages of 18 and 38. Tour prices vary by season, July to September being the highest. Tours including food and occasional hotel nights cost about $1000 for a 10-day tour to $3500 for a nine-week tour of the entire country. Some side trips and cultural events are included in the price, and participants help with cooking and camp chores.

Similar deals are available from Suntreks (☎ (707) 523-1800, (800) 292-9696, fax 523-1911), Sun Plaza, 77 West Third St, Santa Rosa, CA 95401. Suntreks also has offices in Australia (☎ 02 281 8000, fax 02 281 2722), 62 Mary St, Surry Hills, Sydney NSW 2010; Germany (☎ 089 480 2831, fax 089 480 2411), Swdanstrasse 21, D-81667, Munich; and Switzerland (☎ (1) 462 6161, fax 462 6545), Birmensdorferstr 107, PO Box 8371, CH-8036, Zurich. Their tours are for the 'young at heart' and attract predominantly young international travelers, although there is no age limit. Prices range from about $1600 for the three-week trek to about $4500 for their 13-week around-America treks.

Road Runner USA/Canada (☎ (800) 873-5872), 6762A Centinela Ave, Culver City, CA 90230, organizes one and two-week treks in conjunction with Hostelling International to different parts of the USA and across country. They also have offices in England (☎ (892) 542010), PO Box 105, Kelly House, Warwick Rd, Tunbridge Wells, Kent TN1 1ZN and in Australia (☎ (2) 299-8844) Wholesale Pty Ltd, 8th Floor, 350 Kent St, Sydney, NSW 2000.

Maupintours (☎ 800 255-67-162), 1515 St Andrews Drive, Lawrence, KS, offers just about the only full-service tours of the Northwest. They offer a number of slightly varying itineraries that include many of the highlights, including Seattle, the San Juans, Olympic Peninsula, Portland, the Oregon coast and Crater Lake. All meals, lodging and fees are typically included in the price, which are at about $1400 per person.

Local day tours are available from Seattle to Mt Rainier and the islands of the Puget Sound, and from Portland to the Columbia Gorge, Mt Hood, the wine country and the northern Oregon coast. Day tours to Crater Lake leave from Medford and Klamath Falls.

# To/From Abroad

## AIR
### Buying Tickets

Numerous airlines fly to the USA, and a variety of fares are available; in addition to a straightforward roundtrip ticket, it can also be part of a Round-the-World ticket or Circle Pacific fare. So rather than just walking into the nearest travel agent or airline office, it pays to do a bit of research and shop around first. You might start by perusing travel sections of magazines like *Time Out* and *TNT* in the UK, or the Saturday editions of newspapers like the *Sydney Morning Herald* and *The Age* in Australia. Ads in these publications offer cheap fares, but don't be surprised if they happen to be sold out when you contact the agents: they're usually low-season fares on obscure airlines with conditions attached.

The plane ticket will probably be the single most expensive item in your budget, and buying it can be intimidating. It is always worth putting aside a few hours to research the current state of the market. Start shopping for a ticket early – some of the cheapest tickets must be bought months in advance, and some popular flights sell out early. Talk to other recent travelers – they may be able to stop you from making some of the same old mistakes. Look at the ads in newspapers and magazines, consult reference books and watch for special offers.

Note that high season in the USA is mid-June to mid-September (summer) and the one week before and after Christmas. The best rates for travel to and in the USA are found November through March.

Call travel agents for bargains (airlines can supply information on routes and time-tables; however, except at times of fare wars, they do not supply the cheapest tickets). Airlines often have competitive low-season, student and senior citizens' fares. Find out the fare, the route, the duration of the journey and any restrictions on the ticket.

Cheap tickets are available in two distinct categories: official and unofficial. Official ones have a variety of names including advance-purchase fares, budget fares, Apex and super-Apex. Unofficial tickets are simply discounted tickets that the airlines release through selected travel agents (not through airline offices). The cheapest tickets are often nonrefundable and require an extra fee for changing your flight. Many insurance policies will cover this loss if you have to change your flight for emergency reasons. Return (roundtrip) tickets usually work out cheaper than two one-way fares – often *much* cheaper.

Use the fares quoted in this book as a guide only. They are approximate and based on the rates advertised by travel agents and airlines at press time. Quoted airfares do not necessarily constitute a recommendation for the carrier.

If traveling from the UK, you will probably find that the cheapest flights are being advertised by obscure bucket shops whose names haven't yet reached the telephone directory. Many such firms are honest and solvent, but there are a few rogues who will take your money and disappear, to reopen elsewhere a month or two later under a new name. If you feel suspicious about a firm, don't give them all the money at once – leave a deposit of 20% or so and pay the balance on receiving the ticket. If they insist on cash in advance, go elsewhere. And once you have the ticket, ring the airline to confirm that you are booked on the flight.

You may decide to pay more than the rock-bottom fare by opting for the safety of a better-known travel agent. Established firms like STA Travel, which has offices worldwide, Council Travel in the USA or Travel CUTS in Canada are valid alternatives and they offer good prices to most destinations.

Once you have your ticket, write down its number, together with the flight number and other details, and keep the information somewhere separate. If the ticket is lost or stolen, this will help you get a replacement.

Remember to buy travel insurance as early as possible.

### Arriving in USA by Air

Even if you are continuing immediately to another city, the first airport that you land in is where you must carry out immigration and customs formalities. Even if your luggage is checked from, say, London to Seattle, you will still have to take it through customs if you first land in New York.

Passengers aboard the airplane are given standard immigration and customs forms to fill out. The cabin crew will help you fill them out if you have any questions, but the forms are quite straightforward. After the plane lands, you'll first go through immigration. There are two lines: one is for US citizens and residents, and the other is for nonresidents. Immigration formalities are usually straightforward if you have all the necessary documents (passport and visa). Occasionally, you may be asked to show your ticket out of the country, but this doesn't happen very often.

After passing through immigration, you collect your baggage and then pass through customs. If you have nothing to declare, there is a good chance that you can clear customs quickly and without a luggage search, but you can't rely on it. After passing through customs, you are officially in the country. If your flight is continuing to another city or you have a connecting flight, it is your responsibility to get your bags to the right place. Normally, there are airline counters just outside the customs area that will help you. Also see the information under Customs in Facts for the Visitor.

### Air Travelers with Special Needs

If you have special needs of any sort – a broken leg, dietary restrictions, dependence on a wheelchair, responsibility for a baby, fear of flying – you should let the airline know as soon as possible so that they can make arrangements accordingly. You should remind them when you reconfirm your booking (at least 72 hours before departure) and again when you check in at the airport. It may also be worth ringing round the airlines before you make your booking to find out how they can handle your particular needs.

Airports and airlines can be surprisingly helpful, but they do need advance warning. Most international airports can provide escorts from check-in desk to plane where needed, and there should be ramps, lifts, accessible toilets and reachable phones. Aircraft toilets, on the other hand, are likely to present a problem; travelers should discuss this with the airline at an early stage and, if necessary, with their doctor.

Guide dogs for the blind will often have to travel in a specially pressurized baggage compartment with other animals, away from their owner, though smaller guide dogs may be admitted to the cabin. Guide dogs are not subject to quarantine as long as they have proof of being vaccinated against rabies.

Deaf travelers can ask for airport and inflight announcements to be written down for them.

Children under two travel for 10% of the standard fare (or free, on some airlines), as long as they don't occupy a seat. (They don't get a baggage allowance either.) 'Skycots' should be provided by the airline if requested in advance; these will take a child weighing up to about 22 lbs. Children between two and 12 can usually occupy a seat for half to two-thirds of the full fare, and do get a baggage allowance. Strollers can often be taken on as hand luggage.

### Baggage & Other Restrictions

On most domestic and international flights you are limited to two checked bags, or three if you don't have a carry-on. There could be a charge if you bring more or if the size of the bags exceeds the airline's limits. It's best to check with the individual airline if you are worried about this. On some international flights the luggage allowance is based on weight, not numbers; again, check with the airline.

If your luggage is delayed upon arrival (which is rare), some airlines will give a cash advance to purchase necessities. If sporting equipment is misplaced, the airline may pay for rentals. Should the luggage be lost, it is important to submit a claim. The airline doesn't have to pay the full amount of the claim, rather they can estimate the value of your lost items. It may take them anywhere from six weeks to three months to process the claim and pay you.

**Smoking**  Smoking is prohibited on all domestic flights within the USA. Many international flights are following suit, so be sure to call and find out. Incidentally, the restriction applies to the passenger cabin and the lavatories but not the cockpit. Many airports in the USA also restrict smoking, but they compensate by having 'smoking rooms'.

**Illegal Items** Items that are illegal to take on a plane, either checked or as carry-on, include aerosols of polishes, waxes, etc; tear gas and pepper spray; camp stoves with fuel; and divers' tanks that are full. Matches should not be checked.

### Major Airlines

| | |
|---|---|
| Air Canada | ☎ (800) 776-3000 |
| Air France | ☎ (800) 237-2747 |
| Air New Zealand | ☎ (800) 262-1234 |
| American Airlines | ☎ (800) 433-7300 |
| British Airways | ☎ (800) 247-9297 |
| Canadian Airlines | ☎ (800) 426-7000 |
| Continental Airlines | ☎ (800) 525-0280 |
| Delta Air Lines | ☎ (800) 221-1212 |
| Japan Air Lines | ☎ (800) 525-3663 |
| KLM | ☎ (800) 374-7747 |
| Northwest Airlines | ☎ (800) 447-4747 |
| Qantas Airways | ☎ (800) 227-4500 |
| TWA | ☎ (800) 221-2000 |
| United Airlines | ☎ (800) 241-6522 |
| USAir | ☎ (800) 428-4322 |

### Round-the-World Tickets

Round-the-World (RTW) tickets have become very popular in the last few years. Airline RTW tickets are often real bargains and can work out to be no more expensive or even cheaper than an ordinary return ticket. Prices start at about UK£850, A$1800 or US$1300.

The official airline RTW tickets are usually put together by a combination of two airlines, and permit you to fly anywhere you want on their route systems as long as you do not backtrack. Other restrictions are that you must usually book the first sector in advance and cancellation penalties apply. There may be restrictions on the number of stops permitted, and tickets are usually valid from 90 days up to a year. An alternative type of RTW ticket is one put together by a travel agent using a combination of discounted tickets.

Although most airlines restrict the number of sectors that can be flown within

the USA and Canada to four, and some airlines black out a few heavily traveled routes (like Honolulu to Tokyo), stopovers are otherwise generally unlimited. In most cases a 14-day advance purchase is required. After the ticket is purchased, dates can be changed without penalty and tickets can be rewritten to add or delete stops for $50 each.

The majority of RTW tickets restrict you to just two airlines. British Airways and Qantas Airways offer a RTW ticket called the Global Explorer that allows you to combine routes on both airlines to a total of 28,000 miles for US$2999 or A$3099.

Qantas also flies in conjunction with American Airlines, Delta Air Lines, Northwest Airlines, Canadian Airlines, Air France and KLM. Qantas RTW tickets, with any of the aforementioned partner airlines, cost US$3247 or A$3099.

Canadian Airlines offers numerous RTW combinations, such as with Philippine Airlines for C$2790 that could include Manila, Dubai, Pakistan and Europe; another with KLM that could include Cairo, Bombay, Delhi and Amsterdam for C$3149; and a third with South African Airways that could include Australia and Africa for C$3499.

Many other airlines also offer RTW tickets. Continental Airlines, for example, links up with either Malaysia Airlines, Singapore Airlines or Thai Airways for US$2570. TWA's lowest priced RTW, linking up with Korean Air, costs US$2087 and allows stops in Honolulu, Seoul, Tel Aviv, Amsterdam and Paris or London.

### Circle Pacific Tickets

Circle Pacific tickets use a combination of airlines to circle the Pacific – combining Australia, New Zealand, North America and Asia. Rather than simply flying from point A to point B, these tickets allow you to swing through much of the Pacific Rim and eastern Asia taking in a variety of destinations – as long as you keep traveling in the same circular direction. As with RTW tickets there are advance purchase restrictions and limits on how many stopovers

## Air Travel Glossary

**Apex** – Apex, or 'advance purchase excursion' is a discounted ticket that must be paid for in advance. There are penalties if you wish to change it.

**Bucket Shop** – An unbonded travel agency specializing in discounted airline tickets.

**Bumping** – Just because you have a confirmed seat doesn't mean you're going to get on the plane – see Overbooking.

**Cancellation Penalties** – If you must cancel or change an Apex ticket there are often heavy penalties involved, but insurance can sometimes be taken out against these penalties. Some airlines impose penalties on regular tickets as well, particularly against 'no show' passengers.

**Check In** – Airlines ask you to check in a certain time ahead of the flight departure (usually two hours on international flights). If you fail to check in on time and the flight is overbooked the airline can cancel your booking and give your seat to somebody else.

**Confirmation** – Having a ticket written out with the flight and date you want doesn't mean you have a seat until the agent has checked with the airline that your status is 'OK' or confirmed. Meanwhile you could just be 'on request'.

**Discounted Tickets** – There are two types of discounted fares – officially discounted (see Promotional Fares) and unofficially discounted. The lowest prices often impose drawbacks like flying with unpopular airlines, inconvenient schedules or unpleasant routes and connections. A discounted ticket can save you other things than money – you may be able to pay Apex prices without the associated Apex advance booking and other requirements. Discounted tickets only exist when there is fierce competition.

**Full Fares** – Airlines traditionally offer 1st class (coded F), business class (coded J) and economy class (coded Y) tickets. These days there are so many promotional and discounted fares available from the regular economy class that few passengers pay full economy fare.

**Lost Tickets** – If you lose your airline ticket an airline will usually treat it like a travelers' check and, after inquiries, issue you with another one. Legally, however, an airline is entitled to treat it like cash and if you lose it then it's gone forever. Take good care of your tickets.

**No Shows** – No shows are passengers who fail to show up for their flight. Full-fare passengers who fail to turn up are sometimes entitled to travel on a later flight. The rest of us are penalized (see Cancellation Penalties).

**On Request** – An unconfirmed booking for a flight; see Confirmation.

**Open Jaws** – A return ticket where you fly to one place but return from another. If available this can save you backtracking to your arrival point.

you can take. These fares are likely to be around 15% cheaper than RTW tickets.

Circle Pacific routes essentially have the same fares: A\$2999 when purchased in Australia, US\$2449 when purchased in the USA and C\$3309 when purchased in Canada. Circle Pacific fares include four stopovers with the option of adding additional stops at US\$50 each. There's a 14-day advance purchase requirement, a 25% cancellation penalty and a maximum stay of six months. There are also higher busi-

**Overbooking** – Airlines hate to fly empty seats and since every flight has some passengers who fail to show up they often book more passengers than they have seats. Usually the excess passengers balance those who fail to show up but occasionally somebody gets bumped. If this happens guess who it's most likely to be? The passengers who check in late.

**Promotional Fares** – Officially discounted fares like Apex fares which are available from travel agents or direct from the airline.

**Reconfirmation** – At least 72 hours prior to departure time of an onward or return flight you must contact the airline and 'reconfirm' that you intend to be on the flight. If you don't do this the airline can delete your name from the passenger list and you could lose your seat. You don't have to reconfirm the first flight on your itinerary or if your stopover is less than 72 hours. It doesn't hurt to reconfirm more than once.

**Restrictions** – Discounted tickets often have various restrictions on them – advance purchase is the most usual one (see Apex). Others are restrictions on the minimum and maximum period you must be away, such as a minimum of 14 days or a maximum of one year. See Cancellation Penalties.

**Standby** – A discounted ticket where you only fly if there is a seat free at the last moment. Standby fares are usually only available on domestic routes.

**Tickets Out** – An entry requirement for many countries is that you have an onward or return ticket, in other words, a ticket out of the country. If you're not sure what you intend to do next, the easiest solution is to buy the cheapest onward ticket to a neighboring country or a ticket from a reliable airline which can later be refunded if you do not use it.

**Transferred Tickets** – Airline tickets cannot be transferred from one person to another. Travelers sometimes try to sell the return half of their ticket, but officials can ask you to prove that you are the person named on the ticket. This is unlikely to happen on domestic flights, but on an international flight tickets may be compared with passports.

**Travel Agencies** – Travel agencies vary widely and you should ensure you use one that suits your needs. Some simply handle tours, while full-service agencies handle everything from tours and tickets to car rental and hotel bookings. A good one will do all these things and can save you a lot of money but if all you want is a ticket at the lowest possible price, then you really need an agency specializing in discounted tickets. A discounted ticket agency, however, may not be useful for things like hotel bookings.

**Travel Periods** – Some officially discounted fares, Apex fares in particular, vary with the time of year. There is often a low (off-peak) season and a high (peak) season. Sometimes there's an intermediate or shoulder season as well. At peak times, when everyone wants to fly, not only will the officially discounted fares be higher but so will unofficially discounted fares or there may simply be no discounted tickets available. Usually the fare depends on your outward flight – if you depart in the high season and return in the low season, you pay the high-season fare. ∎

---

ness class and 1st-class fares. Departure and airport-use taxes, which will vary with the itinerary, are additional.

Qantas Airways offers Circle Pacific routes in partnership with Delta Air Lines, Japan Air Lines, Northwest Airlines or Continental Airlines. In the off-season, the Australian winter, Qantas occasionally offers hefty discounts on tickets that use Qantas as the primary carrier.

United Airlines flies in conjunction with Cathay Pacific, Qantas, Ansett, Malaysia

Airlines or British Airways. Canadian Airlines has Circle Pacific fares from Vancouver that include, in one combination or another, virtually all Pacific Rim destinations. Canadian's partners include Qantas, Air New Zealand, Singapore, Garuda, Cathay Pacific or Malaysia airlines.

### To/From Canada

Travel CUTS has offices in all major cities. The *Toronto Globe & Mail* and *Vancouver Sun* carry travel agents' ads; the magazine *Great Expeditions* (PO Box 8000-411, Abbotsford BC V2S 6H1) is also useful.

Most connections between the US Pacific Northwest and Canada are through Vancouver, BC. Both Portland and Seattle have frequent and inexpensive flights to Vancouver, which is serviced by both Air Canada and Canadian Airlines. A roundtrip flight between Seattle and Vancouver is usually less than $100.

### To/From the UK & Ireland

Check the ads in magazines like *Time Out* and *City Limits*, plus the Sunday papers and *Exchange & Mart*. Also check the free magazines widely available in London – start by looking outside the main railway stations.

Most British travel agents are registered with the ABTA (Association of British Travel Agents). If you have paid for your flight to an ABTA-registered agent who then goes out of business, ABTA will guarantee a refund or an alternative. Unregistered bucket shops are riskier but sometimes cheaper.

London is arguably the world's headquarters for bucket shops, which are well advertised and can usually beat published airline fares. Two good, reliable agents for cheap tickets in the UK are Trailfinders (☎ 071-938-3366), 46 Earls Court Rd, London W8 6EJ, and STA Travel (☎ 071-937-9962), 74 Old Brompton Rd, London SW7. Trailfinders produces a lavishly illustrated brochure including air fare details.

Virgin Atlantic has a roundtrip high-season fare from London to New York for £448 (US$734), which allows a one-

month maximum stay and requires a 21-day advance purchase. Off-season (winter) flights from London to New York range from £240 (US$393) to £508 (US$833), and to Los Angeles starting at £280 (US$460).

The Globetrotters Club (BCM Roving, London WC1N 3XX) publishes a newsletter called *Globe* that covers obscure destinations and can help you find traveling companions.

### To/From Continental Europe

If you are planning to remain on the Pacific coast, it is definitely worth flying straight to or from the West Coast: you can save hours of flight time and airport dawdling. Flights from London, Copenhagen and Amsterdam fly non-stop into Seattle, which is only 20 minutes away from Portland by air. Vancouver, BC is also convenient, and has links to Frankfurt. San Francisco has direct links to Paris.

It takes between eight to nine hours to fly non-stop between Seattle and London. Compare this with the total travel time if West Coast-bound travelers from Europe hub out of New York or Chicago. The primary European airlines serving Seattle are British Air, SAS and United. Fares fluctuate wildly, but are usually between $900 to $1000 roundtrip between Seattle and London during high season; off-season fares can drop as low as $550 round-trip.

In Amsterdam, NBBS is a popular travel agent. In Paris Transalpino and Council Travel are popular agencies. The newsletter *Farang* (La Rue 8 á 4261 Braives, Belgium) deals with exotic destinations, as does the magazine *Aventure du Bout du Monde* (116 rue de Javel, 75015 Paris, France)

Virgin Atlantic flights from Paris to New York are substantially cheaper; a ticket with seven-day advance purchase ranges from FF3790 (US$773) to FF4530 (US$924)

### To/From Australia & New Zealand

In Australia, STA Travel and Flight Centres International are major dealers in cheap air fares; check the travel agents' ads in the Yellow Pages and call around. Qantas flies to Los Angeles from Sydney, Melbourne (via Sydney or Auckland) and Cairns. United flies to San Francisco from Sydney and Auckland (via Sydney) and also flies to Los Angeles.

In New Zealand, STA Travel and Flight Centres International are also popular travel agents.

The cheapest tickets have a 21-day advance-purchase requirement, a minimum stay of seven days and a maximum stay of 60 days. Qantas flies from Melbourne or Sydney to Los Angeles for A$1470 (US$1088) in the low season and A$1820 (US$1346) in the high season. Qantas flights from Cairns to Los Angeles cost A$1579 (US$1168) in the low season and A$1919 (US$1420) in the high season. Flying with Air New Zealand is slightly cheaper, and both Qantas and Air New Zealand offer tickets with longer stays or stopovers, but you pay more. Full-time students can save A$80 (US$59) to A$140 (US$103) on roundtrip fares to the USA. United also flies to Los Angeles.

Roundtrip flights from Auckland to Los Angeles on Qantas cost NZ$1720 (US$1186) in the low season. (This is the quoted student fare.)

**To/From Asia**
Hong Kong is the discount plane ticket capital of the region, but its bucket shops can be unreliable. Ask the advice of other travelers before buying a ticket. STA Travel, which is dependable, has branches in Hong Kong, Tokyo, Singapore, Bangkok and Kuala Lumpur. Many if not most flights to the USA go via Honolulu, Hawaii.

**To/From Japan** United Airlines has three flights a day to Honolulu from Tokyo with connections to West Coast cities like Los Angeles, San Francisco and Seattle. Northwest and Japan Air Lines also have daily flights to the West Coast from Tokyo; Japan Air Lines also flies to Honolulu from Osaka, Nagoya, Fukuoka and Sapporo.

**To/From Southeast Asia** There are numerous airlines flying to the USA from Southeast Asia; bucket shops in places like Bangkok and Singapore should be able to come up with the best deals. Tickets to the US West Coast often allow a free stopover in Honolulu.

Northwest Airlines flies to Honolulu from Hong Kong, Bangkok, Manila, Seoul and Singapore, with connections to the West Coast. Korean Air and Philippine Airlines also have flights from a number of Southeast Asian cities to Honolulu, with onward connections.

**To/From Central & South America**
Most flights from Central and South America go via Miami, Houston or Los Angeles, though some fly via New York. Most countries' international flag carriers (some of them, like Aerolíneas Argentinas and LANChile, recently privatized), as well as US airlines like United and American, serve these destinations, with onward connections to Seattle. Continental has flights from about 20 cities in Mexico and Central America, including San Jose, Guatemala City, Cancún and Mérida.

**LAND**
Drivers of cars and riders of motorbikes will need the vehicle's registration papers, liability insurance and an international drivers permit in addition to their domestic license. Canadian and Mexican drivers licenses are accepted. Customs officials along the entry points between Canada and Washington can be strict and wary of anything that doesn't look straight-laced. To avoid unnecessary conflicts dress well and be cordial for those few hours between countries.

**SEA**
Chances that you will arrive on a boat and still have time to enjoy being in the USA are few. There are cruises, such as the QE2, that make transatlantic voyages, but the cruise itself is usually the vacation. There is service from the most southwesterly and southeasterly points in Canada into ports in

Seattle and Maine for those that just happen to be in those corners.

Seabourn Cruise Line (☎ (800) 929-9595), 55 San Francisco St, San Francisco, CA 94133, offers cruises from Montreal to New York and between Alaska and Vancouver, BC.

The *Victoria Clipper* catamaran (☎ (206) 448-5000) makes three daily 2½-hour runs between Victoria, BC and Seattle for C$61 (US$45) one way.

## LEAVING THE USA

You should check in for international flights two hours early. During check-in procedures, you will be asked questions about whether you packed your own bags (yes), whether anyone else has had access

to them since you packed them (no) and whether you have received any parcels to carry (no). These questions are for security reasons.

## Departure Taxes

Airport departure taxes are normally included in the cost of tickets bought in the USA, although tickets purchased abroad may not have this included. There's a $6 airport departure tax charged to all passengers bound for a foreign destination. However, this fee, as well as a $6.50 North American Free Trade Agreement (NAFTA) tax charged to passengers entering the USA from a foreign country, are hidden taxes added to the purchase price of your airline ticket.

# Getting Around

This chapter deals with the intricacies of getting around within the Pacific Northwest. Don't automatically assume that, once arriving in the Northwest, ground travel is going to be the cheapest method of transport. The US West is home to a number of inexpensive, no-frills airlines that offer rates that will rival bus and train fares. Ask a travel agent for information about discount airlines.

## AIR

Portland and Seattle are the main hubs for flights to outlying regions in the Northwest. United Express, a division of United Airlines, and Horizon Air are the two most common carriers on these commuter flights. From Portland, flights are available to Pendleton, Klamath Falls, Coos Bay, Salem, Astoria, Bend, Eugene, Corvallis and Medford. Flights leave from Seattle for Port Angeles, Olympia, Yakima, the Tri-Cities, Walla Walla, Spokane, Bellingham and Wenatchee, as well as to destinations in the San Juan Islands. Boise is served by a number of national airlines.

Regular fares on these routes can be expensive if you don't have advance booking, but fares can drop by about half if you are able to fly very early in the morning or late at night, or on specific flights. Ask about special fare flights.

If you are arriving from overseas or another major airport in the USA, it is usually much cheaper to buy a through ticket to small airports as part of your fare rather than separately, unless your travel plans are so spontaneous as to preclude doing so.

Another alternative is an air pass, available from the major airlines that fly between the USA and Europe, Asia and Australia. Air passes are particularly valuable if you're flying between widely separated destinations. (See Visit USA Passes in Getting There & Away.)

## Regional Carriers

The following list includes both major airlines and smaller commuter carriers, some of which also serve Western and Midwestern states such as Arizona, California, Idaho, Kansas, Nebraska, Nevada, Oklahoma, North Dakota, South Dakota and Utah.

| | |
|---|---|
| American | ☎ (800) 433-7300 |
| Delta | ☎ (800) 221-1212 |
| Horizon Air | ☎ (800) 547-9308 |
| Mark Air | ☎ (206) 241-4900 |
| Reno Air | ☎ (800) 736-6247 |
| Southwest Airlines | ☎ (800) 466-7747 |
| United Express | ☎ (800) 241-6522 |
| Western Pacific | ☎ (800) 930-3030 |

## BUS

Since Americans rely so much on their cars and usually fly longer distances, bus transport is less frequent than is desirable, but some good deals are available. Greyhound (☎ (800) 231-2222), the main bus lines for the region, has extensive fixed routes and its own terminal in most central cities, often in undesirable parts of town. However, the buses are comfortable, the company has an exceptional safety record and it usually runs on time.

Greyhound has reduced or eliminated services to smaller rural communities it once served efficiently. In many small towns Greyhound no longer maintains terminals, but merely stops at a given location, such as a grocery store parking lot. In these unlikely terminals, boarding passengers usually pay the driver with exact change.

Green Tortoise (☎ (800) 227-4766) is a fun alternative to Greyhound, if you're traveling between Seattle and San Francisco or points along the way. Fares are lower than Greyhound, and the trip may take a little longer because of sporadic stops for cookouts or skinnydipping.

## Greyhound Fares

Tickets can be bought over the phone with a credit card (MasterCard, Visa or Discover) and mailed if purchased 10 days in advance or picked up at the terminal with proper identification. Greyhound terminals also accept American Express, travelers' checks and cash. Note all buses are non-smoking, and reservations are made with ticket purchases only.

**Special Fares** Greyhound occasionally introduces a mileage-based discount fare program that can be a bargain, especially for very long distances, but it's a good idea to check the regular fare anyway. As with regular fares, these promotional fares are subject to change.

**Ameripass** Greyhound's Ameripass is potentially useful, depending on how much you plan to travel, but the relatively high prices may impel you to travel more than you normally would simply to get your money's worth. There are no restrictions on who can buy an Ameripass; it costs $179 for seven days of unlimited travel year round, $289 for 15 days of travel and $399 for 30 days of travel. Children under 11 travel for half price. You can get on and off at any Greyhound stop or terminal, and the Ameripass is available at every Greyhound terminal.

**International Ameripass** This can be purchased only by foreign tourists and foreign students and lecturers (with their families) staying less than one year. These prices are $89 for a four-day pass for unlimited travel Monday to Thursday, $149 for a seven-day pass, $209 for a 15-day pass and $289 for a 30-day pass. The International Ameripass is usually bought abroad at a travel agency or can be bought in the USA through the Greyhound International depot in New York City (☎ (212) 971-0492) at 625 8th Ave at the Port Authority Subway level, open Monday to Friday from 9 am to 4:30 pm. New York Greyhound International accepts MasterCard and Visa, traveler's checks and cash, and allows purchases to be made by phone.

To contact Greyhound International to inquire about regular fares and routes, call (800) 246-8572. Those buying an International Ameripass must complete an affidavit and present a passport or visa (or waiver) to the appropriate Greyhound officials.

There are also special passes for travel in Canada that can be bought only through the New York City office or abroad.

## TRAIN

Amtrak (☎ (800) USA-RAIL or 872-7255) fares vary greatly, depending on different promotional fares and destinations. Reservations (the sooner made, the better the fare) can be held under your surname only; tickets can be purchased by credit card over the phone, from a travel agent or at an Amtrak depot.

Amtrak provides daily service from Seattle and Portland to towns on both sides of the Columbia Gorge; this is one of the most spectacular train rides you'll find in the USA. On the Oregon side, the *Pioneer* runs between Seattle, Portland, Hood River, The Dalles, Hermiston, Pendleton, LaGrande, Baker City and Ontario. In Idaho, the train stops at Boise, Shoshone and Pocatello where it cuts down to Salt Lake City, UT. The *Pioneer* runs only every other day; check schedules carefully.

A branch of the *Empire Builder* leaves Portland, and crosses to Vancouver, WA before running up the north side of the Gorge to meet the other east-bound half of the train at Spokane (the west-bound *Empire Builder* divides at Spokane for Portland and Seattle; make sure you're sitting in the correct portion of the train!). The *Empire Builder* is expected to change from a daily to an every-other-day service in the near future; check schedules carefully.

The daily *Coast Starlight* connects Seattle to Tacoma, Olympia, Portland and on to Salem, Albany and Eugene; it then sets off for Klamath Falls in southern Oregon. The Seattle branch of the *Empire Builder* heads north to Everett before winding east to Wenatchee and Spokane, and Sandpoint, ID. For more information see the Getting There & Away chapter.

## CAR & MOTORCYCLE

The US highway system is very extensive, and, since distances are great and buses can be infrequent, auto transport is worth considering despite the expense. Officially, you must have an International or Inter-American Driving Permit to supplement your national or state driver's license, but US police are more likely to want to see your national, provincial or state driver's license.

### Rental

Major international rental agencies like Hertz, Avis, Budget and A-1 have offices throughout the region. To rent a car, you must have a valid driver's license, be at least 25 years of age and present a major credit card or else a large cash deposit.

Many rental agencies have bargain rates for weekend or week-long rentals, especially outside the peak summer season or in conjunction with airline tickets. Prices vary greatly in relation to region, season and type or size of the car you'd like to rent.

Basic liability insurance, which will cover damage you may cause to another vehicle, is required by law and comes with the price of renting the car. Liability insurance is also called third-party coverage.

Collision insurance, also called the Liability Damage Waiver, is optional; it covers the full value of the vehicle in case of an accident, except when caused by acts of nature or fire. For a mid-sized car the cost for this extra coverage is around $15 per day. You don't need to buy this waiver to rent the car. Agencies also tack on a daily fee per each additional driver in the car.

Some credit cards, such as the Master-Card Gold Card, will cover collision insurance if you rent for 15 days or less and charge the full cost of rental to your card. If you opt to do that, you'll need to sign the waiver, declining the coverage. If you already have collision insurance on your personal policy, the credit card will cover the large deductible. To find out if your credit card offers such a service, and the extent of the coverage, contact the credit card company.

Be aware that some major rental agencies no longer offer unlimited mileage in non-competitive markets (most of the Pacific Northwest) – this greatly increases the cost of renting a car.

### Purchase

If you're spending several months in the USA, purchasing a car is worth considering; a car is more flexible than public transport and likely to be cheaper than rentals, but buying one can be very complicated and requires plenty of research.

It's possible to purchase a viable car in the USA for about $1500, but you can't expect to go too far before you'll need some repair work that could cost several hundred dollars or more. It doesn't hurt to spend more to get a quality vehicle. It's also worth spending $50 or so to have a mechanic check it for defects (some AAA offices have diagnostic centers where they can do this on the spot for its members and those of foreign affiliates). You can check out the official valuation of a used car by looking it up in the *Blue Book*, a listing of cars by make, model and year and the average resale price. Local public libraries have copies of the *Blue Book*, as well as back issues of *Consumer's Report*, a magazine that annually tallies the repair records of common makes of cars.

If you want to purchase a car, the first thing to do is contact AAA (☎ (800) 222-4357) for some general information. Then contact the Department of Motor Vehicles to find out about registration fees and insurance, which can be very confusing and expensive. As an example, say you are a 30-year-old non-US citizen and you want to buy a 1984 Honda. If this is the first time you have registered a car in the USA, you'll have to fork over some $300 first and then about $100 to $200 more for general registration.

Inspect the title carefully before purchasing the car; the owner's name that appears on the title must match the identification of the person selling you the car. If you're a foreigner, you may find it very useful to obtain a notarized document authorizing your use of the car, since the motor vehicle bureau in the state where you buy the car may take several weeks or more to process the change in title.

**Insurance** While insurance is not obligatory in every state, all states have financial responsibility laws and insurance is highly desirable; otherwise, a serious accident could leave you a pauper. In order to get insurance some states request that you have a US driver's license and that you have been licensed for at least 18 months. If you meet those qualifications, you may still have to pay anywhere from $300 to $1200 a year for insurance, depending on where the car is registered and the state. Rates are generally lower if you register it at an address in the suburbs or in a rural area, rather than in a central city. Collision coverage has become very expensive, with high deductibles, and is generally not worthwhile unless the car is somewhat valuable. Regulations vary from state to state but are generally becoming stringent throughout the USA.

Obtaining insurance, however, is not as simple as walking into an agency, filling out a form and paying for it. Many agencies refuse to insure drivers who have no car insurance (a classic Catch-22!); those who will do so often charge much higher rates because they presume a higher risk. Male drivers under the age of 25 will pay astronomical rates. The minimum term for a policy is usually six months, but some insurance companies will refund the difference on a prorated basis if the car is sold and the policy voluntarily terminated. It is advisable to shop around.

**Drive-Aways**
Drive-aways are cars that belong to owners who can't drive them to a specific destination but are willing to allow someone else to drive it for them. For example, if somebody moves from Boston to Portland, they

may elect to fly and leave the car with a drive-away agency. The agency will find a driver and take care of all necessary insurance and permits. If you happen to want to drive from Boston to Portland, have a valid driver's license and a clean driving record, you can apply to drive the car. Normally, you have to pay a small refundable deposit. You pay for the gas (though sometimes a gas allowance is given). You are allowed a set number of days to deliver the car – usually based on driving eight hours a day. You are also allowed a limited number of miles, based on the best route and allowing for reasonable side trips, so you can't just zigzag all over the country. However, this is a cheap way to get around if you like long-distance driving and meet eligibility requirements.

Drive-away companies often advertise in the classified sections of newspapers under 'Travel'. They are also listed in the yellow pages of telephone directories under 'Automobile Transporters & Drive-away Companies'. You need to be flexible about dates and destinations when you call. If you are going to a popular area, you may be able to leave within two days or less, or you may have to wait over a week before a car becomes available. The routes most easily available are coast to coast, although intermediate trips are certainly possible.

**Shipping a Car or Motorbike**
In general, because good used cars are cheap in the USA, it is usually unnecessary to ship a car, but a surprising number of people take their own transport to the USA and beyond. Jonathon Hewat, who drove a VW Kombi around the world, wrote a book called *Overland and Beyond* (Roger Lascelles, 47 York Rd, Brentford, Middlesex TW8 0QP, UK), which is a worthwhile read for anyone contemplating such a trip.

Air-cargo planes do have size limits, but a normal car or even a Land Rover can fit. For motorcyclists, air is probably the easiest option; you may be able to get a special rate for air cargo if you are flying with the same airline. Start by asking the cargo departments of the airlines that fly to

**Accidents Do Happen**

Accidents do happen – especially in such an auto-dependent country as the USA. It's important that a visitor knows the appropriate protocol when involved in a 'fender-bender'.

• DON'T TRY TO DRIVE AWAY! Remain at the scene of the accident; otherwise you may spend some time in the local jail.

• Call the police (and an ambulance, if needed) immediately, and give the operator as much specific information as possible (your location, if there are any injuries involved, etc). The emergency phone number is 911.

• Get the other driver's name, address, driver's license number, license plate and insurance information. Be prepared to provide any documentation you have, such as your passport, international driver's license and insurance documents.

• Tell your story to the police carefully. Refrain from answering any questions until you feel comfortable doing so (with a lawyer present, if need be). That's your right under the law. The only insurance information you need to reveal is the name of your insurance carrier and your policy number.

• Always comply to an alcohol breathalyzer test. If you take the option not to, you'll almost certainly find yourself with an automatic suspension of your driving privileges.

• If you're driving a rental car, call the rental company promptly. ■

your destination. Travel agents can sometimes help as well.

### Safety

Drivers should be aware that much of the Pacific Northwest region is open-range country in which cattle and, less frequently, sheep forage along the highway. A collision with a large animal (including game animals like deer or moose) can wreck a car and severely injure or kill the driver and passengers, not to mention the animal, so pay attention to the roadside – especially at night. Seat belts are obligatory for the driver and all passengers in all three states.

During winter months, especially at the higher elevations, there will be times when tire chains are required on snowy or icy roads. Sometimes icy or snowy roads will be closed to cars without chains or 4WD. So it's a good idea to keep a set of chains in the trunk. (Note that rental car companies specifically prohibit the use of chains on their vehicles. You are responsible for any damage due to chains.) Roadside services might be available to attach chains to your tires for a fee (around $20). Other cold-weather precautions include keeping a wool blanket, a windshield ice-scraper, a spade or snow shovel, flares and an extra set of gloves and boots in the trunk for emergencies.

Some but not all US states have motorcycle helmet laws. Oregon and Washington both require that anyone (including passengers) riding a motorcycle wear a helmet; in Idaho, it is only mandatory for those under 18 years of age. However, use of a helmet is highly recommended.

Weather is a serious factor throughout the Pacific Northwest, especially in winter. All three states provide road and travel information as well as state highway patrol information by telephone; for these numbers, see the Emergency entry in the Facts for the Visitor chapter and under Information for each state.

To avert theft, do not leave expensive items, such as purses, compact discs, cameras, leather bags or even sunglasses, visibly lying about in the car. Tuck items under the seat, or even better, put items in the trunk and make sure your car does not have trunk entry through the back seat; if it does, make sure this is locked. Don't leave valuables in the car overnight.

### TAXI

Taxis are especially expensive for long distances, but aren't so outrageous if shared among two or three people. Check with the service before setting out regarding fares per-person, return-trip fees and taxes. Check the Yellow Pages under 'taxi' for phone numbers and services. Drivers often expect a tip of about 10% of the fare.

## BICYCLE

Cycling is an interesting, inexpensive and increasingly popular way to travel in the USA, and in the Pacific Northwest especially. Roads are good, shoulders are usually wide and there are many good routes for mountain bikes as well. The changeable weather can be a drawback, especially at high altitudes where thunderstorms are frequent. In some areas the wind can slow your progress to a crawl (traveling west to east is generally easier than east to west), and water sources are far apart. Cyclists should carry at least two full bottles and refill them at every opportunity. Spare parts are widely available and repair shops are numerous, but it's still important to be able to do basic mechanical work, like fixing a flat, yourself.

Bicycles can be transported by air. You *can* disassemble them and put them in a bike bag or box, but it's much easier simply to wheel your bike to the check-in desk, where it should be treated as a piece of baggage, although airlines often charge an additional fee. You may have to remove the pedals and front tire so that it takes up less space in the aircraft's hold; check all this with the airline well in advance, preferably before you pay for your ticket. Be aware that some airlines welcome bicycles, while others treat them as an undesirable nuisance and do everything possible to discourage them.

Motorists are generally courteous to cyclists, though they often drive too fast. Cyclists may encounter the occasional arrested-development imbecile or perpetual adolescent who harasses cyclists to show off, however. Some cities require helmets, others don't, but they should always be worn.

For more on the details of cycling in the Pacific Northwest, see the Outdoor Activities section.

## HITCHHIKING

Hitchhiking is never entirely safe in any country in the world, and has a reputation for being much more dangerous in the USA than in Europe. We don't recommend it, and travelers who decide to hitch should understand that they are taking a small but serious risk. You may not be able to identify the local rapist/murderer, thief, or even a driver who's had too much to drink, before you get into the vehicle. People who do choose to hitch will be safer if they travel in pairs and let someone know where they are planning to go.

Because public transport is so limited in parts of the Pacific Northwest, some visitors may be tempted to hitchhike to areas where access is difficult. Should you hitch, keep a close watch on your possessions; there are recent instances of 'friendly' drivers absconding with an innocent hitchhiker's possessions while the latter visited the toilet during a gasoline stop.

## WALKING

Because of the great distances only a handful of people care to use their feet as a primary means of transportation. However, it is possible to walk from Canada to Mexico via the Pacific Crest Trail, and to cover other interesting areas on foot; for more information, see the Hiking & Backpacking entry in the Outdoor Activities chapter.

# Washington

# Facts about Washington

People here like to joke about being in 'the upper left hand corner'. That's of the USA, of course, as Washington State is squeezed into the far northwest corner of the country, between the Pacific Ocean, Canada and the other lower 47 states. It's not just the unique geographic position that fuels this claim: Washingtonians take a great deal of pride in being at the northern and western extreme of the continental USA. It's easy to assume that if there's a virtue to the country's long westering and northering instinct, then these are the qualities of this progress-oriented state.

Washington likes to keep its distance. Washingtonians have long known that by cloaking the state in tales of rain and gloom, they could keep the rest of the world away from what is undoubtedly one of the most beautiful corners of North America. However, by now there's scarcely anyone who doesn't know that Seattle is recognized as one of the major cultural and trend-setting centers of the USA, and that life in this green state is as sweet as anywhere in this fallen world.

What's not to like? The western part of the state is about equally divided between glaciered peaks and wilderness, dynamic cities and a seascape of misty islands and harbors. To the east are more arid uplands with 300 days of sunshine, and all-season recreation. Does it rain? To the west, but that's the price you pay to live in this well-washed, hospitable and sophisticated state.

## HISTORY

Though Hudson's Bay Company (HBC) factor John McLoughlin had sought to restrict settlement of the greater Oregon territory to the region south of the Columbia River, as pioneers continued to roll into the Pacific Northwest, the easily settled land along the Willamette began to disappear. After 1846, settlers began streaming north. The first American settlement in

**OFFICIAL WASHINGTON**
**Statehood:** November 11, 1889
**Population:** 5,250,900
**Area:** 71,303 sq miles,
   18th largest in the USA
**Capital:** Olympia
**Nickname:** Evergreen State
**Bird:** willow goldfinch
**Fish:** steelhead trout
**Flower:** Western rhododendron
**Tree:** Western hemlock

Washington was at Tumwater in 1845, on the southern edge of Puget Sound. This group of 32 Missourians purposely chose to move to British territory (despite the disapproval of the HBC) because some of the settlers were part African American, and Oregon law, in order to sidestep the contentious issue of slavery, forbade the settlement of African Americans; the settlers expected better treatment from the British. The village of Tumwater was soon thriving with mills and trading posts, and Olympia was founded as the mill town's port.

In 1851, both Seattle and Port Townsend were established, and quickly became logging centers. The forests of the Pacific Northwest began to fall to the sawyer, and lumber was shipped at great profit to San Francisco, the boomtown of the California Gold Rush.

WASHINGTON

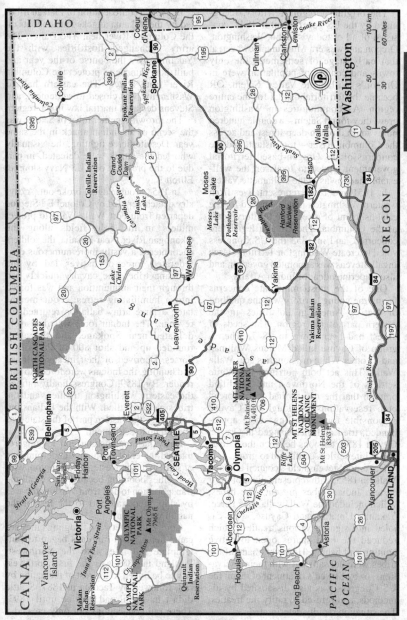

The original Oregon Territory, recognized by the US government in 1848, consisted of all of today's Idaho, Washington, Oregon and western Montana. However, at that early stage of settlement, the only towns and centers of population were in Oregon's Willamette Valley. Salem, OR became the territorial capital for the entire region. As communities in Washington grew, they found Salem – a couple hundred miles south through deep forest and across the Columbia River – too distant, and the concerns of the Oregon-based territorial government tended to focus on the well-established towns of the Willamette Valley.

In 1851 and 1852, representatives from western Washington met and called for the establishment of a separate territory north of the Columbia. The Oregon legislature concurred, and in 1853 the US Congress voted to create Washington Territory. Isaac Ingall Stevens was appointed governor, and also Superintendent of Indian Affairs.

One of the most immediate concerns facing the young territory was the quelling of Native American hostilities in the eastern part of the region. The seeds of unrest had been sown in 1847, when a group of Cayuse killed Marcus Whitman and 11 other White missionaries near Walla Walla. This act both horrified the White settlers of the Northwest and solidified opinion that the natives had to be forced onto reservations. Although the Cayuse responsible for the killings were apprehended, tried and then hanged at Oregon City in 1850, tensions between the natives and White settlers continued to grow.

Governor Stevens held a council at Walla Walla in 1855, with representatives of most eastern Indian tribes present. The tribes, which included the Wallawalla, Nez Perce, Yakama, Umatilla and Cayuse, were cajoled into signing various treaties, which reduced the land shares open to native hunting and fishing. However, many of the tribes were not satisfied with their reservations, or by Steven's treatment of them; the US Congress was also dissatisfied by his methods, and refused to ratify the treaties. The situation rapidly deteriorated.

In 1856, a confederation of Plateau tribes led by the Yakama attacked steamboats on the Columbia River near The Dalles. The army exchanged hostilities with the Yakamas over the course of the year and built Fort Simcoe to protect the Columbia River from attack. The eastern half of Washington was closed to settlement, and Stevens declared martial law in the region.

The thrown-together town of Seattle was the scene of an Indian attack in the same year. Despite fierce fighting, the Nisqually who led the attack were defeated, in part due to the presence of a US Navy sloop in Elliott Bay.

In 1858, trouble again broke out. A cavalry detachment led by Colonel E J Steptoe departed from Fort Walla Walla to protect miners in the gold fields along the Okanogan River. Near Rosalia, the soldiers encountered a vastly more numerous confederated force of natives led by the Spokane tribe. The cavalry quickly ran through their ammunition and was forced into a humiliating retreat. Four months later, a large army battalion returned for revenge. The Indian force was decisively defeated near Spokane, and the army rounded up and shot 800 of the tribes' horses. Deprived of their means of travel and hunting, the Indians were forced to surrender. By 1859, Congress finally ratified the eastern Washington treaties, and the tribes were resettled. With the Indians out of the way, the eastern part of the state was opened up to settlement.

Dairy farming, fishing and logging remained the chief economic underpinnings of settlements in western Washington, with port cities booming because almost all the transportation to and from Washington was by ship; land transport to the rest of the nation was lacking.

Competition between fledgling cities became fierce when railroads began to contemplate rail lines into the Northwest. Portland in 1883 was the first Northwest city to be linked to the rest of the nation by rail, followed by Tacoma in 1887. Seattle didn't have railroad service until 1893. These rail connections not only created a

WASHINGTON

new, readily accessible national market for products of the Pacific Northwest, they also brought in floods of settlers, many of them newly arrived immigrants to the USA.

Washington was finally admitted to the Union in 1889. Seattle's supremacy as the Northwest's greatest seaport was established in 1897, when gold was discovered in the Canadian Klondike and it became the principal port for prospectors and adventurers destined for the Yukon. Seattle boomed; the waterfront was a flurry of departing and arriving ships, honky-tonks, brothels and mercantile outfitters. By 1900, Seattle had surpassed Portland as the largest city in the Northwest.

In many ways, the story of Washington and the 20th century is the story of massive federal works projects and military spending. As early as 1902, the federal government was building dams in the Columbia River basin with the potential to power one third of the USA. The Bonneville Dam, completed in 1937, was the single largest public works project of Franklin Roosevelt's New Deal. Its cheap electrical power proved an enormous boon to the Puget Sound's rapid industrial growth during WW II. In 1947, Bonneville was joined by Grand Coulee Dam, the world's largest hydroelectric and irrigation project.

The naval yards at Bremerton were the Northwest's major ship-building and repair facility during world wars I and II, and home of the Northern Fleet; the city's population grew 235% in the two years following the bombing of Pearl Harbor. The bustling commercial airplane factory south of Seattle owned by William Boeing received the military contracts to build the Air Force's fleet of 13,000 B-17 and B-29 bombers.

Not everyone prospered during the war effort. Japanese immigrants had been moving to the Puget Sound area since the 1880s; a substantial Japanese population also lived in the Yakima Valley, where they operated some of the area's first irrigated farms. In 1942, the federal government removed 18,000 Japanese Americans from their land and homes and interned them in camps in rural western states like Idaho, Wyoming and Montana.

Washington has continued to boom throughout the second half of the 20th century. Seattle, and later Spokane, seemed so certain of their place in the universe that each threw a World's Fair, bringing millions of people to the state.

However, all this success has come at a cost. The massive irrigation projects along the Columbia, and the production of cheap hydroelectricity has led to the near irreversible destruction of the Columbia River ecosystem. The dams have all but eliminated most runs of native salmon, and further disrupted the lives of Native Americans who depended on the river for sustenance and cultural continuity.

The Puget Sound is predicted to have a population of over five million people by early in the 21st century. Many people are finding that the region's much vaunted livability is rapidly disappearing as the entire area becomes one enormous metropolitan area linked by jammed up freeways.

## GEOGRAPHY

The geography of coastal Washington can be described in two words: mountains and water. The mountains in this case are those of the highly glaciated Olympic Range, on the Olympic Peninsula which points like a thumb into the Pacific Ocean. Moist marine air rolls in off the ocean and hits these 8000-foot peaks, dumping immense amounts of precipitation. North America's only temperate rainforests are the result; much of this unique ecosystem is preserved in Olympic National Park.

The Olympic Mountains are surrounded on the north and east by a low-lying basin fed by the waters of the Pacific Ocean. The Strait of Juan de Fuca, Puget Sound, Hood Canal and many smaller bays and inlets reach like tendrils far inland, isolating hundreds of islands and peninsulas. The major population centers of Washington – Olympia, Tacoma, Seattle, Everett and Bellingham – are located along these inlets; all are dependent on deep-water harbors for much of their prosperity.

Marching north and south across the state are the massive volcanoes of the Cascade Range. The southern peaks, including Mt St Helens and Mt Rainier, rise high into the horizon as isolated, snow-clad cones. The North Cascades are different. The most recent volcanoes, like Mt Baker, have pushed up through an already ruggedly mountainous landscape, which once stood offshore as an island before ramming into the North American continent.

The Cascades effectively block the eastward flow of moist Pacific air. Heavy rains fall on the western slopes of the mountains, which create the conditions for thick Douglas fir forests; however, eastern Washington receives much less rainfall. Running east across the northern boundary of Washington is a series of mountainous highlands, which, like the North Cascades, are the buckled remnants of former Pacific islands that have been jammed onto the leading western edge of the continent. Vegetation is comparatively light on these uplands, with ponderosa pines dominant in the forests.

Encircled by the Columbia River, the desert basin of south-central Washington is given life through the river's many irrigation dams. The eastern edge of the basin is an especially barren piece of real estate: it was denuded of much of its topsoil during massive ice-age floods. In the far east flank of the state the land begins to rise toward the foothills of the Rockies, alleviating the effects of the Cascade rain shadow.

## CLIMATE

The Pacific Ocean and the towering Cascade peaks largely determine the climate of Washington. The coast of Washington receives the full brunt of moist, marine air, and coastal towns like Aberdeen receive around 85 inches of rain a year. Temperatures are mild however, with only a 20°F variation between summer and winter average temperatures. However, the heavy rainfall in the Olympic Mountains serves to insulate other parts of western Washington: Sequim, in the rain shadow of the Olympic peaks, receives only 12 inches of rain a year. Throughout coastal Washington, temperatures rarely rise above 80°, or fall below freezing. Seasonal change is gradual, as both spring and fall are periods of cloud and rain.

Rain and snowfall is heavy in the western Cascades, with winter coming early, often in October. Trails may not be free of snow until July. Even in mid-winter, however, temperatures are often mild, around 20° or 30°F; in summer, highs remain in the 70°s.

The climate is very different east of the Cascades. Summer temperatures on the Columbia Plateau reach highs of over 100°F, sometimes for days on end. Rainfall is scant; Yakima receives only 8 inches yearly. Winters can be harsh, with the average January temperature below 20°F.

## POPULATION & PEOPLE

The current population of Washington is 5,240,900, and growing fast. Urban forecasters predict that the population of the Puget Sound area alone will reach 5 million early in the next century. Washington is one of the fastest growing states in the USA, as the region's dynamic economy and easygoing lifestyles lure in young people from around the country.

Like the rest of the Pacific Northwest, Washington is overwhelmingly White (88% in the 1990 census). Only around 10% of the state population is comprised of African, Asian and Hispanic Americans.

The Puget Sound area was one of the most densely populated areas of prehistoric Native America, and a great many Indians still live here. On the 1990 census, 87,000 people identified themselves as Native American. Though still only 1.6% of the state's population, it's by far the largest number of Native Americans in the Northwestern states. The federal government recognizes 26 different reservations in Washington, and many serve as home to more than one tribe. Some reservations, especially along the coast, are very small, consisting basically of just a town and a harbor. The largest reservations are east of the Cascades, where the Yakama and

Colville Confederated Tribes each maintain million-plus-acre homelands.

## ARTS

Seattle is without question the center of the performing art scene in Washington, with thriving theater, classical music and dance companies. However, high rents have served to drive some painters and writers away from the city. You'll find skilled artists living in many rural areas, especially on the Olympic Peninsula and in the San Juan Islands. Don't hesitate to duck into art galleries in out of the way places: you may be surprised by the sophisticated work done by lesser-known local artists.

## Music

Seattle is now probably best known for producing an early '90s rock music phenomenon called 'grunge', a guitar and angst-driven derivative of the punk rock scene. The band Nirvana (before the suicide of lead singer Kurt Cobain) was among the most popular of the many Northwest bands that exemplified the sound, along with other bands like Soundgarden and Pearl Jam. All the attention that Seattle has harvested from the success of these bands has led to an ongoing efflorescence of new rock bands. Seattle and other Puget Sound cities like Bellingham, Tacoma and Olympia, are home to a great number of music clubs that feature local bands, each expressing the suburban teen anxiety that typifies the Northwest sound.

Of course, there was music in Seattle before grunge. A musical generation ago, Seattle was known as the home of Jimi Hendrix, who is buried in the Renton cemetery. Quincy Jones also hails from Seattle; Ray Charles had his first success in the 1950s as a musician on Seattle TV.

## Theater & Film

Seattle has one of the most dynamic theater scenes in the USA. In addition to quality professional theater, the city offers a wide array of amateur and special-interest troupes. Bellingham is known as much for its theater students as its theaters; Western

Washington State University has a noted drama program.

Seattle has come a long ways as a movie mecca since the days when Elvis starred in 1963's *It Happened at the World's Fair*, a chestnut of civic boosterism. Nowadays, Seattle is where directors come to shoot droll and stylish comedies. *Say Anything*, *The Fabulous Baker Boys*, *Singles* and *Sleepless in Seattle*, and TVs *Northern Exposure* and *Frasier* have each done a lot to create Seattle's current reputation as a hip and youthful place to slack off and be trendy.

The creepy, darker side of the Northwest is also on display in films and TV. *Twin Peaks*, the moody and disturbing TV series was shot in Washington, as was the survivalist paean, *First Blood*.

## Visual Arts

Seattle is the center of the art and gallery scene in Washington. In addition to high-quality modern and Western art galleries, a number of galleries are devoted to contemporary Native American carvings and paintings. Seattle is also home to the

Northwest coastal Indian art

## Telephone Area Codes

Effective November 15, 1997, Washington added two new area codes for the Seattle/Tacoma area. The breakdown for the three area codes is Seattle, Richmond Beach, Bainbridge, Mercer and Vashon Islands retain 206; the northern area, from Kent up to Everett, now uses 425; and the region south of Seattle and east of Lake Washington uses the new 253 area code. The rest of western Washington is now reached by using 360. Eastern Washington's area code remains 509. For more information check the local telephone directory. ∎

Seattle Art Museum, in a stylish new building downtown. The collection of native artifacts and folk art is especially impressive. A sizable Asian art collection is located at the Seattle Asian Art Museum in Volunteer Park.

Another specialty of the Puget Sound area is glass-blowing, led by a group of inventive and influential artisans known as the Pilchuk School. The most famous of these artists is Dale Chihuly, whose work can be seen in a number of Seattle galleries, and at a number of places in his hometown, Tacoma. The newly renovated Union Station Courthouse there contains massive works by Chihuly, as does the Washington Historical Society Museum. The San Juan Islands are another hot-bed of artistic activity; several of the islands have co-operative galleries that feature the arts & crafts of island artisans.

## INFORMATION
### Useful Phone Numbers

For a recording of road conditions over mountain passes from October 1 to April 15, call the Washington State Department of Transportation (☎ (206) 434-7277, (900) 407-7277). Call the National Weather Service Public Information Line (☎ (206) 526-6087) for a local weather forecast.

### Time

Washington is in the Pacific Time Zone, which is eight hours behind GMT/UTC, and three hours behind New York City. Washington observes daylight-saving time, which goes into effect from the first Sunday in April to the last Sunday in October.

### Taxes

Washington State sales tax is around 8.2%; some areas add on their own small tax to the standard amount. The bed tax, primarily applicable in Seattle hotels, is 15% (which includes the 8.2%).

Seattle graffiti (TW)

Pike Place Market, Seattle (BM)

Seattle Art Museum (TW)

Crabs at the Pike Place Market, Seattle (TW)

Seattle waterfront (BM)

The Space Needle at sunset, Seattle (KS)

# Seattle

More than any other city in the Pacific Northwest, Seattle epitomizes the area's trend from hick to hip. It wasn't long ago that many people hadn't the foggiest idea where this place was, nor where Washington State was, for that matter. Now it seems everyone knows someone who is living the good life in Seattle, who is up on the music scene or who was there when the coffee craze first started. Music, coffee, plaid and microbrews are recent additions. Before that, this city was conservative and tranquil, relatively provincial in comparison to larger cities. Today it seems larger than life, with more progress and fashions pouring out than ever before, the tallest building on the West Coast shadowing downtown and an overexaggerated sports arena drawing rowdy crowds. But Seattle is really quite small; it's the surrounding neighborhoods that bolster its size and create an impression of living in a city where trees and azaleas outnumber houses.

Seattle's position on the protected waters of the Puget Sound has done more than ensure it a place at the table of international trade. The coastal mountains and the many islands and fingers of land and water that make up the complex geography of the Puget Sound give Seattle one of the most beautiful settings of any city in the USA. From the hills behind downtown, the snow-capped Olympic Mountains rise from the western horizon across the deep blue waters of the sound; ships and ferries wind through scattered, green-clad islands. South and east of the city appear the massive peaks of the Cascades, with Mt Rainier – known in Seattle simply as 'the mountain' – taking up half the horizon.

Seattle's solid success as a trade and manufacturing center, mixed with its beautiful, big-as-all outdoors setting, has made the metropolitan area one of the fastest growing in the USA. Young people especially have found their way to this seaport in search of a city that offers economic opportunity, easy access to recreation and forward-looking politics and culture. In short, if you're looking for lifestyle (and who, in the '90s, isn't?), Seattle has it in spades.

A measure of its success is that Seattle now finds itself a trend exporter. Musical and fashion tastes evolve and permute in the city's many smoky clubs before leaking out to other pace-setting capitals; Seattle has almost single-handedly made coffee a national obsession; its homegrown 'grunge' music has swept the nation, and TV series and movies base themselves in Seattle in order to partake of the city's hip but quirky cultural and social life.

If Seattle has any one defining characteristic, it is that the city is open for business and ready for more – whether that's more talent, a better Italian restaurant, another military contract or software company, or just another caffe latte.

## HISTORY

The Elliott Bay and Lake Washington area was home to the Duwamish, a Salish tribe that fished the bays and rivers of the Puget Sound. Generally a peaceable tribe, the Duwamish befriended early White settlers.

David Denny was a native New Yorker who in 1851 led a group of settlers across the Oregon Trail with the intention of settling along the Puget Sound. Recognizing the seaport possibilities of the Sound, Denny and his fellow settlers staked claims on Alki Point, in present-day West Seattle. The group named their encampment Alki-New York, (the Chinookan word *Alki* means 'by-and-by', which gives a good sense of Denny's aspirations). After a winter of wind and rain, Denny's group determined that their foundling city needed a deeper harbor and moved the settlement to Elliott Bay, across the strait. The colony was renamed Seattle for the Duwamish

WASHINGTON

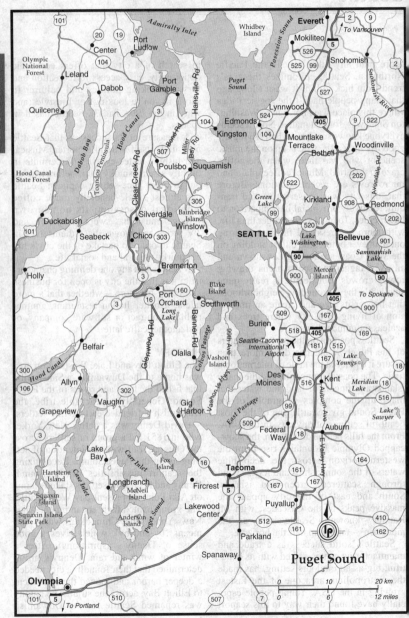

Puget Sound

chief Sealth, who was a friend of an early merchant.

Early Seattle was hardly a boomtown. As a frontier town, the majority of the settlement was comprised of bachelors. One of the town's founding fathers (and sole professor at the newly founded university), Asa Mercer went back to the East Coast with the express purpose of inducing young unmarried women to venture to Seattle. On two different trips, a total of 57 women made the journey back to Seattle and married into the frontier stock, in the process establishing a more civilized tone

in the city (and also inspiring the especially bad 1960s TV show, *Here Come the Brides*).

A spur from the Northern Pacific Railroad's terminus in Portland reached Seattle in 1893, linking the town by rail to the rest of the country. Lumber, shipping and general commerce derived from immigration helped grow the town. The Great Fire of 1889 barely dimmed the city's advance: after 50 blocks of the old wooden downtown burned in a single day, the city rebounded with a new brick and iron city, centered in today's Pioneer Square.

## The Boeing Empire

One of the seminal events in Seattle history occurred in 1916, when William Boeing, a pioneer aviator, began his air-transport empire by designing and producing a pontoon biplane; Boeing went on to establish an airline, Boeing Air Transport, which in 1927 flew the first commercial flight between Chicago and San Francisco. (Boeing Air Transport later became United Airlines.) But it was WW II that really started the engines at Boeing: the factory received contracts to produce B-17 and B-29 bombers, which led the fleet in the US air war against the Axis nations. Immense defense contracts began to flow into Boeing, and by extension into Seattle, fueling rapid growth and prosperity.

WW II brought other developments to Seattle. About 6000 Japanese residents were removed from their jobs and homes and sent to internment camps in Idaho and eastern Oregon. At the same time, the boom in aircraft manufacturing and shipbuilding brought tens of thousands of new workers to the area. Because of Boeing and the shipyards at Bremerton, the Puget Sound became a highly defended area; military bases brought in thousands of new residents. By the end of the war, Seattle had grown to nearly half a million people.

After the war, Boeing diversified its product line and began to develop civilian aircraft. In 1954, Boeing announced the 707, and led the revolution in air transportation. By 1960, the metropolitan population of Seattle topped one million, and Boeing employed one in ten of these; moreover, one in four Seattlites was employed in a job directly affected by Boeing. Boeing was the biggest and almost the only game in town.

However, the fortunes of Boeing weren't always to soar. A combination of overstretched capital (due to cost overruns in the development of the 747) and a cut in defense spending led to a severe financial crisis in the early 1970s. Boeing was forced to cut its work force by two-thirds; in one year, nearly 60,000 Seattlites lost their jobs. The local economy went into a tail-spin for a number of years. Boeing remains, however, an overwhelming force in the economics of Seattle.

**Boeing Factory Tours** North of Seattle near the city of Everett is the facility where most of Boeing's wide-bodied jets – the 747, 767 and the mammoth of the airplane world, the 777 – are produced. Free 90-minute tours of the vast building – apparently the world's largest – and the production areas are offered on weekdays. No photography is allowed in the facility. Tour times change seasonally; call ahead to confirm. Tours are offered on a first come, first serve basis, and are quite popular, so plan to get to the plant with plenty of lead time.

To reach the Boeing factory, follow I-5 north to exit No 189, then head west and drive three miles on Hwy 526. ■

Seattle's first boom came when the ship *Portland* docked at the waterfront in 1897 with its now-famous cargo: two tons of gold newly gleaned from Yukon gold fields. The news of the gold strikes spread immediately across the USA; within weeks, thousands of fortune hunters from all over the country converged on Seattle on their way north. Seventy-four ships left from Seattle for Skagway that summer and autumn.

In all, over 40,000 people passed through Seattle on their way north. The Canadian government demanded that the prospectors bring with them a year's worth of supplies, and outfitting the miners became very big business in Seattle. Most of the goods shipped north to sustain the gold camps also passed through the city. Seattle became the banking center for the fortunes made in the Yukon; and the bars, brothels, theaters and honky-tonks of the Pioneer Square area blossomed, as the entertainment-deprived miners took solace and pleasure along the waterfront.

Many of Seattle's shopkeepers, tavern owners and restauranteurs made quick fortunes in the late 1890s: area merchants grossed an estimated $300,000 in 1897; in 1898, the gross income rose to $25 million. Many of the men who made fortunes in Alaska chose to stay in the Northwest, settling in the thriving port city on the Puget Sound.

The boom continued through WW I, when Northwest lumber was greatly in demand. Shipyards opened along the Puget Sound, bringing the ship-building industry close to the forests of the Northwest, a primary source of lumber.

## CLIMATE

Seattle's reputation for rain is somewhat undeserved. With 38 inches of precipitation a year, Seattle ranks behind many Midwestern and Eastern cities for total precipitation. However, when it comes to damp and cold, there aren't many places in the USA that can top Seattle. The city receives an average of only 55 days of unalloyed sunshine a year; the remaining 310 days

see some form of fog, mist or cloud. This pervasive grayness can make the city's otherwise moderate temperatures – winter highs range between 40° and 50°F, and summer highs are between 75° and 85°F – seem bone-chilling.

The majority of rain falls in the winter, between November and April. Snow is unusual, but when it comes, it really piles up; everyone in Seattle has a story about the last big snowfall. Because of moderate temperatures and quirky weather patterns, snow rarely lasts more than a few hours on the ground.

Summer is very pleasant, though cool. Marine clouds often blanket the Seattle area in the morning but burn off completely by afternoon. A light jacket is often necessary even in the height of summer. Spring and fall are best described as transitional with rain and sun alternating several times a day.

## ORIENTATION

Washington's largest city sits on a slim isthmus between two bodies of water, the Puget Sound and Lake Washington.

Interstate 5 runs north and south through the center of Seattle; I-90 joins it just south of downtown, providing the main link with eastern Washington as it cuts across the center of the state to Spokane. Highway 520 links downtown with Kirkland and Bellevue on two-mile-long Evergreen Point Bridge. Interstate 405, known as the eastside freeway, cuts north-south through the suburbs east of Lake Washington. Seattle is 141 miles south of Vancouver, BC on I-5. Spokane is 280 miles east on I-90, and Portland is 172 miles south on I-5.

### Neighborhoods

Seattle is a very neighborhood-oriented city. Historically, this probably evolved because the difficult marine terrain around the city made it easier to stay close to home, rather than venturing out across lakes and canals.

Lake Union and the Lake Washington Ship Canal divide the city into northern and southern halves. Downtown Seattle and the Capitol Hill and Queen Anne

**Second Only to Los Angeles**
No discussion of getting around Seattle can avoid a mention of Seattle traffic. It can be awful. According to a study in the early 1990s, in the USA only Los Angeles has worse traffic than Seattle. Unfortunately, unless you know the city intimately, there aren't many ways to avoid congestion. With only two bridges across Lake Washington, for instance, you simply have to wait your turn: there's no other practical way to get there. Also, because the Boeing shift changes begin at 2:30 pm, lunch is about the only time it's not rush hour somewhere in Seattle. If you have a choice, avoid traveling on freeways after 3 pm; chances are that traffic is at a standstill. Also, even when traffic is moving, heavy rains can make driving conditions nightmarish. Use caution and have patience. Seattle traffic will demand both. ■

neighborhoods are among those in the south; Ballard, Fremont, Wallingford and the U District are to the north. There are four bridges (besides the freeway bridges) that cross the shipping canal. The westernmost is the Ballard Bridge, linking Ballard and the neighborhood of Magnolia, west of Queen Anne. The Fremont Bridge crosses from Queen Anne to Fremont. East of Lake Union, the University and the Montlake bridges both hook the U District to the neighborhoods south of the canal.

### Downtown

Compared to the rest of the city, downtown orientation is pretty straightforward. The historic downtown area is called Pioneer Square and includes the area between Cherry and King Sts, along 1st to 3rd Aves. The main shopping area of the city lies between 4th and 5th Aves, between Olive and University Sts. Seattle Center, with many of Seattle's cultural and sport facilities as well as the Space Needle, is just north of downtown. Alaskan Way is the Waterfront's main drag; the Waterfront trolley runs the length of it.

### INFORMATION
### Tourist Offices

Visitor Information Center/Downtown Seattle (☎ 461-5840), 800 Convention Place, is at the Washington State Convention & Trade Center, built directly above I-5. You can enter this four-story structure either from Pike St or the Union St underpass.

The AAA office (☎ 448-5353) is at 330 6th Ave N.

### Money

There are a number of options for exchanging money. Thomas Cook Foreign Exchange has an office downtown at 906 3rd Ave (☎ 623-6203) and in Bellevue at 10630 NE 8th Ave (☎ 462-8225). The American Express office (☎ 441-8622) is at 600 Stewart St.

All branches of US, First Interstate and Seafirst banks can exchange foreign currency and travelers checks; however, to buy foreign currency and travelers checks (except Canadian), you'll need to go to the main branches listed below. If you know someone with accounts at one of the following branches, then exchanging the money through their accounts reduces the exchange fees slightly; also, Seafirst charges an additional $6 for exchanging money at its outlying branches; you can avoid paying it by going to the main branch (though your savings will probably be eaten up by parking charges).

In general, the main branches of the following banks offer international currency and business departments that can process transactions more quickly and efficiently

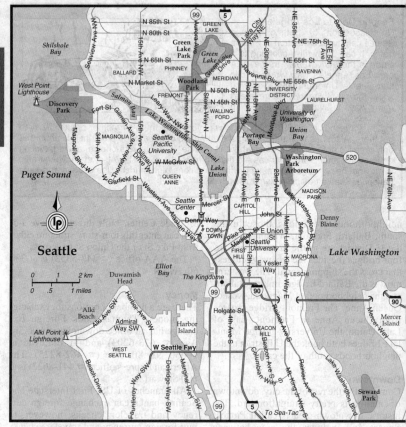

than smaller branch offices. Also, if you plan on heading out into more rural areas in the Northwest, you may want to exchange your money in Seattle, for the same reasons.

First Interstate Bank
    999 3rd Ave (☎ 575-1200)
Seafirst Bank
    701 5th Ave (☎ 358-7800)
US Bank
    1420 5th Ave (☎ 344-3795)

**At the Airport** There are Thomas Cook booths throughout the airport where you can change money. The booth at the main terminal is open from 6 am to 10 pm; in the north esplanade, from 6 am to 8 pm; on the transit level, from 8:45 am to 4:30 pm; and the booth on the concourse level is open from 11 am to 6 pm. Should your flight arrive after hours, you can get some cash from the credit card machines near the booths.

**Post & Telecommunications**
Seattle's main post office (☎ 442-6340) is at 301 Union St, WA 98101. If you're staying near the university, go to University Station (☎ 632-0115), 4244 NE University, WA 98105. On Capitol Hill, go to Broad-

way Station (☎ 324-2588), 101 Broadway E, WA 98122.

All around Seattle are public phones that accept credit cards and US West Telecards, which you can buy at ferry terminals for values of $5.25 to $22 worth of calls.

## Travel Agencies
Council Travel has two offices in Seattle. One is in Capitol Hill in the Alley Market on Broadway (☎ 329-4567). It's open from 9 am to 5 pm Monday to Friday, and Saturday from 10 am to 2 pm for walk-ins only. The other is in the University District (☎ 632-2448) at 1314 NE 43rd St,

right by University Way. It has the same hours as above.

## Bookstores
Seattle is blessed with an abundance of new and used-book stores. Check out the Yellow Pages to find a specialty store that focuses on your interests. Some of the great theme bookstores include The Seattle Mystery Bookstore (☎ 587-5737), 117 Cherry St, Flora & Fauna Books (☎ 623-4727), 121 1st Ave S, or Play's the Thing Bookstore (☎ 322-7529), 514 E Pike St, with theater scripts.

One of the best general bookstores in the Northwest is the Elliott Bay Book Company (☎ 624-6600), 101 S Main St. This rambling bookstore has taken over most of the historic storefronts along a block of Pioneer Square. The interior, all exposed red brick and high ceilings, is absolutely stuffed full of new books and browsing customers. Downstairs is a popular coffeeshop, and Elliott Bay is the local leader in author appearances, with some writer appearing at a reading or signing almost nightly. Check out the listings and ads in the *Seattle Weekly* or call for a current schedule.

The University Bookstore (☎ 634-3400), 4326 University Way NE, is a vast all-purpose bookstore that serves the university. Red & Black Books (☎ 322-7323), 432 15th Ave E, offers a great selection of books on gay, lesbian and feminist issues, and books with a multicultural focus. Beyond the Closet Bookstore (☎ 322-4609), 1501 Belmont Ave, is the city's gay-focused bookstore.

Travelers will want to make a pilgrimage to Wide World Books & Maps (☎ 634-3453), 1911 N 45th Ave. In addition to a great selection of travel guides, this pleasant store offers travel gear. Downtown, the source for maps is Metsker Maps (☎ 623-8747), 702 1st Ave; they also carry a modest selection of travel guides.

## Media
Principal printed news sources are the morning's *Seattle Post-Intelligence*

(usually called the PI), and the afternoon's *Seattle Times*. A good source for entertainment listings is *The Tempo*, the Seattle Times' entertainment supplement distributed on Fridays.

Seattle has a lively alternative publishing scene. The most interesting of the many papers that litter clubs and cafes is *The Stranger*, as close as there is to a weekly voice of Seattle's trendy counterculture. *The Stranger* is a valuable source for film and music info and is a great guide to the club scene; it also features weird local cartoons and the mandatory Savage Love column. The *Rocket* focuses on the music scene. The *Seattle Gay News* covers the gay and lesbian beat.

The *Seattle Weekly* is the baby-boom generation's alternative news weekly, with full listings of arts and entertainment, and investigative pieces exposing city hall bad guys. Check their 'Cheap Thrills' section for free or inexpensive entertainment.

National Public Radio is heard on KUOW at 94.9 FM, and at 88.5 FM on KPLU. You can pick up the Canadian Broadcasting Corporation at 92.3 FM.

### Laundry
Sit & Spin (☎ 441-9484) at 2219 4th Ave in Belltown, is a cafe, art gallery, dance club *and laundry*, leaving you no reason to do your laundry anywhere else. Check local club listings for current acts. On Capitol Hill, go to 12th Ave Laundry (☎ 328-4610), 1807 12th Ave. North of downtown, go to University Maytag Laundry (☎ 526-8992), 4733 University Way.

### Medical Services
If your medical needs aren't grave, then one of the following walk-in clinics should be able to deal with most situations. The Downtown Clinic (☎ 682-3808) is at 509 Olive Way, Suite 217, near the uptown end of the Monorail. The Virginia Mason Fourth Ave Clinic (☎ 223-6490) is at 1221 4th Ave. Both of these offices are open from 8 am to 5 pm Monday to Friday, and Saturday mornings.

For complete medical care, including an emergency room, go to Providence Medical Center (☎ 320-2111) at 500 17th Ave, or to Virginia Mason Hospital (☎ 624-1144), 925 Seneca St.

### DOWNTOWN
The area that most people associate with Seattle is the downtown area – the business district, Pike Place Market, Belltown, Pioneer Square and on the perimeter, the International District. Starting from the visitors center in the Convention Center, the best way to see it all is to walk towards the water down either Pike or Pine Sts.

The first area you will encounter is the new, classy shopping district that revolves around Nordstrom and the Westlake Center, both between 4th and 5th Aves. Here skateboarders and trench-coat-clad professionals tolerate each others' definition of fun. Right in the heart of the skateboard territory, there's a waterwall that you can walk through without getting wet. The Bon Marche at 3rd Ave and Pine St is Seattle's oldest and largest department store.

The **business district** is to the right (just look for the looming buildings). There's not much to see there, except the buildings themselves and some sculpture. Most impressive is the **Columbia Seafirst Center** taking up the block between 4th and 5th Aves and Columbia and Cherry Sts. This Darth Vader of a building is the tallest on the West Coast. The observation deck on the 73rd floor is open weekdays from 8:30 am to 4:30 pm and costs $3.50 per adult. On the first level there's a food court with a plethora of fast food and frazzled bankers. Outside is the *Three Piece Vertebrae*, a sculpture by Henry Moore – a recipient of Seattle's 1%-for-art clause. In the block around 5th Ave and Union St is the top-heavy **Rainier Square building** that looks like a beaver started chipping away at its base. The beauty of the skyline is the blue-and-cream **Washington Mutual Building** at University St and 2nd Ave, which turns colors with the clouds and sunsets.

Check out the ornamental walruses on the **Arctic Building** at 3rd Ave and Cherry St, and the dour terra-cotta head of a Native

American chief at the Skinner Building at University St and 5th Ave. Sixteen of these 800-pound heads once decorated the exterior of the White Henry Stuart Building, the original structure on this site (it was torn down in 1976).

The distinctive, white 42-story **Smith Tower**, at the corner of 2nd Ave and Yesler Way near Pioneer Square, was built in 1914 by L C Smith, a man who built his fortune on typewriters. It was the tallest building in the world outside of New York for many years.

Heading down Pike or Union Sts the blocks between 3rd and 1st Aves are quite run down and are worth extra precautions. Businesses move out frequently, panhandlers hover around bus stops and empty lots call into question the city's prosperity. Unfortunately this is also where the main post office is and where buses en route to Capitol Hill and the University District stop (along Pike St). At the end of Pike St is Pike Place Market. From here, the Waterfront is straight ahead, Belltown and the Seattle Center are to the north and the Seattle Art Museum and Pioneer Square are to the south. (See below for these areas.)

### Pike Place Market
This farmer's market began in 1907. Almost 90 years later, Pike Place is one of Seattle's most popular tourist attractions, and is as noted for its exuberant theatricality as much as for its vastly appealing fish and vegetable market. Pike Place Market features some of the most boisterous fishmongers in the world, whose dare-devil antics with salmon merge gymnastics, theater and cuisine.

Never go to market on the weekends, or a Friday for that matter, unless you enjoy being stuck in human gridlock next to a stack of frozen crab. The best bet for enjoying the wonderful market is to go on a weekday morning. Pike Place is made up of several buildings, the most popular of which are the **Main and North arcades**, with the banks of beautiful fresh produce carefully arranged in artful displays, and the fresh fish, crabs and shellfish piled high

with ice (many fish stands will pack any fish for overnight delivery).

But this is only a small part of today's Pike Place Market. Over half of the open-air stalls are now devoted to locally made arts & crafts, and the three labyrinthine lower levels of the market are devoted to pocket-sized shops of all descriptions, from Indian spice stalls to magicians' supply shops to military button booths. The streets surrounding Pike Place Market continue the warren-like maze of shops, with ethnic food stalls, plant shops, galleries and gift boutiques. If you're looking for souvenirs, head to the Made in Washington Store (☎ 467-0788).

The **Economy Market Building** (once a stable for merchants horses) on the south side of the entrance has a wonderful Italian grocery store, De Laurenti's – a great place for an aficionado of Italian foods to browse and sample. There's also Tenzing Momo, one of the oldest apothecaries on the West Coast – a great place to pick up herbal remedies, incense, oils, books or, on occasion, get a tarot reading.

Across from the Main Arcade is the

'The Pig' at Pike Place Market (CH)

WASHINGTON

WASHINGTON

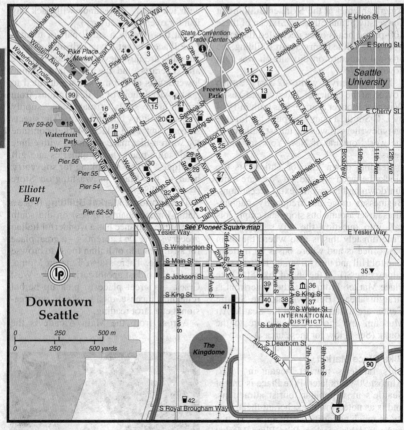

Downtown Seattle

0        250        500 m
0        250        500 yards

Elliott Bay

The Kingdome

INTERNATIONAL DISTRICT

| PLACES TO STAY | | |
|---|---|---|
| 7 | Inn at the Market | |
| 9 | Sheraton | |
| 12 | Inn At Virginia Mason | |
| 13 | Sorrento Hotel | |
| 16 | HI/AYH Seattle | |
| 21 | Olympic Four Seasons Hotel | |
| 22 | YWCA | |
| 23 | Pacific Plaza | |
| 24 | Hotel Seattle | |
| 25 | Stouffer Madison Hotel | |
| 29 | YMCA | |
| 30 | Alexis Hotel | |

| PLACES TO EAT | |
|---|---|
| 1 | Dahlia Lounge |
| 5 | Cafe Sophie |
| 6 | Pink Door Ristorante |
| 9 | Fullers |
| 21 | Georgian Room |
| 30 | Painted Table |
| 27 | McCormick's Fish House & Bar |
| 35 | A Little Bit of Saigon |
| 37 | Sea Garden |
| 38 | Hing Loon |
| 39 | House of Dumplings |

| OTHER | |
|---|---|
| 2 | Westlake Center |
| 3 | Nordstrom |
| 4 | Bon Marche |
| 8 | City Center Mall |
| 10 | Visitors Center |
| 11 | Virginia Mason Hospital |
| 14 | Rainier Square |
| 15 | Post Office |
| 17 | Captain Cook's |
| 18 | Seattle Aquarium, Omnidome Theatre |
| 19 | Seattle Art Museum |
| 20 | Virginia Mason Fourth Ave Clinic |
| 26 | Frye Art Museum |
| 28 | Thomas Cook Exchange |
| 31 | Legacy Ltd Gallery |
| 32 | Metro Bus Customer Service |
| 33 | Metsker Maps |
| 34 | Greg Kucera Gallery |
| 36 | Wing Luke Asian Museum |
| 40 | Uwajimaya |
| 41 | King Street Station (Amtrak) |
| 42 | Hart Brewers Pub |

WASHINGTON

The Jonathan Borofsky *Hammering Man* sculpture towers over visitors at the Seattle Art Museum (TW)

**Sanitary Market** – the first building in which live animals were prohibited – a maze of great little eateries including the Three Sisters Bakery with sit down (but it's always packed) and take out of some of the best breads and sandwiches around. Also, all in a row, there's the Greek Deli, Mee Sum Pastry with great pork buns, a juice bar and Cinnamon Works – all great choices for a quick snack.

For a compulsive browser, amateur chef, hungry traveler on a budget or student of the human condition, Seattle has no greater attraction than Pike Place Market.

The Main Arcade has restrooms. Elevators and stairs lead down to Western Ave and the Waterfront. The stalls close at 6 pm.

**Seattle Art Museum**

Jonathan Borofsky's four-story action sculpture, *Hammering Man*, welcomes visitors to the Seattle Art Museum (☎ 654-3100), 100 University St, where the towering figure waves tools at the museum's front door.

The museum's collection, focusing on world art with an emphasis on Asian, African and Native American folk and tribal art, is greatly enhanced by the recent move to more spacious quarters. Especially good are the displays of masks, canoes and totems from Northwest Coastal tribes. Traveling shows are found in the Special Exhibits gallery; films and lectures take place in the 300-seat auditorium.

The museum is open Tuesday to Sunday from 10 am to 5 pm, with hours extended to 9 pm on Thursday. Admission is $6 for adults, $4 for seniors and students. (Within two days, tickets are also good at the Seattle Asian Art Museum in Volunteer Park.) On the first Tuesday of the month, admission is free.

**Frye Art Museum**

This small museum (☎ 622-9250), 704 Terry Ave, preserves the collection of Charles and Emma Frye. The Fryes collected over 1000 paintings, mostly 19th and early 20th-century European and

American pieces, and a few Alaskan and Russian artworks. It's open Monday to Saturday from 10 am to 5 pm, and Sunday from noon to 5 pm. Admission is free.

## The Waterfront

Visitors can catch the flavor of a major seaport by walking along the Seattle waterfront; they can also do a lot of eating and souvenir shopping in Seattle's tackiest tourist zone. Along the length of the waterfront, amidst the horse-drawn carriages, pedicabs and cotton-candy vendors, are services that offer harbor tours and boat excursions (see Organized Tours, later in this chapter).

Washington State Ferries also depart for Bremerton, Bainbridge Island and Victoria, BC from the piers (see Getting There & Away). The Seattle Aquarium and the Omnidome theater (see below) are on Pier 59. Piers 54, 55, 56 and 57 are devoted to shops, restaurants and novelty venues like the 100-year-old Ye Olde Curiosity Shop (☎ 682-5844), a cross between a museum and a souvenir shop. Pier 58 is now Waterfront Park, a small viewing area with benches.

The **Waterfront Trolley** runs along Alaskan Way, the main thoroughfare along the waterfront. These little streetcars are especially handy for visitors, as they link the area near Seattle Center (from the base of Broad St) to the Waterfront and Pike Place Market, and on to Pioneer Square and the International District. Tickets range between 85c and $1.10, and remain valid for an hour and a half.

Unfortunately, city planners ran a freeway around the city, dividing downtown from the Waterfront. While it in no way infringes upon getting from one place to the other, it is incredibly noisy and the parking areas under the freeway can be a bit scary at night. Luckily, more savvy planners have created several walkways down to the water, the most recent of which are the Harbor Steps leading off from where University St ends at the Seattle Art Museum. In the middle of all is more sculp-ture, this time the rotating *Schubert's Sonata* by Mark di Suvero.

**Seattle Aquarium** This well-designed aquarium (☎ 386-4320, 386-4300), 1438 Alaskan Way, Pier 59, in Waterfront Park, offers a view into the underwater world of the Puget Sound and the Northwest Pacific coast. Exhibits include re-creations of the many environments of bay and ocean, including tidepools, eelgrass beds, a coral reef and the seafloor. The centerpiece of the aquarium is a glass-domed room where sharks, octopi and other deep-water denizens lurk in the shadowy depths. The passages eventually lead outdoors to a salmon ladder, and to views over Elliott Bay and a pool where playful sea otters and seals await your attention.

The Seattle Aquarium is open daily from 10 am to 8 pm Memorial Day to Labor Day, and from 10 am to 5 pm the rest of the year. Entrance is $6.75 for adults, $5.25 for seniors 65 or older and disabled visitors, $4.25 for youths ages six to 18 and $1.75 for children ages three to five. Children under three are free. Combination tickets with the Omnidome theater are available; see below.

**Omnidome Film Experience** Adjacent to the aquarium is this 180° surround-screen theater (☎ 622-1868) on Pier 59. There are usually two shows available; the ongoing favorite is *The Eruption of Mt St Helens*, which features a helicopter ride over an exploding volcano (the film received an Academy Award nomination). Most features are 45 minutes long and begin showing daily at 10 am; call for show times. Tickets for one show are $6 for adults, $5 for seniors and youths ages 13 to 18 and $4 for children ages three to 12. Children under three are free.

A combination ticket to the aquarium and to the Omnidome Film Experience is available at $11 for adults, $8 for seniors; $7.25 for youths ages 13 to 18, $6.25 children ages three to 12 and $4.75 for children ages three to five.

## Pioneer Square

The birthplace of Seattle, this red-brick district of historic buildings and totem-lined plazas is still a real crossroads of modern Seattle. For years this area was in decline until cheap rents and Historic-Register status brought in art galleries, antique shops and cafes. Browsing the Pioneer Square area is rather like visiting a movie set of turn-of-the-century Seattle, except that the food and the shopping are better. Some of Seattle's best antique stores and art galleries are here; a number of restaurants play up the frontier image while serving some of the city's best food — Merchants Cafe (see Places to Eat) is reputedly the oldest restaurant in Seattle and perhaps on the West Coast.

Pioneer Square is most easily reached by walking or by bus (it's in the free-transit zone). For something more touristy-historic, take the Waterfront Trolley from the Waterfront, which will put you smack dab in the heart of the square.

If walking from Pike Place Market, take either Alaskan Way along the Waterfront, or 1st Ave to pass by the art museum's *Hammering Man* and some unusual shops. The Pioneer Square area is bounded roughly by Cherry and S King Sts, 1st and 3rd Aves.

Right at the corner of Cherry St and 1st

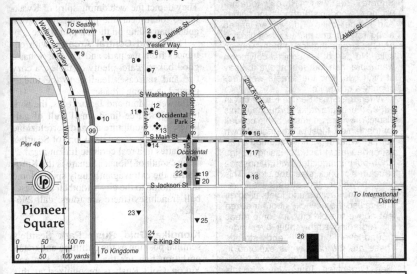

| PLACES TO EAT | 3 | Doc Maynard's Public House (Underground Tour) | 14 | Elliott Bay Book Company |
| 1 | Trattoria Mitchell | 4 | Smith Tower | 15 | Klondike Gold Rush National Historic Park |
| 5 | Merchants Cafe | 6 | Starbuck's | 16 | Comedy Underground |
| 9 | al Boccalino Ristorante | 7 | New Orleans Creole Restaurant | 18 | Linda Farris Gallery |
| 17 | Cafe Hue | 8 | Colourbox | 19 | Torrefazione Italia |
| 23 | Il Terrazzo Carmine | 10 | OK Hotel | 20 | Pacific Northwest Brewing Company |
| 24 | Umberto's Ristorante | 11 | The Central | 21 | Glasshouse Art Glass, Foster/White Gallery |
| 25 | FX McRory's Steak, Chop & Oyster House | 12 | Fireworks Fine Crafts Gallery | 22 | Davidson Galleries |
| **OTHER** | | 13 | Grand Central Arcade | 26 | King St Station (Amtrak) |
| 2 | Pergola | | | | |

Ave you'll come to the original Pioneer Place – a cobblestoned triangular plaza with a totem pole and pergola. The totem pole, so the story goes, was stolen from the Tlingit Indians in 1890 but burned down. When asked if they could carve another, the Tlingit took the money offered, thanking the city for payment of the first totem pole, and waited for a better incentive to carve the one now standing.

The **pergola** may look decorative, but its original purpose was as a cover to an

---

**The Great Fire**

In the early days of Seattle, the Pioneer Square area was a thrown-together village of wooden storefronts, log homes and lumber mills. Tide water lapped along 1st Ave, and many of the buildings and the streets that led to them were on stilts. No part of the original downtown was more than four feet above the bay at high tide, and the streets were frequently a quagmire.

When the Great Seattle Fire struck in 1889, the boardwalks throughout this district provided an unstoppable conduit for the flames. Most of the original town burned. What might have seemed a catastrophe was in fact a blessing, as the city rebuilt immediately with handsome structures of brick, steel and stone. This time, however, the streets were regraded, and ravines and inlets filled in. This raised the new city about a dozen feet above the old city; in some areas the regrading simply built over older ground-level buildings and streets. These are the catacombs explored in the famous Seattle Underground Tour (See Organized Tours, later in this chapter).

The rapid rebuilding of the Pioneer Square area also endowed the district with a rare architectural homogeneity. Almost all of the buildings around Pioneer Square were built between 1890 and 1905, and many of these buildings share something other than simple contemporality: one architect, Elmer Fisher, was responsible for the plans of 50 buildings erected immediately after the fire. ■

---

underground lavatory and to protect those waiting for the cable car that went up and down Yesler Way. Unfortunately, some homeless people and weekend partiers seem to be turning the area back into a lavatory. Incidentally, Yesler Way was originally called Skid Rd – logs would 'skid' down the road linking a logging area above town to Henry Yesler's mill on a pier. With the decline of the area, the street became a haven for homeless people. Soon the nickname 'Skid Row' was being used for equally destitute areas around the country.

Just south of Pioneer Place on Occidental Ave S, **Occidental Park** has a few more totem poles all carved by Duane Pasco. They depict the welcoming spirit of Kwakiutl, a totem bear, the tall Sun and Raven, and a man riding on the tail of a whale.

The **Grand Central Arcade**, with entrances from the park and 1st Ave S, has a good bakery cafe, plenty of tables, a cozy fire and staircases leading to the underground shopping arcade.

Between Main and Jackson Sts, the park turns into a tree-lined 'mall' full of galleries, some sculpture art and Torrefazione Italia, where you can drink one of Seattle's best lattes in a real ceramic Italian *tazza*.

Just south of Pioneer Square is the **Kingdome**, the extravagantly ugly sports dome that is home to the city's football and baseball franchises (there are tours; call 296-3128).

**Klondike Gold Rush Park** Seattle's seminal position as the outfitting and transportation hub for the 1897 Alaskan and Yukon Gold Rush is recognized at this small free national historical park/museum (☎ 553-7220), 117 S Main St. Exhibits document the abundance of gear and food necessary to stake a claim in the Klondike, which brought a boom to Seattle merchants. Gold panning is demonstrated by park rangers; there's a slide presentation about the gold rush as well. Admission is free and hours are from 9 am to 5 pm daily.

**Art Galleries** Stop in to the many galleries downtown to get a better feel for Northwestern art. The Seattle area is known for its Pilchuck school of art glass blowing. Glasshouse Art Glass (☎ 682-9939), 311 Occidental Ave S, and, just upstairs, the Foster/White Gallery (☎ 622-2833), 311½ Occidental Ave S, feature glass works, as well as paintings from mainstream Northwest artists.

Davidson Galleries (☎ 622-1554), 313 Occidental Ave S, is another Pioneer Square gallery with often eclectic groupings of old and new regional artists. Contemporary Northwestern art is on display at Donald Young Gallery, (☎ 448-9484), 2107 3rd Ave, usually Seattle's most experimental gallery; at Linda Farris Gallery (☎ 623-1110), 322 2nd Ave S; and at Greg Kucera Gallery, (☎ 624-0770), 608 2nd Ave, where blue-chip contemporary artists hang with the best of the locals. Legacy Ltd (☎ 624-6350), 1003 1st Ave, is probably the city's best gallery for Northwest Indian and Eskimo art and artifacts. Fireworks Fine Crafts Gallery (☎ 682-8707), 210 1st Ave S, is a great mixture of funky handmade jewelry, furniture, pottery, you name it. This is a good place to actually buy something artsy without spending your annual income.

On the first Thursday of every month, the galleries around Pioneer Square stay open late, enticing people with wine and snacks, and everyone goes to look at everyone else looking at the art. Known as **ArtWalk** or First Thursday, this is the best time to be a part of the whole gallery scene. Of course, any of the above places can be visited on other days as well.

## THE INTERNATIONAL DISTRICT

East of Pioneer Square is the International District, Seattle's Chinatown, where Asian groceries and restaurants line the streets. Chinese were among the first settlers in Seattle, and have been followed by Japanese, Filipinos, Vietnamese, Laotians and others.

The main center of the district is between 5th and 7th Aves and Weller and Jackson Sts. The best way to get there from Pioneer Square is to walk up Jackson St. You'll pass the outwardly handsome **King Street**

**Station**, the old Italianate Great Northern Railroad depot, its stately brick tower long an integral (though now dwarfed) piece of the downtown skyline. It's presently in use as the Amtrak station. Go along Jackson St to 6th Ave and turn right to get to the heart of the small district.

Weller St is a good street to get a glimpse of it all. Besides the many restaurants, there is Pacific Herb & Grocery (☎ 340-6411) at 610 S Weller St between 6th and Maynard Aves. As herbal medicine specialists they can tell you all about the uses of different roots, bones, flowers and teas. Right next door is a tofu shop where you can watch them make the tofu and buy some very cheaply. At about 7th Ave the district fizzles out for a few blocks then picks up at 10th Ave and continues to 12th Ave with a hodgepodge of small malls and parking lots. This area has more Vietnamese influence than the area below.

In case you have forgotten you're on the Pacific Rim, head to Uwajimaya (☎ 624-6248), 519 6th Ave S, the supermarket of the International District. At this large Asian department and grocery store – a cornerstone of Seattle's Asian community – you'll find exotic fruits and vegetables and cooking utensils, and come face to face with what you've always feared was in dim sum.

### The Wing Luke Asian Museum

This pan-Asian museum (☎ 623-5124), 407 7th Ave S, is devoted solely to Asian and Pacific-American culture, history and art. Named after the first Asian elected official in Seattle, the museum examines the often difficult and violent meeting of Asian and Western cultures in Seattle. Particularly good are the photos and displays on the Chinese settlement in the 1880s and the retelling of Japanese internment during WW II. The museum is self-guided and open from 11 am to 4:30 pm Tuesday to Friday, and from noon to 4 pm Saturday to Sunday. Admission is $2.50 for adults, $1.50 for seniors and students and 75c for children ages five to 12.

WASHINGTON

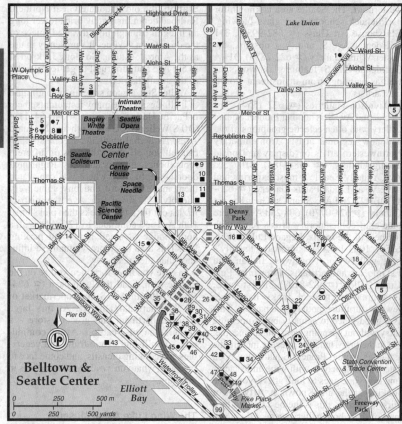

Belltown &
Seattle Center

Elliott
Bay

## BELLTOWN

Immediately north of Pike Place Market, in the area that reaches from Virginia St to Broad St and from Western Ave to 3rd Ave, is a district called Belltown. Long an area of warehouses and office buildings, this neighborhood is now home to trendy coffeeshops, designer shoe stores and many of Seattle's most noted live-music venues. Most of the shops and fancy restaurants are along 1st Ave, while 2nd Ave has a string of bars and nightclubs.

## SEATTLE CENTER

In 1962, Seattle was confident and ready

for company. The self-assured, forward-ho swagger of the city was perfectly captured in the spirit of the 1962 World's Fair. Seattle, the home of hi-tech jumbo jets, saw itself as the city of the future; the Space Needle and the Monorail now evoke a distinctly 1960s notion of tomorrow's world.

The World's Fair, which was also known as 'Century 21 Exposition', was a summer-long exhibition that brought in nearly 10 million visitors from around the world to view the future, Seattle-style. A warehouse area north of downtown was leveled, and a futuristic international enclave of exhibition halls, arenas and public spaces sprang

| PLACES TO STAY | | 6 | Uptown Bakery | 15 | Five Point Cafe |
|---|---|---|---|---|---|
| 3 | Green Tortoise Back-packers' Guest House | 14 | Cafe Minnies | 17 | Timberline |
| | | 27 | Two Bells Tavern | 18 | Re-Bar |
| 8 | Inn at Queen Anne | 29 | Mama's Mexican Kitchen | 20 | Greyhound Bus Depot |
| 10 | Econolodge | 35 | Macrina | 23 | American Express |
| 11 | Seattle Inn | 38 | Vici Pizza | 24 | Downtown Clinic |
| 12 | Travelodge | 39 | Casa-U-Betcha | 25 | Weathered Wall |
| 13 | Best Western Executive Inn | 41 | Chez Banana | 26 | Sit & Spin |
| | | 44 | Queen City Grill | 28 | Rendezvous |
| 16 | Loyal Inn Best Western | 46 | Continental Deli | 30 | Lava Lounge |
| 19 | Sixth Avenue Inn | 48 | Kaleenka Russian Cafe | 31 | Crocodile Cafe |
| 21 | WestCoast Camlin Hotel | 49 | du jour | 32 | Donald Young Gallery |
| 22 | WestCoast Vance Hotel | | | 33 | Penny University |
| 34 | Moore Hotel | **OTHER** | | 36 | Belltown Pub |
| 42 | Commodore Motor Hotel | 1 | Cucina! Cucina! | 37 | Lux Coffee House |
| 43 | Edgewater | 4 | Queen Anne Hall | 40 | Belltown Theatre Center |
| | | 5 | Sorry Charlies | 45 | Belltown Billiards |
| **PLACES TO EAT** | | 7 | Mecca Cafe | 47 | Virginia Inn Tavern |
| 2 | Adriatica Restaurant | 9 | AAA | | |

up. Never mind that today the Seattle Center, as we now term the World's Fair grounds, generates more nostalgia for the Jetsons than thoughts of the future.

Probably no other building in Seattle epitomizes the city as well as the Space Needle, the 605-foot-high futuristic observation station and restaurant. The Monorail, a 1.5-mile experiment in mass transit, was another signature piece of the 1962 fair. The Flag Pavilion & Plaza, and the International Fountain (with jets of water that pulse to the beat of music) point to the cosmopolitan sympathies of the fair. These landmarks have lived on; the Seattle Opera House (home of the opera, symphony and ballet), two playhouses, two sports arenas, the Fun Forest Amusement Park (with carnival rides) and various museums and art spaces are other remnants of the fair.

For information about the Seattle Center complex, call 684-8582 or 684-7200; it's between Denny Way and Mercer St, and 1st and 5th Aves N. A number of fast-food venues, as well as bathrooms and other public facilities, are located in Center House near the Monorail Terminal. No admission is charged to enter the Seattle Center area.

Parking can be tight around Seattle Cen-

ter when more than one large event takes place. There are parking lots on Mercer St, between 3rd and 4th Aves N. There's easy access to the Waterfront Trolley at Broad St and Western Ave, if you want to continue the walking tour of downtown.

### Space Needle

Seattle's signature monument, the Space Needle (☎ 443-2111), 219 4th Ave N, takes advantage of its 520-foot-high observation deck with 360° views of Seattle and surrounding areas to bombard visitors with historical information and interpretive displays. To zip to the top on the elevators (it takes 41 seconds) commands a charge of $6.50 for adults, $5.75 for seniors and $4 for children ages five to 12.

Way back in 1962, the Space Needle surfed the wave of the future with its two revolving restaurants (☎ 443-2100); one is much more expensive than the other, though a meal in either one results in free passage on the elevators for patrons. There's also a lounge at the top, but there's no free passage for mere drinks.

### The Monorail

The futuristic Monorail provides fun and frequent transport between downtown's Westlake Center, at Pine St and 5th Ave, and Seattle Center. Cars run about every 10 minutes, and tickets are 90c for adults, 70c for children and 35c for seniors. The trip takes only two minutes.

### Pacific Science Center

This museum of science and industry (☎ 443-2001), 200 2nd Ave N, once housed the science pavilion of the World's Fair. Today, the center offers virtual reality exhibits, laser shows, holograms, hands-on demonstrations and other wonders of science. Also on the premises is the vaulted-screen **IMAX Theatre** and a planetarium. The Pacific Science Center is open weekdays from 10 am to 5 pm, and weekends from 10 am to 6 pm. Admission to the exhibit space is $5.50 for adults, $4.50 for seniors and children ages six to 13, and $3.50 for children ages two to five. Admission to the IMAX Theatre and Laserium is $2 on top of the general admission price or $5 for a theater ticket only.

### Children's Museum

This learning center (☎ 441-1768) in the basement of Center House offers a number of imaginative activities and displays, many focusing on cross-cultural awareness and hands-on art sessions. The play area includes a child-sized neighborhood, a play center and an area dedicated to blowing soap bubbles. The Children's Museum is open from 10 am to 5 pm Tuesday to Sunday. During summer break, the museum opens Mondays 10 pm to 5 pm. Admission is $3.50 per person, with children under one year free.

Also for kids is the **Seattle Children's Theatre**, in the Charlotte Martin Theatre. Call 443-0807 for performance information. The **Pacific Arts Center** (☎ 443-5437), in the same building, offers children's art classes and exhibits designed for young audiences.

### Northwest Craft Center

Flanking the International Fountain is this gallery (☎ 728-1555), mostly dedicated to ceramics by regional craftspeople. Exhibits

change monthly; there's also a gift shop carrying other handmade crafts from the area.

### CAPITOL HILL

Brass-inlaid dance steps along Broadway propel you into a rumba or a tango (actually, it's public art), but you'll never see a local learning the steps. And that's about as aesthetic as the streets get. Unlike other parts of the city, it's the throngs of people along the streets and not the buildings that really sets Capitol Hill apart from the other neighborhoods. Long a counterculture oasis, there are probably more nose rings and goatees on Capitol Hill than anywhere else in the Northwest. Also the principal gay and lesbian neighborhood in Seattle, the area has a vitality and creativity unmatched.

If you take buses No 7 or 10 from downtown, get off at **Broadway** – the main strip. East John St (the continuation of Olive St) is the main corner of activity. Twice Told Tales (☎ 625-1611), on E John St, is a rambling used-book store with a bubble machine outside. It stays open very late. Head north on Broadway to peruse the multitudes of shops. Espresso Roma (see Coffeehouses under Entertainment) is a gathering point for all sorts and a good place to get the daily fix. Between Harrison and Republican Sts is the Broadway Market with two stories of shops, eateries and a cinema featuring more 'artsy' flicks. Across the street, Dillettante Chocolates, decked in pink and umbrellas, is well known for the truffles and 'adult' milkshakes. A block past that, Pacific Dessert Co is another place for sugar and caffeine highs. The Broadway strip ends at E Roy St and the atmosphere turns to well-maintained houses with manicured lawns. Continue down Broadway until it turns into 10th Ave E and you'll be right by Volunteer Park (see below). Near the corner of 10th Ave E and Galer St is **St Marks Cathedral** (☎ 720-0217), where a chorus performs Gregorian chants (compline) on Sunday nights at 9:30 pm.

Seven blocks east of Broadway is **15th Ave E**, another strip, although much more tame and sparse than the former. The blocks between Thomas and Mercer hold the most interest, with bookstores, wine shops, bakeries and restaurants back to back. At the Internet Cafe, at the corner of Mercer St inside the Seattle Espresso Company, you can caffeinate while you cruise online. (See Coffeehouses for details.)

South of Broadway is the hip **Pike/Pine Corridor** which extends from 12th Ave to about 9th Ave (back near the convention center). Long considered Seattle's gay-bar district, the nightlife hotspot has diversified

to include all-night coffeehouses, live-music clubs and rowdy, smoke-filled bars. If you're looking for late-night action, this is one of Seattle's most lively scenes.

If you're driving, your best bet is to park in the pay lot behind the Broadway Market west of Broadway on E Harrison St.

### Volunteer Park

This stately 140-acre park above downtown Seattle on Capitol Hill began as pioneer Seattle's cemetery. However, as Seattle grew and the need for water became more pressing (particularly after the Great

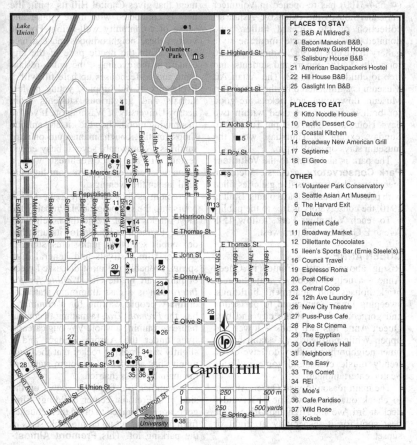

**PLACES TO STAY**
2  B&B At Mildred's
4  Bacon Mansion B&B,
   Broadway Guest House
5  Salisbury House B&B
21 American Backpackers Hostel
22 Hill House B&B
25 Gaslight Inn B&B

**PLACES TO EAT**
8  Kitto Noodle House
10 Pacific Dessert Co
13 Coastal Kitchen
14 Broadway New American Grill
17 Septieme
18 El Greco

**OTHER**
1  Volunteer Park Conservatory
3  Seattle Asian Art Museum
6  The Harvard Exit
7  Deluxe
9  Internet Cafe
11 Broadway Market
12 Dilettante Chocolates
15 Ileen's Sports Bar (Ernie Steele's)
16 Council Travel
19 Espresso Roma
20 Post Office
23 Central Coop
24 12th Ave Laundry
26 New City Theatre
27 Puss-Puss Cafe
28 Pike St Cinema
29 The Egyptian
30 Odd Fellows Hall
31 Neighbors
32 The Easy
33 The Comet
34 REI
35 Moe's
36 Cafe Paridiso
37 Wild Rose
38 Kokeb

Seattle Fire), Volunteer Park, with its water tower and reservoir, was created.

Roads and paths wind around the park, with manicured meadow-like lawns descending to the mansion-rich neighborhoods that flank the area. Because the park has existed in one form or another since 1876, the trees and landscaping here reflect a kind of maximum growth of the Seattle urban ecosystem. Keen seekers of views can climb the 75-foot 1907 watertower for wonderful vistas over the Space Needle and Elliott Bay.

The **Seattle Asian Art Museum** (☎ 654-3100) has re-opened in Volunteer Park and houses the extensive Asian art collection of Dr Richard Fuller, who donated this severe arte moderne-style gallery to the city in 1932. Admission is $6 for adults, $4 for seniors and students, and free to children under 12. The Asian Art Museum is administered by the Seattle Art Museum downtown, and tickets are good for both institutions if used within two days. Hours are 10 am to 5 pm Tuesday to Sunday, except on Thursday, when the museum stays open till 9 pm.

The park is also home to the **Volunteer Park Conservatory**, a classic Victorian greenhouse that features five galleries filled with palms, cacti and tropical plants. Built in 1910, the conservatory is free to the public.

To reach Volunteer Park, follow 15th Ave to E Galer St, and turn west.

### QUEEN ANNE

Rising above Seattle Center is Queen Anne – a neighborhood of majestic red-brick houses and apartment buildings, sweeping lawns manicured to perfection and gorgeous views of the city and bay. Queen Anne has two hubs – lower and upper. While not nearly as established as other neighborhoods, they do have cafes, trendy music clubs and some old-time Seattle entertainment.

The main reason to visit Queen Anne is to check out the view. The observatory deck at 3rd Ave and Highland Drive is the best spot for it, especially at night or sunset.

From downtown take 1st Ave, which will turn into Queen Anne Ave N. Highland Drive can be accessed from here. Along W Olympic Place there's Kinnear Park, a nice expanse of grass and trees where men and dogs stroll along.

Buses No 2 and 13 go near the vista point; buses No 1, 3 and 4 also go up to Queen Anne. Bus No 1 travels on the west side of the hill, No 3 and No 4 go up Taylor St, on the east side.

### FREMONT

Unlike the flashy, urban disenfranchisement that gives Capitol Hill its spirit, life here is conducted with more humor and sense of community well-being. For the visitor, these neighborhoods make a nice change from the hectic pace of the city center; in the evenings, the pubs, restaurants and coffeehouses up here fill with a lively mix of old hippies, young professionals and gregarious students from nearby University of Washington. If you're in a buying mood, shop the kitschy antique shops for that couch, mannequin or retro sundress. A brewpub, several busy ethnic restaurants and a coffeehouse with a dramatic clientele keeps Fremont hopping until late in the evenings.

Fremont is located where Lake Union pours into the shipping canal. Probably the most fun-loving of the northern neighborhoods, Fremont is known for its unorthodox public sculpture, junk stores, summer outdoor film festivals and general high spirits. Probably the most discussed piece of public art in the city, *Waiting for the Interurban* is a cast aluminum statue of ordinary people waiting for a commuter bus; the *Fremont Troll* (a mammoth cement figure consuming a whole VW bug carcass) lives under the Aurora Bridge; and a slightly zany-looking rocket that the community has adopted as its totem stands in the main business district.

In summer, old films are shown on the side of a Fremont-center building; filmgoers are encouraged to bring their couches from home and set up comfortable seats in the parking lot. This **Fremont Almost-**

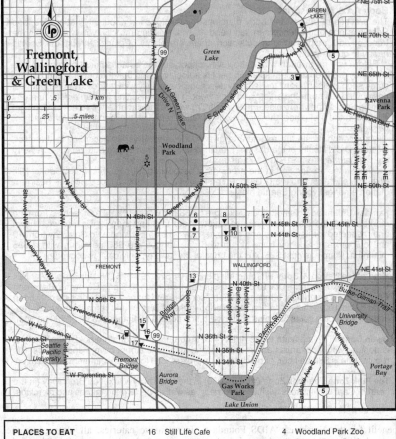

Fremont,
Wallingford
& Green Lake

| PLACES TO EAT | | 16 | Still Life Cafe | 4 | Woodland Park Zoo |
| 6 | Bizzarro | 17 | Costas | 5 | Seattle Rose Garden |
| 8 | India Cuisine | | **OTHER** | 7 | Besa del Sol |
| 9 | Julia's | 1 | Bathhouse Theatre | 10 | Teahouse Kuan Yin |
| 11 | My Brother's Pizza | | Company | 13 | Green Room Cafe |
| 12 | Boulangerie | 2 | Gregg's Greenlake Cycle | 14 | Triangle Tavern |
| 15 | Longshoreman's Daughter | 3 | The Latona | | |

**Free Outdoor Cinema** (☎ 632-0287) is held every Saturday night beginning in June and running into September. They ask for a $5 donation to help pay for the cinema and support charities. The films are held in the U-Park parking lot behind the Red Door Ale House (35th St and Fremont Place).

In the same parking lot the **Fremont Sunday Market** runs from 10 am to 5 pm throughout summer and features an incredible variety of artists and people getting rid of junk. Call 282-5706 for information or to set up your own booth. Also, in August there's the wacky **Miracle on 34th St**, a

### Body Art & Accessories

The practice of tattoos and body piercings has exploded in popularity nationwide, and Seattle is one of the leaders in this trend. If, while visiting the city, you wish to join the trend or add another to your collection, there are plenty of places throughout Seattle happy to oblige you.

Before you go through with it, however, check out the establishment carefully. Make sure they are licensed, that all equipment is autoclaved and that the general atmosphere of the shop is clean. Don't make hasty decisions, especially with tattoos. Think about your design and research the artists and their work. If after consulting with an artist you aren't satisfied, go somewhere else. Finally, if you're wondering about tattoo removal, don't get a tattoo in the first place; the technology of tattoo removal is expensive, painful and not very effective.

Many tattoo artists are reluctant to give hourly rates; it varies according to the color, location and difficulty of the design. Piercings generally run $25 to $30 per hole. Jewelry typically ranges from $15 to $30 and up.

Most shops are located in the areas most associated with youth culture: Capitol Hill, Pike Place Market and the U District. The following list includes those with the best reputation amongst young Seattle hipsters.

**Fantasy Unlimited** This notorious sex store (☎ 682-0167) at 102 Pike St, across from the market, offers more than an immense variety of sex toys and lingerie; it is also well known and respected for its piercing and tattoo services. It's open Monday to Saturday from 10 am to 7 pm and Sunday from 11 am to 6 pm. Tattoos are $85 per hour, with a $35 minimum. Piercings cost $25 plus the price of the jewelry; only cash is accepted.

**Mind's Eye Tattoo & Body Piercing** Mind's Eye (☎ 522-7954), 5206 University Way NE, is open weekdays from 1 to 10 pm and Sunday from noon to 6 pm. Co-owner Reverend Eric Eye does weddings, baptisms, funeral services and tattoos. Although he's only been open since 1992, this is the first tattoo shop in the U District and remains the most reputable. A piercing costs $25 plus jewelry; a tattoo costs a minimum of $35, or $90 an hour.

**Owen Connell** This private tattoo artist (☎ 328-4882) with a signature bold, graphic style, is popular with local artists and musicians and also does album covers and posters. His regular rate is $80 an hour, or he charges by project. Call for an appointment and location.

**The Pink Zone** The Pink Zone (☎ 325-0050) in the Broadway Market on Broadway (in the heart of Capitol Hill), sells "visible queer gear" as well as performing tattoos and piercings.

---

benefit for the Northwest AIDS Foundation. Artists and area businesses make mini-golf courses, breweries pitch in for a beer garden and all have a crazy time for $5. Call 632-0287 for details and dates.

To get to Fremont from downtown, take Westlake Blvd north along Lake Union, and follow signs for the Fremont Bridge. The main strip, Fremont Ave N, is the focal point of the shops and eat-&-drinkeries.

### WALLINGFORD

Wallingford has blossomed from an old working-class neighborhood into a pleasant district of interesting shops, bookstores and inexpensive eateries, all just across the freeway from the university. The main shopping area focuses on the old Wallingford school, at Wallingford St and N 45 St, which has been remodeled into a boutique and restaurant mall. Just down the street are a couple of art and foreign-film cinemas, amid a clutch of ethnic restaurants.

The main hub is along N 45th St approximately between Stone Way and Corliss Ave. There's an incredible mix of stores (including the locally known Erotic Bakery (☎ 545-6969, where phallus-shaped desserts are made to order) and an amazing assortment of comic book stores (quite the

The friendly staff pride themselves on cleanliness and attract a diverse (but generally young) clientele. They are open for tattoos and piercings Monday to Friday from noon to 10 pm, Saturday to 9 pm and Sunday to 7 pm. There's a $30 minimum for tattoos, and hourly rates are $95.

**Rudy's Barbershop** Wildly popular with the gay male crowd and hip others, Rudy's (☎ 329-3008), 614 E Pine St, is open Monday to Saturday from 9 am to 9 pm and Sunday from 11 am to 5 pm. The minimum for tattoos is $50; the rate is $95 to $100 an hour.

**Sin** Next door to Rudy's at 616 E Pine St, Sin (☎ 329-0324) offers piercing as well as S & M clothing and accessories. For the more adventurous urban primitive, branding and scarification services are also available. Sin is open Sunday to Thursday from noon to 8 pm, Friday and Saturday to 9 pm. Piercings cost $25 plus the price of jewelry.

**Tattoo Emporium** At the oldest tattoo shop in Seattle (☎ 622-6895), 1106 Pike St at the corner of Boren Ave, an old-time sailor flash is as common as custom design. There's a $30 minimum and the hourly rate is $110. The shop is open Monday to Saturday from 11 am to 11 pm and Sunday from 1 to 8 pm.

**Tattoo You** This tattoo joint in the Corridor (☎ 324-6443), 1017 E Pike St, is open Wednesday to Saturday from noon to 6 pm. Piercings are $25 plus the cost of jewelry; tattoos are a minimum of $30, depending on the intricacy of the design.

**Vyvyn Lazonga** Vyvyn Lazonga (☎ 622-1535) is one of the first modern female tattoo artists and has nationwide name recognition. The store, at 1516 Western Ave, just below Pike Place Market, is open daily from 11 am to 7 pm and charges a $50 minimum or $100 an hour. ■

rage in Seattle). Teahouse Kuan Yin is a great stop for a pot of exotic tea (see Coffeehouses under Entertainment), and Herbal Altar-Natives (☎ 545-2915) is an extremely weird head shop/gift boutique/coffeehouse with free T'ai Chi lessons, hemp products and a vegan spiritual pasta line (huh?).

To reach Wallingford for downtown, take I-5 north, exit at 45th St and turn west.

### Gas Works Park
Urban reclamation has no greater monument in Seattle than Gas Works Park. On a grassy point on the north end of Lake Union, this factory produced heating and lighting gas from 1906 till 1956. The gas works was thereafter understandably considered an eyesore and environmental menace; however, the beautiful location of the park – with stellar views of downtown Seattle over Lake Union, with sailboats and yachts to-ing and fro-ing from the shipping canal – induced the city government in 1975 to convert the former industrial site into a public park.

Rather than tear down the factory, however, landscape architects preserved much of the old plant. Painted black and now highlighted with rather joyful graffiti, it looks like some odd remnant from a former civilization. Gas Works Park is one of Seattle's best-loved parks; people come here to fly kites, picnic near the lake and simply take in the view. Be sure to climb the small hill to see the clever sundial.

Gas Works Park is at the southern end of Meridian Ave at N Northlake Way.

## GREEN LAKE

Just north of Wallingford are a cluster of neighborhoods flanking the east shores of Green Lake. If you need to get away from the crowds along the lakefront, the requisite coffeeshops and cheap restaurants in the old town (along Ravenna Blvd) make a good getaway. East a few blocks, near NE 65th St and Roosevelt Way NE, are a cluster of New Age bookstores and crystal shops.

### Woodland & Green Lake Parks

This large park complex contains Seattle's highly acclaimed zoo, the civic rose gardens and enormous Green Lake, a favorite with swimmers and windsurfers in summer; the paths that line the lake are very popular with joggers and bikers.

The **Woodland Park Zoo** (☎ 684-4800), 5500 Phinney Ave N, one of Seattle's greatest tourist attractions, is rated one of the top 10 zoos in the country. The Seattle Zoo was one of the first in the country to free animals from their restrictive cages in favor of ecosystem enclosures, where animals from similar environments share large spaces that seek to replicate their natural surroundings. Feature exhibits include Tropical Rain Forest, two gorilla exhibits, an Asian Elephant Forest and an African Savanna. It's open daily from 9:30 am to dusk (roughly 6 pm from March 15 to October 14, or 4:30 pm at other times of the year). The cost is $6.50 for adults, $4.75 for seniors 65 and over, $4 for youth ages six to 17 and $1.75 for children ages three to five. An additional $2.50 is charged for parking.

The 2.5-acre **Seattle Rose Garden** (☎ 684-4040), near the entrance road to the zoo, contains 5000 plants. Varieties include heirloom roses, as well as new strains being tested for All-American Rose selections. Entrance is free.

Down the hill from the zoo is **Green Lake Park**, an incredibly popular park with recreationalists and sunbathers. Two paths wind around the lake, but even these aren't enough to fill the needs of the thousands of joggers, power walkers, bikers and inline skaters who throng here daily. In fact, competition for space on the trails has led to altercations between speeding athletes; the city government has been called in to either re-regulate access to the paths, or build more defined lanes.

Tennis courts, a soccer field, bowling green and baseball diamond are some of the other recreational facilities at the park, as well as boat rentals. There are two swimming beaches along the north end of the lake, but on sunny days, the entire shoreline is massed with gleaming pale bodies.

## THE U DISTRICT

The campus sits at the edge of a busy commercial area known as the U District. The main streets here are University Way, also known as **'the Ave'**, and NE 45 St. On these busy streets are innumerable cheap restaurants and cafes, student-oriented bars, cinemas and bookstores.

### University of Washington

Established in 1861, the University of Washington was first built downtown, on the site of the present Olympic Four Seasons Hotel. There were originally 37 students, overseen by university president and carpenter Asa 'Here Come The Brides' Mercer (who in the 1860s masterminded the scheme to bring marriageable women to Seattle from the eastern USA).

The university moved to its present location along Lake Washington in 1895; much of the 694-acre site was incorporated into the grounds of the Alaska-Yukon-Pacific Exposition, a world's fair-like gathering that built dozens of new buildings in the area and served to landscape the campus.

Today, the university is the largest in the Northwest, with around 33,000 students.

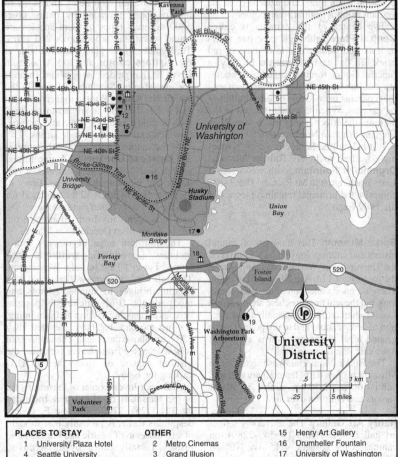

**PLACES TO STAY**

1 University Plaza Hotel
4 Seattle University
  Travelodge
13 University Inn

**PLACES TO EAT**

6 Rosebud Cafe
10 Flowers
12 Taqueria Mexico

**OTHER**

2 Metro Cinemas
3 Grand Illusion
5 Al Young Bike & Ski
7 Burke Museum
8 Varsity
9 Council Travel
11 Allegro Espresso Bar
14 Big Time Microbrew
   & Music

15 Henry Art Gallery
16 Drumheller Fountain
17 University of Washington
   Waterfront Activities
   Center
18 Museum of History and
   Industry (MOHAI)
19 Washington Park
   Arboretum Visitors Center

Noted programs include law and medicine; it's also highly regarded for computer science and liberal arts. 'U Dub', as most people refer to the university, is also notable for a state institution in that over half of its

students are in graduate programs. The university is a lovely, lively place; it is definitely worth touring the campus – maps are available from the visitors center (☎ 543-9198) at 4014 University Way – especially in spring when bulbs and azaleas paint the verdant campus with brilliant colors.

The center of the campus is called **Central Plaza**, although everyone refers to it as Red Square due to its base of red brick. To the east is **Suzzalo Library**, a fanciful Gothic Revival cathedral of books. Beyond the library are the **Quads**, an area that contains many of the original buildings on campus. When the ivy turns red in the autumn, the effect is very much more New England-ish than Northwestern.

Just below Red Square is a wide promenade leading to lovely **Rainier Vista** at **Drumheller Fountain**, with views across Lake Washington to Mt Rainier. These sites comprise the principal remaining legacy of the 1909 Expo.

**Burke Museum** This museum of natural history and anthropology (☎ 543-5590) is on the University of Washington campus near the junction of 17th Ave NE and NE 45th St. There's a good collection of dinosaur skeletons, but the real treasures here are the North Coast Indian artifacts, especially the collection of cedar canoes and totem poles. On the ground level of the museum is a pleasant patio cafe, the Boiserie.

The Burke Memorial Washington State Museum is open daily from 10 am to 5 pm; admission is $2.50 for adults, $1.50 for seniors and children over six.

**Henry Art Gallery** The university's fine-art gallery, the Henry (☎ 543-2280), on campus at the corners of 15 Ave NE and NE 41st St, mounts some of the most intelligent exhibits and installations in Seattle. The focus is on 20th-century art and artists; there's a small permanent collection, but the changing shows – the Henry mounts 35 a year – are usually noteworthy. It's open Tuesday to Sunday from 11 am to 5 pm, and Thursday from 11 am to 9 pm. Admission is $4; U of W students get in free.

**Washington Park Arboretum**
This wild and lovely park (☎ 543-8800) offers a wide variety of gardens, a water-front nature trail and acres and acres of mature forest threaded by paths. Over 5500 different types of plant species are found within the arboretum's 200 acres. Trail guides to the plants are available at the **visitors center** at 2300 Arboretum Drive E; free guided tours of the grounds are available on Sundays at 1 pm. In the spring, the **Azalea Way**, a jogger-free trail that winds through the arboretum, is lined with a giddy array of pink and orange-flowered azaleas and rhododendrons.

At the southern edge of the arboretum is the **Japanese Garden**, a 3.5-acre formal garden with koi pools, waterfalls, a teahouse and manicured plantings. Entry to the Japanese Garden is $2 for adults, $1 for youths 19 and under and seniors; the garden is open daily from 10 am to 6 pm but is closed from December to March.

The northern edge of the arboretum includes a wonderful **wetlands trail** around Foster Island in Lake Washington. The trail winds through wetlands and over floating bridges to smaller islands and reedy shoals. Bird watching is popular here, as is canoeing, fishing and swimming. It's just too bad that busy, elevated Hwy 520 roars above the island. The nature trail is best accessed from the car park near the visitors center, or from the MOHAI parking lot, below.

At the northwest corner of the arboretum is the **Museum of History & Industry** (☎ 324-1125), 2700 24th Ave E, which, despite its name, is probably best thought of as a museum of Seattle and Puget Sound history. Usually called by its acronym, MOHAI is a likable collection of old planes, memorabilia from the Great Fire, and artifacts and lore from Seattle's great seafaring era. On Saturdays, the museum is converted to a soundstage for live recordings of public radio's *Sandy Bradley's Potluck,* a good-natured musical revue that features folk and ethnic acts, as well as sometimes silly but refreshingly ad hoc comedy skits and general chatter. It's a lot of fun, a kind of low-key *Prairie Home Companion* without the Lutheran angst. The show begins at 11 am every Saturday and lasts for an hour. There are no reservations, just show up. Entry is $5.

The Washington Park Arboretum is just south of the University of Washington along Union Bay in Lake Washington. To reach the visitors center and hiking trails at the north end of the park, take Hwy 520 east from I-5, and take the first exit (for Montlake/U of W). This intersection can be confusing: stay in the right lane, and go straight through the first intersection. This lane becomes Lake Washington Blvd. Follow this street for about a quarter mile, and then turn east onto E Foster Lake Rd (not 26th Ave). Follow signs for the visitors center. If your trying to get to MOHAI, follow the signs toward Montlake and the university, but turn immediately on Hamlin St or Shelby St, before crossing the Montlake Bridge.

Access from the south is somewhat less confusing. Follow Madison St from downtown until it intersects with Lake Washington Blvd. Turn north at the junction. Take Arboretum Drive E to the visitors center.

## BALLARD & THE CANAL

Northwest of Seattle, the waters of Lake Washington and Lake Union meet the Puget Sound in the eight-mile-long Lake Washington Ship Canal. The idea of linking the major lakes around Seattle to the salt water bay had been discussed since 1867, but it wasn't until 1911 that the Army Corps of Engineers, under the direction of Hiram Chittenden, began the unification of the waters. First, a channel was cut between Lake Washington and Lake Union, thereby lowering Lake Washington by nine feet. Then the canal was cut through from Salmon Harbor on Lake Union to the Puget Sound, and two locks were installed in 1917.

Today 100,000 boats a year pass through the canal, and the locks, with its fish ladder and beautiful adjacent park, is a popular outing destination for families. This is also a restful spot for anyone needing some relief from the jangling of Seattle caffeine and traffic.

The locks are just west of Ballard, a pleasant little community that is often affectionately referred to as the Viking North. Settled principally by Swedes, Norwegians and Danes in the 1900s, these seafaring immigrants were instrumental in establishing Seattle's fishing fleet. Although boats no longer leave Ballard to fish the high seas (they leave from Fisherman's Terminal, just across the shipping canal), Ballard still maintains a decidedly Nordic air. Scandinavian import shops line the streets, and the **Nordic Heritage Museum** (☎ 789-5707), 3014 NW 67th St, preserves the history of Northern European settlers in Seattle.

While Ballard has been the brunt of many a local's joke, it is fast becoming another hip neighborhood, centered mainly in its historic district along Ballard Ave NW between 20th and 22nd Aves. There are many good taverns and some fun budget gourmet restaurants. Market St is the main commercial drag.

### Hiram M Chittenden Locks

Watching boats traverse the two locks on the shipping canal exerts a strange Zen-like attraction for locals and tourists alike. The process takes between 10 and 30 minutes, depending on whether the large or the small lock is used. Walkways along the locks allow an intimate look at the workings of these water elevators and a good look at the vessels that are coming and going.

On the southern side of the locks is a **fish ladder**, built in 1976 to allow salmon to fight their way to spawning grounds in the Cascade headwaters of the Sammamish River, which feeds Lake Washington. Visitors can watch the fish from underwater glass-sided tanks or from above (nets are installed to keep salmon from overleaping and stranding themselves on the pavement). Visitors can also watch sea lions munch on the salmon while the fish thrash around trying to figure out how to negotiate the fish ladder (just what to do about the salmon-loving sea lions has stymied environmentalists, anglers and the local Fish & Wildlife Department).

On the northern entrance to the lock area is the **Carl English Jr Botanical Gardens**, a charming, small arboretum and specimen garden. Trails wind through gardens filled with mature trees (with identifying labels) and flower gardens; plan on communing with imploring squirrels and haughty Canadian geese. Flanking the gardens is a small museum and visitors center (☎ 783-7059) documenting the history of the locks. Free tours of the locks are offered daily at 1 pm and 3:30 pm June to September. From October to May, tours are offered at 2 pm Saturdays and Sundays only.

The visitors center (☎ 783-5870) at the locks is open from 11 am to 5 pm Thursday to Monday, October to June, and from 10 am to 7 pm daily the rest of the year. Access to all areas at the locks is free; the gardens are closed from 9 pm to 7 am, although the locks remain open 24 hours. The Chittenden Locks are northwest of Seattle, at 3015 NW 54th St, about half a mile west of Ballard off Market St.

### Fishermen's Terminal

Seattle's fishing fleet resides at the Fisherman's Terminal, in a wide abayment in the shipping canal called Salmon Bay. About 700 fishing boats dock here, making this the largest halibut and salmon fleet in the world. One of the reasons for the popularity of Fisherman's Terminal with boat owners is the fact that the facility is in fresh water, above the Chittenden Locks. Fresh water is much less corrosive to boats than salt water.

It's great fun to wander the piers, watching crews unload their catch, clean boats and repair nets. Interpretive displays explain the history of Seattle's fishing fleet, and a statue at the base of the piers commemorates lost seamen.

In the two shed-like terminal buildings are a couple of good restaurants specializing in the freshest seafood in Seattle, a tobacconist, a ship's chandlers and a store devoted to navigational charts and nautical gifts. Stop at the **Wild Salmon Fish Market** (☎ 283-3366) to buy the pick of the day's catch.

The Fisherman's Terminal is on the south end of the Ballard Bridge, at 19th Ave and W Nickerson St.

### Shilshole Bay & Golden Gardens

Continuing about two miles along Seaview Ave from the locks is Shilshole Bay Marina. There's not much here besides the tacky-touristy restaurants and shops that accompany harbors, but the boats are nice. Just a couple hundred yards more is Golden Gardens Park, a beach park with sandy beaches and pebbly shores. There are picnic facilities, bathrooms, basketball hoops, volleyball nets, gangs of Canadian geese and plenty of space to get away from all the activity.

### DISCOVERY PARK

Discovery Park is 534 acres of urban wilderness. Locals love to come here to get away from the ever-present manicure of city gardens and get windswept along the many trails. The visitors center (☎ 386-4236) is open daily from 8:30 am to 5:30 pm. The park runs educational programs ranging from nature walks on Saturdays to day camps for children to birding tours.

The park was originally Fort Lawton, an army base built in 1901 to protect Seattle from unnamed enemies. Fort Lawton didn't see much activity until WW II, when the fort was used as barracks for troops destined for the Pacific. When the fort was declared surplus property in the 1960s, the city of Seattle decided to turn the area into a park (although significant areas of the park are still used for military housing).

Discovery Park has over seven miles of hiking trails. A number of trails lead to the **Daybreak Star Indian Cultural Center**, a community center for Seattle-area Native Americans. Except for a small art gallery, there are few facilities for outside visitors. The vista point here has beautiful views of the Sound, and several steep trails lead down through the forest to narrow, sandy beaches.

A paved road takes an almost three-mile loop of the park, with other trails sprawling from there to other lookouts. About a mile off from the loop trail, a trail skirts the water edge of the park all the way to the **West Point Lighthouse**, a great scenic spot.

For a map of the trail and road system stop by the visitors center near the Government Way entrance. From downtown take Elliott Way north, which will turn into 15th Ave W. Take the Dravus St exit and turn left on Dravus St. Then on 20th Ave W, go right until it turns into Gilman Ave W and then into W Government Way. Or simply take the bus; lines 19 and 33 all leave from downtown and the Seattle Center and go to the park.

## LAKE WASHINGTON

When it gets hot in the summer – yes, Seattle can get hot – people make the pilgrimage to this lake to sprawl out on the small sandy/grassy beaches. Just driving or cycling around the area is a good respite – the houses along Lake Washington Blvd boast of old money or new corporate wealth. This is the neighborhood of Microsoft's top dogs and was home to deceased singer Kurt Cobain.

As you go along Lake Washington Blvd you'll pass Leschi, mainly a resting point for all those cyclists looping the lake or on the Burke-Gilman Trail.

Going north along Lake Washington Blvd, **Denny Blaine Park**, a predominantly lesbian beach, is down a tree-lined boulevard. Continue along the boulevard and you'll end up at Madison St right by the arboretum. If you take Madison St to the right, you'll get to **Madison Park**, another neighborhood with the usual hub of trendy restaurants and cafes, including *Cafe Flora* (☎ 325-9100), 2901 E Madison St, a favorite with vegetarians and non-smokers. At the end of Howe St there's a public beach with picnic tables and a floating dock.

### Madrona

Take Union or Cherry Sts from downtown to get to Madrona, once a never-heard-of neighborhood but now another destination for many, mainly to eat at one of the most popular brunch places in the city, the Hi Spot Cafe. Most everything is on 34th Ave

between Pike and Spring Sts. Besides food, the only real reason to venture this far is to get to Lake Washington. **Wilridge Winery** (☎ 325-3051), 1416 34th Ave, specializes in reds – Cabernet Sauvignon and Merlot mostly. Call them to arrange a tour or make any purchases.

## Seward Park

For something wild, as in wilderness, go to Seward Park, a 277-acre promontory that juts into Lake Washington. The park preserves about the only old-growth forest anywhere in the vicinity of Seattle and is home to wildlife, including a nesting pair of bald eagles. Hikers and bikers will be interested in the 2.5-mile lakeside trail; other trails lead to a fish hatchery, beach access and several picnic areas. Seward Park can be dangerous after dark, so be attentive.

To reach the park, take I-5 south to I-90, exit No 164. Once on I-90, take exit No 1, for Rainier Ave S, or Hwy 900. Stay on Hwy 900 until the intersection with S Orcas St in about two miles. Turn east, and follow the signs to the park.

## ALKI BEACH

For something wild, in its other sense, head out to West Seattle to Alki Beach. At the headland of Alki Point, Seattle's first settlers made their home; today, this two-mile stretch of sandy beach is a madhouse in summer, when in emulation of southern California the volleyball nets go up, mass sunbathing occupies the strand and teens in souped-up cars prowl the streets. Still, it's Seattle's only real beach scene, and the views onto Seattle from Duwamish Head, at the northern end of the beach, are spectacular. You might want to avoid Alki on summer weekends, but the good beachside cafes, the quaint fish & chips joints, the miniature of the Statue of Liberty on the beach and the Alki Point Lighthouse make it a nice getaway most other times.

Take Hwy 99 or I-5 south of Seattle to the West Seattle Freeway; get off at Harbor Ave SW, the beach road that will take you all the way around the promontory.

## HIKING & BIKING

In Seattle, it's possible to hike wilderness trails without ever leaving the city. **Seward Park** offers several miles of trails in a remnant of the area's old-growth forest, and even longer trails are available in 534-acre **Discovery Park**, northwest of downtown (see Seward and Discovery parks sections for more details).

A convenient place to rent a bike is Al Young Bike and Ski (☎ 524-2642), 3615 NE 45th St, near both the university and the Burke-Gilman trail. Near Green Lake, you can rent bicycles, and just about any other form of recreational conveyance including inline skates, at Gregg's Greenlake Cycle (☎ 523-1822), 7007 Woodlawn Ave NE.

### The Burke-Gilman Trail

For a long-distance path that is welcoming to both hikers and bikers, try the Burke-Gilman Trail, a 12.5-mile paved path that runs between Gas Works Park and Log Boom Park on the north end of Lake Washington in the suburb of Kenmore. The trail follows an old rail line along the shores of Lake Union and Lake Washington, all at an easy grade. The views are great, though on weekends the trail can be pretty busy.

### SKIING

Seattle is fortunate to have several ski areas within an easy drive of the city. Closest are the ski slopes at Snoqualmie Pass (see Around Seattle, at the end of this chapter) and Stevens Pass, 78 miles east of Seattle on Hwy 2 (see the Central Washington chapter).

In central Seattle, probably the most convenient place to rent skis is on Capitol Hill at REI (☎ 323-8333), 1525 11th Ave. Convenient to neighborhoods near the university is Seattle Ski Rental Inc (548-1000) at 907 NE 45th St.

If you don't have a vehicle or don't want to face the drive, there are several options for getting to the ski areas. The Pass's ski buses (☎ 232-8182) leave from several locations in the Seattle area for Snoqualmie Pass ski areas. While most seats on the bus are reserved by season-pass

holders, single seats are often available, particularly during the week. A roundtrip ticket costs $16.

### BOATING & KAYAKING

Northwest Outdoor Center Inc (☎ 281-9694), 2100 Westlake Ave N, on Lake Union, offers instruction in sea and white-water kayaking, and rents kayaks on Lake Union. Other services include houseboat and kayak tours, as well as sunset tours through the locks at Ballard.

The U of W Waterfront Activities Center (☎ 543-9433) rents canoes and rowboats for $4 an hour. Bring along an ID – and a passport if you're from out of the country. You have to stay in the Lake Washington area; no cruising through the canal to the Puget Sound. The center is open from 10 am to around 6:30 or 7:30 pm and is in the southeast corner of Husky Stadium parking lot.

In good weather, the surface of Lake Union is covered with sailboats. Join the fun at Sailboat Rentals & Yacht Charters Inc (☎ 632-3302), 1301 N Northlake Way, Lake Union. Rentals include 14-foot to 32-foot models, available by the hour, day or week.

### SWIMMING

There's a pool at the downtown YMCA (☎ 382-5010), 909 4th Ave, open to both men and women. The downtown YWCA (☎ 461-4868), 1118 5th Ave, also offers a pool. Also convenient to downtown is the Queen Anne Pool (☎ 386-4282), 1920 1st Ave W.

There are public beaches at Green Lake Park, Alki Beach and Lake Washington. For information about city pools throughout the city, call the city park bureau at 684-4075.

### GOLF

Seattle's most popular course is Jackson Park (☎ 363-4747), 1000 NE 135th St, on the far northern edge of Seattle. This 18-hole course is best attempted on weekdays, when there are fewer lines at the first tee. Another convenient course is Jefferson Park (☎ 762-4513), 4101 Beacon Ave S, an

18-hole course with short fairways and lots of lovely and mature – but sometimes troublesome – trees and bushes.

Southwest of downtown is West Seattle Municipal Course (☎ 935-5187), 4470 35th Ave SW, with 18 holes, and superior views across Elliott Bay to Seattle.

## CAMPING & OUTDOOR GEAR

REI (☎ 323-8333) is right by the Pike/Pine Corridor at 1525 11th Ave. This is the original store. There are plenty of brochures on trips and day outings as well as a bulletin board with local information.

REI rents all forms of ski packages, climbing gear and camping equipment – call for daily/weekly rates. REI Adventure Travel organizes trips and can be reached at (800) 622-2236. For hard-core climbing and hiking equipment, go the The North Face (☎ 622-4111), 1023 1st Ave, downtown.

The other local outfitting company-made-good is Eddie Bauer (☎ 622-2766), 1330 5th Ave. The flagship downtown store offers a large selection of rugged clothing (including things you don't find in the catalog) plus a new decorator and homewares department.

## COURSES

Seattle's Experimental College (☎ 543-4375) is a funky alternative and continuing-education institution with a variety of one-day and multi-day seminars. If you're interested in taking a massage class or art workshop, or heading off on a kayaking expedition in the Sound, call for their schedule of classes in advance of your trip. They're pretty cheap, lots of fun and a good way to meet locals who share your interests.

## ORGANIZED TOURS
### City Tours

Seattle suffers no shortage of tour organizers. Gray Line of Seattle (☎ 626-5208, (800) 426-7532) has a whole catalog of Seattle-area bus and boat tours. The six-hour Grand City Tour operates from April to mid-October; adult tickets cost $28. Their Seattle City Tour is an abbreviated

version that runs year round, lasts almost three hours and costs $18.50.

Organized walking tours are available through Seattle's Best Walking Tours (☎ 236-2060) for $5 to $10, Seattle Walking Tour (☎ 885-3173) for $8, and Seattle Tours (☎ 660-8687) for $25.

### Boat Tours

Seattle Harbor Tours (☎ 623-4252), Pier 55, does a one-hour narrated tour of Seattle harbor. Prices start at $12.50 for adults, $11.50 for students and seniors and $5.50 for children ages five to 12 (kids under five are free). Their 1.5-hour Lake Washington Cruise runs from May to October; adult tickets on this tour cost $14.80. Inquire about the 2.5-hour cruise through Ballard Locks or the four-hour excursion to Tillicum Village (see Around Seattle).

### Bill Speidel's Underground Tour

Seattle's 'underground' was conveniently forgotten until the late 1960s, when businessman and raconteur Bill Speidel chanced onto the old subterranean store-fronts near his office, and after a few years of courting headlines and permits, he was in business as a tour operator.

Most of these chambers date from the 1880s, before Seattle's fire and the rebuilding of the district elevated the city off the tide flats. Tour guides like to emphasize the 'underground' nature of the tour with whimsical noting of historic bordellos and corrupt politicians, both of which flourished in early Seattle history. An hour-long, three-block subterranean hike through a series of rather ordinary-looking basements follows the 20-minute introduction. Tours start daily from **Doc Maynard's Public House** (☎ 682-4646), 610 1st Ave, a restored 1890s saloon. Schedules vary seasonally, and reservations are recommended. Tickets are $5.95 for adults, $4.87 for seniors, $4.33 for students ages 13 to 17, and $2.71 for children ages six to 12; only cash is accepted.

### Sierra Club Outings

The local branch of the Sierra Club (☎ 523-2019), 8511 15th St NE, is very busy, and with a little planning you can fit an outdoor adventure into your Seattle stay. Their extremely diverse offerings range from beachcombing & botany walks at Alki to enological bike tours of the Yakima valley wine country, and from weekend canoe trips down the Olympic Peninsula's Bogachiel River to weekend day-hiking & car-camping trips along the Pacific Crest Trail. Call for a recording of future events. Most day trips are free; longer trips may have minimal fees.

They also schedule monthly Sierra Singles mixers, where you might meet an unattached outdoorsy type for hiking, biking or whatever.

### SPECIAL EVENTS

#### Chinese New Year

Seattle's first big ethnic festival is Chinese New Year, held in the International District, usually in January; call 623-8171 for more information.

#### Fat Tuesday

The Pioneer Square district embraces its somewhat rowdy reputation on Mardi Gras in February, when the area is convulsed with the Fat Tuesday celebration. Music and revelry in bars and restaurants obviously comprise the main events, although the special Seattle touch is lent by the annual, competitive **Spam-Carving Contest**. Contact the visitors center for more information.

#### Freedom Day Celebration

Seattle's lesbian and gay-pride event is called the Freedom Day Celebration, and is usually held the last Sunday in June on Capitol Hill. The parade begins along Broadway and continues to Volunteer Park, where there are speeches, music and a rally.

#### Northwest Folklife Festival

The Northwest Folklife Festival (☎ 684-7300), 305 Harrison St, takes over Seattle Center during Memorial Day weekend. Over 5000 performers and artists present music, dance, crafts, food and family activities representing over 100 countries. Admission is free.

#### Seafair

Seattle's biggest summer festival is Seafair, an extravagant civic celebration that began as a hydroplane race on Lake Washington. Old families in Seattle jealously maintain their moorages on Lake Seattle in order to have the best possible views of these roaring jet boats. Today, however, all manner of festivities stretch the event to three weeks (from late July through early August) and extend across all of Seattle; events include a torchlight parade, an airshow, lots of music, a carnival and even the arrival of the naval fleet. Lodging is in short supply in Seattle on Seafair weekends, so plan accordingly. Unless you want to watch the hydroplane races, avoid Seattle on this weekend (usually the first weekend in August), and don't plan to cross the I-90 or Hwy 520 bridges while the races are in progress. For more information, contact the festival office at 728-0123.

#### The Bite

Seattle's restaurants and caterers celebrate at the Bite of Seattle, at Seattle Center, usually the second weekend in July. For a single entry fee, guests can sample foods from dozens of Seattle-area chefs, and taste local beers and wines. The evening ends with live music.

#### Bumbershoot

Seattle's biggest arts celebration is Bumbershoot, held at Seattle Center over Labor Day weekend. In addition to an arts-&-crafts street fair, there are special theatrical and musical events (past artists include the Indigo Girls and UB40), and fine arts exhibitions. For more information, call 684-7200.

#### Western Washington Fair

The Puget Sound remembers its agricul-

met Falls, Mt Rainier National Park (WB)

Stream near Blewett Pass (JJ)

rthern Cascades (JJ)

Indian encampment on the Columbia River (BM)

Olympic Mountains from Hurricane Ridge,
Olympic National Park (BM)

Spokane Falls and the Flour Mill (JJ)

View of Diablo from the Incline Railroad (JJ)

tural underpinnings at the Western Washington Fair (☎ 845-1771), 110 9th Ave SW, south of Seattle in Puyallup. Held in mid-September, the fair offers a bewildering array of livestock and agricultural displays, a carnival, home and garden show and live entertainment.

## PLACES TO STAY

The Seattle B&B Association runs a 24-hour availability hotline (☎ 547-1020) and makes referrals to other area B&Bs. Note that reservations cannot be made through the association. For a brochure listing the association's member B&Bs, write to the SBBA at PO Box 31772, Seattle, WA 98103-1772. Traveller's Reservations (☎ 232-2345) offers a reservation service to selected local and regional B&Bs and hotels.

### Camping

Campers intending to visit downtown Seattle face lengthy commutes. Two suburban campgrounds offer the most convenient facilities. In Bellevue, *Trails Inn* (☎ 747-9181), 15531 SE 37th St, offers showers, an indoor pool, playground and laundry, but no tenting facilities. To reach the campground, take I-90 exit No 11, turn south to the frontage road and follow the signs for five blocks. In Kent, south of Seattle, is the *Seattle South KOA* (☎ 872-8652), 5807 S 212th St. A heated pool, car rentals, playground and laundry are some of the facilities.

Tent campers are pretty much limited to *Saltwater State Park*, a busy but pleasant beachfront park on the Puget Sound, south of Seattle. To reach the park, take I-5 exit No 149 west toward Des Moines. At the junction of Hwy 99 (also called Pacific Hwy), turn south and drive to 240th St. Turn west and follow signs to the park.

### Downtown

**Hostels** *Hostelling International – Seattle* (☎ 622-5443), 84 Union St, offers 140 beds in 23 different rooms, including family rooms. Kitchen and laundry facilities are provided, as well as a common area with a TV. Rates are $14 a night. The hostel is in a good location, central to the Waterfront and to Pike Place Market.

Both men and women can stay at the *Downtown YMCA Hotel* (☎ 382-5000), 909 4th Ave; rooms for singles/doubles start at $34/39. There are also beds in a dormitory reserved for card-carrying HI/AYH members; the cost is $18. The *Downtown YWCA* (☎ 461-4888), 1118 5th Ave, has shared or private rooms for women only, starting at $31 and $36.

**Hotels – middle** Most of the following downtown motels offer some kind of parking program with in-and-out privileges, but you'll pay handsomely for it, usually between $9 and $12 a day. If you have a car, you'll need to factor the parking fees into the cost of staying downtown or else stay out at Seattle Center where most lodgings offer free parking.

The *Pacific Plaza* (☎ 623-3900, (800) 426-1165), 400 Spring St, is centrally located, just a block from the Olympic Four Seasons. Nicely remodeled rooms come with a big breakfast (in the breakfast lounge) and cost $74 to $94. The *Inn at Virginia Mason* (☎ 583-6453, (800) 283-6453), 1006 Spring St, is on First Hill, just above downtown near a complex of hospitals. This nicely maintained older hotel caters to families needing to stay near the medical facilities but also offers quiet rooms to other visitors. Rates begin at $85 for both singles and doubles; commercial and AAA discounts apply, and there are discounts if you are staying at the hotel for medical reasons ($62 for singles/doubles). At the *Hotel Seattle* (☎ 623-5110), 315 Seneca St, rooms run $72 to $76.

**Hotels – top end** Most large hotel chains have facilities in Seattle, offering business travelers and conventioneers modern rooms with a wide range of facilities. The best of these in Seattle are the *Sheraton* (☎ 621-9000), 1400 6th Ave, and the *Stouffer Madison* (☎ 583-0300), 515 Madison St.

For a more unique Northwestern experience, stay at one of Seattle's local luxury hotels or one of the many historic grand hotels, many of which have been remodeled and retooled; both options offer gracious comforts of another era. The prices listed are standard midweek rates; at most hotels, there are weekend packages and off-season deals that lower the prices considerably.

The *Inn at the Market* (☎ 443-3600), 86 Pine St, is in fact a new and architecturally interesting hotel, and it's the only lodging in the venerable Pike Place Market. Rooms are large, and most have grand views onto market activity and the Puget Sound. Room prices start at $110. The *Alexis Hotel* (☎ 624-4844, (800) 426-7033), 1007 1st Ave near Madison St, is a modern hotel tucked inside an old architectural exoskeleton. This is a hotel that emphasizes quiet, high-quality service and amenities, so don't expect dramatic views or ostentatious glamour. In addition to the main hotel building, there are condo-style suites for longer stays in the *Arlington Suites* building next door. The suites (without daily maid service) start at $150, while hotel rooms start at $170/185.

The *Sorrento Hotel* (☎ 622-6400), 900 Madison St, was Seattle's finest hotel when it was built in 1909. After a substantial refurbishing, this beautiful hotel, lined with mahogany and hung with chandeliers, is again one of Seattle's best. Rooms start at $140/160. The other doyen of old money and elegance is the *Olympic Four Seasons Hotel* (☎ 621-1700, (800) 821-8106 in Washington, (800) 332-3442 elsewhere), 411 University St. Imposing and luxurious, the Olympic was built in 1924, and subsequent remodels have worked to maintain the period glamour of its architecture. This hotel could have been a set in an extra-suave Cary Grant movie. Rooms range from $195 to $225.

### Seattle Center & Belltown

**Hostels** The *Green Tortoise Backpackers Guesthouse* (☎ 322-1222) at 715 2nd Ave, a couple blocks from the Needle, charges $13 a night for a dorm bed and bathroom.

They also have private rooms for $35 with a bathroom. Reservations are recommended as this place fills fast with travelers from the bus (see Getting There & Away).

**Hotels – bottom end** Two large but modest older hotels offer inexpensive lodgings right downtown; rooms here are best described as no-frills, but there's nothing scary about staying here, and you can't argue with the rates. The *Commodore Motor Hotel* (☎ 448-8868), 2013 2nd Ave, offers a mix of options, including $12 hostel rooms, rooms with bathroom down the hall ($27/31 for singles/doubles), and rooms with full bath facilities ($42/49). It's near Pike Place Market and the Belltown area; the hotel also has its own free parking garage, always a plus in Seattle. The *Moore Hotel* (☎ 448-4851, (800)-421-5508), 1926 2nd Ave, offers rooms with facilities down the hall or in the room; this once-grand hotel has 135 rooms starting at $34/39. Consider that you can afford a suite here for the price of a closet at a remodeled hotel.

**Hotels – middle** Long one of Seattle's landmarks, the *WestCoast Camlin Hotel* (☎ 682-0100), 1619 9th Ave, has recently been remodeled; its beautiful lobby again sparkles. Rates usually start at $83/93, but from October 16 to April 30 (occupancy permitting) the Camlin runs a 'B&B special' – single or double occupancy is $65, and breakfast is thrown in at no charge. The same company now owns the *WestCoast Vance Hotel* (☎ 441-4200), 620 Stewart St, a nicely restored older hotel with rooms at $69/85. The Vance runs a B&B offer similar to the Camlin's (from October 15 to April 15, a special $69 B&B double-occupancy rate kicks in), but the rooms here are smaller.

There's no old-fashioned glamour at the *Sixth Avenue Inn* (☎ 441-8300, (800) 648-6440), 2000 6th Ave, a motor inn centrally located downtown, but there is free parking. Seasonal rates range between $54 and $82 for singles, $66 and $94 for doubles.

Only one Seattle hotel actually faces

onto Elliott Bay, and that's the *Edgewater* (☎ 728-7000, (800) 624-0670), 2411 Alaska Way. When this hotel was first built, people paid a premium to stay in the rooms that literally hang over the bay, in order to fish from the windows. Times have changed, and fishing is no longer allowed. If you came to Seattle to experience the tang of sea air, this might be the hotel for you. Prices range quite a bit depending on if you're right on salt water.

There's a cluster of mid-range motels near Seattle Center. At the *Econolodge* by the Space Needle (☎ 441-0400), 325 Aurora Ave N, youths 18 and under can stay free when accompanied by their parents, which is especially great when you're trying to scrounge enough dough to send your herd up the Space Needle. Single/double rooms start at $54/64. The *Seattle Inn* (☎ 728-7666), 225 Aurora Ave N, offers singles/doubles at $49/64. The *Travelodge* by the Space Needle (☎ 441-7878, (800) 578-7878), 200 6th Ave N, has rooms that start at $65/70. The *Inn at Queen Anne* (☎ 282-7357, (800) 952-5043), 505 1st Ave N, is right across from Seattle Center; rooms cost $55/65. *Loyal Inn Best Western* (☎ 682-0200), 2301 8th Ave, has some kitchenettes; rooms cost $60 to $92. The remodeled *Best Western Executive Inn* (☎ 448-9444), 200 Taylor Ave N, is in the shadow of the Space Needle, with rooms starting at $84/92.

## Capitol Hill

**Hostels** *Vincent's Guesthouse* (☎ 323-7849), 527 Malden Ave E, has dormitory beds going for $12 a night and private rooms are available for $20 to $45. They have a communal kitchen, TV lounge and laundry facilities.

On Broadway, the *American Backpackers Hostel* (☎ 720-2965, (800) 600-2965), 126 Broadway E, is in a better location and offers free breakfast and free downtown pickup. Most of their guests are international travelers and they are very busy so call ahead for reservations, especially if you want a private room. The hostel's dormitory beds are $14 and private rooms are $40. Enter via the alley beside the bubble machine near Twice-Told Tales.

## B&Bs

The *Bacom Mansion B&B/Broadway Gardens* (☎ 329-1864, (800) 240-1864), 959 Broadway Ave E. offers eight guest rooms, six with private baths. Rates at this Tudor-style mansion start at $59.*B&B at Mildred's* (☎ 325-6072), 1202 15th Ave E, is an old Victorian home across the street from Volunteer Park. The three guest rooms each with private baths range between $75 and $85. *Salisbury House B&B* (☎ 328-8682), 750 16th Ave E, is also near the park. The four rooms at this 1904 home range from $67 to $93; all rooms have private bathrooms. On a much larger scale is *Gaslight Inn B&B* (☎ 325-3654),

1727 15th Ave E, with 15 rooms available in two neighboring homes; there's also a pool and hot tub. There are a mix of private and shared facilities; rooms range from $62 to $98. At the *Hill House B&B* (☎ 720-7161, (800) 720-7161), 1113 E John St, there are five guest rooms in a restored 1903 home; three have private facilities. Rates range between $60 to $95.

## Queen Anne

**B&Bs** Just north of Seattle on Queen Anne Hill is a clutch of nice older homes, some now B&Bs; this area is convenient to events at Seattle Center. The *Beech Tree Manor B&B* (☎ 281-7037), 1405 Queen Anne Ave N, is a turn-of-the-century mansion with six rooms ranging from $49 to $79; there's a mix of private and shared facilities. While most B&Bs ban children, the *Williams House B&B* (☎ 285-0810), 1505 4th Ave N, welcomes them. At this Victorian home, there are five guest rooms ranging from $65 to $100, with a mix of private and share baths; most rooms have views of the downtown skyline and the Puget Sound.

**Houseboats** For something uniquely Seattle, consider *Houseboat Hideaways* (☎ 323-5323), at Lake Union's Westlake Marina. Both of the two houseboats sleep one to six people; nightly rates begin at $89. Call or write PO Box 782, Edmonds, WA 98020, for more information.

## The U District

**Hotels** Off I-5 exit No 169 are a number of moderately priced motels near the University of Washington; only three miles from downtown, these accommodations are also close to eating and drinking in the Wallingford/Green Lake area. *University Plaza Hotel* (☎ 634-0100, (800) 343-7040), 400 NE 45th St, is just across the freeway from campus. Room rates vary seasonally and start at $72/88; there's a heated swimming pool, and pets are allowed. The *University Inn* (☎ 632-5055, (800) 733-3855), 4140 Roosevelt Way NE, is adjacent to campus and offers free continental breakfast and

outdoor pool, and children under 18 stay free with parents. Rooms for singles/doubles start at $72/82. Just east of the university, *Seattle University Travelodge* (☎ 525-4612, (800) 578-7878), 4725 25th Ave NE, is close to Children's Hospital, has an outdoor pool and allows pets. Rooms start at $69/79.

## PLACES TO EAT

Seattle offers a bewildering array of inexpensive places to eat; it also boasts the most expensive restaurants in the Northwest. In general, food prices are higher here than elsewhere in the region. This is particularly noticeable in the mid-range of restaurants as a nice, medium-frills meal edges toward and past $20 a person. If you need to justify such reckless expense, remember that Seattle has one of the hottest restaurant scenes on the West Coast.

If you're looking for organic produce and healthy food, check out the listings for Puget Consumers Co-op in the phone book. There are seven locations in Seattle. Convenient to downtown is the Central Coop (☎ 329-1545), 1835 12th Ave E, with a good selection of organic groceries and macrobiotic products.

### Downtown

**Budget** In Seattle, to find cheap eats, it's convenient to remember neighborhoods, not just restaurant names. For a wide selection of fresh produce, bakery products, deli items and take-away ethnic foods, head to Pike Place Market. There's no reason to go away hungry from – or to spend much money at – this cacophonous market. If you want a sit-down meal, some of the market cafes are inexpensive. Try *Lowell's* (☎ 622-2036) for eye-opening breakfasts and cheap-and-cheerful lunches. If for some reason you've been hankering for Bolivian cuisine, hanker no more. *Copacabana Cafe* (☎ 622-6359), 1502½ Pike Place, offers inexpensive Andean dishes like pollo saltado (braised chicken with green peppers and tomatoes) for $9. Lunch dishes hover at $6. However, perhaps the best reason to explore South American cuisine may be this convivial restaurant's great views over the Pike Place Market.

If you want to stick closer to Pioneer Square, get the same quality of food and good prices at *Cafe Hue* (☎ 625-9833), 312 2nd Ave S, the *India Taj* (☎ 233-0160), 625 1st Ave S, or the *Szechwan Garden* (☎ 343-9988) at 88 Yesler Way. Seattle's best bakery is also in Pioneer Square. In addition to peasant-style loafs and baguettes, *Grand Central Baking Co* (☎ 622-3644), 214 1st Ave S in the Grand Central Arcade, offers lunchtime salads and focaccia sandwiches cafeteria-style in its lobby-like dining area.

**Middle** Remember that this is downtown Seattle. In most (but not all) of the following listings, middle-range meals are going to run $15 to $20 a person. If you're looking for a wider selection of good, less expensive food, head to the neighborhoods, like Capitol Hill, the International District or Wallingford. Also, if you're watching your dollars, try one of the following for lunch; you'll easily be able to get in and out for under $10.

In the Pike Place Market, *Place Pigalle* (☎ 624-1756), 81 Pike St, offers great views over the bay and inventive French-influenced dishes. Menus change seasonally and include favorites like grilled chicken breast with Montrachet cheese and lavender vinaigrette for $13.

*Merchants Cafe* (☎ 624-1515), 109 Yesler Way between 1st and Occidental Aves S, serves a wide assortment of salads, hot sandwiches (about $5) and steak, seafood and chicken entrees between $9 and $12. The cafe is open for breakfast (omelets are the specialty), lunch and dinner and has a very reasonable beer and wine list. It's a good place to get a bite to eat or a drink, if only to check out the historic idiosyncrasies of the place, like the stand-up bar, all 30 feet of it, that came from the East Coast via the Horn. According to the restaurant, during the Great Depression, the cafe did its part by selling beers for a nickel and distributing free sandwiches and hard-boiled eggs.

*Trattoria Mitchell* (☎ 623-3883), at 84 Yesler Way between 1st Ave S and Western Ave, serves decent pasta, pizza and calzones for about $6 to $8. Its main attraction is that it stays open until 4 am from Tuesday to Saturday to feed all those joint-cover revelers.

A Seattle institution, the *Pink Door Ristorante* (☎ 443-3241), 1919 Post Alley, titillates first-time visitors by posting no sign. Just head for the pink door with the amazing Italian smells wafting out, and *eccolo!* Lunch is mostly pastas dishes ($7) and an amazing cioppino ($8.50); at dinner, there's a four-course prix-fixe menu. The restaurant is near the corner of Stewart St and Post Alley.

*Cafe Sophie* (☎ 441-6139), 1921 1st Ave, is an old-fashioned, shadowy bistro that seems to have drifted in from someone's fantasy of 1890s Paris. Dishes like grilled duck breast with dried cherry port sauce ($17), salmon with Sauternes wine and scallops ($18), and an outstanding Wiener schnitzel ($14) make this the place to go for interesting continental cuisine. If you make reservations, ask to sit in the 'Library', a cozy room with views over the bay.

When people think about Northwestern food, they often think of old-fashioned oyster bars and cavernous fish houses filled with rowdy yeomen. While the purveyors of Northwest cuisine have tried to expunge this food stereotype, and the frontier yeoman have been replaced with stockbrokers and professional athletes, the turn-of-the-century steak and fish house still exists at a couple of entertaining Seattle restaurants. *McCormick's Fish House & Bar* (☎ 682-3900), 722 4th Ave, offers a full sheet of daily fresh fish specials, mostly grilled with zesty sauces, a fine selection of local oysters, chops and steak, all served in a series of wood-lined, brass-outfitted chambers that gives off the aura of a bustling Victorian men's club. Even more uproarious is *FX McRory's Steak, Chop & Oyster House* (☎ 623-4800), 419 Occidental Ave S. This vast Pioneer Square landmark sits across from the Kingdome, and the bar, always full of jocks, can get completely out of hand after home games. At other times, diners can admire the lovely architecture and enjoy well-prepared steak; the oysters are a must.

For reasons not immediately apparent, Seattle has an inordinate number of Italian restaurants. Two of the best are in the Pioneer Square area. Busy and engaging, *Umberto's Ristorante* (☎ 621-0575), 100 S King St, is known for its outstanding pasta dishes (in the $13 range); however, the grilled meats are truly superior; pork tenderloin with Madeira and wild mushrooms is $17. A shade more expensive and dignified, *al Boccalino Ristorante* (☎ 622-7688), 1 Yesler Way, offers excellent pasta dishes but really delivers with innovative grilled fish and seafood dishes. Unfortunately, you'll have to endure the surly disdain of the waiters, which seems to be compulsory here.

**Top End** If you feel like a splurge or have an expense account, then downtown Seattle has plenty of restaurants to serve you; a full dinner at the following trend-setting restaurants will run at least $25 or $30 a head unless you're quite conservative. Informal attire is usually appropriate at any of the following restaurants.

At *Il Bistro* (☎ 682-3049), 93A Pike St, No 206, in Pike Place Market, the best and freshest of the market is incorporated into daily specials. Trade the charmingly scruffy ambiance of the market for European luxury at *Il Terrazzo Carmine* (☎ 467-7797), 411 1st Ave S. *Campagne* (☎ 728-2800), 86 Pine St, in the Inn at the Market, is Seattle's best traditional French restaurant, with an emphasis on the foods of Gascony.

If Seattle is in fact home to a school of cuisine (as many here fervently presume), then the following restaurants are among the best practitioners. The *Dahlia Lounge* (☎ 682-4142), 1904 4th Ave, usually gets the credit for creating the reality and then the notion of Northwest cuisine. The *Painted Table* (☎ 624-3646), 92 Madison St, is an unpretentious, pretty restaurant in the Alexis Hotel. *Fullers* at the Seattle Sheraton Hotel (☎ 447-5544), 1400 6th

Ave, is often considered the city's single best restaurant. The *Georgian Room* at the Olympic Four Seasons Hotel (☎ 621-7889), 411 University Ave, is one of the most imposing restaurants in the city, with equally stylish, regionally inspired food.

## Belltown & Seattle Center

**Budget** Just north of the market is Belltown, where there's an abundance of delis, inexpensive taverns with pub lunches and low-budget hangouts frequented by arty musicians and starving students. A lot of these venues are little cubbie holes that serve soup, sandwiches and salads to eat in (there are always a few streetside tables) or take away. A favorite for soups is the *Continental Deli* (☎ 728-8759), 2125 1st Ave; at *du jour* (☎ 441-3354), 1919 1st Ave, the views from the back and the fancy salads make this a local hangout.

*Mama's Mexican Kitchen* (☎ 728-6262) at the corner of 2nd Ave and Bell St is always packed. But that's no surprise for a place that serves $5 burritos, huge combination plates and, from 4 to 6 pm on weekdays, $2 margaritas all surrounded in Mexican kitsch artifacts.The pizza's great at *Vici Pizza* (☎ 443-0707), 2218 1st Ave; a slice and a Caesar salad is $4. The venerable *Two Bells Tavern* (☎ 441-3050), 2313 4th Ave, serves one of Seattle's best burgers – and a couple of dozen regional draft beers.

**Middle** There are few livelier Mexican restaurants than *Casa U-Betcha* (☎ 441-1026), 2212 1st Ave, with its wild decorations and enticements to order a margarita. Most importantly, the food's good, a mix of well-prepared traditional dishes and nuevo Mexican, like salmon broiled in banana leaves. Also favoring the Caribbean shores of Mexico is *Chez Bananas* (☎ 441-5657), 113 Blanchard St; dishes like chile rellenos in yaya sauce are $7.50 and Creole scallops are $10.

If you're worried about spices, then the *Kaleenka Russian Cafe* (☎ 728-1278), 1933 1st Ave, might be a better bet. Solid dishes like Siberian beef dumplings are $9; Georgian pressed chicken is $13.

On 1st Ave at Battery St, there's *Macrina* (☎ 448-4032), an artsy bakery that makes some of the best bread in town. They also serve a prix-fixe dinner of fresh Seattle cuisine. Keep going and at the corner of 1st Ave and Denny Way there's *Cafe Minnies,* a '50s-style diner open 24 hours – a blessing after you've been out to 2 am.

The handsomely austere *Queen City Grill* (☎ 443-0975), 2201 1st Ave, offers great seafood from its daily menu, and a solid and eclectic selection of meats and chicken from its seasonal menu. The crab cakes with bell pepper aioli is $15, a free-range chicken grilled with jerk sauce is $15, and a grilled sweetbread salad is $12.

**Top End** No compilation of Seattle restaurants would be complete without a mention of the Space Needle (☎ 443-2100), 219 4th Ave N. Of the two restaurants in the tower, the *Emerald Room* serves its version of Northwest cuisine 500 feet in the air. In fact, the restaurant's not as bad as its reputation, though it is quite expensive. The

Space Needle (TO)

ride up the elevator is free if you have meal reservations.

### International District

Another neighborhood for cheap eats is the International District. The best deals are the many Vietnamese, Thai and Chinese restaurants that line Jackson St between 6th and 12th Aves. In many of these restaurants, you'll have trouble spending over $5 on lunch, and $7 can buy dinner if you're cautious. One of the things you'll notice in the district is that there are places where the tourists go and places where everyone else goes. These suggestions weed out the ones with lines and consequently higher prices and suggests some local favorites.

*Hing Loon* (☎ 682-2828), 628 S Weller St, specializes in seafood dishes. The curry scallops cost $8.75 and are pleasantly spicy. Hot pots cost around $8. Check out the selections on the walls as well. The place is clean, the service fast. It's open daily from 10 am to midnight, and stays open until 2 am on Friday and Saturday nights.

A bit pricier but higher quality is *Sea Garden* (☎ 623-2100) at 509 7th Ave S. Hot pots cost $8 to $9, huge bowls of noodle soup cost between $3 and $5 and double mushroom scallops cost $9.50.

For a cheap snack or meal there's *House of Dumplings* (☎ 340-0774), across from Uwajimaya on S King St. Eight very good vegetable dumplings cost $5.

Up in the more Vietnamese sector, in Asian Plaza on the corner of S Jackson St and 12th Ave, there's *A Little Bit of Saigon* (☎ 325-3663), a huge restaurant serving some great food and 'imporked' beer. Their spring rolls (not fried) are served with peanut sauce and cost $2. A large bowl of rice noodle soup costs $4 and the '7 courses beef, served with all the fixings' is about $7. If you're really adventurous, try one of their desserts in a glass.

### Capitol Hill

**Budget** There's no end to good and inexpensive places to eat along Broadway, especially if you like ethnic food. Student favorites include the *Kitto Noodle House* (☎ 325-8486), 614 Broadway E for Asian noodles, and *El Greco* (328-4604), 219 Broadway E, for Mediterranean dishes. For vegetarian entrees and fresh juices, go to the *Gravity Bar* (☎ 325-7186), 415 Broadway E, in the Broadway Market. A popular place for coffee and dessert is the *Pacific Dessert Co* (☎ 329-6463), 416 Broadway E. Over at 19th Ave E and E Aloha St is the *Surrogate Hostess* (☎ 324-1944), 746 19th Ave E, a hip and health-conscious eatery where food is served cafeteria-style.

**Middle** *Septieme* (☎ 860-8858), 214 Broadway E, is a very trendy, intensely spare and arty cafe with an attitude. The food – all homemade, all simple meaty stuff – is very good. The *Broadway New American Grill* (☎ 328-7000), 314 Broadway E, mixes a rowdy bar scene with good burgers, ribs and other items from the grill.

On 15th Ave between Harrison and Republican Sts, *Coastal Kitchen* (☎ 322-1145) serves up some of the best food in the neighborhood, with their eclectic mix of Cajun, Mayan and Mexican inspirations. They have a great 'Blunch', served between 8:30 am and 3 pm on weekends, including corn griddle cakes for $4.25 and Charleston breakfast shrimp for $7.75. Dinners range from $7 to $13 and include such specialties as crab cakes served with wild greens and grilled bread, chicken in mole negro and hominy with grilled vegetables.

### Queen Anne
Everyone's favorite breakfast diner is the *5 Spot* (☎ 285-7768), 1502 Queen Anne Ave N. Go early, and avoid the weekends when lines snake out the door.

*Pacific Dessert Co* (☎ 284-8100), 127 Mercer St, is famous in Seattle for its fabulous rich cakes and good coffee, and is a popular after-opera spot for the well-dressed Seattle Center crowd.

*Adriatica Restaurant* (☎ 285-5000), 1107 Dexter Ave N at Ward St, always gets a mention when people talk about their favorite Italian restaurants. In an old home overlooking Lake Union at the top of a dizzying flight of stairs, Adriatica offers views to go with its excellent pasta, veal and fish dishes.

The *Uptown Bakery* (☎ 285-3757) is part of the Uptown Cafe, both with open-air seating when the weather's good. They have scrumptious pastries to go with the coffee for $3 to $4 and panini sandwiches for $4.50. They open at 4:45 am on weekdays and stay open until 10 pm. On weekends they open at 5:45 am and stay that way until midnight.

### Fremont
An institution in Fremont, the *Still Life Cafe* (☎ 547-9850), 709 N 35th St, is a great spot to park at a table and drink coffee and nibble this and that. Most dishes are vegetarian; the soups are especially good. The place to be in Fremont is the *Triangle Tavern* (☎ 632-0880), 3507 Fremont Place N. Zippy American dishes make this arrow-shaped cafe a bustling crossroads.

The *Longshoreman's Daughter* (☎ 633-5169), across the street from the Triangle Tavern on NW 36th St, serves hearty plates of seasonal vegetables, seafood, meat and excellent garlic mashed potatoes. For lunch a combo of soup, salad and roasted garlic/parmesan bread costs $5.25. Dinner entrees cover many tastes, from chipotle BBQ chicken for $10 to miso soba for $7. They also have a reasonably priced wine list and are open 7:30 am to 10 pm daily. Down the street is a small walk-in burrito place, *Taco del Mar*, where an overflowing burrito will cost about $4. *Costas*, (☎ 328-3479) on the corner of Fremont Ave N and 34th St, serves good, inexpensive Greek food.

### Wallingford
In Wallingford, N 45th St stretches past a long strip of inexpensive, mostly ethnic restaurants. *India Cuisine* (☎ 632-5307), 1718 N 45th St, is one of Seattle's best tandoor houses. Other good choices

include a Thai cafe, as well as a Mexican and Irish and even Afghani restaurant. Don't pass up the *Boulangerie* (☎ 634-2211), 2200 N 45th St, as close as Seattle gets to a real French bakery.

With a name like *Bizzarro* (☎ 545-7327), 1307 N 46th St, you'd never guess that this Wallingford hotbed is an excellent neighborhood Italian cafe. When you learn that it's housed in someone's garage, then the name makes sense. Vegetarians and breakfast-lovers flock to *Julia's* (☎ 633-1175), 1714 N 44th St.

*My Brother's Pizza* (☎ 547-3663), at N 45th St and Meridian Ave, has some of the best pizza in the city and is often packed, but there is a take-out window. They have a unique way of serving pizza – upside down and in a bowl. A spinach 'dome' pizza costs $5.75. A large pizza pie (could feed four) with all the sausages and pepperoni imaginable costs $17. It's open Monday to Friday from 5 to 10 pm and weekends from 11:30 am to 11 pm.

### The U District

Adjacent to the University of Washington is University Way, where you'd rightly expect to find a lot of inexpensive restaurants and cafes. During the day, it can be hard to park along 'the Ave', as it's called. Head here at night, when the crowds are fewer, and the food is still cheap. *Taqueria Mexico* (☎ 633-5256), 4226 University Way, can accommodate the smallest budget. *Flowers* (☎ 633-1903), 43rd St and University Way, offers vegetarian fare and a juice bar.

North of the university is *Sante Fe Cafe* (☎ 524-7736), 2255 NE 65th, a converted storefront with New Mexican-style food.

### Ballard

OK, so it's a cliché. *Ray's Boathouse* (☎ 789-3770), 6049 Seaview Ave NW, offers views over the Olympics, nautical decor and an exhaustive fresh fish menu: it's what tourists think of when they think of Seattle. But the food's great, and the views wondrous. If you can't get reservations, at least come for a drink on the

deck. Ray's is about a mile west of the Ballard Locks.

### Madrona

The *Hi Spot Cafe* (☎ 325-7905), 1410 34th Ave, has been known since it opened for incredible cinnamon rolls, Torrefazione coffee and filling breakfasts, including creative omelets served with potatoes for $6.50, homemade granola for $2.75 and mimosas for $3. The sandwich and salad lunch ($3 to $6) is just as good, as is dinner with smoked trout salad for $6.25 and polenta sticks with ratatouille for $8.95. They are open from 7 am to 2 pm daily and also from 5:30 to 9:30 pm Tuesday to Saturday. On weekends get there very early for breakfast or wait outside with the neighborhood lab 'Blackie'.

*Cafe Soleil* (☎ 325-1126), down the street at 1400 34th Ave, is another good eatery with outdoor tables and friendly service. Egg frittatas with such tastes as sun-dried tomatoes, black olives and feta cheese cost $5.50.

### ENTERTAINMENT

For a listing of Seattle's live entertainment, consult the *Seattle Weekly*, the *Stranger* or the Friday editions of the daily papers. Tickets for most events are available at Ticketmaster (☎ 628-0888, 292-2787), which has ticket centers in several store chains and some independent stores. Chains include PayLess Drug Stores, Budget Tapes & Discs, Disc Jockey, Tower Records and The Wherehouse. Call to charge tickets by phone or to find the location nearest you. It's open Monday to Saturday from 8 am to 9 pm, Sunday from 10 am to 6 pm.

For rush seats, Ticketmaster has its own Discount Ticket Booth (☎ 233-1111) at Westlake Center. Day-of-performance tickets are extra cheap, but you'll have to pay cash. It opens at 10 am daily. Ticket/Ticket (☎ 324-2744) is another half-price, day-of-show ticket outlet; however, they won't give out ticket-availability information over the phone. There is a location at

Pike Place Market and at the Broadway Market on Capitol Hill.

## Coffeehouses

Seattle often gets the credit for starting the US coffee craze. In the process, Seattle's coffee fanaticism has also served to revitalize the coffeehouse as a social meeting place that offers frequent poetry readings, theatrical entertainment and acoustic music, as well as a place to read, write letters and chat with friends. Coffeehouses also provide an largely alcohol-free place to hang out. It's Cafe Culture for the '90s. There are coffeehouses all across Seattle; here are a few to get you started.

**Downtown & Pioneer Square** The most attractive coffeehouse in the Pioneer Square area is *Torrefazione Italia* (☎ 624-5773), in the Occidental mall. It's open from 7 am to 6 pm Monday to Friday and from 9 am on Saturday; closed Sunday. *Starbucks Coffee* (☎ 382-2656), 102 1st Ave S, across from the beautiful pergola in Pioneer Square, is as central as you can get.

**Belltown** For a break from the grunge bands in Belltown, head to *Penny University*, 2020 2nd Ave, or *Lux Coffee House* (☎ 443-0962), 2226 1st Ave.

**Capitol Hill** Feeling pensive? Go to *Espresso Roma* (☎ 324-1866), 202 Broadway E, where agitprop junkies and worried-looking students mainline caffeine.

If you're near the dance clubs on Pine and Pike Sts, head to *Puss-Puss Cafe* (☎ 720-1883), 514 E Pine St, or *Cafe Paradiso* (☎ 322-6960), 1005 E Pike St, both open very late on weekend nights. Other favorites are *Rosebud Espresso* (☎ 323-6636), 719 E Pike St, and *The Green Man*.

The *Internet Cafe* (☎ 323-7202; internet http://internetcafe.allyn.com) is at the corner of 1st and Mercer Sts inside the Seattle Espresso Company. For $4 you get an hour of full access to Internet, e-mail and World Wide Web service. The cafe also acts as a post office, holding onto mail sent until you read it. It's also an unpretentious place to relax, have some tea or espresso, study, read or learn more about the Internet.

**The U District** Near the university, go to *Allegro Espresso Bar* (☎ 633-3030), 4214 University Way NE, or *Rosebud Cafe* (☎ 633-0801), 1411 NE 45th.

**Wallingford** In the Wallingford area, there's *The Green Room Cafe* (☎ 632-6420), 4026 Stone Way N, billed as Seattle's theatrical coffeehouse, and often stages readings of plays. And for a caffeine switch, try the tea shop next to Wide World Books. *Teahouse Kuan Yin* (☎ 632-2055) at 1911 N 45th St, has an impressive selection of black, oolong, green and herbal teas and paraphernalia to enjoy a pot. It's open from 10 am to 11 pm every day but stays open until midnight on Fridays and Saturdays.

## Cinemas

Although suburban multi-screen cinema complexes are common enough in Seattle, there are still quite a number of small independent theaters that go out of their way to find the unusual and obscure. At opposite ends of Capitol Hill are two of the best art cinemas, the *Egyptian* (☎ 323-4978), 801 E Pine St, and the *Harvard Exit* (☎ 323-8986), 807 E Roy St. Cineastes will like the off-beat fare at both the *Pike St Cinema* (☎ 682-7064), 1108 E Pike St, and the *Grand Illusion* (☎ 523-3935), 1403 NE 50th St in the U District.

Some first-run houses tend toward foreign and smaller independent films. *Broadway Market Cinemas* (☎ 323-0231), Broadway and E Harrison St on Capitol Hill, and the *Varsity* (☎ 632-3131), 4329 University Way NE, and the *Metro Cinemas* (☎ 633-0055), 45th Ave and Roosevelt Way NE, near the university, offer first-run art and foreign films with the regular mainstream smash hits.

The biggest event of the year for film-goers is the Seattle International Film Festival (☎ 324-9996), a three-week-long extravaganza of films from around the world that usually includes many US debuts. The festival is usually held in late May and early June at the Harvard Exit and the Egyptian theatres.

## Theater

Seattle has one of the most vibrant theater scenes on the West Coast. The following equity troupes present a range of classical and modern dramatic theater. Check the newspapers for openings (the PI's *What's Happening* section, which comes out on Fridays, has good theater listings).

*A Contemporary Theatre* (ACT) (☎ 285-5110), 110 W Roy St, near Seattle Center, is in historic Queen Anne Hall. The season runs May to December. The box office is open Tuesday to Friday from noon to 6 pm. *Seattle Repertory Theatre* (☎ 443-2222), 155 Mercer St, performs in the Bagley Wright Theatre at Seattle Center. Next door, the *Intiman Theatre Company*, Seattle's oldest and largest, performs at the Intiman Playhouse at Seattle Center (☎ 626-0782), 2nd Ave N and Mercer St. The *Seattle Children's Theatre* (☎ 441-3322) offers excellent productions for young theatergoers in the Charlotte Martin Theatre at the Seattle Center. *Bathhouse Theatre Company* (☎ 524-9108), 7312 W Green Lake Drive N, take risks with modern adaptations of classics and original contemporary drama. *Empty Space Theatre* (☎ 547-7500), 3509 Fremont Ave, presents off-beat shows and readings. Tickets for all the above venues are available through Ticketmaster. *The Annex Theatre* (☎ 728-0933) and the *Velvet Elvis* (☎ 624-8477) are two alternative-theater venues.

On Pine St west of Broadway, there's the *Odd Fellows Hall* – a huge warehouse turned performance space with numerous shows including the Allegro dance series. Check local newspapers for listings.

*New City Theatre* (☎ 323-6800), 1634 11th Ave, offers a wild mix of cabaret, regular plays, film and performance-art shenanigans. *The Greek Active* is a gay troupe that performs farces (this is the new drag art form) at The Easy (☎ 323-8343) on 916 E Pike St. Both the *Cornish College of the Arts* (☎ 323-1486), at 710 E Roy St and 1501 10th Ave E,

and the *University of Washington School of Drama* (☎ 543-4880) churn out student productions.

## Performing Arts

Under maestro Gerard Schwartz, the *Seattle Symphony Orchestra* (☎ 443-4747) has risen to prominence as a major regional orchestra, and has released a series of critically acclaimed recordings. The symphony performs at the Opera House in Seattle Center. The *Northwest Chamber Orchestra* (☎ 343-0045) is the Northwest's only orchestra that focuses on period chamber music; the group performs at various venues throughout the city.

The *Seattle Opera* (☎ 389-7676) has moved from strength to strength under the directorship of Speight Jenkins. For a regional company, the Seattle Opera isn't afraid to tackle weighty or non-traditional works; productions of Philip Glass and a summer *Ring* cycle have given opera lovers a lot to mull over. However, the company is perhaps most noted for its unconventional stagings of the traditional repertoire. Performances are at the Opera House in Seattle Center. Also performing at the Opera House is the *Pacific Northwest Ballet* (☎ 441-9411), the foremost dance company in the Northwest. *Seattle Men's Chorus* (☎ 323-2992) is one of the nation's most active gay choral groups, with nearly three dozen engagements throughout the year. Their Christmas concert is a popular holiday sell-out.

Summer musical festivals include the Seattle International Music Festival (☎ 622-1392), the Seattle Chamber Music Festival (☎ 328-5606) and the International Chamber Music Series (☎ 543-4880).

## Bars & Brewpubs

There's nothing sedate about nightlife in Seattle. While there's lots of attention paid to live music clubs, the microbrew craze has served to establish neighborhood bars as lively and respectable places to while away the hours.

The main gay-bar district is centered around Pike and Pine Sts and Broadway on

Capitol Hill, with a number of gay-oriented dance clubs as well as coffeehouses. This area is also home to arty live music clubs and taverns, so it's about as close to party central as it gets in Seattle.

**Downtown & Pioneer Square** For a good overview of the 'scene' in Pioneer Square, get the $7 joint cover that lets you into about 10 different clubs, most on 1st Ave S, with live jazz and blues music. You'll be able to tell which places participate by the crowds, the signs and the coffee/pretzel carts outside. On weekdays (Monday to Thursday) they do the same thing but for $3 to $5 depending on the bands playing.

For live music and a fairly intense late night scene, head to gleaming *Pacific Northwest Brewing Co* (☎ 621-7002), 322 Occidental Ave S, near Pioneer Square.

*Hart Brewery & Pub* (☎ 682-3377) at 91 S Royal Brougham Way, right across from the Kingdome, is where Hart Brewers make both Pyramid and Thomas Kemper beers. A sampler of 6 beers costs $6 and is a great introduction to the 24 different varieties on tap. Tours are given daily and cost is $2. It's open from 11 am to 10 pm Monday to Thursday, to 11 pm Friday and Saturday and to 9 pm on Sunday.

For an elegant cocktail with piano glissandos in the background, take the elevator to the *Cloud Room* (☎ 682-0100), 1619 9th Ave, atop the Camlin Hotel.

**Belltown** One of Seattle's most likable bars, the *Virginia Inn Tavern* (☎ 728-1937), 1937 1st Ave in Belltown, manages to service many distinct groups of people at once. Lots of beers on tap, nice interior and friendly help make this a good rendezvous and a great staging area for forays elsewhere. If you can't get in the door, walk down to the *Belltown Pub* (☎ 728-4311), 2322 1st Ave, another friendly bar with tons of atmosphere.

*Belltown Billiards* (☎ 448-6779) is just down the street from the Queen City Grill at 90 Blanchard St. You can eat here if you want – they have a decent Italian menu, but the main draw is playing pool in a swanky

location. This place draws all types, from club rats to corporate brats. There's live jazz on Sundays and Mondays and a Chardonnay happy hour from 4 to 7 pm weekdays with half-price pool. Pool rates are $6 a person, less the more people you have at the table.

The *Lava Lounge*, decorated with tacky black-velvet-style paintings of volcanoes and a grass hut, has shuffleboard tournaments on Sundays and $3 pints of beer. The lounge stays open from 3 or 4 pm to 2 am.

**Seattle Center** *Five Point Cafe*, in Tillicum Square at 415 Cedar St, faces the statue of Chief Seattle. Around since 1929, this is a popular hangout for old-timers as well as bikers and young hipsters. Check out the men's bathroom – while standing at

Statue of Chief Seattle (CH)

the urinal you can get a periscope-view of the Space Needle. The Five Point is open 24 hours a day.

Sure, at *Cucina! Cucina!* (☎ 447-2782), 901 Fairview Ave N, between Capitol Hill and Seattle Center on Lake Union, you can get a meal, but most people go there to drink. In summer there are tables outdoors.

**Capitol Hill** Along 'the Corridor' *Wild Rose* (☎ 324-9210), at Pike St and 11th Ave, is one of few bars for lesbians in the area. They serve sandwiches ($4 to $5) and have a wide selection of microbrews and pool tables. It's open from 11 am to midnight, but the kitchen closes around 9:30 pm.

*Moe's* at Pike St and 10th Ave is a popular spot because you can do just about anything – eat in the restaurant from amoeba-shaped tables, drink lattes upstairs or listen to some bands in the back room. Across the street there's *The Comet* an institution in the world of grunge music, where pool and surly attitudes still mandate. Next door *The Easy* is one of the other lesbian bars in the area (see Dance Clubs, below).

On Broadway at the corner of Thomas St, *Ileen's Sports Bar* (☎ 324-0229) tries really hard to be sporty, but the locals, loyal to the former name of 'Ernie Steele's', maintain the mix of trendy clientele, alternative music and good, cheap drinks. The

smoke, as well as mounted heads of moose and elk, reinforce the non-sportiness. Adjacent is a diner that serves daily specials like pork chops for $6.25, turkey sandwiches for $4 or crab sautée for $5.

The *Deluxe* at the end of the Broadway strip at Roy St does, however, hold a sports bar atmosphere with vinyl booths, tacky pop music, constant games on TV and a standard selection of beers and sophisticated diner food. There's a happy hour from 3 to 7 pm, and if you didn't get enough the first time, there's another at 11 pm to 1 am when the place closes.

**Queen Anne** *Sorry Charlies Restaurant & Piano Bar* (☎ 283-3245) on Queen Anne Ave between Mercer and Republican Sts, is a great example of old-time Seattle tacky diner atmosphere The piano man comes in at 8 pm, Tuesday through Sunday, and everyone joins in. Charlies stays open until 3 am.

Across the street, *The Mecca Cafe* (☎ 285-9728), is one of the latest trend-setting nightspots mixed with a diner atmosphere.

**Fremont & Green Lake** *The Trolleyman Pub* (☎ 548-8000), 3400 Phinney Ave N, at the Fremont Brewery, is Redhook Ale Brewery's main operation.

The *Triangle Tavern* (☎ 632-0880), right at Fremont Place N and 35th St, has eight beers on tap and a lively crowd.

Seattle skyline (TO)

If you're thirsty from too much sun-bathing at Green Lake, head to *The Latona*, at NE 65th St and Latona Ave NE, to find one of the nicest pubs in the area.

**The U District** Just next to the university is rowdy *Big Time Microbrew & Music* (☎ 545-4509), 4133 University Way NE. The *Blue Moon Tavern* at 712 NE 45th St, is a dive of an institution made famous by the people who sat here, like Kerouac and Ginsberg.

### Live Music
The Northwest's gift to the music world, grunge rock, was a passing phase, albeit one of epic proportions. The cult of grunge is dying out more slowly in the rest of the world than it is in Seattle, where it is now generally considered passé. That doesn't mean that grunge bands like Pearl Jam and Mudhoney aren't still extraordinarily popular; they are. It's just that the grunge image lost much of its appeal for its progenitors when impressionable suburban youth all over the country adopted its ratty plaid-shirted style.

You'll still find a cutting-edge music scene in Seattle, with new venues opening at an astonishing rate.

Don't miss *Crocodile Cafe* (☎ 441-5611), 2200 2nd Ave in Belltown, a springboard for local bands, or the extra trendy *Mo'Roc'In Cafe* (☎ 323-2373), 925 E Pike St. Moe's, as it's known, offers three floors of live music, poetry readings, dancing and performance art. There's more multi-venue artistic anguish at the *OK Hotel* (☎ 621-7903), 212 Alaskan Way S, and at *The Weathered Wall* (☎ 728-9398), 1921 5th Ave. Other hot clubs are *Captain Cook's* (☎ 223-9467), 1414 Alaskan Way, and *Colourbox* (☎ 340-4101), 113 1st Ave S. Between Bell and Battery Sts on 2nd Ave, there's the *Rendezvous* (☎ 441-5823), a diner-turned-music-club for bands that really want to make it but can't seem to get into the place up the street.

There is more to the live music scene in Seattle than aspiring to the next generation of grunge rock. For jazz, head to the *New Orleans Creole Restaurant* (☎ 622-2563), 114 1st Ave S, near Pioneer Square. Just down the street is the city's best blues club, *The Central* (☎ 622-0209), 207 1st Ave S. *Kell's Restaurant & Bar* (☎ 728-1916), 1916 Post Alley, in the Pike Place Market area, has live Irish music Wednesday to Saturday evenings.

*The Backstage* at 22nd and Market in Ballard (☎ 781-2805) has always brought in good music, especially blues. The *Tractor Tavern* (☎ 789-3599), 5213 Ballard Ave, is a great space to see/hear live music, which they have almost every night.

### Dance Clubs
The hottest dance clubs in Seattle are mixed gay and straight discos, especially the always amusing *Re-Bar* (☎ 233-9873), 1114 Howell St at Boren St. For something different, head to the *Timberline* (☎ 622-6220), 2015 Boren St, a gay country & western bar with line dancing. For an old fashioned mostly-gay disco scene, head to *Neighbors* (☎ 324-5358), 1509 Broadway (enter in the alley) or *The Easy* (☎ 323-8343), 916 E Pike St.

On weekends, a couple of area restaurants role up the carpets to provide some of the hottest dance scenes in the city. The *Besa del Sol* (☎ 547-8087), 4468 Stone Way N in Wallingford, shifts into high gear as a salsa dance club. *Kokeb* (☎ 322-0485), 926 12th Ave E on Capitol Hill, is normally an Ethiopian restaurant, but on Friday and Saturday nights they put away the spices and turn up the Afro-Pop rhythms.

### Comedy Clubs
Seattle's main venue for stand-up comedy is the *Comedy Underground* (☎ 628-0303, 628-0888), located at 222 S Main St near Pioneer Square. If you've never seen *TheatreSports* (☎ 781-9273), then plan a wild evening of audience inspired madness with these compulsive improvisational actors. The original Seattle troupe is located in Pike Place Market, near the south end of Post Alley. Another improv group, the City Improv, performs at the *Belltown Theatre Center* at 115 Blanchard

St. Both groups perform late night Friday and Saturday only.

## Professional Sports

Seattle has a full compliment of professional sports teams. The Seattle Mariners baseball team (☎ 343-4600) and the Seattle Seahawks (☎ 827-9777), the northwest's only NFL franchise, play in the Kingdome, 201 S King St. Both these teams have traditionally been also-rans in their respective divisions, though things are looking up with recent draft choices. Tickets are pretty easy to come by for the Mariners; the Seahawks command a larger, uproarious audience and tickets are scarce.

Plenty of sports excitement is provided by the Seattle Supersonics (☎ 281-5850), Seattle's NBA franchise. The Sonics, who play at the Seattle Center Coliseum, are major contenders in basketball's Western Division; they play a high-energy, highly aggressive game and have won an exuberant and devoted following. Tickets can be pretty hard to find, so call ahead if possible. Late arrivals may need to depend on scalpers near the Coliseum.

The Seattle Thunderbirds Hockey Club (☎ 448-7825) plays at the Seattle Center Arena from September to March. This isn't the NHL, but you can't beat the enthusiasm and moxie of the team.

Tickets for all the above teams can be obtained through Ticketmaster outlets (☎ 628-0888).

## GETTING THERE & AWAY

### Air

Seattle's airport, known as Sea-Tac, is the largest airport in the Northwest, with daily service to Europe, Asia and points throughout the USA and Canada on most national and regional airlines.

Sea-Tac is also a major hub for small commuter airlines with flights to the San Juan Islands, Bellingham, Wenatchee, Yakima and Spokane. Portland is linked to Seattle with flights almost every half hour; there are hourly flights between Seattle and Vancouver, BC.

Sea-Tac is 13 miles south of Seattle on I-5.

The following airlines have offices downtown:

Alaska Airlines
1301 4th Ave (☎ 433-3100, (800) 426-0333)
American Airlines
1400 6th Ave (☎ (800) 445-4435)
There's also a ticketing desk in the Sheraton Hotel.
Continental Airlines
400 University St (☎ 624-1740, (800) 231-0856)
Delta Airlines
410 University St (☎ 625-0469, (800) 221-1212)
Northwest Airlines
402 University St (☎ (800) 225-2525)
Scandinavian Airlines
1301 5th Ave, Suite 2727 (☎ (800) 221-2350)
United Airlines
1225 4th Ave (☎ 441-3700, (800) 241-6522)

### Bus

Greyhound buses (☎ 628-5526, (800) 231-2222) link Seattle to Portland, Eugene and points in California along I-5 south, as well as to Bellingham and Vancouver, BC on I-5 north. Buses also service the I-90 corridor from Seattle to Spokane and on through northern Idaho and Montana to Chicago. Another bus leaves from Seattle for Yakima, the Tri-Cities and points south along Hwy 97. One bus daily links Seattle to Port Angeles. The depot is at 9th Ave and Stewart St.

If you're heading to British Columbia, consider the Quick Shuttle (☎ (800) 665-2122), which makes five daily express runs between Seattle and Vancouver, BC. Pickup is either at the airport ($29 one way to Vancouver) or the downtown Travelodge, 200 6th Ave N ($23 one way).

Green Tortoise (☎ (800) 867-8647) travels overnight to San Francisco for $49 (call for a spot) and to Portland for $15. The schoolbus-turned-lounge leaves from the Greyhound depot Sunday and Thursday at 8 am.

### Train

Amtrak offers train service into Seattle at King St Station (☎ (800) 872-7245), 303 S Jackson St. Seattle is the terminus of two

Amtrak train lines. The daily *Empire Builder* heads east through Spokane, eventually reaching Chicago; a roundtrip ticket from Chicago to Seattle ranges from $224 to $434, depending on availability. The *Coast Starlight* runs daily between Seattle and Los Angeles, with stops in Tacoma, Olympia, Portland and points south; roundtrip to Portland can be as little as $30 with advance booking; to Los Angeles, fares range between $108 and $314.

## Ferry

Ferries to Washington destinations (Bremerton and Bainbridge Island) are state-operated, and all ferry queries can be routed through a central information line (☎ 464-6400). Reservations for the Washington State Ferry System are taken for vehicles only; call the reservation line (☎ 376-2134, 378-4777).

**To/From Victoria, BC** The *Victoria Clipper* (☎ 448-5000) departs from Pier 69 in Seattle bound for Victoria at 8 am daily. This is a passenger-only ferry; adult fare for the 2½-hour trip costs $55 one-way, $89 roundtrip.

The slower but cheaper *Victoria Line* (☎ (604) 382-8100) originates in Victoria and departs Seattle for a 4½-hour return trip at 1 pm daily. Passengers cost C$25 one-way, C$45 roundtrip, and automobiles (includes driver) are C$49 one-way, C$90 roundtrip.

Reservations for ferries to Victoria, BC are recommended and can be made by calling individual operators. Only cash or traveler's checks are accepted for these fares, and travelers should be prepared to go through Canadian customs upon arrival.

## Car

Most national rental-car firms have booths at the airport. The following also maintain offices in the downtown area.

Allstar Rent-a-Car
    2402 7th Ave (☎ 443-3368)

Avis
    1919 5th Ave (☎ 448-1700)
Budget
    19030 28th Ave S (☎ 682-2277, (800) 527-0700)
Dollar Rent A Car
    710 Stewart St (☎ 682-1316)
Hertz
    722 Pike St (☎ 682-5050, (800) 654-3131)
National Car Rental
    1942 Westlake Ave (☎ 448-7368)
Xtra Car Discount Rentals
    1124 Denny Way (☎ 623-8646)

**RV Rental** Adventure Werks (☎ (800) 736-8897), 3713 Seeley St, Bellingham, specializes in VW-camper rental. Camping packages and mountain bike rental are also available.

There are also a handful of companies that rent motorhomes (RVs):

Eastside Motorhome Rentals
    3625 241st Ave SE, Issaquah (☎ 399-5878)
NW Van & Motor Home Rentals
    14458 Ambaum Blvd SW (☎ 241-6111, (800) 359-4306)
Western Motorhome Rentals
    . 19303 Hwy 99, Lynnwood (☎ 775-1181, (800) 800-1181)

## Weather & Road Conditions

For a report of road conditions, call 455-7700. Call 368-4499 for a traffic report.

## GETTING AROUND
### To/From the Airport

Gray Line runs an Airport Express (☎ 626-6088) every 15 minutes from 5 am to midnight between Sea-Tac and downtown Seattle's major hotels. The cost is $7 one way or $12 roundtrip. There's also the Shuttle Express (☎ 622-1424, (800) 487-7433).

### Bus

Metro Transit (☎ 553-3000) serves the greater Seattle metropolitan area with 130 bus routes. Most of Seattle's buses run through downtown on 4th Ave, or in the Bus Tunnel, which has five entrances in the downtown area. In the immediate downtown area, all bus rides are free from 6 am to 7 pm in the area between 6th Ave and the Waterfront, and between Jackson St in Pioneer Square and Battery St. Note that Seattle Center is outside of the free-ride district.

Regular bus fare is $1.10 during peak hours (5 to 9 am and 3 to 6 pm) and 85c at other times. If you are catching a bus that's heading downtown, you purchase your ticket when you get on; however, if you board a bus downtown and head elsewhere, you pay when you get off. Bus drivers do not make change, so you need exact change. Buy tickets in advance or get a day pass ($3.20 during the week, $1.70 weekends) at the Metro Customer Service office at 821 2nd Ave, or at the Westlake Center bus tunnel station. Pick up a copy of various bus schedules at these offices, and also a Metro bus map for $2.

Frequently used buses include the 71, 72 and the 73 between downtown and the university; bus No 7 climbs up to Capitol Hill and runs along Broadway before eventually ending up at University of Washington; buses No 10 and 43 also go to Capitol Hill. To get to Seattle Center, take buses No 1, 2, 3, 4, 6, 13, 15 or 18. Bus No 26 runs to Fremont, and then through Wallingford to Greenlake.

## Trolley
Seattle Trolley Tours (☎ 626-5212) makes a great form of downtown transport, especially for sightseeing. Visitors are encouraged to get off and on at leisure, and tickets are good for the full day of operation. Stops, indicated by bright yellow sandwich boards, include the Westlake Center, Space Needle, Pike Place, Waterfront, Pioneer Square, International District, Kingdome, Seattle Art Museum and Newmark Center. The trolley runs every 30 minutes. Information centers are located across from the Westlake Center Nordstrom on Pine St and at Pier 57. One-day tickets cost $11 adult or $7 senior and student, and

can be purchased either at the information center or upon boarding. The trolley operates daily from 9:30 am to 6 pm between May 1 and Oct 15.

## Taxis
For a cab, call one of the following: Farwest Taxi (☎ 622-1717), Graytop Cabs (☎ 282-8222), STITA Taxi (☎ 249-9999) or Yellow Cabs (☎ 622-6500).

# AROUND SEATTLE
## South Seattle
**Museum of Flight** Much more interesting than it sounds, this vast museum of aviation (☎ 764-5720), 9494 E Marginal Way S, has over 50 historic aircraft on display. It's on Boeing Field, about 10 miles south of downtown. The museum has no formal ties to Boeing; the entire history of flight, from da Vinci to the Wright Brothers to the NASA space program is presented. Twenty airplanes are suspended from the ceiling of the six-story glass Great Gallery; vintage flyers reside on the grounds outside the buildings; the restored 1909 Red Barn, where Boeing had its beginnings, contains exhibits and displays. There's also a hands-on area where visitors get to work the controls and sit in the driver's seat. Films about flight and aircraft history are shown in the small theatre; there's also a gift shop and cafe.

The museum is open from 10 am to 5 pm daily except Thursday, when the museum stays open until 9 pm. Admission is $6 for adults, youths ages six to 15 are $3, and under six are free. To find the museum, take I-5 exit No 158 south of Seattle; turn west and follow East Marginal Way.

**Rainier Brewing Company Tours** It's a far cry from microbrew, but Rainier Beer (☎ 622-2600), 3100 Airport Way, is a northwest original. Stop by for a free factory tour. It's open from 1 to 6 pm Monday to Saturday.

## In & On the Sound
**Bainbridge Island** The most popular ferry trip for tourists is the Washington State

Ferry between Seattle and Winslow, Bainbridge Island's primary town. Winslow has outfitted itself as a destination for day passengers by establishing an array of shops and restaurants within an easy walk of the dock. However, most tourists take the ferry simply for the ride and the great views of Seattle as the ferry negotiates Elliott Bay. The **Bainbridge Island Winery** (☎ 842-9463) in Winslow is a good destination for cyclists and wine-lovers.

Ferries to Bainbridge Island make trips around the clock, with at least one ferry each hour during the day. Ferries board at Pier 52 for the 35-minute (one-way) trip; one-way fare (seasonal) costs $3.30 for passengers, $5.50 for autos (driver included).

**Bremerton** The other ferry destination from Seattle is Bremerton, the largest town on Kitsap Peninsula, and the Puget Sound's principal naval base. The main attraction here is the Naval Museum (☎ 479-7447), 130 Washington Ave, and *USS Turner Joy* (☎ 792-2457), 300 Washington Beach Ave. This historic US Naval destroyer is on the waterfront park, right next to the ferry terminal. Tours are available from 10 am to 6 pm daily May to October, and Thursday to Monday from 11 am to 4 pm November to April. Tickets cost $3 to $5.

The automobile ferry to Bremerton makes 13 trips daily and leaves from the ferry terminal at Pier 52. There are five weekday and four weekend passenger-only ferries. Boarding and ticket sales for this ferry are at Pier 50. The trip takes about an hour on either ferry, and one-way tickets cost $3.30 for passengers and $5.50 for autos (driver included).

**Tillicum Village** Blake Island is a state park whose only approach is by boat; this made it a safe place to host the 1993 APEC conference, where President Clinton met with 14 Asian leaders. The most popular facility on the island is Tillicum Village (☎ 443-1244) with its Northwest Coast Indian Cultural Center & Restaurant. Boats depart Piers 55 and 56 in Seattle for a tour of the waterfront and the

crossing to Blake Island. Once there, the package includes a traditional Indian salmon bake, traditional dancing and a film about Northwest Native Americans. After the meal, there's time for a short hike or to shop for gifts. Tours last four hours and depart daily from May to mid-October, and on weekends all year. Adult ticket prices range between $45 and $50; children are $20.

### Bellevue
Bellevue was long the suburb that Seattlites loved to disdain. However, the mass immigration to the Seattle area has boosted the population of this city on the eastern shores of Lake Washington to the point that Bellevue is now Washington's third-largest city, an upscale burg with high-cost housing and attractive parks. Civic and social life centers on **Bellevue Square**, the shopping mall that sets the tone for the downtown and the surrounding communities. Even if you don't need to go shopping, the top floor's **Bellevue Art Museum** (☎ 454-6021) is worth a stop.

North of Bellevue on I-405 is **Kirkland**, a city known for its lakefront business district, marinas and antique shopping malls. Some of the best public access to Lake Washington is along Lake Ave; lots of waterfront restaurants are found here, some with docks for their boat-transported customers. **Hales Brewery** (☎ 827-4359), 109 Central Way, is one of the original Seattle microbreweries.

Cross Lake Washington on the Evergreen Point Floating Bridge and turn south onto I-405 for Bellevue, north for Kirkland. Exit at NE 8th St for Bellevue Square.

### Snoqualmie Falls
An hour's drive into the mountains east of Seattle is *The Salish Lodge at Snoqualmie Falls* (☎ 888-2556, (800) 826-6124), PO Box 1109, Snoqualmie, WA. This beautiful resort lodge sits atop 268-foot Snoqualmie Falls and was the locale for many of the scenes from the TV series *Twin Peaks*. The drive into the Cascades, views of the waterfall and short hikes in the area, followed by

WASHINGTON

lunch at the lodge (jokes about cherry pie and a cup of joe are mandatory) make for a nice day away.

The ski resort at **Snoqualmie Pass** is a popular excursion for Seattlites, and includes four different ski areas operated by a company simply called The Pass (☎ 232-8182, for a snow report, 236-1600). The four areas, Alpental, Snoqualmie Summit, Ski Acres and Hyak, vary greatly in difficulty and somewhat in conditions. Alpental is generally considered the most difficult, with steep slopes and 2200 feet of vertical drop. Hyak is over the pass, and usually offers drier and faster snow. Ski Acres offers both downhill and groomed cross-country runs; snow tubing is available at the Snowflake Recreation Area. Snowboards are allowed on all slopes, although Hyak and Snoqualmie Pass have set aside snowboarding areas. Full rental and ski instruction options are available; night skiing is offered throughout the week. One lift ticket is good at all four ski areas; free buses link the runs. Early-week tickets are $14. Weekends and holidays, tickets are $27.

To reach Snoqualmie Falls, drive east on I-90 to North Bend, exit No 31. The falls and resort are four miles northwest of town on Hwy 202.

### Woodinville Wineries

The suburban community of Woodinville, 14 miles north of Bellevue off I-405, is home to two popular wineries and now a brewpub. **Chateau Ste Michelle** (☎ 488-3300), 14111 NE 145th St, was one of Washington's first wineries (though most of their wine production is in the Yakima area). This historic 87-acre estate lends itself easily to picnics and concerts in the summer. It's open for wine tasting from 10 am to 4:30 pm daily. Next door is the **Columbia Winery** (☎ 488-2776), 14030 NE 145th St, with more wine tasting; it's open daily from 10 am to 5 pm; tours are on Saturday and Sunday.

**Redhook Brewery** (☎ 482-3232), 14300 NE 145th St, was one of Washington's first microbreweries. Their new Woodinville brewery and pub, called the *Forecasters Public House*, also offers tours daily.

# Southern Puget Sound

Tacoma and Olympia are the two largest cities as you head south along Puget Sound, and they can make nice alternatives to staying in Seattle. Though it was once the principal city on the sound, Tacoma has suffered a bad reputation for years – partly the result of too many pulp mills. But Tacoma has been cleaning up its act, and today it's much nicer than the many Northwest jokes about it would lead you to believe, with some inexpensive accommodations and the largest city park this side of New York City's Central Park.

Olympia is the state capital, a smaller, cozier city that runs on politics but has a surprisingly hip, alternative side. In addition to being a pleasant place to visit in and of itself, Olympia makes a good base from which to explore the Olympic Peninsula, the Pacific coast beaches and Mt Rainier National Park.

## TACOMA & AROUND

Long the object of every other northwestern city's scorn, Tacoma (population 181,200) has been known for years as a beleaguered mill town with a big dome stadium and a bombed out, though architecturally notable, downtown. It didn't take much of a poet to compose the rhyme 'the Tacoma Aroma', but the epitaph stuck: it's the coy euphemism for that certain, not-wholly-pleasant odor the area's pulp mills lend to the air.

However, Tacoma is turning itself around. People who speak ill of this Puget Sound city probably haven't been there recently, or they didn't bother to look beyond the shopping malls. While nobody was paying much attention, artists who found Seattle too expensive have moved their studios south; community activists have renovated old theater buildings and other once-grand downtown structures – including the fabulous Union Station, which has been gussied up and turned into

a federal courthouse. Antique dealers have also taken over a couple of downtown blocks. Add to this an influx of new residents – who have found that Tacoma has just about the only affordable housing on Puget Sound – and all of a sudden, Tacoma starts looking good.

And nobody ever said there was anything wrong with Tacoma's location. Backed up against the foothills of Mt Rainier, and facing onto the fjords of the Puget Sound and the jagged peaks of the Olympic Mountains, Tacoma offers visitors a number of reasons to visit this one-time center of Northwest commerce and culture, including an excellent zoo and aquarium in one of the nation's largest city parks, the state historical museum, the Tacoma Dome (a sports and music stadium that is the world's largest wooden domed structure) and perhaps the most beautiful high school in the country.

### History

Commencement Bay was visited by Captain George Vancouver in 1792, and thereafter by other early explorers. However, the usual settlement pattern of saw mills and farmlands was barely underway when local land speculators began to wager that Tacoma would end up as the Puget Sound rail terminus for the Northern Pacific Railroad, which by the late 1860s was looking for a Northwest port city. While almost every settlement on the Puget Sound went through boom times as speculation rose about where the railroad would end up, Tacoma had a real advantage: Commencement Bay was deep (at that time much of Elliott Bay in Seattle was a mudflat at low tide) and highly protected by the bluffs along Browns Point and Point Defiance.

Tacoma was indeed named the Northern Pacific's western terminus, and trains reached there in 1887; for the next decade Tacoma was the uncontested dominant city on Puget Sound. Ships from Asia docked at the wharves to unload tea and fabrics; trains brought metals, grain, coal, lumber and hops to be exported to the Far East and the boomtowns of California. The trains also brought settlers and skilled laborers to the Northwest, and the waterfront became a warren of factories and mills.

This period of prosperity and limitless self-confidence is best expressed in the monumental architecture of the young city's civic and commercial buildings. Even after a century's worth of razing and modification, the city center still boasts one of the finest enclaves of historic buildings in the Northwest.

Tacoma saw its prominence on Puget Sound diminish as Seattle became linked to the rest of the nation by rails in 1893. Seattle also boomed as Klondike gold, provisions and miners funneled through its ports. By the turn of the century, Seattle had became the financial and cultural center of Washington, while Tacoma became more and more industrial. The wood-products giant Weyerhaeuser brought its mills – and eventually its corporate head-quarters – to Tacoma in the early 1900s,

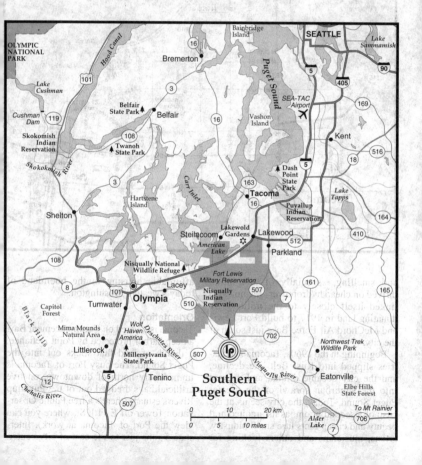

WASHINGTON

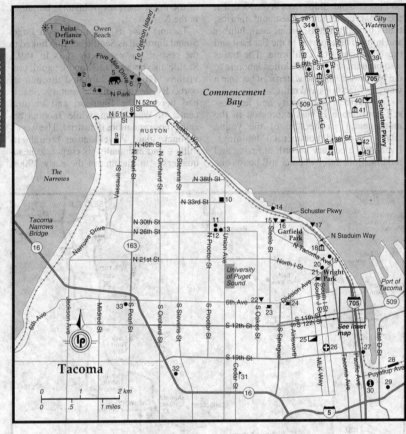

and smelting, especially of aluminum, thrived on cheap hydropower. Tacoma also linked itself closely to the military by donating land in 1917 to build Fort Lewis and McChord Air Force Base just south of the city.

Beginning in the 1960s, Tacoma's industries slipped into Rust Belt-like decline, and the city became diluted and merged into the suburban sprawl of the greater Puget Sound. Today, the city seems at the cusp of a second boom, as its architectural beauty and cheap rents lure small industry, artists, musicians and others looking for affordable housing in the boomland of today's western Washington.

### Orientation

Tacoma is located on Commencement Bay, a deep harbor protected by Point Defiance, a thumb of land that sticks out into the Puget Sound. The busy Port of Tacoma is immediately north of downtown, on five artificial bays dredged out of the Puyallup River's estuary (there's a free Public Observation Tower off E 11th St, where you can view the Port of Tacoma at work). Interstate 5 runs just to the east of city center.

**WASHINGTON**

Tacoma is 32 miles south of Seattle, and 143 miles north of Portland. Highway 16 cuts off from I-5 at Tacoma and crosses the impressive Tacoma Narrows Bridge, leading to Gig Harbor and Bremerton on the Kitsap Peninsula.

A branch of the freeway, called I-705, departs from I-5 at exit No 133 and runs to city center and to the port area. Just to the east is the Tacoma Dome. Point Defiance Park is at the northern end of Tacoma, and is reached from downtown on Ruston Way, which is paralleled by a waterfront walking/biking path. From the end of Pearl St in Point Defiance Park, a ferry departs for Vashon Island.

Pacific Ave, Commerce St and Broadway are the main downtown arterials running north-south; the center of Tacoma is largely encompassed between east-west running 9th and 15th Sts. In general, east-west streets are numbered, north-south streets have names. Another main arterial is Division Ave, which divides north from south in street addresses, and turns into 6th Ave west of downtown.

### Information
**Tourist Office** Look for tourist information at the visitors center (☎ 627-2836, (800) 272-2662) at 24th Ave and B St off I-5 exit No 133.

**Post & Telecommunications** The main post office (☎ 471-6175) is at 4001 S Pine St; more convenient to downtown is the branch at 1102 A St (☎ 471-6101). Tacoma's and Seattle's telephone area codes are still 206, though the rest of western Washington has been changed to 360.

**Bookstores** Book Feire (☎ 759-4680), 3818 N 26th St, is a small full-service bookstore in the Proctor neighborhood.

**Media** To find out what's happening in Tacoma, check out the free *Tacoma's Monthly*. For arts and events, pick up *Choices*. Public radio is heard at 88.5, KPLU FM.

**Laundry** To clean your clothes, head to New Era Laundercenter (☎ 759-3501), 2621 N Proctor St.

**Medical Services** St Joseph's Medical Center (☎ 627-4101) is at 1717 South J St.

### Union Station
Start a tour of downtown Tacoma at Union Station, on Pacific Ave at 19th St. This enormous copper-domed neo-Baroque depot was designed by the same architects who built New York City's Grand Central Station, and it was completed in 1911.

However, by the 1980s, Amtrak had pulled out, Union Station had been boarded up, and the surrounding red-brick warehouse neighborhood had become quite creepy, to say the least. The graceful train depot was renovated in the early '90s and now houses the federal courts. Next door, an entirely new building is being constructed in the same domed style to house the Washington State Historical Society Museum. (The museum is set to move into this new building in 1996.)

Step inside the airy Union Station rotunda, which is dominated by several massive installations of glass art by Tacoma-native Dale Chihuly. Hanging from the center of the rotunda is a translucent, three-story cluster of sensuous, deep-blue grapes; in the north-facing rosette is a collage of poppy red glass. (Chihuly is re-establishing such strong ties in Tacoma that backers are attempting to build him a $5 million studio across the tracks from Union Station.)

**Tacoma Art Museum**

After seeing the glass installation at Union Station, you'll probably want to see more of Chihuly's work. The **Tacoma Art Museum** (☎ 272-4258), at 12th St and Pacific Ave, has a permanent display of some of Chihuly's more intimate works, as well as a gallery devoted to traveling shows. The museum is open from 10 am to 5 pm Tuesday, Wednesday, Friday and Saturday, from 10 am to 7 pm Thursday, and from noon to 5 pm Sunday. Admission is $3 for adults and $1 for children; students and seniors are $2.

**Broadway Theater District**

Things began to look up for Tacoma's arts scene when the ornate **Pantages Theater**, 909 Broadway, was renovated in 1983, and now the blocks surrounding the Pantages are abuzz with a lively gentrification. The Pantages was once an elaborate vaudeville hall, famed for its acoustics; today it's Tacoma's primary performance stage. Together with the refurbished **Rialto Theater** at the corner of Market and 9th Sts

and the **Theatre on the Square**, 915 Broadway, these theaters are the primary components of the Broadway Center for the Performing Arts complex (see Entertainment below).

In the midst of the theater district is the **Children's Museum of Tacoma** (☎ 627-2436), 925 Court C, a hands-on activity center specializing in science & technology exhibits for kids. It's open from 10 am to 5 pm Tuesday to Friday, from 10 am to 4 pm Saturday, and from noon to 4 pm Sunday. Call for extended summer hours. Admission is $3 per person.

Directly north of 9th St on Broadway is **Antique Row**, a two-block-long maze of antique and collectibles shops, which antique lovers shouldn't miss. Along Broadway in the antique district, a **farmer's market** sets up every Thursday from June through September. South on Broadway to 13th St is **Broadway Plaza**, a 1960s urban renewal project in the form of a pedestrian mall.

**Stadium District**

The Stadium neighborhood has always been Tacoma's nicest, and a walk down N Tacoma Ave from Garfield Park turns up a number of nice **Victorian homes**. Turn down Division Ave and head to Wright Park at Division Ave and South G St, where the ornate, domed **Seymour Botanical Conservatory** (☎ 591-5330), 316 S G St, is filled with tropical plants in the middle of a park full of native Douglas firs. The conservatory is open from 8 am to 4:20 pm daily.

The most amazing structure in this genteel old neighborhood is the turreted, ivy-covered **Stadium High School**, at the corner of N 1st St and Broadway, near the historical museum. Construction began in 1891, when the building was conceived as a monumental luxury hotel. However, a series of economic calamities waylaid the hotel's completion, and by 1902 the unfinished Chateau-esque structure was slated to be dismantled. However, alert citizens petitioned to convert the building into a badly needed high school. The result is one of the most eye-catching and architecturally imposing public schools anywhere.

## Washington Historical Society Museum

Located across a playing field from Stadium High School, and overlooking Commencement Bay, this is the state's leading museum of history (☎ 593-2830), 315 N Stadium Way. The primary exhibit is 'Washington: Home, Frontier, Crossroads', a chronological examination of the history of Washington, beginning with Native Americans and moving through the settlement era and up to the present. Particularly well done are the exhibits relating to the Northwest coastal tribes. A new display called 'Baskets' beautifully displays more of Dale Chihuly's large, incredibly luminous glass works. Other galleries are devoted to changing exhibits, often the works of regional photographers. The lobby contains a good bookstore with an excellent selection of Northwest history and travel books, as well as a selection of quality crafts and gifts. It's open from 10 am to 5 pm Tuesday to Saturday, and from 1 to 5 pm Sunday. Admission is $2.50 for adults and $2 for seniors; children are $1 and families are $6; children under five are free.

Plans call for the museum to move sometime in 1996 to a new location directly south of the Union Station. Call ahead for current information.

## Point Defiance Park

One of Tacoma's preeminent attractions, this 700-acre park (☎ 305-1000), flanked by the waters of Puget Sound, contains a wealth of gardens, the city zoo and aquarium, and a number of recreational and historic sites.

The park contains 13.7 miles of hiking trails, which wind through groves of old-growth forests and lead to sheltered beaches. (You probably shouldn't hike the trails alone after dark.) The main paved road through the park is called Five Mile Drive; on Saturday this scenic road remains closed to motor vehicles until 1 pm, though it's open to bicycles, joggers and in-line skaters. Bicyclists are not allowed on any hiking trails, but must stay on the paved bike paths. Popular picnic areas include **Gig Harbor Viewpoint** and **Owen Beach**, which is a favorite of summer sunbathers.

Formal gardens are abundant at Point Defiance Park and are maintained cooperatively by members of local garden clubs, with help from the Metropolitan Park District. Park gardens include the **Japanese Garden**, with a Torii Gate and Shinto Shrine received as a gift from Kitakyushu, Tacoma's sister city, the **Herb Garden** and the **Rhododendron Garden**, a blaze of color in May. Just past the zoo entrance on Five Mile Drive is the civic **Rose Garden**, established in 1895, with more than an acre of bushes, many of heirloom varieties. A new addition is the **Iris Garden**, a small circular bed across from the **Dahlia Trial Garden**. The **Northwest Native Garden**, located near the park's main exit, presents a collection of indigenous plants ranging from trees to grasses.

The **Boathouse Marina** offers moorage and boat rentals, and it sports a restaurant, *The Boathouse Grill* (☎ 756-7336), and a tackle shop. Find additional moorage and shower facilities at Breakwater Marina, east of the Vashon Island ferry dock.

To reach the park from downtown, take Schuster Parkway north and turn onto Ruston Way; it's about five miles to the park. From I-5, take exit No 132 and follow Hwy 16 to 6th Ave. Turn right on Pearl St, and follow Pearl St north three miles to the park entrance.

## Point Defiance Zoo & Aquarium This
award-winning zoo (☎ 591-5337) is often considered one of the best in the USA. It's unusual in that it focuses primarily on species from the Pacific Rim, including polar bears, musk ox and Arctic fox at the Arctic Tundra exhibit. Peer at coastline mammals through the underwater windows at Rocky Shores. No less than 30 huge sharks swim among tropical fish and eels in the lagoon at Discovery Reef Aquarium. A special exhibit, 'Sharks: The Survivors', is

full of facts and activities aimed at destroying negative stereotypes about sharks. Elephants and apes and other zoo favorites are housed in the Southeast Asia complex. It's open from 10 am to 4 pm daily. Admission is $6.75 for adults and $6.25 for seniors; children ages five to 17 are $5 and preschoolers (three to four) are $2.50.

**Fort Nisqually Historic Site** In 1833, the Hudson's Bay Company trading post at Fort Nisqually was established 17 miles south of Tacoma near DuPont. This restoration of the HBC fort (☎ 591-5339) includes the factor's house, granary, trade store, blacksmith shop, laborer's quarters and corner bastions, all furnished to reflect life on the frontier in the 1850s at the height of the old fort's prominence. Nineteenth-century fur-trade artifacts are on exhibit in the small museum. Docents in period clothing demonstrate blacksmithing, spinning, beadwork and black powder.

Fort Nisqually is open from noon to 6 pm daily, Memorial Day through Labor Day, with adult/child admissions at $1.25/75¢. The rest of the year, the fort is open from 1 to 4 pm Wednesday through Sunday, and admission is free.

**Camp 6 Logging Museum** An open-air logging museum, Camp 6 (☎ 752-0047) is a reconstruction of a pioneer logging camp focusing on the steam-powered equipment used from the 1880s to the 1940s. On spring and summer weekends only, ride on a logging train with a steam locomotive. In the summer, indoor exhibits are open from 10 am to 6 pm Wednesday to Friday, and from 10 am to 7 pm Saturday, Sunday and holidays. From January to March and in October, it's open from 10 am to 4 pm Wednesday to Sunday, April to May from 10 am to 5 pm Wednesday to Sunday.

**Never Never Land** If the kids didn't enjoy the steam donkey at Camp 6, then this 10-acre, storyland theme park (☎ 591-5845) in an outdoor forest setting might tickle their fancy. Wooded paths lead to oversized sculpted figures of nursery-rhyme charac-

ters; on summer weekends, kids can meet real costumed characters, such as Humpty Dumpty, Peter Rabbit, the Big Bad Wolf and Little Red Riding Hood. It's open from 11 am to 6 pm daily May to Labor Day, and from 11 am to 5 pm on weekends only in early spring and September. Admission is $2.75 for adults and $1.25 for children.

**Lakewold Gardens**
The Lakewold Gardens (☎ 584-3360), 12317 Gravelly Lake Drive, on a 10-acre estate from the 1900s, is one of the Northwest's finest private gardens. Landscape architects from the Olmsted Bros firm, who also planned New York City's Central Park, were involved in the original planning of the garden, and in the successive 90 years it has evolved into a mature woodland estate. Especially notable are the rhododendrons, which number in the hundreds, exotic trees chosen for their multicolored and many-shaped foliage, and a formal garden with roses, statuary, fountains and parterres.

The garden is open from 10 am to 4 pm Thursday to Monday, April to September; in the off-season from 10 am to 3 pm on Monday, Thursday and Friday. Admission is $6 for adults and $5 for children (under 12) and seniors. To get to the gardens, take I-5 south to exit No 124, which leads onto Gravelly Lake Drive.

**Northwest Trek Wildlife Park**
This wildlife park (☎ 847-1901, (800) 433-8735) allows Northwest native wildlife to roam freely on a 600-acre site. Species like grizzly bears, cougars and wolves live in large natural outdoor enclosures; bison, elk, deer and caribou range pretty much as they see fit in a 435-acre meadow and forest. Trams circle through much of the park, with naturalists leading an hour-long tour. While wildlife parks like this may bring back nightmare memories of mom-and-pop zoos with animals in stinky runs, Northwest Trek is well done and is administered by the Park Bureau of Tacoma. In addition to the wildlife areas, there's a cafe and gift shop on the facility; picnic areas are available.

At the **Cheney Discovery Center**, children learn about environmental issues and watch bees in a glass-sided hive; there's also a supervised touch tank with live reptiles and amphibians.

Northwest Trek is located 35 miles south of Tacoma, north of Eatonville off Hwy 161 at 11610 Trek Drive E (take I-5 south to Hwy 512 east, which leads to Hwy 161 south). The park is open from 9:30 am to dusk daily, March through October. The rest of the year the park is open Friday, Saturday and Sunday only, the same hours. Admission is $7.75 for adults and $6.75 for seniors; youth ages five to 17 are $5.25, and children (three and four) are $3.25.

### Steilacoom

Steilacoom is Washington's oldest incorporated town, founded in 1851 by a New England sea captain. After the establishment of a hotel, store and sawmill, the little town was up and running, and for a couple decades it was an important settlement for newly arriving settlers. It didn't take long for nearby Tacoma to overwhelm the little village, especially after the railroad brought a galloping pace of development to the area.

The old town center boasts 32 buildings on the National Register of Historic Places, most dating from the late 1800s; many buildings are open for viewing. Check out the original furnishings and artifacts of the **Nathaniel Orr Home & Pioneer Orchard** (☎ 584-4133), built between 1854 and 1857, open from 1 to 4 pm on Sundays, April through September. There's a **pioneer museum** in the town hall, open from 1 to 4 pm Tuesday to Sunday, March to October, and open Friday to Sunday the rest of the year except January, when it's closed. Admission to the above museums is by donation.

The **Steilacoom Tribal Cultural Center** (☎ 584-6308), 1515 Lafayette St, commemorates the history of the local Salish tribe. The museum consists of three exhibition galleries, a gift shop and a snack bar serving Native American foods. The center is open from 10 am to 4 pm Tuesday

to Sunday. Admission for adults is $2, for seniors and students $1; families are $6.

Steilacoom is 15 miles south of Tacoma on the Puget Sound. From I-5, take exit No 128, and turn west, following Steilacoom Rd.

### Fort Lewis Military Museum

Fort Lewis is a large army training camp that was established in 1917 as the USA entered WW I. Pacific Northwest military history from Lewis and Clark onward is retold at the Military Museum (☎ 967-7206) in Fort Lewis off I-5 exit No 120.

One of the most notable features of the museum – most of which consists of old uniforms and equipment – is the museum building itself. The chalet-like structure was built in 1919 by the Salvation Army as a 150-room inn to provide R&R for local military personnel and their guests, and it served as the social center of the fort for decades. The museum is open from noon to 4 pm Wednesday to Sunday; admission is free.

### Activities

If you're headed to Point Defiance Park looking for exercise, Bike & Blade rents big and little wheels from a street-side booth along Ruston Way, a block or two north of 30th St. Hiking and camping gear is available for rent or purchase from Backpackers Supply & Outlet (☎ 472-4402), 5206 S Tacoma Ave.

Both convenient and challenging, Allenmore Public Golf Club (☎ 627-7211), 2125 S Cedar St, is a well established 18-hole **golf** course just west of downtown. To **swim**, go to People's Center Pool (☎ 591-5323), 1602 Martin Luther King, Jr Way, open year round.

### Places to Stay

**Camping** Five miles northeast of downtown Tacoma (off Hwy 509) is *Dash Point State Park* (☎ 593-2206), a beachfront state park with both tent sites ($10) and trailer hook-ups ($14). This is a popular place in summer, when the water warms up enough for swimming. Across the Hwy 16 Narrows

Bridge is *Gig Harbor RV Resort* (☎ 858-8138), in Gig Harbor at 9515 Burnham Drive. Hook-ups ($21) and tent sites ($19) are available, as well as a pool, laundry and playground.

**B&Bs** *Bay Vista B&B* (☎ 759-8084), 4617 Darien Drive N (off 46th St), is near Point Defiance and the Vashon Island ferry; it has one suite and a bedroom for $65 to $75. *Commencement Bay B&B* (☎ 752-8175), 3312 N Union Ave, overlooks the bay and offers three guest rooms (two share a bathroom); there's even an office with a modem hook-up for business travelers. Rooms rates range from $70 to $85 in peak season.

For other B&Bs in Tacoma, contact Greater Tacoma B&B Reservations by phone at 759-4088. There's no added charge to make reservations using this service.

**Hotels** If you're on a budget, you can save a little money by staying in Tacoma and commuting half an hour up to Seattle. However, almost all lodgings in Tacoma are now located along the freeway and don't offer much in the way of charm. Just east of Tacoma in Fife there are several, but the *Econo Lodge at the Port of Tacoma* (☎ 922-0550, (800) 424-4777), off I-5 exit No 136 at 3518 Pacific Hwy, has the best rates in the area. There's an outdoor pool and guest laundry, pets allowed; singles/doubles are $30/36.

South of Tacoma, between I-5 exits No 128 and 129, are a clutch of motels. The most attractive of these is the *Best Western Tacoma Inn* (☎ 535-2880), 8726 S Hosmer St, with a courtyard pool, putting green and guest laundry. Rooms begin at $58/64. Next door the *Tacoma Travelodge* (☎ 539-1153), 8820 S Hosmer St, has rooms at $50/60.

About the only place to stay downtown is the *Sheraton Tacoma Hotel* (☎ 572-3200), 1320 Broadway Plaza, a convention-style hotel with rooms starting at $99/$109, and suites from $140.

**Places to Eat**

For something hip and inexpensive, go to *Cafe Wa* (☎ 383-3465), at the corner of 6th and State Sts, for coffee, sandwiches and pizza. At *Leslie's Southern Kitchen* (☎ 627-4282), 1716 6th Ave, a transplanted southerner cooks up catfish and great corn cakes; nearly everything is under $9. This is a great place to come for a hearty breakfast. In Ruston, on the way to Point Defiance Park, *Antique Sandwich Company* (☎ 752-4069), 5102 N Pearl St, is a landmark luncheonette filled with students, young families and seniors who have been regulars for decades.

As in nearby Seattle, Italian food has become the dining standard. The southern Italian meals at *Zeppo* (☎ 627-1009), 100 S 9th St at Dock St, have a contemporary touch; pasta with artichokes and fresh herbs goes for about $15. *Grazie* (☎ 627-0231), 2301 N 30th St, is another Italian hangout with great views of Commencement Bay; northern Italian specialties with veal, chicken and pasta are in the $12 to $16 range.

One of Tacoma's originals, *Harbor Lights* (☎ 752-4600), 2761 Ruston Way, is a former fishermen's eatery. The clientele has changed, but not the excellent quality, the old-fashioned seafood preparations or the enormous workingman's portions. Call ahead for reservations.

Out in Point Defiance Park, the *Boat House Grill* (☎ 756-7336), near the park's Pearl St entrance, has great views over Commencement Bay, and is a great place for a drink and a light meal.

**Entertainment**

**Coffeehouses** *Temple of the Bean* (☎ 383-5720), 817 Division Ave, is right across from Wright Park and has the feel of a neighborhood hangout. *Shakabrah Java* (☎ 572-4369), 2602 6th Ave, offers a fine selection of loose-leaf teas as well as the standard coffee drinks; it has living room with board games. *Cicero's* (☎ 272-2122), 2123 N 30th St, offers a place to swill lattes and enjoy great muffins with the upper middle class.

**Cinemas** For off-beat and foreign films, the restored *Blue Mouse Theatre* (☎ 752-9500), 2611 N Proctor St, is the place to go (the cool neon on the marquee was designed by omnipresent Dale Chihuly). Art films are shown at the *Rialto Theater* (☎ 572-5670), 310 9th St, as part of the Broadway Center series.

**Theater** Tacoma has a long history of live theater. Tacoma Actors Guild (☎ 272-2145) makes its home at the *Theatre on the Square* (☎ 591-5890), 915 Broadway. The *Tacoma Little Theater* (☎ 272-2481), a community theater group since 1909, stages both children and adult productions at 210 N I St. In the summertime, outdoor drama and comedy productions are staged at Celebrations Meadow in Gig Harbor by the Performance Circle (☎ 851-7529).

**Performing Arts** The *Broadway Center for the Performing Arts* (☎ 591-5890), 901 Broadway, brings music, dance and theater to town. Shows are staged at the restored and opulent, 1100-seat Pantages Theater (☎ 591-5894), 901 Broadway, and at the Rialto Theater (☎ 572-5670), 310 9th St at Market St. The *Tacoma Opera* (☎ 627-7789) is a community opera company, with all works sung in English. The *Tacoma Philharmonic* (☎ 591-5890) is a presenting organization that brings outside symphony orchestras to the Pantages. *BalleTacoma* (☎ 272-9631) performs at Pantages, while the local *Tacoma Symphony* (☎ 591-5894) and the *Tacoma Youth Symphony* (☎ 627-2792) both perform at the Rialto.

**Nightlife** *Java Jive* (☎ 475-9844) is on S Tacoma Way along an unattractive strip of car dealerships. Quite the institution in Tacoma, this pre-fab, larger-than-life coffeepot was built in 1927 by veterinarian Dr Button. Primarily a restaurant, the Jive served its days as a speakeasy – the entrance was through the ladies' room. Today the place is a scream of tacky furniture, pool tables, jukeboxes and a menu of cheap sanwiches, burgers and domestic beer.

*Engine House No 9* (☎ 272-3435), 611 N Pine St by 6th St, has a great selection of beers and ciders on tap. A pitcher costs $7.50, a pint about $3. They also have a full menu, including sandwiches, pizzas and salads – none of which are over $6.50. The Engine House (it really was a fire engine house) is open daily from 11 am to 2 am.

*Katie Downs* (☎ 756-0771) along the Waterfront at 3211 Rustin Way, is a popular place to grab a beer (they have 22 kinds on tap) and a pizza or some steamer clams. There is seating on an outdoor deck with a great view of the Sound. Reservations are taken but not for the nighttime, nor for deck seating. It's open daily from 11 am to midnight.

**Spectator Sports** Tacoma Tigers (☎ 752-7700, (800) 281-3834) is a Triple-A farm team of baseball's Oakland As; they play at lovely Cheney Stadium, Hwy 16 at Stevens St. The Tacoma Rockets (☎ 627-3653), of the Western Hockey League, play in the Tacoma Dome, off East D St.

### Getting There & Away
**Air** Tacoma is served by Sea-Tac Airport, 15 miles north on I-5. Sea-Tac is the largest airport in the Northwest, and it's served by a wide selection of domestic and international airlines. For more information on air service to Sea-Tac, see Seattle.

**Bus** Greyhound (☎ 383-4621), 1319 Pacific Ave, links Tacoma to other cities along the I-5 corridor. Also, regional buses leave from the bus station for Port Angeles and Port Townsend; call the Greyhound number for information.

**Train** Four Amtrak trains a day link Tacoma to Seattle and Portland from the depot (☎ 627-8141) at 1001 Puyallup Ave.

**Ferry** Sailings to Vashon Island via the Point Defiance-Tahlequah Ferry run daily from about 5 am to midnight. Vehicle/driver fares are $8 to $10, foot passenger fares are $2.30. For information on Washington State Ferries, call (800) 843-3779.

**Car** For a rental vehicle, contact either Enterprise (☎ 566-6480), 5973 6th Ave, or Budget (☎ 383-4944), 1305 Pacific Ave in downtown Tacoma.

## Getting Around

To get to and from the airport, Capital Aeroporter (☎ 927-6179) offers 15 buses daily between Tacoma-area stops and Sea-Tac. A one-way fare is $13; the downtown stop is at the Sheraton, 1320 Broadway.

The local bus system is called Pierce Transit (☎ 581-8000, (800) 562-8109), with service throughout the Tacoma area. Buses to note are the No 11, which runs from downtown to Point Defiance Park and the Vashon Island ferry, and the No 100, which runs out to Gig Harbor. Pierce Transit also operates a number of express buses throughout the day to Seattle center.

For a taxi, call Yellow Cab (☎ 472-3303).

## OLYMPIA & AROUND

Olympia is a city known to most for its beer and its politics, and as such, it may not initially seem like an obvious magnet for travelers. As Washington's oldest settlement and the state capital, Olympia (population 36,520) could easily be just another one of those sleepy 'insiders only' towns whose most interesting moments were 100 years ago. In fact, Olympia is a vital city – together with sister cities Lacey and Tumwater, the urban area has a population of over 90,000 – with a strong alternative community.

Of course, part of the reason for the vitality of Olympia is the state capital, which keeps political issues in the forefront. But no small part of the equation is Evergreen State College, an innovative public university with 3100 students, which was founded in 1971 at the height of the student movements of the '60s. Classes, programs and degrees are usually interdisciplinary, multi-ethnic and relatively unstructured, attracting students and faculty with progressive, out-of-the-mainstream ideas. When you find that Olympia offers better music, cinema, coffee and just-under-the-surface hipness than you might expect, thank Evergreen.

Olympia makes a good center for exploration of western Washington. Both Mt Rainier and Olympic national parks are within an hour's drive, and Pacific coast beaches are just 60 miles away at Ocean Shores.

## History

The lower reaches of the Puget Sound were home to the Nisqually, a Salish tribe. The Nisqually were unlike most coastal tribes in that they maintained large herds of horses, which they pastured in the lowlands in the Nisqually River valley. Leschi was chief of the Nisqually when the first explosion of White settlers moved into the Puget Sound area; he led a group of local tribes who attacked the early residents of Seattle in 1855. He was hanged in 1858, and the tribe was moved onto a small reservation along the Nisqually River.

The first US settlement in Washington was at Tumwater, along the falls of the Deschutes River. A group of 32 Missourians arrived here in 1845, choosing to settle north of the Columbia in British-dominated territory, as some members of the party were partly African American – including the group's leader, George Bush – and Oregon's territorial laws forbade settlement by blacks. Access to water power and to the harbor at Budd Inlet propelled the new settlement into industrialization. By 1850, the settlement (then called New Market) boasted a grist and saw mill, tannery and other small factories. Brewing was an early industry here as well. The original brewery in Tumwater was called Capital Brewing Company; in 1905, the company was bought out and renamed the Olympia Brewing Company.

Olympia was Washington's principal settlement when the village was named the territorial capital in 1853. The first meetings of the territory's legislature met above a bar, then were moved to a local Masonic lodge. The building of a permanent capitol building was not begun until 1893; however, due to economic vicissitudes, the capitol was not completed until 1928. During much of this time, the old Thurston County Courthouse served as Washington's state capitol.

## Orientation

Olympia is at the southern end of the Puget Sound. Immediately south of Olympia is Tumwater, and east is Lacey; these three separate towns make up an urban entity often referred to as the South Sound. Due to its location, Olympia is a division point for a number of road systems. Interstate 5 loops through, running between Seattle (60

miles) and Portland (114 miles). Highway 101 runs north and west, leading to the Hood Canal and Olympic Peninsula; Port Angeles is 121 miles. Off of Hwy 101, Hwy 8 to Aberdeen (50 miles) also leads out from Olympia.

Olympia is dominated by the Washington State Capitol, which rises on a bluff above Capitol Lake (formed by damming the Deschutes River), Budd Inlet and downtown. Interstate 5 exit No 105 loops around and turns into 14th Ave and leads directly to the capitol and to Capitol Way, the main north-south street through down-

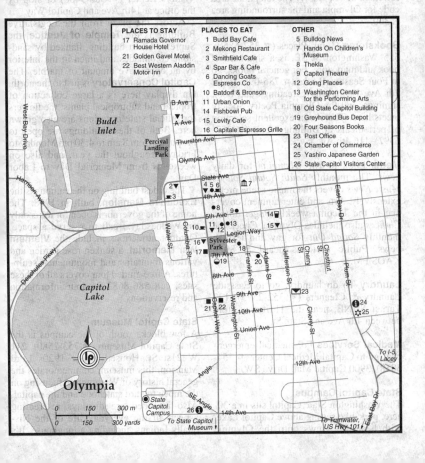

**PLACES TO STAY**
17 Ramada Governor House Hotel
21 Golden Gavel Motel
22 Best Western Aladdin Motor Inn

**PLACES TO EAT**
1 Budd Bay Cafe
2 Mekong Restaurant
3 Smithfield Cafe
4 Spar Bar & Cafe
6 Dancing Goats Espresso Co
10 Batdorf & Bronson
11 Urban Onion
14 Fishbowl Pub
15 Levity Cafe
16 Capitale Espresso Grille

**OTHER**
5 Bulldog News
7 Hands On Children's Museum
8 Thekla
9 Capitol Theatre
12 Going Places
13 Washington Center for the Performing Arts
18 Old State Capitol Building
19 Greyhound Bus Depot
20 Four Seasons Books
23 Post Office
24 Chamber of Commerce
25 Yashiro Japanese Garden
26 State Capitol Visitors Center

Olympia

town. The main commercial area of Olympia is around 4th and 5th Aves along Capitol Way.

## Information

**Tourist Offices** Olympia/Thurston Chamber of Commerce (☎ 357-3362, (800) 753-8474) is at 1000 Plum St SE. The State Capitol Visitors Center (☎ 586-3460) is right off the freeway at 14th Ave and Capitol Way.

**Post & Telecommunications** Olympia's central post office (☎ 357-2286) is at 900 Jefferson St SE, 98507. The telephone area code for Olympia and the surrounding area is 360.

**Bookstores** Going Places (☎ 357-6860), 515 Washington St SE, is a small travel book and map store. For general books, go to Four Seasons Books (☎ 786-0952), 302 7th Ave E; they have readings and book signings, and the Olympia Poetry Society meets here. There's an excellent selection of periodicals at Bulldog News (☎ 357-6397), 116 4th Ave E.

**Media** Look to *The Olympian* for daily news. The monthly *South Sound Sounds Music News* covers the music scene pretty extensively. Arts and entertainment coverage in the Tacoma weekly *Puget Sound Choices* also includes Olympia. Check the monthly *Sound Out* for gay and lesbian news. Public radio is heard at 89.3, KAOS FM.

**Laundry** To do laundry, go to Eastside Laundry & Cleaners (☎ 352-2575), 122 Turner St NE, near the Thriftway store between 4th Ave and State St.

**Medical Services** For medical emergencies, go to Capital Medical Center (☎ 754-5858), 3900 Capital Mall Drive SW.

## State Capitol Campus

The Washington State Capitol sits in a 30-acre, park-like setting above Capitol Lake, with beautiful views onto the Olympic Mountains across Budd Inlet. This campus holds the majority of the state's official buildings, including the vast domed **Legislative Building**, completed in 1927. At the time of its construction, the capitol's 287-foot dome was the fourth largest in the world (exceeded only by the US Capitol, St Paul's in London, and St Peter's in Rome); the chandelier hanging in the rotunda was made by Louis Tiffany. The Legislative Building is open daily; admission is free. Tours are usually offered on the hour from 9 am to 4 pm. To find out about tours and for general information, call the Capitol Visitors Center (☎ 586-3460) or stop by the office at 14th Ave and Capitol Way.

Across the plaza from the Legislative Building is the **Temple of Justice**, the Supreme Court building, flanked by sandstone colonnades and lined in the interior by an oppressive amount of marble. The **Capitol Conservatory** is just to the north. On display here is a large collection of tropical and subtropical plants; the flowers for official state occasions are also grown here. Both of these buildings are open to the public from 8 am to 4:30 pm Monday to Friday throughout the year, and also on weekends from Memorial Day to Labor Day.

The oldest building on the campus is the **Executive Mansion**, built in 1908. The home of the governor is open for tours only on Wednesdays; call to reserve a space. Outdoor attractions include the **Vietnam War Memorial**, a sunken rose garden and various fountains and monumental sculptures. A free guided tour covers all of these sites; call 586-8687 for tour information and reservations.

## State Capitol Museum

A few blocks south of the campus is the State Capitol Museum (☎ 753-2580), 211 W 21st St. Housed in the 1920s Lord Mansion, this museum commemorates the general history of Washington, focusing on the move toward statehood and the capital. Also included are displays re-creating aspects of the everyday life of the Nisqually Indians, including a longhouse. It's open from 10 am to 4 pm Tuesday to Friday, and from noon to 4 pm Saturday and Sunday. Admission is by donation.

## Olympia Brewery

Forget regional microbrews for a moment and tour one of the West's largest breweries. The Olympia Brewery (☎ 754-5177) has been producing beer since 1896 (though in 1993 the brewery was bought by Pabst), and the brewery ranks right with state government as the city's largest employer. The free 40-minute tour through the fermentation tanks to the tasting room and gift shop is actually quite interesting. The brewery is located on Capitol Blvd, immediately east of I-5 exit No 103 in Tumwater; you can't miss it. It's open from 8 am to 4:30 pm daily except major holidays.

## Old State Capitol Building

In 1903, under the leadership of Populist governor John Rogers, the state government recycled the 1891 Thurston County Courthouse by turning it into the state capitol for nearly 25 years, while the current Legislative Building was very slowly being built. In its heyday, the Romanesque Revival structure was even more commanding: its nine-story central tower burned in 1928, and the building's 11 turrets fell off the building during a 1949 earthquake. The old capitol is now the office for the State Superintendent of Public Instruction; it's open for self-guided tours, or groups can call ahead for a guided tour (☎ 753-6725). The old capitol, at 600 S Washington St across from Sylvester Park, is open for visitors from 9 to 11:30 am and from 1 to 4:30 pm Monday to Friday.

## Tumwater Historical Park

This park, at the lowest of the three falls on the Deschutes River, is situated at the site of Olympia's original pioneer settlement and offers a playground, picnic area and nature trail along the river. Although the passage of I-5 through this historic corridor has meant the destruction of many of the

area's old homes and buildings, a few remain. The **Henderson House Museum** (☎ 753-8583), on Deschutes Way in the park, contains artifacts and displays of pioneer life and early industry in Tumwater. Adjacent is **Crosby House**, a museum commemorating one of Olympia's first families. In 1847, 24 members of the Crosby family arrived from Maine, almost doubling the White population of the Tumwater/Olympia area. The Crosby House was built in 1858 and was the home of Nathaniel Crosby III, grandfather of Bing Crosby. Both museums are open from noon to 4 pm Thursday to Sunday.

## Percival Landing Park

When Olympia was established, its narrow harbor was a mudflat during low tides: after years of dredging, Olympia harbor is still small potatoes compared to the engines of commerce at Tacoma and Seattle. This park, on Water St between Thurston St and 4th Ave, is essentially a boardwalk along the harbor, which is used mostly as a marina by pleasure boats. It's a pleasant half-mile walk, especially when the Olympic Mountains sparkle across the bay. At the north end of the boardwalk is an observation tower, from which one can see logs being loaded onto freighters at the Port of Olympia. At the 4th St end of the waterfront is a locally noted statue called *The Kiss*, which you don't need to see to imagine.

The park is the site of a number of festivities, including the Olympia Farmers Market and Harbor Days, when vessels as different as tug boats and Native American cedar canoes fill the harbor.

## Olympia Farmers Market

One of the pleasures of summer in Olympia is the Olympia Farmers Market (☎ 352-9096), in Percival Landing Park. The market offers fresh local produce, crafts and food booths, and opens the first weekend in May for its regular hours (from 10 am to 3 pm, Thursday through Sunday) and remains open until the first weekend of November.

### Yashiro Japanese Garden

This small, relatively new garden is a collaborative effort between Olympia and its Japanese sister city, Yashiro. Highlights include a bamboo grove, pagoda and a pond and waterfall; the grounds include stone lanterns and other gifts from Yashiro. The garden is near Plum St and Union Ave, next to the chamber of commerce building. The garden is open daily during daylight hours. Admission is free.

### Hands On Children's Museum

Kids will be enthralled by this new children's activity center (☎ 956-0818) at 108 Franklin St NE. Exhibits include a simulated tide pool, make-believe seafood diner and 'underseas' film theater – but what kids of today really enjoy is playing on the computers and the multimedia CD-ROM programs. The museum is open from 10 am to 5 pm Tuesday to Saturday. Admission is $2.50.

### Nisqually National Wildlife Refuge

The estuary of the Nisqually River has been set aside as a preserve for wildlife, particularly for waterfowl and shorebirds. The diverse habitat at the refuge, which includes saltwater and freshwater marshes, tide flats, grasslands and woodlands, is home to over 300 species of wildlife; about 20,000 migratory waterfowl winter here.

A number of hikes, ranging from a half mile to over five miles, lead out from the refuge parking area. For more information and a wildlife checklist, stop by the refuge headquarters (☎ 753-9467) at 100 Brown Farm Rd (take I-5 north to exit No 114). The wildlife area is open during daylight hours; there is a $2 entry fee per family.

### Wolf Haven America

Wolf Haven America is a 75-acre wolf rehabilitation center and permanent home for nearly 40 wolves no longer able to live in the wild. Associated with the center is the nonprofit Wolf Haven International (☎ 264-4695, (800) 448-9653), which offers programs, tours and ecology classes at the interpretive center, all designed to

Gray wolves once inhabited most of North America, but are now found only in Canada and the northernmost parts of the USA.

provide a better understanding of the much-maligned wolf.

Tours of the grounds are available on the hour. The center is open daily from 10 am to 5 pm, May through September, and from 10 am to 4 pm Wednesday to Sunday, October through April. Admission is $5 for adults and $2.50 for children ages five to 12. From May through September, there's the special Summer Howl, an evening campfire program from 6 to 9 pm on Friday and Saturday. Admission to Summer Howl costs $6 for adults and $4 for children.

To reach Wolf Haven from Olympia, take I-5 south to exit No 102 and follow signs to Tenino on Capitol Blvd. Continue south (the street becomes Old Hwy 99) about six miles and follow the signs; the center is located 1111 Offut Lake Rd.

### Mima Mounds Natural Area

These geologic curiosities – acres and acres of dimpled prairies – once covered much of the lowlands around the southern Puget Sound. Early explorers assumed that these six to eight-foot-high, 20 to 30-foot-wide, earth mounds were burial chambers; however, modern researchers believe they are the result of ancient pocket gophers or ice-age freeze-thaw patterns. Whatever caused these mounds, they are certainly very odd.

The Nature Conservancy bought one of the last remaining tracts of Mima Mounds (most have been leveled and plowed as farmland) and released the land to the state for preservation. The Mima Mounds Natural Area Preserve encompasses a 500-acre clearing containing thousands of mounds. A number of trails wind through the mounds, including a half-mile nature trail; the preserve is especially interesting during the spring wildflower season, when the area is carpeted with blooms. There's also an informational kiosk and picnic tables. It's only open during daylight hours; no overnight camping.

To reach the Mima Mounds, take I-5 exit No 95 south of Olympia and turn west on Hwy 121 toward Littlerock. From Littlerock, follow 128th Ave SW one mile to the T-junction with Waddell Creek Rd. Turn north one mile to the preserve. For more information on the Mima Mounds Natural Area, contact the Washington Department of Natural Resources at (206) 748-2383.

### Golf

There are a number of good golf courses around Olympia. Two 18-hole courses to check out are Indian Summer Golf Course (☎ 923-1075), 4009 Yelm Hwy SE, in a garden-like setting, and Capitol City Golf Club (☎ 491-5111), 5225 Yelm Hwy SE (take Capitol Way south of Olympia). It's one of the best winter courses in the Puget Sound area.

### Special Events

Olympia starts its spring festival season off with Artburst/Artwalk (☎ 753-8380), an arts & crafts fair held at several downtown locations in late April. Watch for special displays and exhibits, as well as discussions and events.

Throughout the summer, the Music in the Park & Music in the Dark series (☎ 943-2375) takes place in Sylvester Park in front of the Old State Capitol on Washington St and Legion Way. Concerts are

held Friday at noon and Wednesday at 7 pm, mid July to the end of August.

Olympia's big summer festival is Harbor Days (☎ 754-4567), held on Labor Day weekend, when Percival Landing Park becomes the site of various maritime events, like tub boat races and food and craft booths.

### Places to Stay

**Camping** *Olympia Campground* (☎ 352-2552), 1441 83rd Ave SW (off I-5 exit No 101), promises shady sites and good TV reception. Among the full-service amenities are a heated pool, free showers, game room and movie rentals. Tents cost $16, hook-ups cost $21 and camper cabins are also offered. It's open year round. Only blocks away, and with similar facilities, is *American Heritage Campground* (☎ 943-8778), 9610 Kimmie St SW, with more wooded sites for tents ($17), RVs ($23) and cabins. Turn off I-5 at exit No 99 and travel a quarter mile east to Kimmie St. It's open during the summer only.

Forego the RV-park scene for *Millersylvania State Park* (☎ 753-1519), ten miles south of Olympia off I-5 exit No 95. Among the recreation available at the park is hiking, lake fishing and swimming. Tent sites cost $10; RV hook-ups are $14.

**B&Bs** *Harbinger Inn B&B* (☎ 754-0389), 1136 E Bay Drive NE, is a 1910-era home overlooking Budd Inlet. There are four guest rooms, three with private facilities. Children under 10 are not permitted. Rates range between $60 and $90.

**Hotels** Olympia is the state capital, and rooms tend to be expensive if you're not on a lobbyist's expense account. If you're just passing through, there's a clutch of motels out at I-5 exit No 102, including most of the chains. Try the *Tyee Motel* (☎ 943-6448, (800) 648-6440), 500 Tyee Drive, which has a pool and restaurant; single/double rooms range from $49 to $72 depending on the season. The *Best Western Tumwater Inn Motel* (☎ 956-1235), 5188 Capital Blvd, has microwaves, guest

**WASHINGTON**

laundry and free continental breakfast. Rooms are $62/72.

Stay right downtown at the *Golden Gavel Motel* (☎ 352-8533), 909 Capitol Way S, one of the less expensive places to stay at $44/48. Across the street, the *Best Western Aladdin Motor Inn* (☎ 352-7200), 900 Capitol Way S, is where many representatives have their suites while the legislature is in session. There's a heated outdoor pool; rooms are $65, single or double. The *Ramada Governor House Hotel* (☎ 352-7700, (800) 272-6232), 621 Capitol Way S, is Olympia's fanciest lodging, with a heated pool, guest laundry, fitness center, restaurant and convention facilities. Rooms begin in the $120 range.

## Places to Eat

If you're looking for a latte to start the day, head to *Batdorf & Bronson* (☎ 786-6717), 513 Capitol Way S, a comfortable espresso bar with breakfast pastries and a selection of regional papers. There's no better place for a traditional breakfast than the old-fashioned, wood-paneled *Spar Bar & Cafe* (☎ 357-6444), 114 4th Ave E, a diner, cigar shop, newsstand and bar combo that hasn't changed since the 1930s.

If you're assembling organic food to cook yourself, head to *Olympia Food Co-op* at either of two locations: westside (☎ 754-7666), 921 Rogers St N, or eastside (☎ 956-3870), 3111 Pacific St SE. For picnic breads, go to *San Francisco Street Bakery* (☎ 753-8553), 1320 San Francisco St NE. At *Levity Cafe* (☎ 357-7446), 430 Legion Way SE, there's a selection of organic baked goods and wood-fired pizza; try the alder-smoked bread.

Olympia's long-standing vegetarian restaurant is the slightly dowdy *Urban Onion* (☎ 943-9242), 116 Legion Way E. Lunchtime salad and quiche go for $7. *Mekong Restaurant* (☎ 352-9620), 125 Columbia St NW, is the local favorite for Thai food, while *Capitale Espresso Grille* (☎ 352-8007), 609 Capitol Way S, offers a selection of spicy Italian pastas (*penne alla puttanesca* goes for $9).

Since it's the state capitol, there are a number of fine dining establishments – all the better to schmooze in. Upscale Continental cuisine is offered in a refurbished Victorian mansion at *Seven Gables Restaurant* (☎ 352-2349), 1205 West Bay Drive NW. Sauces here are sometimes so French and unusual that the affable wait staff has trouble with their pronunciation; scallops with lime, champagne and red bell pepper goes for $16.

If you're looking for a table with a view, go to the *Budd Bay Cafe* (☎ 357-6963), 525 Columbia St NW, right above the marina on Percival Landing. Dinner entrees include steak, seafood, pasta and prime rib in the $13 range; on Sunday there's a popular champagne brunch. Get an eyeful of Deschutes Falls and the Olympia Brewery at *Falls Terrace* (☎ 943-7830), 106 S Deschutes Way, open for lunch and dinner, serving that Northwestern triumvirate of steak, pasta and seafood, all in the $15 range.

## Entertainment

**Coffeehouses** In Olympia's coffeehouses you're more likely to spot local artists, students and stylishly disenfranchised youth than lobbyists. For late-night espressos and post-concert discussions, the place to go is *Dancing Goats Espresso Co* (☎ 754-8187), 124 4th Ave E. There's more of an edge at *Smithfield Cafe* (☎ 786-1725), 212 4th Ave W, where the clientele seems younger and less Evergreen College influenced.

**Brewpubs** *Fishbowl Pub* (☎ 943-6480), 515 Jefferson St SE, serves their own Fish Tail ales, a tasty alternative to the ubiquitous Olympia Brewery beers. In addition to the British-style ales, there's a snack menu.

**Cinemas** Olympia's art cinema *par excellence* is the *Capitol Theatre* (☎ 754-5378), 206 5th Ave E. This foreign and independent film cinema commands the kind of local devotion you'd expect in a small, intellectual community. For the latest major release films, go to the *Lacey Cinemas* (☎ 459-2093) at 4431 Martin Way E in Lacey.

**Performing Arts** Olympia's primary venue for national touring shows and other cultural activities is the *Washington Center of the Performing Arts* (☎ 753-8586), 512 Washington St SE.

**Live Music** On weekend evenings, the backstage of the *Capitol Theatre* (☎ 754-5378), 206 5th Ave E, is where to catch local bands, delivered fresh from Evergreen College.

**Dance Clubs** For dancing, go to *Thekla* (☎ 352-1855), 116 5th Ave E; its entrance is in the alley (you can't miss the cartoon montage around the door). The music changes nightly, but the clientele remains a friendly gay/straight hodgepodge.

### Getting There & Away
**Air** There is no commercial air service to Olympia. Travelers who wish to fly will need to go to Sea-Tac and call the Capital Aeroporter (☎ 754-7113), which operates 15 buses daily from the Ramada Governor House Hotel, 621 Capitol Way E, in Olympia. One-way fare is $20; reservations are suggested.

**Bus** Six Greyhound buses a day link Olympia to other I-5-corridor cities from its station (☎ 357-5541) at 107 7th Ave E. One-way fare to Seattle is $10. Gray's Harbor Transportation Authority (☎ 532-2770, (800) 562-9730) also offers bus service to Aberdeen on the Pacific coast.

**Train** Amtrak (☎ 923-4602) stops at its station at 6600 Yelm Hwy SE; four trains a day link Olympia with Seattle and Portland. If you call ahead to Olympia's Intercity Transit (☎ 786-1881), a shuttle will meet the train; there is no extra charge for this service.

### Getting Around
Olympia's public transport system is called IT for Intercity Transit (☎ 786-1881, (800) 287-6348)). The downtown transit center is at State Ave and Capitol Way. For a cab, call Capitol City Taxi at 357-4949.

# Northwestern Washington & the San Juan Islands

In the northwestern corner of Washington, the Pacific Ocean washes into the Strait of Georgia, the Strait of Juan de Fuca and the Puget Sound, as well as into a thousand tiny inlets, fjords and channels. Rising above the mist and the blue-green waves is a mosaic of forested islands and peninsulas along the bay-dented mainland. The primary attraction here is the San Juan Islands, which, together with the Oregon coast, is undoubtedly the most beautiful and unique destination in the Pacific Northwest. These remote islands, accessible only by boat or air, range from tightly folded mountain peaks to rolling moors and farmland. Bicycles fill the roads, B&Bs nestle among the trees and sheep and cattle graze in grassy pastures. And everywhere, the Pacific encroaches.

The largest city in this marine-oriented province is Bellingham, a delightful university town with lively street life and good restaurants. For the traveler, Bellingham is a welcome escape from the big city stress of either Seattle or Vancouver, BC, and it is close to recreation on Mt Baker and in North Cascades National Park. Along the lower Skagit River, historic La Conner provides a relaxing respite from highway driving, or for an overnight stay, and in the spring the fertile flood plains of this valley come alive with acres of tulips and other flowers in a not-to-be-missed display.

Whidbey Island contains two of Washington's most popular (read: crowded) vacation spots: the beautiful Deception Pass State Park and the quaint, upscale town of Langley.

## GETTING THERE & AWAY

Though planes fly from Bellingham and Sea-Tac Airport in Seattle to the San Juan Islands, buses are the main regional link to the south. Greyhound service sticks exclusively to I-5 stops. The Airporter Shuttle (☎ (800) 235-5247) is a small private carrier that links Sea-Tac to Whidbey Island, Anacortes and the San Juan ferry terminal ($27 one way, $49 roundtrip), Mt Vernon/Burlington, Bellingham ($29 one way, $52 roundtrip) and Blaine. There are six buses a day; reservations are requested. Although the fares aren't exactly cheap, this is the easiest way to get to slightly off-the-freeway locations in this part of the Northwest.

Amtrak (☎ 800) 872-7245) has not offered train service north of Seattle for nearly 20 years, but as part of the planned high-speed rail service between Eugene and Vancouver, BC, rail service is being reinstituted between Seattle and Vancouver, BC, with stops in Edmonds, Everett, Burlington/Mt Vernon, Bellingham, the border crossing at Blaine and Vancouver, BC.

---

### Smuggling in the San Juans

Because the San Juans and northwestern Washington were remote unpatrolled regions between two nations, there has been a long history of smuggling in the area. In the 1880s, smuggling was mostly of wool bundles and Chinese laborers, who, under the Chinese Exclusion Act of 1882, were forbidden to enter the territory.

During Prohibition in the 1920s, a flood of alcohol flowed from Canada through these US waters. The most famous of these smugglers was Seattle police captain Ray Olmstead, who brought in some 200 cases of booze a day and evaded capture by using a network of canny locals to move his goods for him. ■

WASHINGTON

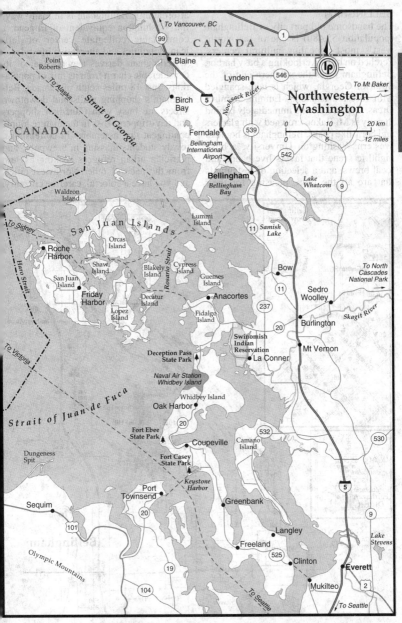

## BELLINGHAM

The handsome old port city of Bellingham (population 55,480) is one of the Northwest's most appealing cultural centers. Perched on hills overlooking a busy harbor, Bellingham faces the southern end of the Strait of Georgia, which is here spangled with forested islands – Lummi, Samish, Orcas, Cypress. Rising immediately behind the city is Mt Baker, crowned with glaciers and horn-like peaks. Bellingham is home to Western Washington University, a busy nightlife scene that favors live bands and local brews, and a selection of restaurants that are all the more pleasing for their affordability. Bellingham is in many ways the Washington equivalent of Eugene: a comfortable collegiate center of left-leaning politics and alternative lifestyles.

Bellingham derives a good deal of its considerable charm from its mix of populations. Just 18 miles south of Canada, Bellingham's shopping malls and downtown streets are busy with Canadian shoppers and day-trippers. Toss in the mature hippie contingent that assembles in coffeeshops, rowdy students massing in brewpubs, and patrician urban refugees seeking asylum from the pace of other Northwest cities, and you have a colorful, carefree citizenry.

WASHINGTON

Bellingham began as four separate communities – Fairhaven, Sehome, Whatcom and Bellingham – each of which developed along deep Bellingham Bay. Fairhaven grew up around speculation that it would be selected as the Great Northern Railroad's Pacific coast port city, and a core of red-brick storefronts and hotels sprang up in the 1880s. When the Great Northern chose Seattle instead, Fairhaven fell into a slumber. Recent renovation has turned the handsome old buildings into a shopping and dining precinct. Whatcom was the site of an early commune, Sehome was the site of a coal mine in the 1860s, and Bellingham was a busy port site. By 1903, the towns had consolidated into a single civic entity.

## Orientation

Bellingham is 18 miles south of the international border crossing at Blaine and 54 miles from downtown Vancouver, BC. From Seattle, Bellingham is 89 miles north on I-5.

Because Bellingham is comprised of what were formerly several separate towns, the street systems are pretty confused. The current city center is west of I-5 exit No 253, which leads to Holly St, a major downtown arterial and one of the few streets to cut through the area without getting caught up in conflicting street grids. Holly St intersects State St, another major arterial that runs south to the Fairhaven district and north to I-5 exit No 254. North of the intersection of State and Holly Sts is a quadrant of streets with a completely different grid; many city offices and businesses are located here.

Be sure to stop and get a map from the visitors center. In many ways, it is probably easier just to park and explore Bellingham on foot. The grid is pretty hard to figure out if you're behind the wheel.

## Information

**Tourist Office** For information about the area, contact the Bellingham/Whatcom County Convention & Visitors Bureau (☎ 671-3990, (800) 487-2032), 904 Potter St, Bellingham, WA 98229. The visitors center is off I-5, exit No 253, but it's a little difficult to locate. To find it, turn north on King St from Lakeway Drive (following signs for I-5 north), and turn immediately right instead of entering the freeway.

For information about the Canadian/US border contact the US Border Patrol at Blaine (☎ 332-8781) or the Canadian Immigration office (☎ (604) 536-7671).

**Post** The Bellingham post office (☎ 676-8303) is at 315 Prospect St, 98225.

| PLACES TO STAY | | | | | |
|---|---|---|---|---|---|
| 1 | North Garden Inn | 26 | Casino Bar & Grill | 15 | Post Office |
| 2 | Shangri-La Downtown Motel | 28 | Juice Oasis | 16 | Whatcom Museum of History & Art, Children's Museum |
| 6 | Aloha Motel | 36 | Tony's Coffee & Tea | | |
| 7 | Bell Motel | 37 | Dos Padres Fine Mexican Food | 17 | Mt Baker Theatre |
| 8 | Coachman Inn | 38 | Cobblestone Cafe | 23 | Whatcom Transport Bus Depot |
| 9 | Bay City Motor Inn | 39 | Bel Porto Cucina Mediterraneo | 27 | Greyhound Bus Depot |
| 14 | Bellingham Hostel | | | 30 | The Royal Room |
| 29 | Travelodge | **OTHER** | | 31 | Three Bs Tavern |
| | | 3 | South Campus, St Joseph Hospital | 32 | Up & Up Tavern |
| **PLACES TO EAT** | | | | 33 | Community Food Co-op |
| 18 | Pacific Cafe | 4 | Visitors Center | 34 | Archer Ale House |
| 19 | Old Town Cafe | 5 | Sunshine Cleaners | 35 | Village Books, Colophon Cafe |
| 20 | The Breakfast Club | 10 | WWU Western Gallery | | |
| 21 | Il Fiasco Cucina Italiana | 11 | WWU Visitors Center | 40 | Speedy O'Tubbs Rhythmic Underground |
| 22 | Cafe Toulouse | 12 | Fairhaven Bike & Mountain Sports | | |
| 24 | Teriyaki Bar | | | 41 | Fairhaven Laundry & Cleaners |
| 25 | Bluewater Bistro | 13 | Alaska Marine Hwy Ferries, San Juan Islands Ferry | | |

**Bookstores** Bellingham's best bookstore is Village Books (☎ 671-2626, (800) 392-BOOK), at Harris Ave and 11th St, which sells new and used books. Like Powell's Books in Portland or Elliott Bay Books in Seattle, Village Books is a real community resource, with lots of author readings and literary activities, to say nothing of being home to the popular Colophon Cafe, the trendy coffeeshop with service on both floors of the bookstore.

**Media** Bellingham offers a number of free publications that profile the local arts and entertainment scene. Pick up a handful in most bookstores or cafes. The best of these is called *Northwest Events* and is published monthly. The daily paper is the Bellingham *Herald*. For public radio, tune to KZAZ, 91.7 FM.

**Laundry** Convenient to Fairhaven and the university is Fairhaven Laundry & Cleaners (☎ 734-9647) at 1414 12th St. There's also Sunshine Cleaners (☎ 733-6610) in the impossible-to-miss Fred Meyer Shopping Center immediately north of I-5, exit No 253.

**Medical Services** For health emergencies, go to St Joseph Hospital (☎ 734-5400) at 2901 Squalicum Parkway, near I-5, exit No 256. The hospital's South Campus (same phone number) is at 809 E Chestnut St and is more convenient to downtown.

### Whatcom Museum of History & Art

The building itself is reason enough to visit this excellent regional museum (☎ 676-6981), 121 Prospect St. It's in the imposing and fanciful red-brick Whatcom City Hall, built in 1892. This large complex now boasts four separate units, whose galleries contain a good collection of artifacts from local native tribes, a collection of vintage toys, a recreation of a 19th-century Bellingham street scene and a large natural history section with hundreds of stuffed birds. Several galleries are devoted to traveling displays of fine art. Next door is the **Children's Museum of the Northwest**

(☎ 733-8769), 227 Prospect St, with interactive displays for the younger set.

The museum is open from noon to 5 pm Tuesday to Sunday. Admission is $2 for adults, $1 for seniors, students and children under 12. Hours for the Children's Museum are from 10 am to 5 pm Thursday to Saturday; admission is $2.

### Western Washington University

Western Washington University (WWU) was founded in 1893 as a normal school and served as a teacher training college before being redesignated as a regional university in 1977. The university is just south of downtown Bellingham, nestled between steep hills. With a student body of approximately 10,500 students, WWU offers a full range of academic programs, though its strengths are in the fine and performing arts. The Visitors Information Center (☎ 650-3424) at the end of South College Drive can tell you more about the university and about daily events or entertainment on the campus.

### WWU Outdoor Sculpture Museum

Bellingham abounds with outdoor sculpture, a heavy concentration of which falls on the WWU campus. In fact, WWU's 17 sculptures comprise the largest collection of outdoor sculpture on the West Coast. Interpretive information, including a free map and brochure of the 'sculpture walk' are available from the Whatcom Museum, Whatcom County Visitors & Convention Bureau, WWU Visitors Center, or the university's Western Gallery. When classes are in session you'll need to obtain a parking permit from the visitors center, open from 7 am to 7 pm Monday to Friday. Audiophone tours are also available from here or from the Western Gallery, open from 10 am to 4 pm Monday to Friday, and from noon to 4 pm on Saturday. Call 650-3963 for more information or to arrange a group tour. Admission is free.

### Activities

Fairhaven Bike & Mountain Sports (☎ 733-4433), 1103 11th St near the Fairhaven district, has plenty of recreation gear for sale and rental, including bicycles, skis, snowboards, hiking and mountaineering equipment, rollerblades and clothing.

The Bellingham area is home to a number of **golf** courses; however, many are private. The Lake Padden Municipal Golf Course (☎ 676-6989), 4882 Samish Way, is a public, 18-hole course owned by the city. It is in a forested park-like area near a busy lake.

## Cruises

Bellingham offers a number of scenic and wildlife cruises into the Strait of Georgia and to neighboring islands. Victoria, BC/San Juan Cruises (☎ 738-8099, (800) 443-4552), 355 Harris Ave, offers narrated day trips out to the San Juan Islands and to Victoria, BC. Tours leave from the Bellingham Cruise Terminal.

## Places to Stay

**Hostels** Just south of the USA/Canada border is HI's *Birch Bay Hostel* (☎ 371-2180), 4639 Alderson Rd No 630, at Bay Horizon County Park in Blaine. The hostel is open from April through September. Rates for members/non-members are $9/12; cyclists get a break at $7. Plan to check out by 9:30 am.

In Fairhaven Park is HI's *Bellingham Hostel* (☎ 671-1750), 107 Chuckanut Drive. Dorm-style accommodations for members/non-members are $10/13.

**B&Bs** *North Garden Inn* (☎ 671-7828, (800) 922-6414; (800) 367-1676 from Canada), 1014 N Garden St, is a historic, 1897 Queen Anne Victorian that sits above downtown, with views of the bay and San Juan Islands, and is within easy walking distance of restaurants and shopping. The 10 guest rooms range from $54 to $74. The *Decann House* (☎ 734-9172), 2610 Eldridge Ave, is a less imposing Victorian home with great bay views on the western side of downtown (follow Holly St west). Rooms cost from $45 to $70.

For more contemporary lodgings, check out *Schnauzer Crossing B&B* (☎ 733-

0055), 4421 Lakeway Drive, named for the owner's two pet dogs. This modern home overlooking Lake Whatcom in eastern Bellingham offers two guest rooms and a cabin, with a private tennis court, extensive gardens and a hot tub. Rates begin at $110.

For a more extensive listing of area B&Bs, contact the Bed & Breakfast Guild of Whatcom County (☎ 676-4560), and ask for their brochure.

**Hotels** The majority of Bellingham's inexpensive motels are along Samish Way, off exit No 252. If you're looking for something cheap, try the *Bell Motel* (☎ 733-2520), 208 N Samish Way, or the *Aloha Motel* (☎ 733-4900), 315 N Samish Way. Both have single/double rooms for $29/39, take pets and offer kitchen units. For a little more comfort, try the *Coachman Inn* (☎ 671-9000, (800) 962-6641; (800) 543-5478 in Canada), 120 Samish Way, with a pool and rooms at $43/45. The *Bay City Motor Inn* (☎ 676-0332, (800) 538-8204), 116 N Samish Way, offers a workout room and a pool table; rooms are $40/45.

Out near the freeway exit No 256, there's a *Quality Inn* (☎ 647-800), 100 E Kellogg Rd, with a pool, laundry, hot tub and rooms for $63/74. The lodging of choice in these parts – if you judge by the number of Canadian license plates – is *Best Western Heritage Inn* (☎ 647-1912, (800) 528-1234), 151 E McCloud Rd, off exit No 256. Rooms (starting at $64/69) are large and nicely furnished, and there's a free continental breakfast.

If you want to enjoy downtown Bellingham, stay at one of the motels located within walking distance of fine restaurants and entertainment. The *Shangri-La Downtown Motel* (☎ 733-7050), 611 E Holly St, is a trifle modest but a good deal at $32 a night. The *Travelodge* (☎ 734-1900, (800) 578-7878), 202 E Holly St, is right downtown and a good deal with rooms under $40 a night.

## Places to Eat

For a town its size, Bellingham has a wide variety of very good restaurants, with most prices well below what you'll find in Seattle.

**Downtown** The Breakfast Club (☎ 676-1070), 301 W Holly St, with omelets, hash browns and such, is a popular place for breakfast. Just down the street is another standby, the Old Town Cafe (☎ 671-4431), 316 Holly St. There's a happy-go-lucky, hippie atmosphere here, where vegetarian dishes are offered at breakfast and lunch, along with fresh pastries and espresso. Look for discounts on bakery goods and tidbits during weekday 'tea time' (from 2 pm), the last hour of the day, when the cafe tries to sell everything off before closing. Cafe Toulouse (☎ 733-8996), 114 W Magnolia St, No 102, is a nice street-side bistro with morning coffee and light lunch fare.

The place to go for organic produce and health foods is the Community Food Co-op (☎ 734-8158), 1220 N Forest St. The co-op's cafe, called the Swan Cafe (☎ 734-0542), is open for three meals a day. For a vegetarian snack, head to The Juice Oasis (☎ 647-4519), 207½ E Holly St.

A popular student haunt is The Teriyaki Bar (☎ 733-0294), 119 W Holly St, which has a drive-up window and also offers delivery, with most dishes under $5. Another inexpensive hangout is the Bluewater Bistro (☎ 733-6762), 1215½ Cornwall Ave, a lively and casual place for pasta, salads and burgers, mostly under $10. Across the street is the Casino Bar & Grill (☎ 733-3500), 1224 Cornwall Ave, which is by night a jazz club and by day a friendly brass-filled dining room serving a light menu with sandwiches, burgers and grilled items.

Bellingham's two best restaurants are downtown. The Pacific Cafe (☎ 647-0800), 100 N Commercial St, brings both Oriental and French influences to bear on local fish, seafood and meat. Specialties include grilled salmon with a ginger-tamarind glaze ($16). Il Fiasco Cucina Italiana (☎ 676-9136), 1309 Commercial St, is a superior Italian restaurant with excellent service and delicious food. Pasta dishes run from $10 to $12, while grilled dishes – like

pork tenderloin with wild mushrooms – are in the $15 range. It's open for lunch weekdays only, dinner daily.

**Fairhaven** Housed inside Village Books in Fairhaven, the Colophon Cafe (☎ 647-0092), 1208 11th St, blends the features of a literary cafe with a multi-ethnic eatery. Espresso and pastries, especially the homemade pies, fuel book-shoppers, while the meals served at lunch and dinner – which include soups, entrees and salads – bring people in from the neighborhood for tasty and inexpensive dining. Also in Fairhaven is Dos Padres Fine Mexican Food (☎ 733-9900), 1111 Harris Ave. Dishes reflect a mix of traditional and nuevo influences; a three-alarm, black-bean enchilada dinner is under $10.

There's also plenty of choice for fine dining in Bellingham. In the Fairhaven district is Bel Porto Cucina Mediterraneo (☎ 676-1520), 1114 Harris Ave, which features upscale Mediterranean-style cuisine. Grilled salmon with black olives goes for $12; there's live music in the evenings. Just down the street is the Cobblestone Cafe (☎ 650-0545), 1308B 11th St, tucked into a little garden. It has a small, continental-influenced menu, but with something for everyone. Steak and vegan entrees share the same menu; lamb brochettes are $15.

## Entertainment

**Coffeehouses** Relax in the locals' favorite coffeeshop at Tony's Coffee & Tea (☎ 733-6319), 1101 Harris Ave, in Fairhaven. Students, unrepentant hippies and housewives come here to do some serious hanging out. In summer, there's a shady garden area to lounge in.

**Bars & Brewpubs** Bellingham's student population supports a number of friendly bars and taverns. In Fairhaven, the Archer Ale House (☎ 647-7002), 1212 10th St, offers lots of regional microbrews on tap, features darts and is smoke-free. Downtown, the Three Bs Tavern (☎ 734-1881) and the Up & Up Tavern (☎ 733-9739), next door to each other at 1234 State St, are both lively student hangouts with pool tables and draft beer.

**Theater** *Mt Baker Theatre*, at 106 N Commercial St, is a grand old historic theater, built in 1925, which is both a cinema (☎ 734-4950) and live performance stage (☎ 734-6080) specializing in national touring acts. WWU's *Performing Arts Center* (☎ 650-3866), on campus, is another performance space featuring local and regional music and dance productions.

**Live Music** On Friday and Saturday, Bellingham musicians emerge from dark garages all over town to play at *The Royal Room* (☎ 738-3701), 208 E Holly St. The Folk Showcase is on Tuesday. There's also a restaurant and billiards. *Speedy O'Tubbs Rhythmic Underground* (☎ 734-1539), 1305 11th St in Fairhaven, is another haven for blues, jazz and regional touring bands. For live jazz, head to the *Casino Bar & Grill* (☎ 733-3500), 1224 Cornwall Ave.

### Getting There & Away

**Air** Bellingham International Airport (☎ 676-2500) is northwest of Bellingham off I-5, exit No 258. The city is served by Horizon Air (☎ (800) 547-9308) and by United Express (☎ (800) 241-6522) with service to Seattle and Vancouver, BC; a roundtrip from Seattle is around $100. Island Shuttle (☎ (800) 475-3829) flies from Bellingham to Victoria, BC and the San Juan Islands with both regularly scheduled flights and charters.

**Bus** Greyhound buses serve Bellingham on the Seattle-Vancouver run. Three buses pass through daily heading north to Vancouver, BC ($13), and four go south to Seattle ($12). There's a special Seattle-bound express on Fridays. The depot (☎ 733-5251) is at 1329 N State St.

**Ferry** Bellingham is the terminal for the Alaska Marine Highway Ferries (☎ 676-8445, (800) 642-0066), which travel once a week up the Inside Passage to Juneau, Skagway and other southeast Alaskan

ports. Passenger fares to Skagway start at $246; add a small car (up to 15 feet) and it's $581. Cabins for the three-day trip can be hard to come by, so reserve well in advance.

San Juan Islands Passenger Excursion Ferry (☎ 671-1137) travels daily from the Alaska ferry terminal in Fairhaven to Orcas and San Juan islands. The roundtrip rate for students is $27, for adults $33, with the option of returning the same or next day. They also run whale-watching tours. $50 covers passage to/from Friday Harbor, with a one-hour stopover in town plus the whale-watching excursion; a stopover on Orcas Island instead will run $40. Bicycles are welcome onboard for $5 roundtrip.

### Getting Around

Bus service on Whatcom Transportation Authority (☎ 676-7433) is modest but functional. The fleet runs mostly on weekdays from around 6 am to 5 pm; service is reduced on Saturdays and nonexistent on Sundays. On weekday evenings the special 'Nightline' bus connects Fairhaven, WWU and Bellis Fair to downtown Bellingham. Bus 1A goes south to the Bellingham Ferry Terminal every hour. Find the main bus terminal downtown on Railroad St, between E Champion and Magnolia Sts.

The system is currently undergoing a facelift, so look for new, state-of-the-art buses and transfer centers. In a pinch, look for schedules in the phone book.

### ANACORTES

Noted principally as the departure point for the San Juan Islands, Anacortes is actually quite a pleasant town, so all is not lost if travelers end up spending a night here. In fact, unintended layovers are not uncommon. Ferries have been known to fill up on summer weekends, and once they're full, they're full. Also, travelers who forget to check the ferry schedule or who suffer at the hands of the Seattle traffic gods sometimes show up too late and must wait until the following day.

The ferry terminal is three miles to the west of Anacortes, and lots of motels and fast-food restaurants line Hwy 20 from the outskirts of Anacortes to the ferry dock. However, if you have time to kill or need to spend the night, head downtown, where there are good restaurants and inexpensive motels. The old downtown buildings are decorated with life-size cutouts of Anacortes residents created from historic photographs. While it sounds kind of cheesy, in fact the effect is pleasant and rather sweet.

## Orientation & Information

Anacortes is itself on Fidalgo Island, separated from the mainland by a narrow channel, 17 miles west of I-5 on Hwy 20. The downtown harbor (as opposed to the Washington State Ferry Terminal) skirts the edge of the business district, giving the town a real maritime air. The chamber of commerce (☎ 293-3832) is at 819 Commercial Ave.

## Places to Stay

There are a lot of motels along the Commercial Ave strip. The best deals are at *Gateway Motel* (☎ 293-2655), 2019 Commercial Ave, and at *Paul's Motel* (☎ 293-3108), 3100 Commercial Ave, which both have single/double rooms for $35/40. A couple notches up in facilities, comfort and price (both start at around $58/65) are the *Anacortes Inn* (☎ 293-3153 or (800) 327-7976), 3006 Commercial Ave, and the *Islands Inn* (☎ 293-4334), 3401 Commercial Ave, which has a good restaurant in the complex. Both have pools.

It's quieter to stay downtown, off the main strip, and it's an easy walk to good restaurants. The *Cap Sante Inn* (☎ 293-0602), 906 9th St, is a cozy motor inn with a guest laundry and rooms at $56/60. The *San Juan Motel* (☎ 293-5105), 1103 6th St, offers kitchenettes and rooms at $35/40.

*Ship Harbor Inn* (☎ 293-5177), 5316 Ferry Terminal Rd, offers the easiest access to the ferries, as it's just above the terminal; what's more, the rooms have fireplaces and are nicer than average. The motel also offers bike rentals for those heading to the San Juans. Double rooms start at $72.

By far the most stylish place to stay in the area is the *Majestic Hotel* (☎ 293-3355), 419 Commercial Ave, which offers 23 antique-filled rooms in a beautifully restored 1889 hotel filled with wood paneling, marble and brass. The cozy downstairs bar is a great place for a drink, and the restaurant is excellent. Rates start at $89 and go to $189.

## Places to Eat

For breakfast, head to *Calico Cupboard Cafe & Bakery* (☎ 293-7315), 901 Commercial Ave, for old-fashioned breakfasts, or load up on French pastries at *La Vie en Rose* (☎ 299-9546), 416 Commercial Ave. There's a little of everything at friendly, boisterous *Gere-a-Deli* (☎ 293-7383), 502 Commercial Ave, from bowls of granola in the mornings to all-you-can-eat pasta on Friday nights. Soups, salads and sandwiches are the staples at lunch. *El Jinete* (☎ 293-2631), 509½ Commercial Ave, is a cozy Mexican restaurant with traditional dishes under $7.

*Brewhouse Brewpub* (☎ 293-2444), 320 Commercial Ave, is a delightful place to sample the local brews and to snack on wood-fired pizza. Located in a handsome old bar, the Brewhouse really packs 'em in at night, and with reason: the food is reasonably priced, and it's a friendly, youthful place to have a drink in a town where most bars are basically locals-only.

The restaurant of note in Anacortes is the *Courtyard Bistro* (☎ 299-2923) in the Majestic Hotel at 419 Commercial Ave. The dining room, refurbished with pastel-colored walls, retains the classy charm that was its birthright in 1889. Dinners are a melange of classic French and fresh Northwest flavors; local fish is featured. Anacortes Bay Bouillabaisse is $16; chicken breast with forest mushrooms is $15.

## Getting There & Away

The closest Greyhound bus service is to Burlington, 17 miles east of Anacortes at the junction of I-5 and Hwy 20. From here, Skagit County Transport buses continue to Anacortes and to the ferry terminal; for schedule information, call 757-8801. If you're flying into the Seattle airport, the Airporter Shuttle (☎ (206) 622-1424) offers six buses a day between Sea-Tac, Anacortes and the San Juan ferries; a single fare is $27, and reservations are appreciated. The Airporter does not make stops in downtown Seattle.

# Lower Skagit River Valley

The Skagit River originates far to the east in North Cascades National Park and flows west to meet the Pacific Ocean near the little port town of La Conner. For much of its journey between the national park and the town of Sedro Woolley, the road and river share a steep-sided glacial valley, a designated 'Wild & Scenic' route that nonetheless is joined by the undulating power lines of three upper Skagit hydroelectric dams.

Out of the canyon, the Skagit River leaves the mountains and flows through a low-lying flood plain. As in Holland, early settlers used dikes to channel the river, retrieving rich farmland from the Skagit's seasonal floods. Today, dairy farms and plant nurseries are the norm: in the early spring, lower Skagit valley fields are a wild display of tulip blooms, as this area is one of the nation's primary sources of spring bulbs. Most towns here – like Sedro Woolley and Mt Vernon – are small and serve local farmers; however, historic streets and boutique shopping make La Conner a major destination.

## SEDRO WOOLLEY
An early settler wanted to name this forested town 'Bug', but the local women lobbied hard for 'Sedro' (Spanish for cedar) and won. Woolley was tacked on when an entrepreneurial Mr Woolley started building a few miles away, where the railroad was set to go through. The towns and their names eventually merged, and Sedro Woolley (population 6920)

developed into a thriving timber town. Though logging has diminished in recent years, it's still a big part of the local economy.

For travelers, the town of Sedro Woolley isn't of consuming interest. It is, however, a good place to stop before heading into North Cascades National Park (see the North Cascades chapter), as it's the last town of consequence for a couple hundred miles on Hwy 20 as it winds east up the Skagit River canyon and into the wilds of the Cascade Mountains.

### Information
The chamber of commerce (☎ 855-1841), 116 Woodworth St, is housed in a caboose at the west end of town. The Mt Baker-Snoqualmie National Forest Ranger Station (☎ 856-5700), 800 State St, is open from 8 am to 4:30 pm Monday to Friday. This is a good place to stop for information about the North Cascades National Park, if you're planning an excursion in that direction.

The post office in Sedro Woolley (☎ 855-1373) is at 111 Woodworth St. The Crossroads Sparkle Shop (☎ 856-0700), a laundromat, is next to Thrifty Foods in Sedro Woolley's Crossroads Square. If you're headed east, this is the last laundromat you may see for a while.

### Places to Stay & Eat
The *Three Rivers Inn & Restaurant* (☎ 855-2626, (800) 221-5122), 210 Ball St (on Hwy 20 near the Hwy 9 intersection), is not bad at all for a bed and a meal. Singles/doubles are $55/57 and up, and there's an outdoor pool. The other motel in town, the *Skagit Motel* (☎ 856-6001), is a few dollars less at $32/45; it's a mile west of town on Hwy 20.

## MT VERNON
The farming center of Mt Vernon (population 20,450) sits along a wide curve in the Skagit River. When White settlers first arrived, they began to build dikes along the Skagit to channel the river out of its wide flood plain and sloughs. However, river travel and farming above the Mt Vernon

area was impeded by enormous natural log jams in the river. After the log jams were removed in the 1870s, the valley opened up for more farming.

The low-lying rich soil and abundant water in the Skagit River valley makes this one of the most productive agricultural areas in the Northwest. The valley is the nation's single largest source of peas and is noted also for its production of strawberries. The most famous crops of the valley, though, are tulips, daffodils and irises, which come into bloom in the spring and are the focus of April's annual Tulip Festival.

### Information

The Mt Vernon Chamber of Commerce (☎ 855-0974) is at 200 E College Way, and the post office (☎ 855-1373) is at 1207 Cleveland St. For medical emergencies, go to Skagit Valley Hospital (☎ 424-4111), 1415 E Kincaid.

### Skagit Valley Tulip Festival

Head to Mt Vernon during the first two weeks of April for the Northwest's most colorful festival. While most people don't really think of this as a 'festival' per se – most simply drive the side roads between Mt Vernon and La Conner armed with a tulip field map – there is an ongoing roster of events: an arts-&-crafts fair, a salmon bake, parade, musical concerts and the like.

When the weather is clear, the roads through the tulip fields are jammed with cyclists. If possible, take in the festival backroads on a weekday, as weekend afternoons bring long lines of cars, bikes and pedestrians sure to spoil the pace of a leisurely drive. For more information about the festival, contact the chamber of commerce.

### Places to Stay & Eat

*West Winds Motel* (☎ 424-4224), 2020 Riverside Drive, is a modest, inexpensive lodging in a town with otherwise rather expensive motels. Pets are allowed, children under 10 sleep for free, and singles/doubles are \$30/38. The *Tulip Valley Inn*

(☎ 428-5969), 2200 Freeway Drive, is a new motel complex with rooms at \$42/55. The *Motor Inn Best Western* (☎ 424-4287), 300 W College Way, with a pool, kitchen units and pets allowed, is a good deal at \$55/58.

Although the intersection of Hwy 538 and I-5 at exit No 227 sprouts forth a large variety of fast food restaurants, Mt Vernon has much better things to offer off the freeway. The *Longfellow Cafe* (☎ 336-3684), 120-B N 1st St, is in a historic old granary, with lunchtime sandwiches, soups, light entrees and evening seafood specials. *Wildflowers* (☎ 424-9724), 2001 E College Way, is Mt Vernon's other restaurant of note. Located in a Victorian home, the restaurant's specialty is elaborate preparations of local seafood (from \$14 to \$22) as well as freshly made breads, salads and desserts.

## LA CONNER

At first glance, La Conner is an unlikely little tourist mecca, just north of the mouth of the Skagit River. However, La Conner's well-maintained and stylish 1880s storefronts and pretty harbor became a magnet for artists and writers during the 1960s and '70s (the likes of Tom Robbins lives here). The galleries and artistic coteries drew attention to the slumbering but handsome town, and soon boutiques, nice restaurants and antique shops took up residence. Not much later, the tour buses began rolling in.

La Conner is very charming and a relaxing stop for anyone whose nerves are jangled by nearby I-5 traffic or for San Juan-bound travelers early for their ferry. Summer weekends bring hundreds of people to town, however, and the narrow streets become absolutely jammed. Time your visit carefully if you want to avoid the crowds.

### Orientation & Information

La Conner is 11 miles west of I-5, and nine miles from Anacortes. Directly across the Swinomish Channel from La Conner is a lobe of Fidalgo Island, home to the

WASHINGTON

Swinomish Indian Reservation. For more information, contact the La Conner Chamber of Commerce (☎ 466-4778), PO Box 1610, La Conner, WA 98257.

## Skagit County Museum

In a modern building well away from the crush of tourists, this museum (☎ 466-3365), 501 4th St, offers well-presented displays of the usual dolls, vintage kitchen tools and medical equipment that you come to expect in regional museums. What makes this museum more interesting is the display of old photos, tools and mementos from the period when dikes were built along the Skagit River to reclaim land. It is open from 11 am to 5 pm Tuesday to Sunday; closed Monday. A $1 donation is requested.

## Skagit Valley Nurseries

The reclaimed farmland along the Skagit River delta is home to a large number of plant nurseries, and if you're a gardener you'll enjoy stopping to browse through the wealth of plants on display and for sale. The oldest of the local nurseries is Tillinghurst Seed Co (☎ 466-3329), 623 E Morris St, which is still doing business out of its 1885 storefront. RoozenGaarde Garden & Store (☎ 424-8531), 1587 Beaver Marsh Rd, near Mt Vernon, is one of the area's largest growers of tulips and daffodils, and it offers cut flowers for sale in the spring and bulbs for sale in the fall. Christianson's Nursery (☎ 466-3821), 1578 Best Rd, offers a wide selection of nursery stock, including roses, rhododendrons, perennials and fruit and berry plants. Contact the chamber of commerce for a complete list of regional nurseries.

## Places to Stay

Don't expect any lodging deals in La Conner: local inns and B&Bs take themselves seriously. A number of the B&Bs are old converted farmhouses in the land between La Conner and Mt Vernon. Ridge-

way B&B (☎ 428-8068, (800) 428-8068), 1292 McLean Rd, is situated in the midst of tulip fields and offers five guest rooms, two with private facilities. Rooms begin at $75. The White Swan Guest House (☎ 445-6805), 1388 Moore Rd, offers three rooms in a Victorian farmhouse and a two-story cottage with full kitchen. Rooms begin at $80.

Hotel Planter (☎ 466-4710, (800) 488-5409), 715 1st St, is a refurbished hotel with renovated rooms and 1907-era charm. Children are allowed on weekdays only; rooms start at $70 a night. La Conner Channel Lodge (☎ 466-1500), 205 N 1st St, is a new lodging right on the channel, though this handsome luxury inn does its best to look in keeping with the rest of turn-of-the-century La Conner. The large and airy rooms have fireplaces and decks and cost in the neighborhood of $132 to $209. The La Conner Country Inn (☎ 466-3101), 107 S 2nd St, is a shingle-sided lodge-like inn just a few steps away from the busy waterfront, and it offers comfortable rooms with fireplaces starting at $78.

## Places to Eat

For breakfast, head to the Calico Cupboard (☎ 466-4451), 720 1st St, a bakery and cafe with fresh baked pastries, omelets and light lunches. Just down the street is Legends (☎ 466-5240), 708 1st St, which offers Native American fast food – salmon tacos for less than $5.

The La Conner Tavern (☎ 466-9932) 702 1st St, is an old-fashioned bar with regional microbrews and burgers. Hungry Moon Delicatessen (☎ 466-1602), 110 N First St, offers sandwiches, desserts and light meals to eat in or take out. Lighthouse Inn (☎ 446-3147), with outdoor seating overlooking the channel, serves grilled seafood, steak and other Northwest fare in the $10 to $12 range; there's also a streetside deli serving sandwiches. Palmers Restaurant & Pub (☎ 446-4133) is the local fine-dining establishment, in the Channel Lodge. French-influenced entreès featuring veal, duck and seafood are in the $20 range.

# The San Juan Islands

The San Juan archipelago contains 457 islands sprawled across 750 sq miles of Pacific waters in the area where Puget Sound and the Straits of Juan de Fuca and Georgia meet. Only about 200 of these islands are named, and of these, only a handful are inhabited. Washington State Ferries provides service to the four largest islands – San Juan, Orcas, Shaw and Lopez – while others are accessible only by private boat or plane.

In the 1860s, the islands were the scene of an odd and prolonged border dispute, called the 'Pig War', between the USA and Britain, when they were claimed by both nations. Though both sides had very little at stake, they nearly came to blows over the shooting of a marauding pig. Eventually, the USA's claim of ownership prevailed without further bloodshed.

Only in the last twenty years have the San Juans been 'discovered', as they were long considered an inaccessible backwater of farmers and fishers, a patchwork of fields, forests, lakes and sheep pastures, with fishing boats setting sail from tiny rock-lined harbors. But today tourism is by far the mainstay of local economies. The islands are now a major holiday destination without lodging enough to handle the crowds during the summer high season. And yet, despite the inevitable adulteration that commercialization brings, the islands retain their bucolic charm and make for a restful, almost unforgettable retreat.

In certain respects, the islands don't even feel like they belong to North America. The sense of remoteness from mainland life is palpable, the pace slower. A rocky field filled with sheep looks like it could be off the coast of Ireland; a steep cliff-lined bay filled with old fishing boats could be in northern Scotland.

The islands are in a rain shadow created by Vancouver Island, and they receive only 25 inches of rain a year and are sunny 250 days a year – substantially better weather

**ORCAS ISLAND**
1  Smuggler's Villa Resort
2  Kangaroo House
3  Orcas Island Medical Center
4  Crescent Beach Kayaks
5  Ship Bay Oyster House
6  Turtleback Farm Inn
7  Rosario Resort & Spa
8  North End Campground
   Midway Campground
   South End Campground
9  Mountain Lake Campground
10 Doe Bay Village Resort
   & Retreat
11 Cafe Olga
12 Spring Bay Inn
13 Deer Harbor Lodge & Inn
14 Deer Harbor Resort & Marina

**SAN JUAN ISLAND**
15 Roche Harbor Resort
16 States Inn B&B
17 Lakedale Campground
18 Island Lodge at Friday
   Harbor
19 Pedal Inn Bicycle Park
20 Olympic Lights B&B

**LOPEZ ISLAND**
21 The Inn at Swifts Bay
22 Lopez Lodge
23 Edenwild Inn
24 Islander Lopez Resort
25 Bicycle Shop on Lopez
26 MacKaye Harbor Inn

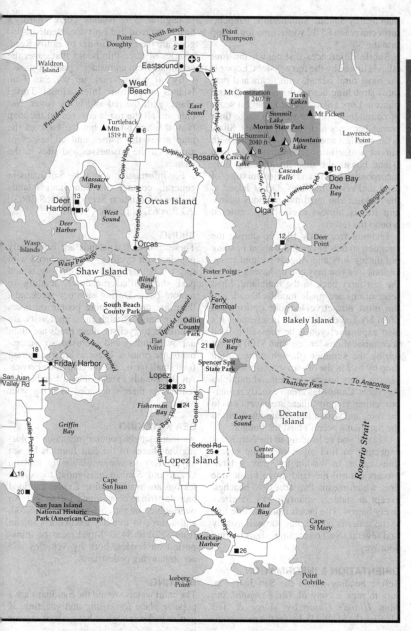

than nearby Seattle. Summertime temperatures can reach 85°F; wintertime lows drop into the 30°s.

Subtle differences distinguish the four islands linked by the ferry system. Lopez is the most rural island, with fields and pastures stretching across the island's central plateau. Lopez also has the strongest sense of community; people seem to make their homes here, not just visit the resorts. Shaw is the smallest and most remote island, with almost no facilities for tourists. San Juan Island boasts the most history, the only incorporated town and a nice mixture of rural and resort facilities. Orcas Island is the rockiest and most mountainous island, and life is almost exclusively centered around the resorts.

Lodging frequently fills up during the summer, so don't even think about heading out during July and August without reservations – or you may end up having to take the last ferry back to the mainland. Most reservations are made months ahead, and the most attractive lodging options are often booked even further in advance. It's also expensive: you'll be pressed to find accommodations for less than $100 a night during the summer (though prices often drop by half in the off-season); during high season, many resorts also demand multiple-day stays. Campsites aren't exactly numerous, either. Happily, there are exceptions to the rule, and with a little planning a trip to the San Juans needn't bust the budget.

Also, if you're heading to the San Juans expecting to find miles of public beach, think again. In Washington, private land-owners control the land down to the tide line, which means that access to beaches, except at state or county parks, is effectively barred. The beach from the tide line to the water *is* public, but you will usually find several 'No Trespassing' signs barring your way.

## ORIENTATION & INFORMATION
Before heading out to the San Juans, be sure to pick a copy of *The Essential San Juan Islands Guide* by Marge & Ted Mueller (JASI, 1994), by far the most com-

plete guide to the islands. There's hardly a turn in the road that isn't documented. Also good are the *Emily Guides* by Emily Reed, a series of three thin books that cover the essentials from an insider's point of view.

By all means, pick up the San Juan Islands map from International Travel Maps, with the red and black cover. Not only are all the roads covered on the map (valuable for bikers) but the back of the map gives the names and addresses of almost all the businesses and sites in the islands.

For information about the San Juans in general, contact the San Juan Islands Visitor Information Service (☎ 468-3663), PO Box 65, Lopez, WA 98261.

## BIKING
These mostly flat islands are immensely popular with cyclists – each is laced with tiny roads that wind through forests and past sheep-filled meadows, leading to remote bays. During summer weekends, there are probably more people on bikes than in cars. Though most motorists are courteous to cyclists, these roads are often narrow, winding and overused, so remember to use caution. Bicycles are transported for a small fee on Washington State Ferries. All the islands except Shaw offer bicycle rentals, so there's no need to bring your own.

## SEA KAYAKING
An increasingly popular means of exploring the shores of the San Juans is by sea kayak. Kayaks are available for rent on Orcas and San Juan islands; tours and lessons are available also. Expect a guided half-day trip to cost around $30 to $40. An overnighter might cost as much as $200, and a three to five-day excursion can run from $220 to $450. Kayaks can be transported on ferries, both by vehicles and accompanying pedestrians.

## BOATING
The calm waters around the San Juans are a popular place for sailing and yachting. If you're lucky enough to have a boat at your

disposal, or if you are planning on using boats as your primary means of transport, obtain a copy of *San Juan Islands, Afoot and Afloat* by Marge & Ted Mueller (Seattle, The Mountaineers, 1988), a handbook for the independent boat traveler.

More likely, travelers will turn to marinas on San Juan, Orcas and Lopez for various rental packages. Marinas usually offer a wide range of boat rentals, beginning with uncomplicated hourly hires of small rowboats and kayaks to lunch or cocktail cruises to more ambitious multiple-day excursions on yachts and sailboats. For the latter, you'll generally choose between a skippered charter (hiring a boat with crew by day or week) or a 'bare-boat' charter, which is self-navigated. Depending on your needs, tastes and size of party, a skippered charter can cost between $100 a day to several thousand dollars a week; meals, bedding and other niceties are usually included. See the individual island listings below for whom to contact about packages.

Prices for bare-boat rentals are equally broad and depend largely on the size and type of boat hired. Bare-boat charters provide all the on-board equipment and gear required or necessary for a safe trip. Food, itinerary, bedding and other personal items are left to you. Before you are allowed to rent a bare-boat charter, companies will probably ask you to participate in a short checkout cruise to familiarize you with the vessel and to ascertain that you are competent to handle the boat. Prices for a bareboat rentals begin at around $100 a day for a basic, comfortable sailboat.

## GETTING THERE & AWAY
### Air
Three airlines fly from the mainland to the San Juans. Harbor Air Lines (☎ (800) 359-3220) offers three flights a day from Sea-Tac Airport to Friday Harbor Municipal Airport, one mile west of Friday Harbor off Spring St. Kenmore Air (☎ (800) 543-9595) flies to Lopez, Orcas and San Juan islands on seaplanes from Lake Union and Lake Washington in Seattle; charter flights

are available. If the ferry seems too slow, West Isle Air (☎ (800) 874-4434) flies between Anacortes and the San Juans, with stops on Lopez, Orcas and San Juan islands; there are also links between Orcas and Friday Harbor. Four flights a day link Bellingham to the three major islands.

### Ferry
**Routes** By far the majority of people who visit the San Juans arrive on Washington State Ferries (☎ (800) 843-3779), the state-owned ferry system that serves the islands of the Puget Sound and western Washington. From the mainland, car ferries leave from Anacortes and depart for the four principal islands. At least one ferry a day continues on to Sidney, near Victoria, BC on Vancouver Island. Additionally, privately owned passenger-only ferries depart from Bellingham in the summer.

If this is your first time on the Washington State Ferries, pick up the small, widely available flyer and take a few minutes in advance to get used to reading the schedules and fares. The system is a little complicated and can be hard to figure out at first.

Generally speaking, there are three different kinds of ferry runs. The **international ferry run** travels between Anacortes and Sidney, with stops at Orcas and/or Friday Harbor, depending on the season and the ferry. Since this is an international run, note that if you board this ferry in the San Juans to return to Anacortes, you will be subject to a customs and immigrations inspection in Anacortes. The Anacortes/Sidney crossing takes three hours. The regular **domestic ferry run** originates in Anacortes and travels to some if not all of the islands. *Not all ferries stop at all four islands*. Make certain that the ferry you take is scheduled to stop at the island you want. Travel time to the closest island, Lopez, takes 45 minutes; the most distant port, Friday Harbor on San Juan, takes 1¼ hours. **Inter-island ferries** travel a circular route exclusively between the four islands.

See also the San Juan Islands Passenger Excursion Ferry under Getting There &

**Ferry Etiquette**
Washington State Ferries is the largest publicly owned ferry system in the USA, with 25 ferries that serve 20 different ports of call in the islands and coastal cities of the Puget Sound. Exploring western Washington is nearly impossible without at some point boarding a ferry, but chances are that most travelers aren't used to the notion of boats as public transport. Here are a few things to consider before boarding the ferries.

**Reservations** Except for the international sailings between Victoria and Seattle and Sidney and Anacortes, which recommend reservations, all other ferry service in the Puget Sound is offered on a first come, first serve basis. Drivers should plan to be at the ferry docks an hour before sailing, and foot passengers at least half an hour in advance, especially on weekends and in high season. If you don't get on the ferry you had planned, you just have to wait for the next. It's not unusual to have to wait for more than one ferry in high season.

**Boarding** After buying your ticket, you will be told to park in specific lanes. These represent the various destinations (especially in the San Juans, where the ferries stop at several islands), or size and weight restrictions. After ticketing and parking, you are free to wander, as long as you heed the call to return to your vehicles to board. You may be asked to back your vehicle onto the boat in some instances. Note that ferries may leave one port of call without being completely full, as they have vehicles to pick up at later destinations.
  Foot and bicycle passengers board first. The crew will indicate when various lanes should drive down the dock and load. After loading, car passengers can leave their vehicles and climb up to seating and eating areas. On some ferries, there's not much but free coffee to drink, while on larger vessels, full food service is available. Smoking is prohibited on the vehicle decks and inside the cabins.
  Pets must stay in vehicles on the lower decks (unless seeing-eye dogs).
  Before boarding, disabled passengers should notify the terminal for specific instructions and assistance.

**Disembarking** When disembarking from ferries at night, don't turn on your headlights until signs say it's OK. A succession of headlights serves to blind the crew whose job is to guide you off the vessel. Drivers should be courteous to pedestrian and local traffic after disembarking. Remember that you are part of a caravan of perhaps 50 or 60 vehicles, and can really clog up local intersections. Slow down and let people cross the street or make turns. ∎

Away for Bellingham. They combine transportation and whale-watching for a memorable passage to the islands.

**Fares** Fares are collected on westbound journeys only; that is, all tickets are considered roundtrip. Hence, if you plan to visit all the islands, it's cheapest to go all the way to westernmost Friday Harbor initially and then work your way back through the other islands, since you won't have to buy another ticket. The exception is the international crossing from Sidney to Anacortes: if you board this ferry, you'll need to pay for the eastbound journey.

Fares between Anacortes and Friday Harbor are $5 for a foot passenger, $17/21 low/high season for a car and driver, and $5 for each additional car passenger. Fares to Orcas/Shaw or Lopez from Anacortes are roughly $2 and $4 cheaper, respectively. Bicycles that are wheeled on in Anacortes incur a $2.75 surcharge, unless they are attached to a vehicle; in this case they ride free. The same rules apply to kayaks. However, foot passengers, bicycles and kayaks ride the inter-island ferries for free. The international ferry between Anacortes and Sidney is $30/36 during the low/high season, one way.

**WASHINGTON**

## Car
There is no public transport on the San Juans Islands. However, most motels and inns will pick up registered guests at the ferry, if they are notified in advance. Lopez, Orcas and San Juan islands each have a taxi service (call to reserve it if you know what ferry you're coming in on). Rental cars are available in Friday Harbor, and of course, bike rentals shops are almost more common than cafes on the islands.

## LOPEZ ISLAND
Lopez is the most agricultural of the San Juan Islands and the closest to the mainland. For both of these reasons, it is somewhat overlooked in the free-for-all that is tourism in the San Juans. However, if you want quiet, pastoral charm and don't need organized fun, it's hard to beat Lopez Island.

One of the first things you'll note as you drive around the island is that all the locals wave as they pass – they don't automatically assume you're a stranger. This friendly, rather agrarian bonhomie makes Lopez seem more like a rather green corner of Iowa than one of the Pacific Northwest's hottest tourist destinations. Lopez has also resisted the commercialization of its farmland rather better than the other islands: here, pastures are for grazing sheep or haymaking – they aren't merely the aesthetic property of quaint country inns and B&Bs.

The island gets rockier and more rural toward the south; near MacKaye Harbor, the stony fields and cliff-lined bay look for all the world like the Hebrides.

### Orientation & Information
The ferry terminal is located at a purely functional harbor on the extreme north end of the island. The closest Lopez comes to a town is Lopez village, no more than a collection of houses and a tiny business district overlooking a shallow bay. Most businesses, including one gas station and a grocery store, are here.

For information about businesses and recreation on Lopez Island, contact Lopez Island Chamber of Commerce (☎ 468-3663), PO Box 121, Lopez Island, WA 98261. If you want a taxi, call Angie's Cab (☎ 468-2227).

### Biking
Except for the long uphill slope leading from the ferry, Lopez is exceptionally flat, making this a good choice for island cyclists. Call ahead and Bicycle Shop on Lopez (☎ 468-3497), off School Rd, will meet the ferry with a bicycle or transport a bike to wherever you are staying on the island. If you are already in Lopez village, rent a bike at Lopez Bicycle Works (☎ 468-2847).

### Charter Fishing
Skippered day and overnight trips are available from Harmony Charters (☎ 468-3310), Mystic Sea Charters (☎ 468-2032) and Kismet Sailing Charters (☎ 468-2435), all of which operate out of Fisherman Bay. Visitors select from a number of organized packages, or they can schedule individualized tours or cruises.

### Places to Stay
**Camping** Just 1.3 miles south of the ferry landing, *Odlin County Park* (☎ 468-2496) is a pleasant waterfront campground, picnic area and public dock. Facilities are minimal – running water, pit toilets – but you can't beat the location. Sites are $10. *Spencer Spit State Park* (☎ 468-2251), five miles southeast of the ferry landing on Baker View Rd, can be reached by both boat and car. This can be a pretty busy place during midsummer, as it is one of the few state parks in the islands. There are nearly 50 sites (no hook-ups), with flush toilets, running water, picnic area and beach access.

**B&Bs** Built to resemble a Victorian mansion, the *Edenwild Inn* (☎ 468-3238) in Lopez village is the most eye-catching building on Lopez Island, with its lovely formal gardens, wide porch and gables. Popular with honeymooners, the mansion has eight guest rooms for $100 and up, some with fireplaces, all with private baths.

On the other side of the island is *The Inn at Swifts Bay* (☎ 468-3636), east on Port Stanley Rd (look for mailbox No 3402 and the banners hanging from the decks). In a quiet corner on a quiet island, this graceful inn offers a hot tub, easy beach access and three acres of surrounding woods for solitude. There are five guest rooms, three with private baths, costing $75 to $155.

Standing stalwart and white at the edge of a shallow bay, the *MacKaye Harbor Inn* (☎ 468-2253), on MacKaye Harbor Rd, is near the south end of the island. This 1920s sea captain's home offers four bedrooms and one suite ($40 to $90); the inn provides bicycles, rowboats and kayaks to guests. It's very popular and heavily booked.

**Hotels** Easily the cheapest place to stay on Lopez Island (and just about on all the islands) is the *Lopez Lodge* (☎ 468-2500), above the video store in Lopez village. Don't go looking for quaint charm: these three rooms are spacious and clean and offer views of the bay for $40 to $90. If you plan to spend most of your time outdoors, then these utilitarian digs might be just the ticket.

*The Islander Lopez Resort* (☎ 468-2233, (800) 736-3434), on Fisherman Bay Rd, south of Lopez village, is as close to a bona fide motel as one will find in the San Juans. The rooms are attractive, there's a hot tub and some have kitchenettes; most rooms have great views over Fisherman Bay. A night here should set you back $75 to $155. Across from the units is a bar and restaurant, which gives onto a marina.

**Places to Eat**

All of the following are less than a block from each other in Lopez village (in fact, they practically constitute Lopez village).

*Holly B's Bakery* (☎ 468-2133) is the early morning latte and pastry stop. Right across the street is *Gail's* (☎ 468-2150), which serves breakfast and lunch daily and dinners from Thursday to Sunday. Summer vegetables are grown in the adjacent garden. Pasta dishes, salads and sandwiches are had at lunch, while at night

steak, seafood and chicken round out the menu; meals begin at $12. In good weather, sit on the veranda below the grape arbor and watch the boats in the harbor. There's more of a pub atmosphere to *Bucky's Lopez Island Grill* (☎ 468-2595), with fish & chips, ribs and burgers.

*Paradise to Go* (☎ 468-4080), at the Edenwild Inn, offers light evening meals, like tortilla pie and salmon loaf, that are priced right (under $10). The most noted restaurant on Lopez is *The Bay Cafe* (☎ 468-3700), in an old storefront, with inventive, ethnic seafood dishes headlining the menu. Prices are in the $12 to $15 range.

**Things to Buy**

Chimera Gallery (☎ 468-3265) in Lopez village is also known as the Lopez Artist Cooperative. This small and amusing gallery features works from local artists and craftspeople, including pottery, hand-blown glass, Northwest Indian carvings, paintings, jewelry, woodblock prints, photography and weaving.

**SHAW ISLAND**

Shaw Island is the smallest of the San Juan Islands with ferry service, and it has the fewest facilities for travelers. South Beach County Park is really the only place to stay, and the only business on the island is a tiny store near the ferry landing. But don't get the idea that Shaw Island is uninhabited: in fact, it is as full of weekend and resort homes as the other islands, and in some ways an address on Shaw is quite fashionable simply because there aren't many tourists clotting up the roads and beaches.

There are good reasons to disembark at Shaw, especially if you're on two wheels. The lack of an organized tourist industry means that the island's roads are mostly free of traffic. The rolling hills are covered with sheep, whose wool plays a large part in one of Shaw's major cottage industries, spinning and knitting.

The one thing that nearly everyone notes about the ferry landing at Shaw is the fact that it is operated by Franciscan nuns. The nuns also operate the small general store and sell gas at the tiny marina near the ferry landing.

## Places to Stay

To reach *South Beach County Park* (☎ 378-4953), head south of the ferry landing on Blind Bay Rd and turn left on Squaw Bay Rd. There are a dozen campsites, with pit toilets only, costing $10 a night. The beach is popular in summer with picnickers and the water is often warm enough for swimming. The only other lodging option is one vacation home rental maintained by *Dockside Properties* (☎ 378-5060, (800) 992-1904), PO Box 1459, Friday Harbor, WA 98250, a San Juan Island-based company.

## ORCAS ISLAND

Orcas is the largest of the San Juan Islands, and in some ways it is the most exclusive. The mountainous landscape isn't particularly friendly to agriculture, the backbone of the local economies on the other islands. However, the rocky promontories and isolated harbors look good in real estate brochures, so retirement homes, resort communities and weekend manses generally take up the void.

In terms of rugged physical beauty, Orcas is probably the most fetching of the islands. Mt Constitution is, at 2407 feet, the highest point in the San Juans, and from its peak there are views stretching from Mt Baker to the Olympic Mountains and Vancouver Island. Mt Constitution is only one of several forested peaks on Orcas, around which the rest of the island folds in steep valleys. Along the rocky coast, narrow cliff-lined inlets do service as harbors for small pleasure boats.

Orcas Island offers a wide array of tourist facilities, including the San Juans' largest state park and campground. However, it still retains a palpable sense of being an insider's destination, perhaps because there really isn't a town on the island. You need to know where you are going before you get there because lodgings, restaurants and recreation are scattered all over. Orcas is the kind of place

The brown pelican, seen in the San Juan Islands, has a flexible beak that allows it to scoop fish out of the water as it skims over the ocean.

where families return to pass the summer generation after generation (some lodgings have a week-long minimum stay in high season), which only adds to the purposeful insularity of the island.

## Orientation & Information

Orcas Island is shaped like a saddlebag, with two distinct lobes very nearly cleaved by East Sound. The ferry terminal is at the tiny community of Orcas Landing, on the western half of the island. Roads lead north and then west to the village of Deer Harbor and, on the other side of Turtleback Mountain, to West Beach. The island's main population center is Eastsound, at the northern extreme of East Sound, where the two halves of the island meet. Most tourist and commercial facilities are available here, including a post office, laundry, bank, grocery store and gas station. The eastern half of the island is essentially comprised of Moran State Park and of resorts scattered along the coastline. The most noted of these is Rosario Resort, whose centerpiece is a mansion and spa built in 1910 by a former mayor of Seattle.

For more information, contact the Orcas Island Chamber of Commerce (☎ 376-2273), PO Box 252, Eastsound, WA 98245. Orcas Island Medical Center (☎ 376-2561) is in Eastsound off Mt Baker Rd.

WASHINGTON

## Orcas Island Historical Museum

This interesting series of six log-cabins-cum-museums (☎ 376-4849) relates the pioneer and local history of Orcas and the San Juan Islands. Besides the usual collection of household goods, tools, weapons and photographs, there's a good display of native artifacts. A curious collection of Chinese 'coolie' hats commemorates the San Juan Islands' role as a passageway for illegal Asian immigrants in the 1880s.

The museum is on N Beach Rd in Eastsound. It's open from 1 to 4 pm Monday to Saturday, Memorial Day to Labor Day, Friday and Saturday only from Labor Day to October 15. At other times you can see it by appointment. Admission is by donation.

## Moran State Park

The fourth-largest state park in Washington, seven-sq-mile Moran State Park (☎ 376-2326) is southeast of Eastsound on Horseshoe Hwy. The park is dominated by **Mt Constitution**, the highest peak in the San Juans at 2407 feet, which is graced with lakes and waterfalls, hiking and mountain bike trails and interpretive displays.

Nearly everyone who visits Orcas Island makes their way up the steep and winding paved road to the summit of Mt Constitution; in summer, this can be a busy place. The road up the mountain turns off Horseshoe Hwy just past Cascade Lake. This five-mile ascent is not a road for trailers or large mobile homes, or for that matter for the vast majority of cyclists, as the grade is a persistent 7% with frequent hairpin turns. At the top, beside an unfortunately situated microwave receiver, is a three-story stone tower whose summit affords great views over all of northwestern Washington.

There are two major bodies of water in the park, **Cascade and Mountain lakes**, which offer campgrounds, good trout fishing, non-motorized boating (both lakes offer boat rentals), picnic areas and swimming beaches.

There are nearly 40 miles of trails in Moran State Park, and about half of them are open seasonally for mountain biking.

Get a trail map from the park headquarters to find out current trails open to bikers.

Both Cascade and Mountain lakes are ringed by hiking trails, and a three-mile trail links the two lakes. This trail passes by the 100-foot **Cascade Falls** and two smaller falls. Cascade Falls is more easily reached from a trailhead off the Mt Constitution road, about half a mile uphill from the junction with Horseshoe Hwy. From here, it's only a quarter mile to the falls.

Trails lead from Cascade Lake's North End Campground and climb 4.3 miles up to Mt Constitution; however, it's a lot easier to catch a ride to the summit and take in the views on the way downhill. A portion of this trail is fairly flat: from the viewing tower, past marshy Summit Lake, to Little Summit, where the trail crosses the road before making the descent to Cascade Lake.

## Biking

For foot passengers getting off at Orcas landing, nothing could be more convenient than Dolphin Bay Bicycles (☎ 376-4157, 376-3093), two blocks from the ferry landing. Rates vary depending on the duration of the rental, and there is no charge for helmets. Racks and touring packs are also available. In Eastsound, head to Wildlife Cycles (☎ 376-4708), just off North Beach Rd, for bike rentals.

## Sea Kayaking

The protected shoreline of East Sound is a good place for beginners to learn the craft of sea kayaking, or for veterans to view wildlife along the rocky coastline. Crescent Beach Kayaks (☎ 376-2464), directly across the road from Crescent Beach near Eastsound, has a limited number of double and single kayaks for rent.

Both of the following kayak outfitters also offer a variety of guided trips in two-person kayaks, from a half day to several days, as well as beginner classes. Contact Shearwater Adventures (☎ 376-4699) in Eastsound for guided half-day trips of Eastsound, the Wasp Islands or the north shore. Island Kayak Guides (☎ 376-4755, 376-

2291), at the Doe Bay Resort & Retreat, offers guided tours of Peapod Island Wildlife Refuge and Gorilla Rock. Beginners will like the introductory trip around Doe Bay and Doe Island. There's also a full-moon evening trip.

In addition to these outfitters, a good number of places with overnight lodgings also facilitate kayaking and offer rental, instruction and excursions.

### Boating & Whale Watching

Deer Harbor Charters (☎ 376-5989, (800) 544-5758), at Deer Harbor Resort, has loads of nautical offerings. Rent a small rowboat with an outboard motor for fishing or exploring, or get outfitted with fishing gear and a guide. Take a sailing excursion, or lounge around the sound on a luxury yacht. Whale-watching excursions will also be replete with sightings of eagles, seals and sea lions, as well as killer whales, minke whales and porpoises. Bareboat charters are also available.

### Places to Stay

**Camping** *Moran State Park* (☎ 376-2326), southeast of Eastsound on Horseshoe Hwy, is the largest camping area in the San Juans. There are over 150 campsites (no hook-ups) in four different lake-side locations: Mountain Lake Campground at Mountain Lake, and North End, Midway and South End campgrounds at Cascade Lake. Sites are $10 and reservations are strongly recommended during the summer.

Tent and RV campers can also stay at *Doe Bay Village Resort & Retreat* on the Horseshoe Hwy at Doe Bay.

**B&Bs** *Kangaroo House* (☎ 376-2175), on N Beach Rd in Eastsound, is a 1907 Craftsman-style B&B set on three acres. There are five guest rooms ($65 to $100), two with private baths. On Crow Valley Rd, off Deer Harbor Rd, is *Turtleback Farm Inn* (☎ 376-4914). This lovely old farmhouse overlooks a wide meadow and lake and offers seven guest rooms ($70 to $150). All have private baths and share a sitting room and dining room.

South of Olga on Obstruction Pass Rd is a unique B&B, the *Spring Bay Inn* (☎ 376-5531). This B&B is run by two former park rangers, who include a program of basic kayak instruction in the price of the stay ($150 to $175). Hungry kayakers returning from a morning tour are greeted with a full breakfast. All equipment is provided. A two-night minimum stay applies during the summer season.

**Hotels** At Orcas Landing, the historic *Orcas Hotel* (☎ 376-4300) was built in 1904 and is listed on the National Register of Historic Places. The old hotel was completely refurbished in 1985, and it now offers a dozen rooms, some with private facilities; rates range between $69 and $170. This handsome inn, with wraparound porches and great views, also has an espresso bar, restaurant and lounge.

Deer Harbor, west of Orcas Landing, is one of the most beautiful harbors on an island known for its beauty. *Deer Harbor Resort & Marina* (☎ 376-4420) seems to own – and rent – pretty much every building in this little hamlet. There's a wide array of accommodations, ranging from cottages to motel-style bungalows ($99 to $169) to small houses right on the water ($229). The resort also offers full boat rental facilities, tennis courts, bike rentals and a small restaurant and market.

Just half a mile from Deer Harbor is the *Deer Harbor Lodge & Inn* (☎ 376-4110), on Deer Harbor Rd. Rooms aren't offered in the old lodge any longer (though the restaurant is open during high season); instead, there are eight rooms in a new, adjacent, log-cabin-like building ($89 for double occupancy).

In Eastsound, the *Outlook Inn* (☎ 376-2200), on Horseshoe Hwy, is now a lodging complex that has at its heart a venerable old hotel from the 1890s. While most rooms in the original hotel share bathrooms (starting at $84), there's a motel-like wing attached to the old hotel with modern rooms (starting at $110). Brand new is a suites-only addition on the bluff just above the old hotel ($225 and up). The restaurant at the

Outlook is notable for the fact that it offers Thai food (including vegetarian dishes) alongside more stalwart Northwest fare. Just next door is the *Landmark Inn* (☎ 376-2423), on the Horseshoe Hwy, another modern lodging with spacious suites.

**Resorts** If you're taking a family or a large group of friends to Orcas, consider the *Smuggler's Villa Resort* (☎ 376-2297, (800) 488-2097) on the northern coast just north of Eastsound on N Beach Rd. The resort is a complex of 20 small and medium-sized, architecturally innovative, two-bedroom homes with fireplaces, right on the beach. Facilities include a marina, an outdoor pool, a tennis court and other recreation facilities. Rates start at $150.

For years, the place for upscale Orcas visitors was *Rosario Resort & Spa* (☎ 376-2222, (800) 562-8820) on Rosario Way, four miles south of Eastsound off Horseshoe Hwy. Built in the 1910s as the middle-age folly of one-time Seattle mayor Robert Moran, the old mansion is the centerpiece of a resort complex that includes almost 180 modern rooms, tennis courts, swimming pools, a marina and elaborate tiled spa facilities in the basement. The old mansion houses a rather fussy and expensive restaurant and lounge, both with exquisite views over East Sound. Accommodations aren't cheap ($95 to $220), and the nouveau riche crowd is quite snooty; however, new management is bent on making this rather tired doyen worth the money.

There are resorts, and then there's *Doe Bay Village Resort & Retreat* (☎ 376-2291, 376-4755), on Doe Bay on the island's easternmost shore, 18 miles east of Eastsound on the Horseshoe Hwy. This slightly shabby, comfortable and welcoming vacation spot is by far the least expensive and most 'alternative' lodging in the San Juans. The resort overlooks Doe Bay, as lovely a spot as any on Orcas, and has at once the atmosphere of an artists' commune, hippie retreat and New Age center. Not coincidentally, Doe Bay possesses the only natural hot springs in the islands and a beachfront sauna.

The lodgings here include campsites, dorm and hostel rooms ($14.50), a tree house and various levels of cabins. Cabins without a bathroom or kitchen start at $41, moving up to $98 as bathrooms, kitchens, wood stoves, beds and extra rooms are added. Rates are for double occupancy; each additional person adds $10.50. All lodging facilities are in a grassy swale with views of the water, with the clothing-optional hot springs off to one side. Off to the other side is the office and restaurant, where healthy meals are served up family-style, according to the whim of the cook.

**Vacation Home Rentals** *Dockside Properties* (☎ 378-5060, (800) 992-1904), PO Box 1459, Friday Harbor, WA 98250, on San Juan Island, has a handful of vacation homes available for rent. Call the 800 number for an illustrated brochure with detailed rates.

### Places to Eat

There are dining rooms at most resorts and marinas, and some are noted above. The following restaurants deserve special notice. At Orcas landing, *The Boardwalk* (☎ 376-2971) is a string of cottages-cum-boutiques with several eating options, including burgers and fish & chips. The *Orcas Hotel* (☎ 376-4300) is open for breakfast, lunch and dinner. The old hotel's dining room combines a pub ambiance with Northwest cuisine. There's also a small coffeeshop tucked into the westside corner of the building for espresso and pastries.

*Doty's A-1 Cafe & Bakery* (☎ 376-2593), off North Beach Rd, is the place to go for that all-important jelly doughnut or deli sandwich; there's also indoor seating for an inexpensive breakfast or lunch. For high-brow cuisine, go to *Christina's* (☎ 376-4904), along Horseshoe Hwy in Eastsound. Fresh seafood is the major item on the highly eclectic, rather French menu (grilled sturgeon with beurre blanc is $19).

Following Horseshoe Hwy two miles

south from Eastsound, the *Ship Bay Oyster House* (☎ 376-5886) is in an attractive, turn-of-the-century sea captain's home. Offerings include oysters, scallops, mussels, shrimp, and catch-of-the-day specials from $12 to $17. Steak, chicken and ribs are also available.

At the Orcas Room at *Rosario Resort* (☎ 376-2222), 1 Rosario Way, there's a lot to like, including the views, the food (French-influenced Northwest cuisine like leg of lamb and veal scallops in the $20 range), and the handsome old mansion. But if you're not in the mood for intimidating waiters and the company of European industrialists, go for a relaxed lunch instead (the Caesar salad is $8).

In the tiny community of Olga, find *Cafe Olga* (☎ 376-5098) in the Orcas Island Artworks building. At this homey restaurant and gallery, light meals and bakery goods are served at lunch and for early dinner.

### Getting Around

The all-in-one transportation service on Orcas Island is Adventure Limo & Taxi (☎ 376-4994), which offers regular taxi service as well as guided tours of island sites. They also rent cars and minivans.

### SAN JUAN ISLAND

Most visitors will find that San Juan Island, of all the islands, offers the most hospitable blend of sophisticated amenities, rural landscapes, bustling harbors and cultural facilities. A large part of the island's draw is Friday Harbor: with a population of 1730 people, it's the only real town in all the San Juan Islands. But follow any of the streets out of Friday Harbor and you're soon on a

---

### The 'Pig War'

San Juan Island was the scene of an odd border dispute between the USA and Britain in the period between 1855 and 1872. In 1846, both nations agreed to split North America along the 49th parallel, with Britain retaining Vancouver Island. However, the ownership of the San Juan Islands was left unresolved, as the treaty divided the islands through 'the middle of the channel'. The British thought the channel in question was Rosario Strait, while the USA believed it was the Haro Strait. In between lie the San Juan Islands.

The dispute wasn't terribly important until American settlement took hold. The British Hudson's Bay Company (HBC) had maintained a fishery and various farms on San Juan Island for many years; then in 1855, a US magistrate attempted to levy import duties on goods from the HBC farms. Official indignation was expressed by both sides, while US settlers continued to stream onto the islands. Finally, in 1859, shots were fired. A pig from the HBC farms had taken to wandering from its pens and rooting in the potato patch of a US settler. The American shot the pig, the British demanded compensation, and, after more mutual indignation, the USA sent troops to occupy the island and found Fort Pickett (now known as the American Camp). The British sent war ships from Victoria, BC, to the island to protect HBC interests.

Cooler heads prevailed in London and Washington, DC, and a treaty declaring joint military occupation was agreed upon. Meanwhile, the dispute was sent to Kaiser Wilhelm I of Germany to arbitrate. In 1872, he judged in favor of the USA, and the international boundary was established through Haro Strait. ∎

central plateau, where small farms, dairies and lakes fill the verdant landscape.

The only other community of any size is Roche Harbor, on a beautiful bay to the northwest. This used to be the center of a lime-processing operation, an early San Juan Island industry. John McMillin, a one-time attorney from Tacoma, built an imposing complex that included lime kilns, a grand hotel, a private estate, workers' cottages, a small railway, a company store, a chapel and a shipping wharf. The lime factory closed in the 1950s, and the extensive buildings are now part of Roche Harbor Resort.

### Orientation & Information

San Juan Island is the most westerly of the San Juan Islands. The ferry terminal is at Friday Harbor on the eastern side of the island. From Friday Harbor, take 2nd St to Tucker Ave, which will turn into Roche Harbor Rd and lead to those resort facilities in 10 miles. The main road from Friday Harbor south is Cattle Point Rd.

For more information, contact the San Juan Island Chamber of Commerce (☎ 378-5240), PO Box 98, San Juan Island, WA 98250. The visitors center at 1st and Spring Sts can fill you in on the San Juan Island National Historical Park.

The post office (☎ 378-4511) is at 220 Blair Ave. For medical emergencies, go to the Inter-Island Medical Center (☎ 378-2141), 550 Spring St. Clean up those dirty clothes at the Wash Tub Laundromat (☎ 378-2070), just off Spring St at Front St, behind the San Juan Inn.

### Friday Harbor

Friday Harbor offers a lively restaurant scene and more culture than you have reason to expect in this distant outpost of the USA. There are several unusual museums and plenty of lodging options and outdoor outfitters to round out your stay.

Friday Harbor is a popular stop for Canadians coming over from Victoria, BC to shop and relax. During summer, there are a number of festivals and events – particularly the Dixieland Jazz Festival – that fill the streets and most available lodging.

**Pig War Museum** For those who can't get enough of the British/US border conflict, this private museum (☎ 378-6495), at Tucker Ave and Guard St in Friday Harbor, might do the trick. Bits of this and that from the period in question are added to mannequin-filled tableaus to relive historic scenes between the troops. The museum is open from noon to 6 pm Memorial Day to Labor Day only; closed Sundays. Admission for $3 for adults and $2 for children and seniors.

**San Juan Historical Museum** In an 1890s farmhouse now on the outskirts of Friday Harbor, this museum (☎ 378-3949), 405 Price St, commemorates early pioneer life on San Juan Island. While the building itself is interesting for its vernacular farmhouse architecture, the displays featuring kitchen and parlor furnishings, like the pump organ and massive wood range, are worth checking out. The museum is open from 1 to 4:30 pm Wednesday to Saturday, May through September. The rest of the year the museum is open the same hours Thursday and Friday only. Admission is by donation.

**Whale Museum** If the San Juan Islands had a mascot, it would surely be the killer whale. Indeed, these 25-foot-long whales are sometimes seen by lucky ferry passengers traveling through the islands. These and other sea mammals have been given their own natural history museum (☎ 378-4710) at 62 1st St. There are a number of whale skeletons and life-size models as well as displays about marine life in general, Native American legends and recordings of ocean mammal songs. Children are welcome; there's even a hands-on children's room with puzzles and the like. If you're truly serious, the museum offers courses concerning marine ecology and natural history.

The Whale Museum is open daily from 10 am to 5 pm Memorial Day to Septem-

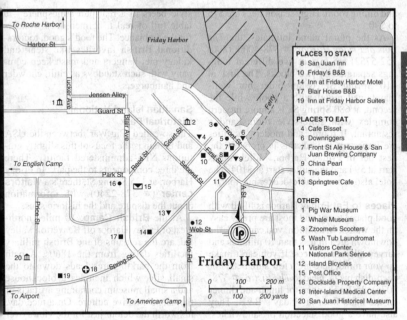

Friday Harbor

| | |
|---|---|
| 0 | 100 | 200 m |
| 0 | 100 | 200 yards |

**PLACES TO STAY**
8  San Juan Inn
10  Friday's B&B
14  Inn at Friday Harbor Motel
17  Blair House B&B
19  Inn at Friday Harbor Suites

**PLACES TO EAT**
4  Cafe Bisset
6  Downriggers
7  Front St Ale House & San
Juan Brewing Company
9  China Pearl
10  The Bistro
13  Springtree Cafe

**OTHER**
1  Pig War Museum
2  Whale Museum
3  Zzoomers Scooters
5  Wash Tub Laundromat
11  Visitors Center,
National Park Service
12  Island Bicycles
15  Post Office
16  Dockside Property Company
18  Inter-Island Medical Center
20  San Juan Historical Museum

ber 30, and daily from 11 am to 4 pm the rest of the year. Admission for adults is $3, children and seniors $2.

**Dixieland Jazz Festival** Friday Harbor's biggest party of the year is the annual jazz festival, held on the last weekend of July. More than a dozen jazz bands play the weekend long on a number of indoor and outdoor stages, with a special kids' concert on Saturday and a jazz church service on Sunday. Food and crafts booths line most downtown streets. Plan well in advance for lodging, as most rooms book up early for the weekend. For more information about the festival, contact the festival office (☎ 378-4224, 378-5509) at PO Box 1666, Friday Harbor, WA 98250.

**Places to Stay** On the hill above the harbor, *Blair House B&B* (☎ 378-5907), 345 Blair Ave, is a woodsy, 1909 home offering five rooms with shared baths and a cottage with private facilities. All rooms share access to a swimming pool and hot tub. Room rates are $75 to $85, while the cottage goes for $95 for two people.

In Friday Harbor, two old downtown hotels have been turned into B&Bs. *Friday's B&B* (☎ 378-5848, (800) 352-2632), 35 1st St, first opened its doors in 1891. Renovated in 1992, the rooms are individually decorated according to a wildlife theme. There's a strong focus on privacy and intimacy here – the walls have even been soundproofed! Friday's now offers seven double rooms with shared bath, three suites with private baths and one kitchenette. Rooms cost $80 to $155; a continental breakfast is included. The Bistro Restaurant is on the main floor.

The *San Juan Inn* (☎ 378-2070), 50 Spring St, is another historic hotel that's been updated with modern conveniences without losing its 1879 Victorian charm. There are four double rooms with private baths and six rooms that share three baths. All rooms share a 2nd-floor sitting room and dining room. High-season rates are $75 to $90.

As the plural name intimates, the *The Inns at Friday Harbor* (☎ 378-4000, (800) 752-5752) are in fact two different lodgings separated by two blocks. The first, at 410 Spring St, is an older but well-maintained motel with a pool, while the second, at 680 Spring St, is a more modern complex with suite-style rooms and a restaurant. If roomy and modern facilities are important to you, this is probably the best bet in Friday Harbor. Motel rooms start at $94 and the suites start at $104. The hotel also runs a double-decker bus tour.

**Places to Eat** Friday Harbor is filled with good places to eat and most are pretty easy on the wallet. In addition, you can walk the downtown area in less than 10 minutes and survey all your choices. If you can't make up your mind, here are a few sure bets. For deep-dish pizza, head to *The Bistro* (☎ 378-3076), 35 1st St, open for lunch and dinner on the main floor at Friday's B&B. They also have a good selection of sandwiches, salads and pasta. *China Pearl* (☎ 378-5254), 51 Spring St, is a good place to go for inexpensive traditional and Sichuan food. There's live jazz on the weekends and karaoke whenever anyone has the nerve.

Down along the waterfront are several supper clubs, such as *Downriggers* (☎ 378-2700) at the base of Spring St, that offer Northwest cuisine – good steak and grilled seafood ($10 to $22) – along with views over the harbor.

*Springtree Cafe* (☎ 378-4848), 310 Spring St, offers casual bistro-style dining in a spare but comfortable cafe. The menu tends toward seafood and vegetarian dishes ($10 to $12), cooked with Northwest élan but with an eye for health. In summer, there's dining in the courtyard. There's more upscale dining at cozy *Cafe Bisset* (☎ 378-3109), 170 1st St, where seafood, steak and pasta ($12 to $15) are served up with continental flair.

*Front St Ale House & San Juan Brewing Company* (☎ 378-2337), 1 Front St, is the island's only brewery serving up British-style beers in a real pub atmosphere – a table full of real fishermen does wonders for the ambiance. The food's good, too: traditional British favorites like steak and kidney pie, bangers and mash keep company with such standbys as chili, chowder and hamburgers.

## San Juan Island National Historical Park

The so-called 'Pig War' between the USA and Britain is the focus of this slightly gratuitous NPS-administered facility. There are three components to the park. In Friday Harbor, at 125 Spring St, there's a **visitors center** (☎ 378-2240) with information about the dispute and the historic sites.

At the **British Camp**, 10 miles northwest of Friday Harbor off Beaverton Valley Rd, are the remains of the British military facilities dating from the 1860s. A path from the parking area leads down to the small site, which includes a blockhouse and a small museum containing artifacts of the island's native culture. On a nice day, it's worth the detour just for the views over Garrison Bay.

On the southern flank of the island is the **American Camp**, five miles south of Friday Harbor off Cattle Point Rd, which has slightly more developed facilities. The sole remains of the 1859 fort are the officers' barracks and a laundress's house, though a series of interpretive trails lead to earthwork fortifications, a British farm from the dispute era and the beach. Near the trailhead is a small visitors center.

## Lime Kiln State Park

Set on the western shore of San Juan Island, off scenic West Side Rd, this is, surprisingly, the only park in the world devoted to whale watching. Most sitings here are of killer or minke whales, who gather to dine on the salmon runs that proceed through Haro Strait. A trail leads from the car park to the main viewing area, which is equipped with picnic tables and interpretive panels explaining the whales' movements and natural history. Be sure to bring binoculars (even though whales are frequently spotted quite close to shore) and a little patience.

## Biking
Bicycle rentals are available from Island Bicycles (☎ 378-4941), 380 Argyle Rd, or Zzoomers Scooters (☎ 378-8811), 65 Front St, both in Friday Harbor. Next to Lopez, San Juan is the flattest island, and it's very popular with the cycling set. While there's great scenery along all the roads on San Juan, the West Side Rd, which edges along the island's western coast, offers some great views.

## Sea Kayaking
For an educational wildlife tour, take one of the day-long kayak trips offered from May to October by Sea Quest Expeditions (☎ 378-5767). Sea Quest grounds itself in conservation and environmentalism, so sightings of killer whales, porpoises, seals and bald eagles get heavily touted as a learning experience. Both Sea Quest and San Juan Kayak Expeditions (☎ 378-4436) offer fully outfitted, two to five-day kayak trips with no previous kayaking experience required; both are in Friday Harbor. Call to set up appointments.

## Boat Charters
Most charter companies offer 30 to 55-foot sailboats for scenic day-trips, instruction and week-long cruises, either skippered or bare-boat. Most rent year round, but keep in mind that you'll save heaps if you make it in the off-season. Powered yachts are also available from Charters Northwest (☎ 378-7196), 189 1st St S. Charter skippered fishing trips and wildlife tours from Trophy Charters (☎ 378-2110). More sailboats are available from Wind'n Sails Charters (☎ 378-5343, (800) 752-4121).

For more charters contact Dolphin Yacht Charters (☎ 378-4829), a charter agency brokering skippered and bare-boat yachts between Seattle and Alaska.

## Whale Watching
In the summer season, San Juan Boat Rentals & Tours (☎ 378-3499, (800) 232-6722) operates three to four-hour whale-watching trips daily from Mid-May through September, with June the best month for sightings. Board the *Blackfish* at Slip M at the Friday Harbor docks. The captain and naturalist have good track records for finding killer whales, and visitors can eavesdrop on the whales using the

The killer whale, also called the orca, is easiest to spot around the islands in June.

cruiser's underwater hydrophone. You'll be sharing it with no more than a dozen other people. Prices range from $29 to $40 depending on the time of year.

In addition to killer whales, Western Prince Cruises' (☎ 378-5315) four-hour wildlife tour promises views of eagles, seals and porpoises. Tours on the twice-weekly *Western Prince* accommodate up to 33 people, and the tour price of $43 includes admission to Friday Harbor's Whale Museum. Reservations are recommended.

### Scuba Diving

For scuba gear, instruction and rental, head for Emerald Seas Aquatics (☎ 378-2772), at the Spring St landing. Chartered half-day dives cost $55. Full-day dives for four to six passengers cost $500 to $600.

### Organized Tours

Sea-queasy sightseers should head to the Inns at Friday Harbor (☎ 378-4000, (800) 752-5752), 410 Spring St. Hop on the hotel's double-decker bus for a guided tour of the area that includes British Camp and Lime Kiln Park.

### Places to Stay

**Camping** Five miles from Friday Harbor, the versatile *Lakedale Campground* (☎ 378-2350), 2627 Roche Harbor Rd, has 115 tent sites, 15 bicycle sites and 19 RV sites (no hook-ups), plus three tent cabins. Sites ($15 to $21) are nestled among woods and grassy fields between the campground's three trout and bass-stocked lakes and are available from April 1 to October 15. There are also showers, boat rental and a grocery store, which has camping equipment and fishing tackle for sale or rental.

Cyclists will love *Pedal Inn Bicycle Park* (☎ 378-3049), 1300 False Bay Drive, a campground exclusively for cyclists. The campground lies south of Friday Harbor. Reach False Bay Drive from Cattle Point Rd, or from False Bay Rd off Bailer Hill Rd. Purchase staple food items from the small grocery store.

The small campground at *San Juan*

*County Park* (☎ 378-2992), 380 Westside Rd N, on San Juan's west shore, offers access to excellent scuba diving and views of Victoria, BC. It gets crowded during the summer, so plan accordingly. Groceries and tackle are available near the boat launch.

**B&Bs** There's a proliferation of B&Bs on San Juan Island. For a more complete listing, contact the chamber of commerce for a brochure by the B&B Association of San Juan Island.

On the far western side of the island is the *States Inn B&B* (☎ 378-6240, 378-4243), 2039 W Valley Rd, which was once a country schoolhouse. It is now on a working horse ranch and the old school has been remodeled into nine guest rooms, all with private facilities; guided horseback rides are available to guests. Rooms cost $80 to $110. On the southern edge of the island is *Olympic Lights B&B* (☎ 378-3186), 4531-A Cattle Point Rd, a restored 1895 farmhouse standing on an open bluff with views south onto the Strait of Juan de Fuca and the Olympic Mountains. There are five guest rooms ($70 to $105) in the sparely elegant inn, with a mix of private and shared baths.

**Hotels** On a quiet side street half a mile from the town center, *Island Lodge at Friday Harbor* (☎ 378-2000, (800) 822-4753), 1016 Guard St, is another modern, comfortable motel facility with a hot tub and sauna; it's also a rare good deal for the San Juans. The spacious motel rooms go for $69, and kitchen suites are $85. As if that weren't enough, the motel also overlooks a llama pasture.

**Resorts** Located on the site of a former lime kiln and country estate, *Roche Harbor Resort* (☎ 378-2155, (800) 451-8910), in Roche Harbor, is just about the nicest place to stay in all the San Juans. Certainly there's no more beautiful harbor, and the slightly weird accouterments left over from the limestone mining days (check out the family mausoleum festooned with arcane

Masonic symbolism) only add to the charm. In 1886, limestone king John McMillin built the imposing *Hotel de Haro* – with its wide, ivy-covered verandahs and formal gardens – as the company hotel. Over 100 years later, it's still taking guests, who enjoy its slightly faded gentility; rooms at this landmark inn begin at $80. A number of refurbished workers' cottages fill a grassy meadow above the harbor, just a few yards from the swimming pool and playground, and rent for $125 to $155. Fully modern condominiums are discretely tucked behind a stand of trees; they begin at $110 to $138. In addition to the lodgings, there's a marina with boat rentals, restaurant, lounge and old general store on the dock. You can even land your private jet on the air strip.

**Vacation Home Rentals** *Dockside Property Company* (☎ 378-5060, (800) 992-1904), 285 Blair Ave, manages around 60 year-round vacation homes, most of which are on San Juan Island. Call to request a brochure with pictures of all the homes and their rates, which start at $500 weekly.

### Getting Around

Friday Harbor Car Rentals (☎ 378-4351) operates out of the Inns of Friday Harbor, 410 Spring St. There are also car rentals at the Friday Harbor airport from Practical Rent-A-Car (☎ 293-6750).

You can also rent mopeds from Susie's Mopeds (☎ 378-5244), at Nichols and A St. Zzoomers Scooters (378-8811) has a location in Friday Harbor, 65 Front St, and at Roche Harbor Resort.

Primo Taxi (☎ 378-3550) is the place to call for a cab.

# Whidbey Island

Green, low-lying Whidbey Island snakes along the northern Washington mainland from the northern suburbs of Seattle to Deception Pass at Fidalgo Island. The sea is never far away on this long, narrow island, but weekend visitors from Seattle can make the attractive harbor towns on Whidbey as congested as the mainland suburbs. Unlike the San Juan Islands, there is no impression of remoteness here. Langley and Deception Pass State Park are immensely popular vacation spots, the metropolitan sprawl of Puget Sound cities is quite close, and Oak Harbor contains an active, modern naval air base. However, if you don't have time for a trip to the San Juans and hanker for a ferry ride and an island seascape, then a detour across Whidbey is a fine introduction to historic maritime Washington – and don't forget to pick up a bottle of loganberry liqueur near Greenbank and a plate of fresh oysters in Coupeville.

## ORIENTATION & INFORMATION

Whidbey Island, at 45 miles long the longest island in the USA, is threaded by Hwys 20 and 525, which links to ferries at Clinton and to the mainland suburb of Mukilteo. At Keystone, the ferry from Port Townsend links Hwy 20 with the Olympic Peninsula. Highway 20 continues north to Oak Harbor and crosses dramatic Deception Pass on two narrow bridges. Anacortes and the San Juan Island ferries are immediately north; I-5 and the North Cascades National Park are to the west.

The only hospital on the island is Whidbey General Hospital (☎ 678-5151, 321-5151) in Coupeville at 101 N Main St (off Hwy 20).

## GETTING THERE & AWAY

Though tourists aren't likely to fly directly to Whidbey Island, commuter flights on Harbor Airlines (☎ 675-6666, (800) 359-3220), Monroe Landing Rd, Oak Harbor, do depart daily from the Oak Harbor Airport for Sea-Tac Airport and the San Juan Islands.

Washington State Ferries (☎ (800) 843-3779) operates ferries between Clinton and Mukilteo and between Keystone and Port Townsend. The automobile/driver fare for the 20-minute Mukilteo-Clinton ferry is $3.75, passengers cost $2.15; the ferry runs every half hour. Respective fares for the 30-minute Keystone-Port Townsend ferry are $5.55/1.65; the ferry runs about every 45 minutes.

There are two Budget car-rental agencies in Oak Harbor, downtown (☎ 675-2000), 133 W Pioneer Way, and at the airport (☎ 675-6666).

## GETTING AROUND
Island Transit buses run the length of the island every hour for free, daily except Sunday, from the Clinton ferry dock to Langley, Freeland, Greenbank, the Keystone ferry dock, Coupeville, Oak Harbor and Deception Pass. For more information call 321-6688.

## DECEPTION PASS STATE PARK
Early explorers of the Puget Sound believed that Whidbey Island was a peninsula, and it wasn't until 1792 that Captain George Vancouver found this narrow cliff-lined crevasse, churned by rushing water, between Fidalgo and Whidbey islands. Passage through the channel was nearly impossible in the days of sailing ships, and it remains a challenge today even to motorized boats: high tides charge through the pass at better than nine knots.

Visitors to the 5.6-sq-mile park (☎ 675-2417) usually begin their acquaintance with this dramatic land and seascape by parking at the shoulders on either side of the bridge and walking across the spans that arch the chasm. The bridge was built during the 1930s by the CCC and was considered an engineering feat in its day. The park itself also spans the channel, with facilities – including campgrounds – on both the north and south flanks of the passage.

More than 3.5 million visitors per year visit Deception Pass, which makes it Washington's most popular state park. Besides the dramatic bridge overviews, there are over 17 miles of saltwater shoreline and seven nearby islands, three freshwater lakes, boat docks, hundreds of picnic sites and 27 miles of forest trails available to both hikers and bikers. The park is espe-cially popular with scuba divers and sea kayakers, who explore the park's reefs and cliff-edge shores.

Especially popular here are the campgrounds. Well over 250 campsites are nestled in the forests beside a lake and a saltwater bay. However, all sites are allocated on a first-come, first-serve basis, which means that competition for the sites on summer weekends can be fierce. Late-arriving cyclists should ride past the dis-heartening rows of cars and ask about walk-in sites. Rates for standard sites during the summer are $11; facilities include running water, flush toilets and snack concessions.

## OAK HARBOR
Boosters of Oak Harbor (population 18,795) have recently gone to a lot of trouble to promote the virtues of this, the largest town on Whidbey Island. However Oak Harbor remains mostly charmless, dominated as it is by the Naval Air Station Whidbey Island. Built during WW II to re-arm planes defending the West Coast from attack, the post currently maintains a staff of 9000 personnel and is largely a flight-training facility for reservists and home to a number of defensive air squadrons. For tours of the base, call 257-2286.

### Orientation & Information
Oak Harbor is 38 miles from the ferry at Clinton, nine miles from Deception Pass and 21 miles from Anacortes. Highway 20 is the main drag through the town, although an old downtown area along the harbor bypassed by the highway, is just east of the Pioneer Way junction. The Greater Oak Harbor Chamber of Commerce (☎ 675-3535), 5506 Hwy 20, can provide tourist information.

### Places to Stay & Eat
Several modern motels are scattered along the strip north of town. However, the most noteworthy is the *Auld Holland Inn* (☎ 675-0724, (800) 228-0148), 5861 Hwy 20, with its operating windmill and old-world Dutch motif. Lodgings are offered complete with

kitchenettes, outdoor pool, sauna, spa and tennis and basketball courts; rooms begin at $55, and children and pets are welcome. Some of best food in Oak Harbor is served in the inn's *Kasteel Franssen Restaurant & Lounge*, which serves Dutch, French and some Northwest cuisine (from $9 to $19) in a pleasantly ersatz Euro-kitsch dining room.

For more up-to-date southern Italian fare, head to *L'Approdo* (☎ 679-8942), at the corner of Hwy 20 and 700 Ave. Live jazz is played nightly in the lounge.

## COUPEVILLE

One of the oldest towns in Washington, Coupeville (population 1522) has an attractive old seafront filled with shops, antique stores and old inns facing onto Penn Cove, noted for its oyster and mussel production. The town's founder, Captain Thomas Coupe, is noted as the only captain to have sailed a four-rigger through Deception Pass; he settled here along the shallow bay and claimed land for a farm. Other seafarers followed suit, and Coupeville, then a farming community, began to thrive. Although the old town, especially along Front St, remains attractive and is great for a stroll or a weekend getaway, the urban sprawl from Oak Harbor and the influx of refugee Seattlites have begun to take a toll.

Stop by the visitors center for a walking tour map of the town's old homes and business district; Coupe's original home is still standing at Grange St and the waterfront. The **Island County Historical Society Museum** (☎ 678-3310), on the waterfront at Front and Alexander Sts, tells the story of the community's shipping and farming history and is open from 11 am to 5 pm on weekdays, and from 10 am to 5 pm on weekends. Admission is $2 for adults and $1.50 for seniors and students.

### Orientation & Information

Coupeville is 10 miles south of Oak Harbor. For more information about the area, contact the Central Whidbey Chamber of Commerce (☎ 678-5434) at 5 S Main St, Coupeville, WA 98239.

### Places to Stay

A number of old Coupeville homes and inns remain in service as B&Bs. The *Inn at Penn Cove* (☎ 678-8000, (800) 688-2683), 702 N Main St, is made up of two side-by-side Victorian farmhouses that offer B&B lodgings just three blocks from the harbor. Rates for the six rooms range from $69 to $105. The *Anchorage Inn* (☎ 678-5581), 807 N Main St, isn't as old as it looks: it is in fact a painstaking reproduction of a Victorian mansion. While history buffs may object, at least all five rooms have private baths and the floors don't squeak. Rooms range from $75 to $90.

*The Coupeville Inn* (☎ 678-6668, (800) 247-6162), 200 Coveland St, is convenient to harborfront shopping and strolling, and some of the inn's rooms offer balconies overlooking Penn Cove. Double rooms cost $55 to $75, which includes a continental breakfast.

For history, you can't beat the *Captain Whidbey Inn* (☎ 678-4097, (800) 366-4097), 2072 W Captain Whidbey Inn Rd, three miles west of Coupeville on Madrona Way. This madrona-log inn overlooking Penn Cove was built in 1907 and is a showcase of old-fashioned – almost medieval – charms. Lodging is in 12 low-slung guest rooms in the main lodge (some with bathroom down the hall), as well as cottages (some with kitchens), and a more modern building with verandahs facing onto a pond. Rates range between $75 and $175, with two to three-night minimum stay on weekends and include a free continental breakfast. For a romantic dinner there's no cozier place than the wood-lined dining room.

On a more functional level, the *Tyee Motel* (☎ 678-6616), 405 S Main St, is a modest, standard motel with rates starting at $43.

### Places to Eat

A good place to go for fresh bread and pastries, as well as deli-style salads and soups, is *Knead & Feed* (☎ 678-5431), below 4 Front St. The *Captain's Galley* (☎ 678-0241), 10 Front St, is the place to head to sample local oysters and mussels; they also have steak and pasta. There are great views over the harbor, and an outdoor deck. The trendy spot for Northwest cuisine is *Christopher's* (☎ 678-5480), 23 Front St, open Wednesday to Sunday only for lunch and dinner.

### Things to Buy

Ten miles south of Coupeville on Hwy 525, off Wonn Rd, is Whidbey's Greenbank Berry Farm (☎ 678-7700). This farm is the world's largest producer of loganberries, a sweet, blackish berry rather like a boysenberry or black raspberry. The farm offers tours through the old farm buildings, and it sells fruit and fixings for picnics on the grounds. The farm is most noted for its loganberry liqueur, called Whidbeys, which is distilled from local berries and is used as an aperitif and to make kirs a la Northwest. As Whidbeys is Washington's only home-grown liqueur, it makes a good gift or souvenir. The winery-style farm is open from 10 am to 5 pm for touring, tasting and picnicking.

### FORT CASEY STATE PARK

Along with Fort Flagler and Fort Worden across Admiralty Inlet and Fort Ebey to the north, Fort Casey was part of the turn-of-the-century military defense system that once guarded the entrance to Puget Sound. These fixed gun fortresses became obsolete after WW I, and the fort is now a historic state park (☎ 678-4519), with facilities for camping and picnicking. Investigating the old cement batteries and underground tunnels that line the coast brings out the explorer in everyone, even those who excuse their delving in the name of gorgeous scenic views. **Admiralty Head Lighthouse** was built in 1861 and now houses the park's interpretive center.

Recreation at the park includes hiking, scuba diving, boat launching and beachcombing. It's a four-mile walk north along the beach to **Fort Ebey State Park**, a WW II-era defensive fort, which has much the same facilities as Fort Casey. For more

information, call the ranger station (☎ 678-4636) in Coupeville.

### Places to Stay

*Fort Casey State Park* offers 35 campsites overlooking Keystone Harbor, busy with ferries to Port Townsend, and Fort Ebey has 50 campsites. Sites are $10, and facilities include flush toilets and running water. There are some beachside sites but no RV hook-ups.

One of the more unique and affordable places to stay in this part of the state is the *Fort Casey Inn* (☎ 678-8792), 1124 S Engle Rd, a series of four officers' duplexes from 1909 that are now rented as overnight accommodations. Each unit has two bedrooms, a kitchen, bathroom and fireplace in the sitting room. Although the rooms are rather plain, they are perfectly comfortable, and the makings for breakfast are provided in each room. Rates begin at $110 for two people and $140 for four.

### LANGLEY

The most popular getaway on Whidbey Island is Langley (population 925), a seaside town that epitomizes the adjectives 'quaint' and 'cute'. However, the feeling is a bit manufactured. Langley *is* an attractive town – its harbor overlooks Saratoga Sound and the distant peaks of the Cascades – and it has a reputation as an artists' colony. But these things merely serve as the bow that wraps Langley's twee commercialism – the upscale boutiques, gift shops and cafes are designed to enchant those whose idea of a rapturous weekend away is not complete without shopping. If you're unencumbered by kids, all the better – very few of the many expensive B&Bs and inns that have recently sprung up here allow children.

### Orientation & Information

Langley is eight miles north of Clinton and the ferry service from Mukilteo, making this the closest of the Whidbey Island communities to the urban areas of northern Seattle. For more information about the Langley area, contact the Langley Chamber f Commerce (☎ 221-6765) at 124½ 2nd St, Langley, WA 98260.

## Places to Stay & Eat

ust about the only reasonably priced place o stay in Langley is *Drake's Landing* ☎ 221-3999), 203 Wharf St, across from he boat harbor. Rooms cost $45 to $55. Children and pets are allowed by arrangement.

Otherwise, expect to spend in the neighborhood of $100 a night. Probably the most noted of the many B&Bs in Langley is the *Eagles Nest* (☎ 221-5331), 3236 E Saratoga Rd, a contemporary B&B perched on a hill, with views of Saratoga Passage and Mt Baker. The four guest rooms range from $95 to $115; children over 12 are allowed.

The trendsetter in style and expense is he contemporary, condo-esque *Inn at Langley* (☎ 221-3033), 400 1st St. The beautifully furnished, waterfront rooms have large windows, whirlpool tubs and fireplaces. Rooms start at $155 to $175. Five-course dinners are served in the gallery-like *Country Kitchen*.

The most popular place to eat in these parts is *Cafe Langley* (☎ 221-3090), 113 1st St, which offers eastern Mediterranean cuisine, often zipped up with fresh Northwest seafood. Lunch can be had for less than $7, dinner for $13 to $16. For a beer and a burger, head up the stairs to the *Star Bistro* (☎ 221-2627), 201½ 1st St, which serves lunch and dinner. It's a relaxed place to have a drink and recover from a shopping spree.

Even more fundamental is the *Whidbey Island Brewery*, (☎ 221-8373), 620 2nd St, whose tasting room is open from noon to 6 pm daily during the summer season, and Thursday to Monday only in the off-season. Beer's the thing here: the modest lunch menu is mostly hot dogs and locally baked focaccia.

# Olympic Peninsula

A remote and rugged area of wild coast-lines, deep old-growth forests and craggy mountains, the Olympic Peninsula sits like a massive thumb sticking into the Pacific to the west of the mainland, surrounded to the north and east by the Strait of Juan de Fuca and Hood Canal, respectively. This moat-like isolation has allowed the Olympic Peninsula to develop its own ecological and human history.

The peninsula contains Olympic National Park, one of the nation's show-case parks, which harbors the continent's only temperate rainforests, but you will also find mile after mile of clear-cut forests. One of the least populated parts of Washington, the peninsula is home to genteel Victorian seaports and a number of Native American tribes.

The Olympic Peninsula also has some of

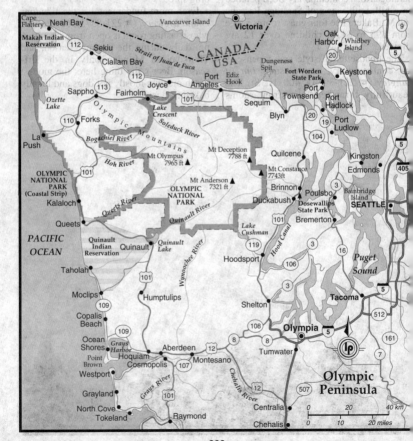

232

he most extreme weather in the USA. Because the towering peaks of the Olympic Mountains trap moist Pacific air, rainfall on the western slopes is massive. At any time of year, visitors should anticipate rain or at least clouds while visiting the Olympic National Park. However, because the Olympics do such a thorough job of wringing out moisture, the land to the east is remarkably dry and sunny. Sequim, only a few dozen miles from the rainforests, receives only 16 inches of rain a year, with 300 days of sunshine.

## HISTORY

Seafaring Native Americans have lived along the Olympic Peninsula for thousands of years, and the rich bounty from the ocean, forest and rivers made native life here relatively comfortable. Tribes like the Makah, Quileute and Quinault became expert seafarers in their cedar canoes, hunting whales and seals, and attained one of the highest levels of cultural sophistication of any Native American tribe.

European sailors had been exploring the Northwest coast since 1592, when Juan de Fuca, a Greek sailing under the Spanish flag, discovered the strait that now bears his name. The first documented contact between the natives on the Olympic Peninsula and European explorers was in 1790, when the Spaniard Manuel Quimper sailed into Neah Bay, traded with the Makahs and claimed the land for Spain. Two years later, a colonizing force arrived from Mexico and established a garrison at Neah Bay, where the Spanish planted gardens and built barns for their goats, cows, sheep and pigs. Soon after, the Spaniards moved the colony to Nookta Bay on Vancouver Island.

The wild mountains and inhospitable coast of the Olympic Peninsula didn't immediately attract settlers, even after nearby Puget Sound was beginning to fill with people. By 1851, Port Townsend was established, and farmers and fishermen began to eke livings from the coastal verge. The expanse of virgin forests on the peninsula began to fall to the sawyer in the 1880s, as mill towns like Aberdeen and Hoquiam sprang up to the south. By the turn of the century, determined pioneers were penetrating the forests of the western peninsula, seeking to clear timber from homesteads in order to till the soil.

The interior of the peninsula remained uncharted until 1885, when an army expedition under the command of Lieutenant Joseph O'Neil explored the northern ranges. The most famous exploration of the Olympics was the so-called Press Expedition, sponsored by the *Seattle Press* newspaper. Scottish explorer James Christie led five men into the Elwha Valley in midwinter, where they spent over five months trying to cross the heart of the peninsula in boats and sleds that they fashioned as they went – though their spirit was unfortunately not equaled by their carpentry skills. Following a long tradition, these explorers named new peaks for their patrons – in this case, newspaper editors.

In general, the inclement weather eventually doomed the efforts of all but the most single-minded of these homesteaders. The peninsula remained wild and isolated until the 1930s, when Hwy 101 pushed through the deep forests, linking longtime coastal communities by road for the first time. Then, in 1938, after a 40-year struggle between conservationists and the industrialists and logging companies, Olympic National Park was established in the heart of the peninsula.

## ORIENTATION

Only one road, Hwy 101, rings the Olympic Peninsula. Even though the road is in excellent condition, it bears repeating that distances are great, and first-time visitors to the peninsula almost always find that it takes a lot longer to get where they're going than expected – always allow extra time.

The most northwesterly point in the continental USA is Cape Flattery near Neah Bay, at the tip of the Olympic Peninsula.

## INFORMATION

There are a number of excellent local publications available that discuss tourist sites, lodging and restaurants on the peninsula.

The Port Angeles *Peninsula Daily News* publishes the free *Olympic Peninsula Visitor Guide* twice a year. Also worth picking up is *Dan Youra's Olympic Peninsula Guide*, which is jammed full of all sorts of information about the peninsula and includes a good map. Priced at $1, the publication is usually available free from visitors centers. To obtain a copy by mail, contact Olympic Publishing (☎ 437-2277), 7450 Oak Bay Rd, Port Ludlow, WA 98365.

## GETTING THERE & AWAY
### Air
Horizon Air (☎ (800) 547-9308) has service to Fairchild International Airport, on the outskirts of Port Angeles, from Portland, Seattle and Victoria, BC.

### Bus
Booking a bus ticket to the peninsula is potentially challenging. Ever since Greyhound's pull-out, local companies scrambling to establish private bus service have floundered about with constantly changing ticket agents, pick-up points and schedules. The Port Angeles Visitor Center (☎ 452-2363) can help if you find the following numbers have all been disconnected.

Port Angeles-Seattle Bus Lines (☎ 457-4580, in Seattle (206) 681-7705) has filled the Greyhound bus void and runs a simple route between Port Angeles and Seattle-area transportation hubs. Buses bound for Sea-Tac Airport and Seattle and Tacoma Greyhound bus stations depart from the Port Angeles Jackpot East at 1315 Front St at 7 am and 2 pm daily. From Sequim, buses headed to Seattle pick up at 7:30 am and 2:30 pm from Thunderbird Travel at 170 E Bell St. Fare is $16 one way and $29 roundtrip. There's no morning bus on Sundays. Olympic Van Tours (☎ 452-3858) has started a similar service; call for details.

To/from Victoria, Grayline Buses (☎ 452-5112) offers sight-seeing tours and overnight packages from Port Angeles. They'll even pick you up at your RV park.

### Ferry
To/from Seattle, the fastest access to the Olympic Peninsula involves taking either the Bainbridge Island/Seattle ferry or the Edmonds/Kingston ferry and driving from there. From Seattle to Port Angeles it's only 77 miles, but because of ferry schedules and traffic, the journey can easily take half a day.

To/from Victoria, BC, the Coho Ferry (☎ 457-4491), also known as Black Ball Transport, provides passenger and automobile service from Port Angeles. The 1½-hour trip costs $25 one way for a car and driver; adult/child passengers cost $6.25/3.15. This ferry makes brief closure in January for maintenance. Also from Port Angeles to Victoria, the Victoria Express (☎ 452-8088, (800) 633-1589) offers one-hour service for passengers and cyclists only. Reservations are recommended. Roundtrip fare for adults is $20, for children $10; seniors receive a 10% discount. Bicycles cost an extra $2. Frequency and schedules vary seasonally for both ferries.

### Weather & Road Conditions
Severe weather can sometimes close down the Hood Canal Bridge. Call 437-2288 for bridge information.

# Olympic National Park

One of the most popular US national parks, Olympic National Park is noted for its wilderness hiking, dramatic scenery and widely varying ecosystems. Beginning at sea level, the heavily glaciered Olympic Mountains rise to nearly 8000 feet in only 25 miles, and were one of the last explored areas of Washington, despite their proximity to major population centers. As early as 1897 there were calls for the Olympics to be preserved as a national park; however, the area was initially declared a forest reserve, and then, in 1909, a national monument by President Theodore Roosevelt.

These designations didn't save large portions of these federal lands from falling into private and state hands. During WW I, almost half of the original national monument was opened up for mining and logging. Earlier attempts to create the Elk National Park, in order to preserve the indigenous Roosevelt elk, failed. President Franklin Roosevelt succeeded in pushing a bill through Congress in 1938 authorizing the Olympic National Forest. The original 1012-sq-mile park consisted of the highest and most rugged peaks of the range; in later years the lowland rainforests and coastal strip were added, bringing the total area to nearly 1406 sq miles.

Olympic National Park is best thought of as a wilderness preserve. Many of the best and most spectacular sights are reserved for long-distance walkers who trek across the park's interior. Camping in the park is easy, with 17 large campgrounds accessible by car and 95 backcountry campgrounds. Magnificent waterfalls, wide alpine meadows sparkling with summer wildflowers, eerie moss-bearded forests dripping with fog, and remote lakes shimmering beneath glaciers are among the destinations available to those willing to get out of their cars and hike a few miles.

## ORIENTATION

Access to Olympic National Park is mostly on foot, as most roads open to vehicles terminate shortly after entering park lands. In the following descriptions, information is laid out by entrance road. Be sure to pick up a current map of the park before heading into the wilderness.

Entrance fees to the park are $5 per vehicle and $3 per person for pedestrians, cyclists and bus passengers. Fees are collected at Hurricane Ridge, Elwha, Hoh, Sol Duc and Staircase entrance points, May to September only, with entrance fees charged for access to Hurricane Ridge on winter weekends and during the Christmas and New Year holidays. Entrance passes are good for one week.

## INFORMATION

For information about the park, contact the Olympic National Park Headquarters (☎ 452-0330, 452-4501), 600 E Park Ave, Port Angeles, WA 98362. If you know what forms of recreation you're interested in, or even what drainages you plan to visit, then let the rangers know: a lot of the free information available is specific to certain valleys and activities. Information on the Olympic National Forest, administered by the USFS, can be obtained from the USFS office (☎ 956-2300) at 1835 Black Lake Blvd NW, Olympia, WA 98512. Many national park visitors centers double as USFS ranger stations, which are where you can pick up free backcountry permits for wilderness camping in the park.

The park headquarters (☎ 452-0330) can provide some road and weather information. Call 452-0329 for weather information on Hurricane Ridge.

---

### The Olympic Mountains

The Olympic Mountains began as sea-floor sediments deep in the Pacific Ocean about 70 million years ago. Undersea volcanoes pushed up through these deep formations to form seamounts, or underwater mountains. As the North American continent edged across the Pacific Ocean, and as the heavier ocean floor slid under the leading edge of the continent, this marine mountain chain was scraped off against the continent's edge.

About 30 million years ago, the ocean-floor plate bearing the old seamount range completely disappeared beneath the continent. With nothing to anchor the jumbled mass of rock, it began to rise. Over the course of millions of years, the old mountains formed at sea level were punched up through the level landmass of the Olympic Peninsula to tower almost 8000 feet above the Pacific.

During the most recent ice age, glaciers flowed down from the Arctic and filled the Puget Sound. The rising Olympic Mountains were filled with valley glaciers; some stretched from the peaks all the way to the Pacific coast. ■

WASHINGTON

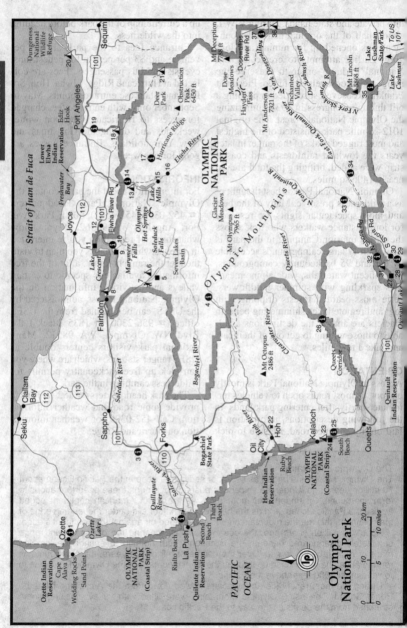

Olympic
National Park

Dungeness
National
Wildlife
Refuge

Sequim

Port Angeles

Ediz
Hook

Strait of Juan de Fuca

Lower
Elwha
Indian
Reservation

Freshwater
Bay

Joyce

Clallam
Bay

Sekiu

Ozette Indian
Reservation

Cape
Alava

Wedding Rocks

Sand Point

Ozette
Lake

OLYMPIC
NATIONAL
PARK
(Coastal Strip)

Rialto Beach

La Push

Second
Beach

Third
Beach

Quileute Indian
Reservation

PACIFIC
OCEAN

Mt Deception
7788 ft

Dosewallips River Rd

Dose
Meadows

Hayden
Pass

Mt Anderson
7321 ft

Lake
Cushman
State Park

To US
101

Mt Lincoln
5868 ft

Enchanted
Valley

East Fork Quinault River

N Fork Skokomish R

Lake
Cushman

N Fork Quinault River

OLYMPIC
NATIONAL
PARK

Deer
Park

Obstruction
Peak
6450 ft

Hurricane Ridge

Elwha River

Lake
Mills

Olympic
Hot Springs

Soleduck
Falls

Marymere
Falls

Seven Lakes
Basin

Lake
Crescent

Elwha River Rd

Fairholm

Glacier
Meadows

Mt Olympus
7965 ft

Olympic Mountains

Queets River

N Shore Rd

S Shore Rd

Quinault Lake

Quinault
Indian
Reservation

Clearwater River

Mt Octopus
2486 ft

Queets
Corridor

Queets

South
Beach

Kalaloch

OLYMPIC
NATIONAL
PARK
(Coastal Strip)

Ruby Beach

Oil
City

Hoh River

Hoh Indian
Reservation

Hoh

Forks

Sappho

Bogachiel River

Bogachiel State Park

Soleduck River

Calawah River

Quillayute
River

20 km

10 miles

Olympic
National Park

WASHINGTON

| | | | | | |
|---|---|---|---|---|---|
| 1 | Ozette Ranger Station, Campground | 13 | Altaire Campground | 25 | Kalaloch Information Station |
| 2 | Mora Ranger Station, Campground | 14 | Elwha Ranger Station, Campground | 26 | Queets Ranger Station, Campground |
| 3 | USFS/NPS Information Station | 15 | Whiskey Bend | 27 | Lochaerie Resort |
| | | 16 | Humes Ranch | 28 | Lake Quinault Lodge |
| 4 | Hoh Rainforest Visitors Center, Hoh Campground | 17 | Hurricane Ridge Visitor Center | 29 | Quinault USFS Office |
| 5 | Sol Duc Hot Springs Resort | 18 | Heart O' the Hills Campground | 30 | Rain Forest Resort Village |
| 6 | Sol Duc Campground | | | 31 | July Creek Campground |
| 7 | Ancient Groves Nature Trail | 19 | Pioneer Memorial Museum Visitor Center | 32 | Quinalt Ranger Station |
| 8 | Fairholm Campground | 20 | Dungeness Recreation Area | 33 | North Fork Ranger Station, Campground |
| 9 | Lake Crescent Lodge | 21 | Deer Park Campground | 34 | Graves Creek Ranger Station, Campground |
| 10 | Storm King Information Station | 22 | Rain Forest Hostel | 35 | Staircase Ranger Station, Campground |
| 11 | Log Cabin Resort | 23 | Kalaloch Campground | 36 | Elkhorn Campground |
| 12 | Shadow Mountain Store | 24 | Kalaloch Lodge | | |

## ACTIVITIES

Olympic National Park is roughly 40 miles in diameter, and few roads penetrate more than a few miles into the park proper. The rest of the park is the province of hikers, especially those willing to traverse the wilderness on one of the many long-distance trails. Pack horses are allowed on nearly all trails and are often used for carrying gear on cross-park expeditions. The 57-mile Olympic Coastal Strip, a parcel of the national body, is accessible only to hikers, who can marvel at the wildlife, ancient petroglyphs and remarkable scenery of this rugged coastline.

Mt Olympus and Mt Deception are the two highest mountains in the park and are popular for **climbing**; both involve considerable cross-glacier traverses and should only be attempted after consultation with authorities and with the appropriate equipment. Though many of the craggy peaks elsewhere require technical climbing skills, it's weather, and not difficulty per se, that often enforces limits on climbers, as conditions can change dramatically in no time at all.

A number of outfitters run **white-water rafting** trips on the park's rivers, including the Hoh, Elwha and Queets. The Olympic Outdoor Center (☎ (800) 659-6095), 26469 Circle Place NW, in Poulsbo (just north of Bremerton), operates several white-water rafting and **sea kayaking** trips, at different times of year, on bays and rivers throughout the peninsula. They also offer equipment sales and rentals and teach classes.

Rivers and lakes in the park are noted for their trout and salmon **fishing**. No license is needed to fish in the park, although other regulations may be in place – check with a park ranger. Canoe and kayak rentals are available at many of the larger lakes.

The park remains open in winter, and the area around Hurricane Ridge is popular for **cross-country skiing** and sledding. Free snowshoe tours are led by rangers on the weekends. Most lower valley trails are passable year round.

### Olympic Park Institute

This environmentally oriented foundation offers seminars in a wide variety of fields, including geology, wildflowers, marine mammals, Northwest Native American art and forest ecology. Most courses involve outdoor field trips and excursions, but are headquartered out of the institute's facility on Lake Crescent. Courses are held in spring, summer and winter, and most take place over a weekend. Fees vary from course to course (anticipate fees from $180) and include food and lodging (the institute owns a lodge and cabins along the lake). For more information, contact

Olympic Park Institute (☎ 928-3720), HC 62 Box 9T, Port Angeles, WA 98362.

## NORTHERN ENTRANCES

The most popular access to Olympic National Park is from the north. Port Angeles and Sequim are good jumping-off points for valley hikes and for visiting Hurricane Ridge and Deer Park. The park's largest lake, Lake Crescent, is popular with anglers and boaters, and it sports two of the park's five lodges.

### Pioneer Memorial Museum & Visitor Center

The park's main information and visitors center (☎ 452-0330) is located at 3002 Mt Angeles Rd in Port Angeles, about one mile south of Hwy 101 off Race St; this same road leads up to Hurricane Ridge (watch for signs). The center offers a children's discovery center, a slide presentation, a bookshop and several interactive displays regarding plant and animal life. A

replica of a prehistoric Makah seal-hunting canoe is worth the stop, especially if you won't make it out to Neah Bay to see the originals at the Makah Museum. Park rangers are on hand to answer any questions. The center is open every day, year round, from 9 am to 4 pm.

### Hurricane Ridge

Beginning at sea level at Port Angeles, the 18-mile Hurricane Ridge Rd climbs up 5300 feet into the Olympic peaks to extensive wildflower meadows and expansive vistas. On a clear day, the rugged peaks and glaciers of Mt Olympus loom spectacularly across the deep, and frequently cloud-filled, Elwha River valley.

The Hurricane Ridge visitors center (☎ 452-0329, for a recorded message about activities and access) is open daily, usually from 9 am to 4 pm, except in midwinter, when it is open only on weekends. The center offers a snack bar, gift shop, toilets and ski (both downhill and cross-country) and snowshoe rentals.

---

### Rainforests & Wildlife

Because of the Olympic Peninsula's geologic isolation – the peninsula was cut off from the mainland by ice-age glaciers – and its current isolation by Puget Sound, a number of plants and animals are unique to the area. In addition to the peninsula's noted rainforests, which include some of the largest and densest virgin forests remaining in North America, there are over 40 sizable river valleys and some 60 glaciers in this rugged range.

**Temperate Rainforests** What produces the rainforests of the Olympic Peninsula is moisture, and lots of it. Rainfall in this area ranges from 140 to nearly 200 inches a year. Coupled with mild temperatures, these conditions allow the trees and plants to grow to massive size. Additionally, the heavily contorted valleys of the west-facing Olympic Mountains trap moist air, producing heavy fogs during summer. This feeds a group of plants called epiphytes, vegetation that hangs from trees and gleans moisture and sustenance from the humid air. The most noticeable of these plants is the club moss, the long, green whiskery growth that attaches itself to branches in the forest. Sword and licorice ferns also sprout along the length of tree trunks, increasing the impression of shaggy vegetative extravagance.

The most common trees in the rainforests are the Sitka spruce, hemlock, red cedar, maple, and red alder, and they can reach mammoth proportions. Trees up to 300 feet tall, with girths of up to 20 feet, are not uncommon. In fact eight species of trees have record-size individual trees on the peninsula.

**Roosevelt Elk** This species of elk is found only in the coastal mountains of the Pacific Northwest, and protection of the herds in the Olympic Mountains was one of the initial reasons for establishing the national park. Roosevelt elk – named after Teddy, not

Hurricane Ridge is a good base for many activities, though there is no camping. In summer, rangers conduct a number of open-air informational discussions and hikes. During the winter, cross-country and downhill skiing and sledding take over; on weekends, rangers lead free guided snowshoe tours.

**Hiking** Hurricane Ridge is one of the highest points accessible to vehicles in the park, so it is understandably a popular trailhead for hikers wanting to explore the park's high country. A number of short hikes lead through meadows to spectacular vista points. **Hurricane Hill Trail**, which begins in the parking area, and the network of trails known as the **Meadow Loops**, beginning at the visitors center, are popular, moderately easy hikes through gorgeous scenery. The first half mile of both of these trails is wheelchair accessible.

From Hurricane Ridge, you can drive a rough and frequently steep 8.4-mile road to **Obstruction Peak**, another vista point

with even better views of the Olympic peaks. Hikers looking for long-distance treks can pick up here the **Grand Ridge Trail**, which leads to Deer Park (see below), and the **Wolf Creek Trail**, an 8.5-mile downhill jaunt to Whiskey Bend, where it picks up the Elwha Trail.

**Skiing** Hurricane Ridge is a great departure point for cross-country skiers, who can explore pristine high meadows and mountain ridges without a dreary uphill slog. The road to the ridge is plowed every weekend, and it stays open during the week, weather permitting. A number of ski trails are indicated in a brochure available from park rangers, or follow trail signs (most of the trails follow the hiking trails). However, unstable snow conditions can make some of these trails dangerous, due to avalanching. Check with park rangers before departing on long trails.

The downhill ski area is open during the Christmas holidays and on weekends only from January through March. Although the

---

Franklin – are larger than the Rocky Mountain wapiti and are more social animals, often running in herds of up to 50 animals. Bull elks can weigh upwards of 1000 pounds. Roosevelt elk are notoriously shy animals, and, even though an estimated 7000 live on the peninsula, it is unlikely that hikers will sight one.

**Mountain Lions** Another conservation success story is the mountain lion. Once considered threatened in much of its natural territory, mountain lions are today becoming more and more common in the Olympics. Although there have been no serious incidents yet in the park, in other areas of the American West there have been a few maulings and killings. Be especially careful not to make sudden movements when hiking alone, and never leave children unsupervised.

**Mountain Goats** These large, white-haired goats were introduced from the Rockies to the Olympic Mountains in the 1920s, where they have thrived. However, mountain goats are now present in the Olympic high country in such numbers that they present a threat to plants of delicate alpine meadows. In recent years, park rangers have been euphemistically 'removing' goats from areas adversely affected by goat overpopulation, which has become an issue of some controversy. ■

ski area doesn't offer many challenges for advanced skiers, the gentle 1600-foot slope is a good place for families or beginners. All-day lift tickets are $15. Folks on inner-tubes and sleds have a separate area behind the ski hill.

## Deer Park

The park's highest access road departs from Hwy 101 five miles east of Port Angeles and climbs up a steep, graveled road to alpine meadows, a campground and a 5850-foot trailhead. There are a couple of good reasons to lurch your way up this 17-mile grade, which closes during snowy weather and is not advised for trailer or RV traffic. From the Deer Park trailhead, the 7.5-mile **Grand Ridge Trail** sets off toward Obstruction Peak, east of Hurricane Ridge. With much of the trail above timberline, it has some of the best views in the park. Deer Park also tends to get far less traffic than Hurricane Ridge, which in summer is almost a carnival of activity. Comparably, visitors and campers here have the wildflowers and vistas to them-selves – and frequently have better weather.

## Elwha River Valley

The Elwha, the largest river on the Olympic Peninsula, and Lake Mills (actually a reser-voir) are popular for trout fishing. Elwha River Rd turns south from Hwy 101 about eight miles west of Port Angeles. Follow it for 10 miles to the Elwha Ranger Station (☎ 452-9191). The road immediately forks. Turn west to reach the Olympic Hot Springs trailhead, turn east and continue to Whiskey Bend to reach the Elwha River and other long-distance trailheads.

**Hiking** The **Olympic Hot Springs** were once commercially developed; however, the pools and cabins from the 1930s resort have long since disappeared and the area's springs have returned to nature. Park super-visors closed the road to the hot springs in order to limit access somewhat and to pre-serve the area. Note that official maps don't even show the hot springs (though it's adja-cent to Boulder Creek Campground). The

2.2-mile hike, which follows the old road bed, is well worth it – a series of hot pools steam alongside the rushing Boulder Creek, all in a verdant deep forest grove. (You'll need a backcountry permit to camp overnight at Boulder.)

From Whisky Bend, the **Elwha Trail** leads up the main branch of the Elwha River and is one of the primary cross-park trails, leading to Dosewallips and, over Low Divide, to the North Fork Quinault River entrance. Day hikers may elect to follow the trail for two miles to Humes Ranch, the remains of a homestead-era ranch.

## Lake Crescent

Lake Crescent is one of the most popular stops in the park, due to its beautiful vistas, its boating and fishing, and for Lake Cres-cent Lodge, one of the park's venerable lakeside resorts. For information about the Lake Crescent area, contact the Storm King Information Station (☎ 928-3380), just east of Lake Crescent Lodge off Hwy 101.

**Hiking** One of the most popular short hikes in the park goes to **Marymere Falls**, a 90-foot cascade that drapes down a basalt cliff. This 1.5-mile roundtrip leads out from the Storm King Information Station along the Barnes Creek Trail. The trail is wheelchair accessible.

For a more energetic hike, climb up the side of **Mt Storm King**, the peak that rises to the east of Lake Crescent. The steep, 3.5-mile trail also splits off the Barnes Creek Trail.

**Fishing & Boating** Lake Crescent was once home to two indigenous trout sub-species, the Beardslee (a cousin of the rainbow) and the *crescentii*, a variation on the cutthroat. Both have become hybridized with introduced hatchery-bred fish. The fishing is good, however, as the lake is very deep with steep shorelines; no bait-fishing is allowed. Boat rentals are available at Lake Crescent Lodge, Log Cabin Resort (see Places to Stay below), and the Fair-holm General Store (☎ 928-3020).

**Paddlewheel Boat Tours** Paddlewheel boats once plied Lake Crescent, serving the many resorts and lodges that lined its shores. Paddlewheel boats again cruise the lake, now offering interpretive tours. Cruises depart from near Crescent Lake Lodge, but ticketing and free parking are available at the Shadow Mountain Store 13 miles west of Port Angeles on Hwy 101. Buses also depart from there at 11:30 am, 1, 3 and 4:30 pm from mid-May to the first weekend of October; from Memorial Day to Labor Day there is also a 6 pm departure. Arrive at the shuttle a half hour before the desired departure time. Tickets for $15 for adults, $14 for seniors and $10 for youth ages 17 and younger. Reservations are recommended (☎ 452-4520).

### The Soleduck River Valley

Just west of Lake Crescent, the Soleduck River flows toward the Pacific coast. The headwaters of the river fall within the national park boundaries and offer a developed hot springs resort and some of the best day hiking in the Olympics. A paved road follows the Soleduck River from Hwy 101 for nearly 14 miles, passing the hot springs and ending at a trailhead. The summer-only Soleduck Ranger Station (☎ 327-3534) is located at the hot springs.

**Sol Duc Hot Springs Resort** Indian legend recounts the battle of two lightning fish who engaged in bitter combat; however, neither won the contest. Each crawled into the earth and shed hot tears, thereby creating Sol Duc and Olympic hot springs. The mineral springs at Sol Duc are much more developed than the natural pools at Olympic. The hot water has been diverted into three large tiled pools and there's also a regular swimming pool to cool off in. Access to the hot springs is $5. In addition to cabins, the resort contains a restaurant and snack bar, a gift shop and a grocery store. In summer there are ranger-led programs and activities.

**Hiking** Two miles past the resort, the Soleduck road terminates, and trails lead into the forest. The most popular hike here is to **Soleduck Falls**, where the Soleduck River drops 40 feet into a narrow gorge. The three-quarter-mile, one-way hike follows a gentle grade through a mossy old-growth cedar forest before crossing a bridge above the falls.

For a more strenuous hike, cross the bridge at the falls and climb the **Canyon Creek Trail** up to Deer Lake. This sometimes steep, three-mile, one-way trail reaches the tree-rimmed lake (where you will indeed often see deer) and joins **High Divide Trail**, which leads to a popular overnight destination, the Seven Lakes Basin.

Another good leg-stretcher is the **Mink Lake Trail**, departing from the resort. This 2.5-mile, one-way trail leads up to marshy Mink Lake, noted for its bird and wildlife viewing.

For a short, interpreted hike through an old-growth forest, take the **Ancient Groves Nature Trail**, located eight miles from Hwy 101 along the Soleduck Rd. Along this one-mile loop trail there are signs labeling tree and plant species and explaining rainforest ecology.

### Places to Stay & Eat

**Camping** Nearly all of the national park campgrounds have running water and toilets and allow pets, but there are no hook-ups for RVs and no showers. Unless otherwise noted, fees are $10 a night. There is no camping allowed at Hurricane Ridge; the closest national park campground is *Heart O' the Hills*, five miles south of Port Angeles on Hurricane Ridge Rd, with 105 sites. The *Deer Park Campground* offers 18 campsites and has no fee. There are two campgrounds just inside the park along the Elwha River: the *Elwha Campground* with 41 campsites and the *Altaire Campground* with 30. The only national park campground on Lake Crescent is *Fairholm Campground*, 28 miles west of Port Angeles on Hwy 101, with 87 campsites. Along the Soleduck River, immediately upstream from the Sol Duc Hot Springs

Resort, is *Sol Duc Campground* with 80 sites.

**Lodges & Cabins** There are two lodges at Lake Crescent. The preeminent one is *Lake Crescent Lodge* (☎ 928-3211), 416 Lake Crescent Rd, which is 20 miles west of Port Angeles off Hwy 101 (look for signs to the lodge). This old-fashioned inn was built in 1915 as a fishing resort. The original shake-sided lodge still stands and operates as the main lodging, restaurant and bar, though a number of lakeside cabins have been added to accommodate more guests. Room rates range between $65 and $117 a night. Call well in advance for accommodations; it's open from the last weekend in April to the end of October.

The *Log Cabin Resort* (☎ 928-3325), 3183 E Beach Rd, is located on the north bank of Lake Crescent and offers cabins, chalets (which sleep six), lodge rooms and RV hook-ups. The restaurant is favored by anglers and other hungry outdoor types. It's closed October 1 to May 15.

Along the Soleduck River is the *Sol Duc Hot Springs Resort* (327-3583). Thirty-two modern and rather unromantic cabins, all with private baths and six with kitchens, are scattered around a meadow. There is also a restaurant, snack bar and grocery store. Room rates range between $75 and $85; the resort and lodging are open from May 15 to October 1.

## EASTERN ENTRANCES

The eastern entrances to Olympic National Park aren't as developed with lodges and interpretive sites as other access points, but they are the closest to major population centers and serve as access points for long-distance hikers from the Puget Sound area.

### Dosewallips River Valley

Pronounced *Dossey-WAL-ups*, this narrow valley is surrounded by some of the highest mountains in the Olympics, including Mt Anderson and Mt Deception. The graveled Dosewallips River Rd follows the Dose-wallips River from Hwy 101 for 15 miles

to Dosewallips Ranger Station, where the road terminates and trails begin.

**Hiking** Day hikers won't find many satisfying short loop trails here, but hiking portions of the two long-distance paths – with increasingly impressive views of heavily glaciered Mt Anderson – is reason enough to visit the valley. From the Dosewallips Ranger Station, a wide trail leads upriver for 1.4 miles to Dose Forks, where the path divides into two major trans-park trails.

The northbound trail is called the **Dose-wallips Trail**, and it climbs up to beautiful Dose Meadows (10 miles from Dose Forks) before crossing Hayden Pass and dropping into the Elwha valley and the Elwha Trail. The southerly trail is called **West Fork Dosewallips Trail** and it leads to Honeymoon Meadows (nine miles from Dose Forks), a spring-filled basin immediately beneath the glaciers of precipitous 7321-foot Mt Anderson. The trail continues up to Anderson Pass and into the East Fork Quinault River trail system.

### Staircase

This is another favorite entrance for hikers, in part because the national park trail system nearly abuts Lake Cushman State Park, immensely popular with families, anglers and boaters from the Tacoma area. The Staircase Ranger Station (☎ 877-5569) is just inside the national park boundary, 15 miles from Hwy 101 at the small town of Hoodsport.

**Hiking** The trail system here follows the drainage of the North Fork Skokomish River, flanked by some of the most rugged peaks in the Olympics, including the aptly named Sawtooth Range. The principal long-distance trail is the **North Fork Skokomish Trail**, which leads up this beautiful, heavily forested valley, eventually crossing into the Duckabush River valley to intercept other trans-park trail systems. Ambitious day hikers might consider following this trail 3.7 miles to find the **Flapjack Lakes Trail**, an easy four-mile climb up to several small lakes that shimmer beneath the awesome crags of the Sawtooth peaks.

A popular short hike follows the south bank of the North Fork Skokomish River along the **Staircase Rapids Trail**, which leads through lush old-growth forest to the rapids. Continue up the trail a short distance to the Rapids Bridge, which crosses over to the North Fork Skokomish Trail and makes for a nice two-mile loop trip.

## Places to Stay

There are two popular state parks along the east edge of the national park; both have running water, flush toilets and some RV hook-ups. Near the mouth of Dosewallips River, near Brinnon along Hwy 101, is *Dosewallips State Park* (☎ 796-4415), a large and attractive park with 130 campsites. Fees range from $7 for a tent-only site to $14 for full hook-ups. Eleven miles up the Dosewallips River in the national forest is *Elkhorn Campground*, a USFS site with running water and a $10 nightly fee. At the end of the road, at *Dosewallips Campground*, there are 32 primitive sites, no fees.

*Lake Cushman State Park* (☎ 877-5491), eight miles west of Hoodsport, is centered on a large reservoir on the Skokomish River, in the scenic southern Olympic Mountains. It's popular with anglers, water skiers and campers. There are 80 campsites, some with hook-ups; running water and flush toilets are provided. Sites are $10 to $14. Past Lake Cushman along the North Fork Skokomish River, inside the national park, *Staircase Campground* has 59 sites.

## WESTERN ENTRANCES

The Pacific side of the Olympics is the most remote part of the park and home to the noted temperate rainforests. Three mighty rivers drain this face of the Olympics; their valleys fill with the full force of the Pacific's clouds and moisture, guaranteeing the annual 12 feet of rain necessary for the region's fabulously luxuriant plant growth.

Only Hwy 101 offers access to this vast, heavily wooded area, which in part accounts for its isolation (foul weather is another reason). By car, it takes a long time to make it around to Queets or Hoh from the Puget Sound area.

## Hoh Rainforest

The most famous of the Olympic rainforests, the Hoh River area offers a variety of hikes and an interpretive center. If you have room for only one stop on the western side, this should be it. The following sites are off Hoh River Rd, a paved all-weather road that winds through clear-cuts before reaching the national park boundary, 12 miles from Hwy 101. While driving toward the visitors center, stop at the **giant spruce tree** just beside the road. This lord of the forest is 270 feet high and over 700 years old. There's a ranger station near the visitors center.

**Information** At the end of Hoh River Rd, the visitors center (☎ 374-6925) offers a series of displays that explain the ecology of the rainforest and describe the plants and animals that make it up. There's also a bookstore. Rangers lead guided walks twice a day during summer; call ahead for times. Just outside of the center is a very short, wheelchair-accessible nature trail through a rainforest marsh. The visitors center is open from 9 am to 4 pm year round except July and August, when it closes at 6:30 pm.

**Hiking** Leading out from the visitors center are several excellent day hikes into virgin rainforest. The most popular of these is the justly famous **Hall of Moss Trail**, an easy three-quarter-mile loop through some of the shaggiest trees you will ever see. Epiphytic club moss, ferns and lichens completely overwhelm the massive trunks of maples and Sitka spruce in this misty forest. The 1.25-mile **Spruce Nature Trail** is another short interpreted loop trail leading out from the visitors center.

The **Hoh Trail** is the major entry trail into the wide, glacier-channeled Hoh River valley, and it is the principal access to the park's highest peak, Mt Olympus. The trail follows an easy grade for 12 miles, and day hikers will find this a very pleasant if undramatic hike: just keep going until you need to turn back. If you are tempted to make this an overnight trip – there are numerous formal and informal campsites along the way – be sure to pick up a back-country permit from the ranger station.

**Climbing** The highest peak in the Olympics at 7965 feet, rugged **Mt Olympus** is the most commonly climbed peak in the range. However, don't let its relative lack of stature fool you. Mt Olympus is the first major peak that Pacific storms encounter. A lot of snow – and harsh weather in general – occurs here. In the continental USA, only Mt Rainier and Mt Baker have more extensive glacial formations.

The Hoh Trail largely ends at Glacier Meadows, 17 miles from the Hoh visitors center. The campground here is frequently used as a base camp for ascents of the mountain. From here on, much of the remaining climb is on glaciers and along craggy escarpments. Most people make the ascent from June to early September, although adventurous souls begin to climb as early as April.

Guided climbs and mountaineering schools are available for would-be climbers and are suggested for novices: each year Mt Olympus claims lives and causes injuries, usually from falls into glacial crevasses or exposure in storms. For information on guided climbs, contact Olympic Mountaineering (☎ 452-0240), 221 S Peabody St in Port Angeles, where climbing equipment can also be rented, or from REI outlets in Seattle. For further reference, get hold of Custom Correct maps for the peak and the book *Climber's Guide to the Olympic Mountains*, published by The Mountaineers.

### Queets River Valley
The Queets River valley is the most remote part of the Olympic National Park. Part of this isolation is intentional: the park service has made access to the valley rather chal-

lenging and trails in the Queets don't link up with any other trans-park trails. This means, however, that the Queets valley is the most pristine area in the park.

The so-called Queets Corridor – the thin finger of land that juts out of the southern end of the park along the river – was added to the park in 1953. The narrow corridor, which nearly reaches the Pacific, is meant to preserve one of the peninsula's river valleys all the way from its glacial beginnings to the coast.

**Hiking** Queets River Rd leaves Hwy 101 and almost immediately drops into the national park. The road follows the Queets River for 13 miles before ending at Queets Campground & Ranger Station. From here, there is one popular day hike, the gentle, three-mile **Queets Campground Loop Trail**.

Experienced or adventurous hikers can elect to ford the Queets River and explore the **Queets Trail**, which leads up the river for 15 miles before petering out in heavy forest. The trail passes through some of the most spectacular old-growth rainforest in the park – the trees are sometimes so large as to be disquieting – and past great fishing holes (the Queets is noted for both salmon and steelhead). However, the fording of the Queets remains an obstacle to many and is safely contemplated by the wary only in late summer or fall.

### Quinault River Valley
The focus of the Quinault valley is Quinault Lake, a beautiful glacial lake surrounded by forested peaks. The resorts and homes along the lakeshore make this a very popular retreat; the charming Lake Quinault Lodge is one of the few original Olympic lodges still in business. Upstream from Lake Quinault, the river divides into the North Fork and East Fork Quinault rivers. Both valleys harbor important trans-park trails.

**Quinault Lake** The second-largest lake in Olympic National Park, this deep-blue gem offers fishing, boating and swimming. Two lodges face onto the lake, and there are three public campgrounds. The lake is accessed by two different roads. The South Shore Rd leads to the tiny village of Quinault, with its lodges and a USFS ranger station, before climbing up into the park proper to the trailhead of the famed Enchanted Valley in the East Fork Quinault valley. The North Shore Rd enters the national park and winds along the lake's north shore, accessing the Quinault Ranger Station before climbing up the North Fork Quinault trailhead. (A bridge links the two roads about 13 miles up the valley.)

Quinault Lake is part of the Quinault Indian Reservation, and fishing is regulated by the tribe; check locally for tribal licenses and regulations. Boat rentals are available from Lake Quinault Lodge and boat slips are offered at both south shore public campgrounds and at Rain Forest Resort.

There is plenty of hiking – a number of short trails begin just below the Lake Quinault Lodge on South Shore Rd. This trail system is accessed by any number of points in the Quinault village area; pick up a free map of the trails from the USFS office. The shortest trail is the **Quinault Rainforest Nature Trail**, a half-mile trail through 500-year-old Douglas firs. This short trail adjoins the three-mile **Quinault Loop Trail**, which meanders through the rainforests before looping back to the lake.

**East Fork Quinault River** Leading to arguably the most famous, and certainly one of the most photographed, parts of the park, the **Enchanted Valley Trail** climbs up to a large meadow (a former glacial lake bed) percolated by streams and springs and resplendent with wildflowers and copses of alder trees. To the north are sheer cliff faces and peaks rising 2000 feet from the valley floor; during spring snow-melt, the three-mile-long precipice is drizzled by thousands of small waterfalls.

The aptly named Enchanted Valley is reached after a long hike from the Graves Creek trailhead at the end of the South Shore Rd, 19 miles from Hwy 101. The first 12 miles of the trail pass through old-growth forests and are narrowly walled in by forested ridges. After attaining the Enchanted Valley, the trail is mostly level for 2.5 miles, before arching up to Anderson Pass (19 miles from Graves Creek). Here, long-distance hikers can continue down the **West Fork Dosewallips Trail** to complete a popular trans-park trek.

**North Fork Quinault River** Another popular cross-park path, the **North Fork Quinault Trail** passes through this valley to join the lengthy Elwha River valley and its trail system. This major trail begins at the end of the North Shore Rd, at the North Fork Campground & Ranger Station, 17 miles from Hwy 101. This trail is not as picturesque as the East Fork, as much of the lower terrain is heavily forested.

## Places to Stay & Eat
**Camping** Unless otherwise noted, the USFS campgrounds have running water and toilets but no RV hook-ups, and are $10 a night. The *Hoh Campground*, adjacent to the Hoh Rainforest Visitors Center, offers 89 sites. The *Queets Campground*, at the end of Queets River Rd, offers 20 primitive sites with no fee. The *North Fork Campground*, on the North Fork Quinault River, has seven sites, and *Graves Creek* campground, at the trailhead for the East Fork Quinault River trail, has 30 sites. There is a nice tenters-only campground called *July Creek*, with 29 sites, on the north shore of Lake Quinault.

There's a hostel on the Hoh River; see Forks, later in this chapter, for details.

**Lodges & Cabins** The famous and entirely charming *Lake Quinault Lodge* (☎ 288-2571, (800) 562-6672), 345 S Shore Rd, was built in 1926, and its classic fireplace lobby has greeted visitors ever since. There are a variety of lodging options. Rooms are available in the old, shake-sided log lodge and in a number of detached cabins and annexes; they begin at $90 and go up to $220 a night for suites. Prices drop by half in the off-season or with promotional specials. Call well in advance for rooms. Facilities include a heated pool, a gift shop and boat rentals. The lodge's lakeview dining room offers lunches from $6 and dinners, which feature local fish, seafood and steak, from $12 to $16. Roosevelt Chicken (baked with ham and provolone cheese), first made for and named after former guest Franklin Roosevelt, is $14.

*Rain Forest Resort Village* (☎ 288-2535, (800) 255-6936), 516 S Shore Rd, about 3.5 miles east of Hwy 101, is a more modern, less charming lodging option with rooms in fireplace cabins or in a motel wing. Room prices range between $85 and $120. The *Salmon House* is the resort's restaurant, with family dining, steak and seafood. Other facilities include a general store, laundry and boat rentals. RV hookups are also available.

On the north shore of Quinault Lake is *Lochaerie Resort* (☎ 288-2215), 638 N Shore Rd, four miles north of Hwy 101. This venerable resort offers lodging in six comfortable cabins ($50 to $60), each named after different Olympic peaks and with its own character.

## OLYMPIC COASTAL STRIP

Fifty-seven miles of the Olympic Peninsula coast were added to the national park in 1953, making this the longest wilderness coastline in the continental USA. Known officially as the Olympic Coastal Strip, this is some of the most rugged and picturesque coastline anywhere: seastacks and islands parade out into the pounding surf, often capped by miniature forests (remnants of when these rocks were still part of the headland). Wildlife, including many marine mammals such as sea otters found almost nowhere else in the USA, is frequently seen. There's a wealth of life in tide pools and on rocky aviaries. Gray whales spout offshore.

The coastline is accessed by roads at only a few places; otherwise this expanse of rock, sea water and sand belongs to hardy trekkers who negotiate the tides, waves and treacherous headlands on foot. Long-distance hiking along the Pacific

Ocean should not be entered into lightly: this is not just a saunter down a sandy strand.

If you are contemplating a long trek along the coast, request information from the NPS, buy good maps and learn to read tide tables. Many portions of the coastline can't be negotiated except at low tide, while other areas can't be rounded on foot at any time. These promontories require strenuous climbs up and down (often on rope ladders, or sometimes just on ropes) and cross-country excursions to the next safe beach-walking area. Fast-moving waves can easily isolate hikers on rocky points or headlands, and the weather can change quickly. In all but the height of summer, hikers need to be prepared for all kinds of weather.

The most popular long-distance beach hike is the section between Ozette and Rialto Beach, a 20-mile trek that usually requires three or four days. Another favorite three-nighter is the beach hike between Third Beach (near La Push) and Oil City, a 17-mile hike along one of the most rugged stretches of Olympic coast. Remember that you'll need a backcountry permit to camp overnight along the coast (except at official campgrounds). Also pick up a copy of The Mountaineers' *Exploring Washington's Wild Olympic Coast* by David Hooper, which admirably describes the challenges and pleasures of these coastal hikes.

Although the Olympic Coastal Strip is, in terms of recreation, set up for long-distance hikers, there are a number of areas where less ardent explorers and beachcombers can sample this wonderful wilderness coastline.

### Ozette

Most noted as the site of an ancient Makah village (see Neah Bay, later in this chapter), the Ozette area is one of the most accessible parts of the Olympic coast. Except on the busiest summer weekends, it's easy to get away from the crowds and experience these beaches as wilderness.

The Hoko-Ozette Rd leaves Hwy 112

about two miles west of Sekiu and proceeds 20 miles down a paved and graveled road to Ozette Ranger Station & Campground (☎ 963-2725) on Ozette Lake. Ozette Lake is the third-largest lake in Washington and is a popular spot for waterskiers and anglers.

**Hiking** From the ranger station, two boardwalk trails lead out to the beach. To the north, the three-mile **Cape Alava Trail** leads to a section of sandy beach with a jumble of offshore rocks and islands, making this a lovely place for a picnic or beachcombing.

It was along this coast that the 15th-century village known as Ozette was unearthed. Nothing remains of the excavation today except a commemorative plaque, though many of the artifacts are on display at the Makah Museum at Neah Bay. The southern **Sand Point Trail** from Ozette Ranger Station leads 2.8 miles to beaches below a low bluff; whale watchers often come here in the migration season.

The two Ozette trails can easily be linked as a long day hike. It's a little over three miles between Cape Alava and Sand Point along the beach, and no dangerous headlands impede hikers, even at high tide, though the rather coarse rocky beach can make this hike strenuous.

The high point of this hike is the **Wedding Rocks**, the most significant group of petroglyphs on the Olympic Peninsula. About a mile south of Cape Alava, the small outcropping contains over 100 superb rock carvings, including noted carvings of whales, a European square-rigger and fertility figures. The site was traditionally used for Makah weddings and is still considered sacred, and not just by Native Americans – a lot of New Age worship goes on here as well.

### Rialto Beach
One of the few Olympic beaches easily accessed by vehicle, Rialto is a popular place for day excursions. Located at the mouth of the Quillayute River across from La Push, the log-littered, stony beach faces

a profusion of flat-topped offshore islands. Hikers with an eye on the tide table can trek up to **Hole-in-the-Wall**, a bluff with a wave-weathered hole in it, about two miles north of the parking area. This is a wild place to visit after a storm, when waves barrel up to the edge of the forest, dragging logs out to sea.

Facilities at Rialto Beach include flush toilets and picnic tables. Mora Ranger Station (☎ 374-5460) can issue backcountry permits and information; in summer there are also naturalist-led walks along the beach.

To reach Rialto Beach, turn west one mile north of Forks off Hwy 101 and follow the La Push road (Hwy 110). In 13 miles the road divides, with Mora and Rialto Beach on the northern fork. It's four miles from there to the beach.

### Ruby Beach to South Beach
This most southerly area of the Olympic Coastal Strip is located between the Hoh and Quinault reservations. The beach along this stretch is generally much less dramatic than that farther north, and there is regular beach access from Hwy 101. Probably the most attractive coastal areas are found at Ruby Beach, where the beach is made up of polished black stones the size of silver dollars, and at Kalaloch (pronounced *Klay-lock*). Other beachfronts (unimaginatively named Beach One through Beach Six) are sandy strands popular with beachcombers. For information about this area, contact the Kalaloch Information Station (☎ 962-2283).

### Places to Stay & Eat
**Camping** With a wilderness permit, there are plenty of informal campsites along the beach at both Cape Alava and Sand Point. At *Lake Ozette Campground*, there are 14 regular sites, but no fee. Along the Quillayute River, three miles east of La Push and Rialto Beach, *Mora Campground* offers 94 regular sites with a $10 fee. No beach camping is allowed along Rialto Beach between the Quillayute River and Ellen Creek, about a mile above the beach

parking area. The *Kalaloch Campground* has 177 regular sites.

There's a hostel on the Hoh River; see Places to Stay under Forks for more information.

**Lodges & Cabins** The *Kalaloch Lodge* (☎ 962-2271), 157-151 Hwy 101 in Kalaloch, is the only lodging and restaurant between Ruby Beach and Queets. Built in 1953 as an anglers' retreat, the lodge was included in the park's coastal strip and is now operated by park concessionaires. In addition to rooms in the old lodge, there are over 40 log cabins scattered along the headlands above the beach. Some cabins and rooms sleep up to six people. In peak season, lodge rooms are $58 to $75, while cabins run between $95 and $145; most rooms are half price during the winter. There's also an RV park and tenting sites in an adjacent campground. The lodge restaurant offers family-style meals in beachview dining rooms (the best views are from the upstairs lounge).

# Northeastern Olympic Peninsula

The northeast corner of the Olympic Peninsula is where most of the region's population lives, along a stretch of the Strait of Juan de Fuca from Port Townsend to Port Angeles. Outdoor recreationalists love this part of the peninsula because of the much-discussed rain shadow: you get the beauty of the Olympics but not much of the rain. Golf, sea kayaking, sailing and fishing are all popular pastimes here.

Port Townsend is one of the oldest towns in Washington and it went through a notable building boom in 1890, followed by an immediate bust, which preserved the town as an architectural showpiece. Most of the town is on the National Register of Historic Places. Port Angeles is just a ferry ride from Canada and is on the doorstep to Olympic Mountain high country. This comfortable port town makes a convenient center for Olympic Peninsula exploration.

## GETTING AROUND
Public transportation between the communities in the northeast peninsula is limited to buses. Since each of the two northern counties, Clallam and Jefferson, has its own system, you have to change lines in order to get from Port Townsend to Port Angeles by bus.

Jefferson Transit (☎ 385-4777) serves Port Townsend and outlying areas in Jefferson County, the easternmost corner of the peninsula. Buses travel as far west as Sequim. Connections can be made from there to Port Angeles and points west on The Bus, Clallam County's intercity transit system. The fare is 50c.

The Bus (☎ 452-4511, (800) 858-3747) travels as far west as Neah Bay and La Push and as far east as Diamond Point. Eastbound, the No 30 bus travels between Port Angeles and Sequim, where you can connect with Jefferson Transit buses to Port Townsend and points east. To head west, take the No 14 bus to Sappho, and from there pick up connections to either La Push or Neah Bay. In Port Angeles, the main transfer center is at Oak and Front Sts, conveniently located near the ferry dock and visitors center. Fares start at 50c for adults. Call for detailed route and schedule information.

## PORT TOWNSEND
One of the best preserved Victorian-era seaports in the USA, Port Townsend (population 7740) is one of the few urban must-sees in a region otherwise dedicated to the marvels of nature. Block after block of elaborate storefronts line the harbor, and on the hill above the port are ornate mansions (many of which are now B&Bs) built for the merchant kings of the early Washington Territory. On a clear day, views from Port Townsend are stunning, as the town looks across deep-blue Admiralty Inlet, filled with sailboats and ferries, to Whidbey Island and on to the white-glaciered mass of Mt Baker.

Port Townsend was first settled in 1851, the same year that Seattle was established, and for years the two struggling port cities maintained a strident competition for supremacy in Puget Sound trade. Then, in 1888, a subsidiary of Union Pacific announced plans to build rails from Portland to Port Townsend. With its dominance in the Puget Sound now seemingly assured, the citizens of Port Townsend went into a frenzy of commercial development, building a handsome retail core along the harbor and establishing opulent uptown mansions for the elite of trade and industry. However, in 1890, the rail link with Portland evaporated, and within three years the city was all but deserted. At the time, a local wag maintained that the town was still standing only because no one had the money to tear the buildings down.

Today, a new generation of merchant kings has restored historic Port Townsend, turning the downtown district into a shopper's destination for antiques, rare books, upscale clothing and regional art. While Port Townsend hovers at the brink of over-commercialization, it remains a great place to spend an afternoon browsing and an unparalleled place to spend a night or two in a B&B or vintage hotel.

## Information

The Port Townsend Chamber of Commerce visitors center (☎ 385-2722), 2437 E Sims Way, Port Townsend, WA 98368, is open from 9 am to 5 pm Monday to Friday, 10 am to 4 pm on Saturday, and 11 am to 4 pm Sunday.

The chamber of commerce puts out a useful map and guide of the downtown historic district, which abounds with Victorian-era architecture. The white birds found painted on the pavement all over town mark the Port Townsend Seagull Tour route, an auto tour of sites and historic structures (see also Special Events, below).

The post office (☎ 385-1600), at Washington and Van Buren Sts, is in an amazing stone edifice which was formerly the Customs House. Port Townsend offers a number of used and rare-book stores. For travel information, go to Imprint Bookstore (☎ 385-3643) at 820 Water St.

Do your laundry at Port Townsend Laundromat/Car Wash (☎ 385-5755), 2115 W Sims Way, and wash your car while you wait. Jefferson General Hospital (☎ 385-2200, (800) 244-8917) is at 834 Sheridan St.

## Fort Worden State Park

Fort Worden (☎ 385-4730), 200 Battery Way (off Cherry St), was built in 1900 as one of three major fortifications on Puget Sound to defend the area from enemy attack. Enormous cement batteries lined the beachfront and the hill behind the fort, while an elegant officers' row, parade ground, gymnasium and balloon hangar were also built on the fort's 433 acres. The army maintained the fort until after WW II, and in 1972 the fort was transferred to the state parks service.

Today, the fort has been converted into a major recreation, lodging and arts center. The extensive grounds and array of historic buildings have been refurbished and returned to period spiff (the park served as the backdrop for the filming of *An Officer and a Gentleman*). The commanding officer's home, a 12-bedroom mansion, is open for tours, and part of one of the barracks is now the **248th Coast Artillery Museum**, which tells the story of early Pacific coastal fortifications. A local arts organization, called Centrum Foundation, leases parts of the old fort for numerous art conferences, workshops and summer music and arts festivals. The old balloon hangar has been converted into a performing arts center.

A number of the officers' quarters are available for rent as vacation homes, and HI runs a youth hostel from one of the barracks. The facilities are also available for conferences and meetings. In addition, there are 80 campsites, boat launches, picnic sites and a beach access. Hikes lead along the headland to Point Wilson Light Station.

The **Port Townsend Marine Science Center** (☎ 385-5582) is on the park's fishing pier and features a touch tank. This

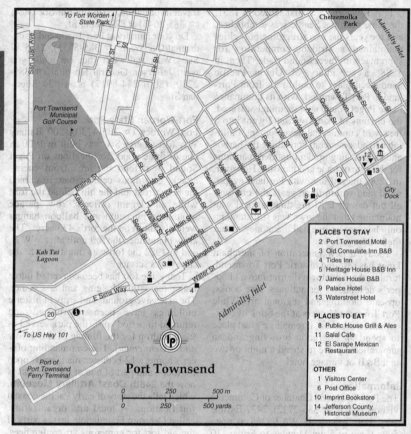

**Port Townsend**

PLACES TO STAY
2  Port Townsend Motel
3  Old Consulate Inn B&B
4  Tides Inn
5  Heritage House B&B Inn
7  James House B&B
9  Palace Hotel
13  Waterstreet Hotel

PLACES TO EAT
8  Public House Grill & Ales
11  Salal Cafe
12  El Sarape Mexican
    Restaurant

OTHER
1  Visitors Center
6  Post Office
10  Imprint Bookstore
14  Jefferson County
    Historical Museum

aquarium is open from noon to 6 pm Tuesday to Sunday, June 15 through Labor Day, Saturday and Sunday only from March 1 through June 14 and from Labor Day through October 31.

**Jefferson County Historical Museum**
The local museum (☎ 385-1003), 210 Madison St, is in the old city hall building, and part of the charm of visiting is snooping around the old courtrooms and jail cells. Displays detail the pioneer and Native American history of Jefferson County with artifacts and scads of photos. The port's maritime history is also well

documented with nautical artifacts. It's open from 11 am to 4 pm Monday to Saturday, and 1 pm to 4 pm on Sunday; admission is by donation.

**Old Fort Townsend State Park**
Constructed in 1856 in response to the Indian War of 1855-6, Fort Townsend, on Old Fort Townsend Rd (four miles south of Port Townsend on Hwy 20), was permanently abandoned in 1895 after a lamp exploded and fire completely gutted the barracks. Although the fort remains historically insignificant, the park sports a pleasant day-use area with picnic facilities and

over six miles of hiking trails, and is a popular spot for crabbing, clamming, fishing and boating.

### Sea Kayaking

Port Townsend is the center for sea kayaking on the Puget Sound, and there are a number of places to rent kayaks and gear and to learn the fundamentals. Kayak Port Townsend (☎ 385-6240) leads full and half-day kayak trips for all experience levels, seven days a week.

### Other Activities

Sea Sport Charters (☎ 385-3575) offers salmon and bottom-fishing excursions and also wildlife tours along the Strait of Juan de Fuca. They operate out of Port Townsend Boat Haven (☎ 385-2355), the local marina. Play nine holes of **golf** at Chevy Chase Golf Club (☎ 385-0704), 7401 Cape George Rd, the state's oldest public golf course, or at Port Townsend Golf Course (☎ 385-0752), 1948 Blaine St. The **swimming** pool at Port Townsend Junior High School (☎ 385-7665) on Walker St at Blaine St, is open to the public.

### Special Events

Those enticed by Port Townsend's Victorian charm will want to be in town for the annual Historic Homes Tours, held once during the spring, the first week of May, and again in the fall, the third week of September. Most of these homes are private residences and are not available for public viewing at any other time. Call the chamber of commerce for more information.

Centrum, a nonprofit arts foundation based at Fort Worden State Park, sponsors an endless stream of arts and music festivals and seminars year round. Call Centrum (☎ 385-3102, (800) 733-3608) for a schedule or write PO Box 1158, Port Townsend, WA 98368.

### Places to Stay

**Camping** RV campers can hook up at *Sea Breeze Center* (☎ 385-0440), 1408 Sims Way, a full-service RV village, or at the

*Jefferson County Fairgrounds* (☎ 385-1013), north of Port Townsend near Fort Worden, where sites are $6 to $8.

Campsites are only one of several accommodation options at *Fort Worden State Park* (☎ 385-4730), 200 Battery Way in Port Townsend. Regular sites are $11 and hookups cost $15. Campers can make reservations by contacting the park directly. Visitors can also pass up the campsites for a stay in one of the park's vacation homes or in the youth hostel (see below). There's more camping at *Old Fort Townsend State Park* (☎ 385-3595) on Old Fort Townsend Rd, four miles south of Port Townsend on Hwy 20, where sites ($10) are lined up on the old parade field (no hook-ups though). It's open from May to mid-September.

**Hostels** There's an *HI/AYH hostel* in the historic barracks at Fort Worden State Park (☎ 385-0655), 272 Battery Way. The hostel should be open year round, even though it has been closed during January and February for maintenance in the past.

**B&Bs** There are dozens of B&Bs in Port Townsend; if you're really into it, contact the chamber of commerce for a full listing. The following are especially nice. The *James House B&B* (☎ 385-1238), 1238 Washington St, offers 12 rooms, some with private baths and many with great views over the harbor. Singles/doubles start at $52/65. The *Heritage House B&B Inn* (☎ 385-6800), 305 Pierce St, is an Italian-ate mansion with six guest rooms (four with private bath) ranging from $60 to $95. The former German ambassador lived at the *Old Consulate Inn B&B* (☎ 385-6753), 313 Walker St at Washington St, a lovely Victorian with a wraparound porch and six rooms (all with private baths) from $69 to $175. Of all the astonishing homes built in Port Townsend, none can top the *Manresa Castle* (☎ 385-5750, (800) 732-1281), 7th and Sheridan Sts (off E Sims Way), built by the first mayor of Port Townsend as a home for his new bride. The 40-room mansion looks like a castle out of a fairy tale, sitting high above the town, with views on all sides. Rooms range from $80 to $175 (for a turret!) in the high season.

**Hotels** Some of the Victorian-era hotels have also been restored. The *Palace Hotel* (☎ 385-0773, (800) 962-0741), 1004 Water St, built in 1890, has been brought back to its original spit and polish. Some rooms have been remodeled into suites with private baths while some rooms are still authentic (bathroom down the hall). Rates range from $54 to $95. Another refurbished inn is the *Waterstreet Hotel* (☎ 385-5467, (800) 735-9810), 635 Water St, with rooms starting at $50.

Not all lodging in Port Townsend is antique. *Port Townsend Motel* (☎ 385-2211, (800) 822-8696), 2020 Washington St, is an attractive motel on the edge of the historic district with single/double rooms starting at $68/78. At the *Tides Inn* (☎ 385-0595, (800) 822-8696), 1807 Water St, the view rooms overlook Admiralty Inlet and Whidbey Island; singles/doubles are $58/78.

**Vacation Home Rentals** *Officer's Row Vacation Homes* at Fort Worden State Park (☎ 385-4730), 200 Battery Way, date from 1904 and were formerly the officers' quarters at Fort Worden. Most of the kitchens are modern, though the houses retain period charm; some have up to six bedrooms. These houses are very popular, and with prices starting at $60, they're a great bargain. Plan to make reservations several months in advance if you want a chance at the prime houses.

**Places to Eat**
The center of Port Townsend is packed with trendy cafes and restaurants. You'll have no problem finding some place to eat. Here are some favorites. For big breakfast omelets or a zippy lunch, head to *Salal Cafe* (☎ 385-6532), 634 Water St. The seafood tacos are notable at *El Sarape Mexican Restaurant* (☎ 379-9343), 628 Water St. *Public House Grill & Ales* (☎ 385-9708), 1038 Water St, offers an informal, pub-like atmosphere, with a menu of grilled items ranging from burgers to steak. For Italian food, head out of town to *Cafe Piccolo* (☎ 385-1403), 3040 Hwy 20, one mile south of Port Townsend, where pizza and pasta are the headliners.

**Getting There & Away**
**Bus** For information about the regional bus system, see Getting Around for the Northeast Olympic Peninsula. The Port Townsend office for Jefferson Transit (☎ 385-4777) is at 1615 W Sims Way.

**Ferry** The Washington State Ferry system (☎ 464-6400) operates about 10 half-hour trips a day to Keystone on Whidbey Island. Rates and schedules vary seasonally, with fares starting at $5.55 for a car and driver and $1.65 for passengers. Service is occasionally disrupted by severe low tides.

**Getting Around**
Port Townsend has a community cycling program. Watch for racks of green bikes, which are free for the borrowing. Just sign one out and bring it back when you're done.

To rent a car, there's a Budget dealer (☎ 385-7766) at 3049 E Sims Way. For a taxi, call Key City Transport (☎ 385-5972).

**SEQUIM**
When they say, 'It's the climate', it's partly because there's not much else to recommend this anomalous little boom town. Directly in the path of the Olympics rain shadow, Sequim (pop 4070) gets less than 20 inches of rain a year, quite a feat on this otherwise sodden peninsula. Initially, irrigation projects brought settlement to this area, then retirees and others looking for sunshine and Shangri-La on the Puget Sound. Predictably, the next step was golf courses, which currently ring the town.

The downtown area is a long and inelegant stretch of old strip malls; nonetheless, boutiques are rapidly squeezing in. Traffic really jams up on Hwy 101 behind Sequim's traffic light, so you may get a chance to window shop from your car.

## Information

The visitors center (☎ 683-6197) is on the east end of town on Hwy 101 at 1192 E Washington St. Direct correspondence to the Sequim-Dungeness Valley Chamber of Commerce, PO Box 907, Sequim, WA 98382.

## Dungeness Spit

Immediately north of town is the Dungeness Spit, a sandy arm that extends 5.5 miles into the Strait of Juan de Fuca; it's the longest natural sand hook in the nation. Now part of Dungeness National Wildlife Refuge, it's a great place to hike and get a closer look at the marine environment of the northern Pacific coast.

The primary wildlife you'll see here are shorebirds, especially herons, various kinds of ducks and loons, and raptors like bald eagles. Seals also crawl up on the sandy beach to sun; watch for them bobbing offshore, looking at you.

To reach the refuge from Sequim, head north up Sequim Ave, which turns into Sequim Dungeness Way, to Dungeness Bay. The Dungeness School House, built in 1892, is on the left side of the road, right before crossing the Dungeness River. Access to the Dungeness Spit is at the Dungeness Recreation Area, a county park. You'll have to park here, as access to the spit is on foot or horseback only. There's a $2 per person fee to enter the refuge and hike the spit. From the park, it's a 12-mile roundtrip walk to **Dungeness Lighthouse**, which was built in 1857 at the end of the spit.

## Olympic Game Farm

If you feel like going on a safari, head to the Olympic Game Farm (☎ 683-4295, (800) 778-4295), 1423 Ward Rd, which offers driving and walking tours through a 90-acre open-air zoo. Most of the 'wildlife' here is semi-domesticated, as many of the animals were trained as 'actors' for wildlife films for Disney Studios. The farm also breeds endangered species (like timber wolves and jaguars) for other zoos. It's open every day from 9 am to 4 pm year round; admission is $5 for adults and $4 for children.

## Sequim Bay State Park

This pleasant state park (☎ 683-4235) is on Sequim Bay, a shallow bay protected by sand spits from the turbulence of the strait, making it a favorite for kayakers and canoers. On the other hand, at low tide, captains of motorized craft are in for a navigational nightmare. There's also camping and picnicking. The park is located four miles southwest of Sequim on Hwy 101.

## Wineries

The near-Mediterranean climate of Sequim has prompted a couple of wineries to spring up. The Neuharth Winery (☎ 683-9652), 148 Still Rd, Sequim, WA 98382, is open daily from 9:30 am to 5:30 pm, May 15 to October 1; the rest of the year from noon to 5 pm, Wednesday to Sunday. It has an attractive tasting room and high-quality wines. The Lost Mountain Winery (☎ 683-5229), 3174 Lost Mountain Rd, Sequim, WA 98382, makes hearty red wines their specialty; call ahead for hours.

## Sea Kayaking

The shallow waters off Dungeness Spit and in Sequim Bay are perfect for exploration by sea kayak. Kayaks & More (☎ 683-3805), 2404 Taylor Cutoff Rd about two miles off Hwy 101, leads a five to six-hour kayak tour to the end of the spit for $50.

## Golf

The sun shines bright in Sequim, and a number of golf courses have sprung up with the retirement community mostly in mind. The only fully public course here is Dungeness Golf Course (☎ 683-6344), 491 Woodcock Rd, an 18-hole course on the road to Dungeness Spit. In addition to a private course, two more large golf resorts are in progress.

## Places to Stay

**Camping** RV hook-ups are $18 at *Conestoga Quarters RV Park* (☎ 452-4637), which is midway between Sequim and Port

Angeles, off Hwy 101 at 40 Siebert's Creek Rd. RVs can also head to the *KOA* outside Port Angeles on Hwy 101.

There are both tent and RV sites ($10/14) at *Sequim Bay State Park* (☎ 683-4235), four miles south of Sequim on Hwy 101. *Dungeness Recreation Area* is adjacent to the Dungeness Spit Wildlife Refuge, and is operated by Clallam County Parks (☎ 417-2291), with 65 campsites ($10), showers and flush toilets, but no hook-ups.

**Hotels** All of the following are along busy Hwy 101, which is essentially all there is to Sequim. They are all in the $59 to $69 range and allow pets. The very red *Red Ranch Inn* (☎ 683-4195), 830 W Washington St, can't be missed on the western edge of Sequim; kids under 12 are free. There's an equally red restaurant on the premises. The *Sundowner Motel* (☎ 683-5532, (800) 325-6966), 364 W Washington St, has some rooms with kitchens. *Sequim Econo Lodge* (☎ 683-7113, (800) 488-7113), 801 E Washington St (Hwy 101), offers free continental breakfast and in-room microwaves and fridges.

Stay outside of town at the *Sequim Bay Lodge Best Western* (☎ 683-0691), 268522 Hwy 101, near John Wayne Marina. Rooms cost $60/70; there's a restaurant and a nine-hole golf course.

**Places to Eat**

For breakfast, the place to go is the *Oak Table Cafe* (☎ 683-2179), 292 W Bell St, for apple pancakes, great omelets and espresso drinks. Sequim's most noted restaurant is *Casoni's* (☎ 683-2415), 104 Hooker Rd, just west of town. Hearty Italian pasta and chicken dishes are the rule here; the homemade cheesecakes are rich and unavoidable. *The Three Crabs* (☎ 683-4264), 101 Three Crabs Rd, at the harbor at Dungeness, is an institution. This is the place to fill up on namesake Dungeness crab. It's worth visiting *El Cazador* (683-4788), 535 W Washington St, a local Mexican chain, if for no other reason than that the Sequim branch is in a renovated grain elevator. For more traditional Northwest-

style cuisine, go to *Buckhorn Grill* (☎ 683-9010), 268522 Hwy 101, at the Sequim Bay Lodge east of town.

**Things to Buy**

Northwest Native Expressions (☎ 681-4640), 1033 Old Blyn Hwy, is a gallery of Native American art located in the tiny S'Klallam Indian community on Sequim Bay. Masks, bentwood boxes and bowls, basketry, blankets and jewelry by artists from many Northwest tribes are on display. There's also a good selection of books and small gifts. Proceeds from sales go to support native tribal cultural programs. The gallery is six miles east of Sequim near Blyn.

**Getting Around**

For buses to/from Sequim, see Getting Around at the beginning of the Northeastern Olympic Peninsula section. In Sequim, the No 40 bus passes through the business district. The corner of Cedar St and 2nd Ave is the transfer point for the No 44 bus, which goes out to Dungeness Bay via Sequim-Dungeness Way, returning via Woodcock Rd.

For a cab, call Sun Taxi (☎ 683-1872).

**PORT ANGELES**

Although Port Angeles (pop 18,270) is mostly known as a place you pass through to get elsewhere – in this case to Canada or to Olympic National Park – it's a pleasant enough town with inexpensive motels and good restaurants and a real nautical air. All in all, it's a good base for exploring the peninsula.

The natural harbor at Port Angeles attracted the attention of land speculators in the 1860s, but President Abraham Lincoln placed the land around the bay under federal ownership as a 'Navy & Military Reserve', in case the USA needed to build defenses against the pesky British installations directly across the strait in Victoria. However, by the 1890s, fear of the British had been largely replaced by the desire to homestead the land, and a flood of squatters moved onto the military reservation and

## Utopia

The land just east of Port Angeles was formerly a utopian colony, established in 1887 by a Seattle attorney named George Smith. The Puget Sound Cooperative Colony was founded on the principle that 'everyone shall act as a civilized being, shall avoid all excesses, be just and undeceiving to all'. With these good intentions, the colony established a school, sawmill and shipyard and cleared land. However, as the town of Port Angeles became more and more of an economic and cultural entity in the late 1890s, the distinction between the citizens of town and colony increasingly blurred and eventually disappeared. ■

settled. Eventually the US government recognized their land claims and opened the remainder of the reservation to settlement.

In the 1910s and 1920s, dams were built on the Elwha River, at the base of the Olympic Mountains. The power was designed to run Port Angeles' saw and pulp mills, which still line the waterfront. However, the dams stopped migration of native salmon and steelhead trout to the upper Elwha, formerly the peninsula's greatest spawning grounds. In recent years, environmentalists have attempted to use the Endangered Species Act to force the state to remove the dams and restore the fish to their native habitat.

### Information

The Port Angeles Visitor Center (☎ 452-2363), 121 E Railroad Ave, Port Angeles, WA 98362, is adjacent to the ferry terminal along the waterfront. Sharing the same office is a visitors center for Victoria, BC (☎ (800) 998-1224). The visitors center for Olympic National Park (☎ 452-0330) is one mile south of town, off Race St at 3002 Mt Angeles Rd.

The post office (☎ 452-9275) is at 424 E 1st St, Port Angeles, WA 97362. Port Book & News (☎ 452-6367), 104 E 1st St, offers a vast selection of magazines and both new and used books. The local travel section is also good. It's open until 9 pm. Peabody Street Coin Laundry, 212 S Peabody St, is open 24 hours a day.

### City Pier

This pier, off the end of Lincoln St, allows pedestrians the chance to venture out into the harbor, where there's an observation tower and picnic area. Also on the pier is the **Feiro Marine Laboratory** (☎ 452-9277, ext 264), operated by the marine studies facility of local Peninsula College. Kids will love the hands-on touch tank filled with the aquatic denizens of the strait. There's a staff person on hand to answer questions and to protect the octopus. The lab is open daily from 10 am to 5 pm from Memorial Day to Labor Day, and Saturday and Sunday from noon to 4 pm the rest of the year; admission is $1 for adults and 50c for children.

### Clallam County Historical Museum

This local museum (☎ 417-2364), 319 Lincoln St, is housed in the handsome old county courthouse and retells the tale of the community's growth. It's largely the tale of logging, milling and shipping, but the building is lovely. The museum is open Monday to Friday from 10 am to 4 pm; admission is free.

### Port Angeles Fine Arts Center

The Olympic Peninsula has a long history as an art-producing area, dating back as far as the Makahs and other artistically inclined natives. Today, dozens of professional artists live on the peninsula, and this small regional gallery (☎ 457-3532), 1203 E 8th St, usually has exhibits of local work. The gallery is high above the city in a five-acre garden with beautiful views over the strait. The center is open Thursday to Sunday from 11 am to 5 pm.

### Waterfront Trail

If you want to limber up before taking on a mountain trail in the Olympics, try the Waterfront Trail, a six-mile trail that stretches along the Port Angeles waterfront out to the end of **Ediz Hook**, the sand spit that loops around the bay. This is a popular picnic spot. A good place to pick up the trail is at the base of City Pier.

WASHINGTON

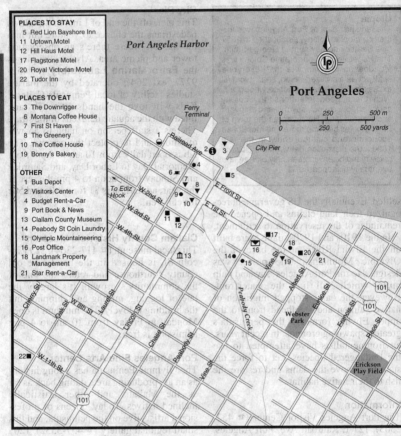

**PLACES TO STAY**
5  Red Lion Bayshore Inn
11  Uptown Motel
12  Hill Haus Motel
17  Flagstone Motel
20  Royal Victorian Motel
22  Tudor Inn

**PLACES TO EAT**
3  The Downrigger
6  Montana Coffee House
7  First St Haven
8  The Greenery
10  The Coffee House
19  Bonny's Bakery

**OTHER**
1  Bus Depot
2  Visitors Center
4  Budget Rent-a-Car
9  Port Book & News
13  Clallam County Museum
14  Peabody St Coin Laundry
15  Olympic Mountaineering
16  Post Office
18  Landmark Property
    Management
21  Star Rent-a-Car

*Port Angeles Harbor*

**Port Angeles**

Ferry Terminal

City Pier

## Activities

A good place to go for outdoor gear and supplies is Olympic Mountaineering (☎ 452-0240), 221 S Peabody St. In addition to selling the necessary gear for most outdoor recreational activities, the store also offers rental stoves, packs, tents, skis and so on. They also offer lessons and classes for many sports, in season.

For guided '**eco-tours**' of Olympic National Park, contact Olympic Van Tours & Shuttles (☎ 452-3858), PO Box 2201, Port Angeles, WA 98362. You can also arrange to be picked up after trans-park

hikes or from Sea-Tac Airport. Contact Rite Bros Aviation (☎ 452-6226, 452-7227), at the west end of Fairchild Airport, for information about **scenic flights** over Olympic National Park and other parts of the peninsula.

The Peninsula Golf Club (☎ 457-6501), 105 Linberg Rd, is a semi-private **golf** course, with some days reserved for members only. Call ahead for reservations.

## Places to Stay

**Camping** *Port Angeles/Sequim KOA* (☎ 457-5916), 80 O'Brien Rd, seven miles east of Port Angeles on Hwy 101, offers both RV and tent sites, with a laundry, showers and a heated pool. Open from April through October; sites begin at $16. *Al's RV Park* (☎ 457-9844), 521 N Lee's Creek Rd, three miles east, provides campers with a quiet off-highway setting. RVs can also camp at *Welcome Inn Trailer Park* (☎ 457-1553), two miles west at 1215 W Hwy 101, for $10 to $15. Five miles west of town, *Shady Tree RV Park* (☎ 452-7054), 47 Lower Dam Rd, welcomes both tents and RVs; sites cost $10/15.

**B&Bs** *Domaine Madeleine* (☎ 457-4174), 146 Wildflower Lane, east of Port Angeles, is a perennial favorite with couples, who come here for the wonderful views of the strait and Vancouver Island, the French-inspired five-acre garden and the comforts of a well-run B&B. There are three guest rooms and one suite, all with views; rooms range from $125 to $165. *Tudor Inn* (☎ 452-3138), 1108 S Oak St, is a 1910 home with five bedrooms, two with private baths, and a library and sitting room for guests. Room rates range from $58 to $90.

**Hotels** Port Angeles sees a lot of travelers due to the ferries, and there are a number of good, reasonably priced motels. Two of the best deals here are the *Traveler's Motel* (☎ 452-2303), 1133 E 1st St, with singles/doubles for $29/34, and the *All View Motel* (☎ 457-7779), 214 E Lauridsen Blvd (off Lincoln St), with rooms starting at $26. Only slightly more expensive is the *Flagstone Motel* (☎ 457-9494), 415 E 1st St, and the *Royal Victorian Motel* (☎ 452-2316), 521 E 1st St. Each of these is near busy Hwy 101.

For a quieter location, head to the *Hill Haus Motel* (☎ 452-9285), 111 W 2nd St, or the *Uptown Motel* (☎ 457-9434), 2nd and Laurel Sts, which sit beside each other on the bluff above downtown. Both have views over the harbor and of the Olympics, and both are clean and friendly. Rooms start in the $50 range.

For something a bit more upscale, go to the *Red Lion Bayshore Inn* (☎ 452-9215),

221 N Lincoln St, right on the waterfront. This is a large development with 187 rooms and the kinds of comforts, like a heated pool, spa and balconies over the harbor, that you'd expect for upward of $90 a night. There's comfort at brand new *Best Western Olympic Lodge* (☎ 452-2993, (800) 600-2993), 140 Del Guzzi Drive, in a country setting one mile east of Port Angeles on Hwy 101. They have a heated pool, Jacuzzi and small conference facilities; rooms begin at $69.

**Vacation Home Rentals** Landmark Property Management (☎ 452-1326), 501 E 1st St, sometimes has private homes available for short-term vacation rentals in the Port Angeles area.

**Places to Eat**
There's a sly kind of countercultural bent to Port Angeles, but it's hard to put your finger on it. Hang out at some of the local cafes and you begin to get a sense of it. For a jolt of espresso and a bagel, go to *Montana Coffee House* (☎ 452-9769), 114 N Laurel St. The extra-narrow *First St Haven* (☎ 457-0352), 107 E 1st St, is the place to go for traditional diner-style breakfasts. If you're on the road out to Seattle, stop at *Bonny's Bakery* (☎ 457-3585), 502 E 1st St. Set in an old church, Bonny's specializes in French pastries, fresh Danishes and cinnamon rolls; there's espresso, too.

*The Coffee House* (☎ 452-1459), 118 E 1st St, is an art gallery-cum-coffeehouse and restaurant that offers a large and eclectic, world-cuisine menu. There are plenty of vegetarian dishes, most less than $10. On weekends, there's local acoustic entertainment. Somewhat oddly, for a restaurant located in the basement of a health-food store and named *The Greenery* (☎ 457-4112), 117-B E 1st St, this isn't a particularly vegetarian restaurant. The prime rib, local seafood and Italian dishes are favorites. You need to enter the restaurant from the alley behind and below the store.

If you're looking for a traditional steakhouse and nightclub, head to *Bushwhacker Restaurant* (☎ 457-4113), 1527 E 1st St.

This is also a good place to find fresh local seafood. Locals are fond of recommending *The Downrigger* (☎ 452-2700), 155 Railroad Ave (on the wharf next to the ferry terminal), which has great views over the harbor and out to Victoria, BC. Go for the views – or a drink – but steer clear of what purports to be cuisine.

### Getting Around
For information about getting to/from Port Angeles by plane or ferry, see the Getting There & Away section at the beginning of this chapter. To get to/from Port Angeles by bus, see Getting Around in the Northeastern Olympic Peninsula section. The bus depot is at the corner of Oak and Front Sts.

Budget Rent-a-Car (☎ 452-4774) has two locations, one directly across from the ferry terminal at 111 W Front St, and one at Fairchild International Airport (☎ 457-4246). Rentals are also available from Star Rent-a-Car (☎ 452-8001), 602 E Front St.

If you need a taxi, call Blue Top Cab Co (☎ 452-2223).

# Northwestern Olympic Peninsula

In the northwest corner of the Olympic Peninsula, Hwy 101 winds through some of the most remote land this side of the Puget Sound. The land that's not part of Olympic National Park is heavily logged and mostly unpopulated, due to extremes of weather and isolation. Four Indian reservations cling to the edge of the continent at the western edge of the peninsula, and each welcomes respectful visitors.

The major town out here is Forks, which has ample numbers of motel rooms and restaurants. If you're traveling in the northwestern peninsula, reservations are a good idea – even in Forks – because it's a long way to the next town. Don't let these considerations inhibit you from visiting other areas: the museum in Neah Bay is world-class, and the bay at La Push is beautiful

and primordial. Just plan ahead. It's worth noting that the restaurants and lodgings in Forks are open year round, while many of the other smaller towns on the northwest corner essentially shut down outside of tourist season.

## CLALLAM BAY & SEKIU
After winding through clear-cuts, Hwy 113 drops onto the Strait of Juan de Fuca at Clallam Bay, a wind-tossed little village alongside a snug cove. Three miles later is Sekiu, on a hillside above a marina. Its strictly utilitarian buildings and harbor resemble a coastal town in Alaska.

Both these places are primarily fishing villages, and there's not much here – besides great views – to attract visitors who aren't interested in charter fishing. Most motels, in fact most businesses in Clallam Bay and Sekiu, offer charter fishing, though the recent bans on salmon fishing have hit these fishing communities hard.

### Places to Stay & Eat
The *Bay Motel* (☎ 963-2444) in Clallam Bay sits right on the water, with rooms beginning at $35. At *Curley's Resort Motel* (☎ 963-2281) on Hwy 112, Sekiu's main street, there's a choice of motel rooms ($30) or cabins ($75). Curley's is next to a restaurant, and also operates a scuba-diving center. Across the street and right on the harbor is *Van Rippers Resort & Charter* (☎ 963-2334), which offers a variety of rooms, mostly in the above price range; one room ($65) sleeps six.

Restaurants out here are seasonal and pretty ordinary; there's a grocery store in Clallam Bay.

## NEAH BAY
The center of the Makah Indian Reservation, this old fishing town features one of the best Native American museums in the USA, but otherwise it has pretty basic amenities for the traveler. It's a long and increasingly winding cliff-side road that links Neah Bay (population 1214) to the rest of the peninsula, and from here roads press even farther west through forests to

Cape Flattery, the most northwesterly point in the continental USA. Neah Bay sits alongside a wide, wind-frothed harbor overlooked by totem poles. There's more than just a sense of history here: in Neah Bay, on the continent's edge, there's a sense of timelessness.

## Orientation & Information

On Hwy 112, Neah Bay is 18 miles west of Sekiu and 75 miles west of Port Angeles. For more information about the Makah Reservation, contact the Makah Tribal Council (☎ 645-2201), PO Box 115, Neah Bay, WA 98357.

## Makah Museum

This transfixing museum and cultural research center (☎ 645-2711), on the east end of Neah Bay off Hwy 112, is one of the USA's greatest collections of Native American archaeology and the sole repository of the Ozette artifacts. Excellent displays interpret the many objects found at the Ozette site and fit them together into a whole that illustrates the day-to-day life of the ancient Makah.

Especially impressive is the ingenious use that the Ozettes made of their environment: everything they needed was fashioned from bone, stone, wood or grasses. Also notable is the intricate use of design: not only would they carve a comb from a piece of bone, its handle would be fashioned to represent a grimacing human face. Not only would they fell cedar trees and cut boards (all without the use of any metal tools), the house planks would be etched with ceremonial shapes like whales and owls.

Among the displays are a number of Makah canoes, complete with whaling weapons, and a replica of an Ozette longhouse, which is filled with the tools, baskets, and goods of everyday life. In the museum theater, the film *A Gift from the Past* is shown twice daily at 10 am and 2 pm, and recounts the discovery, excavation and importance of the Ozette site. The sophistication of ancient Makah life is quite remarkable, and to walk out of the museum and find yourself in the same environment where the ancient Makah lived produces a profound and thoughtful respect.

The museum is open daily from 10 am to 5 pm, June 1 through September 15, and Wednesday to Sunday from 10 am to 5 pm the rest of the year. Admission is $4 for adults and $3 for seniors and children.

## Cape Flattery

Although no roads lead directly to Cape Flattery, the most northwesterly point in the lower 48 states, a mile-long hiking path leads to this dramatic 300-foot promontory. From Neah Bay, take the main street through town and follow a sign stating 'Cove Trails' that points up a hill (at this point stop following the roads that say Cape Flattery Resort). The eight-mile road to the Cape Flattery trailhead is pretty rough but negotiable by most vehicles.

From the top of this wild, wind-buffeted point, cliffs fall away to the raging Pacific. Just offshore is Tatoosh Island, with a lighthouse and Coast Guard station. This is a good place to watch for whales during migration season.

## Places to Stay & Eat

Most facilities were designed with anglers in mind, who used to come here in droves for the salmon fishing. Of the bay-side lodgings, probably the best is *Silver Salmon Resort* (☎ 645-2388), on Bay View Ave (Hwy 112), with rooms starting at $39. On the waterfront is the *Bay View Restaurant* (☎ 645-2872), which is open year round.

The best lodging and dining option for most people is also the most unique: the Air Force built a small airbase near Neah Bay during WW II to defend the mouth of the Strait of Juan de Fuca. Years later, the base was closed, and the land – including five barracks and various recreational facilities – reverted to the tribe. The Makah have converted the styleless base facilities into the year-round *Cape Flattery Resort* (☎ 645-2251), about two miles west of Neah Bay on Hwy 112. In addition to

WASHINGTON

## Ozette: The American Pompeii

The Makah tribe has dwelt at the mouth of the Strait of Juan de Fuca for centuries, and they were among the greatest of the seafaring Northwest Indians. Hunters would put to sea on large dugout cedar canoes to hunt gray whales, which annually migrate past these shores. Sometimes the whalers would paddle out 40 miles into the Pacific in search of their quarry. After harpooning the animal, the Makah hunters would lance the whale with floats made of inflated seal skins to keep it from diving. After the whale was killed, it was towed back to the village, where it was processed into food and its bones were made into tools.

Makah also hunted seals, halibut and other marine fish. From the forests and meadows, the Makah made canoes, baskets, bentwood boxes and other everyday items, all artistically designed and most carved with ceremonial or amusing details.

The reason we know so much about Makah prehistory is due to one of the great accidents of archaeology. Ozette, on the western side of the Olympic Peninsula, was one of the five original ancient Makah villages. It was built on a grassy ledge above the beach and below a steep dirt slope. Apparently, about 500 years ago, after a powerful rain storm the slope above the village gave way and a massive mud slide buried old Ozette.

The Ozette villagers apparently never attempted to retrieve the objects from the settlement, and the site remained undisturbed for centuries. Finally, after another lashing storm in the early 1970s, a hiker along the beach noticed timbers and boards sticking out of a recently exposed hillside. The tribe and archaeologists were both contacted, and a decade-long excavation of the site ensued.

Ozette is often referred to as the American Pompeii, for the wealth of items recovered and the view it gives into the everyday life of the Makah villagers. Entire longhouses, with all the tools, toys, weapons, baskets and implements intact, were uncovered. After the artifacts were cataloged and interpreted (often with the help of Makah elders, who were sometimes the only source of information on the use of certain tools or objects), the Makah erected a huge new museum at Neah Bay to exhibit the artifacts and tell the story of their ancient ancestors. ■

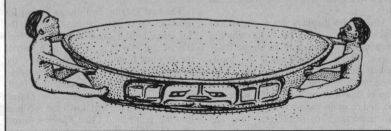

lodging units and dormitory-type accommodations, there's a conference center, bowling alley, gymnasium and restaurant, the *Makah Bay Cafe*. Room rates range between $35 to $55.

## FORKS
Forks is unabashedly a lumber town, but it doesn't seem as down on its luck as many other logging communities in the Northwest. This is by far the largest and friendliest place to stay on the western half of the Olympic Peninsula, as there are lots of hotels and several good places to eat. Forks is convenient to the Hoh rainforests, Neah Bay and the Olympic coastline.

### Orientation & Information
Many roads lead off Forks to interesting places. From Forks, it's 17 miles west to La Push and Rialto Beach, and 57 miles north to Neah Bay. The Hoh Rainforest Visitors Center is 24 miles south on Hwy 101, and Kalaloch is 35 miles south.

The Forks Chamber of Commerce (☎ 374-2531) can be contacted at PO Box 1249, Forks, WA 98331.

### Forks Timber Museum
One mile south of Forks on Hwy 101 next to the visitors center, this museum (☎ 374-9663) remembers the early settlers and loggers of the west end. Included in the collection is a steam donkey – used to transport logs – and pioneer farming implements. The local Native Americans are represented with a dugout canoe. Admission is by donation.

### Places to Stay
**Camping** There's easy access to a number of public campgrounds; check the map from the national park. Most convenient is *Bogachiel State Park* (☎ 374-6356), six miles south of Forks on Hwy 101, with 41 sites, piped water and flush toilets, right on the Bogachiel River. Otherwise, there's *Forks 101 RV Park* (☎ 374-507, (800) 962-9964), a half mile south of town on Hwy 101.

**Hostels** The *Rain Forest Hostel* (☎ 374-2270), HC 80, Box 870, Forks, WA 98331, 23 miles south of Forks on Hwy 101, is a private home with four dorm rooms. Facilities include a full kitchen, common room and fireplace. Lodging is $8 per night.

**B&Bs** *Miller Tree Inn B&B* (☎ 374-6806), 654 E Division St (next to City Hall), offers six guest rooms, two with private baths. This old farmhouse sits on three acres, and rooms begin at $55.

**Hotels** *Forks Motel* (☎ 374-6243, (800) 544-3416), 432 Forks Ave S, is a pleasant place with lots of rooms, a laundry, some kitchenettes and a pool; singles/doubles are $45/55. Across the street is *Pacific Inn Motel* (☎ 374-9400, (800) 235-7344), 352 Hwy 101 S, where kids under 12 are free and there's a guest laundry. Rooms cost $43/48. *Town Motel* (☎ 374-6231), 1080 S Forks Ave, offers large family units and pets are OK. There are some kitchen units; rates begin at $29/35.

### Places to Eat
For breakfast, follow the locals to *The Coffee Shop* (☎ 374-6321), 241 Forks Ave, just next to the Pay & Save supermarket. Mountains of eggs, hash browns and pancakes sustain logger and tourist alike.

At *North South Garden* (☎ 374-9779), 219 Sol Duc Way, expert cooks serve up Asian food, the quality of which rivals that in Seattle or Portland. An extensive selection of both Mandarin and Sichuan food is available, with most dinner entrees ranging from $6 to $9. The *Smokehouse Restaurant* (☎ 372-6258), one mile north of Forks at the La Push junction, is the local steak and seafood house.

## LA PUSH
La Push is a tiny fishing village at the mouth of the Quillayute River and the principal settlement in the Quileute Indian Reservation. La Push looks out onto a jumble of towering, tree-topped islands, which serve to protect its small, busy

harbor. It's worth the 17-mile drive down from Hwy 101 just to watch the fishing boats setting out to sea from this beautiful and rugged bay. The Quileute have done more to attract tourism than many of the tribes on the peninsula by building a somewhat funky resort in La Push, above a magnificent stretch of beach.

### Orientation & Information

The road down from Hwy 101 divides at the point where the Bogachiel and Soleduck Rivers join. The northerly road continues to Mora and Rialto Beach on the Olympic Coastal Strip, while the road to the south continues to La Push. Just outside of town are the trailheads to Third and Second beaches, also part of the park. Both offer a scenic beachfront; however, the coast is so rugged here that it's not possible to walk from one to the other along the Pacific. Third Beach is the starting point for a popular three-day beach hike to Oil City, 17 miles south near Hoh.

For more information, contact the Quileute Tribal Council (☎ 374-6163), PO Box 279, La Push, WA 98350.

### Places to Stay & Eat

At the tribally owned and operated *La Push Ocean Park Resort* (☎ 374-5267, (800) 487-1267), lodgings range from comfortable to pretty rustic and include a motel unit, a lodge and a variety of cabins. The lodge sits above one of the most beautiful beaches in Washington, but before setting out be sure you know what class of lodging you're getting. Ask specific questions – not all cabins have private bathrooms. Rooms range from $36 for Camper's Cabins (no toilet) to $125 for deluxe cabins with stone fireplaces. The resort also offers tent and RV camping for $10 to $12.

There's no restaurant in La Push, though there is a small market, and fresh seafood is available from fishing terminals near the harbor. You may want to request a kitchenette at the resort if you're going to spend any amount of time at La Push.

# North Beach Area

These extensive sandy beaches – there's almost 30 miles of public access shoreline between Moclips and Point Brown – certainly offer beachcombers plenty of opportunity to explore, and in midsummer, temperatures invite sunbathing and dips into the chilly Pacific. These are the closest beaches to Puget Sound population centers, and they can be very busy with family vacationers. In the fall, the beaches come alive with razor-clam diggers, who at low tide hunt the wily and succulent bivalves.

However, there's little else to recommend these beaches. If you're looking for wild and isolated coastline, or a mystic oneness with the sea, this isn't your stretch of beach. Washington State beaches are administered by the state highway department and are maintained as public roadways. Here, vehicles are allowed on the beaches, and you'll have to watch your children and dogs lest they be struck by speeding motorists; hardly anyone obeys the 25-mph speed limit. By late afternoon, after the hot-rod beach bums have had a few beers, lolling on the beach is, at the very least, unpleasant, if not unsafe. If you're heading to the Northwest for a beach holiday, you'll generally be much happier in Oregon, where vehicles are kept off the beaches.

## ORIENTATION

South of Queets, at the southern end of the Olympic National Park Coastal Strip, Hwy 101 heads inland to avoid the Quinault Indian Reservation. The road passes by Lake Quinault, and then heads south to Hoquiam. An alternative route is to take a good, 17-mile-long, paved and gravel road seven miles south of Lake Quinault, which joins Hwy 109 at Moclips. From here, travelers can continue south past modest beachside towns to Ocean Shores, or drive north into Taholah, a fishing village on the Quinault Reservation. It's 24 miles between

Lake Quinault and Moclips, and 23 miles between Moclips and Ocean Shores.

## INFORMATION

For information about this stretch of beach, contact the Washington Coast Chamber of Commerce (☎ 289-4552, (800) 286-4552), on Hwy 109 in Ocean City. For information about the Quinault Reservation, contact the Quinault Indian Nation (☎ 276-8211), PO Box 189, Taholah, WA 98587.

## MOCLIPS

Moclips, just south of the Quinault Indian Reservation, is kind of a dead end for northbound beach holiday makers – from here the road turns inland to Lake Quinault. The isolation suits most visitors. The beach here is more rugged and picturesque than farther south: cliffs line the beach, and a few rocky tide pools sit at tide line. Along Hwy 109, between Moclips and the development at Ocean Shores are a number of desultory beach towns and beach access points. The farther south you go the busier and more developed it gets.

### Places to Stay & Eat

*Pacific Beach State Park* (☎ 289-3553), on Hwy 109 two miles south of Moclips at Pacific Beach, offers 118 tent sites ($10) and 20 RV sites with hook-ups ($14). There's no vehicle access to the beach at this park, which means that you'll usually find more people than pick-ups crossing the sand.

Moclips has a couple of fairly basic oceanfront motels and one charming resort. The best of the motels is the *Hi-Tide Ocean Beach Resort* (☎ 276-4142), 4890 Railroad Ave, which offers new condo-type units above the mouth of the Moclips River. Rates range between $69 and $89.

For something special, go to the *Ocean Crest Resort* (☎ 276-4465), at Sunset Beach, one mile south of Moclips off Hwy 109; this is the nicest place to stay along this stretch of coast. There are a number of lodging options, ranging from studio apartments to two-bedroom suites. All rooms in this rambling complex have cable TV and maid service; kitchenettes and fireplaces are also available. There is a two-night minimum stay on weekends. In addition to the handsome rooms, there's a heated indoor pool, a sauna and an exercise room. The restaurant is noted for its outstanding food – steak and seafood – and for its long views of the Pacific shore. The upstairs lounge is a great place for a snug drink while watching for whales. The resort offers private beach access down a winding, wooded path. Rooms range from $52 to $115; in the off-season, the resort offers three nights for the price of two. Call for other specials.

The only restaurant in the area is at Ocean Crest Resort, and there's a small market in the town.

## OCEAN SHORES

Ocean Shores (pop 2620) is what's left of a huge development gone bust. In the 1960s, developers divided nine sq miles of this land up into lots in anticipation of a land rush. Four-lane roads and an airport went in. The boom never happened, and after a decade the company went bankrupt.

The moral of the story is that it's hard to make a real estate boom out of the most characterless beach in the entire Northwest. The views from this finger of land north of the mouth of Grays Harbor are limited to mile after mile of marshy coastal plains covered with scrubby pines and beach grass, with houses stuck here and there.

However, these aesthetic considerations don't stop Ocean Shores from being a major beach resort. People come for the sandy beaches, and there are certainly a lot of them. These beaches double as sand-lot speedways, so watch out for revved-up pick-ups careening along the shoreline. There are also many motels and beach-type concessions near the 'gates' to Ocean Shores. A bit farther south some quite up-scale resorts face onto the Pacific. From the marina, a summer-only car ferry crosses over to Westport.

## Orientation & Information

Ocean Shores is 18 miles west of Hoquiam on Hwy 109. For more information, contact the Ocean Shores Chamber of Commerce (☎ 289-2451, (800) 762-3224), in the Catala Mall, 899 Point Brown Ave, which is the main street in Ocean Shores.

## Places to Stay & Eat

Ocean Shores Visitors Center offers a reservation service (☎ (800) 562-8612) to the many motels and campgrounds lining the beach.

For camping, go to *Ocean City State Park* (☎ 289-3553), 148 Hwy 115, which offers almost 200 campsites right on the beach.

Following are a couple of dandy motels in Ocean Shores, but there are dozens of others. *Gitchee Gumee Motel* (☎ 289-3323, (800) 448-2433) offers kitchens in non-

smoking and pet-friendly units, and indoor and outdoor swimming pools. Rooms in the high season begin at $55. The *Polynesian Oceanfront Resort* (☎ 289-3361, (800) 562-4836) has a variety of room types, from motel rooms ($49 and up) to a three-bedroom penthouse ($88). Most rooms have balconies and kitchen facilities. There's also an indoor pool and exercise room. Children under 12 are free. *Mariah's Restaurant*, in the complex, is one of the better places to eat in Ocean Shores.

However, seek not cuisine at Ocean Shores. Be happy that the *Homeport Restaurant* (☎ 289-2600), 857 Point Brown Ave, offers chowders, steak, seafood and a salad bar. If you were far-sighted enough to get a kitchen motel unit, then head to *Mike's Seafood* (☎ 289-0532), 830 Point Brown Ave, to buy a crab or some razor clams.

# Southwestern Washington

Separated from the rest of the state by deep forests, I-5 and the Columbia and Chehalis rivers, southwest Washington is an isolated network of mountains, bays and sandy peninsulas that contains some of the state's most appealing beaches and farm country.

The mouth of the Columbia River is the region's prominent geographical feature, and it is responsible for the local climate as well as for most of the area's history. The great river is over five miles wide when it reaches the Pacific Ocean at Cape Disappointment, its valley forming a trough between Oregon's Coast Range and the Olympic Mountains farther north. Through this gap in the coastal mountains, the clouds, rain and winds of the Pacific flow unhindered, spreading far inland, creating one of the mildest climates in the continental USA. Summers are cool, and winters are wet but not cold. The frequent fogs and rains (up to 100 inches yearly) favor dense forests and dairy farms.

The Columbia River, a great navigational river, attracted the first White settlers to the region and is home to Longview, one of the largest timber ports in the world. The old-growth forests of southwestern Washington once rivaled those of the Olympic Peninsula, but they fell to the logger early because of easy access to the river. Industrial logging quickly supplanted farming as the pillar of local economies. However, once-prominent salmon-fishing ports at the mouth of the Columbia River and at Grays Harbor have declined along with the salmon, though Westport is still a center for charter fishing in the Northwest.

In the late 18th century, American and European traders arrived and established long-standing trade relationships with the native Chinook tribes along the river and at Grays Harbor. Lewis and Clark tarried here as well, partaking of Chinook hospitality during the hard winter of 1805. Access to the Columbia River's trade routes was important to the Hudson's Bay Company, which established Fort Vancouver across from the confluence of the Willamette River in 1824. This fur-trading outpost was the first real settlement in the Pacific Northwest, and it became the unwitting nucleus of pioneer migration.

The Columbia River is also responsible for the 28 miles of beaches along the Long Beach Peninsula and for those at Grayland, as its mighty burden of sediment flows out into the Pacific and is swept northward by currents, dumping its sand. Protected by this spit of land, the shoals and backwaters of Willapa Bay are perfect for raising oysters, and this remote corner of Washington is one of the most famed oyster-raising areas in the USA.

## ORIENTATION

Interstate 5 runs along the Columbia and Cowlitz rivers as it threads its way between Portland and Seattle. Between this transportation corridor and the Pacific Ocean runs Hwy 4, which continues to parallel the Columbia from Longview, and Hwy 6, which links Chehalis and Raymond. Both are slow roads that pass lots of clear-cuts and low mountains. This remoteness means that the western parts of this region, in particular the Long Beach Peninsula, are more accessible from Oregon than from the rest of Washington, and historically, Oregonians have played a large role in developing the area as a beach resort. The quickest access to Long Beach from the south is on Oregon's Hwy 30, crossing the river at Astoria.

## CENTRALIA & CHEHALIS

These two old farm and mill communities lodged between logged-off hills on the upper Chehalis River were once separated by five miles of fields, but they have practically grown together to form a single elongated town. While each town boasts a

WASHINGTON

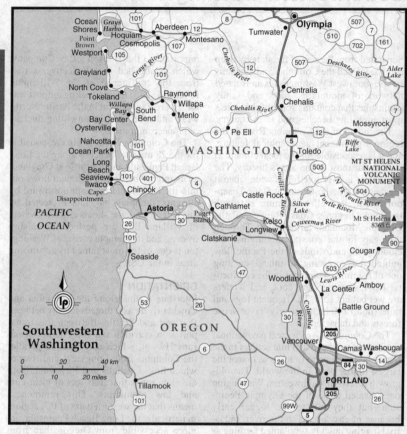

Southwestern Washington

0        20        40 km
0    10    20 miles

historic red-brick center oriented to the railroad tracks, they both also have business districts strung alongside I-5. Centralia (population 12,380) has established a new-found reputation as a shopping destination: there are dozens of factory outlets shops and discount malls just west of exit No 82, and the old downtown is packed with antique malls. Chehalis (population 6710), while hardly a New Age capital, can surprise a visitor with main-street businesses like a metaphysical bookstore and hypnotherapy services.

Centralia has the honor of being the only community in the Northwest founded by an African American, George Washington. Washington was born in Virginia, but he moved out West from Missouri with the Cochran family who first owned him, but who then freed and adopted him. Hoping for greater tolerance on the frontier, Washington arrived in Oregon Country just as the legislature passed a law forbidding settlement by African Americans. He then moved north across the Columbia River, hoping that the British, who still effectively controlled the area, might be more tolerant. Washington was able to establish a land claim in 1852 near the Chehalis River, which now includes most of downtown

Centralia, after he was granted an exemption by the legislature. However, the territory of Washington soon split off from Oregon, thereby nullifying the exemption.

Two White men, traveling through the territory, stopped to spend the night at Washington's farm. Admiring the location and realizing that Washington was constitutionally unable to own the land, the men announced they were going to file a claim for it. Alerted to the situation, the Cochrans rushed ahead and filed a claim first. The Cochrans later deeded the farm back to Washington, who platted his land and sold it for building sites.

## Orientation & Information

Both Centralia and Chehalis are on I-5, exactly halfway between Portland and Seattle, both 84 miles away. Highway 6 cuts off from I-5 at Chehalis, heading west to Raymond (51 miles) and the Pacific Coast.

Both Centralia and Chehalis are a little odd to navigate for first-time visitors. In Chehalis, be prepared for a seemingly

---

### The Centralia 'Wobblies'

Centralia is known for the 'Centralia Massacre'. By the 1900s, Centralia and Chehalis were both booming, with logging, mining and farming in the ascendancy. Since working conditions and pay in the logging and mining camps were poor, unions quickly took root, the dominant one being the Chicago-based International Workers of the World, known as the IWW or the 'Wobblies'. The IWW subscribed to revolutionary goals like a single worldwide

From the IWW Paper, *Industrial Worker*, Dec 26, 1912

union and a worker takeover of the means of production, which was to be achieved by class warfare and armed resistance to the forces of capitalist oppression. The IWW also spoke out against US involvement in WW I, favoring pacifism.

In Centralia, the IWW enjoyed support from the working classes; however, during WW I, the union's practice of labor slowdowns and strikes angered many who felt that these labor agitations were unpatriotic during wartime. In 1919, after the return of local soldiers from Europe, the American Legion held an Armistice Day parade to honor the returned veterans. As they had in the past, the Legionnaires boasted of their intent to raid the IWW union hall, but this time, unlike the past, the IWW intended to meet fire with fire.

As they had threatened, a group of armed veterans assembled in front of the IWW union hall and rushed the building in a raid. Armed IWW supporters fired into the crowd, killing three Legionnaires; a fourth was killed in a later skirmish. In the melee, most of the IWW assailants escaped, though one, Wesley Everest, was apprehended after a long chase. Not knowing who had fired the fatal shots, law enforcement rounded up the local leaders of the IWW and jailed them. That night, vigilante Legionnaires broke into the jail and abducted Everest. The next day, Everest was found beaten, castrated and shot, hanging from a railway bridge. His body was brought back to the jail and put on display in front of the remaining IWW members.

Nine IWW members were tried, found guilty of first-degree murder and sentenced to lengthy jail terms. No investigation or charges ever followed the death of IWW-member Everest.

The IWW union hall still stands at 807 N Tower St; the Lewis County Museum has a good exhibit of the documents and history of this traumatic incident, which is a seminal chapter in the history of the US labor movement. ■

gratuitous one-way system and oddly angled streets; the principal street is called Market St. In Centralia, be prepared for an address numbering system that doesn't follow the numbered streets. Addresses are numbered from Main St; 1st St is actually the 700 block, as far as addresses go.

For information about the area, contact the Lewis County Visitors & Convention Bureau (☎ 525-3323), 500 NW Chamber of Commerce Way, Chehalis, WA 98532.

### Lewis County Historical Museum
The Lewis County Historical Museum (☎ 748-0831), 599 NW Front St, in the old railway depot in Chehalis, offers a wide perspective on the sometimes violent history of the area. In addition to the usual re-creation of a frontier school room, kitchen and doctor's office, there are baskets and artifacts from the local Chehalis tribe, vintage logging equipment and displays relating to George Washington's founding of Centralia. The central exhibit deals with the so-called Centralia Massacre (see the aside on the Centralia 'Wobblies'). The museum does a good job of presenting the case from all points of view. However, most of the exhibits are lengthy documents and texts that have to be read, so plan to spend some time if you want to take in this exhibit.

The museum is open from 9 am to 5 pm Tuesday to Saturday and 1 to 5 pm on Sundays; it's closed on Monday. Admission is $2 for adults, $1.50 for seniors and $1 for children.

### Places to Stay
**Camping** Two nice state parks are within an easy drive of Centralia and Chehalis. *Lewis & Clark State Park* (☎ 864-2643), contains a magnificent stand of old-growth forest. To reach the park, drive 10 miles south of Chehalis on I-5 and take Hwy 12 east for 2.5 miles. Turn south onto Jackson Hwy, which leads immediately to the park. *Rainbow Falls State Park* (☎ 291-3767) is on the Chehalis River, 17 miles west of Chehalis on Hwy 6. Facilities at both parks include running water, flush toilets, picnic

areas and hiking trails; campsites are $10 a night.

**B&Bs** Like many Northwest towns, Centralia and Chehalis have their share of grand old homes built by early logging barons and industrialists. The *Candalite Mansion B&B* (☎ 736-4749), 402 N Rock in Centralia, is a 1903 mansion with six guest rooms, some with private baths. Rooms are $50 to $65.

**Hotels** There are a number of inexpensive motels off I-5 exit No 82 in Centralia, which are handy to the factory outlet stores. The *Park Motel* (☎ 736-9333), 1011 Belmont, has single/double rooms for $37/48. At the *Huntley Inn* (☎ 736-2875, (800) 448-5544), 702 W Harrison Ave, there's an outdoor pool and free continental breakfast. Rooms are $48/49 and children under 12 are free. The *Ferryman's Inn* (☎ 330-2094), 1003 Eckerson Rd, offers a pool, hot tub, guest laundry and continental breakfast. Rates are $40/46. Pets are allowed at all of the above motels.

If you want to stay in Chehalis, head to the *Cascade Non-Smokers' Motel* (☎ 748-8608), 550 SW Parkland Drive, off I-5 exit No 76, where rooms are $42/48.

### Places to Eat
There's a concentration of fast-food and chain restaurants near the outlet stores at I-5 exit No 82. If you head into town to go antique shopping, stop off at the *Antique Mall Cafe* (☎ 736-1183), 201 S Pearl St, for soup, sandwiches and light entrees. In Chehalis, go to *Sweet Inspirations* (☎ 748-7102), 514 N Market Blvd, which serves lunchtime sandwiches and light meals at a refurbished soda fountain. At night, there are better-than-average steak, seafood and chicken dishes in the $12 range. Only slightly more expensive is *Mary McCranks* (☎ 748-3662), four miles south of Chehalis on Jackson Hwy. This old-fashioned dinner house has been serving up tasty, home-style cooking since the 1930s, so long, in fact, that its traditional menu of chicken and dumplings, steak and gravy, and the like,

has come back into style as regional cooking.

# Lower Columbia River

Near Portland, the Columbia River picks up the waters of the Willamette River and turns north to catch the waters of the Lewis and Cowlitz rivers. Downstream from Longview, the river cuts west again, becoming truly enormous. Steep hills and cliffs line the Columbia River, islands and shoals slow the current, and the river continually widens until, near Grays Bay, it occupies a channel over seven miles across.

Throughout most of the history of the Northwest, the Columbia River has been one of the region's principal avenues of entrance and exploration. Historic villages and military forts line its shores, and enormous ships still ply the river, headed from Portland or Longview to ports around the world. While many of the Washington towns along the Columbia River are industrial and don't offer much for the traveler, others retain the charm of small fishing ports. Highway 4 from Longview to the Long Beach Peninsula clings to the cliffs along the river and offers dramatic views of wooded islands and across to the green, deforested hills of Oregon.

## HISTORY

Chinook villages once stretched along the northern bank of the Columbia River. Because the lower Columbia was the crossroads for the transportation of goods north and south, as well as east to the Native American trade center at Celilo Falls, the Chinook became one of the most prominent mercantile tribes in the Northwest.

The first of the White explorers to penetrate from the Pacific Ocean across the bar and up the Columbia River was the American Robert Gray in 1792, closely followed by various British explorers. For the next decade, trade flourished between the Chinook and other tribes along the northern Pacific coast and the British and US traders. Chinook women took the lead in these trading ventures, which elevated them to dominant positions within the tribe.

When Lewis and Clark arrived at the mouth of the Columbia in 1805, they initially worked their way up the Washington side of the river in a dismal winter storm so unsparing that the captains recorded heavy rainfall and gales for 31 days in a row. The US party traded with the Chinooks before crossing over to Oregon.

Disease decimated the Chinook population as contact with Whites increased, leaving the mouth of the Columbia River open to settlement. Ilwaco was the first encampment along the river. Founded in the 1840s, it became the transportation link between the river steamers, ocean-going riggers and the new-born communities of Willapa Bay. Soon the Civil War brought fortifications to the mouth of the river. Fort Canby was established in 1852 and quickly upgraded to prevent Confederate gunboats from entering the river. Later in the century, Fort Columbia was established nearby to provide further protection to Columbia River ports.

As better shipping and rail links provided a market for Northwest products in the 1880s, industrial fishing and canning of salmon became the dominant trade of Ilwaco and Chinook. At its peak, 34 fish-canning operations lined the waterfront of the lower Columbia towns.

## VANCOUVER

Vancouver (population 55,450) and much of quickly urbanizing Clark County is immediately across the Columbia River from Portland, and it is best thought of as a suburb of Oregon's largest city. As anyone who has tried to get across the bridges during rush hour can testify, *a lot* of people commute between homes in southwest Washington and jobs or shopping in Portland. The reason for this border jumping is partly due to the two states' tax codes:

WASHINGTON

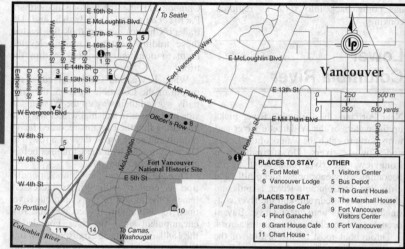

| PLACES TO STAY | OTHER |
|---|---|
| 2 Fort Motel | 1 Visitors Center |
| 6 Vancouver Lodge | 5 Bus Depot |
| | 7 The Grant House |
| PLACES TO EAT | 8 The Marshall House |
| 3 Paradise Cafe | 9 Fort Vancouver |
| 4 Pinot Ganache | Visitors Center |
| 8 Grant House Cafe | 10 Fort Vancouver |
| 11 Chart House · | |

Oregon doesn't have a sales tax and Washington has a marginal property tax. With a little ambition, the savvy local can do a little more driving and pay a little (or a lot) less tax.

Present-day Vancouver is a fairly drab place, despite the fact that it is the oldest settlement in the Pacific Northwest and is currently one of the fastest growing areas of Washington State. Vancouver's major appeal to travelers is reconstructed Fort Vancouver, the old Hudson's Bay Company trading post. The adjoining US Army's Officers' Row is also a lovely place for a stroll. However, most travelers will find dining, lodging and nightlife options more appealing in nearby Portland.

## Orientation

Vancouver is on the northern bank of the Columbia River, not far from the confluence of the Willamette River. Vancouver is 164 miles from Seattle on I-5, but only eight from downtown Portland across I-5's Interstate Bridge. A second freeway, I-205, leaves I-5 just northeast of Vancouver and links eastern Vancouver communities with east Portland, Portland International Airport (PDX), and with I-84 eastbound

before rejoining I-5 south of Portland. Highway 14 follows the north bank of the river, joining the two freeways and continuing east to Camas, Washougal and the Columbia River Gorge.

Downtown Vancouver is directly west of I-5. The principal streets through downtown are Main St and Broadway, which parallel the freeway.

## Information

For information about the Vancouver area, contact the Vancouver/Clark County Visitors & Convention Services (☎ 693-1313, (800) 377-7084), 404 E 15th St, Suite 11, Vancouver, WA 98663.

The headquarters for the Gifford-Pinchot National Forest (☎ 750-5000), which administers most of the forests in southwest Washington, is at 6926 E 4th Plain Blvd.

The post office (☎ 695-4462) is at 2700 Caples Ave. For clean clothes and that just-tanned look, go to Wash 'n Tan (☎ 693-2954) at the corner of Fourth Plain Blvd and Kauffman St, which features drop-off service, dry cleaning and tanning booths. The Southwest Washington Medical Center (☎ 256-2000) is at 3400 Main St.

## Fort Vancouver

Administered by the NPS, the reconstruction of Fort Vancouver (☎ 696-7655), the Hudson's Bay Company trading post, is an engaging stop for families or anyone curious about Northwest history. A living history program with instructive docents in period costume, an interpretive center and museum, and the buildings and stockaded grounds provide a vital insight into life on the Pacific frontier. Even if you're just looking for a place to park the car and stretch your legs or have a picnic, this is a good stop: between the old parade grounds, the Officers' Row and the fort area, this a major green space with lovely trees and manicured lawns.

## Fort Vancouver National Historic Site

In 1948, archaeologists began to excavate the site of old Fort Vancouver, and with contemporary drawings and material gleaned from the site, they reconstructed several portions, with other buildings slated for reconstruction. A 15-foot-high stockade with a three-story corner turret

**WASHINGTON**

### Fort Vancouver: On the Edge of the Frontier

Fort Vancouver was founded in 1824 as the British administrative headquarters and principal trading post in the Oregon Country, which then included all of present-day Oregon, Washington, Idaho and parts of Montana and British Columbia. The stockaded fort – which did not serve a military function – was also the center of civilized life in the region, and saw the Northwest's first farms, dairy operations, orchards, saw mills, foundries, hospital and commercial bakery.

The Hudson's Bay Company (HBC) employed its own trappers – who trapped beaver, mink, otter and wolf, among other animals – and traded with Native American hunters for furs. The principal items of trade included blankets, glass beads and fabric, all produced in Europe. The local smithy, bakery, farms and gardens soon created other items for trade and sale, mainly to other HBC forts and to the increasing number of Americans settling in Oregon.

Life at Fort Vancouver was conducted with a great deal of civility. Dr John McLoughlin, a Scots-Canadian physician, was the chief factor (or presiding officer), and he and his Iroquois wife lived in a large white clapboard home with all the niceties and elegance of a contemporary home in Boston or Britain. There were separate dining rooms for male guests and for their wives. Employees lived in barracks within the stockade, while the substantial numbers of hangers-on – farmers, day laborers and Indian traders – lived outside the barricade. Farms spread out for 20 miles along the flat Columbia flood plane and extended 10 miles inland. The population of the fort and environs, at its height, was about 1000 inhabitants.

When pioneers arrived at the end of the Oregon Trail in the early 1840s, most were penniless, hungry and facing a long dreary winter. For reasons that are at best conjectural, McLoughlin seemed attracted to the American pioneers, and he welcomed them to Fort Vancouver, where – despite strict HBC regulations to the contrary – he extended them credit, sold them seed grain and livestock, and helped them settle along the Willamette River. McLoughlin's generosity landed him in trouble with his superiors. When Britain ceded the Oregon Country to the USA in 1846, eventually moving the HBC headquarters to Fort Victoria in British Columbia, McLoughlin was relieved of his duties, and he chose to stay in US territory and moved to Oregon City.

Fort Vancouver remained an HBC property until 1860, although the heyday of the fur trade was long over. Much of the fort burned down in 1863. Meanwhile, the US Army established an adjacent garrison called Vancouver Barracks, and in time this served as the military headquarters for the army's Department of the Columbia. The clapboard barracks along the current parade grounds and the beautiful homes along Officers' Row date largely from the 1870s and 80s, though the Vancouver Barracks remained in military operation through both world wars. Vancouver Barracks was decommissioned in 1947. ■

Sandhill cranes stop north of Vancouver on their migratory route.

encloses an area of roughly 700 by 300 feet. Inside the stockade are reconstructions of the Chief Factor's residence, bakery, foundry, trade shop, kitchen and other buildings. Children will enjoy climbing up into the bastion for views of the fort, Columbia River and Mt Hood.

The reconstructed fort is open daily from 9 am to 5 pm Memorial Day to Labor Day, and from 9 am to 4 pm the rest of the year. Tours leave on the hour and group tours can be booked on the half hour. Call 696-7655 to schedule. Cultural demonstrations by interpreters in period dress are presented daily in the fort's kitchen, and Thursday to Monday also in the forge. Other demonstrations are available on summer weekends. Entrance fees for adults/families are $2/4, and children under 17 are free. The visitors center, on E Reserve St, is free and features a small museum, gift shop and interpretive information, including a 15-minute film.

**Officers' Row** On the north side of E Evergreen Blvd and the old parade grounds is Officers' Row, a park-like boulevard of historic and glamorous officers' homes built between 1850 and 1906 by the US Army. These handsome buildings are owned by the city of Vancouver and are rented out as offices and apartments. Two of the buildings are open to the public. **The Grant House** (☎ 694-5252), 1101 Officers' Row, is the oldest – built in 1850 from

logs and later covered with clapboard – and it now houses a cafe and the Grant House Folk Art Center, a small exhibition space and gallery. **The Marshall House**, built in 1886 and home in the 1930s to General George Marshall, is a grand, Queen Anne-style mansion. Tours are available; call 693-3103 for schedules.

### Places to Stay

Although Vancouver is a fairly large city – it's Washington's fourth-largest metropolitan area – most people visit it as a side trip from Portland. If you want to stay north of the Columbia River, Vancouver offers a couple of inexpensive lodging options, though both back up to the freeway. The *Fort Motel* (☎ 694-3327), 500 E 13th St, is in downtown Vancouver and is handy to tours at its namesake Fort Vancouver. The *Vancouver Lodge* (☎ 693-3668), 601 Broadway, is also downtown. Both offer kitchenettes and non-smoking rooms and take pets; singles/doubles start at $37/44.

### Places to Eat

Restaurants in Vancouver offer a bit more selection. *Paradise Cafe* (☎ 696-1612), 1304 Main St, is an espresso bar with a good selection of pastries, salads and light entrees for lunch. Eat in the splendor of old Officers' Row at the *Grant House Cafe* (☎ 699-1213), 1101 Officers' Row. For weekday lunches, salads and sandwiches are offered, while on Thursday to Sunday night the restaurant is open for dinner with a menu offering steak, lamb and seafood à la Northwest ($12 to $15). *Pinot Ganache* (☎ 695-7786), 1004 Washington St, offers a wide variety of dishes in a busy bistro atmosphere. One of Vancouver's most popular places to eat is right on the banks of the Columbia River. Although the food at the *Chart House* (☎ 693-9211), 101 E Columbia Way, doesn't involve any surprises – chicken, pasta and steak – on a warm evening this is a great place to enjoy a drink or dinner on the waterside deck and watch the sunset.

### Things to Buy
Most of the woolen products from the renowned Pendleton Woolen Mill are made not in Pendleton but in Washougal, 16 miles east of Vancouver on Hwy 14. Free tours of the mill (☎ 835-2131), 2 17th St in Washougal, are offered Monday to Friday at 9, 10 and 11 am, and at 1:30 pm. The outlet store here sells fabric, clothing and blankets at substantial discounts.

### Getting There & Away
Vancouver's public transport system is called C-Tran (☎ 695-0123), and it offers service throughout Clark County. Buses No 5, 14 and 134 run down I-5 to Portland. The downtown bus mall is along 7th St between Broadway and Washington St.

## LONGVIEW & KELSO
After driving through the mossy woods or from the west along the Columbia River, it's a little surprising to come upon Longview (population 32,650) and its twin, Kelso (population 11,850). These thoroughly industrial small towns are at the westward turn of the Columbia, where it meets the Cowlitz River.

The confluence of these rivers was an important site in the early history of the Northwest, when most transportation was by water. The Cowlitz River was navigable by boat up to Cowlitz Landing near Toledo; from there Hudson's Bay Company trappers continued overland to the lower Puget Sound. Later, after Kelso developed as a lumber mill center, the Cowlitz River served as the avenue for log flotillas.

Longview was founded as a planned community – one of the first in the American West – for employees of the Long-Bell Lumber Company, which built a huge mill here in 1924. The town was laid out in a series of concentric rings, through which meanders a man-made lake and park. Take a walk along Broadway St or through Sacajawea Park to get a sense of the grand aspirations of Longview's civic planners.

Longview is where the majority of the logs cut from the southwest Washington forests go to be milled and shipped overseas. Despite attempts to ban the shipping of raw logs from Northwest forests (in order to keep mill jobs stateside), nearly two million tons of logs leave the port of Longview each year, bound mostly for Japan. Cross Longview's high arching bridge over the Columbia River and look down to see acres and acres of unmilled logs awaiting export.

If you're driving I-5, you'll note that near Castle Rock there are huge piles of white soil overgrown with gorse along the Cowlitz River. These immense dikes are volcanic dust from Mt St Helens, which were dredged from the Toutle and Cowlitz rivers shortly after the volcano erupted in 1980.

### Orientation & Information
Interstate 5 cuts through the eastern edge of Kelso, which is 47 miles north of Portland and 145 miles south of Seattle. Highway 4 cuts west from Kelso and Longview, heading to the Long Beach Peninsula, 76 miles distant. Highway 433 cuts across the Columbia here to meet up with Oregon's Hwy 30, which links Portland and Astoria.

For further information on the area, contact the Longview Area Chamber of Commerce (☎ 423-8400), 1563 Olympia Way, Longview, WA 98632. The Kelso post office (☎ 425-0770) is at 304 Academy St; the Longview post office (☎ 423-1010) is at 1603 Larch St.

## Places to Stay

There are a number of motels and fast-food restaurants in Kelso, just off I-5 exit No 39. Convenient to the freeway is the new *Comfort Inn* (☎ 425-4600), 440 Three Rivers Drive, with indoor pool, spa and free continental breakfast. Rooms are $51/56 for a single/double. The *Best Western Aladdin Motor Inn* (☎ (800) 764-7378), 310 Long Ave, has kitchen units, a pool and on-premises restaurant and lounge; rates are $50/54. Save some money by driving into downtown Longview to the *Town House Motel* (☎ 423-7200), 744 Washington Way, where pets are welcome; rates are $34/36. The *Monticello Hotel* (☎ 425-9900), 1405 17th Ave, was built in 1923 as Longview's showcase hotel. Today, the handsome hotel has been converted into offices, but the motel wing still takes guests, where rooms – some with fireplaces – go for $34/40.

## Places to Eat

The inevitable and easily spotted fast-food emporiums are near the freeway. For coffee, soup and sandwiches, stop by the *Bookshop Cafe* (☎ 425-8707), 1203 14th Ave. The dining room at the Monticello Hotel serves three meals a day in its slightly faded dining room; seafood and steak are the main draw. For the area's best meal head to *Henri's* (☎ 425-7970), 4545 Ocean Beach Hwy, on Hwy 4 toward Cathlamet. The steak, seafood and lamb dishes ($12 to $16) are meant to be continental, but in this blue-collar town, size of portion matters more than refinement.

## CATHLAMET

The old logging and fishing town of Cathlamet (population 508) occupies a position above the Columbia River and Puget Island, a low-lying agricultural island dedicated to dairy farms. The little-changed downtown area is a pleasant stop for travelers looking for a break from the persistent curves of Hwy 4. The harbor is usually filled with pleasure boats, whose crews tie up here to enjoy the tranquility and historic atmosphere.

Cathlamet was originally the site of a Chinook village; the first White settler arrived in 1846. Cathlamet prospered early as a salmon-packing center and boomed in the 1910s as a logging and mill town. Not much has changed the handsome, red-brick center of town since these heydays.

A bridge leads from Cathlamet to Puget Island, the largest island in the Columbia River Gorge. This flat, rural island is popular with cyclists. Follow Hwy 409 across the island and take a car ferry – the last on the lower Columbia – to Oregon (see Getting There & Away).

Cathlamet is 26 miles west of Longview and Kelso on Hwy 4; from Cathlamet, it's 40 miles to Long Beach.

## Places to Stay & Eat

If you're looking for a quiet retreat, consider the *Country Keeper B&B* (☎ 795-3030), 61 Main St, in a 1907 mansion that once served as the county library. The four guest rooms (two with private baths) are filled with antiques; rooms begin at $75. Some of the cheapest rooms hereabout are at *Nassa Point Motel* (☎ 795-3941), three miles east of Cathlamet on Hwy 4. With the Columbia River practically in the front yard, this is a popular stop for anglers, windsurfers and boaters. Rooms start at $25 a night.

There are several homey cafes in Cathlamet, and the best of the lot is *Birnie's Retreat* (☎ 795-3432), 88 Main St. It's open for three meals a day, and at night it offers a selection of seafood and Cajun dishes.

## Getting There & Away

Ferries (☎ 849-4277) leave from Puget Island on the hour, and from near Westport, OR at 15 minutes after the hour. The fare is $2 for a car and driver, 50c per additional passenger, and $1 per cyclist or foot passenger. The passage takes 15 minutes.

## CHINOOK

The small town of Chinook is named for the Native American tribe whose villages once lined these shores, but the community might well have been named for the

Chinook salmon. By the 1880s, Chinook was one of the region's major fish-canning centers, and this affluence is easily seen in the handsome turn-of-the-century fishermen's homes and the false-fronted downtown.

Chinook is still an active fishing port, but most travelers will remember Chinook for its HI/AYH hostel, one of the few along the northwest Pacific coast. Chinook is five miles west of the base of the Astoria Bridge on Hwy 101 and nine miles southeast of Long Beach.

### Fort Columbia State Park
Fort Columbia State Park (☎ 642-3078), on a rocky bluff above the Columbia River one mile south of Chinook, is a well-preserved military fort built between 1898 and 1905 during the Spanish-American War. Although the fort maintained its defensive purpose through WW II, it was demilitarized shortly thereafter.

The fort is largely unchanged from the glory days of 1900, with the barracks now serving as an interpretive center and museum. Other buildings open to the public include Columbia House, the commanding officer's residence. The old hospital is now operated as a hostel. Trails lead to cement artillery fortifications and batteries, which once housed guns that protected shipping channels on the Columbia River.

Park hours are from 8 am to dusk daily May 15 to October 1; it is closed Monday and Tuesday the rest of the year. The interpretive center is open from 10 am to 5 pm Wednesday to Sunday, May through October; admission is free.

### Places to Stay & Eat
The *Fort Columbia Hostel* (☎ 777-8755) at Fort Columbia State Park, is one mile south of Chinook on Hwy 101. The hostel offers a fully equipped kitchen, an all-you-can-eat pancake breakfast for 50c, and a combination of family and dorm-style rooms in the fort's old hospital. Facilities include a game room, lounge area and fireplace. There are hiking trails nearby. Rates are $8.50 for HI/AYH members, $11.50 for non-members.

Chinook's most noted restaurant, and in fact a favorite throughout the Northwest, is *The Sanctuary* (☎ 777-8380), Hwy 101 at Hazel St. In an old Methodist church built in 1906, the Sanctuary prepares local seafood, steak and pasta ($10 to $17) in an eclectic multi-ethnic manner that's always interesting and often excellent. Pizza is available in the Sanctuary's Garden Annex.

## ILWACO
The major fishing port on Washington's southern coast, Ilwaco (population 890) still bustles with charter and commercial fishing. The early growth of the salmon-canning industry here was aided by the development of salmon traps, a method of catching the fish that was made illegal in the 1930s.

Unlike the flat Long Beach Peninsula that stretches to the north from here, Ilwaco is hemmed in by rocky hills. West of town, on a rugged promontory above the mouth of the Columbia River, are the remains of Fort Canby, a Civil War-era military fort that was designed to protect Columbia River shipping from Confederate interference. After WW II, part of the fort's land passed into the hands of the state, which dedicated it to the city as a park.

### Fort Canby State Park
Although little remains of the original fort, this state park (☎ 642-3078) is of considerable interest for its Lewis & Clark Interpretive Center, nice beach area and hiking trails to dramatic lighthouses.

Although established in 1852, Fort Canby wasn't heavily fortified until the 1860s, during the Civil War. The fort was upgraded dramatically during WW II, when it and Fort Stephens on the Oregon side of the Columbia River stood as the principal defenders of the river from enemy infiltration. The mouth of the Columbia River was webbed with mines during the war. Although no shots were fired from Fort Canby, a Japanese submarine did manage to penetrate close enough to the Oregon side to fire on Fort Stephens in 1942.

The rugged coastline of Fort Canby State Park (DS)

Lewis and Clark camped near here in 1805 and climbed up onto the bluff for their first real glimpse of the Pacific Ocean. The **Lewis & Clark Interpretive Center** offers a timeline of their entire journey that discusses the reasons for the expedition, followed by a retelling of their adventure with diary entries, mementos and illustrations. A multimedia theater shows short films about the journey. The center also documents the history of navigation on the Columbia, especially focusing on the dangerous Columbia bar, seen from the building's expanse of windows.

From the interpretive center, a hiking trail leads 1.8 miles to **Cape Disappointment Lighthouse**. On a steep bluff above the Columbia, the lighthouse was built in 1856, the first lighthouse in the Northwest. A second lighthouse, **North Head Lighthouse**, is off the park's main access road and is accessed by a short hiking trail from the parking area. Neither lighthouse is open for tours.

**Waikiki Beach** is immediately south of the camping area, or it can be reached by turning west on Jetty Rd. Continue on this road until you reach the end of the riprap jetty, a half-mile-long rock spit that extends out into the Pacific.

Fort Canby State Park is open daily, with no admission charged for day-use areas. The Lewis & Clark Interpretive Center is open from 10 am to 5 pm daily, and donations are appreciated. See Places to Stay & Eat for camping information. To reach Fort Canby, follow Hwy 101 through Ilwaco and turn onto Robert Gray Drive at the flashing light. The interpretive center is 3.5 miles south of the intersection.

### Ilwaco Heritage Museum
Ilwaco's maritime past is on display in this good regional museum (☎ 642-3446), 115 SE Lake St. There are displays on the local Chinook, and other exhibits explain the history of the local cranberry and logging industry. A toy-sized version of the old Clamshell Railway that ran from Ilwaco to Nahcotta in the late 1880s still runs on a 50-foot scale model of the Long Beach Peninsula in the line's old former depot,

also a part of the museum. The museum is open from 9 am to 5 pm Monday through Saturday, and 10 am to 4 pm on Sunday, Memorial Day through Labor Day. The rest of the year it's open from 10 am to 4 pm Monday to Saturday, and 10 am to 2 pm on Sunday. Admission is $1.25 for adults, $1 for seniors and 50c for children.

### Charter Fishing
Ilwaco offers plenty of charter-fishing options, including salmon (during season), sturgeon, tuna and bottom fish. Contact one of the following for prices and packages, or contact the Long Beach Peninsula Chamber of Commerce (☎ 642-3145, (800) 642-2400) for a full listing of outfitters. Sea Breeze Charters (☎ 642-2300), Beacon Charters (☎ 642-2138) and Ilwaco Charter Service (☎ 642-3232) are all along the harbor, off Howerton Ave.

### Places to Stay & Eat
*Beacon Charters & RV Park* (☎ 642-2138), along the waterfront, also offers RV sites with showers and some full hook-ups for $13 to $15. *Fort Canby State Park* (☎ 642-3078) offers over 250 campsites, with piped water, flush toilets and access to beach recreation. Sites are $10 and $14.

The *Inn at Ilwaco* (☎ 642-8686), 122 Williams St NE, on a wooded rise above town, was once the Ilwaco Presbyterian Church but is now a handsome inn with nine guest rooms in the old parsonage and vestry. The church proper is a community arts center. The rooms range from $55 to $80.

*Kola House B&B* (☎ 642-2819), 211 Pearl Ave, has five rooms, one with a fireplace and sauna. There's also a hot tub in the basement. Book early for the small cabin. Rooms cost $65 to $75.

*Heidi's Inn* (☎ 642-2387), 126 Spruce St, is a modest but comfortable motel with kitchen units and a guest laundry; pets are OK. Single rooms start at $42 and apartment-like kitchenettes at $45, with discounts offered for midweek or week-long stays. The *Tidewind Cafe* (☎ 642-2111) overlooks the harbor off Howerton St, and

offers home cooking and breakfast anytime.

# Long Beach Peninsula & Willapa Bay

The Long Beach Peninsula, the thin sand spit just north of the mouth of the Columbia River, claims to have the world's longest beach. And with 28 unbroken miles of it, the boast has to be taken seriously. However, the beautiful beach is disappointingly adjoined with 28 miles of rather lackluster development, and the beach itself is overrun with pickup trucks (as Washington State beaches are considered highways). Purists might prefer the Willapa Bay side of the peninsula, with its old towns, oyster beds and wildlife viewing.

The beach resorts here have a long pedigree, dating from the 1880s, when Portland families journeyed down the Columbia River by steamboat to summer at the coast. A rail line, referred to as the Clamshell Railway, linked the oyster beds at Nahcotta to boats at Ilwaco in 1888. While the oyster beds on the bay side of the Long Beach Peninsula were the main economic force, the railroad also carried summer holiday-makers to the sandy beaches on the Pacific side of the spit. Soon the beach towns of Seaview and Long Beach sprang up, and across the bay beach resorts at Tokeland and North Cove were established.

Willapa Bay is known to oyster-lovers around the country for the excellent bivalves that grow in this shallow inlet, which is fed by six rivers. The first industry founded here was oyster production, and while logging and dairy farms have each had their day, oyster farming remains the area's major industry.

### GETTING AROUND
Pacific Transit System (☎ (206) 642-9418, (360) 875-9418) is the local bus company,

WASHINGTON

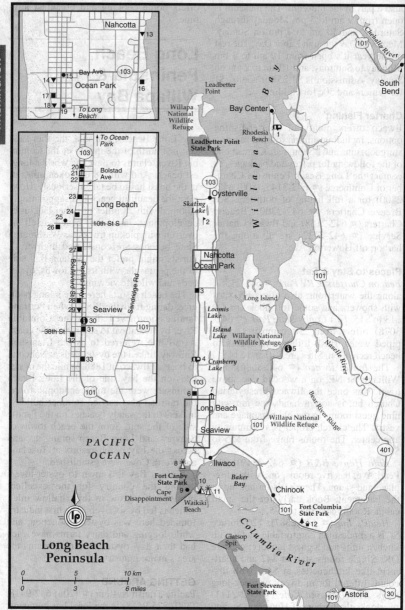

**Long Beach Peninsula**

Nahcotta

13

Bay Ave
103
Ocean Park
14 15
16
17
18 19
To Long Beach

To Ocean Park
103
20
21 Bolstad Ave
22
23
Long Beach
24
25 10th St S
26
27
Pacific Hwy
28
29 Seaview
Sandridge Rd
30
38th St
31
32
101
33
101

Chehalis River
101
South Bend

Willapa Bay

Leadbetter Point
Willapa National Wildlife Refuge
Bay Center
Rhodesia Beach
1
Leadbetter Point State Park
103
Oysterville
Skating Lake
2
101
Nahcotta
Ocean Park
3
Long Island
Loomis Lake
Island Lake
Willapa National Wildlife Refuge
5
Nuselle River
4 Cranberry Lake
103
7
6
Long Beach
101
Willapa National Wildlife Refuge
Bear River Ridge
Seaview
4
401

PACIFIC OCEAN

8
Ilwaco
Fort Canby State Park
10
Baker Bay
9
Cape Disappointment
11
Waikiki Beach
Chinook
Fort Columbia State Park
12
101

Columbia River

Clatsop Spit

Fort Stevens State Park
101
Astoria
30

0        5        10 km
0        3        6 miles

and it runs buses throughout Pacific County, from Westport to towns along the Long Beach Peninsula. Pacific buses also run as far south as Astoria, OR.

For a cab on the Long Beach Peninsula, call Beach Cab (☎ 642-3905).

## LONG BEACH & SEAVIEW

Long Beach and Seaview (combined population 1290) comprise the major population center on the peninsula. Both began as beach resorts in the late 1880s. A few old inns from this era have been beautifully restored, but most visitors will probably find that much of the local charm has been overrun by aggressive commercialization. Highway 103 stretches out to form the main – and nearly the only – street for both Long Beach and Seaview, and it's lined with the sorts of T-shirt shops, artsy boutiques, fast-food mills and bumper car arenas that somehow always find their way to beach towns. However, you can't argue with the expanse of beach that year after year brings in multitudes of sunbathers and vacationers during the summer high season.

### Orientation

The Long Beach Peninsula has two main arteries. On the west side of the peninsula is Hwy 103 (also known as Pacific Hwy), which runs from Seaview to Leadbetter Point State Park. On the east, or bay, side,

an alternative route called Sandridge Rd runs from just east of Seaview to Oysterville. Both of these roads are heavily used and slow going, especially during the high season. Many local access roads cross the peninsula, linking these arterials. From Portland to Long Beach is 126 miles; from Seattle, it's 146 miles.

### Information

The Long Beach Peninsula Visitors Bureau (☎ 642-2400, (800) 451-2542) can be reached at PO Box 562, Long Beach, WA 98631. This office can also help you get reservations for area motels and lodgings. There's a visitors center at the corner of Hwy 101 and Pacific Hwy (or Hwy 103) in Seaview.

The local *Chinook Observer* (☎ 642-8181) puts out an excellent annual guide to services, activities and business on the peninsula. The *Visitor's Guide* is available free at visitors centers, or get one by mail by sending $2 to the *Chinook Observer*, PO Box 427, Long Beach, WA 98631.

The peninsula's only hospital is Ocean Beach Hospital (☎ 642-3181) at 1st and Fir Sts in Ilwaco.

### Beaches

Primary beach-access sites in Long Beach are west off 10th St and Bolstad Ave. An all-abilities quarter-mile-long boardwalk links the two access points. In Seaview, the

| PLACES TO STAY | | | | |
|---|---|---|---|---|
| 1 | Bay Center KOA | 28 | Shelburne Inn | |
| 3 | Klipson Beach Cottages | 31 | Poulsbo B&B | |
| 4 | Anderson's RV Park | 32 | Sou'Wester Lodge | |
| 6 | The Breakers | 33 | Gumm's B&B | |
| 10 | Fort Canby Campground | | | |
| 12 | Fort Columbia Hostel | **PLACES TO EAT** | | |
| 16 | Moby Dick Hotel | 13 | The Ark | |
| 17 | Sunset View Resort | 14 | BJ Squidley's | |
| 20 | Arcadia Court | 18 | Bay St Cafe | |
| 22 | Our Place at the Beach | 26 | Lightship Restaurant | |
| 23 | Shaman Motel | 28 | Shoalwater Restaurant | |
| 24 | Boardwalk Cottages | 29 | 42nd Street Cafe | |
| 26 | Nendel's Inn | | | |
| 27 | Scandinavian Gardens Inn B&B | **OTHER** | | |
| | | 2 | Surfside Golf Course | |

| | |
|---|---|
| 5 | Willapa National Wildlife Refuge Headquarters |
| 7 | Cranberry Museum & Gift Shop |
| 8 | North Head Lighthouse |
| 9 | Lewis & Clark Interpretive Center |
| 11 | Cape Disappointment Lighthouse |
| 15 | Jack's Country Market |
| 19 | P&K Crab & Seafood Market |
| 21 | World Kite Museum & Hall of Fame |
| 25 | Skippers Horse Rental |
| 30 | Visitors Center |

primary public access point is off 38th St. The beach in this area is now closed to vehicles from April 15 to Labor Day weekend. The beach north of Bolstad Ave to Ocean Park is open to vehicles year round; additionally, during razor clam seasons, vehicles are permitted on all beaches.

**Note** Remember that surf-swimming here is dangerous and is prohibited along the beach due to strong waves and quickly changing tides.

### World Kite Museum & Hall of Fame
Long Beach is noted worldwide for its kite festival, so it was just a matter of time before someone opened a kite museum here (☎ 642-4020), 104 Pacific Hwy N. In case you think that a museum devoted to the history and artistry of kites is a bore, think again. Kites have been used for scientific research, aerial photography, mail delivery and reconnaissance – as well as for amusement – for centuries. The whole story's here, along with the largest, smallest and wackiest kites.

The museum is open daily from 11 am to 5 pm June to August; September and October it's closed Tuesday to Thursday. The rest of the year, it's open from 11 am to 4 pm, weekends only. Admission is $1 for adults, 50c for children and $3 for families.

### Cranberry Museum
The Long Beach Peninsula is a major producer of cranberries. Many of the roads that cross the peninsula pass by cranberry bogs, which are colorful in spring when the bushes are in flower and again in fall as the fields are flooded and the bright red berries float to the surface. Tour cranberry bogs and a historic cranberry research center at this informal museum and gift shop, along Pioneer Rd north of Long Beach. The museum is open from 10 am to 3 pm Friday, Saturday and Sunday. Admission is free.

### Activities
Sports rental outlets are scattered around the various communities on the peninsula. Willapa Bay Excursions (☎ 665-4449), 270th St and Sandridge Rd in Nahcotta, rents kayaks and bikes and also offers tours of the peninsula. A number of outfitters offer **horseback riding** along the beach. Skippers Horse Rental (☎ 642-3676), along 10th St S, in Long Beach, is open year round.

### International Kite Festival
Thousands of people descend on Long Beach each year for the Washington State International Kite Festival, which is billed as the largest kite festival in the western hemisphere. The festival is held during the third week of August and includes participants from all over the world. Events include stunt-kite flying and competitions between individuals and teams. Each year, festival-goers seek to gain new world records, perhaps involving the greatest number of kites in flight at one time, the largest kite flown, the longest flight time for a kite and so on.

Long Beach is busy during the festival – approximately 150,000 people visit during the week-long event – so make plans early to attend.

### Places to Stay
Long Beach and Seaview offer quite a mix of old-fashioned inns, resort condos and cheesy motels. The places listed below are all good choices; for more options, contact the chamber of commerce (☎ 642-2400, (800) 451-2542), which offers a room-reservation service.

**Camping** *Anderson's RV Park* (☎ (800) 645-6795), 3.5 miles north of Long Beach on Hwy 103, offers 60 hook-ups with hot showers. The *Sou'Wester* (☎ 642-2542), also offers sites for both tenters and RVs, with hot showers and laundry, from $14.50 to $20. For more information, see Sou'Wester Lodge below.

**B&Bs** *Poulsbo B&B* (☎ 642-4393), 3911 N Place, was built in 1887 by a German sea captain. The house is surrounded by a nice garden and offers five guest rooms with shared facilities. Rooms start at $65 a night. *Gumms B&B* (☎ 642-8887), Hwy 101 at 33rd St, offers four guest rooms and a hot tub; rooms are $65 to $75. The *Scandinavian Gardens Inn B&B* (☎ 642-8763), 1610 California St S, offers four guest rooms and a suite, each with private bath. Facilities include a sauna and spa. Rooms range from $65 to $110 and a Scandinavian-style breakfast is served.

For more information on B&Bs, contact the B&B Association of the Long Beach Peninsula (☎ 642-8484), PO Box 1012, Long Beach, WA 98631.

**Hotels** Just a quick walk from the beach, *Arcadia Court* (☎ 642-2613), N 4th at Boulevard St, offers eight well-kept cabins, most with kitchen facilities; pets are OK. Prices start at $49 a night. At *Boardwalk Cottages* (☎ 642-2305), 800 S Boulevard St, all units have kitchens; one/two-bedroom cottages are $65/70.

One of the better deals in motels in Long Beach is *Our Place at the Beach* (☎ 642-2777), 101 N Boulevard St, a small older motel with some kitchen units, a fitness center, hot tubs and a sauna. They have senior and AAA discounts, and pets are allowed. Single/double rooms are $50/55. Slightly newer and spiffier is the *Shaman Motel* (☎ 642-3714, (800)753-3750), 115 3rd St SW, which offers large rooms in a motel complex. Some units offer ocean views and fireplaces; there's a swimming pool and pets are OK. Rates are $74/79.

Long Beach's only real beachfront lodging is *Nendel's Inn* (☎ 642-2311, (800) 547-0106), 409 10th St SW, which abuts the boardwalk and the beach. Facilities include a good restaurant, lounge and hot tub. During the high season, rooms begin at $80, but drop to about half during winter. *The Breakers* (☎ 642-4414, (800) 288-8890) is a condominium resort one mile north of Long Beach on Hwy 103. The Breakers offers suite-style rooms with fireplaces, kitchens and balconies, with an indoor pool and spa on the premises. Standard units are $57, rooms with kitchenettes

are $77. You'll find cheap off-season rates and midweek discounts here too.

*Sou'Wester Lodge* (☎ 642-2542) on 38th St (or Beach Access Rd) is a historic three-story lodge built in 1892 by an Oregon senator. The Sou'Wester is heavy on irreverence: the owners insist that the establishment is a B&(MYOD)B, or 'bed and make your own damn breakfast'. Unlike the upscale Shelburne Inn, which it otherwise resembles, the Sou'Wester has a self-amused air of funkiness, eclecticism and nonchalance. In the original lodge, there are both simple bedroom units that share kitchen, bathroom and living area ($51 to $54) and apartment-style units ($61 to $99). There are also a number of cabins ($50 to $70) and TCH units, or Trailer Classics Hodgepodge – a collection of 1950s Spartan house trailers, each one renovated and individually decorated a la Sou'Wester ($31 to $81).

If the Sou'Wester isn't quite your style, then head to the *Shelburne Inn* (☎ 642-2442), 4415 Pacific Hwy, a Historic-Register building and one of the original lodgings on the Long Beach Peninsula. Built in 1896 as a stage coach inn, this hotel is also home to one of the top restaurants in the Northwest. The entire building is a jewel of late 19th-century artisanship that has been carefully preserved and refurbished with period fixtures. Each of the 15 guest rooms has a private bath and is decorated with antiques. Rooms vary greatly in size, and range from $95 to $155 a night, including breakfast.

### Places to Eat
There are any number of fast-food restaurants, chowder houses and assorted eateries along the Hwy 103 stretch. The area has several restaurants of note, however. The *42nd Street Cafe* (☎ 642-2323), 42nd St and Pacific Hwy, serves old-fashioned home-style food, like pot roast and pan-fried chicken, as well as hearty preparations of local seafood and oysters. Most dishes range from $10 to $12.

The *Lightship Restaurant* (☎ 642-3252) offers great views of the beach (from the top floor of Nendel's Inn), with fresh local seafood, steak, prime rib and homemade desserts.

Most people consider the *Shoalwater Restaurant* (☎ 642-4142), 4415 Pacific Hwy at the Shelburne Inn, one of the show-places of Northwest cuisine. The dining room, dominated by arched stained-glass windows and old wainscot panels, is certainly one of the most charming you'll find. Local seafood, fish, poultry and lamb are served with a consistently inventive flair; dishes are in the $20 range. Lunches are available only in the pub, and breakfasts are for guests only.

## OCEAN PARK

Ocean Park began its existence as a Methodist church camp in the 1880s. Camp meetings gave way to a Christian resort community in the 1890s (when permanent homes were first built here), and restrictive covenants limited sales of alcohol and gambling. Even though times have changed and Ocean Park seeks to attract as many weekenders as possible, the sale of alcohol is still limited to the parts of town south of Bay Avenue.

Today, Ocean Park is a quieter, less-developed version of the resort towns to the south. It feels much more like a town where people live rather than just visit. However, in terms of lodging, restaurants and activities, there is decidedly less choice – a trade-off that may be attractive if you want to avoid the manic congestion of Long Beach.

### Orientation & Information

Ocean Park is 10 miles north of Long Beach along Hwy 103. From Ocean Park it's only one mile across to Nahcotta, on the Willapa Bay side of the peninsula. Contact the Ocean Park Chamber of Commerce (☎ 665-4448, (800) 451-2542) at PO Box 403, Ocean Park, WA 98640.

### Activities

Surfside Golf Course (☎ 665-4148), 31508 J Place, is a challenging nine-hole course north of Ocean Park. You can rent bikes at

Surfside Mini Mart (☎ 665-6880), north of Ocean Park on I St.

### Places to Stay & Eat

*Klipson Beach Cottages* (☎ 665-4888), 22617 Pacific Hwy, south of Ocean Park, are attractive cabins with decks, kitchens, barbecues and fireplaces or wood stoves. Weekday/weekend rates for single rooms start at $70/80. *Sunset View Resort* (☎ 665-4494, (800) 272-9199), 256th St and Park Ave, is a handsome motel resort with ocean views, hot tubs and easy beach access, tucked in the dunes just south of Ocean Park. Rooms start at $50.

Most of the food in Ocean Park is perfunctory. You'll find a good deli – and just about everything else – at *Jack's Country Market*, at Hwy 103 and Bay Ave. Stop by *P&K Crab & Seafood Market* (☎ 665-6800), Hwy 103 and 254th St, for fresh crab, clams and other seasonal seafood. Most restaurants are associated with taverns, and offer burgers, pizza and such. Probably the best and most lively of these is *B J Squidleys* (☎ 665-5261), Hwy 103 and 259th St. For something a little more refined, go to *Bay St Cafe* (☎ 665-4224), at the corner of Ocean and Park Sts, which offers steak and seafood specials.

## OYSTERVILLE & NAHCOTTA

The charm of these old settlements – the only settlements on the bay side of the Long Beach Peninsula – derives not just from their history but also from the absence of the carnival atmosphere of the beachfront towns. Here, wildlife viewing, oyster harvesting and gracious dining occupies the time of residents and visitors alike. Oysterville stands largely unchanged since its heyday in the 1880s, when the oyster boom was at its peak. The entire town was placed on the National Register of Historic Places in 1976.

Just off Hwy 103, Oysterville is filled with well-preserved Victorian homes. The oldest, built in 1863, is the **Red Cottage**, near Clay St and Territory Rd. The **Big Red House**, the original home of Oysterville co-founder R H Espy, was built in

1871, and it stands at Division St and Territory Rd. If you walk down Clay St toward the bay and look back, you can see the house facades that were once the townfront: since at first there was no overland transport, the town was originally oriented toward the bay. Other historic buildings include a one-room schoolhouse and the 1892 **Oysterville Church**, which is open daily during the summer and on weekends the rest of the year; pick up a copy of the historic walking tour brochure here. A family-owned oyster plant still operates at the docks on Pacific St; if you have access to a kitchen or even a campfire, pick up some oysters for later.

### Leadbetter Point State Park

This 807-acre park is a kind of buffer between the straggling developments of Long Beach Peninsula and a section of the Willapa National Wildlife Refuge, which is here a narrowing band of dunes increasingly breached by Pacific waves. The park offers a couple of informal hiking trails through forest and marshes, with good bird-watching. However, most people meander down to the shores of Willapa Bay. At low tide, mile after mile of reed-covered shoals are exposed, riven with narrow channels.

Stroll north along the lowering dunes and keep an eye open for unusual birds. This is one of the best places to watch for shorebirds in the Northwest. Snowy plovers, Lapland longspurs, sooty shearwaters and brown pelicans are just some of the varieties that an alert bird-watcher can spot here.

### Jazz & Oysters

Jazz & Oysters is one of Oysterville's big summer events, held in mid-August. Besides live jazz on the grounds of the

---

### The Oysters of Willapa Bay

In 1854, entrepreneurs R H Espy and I A Clark journeyed to the mouth of the Columbia River, looking for a place to begin an oyster business. They asked Chinook Chief Nahcati for advice, and he directed them north to what was then called Shoalwater Bay, where for centuries the Chinook had harvested wild oysters. As they canoed to the spot where they were to rendezvous with Chief Nahcati, the two men got lost in a sudden fog. The chief, who had seen them approaching, began beating a hollow log to guide them, and the entrepreneurs arrived safely. Finding that the oysters were indeed abundant, they began a settlement near the Chinook camp.

At that time, native oysters filled the bay. The Chinook harvested oysters seasonally and dried the flesh of the bivalves for use throughout the year. Dried oysters were so prevalent and popular with coastal tribes that they functioned in trade as a form of currency. The oyster business started by Espy and Clark experienced immediate success: wealthy prospectors in San Francisco would pay over $40 a plate for fresh oysters. Ice-filled freighters began calling at Oysterville and later Nahcotta (which had a deeper port), transporting the oysters to the booming Gold Rush center. Within two years, Oysterville grew to 500 inhabitants and became the seat of Pacific County. By 1888 the 'Clamshell Line', a branch of the Ilwaco Railway & Navigation Company, reached Nahcotta and linked these oyster-producing towns to the Columbia River navigation system.

However, the native oysters weren't able to sustain such over-harvesting, and the oyster boom went bust. By 1893, Oysterville's future was so blighted that partisans of South Bend, across Willapa Bay, rowed over and stole the county documents, thereby establishing that town as the new county seat.

The oyster industry was in major decline until the 1940s, when Japanese oysters were imported and intensive oyster farming techniques were introduced. Oysterville and Nahcotta are once again major producers of oysters; watch for shallow-bottomed oyster boats harvesting shellfish at high tides and note the gleaming pile of white shells beside the wharfs. ∎

historic Oysterville Schoolhouse, there's grilled oysters and other seafood for sale. For information, call 642-2400.

## Places to Stay & Eat

*Moby Dick Hotel* (☎ 665-4543), in Nahcotta, is an old coast guard barracks turned B&B. It's agreed that the Moby Dick doesn't look like much from the outside, but it's actually a nice place to spend the night. There are 10 rooms, with rates starting at $75.

*Nahcotta Natural* (☎ 665-4830), 270th St and Sandridge Rd in Nahcotta, is a good health-food store with local crafts, espresso and a selection of sandwiches and soup at lunch. It's in the old Clamshell Line train depot.

*The Ark* (☎ 665-4133), on the oyster wharf in Nahcotta, is considered one of the best restaurants in the Pacific Northwest. The dining room is unostentatious but comfortable – however, what's been bringing diners here for the last two decades is their sophisticated yet adventurous way with fish. The restaurant was begun with help from local-boy-made-good James Beard, whose culinary convictions wed classical French techniques to fresh and sometimes unusual local products. The result is grilled fish, like salmon, sturgeon, swordfish – or whatever comes off the fishing boats – with rarefied sauces, fresh wild mushrooms, local vegetables, nuts and oysters: raised within yards of the restaurant, and pan-fried for an all-you-can-eat feast, this simple delicacy alone ensures the Ark's reputation. The pastries are usually rich with local fruit and heavy with cream. It's worth keeping in mind that the Ark's bakery is open daily for goodies like cookies, cinnamon rolls and whole-wheat breads. Entree prices range from $15 to $20, but for a full dinner plan on $25 to $30.

## WILLAPA NATIONAL WILDLIFE REFUGE

Willapa Bay is an extremely shallow body of water, and during low tides the salt water retreats, leaving only a few channels filled with water, surrounded by miles of mud flats, salt marshes and reedy estuaries. The bay provides a habitat for a great diversity of wildlife, notably shorebirds in migration (256 varieties have been sighted in Willapa Bay and 86 species are known to nest here), as well as birds of prey and songbirds. **Long Island**, an eight-mile-long rocky island in the bay, is home to many large mammals, like Roosevelt elk, black bear, otter and coyote, which are now rare on the mainland near the bay.

There are five parts to the refuge, including Long Island, an area at the mouth of the Bear River and the extreme tip of the Long Beach Peninsula, beyond Leadbetter Point State Park. To reach Long Island you'll need a canoe or kayak; there's a boat dock across from the headquarters. Be sure to inquire about tides before embarking, as it's easy to get stranded during low tide. Long Island offers seven primitive campgrounds as well as a network of hiking trails. Contact the refuge for a map.

The headquarters for the refuge is across from Long Island off Hwy 101, eight miles northeast of Seaview, and can be contacted by writing to Willapa National Wildlife Refuge (☎ 484-3482), Ilwaco, WA 98624. For kayaks and canoes, contact Willapa Bay Kayak Rentals (☎ 642-4892) in Nahcotta near Ocean Park.

## BAY CENTER

While the village of Bay Center is undeniably on the bay, it's not particularly the center of anything. However, it does possess a colorful harbor and beach access. While not especially geared to tourism, its drowsy pace and old architecture make it a pleasant stop for a look-see and a plate of oysters.

Bay Center, an old oystering town from the 1850s, is 12 miles southwest of South Bend off Hwy 101 at the mouth of the Palix River.

### Rhodesia Beach

Bay Center sits on the sand spit formed by the Palix River, which juts out into Willapa Bay. The bay side of the spit is known as

Rhodesia Beach and is one of the more attractive beaches along the bay. Clamming is popular here during the appropriate season, as are kite-flying, swimming and sunbathing.

## Places to Stay & Eat

*Bay Center KOA* (☎ 875-6344), off Hwy 101 at Bay Center, is the largest campground on Willapa Bay, offering full-service tent and RV camping, hook-ups with cable TV, bicycle shelter for cyclists, laundry and so on. There's swimming and clam digging in season. It's open from March to November; sites range between $15.50 and $20.50.

The *Blue Heron Inn* (☎ 875-9990) is in Bay Center and offers a lively bar and restaurant scene with fresh salmon, crab and oysters. If you're already full of oysters, there's also standard pizza and burger fare.

## SOUTH BEND & RAYMOND

The little towns around Willapa Bay are some of Washington's earliest, and they have changed little over the last 50 years. South Bend (population 1550) is fond of calling itself the Oyster Capital of the World; with the world's largest oyster plant and six major oyster companies here, it's hard to dispute the title.

The first things you'll notice as you enter South Bend are the mountains of oyster shells piled by the aging harbor and the briny scent of the sea. The next thing you'll notice is the opulent Pacific County Courthouse, a Jeffersonian monument exemplifying the region's turn-of-the-century pride. Raymond (population 2800), four miles up the bay from South Bend, is another historic waterfront at the mouth of the sluggish Willapa River.

## Orientation

South Bend and Raymond are near the confluence of the Willapa River and Willapa Bay, along Hwy 101. From Raymond, Hwy 101 cuts through a low range of heavily lumbered mountains before reaching Aberdeen, 22 miles north. Highway 6 runs

between Chehalis and Raymond, a pleasant 52-mile drive through low-lying farm and dairy land.

Highway 101 is the main street of South Bend, though it's referred to as Robert Bush Drive. Most of Raymond's historic town center is a few blocks west of Hwy 101, near the harbor.

## Information

For information on the Willapa Bay area, contact the South Bend Chamber of Commerce (☎ 875-5231), PO Box 335, South Bend, WA 98586, or visit the information booth at the corner of Hwy 101 and A St. Contact the Raymond Chamber of Commerce (☎ 942-5419), PO Box 86, Raymond, WA 98577, or stop at the visitors center at Commercial and 5th Sts.

For medical emergencies, head to Willapa Harbor Hospital (☎ 875-5526), at Alder and Cedar Sts, in South Bend.

## Pacific County Museum

This community museum (☎ 875-5224), 1008 W Robert Bush Drive in South Bend, is a repository of local history spanning the periods of Native American prehistory through the pioneer fish and oyster industry of the mid-1800s. The museum has an especially good selection of historic fishing and logging equipment. The museum's bookstore is a good place to pick up tourist information and regional histories, often written by local writers. The museum is open from 11 am to 4 pm Monday to Sunday. Admission is free.

## Activities

Willapa Harbor Golf Course (☎ 942-2392), between South Bend and Raymond off Hwy 101, is a challenging nine-hole course beside Willapa River.

## Special Events

South Bend's big event is the Oyster Stampede, held on Memorial Day weekend. There are tons of oysters to sample in the large tent along the harbor. If you're handy with an oyster knife, consider competing in the oyster shucking contest. For more information call the chamber of commerce (☎ 875-5231).

Raymond pulls out the stops for the Willapa Harbor Festival, held the first weekend of August. Formerly known as the Loggers Festival, event sponsors have toned down the logging theme and instead focus on parades, a salmon barbecue, a quilt and flower show and musical events. For more information contact the Raymond Chamber of Commerce (☎ 942-5419).

### Places to Stay

*Bruceport Park* (☎ 875-6025), six miles west of South Bend on Hwy 101, offers tent and RV camping with showers, laundry, a convenience store and beach

access. Sites are $10.50 with hook-ups, $8.50 without.

*Maring's Courthouse Hill B&B* (☎ 875-6519, (800) 875-6519), 600 W 2nd St, South Bend, is an 1892 vintage home just a block from the Pacific County Courthouse, with riverview rooms. The three guest rooms, two with private bath, range from $45 to $90.

It's nothing fancy, but the *H & H Motel* (☎ 875-5523), E Water and Pennsylvania Sts, north of South Bend on Hwy 101, is a perfectly adequate motor inn, with a good bar and diner next door. Single/double rooms are $34/42.

### Places to Eat

In South Bend, expect to find oysters on

**The Grave of Willie Keil**
One of the more macabre tales of the Oregon Trail days is the story of Dr William Keil, the charismatic leader of the utopian Aurora Colony in the Willamette Valley. Keil and his followers moved from New England to Missouri in the 1850s, where they established a commune called Bethal Colony. However, the climate and their reception by the local people filled Keil with foreboding. The group decided to emigrate in 1855 to the Oregon Country, where they planned to re-establish their colony on Willapa Bay.

As plans to begin the 2000-mile journey started to take shape, Keil promised his 19-year-old son Willie that he could lead the wagon train on the trip west from Missouri. However, Willie died of malaria four days before departure. Dr Keil was able to fulfill his promise anyway: he had his son's body sealed in a zinc-lined coffin filled with whiskey, and he placed it in a hearsified wagon at the head of the train of 250 people. Willie's brandied body was finally buried at its present location along Hwy 6, one mile west of Menlo, the night of the party's arrival on November 26, 1855. Visit the grave site, now a state monument, and reflect on the determination of the Oregon Trail pioneers.

Although a handful of the colonists chose to remain on Willapa Bay, most, including Dr Keil himself, found the climate here too damp and instead moved south of Portland to establish the Aurora Colony. ■

every menu. For a quick beer and an oyster shooter, go to *O'Sheridan's Tavern* (☎ 875-5791), 1011 W Robert Bush Drive, an old saloon turned oyster bar. *Gardners'* (☎ 875-5154), 702 W Robert Bush Drive, is a bit more homey, with seafood and pasta dishes mostly under $10. It's open for dinner Thursday to Sunday and for lunch on Thursday and Friday. Fine dining in South Bend means *Boondocks Restaurant* (☎ 875-5155), at the corner of Willapa St and Robert Bush Drive. Oysters join steak, prime rib and other grilled items; prices range from $10 to $15.

## TOKELAND

The tiny community of Tokeland is on a spit of sand that reaches out into the north end of Willapa Bay. Although the resort community here reached its peak almost a century ago, and has been in gentle decline pretty much ever since, there's a good reason to turn off Hwy 105 and make your way to the old village. The *Tokeland Hotel* (☎ 267-7006), 100 Hotel Rd, is a handsome old resort hotel established in 1885, and, notwithstanding a few updates in plumbing, it's still offering the same rooms and hospitality as the day it opened. The rooms are small and bathrooms are down the hall, but the charm and authenticity of this well-kept old inn will delight most visitors. Well-behaved pets also get an invite. Single/double rooms are $55/65. Three meals a day are served in the dining room.

# Grays Harbor Area

The large, highly protected bay known as Grays Harobr was a natural for both native and early White settlement. The bay, which receives the waters of six major rivers, saw the development of Aberdeen and Hoquiam in the late 19th centruy. During these early years of Washington, when most commerce was maritime, the mills, factories and shipping lines of Grays Harbor were amongst the most important in the Northwest. Now a sleepy backwater, the Grays Harbor area

is doing its best to lure in tourism by stressing charter fishing and access to the beaches along the Pacific coast.

## ABERDEEN & HOQUIAM

In some cities, history looks distinguished, in others, is just looks old. There's as much history here as anywhere in Washington, but unfortunately the faded old mill towns of Aberdeen (population 16,665) and Hoquiam (population 8970) have seen better days. The good news is that beneath the shabby exterior are some inexpensive rooms, a few good restaurants and pleasant, hard-working people.

Originally, Grays Harbor was home to the Chehalis tribe, who maintained villages along the bay and the riverbanks. The first White explorer to discover this large harbor was the American Robert Gray, in 1792, but White settlement didn't arrive until 1848.

The industrial engines of Aberdeen were fired in 1877 when a salmon packing plant opened. Hoquiam's first lumber mill opened in 1882. By 1910, 34 lumber mills ringed Grays Harbor, with dozens of ships docked and waiting to freight the lumber to other parts of the nation. Aberdeen and Hoquiam were especially known for their large immigrant populations, who worked the shipyards, fishing boats, forests and mills, as well as for their wealthy captains of industry, whose elaborate homes still watch over Grays Harbor. The boom went bust during the 1930s, and these once-thriving port cities have been in gentle decline ever since. A recent effort to lure retirees and new small business ventures to the area has partially succeeded. Hoquiam/Aberdeen has been selected as one of the top 10 'micropolitan areas' in the USA.

### Orientation

Aberdeen is at the extreme eastern end of Grays Harbor, on the banks of the Chehalis and Wishkah rivers. Hoquiam is just to the west, on the banks of the Hoquiam River. A third population center, Cosmopolis (pop 1372), sits across the Chehalis River from Aberdeen. Getting around in this thrown-together urban area can be pretty confusing, as each community has a different street grid. Stop and get a free map from the visitors center if you're going to spend any time here.

Aberdeen is 50 miles from Olympia. From Hoquiam, it's 38 miles north to Lake Quinault in Olympic National Park.

### Information
The Grays Harbor Chamber of Commerce & Visitors Center (☎ 532-1924, (800) 321-1924), is at 506 Duffy St (off Hwy 101), Aberdeen, WA 98520, on the strip linking Aberdeen and Hoquiam. The *Daily World*

is the local paper. The Aberdeen post office (☎ 532-4811) is at 115 K St. In Hoquiam, the post office (☎ 532-4280), is at the corner of M and 8th Sts.

The Grays Harbor Community Hospital (☎ 532-8330) is at 915 Anderson Drive in Aberdeen (take Hwy 101 toward Hoquiam, turn right onto Oak St, which turns into Anderson Drive). Aberdeen's Loads of Fun (☎ 532-4609) at 600 W Market St, is the local laundry.

### Grays Harbor Historic Seaport
This nonprofit association (☎ 532-8611), 813 E Heron St, has taken over a portion of

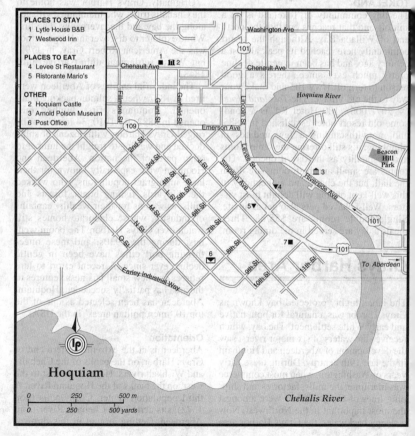

**PLACES TO STAY**
1  Lytle House B&B
7  Westwood Inn

**PLACES TO EAT**
4  Levee St Restaurant
5  Ristorante Mario's

**OTHER**
2  Hoquiam Castle
3  Arnold Polson Museum
6  Post Office

Hoquiam

*Hoquiam River*

Beacon Hill Park

To Aberdeen

*Chehalis River*

0     250     500 m
0     250     500 yards

Aberdeen's old harbor, and is dedicated to the region's maritime history. In honor of Washington's centennial in 1989, the group designed and built a full-scale replica of *Lady Washington*, one of the ships piloted by Captain Robert Gray when he first sailed into Grays Harbor in 1792. Other Historic Seaport projects include building a replica of Gray's other ship, the *Columbia Redivida* and developing a wetlands interpretive center.

For the traveler with a little time and curiosity, the *Lady Washington* offers a chance to sail on an 18th-century sailing vessel. This isn't a museum piece: the ship is usually on the go and is used for sail training, day excursions and other hands-on sail programs – it has sailed as far as Hawaii, and interested individuals can sign on as crew or as passengers on extended trips.

Much of the year, the *Lady Washington* sits at harbor in Aberdeen, where it is open for tours; call for the schedule and for a list of programs. The ship also sails up to Seattle during the summer, so be sure to call before heading out to Aberdeen.

### Arnold Polson Museum
Built in 1923 by one of the timber barons

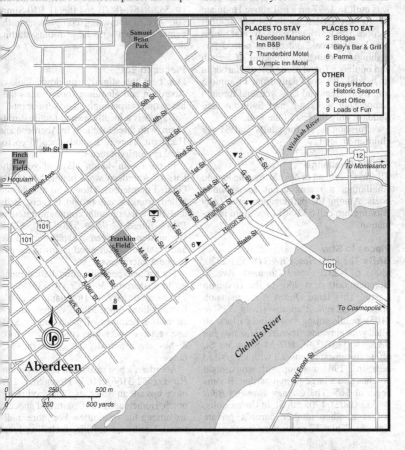

PLACES TO STAY
1  Aberdeen Mansion Inn B&B
7  Thunderbird Motel
8  Olympic Inn Motel

PLACES TO EAT
2  Bridges
4  Billy's Bar & Grill
6  Parma

OTHER
3  Grays Harbor Historic Seaport
5  Post Office
9  Loads of Fun

Samuel Benn Park

Finch Play Field

Franklin Field

To Hoquiam

To Montesano

To Cosmopolis

Aberdeen

Wishkah River

Chehalis River

0   250   500 m
0   250   500 yards

of Hoquiam, this 26-room mansion-cum-museum (☎ 533-5862), 1611 Riverside Ave in Hoquiam, is filled with period furniture, clothing, a doll collection and logging implements. Next door is the civic rose garden. The museum is open June 1 through Labor Day weekend, Wednesday through Sunday from 11 am to 4 pm; the rest of the year the same hours but weekends only. Admission for adults is $2, children 50c.

### Hoquiam Castle

Less a museum than a showcase of late Victorian-era taste, the so-called Hoquiam Castle (☎ 533-2005), 515 Chenault Ave, was built in 1897 on a hill above Hoquiam by Robert Lytle, another local lumber tycoon. The lavish cut glass, formal rooms paneled with oak and ornate period furnishings demonstrate the kind of wealth and opulence found along Grays Harbor in its heyday. It's open daily from 11 am to 5 pm, from Memorial Day weekend through Labor Day weekend, and Saturday and Sundays only the rest of the year.

Admission is $4 for adults and $1 for children under 11.

### Pacific Challenge

The first weekend of May brings the Pacific Challenge, a racing event for wooden boats. Among the participants is the *Lady Washington*; call 532-8611 for more information.

### Places to Stay

**B&Bs** The *Lytle House B&B* (☎ 533-2320, (800) 677-2320), 509 Chenault Ave in Hoquiam, sits next door to the Hoquiam Castle. This large Queen Anne mansion offers eight guest rooms (from $75 to $105), public sitting rooms and parlors, all filled with antiques. *Aberdeen Mansion Inn B&B* (☎ 533-7079), 807 M St at 5th St, offers five guest rooms, all with king-sized beds, in a 1905 mansion with wraparound porches and a large formal garden. Rooms begin at $65. The *Cooney Mansion B&B* (☎ 533-0602), 1705 5th St, in Cosmopolis, is yet another lumber baron's private Xanadu. This 37-room Craftsman-style

mansion offers nine guest rooms (from $5 to $120), five with private baths, with th modern luxury of a hot tub, sauna and exer cise room.

**Hotels** The place to stay in Aberdeen i *Olympic Inn Motel* (☎ 533-4200, (800 562-8618), at 616 W Heron St. Th Olympic offers senior and commercia rates, kitchen units and laundry, and mo units are non-smoking; rooms begin at $5! The *Thunderbird Motel* (☎ 532-3153), 41 Heron St, is right in the center of town with singles/doubles for $36/47. Over i Hoquiam, the best bet is the *Westwood In* (☎ 532-8161, (800) 562 0994), 910 Simp son Ave, a sprawling complex near th center of town with large rooms startin at $50.

### Places to Eat

Don't let the slightly run-down look o Aberdeen and Hoquiam fool you, as the have some surprisingly good restaurants.

*Duffy's* is a locally owned family dinin chain, with three locations in Aberdeen an Hoquiam. They're a good place to go fo breakfast or light meals.

In the rootin'-tootin' days of yore, th bars in Aberdeen were haunted by Bill Gohl, a murderous fellow who robbed an killed drunken sailors and loggers. Bill and the era are both commemorated *Billy's Bar & Grill* (☎ 533-7144), 322 Heron St in Aberdeen, a handsome old ba and restaurant with good sandwiches an regional microbrews.

For an unexpectedly good Italian mea go to *Ristorante Mario's* (☎ 533-1401 716 Simpson Ave, in Hoquiam, in an ol formica-lined diner. Mario's offers savor enormous helpings of pasta (under $1( and regional specialties (veal and seafoo dishes are especially good) in the $1 range.

Aberdeen's best restaurant is also Italia *Parma* (532-3166), 116 W Heron St, is a b more upscale in decor, and the food is to notch. Homemade bread, pasta and gnocch are among the specialties. For more trad tional Northwest cuisine, including loca seafood, go to the *Levee St Restaurant* (☎ 532-1959), 709 Levee St in Hoquiam, right on the waterfront, or *Bridges* (☎ 532-6563) 112 North G St in Aberdeen.

### Getting There & Away
Gray's Harbor Transportation Authority (☎ 532-2770, (800) 562-9730), 3000 Bay Ave in Aberdeen, operates the local bus system and provides the public link to Puget Sound cities. There are six buses a day between Aberdeen and Olympia, and the fare is only $1.

## WESTPORT
The stretch of beach between Westport (population 1970) on Grays Harbor and North Cove at the mouth of Willapa Bay is a study in drabness. There are miles of beach here, certainly, and the pace is slower and the atmosphere more tranquil than at Ocean Shores to the north or on the Long Beach Peninsula. However, it seems like beach resorts ought to be more fun than this. Mile after mile of flat beach is flanked by scrubby pines and beach grass, with near-derelict cottages and RV parks inserted. This is a forlorn kind of place, in keeping with the Pacific pall that's common here much of the year. If you're fond of ennui, this might be your beach.

Westport was for years the largest whaling port on the West Coast and the largest charter fishing center in the Northwest. However, whaling ended long ago and current restrictions on salmon fishing have crippled the economy of this fishing community. Quite a lot of charter fishing still goes on – as there are plenty of other fish in the sea – and boats run whale-watching expeditions during migration. However, without the huge runs of salmon in Grays Harbor, the backbone of the fishing industry seems to have disappeared.

### Orientation & Information
The area known as South Beach is the sandy headland from Westport to North Cove – in other words, the thrust of land between Grays Harbor and Willapa Bay. Westport is at the northern tip of a sandy peninsula and is really the only town in this area, although civilization clings desultorily to Hwy 105 as it rounds the cape toward the south. Westport is 22 miles southwest of Aberdeen.

The Westport-Grayland Chamber of Commerce (☎ 268-9422) can be contacted at PO Box 306, Westport, WA 98595.

### Westport Light State Park
Head out West Ocean Ave to Westport Light, the tallest lighthouse on the West Coast at 107 feet, and one of the few lighthouses in the nation that retains most of its original lighting system. Today, a 1000-watt electric lamp burns through an 1895 French-built Fresnel lens. Note that Westport Light isn't in the day-use park itself but on the Coast Guard property that's immediately adjacent; there are no tours. The year-round park has well wind-screened picnic sites and access to a stretch of beach that's closed to motor vehicles from April 15 to Labor Day.

### Westport Maritime Museum
A former coast guard station turned museum (☎ 268-0078), 2201 Westhaven Drive, boasts some great period photos and artifacts of seafaring days gone by. A complete skeleton of a gray whale is outside and can be viewed anytime. From April to May the museum is open from noon to 4 pm, weekends only, and June to September it's open Wednesday to Sunday. At other times it can be visited by appointment only. Admission is by donation.

### Charter Fishing
Charter fishing is not what it once was in Westport, but it is still going strong. Though Northwest salmon populations have declined rapidly, not all runs of salmon are equally threatened, so salmon fishing is regulated and restricted on a seasonal basis. If you want to fish for salmon, call one of the following charter fishing operations to find out if a season is going to open in the near future.

However, charter boats head out regularly in search of bottom fish, tuna, shark, halibut and rockfish – all worthy quarry for the angler, offering much the same thrill and adventure as salmon fishing. Most charter companies also run whale-watching excursions in the spring. Some sort of discount is usually available in the form of package deals with lodging, or group and weekday discounts, so don't be shy about asking. Keep your eyes peeled for discount coupons in local papers and tourist brochures.

For information about charter fishing from Westport, contact one of the following outfitters, or request a full listing of outfitters from the chamber of commerce. Westport Charters (☎ 268-9120, (800) 562-0157) is a well-established outfit with a fleet of nine vessels. Bran-Lee Charters (☎ 268-9177, (800) 562-0163) on Westhaven Drive, runs a $50 full-outfit bottom-fishing special. Deep Sea Charters (☎ 268-9300, (800) 562-0151) is right across from Float 6. Coho Charters (☎ 268-0111, (800) 572-0177), 2501 N Nyhus, is part of a large year-round motel and RV park complex (see below).

## Places to Stay

**Camping** RV campers are welcome at the *Coho Charters Motel & RV Park* (see below), where full hook-up sites are $15; no tents. Tent campers will want to go to *Twin Harbors State Park* (☎ 268-9717), three miles south of Westport on Hwy 105, a vast campground with 321 sites. Facilities include piped water and flush toilets; prices begin at $10.

**B&Bs** *Glenacres Inn B&B* (☎ 268-9391), 222 N Montesano St, is a historic inn built in 1898 on a wooded estate. Facilities include an outdoor hot tub and gazebo. There are five B&B rooms in the main lodge, as well as motel-like rooms in a separate building and a row of cottages. Rooms cost $59 to $72 in high season. Kitchen-equipped cottages – where pets are allowed – are available for $45 to $170.

**Hotels** The most inexpensive places to stay in Westport are back away from the harbor

along Hwy 105, known here as Montesano St. *McBee's Silver Sands Motel* (☎ 268-9029), 1001 S Montesano St, has 19 small motel units that don't offer much above the basics but are cheap, with rooms from $36; they will accommodate pets with prior notice. The *Frank L Motel* (☎ 268-9200), 725 S Montesano St, is comfortable and clean and offers kitchenettes; pets are allowed. You can cook clams, crabs and oysters on the patio barbecue. Rooms rates are $38/41 for singles/doubles. *Hazel-H Motel* (☎ 268-9711), 830 N Montesano St, is another small motel with four kitchen-equipped units available. Single/double rooms are $45/50.

*Coho Charters Motel & RV Park* (☎ 268-0111, (800) 572-0177), 2501 N Nyhus St, is only one block away from the beach and harbor. The motel rents crab pots, sells bait and offers charter packages. Rooms are $42/45. *Islander Charters & Motel* (☎ 268-9166, (800) 322-1740), 421 E Neddie Rose Drive, is right on the harbor with oceanview and kitchen-equipped rooms; there's also an outdoor pool, restaurant and charter office. Rooms start at $42/45 and pets can stay for $10 extra.

*Chateau Westport* (☎ 268-9101, (800) 255-9101), 710 W Hancock St at Forrest St, a resort motel on the beach, is the fanciest lodging in the area. There's an indoor pool, most rooms come with balconies and kitchens are available. Oceanview rooms start at $65. A substantial discount is offered in the off season.

## Places to Eat

Along the harbor are a lot of fish & chips restaurants and other take-away food establishments. For the best views and food, try the following. The *Islander Restaurant* (☎ 268-9166), 421-E Neddie Rose Drive, is the harborview dining room of a motel complex. That being said, the food – mostly burgers, steak and local seafood costing between $10 and $15 – isn't bad. Only a few yards away is *Pelican Point* (☎ 268-1333), 2681 Westhaven Drive, which is Westport's fine-dining establishment, or as close as it gets around here.

Expect seafood, steak and ribs from $12 to $17. It's open for lunch and dinner.

### Getting There & Away

**Bus** Grays Harbor Transit (☎ 532-2770, (800) 562-9730) is the county-operated bus system. Southbound buses from Aberdeen connect at Westport with Pacific Transit System buses serving South Bend, Raymond and the Long Beach Peninsula. Grays Harbor Transit also represents the only bus service to Aberdeen and Olympia.

Other buses travel up Hwy 101 to the south end of Olympic National Park via Quinault, and to communities on the north side of Grays Harbor.

**Ferry** In the summer only, a passenger ferry crosses from Westport to Ocean Shores six times daily. The fare is $8 roundtrip, $4.50 one way, with children under six free. Call Bill Walsh at Westport/Ocean Shores Ferry (☎ 268-0047 in Westport, 289-3391 in Ocean Shores) for information.

# Southern Cascades

The mightiest and the most explosive of the Northwest's peaks are found in southern Washington. Mt Rainier, one of the highest peaks in the USA, towers above Tacoma and the Puget Sound. One of the first national parks, this massive peak is extremely popular with hikers, climbers, skiers and onlookers, who wind along the area's roads in summer and fall, exultant with the majestic surroundings.

A mountain experience of a completely different sort comes at Mt St Helens, the sawed-off peak whose 1980 eruption showed the world what tremendous forces lay hidden in Northwest landscapes. Two viewpoints and a new interpretive center provide a look at the devastation wrought by the explosion of this volcanic peak.

Tucked into a little-visited corner of southern Washington is Mt Adams, in many ways the neglected sibling in this family of peaks. Fans of the mountain's many marvels hope it stays that way. An easy summit climb, wildflower meadows, berry fields and – most uniquely – relative solitude, recommend Mt Adams to the explorer who likes a little wilderness in their outdoor experience.

Geologically speaking, the Cascade peaks are all very young. Mt Rainier began erupting about a million years ago, although it and Mt Adams have been very active in the last 20,000 years. Youthful Mt St Helens is still in the process of expressing itself.

Mt Rainier is big enough, it is often said, to create its own weather, which basically means *bad* weather. Sometimes it seems to snare any passing cloud and make a storm out of it. In fact, weather is very changeable on and near all the Cascade peaks. Lovely summer days can turn blustery in an instant, so pack a warm sweater and rain gear. Summer temperatures average in the mid-70s; in the winter, temperatures run toward the mid-20s, and snowstorms are common.

Summer comes late to the southern Cascades, but it comes with a bang, as high-elevation meadows explode with wildflowers. By mid-August, the huckleberries are ready for picking, and it's almost worth a special trip – the Mt Adams area has huckleberry fields designated especially for harvesters. And while most visitors never see the black bears and cougars that live in the backcountry, day hikers have a good chance of spotting hoary marmots, pine martens and mountain goats.

# Mt Rainier National Park Area

Mt Rainier, at 14,411 feet, is the Cascades' highest peak, and it is imbued with more myth than any other mountain in the Northwest. Seattlites simply call it 'the Mountain' and judge the weather by its visibility. If you can see the peak for a few days running, the weather is good. But the flat, flying-saucer shaped, lenticular clouds that hover around the summit often herald fierce mountain storms – even on days when hikers at Paradise or Sunrise are enjoying good weather. With its 26 glaciers, Mt Rainier is the most heavily glaciated peak in the USA outside of Alaska.

The Nisquallies, Yakamas, Puyallups and other local native people knew this volcanic peak as Tahoma. They made regular trips to its foothills to hunt, fish and pick huckleberries, but they were generally uneasy about climbing the mountain.

When British captain George Vancouver spotted the peak from the Puget Sound in 1792, he named it for his friend Rear Admiral Peter Rainier. This name was not easily accepted by all Euro-Americans who moved to the northwest; even in the late

1800s, many felt Tahoma was a far more appropriate name.

When Mt Rainier was declared a national park in 1899, some of the land was obtained by a swap with the Northern Pacific Railroad. Railroad lands were originally granted by the federal government as an incentive for railroad companies to build a transcontinental line. Northern Pacific swapped some of its grant lands within the new park for timber-rich land elsewhere, which they subsequently sold to timber companies. During the 1930s, Depression-era CCC workers built many of the still-existing park structures and trails.

Mt Rainier is still a fairly potent volcano. It was created by repeated episodes of lava and mudflow and many eruptions of ash and rock. Before blasting its top some 5800 years ago, Mt Rainier reached as high as 16,000 feet. The two-mile crater from that eruption was joined by another large crater after a blast 2500 years ago; these two craters mark Mt Rainier's summit now, where gas from mountaintop steam vents creates toasty fern caves.

## ORIENTATION

Mt Rainier – so visible from the windows of Seattle – is actually 95 miles southeast

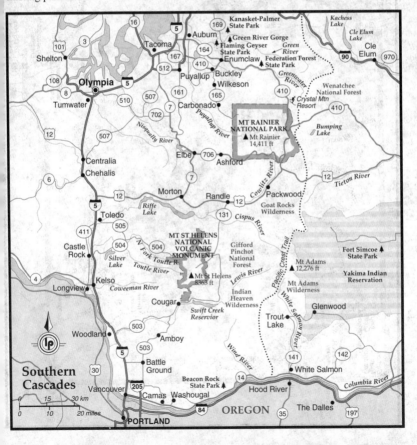

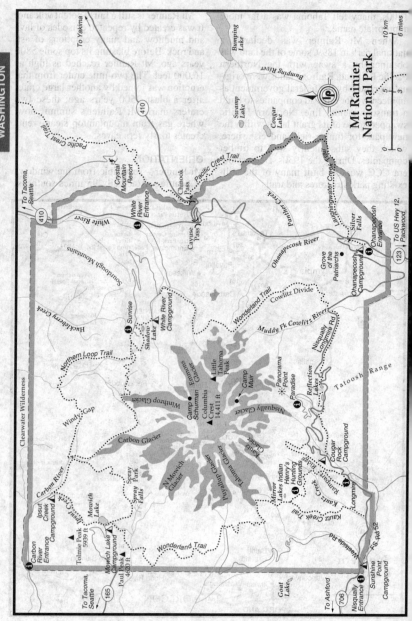

Mt Rainier
National Park

10 km
6 miles

To Yakima

Bumping
Lake

Bumping River

Swamp
Lake

Cougar
Lake

410

Pacific Crest Trail

Crystal
Mountain
Resort

To Tacoma,
Seattle

Chinook
Pass

Pacific Crest Trail

Laughingwater Creek Trail

Silver
Falls

To US Hwy 12,
Packwood

Ohanapecosh
Entrance

White River
Entrance

White River

Cayuse
Pass

Panther Creek

Ohanapecosh River

123

Ohanapecosh
Campground

410

Sourdough Mountains

Grove
of the
Patriarchs

Huckleberry Creek

Wonderland Trail

Cowlitz Divide

Muddy Fk Cowlitz River

Nisqually-Longmire Rd

Sunrise

Shadow
Lake

White River
Campground

Northern Loop Trail

Emmons
Glacier

Little
Tahoma
Peak

Camp
Muir

Panorama
Point

Paradise

Reflection
Lakes

Tatoosh Range

Clearwater Wilderness

Windy Gap

Winthrop Glacier

Camp
Schurman

Columbia
Crest
14,411 ft

Nisqually Glacier

Carbon Glacier

Kautz Glacier

Cougar
Rock
Campground

N Mowich Glacier

Spray
Park

Spray
Falls

Tahoma Glacier

Puyallup Glacier

Mirror
Lakes

Indian
Henry's
Hunting
Grounds

Kautz Creek

Longmire

Carbon River

Ipsut
Creek
Campground

Ipsut Creek

Mowich
Lake

Tolmie Peak
5939 ft

Mowich Lake
Campground

Paul Peak
4620 ft

Kautz Creek Trail

Wonderland Trail

Nisqually Rd

Westside Rd

FS Rd 52

Carbon River
Entrance

165

To Tacoma,
Seattle

Goat
Lake

Sunshine Point
Campground

Nisqually
Entrance

706

To Ashford

of that city. There is no ring road encircling the park; the four entrances by and large mark separate roads. The main entrance road, Hwy 706 (also known as the Nisqually-Longmire Rd), comes in through the town of Ashford, near the park's southwest corner, and follows the Nisqually River into the park. Past the Nisqually entrance is Longmire, which contains the only hotel open year round, and Paradise, where Mt Rainier's other hotel operates during the summer.

East of Paradise, near the park's southeast corner, Hwy 706 runs into Hwy 123; drive south and you'll arrive at the Ohanapecosh entrance. Drive north and Hwy 123 becomes Hwy 410 about halfway up the eastern park boundary at the Cayuse Pass. Just north of that junction, the White River entrance road cuts west off Hwy 410, running along the White River and ending at Sunrise, known for its great views. Highway 410 bends around and becomes an east-west road across the northern outskirts of the park, passing through the town of Enumclaw before reaching the Tacoma suburbs.

The most remote entrance to Mt Rainier National Park is the Carbon River entrance, south of Hwy 410 in the northwest corner. Another road near the Carbon River entrance leads to Mowich Lake but is not an official entrance road.

## INFORMATION

For information on the park, call or write the superintendent's office (☎ (206) 569-2211) at Mt Rainier National Park, Ashford, WA 98304.

Park entrance fees are $5 per car and $3 for pedestrians and cyclists. All roads but the Hwy 706 Nisqually entrance road to Paradise close down in the winter. Pay phones are available at all the park's fee campgrounds as well as at ranger stations and visitors centers.

Mt Rainier National Park publishes two newspapers a year, *Tahoma* and *Snowdrift*, which are dispensed upon entry to the park and are available at all visitors centers. These have current information on natural-ist walks, evening campground programs and park news.

## HIKING & CLIMBING

Hiking opportunities range from short walks on interpretive nature trails to extended backcountry jaunts. Once hikers have had a taste of Rainier's trails, many pine to circumnavigate the mountain on the

---

### Because It's There: Climbing Mt Rainier

The first documented climb to the summit of Mt Rainier was accomplished in 1870, when Sluiskin, a Yakama guide, led Hazard Stevens and Philemon Van Trump as far as present-day Paradise, there refusing to go any farther (Native American legend had it that a fiery spirit lived in the mountain). Stevens and Van Trump continued, without their guide, up past Camp Muir and along the Gibraltar Ledge to the summit, where they spent the night in a sulpherous hot-springs cave. When they returned to base camp, Sluiskin initially took them for ghosts.

James Longmire, one of two members of that first climb who had turned back early, settled near a mineral springs at the base of the mountain in the 1880s. Once he established a trail, Mt Rainier began to be visited by aspiring mountain climbers. In 1884 he opened a mineral spring resort and began building access roads for visitors to his establishment, and up the mountain to Paradise.

In 1890, Fay Fuller, a Puget Sound schoolteacher, became the first woman to climb Mt Rainier. Fuller climbed in bloomers, a straw hat and leather oxfords, which she customized by driving 'long caulks and brads' into the soles. She spent a night in an ice cave in the summit crater with her five male climbing partners, and later wrote that she expected many women to follow in her footsteps, which indeed they did. Early in the 20th century husband-and-wife climbing teams were fairly common, and later Mountaineers' expeditions to the Cascades summits were close to 50% women. ■

**WASHINGTON**

**Wonderland Trail**, a 93-mile loop around the mountain. The trail changes elevation at nearly every turn, passing through lowland forests and subalpine meadows. It's a good 10-day trek, with campgrounds spaced about every 10 miles. Camping is restricted to the designated campgrounds. Remember, before any overnight backpacking trip, it's necessary to stop by an NPS ranger station or visitors center and obtain a backcountry permit. There are five regular campgrounds (a total of 577 sites) in the park; all have running water and either flush or pit toilets, but no RV hook-ups.

Climbers must also register with the NPS. Guided climbs are available through Rainier Mountaineering, based in the summer at the Paradise Guide House (☎ 569-2227) and during the winter at 535 Dock St, suite 209, Tacoma, WA 98402 (☎ 627-6242).

### ORGANIZED TOURS
Gray Line (☎ (206) 626-7532, (800) 426-7532) runs bus tours of the park, which leave from the Seattle Sheraton Hotel. The 10-hour tour leaves the hotel at 8:15 am daily during the summer and costs $39.

### ASHFORD
Ashford on Hwy 706 is one of the main entry points to the Mt Rainier area and is a good place to stock up on food and provisions before hitting the high country. It is also one of the few nearby towns that offer much in the way of lodging and restaurants. Ashford is five miles west of the Nisqually entrance to the park.

A well-developed network of cross-country ski trails has several access points off Hwy 706 near Ashford. Stop by the Mt Tacoma Trails office (☎ 569-2451), at Whittaker's Bunkhouse, for a trail map.

Climbers, hikers and auto tourists all get a little stiff and sore, but there are two spots halfway between Ashford and the park entrance where you can soak in hot tubs. Wellspring (☎ 569-2514) has hot tubs and a sauna for $10 an hour. Massages for a half/full hour are $25/45. Less than a mile to the east, Stormking (☎ 569-2964) has

hot tubs for $10 an hour and hour-long massages for $35. At either spot, reservations are recommended, especially for a massage.

### Places to Stay
There is one main road in Ashford – Hwy 706 – and everything is on it. *Growly Bear B&B* (☎ 569-2339), an attractive homestead house built in 1890, is a mile from the park entrance and has rooms from $50 to $90. *Jasmer's Cabin B&B* (☎ 569-2682) is in the quiet heart of Ashford.

*Whittaker's Bunkhouse* (☎ 569-2439) is a motel with simple rooms for $55; the building was originally used as a logger's bunkhouse. Mountain climbers often go for an $18 bunk in the six-person bunkroom. Guests may run into the owner, renowned mountaineer and raconteur-extraordinaire Lou Whittaker, at the bunkhouse espresso bar in the morning.

*Alexander's* (☎ 569-2300, (800) 654-7615), a comfortable and graceful old country inn, has shared-bath rooms for $50 and up; rooms with private bath start at $59. The restaurant here is also noteworthy (see Places to Eat).

*Nisqually Lodge* (☎ 569-8804) is about the only motel in Ashford where you'll find TVs and telephones in the rooms, and there's also an outdoor hot tub. Rates start at $67.

Both the *Cottage at the Berry* and the somewhat larger *Cabin at the Berry* (both ☎ 569-2628) are near the Wild Berry restaurant just west of the park entrance. For one or two people, the cottage costs $60; three to five people pay $70. At the cabin, rates start at $60 for one or two and top out at $115 for a full house of five to eight people.

### Places to Eat
Many of Ashford's restaurants are associated with lodgings; the restaurant at *Alexander's* serves elegant dinners – its prices are on par with the park lodges' but the food is a far sight better. Expect to pay

about $16 for a salmon dinner, though early evening specials can be had for less than $10.

For a casual lunch or dinner, the *Wild Berry* (☎ 569-2628) is a local institution known for friendly service and generous portions of hearty food, such as stew for about $8. The Wild Berry cooks lots of pizzas, but they're not necessarily turned out fast.

## NISQUALLY ENTRANCE

This southwestern corner of Mt Rainier National Park is its most visited corner: it has the park's only lodging, a road that's plowed all winter long and plenty of lovely countryside, from lush old-growth forests near Longmire to alpine meadows at Paradise, 5400 feet above sea level.

Highway 706 enters the park along the Nisqually River, which has its headwaters in the Nisqually Glacier above Paradise. Just inside the entrance, the Westside Rd heads off to the north, and car traffic must stop after three miles but cyclists and hikers can keep on going. Cyclists must stick to the old roadbed, but hikers can strike out on trails, most of which lead up drainages toward the mountain. If you plan to camp anywhere along the Westside Rd, be sure to pick up a backcountry permit at Longmire. It's also a good idea to inquire about road and trail conditions; flood damage has closed much of the road and some trails in recent years.

Or, continuing east on Hwy 706, the first good views of the mountain come at Kautz Creek, one of the several glacier-fed streams that contribute to the Nisqually River. After passing Longmire, the road begins to climb steadily, passing several good viewpoints and some sharp hairpin turns on the way to Paradise. Allow *at least* 45 minutes to drive from the park entrance to Paradise – and that's without making any stops.

From Paradise, the road heads east through waterfall-bedecked Stevens Canyon on the way to the Ohanapecosh entrance.

## Information

Backpackers and hikers should stop by the Longmire Hiker Information Center (☎ 569-2211, ext 3317) for trail information and backcountry permits. Park rangers at the Jackson Visitor Center (☎ 569-2211, ext 2328) at Paradise dispense trail maps and can recommend good hikes and campsites. This is another place to get backcountry permits and to register if you're climbing the mountain.

## Longmire

James Longmire, who in the 1880s moved near the mountain, noticed a mineral springs and a lovely meadow near the base of Mt Rainier during an 1883 climbing trip. He and his family returned the following year and established Longmire's Medical Springs, and in 1890, he built the Longmire Springs Hotel. When Mt Rainier became a national park in 1899, the Longmire area was the hub of activity and the original park headquarters.

The **Longmire Museum** (☎ 569-2211, ext 3314), open from 9 am to 5:30 pm daily, has exhibits on natural history, Native American culture and early White exploration of the area. Admission is free. To stretch your legs from the long drive in, wander the **Trail of the Shadows**, a 1.8-mile trail across the road from the Longmire Lodge. As steeped in history as it is in nature, the trail passes the mineral springs that spurred the hot springs resort in 1884, when the water ran considerably warmer than it does now, and a cabin built in 1888 by Longmire's son.

## Paradise

Late-summer visitors to Paradise can expect dazzling wildflowers. First to bloom, even before the snow has completely melted, are avalanche lilies, glacier lilies and western anemones. They're followed by lupine, mountain bog gentian and paintbrush, creating broad washes of blue and red across the slopes. The Nisqually Glacier dips down toward Paradise; follow the **Skyline Trail** to the Glacier Overlook for a good look at the glacier and Nisqually

Mt Rainier (DS)

Icefall, huge chunks of ice moving slowly down the glacier.

Even if you're not staying at the **Paradise Inn** (see Places to Stay below), the lobby of this classic national park lodge is worth a visit. Huge fireplaces anchor each end of the lobby, massive timbers hold up the ceiling, and comfortable leather sofas and chairs make relaxing with a good mystery novel as alluring as hiking Paradise's trails.

A shop in the Jackson Visitor Center sells books on Rainier and the Cascades, and there's a post office in the lobby of the Paradise Inn.

### Hiking

A couple of trails lead to **Indian Henry's Hunting Grounds**, a magnificent flower-lit meadow with (on the right days) perfect views of Mt Rainier reflected in Mirror Lake. It's a 5.5-mile hike in through meadow after meadow from the Kautz Creek trailhead, which is 3.5 miles from the park entrance, about halfway between the entrance and Longmire. Another route to Indian Henry's Hunting Grounds starts near Longmire and follows the Wonderland Trail over **Rampart Ridge** – this 6.5-mile hike to the meadows is not easy, as the 2400-foot elevation gain is accomplished with lots of ups and downs.

Paradise is laced with trails, many of them paved for the first mile or so, and it's easy enough to wander out from the parking lot and make up an impromptu loop just by following the trail markers. But for a decent leg-stretch and a close-up look at wildflowers, marmots and the Nisqually Glacier, hike the six-mile **Skyline Trail**, starting at the Paradise Inn and climbing about 1600 feet to **Panorama Point**, with good views of Rainier and the neighboring Tatoosh Range. The trails are usually crowded near the lodge, but traffic drops off after the first hill leaves unconditioned hikers sucking thin air. For a steep shortcut on the return part of the loop, hike down **Golden Gate Trail**.

Ambitious day hikers can continue up the mountain from Panorama Point and follow the **Pebble Creek Trail** to the snow-field track leading to **Camp Muir**. Camp Muir is the main overnight bivouac spot for climbing parties, and it has stupendous views south to Mt Adams, Mt St Helens and Mt Hood. Camp Muir is at 10,000 feet, so it's not a hike to be taken lightly, and it requires sufficient clothing for all sorts of weather and a good supply of food and water.

A lower elevation trail, the **Lakes Trail**, starts at Paradise and heads a little way down the mountain, making a five-mile loop through subalpine meadows and passing Reflection Lakes, with views of the Tatoosh Range. In the fall, trailside huckleberry bushes redden, making this a lovely, not overly strenuous, hike.

### Skiing
During the winter, the road is plowed as far as Paradise, and people take to the trails on cross-country skis and snowshoes. There is also a designated 'snow play' area, which is groomed for inner tube riders.

It can be a hairy drive up the mountain in bad weather, though. If it seems safer to stay at lower elevations, ski the Westside Road, just inside the Nisqually entrance (though you may encounter snowmobilers).

The Longmire Ski Touring Center (☎ 569-2411), with trail information and cross-country ski and snowshoe rentals, is open at Longmire from mid-December to April.

### Climbing
The most popular route to the summit of Mt Rainier starts at Paradise and involves a brief night's rest at Camp Muir before you rise between midnight and 2 am to don crampons, rope up, climb over Disappointment Cleaver and ascend the Ingraham Glacier to the summit. All climbers going higher than Camp Muir must register at the Paradise Ranger Station. Inexperienced climbers should not attempt this rigorous ascent independently; climb instead with the guide service.

Rainier Mountaineering (☎ 569-2227, 627-6242 in the winter) offers climbing classes, guided climbs to Mt Rainier's summit and a variety of specialized seminars. Unless you are an expert mountain climber, it is prudent to spend $381 for a day of climbing school and a two-day summit climb. Rainier Mountaineering's base is the Guide House across from the Paradise Inn. Rent ice axes, crampons and plastic mountaineering boots from the Guide House, open daily from 9 am to 5 pm.

### Other Activities
Park naturalists present slide shows at the Paradise Inn and the Cougar Rock Campground amphitheater every summer evening at 8:30 or 9 pm. Check the bulletin boards at the inn and campground for a schedule of topics.

Children ages six to 11 can join a park ranger for 'Junior Ranger' hikes and nature activities at the Cougar Rock Campground. The 1.5-hour program is repeated several times a week; check the campground bulletin board for the schedule.

Movies and slide shows about the mountain and the preservation of Paradise's meadows are shown throughout the day at the Jackson Visitor Center.

### Places to Stay
**Camping** *Sunshine Point Campground*, just inside the park near the Nisqually entrance, is one of the park's smaller campgrounds. Its 18 riverside sites go for $6 a night, and it's the only campground open year round. *Cougar Rock Campground*, 2.5 miles uphill from Longmire on the way to Paradise, has 200 sites, costs $8 and is open until mid-October.

**Lodges** Of the park's two lodges, *Paradise Inn* (☎ 569-2413) and the *Longmire National Park Inn* (☎ 569-2411), Paradise is grander and has the more spectacular setting. But Longmire is cozier and, conveniently for cross-country skiers, is open year round. The season at Paradise runs from late May to early October. Call for reservations at either place (☎ 569-2275). Rooms at either lodge start at about $60, and they fill up fast. It's best to book way in advance, but cancellations occur frequently, so it pays to keep calling even if initially there are no openings. It's also a good idea to ask for a confirmation, as booking foul-ups happen easily. If the park lodges are full, the closest accommodations outside the park are in Ashford.

### Places to Eat

A snack bar at the Paradise Inn and a cafeteria in the Jackson Visitor Center at Paradise offer the most basic sustenance. But even cafeteria chili is welcome after a winter snowshoe expedition. The visitors center cafeteria is open daily from May to September and on weekends and holidays the rest of the year.

The dining room at *Paradise Inn* (☎ 569-2413) is pretty good if you're just there for one or two meals. After that, even the salmon seems a little institutional and requires some vigorous hiking to make it seem worth the $15 or so it'll set you back. The Paradise Inn is open from late May to early October. Down the hill at Longmire, Glacier Park Services, the park concessionaire, serves essentially the same meals at the *Longmire National Park Inn* (☎ 569-2411); they serve three meals a day and are open year round.

### PACKWOOD

Packwood, with its abundance of motels and restaurants, is a convenient base for exploring the east side of Mt Rainier and for launching a trip into the Goat Rocks Wilderness Area to the south.

Twelve miles southwest of Ohanapecosh on Hwy 12, Packwood is the closest real town to the Ohanapecosh and White River entrances to Mt Rainier National Park. It's also on the well-traveled route between Mt Rainier and Mt St Helens, with the less visited Mt Adams also in the neighborhood. To reach Mt St Helens, head west on Hwy 12 to Randle, then south on Hwy 131 to the turnoff for the Windy Ridge viewpoint. You can get to trailheads on the north side of Mt Adams by heading south on USFS Rd 21, a few miles south of Packwood.

The Packwood Ranger Station (☎ 494-5515), on Hwy 12 near the north end of town, is a good source of information on the Goat Rocks Wilderness Area.

### Places to Stay

*Packwood RV Park & Campground* (☎ 494-5145) has a few tent sites and full amenities, including a laundromat, a store and a cafe. It's right in the heart of Packwood, set back just a bit from Hwy 12. Rates run from $10 to $15. *La Wis Wis* (☎ 494-5515), a USFS campground on Hwy 12 halfway between Packwood and Ohanapecosh, is a good place to look for a campsite in the summer when the national park fills up. It has about 100 sites with running water and flush toilets for $8 or $10.

*Old Hotel Packwood* (☎ 494-5431) is a renovated log hotel with a big porch and shared baths for most of the rooms; singles/doubles are $20/38. Unfortunately, the place hasn't changed much since it was built in 1912. The *Tatoosh Motel* (☎ 494-5321), on the west side of town, has homey duplex cabin-type units; several have kitchenettes and there is an outdoor hot tub. Single/double rooms are $42/45.

Another good choice in Packwood is the *Mountain View Lodge Motel* (☎ 494-5555), where doubles start at $29. It's on the east side of town. The *Inn of Packwood* (☎ 494-5500) has an indoor pool and an outdoor spa, and singles/doubles for $39/55. The *Cowlitz Lodge* (☎ 494-4444), also right on Hwy 12, has rooms from $50, a free continental breakfast and a hot tub.

## Places to Eat

Packwood is home to a number of drive-ins and unprepossessing diners. Probably the best of the lot is *The Club Cafe* (☎ 494-5977), a chicken-fried-steak kind of place. A bit more upscale is *Peter's Inn* (☎ 494-4000), a steakhouse with a good salad bar.

## OHANAPECOSH ENTRANCE

Ohanapecosh means 'Clear Waters' to the local Native Americans, and this southeastern entry road certainly provides beautiful views of the rushing Ohanapecosh River. There are also a couple of popular trails into the dense forests here.

From Ohanapecosh, there's good access (via Hwy 12) to the Goat Rocks Wilderness Area and Mt St Helens. To reach Mt St Helens, take Hwy 12 west to Randle, then head south on Hwy 131, which shortly becomes USFS Rd 25. This will put you on the east side of Mt St Helens.

## Information

The Ohanapecosh Visitor Center (☎ 569-2211, ext 2352), on Hwy 123 at the park's southeastern corner, is open daily from 9 am to 6 pm during the summer. The displays here focus on tree identification and the local old-growth forest. Rangers also offer information on hiking trails.

## Hiking

The 1.5-mile trail into the **Grove of the Patriarchs** is one of Mt Rainier's most popular hikes, and it's worth the walk for a look at some truly large trees. The mostly level trail crosses the Ohanapecosh River to a small island where 1000-year-old Douglas firs and cedars grow. Find the trailhead just north of the Ohanapecosh Visitor Center.

Just outside the Ohanapecosh Visitor Center, the half-mile **Ohanapecosh Nature Trail** winds through the forest and visits a small natural hot spring. The hot spring is more of a seep than a wallow, but there is a tiny trailside bench that allows weary hikers to soak their sore feet in a six-inch-deep pool. Below the springs, bright green grass grows lushly in a meadow that was once the site of a hot-springs spa.

If the Ohanapecosh Nature Trail seems like just a starting point for a hike, follow the signpost just past the hot springs for the **Silver Falls Loop**. The easy three-mile loop visits noisy Silver Falls and, at its north end, can hook up with the trail to the Grove of the Patriarchs.

The **Pacific Crest Trail** runs along the eastern edge of Mt Rainier National Park, and trailheads at Ohanapecosh and Chinook Pass, on Hwy 123 a few miles south of the park's White River entrance, provide local access to the high mountain trail. It's best to make this fine 19-mile stretch into a two-day, north to south backpack, starting at Chinook Pass. Plan for cool weather; the trail runs at 5000 feet and above, with peeks at Mt Rainier and plenty of wildlife and late-season huckleberries.

## Places to Stay & Eat

The 208-site *Ohanapecosh Campground* charges $10 a night and is open from June to late October. If it's full, head out of the park and go south a few miles to *La Wis Wis Campground*, a Gifford Pinchot National Forest campground (see Places to Stay under Packwood, above).

There are no food services at Ohanapecosh. The closest place for groceries or a meal is in the town of Packwood, about 12 miles to the southwest on Hwy 12.

## WHITE RIVER ENTRANCE

Some of the best views of Mt Rainier – with Emmons Glacier sliding down its face, Little Tahoma peak in the foreground, and the craggy Goat Rocks Wilderness Area off to the southeast – are from Sunrise. Sunrise's 6400-foot-high open meadows are scattered with trees and laced with hiking trails. Since it's on the mountain's east side, the whole White River-Sunrise area benefits from Mt Rainier's 'rain shadow' and receives less precipitation than the damp west side.

Basic visitor facilities, including meals and restrooms, are available at the Sunrise

Lodge. There's also a visitors information desk to answer questions and issue permits.

### Orientation & Information

The White River entrance road, off Hwy 410, follows the river valley to the White River Campground on a spur off the main road about seven miles from the park entrance. The main road leaves the river and begins climbing after the turnoff for the campground, ascending another 2400 feet in the 10-mile stretch to Sunrise.

The ranger station (☎ 569-2211, ext 2356) at the White River entrance dispenses backcountry permits and hiking information. It's open Sunday to Thursday from 8 am to 4:30 pm, Friday from 8 am to 9 pm and Saturday from 7 am to 7 pm. Sunrise Visitor Center (☎ 569-2211, ext 2357) is open Sunday to Friday from 9 am to 6 pm, and on Saturday from 9 am to 7 pm.

### Sunrise Goat Watch

Park naturalists lead a 1.5-mile hike each Sunday afternoon from the Sourdough Ridge trailhead at Sunrise to explore the mountain goat habitat. If this doesn't fit your schedule, make it a self-guided walk. Pick up the trail at the picnic area behind the visitors center and either hike the nature trail loop (there is some uphill walking) or blast off onto a longer trail along Sourdough Ridge.

### Hiking

It doesn't take long for hikers to become enraptured with the White River-Sunrise area. The only glitch may be the crowds. Try to hike on a weekday, and hit the trail early in the morning.

A trailhead directly across the parking lot from the Sunrise Lodge provides access to several short walks and a plethora of longer hikes. It's an easy stroll to the Emmons Vista, with good views of Mt Rainier, Little Tahoma and the Emmons Glacier. For a longer, but level, walk, turn right just before the Emmons Vista onto the **Sunrise Rim Trail**, which takes about 1.5 miles to reach Shadow Lake and Sun-

Clark's nutcracker can be found in the high mountains. Its white patches on black wings make it distinctive.

rise Camp, a walk-in backcountry campground. From here, an old service road provides a short route back to the lodge parking lot.

Three miles from the White River entrance, the trail to **Summerland** takes off along Frying Pan Creek. The 4.3-mile hike climbs gradually through forest, then through brush, before reaching Summerland's open subalpine meadows with views of Mt Rainier and pointy, glacier-chiseled Little Tahoma peak. Mountain goats and elk are often visible from this extremely popular trail.

To get to **Emmons Glacier**, a less spectacular, but perfectly pleasant, trail starts from the far end of the White River Campground and follows a fork of the White River for 3.5 miles to Glacier Basin, a meadow surrounded by slopes that are home to mountain goats and form a corridor for mountain climbers. For a view of Emmons Glacier, the largest glacier in the lower 48 states, turn off the **Glacier Basin Trail** after one mile and hike another half mile along the glacier's lateral moraine to the overlook. (Actually, the official viewpoint doesn't have much over the many informal tracks up to the moraine's crest that precede it.)

Though most people drive from White River to Sunrise, sturdy hikers can leave their cars at the White River Campground and take the three-mile trek from the campground's 'C' loop up the Wonderland Trail to the **Sunrise Rim Trail**. The steep trail is forested for the first couple of miles, then it breaks into steep-walled subalpine meadows and good mountain views. At Sunrise, the trail hooks up with a bevy of nature trails.

### Climbing
From the White River Campground, climbers hike the Glacier Basin Trail to the Inter Glacier, then rope up into teams and continue to the 9500-foot bivouac at Camp Schurman, where rocky Steamboat Prow juts up and separates the Emmons and Winthrop glaciers. Most climbers follow Emmons' crevasse-free 'corridor' as far as possible, then skirt crevasses, including the gaping bergschrund where the top of the glacier pulls away from the mountain's ice cap, to reach the summit.

### Places to Stay & Eat
The 117-site *White River Campground* is 10 road miles or 3.5 steep trail miles downhill from Sunrise. Campground fees are $8, which buys flush toilets, running water and crowded, though not unpleasant, camping spaces. It's open only in summer.

For campers who are willing to pack their gear 1.5 miles and can dispense with such amenities as running water, *Sunrise Camp* is just down the Sunrise Rim Trail from the lodge parking lot. This is backcountry camping, so a permit is required.

There is no indoor lodging at Sunrise. The closest motel rooms are at *Crystal Mountain Resort* (see Crystal Mountain Resort later in this section) or in Enumclaw or Packwood.

The *Sunrise Lodge* restaurant is open for meals from 10 am to 7 pm daily from late June through early September. Don't expect anything fancy – it's a hamburger and hot dog sort of place.

### CARBON RIVER ENTRANCE
This remote northwest corner of Mt Rainier National Park is a dense green pocket, made all the more striking by the intensive clear-cutting that has gone on in the Carbon River valley outside the park boundaries. There's lots of water, mushrooms, moss and hikes to waterfalls. There's also the park's lowest-reaching glacier, a river cloudy with glacial till, and a remarkable inland rainforest. The Carbon River area has very few glimpses of Mt Rainier; for big mountain views, head to Mowich Lake.

### Orientation
To get to Carbon River and Mowich Lake from the I-5 corridor, it's easiest to take Hwy 167 south to Puyallup and from there pick up Hwy 410 east to Buckley. From there take Hwy 165 south past the small towns of Wilkeson and Carbonado; the road forks a few miles past Carbonado. The left fork follows the Carbon River and is paved to just inside the park entrance. The right fork is paved for a couple of miles, and then becomes a well-graded gravel road, which climbs above the Carbon River valley and terminates about 18 miles from the fork at Mowich Lake. Neither road is plowed in the winter.

Beginning in the summer of 1995, construction on the O'Farrell Bridge, which spans the Carbon River near the fork on Hwy 165, will make it more challenging to reach this corner of the park. Call 569-2211 for construction schedules.

### Information
The Carbon River Ranger Station (☎ 569-2211, ext 2358) is open from 9 am to 5 pm daily during the summer; it's just inside the park entrance. This is the only reliable place in the park's northwest corner to get a backcountry permit. During the summer, a park service volunteer patrols the Mowich Lake Campground and can answer questions about the local trails.

### Carbon River Rainforest
Though there are plenty of times when all of Mt Rainier seems like a rainforest, the

short Carbon River Trail just inside the park entrance loops through the only true inland rainforest in the park, indeed in all of North America. Huge-leafed plants grow alongside the boardwalk that elevates the trail from the frequently steaming ground below, and the moist air condenses into droplets hanging from big Douglas firs and cedars.

## Hiking

At 3820 feet, the **Carbon Glacier** reaches a lower elevation than any other glacier on Mt Rainier. A trail starts at the Ipsut Creek Campground, and 3.5 miles away it passes the glacier's leading edge. Hikers are warned not to approach the glacier too closely, as rockfall from the glacier's surface is unpredictable and dangerous. The same trailhead also provides access to the Wonderland Trail, which crosses Ipsut Pass on the way to Mowich Lake (a 5.3-mile hike from the Ipsut Creek trailhead).

A 35-mile, three or four-day trip, the **Northern Loop Trail** passes through some of the park's least traveled areas. The loop starts at Ipsut Creek and follows the Carbon River Glacier Trail for a couple of miles before taking off to the east and passing through Windy Gap on its steep, up-and-down path toward Sunrise. Just west of Sunrise, the Northern Loop Trail joins up with the Wonderland Trail, which returns hikers to Ipsut Creek or continues around the mountain.

To reach **Summit Lake**, just outside the park's Carbon River entrance, turn north on USFS Rd 7810 and follow it to the end. The 2.5-mile trail to Summit Lake is in the Clearwater Wilderness Area. Like the national park, this wilderness area has areas of old-growth forest. Mt Rainier's north face, including the nearly un-climbable Willis Wall, a sheer wall of loose rock and ice, comes into good view at Summit Lake.

From trailheads at Mowich Lake, one extremely popular trail heads south and passes **Spray Falls** on its way to **Spray Park**, flush with wildflowers late in the summer. It's just under three miles to Spray Park. As popular as this trail is, it's not all

that easy. A dizzying run of switchbacks just past the falls pulls the trail out of the forest to the Spray Park meadows.

For views of Mt Rainier, try going to **Tolmie Peak lookout**. Head north on the Wonderland Trail from Mowich Lake, then turn off at Ipsut Pass and climb to the lookout at 5939-foot Tolmie Peak. If the final chug up Tolmie Peak seems too daunting, Eunice Lake at its base is a perfectly good place to relax.

The **Paul Peak Trail** hooks up with the Wonderland Trail three miles from its trailhead on the Mowich Lake Rd. It joins the Mowich River Trail in 5.8 miles. Try this trail on summer weekends when hikers choke Spray Park.

## Places to Stay & Eat

*Ipsut Creek Campground*, at the end of the Carbon River Rd, has 29 sites for $6 a night, and is open only in summer. There's also the small, free walk-in *Mowich Lake Campground* just past the Mowich Lake parking lot, but the campground itself is far less inviting than its surroundings, and there's no water. The *Mountain View Inn* (☎ 829-1100), at the junction of Hwys 165 and 410 in Buckley, is the closest motel.

The closest place to the Carbon River area to buy food is the small town of Wilkeson, about 18 miles from the park entrance. There are a couple of small stores and a restaurant, the *Pick & Shovel*.

## ENUMCLAW

Seattlites almost always pass through Enumclaw on their way to Mt Rainier, and it's where the mountain really starts to tower and the towns quit seeming like passably attractive suburbs of Seattle. Even though there are places to drink espresso and get a decent lunch in Enumclaw, it's a pretty rural place and is justifiably called a gateway to Mt Rainier National Park. It's a good place to stock up on food before getting to remote northern areas of the park.

Highway 410 from Enumclaw leads to the park's White River entrance; Hwy 165, accessible to the southwest of town, is the route to the Carbon River entrance. White River Ranger Station (☎ 825-6585), on Hwy 410 just east of downtown, has information on trails in Mt Rainier National Park and the surrounding national and state forest lands.

## Places to Stay & Eat

The *Kanaskat-Palmer State Park* (☎ 886-0148), 11 miles northeast of Enumclaw via Farman Rd, has 50 campsites (and showers!) for $10 to $14. It's a popular put-in spot for floating the Green River Gorge.

*The White Rose Inn* (☎ 825-7194, (800) 404-7194), 1610 Griffin Ave, is a B&B with rooms at $90, all with private baths.

*Best Western Park Center Hotel* (☎ 825-4490), 1000 Griffin Ave, has singles/doubles for $60/65. It's downtown on Enumclaw's main street (paralleling Hwy 410, one block to the north).

*Baumgartner's Deli* (☎ 825-1067), 1008 E Roosevelt (also known as Hwy 410), is known to locals and park-goers as a place for delicious sandwiches and cheesecake. Have them make a couple of extra sandwiches to eat on the trail – and save those energy bars and dehydrated dinners for another trip.

## GREEN RIVER GORGE

This river preserve, 12 miles north of Enumclaw on Hwy 169, has hiking trails, caves and fossils, not to mention great canoeing (there are several put-in spots). At Flaming Geyser State Park (☎ 931-3930), a subset of the recreation area, methane fuels two geysers, which were originally test holes for gas and coal exploration. There is a six-inch flame on one geyser; the other one bubbles away in a spring, where its methane has dyed the creekbed gray. There are more opportunities for floating or fishing the Green River at Flaming Geyser State Park.

## FEDERATION FOREST STATE PARK

Federation Forest State Park's 612 acres of virgin forest provide a respite from the heavily logged Weyerhaeuser land nearby and is a pleasant spot for a low-key picnic

or nature walk. The park, 17 miles east of Enumclaw on Hwy 410, has an interpretive center and a couple of miles of trails, partly incorporating the historic Naches Trail. The Naches Trail, between Fort Walla Walla and Fort Steilacoom, was used by pioneers from 1853, when the Longmire party crossed the mountains, until about 1884, when easier routes across the Cascades gained favor.

## CRYSTAL MOUNTAIN RESORT

One of the largest and most popular ski areas in Washington, Crystal Mountain Resort (☎ 663-2265, (800) 852-1444) offers year-round recreational activities. This downhill ski resort is just outside the boundaries of Mt Rainier National Park on the northeast corner. It's six miles north on Hwy 410 and about 36 miles east of Enumclaw.

Downhill skiers give Crystal Mountain high marks for its variety of terrain, which includes some very steep chutes and remote, unpatrolled backcountry trails. The vertical drop is 3120 feet and is served by 10 lifts. There are also 34 backcountry trails for advanced skiers. Lift tickets range from weekend rates of $31 to early week rates of $15. There's night skiing Friday through Sunday till 10 pm. The resort offers a full range of rentals (including cross-country skis) and ski instruction classes. Snowboarding is very popular.

During the summer, a $7 chairlift ride leads to several fairly easy hiking and mountain biking trails. Resort staff can provide complete trail information. The popular lift-top restaurant offers a good view of Mt Rainier.

You can rent a mountain bike at the resort's sport shop (☎ (800) 766-9297) for an hour for $5 or for a half/whole day for $15/20. Just downhill from the base of the lifts, a swimming pool and hot tub ($2 admission) may be enticing to park-goers who have been camping a little too long and hiking a little too vigorously.

Call 626-5208 for information on transportation between Seattle and Crystal Mountain.

### Places to Stay & Eat

As you might expect, the accommodations are all managed by the resort, and they offer a bewildering array of package deals, with cut-rate prices during the off-season. Since there are so many price variations, it's best just to call either the *Alpine Inn* (☎ 663-2262) or the telephone operator who services all the other lodgings (☎ 663-2558) and ask their advice. In a nutshell, the *Alpine Inn* is the budget place, with no-frills rooms from $40 (shared bath) or $50 (private shower). The *Village Inn*, from $65 to $77, and the *Quicksilver Lodge*, a touch fancier at about $95, have rooms with TV, VCR and refrigerator. Groups of four or more should look into renting a condominium: one-bedroom apartments at *Silver Skis Chalet* or *Crystal Chalets* start at about $115.

A full range of cafes, restaurants and bars cater to skiers. During the winter, the restaurant in the *Alpine Inn* (☎ 663-2262) has the best food, but it closes down in the summer. If you're here then, go to the *Summit House* (☎ 663-2300) at the top of the lift, which replaces its wintertime cafeteria food with sit-down 'sunset dinners' in the summer.

### GOAT ROCKS WILDERNESS AREA

The Goat Rocks Wilderness Area is wonderful high country, with great craggy rocks, mountain goats and views of the surrounding Cascade peaks. Goat Rocks was originally a 12,000-foot-high volcano; long extinct, it has eroded into several peaks averaging 8000 feet. Since it's largely above the timberline, hiking season starts late (July) and ends early (late September). The **Pacific Crest Trail** (PCT) passes through the most spectacular section of the wilderness area. It's a huge hike, 25 to 30 miles total, with the best parts coming about halfway in, making for no easy in-and-out trip.

However, for experienced hikers, there is a shorter way to get to the heart of the Goat Rocks. From Packwood, drive a few miles west on Hwy 12, then turn south on USFS

Rd 21, take a left just past Hugo Lake onto USFS Rd 2150, which goes to the trailhead at Chambers Lake, some 21 miles from Packwood. Begin hiking at Chambers Lake to Snowgrass Flat (trail No 96), then cut over on a side trail to the PCT. It's about five miles from the trailhead to the PCT, and at that point you're within a mile of good camping spots near some glaciers. The Goat Rocks themselves are stunning, and another three miles up to Elks Pass on the PCT leads to magnificent mountain vistas.

To make a loop back to Chambers Lake, cut cross-country from the glacier-side camp over to Goat Lake. Pick up trail No 86 at Goat Lake; it turns into trail No 95 and returns via a very nice but rugged trail back to the Chambers Lake trailhead. Water is limited along this route; take a good filter and get streamflow or snow off the glaciers.

For more hikes in Goat Rocks, see *100 Hikes in the South Cascades and Olympics* by Ira Spring & Harvey Manning (The Mountaineers, Seattle, 1992).

### RANDLE

Randle, a crossroads town between Mt Rainier and Mt St Helens, doesn't pretend to be anything fancy or upscale. Stay here if 'convenient' and 'cheap' are important words in your vocabulary.

*Maple Grove Campground & RV Park* (☎ 497-2741) is on Hwy 12 in Randle and has sites for $10 to $15 a night.

*Tall Timber Motel* (☎ 497-2991), on Hwy 12 in Randle, has an attached coffee-shop and single/double rooms for $40/45. *Medici Motel* (☎ 497-7700), three miles south of Hwy 12 on Hwy 131, is a modest place with kitchenette rooms for $35. Two of the four rooms share a bath.

Randle's *Big Bottom Cafe* (☎ 497-9982) may seem a little intimidating – the parking lot is full of huge American pickups and the bar is full of giant men – but it is *the* place to get a decent steak in town, and they are used to serving people who are just passing through.

# Mt St Helens

Where were you when Mt St Helens blew? For most people in the Pacific Northwest, the events of May 18, 1980, are as welded into memory as the dates of the bombing of Pearl Harbor and the assassination of John F Kennedy. Mt St Helens erupted with the force of 21,000 atomic bombs, leveling hundreds of sq miles of forest and spreading volcanic ash across the Northwest and as far northeast as Saskatchewan province, Canada. After the smoke cleared, Mt St Helens, once a comely and symmetrical 9677-foot Cascade mountain covered with glaciers, had blown 1300 feet off its peak, and a mile-wide crater yawned on its north side. Spirit Lake, once a resort destination below the peak, was totally clogged with fallen timber and debris, and the rivers that flowed off the mountain were flooded with mud and ash flows.

In 1982, 172 sq miles around the mountain were included in the **Mt St Helens**

## When Mt St Helens Erupted

The most recent Mt St Helens eruption was first anticipated in March 1980, when small steam clouds began to build above the mountain and earthquakes rocked the area. Initially, geologists thought that the pyrotechnics were simply the result of ground water reaching the molten core of the mountain and not of rising lava. In fact, it wasn't until late in the process that scientists realized that a major eruption was imminent.

Even though the state police worked to evacuate the Mt St Helens area prior to the eruption, some people who had always lived near the mountain simply chose to stay and take their chances, while others ignored the warnings and snuck in to watch the volcano. The most famous of those who stayed behind was Harry Truman, the proprietor of a resort on Spirit Lake. He was among the people killed on the mountain when the blast took place.

The 1980 Mt St Helens eruption was one of steam, not lava. The molten rock that rose to the surface of the volcano was heavily infused with water, which at temperatures of 750°F, is capable of enormous explosive power. As this piston of lava pushed closer and closer to the surface, it created a bulge on the north side of the peak, which grew larger and more unstable with each passing day. On May 18, the rock finally gave way: the entire north face of Mt St Helens slid down the mountain in what geologist believe was the largest landslide in recorded history. The landslide carried mud, snow, ice and rock at speeds of 200 mph, dumping them into Spirit Lake and 17 miles down the North Fork Toutle River valley. The mudflows were over 800°F; they turned Spirit Lake into a boiling cauldron that instantly killed all fish and animal life.

Without the rock cover to hold them back, super-heated steam and gases finally broke through to the surface of the volcano, blasting a 15-mile-high cloud of ash and rock into the air at speeds of 500 mph. The blast, carrying scorching temperatures and poisonous gases, hurtled through the forests north of the crater at speeds of 200 mph, leveling 150 sq miles of forest in an instant.

The amount of mud and ash that was eventually carried downriver was enormous; watch at I-5 exit No 52 for 100-foot-high banks of dredged white ash along the Toutle River, now covered with gorse. Even navigation on the Columbia River was affected, as huge deposits of mud and ash closed the shipping channels between Portland and the Pacific for weeks.

In the end, 59 people were killed in the blast; another 190 who were within the affected zone lived through the eruption. Almost 1000 people were left homeless, mostly along the Toutle River. Downwind from the eruption, several inches of ash settled between Yakima and Spokane, disrupting businesses, schools and life in general for many weeks. Many years later, drifts of ash left by the region's snowplows were still visible beside roads. Mt St Helens has remained calm since 1980, but geologists concur that another explosion is only a matter of time. ∎

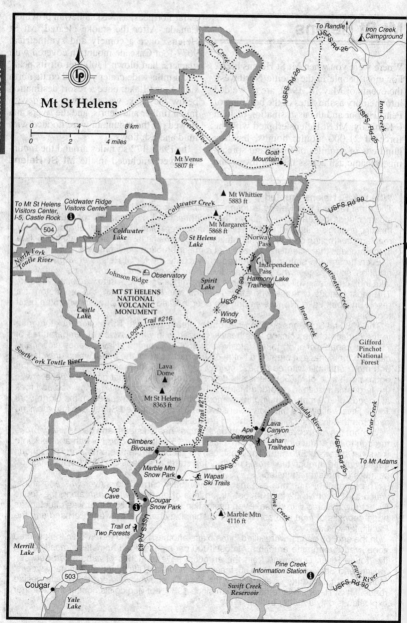

WASHINGTON

# Mt St Helens

0        4        8 km
0        2        4 miles

To Randle

USFS Rd 26

Iron Creek
Campground

Goat Creek

USFS Rd 26

USFS Rd 25

Iron Creek

Green River

Mt Venus
5807 ft

Goat
Mountain

To Mt St Helens
Visitors Center,
I-5, Castle Rock

Coldwater Ridge
Visitors Center

504

Coldwater Creek

Mt Whittier
5883 ft

USFS Rd 99

Coldwater
Lake

Mt Margaret
5868 ft

St Helens
Lake

Norway
Pass

North Fork
Toutle River

Johnson Ridge

Observatory

Spirit
Lake

Independence
Pass

Harmony Lake
Trailhead

MT ST HELENS
NATIONAL
VOLCANIC
MONUMENT

USFS Rd 99

Windy
Ridge

Clearwater Creek

Bean Creek

Gifford
Pinchot
National
Forest

Castle
Lake

Loowit Trail #216

South Fork Toutle River

Lava
Dome

Mt St Helens
8363 ft

Loowit Trail #216

Muddy River

Ape
Canyon

Lava
Canyon

Lahar
Trailhead

Clear Creek

USFS Rd 25

Climbers'
Bivouac

USFS Rd 83

To Mt Adams

Marble Mtn
Snow Park

USFS Rd 83

Wapati
Ski Trails

Ape
Cave

Cougar
Snow Park

Marble Mtn
4116 ft

Pine Creek

Trail of
Two Forests

USFS Rd 83

Merrill
Lake

503

Cougar

Yale
Lake

Pine Creek
Information Station

Swift Creek
Reservoir

Lewis River

USFS Rd 90

**National Volcanic Monument**. The USFS has recently completed a second access road and visitors center in the blast area, and trails have reopened much of the mountain to hikers and skiers. More than a decade later, nature is already beginning to restore life to the mountain.

Native American legends depicted Mt St Helens as the youngest of the fire mountains of Oregon and Washington, and it likely is. Much of the volcano is less than 2000 years old. The mountain was known to have erupted several times in the 19th century, and significantly in 1857. Radio-carbon studies of trees in nearby forests suggest that there is a pattern to the volcano's eruption. After several centuries of quiescence, the mountain explodes several times in decade-spaced intervals, and again falls into a – geologically – short slumber.

The devastation wrought by the eruption is an incredible sight, and one that will haunt your thoughts for days. A trip to either the east or westside crater viewpoints is strongly recommended; if you can, take the time to hike and explore this unique area.

## ORIENTATION

Mt St Helens is directly east of Castle Rock in a remote part of the Gifford Pinchot National Forest. The area was never particularly well served by roads, and the eruption destroyed the few that existed. Today, there are two principal entry routes into the region. The **Windy Ridge viewpoint**, on the northeast side of the mountain, was the first opened and is accessed by long drives on winding USFS roads. The newest entry point is the **Coldwater Ridge Visitor Center**, on the northwest side of the mountain. This viewpoint is easily accessed from I-5 off Hwy 504 and is open year round.

Mt St Helens can be visited as a day-trip from either Portland or Seattle. The town of Castle Rock is about one hour's drive north of Portland on I-5; it's another hour from Castle Rock east to Coldwater Ridge. Castle Rock is a little over two hours south of Seattle. To reach the Windy Ridge area from I-5 requires two more hours.

## INFORMATION

There are two major information centers on the way to Mt St Helens. If you are heading to the Windy Ridge area from the south on Hwy 503, stop at Mt St Helens Volcanic Monument headquarters (☎ 247-5473), 42218 NE Yale Bridge Rd, Amboy, WA 98601. Just off I-5 exit No 49 near Castle Rock, on the way to Coldwater Ridge, is the Mt St Helens Visitor Center (☎ 274-2103), 3029 Spirit Lake Hwy (also known as Hwy 504), Castle Rock, WA 98611. Both offer lots of free information on the mountain and recreation, as well as films and slide shows about the eruption. The Castle Rock visitors center has a particularly impressive series of exhibits about the Cascade volcanoes and post-eruption ecology. You could easily spend an hour just at this visitors center.

Many people also time their visits to take in the film *The Eruption of Mt St Helens* at the Omnimax Theatre (☎ 274-9844) in Castle Rock (on Hwy 504, five miles west of the visitors center). Although not a sanctioned part of the national monument's displays, seeing the eruption in a wraparound theater is pretty exciting and a good reminder of the forces that formed today's Mt St Helens. Call ahead for scheduled showings and ticket prices.

## COLDWATER RIDGE VISITORS CENTER

This center (☎ 274-2131), 45 miles east of Castle Rock and I-5 on Hwy 504, was completed in 1993. After leaving Castle Rock, Hwy 504 climbs steadily to Coldwater Ridge, a 5000-foot-high spur with views directly into the mouth of Mt St Helens' north-facing crater.

The interpretive center is a modern, glass-spined lodge overlooking Coldwater Lake, a long and narrow body of water created by the massive landslide in 1980. The facility provides a wonderful glassed-in viewing area, a theater where a dozen video screens re-create the explosion of Mt St Helens and the rebirth of nature on the mountain, and rooms with interactive displays focusing on the cycles of nature. A

**WASHINGTON**

rather creepy android gives final benediction to hikers before they set out. There's also a bookstore and a cafeteria. A short nature trail called the **Winds of Change** leads from the visitors center and demonstrates the re-growth of vegetation in the area. Interpretive talks and hikes are offered year round; call ahead for a schedule.

Roads lead from Coldwater Ridge Visitors Center down to the lake, and they will eventually continue up to Johnson Ridge Observatory, another visitors center and viewing area that will be completed in 1996 and will look directly into the mouth of the crater. The Coldwater Ridge Visitors Center is open from 9 am to 6 pm from April 1 to September 30, and from 9 am to 5 pm the rest of the year. (Johnson Ridge will have the same hours.) No admission is charged.

## WINDY RIDGE VIEWPOINT

A somewhat more remote vista point is on the northeastern side of the mountain, along Windy Ridge. Partisans often hold that this viewpoint is more impressive than that at Coldwater Ridge; while this is probably true, you will also you spend more time on winding roads to get there.

Windy Ridge is at the terminus of USFS Rd 99, at a car park overlooking log-jammed Spirit Lake and looking directly at the lava dome in the mouth of the crater. The reality of the volcano's power and destruction is everywhere apparent: the road passes by entire forests that were blown down by the tremendous blast of the eruption; boulders and ash are strewn about the mountainside. Trails lead to other viewpoints and down to Spirit Lake. There are toilets and a snack bar at the viewpoint, but no phone or visitors center. Rangers offer interpretive talks and hikes on summer weekends.

To reach Windy Ridge from the north, turn onto USFS Rd 25 at Randle, on Hwy 12 (48 miles east of I-5 exit No 68). Travel 20 miles to the junction of USFS Rd 99. Follow this frequently winding, and – in summer – heavily traveled, gravel road for

another 17 miles to the viewpoint. From the southwest, turn east off I-5 at Woodland (exit No 21) onto Hwy 503, which leads to USFS Rd 90 and the Pine Creek Information Station at the intersection with USFS Rd 25 (in total about 45 miles). Follow USFS Rd 25 for 25 miles, and turn west on USFS Rd 99; the viewpoint is 17 miles distant. Allow at least 1¼ hours for the drive from either Randle or Pine Creek.

## APE CAVE

The longest lava tube in the continental USA, the Ape Cave is also, at 12,810 feet in length, one of the longest underground hiking trails in the USFS trail system. Lava tubes are formed when the exterior of a deep lava flow hardens while the interior continues to flow. Eventually the liquid lava empties out of the crust, leaving a hollow tube with lava walls. In the case of the Ape Cave, the lava flowed down a deep watercourse; the top of the ravine sealed, but the lava continued to flow underground.

Hikers can walk and scramble the length of the Ape Cave on two trails, both beginning at an informational kiosk just off USFS Rd 8303. The three-quarter-mile **Lower Ape Cave Trail** follows the cave downstream from the main entrance. This part of the cave has a dry sandy bottom and nearly 20-foot-high ceilings, and it is by far the easier walk. There is no exit at this end of the cave, so you need to retrace your steps to get out. The 1.5-mile **Upper Ape Cave Trail** requires a lot of scrambling over rock piles and narrower passages. The trail eventually exits at the upper entrance. Hikers can rent lanterns at the Ape Cave headquarters for $3.

Free half-hour, ranger-led explorations of the Ape Cave are offered from June 15 through September 5. Monday through Friday these Ape Cave lantern walks are offered at 12:30, 1:30 and 2:30 pm. On weekends, the tours are held on the half hour from 11:30 am to 4:30 pm.

Also in the Ape Cave area is the wheelchair-accessible **Trail of Two Forests**, a quarter-mile boardwalk along a stream and a lava cast forest. Interpretive displays explain the process of reforestation at this ancient lava flow.

By the way, the reference to 'ape' in the name of this cave and a nearby canyon has nothing to do with primates. A group of boy-scout adventurers took to calling themselves the Mt St Helens Apes after a purported sighting of Big Foot in Ape Canyon in 1924. Members of this group discovered this cave in 1946, hence the name.

## HIKING

A number of short interpreted hikes leave from Coldwater Ridge and the lake, though to reach the principal Mt St Helens trail network from here requires a long slog across desolate pumice fields and mudflows, which can be oppressively hot on a sunny day. Hikers are better advised to begin hikes from Windy Ridge or the south side of the mountain. In any case, take along plenty of water, as there is very little natural water along these barren, dry trails.

Named after the female spirit that inhabits Mt St Helens in Native American myth, the **Loowit Trail No 216** is a 27-mile trail system that circles the mountain. Because of the extremely rugged terrain, be sure to check with rangers before setting out for an extended hike, as washouts and landslides are common. The most popular portion of the trail crosses the face of the crater on the mountain's north side. The easiest access to the Loowit Trail is from Windy Ridge viewpoint.

The **Lahar Trailhead** in Ape Canyon provides access to a number of different hikes into wild volcanic landscapes, including a barrier-free path along a recent mudflow to a waterfall vista. The all-abilities trail is the beginning portion of the 2.4-mile **Lava Canyon Trail**; however, after the first half mile the trail drops down into a steep canyon scoured out by the Mt St Helens eruption. The trail is for the intrepid, but it's great fun. A second trail ascends along a wooded ridge top beside a barren mudflow. The **Ape Canyon Trail** passes through patches of old-growth forest before reaching a deep and narrow chasm cut in the flanks of the mountain. At 5.5

miles, the trail ties into the Loowit Trail No 216.

The long access roads leading into Spirit Lake and Windy Ridge offer several trailheads, including access to the following day hikes. The most popular hike in the area is called the **Harmony Lake Trail**, which leads down past scorched tree stumps to the shores of Spirit Lake. Although the hike is just over a mile in length, it is fairly steep going. The trailhead is about two miles north of Windy Ridge viewpoint on USFS Rd 99.

The views from **Norway Pass** are among the best in the monument, with Mt St Helens and its open-jawed crater rising directly above the timber-cluttered Spirit Lake. To reach this overview, take the 2.5-mile **Norway Pass Trail** from the trailhead on USFS Rd 26, one mile north of the junction of USFS Rds 99 and 26. Hikers with a shuttle can make a loop by returning along the **Independence Pass Trail** from Norway Ridge. This 3.5 mile trail begins on USFS Rd 99 at the Independence Pass trailhead, 2.5 miles south of the junction of USFS Rd 99 and 26.

From Windy Ridge viewpoint itself, the **Truman Trail** leads directly toward the mountain, offering the quickest approach to the crater itself and to the around-mountain Loowit Trail. Even so, it's a hot and desolate four-mile trudge before reaching the crater.

## SKIING

The southern part of the monument has a number of snow parks off USFS Rd 83. In winter, Cougar Snow Park accesses a number of snowed-in USFS roads near the Ape Cave; Marble Mountain Snow Park offers access to more snowbound roads and to Wapiti Meadows, with many miles of groomed trails. (The NPS does not rent cross-country skis in this area, but Jack's Restaurant does.)

## CLIMBING

Because Mt St Helens is a very delicate and sometimes dangerous mountain, climbers must obtain a permit to ascend the peak between May 15 and October 31. The permits are free, but because the number is limited to 100 hikers per day, competition is fierce for summer weekends. Permits are available by contacting the monument headquarters in Amboy (see the preceding Information section); one permit can cover up to 12 people, and the permit is good for 24 hours. For up-to-the-minute information on climbing Mt St Helens, call the Climbers Hotline at 750-3961.

Permits for an additional 40 climbers are available on a first-come, first-serve basis from Jack's Restaurant & Store (☎ 231-4276), five miles west of Cougar on USFS Rd 90, which serves as a de facto headquarters for Mt St Helens climbs. The day before you want to climb, you need to sign up at Jack's; they start taking names at 11 am and issue the permits at 6 pm, and you must be present to receive them. All climbers are required to sign in at the climber's register at Jack's both before and after the climb.

Most climbers leave from the trailhead 216B at the end of USFS Rd 830, off USFS Rd 83, a total of 14 miles northeast of Cougar. No technical climbing abilities are needed, particularly in late summer after all the snow has melted. However, the climb isn't fun and games, as most of the quite steep ascent involves struggling up loose pumice fields. The five-mile trail ends at the summit cliffs, with astonishing views down onto the smoking lava dome and the incinerated viscera of the mountain. Be very careful of the lip of the crater, as the rock here is very unstable. Allow at least eight hours to make the roundtrip. Early in the season, bring along a sheet of plastic and slide down the snow fields for a fast descent.

### PLACES TO STAY & EAT

Mt St Helens is a pretty remote area and facilities are quite limited. There are a couple of diners and motels in Castle Rock, and a rustic lodge at Cougar, but most people will choose to camp or to make this a day-trip from a larger center.

Campgrounds aren't all that easy to find

in this burned-up landscape, either. Campsites are most abundant on the south side of the monument, away from the main force of the explosion. *Yale Lake* and *Swift Reservoir,* on the Lewis River, are both just south of the mountain and offer five lakeside campgrounds popular with motor boaters. Since the slopes along the Lewis River have recently been clear-cut, this is a fairly unenthralling place to get away from it all. To the north of Mt St Helens (on USFS Rd 25 near the junction with USFS Rd 26) is *Iron Creek Campground,* the only campground in the monument itself. Facilities include running water and pit toilets. The $6 sites, of which there are nearly 100, go quickly in summer, and can be reserved by calling MISTIX (☎ (800) 283-2267).

To the east at Castle Rock is *Seaquest State Park,* open year round with nearly 100 campsites offering running water and flush toilets. Seaquest is directly across from the entrance to the Mt St Helens Visitor Center, five miles west of I-5 exit No 49 on Hwy 504.

The nicest place to stay in Castle Rock is the *Mt St Helens Motel* (☎ 274-7721), 1340 Mt St Helens Way NE, where single/double rooms are $44/48. There are a number of family restaurants adjacent.

# Mt Adams

Mt Adams, at 12,276 feet, is the second-highest peak in Washington, and it towers over the beautiful and mostly undeveloped meadows and valleys of south-central Washington. It is one of the most beautiful of the Cascade peaks, with some enchanting hikes and an easy ascent to the mountain's summit. However, Mt Adams also has the distinction of being one of the least visited and under-utilized mountain areas in the Northwest. Oregonians, who have the easiest access to Mt Adams from Portland and I-84, prefer to visit their own peaks, particularly Mt Hood, and getting to Mt Adams from most parts of Washington requires a lot of driving, much of it right past other alluring mountains. Also, the entire eastern slope of Mt Adams is enclosed in the Yakama Indian Reservation, and with a couple of significant exceptions, the land is not open to non-tribal members.

What this means is that hikers and campers will find Mt Adams relatively secluded, certainly compared with the throngs visiting its more popular and famous siblings. During the winter, snowed-in logging roads yield miles of cross-country ski trails near Trout Lake. Routes are well-signed and trail maps are available at the ranger station.

The **Mt Adams Wilderness Area**, a 66-sq-mile preserve, includes the mountain's summit and the western half of the mountain. While hiking, climbing and cross-country skiing are popular pastimes here, a more unique activity in the Mt Adams area is huckleberry picking. The high meadows around the mountain are famed for their late summer crop of this wild blueberry.

Mt Adams was known to early native tribes as Klickitat or Pah-to. Many myths and legends pit the spirit of Mt Adams against that of Mt Hood, directly south in Oregon. Inevitably, their conflicts ended with each shooting fire and smoke at the other. Mt Adams is considered a sacred site to the Yakama tribe.

Mt Adams is also geologically unique among Cascade peaks, as it is composed of a number of separate volcanic cones, each of which erupted at different times, whereas most volcanoes erupt from a single core. These multiple cones lend Mt Adams its distinctive broadly domed appearance. Mt Adams first began erupting about 450,000 years ago, though the peak we see today was largely formed about 15,000 years ago, toward the end of the most recent ice age. Ten major glaciers still cling to the mountain.

## ORIENTATION

The easiest access to Mt Adams is from the Columbia River Gorge, from either I-84 or Hwy 14. From Hood River or White Salmon to the south, take Hwy 141 north

Mt Adams (BM)

(about 25 miles) to Trout Lake, a tiny community that's nonetheless the head of recreation in the area. In summer, USFS Rd 23, a fair graveled road, is open between Randle, south of Mt Rainier on Hwy 12, and Trout Lake (a three-hour drive).

## INFORMATION

For information on hiking or climbing, consult the Gifford Pinchot National Forest ranger stations, which are at 2455 Hwy 141 in Trout Lake (☎ (509) 395-2501) and in Randle (☎ 497-1100). If you plan to pick huckleberries or mushrooms in the national forest, stop here to get permits. Maps of the Mt Adams Wilderness Area and the Indian Heaven Wilderness Area can be picked up for $1 each. They can also be mail ordered through the Forest Supervisor, Gifford Pinchot National Forest, 500 West 12th St, Vancouver, WA 98660.

## HIKING

Two famous trails capture the beauty and vastness of Mt Adams. The slightly misnamed **Around the Mountain Trail**, also known as Trail 9, skirts the southern base of the mountain for 8.3 miles between the

Bird Creek area, at the trailhead off USFS Rd 8290, and the **Pacific Crest Trail** (PCT), which enters the wilderness from the southwest. The PCT continues around to the north side of Mt Adams and branches north before entering the Yakama Indian Reservation. These two trails manage to traverse about half of the mountain's girth, mostly at timberline and mostly at a gentle grade. The views of surrounding Cascade peaks are incredible. It's about 25 miles from the Bird Creek trailhead to the northern border of the wilderness area (via the PCT). There are no base trails on the mountain's east side, which belongs to the tribe.

To those who know it, the **Bird Creek Meadow Trail** is one of the best loved hikes in the Northwest. The three-mile loop trail leads from the Bird Creek trailhead and gently climbs to an alpine meadow showered by waterfalls and ablaze with wildflowers. Looming above are the cliffs and glaciers of Mt Adams' summit. After ascending to a ridge-top viewpoint, the trail loops back beside tiny lakes and yet more wildflowers. The best time to hike the trail is in July, when blooms are at their peak and most of the trails will be free of ice.

Both of the above trails begin in a small, western portion of the Yakama Indian Reservation that is open to non-Yakamas. However, to hike or camp in this area requires paying a $5-per-vehicle fee to the tribe. The Around the Mountain Trail can also be accessed from the Morrison Creek or Cold Creek campground trailheads, outside the reservation, but Bird Creek Meadows is entirely within the reservation and subject to the fee.

## CLIMBING

Mt Adams is known as one of the easiest Cascade peaks to climb, and it's often used as a trial peak for beginners. Although most climbs on Mt Adams are non-technical slogs up a glacier, even these require basic climbing gear. Altitude sickness and severe weather changes are the biggest threats to novice climbers.

The easiest approaches (Grade II) are from the south, via Cold Creek Camp-

ground, and up the South Spur to the summit. These approaches are good between May and August. There's a more difficult route (Grade III) from the north over Adams Glacier via Takhlakh Lake Campground. Climbers should sign in and out at the USFS ranger station at either Trout Lake or Randle.

## PLACES TO STAY & EAT

Though there are some lovely campgrounds on Mt Adams, be prepared for insect pests during the summer. Near Bird Creek Meadows are three lakeside campgrounds in the Yakama Indian Reservation (☎ (509) 865-5121, ext 657). Sites are $10 a night in addition to the $5 entrance fee

---

**Stalking the Wild Huckleberry**

The huckleberry is a wild blueberry, admired for its tangy flavor. It can be eaten fresh, made up into pies, jams and any number of ice-cream and chocolate confections. The huckleberry was an integral part of the Native American diet. Tribes made summer excursions to the high mountain meadows where these low, brushy huckleberry plants flourish; the berries were often dried for winter use.

Southwest of Mt Adams are some of the largest and most productive wild huckleberry meadows in the Northwest. The elevation is high – usually above 4000 feet – but quite flat due to the underlying lava flows. This land of marsh and lake is perfect for huckleberries – as it is for mosquitoes, so be warned.

Huckleberry season is usually August through September, and a number of USFS-administered areas are open for berry picking. Free USFS permits are necessary, and rangers will also offer advice and maps indicating where the harvest is most productive. Traditionally, the best berry picking is in the Sawtooth Berryfields, an area immediately north of the Indian Heaven Wilderness Area. Follow signs for the Surprise Lakes or Cold Springs campgrounds, off USFS Rd 24, about 21 miles west of Trout Lake. ∎

and all have running water and pit toilets. The campgrounds at *Bird Lake*, 20 sites, and *Mirror Lake*, 12 sites, are about 16 miles east of Trout Lake on USFS Rds 82 and 8290. Two miles farther down this rough road is *Bench Lake Campground*, with 44 sites and great views of Mt Adams; the final stretch of the road is especially steep and rutted.

There's another cluster of lakeside USFS campgrounds about 25 miles north along Hwy 23. The nicest of these is *Takhlakh Lake Campground*, which has 54 sites with running water and pit toilets. It costs $5 a night. From here, you can hike into the *Chain of Lakes Campground*, less than a mile away, for more seclusion; this primitive campground has three sites and is free.

There are two B&Bs in Trout Lake, both with restaurants. The *Trout Lake Country Inn* (☎ (509) 395-2894), 15 Guler Rd, is also a weekend dinner theater. Rooms cost $60, and the dinner theater on Saturday nights costs $17. Also in Trout Lake, *Mio Amore Pensione* (☎ 395-2264) is on Little Mountain Rd off Hwy 141. Rooms run $60 to $135. The North Italian dinner costs $25; the dining room is open to non-guests, but reservations are required.

*Flying L Ranch* (☎ 364-3488), 25 Flying L Lane in Glenwood, is about 18 miles from Trout Lake off Glenwood Rd. Rooms in the lodge and guesthouse cost $65 to $90; cabins are $100. Prices include breakfast and use of a common kitchen. Recreation packages are available in the summer.

The other option for food in Trout Lake is *Bonnie's Place Cafe* (☎ 395-2747), 2376 Hwy 141, a traditional diner. *Tsugali's Deli* (☎ 395-2269), 2385 Hwy 141, offers picnic supplies and heaping scoops of huckleberry ice cream.

# Northern Cascades

The Cascade Range starts in Canada and runs all the way south to northern California, but the North Cascades refer specifically to the rugged, chiseled alpine peaks in northern Washington. Indeed, with their hanging glaciers and valleys, their icefalls and cirque-cradled lakes, these particular mountains are so thoroughly alpine in character that it's tempting to call them, as John Muir did, the 'American Alps'.

Rocky, glaciated and wild, the North Cascades are well known to Northwest climbers, hikers, bicyclists, anglers and auto tourists, all of whom tend to give a little sigh of awe before they launch into descriptions of this majestic land. However, don't expect to happen across a motel or lodge, or even much of a cabin resort, between Marblemount and Mazama. Due to the lack of facilities, most people merely drive through, but as with the Olympic Mountains, the most beautiful and dramatic sights of this rocky terrain are found off road – by hiking one of the numerous trails or climbing to the crests of the mountain's ridges. Campgrounds, both formal and de facto, abound in the North Cascades. And it's best to come prepared with enough food to see you through your stay, be that a bag of chips to nibble as you drive or a week's worth of camp chow.

Mount Baker, just west of the national park, is extremely popular, not only because it offers some of the best hiking, climbing and skiing in the state but because there's a little more in the way of accommodations and even a few good restaurants nearby. Farther south, the area around Darrington is another major access to the North Cascades; it has plenty of hiking, and climbers head for Glacier Peak.

The Cascades are the spine of the Northwest, wringing out Pacific storm fronts like a wet sponge. They divide the land and the state, creating wet, forested slopes and valleys to the west and leaving the plains to the east bone dry. Go prepared for snow, expect rain, and given some luck, the sun will shine long enough to see the peaks. If anything, the weather is changeable. Hikers should take this seriously, and pack for rain and cold weather even in summer.

On the east side of the mountains, the Stehekin River flows down out of the mountains and feeds into Lake Chelan, the third-deepest lake in the USA and another beautiful center for recreation or relaxation in this gorgeous corner of the state. Cross-country skiers flock to the Methow valley in the winter from miles around – the trails here are excellent and the weather is generally much better than at Mt Baker.

## HISTORY

Native people, like most modern folks, didn't make year-round homes in the North Cascades. Though Native Americans traveled to the North Cascades in the summer for roots, berries, hunting and fishing, they didn't really stick around once the snow began to pile up. Trails first traveled by Native Americans between the Puget Sound and the Columbia Basin are still hiked today; the popular Cascade Pass trail was one link in this traders' route.

When Whites arrived, it took them about 70 years to find a way into and through the mountains. The first to make it through was a cartographer in the army's employ. Miners kept hoping to strike it rich in the mountains, but few managed to eke out any type of living from the rocky, remote streams.

It took power-thirsty Seattle to put any kinds of reins on this rugged country. The abundant water cascading down steep drops caught the eyes of engineers, and in the 1920s and '30s a series of dams were built along the Upper Skagit River, turning this section of the river into reservoirs and stringing the valleys with power lines. The

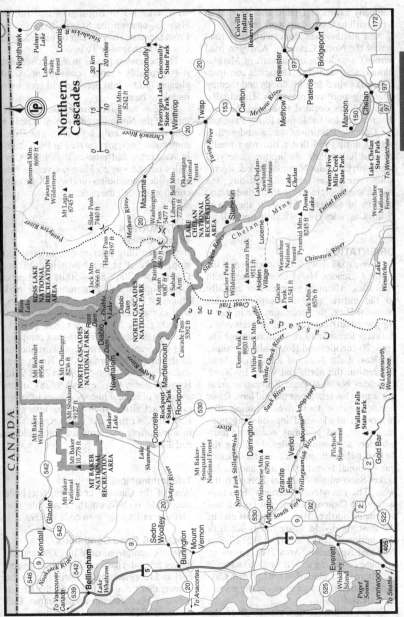

Northern Cascades

company towns of Diablo and Newhalem were built to house dam workers.

And all this was done without a road across the North Cascades. A wagon road across Cascade Pass, southeast of Marblemount, was started in 1896, but construction was halted first by floods and then by changing political pressures. Eventually, road builders decided to extend the road that reached to Diablo over Rainy Pass, and the Cascade Pass route was abandoned. It wasn't until 1968 that a dirt road finally crossed Rainy Pass; during the same year the North Cascades National Park & Recreation Area was created, shifting the region's economic focus from timber and mining to tourism. In 1972, the paved North Cascades Hwy officially opened.

## ORIENTATION

Only one road, Hwy 20 (also known as the North Cascades Hwy) crosses the North Cascades. Although people refer casually to the entire area as North Cascades National Park, the mountains are in fact a jigsaw of different parks, wildernesses, national forests and recreation areas. The Hwy 20 corridor and Ross Lake constitute the Ross Lake National Recreation Area, flanked on the north and south by North Cascades National Park. Recreation areas are somewhat less protected and have fewer restrictions on their use, meaning that hikers can take leashed dogs on recreation-area trails, and you may encounter four-wheelers and snowmobiles. Flanking the 781-sq-mile national park are the Okanogan National Forest to the east and the Mt Baker-Snoqualmie National Forest to the west. The Pasayten Wilderness Area falls within the Okanogan National Forest, and is situated north of Hwy 20 and just east of the Cascade divide. Immediately south of the national park is the Lake Chelan National Recreation Area. The upshot of all these confusing administrative factors is that there is no admission fee to North Cascades National Park or to any of the associated areas.

To get to the North Cascades from the west, take I-5 to Burlington and follow Hwy 20 east up the Skagit River valley. From the east, Hwy 20 can be picked up at Omak, Okanogan or Twisp.

The nearest airport is in Wenatchee, but it's probably more convenient (and cheaper) to fly into Sea-Tac and pick up a rental car there.

There is no public transportation to or through the North Cascades. You'll need a car or, for the hardy, a bicycle. The Bike-centennial Trail, inaugurated in 1976, starts in Anacortes and crosses the North Cascades on the way to Maine. Cyclists ride alongside automobiles on Hwy 20, the only corridor through the park.

## INFORMATION
### Tourist Offices

If you can only tolerate one information stop, make it at the Newhalem Visitor Center (☎ (206) 873-4500), right next to the Newhalem Campground. The park offices (☎ 855-1331) are in Sedro Woolley, well to the west of the mountains, at 800 State St (Hwy 20). You can pick up back-country permits here for off-road camping.

If you want a more in-depth introduction to the area's wilderness, the North Cascades Institute (☎ 856-5700, ext 209), 2105 Hwy 20, Sedro Woolley, WA 98284, offers a variety of natural history classes incorporating activities such as backpacking, kayaking, writing and photography. The institute offers programs for both children and adults.

### Telecommunications

West of the Cascade crest, the telephone area code is 360; on the east side (the Methow valley), the area code is 509.

### Weather & Road Conditions

Hwy 20, completed only in 1972, usually closes around Thanksgiving (late November) and reopens around April. During the winter, don't count on driving the stretch between Marblemount and Mazama. Call (900) 407-7277 for road information.

## MT BAKER

At 10,778 feet, Mt Baker looms over much of northern Washington, providing a craggy, glacier-hung backdrop to Bellingham. The peak was heavily glaciered during the last ice age; after these large glaciers retreated, the mountain was incised with cirques and deep notch-like valleys. Glaciers are still gnawing away at Mt Baker; 10,000 acres of permanent snowfields still cling to the mountain's flanks.

This rugged birthright makes Mt Baker and nearby 9127-foot Mt Shuksan popular destinations for hikers, skiers and climbers. It also means that many of the trails up and around Mt Baker and the surrounding peaks require pretty steep ascents and descents. Also, Mt Baker's far northwest location (only 15 miles south of the Canadian border) means that precipitation, mostly snow, positively dumps here. Hiking trails may not be free of snowpack until August. All that snow is good news to skiers: the Mt Baker Ski Area has the deepest base in the state, and informal cross-country trails open up the wilderness to adventurous Nordic skiers.

The rugged and snow-bound territory around Mt Baker wasn't of much interest to either natives or to White settlers until rumors of gold brought prospectors swarming into the North Fork Nooksack River in the 1890s and 1900s. Although hard rock mining did briefly flourish in the area, difficult climate made transportation and exploration difficult. Logging soon replaced mining as the primary economic force in the area.

Mt Baker was first climbed in 1868, and by 1911 ascents of the mountain were common enough for the Bellingham Chamber of Commerce to sponsor a marathon race that included a climb up and down the peak. The annual race was canceled two years later, when one contestant fell into a glacial crevasse and had to be rescued.

Although there were frequent calls throughout this century for the Mt Baker area to be declared a national park, it

---

### The North Cascades Volcanoes

Washington's North Cascades started off as the southern tip of a volcanic microcontinent that included part of present-day British Columbia. Tropical fossils in the North Cascades hint that the erstwhile island had its start in the South Pacific, then drifted north and ran into the Okanogan, which then formed the western edge of North America. As the two bodies of land joined, rocks crumpled to form long north-south ridges, stretching and faulting along the same axis. Volcanoes, present before the micro-continent ever drifted into North America, continued erupting.

But not all the intensely hot rocks spewed out; many were subjected to great pressures and crystalized beneath the earth's surface to form granite. Much of this granite was ultimately pushed upward into new mountains. The metamorphic forces of pressure and heat turned much of the granite into gneisses, which form the North Cascades' characteristic spires and horns. These were carved during several waves of ice ages, beginning about 500,000 years ago. Glaciers carved out long, straight, U-shaped river valleys with exceptionally steep walls, giving the Cascades their distinctive chiseled look. Even today, 318 glaciers continue to work on the rocks. For a good look at rocks and informative park displays, pull off at the Diablo Lake Overlook, milepost 132.

The highest of the North Cascade peaks, Mt Baker is on the edge of the Northern Cascade province. As the Cascade Range began to rise, volcanoes shot up through this older formation. Mount Baker began to erupt about one million years ago, although Mt Baker's present cone was probably built in the last 20,000 years.

Mt Baker is still an active volcano. A summit cinder cone and a 12-mile-long lava flow down Sulfur Creek are probably only 1000 years old, and eruptions of ash were reported in 1843 and 1859. More recently, Mt Baker produced significant steam and ash eruptions in 1975, leading to speculation that the volcano was building up to a major eruption. ■

WASHINGTON

wasn't until 1984 that the region was made a wilderness area.

The peak itself, and 184 sq miles of surrounding public land, are enclosed in the Mt Baker Wilderness Area; adjacent to this is the 8600-acre Mt Baker National Recreation Area. Paved Hwy 542, which climbs up to 5200 feet to a breathtaking vista called Artist Point, has been designated a National Forest Scenic Byway. However, the final 10 miles are very steep and narrow – you may find that some of the switchbacks are themselves breathtaking. If you are pulling a trailer, it's a good idea to leave it at the base of the mountain.

The little community of Glacier (population 200) is basically a smattering of motels and restaurants designed to service skiers. No gasoline is available, so tank up at Kendall.

## Orientation

Generally speaking, there are two ways to get to Mt Baker. The most popular is on Hwy 542, which travels east from Bellingham via Kendall. It's 62 miles from Bellingham to Mt Baker Ski Area. This road is open year round and offers the highest-altitude access point. A second access road, Baker Lake Rd off of Hwy 20 at Concrete, dead-ends at the northern end of the Baker Lake (see below).

## Information

The wilderness area is administered by the Mt Baker-Snoqualmie National Forest ranger station (☎ 856-5700) at 2105 Hwy 20, Sedro Woolley, WA 98284; contact this office for more information about the wilderness, hiking and ski trails.

Additionally, the Glacier Public Service Center (☎ 599-2714), just east of Glacier, is open from 9 am to 5 pm daily, June 15 to September 15, and Thursday through Sunday the rest of the year. At this handsome CCC-built stone lodge is a small bookshop, interpretive displays on the park, and a ranger to answer questions; you can also call here to find out about road closures.

## Mt Baker Hwy Scenic Byway

Even if you're a travel purist and spurn popular vista points, you'll probably want to join the parade of RVs and drive Hwy 542 up to Artist Point, with its incredible views onto Mt Baker and Mt Shuksan. It's a great introduction to this magnificent area, with hiking trails splitting off from the highway to lead to less thronged viewpoints and hidden lakes. This route is open all winter as far as Mt Baker Ski Area; the remaining 2.6 miles to Artist Point are open from mid-July to late October, or until snowfall. Also bear in mind that the final 10 miles of the highway climb 3200 feet. This is a steep and very winding road.

From Glacier, the first 14 miles climb through old-growth fir forests along the North Fork Nooksack River. One stop along this stretch of road ought to be **Nooksack Falls**, which drops 175 feet into a deep gorge. After Silver Fir Campground, the road begins to climb in earnest. Mt Shuksan looms to the east, its glaciers seemingly held back by horn-like peaks. At **Heather Meadows**, the upward climb slows for a moment; the Mt Baker Ski Area is here, and just up the road is **Austin Pass**, a picnic area and the beginning point of several hiking trails.

The road ends at **Artist Point**, at 5200 feet, with views onto the face of both Mt Baker and Mt Shuksan across a tiny reflecting pond. To the north rear rugged peaks in Canada. This is a magical spot, like being at the top of the world.

## Hiking

Many hiking trails around Mt Baker require fairly strenuous climbs up glacier-carved valleys to viewpoints and wildflower meadows; however, several hikes leave from trailheads at the end of lengthy backroad drives and reach the high country in relatively short order.

**Heliotrope Ridge** Most climbers ascend to the top of Mt Baker from Heliotrope Ridge and onto Coleman Glacier. The three-mile, one-way trail to the edge of the glacier is also popular with day hikers in August, when the meadows, at 6200 feet, are ablaze with wildflowers.

To reach this trail, designated as No 677, turn south onto USFS Rd 39 one mile east of Glacier. This unpaved road climbs up the side of Mt Baker for eight miles to the trailhead. After hiking two miles through forest, the trail reaches timberline and then crosses several glacial streams and wildflower meadows. The trail then climbs up onto a moraine and suddenly overlooks Coleman Glacier. The views onto the face of Mt Baker and onto the massive, deeply rivened glacier are incredible. Unless you have climbing gear, don't attempt to make your way onto the glacier or to climb any higher along the frequently snow-packed morainal ridge.

**Excelsior Mountain** From this 5700-foot peak, hikers and Mt Baker view each other eye to eye across the narrow North Fork Nooksack valley. Several steep trails lead to this vantage point from Hwy 542; the following route lets your vehicle do most of the climbing. Drive two miles east of Glacier, and turn at the Douglas Fir Campground onto USFS Rd 31, also called Canyon Creek Rd. Follow this road for almost 15 miles around to the back of Excelsior Mountain. Park at the head of trail No 625, and hike 2.5 miles past Damfino Lakes and meadows to Excelsior Pass. A quarter mile to the east, at the end of an easy path, is Excelsior Peak.

**Lake Ann** One of the most popular hikes in the area is the eight-mile, roundtrip hike up to Lake Ann, shimmering beneath the massive hanging glaciers of Mt Shuksan. The trail to Lake Ann leaves from Austin Pass Picnic Area.

**Chain Lakes Loop** Beginning at the Artist Point parking lot and circling a high plateau, this beautiful six-mile loop trail passes a half dozen icy lakes surrounded by huckleberry meadows. The trail begins at the west end of the parking lot, and the tree-shaded trailhead is sometimes covered

by snow: take the trail that drops into the forest, not the trail that climbs the plateau.

The trail passes Mazama, Iceberg and Hayes lakes, then climbs a ridge to drop onto the first of the two Bagley lakes. Between the two lakes, a trail cuts south and climbs up to Hwy 542, and a short climb up the road returns hikers to their vehicles at Artist Point. Hikers can also continue on the loop trail past the second Bagley Lake, shortly arriving at Mt Baker Ski Area.

### Skiing
Mt Baker Ski Area (☎ 734-6771) offers 1500 feet of alpine ski runs on the dry, eastern side of the mountain. The lodge offers complete rental and instruction facilities. Lift tickets are $27.50 weekends and holidays and $18 midweek. The ski area also offers groomed cross-country trails. Call 671-0211 for a snow report.

The heavy falls of fine, dry snow make Mt Baker the most popular cross-country ski destination in Washington. From the ski area, snowed-in Hwy 542 up to Artist Point and the trail around the Chain Lakes open up great vistas of the snowy peaks. Another popular cross-country ski trailhead is at Silver Fir Campground, where trails lead up meadows along Anderson Creek.

Cross-country ski rentals are available from the ski shop at the Mt Baker Ski Area or from The Outpost or the Base Camp in Bellingham (see Bellingham). State sno-park permits are mandatory at plowed trailheads and are available at local businesses.

### Climbing
The two principal routes up Mt Baker ascend Coleman Glacier, on the northwest side of the mountain, and Easton Glacier, on the south side. Both require two days, with a night spent camping at the base of the glaciered peak.

The easiest route is from the south, up Easton Glacier from the Shreiber Meadow trailhead. Although technical equipment is highly recommended, snowmobiles have been known to ascend Mt Baker along this route. The northern ascent begins at the

Heliotrope Ridge trailhead (see Hiking above) and continues across Coleman and Roosevelt Glaciers for a final steep and icy climb up the North Ridge to the summit.

In addition to the usual dangers from altitude sickness and glacial crevasses, Mt Baker offers the threat of extremely changeable weather. As the peak is only 35 miles from sea level in Puget Sound, moist air can belt across the hills and shroud the peak in clouds and storms in minutes. Take navigational tools along on any high elevation hike, and know how to use them.

Novice climbers should consider classes and guided climbs with the American Alpine Institute (☎ 671-1505), 1515 12th St, Bellingham, WA 98225. AAI is one of the nation's best climbing schools, and they offer a variety of weekend classes as well as longer programs focusing on rock, ice and snow climbing. A three-day ascent of Mt Baker, including instruction in glacier travel, costs $315 to $495, depending on the number of students per guide. They lead two to three climbs weekly during the climbing season (mid-May to September).

### Rafting
White-water rafters put in just above Douglas Fir Campground and raft the North Fork Nooksack, a class III river, to Maple Falls, a total of 10 miles. For a guided raft trip, contact Blue Sky Outfitters (☎ 931-0637), PO Box 124, Pacific, WA 98047.

### Places to Stay & Eat
Several attractive USFS campgrounds are positioned along Hwy 542 and the North Fork Nooksack River. *Douglas Fir Campground* is two miles east of Glacier and *Silver Fir Campground* is 12 miles east of Glacier. Sites at these campgrounds cost $10 and have drinking water and pit toilets.

*Glacier Creek Motel & Cabins* (☎ 559-2991), 10036 Mt Baker Hwy in Glacier, offers lodging either in motel rooms ($42 to $54) or in creek-side cabins, which start at $50 and are $55 with a kitchen. Pets are allowed in the cabins only.

The *Snowline Inn* (☎ 228-0119), 10433 Mt Baker Hwy in Glacier, is on the road to the ski area and offers condominium rooms, all with full kitchen facilities. One-bedroom units start at $40; larger loft units start at $75.

Food is surprisingly good in Glacier. *Milano's Pasta Fresca* (☎ 599-2863), 9990 Mt Baker Hwy, offers fresh pasta – no surprise – in an attractive bistro atmosphere; dinner entrees run $9 to $11. The *Chandelier* (☎ 599-2233), east of Glacier, offers family-style cooking (dinners from $8 to $15) and late-night dancing. The best food in the area is at *Innisfree Restaurant* (☎ 599-2373), 9393 Mt Baker Hwy. Fresh seafood and local trout lead the nightly changing menu, which usually includes lamb and vegetarian dishes.

## DARRINGTON
At another major access point for trekking the Cascade Range, Darrington (population 1085) is a rain-drenched timber town trying its hand at tourism. From here, most people head to the Glacier Peak Wilderness Area and to 10,541-foot Glacier Peak itself. Darrington is also the northern terminus of the **Mountain Loop Hwy** (USFS Rd 20), a woodsy corridor that links Hwys 92 and 530, and which is strewn with trailheads and peppered with the dregs of old mines. Miners went after galena ore, a conglomeration of silver and lead, but the plethora of faulted rock in the nearby hills made it difficult to follow veins very far.

Besides its hiking trails and its timber, Darrington has long been known for its July bluegrass festival – the legacy of the area's many settlers from North Carolina, who brought not only the tunes but bootleg whiskey good enough to make performers out of everyone.

### Orientation & Information
Darrington is 19 miles south of Rockport on Hwy 530, and 28 miles east of the Arlington off I-5. If you're traveling from the Seattle area, this is a good alternative approach to North Cascades National Park. Even more scenic is Hwy 92 and the Mountain Loop Hwy. To reach it, get off I-5 at Arlington (Hwy 530), then head south on

At 10,541 feet, Glacier Peak towers over its Cascade neighbors. (WB)

Jordan Rd to Granite Falls and Hwy 92. Turn east on Hwy 92, and turn north at the Sauk River for the Mountain Loop Hwy till it rejoins Hwy 530 at Darrington.

Stop by the Darrington Ranger Station (☎ 436-1155), 1405 Emmons St, for hiking information. If you're driving the Mountain Loop Hwy, the USFS has an information station in Verlot (☎ 691-7791).

### Hiking & Climbing

One deservedly popular local hike is to **Kennedy Hot Springs** in the Glacier Peak Wilderness Area. Head south from Darrington on USFS Rd 20; after eight miles, at the White Chuck Campground, turn onto USFS Rd 23 and continue to the road's end. Park and start hiking along the White Chuck River Trail (No 643). The 96°F springs is five miles in from the trailhead.

To climb **Glacier Peak**, follow the White Chuck Trail another 1.5 miles past the hot springs to the Pacific Crest Trail. Turn north and hike about half a mile to the Glacier

Trail and Sitkum Ridge and the timberline base camp. It's a long approach – about 10 miles all told – before you get onto the Sitkum Glacier, a relatively untechnical but steep route to the 10,541-foot summit.

### Special Events

Darrington holds a Bluegrass Festival (☎ 436-1724) in mid-July. Food and crafts are sold at the festival, and camping is permitted. It's worth dropping down from the North Cascades just for this festival, which draws participants and spectators from around the Northwest.

### Places to Stay & Eat

There are about a dozen USFS and state-run campgrounds along the Mountain Loop Hwy, most of them on the South Fork of the Stillaguamish River east of Verlot. The campgrounds with running water charge an $8 fee; these include (from the west) *Turlo Campground*, *Verlot Campground* and *Gold Basin Campground* (the area's largest campground). Free campgrounds, with no running water, are *Red Bridge Campground* and *Boardman Creek Campground* on the South Fork of the Stillaguamish, and *Bedal Campground*, *White Chuck Campground* and *Clear Creek Campground* on USFS Rd 20 along the Sauk River. There are also several group campgrounds, which must be reserved in advance by telephone (☎ 436-1155).

Though most visitors are after campsites rather than rooms, a couple of B&Bs in Darrington provide lodging for those who are launching trips into the North Cascades or the Mt Baker-Snoqualmie National Forest. *Bradley's Bed 'n Bath* (☎ 436-0120), 716 Sauk Ave, built in 1906 as a boardinghouse for local schoolteachers, has three $48 rooms with no private baths. *Hemlock Hills B&B* (☎ 436-1274), 612 Stillaguamish, has two rooms, $55 each, with a shared bath; on clear days it has views of the mountains.

The *Stagecoach Inn* (☎ 436-1776, (800) 428-1776), 1100 Seaman, is Darrington's only real motel, with rooms for $49.

There's kind of a paucity of restaurants in Darrington, so it helps that the Stagecoach serves a continental breakfast. Your best bet for a meal is to cook it yourself or drive back to Arlington.

## BAKER LAKE & LAKE SHANNON

To get to North Cascades National Park proper, you need to take Hwy 20, and the first town you meet on Hwy 20 is Concrete (population 730); just north of Concrete is Baker Lake and Lake Shannon. Baker Lake is a natural lake that was enlarged by the backwaters from Upper Baker Lake Dam in the early 1960s. Below it is Lake Shannon, which is held back by Lower Baker Lake Dam. Washington's largest colony of nesting osprey is found at Lake Shannon.

Baker Lake is a popular place to launch a boat and fish for Kokanee salmon or lake and rainbow trout; there are also several hiking trails. Baker Lake Rd runs along the west side of the lake, passing several campgrounds and the **Shadow of the Sentinels**, a nature trail through old-growth

Douglas firs, before ending at USFS Rd 1168, which leads to the **Baker River Trail**. This relatively flat trail runs three miles up the jade green river past huge old cedars and beaver ponds; it makes a good family hike.

### Baker Hot Springs

This free, hike-in hot pool is about three miles west of the Park Creek Campground on Baker Lake's north end. Take USFS Rd 1144 (just past the campground) for 3.2 miles to a large parking area. A short trail from the north end of the parking lot leads to the 109°F natural pool. Don't expect to see bathing suits.

### Climbing

North Cascades climbers get to choose from glaciers, rock and ice; many climbs, including Mt Shuksan, a 9127-foot peak north of Baker Lake, contain a mix of all three. Shuksan is an exception among the local peaks in that its approach is easy; most North Cascades climbs require several days to climb, largely because the approach hikes are quite long. Reach the Sulfide Glacier route by driving almost all the way up Baker Lake Rd, turning onto Shannon Creek Rd (USFS Rd 1152) at the campground and, after three miles, taking the high road until it ends (4.5 miles). Hike the **Shannon Ridge Trail** to timberline. This route is best climbed during the summer, and it's a favorite with ski mountaineers. For complete route information, see Fred Beckey's *Cascade Alpine Guide, Volume three*.

### Places to Stay

**Camping** Baker Lake offers seven campgrounds, mostly on the lake's west bank. If it's hot out, bear in mind that *Horseshoe Cove Campground* has a swimming beach, and that glacier-fed Baker Lake warms up enough for swimming in the summer; there is running water, mostly pit toilets and sites cost $10. In addition to the USFS campgrounds, Puget Power maintains a free campground, *Kulshan Campground*, at the Upper Baker Dam. On the east side of

Baker Lake, *Maple Grove Campground* is
at the end of the East Bank Trail, an easy
four-mile hike past burn scars from Mt
Baker's 1843 eruption. *Maple Grove
Campground* is accessible only by foot or
by boat, has no water and is free. For reservations at the local USFS campgrounds,
call the ranger station in Sedro Woolley
(☎ 856-5700).

**Hotels** The closest motel lodgings are at
Concrete. The *North Cascade Inn* has a
motel (☎ 853-8870) and an antique-
bedecked restaurant (☎ 853-8771) with
especially good pie; it's on Hwy 20 just
west of Concrete. Rooms start at $40.

**Resorts** *Baker Lake Resort* (☎ 853-8325)
is open year round at milepost 20 on Baker
Lake Rd; it has cabins, campsites, boat
rentals and a small store. Cabins are $40 to
$85, with the less expensive ones sharing
bathroom facilities. All the cabins include
kitchenettes, but guests are expected to
bring their own linens and towels.

### Places to Eat
Aside from the small store at Baker Lake
Resort, there is no place to buy food along
the lakes. Stock up or chow down in Concrete, where the *Baker St Bar & Grill*
(☎ 853-7002) brings microbrew beers and
tasty, trendy food to Concrete's main drag.
Every year, on the 4th Saturday of July, the
restaurant sponsors a Skagit River raft race
from Rockport to Concrete, where style is
as important as speed. *Annie's Pizza Station* (☎ 853-7227), on Main St in uptown
Concrete, serves pizza and sandwiches
from a renovated gas station.

## ROCKPORT
Rockport (population 300) is a pretty town
set where the Sauk River joins the Skagit
River; Hwys 20 and 530 also meet here.
Rockport has become known as one of the
Northwest's best bald eagle viewing sites,
and it's also popular with river rafters and
anglers.

Before tourists began traveling the North
Cascades Hwy, Rockport was a way station

for miners, who in the 1880s traveled
upriver on steamboats to Rockport, then
continued up the Skagit River to the mines.
However, mining ultimately proved less
profitable than milling the local cedar trees,
which were turned into shingles in nearly
every Skagit River town.

The post office (☎ 853-8201) is at 5085
Railroad Ave. You may also want to take
advantage of the Wilderness Village Laun-
dromat (☎ 873-2571) east of Rockport on
Hwy 20, next to the Wilderness Village RV
Park.

### Howard Miller Steelhead Park
The riverside setting, near the confluence
of the Sauk and Skagit Rivers, and the
name of this park will lure anglers, but even
passersby can stop and take a look at the
30-foot-long cedar dugout canoe. Native
Americans traveled the local rivers in such
canoes, which they poled from a standing
position, rather than kneeling to paddle.

### Upper Skagit Bald Eagle Area
The bald eagle area is essentially the 10-
mile stretch of the Skagit River between
Rockport and Marblemount. After salmon
spawn, their spent carcasses become meals
for the many eagles who winter here.
January is the best time to view the eagles,
though they may be present from November through early March. Howard Miller
Steelhead Park makes a good base for a
morning of eagle-watching.

### Hiking
The **Sauk Mountain Trail** leads to an old
fire lookout with great views of Mount
Baker and the North Cascades. This 2.1-
mile hike from USFS Rd 1030, which is
well marked by signs near Rockport State
Park, climbs 1200 feet, is not too steep for
average hikers and passes wildflowers
galore in the spring and a side trail to Sauk
Lake.

### Rafting & Floating
This part of the Skagit River is an easy
float. Reach the standard put-in spot by
taking Cascade River Rd out of Marble-

mount and turning left just after the bridge over the Skagit River. Take out at Howard Miller Steelhead Park. Several outfitters run **eagle-watching float trips**. Call North Cascades River Expeditions (☎ (800) 634-8433), Orion Expeditions (☎ 322-9130, (800) 553-7466), DownStream River Runners (☎ (800) 234-4644) or North Cascade Outfitters (☎ (509) 997-1015). Eagle-watching trips usually run from mid-November to January and cost about $50 per person, with discounts for groups.

### Special Events
The Upper Skagit Bald Eagle Festival (☎ 853-7009) is held each January in Rockport and nearby towns.

### Places to Stay
**Camping** *Wilderness Village RV Park* is east of Rockport along Hwy 20. Prices range from $6 for a tent site to $12 for an RV hook-up, and it has all the expected amenities of a private campground.

The riverside *Howard Miller Steelhead Park* (☎ 853-8808) has an expanse of grassy sites for tents ($8) and RVs ($12); this county-owned campground, where Hwy 530 joins Hwy 20, is open year round – handy for winter steelhead anglers – and it has showers. *Rockport State Park* (☎ 853-8461) is about a mile west of Howard Miller, just north of Hwy 20. It's not on the river, but it's set in a lush old-growth forest with several hiking trails. Fees range from $5 to $14, and there are A-frame shelters and showers. Camping season runs from April to October.

**Hotels** *Totem Trail Motel* (☎ 873-4535) has rustic cabin units, with rooms from $42, and a restaurant and lounge alongside Hwy 20. The area's nicest cabins are at *Clark's Skagit River Cabins* (☎ 873-2250), between mileposts 103 and 104, by the funky Eatery Drive-In Restaurant & Museum. Cabins go for $50 to $100 a night (winter rates are somewhat lower); tent and RV spaces run $10 to $15.

**Lodges** *Cascade Log Cabins* (☎ 873-4106), on Hwy 20 about five miles east of Rockport, has cedar log cabins with kitchens for $50; there's a trail from the cabins to the river.

### Places to Eat
Head several miles east of Rockport for a berry shake at *Cascadian Farms* (☎ 853-8629), a tiny roadside stand with coffee, homemade ice cream and local organic berries, juice and pickles. For convenience sake, there's a restaurant at the *Totem Trail Motel* (☎ 873-4535), along Hwy 20, though savvy travelers hold their hunger until Marblemount.

## MARBLEMOUNT
Marblemount (population 200), founded in the mid-1860s as a supply point for gold prospectors, is the region's oldest town. For a time, marble was quarried from the slopes, but it proved to be as unprofitable as the gold panning.

Stop and fill the car with gas and snack food at Marblemount – it's the last real town on Hwy 20 for 69 miles (and it has the last tavern for 89 miles). In the winter, Hwy 20 is plowed as far east as Marblemount; the stretch between Marblemount and Mazama is usually closed between mid-November and early April. The highway turns north just past Marblemount, and Cascade River Rd heads east across the Skagit River, past a fish hatchery and some campgrounds, to the Cascade Pass trailhead, some 25 miles from Marblemount.

### Information
The North Cascades National Park Complex Backcountry Ranger Station (☎ 873-4500) issues backcountry permits and answers questions about trails. Call (206) 434-7277 or (360) 757-8907 for road information if you want to travel past Marblemount near the beginning or end of winter. The post office (☎ 873-2125) is at 5868 Hwy 20.

### Cascade Pass
The 3.5-mile hike to Cascade Pass is

perhaps the best loved in these mountains, and for good reason. Close-up views of a glacier greet hikers as soon as they hit the trail, avalanches thunder down from nearby Johannesburg Mountain, and the relatively easy trail up forested switchbacks pops out at a huge wildflower meadow at the pass. Most hikers turn around at Cascade Pass (due to overuse, no camping is allowed here), but the trail continues to the Stehekin Valley. In fact, this is the most popular land route into Stehekin, the isolated village at the head of Lake Chelan, and it's a route historically used by Native Americans and early White explorers crossing the Cascades. Another option from the pass is to hike an additional two steep miles up the Sahale Arm, for more wildflowers and some of the North Cascades' best views of peaks and spires. Expect to find plenty of other hikers on this trail, which is a 25-mile drive from Marblemount along Cascade River Rd; no dogs allowed.

### Places to Stay & Eat
Campgrounds around Marblemount include three free spots along the Cascade River, none with drinking water. *Cascade Island State Park* campground is two miles east of town. *Marble Creek Campground* and *Mineral Park Campground* are USFS campgrounds on the Cascade River Rd, eight and 16 miles east of Marblemount, respectively.

The *Mountain Song Cafe* (☎ 873-2461) is usually filled with climbers on their way to and from the North Cascades. They know this is the place for a carbo fix (you can even order a pie and potato combo plate for breakfast). The buffets – $3.25 for breakfast and between $5 and $6 for lunch and dinner – are healthy, satisfying bargains. Dinner entrees are $8.75 and include dishes like Indonesian satay and snapper with pineapple-cilantro salsa. However, the Mountain Song closes down with the highway (around November through March).

During the winter, grab a meal at the *Log House Inn* (☎ 873-4311), Marblemount's less hip restaurant.

# North Cascades National Park

For the backcountry hiker and adventurer, North Cascades National Park is paradise. The North Cascades Hwy is really the only road, and there are precious few facilities. Though there are plenty of scenic pull-offs along the highway and easily accessible, short interpretive hikes, a whole new world of craggy, rugged mountains awaits those who venture a few miles off the road to the first pass. Come with a backpack, pick up a map and backcountry permit at one of the visitors centers or ranger stations, and strike out into some of the most dramatic scenery Washington offers.

The Hwy 20 corridor and Diablo and Ross lakes are actually in the Ross Lake National Recreation Area, while North Cascades National Park straddles this strip to the north and south. Newhalem, a utilitarian dam-workers' town, is the jumping-off point for recreation in the area, and the visitors center here is definitely worth a stop. Many people also come for tours of the Diablo and Ross Dams, for rafting the Skagit River and for fishing in the river and lakes.

On the east side of the park, the North Cascades Hwy crests two passes, the 4860-foot Rainy Pass and, five miles to the east, the slightly higher 5477-foot Washington Pass. A big hairpin loop in the highway at Washington Pass is a striking marker of the climatic change between west and east, and two geological landmarks of the North Cascades – Early Winters spires and Liberty Bell Mountain (a favorite of rock climbers) – are visible from the Washington Pass overlook, just west of the hairpin.

The relatively large expanse of wilderness and the alpine character of the North Cascades make this home to a variety of wildlife. Small populations of gray wolves and grizzly bears keep a foothold in the North Cascades' remote backcountry. Black bears are more common, as are mountain lions. Marmots laze around on sunny rocks, occasionally standing up to give a shrill yell at intruders. These large rodents spend most of the summer eating, and by the time a marmot enters its winter burrow, 50% of its body weight may be fat. Mountain goats, actually members of the antelope family (with pliable split hooves and muscular forelegs), live on rugged mountain slopes, where they can climb amazingly steep rock walls.

## INFORMATION
### Tourist Office
The North Cascades Park Visitor Center (☎ (206) 386-4495), on Hwy 20 near Newhalem, has information on trails and camping, as well as exhibits explaining the area's plants, animals and rocks. The center opened in 1993, and some of the exhibits are quite imaginative, stressing sensitivity to the environment. A walk-through exhibit mixes informative placards about the park's different ecosystems with nature videos. And the New Agey slide show, meant to send viewers into a meditative trance, is better than it sounds. In back of the building, a short, wheelchair-accessible boardwalk leads to magnificent views of the mountains. Nearby Newhalem Creek Campground also hosts ranger talks nightly during the summer.

Check the National Park publication, the *North Cascade Challenger*, for current information on ranger-led hikes, campground fees and other park-related news.

### Telecommunications
The area code for Newhalem and Diablo is 206, since Seattle City Light, who operates the dams, is based in Seattle.

## LADDER CREEK FALLS
A splendid garden and a waterfall hide behind Newhalem's old-fashioned hydroelectric dam. Ignore the buzzing power lines and cross either of the two footbridges over the river and follow Ladder Creek loop trail through terraced gardens planted largely with native Northwest plants. The garden's original planner, engineer and

dam builder, James Ross, first used tropical plants and moved them all into greenhouses during the winter. Mist from Ladder Creek Falls, cut deep into a rock chasm, sprays hikers, and at night the falls are illuminated, legacy of James Ross' commitment to hydroelectric power. The light show is free, and it constitutes pretty much the high point of local nightlife. There's a small visitors center with interpretive displays inside the Gorge Powerhouse.

## ROSS & DIABLO LAKES
Ross Lake is 24 miles long, stretching all the way across the Canadian border, but there are no roads along it from the south. To get to any of the lakeside trailheads, or to the lake's resort (see Places to Stay below), you must take the resort-run water taxi. Trout live in Ross Lake, and boat rentals for fishing can be had at the resort.

Just below Ross Lake, blue-green Diablo Lake is held back by the 389-foot-high Diablo Dam, which, when it was completed in 1930, was the world's highest arch-type dam. Perhaps more interesting than its size is the amount of trouble James Ross and the city of Seattle went to for its construction. Since there was still no road here in the '20s, a narrow-gauge railroad ferried workers and their supplies from Rockport through the rocky Skagit River canyon to Diablo, where, one by one, the railroad cars were hoisted 560 feet up the steep hillside to the dam by an incline lift, which consisted of two parallel sets of tracks and a counterweight. At the top of the hill, a locomotive carried the railroad cars a few hundred yards to Diablo Lake, which they crossed on a barge to the Ross Dam construction site.

In another bit of area history, Jack Kerouac spent the summer of 1956 as a fire lookout on Desolation Peak north of here – he hated it.

Skagit Tours (☎ (206) 684-3030) operates several tours of Diablo and the vicinity. On the popular, 4½-hour deluxe tour, visitors are hauled up the hillside on the Incline Railroad, shown around the hilltop hydroelectric project, ferried across Diablo

Lake for a walk through the turbines of Ross Dam, and returned to Diablo for a big fried chicken dinner. The deluxe tour costs $24.50 ($22 for seniors, $12.50 for children ages six to 11), and reservations are required. The tour provides a good insight into local history and geography.

Less ambitious is the 90-minute, $5 tour, which eliminates the boat ride to Ross Dam and the chicken dinner and substitutes a walk across the top of Diablo Dam. Reservations are not required for this tour, which leaves at 11 am and 1:15 pm daily from mid-June to Labor Day.

Even the thriftiest of travelers can stop for a ride up the **Incline Railway**. This brief ride costs 25c, and it's an easy way to get some views.

## HIKING

Hiking the northern Cascades is a wonder of riches, and the essential reference guide is *100 Hikes in the North Cascades* by Ira Spring and Harvey Manning (The Mountaineers, Seattle, 1994). Listed below are only a smattering of what's available; stop by the visitors center for a full listing and advice on an appropriate trek.

From the Newhalem Creek Campground, 40 yards past the Newhalem Creek bridge, the less-trafficked **Lower Newhalem Creek Trail** passes hemlocks, cedars and firs on its nearly half-mile path to a creekside glade.

From the south end of the Colonial Creek Campground (four miles east of Diablo Dam), the long **Thunder Creek Trail** leads to a number of interesting sights. Park Creek Pass, 19.5 miles from the trailhead, offers views and a passageway to the Stehekin River. It's only a 1.3-mile jaunt from the campground to Thunder Creek, where a surprising number of wildflowers flourish in the dank creek-bottom forest. To reach the **Thunder Woods Nature Trail**, head 300 yards down the Thunder Creek Trail, then turn off for the sometimes steep 1.8-mile loop. A little over a mile down the Thunder Creek Trail, there's a junction for **Fourth of July Pass** and **Panther Creek Trail**. A moderately

steep trail reaches Fourth of July Pass in 3.2 miles. Panther Creek Trail continues five miles back to Hwy 20, east of Colonial Creek Campground.

From its Hwy 20 trailhead (milepost 134), the **Ross Dam Trail** descends one mile to Ross Dam, crosses over the top of the dam, and follows the west bank of Ross Lake to Ross Lake Resort (1.5 miles), Big Beaver Creek and backcountry.

After a quick descent from the highway (milepost 138) to Ruby Creek, the **East Bank Trail** cruises along the creek and Ross Lake north to the Pasayten Wilderness. There aren't big expansive views, but

---

**A Tale of Two Forests**

The North Cascades contain a rich variety of flora, which varies dramatically between the wet west and drier east slopes, as well as with elevation. The lower elevation, west-side slopes are forested with Western hemlocks and Western red cedar, like those on the short Happy Creek Forest boardwalk near Ross Lake and the Thunder River Trail at Colonial Creek Campground. Higher up, Douglas firs and Pacific silver firs join these trees. Such a forest can be seen on Hwy 20 at Rainy Pass. As the elevation increases, mountain hemlock and Pacific silver fir predominate until, at subalpine levels (such as at Washington Pass or along the Cascade Pass Trail), subalpine fir replaces silver fir. The wildflower meadows at Cascade Pass and Sahale Arm are examples of the highest, west-side subalpine zones. Above them, many rocky Cascade peaks are cloaked only with snow and ice.

On the east side of the Cascades, in places like Blue Lake and Cutthroat Pass, subalpine larch and whitebark pine grow in the high, relatively dry subalpine forest. The Douglas fir and lodgepole pine forest along the Stehekin River is characteristic of east-side mid-elevation growth, and lower on the Stehekin and at Bridge Creek, the lowlands forest is comprised of ponderosa pine and Douglas fir, which is particularly abundant due to years of fire suppression. ∎

if you're in the mood for a dark forest hike, this is the ticket. It's also one way to get to Hozomeen, a remote lakeside campground 28 miles to the north, near the Canadian border.

At Rainy Pass, the **Pacific Crest Trail** crosses Hwy 20. To sample the trail, strike out north from here for 6820-foot Cutthroat Pass (four miles). Several more leisurely hikes also start from Rainy Pass. Try the easy two-mile trail to green, cirque-cradled **Lake Ann**, from which it's another mile to **Heather Pass**, with yet an additional mile to 6600-foot **Maple Pass**.

Just to the west of Washington Pass, between mileposts 161 and 162, **Blue Lake Trail** is an ambling two-mile climb through subalpine meadows to Blue Lake, at 6250 feet. Snow blocks the trail's upper reaches until at least July, and once it melts, there can be lots of bugs and almost as many hikers. Nevertheless, the views onto Whistler Mountain, Cutthroat Peak and Liberty Bell Mountain make a hiker willing to put up with a few inconveniences.

### RAFTING & FLOATING

You can book rafting trips on the Skagit River with Alpine Adventures (☎ (800) 926-7238), Osprey River Adventures (☎ (509) 997-4116) or Northwest Wilderness River Riders (☎ (206) 448-7238).

Expect to pay around $75 for a day on the river, and though the dam-controlled water levels make the Skagit runnable year round, outfitters tend to concentrate on summer white-water trips.

Floaters usually put in at Goodell Creek Campground and float to Bacon Creek or Copper Creek, about 10 miles downstream. The stream conditions depend on what's going on at the dams upstream, but it's usually a Class II or III trip. The waters are a little quieter downstream from Marblemount.

### PLACES TO STAY & EAT
### Camping

*Newhalem Creek Campground*, a big USFS campground near the North Cascades visitors center, is open mid-June to Labor Day. There are 127 sites, no hook-ups and the fee is $10; amenities include flush toilets, running water and regularly scheduled talks and hikes with park naturalists. The smaller, less-developed *Goodell Creek Campground* is open year round on the Skagit River west of Newhalem, near milepost 119. Expect to find pit toilets, drinking water and a $7 fee. *Gorge Creek Campground* has no amenities and only a few spaces, but it's a reasonable alternative to the big, crowded park campgrounds. It's right off the highway on the road to Diablo.

---

#### Wheelchair-Accessible Trails

While ardent hikers may not feel a trek has even begun until after the first few miles, the North Cascades offer plenty of short, beautiful trails that are accessible to hikers of all abilities. At the back of the North Cascades National Park Visitor Center in Newhalem, a short boardwalk leads to views of the Picket Range, some of the most spectacular peaks in the North Cascades.

To get a feel for the frequently drippy west-side forests, try the half-mile **riverside nature trail**, which skirts Newhalem Campground. This 'To Know a Tree' trail is graded and graveled for wheelchair use.

At the end of Main St in Newhalem, the **Trail of the Cedars** is a half-mile loop across a suspension bridge to the Skagit River's forested south shore.

A boardwalk trail, the **Happy Creek Forest Walk** makes a three-mile loop through old-growth forests off Hwy 20, milepost 134, right between Diablo and Ross Lakes (about eight miles east of Diablo). Even to seasoned nature-trail walkers, the interpretive signs are quite good.

At Rainy Pass on Hwy 20, milepost 161, there is the **Rainy Lake Trail**, a mile-long paved trail through the woods to Rainy Lake. ■

The *Colonial Creek Campground* near Diablo has 167 sites – flush toilets, running water, no hook-ups – on the Thunder Arm of Diablo Lake on either side of the highway. On the south side, several walk-in sites set on a bluff among big trees offer a chance to get away from the cars; the lakeside spots are the most coveted and the most crowded.

## Lodges

The floating cabins at secluded *Ross Lake Resort* (☎ (206) 386-4437), on the west side of the lake just north of Ross Dam, were built in the 1930s for loggers working in the valley soon to be flooded by Ross Dam. There's no road to the resort – guests can either hike the two-mile trail from Hwy 20 or take the resort's tugboat taxi and truck shuttle from the parking area near Diablo Dam. The houseboat cabins are rustic, but they do have plumbing, electricity and kitchenettes. Guests in the smallest, least expensive cabins share a bathroom with one other cabin. Since there's no restaurant, guests should remember to bring food for all their meals. Cabins range from $51 to $99 a night (the most expensive are bunkhouse cabins with room for six). The resort rents canoes, kayaks and motorboats ($20 to $46 a day), and operates a water taxi service for hikers destined for trailheads around the lake.

If you need to pick up some food, stop by the store in Newhalem.

# Methow Valley

East of Washington Pass, the land dries up a bit and the sky is typically less choked with clouds. The Methow (pronounced *MET-how)* River valley is the land of cross-country skiing, where the snow is more powdery than the 'cement' that falls west of the Cascades. Recreationally, the Methow comes into its own in the winter, but summer's no let-down. When snow melts, the valley becomes spectacularly green,

and there's plenty of hiking, mountain biking, rafting and fishing.

The Upper Methow River flows through a straight, steep-walled valley cut by a glacier during the most recent ice age. The valley begins to widen around Mazama and becomes fairly open by the time it hits Winthrop and Twisp. Off to the southwest is the Sawtooth Ridge and the Lake Chelan-Sawtooth Wilderness Area. To the north and east, the Okanogan hills reach into Canada. At Pateros, the Methow River flows into the Columbia River.

Native Americans lived along the Methow, Twisp and Chewuch rivers going back some 9000 years. In 1811, David Thompson, the North West Company trader and geographer, visited the Salish-speaking Methows along the river named for them and observed tribal members fishing for salmon at the river's mouth. Never a large tribe, the Methows were more or less swallowed up when they were sent to the Colville Reservation in 1883.

For Whites, 1883 marked the beginning of Methow valley settlements. Gold was the original lure, commerce proved more permanent, but nothing really boomed until Hwy 20 opened in 1972, bringing a steady stream of visitors. Winthrop has especially tried to capitalize on tourism, turning itself into a living version of the 'Old West' – you will also find most of the area's accommodations here.

## ORIENTATION & INFORMATION

Winter snows block the highest stretch of Hwy 20 between Marblemount and Mazama from late November (pg 172) to early April. To check on its status, call (900) 407-7277. Methow-bound skiers make their approach from western Washington by taking Hwy 2 to Wenatchee, then heading north on Hwy 97 past Lake Chelan to Pateros, where Hwy 153 traces the Methow River northwest to Twisp and Hwy 20.

Methow Valley Central Reservations (☎ 996-2148, (800) 422-3048) runs a very helpful reservation service, which books accommodations in the region's inns,

WASHINGTON

lodges, B&Bs and cabins, as well as in vacation home rentals.

## MAZAMA

There's not much to the town of Mazama (population 60) – really just a couple of gas pumps and one of the state's busiest pay phones in front of the general store – but there are several small resorts in the area. The village of Early Winters, a stone's throw up the highway from Mazama, is still small and exceedingly quiet, but that may be changing soon: a long-proposed, much-fought-over ski resort has been approved for construction on Sandy Butte, southwest of Mazama, and development is bound to follow.

The USFS runs a visitors center (☎ 996-2534) near milepost 178 on Hwy 20 in Early Winters. Though 911 will summon police or an ambulance, call 997-2106 to report a fire.

## Harts Pass

Near the end of what may be the state's most terrifying road – a steep one-laner with long, deadly drop-offs and no guard rails – is Harts Pass (6197 feet): suck in your breath and drive, for the views from the top are outstanding. Catch the road to Harts Pass by heading northwest on Lost River Rd (aka Mazama Rd) past the Mazama Country Inn to USFS Rd 5400. The road is paved for the first 12 miles, and the last dozen miles are gravel. At Harts Pass, there's still more of a climb for the intrepid driver; head another 2.5 miles up to Slate Peak, where, a short hike from the road's end, the view from an abandoned fire lookout is a true panorama. At its 7800-foot terminus, this is the state's highest roadside spot. Slate Peak is also the site of the northernmost road access to the Pacific Crest Trail in the USA; north of the road's end, the Pasayten Wilderness reaches to Canada.

---

### Cross-Country Skiing in the Methow Valley

This is what the Methow valley is famous for – good, dry snow and plenty of places to ski. The Methow Valley Sports Trails Association (MVSTA) (☎ 996-3287, (800) 682-5787) has built and maintains an extensive system of cross-country ski trails – over 90 miles worth. When there's no snow, these trails double as mountain biking and hiking routes. Trail passes and maps are available at most local businesses; passes cost $10 weekdays, $12.50 weekends or $25 for three days, and they are not required for hikers and mountain bikers. Arrange a shuttle to or from a trailhead by calling 996-2324.

Around Mazama there are two main ski hubs: one is off Hwy 20 near the Mazama Country Inn (☎ 996-2681), which sells passes and maps and rents equipment in season, and the other is just west of the Early Winters ranger station (closed in the winter), near the end of the plowed stretch of Hwy 20. Where the highway is left unplowed, cross-country skiers are joined by dogsledders and snowmobilers.

Another good place to ski is on MVSTA's Rendezvous trails, which follow the Methow River between Mazama and Winthrop. Near Mazama, the trailhead is in a parking lot on Lost River Rd, just southeast of town. The trails, which are dotted with skiers' huts, link up with another trailhead in a parking lot at Cub Creek, some 17 miles away. The Cub Creek trailhead is about five miles up Chewuch River Rd from Winthrop. Obviously, most people don't ski the 17-mile stretch; many loops can be fashioned from either trailhead, and there's ample opportunity to practice telemark skiing.

Another big trail network is up on Sun Mountain, just below the lodge (☎ 996-2211, (800) 572-0493). If you aren't a lodge guest, park at the day-ski lot, just above Patterson Lake. The elevation here is 2600 feet, nearly 1000 feet higher than Winthrop, and the trails climb up to 3600 feet on the Thompson Ridge Rd trail.

In Winthrop, rent skis and purchase trail passes from Winthrop Mountain Sports (☎ 996-2886), 257 Riverside Ave. Rendezvous Outfitters (☎ 996-3299), PO Box 728, Winthrop, WA 98862, leads hut-to-hut, cross-country ski trips and maintains four skiers' huts in the Rendezvous trail system. Each hut sleeps eight people at $25 per person, or it's $140 to book the entire hut. Freight haul is available for $70 a leg. ■

## Hiking

Several trails have their start on Harts Pass Rd (USFS Rd 5400). For a lowlands amble and perhaps some fishing along the Methow River, turn off Harts Pass Rd at the River Bend Campground and catch the trail about one mile past the campground. The trail follows the Methow for six miles, then climbs two more miles to meet the **Pacific Crest Trail**, where a turn to the south will lead to the highly scenic Methow Pass, Snowy Lakes Pass and Golden Horn.

Hikers, mountain bikers and horseback riders can follow the meanders of the Methow River between Mazama and Winthrop along the **Methow River Trail**, which continues down the valley floor to Twisp. River access is easy, and the trail is right along its banks.

## Outfitters & Guide Services

In general, though outfitters may be based in one Methow valley town or another, their active range is valley-wide. Early Winters Outfitters (☎ 996-2659, (800) 737-8750) offers horsepacking trips, cattle drives and fishing and hunting trips out of Mazama. An hour-long horseback ride is $15, an all-day ride is $75, and pack trips into the Pasayten Wilderness Area run $95 for hikers, $125 for horsepackers.

## Places to Stay

**Camping** Three USFS campgrounds are just off Hwy 20 on Early Winters Creek. *Lone Fir Campground* (milepost 168) has pit toilets, running water and an $8 fee. *Klipchuck Campground* (milepost 175, then about a mile up the side road) and *Early Winters Campground* (milepost 177) have similar amenities.

**B&Bs** B&B accommodations are available at *Chokecherry Inn B&B* (☎ 996-2049), on the Methow River about three quarters of a mile east of the Early Winters ranger station. The two rooms have private baths, and there's a hot tub on the deck. Rooms run $68.

**Lodges** *Mazama Country Inn* (☎ 996-2681, (800) 843-7951), off Hwy 20 in Mazama, is the nicest, though most expensive, lodge in the Upper Methow valley. Rooms in the lodge start at $75; cabins with kitchens run up to $170. Ski trails radiate out from the lodge, and the restaurant serves the best food for miles around. In the winter, all meals are included in room rates; during the summer, meals are served but not included. This is the only restaurant in town, so call ahead for reservations.

*Early Winters Cabins* (☎ 996-2355, 996-2843), off Hwy 20 just south of Mazama, are a little more rustic – in the winter, guests must chop their own wood to burn for cabin heat. Rates run $55 to $75 for these woodsy, creekfront cabins.

*North Cascades Basecamp* (☎ 996-2334), 255 Lost River Rd, is a small inn with six lodge rooms (all with shared baths) and a housekeeping cabin, a hot tub, trails and a pond. This is a good place to bring kids, as several of the rooms have bunk beds or twin beds in addition to a double or queen, and there's a playroom in the lodge. Lodge rooms run $120 for doubles, with a $23 to $40 surcharge for each extra person, depending on their age. Rates include all meals. During the summer, the lodge offers a less expensive B&B rate, with rooms starting at $65. The cabin sleeps up to six for $150 a night, no meals included. All accommodations are slightly less expensive on weekdays or with stays of longer than three days.

At *Brown's Farm* (☎ 996-2571), on Wolf Creek Rd between Mazama and Winthrop, fresh eggs come with a cabin rental. Cabins with complete kitchens start at $55.

**Vacation Home Rentals** Call Methow Valley Central Reservations (☎ 996-2148, (800) 422-3048) to book one of the many rental homes, ranging from cabins to apartments to ranches, available in the Methow valley.

## WINTHROP

Winthrop (population 400) has been done over as an upscale Western town, where espresso is sold from false-fronted shops and flower baskets line the streets. As with its sister theme town, Leavenworth, it's easy to curl a lip or roll the eyes when describing Winthrop, but the fact is, it works. What was once a struggling east-slope town is now a thriving part of the new Old West.

The town was first settled in 1891 by Harvard-educated Guy Waring, who built a trading post at the confluence of the Chewuch and Methow rivers. After a couple of visits to Winthrop, Waring's Harvard classmate Owen Wister settled down and wrote the best-selling book *The Virginian*, whose characters are supposedly based on Winthropians.

When the North Cascades Hwy opened in 1972, Winthrop was ready and waiting, with many of its frontier-era buildings spiffed up for the tourist trade. You know what to do: stroll the wood-plank sidewalk downtown and browse the gift shops. Be sure to stop and watch the blacksmith if he's at work forging wrought-iron hooks and trivets. Early in the century, Guy Waring owned every building on the main street except the log town hall; several of these buildings are still standing, though many have changed function. One, the Duck Brand Saloon, was built by Waring and bears the name of his cattle brand. The Duck Brand Saloon that serves up beer and nachos today is not the original; the first Duck Brand is now the community center. What is now the Winthrop Palace Restaurant, at 149 Riverside Ave, was built in 1909 as the Winthrop Hotel.

### Orientation

At Winthrop, the Chewuch River flows in from the north to join the Methow River, which runs down the sparsely-treed eastern flanks of the Cascades toward the Columbia River. The highway makes a 90° turn as it enters Winthrop from the west, and in the town center is sometimes referred to as Riverside Ave.

### Information

The Winthrop Chamber of Commerce

(☎ 996-2125) is on Hwy 20, right where it turns the corner in downtown. A USFS ranger station (☎ 996-2266) is on the west side of town, up the hill from the baseball diamond on West Chewuch Rd.

The post office (☎ 996-2282) is at 1110 Hwy 20. Trail's End Bookstore (☎ 996-2345) is at 156 Riverside Ave, next to the Trail's End Motel. For ambulance services, call 996-2888. Reach police at 911 or 996-2160, and report fires by calling 997-2106. The local road report number is 976-7623.

### Shafer Museum

Guy Waring built the log house that is now the centerpiece of the local historical museum (☎ 996-2712) on Castle Ave at Bridge St, one block up the hill from Riverside Ave. The well-built log home, known to Winthropians since its construction in 1897 as 'The Castle', was Waring's payback to his wife for moving west. It's open from 10 am to 5 pm, Memorial Day to Labor Day, and donations are appreciated.

### Cascade Smoke Jumpers Base

Before a local cobbler teamed up with the USFS to make padded, multipocketed jumpsuits, nobody had jumped from a plane to extinguish a forest fire. Now that smoke jumpers have become elevated to heroes of modern western mythology, the Cascades Smoke Jumpers Base is open for tours. It's halfway between Winthrop and Twisp on Eastside Winthrop-Twisp Rd. Call ahead to the Twisp Ranger Station (☎ 997-2131) to check on the schedule, but visitors are usually welcome from 8 am to 5 pm, June to October. Admission is free.

### Pearrygin Lake State Park

If downtown Winthrop's crowds close in on you, skip out of town to Pearrygin Lake, where the state park has a swimming beach and boat launch on the pretty aqua-colored lake, which is actually warm enough to swim in during the summer. During the winter, snowmobilers come here to get away from the cross-country skiers. The park also has facilities for tent camping and RVs, and the lake is stocked with trout. It's just under five miles northeast of town on Pearrygin Lake Rd (follow the signs from Hwy 20).

### Biking
Mountain bikers hit the ski trails once the snow clears in the summer. One popular ride from Winthrop is an easy 12-mile loop to Pearrygin Lake. Start by following the well-marked road to Pearrygin Lake State Park. After four miles of paved-road cycling, continue straight up the dirt Pearrygin Lake Rd rather than turning right to follow the paved entrance to the state park. The road climbs gently for two miles, affording good views of the valley and surrounding mountains. At the T-intersection, turn right and coast, hitting pavement again at the Bear Creek Golf Course. At the valley floor, turn right and pedal three miles back to town.

Both Winthrop Mountain Sports (☎ 996-2886) and the Virginian Resort (☎ 996-2535) rent mountain bikes. You can pick up a booklet describing local mountain bike routes at Winthrop Mountain Sports and at the ranger station.

### Other Activities
While cross-country skiing is the main draw (see aside, above), the summer still finds plenty to do around here. **Fishing** for trout and steelhead is popular in the Methow River, and Moccasin Lake, a mile-long hike from Patterson Lake Rd (the trailhead is about halfway up the road to Sun Mountain Lodge), has very good fly-fishing. Aspiring rock climbers can find instruction from the folks at Winthrop Mountain Sports (☎ 996-2286, (800) 719-3826).

If **golf** is more your speed, Bear Creek Golf Course (☎ 996-2234) has nine holes and charges $10 weekdays, $11 on weekends. The course is noted for its lovely surroundings and for the wild animals that may stroll across the fairway. And **horseback riding** is also popular in the Methow valley – the Chewuch River Ranch (☎ 996-2497) has hour-long rides for $18, half-day lunch rides for $55, and overnight rides for $110.

### Special Events
Winthrop's Memorial Day weekend rodeo makes you remember that Winthrop really is a western town, and not just a made-up one. The summer season is highlighted by the Winthrop Rhythm & Blues Festival (☎ 996-2111) – national acts come to town for three days in late July, and the concerts, held downtown and at Twin Lakes, can get pretty wild.

Call the Methow Valley Sport Trails Association (☎ (800) 682-5787) for details on their early-October Methow Valley Mountain Bike Festival.

And, if you're in town over President's Day weekend, be prepared for the big snowshoe softball tournament.

### Places to Stay
**Camping** Right on the northeast edge of Winthrop, *Pine Near Trailer Park* (☎ 996-2391) is a small, private campground with room for tents as well as trailers ($10 to $12). There's also a large *KOA* (☎ 996-2258) just east of town on Hwy 20 with fees ranging between $15 and $20. It's on the Methow River, which means it's more pleasant than the average KOA.

*Pearrygin Lake State Park* (☎ 996-2370) is five miles northeast of town on Pearrygin Lake Rd. Showers, boat launch, swimming and fishing make this a popular and usually crowded spot; campsites are $10.

*Derry's Resort* (☎ 996-2322), also on Pearrygin Lake, has cabins, campsites (geared toward RVs but tents are okay), boat rentals and laundry facilities. Campsites run $12 to $17.

**B&Bs** *Farmhouse Inn* (☎ 996-2191), off Hwy 20 just south of town, is operated by the owners of the Duck Brand Hotel and Cantina (see below). Three rooms at the six-room inn have private baths, the other three rooms share two baths. Rooms run $53 to $64.

**Hotels** *Trail's End Motel* (☎ 996-2303), 130 Riverside Ave, a small false-fronted, downtown motel, falls into the budget category during the winter, when double rooms drop to $40. Summertime rates are about $15 higher. There's a bookstore next door and a cafe in the same complex.

*Winthrop Inn Motel* (☎ 996-2217, (800) 444-1972) has a heated pool and hot tub, with single/double rooms starting at $60/65. It's right on Hwy 20 by the Methow River and has good access to cross-country ski trails. *Marigot Motel* (☎ 996-3100, (800) 468-6754), 960 Hwy 20, is a large motel on the south side of town, with a hot tub and washers and dryers; double rooms start at $65 and go to $75 on weekends. Pets and smokers are allowed in specific rooms.

The *Hotel Rio Vista* (☎ 996-3535), 285 Riverside Ave, has a typical Winthropian false front and is right downtown. Each room has a deck with a view of the Methow and Chewuch rivers. Double rooms run $80 in the summer (May to October), and $70 in the winter (with winter midweek specials). At the *Duck Brand Hotel* (☎ 996-2192), 248 Riverside Ave, several rooms are above the very popular restaurant, which can make for noisy evenings (till the restaurant closes at 9:30 pm). Rates are $59/71 for singles/doubles.

*Winthrop Mountain View Chalets* (☎ 996-3113, (800) 527-3113), on Hwy 20 at the south end of town, has simple two-person cabins with microwave ovens and nice decks (but no phones in the rooms) for $55 a night.

The *Virginian Resort* (☎ 996-2535, (800) 854-2834), 808 Hwy 20 just south of town, has comfortable riverside motel rooms and kitchenette cabins, a heated outdoor pool and mountain bike rentals. Rooms start at $50 and top out around $75. Cabins run $65 to $75. Pets are allowed in some rooms. The adjoining restaurant serves reasonably good Northwest cuisine.

**Resorts** *Sun Mountain Lodge* (☎ 996-2211, (800) 572-0493), nine miles southwest of town via Twin Lakes and Patterson Lake Rds, is the region's premier resort. Its rather grand mountaintop setting offers expansive views of the Methow valley. The

high-gloss rustic lodge has very comfortable rooms and a great restaurant. Cabins, a little ways down the hill at Patterson Lake, are somewhat removed from the hub of activity. Hiking, mountain bike and cross-country ski trails lead out from the lodge. The resort also has horseback riding, canoeing, sailing, tennis courts and a pool. In short, it's kind of a recreational fantasyland: splendid, very comfortable and with lots of good food waiting at the end of the day. Room rates vary widely according to the season and the type of accommodations. During the winter, lodge rooms run about $105; during the summer, expect to pay $130. Spring and fall rates are substantially lower (about $70 a night), and midweek stays always bring a price break of $15 to $20. The Patterson Lake cabins sleep four and run $115 in winter, $135 in summer, and $80 in the spring or fall.

*WolfRidge Resort* (☎ 996-2828, (800) 237-2388) is on Wolf Creek Rd, 5.5 miles northwest of town; reach it via Twin Lakes Rd, which is just south of downtown and doubles back north. It has a wide variety of accommodations, ranging from hotel rooms to log townhouse suites; there's a heated outdoor pool and hot tub and cross-country ski trails. Pets can be accommodated with notice. Rates start at $55 for a hotel room and run to $139 for a two-bedroom townhouse.

*Westar Lodge & Retreat* (☎ 996-2697) is four miles north of town on West Chewuch River Rd. The Westar is geared toward housing groups, and it's a good place to come with a handful of friends for a cross-country ski vacation.

*Chewuch River Guest Ranch* (☎ 996-2497), six miles north of Winthrop on East Chewuch River Rd, specializes in horseback riding, both for ranch guests and day riders. Several guest rooms are available for $55, and a two-bedroom house rents for around $80 a night (less during midweek).

*Spring Creek Ranch* (☎ 996-2495, 996-2510), across the Methow River from downtown at 491 Twin Lakes Rd, is a nicely renovated, 1929 farmhouse with kitchen facilities and a washer and dryer;

's $120 for a double and $10 for each xtra person.

**ki Huts** A series of four ski huts, accessile only from trails, dot the Rendezvous rea outside Winthrop. Call the Methow 'alley Central Reservations (☎ (800) 422-048, 996-2148) to book a bunk ($25) or an ntire eight-person hut ($140). If you're not p to skiing with a pack, freight haul is vailable for $70 a leg. They are also workng on a midweek inn-to-inn ski package, vhere skiers stay at a different inn or B&B ach night, again with an optional freight aul. Call the reservations service to disuss various options and prices.

**▶laces to Eat**

f you just want a drink, the *Winthrop* *3rewing Company* (☎ 996-3174) has a iverfront deck and microbrews on tap in he little red schoolhouse on Winthrop's iain street. *Pasayten Burger Company* ☎ 996-2444), 162 Riverside Ave, has a /ide range of burgers for $4 and up. *Three* *'ingered Jack's* (☎ 996-2411), 176 Riveride Ave, is supposedly the site of the tate's first legal saloon; they serve three neals a day, with nightly dinner specials such as prime rib for $9.95). The lively, aux-Western *Cantina* (☎ 996-2192), in the )uck Brand Hotel, 248 Riverside Ave, erves up everything from Mexican food to pple pie.

At the *Winthrop Palace* (☎ 996-2245), 49 Riverside Ave, you're dining in the rstwhile Winthrop Hotel, which, from the ooks of it, wasn't a bad place to spend a iight in 1909. Both the setting and the food ere are a little bit fancier than the other lowntown Winthrop restaurants, which is 'ot really saying much. Open for three neals a day.

If fancy is what you want, the restaurant t *Sun Mountain Lodge* (☎ 996-2211) is as lose as you're going to find in this town. 'he food, which focuses on Northwest uisine, really is worth the drive, and the 'unday brunch draws hungry hikers and ross-country skiers from all over the

Methow valley. It's far and away the region's best restaurant – and the dress code is casual.

## TWISP

Twisp (population 900) isn't loaded with prepackaged entertainment, but if small and unpretentious strikes a chord, spend a night in Twisp, a more genuine version of the West than its false-fronted neighbor. Originally, Native Americans set up fishdrying camps at the junction of the Methow and Twisp Rivers, and the women who prepared the salmon were often plagued by yellow jackets, or *twips*, setting the stage for one of Washington's most charming town names.

### Orientation

Past Twisp, Hwy 20 turns east through the Okanogan National Forest to the towns of Omak and Okanogan in the Okanogan Valley. Hwy 153 splits off and follows the Methow River south, joining Hwy 97 and the Columbia River at Pateros. Highway 153 is the most convenient way to drive between Lake Chelan and the North Cascades, and it's the route used by Methowbound cross-country skiers when the North Cascades route shuts down in the winter.

### Information

Twisp Chamber of Commerce (☎ 997-2926) is in the Methow Valley Community Center, on Hwy 20 at the north edge of town, next to the tennis courts. Twisp ranger station (☎ 997-2131), 502 Glover St (Twisp's main street), has information on trails and campgrounds in the Okanogan National Forest.

You'll find the post office (☎ 997-3777) at 205 Glover St. For medical emergencies, call 997-2106 for an ambulance (or fire). The Methow Valley Family Practice (☎ 997-2011) has offices at 541 E 2nd Ave, but the nearest hospitals are in Omak (☎ 826-1760) and Brewster (☎ 689-2517), each about 35 to 40 miles from Twisp.

There is no public transportation to Twisp.

**WASHINGTON**

## Farmer's Market

Every Saturday morning from late spring through early fall a Twispian mix of red-necks, hippies and redneck hippies gather at the Methow Valley Community Center, next to the tennis courts on Hwy 20, for a farmer's market. Stop by for baked goods, produce or a handcrafted knife.

## Confluence Gallery

For a small town, Twisp has a pretty lively cultural scene, anchored in large part by the Confluence Gallery & Art Center (☎ 997-2787), 104 Glover St. The gallery mounts a new exhibit every six weeks or so, with a focus on work by regional artists. Folk art, Native American art and quilts have been the focus of several recent exhibits. They also sponsor events, including talks by artists, writers and performers on the first Tuesday of every month.

## Hiking

Trails abound along the Twisp River. Follow Twisp River Rd west of town for about 11 miles, and veer left onto USFS Rd 4420 (West Buttermilk Creek Rd) to reach a trail up **Eagle Creek**, which sprouts a trail up **Oval Creek** two miles from the trailhead. The seven-mile Eagle Creek Trail is fairly level; there's more uphill on the Oval Creek route, but it does have the reward of three high mountain lakes start-ing about 6.5 miles in. Both of these trails can be the first leg of a backpacking trip into the Lake Chelan-Sawtooth Wilderness Area. There are many trails in the area, with many opportunities to hike over to Lake Chelan. If, at the end of the Twisp River Rd, you follow USFS Rd 44, you'll pass several campgrounds, each with hiking trails nearby (see Camping below). Pick up a wilderness area map at the Twisp ranger station (☎ 997-2131).

There is a wheelchair-accessible paved walkway surrounding **Black Pine Lake**, a remote lake southwest of Twisp. From Hwy 20, follow the Twisp River Rd 11 miles to USFS Rd 300, which heads south and reaches Black Pine Lake after 6.5 miles.

## Rafting & Floating

Rafters divide the Methow River into two floatable stretches. The upper stretch, from the town of Carlton to McFarland Creek (three miles north of Methow) provides an easy-going float; the lower Methow, from McFarland Creek to Pateros, runs through the Black Canyon with more challenging white-water. Osprey River Adventures (☎ 997-4116) runs white-water trips on the Methow River for $45 ($40 for children under 12). The Osprey River folks also raft the Skagit River.

## Other Activities

There is plenty to see and do outdoor around Twisp. If you don't mind a few snowmobiles, **cross-country skiing** i easy along the flat Twisp River Rd, just ou of Twisp. Just drive to the end of the plowed road, and ski as far as you like Nearer to downtown, trails start at the Idle A-While Motel and tool around Twisp and along the Methow River. North Cascade Outfitters (☎ 997-1015) offers **horseback riding**: a 1½-hour ride costs $15, and a 2½-hour rides costs $25. Customized pack trips are also available. Or for something a little different, Malamute Express (☎ 997-6402) runs **dog-sledding trips**; a half day costs $112, a full day with lunch cost $224.

## Places to Stay

**Camping** As with most of the recreation around Twisp, the Twisp River is the place to look for campsites. Four maintained campgrounds are open late May to early September in the Okanogan National Forest (☎ 997-2131), and all are at trail heads into the Lake Chelan-Sawtooth Wil derness Area. To reach them, head 11 mile west of town on the Twisp River Rd, then continue on USFS Rd 44 (which will turn into USFS Rd 4440). *War Creek Camp ground* is 3.5 miles from the start of USFS Rd 44 and has running water and a $7 fee *Poplar Flat Campground* is the next river side campground, about 9.5 miles up USFS Rd 44. It is $5 a night and also has water The last two have no water and are free

*South Creek Campground* is about 1.5 miles from Poplar Flat and *Roads End Campground* is 13.5 miles up USFS Rd 44.

**B&Bs** *Methow Valley Inn B&B* (☎ 997-3014), near the Methow and Twisp rivers (follow the sign at the main Twisp intersection), has rooms from $50 to $65, with private baths in the more expensive rooms. Both children and pets can be accommodated here, but make sure to arrange it first.

**Hotels** You won't find anyplace particularly fancy or upscale to stay in Twisp, but there are several reasonably priced, basic motels, virtually all of which allow dogs. The *Sportsman Motel* (☎ 997-2911), 11010 E Hwy 20, has perfectly good knotty-pine rooms; singles/doubles are $31/36.

At the *Idle-A-While Motel* (☎ 997-3222), 505 N Hwy 20, kitchenette cottages and regular motel rooms start at $40/44. It's not a bad place to while away a quiet Twisp evening – the motel has a hot tub and sauna, and VCRs and movies are available for rent. Dogs are $1 extra, and there's easy access to cross-country ski trails in the winter.

*Twisp River Lodge* (☎ 997-7343), 125 N Methow Hwy, is another reasonable option in Twisp, with rooms from $35/38.

A few miles southeast, in Carlton on Hwy 20, the *Country Town Motel* (☎ 997-3432) is one of the nicer motels between Winthrop and Chelan. There's an outdoor pool, a hot tub and a tiny golf course. Rooms are $50, and the motel is right across the road from the Methow River and the town's only other attraction, a guy who does chainsaw sculptures, seemingly 24 hours a day.

### Places to Eat
The *Roadhouse Diner* (☎ 997-4015) has good breakfasts (they also serve lunch and dinner) on Hwy 20 in Twisp, but the real treat is the *Cinnamon Twisp Bakery* (☎ 997-5030), on Glover St, with excellent cinnamon twists and bagels. For homemade pizza and calzone, try *Hometown*

*Pizza* (☎ 997-2100), also on Glover St downtown.

The *Queen of Tarts* (☎ 997-1335), in the Confluence Gallery, 104 Glover St, is a good place to stop for lunch or coffee. Like the gallery, it closes down at 3 pm.

### PATEROS
At Pateros (population 580), the Methow River flows into the Columbia, and the wide open, dry feeling of being east of the Cascades comes on strong. Like Twisp, Pateros is genuinely western – drive by early on a Saturday night and you may find people practicing their western dancing in front of the fire house.

Before dams took over the Columbia River, wild rapids rocketed past Pateros. When Wells Dam was built in 1968 and created Lake Pateros, the rapids were flooded and most of the town was forced to relocate to higher ground.

Pateros is 33 miles southeast of Twisp on Hwy 153, and about the same distance south of Okanogan on Hwy 97. The main attraction is **Alta Lake**, which is just southwest of Pateros (take Alta Lake Rd south from Hwy 153). It's home to a state park and a couple of small resorts, one of which has an 18-hole golf course. Boaters and anglers like the lake, which is stocked with rainbow trout, and there is a swimming beach. If you happen to be passing through over the third weekend in July, stick around for the Apple Pie Jamboree.

### Places to Stay & Eat
There is plenty of camping at *Alta Lake State Park* (☎ 923-2473) for $10, as well as RV sites, which can also be found at *Riverfront Park* in central Pateros for $5 a night.

*Amy's Manor B&B* (☎ 923-2334) is a touch of elegance in this plain town. The hillside B&B is on a 170-acre estate with tennis courts, gardens and great views, just northwest of Pateros on Hwy 153. Singles/doubles cost $50/60.

It's not often that motor inns have boat docks, but at the *Lake Pateros Motor Inn*

(☎ 923-2203, (800) 444-1985) boaters can pull up and spend the night. The inn is off Hwy 97, just north of the Hwy 153 junction on Lake Pateros. This is a pretty nice place to stay, with an outdoor pool and riverfront rooms; singles/doubles are $52/$56, and leashed dogs are permitted.

*Alta Lake Resort* (☎ 923-2359) is connected with the golf course just north of Alta Lake and is, not surprisingly, particularly geared to golfers. Rooms for two start at about $50; add $10 for a kitchenette. *Whistlin' Pine Resort* (☎ 923-2548), also on Alta Lake, has rustic two or four-person cabins for $30/40; tent and RV sites are from $13. Whistlin' Pines is as close as you'll find to a dude ranch around here, as they offer horseback riding and fishing.

There aren't many places to eat in Pateros. Your best bet for dinner is the *Cafe Bienville* (☎ 923-2228), nine miles north in Methow. This little cafe serves up Cajun food from an unlikely roadside spot on Hwy 153. Full meals run from $15 to $20 (and they don't take credit cards). It's easy to catch the place closed or full up, so call ahead for reservations.

# Lake Chelan

The glaciers that carved Lake Chelan were powerful excavators, leaving the third-deepest lake in the USA, after Oregon's Crater Lake and Lake Tahoe, on the California/Nevada border. Both glaciers and mountain streams feed water into Lake Chelan, which is 55 miles long and 1500 feet deep.

Chelan, at the southeastern tip of the lake, is the primary base for transportation, accommodations, restaurants, recreational services and entertainment. Up the lake, mountains rise and the trees fill in the lakeshore; by the time you reach Stehekin, a remote village near the lake's head, mountains jut up beyond the dense forest . Lake Chelan is central Washington's playground. Anything you can do in or on

water – swimming, fishing, sailing, canoeing, kayaking, water-skiing and jet skiing – is permitted. Windsurfers will have the most luck up the lake, near Stehekin or Lucerne, where the wind is stronger.

A guarded swimming area, picnic areas and a boat launch, in addition to nearly 150 campsites, make **Lake Chelan State Park** a busy lakeside spot. To get there, head west of Chelan on S Shore Rd for nine miles, or cut north on the Navarre Coulee Rd (Hwy 971) from Hwy 97 between Entiat and Chelan.

There are other boat launches at Twenty-Five-Mile Creek State Park, Don Morse Memorial Park, Old Mill Park and Manson Bay Park. Up the lake, beyond the reach of roads, are another 11 boat docks, most associated with campgrounds. The lake is open to all manner of watercraft.

## ORIENTATION
The town of Chelan serves as the gateway to Lake Chelan. Stehekin, at the north end of the lake, is on the southern edge of the North Cascades, and is connected to Chelan by *The Lady of the Lake II*, a passenger boat that runs regularly up and down the lake. Other than a boat, only a float plane or hiking trail will get you to Stehekin.

South Shore Rd follows Lake Chelan's western shore up as far as Twenty-Five-Mile Creek State Park; on the opposite side of the lake, the road stops at Greens Landing, a few miles past the town of Manson.

## GETTING THERE & AWAY
### Air
Pangborn Memorial Airport, 38 miles south at Wenatchee, is the nearest airport, and is serviced by Horizon Air (☎ (800) 547-9308).

### Bus
Empire Bus Lines runs between Canada and Wenatchee, with stops in Chelan. Free Link buses (☎ 662-1155) connect Chelan with Wenatchee and Leavenworth.

## GETTING AROUND
### Air
Chelan Airways (☎ 682-5555) operates a daily seaplane service to Stehekin, and all points in between. The fare is $80 roundtrip to Stehekin, $100 roundtrip to Domke Lake, a mile south of the Lucerne boat landing.

### Ferry
The Lake Chelan Boat Company (☎ 682-2224), 1418 W Woodin Ave, controls boat service up and down Lake Chelan. A ride on the *Lady of the Lake II* is the most common way to get around, and is popular with tourists who simply want to cruise the lake with a 90-minute stop in Stehekin. Another option is the *Lady Express*, which cuts the four-hour (one-way) boat trip down to just over two hours. Boats leave Chelan every morning at 8:30 am, and the last boat leaves Stehekin at 2 pm during the summer, returning to Chelan by 6 pm. Bring a bicycle along for $13 roundtrip (or rent one in Stehekin). If your destination is Holden Village or one of the lakeside campgrounds, check with the tour company as to which boat best suits your needs.

Fares vary seasonally and in the high season can cost up to $39 for a roundtrip ticket; children under age 11 pay half price. Complete timetable and fare information is also available from the Lake Chelan visitors center. The boats do not transport cars. Dogs aren't permitted on the tour boat from April 1 to October 15, but there is a kennel in Manson, the Animal Inn Boarding Kennel (☎ 687-9497), 712 Wapato Way. During the off-season, a caged pet can ride for $24 roundtrip.

## CHELAN
This town (population 3000) at the southeastern tip of Lake Chelan is flush with lakeside condos and views of the North Cascades. Chelan is the hub of commercial and resort traffic on the lake, and is only appealing in a strictly functional way. The town is flanked by dry hills with scattered pines, lots of scrabble and scree, yellow balsamroot in spring and apple trees galore.

The apples grown here are supposedly the state's finest, and no one who stops by a roadside fruit stand in late October is apt to argue the point.

### Orientation
Chelan is 37 miles northeast of Wenatchee via Hwy 97 and 54 miles southwest of Omak on the same road. From Seattle, it's 166 miles via Stevens Pass and 173 miles via Snoqualmie Pass.

### Information
If it's tourist information you seek, don't miss the Lake Chelan Chamber of Commerce visitors center (☎ 682-3503, (800) 424-3526), 102 E Johnson Ave. Their glossy visitors' guide is useful and comprehensive. Write to PO Box 216, Chelan, WA 98816. The Chelan Ranger Station (☎ 682-2576), 428 Woodin Ave, provides copious amounts of information on the Wenatchee National Forest, Lake Chelan State Park, the Lake Chelan National Recreation Area, near Stehekin, and North Cascades National Park.

The Chelan post office (☎ 682-2625) is at 144 E Johnson Ave. Lake Chelan Community Hospital (☎ 682-2531) is at 503 E Highland.

### Downtown Chelan
The **Campbell House Hotel**, at Chelan and Sanders, first did business in 1900, and some of the Campbell family furniture, which journeyed with its owners from Iowa to Chelan, is still in the hotel. The hotel now serves as the restaurant at Campbell's Resort & Conference Center (see Places to Stay). Another historic structure is **St Andrews Church**, a log building with stained glass windows at 120 E Woodin Ave.

Catch **Riverwalk Park's** mile-long paved path at Emerson and Wapato Sts, and stroll along the short Chelan River.

### Manson
The rural community of Manson (population 1800) makes a scenic drive or bike ride from Chelan. It's eight miles from Chelan

WASHINGTON

via Columbia St, which becomes Hwy 150 (also known as the Manson Hwy), through apple orchards and past views of the lake. From Manson, head out Wapato Lake Rd (turn at the golf course) past Roses Lake, Wapato Lake, and Dry Lake. Manson Bay Park has a swimming and picnic area on Lake Chelan. There's also a boat ramp and picnic area at Old Mill Park, two miles east of Manson on Hwy 150.

Flies are used to catch trout in Wapato Lake.

### Biking

Mountain bikers should stop by the ranger station (☎ 682-2576) at 428 Woodin Ave and pick up a map of USFS roads open to cycling. Road cyclists can ride a loop up to Manson (see above).

### Skiing

There are plenty of good places to go **cross-country skiing** around Chelan, though most are run as off-season business ventures and lack that true wilderness getaway feel. Rentals from Lake Chelan Sports (☎ 682-2629), 132 E Woodin Ave, start at $12 a day. Lakeland Ski (☎ 687-3204), 45 Wapato Way in Manson, also rents skis, and is convenient to Echo Valley and Echo Ridge, two small local ski areas (see below).

Bear Mountain Ranch Nordic Center (☎ 682-5444), on Country Club Rd, five miles west of Chelan off Alt Hwy 97, maintains 34 miles of cross-country trails with telemark areas and good views of the lake. The trails are open late December to mid-March, Wednesday to Sunday and holidays from 9:30 am to 4 pm. Rentals are available, and a trail fee is charged.

When snow makes it impossible to tee off, meet your golf partner for cross-country skiing (or sledding) at the Lake Chelan Municipal Golf Course, 1501 Golf Course Drive. The Lake Chelan Nordic Club (☎ 682-3503) looks after the three miles of groomed Nordic trails, and is open from Christmas to mid-February.

For **downhill skiing** and snowmobiling check out the Echo Valley Ski Area (☎ 682-2576), off Hwy 150 between Chelan and Manson, on Cooper Rd. Volunteer mem-

bers of the Chelan Lake Ski Club are in charge of operating the three tow-ropes and one pommel lift. Echo Valley is open from Christmas to the end of February, on Wednesday, Saturday and Sunday. Its next-door neighbor, Echo Ridge, offers considerably more in the way of cross-country trails. It's also another place to drag your snowmobile. A $6 donation is requested, which goes toward snow plowing and trail grooming. Contact the Lake Chelan Ski Club (☎ 687-3167) for information on either of these areas.

### Fishing

In Lake Chelan, fish for lake, rainbow and cutthroat trout, Kokanee and Chinook salmon, ling cod and smallmouth bass. Just north of Manson, Wapato Lake has good early summer fly-fishing for rainbow trout, and a fair number of bluegill and largemouth bass. Nearby Roses Lake is open from December 1 to March 31 for rainbow trout, brown trout and catfish. Antillon Lake, another three miles north from Wapato Lake, is popular with families, as the resident bluegills, pumpkinseed and crappies are fairly easy to hook. Contact Rush's Fishing Guide Service (☎ 682-2802), PO Box 1481, Chelan 98816, for guided fishing excursions. Graybill's Guide Service (☎ 682-4294) specializes in salmon, steelhead and lake trout fishing.

### Swimming

Don't even think your kids are going to let you sneak past Slidewaters Water Park (☎ 682-5751), 102 Waterslide Drive. A day-long pass costs $10.95, or $7.95 for children ages four to seven. After 5 pm, the rates drop to $7.95 and $4.95.

If you prefer, you can skip the slide and take a swim in Lake Chelan. There are public beaches at Lakeside Park near the west side of Chelan, Don Morse Memorial Park, Manson Bay Park, just east of the lake's south end, and Lake Chelan State Park.

### Golf
Lake Chelan Municipal Golf Course (☎ 682-5421), 1501 Golf Course Drive is the public 18-hole hangout. The course is on a bluff overlooking the lake, surrounded by lovely scenery. There's also a small, inexpensive nine-hole course at 455 Wapato Lake Rd in Manson, called 'MA8+1' (☎ 687-6338). Central Washington's most deluxe course is Desert Canyon (☎ 784-1111, (800) 852-5238), about 17 miles south of Chelan in Orondo.

### Hang-Gliding
The warm thermals rising from the Columbia Basin provide good conditions for hang gliders, and it's not unusual to see gliders launching off 3800-foot Chelan Butte, just southwest of town. Take Chelan Butte Rd at the west end of town, near Lakeside Park.

### Sports Rentals
Ship'N Shore Boat Rental (☎ 682-5125), 1230 W Woodin Ave, rents ski boats and jet skis, as does neighboring Chelan Boat Rentals (☎ 682-4444), 1210 W Woodin Ave. RSI Sports (☎ 784-2399, (800) 786-2637) delivers jet skis and boats to your site.

### Apple-Packing Tours
If you need a break from a life of leisure, tour one of Chelan's apple-packing sheds. Blue Chelan (☎ 682-4541), Trout (☎ 682-2591), and Beebe (☎ 682-2526) all offer tours.

### Special Events
Manson's Apple Blossom Festival is highlighted by a parade and a chicken noodle dinner in mid-May. Various hang-gliding events are held in Chelan throughout the spring and summer. Chelan's best festival is the mid-July Bach Feste, a 10-day series of concerts. Call the visitors center (☎ 682-3503, (800) 424-3526) for exact schedules of all special events.

### Places to Stay
If Chelan is fully booked or seems too expensive, look in Wenatchee, where there are plenty of motel rooms for less than $50. Free public transportation links Wenatchee with Chelan.

The tourist season peaks in the summer and in most places off-season rates drop at least a little bit. Prices in the listings below reflect the high-season summer months, and winter visitors to Chelan can count on room rates being considerably cheaper – up to 40% or even 50% lower at motels.

**Camping** If you're aiming for a spot on Lake Chelan, *Lake Chelan State Park* (☎ 687-3710), on S Lakeshore Rd, nine miles west of Chelan is a large campground with nice lakeside spots for $10 a night. Reservations are required during the summer (they're pretty serious about this), with an additional $5 reservation fee. Call ahead or write them at Route 1, PO Box 90, Chelan, WA 98816. If you don't have reservations, try *Twenty-Five-Mile Creek State Park* (☎ 687-3610), 20 miles west of Chelan on S Shore Rd, just about at road's end. Even though it's fairly remote, the campground can fill up early on summer weekends.

*Lakeshore Park* (☎ 682-5031), on Manson Rd in downtown Chelan is primarily an RV park, with sites from $10 to $25. Reservations are recommended during the summer. *End of the Road RV Park* (☎ 687-9592), eight miles from Chelan on Manson Rd (Hwy 150) has eight RV sites (nothing for tenters) scenically situated next to a car wash.

Campgrounds are not limited to Lake Chelan. *Beebe Bridge Park* (☎ 664-6380) is on the Columbia River four miles east of Chelan on Hwy 97 and has showers, a swimming beach, a boat launch with short-term moorage and tennis courts. There are also a couple of campgrounds on the road to Wenatchee: *Daroga State Park* (☎ 884-8702), eight miles north of Orondo on Hwy 97, and *Orondo River Park* (☎ 884-4700), three miles north of Orondo on Hwy 97.

To take a break from resort-town pampering, pitch a tent at a primitive USFS campground. There are only a handful of sites at these campgrounds, most of which don't have water or any camping fee. Head up Twenty-Five-Mile Creek on USFS Rd 5900 and choose between four campgrounds; the fresh spring water is at *Handy Springs Campground*, 18 miles up the road.

**B&Bs** *Brick House Inn B&B* (☎ 682-4791), 304 Wapato Way, is a downtown-Chelan Victorian home. Both children and pets are permitted, and singles/doubles start at $55/65. *Highland Guest House* (☎ 682-2892, (800) 681-2892), 121 E Highland Ave, is a 1902 Victorian with good views. Rooms start at $80 but drop to $60 in the winter. *Mary Kay's Romantic Whaley Mansion Inn* (☎ 682-5735, (800) 729-2408), 415 S 3rd Ave is elegantly decorated, and rooms easily clear the $100 hurdle.

Up the lake, *Holden Village B&B* (☎ 687-9695), on Twenty-Five-Mile Creek at the end of S Shore Rd, offers inexpensive no-frills rooms from $30/40 during the summer, with lower winter rates and a three-bed dorm with bunks for $15 each. Many of the guests here are headed to Holden Village, a church-based retreat up the lake, but the B&B is open to anyone who's willing to change their own bed linens in the morning.

In Manson, *Hubbard House B&B* (☎ 687-3058), 911 Wapato Way, is a 1920 French Normandy home with private lake access. Rooms with shared bath start at $70; a large room with private bath goes for $90. Manson's other B&B, the *Proctor House Inn* (☎ 687-6361), 495 Lloyd Rd, is a large hilltop house with views of the Chelan valley. Rooms peak at $85 to $115 during the summer.

**Hotels** *Parkway Motel* (☎ 682-2822), 402 N Manson Rd, across from Lake Shore Park, allows pets in the off-season and charges only $35 for a basic room or $55 for a kitchenette. *Mom's Montlake Motel* (☎ 682-5715), 823 Wapato Way, is one block off the main drag at the east end of town, and is a quiet, inexpensive place. Single/double rooms start at $42/48.

The box-like *Apple Inn Motel* (☎ 682-4044), 1002 E Woodin Ave, has a heated outdoor pool and indoor hot tub. In the summer, rooms start at $49, or $55 with kitchenette. The *Midtowner Motel* (☎ 682-4051), 721 W Woodin Ave, isn't on the lake, but it's a well-rounded place, with indoor and outdoor pools, a hot tub, laundry facilities and kitchenette rooms. All this (and they also allow pets) for a mere $50/65.

*The Cabana Motel* (☎ 682-2233), 420 Manson Rd, is across from the city park and marina. Doubles start at $63, or $79 for a poolside kitchenette double; pets are OK.

Up the road in Manson, the *Mountain View Lodge* (☎ 687-9505, (800) 967-8105), 25 Wapato Point Parkway, has a heated pool, a hot tub and a picnic area, and houses more than the occasional tour group. Rooms start at $69/80.

**Resorts** Though they're not quite full-fledged destination resorts, all these 'resort motels' offer more than the average motel. They're all on the lake, have private beaches with boat moorage and are equipped to deal with small conventions or large families.

The sprawling *Campbell's Resort & Conference Center* (☎ 682-2561, (800) 553-8225), 104 W Woodin Ave, has swallowed up the historic Campbell Hotel, established in 1901. This is Chelan's premier resort. During peak season rooms start at $98. Rooms or cottages with kitchens start at $138. *Caravel Resort* (☎ 682-2582, (800) 962-8723), 332 W Woodin Ave, is lakeside and right on the edge of town; rooms start at $92. *Westview Resort Motel* (☎ 682-4396, (800) 468-2781), 2312 W Woodin Ave, on the outskirts of town by

Lakeside Park, has an outdoor pool and spa, private beach and dock. Summer rates start at $98 for doubles.

*Darnell's Resort Motel* (☎ 682-2015, (800) 967-8149), 901 Spader Bay Rd, off the road to Manson on the north side of Chelan, is another upscale lakeside motel, with an emphasis on family vacationers. Besides the beach, there are paddleboat rentals, tennis courts, an exercise room, a nine-hole putting golf course and bicycles. Rates start at $75 for a double. There are also two-bedroom units which sleep six for $165 to $220.

*Watson's Harverence Resort* (☎ 687-3720, (800) 697-3720), has lakefront cottages on S Shore Rd, near Lake Chelan State Park. Cottages for four people run $125 during July and August. Boat storage and moorage are also available. *Kelly's Resort* (☎ 687-3220) is about five miles past Lake Chelan State Park on Hwy 971 (S Shore Rd). Woodsy cottages across the road from the lake start at $75 for two people. Larger cottages run $97 for four adults, with weekly and family rates available.

**Houseboats**   Panorama   Enterprises (☎ 242-9590, (800) 800-0409) can set you up with a houseboat rental. The cost is $1995 for a week, or $1435 for four days, with discounts in the off-season. The boats sleep 10 people.

**Vacation Home Rentals**  Chelan Vacation Rentals (☎ 682-4011, (800) 356-9756) has condos in a development with pool, hot tub and racquetball courts. Golf packages at Desert Canyon are also available.

### Places to Eat
Early in the morning, *Flying Saucers Espresso* (☎ 682-5129), 116 S Emerson St, is the place to engage in local gossip and swill espresso. If it's hip you're craving, there's a touch of it here, and a good dose of local color, but never so much of either as to make an outsider feel unwelcome. There's an astounding variety of home-made muffins, as well as cookies and pas-

tries for later in the day. If you'd rather eat a full breakfast, cross the street and head upstairs to the *Emerson St Cafe* (☎ 682-2750), 113 S Emerson St, and try the Northwest Scramble ($5.75). Lunch (good pastas) and dinner are also served here.

*Dagwood's* (☎ 682-8630), 246 W Manson Hwy in Chelan Plaza, has good sandwiches (gyros for $4.25), smoothies and ice cream. They're open from 8 am to 10:30 pm, and it's a comfortable place to eat a muffin for breakfast or a salad for dinner.

*Goochi's* (☎ 682-2436), 104 E Woodin Ave, tries for a brewpub atmosphere (though big-screen TV is not a typical brewpub installation) and does have many Northwest microbrews on tap. Burgers ($5 to $7.50) highlight the lunch menu, and for dinner, it's the sort of place where you follow your oyster shooters with a steak (about $15). Even if you're not up for a drink, stop in for a look at the cherrywood bar, brought around Cape Horn from Europe in the late 1800s, and previously installed in a Montana bar. *Campbell House Restaurant* (☎ 682-4250), 104 W Woodin Ave, is the fanciest dining spot in town, and though the meals aren't generally what you'd call innovative, vegetarians will have to give the place credit for serving a stuffed squash entree ($10.25). At *Chelan House* (☎ 682-2013), 502 E Woodin Ave, the dinner theater is played up; the dinner itself is the standard American meat with salad bar. It does, however, open at 5:30 am for breakfast.

There are a couple of decent places to eat in Manson. *Uncle Tim's Pizzeria* (☎ 687-3035), 76 Wapato Way, has huge, meaty pizzas and several pasta dishes (with prices topping out at $9.95 for shrimp tortellini). For Mexican food, *El Vaquero* (☎ 687-3179), 75 Wapato Way, is more authentic and tastier than the other nacho joints in the area, and it's easy to eat your fill for less than $10.

### Entertainment
Catch a movie at the *Ruby Theater* (☎ 682-5016) 135 E Woodin Ave. The theater dates

from 1913, and is named for the original owner's daughter.

If dinner theater sounds like fun, *Chelan House* (☎ 682-2013), 502 E Woodin, is the best show in town. There's also a new *Performing Arts Center* where the Chelan Valley Players (☎ 682-3520) stage shows.

*Goochi's* (☎ 682-2436), 104 E Woodin Ave, hosts a comedy night every Wednesday, and on Thursday nights brings in blues bands from around the Northwest.

### Getting There & Away

See Getting There & Away and Getting Around for the Lake Chelan area for more detailed information on transportation options.

**Air** Chelan Airways (☎ 682-5555) operates a daily seaplane service between Chelan and Stehekin; the fare is $80 roundtrip. The airfield is northeast of town on Alt Hwy 97.

**Bus** Empire Bus Lines (☎ (800) 351-1060) run buses between Canada and Wenatchee, with stops in Chelan.

### Getting Around

There's a Link bus up to Manson from Chelan. During the summer, a shuttle runs up to Lake Chelan State Park, and a wintertime bus (equipped with ski racks) stops at the Mission Ridge Ski Area in Wenatchee. Buses stop throughout the small downtown; a convenient place to catch them is in near the visitors center.

### HOLDEN VILLAGE

Holden Village (☎ 687-3644), a retreat center operated by the Lutheran church, offers programs on theology, literature, the environment, Bible study, race and culture, as well as arts and crafts, for people of all religious backgrounds. Holden Village is open year round, and during the winter, the schedule is less structured. Several trails lead into the adjacent Glacier Peak Wilderness Area. Holden Village is connected by a road to the Lucerne boat landing, and most visitors arrive on the *Lady of the Lake*

*II* tour boat. (You can't drive there.) Rates are $40 per person per night, or $215 a week, which includes all meals and seminars. For information, write to the Registrar, Holden Village, Chelan, WA 98816.

### STEHEKIN

Of all the wonderful spots in the North Cascades, Stehekin (population 70) is especially charmed. Part of the charm is from its remoteness, as the tiny community is only accessible by boat, plane or a long hike, most often across Cascade Pass. An equal amount of charm accrues from the beauty of its location at the head of Lake Chelan, on the southern edge of the North Cascades. Plenty of hiking trails lead into the mountains. If possible, stay here for a day or two rather than making a quick up-and-back tour-boat excursion.

Virtually all the tours, activities, places to eat and accommodations are limited to the summer season, which runs from mid-June to mid-September. In the winter, the North Cascades Stehekin Lodge has a few kitchenette units available, but visitors should bring their own food from Chelan.

Stehekin is roughly translated as 'the way through', and though Native Americans didn't have villages at the north end of Lake Chelan, they did use nearby Cascade Pass as a route across the Cascades.

Miners after North Cascades gold figured a boat ride up Lake Chelan was easier than foot travel across the mountains, and prospectors began tramping through the area in the 1850s. Even Clara Barton, founder of the American Red Cross, visited Stehekin on a wood-fired steamboat in 1891 and filed a mining claim. However, Barton's visit was far upstaged when, in 1944, young Elizabeth Taylor filmed *The Courage of Lassie* in Stehekin. Subsistence farmers began putting down roots in the 1880s, and, in 1905, a six-story Swiss-style hotel opened, catering to hunters and anglers. In 1927, a dam at the lake's foot raised the water level by 21 feet, flooding many buildings, including Stehekin's original 1892 hotel.

## Orientation

Stehekin Valley Rd, Stehekin's only road, is referred to most often as just 'the road'. From the landing, the road continues to the northwest for 23 miles, only five of which are paved. Heading east, the road dead ends after four miles. Destinations at the landing are all within walking distance, and it's easy to rent a bike or catch a bus to travel up the road.

## Information

**Tourist Offices** The Courtney Log Office, 150 yards past the post office has information about the valley and can organize bookings for trips. Golden West Visitor Center houses the NPS Information Center, which is also an interpretive museum and art gallery. It's open daily from 12:30 to 2 pm (the hours of the tour boat's layover in Stehekin) March 15 to May 14, from 7:30 am to 4 pm May 15 to September 15, and from 10:30 am to 2 pm September 16 to mid-October.

There's also an NPS ranger station in the same building as the North Cascades Stehekin Lodge restaurant, which serves as the off-season information center. Backpackers need an overnight camping permit, which can be obtained from the Chelan USFS Ranger Station. A limited number of permits are issued free, on a first-come first-served basis, no more than 24 hours before departure.

**Post & Telecommunications** The post office is in the lower level of the ranger station.

Telephone service in Stehekin is via expensive radio-telephone, so most business listings are for answering services or voice mailboxes in Chelan. One regular credit card phone for outgoing calls is in front of the public laundromat and shower house. Other telephone arrangements can be made at the Courtney Log Office, or the North Cascades Stehekin Lodge.

**Media** The *Stehekin Choice*, put out every two months, is a great way to gain insight

into the life and culture of the 70 or so people who live here year round.

**Laundry** There's a public laundry and shower house building on the main road, about 50 yards beyond the post office.

**Medical Services** The nearest hospital is in Chelan. The valley has its own network of individuals and park-service personnel certified in first-aid, so ask locals for a reference. Contact the ranger station in an emergency. Most businesses and NPS employees carry radios for this purpose.

## Hiking

**Buckner Orchard** The way to Buckner Orchard, one of the Stehekin area's oldest settlements, makes for a nice walk. Once there you'll find a homestead cabin built in 1889, plenty of old farm equipment and trees that keep on bearing apples. Head 3.4 miles up the northwest branch of Stehekin Valley Rd, turn left at the far end of the Rainbow Creek bridge and look for a sign about 20 yards off the road, marking the Buckner Orchard Walk, an easy one-mile roundtrip to the apple orchards.

From just past the bridge, there's also a short path leading to the 312-foot **Rainbow Falls**.

**Lakeshore Trail** An easy trail starts at the Golden West Visitor Center and heads south near Lake Chelan's shore. There's a campground just a short way down the forested trail. It's possible to make this into a backpacking trip: Moore Point is seven miles from the trailhead while Prince Creek is 17 miles.

**Stehekin River Trail** A relatively flat trail starts at Harlequin Campground (4.5 miles northwest from the landing) and heads upriver through the forest, past many fishing holes. It's a cool, shady walk on a hot day.

**Rainbow Creek Trail** A steady uphill hike from a trailhead 2.5 miles from the landing leads to great lake and valley views.

There's a campground two miles from the trailhead at Rainbow Bridge, and 4.4 miles in, hikers must ford Rainbow Creek. Hike for 10 miles, and you're at McAlester Pass.

Rainbow Loop Trail starts at the same trailhead, splits off to the left just past the Rainbow Bridge campground, and heads back downhill to the valley floor. This five-mile version includes the initial climb to great views, with a fairly quick return to the valley.

**Purple Pass Trail** Head east from the Golden West Visitor Center and immediately begin climbing toward 6884-foot Purple Pass, 7.4 miles away. Since it starts at the landing, hikers who are looking for a short, vigorous hike with good views of the lake and mountains can grunt uphill for a hour or so, and then return for the afternoon boat to Chelan.

### Biking
You can rent a bike from the store at the North Cascades Stehekin Lodge or from Discovery Bikes at the Courtney Log Office. Six-speed beach cruisers cost $3.50 an hour or $15 a day at the lodge. Discovery Bikes has mountain bikes for $3.50 an hour or $10 a day.

A popular option for day-trippers is a $12 self-guided bike tour from Stehekin Day Tours (☎ 682-4584). A bus shuttles cyclists and their bikes (rental included in price) up the road to the Harlequin Campground and drops them off to ride back to the boat landing. Everything's timed so that you can arrive on a morning boat, take the bike ride, and then catch the 2 pm boat back to Chelan.

### Fishing
The Stehekin River is open for catch-and-release fishing from March 1 to June 30, with the regular fishing season running from July 1 to October 30. Both cutthroat and rainbow trout live in the upper river and the creeks feeding into it. Chinook salmon begin the run from Lake Chelan up

the Stehekin in late August, and continue through September. Chinook anglers must have a stamp from the Department of Fisheries, as well as a regular fishing license. Stop by McGregor Mountain Outdoor Company, at the landing, for fishing advice, supplies and licenses.

### Boating
Rent a 10-foot boat from the North Cascades Stehekin Lodge for $8 an hour or $32 a day and cruise the lake. Alternatively, sail Lake Chelan with Woodwind Charters, which runs 1½-hour trips up to three times a day ($15 for adults, $7.50 for kids). Check at the North Cascades Stehekin Lodge for a sailing schedule.

The Stehekin Adventure Company (one of the Courtney family's many ventures) runs raft trips on the Stehekin River in the spring and summer (☎ 682-4677); adults are $40, children $30.

### Horseback Riding
Stehekin Valley Ranch's Cascade Corrals (☎ 682-4677) has twice-daily horseback rides, leaving at 8:30 am and 2:15 pm and lasting for 2½ hours. The cost is $30 per person and reservations are required. (Call the ranch or stop at the Courtney Log Office).

### Organized Tours
Stehekin Discovery Tours (☎ 884-4844) operates out of the Courtney Log Office. Two-hour van tours cost $10 ($5 for children ages seven to 12) and leave at 9:30 am and 2:30 pm daily in season. A bicycle breakfast tour to the Stehekin Valley Ranch departs at 7:30 am every morning. The $15 fee includes rental and trip, but breakfast is extra.

Stehekin Day Tours has a bus waiting for the morning boats, and for $21 it shuttles visitors to the Stehekin Valley Ranch for lunch, then takes a leisurely scenic trip back to the boat landing, arriving in time for the 2 pm return boat to Chelan.

North Cascades Stehekin Lodge leads a daily bus trip to Rainbow Falls. Buses leave upon arrival of the *Lady Express* (around 10:45 am) and the *Lady of the Lake II* (around 12:30 pm). The 45-minute tour costs $3.75. There's sometimes a third tour at 1:15 pm.

Buckner Orchard Walks emphasize pioneer lifestyles with stops at the one-room Stehekin School and the Buckner Orchard. Walks leave at 2:30 pm daily from the landing, and cost $5 for adults, $3 for children ages seven to 12. Make reservations at the Courtney Log Office.

Be sure to check at the Golden West Visitor Center for the current listing of interpretive nature walks and hikes led by the NPS.

## Places to Stay

**Camping** First you'll need to obtain a camping permit from the NPS Information Center. Permits are free and are issued within 24 hours of departure. The NPS maintains 11 primitive campsites along the road up the valley, as well as a good number of hike-in campgrounds. *Purple Point Campground* is right at the landing, 200 yards upvalley from the dock. *Weaver Point Campground* is a boaters' campground, one mile from the landing by boat.

Up the road at Harlequin Bridge, *Harlequin Campground* is four miles from the landing. There are great views of the river. You'll have direct access to trailheads for Agnes Gorge and the Pacific Crest Trail at *High Bridge Campground*, 11 miles from the landing. At the end of the line is *Cottonwood Campground*, 23 miles from the landing, the last campground accessible from the road. The road is clear all the way up to Cottonwood only from around the end of June.

**B&Bs** *Silver Bay Inn* (☎ 682-2212), Box 43, Stehekin, WA 98852, has one large, solar-heated B&B room and several housekeeping cabins (see below) two miles up the road near the Stehekin Pastry Company. There is a two-night minimum stay; rates run around $80, with seasonal variations.

**Hotels** *North Cascades Stehekin Lodge* (☎ 682-4494), PO Box 457, Chelan, WA 98816, is in town on the lakefront. Rooms start at $55, kitchenettes at $68. This is the 'modern' (ie non-rustic) place to stay in Stehekin.

**Lodges** *Courtney's Stehekin Valley Ranch* (☎ 682-4677), PO Box 36, Stehekin, WA 98852, provides lodging in rustic cabins. The cost is $55 per person, and includes all meals (lunch the day you arrive and leave), and transportation around the lower valley. *Silver Bay Guest Cabins* (☎ 682-2212), PO Box 43, Stehekin, WA 98852, are a handful of lakeside cabins. There is a five-night minimum stay in the cabins, and rentals run $85 to $130 a night.

*Rustic Retreat* is available for rental from April 15 to October 1. $55 covers four people. Bicycles can be borrowed. Write to PO Box 84, Stehekin, WA 98852 for information.

**Vacation Home Rentals** Contact Mike and Nancy Barnhart (☎ 884-1730), PO Box 25 Stehekin, WA 98852, for information on how to rent the *Flick Creek House*, the *Totem House* or *The Stehekin House*. Craig and Roberta Courtney (☎ 682-4677), PO Box 67, Stehekin, WA 98852, rent out the *Stehekin Log Cabin*. It costs $80 per day for two people, or $425 for the week. It's not as cheap as you'd think, since there's a 25% non-refundable 'booking fee' added to the total calculated rent.

The *Stehekin Cedar Home* is available for monthly lease at $1000 for the first month, $900 thereafter. Write to Walter Winkel, PO Box 14, Stehekin, WA 98852. The *Stehekin Mountain Cabin* rents for $60 to $75 per night, or $360 per week. Write to Don and Roberta Pitts, PO Box 272, Stehekin, WA 98852.

## Places to Eat

The *Stehekin Restaurant*, opposite the public docks, is the restaurant adjoining the *North Cascades Stehekin Lodge*. Breakfasts run $5, and dinners, including grilled halibut and blackened chicken, are around $12. At the *Stehekin Valley Ranch* reservations are required, unless you're part of a tour, and there's a different set dinner menu each day ($12 to $15). If you're cooking your own meals, there's a very limited stock of groceries at the landing, so you'd be wise to stock up in Chelan. The *Silver Bay Inn* serves breakfast, and the *Stehekin Pastry Company*, two miles upvalley from the landing, serves good pastries, espresso and ice cream.

### Entertainment
The NPS offers programs every evening between June 15 and September 15. Presentations on topics of natural and human history start at 8 pm at the Golden West Visitor Center. Local residents sometimes supplement the programs with presentations on local cultural history.

There are also short talks in the afternoon at 1:15 pm, when most people are outside playing. Keep your eyes peeled for the NPS employee-cum-Elvis impersonator who drops in from time to time.

### Getting There & Away
**Air** Chelan Airways (☎ 682-5555) provides air service to Stehekin from Chelan by seaplane. The cost is $80 for a roundtrip ticket.

**Ferry** The most common way of getting to Stehekin is on either the *Lady of the Lake II* or *Lady Express* from Chelan. At least one boat makes the trip daily, year round. Fares and timetables vary seasonally, and a roundtrip ticket can cost as much as $39 in the high season. Tickets can be purchased upon boarding, although advance purchase is recommended in the summer. Contact the Lake Chelan Boat Company (☎ 682-2224), PO Box 457, Chelan, WA 98816, for more information.

**Car** Although there are roads and cars in Stehekin, there are no roads to Stehekin. Those wanting to barge their vehicle in for a long-term stay may do so from Chelan. Contact the Tom Courtney Freight & Barge

Service (☎ 682-4963 Stehekin, 682-2493 Chelan), at Lake Chelan Marina, 2338 Woodin Ave, in Chelan. There's also the Lake Chelan Boat Company Barge Service (☎ 682-2519), PO Box 186, Chelan, WA 98816.

**Hiking** The **Pacific Crest Trail** passes by Stehekin, making it possible to hike from Rainy Pass on Hwy 20, to Cottonwood Campground at the end of the Stehekin Valley Rd, where you could then, depending upon the time of the year, be picked up by the NPS shuttle van. Reservations must be made for a van pickup (see the next section). Alternatively, you could hike 23 miles down the road into Stehekin (there are other campgrounds along the road; see Camping in the preceding Places to Stay section).

### Getting Around
**Bus** The NPS operates a shuttle van up and down Stehekin Valley Rd twice daily, from the boat landing to Cottonwood Campground (weather permitting). It costs $5 each way, and passengers get a narrated tour. Reservations may be made up to two days in advance in person at the ranger stations at Stehekin, Chelan, Marblemount, the North Cascades visitors center (in Newhalem) or the Sedro Woolley Information Station. For those hiking in to Stehekin from other places, reservations can be made more than two days in advance by calling the Golden West Visitor Center (☎ 856-5703, ext 14), open from 7:30 am to 4 pm daily. Note that you will have to reconfirm these arrangements within two to four days of your ride, or you will be axed from the list.

The Stehekin Adventure Company supplements the NPS shuttle during the summer, and runs four buses daily from the landing as far as High Bridge for $4 each way. The bus accommodates both bikes and backpacks. The bus has a 'bakery special', and charges $1 each way for those going only as far as the Stehekin Pastry Company.

**Bicycle** Bicycles are the easiest way to get around. Some lodges rent bicycles, while others simply let their guests borrow them. Rentals are available from the North Cascades Stehekin Lodge, which is directly across from the docks, and from Discovery Bikes, at the Courtney Log Office. The Lake Chelan Boat Company (see Ferry in the Getting There & Away section, above) charges $13 roundtrip for bike transport, if you'd prefer to bring your own.

## Wenatchee River Valley

# Central Washington

If there are any defining images of central Washington, they may well be an apple tree and an irrigation ditch. There wouldn't be much out here it if weren't for the dams on the Columbia and Yakima rivers. The resulting irrigation projects have turned this from a barren desert into one of the nation's greatest agricultural areas. There is still plenty of outback country here too, where farmers get by with dry-land wheat farms and a next-year mentality.

Central Washington's geography is dominated by the Columbia River and its dams. During the Ice Age, glaciers crept down from the north and overtook the Columbia River's channel, forcing the river water to cut a new southerly path. When the glaciers receded, the river went back to its original streambed, leaving a large area of central Washington with a big, dry river channel, known today as the Grand Coulee. This chapter covers this region, bounded by the peaks of the Cascade range to the west and stretching from the Grand Coulee Dam in the northeast to the Yakama Reservation in the southwest.

The long rain shadow cast by the Cascades over the entire area makes for a dry climate and warm summer temperatures. This lack of Pacific-slope gloom has changed a number of communities from agricultural trading centers or mining ghost towns into retirement and recreational communities. The city of Yakima has grown in stature and sophistication as retirees have settled here, and the local wine-making industry now attracts national attention. The Yakima valley is home to the Yakama Indian Reservation and more apple orchards than you ever imagined possible.

Despite, or perhaps because of, the general aridity of the region, lakes are some of the prime destinations for travelers. The Bavarian village of Leavenworth (the concept may be a little hokey, but the setting is lovely) makes its mark as a faux-Alpine

burg; it's a hub for lots of cross-country skiing, summer hiking and water sports on nearby Lake Wenatchee. The Potholes is a curious area south of Moses Lake created when irrigation dams flooded desert sand dunes, which remain as islands above the lakes. Birds flock here, as do canoers and anglers.

Two highways cross the Cascades from the west side into central Washington. Highway 2 heads east from Everett and crosses Stevens Pass to Leavenworth, then heads on to Spokane. From Seattle, I-90 cuts across Snoqualmie Pass and leads to Ellensburg, where I-82 splits off to head south to Yakima. From Ellensburg, I-90 continues west to Moses Lake and Spokane.

# Wenatchee River Valley

As the Wenatchee River makes its way east from Wenatchee Lake to the Columbia River there are remarkable changes in both geography and culture. The area around Wenatchee Lake and Leavenworth is absolutely alpine, craggy and wild. Leavenworth itself is an odd, faux-Bavarian town, remodeled to fit into its landscape and lure visitors who wouldn't come for the great mountain and river recreation alone.

Cashmere, halfway between Leavenworth and Wenatchee, is a quiet riverside town, known mostly for its candy factory. By the time the Wenatchee River pours into the Columbia River at Wenatchee, the scenery is dominated by apple trees. Wenatchee is the area's urban hub, with an easygoing sort of bustle and lodging that's less expensive than up the road in touristy Leavenworth.

## LEAVENWORTH

There are two ways of thinking about Leavenworth (population 1700). Some people see it as the town that went Bavarian back in the '60s – the place where downtown shopkeepers pull on lederhosen and dirndl skirts every morning. Others visualize white-water rafting and hiking trails. No matter what your point of view, there's so much going on here that just about everybody will find *something* of interest. The spectacular mountain setting – it perches 1164 feet above sea level on the east slope

of the Cascades, with the Wenatchee River rushing through town – is bound to appeal.

In the fall, salmon travel to their spawning grounds up the Wenatchee River. The Wenatchee is the only river in the state with three fairly strong wild salmon stocks: approximately 5000 spring Chinook, 9000 summer Chinook, and 40,000 sockeye salmon spawn up the Wenatchee every year.

Wildfires ripped through several nearby canyons and came close to Leavenworth's downtown during the summer of 1994. Stop by the ranger station to determine the

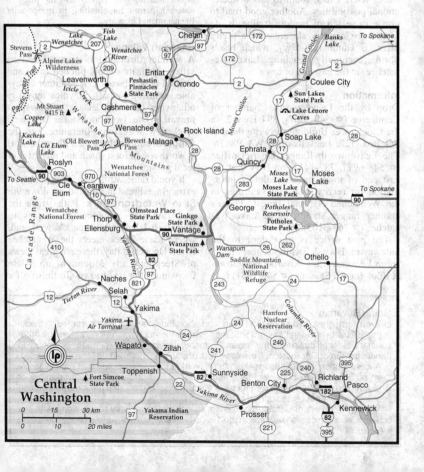

WASHINGTON

status of trails in Icicle and Tumwater canyons.

## Orientation

Leavenworth is 125 miles east of Seattle on Hwy 2, and 46 miles north of I-90. From I-90, you can take Hwy 970 north from Cle Elum or Hwy 97 from Ellensburg (55 miles).

Discover the heart of Leavenworth by cutting south from Hwy 2 onto Front St, which leads into the Bavarian Village.

Icicle Rd, on the west side of town, traces Icicle Creek south to lots of recreational possibilities. Another good road to cruise in search of random trailheads, de facto cross-country ski areas or a pretty drive, is Chumstick Hwy, which heads north (eventually reaching Lake Wenatchee) at the east end of town.

## Information

Drop by the Leavenworth Chamber of Commerce (☎ 548-5807), 894 Hwy 2, in the Clocktower Building, or write them at PO Box 327, Leavenworth, WA 98826. The Leavenworth Ranger District office (☎ 548-6977, 782-1413) on Hwy 2 at the east end of town, has a wealth of information on recreational opportunities in the Wenatchee National Forest. There's another ranger station up at Lake Wenatchee (☎ 763-3103).

The post office is next door to the Safeway on Hwy 2. Two bookstores operate in Leavenworth's Bavarian downtown. A Book for All Seasons (☎ 548-1451) is at

906 Front St, and A Village Books & Music (☎ 548-5911) is around the corner at 215 9th St.

Cascade Medical Center (☎ 548-5815) is downtown, near Waterfront Park, at 817 Commercial St.

**Note** In 1994 an outburst of forest fires in Central Washington sent people living in places like Leavenworth into a panic. Although the town and many popular recreation areas were spared, several trails were badly burned and remain closed. Recreationalists should be sure to stop in at the ranger station to check the status of trails before heading out. This is also the place to obtain a permit for climbing in the popular Enchantment Lakes area.

## Bavarian Village

A wander through this ersatz Bavarian village, with its steeply pitched roofs and painted flower boxes, can be either enjoyable, amusing or both. (Cynics may say otherwise, but we'll let a generous spirit prevail.) The two bookstores are well stocked with regional literature, and the **Gingerbread Factory** (see Places to Eat) is worth a stop for a snack and an earful of local gossip.

If you'd rather stroll than shop, pocket an extra gingerbread muffin and cut down 9th St to **Waterfront Park**. Paths trace the riverfront and a footbridge crosses to Blackbird Island at the park's west end, where Icicle Creek meets the Wenatchee River. On a clear day, there are great views of Sleeping Lady Mountain, up Icicle Canyon southwest of town. To finish off a

---

### Going Bavarian

Leavenworth grew up as a railroad town, and when the Great Northern rerouted its tracks in the 1920s, bypassing Leavenworth, the town foundered. It wasn't long before the other substantial local business, the sawmill, closed, leaving the town badly equipped to handle the Great Depression. Downtown was pretty much boarded up for a few decades.

A local tourism committee, seeking to rejuvenate their town, noted that the California town of Solvang had done well by emphasizing its Danish heritage. A fair number of Russian Germans had pioneered much of eastern Washington, and the mountain setting seemed alpine enough to support a little Bavaria.

Though it took considerable boosterism to get the community to go along with the scheme, economics won out, and in the 1960s Leavenworth's downtown began to lay on the frills. ■

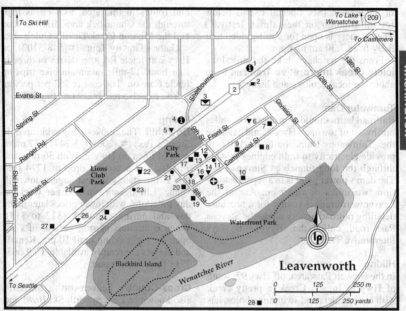

WASHINGTON

**Leavenworth**

Blackbird Island

Wenatchee River

Waterfront Park

City Park

Lions Club Park

To Ski Hill

To Seattle

To Lake Wenatchee

To Cashmere

| PLACES TO STAY | |
|---|---|
| 7 | Pension Anna |
| 8 | Mrs Anderson's Lodging House |
| 9 | Obertal Village Motor Inn |
| 10 | Edel Haus Inn |
| 13 | Edelweiss Hotel |
| 17 | Reiner's Gasthaus |
| 19 | Blackbird Lodge |
| 20 | Kinney Condos, Eighth St Pensione |
| 24 | Tyrolean Ritz |
| 27 | Enzian Motor Inn |
| 28 | Run of the River |

| PLACES TO EAT | |
|---|---|
| 2 | Leavenworth's Finest Espresso |
| 5 | Leavenworth Pizza Co |
| 6 | Burgermeister Bier Garden |
| 12 | Andreas Keller |
| 16 | Gingerbread Factory |
| 16 | Walter's Other Place |
| 18 | Terrace Bistro |
| 26 | Gustav's |

| OTHER | |
|---|---|
| 1 | Ranger Station |
| 3 | Post Office |
| 4 | Chamber of Commerce |
| 11 | A Village Books & Music |
| 15 | Cascade Medical Center |
| 21 | Nussknacker Haus |
| 22 | Leavenworth Brewery |
| 23 | A Book for all Seasons Bookstore |
| 25 | Swimming Pool |

walking tour, return to town via 8th St for more food and gifts.

**Leavenworth National Fish Hatchery**
When the Grand Coulee and Chief Joseph dams blocked salmon from migrating to their upstream spawning grounds, the government tried to ameliorate the loss of these populations by building hatcheries downstream from the dams. At the Leavenworth

Hatchery (☎ 548-7641), off Icicle Rd at 12790 Fish Hatchery Rd, about 2.5 million spring Chinook salmon are reared each year. The hatchery also raises some steelhead trout, a related anadromous fish. Both species of fish are released to migrate to the ocean in mid-April, when the rivers are running full force. The chinook begin returning to spawn at the hatchery around August 10, and continue into the first week

WASHINGTON

of September. (See Special Events below for information on the salmon festival.) The hatchery is open for a self-guided tour daily from 7:30 am to 4 pm.

From the hatchery, hike the mile-long **Icicle Creek Interpretive Trail** and learn about the local ecology and history.

## Tumwater Dam

Railroad buffs should stop about four miles northwest of town, on Hwy 2, and examine the Tumwater Dam, built in 1907 to provide electricity to train engines passing through the long tunnels at Stevens Pass. The dam's power plant is in a separate location two miles downstream. Ask at the Leavenworth ranger station for a brochure detailing railroad history along the Stevens Pass road, called the 'Bygone Byways Interpretive Trail'.

## Hiking

In the Blewett Pass area, off Hwy 97, south of Hwy 2, Ingalls Creek, a pretty creek with big boulders and swimming holes, has a trail running along it for miles and miles starting at Ingalls Creek Rd, about seven miles south of Hwy 2. Several side trails feed into the Ingalls Creek Trail.

The three-mile **Swauk Forest Discovery Trail**, at the Blewett Pass summit, passes through a 'managed' forest. Pick up a brochure at the ranger station to read about natural processes and management decisions that have shaped the forest here.

## Biking

Road bikers can decide if they're up to the 50-mile Leavenworth-Lake Wenatchee Loop. The hilly ride goes up Chumstick Hwy to the lake, then returns to town via Hwy 207 and Hwy 2. It's not for the easily fatigued. When there's no snow on Ski Hill, this area just northwest of town becomes 'mountain bike hill'. Two loop trails, used for cross-country skiing in the winter, are open to bikers and hikers in the summer.

Several roads in the Icicle Creek area, off Icicle Rd, have become popular mountain biking destinations. The USFS ranger station has information on suggested loops

and routes in this area, as well as trips through the Chumstick area, Blewett Pass and the Mission Creek/Devil's Gulch area.

Gator's Gravity Tours (☎ 548-5102), on Hwy 2 at Icicle Rd, specializes in three to four hour, 17-mile mountain bike trips up Icicle Canyon. The cost is $52 per person.

You can also rent bikes on Hwy 207.

## Skiing

**Downhill** The closest big ski area is Stevens Pass (☎ (206) 973-2441), 37 miles west of town on Hwy 2. With 36 runs and 11 lifts, and a vertical drop of 1774 feet, this is the state's second-largest downhill venue. Lift tickets run $30 per weekend day for adults, with lower prices later in the day and during midweek ($12 to $18). When conditions permit, several lifts are open for night skiing until 10 pm. Rentals and classes are readily available. Call 663-7711 for a snow report.

**Cross-Country** Leavenworth's Ski Hill, also known as Leavenworth Ski Bowl and Bavarian Village Family Ski Area (☎ 548-5807) is a small place a mile north of town up Ski Hill Drive, with daytime downhill skiing for beginners, and 25 miles of cross-country ski trails, including a link to downtown Leavenworth. One short stretch of groomed trail is lit for night skiing.

Once there's snow on the ground, Lake Wenatchee becomes a great cross-country ski area, with 20 miles of marked and groomed trails. There's another 36 miles, including a See & Ski interpretive area, in the Lower Chiwawa River area, off the Chumstick road (called Hwy 209 or the Chumstick Hwy), just north of the hamlet of Plain (between Leavenworth and Lake Wenatchee). Get maps and details from the ranger station in Leavenworth.

Cross-country skiers can expect to see snowmobilers at another popular trail area – Blewett Pass, on Hwy 97 south of Hwy 2. Roadside signs indicate sno parks (buy a sno-park pass at any local grocery or sporting goods store) and trails; information is available from the Leavenworth Ranger District office.

Stevens Pass maintains 16 miles of groomed cross-country ski trails. A daily pass costs $6 for adults and $5 for children and seniors. Rentals and snacks are also available at the Nordic Center, which is five miles east of the downhill ski area and is open Friday to Sunday and holidays, 9 am to 4 pm.

## Climbing

Castle Rock, just east of Hwy 2 in Tumwater Canyon, is only about three miles from town and, partly because of its easy access, is a popular rock-climbing area. Serious climbers will no doubt focus on the Alpine Lakes Wilderness Area (see below).

## Fishing

Rainbow and cutthroat trout are found in many lakes and streams (try some of the streams that feed the Chiwawa River), and the Wenatchee River is a good place to fish for winter steelhead. Both Lake Wenatchee and Fish Lake, a smaller lake just northeast of Lake Wenatchee, are popular lake fishing spots.

## Rafting

Leavenworth's close proximity to the Wenatchee River makes it a popular destination for adventure-deprived urbanites. The Classes I to III rapids provide many trip possibilities. The uppermost stretch of the river, from Lake Wenatchee to Tumwater Campground, is an easy 19-mile, day-long float in a kayak or raft. It can be run from March to November; the water is highest in May and June, when snowmelt contributes generously. It's also a nice September and October trip, when there's more wildlife, including salmon, in and around the river. All but expert kayakers should be sure to pull out at Tumwater Campground, as the next stretch of the Wenatchee roils with rapids, big drops and sucking holes. The river is pretty wild all the way from Tumwater to Leavenworth, where it hits the river's third stretch, the 18.5 miles from Leavenworth to Monitor. This is the section that most outfitters run, and its waves and holes earn it a Class III rating.

Northern Wilderness River Riders (☎ 548-4583), 10645 Hwy 209, runs a five-hour, 18.5-mile trip from Leavenworth to Monitor. Prices range from $45 to $75. Leavenworth Outfitters (☎ 763-3733, (800) 347-7934), 21312 Hwy 207, runs a similar Wenatchee River trip, as well as easy float trips. Prices range from $16 (for a short float trip) to $60 (for a white-water shoot). Ask about float, fishing and canoe trips.

High Mountain Recreation Inc (☎ 548-4326, (800) 423-9380), 405 W Hwy 2 (at the Alpen Inn), makes two runs daily down the river. Other companies running the Wenatchee include: Alpine Whitewater (☎ (800) 926-7238), All Rivers Adventures (☎ 782-2254, (800) 743-5628) and Osprey Rafting Co (☎ 548-6400, (800) 743-6269).

### Sleigh & Hay Rides

Capitalizing on the Bavarian theme, Red-Tail Canyon Farm (☎ 548-4512, (800) 678-4512), 11780 Freund Canyon Rd, gives rides in old-fashioned sleighs during the winter months, and hay rides at all other times of the year. The cost is $10 for adults, $5 for children ages three to 12; reservations are recommended. In addition to sleigh rides, Eagle Creek Ranch (☎ 548-7798, (800) 221-7433), at the end of Eagle Creek Rd (two miles north on Hwy 209), also gives buggy and wagon rides.

### Other Activities

Good views of the mountains and the Wenatchee River are reason enough to **golf** at the 18-hole course at Leavenworth Golf Club (☎ 548-7267), 9101 Icicle Rd. The public pool (☎ 548-4142) at 500 Hwy 2, by the Lions Club Park, is open for swimming during the summer.

Leavenworth Ski & Sports Center (☎ 548-7864) is conveniently located near Icicle Rd on Hwy 2 and rents skis, bicycles, inner tubes and golf clubs. They also offer instruction and guided tours for skiers, rafters and mountain bikers. Leavenworth Outfitters (☎ 763-3733, (800) 347-7934), 21312 Hwy 207, rents skis and offers a rental service for canoes, rafts and mountain bikes (delivery to the site is included in the rental fee). Gator's Gravity Tours (☎ 548-5102) rents mountain bikes, tandem bikes and scooters. Up at Lake Wenatchee, Ride-n-Glide Sport (☎ 763-2220), 21328 Hwy 207, rents mountain bikes.

### Organized Tours
High Mountain Recreation Inc (☎ 548-4326, (800) 423-9380), 405 W Hwy 2 at the Alpen Inn, arranges tours of Leavenworth. Popular destinations include the Icicle Creek Interpretative Trail loop, the Leavenworth National Fish Hatchery, the Leavenworth Brewery and other Bavarian Village businesses, the Aplets & Cotlets candy factory in Cashmere and Ohme Gardens in Wenatchee. They also arrange horseback riding, mountain biking, snowmobiling trips and cross-country and downhill skiing. They can also set up a two to five hour dog-sledding tour.

The Eagle Creek Ranch (☎ 548-7798), PO Box 719, Leavenworth, WA 98826, has a variety of pack, hike/pack, drop camp combination trips, with prices starting at $100 per person per day. Trail rides range from 1½ to six hours and cost $20 to $75. Icicle Outfitters & Guides Inc (☎ (800) 497-3912), PO Box 322, Leavenworth, WA 98826, offers more extensive four to seven-day pack trips starting at $375 per person.

### Special Events
Festivals are a part of life in any theme town, and Leavenworth doesn't skimp on them. Whenever there's a festival, lodgings fill up, so don't count on rolling into town without a reservation during the Mai Fest or Christmas-tree-lighting weekends. Call the chamber of commerce (☎ 548-5807) to check if anything's scheduled for the time of your visit or to pin down exact dates for any of the following festivals.

Spring comes late to Leavenworth, but by mid-May it's time to dance around a May pole, listen to 'oompah' music and flirt with strolling accordion players. During the Mai Fest there's a parade and a Saturday night street dance, both of which jam the streets of the Bavarian Village.

Though some locals call the Mai Fest 'snooty', plenty of people make annual oompah pilgrimages.

The International Folk Dance Festival is just a one-day festival in mid-June, but the costumes are great and the dances exciting. Summer at Leavenworth climaxes in mid-August with the Leavenworth International Accordion Celebration. Look for accordion competitions, workshops and dances. Applications are available through the chamber of commerce, and if you start practicing now, who knows what fame awaits.

The Leavenworth Fish Hatchery is the site of the Wenatchee River Salmon Festival in early to mid-August, which celebrates the return of thousands of salmon to the Wenatchee River. Field trips, including wetlands ecology tours and fishing clinics are part of the festival, and there's a crafts fair scheduled to coincide with the salmon events.

Leavenworth looks great at Christmas time, and makes the most of the season by holding Christmas-tree-lighting festivals during the first two weekends of December. There's usually a good bit of snow on the ground, and plenty of opportunity for organized snowman-building contests, sledding in the park and hay rides.

### Places to Stay
If Leavenworth is all booked up or seems too expensive, try Wenatchee, where there are plenty of motel rooms for less than $50. There's free public transportation linking Wenatchee with Leavenworth (see the Wenatchee section for more information).

The tourist season peaks in the summer and picks up again around Christmas. At most places, off-season rates drop at least a little bit.

**Camping** There are scads of campgrounds around Leavenworth, making it easy to avoid expensive in-town accommodations. Of course, winter is hard and long hereabouts, so don't plan on too much early or late-season camping; campgrounds are generally open from May to late October. There are three main camping corridors: Icicle Rd, Blewett Pass (on Hwy 97 south of Hwy 2) and Lake Wenatchee (see the following Lake Wenatchee section). Although public campground spaces generally can't be reserved, the ranger station on Hwy 2 (☎ 782-1413) can help you select a campground.

*Pine Village KOA Kampground* (☎ 548-7709) is on the east side of Leavenworth, just north of Hwy 2, at 11401 River Bend Drive. Campsites are in the $15 to $25 range, cabins are $35 to $40.

As you head out of Leavenworth up Icicle Rd, the first campground you come to is a private one, *Icicle River RV Park* (☎ 548-5420), 7305 Icicle Rd, which charges $22.50 for a full hook-up. Between the RV park and the road's end, there are seven USFS campgrounds. All these campgrounds have running water, pit toilets and fees from $7 to $8. *Black Pine Creek Campground*, 15 miles from Hwy 2 at the end of Icicle Rd, has facilities for horse packers and charges $5.

Several USFS campgrounds and an RV park are along Hwy 97 near Blewett Pass. *Blu Shastin RV Park* (☎ 548-4184) is closest to Leavenworth in a tranquil creekside spot at 3300 Hwy 97. It's seven miles south of the intersection of Hwys 2 and 97, is open year round, charges $14 to $18 and has such amenities as a laundromat and swimming pool. *Bonanza Campground* is 14.5 miles south of Hwy 2 and has hand-pumped water but no garbage service (you have to haul it out yourself). There is no camping fee. Further south on Hwy 97, *Swauk Campground* is another no-frills USFS campground near Blewett Pass.

**B&Bs** *Mrs Anderson's Lodging House* (☎ 548-6173, (800) 253-8990), 917 Commercial St, is right downtown. At $44/49 for a single/double with shared bath, $69 for private bath, these are some of the least expensive rooms you'll find in Leavenworth. Fortunately, the place has some charm and has been providing room and board for many years.

Another downtown inn, the *Edel Haus*

(☎ 548-4412), is an attractive Bavarian-style place at 320 9th St, just across from Waterfront Park. Breakfast is not included in the $70 to $95 rate, but you do get a 50% discount on lunch or dinner at the inn's restaurant (which is, incidentally, one of the best in town).

*Run of the River* (☎ 548-7171, (800) 288-6491), 9308 E Leavenworth Rd, has good views of Icicle Canyon. This log B&B inn forgoes Bavarian style in favor of traditional Northwest hewn-log decor. Rooms run $90 to $140; all have private baths and are equipped with binoculars for bird and wildlife viewing. The inn also has a fleet of mountain bikes for guests' use. *All Seasons River Inn* (☎ 548-1425, (800) 254-0555), 8751 Icicle Rd, has rooms with private baths and riverfront decks from $95 to $125. You can go hiking and cycling close by, and the inn can provide bikes.

If you'd rather stay outside of town, the *Old Blewett Pass B&B* (☎ 548-4475), 3470 Hwy 97 S, is a historic roadhouse with rooms from $75. Up by Lake Wenatchee, *Pine River Ranch* (☎ 763-3959, (800) 669-3877), 19668 Hwy 207, is a lovely old farmhouse with four B&B rooms (private baths) and a cottage outfitted with two suites, from $74 to $125.

**Hotels** Budget lodgings are hard to come by in Leavenworth. Perhaps the best bet is the *Edelweiss Hotel* (☎ 548-7015), 843 Front St, with modest rooms with shared bath for as little as $18. If a private bath is important to you, cough up $43/54 for a single/double. Down the road a bit, the *Wedge Mountain Inn* (☎ 548-6694, (800) 666-9664), next to the Big Y Cafe at the junction of Hwys 2 and 97 has rooms starting at $49/58, with a pool and laundry facilities.

Three miles east of Leavenworth, on the way to Wenatchee, the *River's Edge Motel* (☎ 548-7612, (800) 451-5285), 8401 Hwy 2, has a nice setting on the Wenatchee River. Several rooms are equipped with kitchens, and they all have balconies overlooking the river. There's also a pool and hot tub. Standard rooms start at $58/68.

If you want to get into the thick of things, *Tyrolean Ritz* (☎ 548-5455, (800) 854-6365), 633 Front St, is a small hotel right in the heart of downtown Leavenworth with rooms starting at $60. Ask here if you want to bring your dog; it's one of the few small, personable hotels that takes dogs (a $10 deposit is required).

The *Obertal Village Motor Inn* (☎ 548-5204, (800) 537-9382), 922 Commercial St, is a European-style motel with slightly frou frou decor. Rates start at $61/75 (with senior and AAA discounts available), and pets are allowed with a $10 deposit.

A particularly charming small inn, the *Pension Anna* (☎ 548-6273, (800) 509-2662), 926 Commercial St, is next door to the *Obertal*. The Austrian decor is well executed, and the proprietors recently bought and renovated an old chapel, which is now a suite. Rates start at $75 for a basic room, and go up to $165 for the church suite. Another non-kitschy European-style inn is the *Blackbird Lodge* (☎ 548-5800, (800) 446-0240), 309 8th St, overlooking Blackbird Island. Rooms start at $75 on weekends and $69 on weekdays.

*Enzian Motor Inn* (☎ 548-5269, (800) 223-8511), 590 Hwy 2, a large, meticulously detailed motel, has an exercise room, indoor and outdoor pools and hot tubs, cross-country skis to lend to guests and singles/doubles from $76/86. Give this place a second look – it's much nicer than the standard chain motel.

The *Best Western Icicle Inn* (☎ 548-7000, (800) 528-1234), 505 Hwy 2 (at Icicle Rd), may not be as charming as the Enzian, but it's a comfortable motel with a pool, hot tub and exercise facilities. Expect to pay $79/89.

**Lodges** The *Cougar Inn* (☎ 763-3354) at Lake Wenatchee has cabins for $45 and lodge rooms starting at $75/85 for singles/doubles, and is locally known for its restaurant (see Places to Eat below). *Mountain Springs Lodge* (☎ 763-2713, (800) 858-2276), 19115 Chiwawa Loop Rd, is not far from Lake Wenatchee. Its rooms and lodges (they don't call them cabins here)

are more upscale than the *Cougar Inn*, and there's a hot tub. Both of these places have good access to hiking and cross-country ski trails.

On the road to Blewett Pass, *Ingalls Creek Lodge* (☎ 548-6281), 3003 Hwy 97, has a few lodge rooms from $35/45. The adjacent *Ingalls Creek Trading Post* (☎ 548-5142), 3057 Hwy 97, has more basic rooms with shared bath for $45. Both of these places are right near the Ingalls Creek Trail.

**Resorts** *Mountain Home Lodge* (☎ 548-7077), in a meadow surrounded by trees high on Mountain Home Rd, three miles east of Leavenworth, is a small and very attractive country inn, especially popular with cross-country skiers. During the winter, guests are snowcatted in to the lodge, and all meals are included in the $168 to $258 fee (two nights minimum). In the summer, rates are about $100 less, but meals are extra. Trails are close at hand, and the lodge has an outdoor pool, hot tub and tennis courts.

**Vacation Home Rentals** Three booking services, all with toll-free numbers offer a bevy of vacation home and condo referrals, among them Bedfinders (☎ 548-4410, (800) 323-2920), Destination Leavenworth (548-5802, (800) 962-7359) and Leavenworth Vacation Getaways (☎ 548-4171, (800) 548-4808).

Several condos and apartments are available around Leavenworth, and they're particularly suited to larger groups. At the *8th St Pension* (☎ 548-4662), 219 8th St, a two-bedroom apartment rents for $125 and sleeps six. Next door the *Kinney Condos* (☎ 548-5585, (800) 621-9676), 217 8th St, can also house groups.

### Places to Eat
Leavenworth has plenty of places to eat, especially if you like sausage and Wiener schnitzel. Drive towards Wenatchee to find roadside stands brimming with fresh fruit, especially locally grown apples and pears.

**Bavarian Theme Restaurants** There are plenty, but try *Reiner's Gasthaus* (☎ 548-5111), 829 Front St, where Hungarian goulash is a good alternative to sausage and schnitzel. *Gustav's* (☎ 548-4509), 617 Hwy 2 (right where Front St splits off) has lots of beers on tap to complement the sausages and burgers. *Andreas Keller* (☎ 548-6000), 829 Front St, has the full array of sausage, sauerkraut and German potato salad. It may only be outdone by its neighbor, *Burgermeister Bier Garden* (☎ 548-6625), 921 Front St, where there's dancing to go along with the Bavarian menu. *Cafe Christa* (☎ 548-5074), 801 Front St, is upstairs.

**Budget** East of Leavenworth, where Hwy 97 meets Hwy 2, stop and eat at the *Big Y Cafe* (☎ 548-5012) – everybody else does. It's open 24 hours and is best for a basic breakfast . If you need a jolt to even make it to the Big Y, pull off at *Leavenworth's Finest Espresso* (☎ 782-4969), a drive-up joint on Hwy 2 at the west end of town. They really do have the best java in little Bavaria.

The *Gingerbread Factory* (☎ 548-6592), on Commercial St, known to locals as the GBF, is a funny mix of tourist spot and locals' hangout. Gingerbread and other sweet baked goods are about all the food that's offered, but evening poetry readings add extra flavor. For more nutritious baked goods, head to *Homefires Bakery* (☎ 548-7362), 13013 Bayne Rd, right off Icicle Rd near the fish hatchery. Stop by from 9 am to 5 pm Thursday to Monday, for homemade bread, cinnamon rolls and cookies.

*Leavenworth Pizza Company* (☎ 548-7766) is housed in the Clocktower Building at 894 Hwy 2. It's a reasonably good and inexpensive place for a post-hike pizza and beer.

*Park Place Cafe* (☎ 548-6182), 902 Front St in with the Motteler Village shops, has Mexican food; locals say it's the only decent Mexican food in town.

**Middle to Top End** *Edel Haus Inn* (☎ 548-4412), 320 9th St, has some of Leavenworth's best food, including good salmon dinners, in a quietly elegant dining room downstairs from a B&B. Entrees from \$8 to \$18 (grilled salmon is \$13.95), and it's easy to run up a substantial bill. Lunches run about \$8.

At *Walter's Other Place* (☎ 548-6125), 820 Commercial St, the dinners run around \$10 and feature both Greek and Italian cuisine (eat either moussaka or lasagna for \$9.95). Walter's first restaurant, the *Terrace Bistro* (☎ 548-4193), 200 8th St, is around the corner, up the alley and upstairs. During the summer, get a table on the balcony and gaze down at downtown Leavenworth. It's a fine-dining place, where Euro-food means more than just bratwurst (grilled halibut with a lime glaze costs \$15.95), and is about as hoity-toity as you'll find in all of central Washington. Bratwurst sandwiches do show up on the lunch menu (\$4.95).

Up by Lake Wenatchee, the *Cougar Inn* (☎ 763-3354), 23379 Hwy 207, is known for its Friday night seafood buffet and its Sunday brunch buffet.

### Entertainment

**Brewpubs** *The Leavenworth Brewery* (☎ 548-4545), 636 Front St, brews its own, including root beer. Beer names are half the fun here – order up a Dirty Face Stout, Whistling Pig Wheat, Barking Dog Bitter or Blind Pig Dunkelweizen. Pub food and full dinners are served (dinners cost just under \$10, beer-braised German sausage is \$7.95), and people do come here to eat as well as drink. Live music is performed on the weekends and free brewery tours start daily at 2 pm.

### Things to Buy

If a stroll around Leavenworth inspires you to buy a dirndl skirt, stop by the Nussknacker Haus (☎ 548-4708), 735 Front St. Though they sell clothing, their specialty is actually nutcracker dolls. Less Bavarian, but still a good place to shop for household gifts, is Cabin Fever Rustics (☎ 548-4238), 923 Commercial St.

### Getting There & Away

There is no direct air, train or Greyhound

service to Leavenworth. For air connections, Horizon Air flies into the Wenatchee Pangborn Memorial Airport, 21 miles east of Leavenworth. If you don't have your own wheels, you'll have to take a Link bus from Wenatchee, where Amtrak and Greyhound stop.

Link buses (☎ 662-1155) run on 20 different routes in Chelan and Douglas counties (essentially from Lake Wenatchee to Lake Chelan, every day but Sunday. Buses are free (yes, free) and run roughly every 45 minutes. There are several stops along Hwy 2 in Leavenworth, and some buses have bike racks in the summer and ski racks in the winter.

### Getting Around

For those setting forth on their own, rafting, hiking or mountain biking, Gator's Gravity Tours (☎ 548-5102), at Hwy 2 and Icicle Rd, solves the problem of how to get back to the car. Gator's offers a variety of shuttle services, and will drop you off at the trailhead, store your car and deliver it to a predetermined place, or pick up your raft and crew at the end of a shoot. If you just need a way to cruise around the area, Gator's also rents scooters. Leavenworth Outfitters (☎ 763-3733, (800) 347-7934) offers livery service with any mountain bike, raft or canoe rental.

### LAKE WENATCHEE

Lake Wenatchee, 23 miles north of town, is much closer to Leavenworth than it is to Wenatchee. There are two good routes to the lake: either head north on Chumstick Rd or take Hwy 2 west of town, then turn north onto Hwy 207. Once you get there, be prepared for a full array of activities. During the summer, there's swimming, boating, and fishing, hiking the 4.5 mile trail up Dirtyface Peak, signing on with one of the raft companies on Hwy 207 for a float trip, or cycling around the lake.

In the winter, the lakeside becomes the domain of cross-country skiers. The best part here is that you don't have to drive up in the snow – just catch a free Link bus

(☎ 662-1155, (800) 851-5565) from downtown and throw your skis on the rack.

There's a ranger station (☎ 763-3103) in Lake Wenatchee.

### Places to Stay

*Lake Wenatchee State Park* (☎ 763-3101) is a large campground right on the lake, with showers, a restaurant, a swimming beach, horseback rides and some wheelchair-accessible sites. Campsites cost $10, and hardy campers can pitch a tent (or pull an RV up) year round. It's convenient and convivial. If you want more serenity, head around to the lake's south shore to *Glacier View Campground* (☎ 763-3103), a smaller, lakeside USFS campground with pit toilets, running water and $7 sites.

*Nason Creek Campground* (☎ 763-3103), while not on the lakeshore, is less than a mile away on Hwy 207 between Lake Wenatchee and Hwy 2. For the $8 fee, you get flush toilets, running water and easy access to the Nason Ridge trail. *Tumwater Campground* on Hwy 2, 10 miles west of Leavenworth, is a convenient spot between the town and Lake Wenatchee. It's about what you'd expect from a busy roadside spot: flush toilets, running water, an $8 fee and crowds. There are several hiking trails nearby, including one up Chiwaukum Creek (see Hiking above).

There are plenty of USFS campgrounds up the drainages that feed into Lake Wenatchee. Don't expect to find running water at any of them, but then again, these places are free and most have hiking trails nearby. Head up the Little Wenatchee River on USFS Rd 6500, or follow White River Rd from the head of the lake. Up the Chiwawa River, *Goose Creek Campground* ($8, with water) is near ORV trailheads and draws lots of dirt bikers.

### ALPINE LAKES WILDERNESS AREA

Alpine Lakes, 614 sq miles of pieced-together wilderness, got its patchwork shape from a history of mining and railroad land grants. It is best known for its Enchantment Lakes area, which is accessible from Icicle Canyon. Due to heavy use of this fragile area, the USFS requires $5 permits for overnight trips to the Enchantment Lakes. There's lots of competition for these permits; contact the Leavenworth ranger station well in advance of a visit, and hope for the best. Free permits are issued for travel in other parts of the wilderness area; the number is not currently restricted, and they're available at all local ranger stations and trailheads. Some of the best hikes in this lovely area are described below.

An easy trail along **Icicle Creek** begins at the end of Icicle Rd and follows the valley bottom through an old-growth forest. French Creek flows into Icicle Creek about 1.5 miles up the trail. The trail continues deep into the Alpine Lakes Wilderness Area, but French Creek makes a good turnaround for an easy hike.

Walk up Icicle Creek, past waterfalls, pools and little beaches on the easy three-mile **Icicle Gorge** loop trail. Catch the trail at the Chatter Creek Guard Station on Icicle Rd. If you want a longer hike, there are plenty of trails in the area that can be strung together to construct longer day hikes or backpacking trips into the Alpine Lakes Wilderness Area. Pick up a forest map at the ranger station and, if necessary, a permit for an overnight stay.

Call the Leavenworth ranger station well in advance if you want an overnight permit for the Enchantment Lakes area. You can reach one of the **Enchantment Lakes** trailheads by heading out of Leavenworth on Icicle Rd (USFS Rd 7600) to Snow Creek, just a couple of miles past the fish hatchery. Hike in (it's uphill) past Nada and Snow lakes (5.5 and 6.75 miles, respectively), and continue to climb to the basins dotted with the high Enchantment Lakes (10 miles).

Another entrance to the Alpine Lakes Wilderness Area begins on a dirt road just north of Tumwater Campground on Hwy 2. Turn west from the highway to the **Chiwaukum Creek** trailhead and hike 1.5 miles on the road before reaching the wilderness boundary. Once you're on the trail, a pine and Douglas fir forest shades the creek as far as a trail junction 5.5 miles in. The right-hand fork (trail 1591) continues up Chiwaukum Creek through increasingly patchy forest, giving way to meadows and, ultimately, to Chiwaukum and other alpine lakes. The hike to the trail's fork is a reasonable day hike; allow at least two days for a trip to the lakes. Either way, pick up a wilderness permit at the Leavenworth Ranger District office.

### Climbing

Challenging rock climbing in the Enchantment Lakes area of the Alpine Lakes Wilderness requires a USFS permit. You can obtain one at the Leavenworth ranger station. To reach climbs on the Snow Creek Wall, including Orbit (rated 5.8) and Outer Space (5.9), follow the trail into the Enchantment Lakes area, but rather than climbing all the way to the lakes, turn off onto the climbers' path where the trail and Snow Creek approach the steep wall.

### Henry M Jackson Wilderness Area

Up near the Cascades crest, the Henry M Jackson Wilderness Area lies north of Hwy 2 and south of the Glacier Peak Wilderness Area. Here, up the headwaters of **Little Wenatchee River**, are lots of great hikes. From Leavenworth, trailheads are best reached via Lake Wenatchee River. From Lake Wenatchee, continue on Hwy 207 past the head of the lake to USFS Rd 6500. Follow this road up the Little Wenatchee, take the right fork at Riverside Campground and continue to Little Wenatchee Ford Campground at road's end, where there are four trails to choose from. These include one that follows the Little Wenatchee for about five miles, before climbing to a meadow. Three of the four trails here – Cady Pass, Cady Ridge and Little Wenatchee – eventually hook up with the **Pacific Crest Trail**, making good loops for a two or three-day backpacking trip. The fourth trail branches off the Little Wenatchee trail after about a quarter of a mile and heads up to great views at the top of Poe Mountain. Keep an eye peeled along the roadside for soapstone deposits; if you want to pocket more than a rock or two, get a $13 mineral permit from the Lake Wenatchee ranger station.

## CASHMERE

What Leavenworth has done with Bavaria, Cashmere (population 2500) is attempting with early Americana. The theme isn't quite as successful (or overpowering, depending on your perspective), and mostly Cashmere seems like a quiet, pretty riverside town driven by apples.

Though Cashmere is only 10 miles east of Leavenworth, it's decidedly a river-valley town rather than a mountain town. Apple orchards cover the rolling hills; for an apple-scented backroads drive, take any of the side roads north from Hwy 2. Dryden Rd, about two miles west of Cashmere, follows the north bank of the Wenatchee River through orchards.

### Orientation & Information

Two bridges cross the Wenatchee River from Hwy 2 into Cashmere. Check out the apple sculptures adorning the westernmost bridge. Once you're in town, it's hard to miss two factories – one producing apple juice and the other, Aplets & Cotlets candy. One block north of Aplets & Cotlets, Cottage Ave is the town's main Early-American-style drag.

You'll find the chamber of commerce (☎ 782-1511) at 99 N Division St, and the post office on Elberta Ave at Woodring St. Sunset Laundry (☎ 782-2587) is at 204 Sunset Ave, a couple of blocks west of Division St.

### Aplets & Cotlets Candy Factory

Aplets & Cotlets are sugary confections with some fame in the Northwest (every office must get a box of them at Christmas); they're sort of like ultra-sticky gum drops (but more expensive) made from boiled-down fruit, with walnuts mixed in. The factory tour in Cashmere (☎ 782-2191), 117 Mission St, is the town's biggest attraction. From April to December, hours are from 8 am to 5:30 pm Monday to Friday, and 10 am to 4 pm Saturday and Sunday.

January to March it's open from 8:30 am to 4:30 pm Monday to Friday. Tours take place every 20 minutes. They're free, and of course there are samples at the end.

### Pioneer Village

Sure, you stopped in Cashmere for the free candy, but there's really more to see. Eighteenth-century log buildings have been resurrected from sites all over the county and pieced together into a village at the Chelan County Historical Museum & Pioneer Village (☎ 782-3230), 600 Cottage Ave. The museum itself has a surprisingly good Native American collection. It's open April 1 to October 31 Monday to Saturday from 10 am to 4:30 pm, and Sunday from 1 to 4:30 pm. Admission is $3 for adults, $1 for children.

### Peshastin Pinnacles

A nice day will find rock climbers creeping up the 200-foot sandstone spires here (☎ 664-6373). Hikers can get to the top via steep, but quite manageable, trails. Either way, you're rewarded with great views of the Wenatchee River valley. The pinnacles are north of Hwy 2, just west of Cashmere. Trails are clearly marked from the parking area.

### Places to Stay & Eat

*Cashmere's Village Inn Motel* (☎ 782-3522, (800) 793-3522), 229 Cottage Ave, is a stone's throw from anything in downtown Cashmere and has rooms from $40. The *Cashmere Country Inn* (☎ 782-4212), 5801 Pioneer Ave, is a 1907 farmhouse with private baths for all five guest rooms, a pool and a hot tub. Rates range from $75 to $80, including a full breakfast.

*Saddletree Cafe* (☎ 782-3658), 201 S Division St, is open for breakfast and lunch every day, and for dinner on some days (call for the current dinner schedule). It's a good place for breakfast eggs, but diners in the know will follow every meal with a slice of homemade pie. *Pewter Pot Restaurant* (☎ 782-2036), 124½ Cottage Ave, is another good spot for home cooking, and a little more on the fancy side than you might expect. Dinners run $6 to $14. The house specialties are solid, old-fashioned meals like turkey with all the trimmings, beef Wellington, and New England boiled dinner. Right down the street, *Siraco's* (☎ 782-3444), 106 Cottage Ave, is another well-established Cashmere restaurant, open for breakfast, lunch and dinner.

## WENATCHEE

All over the Northwest, folks hearing 'Wenatchee', will predictably free-associate the name with 'apples'. That's the way it's been since central Washington's semi-arid lands were 'reclaimed' for apple orchards between 1890 and 1900, and that's the way it's likely to stay. As if to prove it, there's the Washington State Apple Commission's visitors center right there as you roll into Wenatchee (population 22,080), toasting you with swigs of cider.

Although the Wenatchee River valley has a history of Native American settlement stretching back at least 11,000 years, the area's development as an agricultural center began quite recently. A Father DeGrassi who taught farming to the Wenatchee tribe is credited as being the first person to irrigate the valley. More small-scale irrigation projects started before the turn of the century, when farmers began to divert river water through ditches to their fields. In 1903 the Highline Canal carried water from west of Cashmere all the way to East Wenatchee. Within a few years, young fruit trees were growing everywhere that ditch water could reach. Once the trees matured, Wenatchee became the certified center of the apple world.

## Orientation

Wenatchee is in almost the exact center of Washington. The Wenatchee River comes into town from the northwest, the Columbia from the north, with the confluence of the two rivers at the north end of town. To the east and west are hills topped with the remains of ancient volcanoes (Saddle Rock, Black Rock and Castle Rock). Highway 97 and Hwy 2 (called Wenatchee Ave in town) go up the east side of the Colum-

bia, while Alt Hwy 97 goes up the west side. The Malaga-Alcoa Hwy heads southeast from downtown to a huge Alcoa aluminum plant on the Columbia River. Two bridges and a pedestrian bridge over the Columbia connect Wenatchee with East Wenatchee. The big river valleys lend an openness to the landscape in striking contrast to the tight Cascade canyons in Leavenworth, 22 miles west.

## Information

Stop by the Wenatchee Area Visitor & Convention Bureau (☎ 622-4774, (800) 572-7753), 2 S Chelan Ave, or write to PO Box 850, Wenatchee, WA 98801. The USFS has an office (☎ 622-4335), at 301 Yakima St. The downtown post office is on Chelan Ave between Yakima and Kittitas Sts.

The *Wenatchee World* is published daily except Sunday in, as it says on the masthead, 'the Apple Capital of the World and the Buckle of the Power Belt of the Great Northwest'. Several translators broadcast Northwest Public Radio at FM 90.1, 90.3, 90.7 and 91.3. Laundry gets done at Wash Works Laundromat (☎ 662-3582), 907 S Wenatchee Ave. Central Washington Hospital (☎ 662-1511), 1300 Fuller St, has 24-hour emergency care.

## North Central Washington Museum

The North Central Washington Museum (☎ 664-5989), downtown at 127 S Mission St, distinguishes itself from other historical museums by its apple exhibits, model trains and good visiting exhibits (summer 1994 brought a wonderful show of Dale Chihuly's glass). It's open daily except major holidays, Monday to Friday from 10 am to 4 pm, and weekends from 1 to 4 pm. It's closed on weekends in January. Suggested donation is $2 for adults and $1 for children (ages six to 12).

## Washington Apple Commission Visitor Center

Go for a taste of apple culture and maybe a nibble of the valley's latest crop at the Washington Apple Commission Visitor

Center (☎ 663-9600), 2900 Euclid Ave, near the Wenatchee Confluence State Park at the northern edge of town. It's obviously an industry effort, but if you're into technical tourism, this is the place to learn how apples are grown, picked and processed. Hours are from 8 am to 5 pm Monday to Friday. The center is also open on weekends from May to December from 9 am to 5 pm on Saturday and 11 am to 5 pm Sundays and holidays.

### Ohme Gardens

These terraced woodland gardens (☎ 662-5785) at 3327 Ohme Rd are carved into a bluff at the northern edge of town high above the confluence of the Wenatchee and Columbia rivers. You can get to the Ohme Gardens via Alt Hwy 97. This green patch amid all the brown landscape is, as clearly as the valley's apple trees are, a testament to irrigation. The gardens are open daily April 15 to October 15, from 9 am to 7 pm during the summer, and 9 am to 6 pm before Memorial Day and after Labor Day. Admission costs $5 for adults and $3 for children (ages seven to 17), which seems a little steep, but it's easy to spend a couple of peaceful hours wandering through the gardens and peering down at the Columbia River. As an added bonus, when Wenatchee parches in the summer, this spot is a little cooler and breezier.

### Rocky Reach Dam

Six miles north of town on Hwy 97, Rocky Reach Dam has fish-viewing windows, a playground and large picnic area and two museums – one historical, the other paying homage to electricity. The historical museum, which is under water in the belly of the dam, is a little creepy, though moderately interesting. Behind the dam, the Columbia widens into flat and glassy Lake Entiat. Of all the exhibits at Rocky Reach, the thing the kids will remember is chasing the resident rabbits across the lawn.

### Wenatchee Park & Entiat

This city park stretches along the Columbia on the edge of downtown Wenatchee.

Seven miles of trails on the Wenatchee side of the river link up with a four-mile trail along the Columbia's east bank. It's rather industrial down by the park, so don't be surprised to hear machinery clanking as you stroll or cycle along the river. Any number of downtown streets lead to the park: head down 5th St to come out by the skating rink, or go down Orondo Ave to reach the boat launch. Once on the trail, head north to Wenatchee Confluence State Park, or south to reach a footbridge across to East Wenatchee.

In Entiat, Entiat City Park is another place popular with boaters and swimmers.

### Hiking

The small town of Entiat, 15 miles north of Wenatchee, is the eastern access point to the **Glacier Peak Wilderness Area** (Darrington is the western entrance). It's 38 miles from Hwy 97 at Entiat to the road's end, with many campgrounds along the way (see Places to Stay). Over 211 sq miles burned in the Entiat drainage during 1994; this Tyee Creek fire was the largest single fire ever in the Wenatchee National Forest. Consequently, many trails in this area are likely to be closed for a while. Stop by the Entiat Ranger Station (☎ 784-1511) at 2108 Entiat Way, for hiking and camping advice.

Mission Ridge Ski Area is another summertime hiking area.

### Skiing

Mission Ridge (☎ 663-7631), 13 miles southwest of Wenatchee on Squilchuck Rd, has a vertical drop of 2200 feet, and 33 runs with four lifts and two tow ropes. It's open from late November to late April; adult lift tickets are $20 a day. There are also some cross-country and telemark trails at Mission Ridge, including some that are lit for night skiing. A free Ski Link bus (☎ 662-1155) runs between Wenatchee and the ski area.

### Golf

Golfers should have no problem keeping busy in the Wenatchee area. Check out the

18-hole Three Lakes Golf Course (☎ 663-5448) south of Wenatchee near Malaga. Fees are steep ($45 to $50) at the Desert Canyon (☎ 784-1111), a particularly challenging 18-hole course midway between East Wenatchee and Chelan in Orondo. There's also Marine Golf (☎ 884-4971) on Rock Island Rd E in East Wenatchee, and Rock Island Golf Course (☎ 884-2806), a long nine-hole course at 314 Saunders Rd in Rock Island.

## Other Activities

There's a pool at the YWCA at 1st and Chelan Sts. For **river swimming**, follow the signs at the north end of town through a few tricky intersections to the Wenatchee Confluence State Park. Besides a swimming beach, there are athletic fields, tennis and basketball courts, a campground and a boat launch ($4 launch fee). The Riverside Trail leads south into downtown.

If you feel like **ice-skating**, the Wenatchee Ice Area (☎ 664-5994) is down by Riverfront Park at 2 5th St. Admission is $2.50, skate rental is $1.50. Rent city or mountain bikes at Second Wind (☎ 884-0821), 85 NE 9th Ave in East Wenatchee. Arlberg Sports (☎ 663-7401), 25 N Wenatchee Ave, rents rollerblades.

## Special Events

Wenatchee's big hoopla is the Washington State Apple Blossom Festival (☎ (800) 572-7753), held in early May. Parades, a crafts show, a carnival, concerts, dances, a swim meet, a 10 K run and the crowning of the Apple Queen make the first week of May a busy time in Wenatchee. The other big event in Wenatchee, the Ridge to River relay race, is held just before the Apple Blossom Festival, around the third weekend in April.

## Places to Stay

**Camping** *Wenatchee Confluence State Park* (☎ 664-6373) marks the junction of the Wenatchee and Columbia rivers. Follow signs from Hwy 2 or 97 at the north end of town; the park is on Olds Station Rd and can be reached in a well-marked but roundabout way. The campground is in a big open field by the river and can be windy. The $11 to $16 fee covers the use of showers, flush toilets and a boat launch. *Wenatchee River County Park* (☎ 662-2525) is about five miles northwest of town, on the south side of Hwy 2 by the Wenatchee River. Manicured grassy lawns surround the campsites, which go for $12 to $17.

About six miles north of town on Hwy 2, *Lincoln Rock State Park* (☎ 884-3044) is another full-service, riverside campground (it's actually on Lake Entiat, part of the Columbia River). Supposedly, a rock across the river from the park looks like Abraham Lincoln. To reserve a site at Lincoln Rock write the park at Route 3, Box 3137, East Wenatchee, WA 98802-9566 or call (206) 753-2027; a $5 non-refundable deposit will be charged in addition to the regular camping fee. Rates run $10 to $15, and there are a few wheelchair accessible sites.

*Entiat City Park* (☎ 784-1500), 16 miles north of Wenatchee on Hwy 97, is on the west bank of Lake Entiat in the town of Entiat. The waterfront sites are particularly attractive to boaters and swimmers. There is a laundromat at the campground. Fees are $10 to $12.

The four USFS campgrounds up the Entiat River, five to 25 miles from Entiat on USFS Rd 371, are in an area ravaged by fire in 1994. Call the Entiat Ranger Station (☎ 784-1511) to see if *Silver Falls*, *North Fork*, *Lake Creek* or *Fox Creek* campgrounds have been opened, and whether water and camping fees have been reinstated.

**B&Bs** *Warm Springs Inn* (☎ 662-8365, (800) 543-3645), 1611 Love Lane (west of town off Hwy 2) isn't right in Wenatchee, but there's nothing wrong with its countryside location on the Wenatchee River. Rooms start at $65. *Rose Manor B&B* (☎ 662-1093), 156 S Emerson, is a huge old home close to downtown. Three of the five rooms have private baths, and some have telephones and TVs. A basic room is $50, a suite with all the extras is $80.

Children are welcome at the antique-filled *Cherub Inn B&B* (☎ 662-6011), 410 N Miller, and they'll be glad to hear that there's a pool. The proprietors offer airport pick-up. Rooms start at $75.

**Hotels** If ever there was a motel strip, N Wenatchee Ave is it. Some of the city's best motels are here, cheek by jowl with no-frills budget motels. Wenatchee does bake in the summer, and even many of the less expensive places have swimming pools. Pools can be had at almost all of the motels listed below.

*Scotty's Motel* (☎ 662-8165, (800) 235-8165), 1004 N Wenatchee Ave, has a hot tub and sauna and a ski wax room. Rooms start at $35. *Avenue Motel* (☎ 663-7161, (800) 733-8981), 720 N Wenatchee Ave, has a hot tub, and basic single/double rooms cost $40/45; it's $5 more for kitchenettes. *Econo Lodge* (☎ 663-8133, (800) 424-4777), 700 N Wenatchee Ave, is one of the city's least expensive motels, with rooms from $30/36. Small dogs are permitted with a $5 surcharge.

*Welcome Inn* (☎ 663-7121), 232 N Wenatchee Ave, is a fairly basic, though well-situated motel with rates starting at $40. *Holiday Lodge* (☎ 663-8167, (800) 722-0852), 610 N Wenatchee Ave, isn't much more expensive, and has a hot tub, sauna, exercise room and laundry facilities for $36/45.

*Orchard Inn* (☎ 662-3443), 1401 N Miller, is one block off busy Wenatchee Ave. It's a large motel with an indoor pool and hot tub. Rooms start at $42/50 and pets are OK if you pay a deposit.

When locals need to house visitors, they often look to the well-established *Chieftain Motel & Restaurant* (☎ 663-8141, (800) 572-4466), 1005 N Wenatchee Ave, where rooms start at $45/55. Pets are OK by pre-arrangement. The adjoining bar and restaurant are worth eating at (check out the late-night bar menu).

*WestCoast Wenatchee Center Hotel* (☎ 662-1234, (800) 426-0670), 201 N Wenatchee Ave, has a fitness center and indoor/outdoor pool. It seems like an expense-account place, and indeed is the home of the Wenatchee convention center, but with rooms starting at $65, it's pretty reasonable. There's more of the same at the *Red Lion Inn* (☎ 663-0711, (800) 547-8010), 1225 N Wenatchee Ave, where rooms also start at $65.

The *Best Western Rivers Inn* (☎ 884-1474, (800) 922-3199), 580 Valley Mall Parkway in East Wenatchee, across from the region's largest mall, is an indication that for many people who live in rural central Washington, Wenatchee is a place to come shopping. The continental breakfast is free, and rooms start at $47/52.

### Places to Eat

Budget-conscious street-food connoisseurs will look for Mexican food trucks to appear along Wenatchee Ave at lunchtime. There's seemingly little rhyme or reason as to where or when they'll show up, and the written menu doesn't always reflect what they're serving, but count on being able to get a couple of beef tacos with fresh toppings for $1.

If you're in the mood for a decent milkshake, stop by *Bellmore's Owl Drug Co* (☎ 662-7133), 30 S Wenatchee Ave, right downtown.

*Dusty's In-N-Out* (☎ 662-7805), 1427 N Wenatchee Ave, is a classic drive-through or sit-down joint with Dusty burgers and Dusty dogs. Not much costs more than $2. Dusty's has been in business since 1949, and has more character, if not necessarily more nutritious food, than chain fast-food joints.

For a more nutritious lunch, the *Greenhouse* (☎ 663-7932) 10 N Chelan Ave, serves salads and sandwiches near the courthouse and the library. Another lunchtime soup and salad spot is *Lemolo's* (☎ 664-6576), 114 N Wenatchee Ave. *Bob's Classics Brass & Brew* (☎ 663-3954), 110 2nd St, has the best burgers in town and huge helpings of fries. Burgers start around $4.

The Vietnamese restaurant *Cuc Tran* (☎ 663-6281), 7 N Wenatchee Ave, is convenient, offers tasty food and is easy on the pocketbook. For more South-East Asian cuisine head up to Mission St, where the *Thai Restaurant* (☎ 662-8077), 1211 N Mission St, is very popular with the locals.

*Windmill* (☎ 663-3478), at 1501 N Wenatchee Ave, is an excellent, well-established steak house, while *Visconti's* (☎ 662-5013), 1737 N Wenatchee Ave, serves spaghetti dinners for $9.95, and is the best traditional Italian restaurant in town.

*Wenatchee Roaster & Ale House* (☎ 662-1234), 201 N Wenatchee Ave, one of Wenatchee's fancier restaurants, peers down condescendingly at the competition from the top of the convention center. However, Wenatchee's true top-end restaurant is *Steven's at Mission Square* (☎ 663-6573, (800) 880-0304), 218 N Mission St, which shows itself to be a destination restaurant with its 800 number. It is a good idea to book a couple of days in advance here. Expect good, fresh pasta and seafood dinners.

Wenatchee's other really nice spot, the *Horan House* (☎ 663-0018), is tucked down by the river at 2 Horan Rd. They sometimes do some special meals, like a Shakespearean dinner.

In East Wenatchee, look for Japanese and Italian restaurants on Valley Mall Parkway – *Sakura* (☎ 884-8831), 703 Valley Mall Parkway, and *Garlini's* (☎ 884-1707), 810 Valley Mall Parkway.

If you're heading south along the Columbia River from Wenatchee, save room for pie at *Marcel's* (☎ 787-2808), 10 B SE, in Quincy.

### Entertainment

During the summer look for lunchtime entertainment every Wednesday at noon at the downtown convention center fountain (☎ 662-4411), 121 N Wenatchee Ave. In the evening look toward *McGlinn's* (☎ 663-9073), 111 Orondo Ave, which serves

microbrews and espresso the two staples of the northwestern diet. It's a big after-work place.

### Getting There & Away

**Air** Horizon Air (☎ (800) 547-9308) serves the Pangborn Memorial Airport (☎ 884-2494) in East Wenatchee, with flights operating to and from Seattle and Spokane.

**Bus** The Greyhound station (☎ 662-2183) is at 301 1st St. Empire Lines, which serves small towns in eastern Washington, uses the same station (and the same telephone line). You can also get to nearby towns on Link buses (see the following Getting Around section).

**Train** Amtrak's *Empire Builder* stops in Wenatchee on its way between Seattle and Chicago four times a week. One-way fare from Seattle is $31, roundtrip is $62 or less, depending on what sort of deal Amtrak has going at the time. The train station is at the foot of Kittitas St.

**Car** At the airport, rentals are available from Budget (☎ 663-2626, (800) 662-2838), National Car Rental (☎ 884-8686) and Hertz (☎ 884-6900). U-Save Auto Rental (☎ 663-0587, (800) 972-2298) is in town at John Clark Motors, 908 S Wenatchee Ave.

### Getting Around

**Bus** Undoubtedly the best public transport deal in the Northwest, Link (☎ 662-1155) operates 20 lines around town and to adjoining communities such as Leavenworth, Cashmere and Lake Chelan. There's no fare, and buses run until 8 pm daily except Sunday. Skiers should inquire about the Ski Link service to Mission Ridge, as these buses have specially mounted ski racks.

**Taxi** Three cab companies vie for your business in Wenatchee: Courtesy Cab (☎ 662-2126), Jerry's Cab (☎ 663-6040) and Woody's City Cab (☎ 884-0358).

WASHINGTON

# Moses Lake & the Potholes

As a vacation destination, Moses Lake appeals mostly to local motorboaters, but it can be a convenient place to spend the night along I-90 (it's about halfway between Seattle and Spokane) or take an afternoon dip in the big community swimming pool.

The Potholes, an even more obscure destination to the average traveler, attract avid birdwatchers from all over the Northwest.

### SOAP LAKE

The Grand Coulee peters out at Soap Lake, ending the dramatic river-cut geology and entering a vast flat region. The funny-smelling water in Soap Lake itself is mildly slippery, and white foam gathers at the shoreline. The lakeside town (population 1149) is an odd assortment of dilapidation, antiques and upscale lodgings.

The town of Soap Lake, which lies north of Moses Lake, is south of Hwy 2 and north of I-90 near the crossroads of Hwys 17 and 28. The Soap Lake Visitor Information Center (☎ 246-1821) is near the foot of the lake at 300 Beach St E. Other than taking a dip in the pungent lake, there's not much to do in these parts.

Indians camped on the banks of **Soap Lake** each summer to gamble, race horses and soak in the lake water. Early in the 1900s, pioneers began frequenting the lake, and it became something of a medical resort. The chamber of commerce keeps a file of letters attesting to the water's ameliorative effect on psoriasis, arthritis and various circulatory disorders.

Soap Lake contains 17 minerals and, according to the lakeside sign, an 'ichthyological-like' oil, making it similar in content to that of Germany's Baden Baden. Drink your fill at the water fountain next to the Inn at Soap Lake or take a swim through the fish oil at the public beach

adjacent to the visitors center at the south end of the lake.

### Places to Stay

*Smokiam Campgrounds* (☎ 246-1211) is right in town on the lakefront, charges $10, and is best suited for RV campers.

*Notaras Lodge* (☎ 246-0462) is a rustic log lodge, and aside from the lake, is the only thing most Northwesterners have ever heard of in Soap Lake. Norma Zimmer, the Lawrence Welk Show's Champagne Lady, used to stay here a lot. Decorated theme rooms maintain a fine line between eccentricity and dopiness. Soap Lake water is piped into the tubs. Rooms run from $38/45, whirlpool suites from $83/90.

*Inn at Soap Lake* (☎ 246-1132), 226 Main Ave E, is a big stone building next to Notaras Lodge. Single/double rooms at this surprisingly elegant, Euro-style hotel start at $40/45. Soap Lake water fills the bathtubs.

Besides these two showpieces, there's a handful of other motels in town. Among them, the *Tolo Vista Motel* (☎ 246-1512), 22 Daisy St N, has comfortable log cabins with mineral baths at $35 and up. *Lake Motel* (☎ 246-1611), just south of Soap Lake at 322 Daisy St S, has doubles for $20 and a swimming pool.

### Places to Eat

After a hot drive down the Grand Coulee, ice cream may be all that you care to eat, and there's that and more in Soap Lake. *Nan's Ice Cream Parlor & Pizza* (☎ 246-0470) is at 27 Daisy St. *Doc's Homeplate Cafe* (☎ 246-1256), 332 E Main Ave, an appealing spot in the heart of downtown Soap Lake, has a bar alongside the cafe.

*Don's Restaurant* (246-1217), across from the Notaras at 14 Canna St N, is the best bet for dinner. They put a Greek twist on American food.

### Getting There & Away

There's a Greyhound stop at 741 Basin St NW (☎ 754-3322).

## EPHRATA

Ephrata (population 5349) is not a particularly exciting place, but with a few motels and restaurants, it can be a practical place to spend a night if you're passing through on your way to Grand Coulee Dam or Spokane.

Ephrata is six miles southwest of Soap Lake on Hwy 28. The Ephrata Chamber of Commerce (☎ 754-4656) is at 12 Basin St SW. There are hot springs in Ephrata as well as the Grant County Museum, but that's about it.

### Places to Stay

You can camp at *Oasis Park* (☎ 754-5102), just west of town at 2541 Basin St SW, an RV park with some tent sites, a swimming pool and a kids' fishing pond. It costs about $10 a night.

All of Ephrata's indoor lodgings are within a few blocks of each other on Basin St, the main drag. *Lariat Motel* (☎ 754-2437), 1639 Basin St SW, has a swimming pool – an important consideration in Ephrata in the summertime. Pets are allowed, and rooms start at $27/29 for singles/doubles. The *Travelodge* (☎ 754-4651), 31 Basin St SW, also has a pool; rooms run $55/65 for singles/doubles.

*Columbia Motel* (☎ 754-5226), near the turnoff to Moses Lake at 1257 Basin St SW, has kitchenette rooms for $36/40 for singles/doubles. Pets are OK. *Sharlyn Motel* (☎ 754-3575), 848 Basin St SW, is small but decent, with rooms from $35/50 for singles/doubles.

### Places to Eat

There's nothing fancy here, but at the *Reel Pizza Place* you can take in a movie while you eat. Try *Bamboo Shoot* (☎ 754-5539), 263 Basin St NW, for Chinese-American food, or *El Charro* (☎ 754-3920), 33 Basin St NW, for Mexican-American. For strictly American chow, eat at the *Oak Tree Inn* (☎ 754-9402), 514 N Basin St.

### Getting There & Away

Amtrak's *Empire Builder* line stops in Ephrata four times a week, but the station

at 24 Alder St NW is unstaffed. The eastbound train stops at 10:22 pm, and the westbound one comes through at 3:15 pm. Call Amtrak at (800) 872-7245 for information.

## MOSES LAKE

The town of Moses Lake (population 11,235) sprawls and is not burdened with an excess of charm. Most travelers know it as a stop on I-90 between Seattle and Spokane. There are a couple of reasons besides hunger, fatigue and need of gas or a bathroom to stop in Moses Lake. The lake itself is appealing mostly to motorboaters, but there's also a swimming beach. More subtly interesting are the Pothole Lakes southwest of town, and more blatantly fun for hot, car-weary kids is the giant aquatics center in downtown Moses Lake.

### Orientation & Information

Moses Lake is 178 miles east of Seattle, and 105 miles west of Spokane on I-90.

Highway 17 comes down from Soap Lake and Ephrata, and cuts northwest-southeast through Moses Lake on the way south to Eltopia, where it joins Hwy 395 to the Tri-Cities. Highway 17 is called Pioneer Way in town. The main part of downtown Moses Lake is squeezed between the lake's Parker and Pelican horns, which extend east from the main body of water. Broadway backs up onto the Parker Horn of Moses Lake.

The Moses Lake Visitor & Information Center (☎ 765-7888) is at 324 S Pioneer Way. The main post office is on 3rd Ave between Ash and Beech Sts. Bob's Laundry (☎ 766-0464) is next to the Excell Shopping Center at 415 E 5th Ave. The Samaritan Hospital (☎ 765-7888) is at 801 E Wheeler Rd, just east of downtown.

### Moses Lake & Parks

The sinuous 17-mile-long Moses Lake draws lots of boaters and jet skiers. The natural lake was augmented by water from the Columbia Basin Irrigation Project, which also feeds the Potholes Reservoir to the south.

Boats ply the lake, anglers go after warm-water fish, including crappie and catfish, and swimming beaches buzz with activity on hot weekends. Most of the activity is centered on Moses Lake State Park, a day-use park west of town off I-90, Cascade Park off Valley Road and Montlake Park on the east side of the Pelican Horn at Linden and Beaumont Rds. All these parks have swimming beaches and boat launches. There are more boat launches at Connelly Park on the north end of town off Hwy 17, and at Lower Peninsula Park, Peninsula Drive and Battery Rd.

Downtown on the lakefront is McCosh Park, at Dogwood and 4th Sts, a developed city park that's a nice place for a picnic. There's no beach access, but there are basketball and tennis courts, and a spectacular outdoor pool with a huge water slide. It's a heated outdoor pool, and it closes down in the winter. Admission is $2.50 for adults, $1.50 for kids.

## Museums

A couple of small museums are worth a visit if you don't want to hang out at the lake or the public pool. Admission is free at both places. **Adam East Museum & Art Center** (☎ 766-9395), at 122 W 3rd Ave, features Native American artifacts and area exhibits. It's open from noon to 4 pm Tuesday to Thursday, and 11 am to 5 pm Friday and Saturday. **Monte Holm's House of Poverty & Main Road Railroad** exhibits refurbished gas engines, antique cars, fire engines and local historic relics. This private museum (☎ 765-6342), at 228 S Commerce St, is open from 8 am to 3:30 pm, Monday to Friday.

## Potholes Wildlife & Recreation Area

If you like odd geography, or yearn to see ruddy ducks swimming past sand-dune islands, spend a morning knocking around the Potholes or the Wildlife Area south and west of Potholes Reservoir. The reservoir, held back by O'Sullivan Dam, is just south

of town on Hwy 262. (Those seeking knowledge of irrigation systems will find a prime example of an irrigation canal flowing from the foot of the Potholes Reservoir.)

The land is surprisingly lush and green, with lots of water and wetlands surrounded by sand dunes, which sometimes pop up through the streams as islands. The Columbia Basin Irrigation Project is responsible for this weird ecology – O'Sullivan Dam and various irrigation schemes have filled any shallow spot with irrigation water, which courses through the native desert and turns some of the high sand dunes into islands. Canoeists can put in at Potholes State Park and paddle the waterways. Bird watchers figure this to be a real oasis; come prepared to spot waterfowl, geese, avocets, herons, egrets, songbirds and burrowing owls. The Potholes aren't particularly well known, but most serious Northwest birders have made springtime pilgrimages.

Lots of the **hiking** here is on causeways running alongside water ditches. Hike beside the Frenchman Hills Wasteway, which leads water away from the Potholes Reservoir. There's a path leading out from the boat launch at Potholes State Park.

Alternatively, head four miles west of the state park, and turn north on C Rd SE and drive to the end of the road to get to some big sand dunes surrounded by pothole lakes and marshes. Foot travelers should watch out for rattlesnakes.

The best access to Potholes Reservoir is from the south. From Moses Lake take Hwy 17 southeast to Hwy 262. Turn west on Hwy 262, which runs along the foot of the reservoir past O'Sullivan Dam, Potholes State Park and other informal access points.

The local Audubon chapter has mapped out an 80-mile **scenic drive** past potholes, coulees and sand dunes, and it's well worth taking in at least part of it. Essentially, it describes a big rectangle bordered on the north by I-90's frontage road, on the west by Dodson Rd, on the south by Frenchman Hills Rd and Hwy 262, and on the east by Rd M (which runs into Hwy 17 just south of Moses Lake. The Moses Lake Visitor & Information Center (☎ 765-7888), 324 S Pioneer Way, should be able to provide you with a copy of the Audubon 'scenic drive' brochure.

## Places to Stay

**Camping** *Big Sun Resort* (☎ 765-8294), just off I-90 near Moses Lake State Park (a day-use park), is an RV park with a few tent sites, lake access and boat docks.

*Potholes State Park* on Hwy 262 on the south side of the Potholes Reservoir, is open year round, with sites from $7 to $13, and is a good base for bird watchers or canoeists bent on exploring the Potholes. The other prime Potholes spot is *Mar-Don Resort* (☎ 346-2651), near the O'Sullivan Dam on Hwy 262, where tent and RV sites run $12 to $18. (They also run a motel – see the next section.)

**Hotels** Most of Moses Lake's motels are clustered around the freeway exits, but there are a few places to stay downtown. Virtually all of these motels have pools, and they'll generally allow pets.

Downtown, the *Travelodge* (☎ 765-8631) is at 316 S Pioneer Way at 3rd St. Singles/doubles start at $39/44. *Maples Motel* (☎ 765-5665) is near downtown parks at 1006 W 3rd St; singles/doubles cost $35/45.

*Sage 'N' Sand Motel* (☎ 765-1755, (800) 336-0454) is south of downtown at 1011 S Pioneer Way, with rooms starting at $35. Out by the freeway, at the intersection of I-90 and Hwy 17 (exit No 179), the *Shilo Inn Motel* (☎ 765-9317, (800) 222-2244), 1819 E Kittleson St, charges $60 to $95, and is pretty fancy by local standards.

Several chain motels are just off I-90 near exit No 176. The *Motel 6* (☎ 766-0250) at 2822 Wapato Drive has singles/doubles starting at $27/34. *Super 8* (☎ 765-8886, (800) 800-8000), 449 Melva Lane, charges $38/46 for singles/doubles. *Best Western Hallmark Inn on the Lake* (☎ 765-9211, (800) 235-4255), 3000 Marina Drive,

is one of Moses Lake's better motels, with boat docks, a pool and tennis courts; singles/doubles start from $52/56.

Also near exit No 176, *Lakeshore Motel* (☎ 765-9201), 3206 W Lakeshore Drive, has a marina with rowboat rentals and a pool; singles/doubles start at $22/35.

The *MarDon Resort Cafe Lounge* (☎ 346-2651) on Hwy 262 down by the Potholes Reservoir, is big enough to pass for a town in these parts. There's a fairly basic motel with rooms starting at $35, RV camping and a restaurant. For as remote as the Mar-Don is, it draws quite a crowd.

## Places to Eat

The *4 B's* (☎ 765-8385), 3001 W Broadway, is part of a Montana-based restaurant chain known for inexpensive 24-hour dining that's a cut above Denny's. *Paddywhacker's* (☎ 765-8182), at 1075 W Broadway, is a burger place with outside seating.

*Michael's on the Lake Restaurant* (☎ 765-1611), 910 W Broadway, is a little classier, with a deck overlooking the lake at, but it's not particularly expensive (a salmon dinner runs $10.95).

Moses Lake is mostly an American-food sort of place, but there is *Thai Cuisine* (☎ 766-1489) in the shopping center on Pioneer Way.

## Entertainment

Free summertime concerts and other events are held at McCosh Park at Centennial Theater (☎ 766-9240), the city's new outdoor amphitheater.

## Getting There & Around

Horizon Air's (☎ (800) 547-9308) Metro 18 prop jets share the Grant County Airport north of town with a fleet of big Federal Express and JAL cargo planes. You can fly in from Portland, Seattle or Spokane.

Greyhound (☎ 765-6441, (800) 231-2222) stops at 630 E Broadway. Get around town in a taxi from Moses Lake Cab (☎ 766-7803).

WASHINGTON

# Yakima Valley

The Yakima River rises from the slopes of Snoqualmie Pass, far to the west. By the time the river gets to Yakima, most of its mountain freshness is gone and dams have slowed it down, diverting its waters into immense irrigation projects. When viewed on a sweltering hot day (of which there are many), the Yakima seems as life-giving as the Nile. The river flows through scorched ochre-colored hills, but where its water touches the soil, a bounty of life springs forth.

The Yakima valley is the single largest producer of apples in the world, though hops, cherries, peaches and other tree fruits, as well as vegetables, are also found in abundance. In the last 20 years, wine grapes have taken their place on the hillsides, making this one of the Northwest's major wine areas.

There's no getting around the fact that it's hot and dry here: Only eight inches of rain fall a year, summer highs hover around 100°F and there are over 300 days of sunshine yearly. These climatic extremes make this area a mecca for sun-lovers. Yakima is noted as a retirement center, especially for the career military, while the sunny weather and access to skiing and fishing serve to attract young recreation enthusiasts. The preponderance of orchard work has brought in a large Hispanic population; people of Hispanic origin compose 30% of the valley's population. The vast Yakama Indian Reservation to the southwest adds a strong Native American presence to the population mix.

At Yakima, the Yakima River suddenly passes out of the Yakima canyon into a wide basin surrounded by brown hills. South of the city is the Yakama Indian Reservation and mile after mile of orchards and farms, which flank the Yakima River to its confluence with the Columbia at Richland. Interstate 82 runs the length of the Yakima valley. Paralleling the freeway for much of the way is Hwy 12, also known

somewhat fancifully as the Wine Country road. At Toppenish, Hwy 97 splits off, heading south to Oregon and I-84. Seattle is 142 miles west of Yakima; Richland is 76 miles east.

## ELLENSBURG

Even if you're not going to stop in Ellensburg (population 12,361), at least slow down for it: it's the site of the state police training academy. Students like to practice catching speeding motorists and writing up tickets.

The other college in town, Central Washington University (CWU), is large enough to give a relaxed collegiate feel to this agricultural hub town. Ellensburg's well-preserved downtown has lots of brick buildings, which were built after a fire burned nine downtown blocks and over 200 homes in 1889. Ellensburg then thought itself on the way to becoming both the 'Pittsburgh of the West' (because of nearby iron ore and coal deposits) and the capital city of Washington. For better or worse, the iron and coal proved to be very low grade, and Olympia got the state capitol building, leaving Ellensburg the state normal school as a consolation prize. Today, Ellensburg is a pleasant enough place to while away an afternoon or spend a night, with the old brick downtown and a couple of good restaurants, not to mention the signing chimps at the university's primate center.

### Orientation

The Yakima River runs down the west side of Ellensburg; the Yakima canyon is bordered by scenic Hwy 821.

Interstate 90 sticks close to the Yakima River and runs more or less west of town. Hop off either northwest (called the West Ellensburg interchange) or southeast (South Ellensburg interchange) of town and let the flow of traffic take you to Main St. Main St forms a T-junction with 8th St, which runs east to the university.

### Information

For visitor information contact the Ellensburg Chamber of Commerce (☎ 925-3137),

436 N Sprague, Ellensburg, WA 98926, or 712 S Main St. You'll find the main post office (☎ 925-1866) at Pearl St and 3rd Ave. You'll find a couple of good book-stores in town. Old Fools Bookstore (☎ 925-4480) is a good new and used book-store at 112 E 3rd Ave. Four Winds Book-store & Cafe (☎ 962-2375), 112 E 3rd Ave, is kind of a student hangout with new and used books and a heavy New Age empha-sis. Catch the *Daily Record* for local news.

One laundromat, Model-Ke Cleaners (☎ 925-5389), is downtown at 207 N Pine St, and another, College Coin Laundry (☎ 962-6000), is close to the university at 8th and Walnut Sts. Kittitas Valley Com-munity Hospital (☎ 962-9841) is at 603 S Chestnut St.

### Historic District
The chamber of commerce has maps of the downtown historic district, which is roughly contained between 5th and 3rd Aves on one side, Main and Pine Sts on the other. The historic district is peppered with antique shops and galleries, making it a tempting place to spend an afternoon. Then there's the **cowboy sculpture** at 5th Ave and Pearl St and the oversize, cartoony **Ellensburg bull** lounging on a bench in the historic district. **Dick & Jane's Spot**, out front at 101 N Pearl St, is a home-owner's version of the 24-Hour Church of Elvis, UFO Museum, Our Lady of Eternal Combustion, etc.

### Museums
The **Kittitas County Museum** (☎ 925-3778), 114 E 3rd Ave, in the 1889 Cadwell Building, is known mostly for its gemstone and petrified wood collections, as well as its horseshoe-arched windows. From May through August the museum is open Tuesday to Saturday from 11 am to 4:30 pm. The rest of the year it's open Tuesday to Friday from 11 am to 3 pm. See the **Clymer Museum** (☎ 962-6416), 416 N Pearl St, for a collection of native-son John Clymer and other Northwest artists' works. It's open from 10 am to 5 pm Monday to

Friday, and from noon to 5 pm Saturday and Sunday.

The very engaging **Children's Activity Museum** (☎ 925-6789), 400 N Main St, has a miniature city to play in, a puppet theater and other incredibly popular hands-on activities. Visit from 10 am to 5 pm Thursday to Saturday, and 1 pm to 5 pm on Sunday.

### Central Washington University
As with most small town college campuses, this one is a good place for a student-watching stroll, but there are a couple of other attractions here as well.

**Primate Center** CWU has gained some renown for its studies of chimpanzee-human communication. Yes, this is the home of the chimps who communicate using American Sign Language. The public is welcome to tour the research center at 13th Ave and D St. Call 963-3001 or (800) 752-4380 for information about scheduled tours or register for a workshop with the signing chimps.

**Japanese Garden** Formal Japanese dry landscape gardens offer a restful place for a stroll on the CWU campus. Find the gar-den's entry gate on the Walnut St Pedes-trian Mall. It's open year round, from daybreak to dusk. There's no admission other than your contribution to a donation box.

### Olmstead Place State Park
A family farm is preserved at this heritage park, 4.5 miles southeast of Ellensburg off I-90, where you'll find a log cabin, pioneer barns and other farm buildings dating from 1875 to 1890. The buildings are open to the public on summer weekends. Contact the park ranger (☎ 925-1943) for more infor-mation.

### Thorp Grist Mill
This historic grist mill was once a de facto meeting place for local farmers and is now a rural museum with a multimedia pre-sentation shown in a grain storage bin. The

mill is open for viewing during the summer, and at other times by appointment. Thorp Mill Historical Preservation Society (☎ 964-9640) has more information. West of Ellensburg, take exit No 101 off I-90, and travel through Thorp to reach the mill and stream park.

### Yakima Canyon
South of Ellensburg, Hwy 821 follows the Yakima River through Yakima canyon. The 25-mile backroad is a winding scenic route to Yakima and, unless you hit it on a busy weekend, is quiet enough for a bike ride.

**Hiking** Though floating may be the ideal way to see the Yakima canyon, there are hiking trails around and above the river. At the Untanum Creek Recreation Area, about 12 miles south of Ellensburg on Hwy 821, a suspension footbridge crosses the river to trails leading up to a ridge-top viewpoint and along Untanum Creek. (Remember: this is rattlesnake country.)

**Fishing** The Yakima River is also a big deal for fly fishing. Contact the Evening Hatch (☎ 962-5959), for fly-fishing guide service. Other types of fishing trips can be arranged through Helland's Guide Service (☎ 925-6650), Route 1, Box 252, Ellensburg, WA.

**Rafting** Some people put their inflatable rafts in around Ellensburg and float down the Yakima River. Supreme Court Justice William O Douglas did. In the '60s he joined a concerned citizens group called the Yakima River Conservancy on a float down the river to rally support for their scenic preservation plan.

It's possible to access the river on its designated scenic stretch along Hwy 821, south of Ellensburg, and spend three to four hours on a float to the Roza Dam. There's also a public put-in north on Hwy 10, below Cle Elum, for a lazy 15-mile, five to six-hour float to the diversion dam near Thorp. River Raft Rentals (☎ 964-2145), seven miles west of Ellensburg on Hwy 10, does raft rentals.

During mating season, it is not unusual for a bull elk to command a harem of up to 60 cows.

**Paragliding** The hot afternoon sun creates strong thermal updrafts, which keep paragliders well aloft above the Yakima River canyon. North American Paragliding (☎ 925-5565) has sales, service and tours.

### Elk Feeding
Once the snow covers the natural forage, the Department of Wildlife takes it upon itself to feed approximately 750 elk each day at Joe Watt Canyon, 15 miles north of Ellensburg. To watch this spectacle, put on some warm clothes and show up at the feeding station promptly at 8 am. From Ellensburg take exit No 102 off I-90 west, cross left over the freeway and at the top of the hill turn right onto Old Thorp Cemetery Rd. Continue to Joe Watt Canyon Rd and turn left. The feeding station is at the end of the road, about one mile away.

### Special Events
The Annual National Western Art Show & Auction (☎ 962-2934), held each May, brings some of the best Western artists to the local Best Western to sell their paintings, prints, sculpture and jewelry. Ask for details at the Clymer Museum (see museums above).

The Whisky Dick Triathlon in late July starts off with a mile-long swim in the Columbia River, followed by a 26-mile bike ride up steep Whisky Dick Ridge and an 8.9-mile run back to Ellensburg.

Ellensburg's ultimate festival, the Ellensburg Rodeo (☎ 962-7831, (800) 637-2444), starts on the Thursday of Labor Day weekend and runs for four days at the Kittitas County fairgrounds. It's ranked among the top 10 rodeos in the nation and is one of central Washington's biggest events. Come prepared to see some hard riding and roping: participants take this rodeo very seriously, as there is big money at stake.

The Kittitas County Fair takes place at the same time as the rodeo and is also held at the same location.

## Places to Stay

**Camping** KOA Campground (☎ 925-9319), off I-90 at the West Ellensburg interchange, has the only camping around Ellensburg. Fortunately, it's on the Yakima River. Sites start at $15, and it's a typically spiffy KOA, with a laundromat, pool, playground and showers; it's open April to mid-October.

**B&Bs** Murphy's Country B&B (☎ 925-7986), 2830 Thorp Hwy S, is a restored farmhouse just southwest of town across from the golf course. The two guest rooms go for $55/60 for singles/doubles.

**Hotels** The Rainbow Motel (☎ 925-3544), 1025 Cascade Way, is a pretty basic place, but it does have laundry facilities and some of the cheapest rooms in town (from $32/46 for a single/double). I-90 Inn Motel (☎ 925-9844), near the West Ellensburg I-90 interchange at 1390 Dollarway Rd, is convenient and inexpensive, with rooms starting at $34/42.

Thunderbird Motel (☎ 962-9856, 925-5700), 403 W 8th St, is a big motel with an outdoor pool. Single/double rooms cost $35/44, and pets are allowed.

Near the freeway's South Ellensburg exchange there's a Super 8 Motel (☎ 962-6888, (800) 800-8000) at 1500 Canyon Rd.

Rooms start at $37, and there's a pool. The Best Western Ellensburg Inn (☎ 925-9801, (800) 321-8791) is nearby at 1700 Canyon Rd. With singles/doubles starting at $45/50, and an indoor pool, fitness center and hot tub, this is Ellensburg's most deluxe motel.

## Places to Eat

In addition to all the usual fast-food restaurants, any college town in Washington is bound to have a few hip coffee joints. In Ellensburg, D&M Coffee Station is one of the best. It's an old gas station turned espresso shop, with brightly painted gas pumps and a deck out back. It's at 408 S Main St near the turnoff for the hospital.

The cafe at the Four Winds Bookstore (☎ 962-2375), 200 E 4th Ave, is a good place for a casual lunch. They serve soup, sandwiches and lots of coffee.

Valley Cafe (☎ 925-3050), 105 W 3rd Ave, is a striking art-deco cafe that turns out remarkably good food. At lunch, a bowl of cioppino goes for $7.95 and a spinach salad for $4.95. Order a huge boxed lunch from their take-out menu for $7.25, or stop by the take-out shop next door to the restaurant for a muffin or cinnamon roll.

Giovanni's on Pearl (☎ 962-2260), 402 N Pearl St, has old-fashioned decor and elegant dinners (be prepared to pay at least $15 for an entree). Despite the name, it's not strictly Italian food (try the Ellensburg lamb).

Bar 14 Ranch House Restaurant (☎ 962-6222), 1800 Canyon Rd, is a steak place conveniently close to freeway exit No 109.

If you're heading north of town on Hwy 97, the Mineral Springs Resort Restaurant (☎ 857-2361), between Ellensburg and Blewett Pass, has huge portions and great pie (skip the ice cream). The water here is local mineral water, and it's strong enough to overpower the tea flavor of iced tea.

## Things to Buy

Jewelry made from Ellensburg blue agate makes an appropriate souvenir. This stone is unique to the Ellensburg area, but most of the prime agate territory is on private land. Fortunately, Ellensburg is studded with gem shops, all peddling blue agates. They're the focus at the Ellensburg Agate Shop (☎ 925-4998), 201 S Main St.

Gallery-hoppers should start at the Community Art Gallery (☎ 925-2670) 408½ N Pearl St, featuring contemporary arts and crafts.

### Getting There & Away
The Greyhound station (☎ 925-1177) is at 8th Ave and Okanogan St.

## AROUND ELLENSBURG
### Roslyn
Roslyn (population 859), a tiny town on Hwy 903, is a couple of miles off I-90, about 25 miles northwest of Ellensburg. This is (and they won't let you forget it) where the TV show *Northern Exposure* was filmed; on TV, it's supposed to be a small town in the Alaskan bush. Watch where you walk in Roslyn to avoid being mowed down by a tour bus or a fellow visitor with a video camera glued to his face.

The *Roslyn Cafe* (☎ 649-2763), at 2nd St and Pennsylvania Ave, is the place to eat, and the *Brick Tavern* (☎ 649-2643), a block down at 1 Pennsylvania Ave, is the place to drink. (It's one of the several places that claim to be Washington's oldest saloon, but gains more cachet for its 'dogs welcome' policy.) Ask for a glass of Roslyn Beer, brewed ultra-locally at the Roslyn Brewing Company (☎ 649-2232), 33 Pennsylvania Ave. The brewery is open to visitors on weekends from noon to 5 pm.

On your way to Roslyn from Ellensburg, you'll pass Cle Elum, home of the Cle Elum Bakery (☎ 674-2233), E 1st St. This bakery is a ritual stop for many I-90 travelers, but other than that, Cle Elum is a pretty quiet logging town with lots of empty storefronts. Of Cle Elum's several motels, *Cedar's Motel* (☎ 674-5535) isn't a bad choice. *MaMa Vallone's* (☎ 674-5174) is the town's somewhat renowned steak house and B&B inn at 302 E 1st St.

### Vantage
Interstate 90 crosses the Columbia River (called Wanapum Lake here, thanks to the Wanapum Dam) at the town of Vantage, a good place to stop the car and wander if the freeway is getting to you. It's 42 miles southwest of Moses Lake and about 30 miles east of Ellensburg.

Fossilized trees and leaves dot the trails at the **Gingko Petrified Forest State Park & Interpretive Center**, and there are many species besides gingkos. A three-quarter-mile interpretive trail and a three-mile hiking trail pass Douglas fir, spruce, maple, elm, gingko and gum trees, safely preserved behind steel grates. The trailheads are a couple of miles north of the freeway, but there's a small visitors center on the west side of the freeway bridge. Take a moment to walk around here – several pictographs have been salvaged from the Wanapum Dam's backwaters, and are displayed on the river side of the visitor center. The park is about one mile north of I-90 at Vantage, on the west bank of the Columbia River.

The **Wild Horse Monument** is across the Columbia from Vantage, and has good views of river. Don't expect to see wild horses here, it's just a statue.

To reach the **Wanapum Dam** (☎ 754-35410), with its fish-viewing windows and exhibits of Native American history, head south along the east bank of the Columbia River on Hwy 26 (which becomes Hwy 243). The dam is five miles south of I-90.

### Places to Stay & Eat
There's camping at *Wanapum State Park* (☎ 856-2700), three miles south of the freeway on the west side of the Columbia. The other option is the *Vantage KOA & Motel* (☎ 856-2230), on the west side of the I-90 bridge, just north of the freeway. This is the closest lodging for people attending concerts at the Gorge Amphitheater (☎ 785-6685) in nearby George, so concert-goers should reserve early. During the peak summer season, motel rooms start at $41/45 and houses at $65. Campsites start at $15 and, believe it or not, the KOA is better for

tent campers than the RV-oriented state park campground.

If you're really concerned about dining, hop on over to Ellensburg, but if you just need sustenance, there are a couple of restaurants in Vantage, including the riverside Wanapum Inn (☎ 856-2244).

## YAKIMA & AROUND

Yakima (population 59,580) is the preeminent city of central Washington, and the trading center of an immense agricultural area. The city reflects this prosperity with a converted downtown-cum-mall development, massive commercial strips and some very conspicuous golf courses. Yakima likes to boast that it is the 'Palm Springs of the North'.

Yakima does offer several noteworthy restaurants, and an abundance of cheap motel rooms. The riverside Greenway, arboretum and adjacent parks make a good place to unload hot passengers and stretch weary muscles.

### Orientation

Interstate 82 runs along the east of the main downtown area of Yakima; exit No 33 leads to Yakima Ave which runs east-west and is the quickest route to downtown. The main north-south strip running through town is 1st St which can be accessed from the N 1st St exit off I-82. Yakima Ave and Front St (essentially the train tracks) divide the city into directional quadrants.

There are both numbered streets and avenues in Yakima, so pay attention when people give addresses (numbered streets are east of the tracks).

### Information

The Yakima Valley Visitors & Convention Bureau (☎ 575-1300) is at 10 N 8th St, Yakima, WA 98901. The main post office (☎ 454-2450) is at 205 W Washington Ave. The Booknook (☎ 453-3762), 722 Summitview Ave, is Yakima's best bookstore, with a good general selection tied to New Age and self-help titles. The daily paper is the *Herald Republic*.

K's Coin Laundry (☎ 452-5335) is at the corner of N 6th Ave and Fruitvale Blvd. Memorial Hospital (☎ 575-8000) is at 2811 Tieton Drive. For a local road report, call 457-7100.

### Downtown Yakima

Yakima is the seat of local government, and many of the prominent older buildings in the downtown core are courthouses and such. Two particularly attractive buildings are the **Larson Building**, at Yakima Ave and 2nd St, an art-deco marvel with 13 different shades of brick in its facade; check out the lobby. The grand, Italianate **Capitol Theatre**, at 19 S 3rd St, is another landmark of Yakima's boom years. Built in 1920 as a movie theater, the theater is now a performing arts center.

A single block makes up Yakima's much-touted historic district. North Front St does contain several good restaurants, a wine-tasting room, some boutiques and an espresso shop. Of more interest is the old Northern Pacific Depot across the street. Most of it has been converted into Grant's Brewery Pub, the brewpub of the Northwest's oldest microbrewery.

Across the railroad tracks is a mish-mash of tourist-oriented boutiques. **Yesterday's Village** is an antique mall in an old apple warehouse, and **Track 29** is the series of gift stalls housed in old rail cars. Also a part of this development is the **World Famous Fantastic Museum** (☎ 575-0100), 15 W Yakima Ave, a goofy collection of celebrity exotica, like a pink Cadillac that once belonged to Elvis.

### Yakima Greenway & Parks

The Yakima Greenway is a series of parks and recreation areas that stretches the length of the Yakima River throughout the city. A walking, hiking and biking path follows the river for seven miles, passing through natural wetlands and native vegetation. At the southern end of the Greenway is the **Yakima Arboretum**, a landscaped garden containing over 400 species of trees and shrubs. Stop at the Jewett Interpretive Center (☎ 248-7337) for a walking-tour brochure. The arboretum is just east of I-82

WASHINGTON

exit No 34. Directly across the river from the arboretum is **Sportsman's State Park**, with picnic tables, camping and special fishing ponds just for children (adults can fish in the river). At the northern end of the Greenway is **Chesterly Park** (N 40th Ave and River Rd), a large park with playing fields and sports facilities. It's another good access point to the Greenway path.

### Yakima Valley Museum

This excellent regional museum (☎ 248-0747), 2105 Tieton Drive, together with adjacent Franklin Park, makes a great stop for visitors. The centerpiece of the museum is its collection of horse-drawn conveyances, the largest such on the US West Coast. Other features of note include artifacts and exhibits about native Yakama culture and a replica of the office of late US Supreme Court Justice William O Douglas. Douglas, Yakima's most noted native son, was the eminent jurist and US Supreme Court justice appointed to the court by Franklin D Roosevelt in 1939. He served until 1975, making him the longest serving justice in the court's history. Although he's honored here and elsewhere around town with plaques and commemoratives, during

**WASHINGTON**

his tenure on the court, his progressive politics usually rankled his home-town neighbors.

Not surprisingly, another section of the museum tells the story of apple production in the Yakima valley. The museum is open Tuesday through Friday from 10 am to 5 pm, and Saturday and Sunday from noon to 5 pm. Admission is $2.50 for adults and $1.25 for seniors and children.

Next door to the museum is **Franklin Park**, with a playground, picnic tables, and – an important feature in sun-baked Yakima – a swimming pool.

### Indian Painted Rocks

The Yakima River cuts narrow passages through the hills that flank the city. For the Native Americans who lived in the valley in prehistoric times, these cliff-lined ravines were natural avenues of transportation, as they are today. At the northern edge of Yakima, along an old foot trail, a large number of pictographs can still be seen. Many are of stylized humans, with fantastic headdresses. It's easy to imagine that these images conveyed either a warning or a mark of territory to the natives who passed through this narrow gap.

To visit the Indian Painted Rocks, drive north from Yakima on N 40th St and turn left onto old Hwy 12, now called Powerhouse Rd. In about a mile, watch for a small plaque near a roadside parking area. Wooden steps lead up to the edge of the cliffs; watch for snakes.

### Skiing

White Pass Ski Area is 50 miles east of Yakima on Hwy 12, on the southeast side of Mt Rainier. This popular ski resort offers 14 runs with a total vertical drop of 1505 feet. Lift tickets range between $18 weekdays and $29 on the weekend. There are also nine miles of groomed cross-country trails. Call 453-8731 for general information, or 672-3100 for the Snowline.

### Fishing

The Yakima River above Roza Dam in the rugged Yakima canyon is a spectacular place to fly fish for trout. A good spot to start out is at Umtanum Creek, where a footbridge gives access to both sides of the river. For flies and gear, as well as guided fly-fishing trips, contact Gary's Fly Shoppe (☎ 457-3474), 1210 W Lincoln Ave.

### Rafting & Floating

Between Ellensburg and Roza Dam the Yakima River is gentle enough for novice floaters, but with scenery impressive enough to make this an enjoyable trip. To plan your own trip, contact Rent-A-Raft (☎ 453-1167), 201 S 1st St.

### Swimming

If it's summertime, it's going to be hot. Head to Lions Pool (☎ 575-6046), at 5th Ave and Pine St.

### Golf

The Apple Tree Golf Course (☎ 966-5877), 8804 Occidental Ave, offers 18 holes nestled in an apple orchard (what else?) and is Yakima's newest course. The signature 17th hole is an island shaped like an apple. Suntides Golf Course (☎ 966-9065), 231 Pence Rd (Hwy 12), is the other 18-hole public standby.

## Wine-Tasting

There are nearly 25 long-established wineries between Yakima and Benton City. Most have tasting rooms with a full array of local wines and gift packages. For a free map and guide to all the wineries in the valley, send a stamped, self-addressed envelope to the Yakima valley Wine Growers' Association, PO Box 39, Grandview, WA 98930.

There are a couple of wineries in Zillah worth visiting. **Bonair Winery** (☎ 829-6027), 500 S Bonair Rd, is open for tasting from 10 am to 5 pm daily, and until 4:30 pm on weekends during the winter. The cabernet is notable. You can picnic in the gazebo.

The second, **Covey Run**, (☎ 829-6235), 1500 Vintage Rd, is open Monday to Saturday from 10 am to 5 pm, and Sunday noon to 5 pm, April 1 to October 30; the rest of the year it's open from 11 am to 4:30 pm, Monday through Saturday, and noon to 4:30 pm on Sunday. Covey Run has a lovely tasting room and is a popular wedding location. As far as the wine goes, stick with the Semillon.

**Stewart Vineyards**, (☎ 854-1882), at 1711 Cherry Hill Rd in the town of Granger, is one of the best in the Yakima valley; just about everything is good here, even the Riesling. Tasting room hours are from 10 am to 5 pm Monday to Saturday, and noon to 5 pm on Sunday.

One of the most noted Washington wineries, especially for its cabernet, is **the Houge Cellars** (☎ 786-4557), Wine Country Rd in Prosser, which also makes one of the best chardonnays east of the Cascades. Their tasting room hours are from 10 am to 5 pm daily. The **Yakima River Winery** (☎ 786-2805) is also in Prosser. This one is 1.5 miles west on N River Rd, which is right off Wine Country Rd. The tasting room is open from 10 am to

5 pm daily. Ask to try John's Port and the Lemberger, an otherwise obscure red varietal that likes the heat of central Washington. A final choice for the Prosser area is **Hinzerling Winery** (☎ 786-2163) at 1520 Sheridan Rd. It's open March to Christmas Eve for tasting from 11 am to 5 pm Monday to Saturday, and 11 am to 4 pm on Sundays. There are picnic facilities. The cabernet from Hinzerling is about as good as Washington red wine gets.

In Benton City, visit **Oakwood Cellars** (☎ 588-5332) or **Kiona Vineyards Winery** (☎ 588-6716). Oakwood is on De Moss Rd, off Hwy 224 and is open from 6 pm to 8 pm Wednesday to Friday, and noon to 6 pm weekends for tasting. It's closed weekdays from November to February. Try the Riesling. Kiona, off Sunset Rd, near Hwy 224, is one of the best for red wines, especially the cabernet and Lemberger. The tasting room is open from noon to 5 pm daily.

## Organized Tours

Yakima Interurban Trolleys (☎ 575-1700) offers trips to Selah on a historic trolley. Trips leave from the Yakima Electric Railway Museum at S 3rd Ave and W Pine St, which is open for self-guided tours free of charge. The trolley trip and tour, however, costs $4 for adults, $3.50 for seniors and $2.50 children ages six to 11. Children under six are free if they sit on someone's lap. Tour times are seasonal. Call in advance.

## Special Events

The Central Washington State Fair (☎ 248-7160) runs from the end of September to the first week in October and is known as one of the Northwest's best agricultural exhibitions. If you've passed them up everywhere else, this would be the one place to give in and try it. The fairgrounds are at Nob Hill Blvd and S 10th St.

There's a large Mexican population in the valley, and the Cinco de Mayo Fiesta is understandably a big celebration hereabouts. Usually held on the first weekend of May, the largest Cinco de Mayo celebrations are in Sunnyside and Wapato.

For something a little different, try the Country Christmas Lighted Farm Implement Parade in Sunnyside. Farmers dress their combines and threshers with festive lights and drive through town; watch for Rudolph and his nose so bright as he mingles with the mower blades, a favorite holiday jest. For more information contact the Sunnyside Chamber of Commerce at 837-5939.

## Places to Stay

**Camping** There are campsites at *Sportsman State Park*, just across the Yakima River on Hwy 24. About half the sites have RV hook-ups, and there are hot showers and flush toilets. The *Yakima KOA* (☎ 248-5882), 1500 Keyes Rd, offers 140 full-hook-up sites, with a laundry, play area, showers and game room. The KOA is one mile east of town on Hwy 24.

**B&Bs** Yakima's early and continued prosperity is reflected in the stately homes throughout the city; a goodly number of them have been turned into B&Bs. The imposing stone-fronted *'37 House* (☎ 965-5537), 4002 Englewood, sits on almost 10 acres of garden; the six guest rooms each have a private bath. Rooms range from $75 for a queen bed to $151 for a master suite. Slightly more modest but also comfortable is the *Irish House B&B* (☎ 453-5474), 210 S 28th Ave, an old Victorian home in a quiet residential neighborhood with three bedrooms. Rooms range between $55 to $60. *Birchfield Manor* (☎ 452-1960), 2018 Birchfield Rd, east of Yakima off Hwy 24, one of the best places to eat in the area, also offers five guest rooms, all with private baths, with rates ranging from $60 to $90.

**Hotels** If you're looking for the motel strip, head to N 1st St, where there's a major concentration of inexpensive motels and fast-food outlets. All of the following have pools and kitchenettes. *Econo Lodge* (☎ 457-6155), 510 N 1st St, takes pets; singles/doubles are $36/40. Check out the *Bali Hai Motel* (☎ 452-7178), 710 N 1st St, which charges $30/36, if for no other reason than its cool neon. The *Palomino Motel* (☎ 452-6551), 1223 N 1st St, takes pets and has singles/doubles for $38/41. *Motel 6* (☎ 454-0080), 1104 N 1st St, has rooms from $33/38. A bit more upscale is the *Red Lion Inn Yakima Valley* (☎ 248-7850, (800) 547-8010), 1507 N 1st St, which caters to business travelers and has meeting rooms, two pools and airport pickup. Rooms begin at $82/92.

Stay closer to downtown at the *Travelodge* (☎ 453-7151), 110 S Naches Ave, on a quiet side street; AAA, senior and commercial rates apply, while standard singles/doubles are $44/52. Yakima's downtown Convention Center is right next to *Cavanaugh's at Yakima Center* (☎ 248-5900, (800) 843-4667), 697 E Yakima Ave, which offers rooms for $67/77. Just off I-82 at exit No 33 is the *Best Western Rio Mirada Motor Inn* (☎ 457-4444), 1603 Terrace Heights Drive. All rooms have views of the Yakima River and easy access to the Greenway; there are also exercise facilities. Rates are $56/61.

## Places to Eat

For a good breakfast, head to *Cafe European* (☎ 248-5844), 3105 Summitview Ave, with great omelets and fresh pastries from the bakery next door. It's also good for lunch and supper, when grilled dishes take on spicy accents. Dishes like halibut with black-bean salsa and cumin oil is $16, rib-eye steak with Zinfandel shallot sauce is $17. Expect lines out the door on weekends.

For a more traditional breakfast without fear of lines, go to *Mel's Diner* (☎ 248-5382), 314 N 1st St. If you just need coffee, go to the *Lincoln Ave Espresso Bar* (☎ 576-6086), 1801 W Lincoln Ave, which offers drive-through service; or give them a call and they'll deliver lattes to your motel room for free.

Everyone's favorite Mexican restaurant is *Santiago's* (☎ 453-1644), 111 E Yakima Ave, where both traditional and specialty dishes are served in a stylish, somewhat boisterous, atmosphere. *Mustard Seed Oriental Cafe* (☎ 576-8013), 402 E Yakima Ave, is the best of Yakima's Oriental restaurants, with subtly spicy Chinese and Japanese food; it's one of the better places for vegetarians in a meat-prone town. The *Deli de Pasta* (☎ 453-0571), 7 N Front St, is a casual Italian bistro, which lets diners match a variety of fresh pasta with the sauce of their choice – try the creamy lemon linguini. Lunch prices are in the $7 range and full dinners with salad and breadsticks run $13.

Yakima also boasts several restaurants that offer quality local wines and the kind of cuisine and high prices that you might not expect to find east of the Cascades. *Gasperetti's Restaurant* (☎ 248-0628), 1013 N 1st St, is an outstanding northern Italian restaurant with an excellent wine list. Pasta dishes like penne with shrimp and tomato-pepper salsa are $12.50; meat dishes like scaloppini alla romana (veal with prosciutto and wine sauce) goes for $22. *The Greystone* (☎ 248-9801), 5 N Front St, in the historic district, is one of Yakima's original bars converted into a fine restaurant. Three-course dinners start at around $17; the excellent rack of lamb goes for $24. Drive out into the country to find *Birchfield Manor* (☎ 452-1960), 2018 Birchfield Rd, east of Yakima off Hwy 24. French-influenced cuisine and an extensive local wine list make this country inn a favorite with serious eaters. Dinner is served Thursday, Friday and Saturday only; reservations are required.

### Entertainment
**Brewpubs** The Northwest boom in microbreweries began in Yakima in 1982, when *Grant's Brewery Pub* (☎ 575-2922), 32 N Front St, first released its British-style ales. Since that day, Grant's has remained in the forefront of regional brewing, and has expanded from the former brewery into the old train station across the street. Grant's ales are amongst the very best of Northwest beers: try the Scottish Ale and the IPA (India Pale Ale). There's also a light menu with sandwiches and homemade soups.

**Cinema** First-run films are shown at *Cinema West* (☎ 248-0234), 2706 W Nob Hill Blvd, and the *Mercy 6-Plex* (☎ 248-0242), Valley Mall Blvd in Union Gap.

**Baseball** The Yakima Bears Baseball club (☎ 457-5151) is a class-A team. Games are played at the Central Washington Fairgrounds. The Yakima Sun Kings Basketball club (☎ 248-1222) is a CBA team and play in the SunDome at the fairgrounds.

### Things to Buy
If you're beginning to like the looks of those pearl-snap shirts and Wranglers jeans, head to Western Outfitters (☎ 248-5400) at 24 S 1st St, a large western clothing store. You'll find everything from cowboy hats to cattle prods. Ouch Cactus Greenhouse (☎ 877-4740), 375 Parker Bridge Rd, just south of Yakima in Wapato, is a collector's outlet for cactus, succulents, bonsai trees and carnivorous plants. The selection of cactus is enormous, as are some of the individual plants. The owners' personal display of live scorpions, poisonous snakes and alligators sets the ambiance.

If you don't have time to make the rounds of Yakima Valley wineries, head to The Wine Cellar (☎ 248-3590), 15 W Yakima Ave, at Track 29. A number of local wines are usually available for sampling, or packed for shipping.

### Getting There & Away
**Air** Commercial flights operate out of Yakima Air Terminal (☎ 575-6149), 2300 W Washington Ave. Horizon Air (☎ (800) 547-9308) links Seattle, Yakima and Spokane, while United Express (☎ (800) 241-6522) flies between Seattle and Yakima only.

**Bus** The Greyhound bus station is at 602 E Yakima Ave at the corner of 6th St, and is open from 8 am to 5 pm daily. A trip to Seattle costs $22 one way, $42 roundtrip. From Yakima, buses continue on to Portland, Walla Walla, Bend, the Tri-Cities and Spokane.

Car Rentals are available from Agency Rent-A-Car (☎ 575-0939), 5 N 9th St and Economy Auto Rentals (☎ 452-5555), 3811 Main St.

## Getting Around

Bus Yakima Transit (☎ 575-6175) runs Monday to Saturday, until around 6:30 pm. The transit center is on the corner of S 4th St and E Chestnut Ave. Adult fare is 35c; exact change is required. Bus No 9 runs hourly down S 1st St on its way to and from the airport.

Trolley The Yakima Downtown Trolley (☎ 575-6175) runs from Monday to Saturday on two routes through the city center. The fare is 25c. The 'red line' trolley passes east-west down Yakima Ave every 15 minutes, between 11th Ave and 9th St. The 'green line' does a north-south run every 20 minutes, making a loop on 1st and 3rd Sts between the historic district on Yakima and Tamarack Aves.

Taxi If you're after a taxi, call Diamond Cab at 453-3113.

## YAKAMA INDIAN RESERVATION

Directly south of Yakima, the Yakima River passes through a narrow gap in the hills before coursing out into the wide, amazingly fertile lower Yakima valley. Apples, hops, vegetables and grapes are everywhere. Stop by roadside stands or wineries to sample the local bounty.

The Yakima valley is also home to the Yakama Indian Reservation, Washington state's largest. At Toppenish, the Yakamas have built a pleasant interpretive center that seeks to explain and demonstrate the tribes' ancient cultural traditions. At Fort Simcoe are the remains of an army outpost constructed in 1856 to quash Yakama resistance to life on the reservation.

During WW II, when American farm labor was in short supply, Mexican and other Latin American workers were brought into the Yakima valley by the federal government to work as temporary farm hands. Many families remained, and

WASHINGTON

### Yakama Indians

The Yakama Indians were one of the most populous and powerful of the inland plateau tribes. They depended for subsistence on the Yakima River, a major salmon fishery. Although the Yakamas were among the first Native Americans in the Northwest to have horses, they didn't use the horse extensively for hunting, preferring fishing to hunting big game.

The Yakamas were among the natives that met Lewis and Clark at Celilo Falls in 1805; they were also among the 14 tribes that signed an 1855 treaty creating the Yakama Reservations. These tribes, which also included Klickatats and Wenatchees, went on to form the Yakama Nation.

However, the treaty was not ratified by the US Congress, and White settlers and miners continued to stream across the Yakama homelands. Conflicts between the Yakamas and the army escalated. In late 1855, the so-called Yakima War began, which involved Yakama attacks on settlements in the Columbia River Gorge and reprisals by Federal troops and Willamette Valley volunteers. The Yakamas were consigned to US Federal control after the army defeated a war party at a key battle at Union Gap in 1856. Fort Simcoe was established to maintain control over the reservation.

The Indian Agent responsible for the Yakamas throughout much of the later 1800s was a Methodist preacher who was a strong advocate of turning the Yakamas from fishers into farmers. Thus, a major fishing area on the Yakima River was sold out from the reservation, and the money used to establish the reservation's first irrigation canal. After the reservation was allotted to individual Yakamas in homestead-sized units, according to the Dawes Act, much of the most fertile and easily irrigated land passed into the hands of White farmers. ■

currently over a third of the population in the Yakima valley is Hispanic.

The Yakima valley is filled with irrigated fields and little towns dedicated to serving the needs of farmers. Toppenish (population 7419) is the primary town in the Yakama Reservation. It's also doing its best to make itself a tourist destination on the basis of its historic murals. Sunnyside (population 11,238) is another town in the valley with tourist facilities. The Toppenish Chamber of Commerce (☎ 865-3262) can be contacted at PO Box 28, Toppenish, WA 98948.

### Downtown Murals

Most buildings in downtown Toppenish are now covered with a variety of large murals, depicting some event or episode from Yakama or Northwestern history. Several contain clever visual tricks. On the first weekend of June is the Mural-in-a-Day Festival, during which a group of painters work together to complete a mural in an eight-hour period. However, given that the city appears dedicated to covering every available surface with a mural, visitors on *any* day during the summer months can usually find a painter in action. Get information on murals in progress from the Toppenish Mural Society's visitors center at 11-A S Toppenish Ave.

### Yakama Indian Nation Cultural Center

At this 12,000-sq-foot interpretive center and museum (☎ 865-2800), displays, dioramas and audio-visual exhibits explain the traditions and culture of the Yakama people. The museum focuses on the challenge of Spilyay, the trickster Coyote whose legends taught the Yakama how to understand and interact harmoniously with nature. Most of the displays detail the seasonal and daily life of the tribe, from fishing at Celilo Falls to a re-creation of a tule mat longhouse. The usual collections of arrowheads and tools aren't much in evidence here. Instead, the dioramas and exhibits, with their accompanying music and sound effects, are meant to evoke a mood or impression of traditional life and spirituality.

The center also houses collections of traditional basketry, as well as a theater, gift shop, ceremonial longhouse, library and restaurant. The cultural center is immediately north of Toppenish on Hwy 97; it is designed to look like a traditional tepee, so you can't miss it. The center is open March to December from 8 am to 5 pm Monday to Friday, Saturday 9 am to 5 pm, and Sunday 10 am to 5 pm. Admission is $2 for adults and $1 for children and seniors.

### Toppenish Museum

If you want to see the kinds of Native American artifacts that are largely absent from the tribe's cultural center, go to the Toppenish Museum (☎ 865-4510) on the 2nd floor of the public library at S Elm and Washington Ave. The high point of this community museum is the Estell Reel Meyer Indian Artifact Collection. Ms Meyer was one of the first women ever to be employed by the Federal government, and as Federal Superintendent of Indian Affairs from 1898 to 1910 collected native crafts and artifacts in her travels. The museum is open from 2 pm to 5 pm Tuesday to Saturday.

### American Hop Museum

This brand new museum pays tribute to the fact that 75% of the US hops crop is grown in the Yakima valley. The museum's focus is on hop-growing from 1805 to present. It's in the restored Hop Growers Supply building at 22 S B St in Toppenish.

### Fort Simcoe State Park

The site of Fort Simcoe long served as a camp for the Yakamas, who stopped at the natural springs here on their way to their fishing camps at Celilo Falls. After the Yakama War, the army built this fort at the springs in order to keep the peace and to settle ongoing treaty violations. At its peak, Fort Simcoe consisted of officers' quarters, a blockhouse, an enclosing stockade and an enlisted mens' barracks. After the treaty creating the Yakama Reservation was ratified in 1859, Fort Simcoe was decommissioned and used as a boarding school for Native American children until 1923.

Today, Fort Simcoe State Park takes in 200 acres of the old fort grounds. The blockhouse and barracks have been rebuilt, and the original white clapboard officers' quarters have been restored and opened for tours. The old Indian Agency building is now an interpretive center that retells the story of the fort and the wars.

Almost as striking as the old fort buildings is the surprising midsummer green of the grounds and the ample shade from old oak trees. It's no wonder that both the Yakamas and the army coveted this oasis in the midst of scorched desert hills. The state park is understandably a popular place for summer picnics, with the grounds open from Memorial Day to Labor Day. Fort Simcoe is 27 miles west of Toppenish, at the end of Hwy 220.

### Special Events
The Yakama Nation Cultural Powwow & Rodeo is held in Toppenish in either late June or early July, and is the Yakama tribe's largest celebration. The four-day festival includes dancing, a parade and an 'Indian Village' with tepees, Indian food booths and stick games. For information, contact 865-5315.

### Places to Stay & Eat
The Yakama Tribes operate the *Yakama Nation RV Resort* (☎ 865-2000, (800) 874-3087) adjacent to the Cultural Center at 280 Buster Rd, north of Toppenish. In addition to RV hook-ups, there is a separate

tenting area and tepees for rent. Facilities include a swimming pool, laundry, showers and playground.

Toppenish and Sunnyside offer the usual kind of roadside motels. In Toppenish, go to the Oxbow Motor Inn (☎ 865-5800), 511 S Elm St, with its own mural! Singles/doubles are $35/40. The Toppenish Inn (☎ 865-7444), at the junction of Hwys 97 and 22, offers free continental breakfast, a pool and brand new rooms for $50/56. In Sunnyside, stop at the *Nendel's Inn* (☎ 837-7878), 408 Yakima Valley Hwy, with a pool, air conditioning and pets allowed; rates are $44/48.

If you're hungry in the Yakima valley, do as the locals do and eat Mexican. There are good, inexpensive places to eat at just about every junction. In Toppenish, try the *El Paso Cafe* (☎ 865-2066), 5 W 1st Ave or *La Hacienda Gardens* (☎ 865-1992), 207 Toppenish Ave.

### Things to Buy
For the unlikely, go to the Hangups Gallery (☎ 786-1149), 1130 Meade Ave, in Prosser. Contemporary art, watercolor, mixed media, basket weaving and Japanese washi designs are featured, though the work of a WSU Emeritus Professor of Entomology, who incorporates dead bugs into his glass on metal enamel jewelry, belt buckles and sculptures might be just the souvenir you've been looking for.

### Getting There & Away
Greyhound buses connect all the stops along the Yakima valley between Yakima and Richland.

# Northeastern Washington

Northeastern Washington's mountains – the Kettle River and Selkirk ranges – are the far western foothills of the Rockies. Ground down by several successive waves of glaciers, these forested slopes are now more rolling hills than jagged peaks. The Columbia River winds south through these mountains, widening into Roosevelt Lake as it turns west and backs up behind the Grand Coulee Dam. The Columbia then turns south again before its final journey to the sea, and the river here marks the far northern boundary of the great western desert. South of the Columbia, the land is flat and dry, the immense, lonesome geography of the mythic West.

Northeastern Washington lacks the developed recreation that's abundant in the western part of the state, but there are many good places to hike, fish and cross-country ski, especially in the Okanogan and Colville national forests. The rugged, dramatic landscape of the Columbia Basin, scoured by ice-age floods, provides a suitably dramatic setting for the Grand Coulee Dam, one of the world's largest producers of hydroelectric power and a towering structure. Roosevelt Lake is a popular vacation spot for boating and fishing. The best place to begin exploring these regions is Spokane, which is the largest city for many a dry mile and a shopping mecca for the smaller communities of the Inland Northwest. It is also the only place where you have a chance of seeing the opera or eating a good Thai meal.

In terms of weather, the Cascade Mountains take the brunt of Pacific storms, which is why the land to the east receives so little rainfall. But at the state's northeastern edge, the Selkirks catch storms anew, receiving up to 80 inches of precipitation a year and creating an undeniable winter. Spokane misses the heavy rain and snow that falls in the nearby mountains, but it still gets its fair share.

## HISTORY

Originally, Native Americans lived mainly around and off the Columbia River and its tributaries. Places like Kettle Falls and Spokane Falls were especially good spots for salmon fishing, and communities grew up around them. David Thompson, a Canadian explorer and fur trader, was the first White person to navigate the entire length of the Columbia River, and his reports and his excellent maps of the Inland Northwest laid the way for more fur traders.

Eventually, the Native American tribes were confined to the Colville and Spokane reservations. These reservations were large at first, but disease decimated the native populations and European settlers took back more of the land as mineral resources, especially gold, were found in the remote hills to the north. Life was pretty rugged, even after the Northern Pacific Railroad came through in 1881, spurring Spokane's growth. It wasn't until the Columbia Basin Irrigation Project in the 1930s, whose centerpiece was the building of the Grand Coulee Dam, that life began to change significantly. The irrigation project turned the nearby desert into wheat fields, and the electricity these dams produced helped support Washington's post-WW II industrial boom.

## ORIENTATION

Highway 2 runs across the southern edge of northeastern Washington, and it's roughly paralleled by Hwy 20 to the north. Bicycle tourists use Hwy 20 pretty heavily in the summer; it's part of a coast-to-coast route across the northern tier of the USA.

Highway 97 courses down the Okanogan valley and joins up with the Columbia River near Brewster and the Chief Joseph Dam. Even more remote, Hwy 21 cuts north-south through the Colville Indian Reservation between Hwy 2 at Wilbur and the Canadian border.

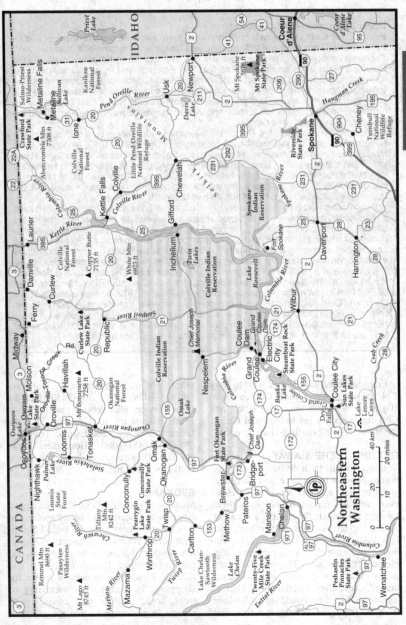

Northeastern Washington

### David Thompson – Early Explorer

Before Lewis and Clark came to the Northwest, there was the Canadian explorer and fur trader David Thompson, and to Northwest and Canadian historians and 'buckskinners', Thompson is something of a cult hero. He not only was the first explorer to paddle the Columbia River in its entirety and the first White person that many Inland Northwest Native Americans had ever met (confirming rumors of white-skinned people) but he traversed the wilderness for 27 years and never killed anybody nor lost anyone in his party to accident or attack. Though he was employed by the North West Company as a fur trader, he was an intellectual man who treated the Native Americans he met and the land itself with respect and dignity.

Thompson first crossed the Rockies in the early 1800s, setting up a trading post, the Kootenae House, at the Columbia's headwaters in Canada; in 1810, along with Jaco Findley and Finan McDonald, he established the Spokane House on the Spokane River, which was the first trading post in present-day Washington, preceded in the Northwest only by the Pacific Fur Company in Astoria, OR. Every year Thompson made an incredible 3000-mile journey by canoe, horseback and foot from Kootenae House to Lake Superior with the six tons or so of furs he had collected.

But no one would probably know or care much about Thompson if he hadn't been such a good writer, map maker and surveyor. He made sense of an extremely confusing and difficult terrain, paving the way for other trappers, and he was the first person to document certain plants and animals; he also took the time to meet and get to know the native tribes, recording some of their rituals and practices in detail. Other trappers and explorers traversed this terrain, but none did so with as much skill and attention.

Eventually, the Hudson's Bay Company took control of the Northwest, and Spokane House was mothballed because of its distance from the Columbia River, being replaced by Fort Colvile just north. Thompson retired to Montreal in 1812, where he died in 1857. Lewis and Clark, who began their much-heralded two-year exploration in 1804 from the other end of the Columbia River, have received most of the glory, but as many a fervent Northwest historian will tell you, Thompson deserves at least as much credit, if not more. (To read further, pick up a copy of *Sources of the River* by Jack Nisbet.) ∎

From Spokane, take Hwy 2 west to Hwy 174 to get to the Grand Coulee Dam. Highway 395 north traces the Kettle and Colville rivers. To get to the Pend Oreille River, take Hwy 2 north to Hwy 20 north.

### GETTING THERE & AWAY

Whether by air, train or bus, most transportation heads to Spokane, and from there you can pick up other local buses. However, Amtrak's *Empire Builder* only slinks through Spokane in the middle of the night.

Bus service is essentially inbred with Greyhound (☎ (800) 231-2222), who bought out a bunch of local carriers to supplement their service. The result is a confusing mishmash of companies with names that all sound alike, and that all sell tickets for one another. Greyhound serves Spokane from Portland and Seattle, and from few other places. Northwestern Trailways (☎ 838-4029, (800) 366-3830) has the same service, plus service east to Boise. From Ellensburg to Osoyoos into the Okanogan valley, take Empire Trailways (☎ (800) 351-1060). Borderline Stage (☎ 624-7192) serves Colville and Kettle Falls from Spokane.

### SPOKANE

Spokane (population 375,000) is the largest city between Seattle and Minneapolis, and it is the trade center for the Inland Northwest, an area comprising eastern Washington, northern Idaho, western Montana and parts of Oregon, British Columbia and Alberta. In addition to being a mecca for shopping, Spokane has an abundance of trees, some popular golf courses, and several large city parks that are great for hiking, biking and a number of other activities.

Spokan Indians, whose name means 'children of the sun', settled and fished from Spokane Falls. They spoke a Salishan language, and after procuring horses, they crossed the Rockies to hunt with their neighbors, the Kalispels, Flatheads and Nez Perce.

Though Spokane was the location of Washington's first trading post in 1810, it was eventually replaced by Fort Colvile, which was more conveniently located on the Columbia River. Indian wars slowed the region's development; it wasn't until 1879

that White settlers staked claims near the falls. The Northern Pacific came through in 1881, when the town's population was 500. In 1889, the burgeoning business area was destroyed by fire. A tent city was quickly constructed, and merchants continued operations while the downtown area was rebuilt, this time in brick rather than wood.

Spokane grew up to be a market center, and today it is inordinately proud of its skywalk, an above-ground, covered walkway between a number of downtown buildings. The area around the river was run down and the river polluted until 1974, when Spokane hosted the World's Fair &

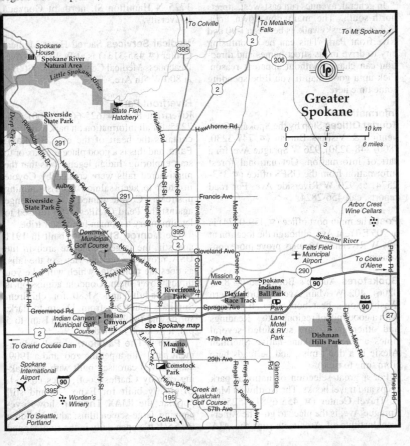

Greater Spokane

Exposition. In anticipation of that event, the city cleaned up and revitalized the area, turning 100 acres into the now attractive Riverfront Park.

## Orientation

Spokane is just 18 miles from the Idaho border and is 110 miles south of Canada. Interstate 90 is the main east-west route through town; Sprague Ave, just north of the freeway, divides north addresses from south. Division St is the main north-south street, and it divides east from west and becomes Hwy 2 north of town. It's a long, nasty drag, but often unavoidable.

In general, avenues run east-west, streets north-south. The main downtown area, including the skywalk, is between I-90 and Riverfront Park. This can be a confusing city to drive in, as street names and direction can change without apparent reason. Pick up a good map if you'll be spending some time here.

## Information

**Tourist Offices** Stop by the Spokane Convention & Visitors Bureau (☎ 747-3230, (800) 248-3230), 926 W Sprague Ave, for a raft of information. Get national forest information from the USFS office (☎ 353-2574) at 920 W Riverside Ave. For road reports, call 456-2824.

**Post** The main post office (☎ 459-0274) is at 703 E Trent Ave, although the location at 904 W Riverside Ave may prove more convenient.

**Bookstores** Auntie's Bookstore (☎ 838-0206), 402 W Main Ave, is northeastern Washington's best bookstore. It's large, with a good mix of regional titles. Readings and other events are scheduled several times a week (Spokane-native Sherman Alexie is a don't-miss, and he reads here from time to time).

For a great selection of national park maps and travel books, The Northwest Map & Travel Center (☎ 455-6981), 525 W Sprague Ave, is the place to go. The American Institute of Architects runs the AIA Bookstore (☎ 747-5498) at 335 W Sprague Ave. It's only open from 10 am to 2 pm on weekdays.

**Media** The *Spokesman-Review* is the local daily newspaper, and the *Inlander*, a free weekly, covers the arts and can be found in stacks in shops all over town. The public radio station is at 91.1 FM.

**Laundry** Most of the laundromats are away from the city center. Monroe St Self Service Laundry (☎ 327-1769), 2407 N Monroe St, is fairly convenient, as is the Hamilton St Wash & Dry (☎ 487-6184), 1725 N Hamilton St, north of Gonzaga University.

**Medical Services** Sacred Heart Medical Center (☎ 455-3131) is at W 101 8th Ave. Deaconess Medical Center (☎ 458-5800) is at 800 W 5th Ave.

## Riverfront Park

Riverfront Park (☎ 625-6600, (800) 336-7275, for all information on park activities) contains the heart of the city, **Spokane Falls**, and this is a good place to relax or to start exploring. Indian legend says that the multi-tiered falls were created by Coyote in order to keep salmon from swimming upstream – Coyote wanted to exact revenge against the Pend Oreilles, who refused to let him marry a woman from their tribe.

The **Monroe St Bridge**, built in 1911 and still the largest concrete arch in the USA, provides excellent views of the falls, as does the **gondola**, which will take you directly over them. Gondola admission is $3 for adults and $1.80 for children. Summer hours are from 11 am to dark; spring and fall hours are from 11 am to 5 pm; it's closed in winter.

There is **The Pavilion**, a small amusement park with a petting zoo, and a 1909, hand-carved carousel, built with painstaking care by Charles Looff; rides cost $1. Originally built for Expo '74 and still popular, the **IMAX Theater** shows eye-popping, large-screen films; adults/children are $5/4. It's open daily in the summer and weekends only in the winter. In the winter the Pavilion becomes the **Ice Palace**, an ice skating rink. Pavilion rides and other activities are all charged separately, or you can get comprehensive day passes for $9.95 a person; call for other rates and specials.

Connected to the park by a footbridge across the river, the **Flour Mill**, 621 W Mallon Ave, was built in 1890 and was then the region's most modern mill. Remodeled in 1973, the mill now houses shops and restaurants. The **Spokane County Court House**, just a few blocks away at Broadway and Madison St, is almost an apparition. Built in the 1890s by a self-trained architect, the French Renaissance structure was inspired by the chateaus at Chambord and Azay-le-Rideau in France's Loire Valley.

On the southern edge of the park, on Spokane Falls Blvd at Post St, statues of runners pay playful tribute to the Bloomsday runners (see Special Events later in this section).

### Centennial Trail

This 39-mile-long greenway trail is centered on Riverfront Park and runs east to the Idaho state line and northwest to Riverside State Park. For more information, contact the Friends of Centennial Trail (☎ 624-3430), 609 W Spokane Falls Blvd, or the office of Centennial Trail (☎ 625-6984), 808 W Spokane Falls Blvd.

In downtown Spokane, many people stroll, run, rollerblade, skateboard or bike along this greenway. Unfortunately, it's not the safest place for a woman to walk in the evening. As you leave the city, the trail becomes less urban and more suited to hiking and cross-country skiing. There are several put-in sites for canoes and kayaks along the river. Designated portions are open for mountain biking and horseback riding.

### St John's Cathedral

The stunning and ornate St John's Cathedral (☎ 838-4277), 127 E 12th Ave, built in 1927, is a classic example of English Gothic architecture. Free cathedral tours are given Tuesday, Thursday, Saturday and Sunday between noon and 3 pm.

### Browne's Addition

Head west from downtown on Riverside Ave or W 2nd Ave for about half a mile to the historic Browne's Addition neighborhood. It's a good place to wander, with lots of trees and big houses. Many homes here were designed by architect Kirtland K Cutter. The most famous was built for mining magnate Patsy Clark, and it's now Patsy Clark's mansion, Spokane's fanciest restaurant (see Places to Eat). **Coeur d'Alene Park**, Spokane's oldest public park, was donated to the city in 1882 and is across the street from Patsy Clark's. It's a pleasant park with a wading pool and plenty of swings for kids.

### Cheney Cowles Museum

The Eastern Washington State Historical Society runs this well-curated, historical museum (☎ 456-3931), 2316 W 1st Ave, which also has rotating exhibits. Hours are Tuesday to Saturday from 10 am to 5 pm, and Sunday from 1 to 5 pm. Admission is free on Wednesday nights from 5 to 10 pm. Regular admission for adults is $3, children and seniors $2.

If you just can't get enough Spokane history, next door is the 1898 **Campbell House**, the Tudor-style estate of mining tycoon Amasa Campbell, which was built during Spokane's 'Age of Elegance'. Admission is included with the Cheney Cowles Museum.

### Peaceful Valley

One of Spokane's funkiest and most charming residential neighborhoods is just south of the river on the northwestern edge of downtown. If you're walking, start at the **Carnegie Library** (which now contains offices) at 1st and Cedar Sts and cut down the flight of cement steps to Peaceful Valley, a pocket-sized community of simple turn-of-the-century homes, many with handcarved trim and flourishing vegetable gardens. The alternative edge to this

WASHINGTON

**PLACES TO STAY**
4 Marianna Stoltz House
13 Cavanaugh's Inn at the Park
17 Sheraton Spokane Hotel
18 Courtyard Marriott
41 WestCoast Ridpath Hotel
44 Suntree 8 Inn
45 Travelodge of Spokane
50 Fotherlingham House Victorian
51 Nendel's Valu Inn
53 Downtowner Motel
59 Best Western Tradewinds Downtown
61 Shilo Inn
62 Cobblestone Inn
64 HI/AYH

**PLACES TO EAT**
1 Azar's
9 Milford's
10 Espresso Delizioso Cafe
24 The Olive Garden
29 Luigi's Italian Restaurant
30 The Onion
33 Great Harvest Bread Company
34 Fugazzi
35 Rock City Grill
37 Thai Cafe
46 Fitzbillies Bagel Bakery
47 The Elk
49 Patsy Clark's
52 Old Spaghetti Factory
56 Java Junky's

**OTHER**
2 Monroe St Self Serve Laundry
3 Mountain Gear
5 Hamilton St Wash & Dry
6 All Star Car Rental
7 Spokane County Court House
8 REI
11 YWCA
12 Flour Mill
14 JS Pumps
15 YMCA
16 IMAX Theater
19 Post Office
20 Quinn's Bike Rental
21 Carousel
22 Opera House/Convention Center
23 Cedar St Market Co-op
25 Fort Spokane Brewery
26 Auntie's Bookstore
27 USFS Office
28 Post Office
31 Birkenbeinder Brewing Company
32 Visitors Center
36 Bloomsday Lilac Association
38 Outback Jack's
39 AIA Bookstore
40 Budget Rent-A-Car
42 Northwest Map & Travel Center
43 Magic Lantern Theatre
48 Cheney Cowles Museum
54 Big Dipper
55 Amtrak Station
57 Payless Car Rental
58 U-Save Car Rental
60 Deaconess Medical Center
63 Sacred Heart Medical Center
65 St John's Cathedral

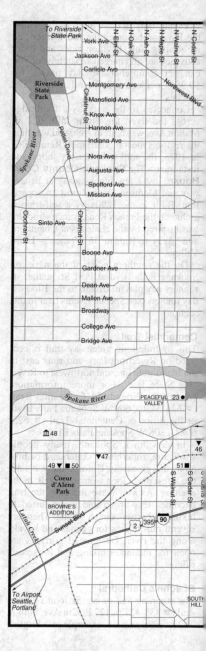

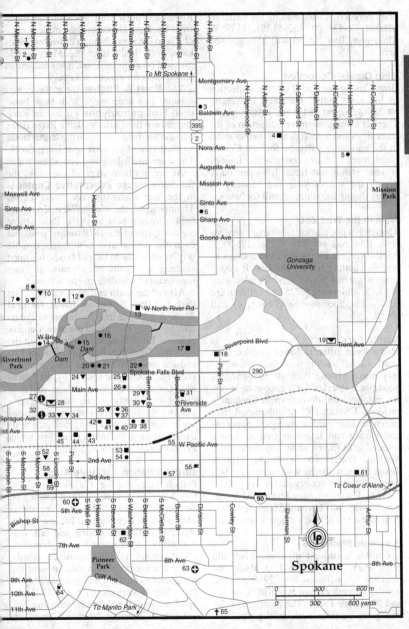

N Madison St
N Monroe St
N Lincoln St
N Post St
N Wall St
N Howard St
N Stevens St
N Washington St
N Galispel St
N Normandie St
N Atlantic St
N Division St
N Ruby St
N Lidgerwood St
N Astor St
N Addison St
N Standard St
N Dakota St
N Cincinnati St
N Hamilton St
N Columbus St

1
2

To Mt Spokane

Montgomery Ave

3
Baldwin Ave
395
2
4

Nora Ave

5

Augusta Ave

Mission Ave

Mission
Park

Maxwell Ave

Sinto Ave
6

Sharp Ave

Sharp Ave

Boone Ave

Gonzaga
University

8
10
7  9
11  12

W North River Rd
13

15  16
14
Dam

17

Riverpoint Blvd
19  Trent Ave
18

Riverfront
Park
Dam

20  21
22
Spokane Falls Blvd
290

24
25
26

Main Ave
Bernard St
Browne St
Pine St

27
28
29
30

31
Riverside
Ave

32
Sprague Ave
33  34
35  36
37
42
41  40
39  38

45  44
43

S Jefferson St
S Madison St
S Monroe St
S Lincoln St
Post St

52
58
59

53
54

2nd Ave

55  W Pacific Ave

56

57

3rd Ave

60
5th Ave

S Wall St
S Howard St
S Stevens St
S Washington St
S Bernard St
S McClellan St
Brown St
Division St
Cowley St

61

To Coeur d'Alene

90

Sherman St
Arthur St

Bishop St

7th Ave

62

8th Ave
63

Spokane

8th Ave

Pioneer
Park

9th Ave
Cliff Ave
64
10th Ave
11th Ave

To Manito Park

65

| 0 | 300 | 600 m |
| 0 | 300 | 600 yards |

neighborhood is sustained by the Cedar St Market Co-Op (☎ 455-5125), 1339 W Main Ave. Bus No 30 will also get you here.

## Bing Crosby Collection
Bing Crosby donated this large collection to his alma mater, Gonzaga University (☎ 328-4220, ext 3847) 502 E Boone Ave. There is a comprehensive collection of his recordings and a good deal of memorabilia in the university's Crosby Student Center. In addition, a bronze statue of the famous crooner stands out front. It's open daily during the school year and Monday to Friday during the summer; call for hours.

## Walk in the Wild Zoo
Though it's not particularly large or extensive, this zoo (☎ 924-7221), 12600 E Euclid Ave, has all the requisite animals as well as a petting zoo for children. It's open from 10 am to 4 pm daily; adults admission is $3.75, seniors are $3.25 and children are $2.25. The zoo may be closing, so call ahead.

## Manito Park
Half a dozen different flower gardens, a big pond, a small wading pool and a conservatory make Manito Park (☎ 625-6622) a good place to relax for a couple of hours. It's not far from downtown in Spokane's residential South Hill neighborhood. Between the lilac garden, rose garden, perennial garden and Japanese garden, there's something to fit just about any floral taste. Spokane Pottery (☎ 747-6664), 2100 S Tekoa St, near the park conservatory, is a large production pottery maker.

From downtown, take Stevens St south, which turns into Bernard St, to 21st Ave, then take a left to reach the park entrance.

## Riverside State Park
Six miles northwest of town, Riverside State Park (☎ 456-3964) is along the Spokane River (follow Hwy 291 north and it will pass park entrances at Rifle Club Rd and Nine Mile Falls). The highlight of the nearly 12-sq-mile park is the Spokane River Centennial Trail, stretching 39 miles from Spokane House at the northern edge of Riverside Park, through downtown Spokane, to the Idaho state line. Many people hike and bike this trail, and it has numerous put-in spots for canoes or kayaks.

The **Bowl & Pitcher** (near the campground) is a deep gorge with huge boulders. Find **petroglyphs** on Indian Rock near where the Little Spokane River flows into the Spokane, or search the **fossil beds** on west side of the river near Deep Creek. There are also hiking and equestrian trails.

At the northern edge of the park, the **Spokane House Interpretive Center** is at the site where the fur trader David Thompson of the North West Company built a trading post in 1810. Today, there are few traces of the 1810 trading post, and even the interpretive center has trouble staying open due to lack of funds. It's open summer weekends most years; at other times, call to schedule an appointment.

Also at the north end of Riverside State Park is **Little Spokane River Natural Area**. A six-mile trail for hikers or cross-country skiers runs along the exceptionally peaceful Little Spokane River between the Spokane Trout Hatchery (on Waikiki Rd) and the mouth of the river. This is also a good place to canoe (put in by the hatchery). Great blue herons nest here, and bald eagles commonly winter at the river's mouth. No pets, bicycles or motorized vehicles are permitted along the Little Spokane. Camping, swimming and floating on innertubes are not allowed either.

## Turnbull National Wildlife Area
Pothole lakes dot the 17,000-acre migratory waterfowl refuge, south of Cheney on Badger Lake Rd. Although Turnbull is known for its teeming bird life, especially abundant during the spring and fall, it is also home to threatened water howellia, which grows in clay-bottomed ponds. There's a six-mile auto tour around the refuge and a couple of hiking trails. Stop by the refuge headquarters (☎ 235-4723) for up-to-the-minute wildlife information.

To reach Turnbull, head to Cheney via

I-90 west. Turn south off Cheney's main drag (Hwy 904) onto the Cheney-Plaza Rd and head about 4.5 miles south to the refuge.

## Wineries
Several Spokane wineries have tours and tasting rooms. **Arbor Crest Winery** (☎ 927-9463), 4705 N Fruit Hill Rd, overlooks the Spokane River, **Latah Creek Wine Cellars** (☎ 926-0164), 13030 E Indiana Ave, is alongside I-90 east of the city, and **Worden's Winery** (☎ 455-7835), 7217 W 45th Ave, exit No 276 from I-90, is the region's largest and oldest.

## Skiing
Mount Spokane Ski Area (☎ 238-6281), 31 miles northeast of town, is a pretty low-key place for a **downhill ski** area. There isn't much resort hype here. The small lodge and rental shop concentrate on 5878-foot-high Mt Spokane and the ski area's 2100-foot vertical drop. To reach Mt Spokane, head north on Division St/Hwy 2, turn east on Hwy 206 and follow it to its end, about three miles past Mt Spokane State Park. Adult lift prices are $15 Thursday to Sunday, and $12 on Wednesday. The lifts shut down on Monday and Tuesday.

**Cross-country skiers** should pick a trail just down the hill from the downhill slopes. There are several trails in and just past Mt Spokane State Park.

## Swimming
The YMCA (☎ 838-3577), 507 N Howard St, in Riverfront Park, and the YWCA (☎ 326-1190), 829 W Broadway, just across the river from the YMCA, both have indoor pools.

## Golf
Spokane is known in golfing circles for its profusion of courses and its enthusiastic golfers. There are more than a dozen golf courses in the Spokane area, including several fine public courses.

Downriver (☎ 327-5269), 3225 N Columbia Circle ($17 for non-residents), and Indian Canyon (☎ 747-5353), 4304 W West Drive ($21), are both hilly, 18-hole

courses near the west end of town. The Creek at Qualchan (☎ 448-9317), 301 E Meadow Lane Rd (exit No 279 on I-90), is a newer, challenging 18-hole course ($21) along Latah Creek south of town. Just south of the creek at Qualchan, Hangman Valley (☎ 448-1212), off S Baltimore Rd at 2210 E Hangman Valley Rd, is a rolling county course ($17). The Spokane visitors center dispenses a map with complete listings for eastern Washington and northern Idaho.

## Horseback Riding
Several stables around town offer horseback riding. Indian Canyon Riding Stables (☎ 624-4646), 4812 W Canyon Drive, is in Indian Canyon Park near the golf course. Trailtown Riding Stables (☎ 456-8249) operates out of Riverside State Park.

## Other Activities
The 39-mile-long Centennial Trail is, for most of its run, separated from auto traffic, making it a great place for walking, **hiking** or casual bike rides. Rent bicycles from Quinn's (☎ 456-6545), 507 N Howard St, in Riverfront Park. To outfit yourself for more intense outdoor recreation, go to REI (☎ 328-9900), 1125 N Monroe St, or Mountain Gear (☎ 325-9000), 2002 N Division St.

## Tours
Take it all in by car on the **Spokane City Drive**. The visitors center will give you a map, but the drive officially starts at Stevens St and Riverside Ave, and it's easy enough to spot the arrowhead-shaped logo on a sign and pick up the route at any point. For sightseeing tours, call Gray Line (☎ 624-4116) or Karivan Tours (☎ 489-8687).

## Special Events
If Spokane is famous for any one thing, it's probably the Bloomsday Run (held the first Sunday in May). It's the world's largest timed road race, attracting up to 60,000 participants. Runners, walkers and wheelchair racers all trace the 12 K (7.46 mile)

course, and all must pre-register through the Bloomsday Lilac Association (☎ 838-1579), 421 W Riverside Ave. With all these runners gathered in one spot, it's no surprise that there's a big fitness and running trade show held the same weekend.

In mid-May, shortly following Bloomsday, the lilacs start blooming and Lilac Festival activities commence. What was once a simple flower show is now highlighted by a carnival, a variety show, and a big torchlight parade on the third Saturday in May. To see the lilacs, visit Manito Park's Lilac Garden.

The St Patrick's Day parade, held on the Saturday nearest St Patrick's Day (March 17), is also a big deal here.

## Places to Stay

Since people from all over the region come here regularly to spend a weekend shopping, Spokane has plenty of inexpensive and moderately priced lodgings.

**Camping** *Riverside State Park* (☎ 456-3964) has 101 sites (no hook-ups) and hot showers for $11 a night. This is a pleasant place to stay and remarkably convenient to downtown Spokane. Spokane's premier RV park, *Park Washington Ponderosa Hill* (☎ 747-9415), 7520 S Thomas Mallen Rd (exit No 272 from I-90), has pleasant wooded sites for $23, a few tent sites, and is adjacent to a golf course and hiking trails. More RV hook-ups can be found at the *Park Lane Motel & RV Park* (☎ 535-1626), 4412 E Sprague Ave. Sites start at $21.50. The *Spokane KOA* (☎ 924-4722) is open seasonally March to mid-November, and rates start at $17 to $22. Take I-90 east of Spokane for 13 miles to exit No 293, then drive south 1.3 miles on Barker Rd.

**Hostels** *Hostelling International Spokane* (☎ 838-5968), 930 S Lincoln St, is nestled in the quiet South Hill neighborhood. The 22-bed hostel has separate men's and women's dorms, a couple of rooms for families and couples, and kitchen and laundry facilities. It's a good idea to re-

serve in advance. Rates for members/nonmembers start at $10/13.

**B&Bs** Spokane B&B Association (☎ 624-3776) can give you a complete listing of B&Bs in Spokane. Some of the most notable ones are listed below.

In Browne's Addition, *Fotheringham House Victorian B&B* (☎ 838-4363), 2128 W 2nd Ave, dates from 1891 and retains many period touches. Two of the three rooms share a bath and cost $65; the room with a private bath goes for $70. *Cobblestone Inn* (☎ 624-9735), 620 S Washington St, has two guest rooms; one is $55/65 for singles/doubles, the other $75/85. The Cobblestone also runs a bakery, which means good breakfast breads for guests, but anyone can stop by – there's a place to sit and eat pastries.

*Marianna Stoltz House* (☎ 483-4316), 427 E Indiana Ave, north of Gonzaga University, offers TVs, telephones and privacy. It caters to business travelers, and rooms are from $50/60.

**Hotels** There are a number of cheap motels on Division St north (Hwy 2) near the shopping strip. For about $35 a night, try the *Liberty Motel* (☎ 467-6000), 6801 N Division St, and the *Royal Scot Motel* (☎ 467-6672), 20 W Houston Ave. *Best Western Tradewinds North* (☎ 326-5500), at 3033 N Division St near Euclid Ave, is a little nicer, with rooms for $56/62 and an indoor pool. For around $63 a night, there's the *Quality Inn* (☎ 467-4900), 7919 N Division St, which has a 24-hour pool and hot tub, and the *Comfort Inn* (☎ 467-7111), 7111 N Division St.

Several places downtown have rooms for around $34/39 and allow pets, such as the *Downtowner Motel* (☎ 838-4411), 165 S Washington St, and the *Suntree 8 Inn* (☎ 838-8504, (800) 888-6630), 123 S Post St. *Nendels Valu Inn* (☎ 838-2026, (800) 547-0106), 1420 W 2nd Ave, is conveniently located on the edge of downtown near Browne's Addition.

*Travelodge of Spokane* (☎ 456-8040, (800) 255-3050), 827 W 1st Ave, has an outdoor pool, hot tub and sauna, and double rooms from $42. *Best Western Tradewinds Downtown* (☎ 838-2191), 907 W 3rd Ave, has rooms starting at $40/44, allows pets with a deposit, and has an outdoor pool and a weight room.

Two decent, inexpensive motels near the airport, with doubles for $36, are the *Cedar Village Motel* (☎ 838-8558), 5415 W Sunset Blvd and the *Motel 6* (☎ 459-6120), 1508 Rustle St (just off Sunset Blvd, near the Holiday Inn).

*Holiday Inn West* (☎ 747-2921), 4212 W Sunset Blvd, near I-90 exit No 277, is on the way to the airport. It has an outdoor pool, and pets are welcome. Double rooms run $66. *WestCoast Ridpath Hotel* (☎ 838-6101, (800) 426-0670), 515 W Sprague Ave, is a huge old hotel. Their outdoor pool is open year round. Rooms start at $65. The *Courtyard Marriott* (☎ 456-7600, (800) 321-2211), 401 N Riverpoint Blvd, is geared toward business travelers and offers discounted weekend rates. There's an indoor pool, hot tub and exercise room. Regular rates start at $70. The *Shilo Inn* (☎ 535-9000), 923 E 3rd Ave, has an indoor pool and rooms from $65.

For some of the nicest digs in town, try *Cavanaugh's Inn at the Park* (☎ 326-8000, (800) 843-4667), 303 W North River Rd, pleasantly located on the Spokane River near Riverfront Park. There are indoor and outdoor pools, kitchen units and an airport shuttle; pets are allowed. Regular single/double rooms begin at $90/99, but there are plenty of special rates. The *Sheraton Spokane Hotel* (☎ 455-9600, (800) 848-9600), 322 N Spokane Falls Court, has a full range of amenities and rooms starting at $108/118.

### Places to Eat
Spokane has a number of good, inexpensive restaurants. But enjoy the range of ethnic cuisines while you're here because Spokane is as cosmopolitan as it gets in this part of the country.

**Budget** *The Elk* (☎ 456-0454), 1931 W Pacific Ave, is an old drugstore turned cafe.

It's a sunny, friendly spot and has particularly good breakfasts. It's open from 9 am to 9 pm Monday to Saturday, till 3 pm on Sunday. *Fitzbillies Bagel Bakery* (☎ 747-1834), 1325 W 1st Ave at Carnegie Square, is a 'New York-style' deli with good bagels and dense 'billie bars' (a Pacific Northwest twist on the bagel, changing its shape and loading it with whole wheat, raisins and nuts). Lunches are about $4.50.

*Great Harvest Bread Company* (☎ 624-9370), 816 W Sprague Ave, is a wholewheat bakery with lunchtime soup, salads and sandwiches. It's open Monday to Friday, 6:30 am to 5:30 pm. Greek, Middle Eastern and American breakfast, lunch and dinner are served at *Azar's* (☎ 326-7171), 2501 N Monroe St.

*Thai Cafe* (☎ 838-4783), 410 W Sprague Ave, is open for lunch and dinner on weekdays, dinner only on Saturdays. Pad Thai is $5. The other Thai restaurant of note, *Riverview Thai Restaurant* (☎ 325-8370), in the Flour Mill at W 621 Mallon Ave, has well-seasoned entrees for just over $5 and a better, quieter atmosphere than most budget eateries.

There's nothing special about the burgers, chili and salads at *The Onion* (☎ 624-9965), 302 W Riverside Ave, but the place is a Spokane institution, and kids enjoy the rollicking waiters. There's an interesting edge to *Java Junky's* (☎ 458-2326), a 24-hour espresso joint at 221 S Division St, where Spokane's disaffected youth mix with the latte-swilling mainstream.

**Middle** You can eat cheaply at *Espresso Delizioso Cafe* (☎ 326-5958), 706 N Monroe St, if you stick to soup and salad, but it's tempting to delve deeper into the eclectic menu. This casually elegant brick-walled restaurant is low-key and unstuffy; the wait staff model Spokane's version of sophisticated grunge dressing. There's often live folk music.

Across from Espresso Delizioso Cafe, *Milford's* (☎ 326-7251), 719 N Monroe St, is Spokane's best seafood restaurant. Seafood dinners here run $15, and it's easy

WASHINGTON

to spend a lot more. On Monday nights, two pounds of steamer clams go for $9.95.

Downtown across from Riverfront Park, *The Olive Garden* (☎ 624-1853), 221 N Wall St (at Spokane Falls Blvd), is a clean-cut place serving large portions of fairly predictable Italian food. Dinners are around $10, lunches about $6. The *Old Spaghetti Factory* (☎ 624-8916), 152 S Monroe St, is a good place to take kids. For a more atmospheric Italian restaurant (red-checkered tablecloths and candles), try *Luigi's Italian Restaurant* (☎ 624-5226), 113 N Bernard St. New-wave Italian crops up at *Rock City Grill* (☎ 455-4400), 505 W Riverside Ave, where a one-person arti-choke heart and shiitake mushroom pizza goes for $8.95.

There's more trendy lunch and dinner food (seafood tostada with black beans and mango salsa) at *Fugazzi* (☎ 624-1133), 1 N Post St.

**Top End** *Patsy Clark's* (☎ 838-8300), in a huge historic house at 2208 W 2nd Ave, is as formal a place as you'll find in Spokane. People throng to the Sunday brunch, and it's the most popular special-occasion restaurant in town. Dinner entrees run from $13 to $19.

### Entertainment
**Brewpubs** *Fort Spokane Brewery* (☎ 838-3809), 401 W Spokane Falls Blvd, brews several ales. It's well situated just across the street from Riverfront Park, and it serves surprisingly good food (sandwiches for about $5). Check out the graceful old bar and the stamped tin ceiling near the entrance. Brewery tours are offered Monday to Friday, from 11 am to 5 pm. Blues bands play here three or four nights a week (always on Sunday).

The new *Birkenbeinder Brewing Company* (☎ 458-0854), 35 W Main Ave, brews 10 to 12 of their own beers on the premises, and serves up to 16 different beers on tap.

**Cinemas** *Magic Lantern Theatre* (☎ 838-4919), 123 S Wall St, is the place to go for arty, foreign films.

**Performing Arts** For round-the-clock information on the arts, call the Spokane Arts Commission (☎ 747-2787).

*Spokane Opera House* (☎ 353-6500), 334 W Spokane Falls Blvd, is part of the convention and international trade center, next to Riverfront Park. The local opera company doesn't sing here, but various traveling shows do use the opera house. The Spokane Symphony (☎ 624-1200) per-forms at *The Met* (☎ 455-6500), 901 W Sprague Ave, which also has operas, plays and other musical events in a fairly intimate setting.

**Live Music** *Big Dipper* (☎ 747-8036), 171 S Washington St, features rock and reggae bands from around the Northwest. There's also grunge-tinged rock at *Outback Jack's* (☎ 747-7539), 321 W Sprague Ave. J S Pumps (☎ 325-9084), 415 N Monroe St, is about the only gay and lesbian club you'll find in eastern Washington. Expect disco and drag. For blues, try the *Fort Spokane Brewery* (☎ 838-3809), 401 W Spokane Falls Blvd. *The Inlander*, the free weekly, has extensive music listings.

**Spectator Sports** The Spokane Indians (☎ 535-2922) play minor league baseball at the fairgrounds, 602 N Havana St (take Sprague Ave east and turn north on Havana St), and the Spokane Chiefs (☎ 328-0450) are a minor league ice hockey team based at the Veterans Memorial Arena, 909 N Howard St.

Playfair Race Course (☎ 534-0505) hosts the horses during the summer and fall, just east of downtown at N Altamont St and E Main Ave.

### Getting There & Away
**Air** Horizon, Southwest, Alaska, Delta, Northwest, United and United Express fly into Spokane International Airport. From Seattle or Portland, it's increasingly easy to find a roundtrip fare for under $100; South-west has fares as low as $58 roundtrip.

The airport is on the southeast outskirts of the city at the junction of I-90 and Hwy 20.

**Bus** All buses serving Spokane share the new Spokane Intermodal Transportation Depot at 221 W 1st Ave, at the train station. From here Greyhound (☎ 624-5251, (800) 231-2222) runs to Seattle and Portland and to points east along I-90. Northwestern Trailways (☎ 838-4029, (800) 366-3830) also runs to Seattle and Portland and makes trips to Pullman, Boise, ID and Reno, NV. Borderlines Stage (☎ 684-3950) has a weekday service to Colville and Kettle Falls. Empire Lines (or Empire Trailways) (☎ 624-4116) also has a ticket agency here for their Ellensburg-Osoyoos route through the Okanogan valley.

**Train** Amtrak's passenger station (☎ 624-5144, (800) 872-7245) is at 221 W 1st Ave. The *Empire Builder* comes through four times a week in each direction. From Spokane, westbound trains continue on to Seattle and Portland, OR, and eastbound trains head to Chicago, IL. The westbound train comes through Spokane at 2:40 am; the eastbound train leaves at 1:35 am. The ticket counter is open on weekdays from 11:30 am to 5:30 am the following morning; weekends it's open from 7:30 pm to 5:30 am the next day.

**Car** Avis (☎ 747-8081), Dollar (☎ 747-2191), National (☎ 624-8995) and Thrifty (☎ 924-9111) rent cars at the airport; Budget (☎ 838-1434) also has cars at the airport and downtown (☎ 624-2255) at 430 W 1st Ave. Other rental agencies in the downtown area include Payless (☎ 838-2089), 203 W 3rd Ave, and U-Save (☎ 455-8018), 918 W 3rd Ave. All Star (☎ 747-8015), 1306 N Division St, is not far, and Rent-A-Wreck (☎ 535-7696), 306 N Freya St, is east of downtown. Rates start at just under $20 a day for a compact car at the economy agents like Dollar and U-Save.

### Getting Around
**To/From the Airport** The Spokane International Airport is seven miles west of downtown off of I-90, but there's no transit bus service into the city. Several hotels

have frequent airport shuttles, and it's easy enough to hop one of these shuttles into downtown Spokane.

Airport Shuttle Service (☎ 535-6979) picks up/drops off door-to-door in the Spokane center. Fares are $8.75 for the first passenger and $3 for each additional person; pickups must be scheduled in advance.

**To/From the Train Station** It's easy to catch a transit bus from nearly any street corner near the Amtrak station, but if you're arriving by train, chances are it's the middle of the night. Since this isn't the best place to hang around outside after hours, you'll probably want to catch a cab.

**Bus** Spokane Transit (☎ 328-7433) runs buses along many routes through town. Pick up schedules at the visitors center.

**Taxi** Several cab companies cruise Spokane. Call Inland Taxi (☎ 326-8294), Spokane Cab (☎ 535-2535) or Yellow Cab (☎ 624-4321) for a ride.

## COLVILLE INDIAN RESERVATION
Eleven different bands make up the Colville Confederated Tribes: the Wenatchee, Entiat, Chelan, Methow, Okanogan, Nespelem, Sanpoil, Lakes, Moses, Palouse and Nez Perce. Up until the mid-1800s, the ancestors of the Colville Confederated Tribes were nomadic, and many tribes fished and traded around the Kettle Falls area. When White fur traders began working the Northwest, it didn't take long before a fur trading post, Fort Colvile, was established at Kettle Falls. Trading was active from 1826 to 1887, and as the years passed, Whites began referring to all the local Native Americans as 'Colvilles'. In 1872, the Colville Indian Reservation was formed.

Today, the reservation covers 2300 sq miles, about half the size of the original reservation, and there are about 7700 tribal members. The tribal headquarters is near Nespelem, north of Grand Coulee Dam.

Tribal industries revolve around timber, and there is a fish hatchery, which stocks all of north-central Washington's lakes and streams.

## Orientation & Information

The Colville Reservation is bordered by Hwy 97 on the west, the Columbia River and Lake Roosevelt to the south and east, and the Okanogan National Forest to the north. Highway 21 runs through the center of the reservation from Wilbur to Republic, but most sites and towns are located along Hwy 155, which goes from Omak to the Grand Coulee Dam.

Though the reservation isn't set up for tourists, respectful visitors are welcome. The tribal headquarters (☎ 634-4711) is just south of Nespelem on Hwy 155. Visitors should stick to the roads and not wander off on unauthorized hikes. Some of the reservation's lakes and streams are open to public fishing; get permits at the Tribal Fish & Wildlife Office (☎ 634-8845) at tribal headquarters. Except for the reservation's houseboat rentals at Keller Ferry (see Grand Coulee Dam above), there are no places for visitors to stay or eat on the reservation. However, it's easy to make a day trip from Omak or the dam area.

## Chief Joseph's Grave

Chief Joseph, the Nez Perce leader, and his band were sent to the Colville Reservation several years after their long march across eastern Oregon, Idaho and Montana was halted by the Army in 1878 (see aside Chief Joseph & the Nez Perce, in the Northeast Corner & John Day Country chapter of the Oregon section). The Nez Perce were assigned first to Oklahoma, but public outcry made the government reconsider these arrangements. In 1884, Chief Joseph and his band were sent to the Colville Reservation. They were prohibited from returning to the main Nez Perce Reservation in Lapwai, ID because they refused to profess Christianity. Joseph died in 1904 and is buried at Nespelem. Find his grave at the northeast edge of town.

## St Mary's Mission

Near the reservation's northwest corner five miles southeast of Omak on Hwy 155 St Mary's (☎ 525-3320) has been an active mission since 1896. Most of the missionary work now centers around the boarding school, but there's also a church, built in 1910, which is open to visitors.

## Chief Joseph Dam

Named after the Nez Perce leader, Chief Joseph Dam is on Hwy 17 near the reservation's southwest corner. The dam was constructed by the Army Corps of Engineers and it is operated by the corps and the Bonneville Power Administration (BPA primarily to generate hydroelectric power which it does very well, sending its electricity to much of the West. Like the Grand Coulee Dam, Chief Joseph Dam was built without fish ladders, which put an end to salmon migration further upstream. Rufus Woods Lake, the dam's 51-mile-long backwaters, stretches to Grand Coulee Dam and is popular with boaters, waterskiers and anglers.

The dam's visitors center (☎ 686-5501 ext 665) houses exhibits on hydropower wildlife migration and local archaeology There's also a nine-minute slide show or the dam. The center's hours are from 9 am to 6 pm daily, April through October.

## Fort Okanogan Interpretive Center

The Colville Confederated Tribes and Washington State operate a park and museum at the site of old Fort Okanogan The Fort Okanogan Interpretive Center (☎ 923-2473), at the junction of Hwys 97 and 17 east of Brewster, sits on a bluff overlooking the confluence of the Okanogan and Columbia rivers. The museum tells the story of the Native Americans who originally lived here and of three fur-trading companies who successively occupied this site in the early 19th century. The interpretive center is open Wednesday to Sunday from 9 am to 6 pm, June through August only. Admission is free. Picnic facilities are available on the grounds.

## Special Events

The Fourth of July Powwow in Nespelem draws participants from across the Northwest. There's also a powwow at the Omak Stampede in August. Contact the tribal offices for more information.

## GRAND COULEE & AROUND

The Grand Coulee Dam, with its three powerhouses, is the world's third-largest hydropower producer (after Guri Dam in Venezuela and Itaipu Dam between Paraguay and Brazil), and it also pumps water for irrigation into Banks Lake, a holding reservoir for the Columbia Basin Irrigation Project. Grand Coulee is the only one of the Columbia River's 11 dams operated by the US Bureau of Reclamation, an agency formed in 1902 to help sustain the economy and improve life in western states by providing reliable sources of water and electricity. The Grand Coulee Dam produces about a quarter of the hydropower generated along the Columbia.

Three small, rather drab towns cluster around the dam, and it's easy to get a little disoriented. Grand Coulee (population 1018) and Electric City (population 915) are just above the dam, and directly below is Coulee Dam (population 1106), the most interesting of the three. The Colville Indian Reservation has its southern boundary in Coulee Dam and extends northward past Omak. West of the dam there is little other than wheat fields for miles, but be sure to take in the Grand Coulee itself south of the dam, which along with Roosevelt Lake offers plenty of outdoor recreation.

## Orientation

Grand Coulee Dam is 90 miles from either Spokane or Wenatchee, and 225 miles from Seattle. From Hwy 2, turn north either at Wilbur (Hwy 174) or at Coulee City (Hwy 155).

The free Keller Ferry crosses Lake Roosevelt and provides access to the scenic north-south Hwy 21, which passes through the Colville Reservation to the town of Republic on Hwy 20. Catch the ferry by heading north from Wilbur (or south from Republic) on Hwy 21. The ferry operates daily from 6 am to 11 pm.

## Information

The Grand Coulee Visitor Arrival Center (☎ 633-9193, 633-9265), on Hwy 155 between Coulee Dam and Grand Coulee, has plenty of information on the area around the dam. It's open daily from 9 am to 5 pm, and evenings during the summer. The Grand Coulee Dam National Recreation Area headquarters (☎ 633-9441), 1008 Crest Drive in Coulee Dam, can provide details about the numerous Roosevelt Lake campgrounds. South of Banks Lake, the Dry Falls Interpretive Center (☎ 632-5214) has exhibits and an information desk on Hwy 17 just south of Hwy 2.

Coulee Community Hospital (☎ 633-1911) is just northwest of Grand Coulee on Hwy 174 toward Bridgeport. Wash your clothes in Grand Coulee at T&T Enterprises (☎ 633-2695), next to the bowling alley at 421 Midway.

## Grand Coulee Dam

The visitors center (☎ 633-9265) on Hwy 155 near Coulee Dam, has historical exhibits of the dam construction and lots of great WPA-era photos. If you're lucky, someone who worked on the dam will be visiting at the same time and will be regaling people with stories, a not uncommon occurrence. There's also a vaguely propagandistic film about hydropower (featuring lots of Woody Guthrie music) running almost constantly. The visitors center is open daily from 9 am to 5 pm (open evenings during the summer).

Guided tours of the dam include the pump-generator plant, the spillway and two power plants. A simpler, 30-minute self-guided tour involves taking a glass-walled elevator down a 45° incline outside the dam and looking into the hydropower units.

It would be hard to visit Coulee Dam without seeing the dam's nightly **laser show**, which runs from Memorial Day through September and illustrates the history of the Columbia River and its dams. It starts after dark, around 9:30 or 10 pm, switching to 8:30 pm during September. The best views are from the visitors center or the park below it.

## Colville Confederated Tribes Museum

The tribal museum and gift shop (☎ 633-0751), 516 Birch St in Coulee Dam, has dioramas of traditional fishing and village life flanked by collections of baskets, spears and other art and artifacts. A gift shop sells books, beadwork and other crafts. The museum is open daily from 10 am to 6 pm May through September. From October through December, it's open Monday to Saturday, and from January through April, Tuesday to Saturday.

## Lake Roosevelt

A 130-mile-long reservoir held back by the Grand Coulee Dam, Lake Roosevelt is a major recreational area with 35 campgrounds along the 660 miles of shoreline. Management of the lake and the campgrounds is divided between the NPS and the Colville Confederated Tribes and the Spokane Tribe. The Colville Confederated Tribes operate a luxury houseboat rental service at Keller Ferry, directly north of Wilbur on Hwy 21. Roosevelt Lake is perhaps most popular with anglers – in addition to prize white sturgeon, which average 100 to 300 pounds, there are walleye, rainbow trout and Kokanee salmon landlocked by the dam.

NPS rangers lead **canoe trips** with a focus on wildlife viewing on Crescent Bay Lake, near Roosevelt Lake just south of Grand Coulee. Budget cuts may end this activity; call the Coulee Dam National Recreation Area (☎ 633-9441) or stop by the dam's visitors center to check on its status.

**Spring Canyon**, off Hwy 174 about three miles east of Grand Coulee, has a boat launch, campground and nature trail exploring the prairie ecosystem.

## Fort Spokane

The army built this post at the confluence of the Spokane and Columbia rivers, east of

---

### Building the Grand Coulee Dam

Dam construction began in 1933, and in 1934 two large towns were hastily constructed below the dam site. On the left bank, Government Town housed engineers in rows of small tidy houses. Across the river, workmen lived in barracks and some small houses in Mason City, one of the first towns built without chimneys, since it used electric heat. Mason City, like any frontier town, was a wild place. Between the dam site and the Canadian border, five camps housed WPA workers, who spent their days clearing brush and buildings from the area set to be flooded by the backwaters of the Grand Coulee Dam. WPA workers were paid $40 to $95 a week, and they were charged 50¢ a day for room and board.

It took nine years to complete the dam. A truly massive structure that dwarfs the Great Pyramid of Egypt, it's big enough to see from the space shuttle, and generates more power than a million locomotives. The dam also changed the landscape in a way that far exceeds the size of the structure itself, putting huge lakes in the middle of the desert and replacing sagebrush with wheat fields.

Grand Coulee Dam was built without fish ladders, a decision that brought about the extinction of salmon and other anadromous fish upriver from the dam. But when you're here, it's easy to see why this was done. The steep 550-foot dam wall is just too big and too steep, and no conventional fish ladder is possible.

The Colville Confederated Tribes lost their best riverfront land when the dam was built, and for years received no compensation from the government. In 1994, a settlement was reached, awarding the tribes an initial payment of $59 million and future yearly payments of at least $15.25 million. This is only a small fraction of the income produced by the dam, which pulls in over $400 million a year for its power generation and cheaply irrigates over half a million acres, all on the non-Indian side of the Columbia River. ■

## The Making of the Coulees

One of the most spectacular geological events in northeastern Washington occurred about 10,000 years ago, when glaciers filled the Pend Oreille River valley and much of northern Idaho, creating a huge ice dam that held back a glacial lake so large it covered most of western Montana. It also blocked the Columbia River, forcing it into a new channel. When the dam finally gave way (bobbing up like an ice cube in a glass of water), torrents of water rushed over eastern Washington, scouring topsoil and enlarging river channels. When the glaciers receded, the Columbia returned to its original channel, leaving a network of dry riverbeds, called coulees. Grand Coulee is the largest of these. Moses Coulee, which crosses Hwy 2 about 12 miles west of Coulee City, is another. The Grand Coulee starts near the dam and extends south past Dry Falls, through Sun Lakes State Park, till it peters out somewhere north of Soap Lake. ■

where the dam now sits, in 1880 to quell any disturbances that might arise between White settlers and local Native Americans recently confined to reservations. Both sides were supposed to stay clear of each other, and during the fort's tenure, which ended in 1898, there were no hostilities. At its peak in the 1890s, Fort Spokane contained close to 50 buildings.

Fort Spokane (☎ 725-2715) is on the shores of Lake Roosevelt (take Hwy 25 north of Hwy 2). Several of the original buildings remain, though many visitors come here just to camp, swim at the beach or boat on the lake. The USFS office here is open from 7:30 am to 4 pm Monday to Friday.

### Banks Lake

The 31-mile-long Banks Lake is a reservoir filled with water shuttled over from the Columbia River via Grand Coulee Dam. At the southern end of Banks Lake, near Coulee City, Dry Falls Dam controls the flow of water out of Banks Lake into the Main Canal, which sends irrigation water out to Columbia Basin farms and orchards.

Steamboat Rock, a 700-foot-high basalt butte rises out of Banks Lake and dominates **Steamboat Rock State Park**. The park (☎ 633-1304) contains a swimming beach, campground and nine-hole golf course.

A sometimes steep **hiking** trail, which bursts with wildflowers in the spring, leads from the campground to the top of the butte, providing a wonderful view down the Grand Coulee (watch out for rattlesnakes here). The Northrup Canyon Trail begins in a sheltered canyon across the road from the state park and passes through Grand County's only forest. Northrup Lake, at the top of the canyon, is stocked with trout. Some homestead cabins remain near the trail. Check in at the Steamboat Rock ranger station before hiking this trail.

### Dry Falls

Dry Falls, which cuts across the Grand Coulee, is 3.5 miles wide and over 400 feet high. These scalloped cliffs are the remnants of what was once the world's largest waterfall. An interpretive center about two miles south of Hwy 2 on Hwy 17 has exhibits depicting the region's geological history.

The coulee at the bottom of the falls is dotted with lakes, which are stocked with trout and popular with flycasters. Reach these lakes via **Sun Lakes State Park** (☎ 632-5583), four miles south of Hwy 2 on Hwy 17, a large park with camping, cabins, a golf course, horseback riding and boat and bicycle rentals.

Ten miles south of Dry Falls, the **Lake Lenore Caves** were formed as the force of water from melting glaciers plucked chunks of basalt from the coulee walls. Prehistoric hunters used these caves as shelters, and Native Americans left pictographs, many of which are still visible near the caves' entrances. A trail from the north end of Lake Lenore leads to the caves.

## Fishing

Good fishing abounds in the lakes near Grand Coulee Dam. Lake Roosevelt and Banks Lake are most popular, though Lake Rufus Woods, below Grand Coulee Dam, also attract anglers (launch a boat from the Elmer City launch, a few miles north of Coulee Dam). Buffalo and McGinnis Lakes, on the Colville Reservation, require a tribal fishing permit, available at businesses on the reservation and in Grand Coulee. Rent boats on Roosevelt Lake at Keller Ferry. The lakes at the bottom of Dry Falls, at Sun Lakes State Park, are tremendously popular for fly-fishing.

## Other Activities

The various parks and recreation areas in this area offer plenty to do, though fishing is the biggest draw. You can go **hiking** around Steamboat Rock, and there is an easy, 6.5-mile **biking** trail, the Down River Trail, that follows the Columbia River north from Grand Coulee Dam. Catch the trail at Mason City Park, across from the Coulee Dam Shopping Center. You can **swim** from beaches on Banks Lake at both Steamboat Rock and Coulee Playland Resort (see Places to Stay below). The town of Coulee Dam also has a public pool (☎ 633-3050), 300 Lincoln Ave, which is open during the summer months. To do a little **horseback riding**, go to Spirit Ridge RV Park (see Places to Stay below), near Elmer City on Hwy 155, or to Sun Lakes State Park, just south of Dry Falls on Hwy 17. There are nine-hole **golf** courses at Banks Lake Golf & Country Club (☎ 633-0163), on Airport Rd just west of Electric City, and at Sun Lakes State Park (☎ 632-5738).

## Places to Stay

**Camping** There are 35 park campgrounds on Lake Roosevelt; camping fees are $10 in season and free in the off-season. They all have running water and flush toilets, but no showers and no hook-ups. *Spring Canyon Campground* is the closest to Grand Coulee Dam. It's on Hwy 174 about three miles east of Grand Coulee. *Keller Ferry Campground* is near the ferry across Lake Roosevelt and the Colville Confederated Tribes' marina. *Fort Spokane* has a large campground with a swimming beach and boat launch; it's off of Hwy 25 north of Hwy 2. To get further details, call the park headquarters (☎ 633-9441).

*Spirit Ridge RV Encampment* (☎ 633-1933, (800) 548-1408) is north of Coulee Dam on Lower River Rd (off Hwy 155) between Elmer City and Nespelem. Besides rather deluxe RV facilities ($18), there are tepee rentals ($15 to $18) and tent sites ($10). *Crescent Oaks RV Park* (☎ 647-5608), on Hwy 2 in Wilbur, a half mile west of the Hwy 21 junction, has grassy RV sites near a wheat field for $11.

*Steamboat Rock State Park* (☎ 633-1304), on Banks Lake, has a handful of $8 tent sites and a bunch of $12 RV sites. On summer weekends, it's wise to reserve a spot. Also on Banks Lake, *Coulee Playland Resort* (☎ 633-2671) has RV and tent sites starting at $10. Both of these places are on Hwy 155, southwest of Electric City.

*Sun Lakes State Park* (☎ 632-5583), on Hwy 17 south of Hwy 2, has campsites ($10 to $16) and cabins (from $56) set in the Grand Coulee just below Dry Falls. The setting is striking and the campground full of amenities like boat rentals, a snack bar and golf course.

**B&Bs** In Coulee Dam, the *Four Winds B&B* (☎ 633-3146), 301 Lincoln Ave, was an old workers dorm. Rates start at $45/55 for singles/doubles; some rooms can accommodate up to four people.

**Hotels** Of the three towns near the dam, Coulee Dam is the best bet for a motel room. *Ponderosa Motel* (☎ 633-2100), 10 Lincoln Ave, has a pool and a view of the dam, which is essentially right across the street. *Coulee House Motel* (☎ 633-1101), at the corner of Birch and Roosevelt, also overlooks the dam (with excellent seats for the nightly light show) and has a sauna, spa and huge pool. Both motels have singles/doubles starting at $48/64.

In Coulee City, the *Lakeview II Motel*

(☎ 632-5792), 9811 Fordair Rd NE, is set in a thicket of trees across a sagebrush field from the lake. The hotel sports a spa and sauna, and decent rooms for $30/35. The *Blue Top Motel* (☎ 632-5596), 109 N 6th, is basic and cheap, starting at $29/35; a few rooms have kitchenettes, and pets are welcome. *Ala Cozy Motel* (☎ 632-5703, (800) 321-7649), 9988 Hwy 2 E, has an outdoor pool and spa, miniature golf and views of Banks Lake; rooms are $35/40.

**Lodges** *Sun Lakes Park Resort* (☎ 632-5291), 34228 Park Lake Rd in the state park, has rustic cabins and a handful of mobile homes. Lodgers enjoy a heated pool, nine-hole and miniature golf courses and activities on Sun Lake. Cabins have kitchenettes, but you'll need to supply your own cookware and dishes. Towels and bedding are supplied. Rates for cabins start at $56, mobile homes at $89.

**Houseboat Rentals** Roosevelt Recreational Enterprises (☎ 633-0136, (800) 648-5253), run by the Colville Confederated Tribes, rents houseboats at Keller Ferry. Houseboats vary in features and capacity, but can usually accommodate up to 10 or 13 people. Rates also vary considerably. Weekend stays start at $995 in peak season, and drop to $725 in the off-season, with considerable breaks given for weekday and longer stays.

**Places to Eat**

Pickings are slim for food around the Grand Coulee Dam. In Grand Coulee, *Siam Palace* (☎ 633-2921), 213 Main St, serves Chinese, Thai and American food. *Melody Restaurant* (☎ 633-1151), 110 Roosevelt Way in Coulee Dam, is part of the *Coulee House Motel* and serves American fare. It's open from early morning till late evening, with a deck looking out on the dam.

In Coulee City, the *Crossing Cafe* (☎ 632-5667), at 5th and Main Sts, serves Korean and American food, while right next door, *Steamboat Rock Restaurant* (☎ 632-5452) serves steak and seafood. If you're staying at nearby Sun Lakes State

Park and get tired of camp cooking, try the *Dry Falls Cafe* (☎ 632-5634) at the intersection of Hwys 2 and 17. They have a $2 breakfast special on weekdays.

# Okanogan River Valley

The Okanogan River courses south from the British Columbia Rockies and joins the Columbia near the tiny orchard town of Brewster, a few miles downstream from Chief Joseph Dam. The Okanogan is a slow-moving river, and the surrounding valley is dry and fairly lightly settled, functioning mostly as a transportation corridor. The Colville Indian Reservation lies to the east of the Okanogan River, with its northern border just north of Omak and its southern and eastern borders delineated by the Columbia River. On either side of the valley, hills rise into various scattered parts of the Okanogan National Forest, where grasslands and cultivated orchards give way to ponderosa pine and Douglas-fir.

Okanogan is Salish for 'rendezvous'. Native Americans lived here for thousands of years before a succession of White explorers, prospectors, miners, trappers, ranchers, homesteaders, loggers, farmers, missionaries and fruit-growers displaced them. North West Company fur traders, led by David Thompson, traveled through in 1811, and were followed the same summer by Americans from Astor's Pacific Fur Company. The American traders stuck around and built a trading post on the Okanogan River just up from the Columbia. This 'Fort Okanogan' was soon inherited by the Hudson's Bay Company, who used it to channel furs coming down the Okanogan River from Canada onto boats bound for HBC's Vancouver, WA headquarters.

Prospectors traipsed the 'Cariboo Trail' up the Okanogan valley to British Columbia's Cariboo gold fields in the 1850s. They were followed by cowboys driving cattle up from the Yakima valley to the mining camps. Today, Hwy 97 sticks pretty close to the old trail as it runs up the Okanogan from Brewster to the Canadian border.

## OKANOGAN & OMAK

Okanogan (population 2390) and Omak (population 4150) have very nearly merged to become one town, but they have very distinct characters. Okanogan is the county seat, and its relatively dignified town center befits this role. Omak is the bustling retail center of the valley, and it's best known for its annual rodeo, the Omak Stampede. To the west, lakes and apple orchards dot the foothills of the Cascade Mountains, while to the east the hillsides are generally dry and grassy.

The **Okanogan County Museum** (☎ 422-4272), 1410 N 2nd St, has surprisingly interesting exhibits, including frontier photographer Frank Matsura's glass-plate photo collection and a quilt display. It's open daily from 10 am to 4 pm late May to early fall. Admission is $1.

### Orientation & Information

Two roads, Hwys 97 and 215 (the commercial strip), connect Omak and Okanogan.

The Omak Visitor Information office (☎ 826-4218, (800) 225-6625) is next to the stampede grounds on Hwy 155 just east of downtown. Information is also dispensed at the rest stop on 2nd St (Hwy 20) in Legion Park in Okanogan. The Okanogan National Forest (☎ 826-3275) has its headquarters at 1240 S 2nd St.

The Mid-Valley Hospital (☎ 826-1760), 810 Valley Way, is at the south end of Omak, which is also where you'll find the Log Cabin Public Coin-Op Laundromat (☎ 826-4462), at the Log Cabin Trailer Court, 509 Okoma Drive (also known as Hwy 215). It's open long hours every day. Call Omak Cab (☎ 826-4123) should you need a lift.

### Omak Stampede

The Omak Stampede (☎ 826-1983) is one of the West's biggest rodeos, with one of the most dramatic and controversial events, the Suicide Race, where horses and their riders pitch down a steep hillside and across the Okanogan River. Horses sometimes die attempting this feat, which has led to protests from animal rights activists.

At the adjacent Indian Encampment, Native Americans dance, drum and play stick games. There's also country music, a parade and a barbecue. The Stampede is always held the second weekend of August.

### Activities

There is some pleasant **hiking** in the national forest to the west, between Okanogan and Twisp. The USFS headquarters in Okanogan dispenses trail information. **Biking** is also popular, as Hwy 20 is a long-distance bike-touring route, and there are plenty of back roads up into the Okanogan hills worth cycling. Rent a bike at The Bike Shop (☎ 422-0710), 137 2nd Ave in Okanogan.

There is also **skiing** at nearby Loup Loup Summit. The Loup Loup Ski Bowl (☎ 826-2720), just off Hwy 20, 18 miles west of Okanogan, is usually open December to March. It's a small ski area with a 1240-foot vertical drop, two lifts and a rope tow, as well as 18.6 miles of cross-country ski trails.

### Places to Stay & Eat

The American Legion Park (☎ 422-3600), on the river in downtown Okanogan, has mostly RV sites and costs $7 a night.

In Okanogan, the Cariboo Inn (☎ 422-6109), 233 Queen St, is an older downtown hotel with rooms from $22 and a restaurant. U&I Motel (☎ 422-2920), 838 2nd St, has a nice riverside setting and is a bargain at $26/33 for single/double rooms. At the south end of town, Ponderosa Motor Lodge (☎ 422-0400), 1034 S 2nd St, is a standard small town motel with rooms from $27/32. Cedars Inn Motel (☎ 422-6431), on Hwy 97 near Okanogan, has an outdoor pool and a restaurant and costs $44/51. All of the motels except the Cariboo Inn have a few rooms with kitchens.

In Omak, the *Stampede Motel* (☎ 826-1161), on W 4th St, has rates from $30/36 for single/double rooms. At *Leisure Village Motel* (☎ 826-4442), 630 Okoma Drive, rooms run $33/44, plus about $5 extra for a kitchen. *Motel Nicholas* (☎ 826-4611), 527 E Grape Ave, has refrigerators in the rooms and charges $35/40. All the motels listed take pets.

Without a doubt, the best restaurant in the area is Omak's *Breadline Cafe* (☎ 826-5836), 102 S Ash. It's possible to get vegetarian dinners, mostly pasta, for under $10 – and, of course, there are plenty of burgers and steaks. The cafe occasionally hosts some alternative, folksy entertainment; it's open for breakfast, lunch and dinner, and is closed Sunday.

### Things to Buy
Detro's Triangle L Western Store (☎ 826-2200) on Main St in Riverside, seven miles north of Omak, is a large and authentic source for cowboy hats, boots, jeans and saddles.

### Getting There & Away
The Empire Lines (Empire Trailways) (☎ 422-3373, (800) 351-1060) bus passes through once a day along Hwy 97. In Okanogan, buses depart from the ticket agency at 1345 2nd St. In Omak, the bus stops at the Gull service station (☎ 826-0302), 607 Wacoma Drive.

## CONCONULLY
The lakeside hamlet of Conconully (population 172), in the eastern foothills of the North Cascades 18 miles northwest of Omak, is a good place to go for a respite from scorching summer days in the Okanogan valley. The name 'Conconully' comes from the Salish word *konekol't*, meaning money hole; it was named after a creek full of beaver whose pelts were used as money at the local trading post. Most visitors come for Conconully State Park. From Omak, take Kernel Rd (near the north end of town) to the west and follow signs to Conconully.

### Conconully State Park
Conconully Lake is a reservoir formed by an irrigation project in the early 1900s, and since then it has been the focus of activity in the area. The state park (☎ 826-7408) has a nice campground, a boat ramp, a lake full of trout, snowmobile trails and a replica of a sod-roofed cabin similar to the one used as Okanogan County's first courthouse.

A couple of **hiking** trails, the Tiffany Lake Trail and the Clark Ridge Trail, start just past the Salmon Meadows campground, 8.5 miles northwest of Conconully on USFS Rd 38. The trails head into the Tiffany Roadless Area and can be fashioned into a loop to make a nice overnight backpack.

### Places to Stay & Eat
*Conconully State Park* (☎ 826-7408) has showers and charges $10 for a campsite. It can be a surprisingly busy place on a summer weekend. There's a string of smaller campgrounds several miles northwest of Conconully Lake on USFS Rd 38. *Cottonwood*, *Oriole* and *Salmon Meadows* campgrounds all have running water and charge $5. If you're really looking for some quiet, keep going northwest for about 30 miles to *Tiffany Springs* campground. It's on USFS Rd 39 (via Rd 38). Bring your own water.

The resorts around Conconully aren't fancy, but they're generally more pleasant than staying in Omak. There aren't proper street addresses here, but nothing's too hard to find.

The lakeside *Conconully Lake Resort* (☎ 826-0813) is open from mid-April to mid-November and has cabins from $25 ($45 for a private bath). *Liars Cove Resort* (☎ 826-1288) has RV sites and some cabins by the lake. *Jack's RV Park & Motel* (☎ 826-0132) has a laundromat, heated pool and hot tub; motel rooms go for $48. *Conconully Motel* (☎ 826-1610) is small, with rooms starting at $35.

Up the road from Conconully, the *Salmon Meadows Lodge* (☎ 826-2604) is a historic lodge owned by the USFS. They rent it out to groups (of whatever size, there are 26 beds) for $75 a night. It's pretty rustic, but it's very popular. During the winter it's accessible only by snowmobile or skis.

For a meal, try *Mr Magoo's* (☎ 826-0132), where you can find waffles, fish & chips and espresso. *Salmon Creek Inn* (☎ 826-1037) serves Mexican and standard American fare in an older false-fronted building.

## TONASKET

Tonasket (population 985) doesn't hold much interest in and of itself, but there's great, lake-speckled country to both the east and west in and around the Okanogan National Forest.

For general information, the chamber of commerce (☎ 486-2931) is at 4th St and Whitcomb Ave. The Tonasket Ranger Station (☎ 486-2186), 1 W Winesap, can guide you to camping and recreation in the area. If you're taking the bus, pick up the Empire Lines (☎ (800) 351-1060) at Pardner's Mini Mart, 606 S Whitcom Ave.

### Places to Stay & Eat

*Tonasket City Park* is a roadside RV park with hook-ups for $5. It's north of town on Hwy 97.

*Orchard Country Inn B&B* (☎ 486-1923) has both B&B rooms with private baths (singles/doubles are $36/50) and a few hostel bunks. It's a spacious 1920s country house in Tonasket at the corner of 1st and Antoine Sts. *Red Apple Inn* (☎ 486-2119) is a basic motel on Hwy 97 at 1st St that has kitchenettes. Rooms start at $36/43.

*Hidden Hills Resort* (☎ 486-1890, (800) 468-1890), 144 Fish Lake Rd, is a little different and a bit more expensive, with hotel rooms starting at about $60/70. It's an old-fashioned inn, attempting to recreate an 1890s atmosphere with modern amenities. The inn's restaurant serves satisfying home-cooked meals. Hidden Hills can be reached from Conconully by heading north along the Sinlahekin Rd, or by turning west off Hwy 97 onto Pine Creek Rd (which becomes Fish Lake Rd). Pine Creek Rd is

about five miles north of the community of Riverside and about 10 miles south of Tonasket.

Tonasket's *Okanogan River Natural Foods Co-Op* (☎ 486-4188), one block west of Hwy 97 at 21 W 4th St, is a good place for campers to stock up. It's also a de facto community center – stop in to find out about the barter fair that's held around here every summer.

There are several passable places to eat in Tonasket. *Don's Drive Inn* (☎ 486-2122) pleases crowds on pleasant summer nights at 101 N Hwy 97. *Shannon's Old Fashioned Ice Cream Parlor* also serves sandwiches and espresso, and the *Roundup Cafe* (☎ 486-2695), 319 S Whitcomb Ave, is a decent downtown place for breakfast.

## MANY LAKES RECREATION AREA

The Many Lakes Recreational Area is dotted with lakes that are excellent for **fishing**. All of the lakes are on the road to Loomis (take 4th St out of Tonasket), which is about 17 miles west; a number of resorts on this road cater to anglers. **Whitestone Lake**, 5.5 miles north of Tonasket, has good warm-water fishing for largemouth bass and crappie. **Spectacle Lake**, just past Whitestone Lake has rainbow trout. Past Loomis is **Palmer Lake**, where bass are a big attraction, along with rainbow and brown trout and Kokanee salmon. **Chopaka Lake**, 6.3 miles north of Loomis, is open to fly fishing only.

### Places to Stay & Eat

Near Loomis in the Many Lakes Recreational Area, most of the resorts listed below have places to park an RV or pitch a tent for $10 to $15. There are primitive public campgrounds at Palmer and Chopaka lakes, but neither have running water.

The Many Lakes area has several small resorts. Don't expect anything fancy: rustic kitchenette cabins are the standard. *Rainbow Resort* (☎ 223-3700), 761 Loomis Hwy, has cabins starting at $35 and RV hook-ups; it's closed from November through March. *Spectacle Falls Resort*

(☎ 223-4141), 879 Loomis Hwy, is just up the road. *Chopaka Lodge* (☎ 223-3131), 1913 Loomis Hwy on Palmer Lake, has cute cabins for less than $40. *Sun Cove Resort* (☎ 476-2223), on Wannacut Lake, has lots of activities, including horseback riding and boating, and a heated pool. Cabins run about $50, with special rates for larger groups or extended stays. Reach Wannacut Lake by turning north off Loomis Rd between Whitestone and Spectacle Lakes onto the Wannacut Lake Rd.

In Loomis, the *Palmer Mountain Restaurant* (☎ 223-3311) is a good place to eat.

## OKANOGAN NATIONAL FOREST

East of Tonasket, the national forest contains **Mt Bonaparte** and **Bonaparte Lake**, where there are several campgrounds, a resort, and some excellent **hiking**. Call the Tonasket Ranger Station (☎ 486-2186) for more information. One easy mile-long hike starts at the Lost Lake campground and ends up at the **Big Tree Botanical Area**, home to two 600-year-old Western larch trees. Another short trail from the Lost Lake campground goes to **Strawberry Mountain**, featuring views of the surrounding area and Canada.

For a more challenging, eight-mile roundtrip, drive six miles west from Lost Lake on USFS Rd 33, then turn south onto USFS Rd 300, which ends in a little over a mile at the trailhead for **Mt Bonaparte**, a far-western outrider of the Rocky Mountains. The trail heads up forested slopes to the 7258-foot summit, where there's a fire lookout with great views. Another trail up Mt Bonaparte starts at the Bonaparte Lake campground.

Bonaparte Lake has good trout fishing during the summer, and nearby is the three-mile **Virginia Lilly Interpretive Trail**, flush with old-growth trees and birds. To reach it, take USFS Rd 20, which forks off Bonaparte Lake Rd less than a mile past the lake, and turn onto USFS Rd 3240. You can go **cross-country skiing** in the Okanogan Highlands near Havillah, which has nine miles of loop trails.

### Places to Stay & Eat

The Bonaparte Lake area contains three excellent lakeside campgrounds. All sites are $6, with running water and flush toilets, except that Beth Lake has no fee and running water only in the summer. *Bonaparte Campground* has sites on Bonaparte Lake; to get there take Hwy 20 about 20 miles east of Tonasket, then go another six miles north on USFS Rd 32. There are several walk-in sites set aside for bicyclists here. Continue about four miles north on USFS Rd 32 past Bonaparte Lake, then turn northwest onto USFS Rd 33 for about another four miles to reach *Lost Lake Campground*. *Beth Lake Campground* is also off USFS Rd 32, northeast of Bonaparte Lake. Turn northwest at Beaver Lake, and head less than two miles up County Rd 9480 to reach tiny Beth Lake and the campground.

In the Okanogan National Forest, *Bonaparte Lake Resort* (☎ 486-2828), 695 Bonaparte Lake Rd, has campsites, cabins from about $25 and a pretty good restaurant. Reach it by traveling east on Hwy 20 to Bonaparte Lake Rd (USFS Rd 32), then north for six miles. Cabins are heated by wood, and during the winter they have no running water. The restaurant at the resort offers decent dining, with dinner from $7 to $12.

## OROVILLE

Oroville (population 1515) is four miles south of the USA/Canada border crossing. The town is on the south shore of **Osoyoos Lake**, the town's main attraction, which has picnicking, swimming and camping. The apple orchards here are a legacy of Hiram 'Okanogan' Smith, an early settler who carried apple trees down from Fort Hope, BC in his backpack and planted them here in 1861. He also came to mine for gold. If you have a little extra time, stop by the tiny town of Molson, which is now an open-air museum.

A Washington State information center (☎ 476-2739) on Hwy 97 north of Oroville is open daily in summer and on weekends during winter. The border crossing is open 24 hours; call the US customs and immigration office at 476-2581; for the Canadian side, call (604) 495-6531.

## Molson Open-Air Museum

Molson is an exceedingly small town fifteen miles east of Oroville with a long and unusual history. It's now an open-air historical museum, consisting of a bunch of old buildings, two housing small museums, and farm implements on a roadside field. Molson began as a turn-of-the-century gold-mining boomtown; no gold was ever found, but homesteaders still came to farm the land. Then one day a stranger came to town and bought the land out from under everyone, instigating a long-running feud that eventually doomed this tiny community. A few people still have farms and ranches in Molson, but today it is little more than a ghost town.

## Places to Stay & Eat

*Lake Osoyoos State Park* (☎ 476-3321) is open year round, with $10 campsites. When the weather's nice, it's the best place in town.

*Camaray Motel* (☎ 476-3684), 1320 Main St, has a pool, allows pets, and singles/doubles are $30/37. For a few dollars more, the *Red Apple Inn* (☎ 476-3694) is just north of town on Hwy 97; some rooms have kitchenettes.

*Cricko's Mexican Restaurant* (☎ 476-2037), 1321 Main St, has decent, home-cooked Mexican dinners for less than $10. Even cheaper is the *Jesus Touch Me Taco-Burrito Shop* just west of Hwy 97 on road to Nighthawk. *Hometown Pizza & Bakery* (☎ 476-2410), 806 Central, makes pizzas from scratch.

## Getting There & Away

The Empire Lines Ellensburg-Osoyoos bus stops at the Eisen's Quickie Mart (☎ 476-2354), 1501 Main St, which serves as the local ticket agency.

# Colville National Forest

The Colville National Forest spans two mountain ranges, the Kettle River and the Selkirk, in the northeastern corner of Washington, with the Columbia River slowing and widening into Lake Roosevelt between them. Most of the activity in the Kettle River Range, also known as the Okanogan Highlands, centers around Republic and Curlew Lake State Park, with the town of Curlew making an interesting stop to the north on Hwy 21.

The Pend Oreille (pronounced *Pond-er-ray*) River flows north through the Selkirk Mountains into Canada, where it joins the Columbia. Most of the recreation centers around fishing, especially lake fishing. The Salmo-Priest Wilderness Area is some of the state's wildest country; it's crossed by hiking trails but has little in the way of facilities. Colville and Metalline Falls make good bases for exploring the Selkirks and the Pend Oreille River area, while Kettle Falls, on Lake Roosevelt, is replete with Columbia River history.

## REPUBLIC

Downtown Republic (population 1005) is largely false-fronted, and even though some of these building facades are fairly recently built, there are enough old ones to keep the effect from being phony. A gold rush started things up in the 1896, and mining has continued, in fits and starts, to this day, as two mining companies are still the biggest industries in the county. Several timber companies are also nearby, fueled by trees from the Colville National Forest. Republic is an attractive western town and a comfortable place to poke around the old-fashioned drug store and load up on bulk groceries and local news at the food co-op.

## Orientation

The Sanpoil River runs north-south through Republic (followed by Hwy 21) from Curlew Lake to the Keller Ferry crossing at Lake Roosevelt. The Keller Ferry runs daily from 6 am to 11 pm. The state's highest pass, Sherman Pass (5575 feet) is on Hwy 20 between Republic and Kettle Falls. Be sure to carry chains if you're driving this stretch between October and April – snowfall can be heavy here.

### Information
Tourist information is available from the Stonerose Interpretive Center/Republic Historical Center (☎ 775-3387) at 61 N Kean St. The ranger station (☎ 775-3305) at 180 N Jefferson, has information on hiking trails in the nearby Colville National Forest.

The Ferry County Memorial Hospital (☎ 775-3333) is at 470 N Klondike Rd in Republic, and there is a laundromat between 8th and 9th Sts near the Frontier Motel. There is no public transportation to Republic.

### Stonerose Fossil Center
The area around Republic contains a good selection of plant fossils from the Eocene Epoch some 50 million years ago, and the Stonerose Fossil Center (☎ 775-2295) offers a good introduction to local fossil finds. It's on the west side of town at 6th and N Kean Sts, across from the town park. The oldest known ancestor of the rose family was found near here, which why it is now called the Stonerose site. The center runs tours, which include the opportunity to dig for fossils, twice a day at 10 am and 2 pm from Tuesday to Sunday, May to October.

### Curlew Lake State Park
The state park (☎ 775-3592) is off of Hwy 21 about nine miles north of Republic. Curlew Lake makes for good canoeing and boating; several of the lakeside cabin resorts offer rentals. There's a nice campground, some pleasant swimming and good fishing for trout and bass. During the winter, you can do a little ice fishing, and cross-country skiers can enjoy the open hills around the lake and to the east along the USFS roads.

### Hiking
By far the most interesting hike in the area is the Kettle Crest Trail, which crosses Hwy 20 at Sherman Pass (Washington's highest paved road pass) some 20 miles east of Republic. North of the highway, the trail passes through thick forest, with plenty of spur trails leading through wildflowers in the spring. South of the highway, the trail passes through part of the huge 1988 White Mountain burn, which charred 20,000 acres. For several miles, hikers can witness a dramatic stage of forest succession, while interpretive road signs explain the rejuvenative effects of fire. Well into spring, snow lingers on the high ridges of the Kettle Crest Trail, and it is popular with cross-country skiers. There is also a primitive campground here.

### Places to Stay
**Camping** Scenic *Curlew Lake State Park* (☎ 775-3592) has tent sites (including a handful of very nice walk-in sites) for $10; RV hook-ups are $14. Most of the Curlew Lake lodges listed below also have RV and tent sites. Campsites are available at the *Triangle J Ranch* for $6 per person per night (see below).

Near Sherman Pass, about 20 miles east of Republic, *Kettle Range Campground* (☎ 738-6111) makes a good base for day hikes along the Kettle Ridge Trail. It's a small, primitive, free USFS campground.

**Hostels** During the summer, the *Triangle J Ranch* (☎ 775-3933), 423 Old Kettle Falls Rd, fills up with bicycle tourists; in the fall, hunters bed down here. Hostel facilities include a four-bed dormitory and a bunkhouse. Use of a big hot tub and an outdoor swimming pool are included in the $10-a-night fee, and an extra $2.50 will buy a breakfast. For a private room and breakfast, the *Triangle J* offers B&B rooms for $40.

**Hotels** *Frontier Inn Motel* (☎ 775-3361), 979 S Clark Ave, is on Republic's main drag, and at the other end of town is the *Klondike Motel* (☎ 775-3555), 950 N Clark St. Both have single/double rooms from $35/45.

**Lodges** Curlew Lake has several small cabin resorts, all of which rent boats and permit leashed dogs. On the east side of the lake, *Pine Point Resort* (☎ 775-3643) is a particularly charming spot, with kitchenette cabins starting at $50 a night. Spaces for RVs ($12 to $15) or tents ($10 to $15) are also available. It's 10 miles north of Republic on Hwy 21; open from mid-April to October 31.

*Fisherman's Cove Resort* (☎ 775-3641), just north of Pine Point on Hwy 21, is currently open year round (but call to check) and has cabins with a shared bathhouse starting at $25. Cabins with private baths and kitchens run about $60.

On the west side of Curlew Lake, eight miles north of Republic on W Curlew Lake Rd, *Collins Black Beach Resort* (☎ 775-3989) has cabins and a few motel rooms starting at $30; open April through October. *Tiffany's Resort* (☎ 775-3152) is about four miles further north. Cabins here start at $40, and there are some tent and RV sites.

**Places to Eat**
In Republic along the main drag, *Ferry County Co-Op* (☎ 775-3754), 34 N Clark Ave, has organically grown staples and healthy baked goods, and the *Wild Rose Cafe* (☎ 775-2096), 644 S Clark, is a cheery spot for breakfast, lunch or dinner. (Don't plan on eating late – dinner shuts down well before 9 pm.)

Curlew, however, serves the best meal, and it's worth driving the 20 miles from Republic to the Riverside Bar & Grill (see Curlew, below).

**Things to Buy**
Right at the western edge of the Colville Forest, between Republic and Kettle Falls on Hwy 20, the Tin-Na-Tit Din-Ne-Ki Indian Art Gallery (☎ 775-3077) almost literally screams for you to stop. It's a little

over the top, but there is some spectacular jewelry and art for sale here. From January to April 15, the shop is open only by appointment.

**CURLEW**
The little town of Curlew, 21 miles north of Republic, is worth a visit, even if it's just for dinner. Besides a good restaurant, local attractions include the Ansorage Hotel, the Antique Car & Truck Museum and the graves of Ranald McDonald and Chief Tonasket.

There are two USA/Canada border crossings in this area: Danville, north of Curlew on Hwy 21, is open from 8 am to midnight. Northwest of Curlew, the Midway/Port of Ferry crossing, is open from 9 am to 5 pm.

---

**Ranald McDonald's Grave**

Don't smirk – *this* Ranald McDonald may be little known, but he had a wild life. McDonald was born in 1824 to a Scottish Hudson's Bay Company factor and a Chinook Indian, the daughter of Chief Comcomly (who did business with Lewis and Clark and the Astorians). As a youngster McDonald met several Japanese sailors whose ship had drifted off course and landed near Cape Flattery. He became fascinated with Japan, which at that time was closed to Westerners, and learned the language from the shipwrecked sailors, then living at Fort Vancouver. McDonald became a sailor himself, and on one voyage deliberately shipwrecked in Japan. He managed to travel throughout the country as an English teacher and de facto diplomat.

After traveling all over the world, McDonald retired to northeastern Washington, where he died in 1894. He's buried about 10 miles from Curlew. To reach the cemetery from Curlew, turn west off Hwy 21 onto W Kettle River Rd, follow it 9.5 miles, turn east and cross the river. Then turn north just after the bridge and head just over one mile up to the cemetery on the bluff over the Kettle River. The cabin where McDonald died (he was visiting his niece here) is on private land across the river. ■

Leavenworth's Bavarian Village (JJ)

tem pole, La Push (BM)

La Conner harbor (BM)

Whatcom Museum of Art & History, Bellingham (BM)

Walla Walla (BM)

## Ansorage Hotel

The Ansorage Hotel (☎ 779-4955) is, unfortunately, no longer a working hotel but a museum filled with period furnishings. Built in 1903, this impressive building housed travelers and prospective homesteaders fresh off the Great Northern Railroad. It's open summer weekends from 1 to 5 pm.

## Car & Truck Museum

A testament to personal vision, this homespun museum (☎ 779-4204, 779-4987) is six miles south of Curlew on Hwy 21. See the world's smallest legal car, the 'Orange Peel', some rare autos and several cars owned by celebrities. It's open daily from noon to 6 pm, May through Labor Day, daily from 2 to 6 pm. It's also sometimes open during September. No fee, but donations are appreciated.

## Places to Stay & Eat

The *Blue Cougar Motel & Cafe* (☎ 779-4817), 2141 Hwy 21 N, has two rooms for $30 each.

The *Riverside Bar & Grill* (☎ 779-4813), 813 River St, turns out remarkably good dinners, with specials like grilled halibut and pineapple salsa for about $10. The regular menu features Mexican and American fare. Dinner is served Wednesday to Sunday only. Call for reservations before making the drive.

## KETTLE FALLS

Kettle Falls (population 1382) is set in an attractive valley, but there isn't much to keep a traveler here besides an interest in Columbia River history, of which there are several noteworthy examples. For at least 9000 years, Kettle Falls was one of the Columbia River's richest fisheries. Native Americans from several different tribes came here each summer to fish and eat salmon, taking as many as 3000 fish a day.

The Hudson's Bay Company took note of all the Native Americans gathering at the falls and reckoned it would be a good spot for a fur trading post. Fort Colvile

started operations in 1825, and itself became a hub of activity. Catholic missionaries opened St Paul's Mission just up the hill from the trading post in 1848. Fort Colvile closed in 1871.

However, many historic sites – including the original town of Kettle Falls and Fort Colvile – were flooded by Lake Roosevelt when the Columbia River was stopped up by the Grand Coulee Dam in 1939. The town's present site was called Myers Falls until all the transplants from Kettle Falls inundated it.

## Orientation

Kettle Falls is 80 miles north of Spokane on Hwy 395, and 31 miles south of the Canadian border. The Columbia River's Lake Roosevelt is just west of town, and at the river's west bank, Hwys 20 and 395 meet.

The nearest border crossing, Laurier/Cascade on Hwy 395, is open 8 am to midnight. On Hwy 25, the Paterson crossing is west of the Columbia River and is open from 8 am to midnight. The Boundary/Waneta crossing is on the river's east bank and is open from 9 am to 5 pm.

The free Inchelium-Gifford ferry crosses Lake Roosevelt 23 miles south of Kettle Falls. It runs from 6 am to 9:30 pm daily. This is also a good place to spot bald eagles, which winter around Lake Roosevelt.

## Information

The Coulee Dam National Recreation Area office (☎ 738-6266), near St Pauls Mission at 1230 Boise Rd, has information about Lake Roosevelt. The ranger station (☎ 738-6111) at 255 W 11th can provide information on recreation in the Colville National Forest. If you just need information on the water level in Lake Roosevelt, call ☎ (800) 824-4916. Boat rentals are available at the Kettle Falls Resort & Marina (☎ 738-6121).

## Kettle Falls Historical Center

A compelling interpretive exhibit chronicles over 9000 years of human occupation. One focus of attention is a giant photo mural showing the pre-dam Columbia as it crashed through Kettle Falls. It's a bit disconcerting to look at the riffling, churning water in the photo and then to look out onto the flat lake that is now the river. The historical center (☎ 738-6964), just north of Hwy 395 on the east side of the Columbia River, is open Wednesday to Saturday from 11 am to 5 pm, mid-May to mid-September.

## St Paul's Mission

Though Hudson's Bay officers from Fort Colvile, the local fur trading post, preached to the Native Americans who came by to trade, there was no formal mission here until 1848, when Catholic missionaries opened St Paul's Mission. St Paul's was a going concern until 1869. The building itself has been totally restored and is an example of tidy French-Canadian-style log architecture. The logs have been squared up and their tongued ends fitted neatly into slots carved into the corner posts.

St Paul's Mission (☎ 738-6266) is on the east side of the Columbia north of the Kettle Falls Historical Center. It's on a dirt road that was once the trail used to portage around the actual falls. Fortunately, the mission was perched high enough on a bluff to be spared the high waters of Lake Roosevelt. Visitors can take themselves on a free self-guided tour. The mission is open daily, year round.

## Myers Falls Interpretive Center

One of Washington's oldest grist mills and power-generating sites is just outside Kettle Falls. From downtown Kettle Falls, head south on Main St and follow the signs to Myers Falls about one mile out of town, on Juniper St. The falls were the site of a grist mill in 1816, a lumber mill in 1890, a brick factory in 1900 and a power plant in 1903. All were tied to the Myers Falls Dam, a small power dam on the Colville River. Along with a simple interpretive display, the falls are still nice, and it's a cool, shady spot for a picnic. This is a very informal, do-it-yourself site, with no fees, no hours, no attendants and no phone.

## Log Flume Heritage Site

The Log Flume Heritage Site is in the middle of ponderosa pine forests west of the Columbia River on Hwy 20 (at Sherman Creek, milepost 335). It's a nice drive, and the site provides a little snapshot of logging history. In the 1920s, as Washington timber was being shipped worldwide, one traditional logging technique, the low-tech waterpower and horse method, was being challenged by a new technique using steam locomotives and trucks. There are several interpretive displays along a winding, wheelchair-accessible trail.

## Camp Growden

At another stop on Hwy 20 west of Kettle Falls (milepost 331), an old CCC work camp, Camp Growden, recalls the years from 1934 to 1941. It's a peaceful place for a picnic and a short walk on the trail. It's also a good place to look for wildlife, including the occasional moose.

## Places to Stay & Eat

In town, the park service's *Kettle Falls Campground* is near the mill; it's open year round and charges $10 in the summer only. It has flush toilets, running water and a boat launch. There are two primitive USFS campgrounds that are only open in the summer, when they are free, with pit toilets and running water: *Canyon Creek Campground* is just west of Kettle Falls on Hwy 20; *Trout Lake Campground* is five miles north of Hwy 20 on Trout Lake Rd (milepost 337)

*My Parents' Estate B&B* (☎ 738-6220) is about a mile east of Kettle Falls on Hwy 395. Prior to its incarnation as a B&B, this was a Catholic mission and convent and a boys' school. The grounds cover 47 acres, and there's a gymnasium. Rates run $65 to $100.

*Barney's* (☎ 738-6546), just west of the river where Hwy 395 hits Hwy 20, operates a small motel alongside their large cafe on the west bank of Lake Roosevelt. Barney's complex is so well established that its location is locally known as 'Barney's Junction'. The motel is neither fancy nor expensive, with rooms starting at $25. In downtown Kettle Falls, at E 3rd St and Hwy 395, the *Double H Motel* (☎ 738-6514) runs about $10 more per night for rooms with microwave ovens and refrigerators. The *Grandview Inn Motel & RV Park* (☎ 738-6733), at the junction of Hwys 395 and 25, has a nice grassy lawn overlooking Lake Roosevelt and rooms from $32/36 for a single/double.

*Barney's Restaurant & Lounge* (☎ 738-6546) is the place everybody eats in Kettle Falls. But there is also *Cafe Italiano* (☎ 738-6480) downtown at 560 Myers St or *Freddie's Cafe* (☎ 738-6714) in town on Hwy 395. The *Hudson Bay Steak & Seafood Co* (☎ 738-6164), near Barney's at 3986 Hwy 20, is the spot for a fancier dinner.

There are lots of fruit orchards and fruit stands around Kettle Falls, primarily south of town on Peachcrest Rd. Stop by for a bag of peaches, cherries, raspberries, pears or apples.

### Getting There & Away
Borderline Stage buses make a trip between Kettle Falls and Spokane once daily on weekdays. Pickup is at the Yellow Pine Grocery. The bus from Colville bypasses Kettle Falls if there aren't any passengers, so be sure to call the office in Colville (☎ 624-7192) for more information.

## COLVILLE
Colville (population 4420) is a town of some substance – there's even a McDonald's sign beckoning along the highway. Indeed, it is northeastern Washington's largest town after Spokane and the seat of Stevens County. It's an attractive timber town, with many gracious older homes and gardens around downtown. Colville dates from 1883, when locals appropriated the buildings from nearby Fort Colvile, which was closed, carting everything a few miles away to a townsite along the Colville River. However, today most travelers will probably only stop here as a base before exploring the Colville National Forest; the USFS

headquarters are here and can provide information on hiking and camping.

### Orientation & Information
The Okanogan Highlands rise to the west of town, and the Kalispell Mountains are to the northeast. Downtown Colville is built on a bench just east of the Colville River. Highway 20 runs east-west through town, and Hwy 395 heads south out of Colville toward Spokane, 71 miles away. Colville is just eight miles east of Kettle Falls.

There's a tourist information center (☎ 684-3517) at 955 S Main St. The Colville National Forest Ranger Station (☎ 684-3711) is at 695 S Main St.

Coin-Op Laundry (☎ 684-2137) is on the main drag, at Main and Dominion Sts .Mt Carmel Hospital (☎ 684-2651), 982 E Columbia Ave, has 24-hour emergency care.

### Keller House
Keller House (☎ 684-5968), a historic house and museum complex on a hill above town at 700 N Wynne St, is the only real tourist attraction in Colville. The house itself, built in 1910, is a rather large bungalow with nice Craftsman details. A lookout, carriage house, log house and some farm machinery have been imported from around the county and flank the Keller House, which is open from 10 am to 4 pm Wednesday to Sunday, May to September. Admission is free.

### Little Pend Oreille Wildlife Area
Bird watchers should swing down to the Little Pend Oreille Wildlife Area, where McDowell Lake attracts waterfowl and it's possible to see black bears, especially in the spring or fall. To reach the refuge headquarters (☎ 684-8384), take Hwy 20 for about eight miles east of Colville, then turn south on Narcisse Creek Rd. There are several rudimentary campsites around the 63-sq-mile wildlife area; a stop at the headquarters will set you up with seasonally appropriate camping, hiking and wildlife viewing information.

## Skiing

Eastern Washington downhill skiers head to 49 Degrees North (☎ 935-6649, or 458-9208 for a snow report), south of Colville near Chewelah. It's a small ski area with four chair lifts, an 1845-foot vertical drop and some childcare services. Even during prime time, lift tickets are less than $25, and weekdays are much cheaper. There are also 9.3 miles of cross-country trails. The ski area is closed Wednesday and Thursday, except during holidays.

The snowmobile's reign may be nearing an end in the Colville National Forest, which is gaining a reputation for good cross-country skiing. Cross-country skiers can find miles of informal trails in the national forest (☎ 684-4557) and the Little Pend Oreille Wildlife Area. Contact the ranger station (☎ 684-3711) for an update on groomed trails.

## Colville Rendezvous

The Colville Rendezvous, held the first weekend of August at the city park, is a fun weekend festival with crafts booths, a wide variety of bands (from bagpipes to country to Dixieland), games and a beer hall.

## Places to Stay & Eat

Camp for free alongside Mill Creek at the *Douglas Falls Campground* (☎ 684-7474), seven miles north of town on Colville-Aladdin Rd, which is off Hwy 20 just east of town. It's only open in the summer, with pit toilets and a water pump. Campsites at the Pend Oreille Wildlife Area (☎ 684-8384) are also free and decidedly primitive, with pit toilets and no water; they are open late spring to the first snows.

*Carefree Guest Ranch B&B* (☎ 684-4739), 786 B Arden Butte Rd, is seven miles south of town. It's an attractive place with horseback riding and a hot tub; double rooms cost about $70 to $80. *Ben's Panorama Motel* (684-2517), 915 S Main St, a large place at the south end of town, has an indoor pool and hot tub. Rooms start at $35/48 for singles/doubles. The smaller *Downtown Motel* (☎ 684-2565), 369 S

Main St, is slightly less expensive with rooms at $32/37.

There are two nice places about 25 miles east of Colville on Lake Gillette. *Lakeside Manor B&B* (☎ 684-8741), 2425 Little Pend Oreille Lake, has two scenic rooms and a hot tub for $75. *Beaver Lodge Resort* (☎ 684-5657), 2430 Hwy 20 E, has cabins for $35 and campsites near the Pend Oreille Recreational Area. A small restaurant and boat rentals round out the resort.

Even though it's no culinary mecca, Colville is not a bad place to stop for a meal. There are several cafes in town, including *Cookie's Cafe* (☎ 684-8660), Oak and 2nd Sts, in the Pinkney city mall, a good breakfast or lunch spot. *Wong's Tea House* (☎ 684-3290), on the west side of town at 695 N Highway St, serves American and Chinese food. Campers can stock up at the *North County Co-op* (☎ 684-6132), 282 W Astor, a good food co-op open to non-members.

## Getting There & Away

Borderline buses make the trip to Spokane once on weekdays. Pick up is from the local ticket office (☎ 624-7192) at 127 E Astor.

## METALINE FALLS

Metaline (population 188) and Metaline Falls (population 235), small towns separated by the Pend Oreille River, are in the very northeast corner of the state. It's remote, lovely country, with access to the Salmo-Priest Wilderness Area, which is home to a few grizzly bears and rare woodland caribou. Metaline Falls is an exceptionally pretty town that used to house a cement factory, which for years covered everything in a thin layer of dust.

Like so many falls in the area, Metaline Falls itself was flooded by a dam – this one the Boundary Dam, up near the Canadian border, which was built in the 1960s. The dam itself is worth a visit, even if you normally eschew dam tours. Keep your eyes peeled for mountain goats, bighorn sheep and moose on the road to Boundary. There's a viewing site at Flume Creek about three miles up Boundary Dam Rd from Metaline.

## Orientation & Information

Metaline Falls is 97 miles north of Spokane and 10 miles south of the Canadian border. From Hwy 20, take Hwy 31 north, which reaches Metaline first and then, across the river, Metaline Falls. A visitors center has been set up in an old railroad car in the town park, across from Katie's Oven Bakery. There's a USFS ranger station (☎ 446-2681) at Sullivan Lake with information about all of the hiking and campsites in this part of the national forest.

## Boundary Dam

The 340-foot-high Boundary Dam (☎ 446-3073), just south of the USA/Canada border, spans two huge rocky cliffs. Its inner workings are pocketed in caverns and connected by tunnels hewn from the limestone. Those who aren't easily spooked should take the dam tour, offered during the summer from 10 am to 5:30 pm. Turn off Hwy 31 just north of Metaline, before the road crosses the river to Metaline Falls, and follow Boundary Rd (also known as County Rd 62) 11.5 miles to the dam's access road.

Near the dam on this side of the river is **Crawford State Park** (☎ 446-4065). The highlight of this park is **Gardner Cave**, a 1055-foot-long limestone cave. Guided tours of the cave's stalactites and stalagmites leave four times daily from Wednesday to Saturday. The park and cave close down from September 15 to May 1.

On the river's east bank, the **Boundary Vista House** is perched on the canyon wall 500 feet above the water. It's the best place around for a panoramic view, and not a bad place to camp for the night. To get there, you must drive north on Hwy 31 from Metaline Falls to Crescent Lake, turn west onto the access road, and drive two miles to the Vista House.

## Box Canyon Dam

Though less impressive than Boundary Dam to the north, Box Canyon Dam (☎ 446-3083) does have a visitors center with tours and a riverside park. People also fish for trout in the reservoir behind the dam.

## Sullivan Lake

Southeast of Metaline Falls, Sullivan Lake can also be reached by crossing the Pend Oreille River at Ione and heading northeast. Campgrounds at both the north and south ends of the lake are connected by a three-mile hiking trail that runs along the lake's east shore. Anglers know Sullivan Lake for its brown trout – the 22-pound state-record brown trout came from here. Continue east along USFS Rd 22, at the lake's north end, to reach more hiking trails.

## Hiking

Stop by the ranger station (☎ 446-2681) at Sullivan Lake to check in and get a map before doing any hiking in this area. The **Shedroof Divide National Recreation Trail** is a 22-mile-long trail through the Salmo-Priest Wilderness Area; it starts east of Sullivan Lake on USFS Rd 22, just past Pass Creek Pass. From here, it's a fairly rugged trail north with lots of good views and wildlife. Several other trails in the area offer the opportunity to make a loop hike, lasting either a day or overnight. Otherwise, most backpackers hike the trail one way. To reach the northern end of the Shedroof Divide Trail, cut north from USFS Rd 22 onto USFS Rd 2220 about six miles east of Sullivan Lake. Follow USFS Rd 2220, a good gravel road, some 12 miles to the Shedroof Divide trailhead (trail No 535).

The trailhead for the **Hall Mountain** hike is also east of Sullivan Lake on USFS Rd 22; turn south on Johns Creek Rd and take this rough road to the end. Bighorn sheep live on Hall Mountain, and the 2.5-mile hike to the summit sometimes rewards hikers with good wildlife viewing.

**Abercrombie Mountain**, at 7308 feet,

is the highest peak in the Washington Selkirks. From the top, there are views into both the Pend Oreille and Columbia river drainages. It's a four-mile hike up the mountain along the Flume Creek drainage, with over 2000 feet in elevation gain. Reach the trailhead by turning off Boundary Rd at Flume Creek north of Metaline; take USFS Rd 350 and continue about seven miles to the end of the dirt road.

### Places to Stay & Eat

There's free camping at *Campbell Park* by Box Canyon Dam, about halfway between Ione and Metaline. The two USFS campgrounds at Sullivan Lake, *Sullivan Lake Campground* at the north end and *Noisy Creek Campground* at the south end, accept some advance reservations (☎ (800) 280-2267). Sites are $6 (but $9 for lakeside), and they have running water, some flush toilets and pit toilets, but no hookups.

The *Washington Hotel* (☎ 446-4415), above *Katie's Oven Bakery* in Metaline Falls, is a classic, old small-town hotel. Built in 1910, it has simple rooms, baths down the hall, and an artist's studio at the foot of the steps. Double rooms go for $25.

There are also several small motels in the area, most offering basic accommodations and rooms for less than $30. *Z-Canyon Motel* (☎ 446-4935), on Hwy 31 in Metaline, and the *Circle Motel* (☎ 446-4343), just north of Metaline Falls on Hwy 31, are two to try.

In a town not noted for culinary extravagance, *Katie's Oven Bakery* (☎ 446-4806) stands out as the place to eat whenever possible. While it may mean a diet heavy on cinnamon rolls, it'll be worth it. There are a couple of burger stands in the area, and satisfying meals down the road in Ione.

### Entertainment

The *Cutter Theatre* (☎ 446-4108), housed in an old school built around 1910 by noted Spokane architect Kirtland Cutter, has recently been restored. Shows range from goofy melodramas to oboe and horn duets. As with everything else in Metaline Falls, it's easy on the wallet – performances run about $5.

## IONE

Several weekends a year, a train runs along the Pend Oreille River between Ione's historic rail depot and Metaline Falls. The two-hour trip is exceptionally scenic and allows passengers the chance to come to grips with their fear of heights *and* of the dark – the tracks cross Box Canyon on a 156-foot-high trestle and pass through an 821-foot-long tunnel. The $4 trips are usually scheduled for Father's Day weekend (mid-June), Fourth of July weekend, the last weekend in July, Labor Day weekend (early September), and a couple of 'autumn colors' weekends in late September and early October. Call Lion's Excursion Train (☎ 442-3397) for exact scheduling; reservations required.

The USFS *Edgewater Campground* is on the east bank of the Pend Oreille, two miles north of Ione; it's primitive, no fee. There are a couple of small motels in Ione, most notably the *Pend Oreille Inn* (☎ 442-3418), also known as *Del's Motel*. It's on the river, albeit right across from the mill. Next door, *Del's Restaurant* is operated by the same folks and is the best place to eat in town. Bargain hunters should stop at *Dos Amigos* (☎ 442-3806), which has daily specials for under $4.

## USK

People come to Usk to hunt and fish. **Brown's Lake** is a fly-fishing-only lake with cutthroat trout. No motorized boats are allowed. Cross the Pend Oreille River at Usk and head five miles north, then six miles northeast to the USFS campground on lake's south shore.

**Davis Lake**, 5.5 miles south of Usk on Hwy 311, is popular with anglers early and late in the season, when they haul in largemouth bass, Kokanee salmon, rainbow trout and Eastern brook trout.

The *Inn at Usk* (☎ 445-1526), is an old country inn with rooms for less than $25 and a few tent sites, and they rent canoes. It rivals the *Washington Hotel*, up in Metaline Falls, as the best place to stay in Pend Oreille country. *X-roads Cafe* (☎ 445-1515), at the junction of Hwys 211 and 20, is Usk's restaurant of note.

WASHINGTON

# Southeastern Washington

Southeastern Washington is the state's loneliest corner, filled with the big wheat farms of the Palouse around Pullman, the stark Channeled Scablands of the desert and the asparagus and onion fields around Walla Walla. There isn't a lot to see or do – the Hanford Nuclear Reservation and Fort Walla Walla being the main tourist attractions – and many of the small towns are little more than a grain elevator and, if you're lucky, a gas station/cafe. The nicest place to stay for a day or two is Walla Walla. Though people aren't much geared toward the tourist trade, they're generally rather pleased and surprised when someone makes a point of visiting.

The Cascade rain shadow looms over this part of Washington: less than 10 inches of rain falls annually in this barren desert landscape. Most of the land in southeastern Washington is underlain by enormous foundations of lava that flooded here over the millennia from volcanic ruptures near Oregon's Wallowa Mountains. Under Pasco, the lava fills a basin a mile and a half deep. The thin soils that managed to form on this volcanic plateau were swept away during the Spokane Floods, when ice dams in Montana gave way at the end of the last ice age and swept across the Columbia Plateau. It's still easy to see the path of the floods in the area north of Ritzville, where the denuded lava flows and gouged-out ponds form a curious geologic area called the Channeled Scablands. However, on the eastern edge of Washington is the Palouse region, an extremely fertile area defined by rolling loess hills planted in wheat and legumes.

## TRI-CITIES

Pasco (population 21,370), Kennewick (population 45,110) and Richland (population 34,080), known as the Tri-Cities, sprawl along the arid banks of the Columbia River between the confluence of the Yakima and Snake rivers, and they constitute Washington's fourth-largest population center. While the Tri-Cities aren't exactly a tourist destination, chances are pretty good that if you're traveling through this part of the state, you'll end up stopping to eat or sleep here, as they're at the intersection of several long, usually hot roads. In general, Richland is the nicest city of the three.

The Yakima, Columbia, Snake and Walla Walla river valleys were each important to prehistoric Native Americans, and the area of their confluence was a crossroads of culture, transport and trade. Lewis and Clark were the first White explorers to make their way through this region in 1805, when they floated down the Snake River to join the Columbia River near Pasco. One of their campsites is now contained in Sacajawea State Park outside of Kennewick. They made their way back to this area the following year, passing the towering basalt cliffs at Wallula Gap and continuing up the Walla Walla River on their way to the Missouri River.

The Hudson's Bay Company built the first Fort Walla Walla near Wallula Gap in 1818, at the mouth of the Walla Walla River at the crossroads of ancient trails leading into Idaho. The trading post remained open until 1855; shortly thereafter Wallula became the steamboat terminus of the upper Columbia, bringing goods from Portland up to Walla Walla and the Idaho gold camps. However, real settlement awaited the overland railroads, which pushed across the Columbia Plateau in 1880. Kennewick grew up around the region's first Columbia River irrigation projects in the 1900s.

However, what put these cities on the map was the Hanford Nuclear Reservation, which was built north of Richland in the 1940s. Hanford was a plutonium-refining plant for the Manhattan Project, and after

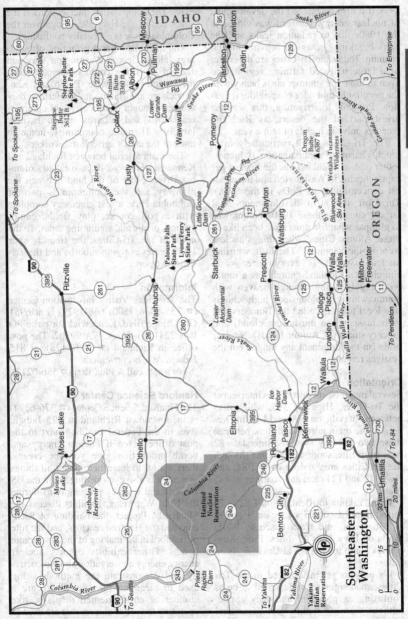

Southeastern Washington

WW II it also researched the development of nuclear energy. Hanford was closed in the 1980s due to radiation leaks and the bank-breaking costs of environmental cleanup. Today, the Tri-Cities are the center of a large irrigated farming region, and even in town the summer air is heavy with the peculiar humid odor of sprinkler irrigation. Previous to irrigation, this was the driest part of the desert, as Richland receives only six inches of rain a year.

The Tri-Cities don't particularly offer much charm or sophistication (which is rather odd, as Richland has the highest per capita income in Washington and the greatest concentration of PhDs in the USA). Turn off the strip developments that largely comprise these 1950s boomtowns to glimpse what life must have been like in these 'Atomic Cities' when things nuclear were in the vanguard. The little whirling nuclear symbol is everywhere – on churches (a Richland church has a mural with angels flying through heaven with atomic whirligigs alongside), high schools (the local team is called the Bombers and their mascot is a mushroom cloud) and grocery stores (ie, Atomic Foods). Nuclear pride isn't so dominant any longer, but the vestiges remain.

### Orientation

Several major Northwest routes intersect at the Tri-Cities. Highway 395, which runs between Ritzville on I-90 and I-84 in Oregon, is the main north-south link between these two freeway systems. Interstate 82 runs from Ellensburg and Yakima through the Tri-Cities area and down to I-84, and Hwys 12 and 124 meet and continue east to Idaho.

From Yakima to Richland on I-82 is 76 miles; from Pasco to Spokane on Hwy 395 is 136 miles; and from Pasco to Walla Walla on Hwy 12 is 47 miles. From Kennewick south to Oregon, at Umatilla, is 30 miles.

It's easy to get misdirected in the Tri-Cities; road signs seem designed to be as confusing as possible, and they appear without warning within feet of critical exits. The octopus-like intersections at the south end of the Hwy 395 bridge over the Columbia River is especially confusing.

Only Richland has a gathering of buildings (along George Washington Way and Jadwin Ave) that could be considered a town center. Otherwise, Pasco and Kennewick are amorphous and centerless; they are best thought of as a series of commercial strips and suburbs. Pasco is now largely a Hispanic community, home to most of the area's agricultural workers.

The main arterial between Richland and Kennewick is Hwy 240, also called Columbia Drive. Most of the land between the highway and the Columbia is part of Columbia Park, a vast greenway complete with a golf course, play fields, campground, picnic and swimming areas. To the north of the Tri-Cities, the freeway spur I-182 serves outlying suburbs and the Tri-Cities Airport.

### Information

The Tri-Cities Visitor Information Center (☎ 735-8486, (800) 666-1929) is at 6951 Grandridge Blvd, Kennewick, or write PO Box 2241 Tri-Cities, WA 99302. The post office in Richland (☎ 943-1128), at 815 Jadwin Ave, is convenient.

For a cab, call A Plus Taxi (☎ 586-0212).

### Hanford Science Center

The Hanford Science Center (☎ 376-6374) is in downtown Richland at 825 Jadwin Ave, in the Federal Building next to the post office. Even if nuclear energy and bomb production give you the creeps, there's a lot to learn here about all things atomic; it is also eye-opening about the US Government's policy presumptions during the Cold War years. Exhibits discuss the Manhattan Project, the building of Richland and the Hanford reactors, and the role of Hanford in the making of the first atomic bombs. Other exhibits discuss nuclear energy, energy conservation and radioactivity and demonstrate the methods being used to clean up the site. There are a number of child-oriented displays, like operating the robot pincers that are used to pick up radioactive materials. The center is open from 8 am to 5 pm Monday to Friday, and from 9 am to 5 pm Saturday; admission is free.

For more Hanford fun, follow Hwy 240 north from Richland into the Hanford Nuclear Reservation proper. Eleven miles north is the **Washington Public Power Supply System Visitor Center** (☎ 372-5860) beside an evil-looking containment tank and nuclear power plant. The visitors

center explains the difference between fusion and fission and the allure of nuclear energy. It's open from 11 am to 4 pm Thursday and Friday, and from noon to 5 pm Saturday and Sunday.

### Wineries

The hot, dry summers of the eastern Yakima valley near Richland give a soft finish to hearty grapes like cabernet and merlot. Who would expect that some of

---

### Hanford: Of Atomic Bombs & Nuclear Waste

In 1942, the US Government established the Hanford Engineering Works as part of the Manhattan Project, the top-secret, WW II program to develop the first atomic bomb. This site was ideal because of its remoteness from population centers and its proximity to the Columbia River's water and hydroelectric power. Richland was founded at the same time as an 'Atomic City'. The plutonium reactors that were built at Hanford, the world's first, produced the payload for the atomic bomb that fell on Nagasaki in 1945.

During the Cold War that followed, the Department of Defense and the Department of Energy pumped billions of dollars into plutonium production and the development of nuclear energy at Hanford, and the Tri-Cities boomed. In the early 1960s, when Hanford was working at full capacity, it had a total of nine atomic reactors, employed some 45,000 workers and produced almost 800 tons of plutonium a month – almost single-handedly fueling the massive US nuclear arms build-up in the race with the Soviet Union. Comforted by official reassurances that every precaution was being taken with safety, residents and workers felt quite proud of their patriotic efforts.

However, despite the government's zealous commitment, safety oversights and poor planning eventually doomed their efforts. Billions of gallons of radioactive waste were simply buried in underground storage tanks, many of which are now leaking. Until Hanford was closed as a reactor site in the 1980s, the Columbia River was considered the most radioactive river in the world. In 1986 the Department of Energy revealed that, in addition to over a hundred accidental radiation releases over the years, in 1949 there was one deliberate release, called the Green Run, which was done to test radiation monitoring equipment. As might be expected, severe health problems are rampant in the area, and though many lawsuits have been filed against the plant, few expect to win their cases. The deactivization and environmental cleanup has been extremely difficult and costly, attracting billions of dollars in federal tax money, but officials admit that almost nothing has been cleaned up so far. Some now feel the best plan is to let the buildings sit for another half century until the radioactive isotopes decay enough so that workers will not be endangered as they dismantle the buildings. Ironically, the cleanup now employs more people than Hanford ever did as an active nuclear facility.

Another odd twist in the Hanford saga is that the reservation also contains some of the most pristine wilderness in Washington, the result of the secrecy and security surrounding the plant. Since Hanford's operations use only 6% of the land, the government is now divesting itself of some of the rest, and the western side has been included in the Arid Lands Ecology Reserve – 120 sq miles of native sagebrush grasslands, a rarity in intensely irrigated central Washington. Plant life here includes bluebunch wheat grass, lupine and balsam root, and the reserve is home to Swainson's and ferruginous hawks, golden eagles, sage sparrows, sagebrush voles and a large and unusual population of desert elk. Though currently a de facto national park, the land's ultimate fate will be the decided by contentious debates between environmentalists, the Yakama Nation, land developers and the federal government. ∎

Washington's finest wines grow within sight of the plutonium reactors at Hanford?

The **Kiona Vineyards Winery** (☎ 588-6716) can be contacted at Rte 2, Box 2169E, Benton City, WA 99320. They are open daily from noon tyo 5 pm. Try the lemberger, often described as the zinfadel of Washington. Contact the **Oakwood Cellars** (☎ 588-5332) at Rte 2, Box 2321, Benton City, WA 99320. They are open from 6 to 8 pm Wednesday to Friday and from noon to 6 pm on Saturday and Sunday, March through October. The rest of the year, weekend hours only. Big round cabernets and merlots are the attraction here, as well as a pretty good chardonnay.

### Places to Stay

Most lodging in the Tri-Cities are national motel chains along the major arterials. There are a number of older motels along the Hwy 395 strip in Kennewick; try the *Tapadera Budget Inn* (☎ 783-6191), 300-A N Ely, at the corner of Hwy 395 and Clearwater, with a pool and single/double rooms for $37/45. One of the nicer places to stay in Kennewick is the *Ramada Inn* (☎ 586-0541), 435 Clover Island Rd; rooms start at $68/73. This motel complex is on an island in the Columbia, which is linked to the shore by a short bridge.

All the following Richland motels offer pools, a necessity here in summer. For a nice but inexpensive place to stay, check out the *Bali Hi Motel* (☎ 943-3101), 1201 George Washington Way, with rates around $35/39. For an extra $5, your pet can stay as well. *Nendel's* (☎ 943-4611, (800) 547-0106), 615 Jadwin Ave, offers a complimentary continental breakfast and some kitchenettes; rooms start from $37/43, and pets are $5. The *Best Western Tower Inn* (☎ 946-4121), 1515 George Washington Way, has a sauna, children's playground and rooms at $55/65.

The choicest lodgings in Richland, and in the Tri-Cities, are along the Columbia River near Columbia Park; both the following are large convention-style hotels that have better than average restaurants. The *Red Lion Hanford House* (☎ 946-7611),

802 George Washington Way, offers access to the paths along the river, with rooms at $79/89. The *Shilo Inn Rivershore* (☎ 946-4661), 50 Comstock St, is next to the golf course and tennis courts; rates are $65/69.

### Places to Eat

Travelers along Hwy 395 swear by the breakfasts at the *Country Gentleman* (☎ 783-0128), 300 N Ely in Kennewick; otherwise, you'll have no trouble spotting some tolerable fast food along this ugly five-mile-long commercial strip.

As in lodging, the nicer places to eat in the Tri-Cities are in Richland. You know this isn't just any eastern Washington town when you can head to *Some Bagels* (☎ 946-3185), 1317 George Washington Way; you can also fill up on lattes here. *Jennifer's Bread & Bakery* (☎ 946-5514), 701 George Washington Way, serves up breads and pastries and light lunch fare.

One of the better restaurants in Richland is *Giacci's Italian Specialties* (☎ 946-4855), 94 Lee Blvd, with sandwiches, pasta and salads; in summer, there's outdoor seating. Otherwise, cruise the drag and find a fast-food restaurant, or head to the Shilo Inn or Red Lion hotel dining rooms, listed above.

### Getting There & Away

**Air** Horizon (☎ (800) 547-9308) and Delta (☎ (800) 221-1212) flights link the Tri-Cities to Seattle, Portland and Spokane. One-way weekday flights to/from Portland or Seattle are in the $150 range, or $80 on the weekend. The Tri-Cities Airport (☎ 547-6352) is just north of Pasco off I-182.

**Bus** Greyhound (☎ (800) 231-2222) passes through Pasco on its run between Portland and Spokane. The bus depot (☎ 547-3151) is at 115 N 2nd St at Clark St.

**Train** Amtrak's *Empire Builder* (☎ (800) 872-7245), on its Portland route, passes through Pasco four days a week. The depot (☎ 545-1554) is at W Clark and N Tacoma Sts. A ticket between Portland and Pasco costs $53 one way; from Spokane to Pasco costs $28.

## WALLA WALLA

Perhaps it's the awkward, unlikely redundancy of the name itself, or the fact that the state penitentiary is located here (inmates crank out more than 2.5 million license plates a year), but Walla Walla (population 28,820) undeservedly suffers a reputation as Washington's town on the backside of beyond. For Puget Sound urbanites, Walla Walla is shorthand for all that's rural and out-of-the-way in eastern Washington.

However, the reality is quite different. Walla Walla possesses a lovely downtown, with one of the most significant enclaves of historic architecture in eastern Washington (it's one of the oldest towns in the state). For its size, Walla Walla has plenty of sophistication, good restaurants, pleasant parks and an academic character, lent by two small but noted colleges. It's also the financial center for this part of the state;

you'll be surprised by the number of banks, stock brokers, furniture stores, art galleries and tuxedo-rental businesses that line the main streets. Located in a rich agricultural area, Walla Walla is world famous for its sweet onions, but you'll also find peas, asparagus, grapes and apple orchards. Nearby is Pendleton, OR, the Blue Mountains, the Palouse, and the Wenaha-Tucannon Wilderness, making Walla Walla an easy and pleasant place to spend a day or two.

The area around Walla Walla was first settled in 1836 with the establishment of the Whitman Mission. But Marcus Whitman's efforts to preach to the local Native Americans eventually ended in a bloody confrontation that started the Cayuse War (see aside The Whitman Massacre, below), and in the early 1850s the area was closed to settlement until treaties with the Cayuse Indians were signed. In 1862, gold was discovered in Idaho and Montana, and the tiny outpost of Walla Walla found itself along

### The Whitman Massacre

Walla Walla is the location of one of the seminal confrontations between early White settlers and Native Americans. In 1836, Marcus and Narcissa Whitman, missionaries from the American Board, established a church mission and farm at Waiilatpu, just west of present-day Walla Walla, in order to minister to local Indians. Relations with the local natives were initially friendly; however, Oregon Trail emigrants often made a detour north to Waiilatpu after the difficult Blue Mountain crossing in order to replenish stores and to rest livestock. As increasing numbers of White settlers began to move across traditional Native American hunting grounds, tensions began to build.

In 1847, an outbreak of measles ran through a Cayuse Indian village, killing many children. Although a doctor, Whitman was unable to halt the advance of the disease, which seemed to kill only the local Native Americans, who had no natural immunities to it. The Cayuse blamed Whitman for spreading the disease, and in late fall, Cayuse braves attacked the mission, killing Whitman, his wife and 12 others. Fifty-three settlers, mostly women and children resting at the mission from the rigors of the Oregon Trail, were taken captive.

The Whitman Massacre, as the killings were known, set in motion the Cayuse War, the first of many conflicts between Native Americans and US settlers in the Oregon Territory; the killings also hastened the approval of territorial status for Oregon. By 1848, Oregon was an official US territory, enabling federal troops to be dispatched in order to apprehend the killers and to protect the settlers from further violence. After two years of skirmishes, four Cayuse braves surrendered and were tried and hanged for the killings.

The Whitman Mission was abandoned, and the region was soon closed to settlement by Washington's Governor Isaac Stevens. Treaties between the US Government and the eastern Washington tribes were signed in 1855, and in 1856 the US Army built Fort Walla Walla in order to enforce their terms. ■

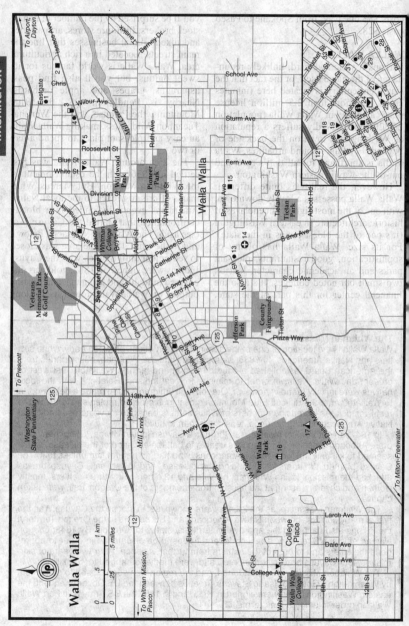

Walla Walla

| PLACES TO STAY | | | | | |
|---|---|---|---|---|---|
| 2 | Colonial Motel | 6 | Homestead Restaurant | 8 | The Pastime Bar |
| 7 | Green Gables Inn | 12 | Crossroads Cafe | 9 | Poplar St Cinema |
| 10 | City Center Motel | 19 | Jacobi's Cafe | 11 | USFS Ranger Station |
| 15 | Stone Creek Inn | 20 | El Sombrero | 13 | Coin-Op Laundry of |
| 17 | Fort Walla Walla | 25 | The Turf | | Walla Walla |
| | Campground | 26 | Merchants Ltd & French | 14 | Walla Walla General |
| 18 | Comfort Inn | | Bakery | | Hospital |
| 23 | Tapadera Budget Inn | 27 | Red Apple Restaurant & | 16 | Fort Walla Walla Museum |
| 31 | Best Western Pony Soldier | | Lounge | 21 | Greyhound Bus Depot |
| | Motor Inn | 32 | Clarette's Restaurant | 22 | Chamber of Commerce |
| 33 | Travelodge | | | 24 | Post Office |
| | | **OTHER** | | 28 | Carnegie Art Center |
| **PLACES TO EAT** | | 1 | Enterprise Car Rental | 29 | Pete's Ski/Sport |
| 5 | Asian Gardens | 3 | Blue Mountain Tavern | 30 | Paula Ray Gallery |
| | | 4 | Speed Wash Self Service | | |
| | | | Laundry | | |

the main transportation line between Portland and the gold fields. The town boomed more or less immediately, with merchants and provisioners setting up highly profitable businesses. Farmers also found a ready market in the mining camps for fresh vegetables, and the fertile valley began to fall to the plow. By 1870, Walla Walla was the largest town in Washington Territory. In 1875, a narrow-gauge rail linked Walla Walla to the steamboats at Wallula on the Columbia River.

As the Rocky Mountain Gold Rush played out, agriculture took over as the mainstay of the local economy. Walla Walla lost its preeminence in eastern Washington after the Northern Pacific Railroad rolled into Spokane in 1883; however, with its colleges (Whitman, established in 1859, is the oldest college in Washington), and its financial institutions, Walla Walla remains a cultural and economic center for much of eastern Washington.

### Orientation
Walla Walla is in a fertile basin where several smaller streams meet the Walla Walla River. Rising behind the town are the Blue Mountains; only six miles south is the Oregon border, with Pendleton, OR 33 miles further south on Hwy 11. The main road through the area is Hwy 12, which leaves the Columbia River near Wallula. From Pasco to Walla Walla is 47 miles; to Lewiston, ID is 87 miles.

The principal streets in town are Rose and Main Sts; Main follows the course of the ancient Nez Perce Trail. Separated from Walla Walla by parks and suburbs is College Place. Technically a separate town, College Place is the home of Walla Walla College, a four-year, Seventh-Day Adventist liberal arts institution founded in 1892.

### Information
Weekend travelers need to be aware that Walla Walla almost totally closes on Sunday. You'll find it difficult even to find a place to eat on the Sabbath.

The Walla Walla Area Chamber of Commerce (☎ 525-0850) is at 29 E Sumach St, Walla Walla, WA 98362. For information on the Walla Walla district of the Umatilla National Forest, drop by the ranger station (☎ 522-6290) at 1415 W Rose St.

The post office (☎ 522-0224) is at 128 N 2nd Ave, Walla Walla, WA 98362. The free weekly *What's Up?* has listings for local entertainment and nightlife. Public radio is heard at 97.9 FM.

Wash your clothes at the Speed Wash Self Service Laundry (☎ 525-9856), 2023 Isaacs Ave, or the Coin-Op Laundry of Walla Walla (☎ 525-9810), 929 S 2nd Ave. Walla Walla General Hospital (☎ 525-0408) is at 1025 S 2nd Ave.

### Historic Walking Tour
Park the car and take a few minutes to acquaint yourself with the lovely 19th-

century buildings and tree-lined streets of Walla Walla. The center of the old town is at 2nd Ave and Main St. In each direction are several blocks of 1890s-era commercial buildings; many still house prominent downtown businesses. Check out the grand **Ellis Hotel**, at the corner of 2nd Ave and Main St, and the **Barrett Building**, between 1st and 2nd Aves on Main St. The **Liberty Theatre**, immediately across the street, is a monument to early Hollywood Orientalism.

To explore the fine old homes of Walla Walla, continue south on 1st Ave one block, past the 1880s **Baumeister Block** and the art moderne **Northwest Bell building**, to Poplar St. Turn east on Poplar St and continue through a residential neighborhood with large and sometimes fanciful homes. After one block turn south on Palouse St; after another block turn east on Birch St, which ends at Park St. Go north on Park St, which leads over Mill Creek and to the shady campus of **Whitman College**.

---

**Walla Walla Sweet Onions**

The Walla Walla valley is noted for many crops, including lentils, peas and asparagus, but none are more closely linked with the area than onions. Walla Walla Sweets are renowned throughout the West as the sweetest and most succulent of all yellow onions. In the summer, roadside stands spring up, and many families buy the fresh onions by the bushel from local farmers. Tradition holds that Walla Walla Sweets are so mild that they can be eaten like apples.

Walla Walla onions are in fact a strain of Armenian onions that reached the Walla Walla valley in 1916 via a Corsican immigrant. The rich volcanic soils of the Walla Walla valley produced onions that were remarkably low in sulfur, the agent that normally makes onions hot and pungent. Local farmers carefully selected the sweetest of individual plants, and by 1925, the Walla Walla Sweet was on its way to becoming the standard onion of the Northwest. ∎

---

Whitman College was established in 1859 as a seminary, and it became a four-year accredited college in 1882. The oldest remaining building on campus is the **Memorial Building**, 345 Boyer Ave, a Romanesque-revival landmark built in 1899. Behind the Memorial Building stretch a series of quads, reminiscent of Ivy League colleges. Walking west along Boyer Ave will bring you back to Main St and downtown.

### Fort Walla Walla Park

Built in 1856 as an army fort, the site of Fort Walla Walla is now a large park and nature preserve with an assortment of playing fields, recreation and picnic areas, a campground and the **Fort Walla Walla Museum** (☎ 525-7703), on Myra Rd south of W Poplar St. There are two portions to the museum. The pioneer village is a collection of 14 historic buildings, including a blacksmith shop, schoolhouse (1867), log cabins and a railway station, arranged around a central meadow. In the fort's old cavalry stables is the museum proper, with collections of farm implements, horse-drawn conveyances, ranching tools and a building filled with old furniture, clothing, Native American artifacts and other mementos of old Walla Walla. (Check out the display relating the story of a once-lowly Corsican onion.) It's a good museum, definitely worth a stop. There is also a campground (see Places to Stay).

The museum complex at Fort Walla Walla is open from 10 am to 4 pm Tuesday to Sunday April through September, and it's open weekends only in October. Admission is $2.50 for adults and $1 for children.

### Whitman Mission National Historic Site

The site of the 1836 Whitman Mission, seven miles west of Walla Walla off Hwy 12, was declared a National Historic Site in 1897, the 50th anniversary of the slayings of the 14 missionaries. The monument is situated atop a bluff overlooking the original mission grounds, which are preserved in a park-like grove of trees. None of the original buildings remain; foundations indicate where various buildings once stood, and an interpretive trail leads through the site. Just off the trail leading to the monument are the graves of the Whitmans and the others who were killed in 1847.

In the visitors center (☎ 529-2761), thoughtful exhibits and a short film detail the story of the Whitmans, the local Native Americans, the Oregon Trail pioneers and the events that led up to the deaths of the missionaries. Maps of the grounds can be picked up at the visitors center, which is open daily from 8 am to 4:30 pm year round except major holidays; admission is $2 for adults and $4 for families.

## Wineries

While hardly the center of the Northwest wine industry, the fertile valley of the Walla Walla River produces some of the most respected of Washington's red wines. Unfortunately for wine tasters, the most renowned of local vintners, **Leonetti Cellars**, doesn't offer a wine-tasting room; pick up a bottle or try the cabernet sauvignon in a local restaurant.

The toast of the local wineries are found around Lowden, roughly 13 miles west of Walla Walla on Hwy 12. **L'Ecole No 41** (☎ 525-0940) is at 41 Lowden School Rd, Lowden, WA 99360, in an old schoolhouse. They are open from 11 am to 4 pm, Wednesday to Sunday; try the semillon and merlot.

**Waterbrook** (☎ 522-1918), Rte 1 Box 46, McDonald Rd, Lowden, WA 99360, is open daily from noon to 5 pm. Just south of Lowden off Frog Hollow Rd, their specialties are merlot and chardonnay. **Woodward Canyon Winery** (☎ 525-4129), Rte 1 Box 387, Hwy 12, Lowden, WA 99360, is open daily from 10 am to 5 pm, Memorial Day to Labor Day, and from 10 am to 4 pm the rest of the year. They have one of Washington's best chardonnays and cabernet sauvignons.

## Activities

Veteran's Memorial Golf Course (☎ 527-4507), 201 E Rees Ave, is right off Hwy 12, east of Walla Walla; it's consistently ranked in *Golf Digest's* list of the nation's top 100 **golf** courses. Head to Pioneer Park, at Alder and Division Sts, to find an outdoor **swimming** pool (☎ 527-4527). For rental skis, go to Pete's Ski/Sport (☎ 529-9804), 124 E Main St.

## Special Events

The Walla Walla Sweet Onion Harvest Festival, held in July at Fort Walla Walla, celebrates the onion that has done so much to bring Walla Walla to everyone's lips. Besides the food booths and recipe contests, there's other fun things to do with onions, like use them in a 'shot put' contest. Live music is provided by local old-time fiddle bands.

One of Walla Walla's biggest events is the Balloon Stampede, held in mid-May at Howard Park. Besides the hot-air balloon gathering, attended by over 40 balloonists, there's a rodeo, carnival, pari-mutuel racing, sheep dog trials and tons of food and crafts booths. For more information, contact the chamber of commerce.

The Walla Walla Mountain Man Rendezvous, held in July at Fort Walla Walla, is a summer festival of pioneer skill and daring-do. Competitive events include black-powder musket shooting and tomahawk throwing. Expect to see lots of buckskin and firearms.

## Places to Stay

**Camping** *Fort Walla Walla Campground* (☎ 527-3770), 1530 Dalles Military Rd, is in the park near the museum. Facilities include full hook-ups for RVs, tent sites, flush toilets and showers; it costs $8.50 to $11 a night.

**B&Bs** *Green Gables Inn* (☎ 525-5501), 922 Bonsella St, is a handsome, 1909 Craftsman home with nice gardens on two lots in a quiet neighborhood. Rooms start at $65. *Stone Creek Inn* (☎ 529-8120), 720 Bryant Ave, is a fantastic old mansion once owned by a Washington territorial governor. The 1883 home sits on several acres of manicured lawns beside a creek. Rooms cost $75.

**Hotels** You don't have to spend much money to stay in a nice motel in Walla Walla; your pet is welcome at most of the following, and pools are available, too.

One of the best deals is the *Tapadera Budget Inn* (☎ 529-2580, (800) 722-8277), 211 N 2nd Ave. Right downtown, its rooms cost $31/40 and include continental breakfast. Out toward Fort Walla Walla is the well-maintained but not quite aptly named *City Center Motel* (☎ 529-2660, (800) 453-3160), 627 W Main St, with rooms for $37/41. Just a block from Whitman College, the *Travelodge* (☎ 529-4940), 421 E Main St, costs $48/56 a night. On the eastern edge of town, the *Colonial Motel* (☎ 529-1220), 2279 E Isaacs Ave, will run you $32/38.

For a little more comfort, go downtown to the *Best Western Pony Soldier Motor Inn* (☎ 529-4360, (800) 634-7669), 325 E Main St, which offers spa and exercise facilities, a pool and a guest laundry for $63/74 a night. The *Comfort Inn* (☎ 525-2522), 520 N 2nd Ave, with rooms for $56/67, offers the same facilities near the freeway and close to downtown.

**Places to Eat**
Walla Walla is an unlikely but delightful haven for vegetarians. In part because of Walla Walla College, many of whose students don't eat meat, most restaurants in Walla Walla offer plenty of vegetarian selections. One vegetarian restaurant is near the campus: *Crossroads Cafe* (☎ 522-3007), 44 N College Ave in College Place, offers lunch, dinner, espresso and food for take-out.

For breakfast head to *Merchants Ltd & French Bakery* (☎ 525-0900), 21 E Main St, a great deli, coffeehouse and bakery. Enjoy a morning pastry and latte from a sidewalk table. With its selection of cheeses and salads, this is also a good place for picnic provisions. For a more traditional

breakfast, go to *Clarette's Restaurant* (☎ 529-3430), 15 S Touchet St, next to Whitman College. This is one of the very few places open on Sundays, and it is usually very busy. If you stay up late or get up early, go to *Red Apple Restaurant & Lounge* (☎ 525-5113), 57 E Main St. It's a little run down, but the food is good, and it's open 24 hours a day.

For Mexican food, go to *El Sombrero* (☎ 522-4984) at Oak St and 2nd Ave. The *Asian Gardens* (☎ 529-4024), 1708 E Isaacs Ave, has cheap Chinese; the daily lunch buffet is under $5.

*Jacobi's Cafe* (☎ 525-2677), 416 N 2nd Ave, has a number of things going for it. It's in the converted old train depot, a nice setting whether you dine inside or, in the summer, outside. The dinner menu is extensive, with a lot of vegetarian and inexpensive options – most under $10 – including Mexican food, lots of filling appetizers, salads and pizza, and a number of regional microbrews are on tap. However, the youthful wait staff at this college hangout seem to wait on customers more by accident than by design, hanging out instead with their friends in the bar.

One of the friendliest and most pleasant places to eat and have a microbrewed beer or glass of local wine is *The Turf* (☎ 522-9807), 10 N 2nd Ave, a small little hole-in-the-wall with sandwiches (a Gardenburger is $5, as is a hot pastrami sandwich). Expect a friendly welcome.

For a hearty dinner with some refinement, go to the woodsy *Homestead Restaurant* (☎ 522-0345), 1528 E Isaacs Ave, where there's steak, local grilled lamb chops with course-ground mustard ($15), Pacific coast seafood like pan-fried Quilicene oysters ($14) or one of a number of vegetarian dishes like stuffed peppers ($9). It's also open Sunday morning for brunch.

**Entertainment**
Students from Whitman College hang out drinking at *Jacobi's Cafe*, 416 N 2nd Ave, where microbrewed ales are served up in yard-long tankards. For live music, go to the *Blue Mountain Tavern* (☎ 525-9941),

2025 E Isaacs Ave, a pleasant old bar that offers blues and other live music.

If you hanker for something a little more subversive, head to the *Pastime Bar* (☎ 525-0873), 215 W Main St. This old bar hasn't changed much since it was established in 1927; not a normal tourist attraction or a student hangout, it's populated with ranchers, scruffy day laborers and the rest of the local population that doesn't quite fit in with the new, smart and sanitized Walla Walla.

For art or foreign films, check what's playing at *Poplar St Cinema* (☎ 522-3333), 116 S 3rd Ave.

*The Little Theater* (☎ 529-3683), 1130 E Sumach St, is a well-established community theater group that stages four productions a year. At Whitman College, student productions are presented in the *Harper Joy Theatre* (☎ 527-5180).

## Things to Buy

For proof of Walla Walla's tasteful prosperity, you need go no further than the downtown art galleries: these aren't quite what you expect in a farm town. Check out the latest show of regional artists at Paula Ray Gallery (☎ 525-3371), 33 S Palouse St. At Western Images Gallery (☎ 522-8470), 31 E Main St, the selection includes wildlife and blue-chip western art.

If you're looking for a gift or a souvenir, go to the Carnegie Art Center (☎ 525-4270), 109 S Palouse St, the regional arts and crafts center in the old community library.

## Getting There & Away

**Air** Horizon Air (☎ 525-2070, (800) 547-9308) has seven to eight flights a day to Seattle from the Walla Walla Regional Airport (☎ 525-0207), which is northeast of town off Hwy 12.

**Bus** There's one Greyhound bus daily going each way between Walla Walla and Pasco, with various connections to Portland, Spokane, Seattle, Pendleton, OR and Boise, ID. The station (☎ 525-9313) is at 315 N 2nd Ave.

**Car** Budget (☎ 525-9043) and Sears Rent-A-Car (☎ 525-8811) are both at the airport. Rental agencies in town include Enterprise (☎ 529-1988), 491 N Wilbur Ave, and Lightfoot's U-Save Auto Rentals (☎ 525-1680), 2933 E Isaacs Ave.

## Getting Around

The local bus service is operated by Valley Transit (☎ 525-9140), whose main transit center is at 4th Ave and W Main St. Schedules and maps are available from the main office at 1401 W Rose St.

Call ABC Taxi (☎ 529-7726) or A-1 Taxi (☎ 529-2525) for a lift.

## DAYTON

Dayton (population 2490) is an attractive older town on the southern edge of the Palouse region. Streams flowing out the Blue Mountains cut deep canyons in the lava flows, and though the sun bakes the farmland on the plateaus, down in the shady, well-watered valley things are garden-like and hospitable. The little-known and remote Wehana-Tucannon Wilderness Area is contained within the Umatilla National Forest here, along the Oregon/Washington state line.

The main businesses in Dayton are asparagus processing and raising peas for seed. The very handsome old Dayton train depot, a gingerbread structure built in 1881, now serves as the local community arts building. Stop by and pick up a walking tour map and check out the other historic buildings in town. Of particular note is the old courthouse, built in 1886 and still in use.

Highway 12 between Walla Walla and Clarkston is the exact return route of Lewis and Clark, and it basically follows a north-south course through Dayton, which is 31 miles northeast of Walla Walla and 66 miles southwest of Clarkston. The chamber of commerce (☎ 382-4825) has an office at 166 E Main St. As you drive in on Hwy 12, note the human figure etched in the hillside, which is meant to resemble an English chalk man. As a high school project, it sure beats a big 'D' on the sidehill.

### Wehana-Tucannon Wilderness Area

Part of the Umatilla National Forest, this wilderness area is home to elk, black bear, bighorn sheep, cougar and bobcat. (Expect to meet hunters in the fall.) Rivers and streams here have cut deep canyons into the basalt lava flow, forming broad tablelands with narrow-valleyed bottomlands.

To reach the wilderness area, follow Hwy 12 northeast from Dayton for 10 miles and turn east onto the Tucannon River Rd. Keep on this road until its end (bear left at the junction two miles past Camp Wooten State Park). From here, there's a hiking trail along the Tucannon River, another up Panjab Creek, and many opportunities for days-long backpacking trips or shorter loop hikes. Contact the ranger stations in Pomeroy (☎ 843-1891) or Walla Walla (☎ 522-6290) for details on trails.

### Skiing

Bluewood Ski Area (☎ 382-4725) in the Blue Mountains is 22 miles southeast of Dayton (turn down 4th St, also known as N Touchet Rd). It has 26 runs, the longest of which is 2.5 miles long, with a vertical drop of 1125 feet. Though not a big resort, there are rentals and a cafeteria at the ski area.

### Places to Stay & Eat

*Lewis & Clark Trail State Park* (☎ 337-6457) five miles southwest of town on Hwy 12 has 25 campsites for $10, with showers and flush toilets but no hook-ups.

*Purple House B&B* (☎ 382-3159), 415 E Clay St, in a lovely old home, has noteworthy breakfasts; dinner by arrangement and a swimming pool; a small pet is okay. Expect to pay $85 to $125.

*Blue Mountain Motel* (☎ 382-3040), 414 Main St, is a no-frills but perfectly adequate place with single/double rooms for $30/34. Rooms at the *Weinhard Hotel* (☎ 382-4032), 235 E Main St, built by brewer Henry Weinhard's nephew, start at $55.

*Patit Creek Restaurant* (☎ 382-2625), 725 E Dayton Ave, an unassuming place just northeast of town on Hwy 12, turns out some of eastern Washington's best meals. It's open for lunch from 11:30 am to 1:30 pm and for dinner from 4:30 to 8:30 pm, Tuesday to Friday; dinner only on Saturday. Set aside $20 per person for dinner, and to be safe, call ahead for a reservation.

If you'd rather eat cheap, *Panhandlers Pizza & Pasta* (☎ 382-4160) is at 404 Main St. And, if you're just passing through Dayton, do stop by the *Elk Drug Store* (☎ 382-2536), 270 Main St, and have a shake at the soda fountain.

## PULLMAN & THE PALOUSE REGION

The Palouse Hills are an extremely fertile region, and the saying goes that for every ten miles you travel east, an additional inch of rain falls. While the richness of the soil and the climate are great for agriculture and it's fascinating country to pass through, there's not much to *do* here. Pullman (population 23,480) is the largest and most interesting town, and it's pretty much defined by Washington State University (WSU), Washington's major agricultural school. With over 17,000 students and faculty, the college pretty much sets the pace when it's in session.

Sometime before the last ice age, prevailing southwesterly winds blew across the lava-covered Columbia Plateau, blowing dust for thousands of years north onto its eastern edge. Dunes gradually accumulated into steep-sided rolling hills, and the resulting soil, called loess, is very fertile. Today, the soft, sensuous Palouse Hills are planted with acre after acre of wheat and legumes. The Palouse is worth a drive or bicycle tour in the spring, when the fields are amazing shades of green, or at harvest time, when wheat is shipped down the Snake River on barges. Farming methods now aim at conserving the rich loess soil, and the rolling, seemingly endless green hills are girdled by swaths of stubble wheat that keep the soil from blowing away.

Originally, Palouse Indians lived along the lower Snake River, where they fished for salmon. They also traveled to collect roots and berries and developed the appaloosa horse (see the Appaloosa Museum in

Moscow, ID). The Palouse did not easily submit to treaties with the Whites, and after they defeated army troops at Steptoe Butte, the US Army went after them with a vengeance. Most Palouse refused to go to reservations, and as Whites moved in, they lived under increasingly marginal circumstances. French-Canadian trappers began working here in the early 1800s, and gold miners swarmed in around the 1860s. By the 1870s, homesteaders were farming and ranching in the area around Pullman and Moscow, ID.

## Orientation

Pullman, seven miles west of the Idaho state line and 76 miles south of Spokane, spreads out from the south fork of the Palouse River. Highway 27, known in town as Grand Ave, cuts through Pullman on its north-south route; Hwy 270, the east-west road, follows Davis Way at the west end of town, Main St to the east. The large WSU campus, bisected by Stadium Way, takes up a big chunk of town. Downtown proper is just west of the campus, near the intersection of Main St and Grand Ave.

Southwest of Pullman, the Palouse plateau drops off fairly dramatically to the Snake and Clearwater rivers. The Snake River cuts its channel about 10 miles southwest of town.

To the south, it's a nice drive between Pullman and Lewiston, ID, and the Snake River, along the Old Lewiston Grade Hwy.

## Information

Pullman Chamber of Commerce (☎ 334-3565, (800)365-6948), 415 N Grand Ave, Suite A, is happy to dispense information and discount coupons. The main post office (☎ 334-3212) is on S Grand Ave just south of Crestview St.

The area's best bookstore, Book People of Moscow (☎ (208) 882-7957), is a few miles east in Moscow, ID at 512 S Main St. In Pullman, there's the university bookstore, Student's Book Corp (☎ 332-2537), in the student union building at 700 NE Thatuna St. Brused Books (☎ 334-7898) is a used-book store at the corner of Main St

and Grand Ave. The *Daily News* publishes in both Moscow and Pullman. Read the *Evergreen Daily* for campus news. Public radio comes in at 1250 AM or 91.7 FM.

Drag your dirty clothes over to Betty's Brite & White Laundromat (☎ 332-3477), 1235 N Grand Ave. Pullman Memorial Hospital (☎ 332-2541) is a full service hospital at 1125 NE Washington St.

## Washington State University

In the late 1800s, local business leaders took advantage of the area's rich agricultural and ranching background to get the state land grant university, and WSU, originally the Washington Agricultural College, opened in 1892 with 21 students. Still largely known for its agriculture department, WSU has some features not found at every university. For instance, bighorn sheep and a grizzly bear live on campus.

A little surprisingly, WSU's **Museum of Art** (☎ 335-1910), in the Fine Arts Center on Stadium Way and Wilson Rd, mounts some lively, well-curated shows, featuring Northwest artists, traveling exhibits and work by students and faculty. There's a vital, unstodgy feeling here, and for those not interested in college sports, it can be one of the most exciting spots in Pullman. Admission is free; hours are from 10 am to 4 pm Monday to Friday, from 1 to 5 pm Saturday and Sunday, and Tuesday evening from 7 to 10 pm.

Other WSU museums are much smaller and more narrowly defined. The **Jacklin Collection** (☎ 335-3009), in room 124 of the Physical Sciences Building, has a huge collection of petrified wood and some dinosaur bones; it's open from 8 am to 5 pm Monday to Friday. Fossils documenting stages of human evolution share the space with a Bigfoot display at the **Museum of Anthropology** (☎ 335-3441) in College Hall; it's open from 9 am to 4 pm Monday to Thursday, and from 9 am to 3 pm Friday, and is closed June 15 to August 15.

If you want the structure of an organized campus tour, you can join the hour-long walking tours (☎ 335-3581) that leave at 1 pm Monday to Friday from room 442 of

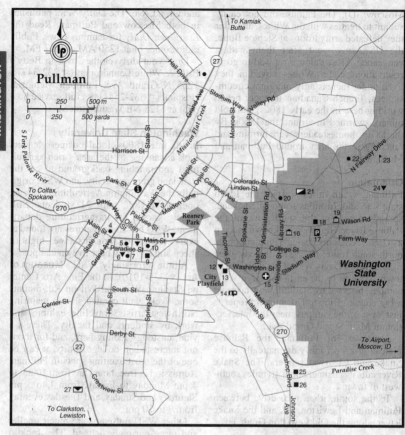

the Administration Building. If you want to park on campus, be sure to stop by the Parking Services office at the corner of Troy Lane and Wilson Rd (next to the Fine Arts Center) for a free parking permit.

### Kamiak Butte

Hike the 3.5-mile Pine Ridge Trail through a mixed conifer forest (the most trees you'll see in the Palouse) to the top of 3360-foot-high Kamiak Butte. From the top of the butte, there are grand views of the Palouse and south to Oregon's Wallowa Mountains. Thanks to all the trees, this is a good spot for bird watching. Warbler, nuthatches and

pygmy and great horned owls thrive in these dense woods.

The geology of Kamiak Butte is virtually identical to Steptoe Butte (see below), and the county park toward the butte's base has camping (and even some shade). It's 10 miles north of Pullman on Hwy 27.

### Three Forks Pioneer Museum

A local farmer has salvaged old buildings and antiques and pieced together an old western town on a corner of his spread. To reach the museum, also known as Rossebo's Farm (☎ 332-3889), head two miles north on Hwy 27, turn west onto the

| PLACES TO STAY | | 11 | Rathaus | 15 | Memorial Hospital |
| --- | --- | --- | --- | --- | --- |
| 9 | Manor Lodge Motel | 12 | Banjara | 16 | WSU Museum of Anthropology |
| 13 | Nendel's Motor Inn | 24 | Ferdinand's | | |
| 14 | Pullman RV Park | | | 17 | Parking Services |
| 18 | Compton Union Bldg | **OTHER** | | 19 | WSU Museum of Art |
| 25 | Quality Inn Paradise Creek | 1 | Betty's Brite & White | 20 | Student's Book Corp |
| 26 | Holiday Inn Express | | Laundromat | 21 | WSU Swimming Pools |
| | | 2 | Chamber of Commerce | 22 | Beasley Performing Arts Coliseum |
| **PLACES TO EAT** | | 4 | Brused Books | | |
| 3 | Swilly's | 5 | Bikes & Skis | 23 | WSU Golf Course |
| 6 | Seasons | 7 | Old Post Office Theatre | 27 | Post Offce |
| 8 | Combine Mall Bakery | 10 | Audian Theater | | |

Pullman-Albion Rd. After two miles turn north on Anderson Rd and go 2.8 miles to Rossebo Farm. The museum is generally open on Sunday afternoons; admission is $2.

### Activities

WSU's two indoor **swimming** pools are open to the public. Call 335-9666 for schedule information. Reaney Park, at Reaney Way and Gray Lane, has two outdoor pools.

WSU's tidy nine-hole **golf** course (☎ 335-4342) is open to the public. It's at the northeast end of the campus.

Take an 80-mile loop **biking** trip through the Palouse to the Snake River. From Pullman, take the Wawawai-Pullman Rd southwest to the Wawawai River Rd, which follows the Snake River to Lewiston, ID. From Lewiston, it's an uphill haul on Hwy 195 back to Pullman. Pick up a rental bike at Bikes & Skis (☎ 332-1703), E 219 Main St.

### National Lentil Festival

The third weekend of September brings Pullman's National Lentil Festival (☎ 334-3565), with entertainment, crafts, a quilt show and a myriad of legume-oriented food booths. Stop by Reaney Park for lentil pancakes, lentil lasagna or lentil ice cream.

### Places to Stay

**Camping** *Pullman RV Park* (☎ 334-4555) has sites for $10 in the city park, right where South St runs into the south fork of the Palouse River. Tent campers should head 10 miles north of town to *Kamiak Butte County Park* (☎ 397-6238) on Hwy 27; campsites cost $5 and have running water and flush toilets. *Boyer Park & Marina* (☎ 397-3791), west of town on the Snake River, is just downstream from Lower Granite Dam; it has a swimming beach, boat launch, showers and laundry facilities. Standard tent sites start at $8, hook-ups at $10; it's $4 more on Friday and Saturday.

**Hotels** Though there are accommodations on the WSU campus, it's not the cheapest place in town: the *Compton Union Building* (☎ 335-9444) rents a single/double room with private bath for $45/60. *Manor Lodge Motel* (☎ 334-2511), on Paradise St near Main St, is Pullman's least expensive motel, with rooms starting at $20/22. Pets are allowed for an extra $2.

Another inexpensive and fairly pleasant place to stay is the *Hilltop Motor Inn* (☎ 334-2555), 928 SW Olsen St, which is off of Davis Way up the hill from town. The $30/42 cabins or rustic rooms are part of the Hilltop restaurant complex. Let them know if you need a ride to and from the airport.

*Nendel's Motor Inn* (☎ 332-2646), 915 SE Main St, is just on the edge of campus and has airport transportation and an outdoor pool. Rooms run $45/47 and up.

A couple of fancier motels are near the river on SE Bishop Blvd. *Holiday Inn Express* (☎ 334-4437, (800) 465-4329), 1256 SE Bishop Blvd, has an indoor pool and rooms for $64. Pets are permitted for a fee. *Quality Inn Paradise Creek* (☎ 332-0500, (800) 669-3212), 1050 SE Bishop Blvd, is the nicest place to stay in Pullman. The pool is outdoors, but there's an indoor sauna and hot tub. Rooms start at $58/65, which includes continental breakfast in the lobby.

## Places to Eat

Benefit from all those dairy students at *Ferdinand's* (☎ 335-4014), the on-campus WSU Creamery. Besides Cougar Gold cheese (good sharp cheddar) and tasty milkshakes, they serve decent espresso weekdays from 9:30 am to 4:30 pm from the Food Quality Building on S Fairway Lane. This is one thing that Pullman's famous for; don't miss it.

A number of places in town have cottoned on to the fact that you can sell students a lot of espresso. For a quick latte, try *Grand Ave Espresso*, at the corner of Main St and Grand Ave. Supplement the java with some food at the *Combine Mall Bakery* (☎ 332-1774), 215 E Main St, a pleasant place to hang out with a roll and coffee. For more of a meal, try *Swilly's* (☎ 334-3395), 200 NE Kamiaken St. It's an easygoing spot with good food and a passably trendy atmosphere.

One of eastern Washington's only Indian restaurants, *Banjara* (☎ 334-6342), is at 905 SE Main St. For a standard student hangout, go for pizza and beer at the *Rathaus* (☎ 334-5400), 630 E Main St.

*Hilltop Restaurant* (☎ 334-2555), part of the Hilltop Motor Inn off Davis Way, is a fairly sedate steak and seafood house with a good view of town. It's one of Pullman's two well-established nice dinner places. The other place, *Seasons* (☎ 334-1410), 215 SE Paradise St, is a fancy cliffside restaurant in an old house up a flight of stairs. The setting is comfortably elegant, dinner entrees run from $9 to $17 and the food is Pullman's best.

## Entertainment

The *Beasley Performing Arts Coliseum* (☎ 335-3525), on campus, brings in some biggish names, including rock shows to appease the student population. But the real entertainment here is college sports, especially football. The Cougars play in the Pac-10 football league and usually field strong teams.

Pullman has three movie theaters: the *Old Post Office Theatre* (☎ 334-3456), 245 SE Paradise St, the *Audian Theatre* (334-3111), 315 E Main St, and the *Cordova Theatre* (☎ 334-1405), 135 N Grand Ave.

## Getting There & Away

**Air** The Pullman-Moscow Regional Airport (☎ 334-4555) is east off Farm Way toward the Idaho state line. Horizon (☎ (800) 547-9308) flies in from various Northwest cities.

**Bus** Link Transportation (☎ (208) 882-1223, (800) 359-4541) runs buses between Pullman and Spokane. If you're staying in town, they'll pick you up or drop you off at your motel.

## Getting Around

Pullman Transit (☎ 332-6535) runs buses around town and campus. Call 334-2200 for information about bus service between Pullman and Moscow.

## COLFAX & AROUND

Colfax (population 2790), in a deep ravine along the Palouse River amid rolling wheat fields, has a handsome brick and stone downtown in the middle of a long commercial strip. Antique stores have taken over a fair number of the old storefronts, making it a pleasant spot to while away a couple of afternoon hours.

For tourist information, call the Colfax Chamber of Commerce (☎ 397-3712). This corner of Washington lacks national forest land, but Whitman County Parks & Recreation (☎ 397-6238) has its headquarters at 310 N Main St. The Colfax Golf Club (☎ 397-2122) is along the Palouse River off Cedar St.

## Perkins House

Perkins House, a Victorian house built in 1884 by the town's first permanent resident, has been restored and is open as a museum at 623 N Perkins Ave. Before he was able to manage the big brick Victorian, Perkins lived in a log cabin; it's still standing out behind the main house. The museum (☎ 397-3259) is open from 1 to 5 pm Thursday and Sunday, June to September; admission is free.

## Steptoe Butte State Park

Steptoe Butte is just about the only public land in the Palouse, and it's a good place to get a bird's-eye view of the country. A road leads to the top of the 3612-foot-high butte, where hawks hover and the Rockies are visible off to the east and the Blue Mountains to the south. To the west, the Columbia Plateau appears to extend forever.

Steptoe Butte is an outcropping of Precambrian rock, once an island just off the western edge of the North American continent. Lava flows covered all the lower ground around the butte 10 to 30 million years ago. Loess then blanketed the land, creating the Palouse Hills, none of which comes close to the height of the rocky butte.

In more recent history, Palouse Indians defeated Lieutenant Colonel Edward Steptoe and his troops here in 1858.

Steptoe Butte is 15 miles north of Colfax, on Hwy 195 and then Hume Rd. You'll have no trouble finding the butte, as it dominates the skyline. Although Steptoe Butte is a state park, no camping is permitted.

### Places to Stay & Eat

*Siesta Motel* (☎ 397-3417), at Main and Thorn Sts, is a reasonable place to spend the night in Colfax, with rooms starting at $23. *Hanford Castle B&B* (☎ 285-4120), less than 10 miles north of Steptoe Butte in Oakesdale, off Hwy 271, is a huge brick Victorian house perched on a Palouse hilltop, surrounded by wheat.

*Diana Lee's* (☎ 397-2770), 300 S Main St in Colfax, serves etoufee and cajun food and is the best place in town to eat, even if one of their specialties *is* vinegar pie. There's a proliferation of Chinese restaurants in Colfax; try the *New China* (☎ 397-3683), 204 N Main St. *Redline Pizza* (☎ 397-6116), 117 S Main St, is a youthful hangout with decent pizza.

### Getting There & Away

Link Transportation (☎ (208) 882-1223, (800) 359-4541) has a bus stop at 610 S Main St in Colfax and runs between Pullman and Spokane.

## SNAKE RIVER COUNTRY

Somewhere between Dusty and Washtucna (population 266) the Palouse leaves off and the Channeled Scablands begin; just west of Washtucna, Hwy 26 climbs up on top of the Columbia Plateau. This is pretty desolate country, and since it's not on the way to anything, it's easy to miss one of eastern Washington's geological highlights, Palouse Falls. If you have a boat, Lyons Ferry State Park is a popular place to put in and cruise the Snake River.

### Palouse Falls State Park

These dramatic falls drop a spectacular 198 feet from arid Channeled Scablands punctuated with basalt spires into a rock gorge. The falls formed when floodwaters from Glacial Lake Missoula diverted the Palouse River's course. The native Palouse referred to the local falls as 'the hole in the ground', and that's indeed what it looks like, albeit an incredibly beautiful hole. It's especially impressive in the spring and early summer, when stream flow is high.

From the foot of the falls, the Palouse River cuts a channel to its confluence with the Snake River, some five miles to the south.

A trail starts in the parking lot and leads to an upper pool up above the falls. A number of other trails wind around the plateau and down to the river gorge. It's a fun place to hike, but watch out for rattlesnakes. Scan the canyon below the falls for prairie falcons, golden eagles, Swainson's hawks and other raptors who nest here.

To get to the state park (☎ 646-3252) from Colfax, head west on Hwy 26 to

Washtucna, then turn southwest on Hwy 260 and, after about six miles, southeast on Hwy 261.

If you're approaching from the south, turn off Hwy 12 onto Hwy 261 toward Starbuck (where most of the roadsides now have a terminal 's' spray painted on) and follow that road across the Snake River to the falls.

### Lyons Ferry State Park

Lewis and Clark, David Thompson and a plethora of missionaries passed by this river junction, but they were hardly the first. Palouse Indians, whose fish-drying scaffolds Lewis and Clark noted, were also relative latecomers.

Marmes Rock Shelter, a small, now-flooded cave about a mile up the Palouse River from its confluence with the Snake, has yielded evidence of the earliest-known North American settlement. Pieces of charred human bone (from a cremation hearth), tools and jewelry date back 10,000 years, almost to the last ice age. Get a glimpse of the site either from the river or from the paved road behind the park caretakers' houses.

The Marmes shelter and other, more recent, sites were discovered as part of an archaeological survey done prior to the construction of the Snake River dams. Construction of Lower Monumental Dam flooded the Marmes site and a sacred Palouse Indian site, but it created a recreational hot spot. There's a boat launch at the state park (☎ 646-3252), and plenty of people take their speedboats out here. The old Lyons Ferry, used for years to cross the Snake, is now a fishing pier. (The Lyons Ferry Bridge spans the Snake here.)

### Places to Stay & Eat

The campsites at *Palouse Falls State Park* (☎ 646-3252) are $7 and are best suited to tenters. At *Lyons Ferry State Park* (☎ 646-3252) the campground is nothing much for tenters, but convenient for boaters with campers or RVs. Sites run $7, and there's a

---

### Salmon & the Snake River Dams

Lower Granite, Little Goose, Lower Monumental and Ice Harbor dams control the Snake River between Lewiston, ID, and the Tri-Cities, where the Snake flows into the Columbia River. These dams, built in the late 1960s and '70s and operated by the Army Corps of Engineers, were the last dams to go in on the Columbia River system. Rather than generating energy or irrigation water, they were designed to control river levels, enabling ships to make it upriver. Because of these dams, Lewiston, ID, is now a seaport.

The tradeoff for this shipping channel has been salmon. Even with all the Columbia River dams, salmon stocks were in pretty good shape before the Snake River dams went in. Now their numbers have dropped perilously, despite fish ladders on all the dams between here and the ocean. There's serious talk among environmentalists about removing these dams. There's good highway and rail access to Lewiston, ID, and, to many, the loss of shipping is minor compared to the loss of native fish.

At Lower Granite Dam, 16 miles southwest of Pullman, smolt (juvenile salmon on their way to the ocean) are loaded onto barges that will ferry them around the dams, dropping them back into the river below the Bonneville Dam, the last dam on the Columbia. This keeps the fish from being diced by dam turbines, but there are indications that it also disrupts the instinct that allows the fish to return to their home streams to spawn.

There are visitors centers with fish ladders and viewing windows at each of the dams. Stop by and look for spring Chinook starting in April and continuing through the summer, fall Chinook in September, and steelhead in the fall. ∎

little marina across the river with a grocery and boat rentals.

At Washtucna, *McKenzie's 7-C Drive In* (☎ 646-3245) is worth a stop for a milkshake. It's near the crossroads turnoff for Palouse Falls. Other than that, plan on cooking your own food over a camp stove or driving through.

## RITZVILLE

Ritzville (population 1740) is mostly an agricultural hub (they call it the heart of the wheat belt) and transportation junction. It's where I-90 meets Hwy 395, which cuts south to the Tri-Cities and Oregon. Ritzville is a pit stop – take advantage of it, freshen up a bit and admire the scenic rolling fields of wheat, barley and canola, and the rich Palouse soil covering much of the land.

If you want to take a quick break from driving, browsing the three-block historic area downtown, just north of exit No 220 from I-90, is pleasant enough. Summertime visitors can stop by the **Burroughs Wheatland Museum** (☎ 659-1656), 408 W Main St, housed in a physician's home and exhibiting his medical paraphernalia, and the Ritzville **Railroad Depot Museum** (☎ 659-1936), 201 W Railroad Ave, which is also home to a small visitors center. If you're in town overnight, check to see if anything's going on at the renovated New Ritz Theatre (☎ 659-1950), 107 E Main St. The city park, just across from a public nine-hole golf course, has a swimming pool and tennis courts and is a good place for a picnic.

### Places to Stay & Eat

Since it's at a big crossroads, Ritzville has a fair crop of motels and one B&B. The *Portico B&B* (☎ 659-0800), 502 S Adams, is in a lovely Victorian mansion. It's about the nicest place in Ritzville, and the most expensive, at $59 or $74 for a room.

*Best Western Heritage Inn* (☎ 659-1007, (800) 528-1234), 1405 S Smitty's Blvd (near exit No 221), is a good bet for a freeway-side motel room, if you're willing to pay $53/60 for a single/double room. There's an outdoor pool and a coin-op laundry.

Downtown, the *IMA Colwell Motor Inn* (☎ 659-1620, (800) 341-8000), 501 W 1st St, is also a reasonably nice motel with a pool and a laundry and rooms starting at $30/40. Nearby are the *Top Hat Motel* (☎ 659-1100), 210 E 1st St, with rooms for $24/31, and the *Westside Motel* (☎ 659-1164), 407 W 1st St, costing $32/38.

There are no hidden culinary gems in Ritzville, but you can get a meal here at almost any time of day. *Perkins Restaurant* (☎ 659-0192), 1406 S Smitty Blvd, is right off freeway exit No 221 by the *Best Western*. Downtown, there's *Jake's Cafe* (☎ 659-1961), 408 W 1st St, and the *Circle T Restaurant & Lounge* (☎ 659-0922), 214 W Main St.

### Getting There & Away

Greyhound (☎ 659-1792) stops at 1176 S Division. Buses headed in all directions pass through here on their way to Seattle, Portland, Spokane, Boise, Montana and other destinations east.

WASHINGTON

# Oregon

# Facts about Oregon

Few states can boast such a varied landscape as Oregon. Beginning with the distinctively rugged Pacific coast, passing over rich valleys to glaciered volcanic peaks and on to rolling expanses of high-desert plains cut by deep river canyons and spiked with errant mountain ranges, the land is epic in its breadth and drama.

But what makes Oregon more than a scenic abstraction is the attitude of its citizens. Oregonians are fiercely proud of and involved with their state, its cities, culture and wild areas. Whether it's grand opera in Portland, rock climbing at Smith Rock or shooting Widowmaker Rapids on the Owyhee River, you're expected to get out there and enjoy yourself.

Oregon's unique character as a state can be traced to its history. While the growth of West Coast neighbors Washington and California derived from the tempests of gold fever, Oregon was settled by the greatest human migration in US history. Over the 2000-mile-long Oregon Trail during the 1840s and 50s came 50,000 young, sturdy and idealistic farmers, traders and their families, looking not for gold but to create enduring settlements. This pioneer purposefulness is still felt in the attitudes that Oregonians bring to land-use legislation, cultural institutions, civic planning and environmental concerns.

And the movement to Oregon is scarcely over. The same vague agrarian ideals still lure people to the state, currently one of the fastest-growing in the country.

## HISTORY

After the pivotal vote at Champoeg in 1843, where the citizens of Oregon – then an ad hoc collection of New England missionaries and French and British trappers – voted to organize a local government on the US model, the path to territorial status and statehood should have been assured. However, partisan rankling in Washington

**OFFICIAL OREGON**
**Statehood:** February 14, 1859
**Area:** 98,386 sq miles,
9th largest in USA
**Population:** 3,038,000
**State Capital:** Salem
**Nickname:** The Beaver State
**State Animal:** beaver
**State Bird:** Western meadowlark
**State Fish:** Chinook salmon
**State Flower:** Oregon grape
**State Stone:** thunderegg
**State Tree:** Douglas fir

DC delayed the action until 1848, when Oregon officially became a US territory.

The years leading up to Oregon's statehood were also the years in which the issues of the Civil War began to play out across the USA. The admission of Oregon to the Union became a political football between advocates and opponents of slavery, with southern senators in the capitol blocking consideration of statehood unless Oregon was admitted as a slave state. However, in 1859 when Oregon became the 33rd state to enter the Union, it voted overwhelmingly to do so as a free state.

The Oregon Trail, a six-month journey across the continent filled with hardship and danger, ultimately ended at Oregon City, in the Willamette Valley. Remarkably few travelers along the Oregon Trail chose

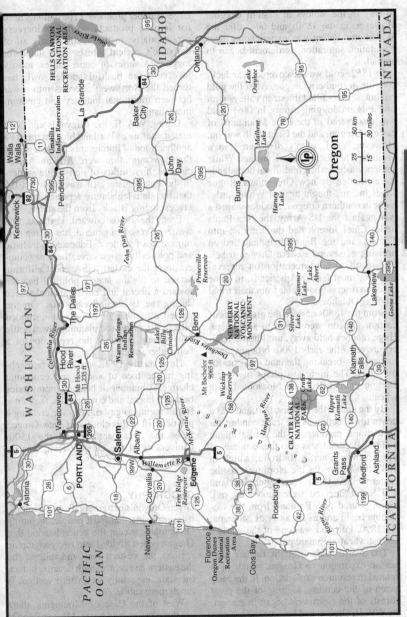

OREGON

OREGON

to stay in the valleys of eastern Oregon. However, in the 1850s and 60s, after the Willamette Valley was experiencing near population saturation, settlement began to spread.

In 1852, gold was discovered near Jacksonville in southern Oregon. After the gold ran out, settlers filled the steep valleys with orchards and logging camps. In 1861, gold was discovered in the Blue Mountains of eastern Oregon, and the Gold Rush was on. However, gold wasn't discovered in a vacuum. The Native Americans and White settlers clashed when traditional homelands were invaded by new Oregonians. Rogue River Indians fought against White settlement in southern Oregon, Modocs waged a war against the US Army, the Nez Perce under Chief Joseph fled the army up into Canada, and the Bannock Indians led an uprising of several eastern Oregon tribes. The result was incarceration on reservations for most Native Americans, in some cases on reservations as far from their tribal lands as Oklahoma.

From the 1880s onward the grasslands of eastern Oregon were open to settlement. Huge ranches held sway, until homesteaders arrived – the early 1900s brought many thousands – breaking the land into one-sq-mile lots. The high lava plains of central Oregon were tilled, and blossomed with wheat.

By the end of the century, Portland was a boom town, acting as the trade conduit for agricultural products of the fertile inland valleys. Portland was also the terminus of the Northern Pacific Railroad, which in 1883 linked the Pacific Northwest to the eastern USA; three years later, Portland and San Francisco were linked by rail. Grain poured into Portland from the Columbia basin and as far away as Montana. By 1890, Portland was one of the world's largest wheat-shipment points.

The world wars brought further economic expansion to Oregon, much of it related to resource exploitation. In the early years of the century, logging of the great forests of the Northwest began in earnest; by WW II, Oregon had become the nation's largest lumber producer. (The nation's need for lumber products seems to increase exponentially; in the 1980s, nearly all of the state's ancient forests were slated for logging. A series of court battles, mostly involving the bashful spotted owl, has turned the Northwest's forests into a war between traditional industry and environmentalism.)

During WW II, the shipyards and light manufacturing of Portland brought the state another flood of immigrants. A large part of this new migration were African Americans, the first influx of non-White settlers in the state's history (it was only in 1926 that the state legislature repealed an 1844 law excluding Blacks from the state).

From the 1960s onward, Portland, and western Oregon in general, has seen a new migration of settlers. Educated, idealistic and politically progressive, these newcomers from the eastern USA and California served to tilt the state's political balance toward a liberal and environmental stance during the 1970s and early 80s. Oregon passed a number of conservation-minded bills (a strict land-use planning law, a bottle bill) which gained it the reputation of a bellwether state.

However, the 1990s see Oregon retrenching in the face of social and economic change. A number of heated controversies between liberal and conservative factions – from logging to gay rights – are creating a political rift in this close-knit state. Oregon faces the 21st century, and the 150th anniversary of the Oregon Trail, wearily divided.

## GEOGRAPHY

Given Oregon's extremely diverse geology, it is surprising that most people, including Oregonians, accept the generalization that Oregon is best divided into two geographic regions: the western coast and valleys, and the eastern and central high deserts. In fact, the state, especially its eastern section, is much more subtle.

West of the Cascade Mountains, there are three major land types. Most striking is

Wallowa Mountains (BM)

Willamette Valley vineyards (BM)

Willamette Valley vineyards under snow (BM)

Sauvie Island Wildlife Refuge (BM)

River recreation (BM)

the Oregon coast, with densely forested (though heavily *de*forested) mountains abutting the Pacific with rocky cliffs and sandy beaches. Inland, between the coast mountains and the Cascades, the Willamette Valley cuts a wide and fertile valley in the northern part of the state. Directly south of the Willamette Valley, the Umpqua River and the Rogue River valleys drain a tightly contorted series of mountain canyons, which flow directly into the Pacific Ocean.

East of the Cascades, the landscape shifts from green valleys to arid uplands. In central Oregon's Deschutes River valley, sage and juniper-tree savannas drop away into immense canyons carved through lava flows. The Ochoco and Blue mountains amble through central and eastern Oregon. These low-slung peaks are drained by the spectacular John Day and Grande Ronde rivers. Further east are the Wallowa Mountains, an island of glaciated, Alps-like high country.

Southern Oregon is divided into two major regions. The salt lakes and barren mountain ridges of Lake and Klamath counties are part of the Great Basin Desert, whose watersheds find no outlet. In the southeast corner of the state, the Owyhee River flows from mountain sources in Idaho to trench its way through an arid lava plateau.

## CLIMATE

Oregon's reputation as a rain-soaked woodland is somewhat undeserved. Portland receives 37 inches of rain a year, less than Atlanta, Houston or Baltimore. However, much of the year is sunless, as marine clouds from the Pacific blanket the inner valleys. Coastal Oregon receives more rain, with Astoria receiving 77 inches.

Southwest Oregon in summer is both warmer and dryer than the coast and the Willamette Valley, with daytime highs in the 90s and about 20 inches of rain yearly.

East of the Cascades, the weather is another story. The mountain range effectively blocks wet Pacific air flows, and

much of central and eastern Oregon is arid, a persistent drought in recent years dramatically reducing annual moisture. Bend receives as little as 12 inches of precipitation annually, much of it in snowfall.

Winters east of the Cascades are quite cold and clear, and snowfall can be heavy. Skiers treasure the abundant powdery snow of Mt Bachelor near Bend, and Anthony Lakes, near Baker City.

The state's highest temperatures are found further to the east, with average summer highs in the Umatilla and Snake River basin regions approaching 100°F. Even in a good year there's not much precipitation out here: a scant eight inches of rain is the norm in southeast Oregon.

## GOVERNMENT

In the national government, Oregon has five congressional delegates and two senators. Generally speaking, national politicians in Oregon don't stray far from populist, progressive well-springs; there's often not a great deal of difference between the mainstream political parties. The state's national senators are both Republicans, but as centrists are as often as not at odds with the national party. In their turn, the house members – four of five are Democrats – have found it difficult to get along with an administration of their own party.

Oregon voted Democratic in the 1988 and 1992 general elections.

Among the major issues currently facing state government are dwindling tax revenues due to voter-imposed property tax limitations. While legislators struggle to find a politically palatable way to increase other forms of taxation, the state's institutions – especially its school and university system – are being gutted, and the means for funding the state's ground-breaking universal health plan are scarce.

## POPULATION & PEOPLE

The current population of Oregon is 3,038,000. Three quarters of this number live in the Willamette Valley, with the Port-

## Is Oregon Conservative or Liberal?

Most people would characterize Oregon's culture in terms of its politics: words like politically progressive, liberal, environmentally aware and ex-hippie capture the image that many hold of the state. However, anyone who has followed the politics in recent years knows that there's another side to Oregon that is very socially conservative, reactionary and hostile to environmentalism. Both of these archetypes are true of the state's culture at the same time. What makes Oregon such a unique state is that the same idealism informs both liberal and conservative elements in the Oregon cultural mix. In some sense, this contradiction is at the heart of what it is to be an Oregonian.

Elements that give the state's progressive reputation are in evidence everywhere. Land-use laws strictly limit urban growth; all Oregon beaches are public property; bike paths, parks and public art are scattered across the state. A live-and-let-live attitude toward minorities and alternative lifestyles typifies the larger cities, and out-of-the-way towns have thriving artistic and countercultural communities.

However, the same urban centers that are models of tolerance also harbor some of the fastest-growing cells of neo-Nazi youth in the USA, communities vote to limit the civil rights of their citizens, and conservative tax revolts have resulted in the evisceration of public institutions and educational facilities. A narrow hatred of spotted owls and environmentalists is a pervasive passion for many individuals in rural communities, and the Oregon Citizen's Alliance's campaign against gays and lesbians has succeeded in dividing families and communities on highly emotional social issues.

Which of these is the real Oregon? The truth is that both urges – to change Oregon in order to save it, and to save Oregon by halting change – derive from the same impulse. Most Oregonians believe in the intrinsic worth and value of the state, its institutions and its land. Both sides are ready and willing to fight in the public forum to preserve the state that they see threatened. The desire to save Oregon from itself is the one value that unites both sides in this ideological battle. ■

land metropolitan area home to about 1.5 million people. In the early 1990s, the state was growing at a rate of 3% a year, and urban forecasters expect the state to gain about a million more residents in the next 15 years; half of these new residents will settle in the Portland area. However, the fastest growing part of the state is the Bend area, in central Oregon.

Not every part of Oregon is growing. According to the 1990 census, 12 Oregon counties saw a decline in population; these counties were generally in the eastern part of the state.

## Ethnicity

According to the 1990 census, the Oregon population is 93% White, with the combined number of African Americans and people of Hispanic and Asian descent coming in at around 6%. Native Americans comprise only 1.4% of the state-wide population. Portland has been alternatively acclaimed and ridiculed as the 'Whitest' city in America: according to some news analyses, Portland has the highest percentage of White to minority citizens of any large US city. Eighty-five percent of the Portland population is White, with

African-Americans comprising 8% and Asians 5.3%.

## Native Americans

An estimated 38,500 Native Americans reside in Oregon, 89% of whom live in metropolitan areas. The remaining 11% reside either in rural areas or on one of Oregon's five Indian reservations. The federal government recognizes nine tribes in Oregon, the Burns Paiute Tribe, the Confederated Tribes of Coos, Lower Umpqua and Siuslaw Indians, the Confederated Tribes of Grande Ronde, the Confederated Tribes of Siletz, the Confederated Tribes of Warm Springs, the Confederated Tribes of Umatilla Indian Reservation, the Cow Creek Band of the Umpqua Indians, the Klamath Tribe, and the Coquille Tribe. Many other Indian tribes reside in Oregon without federally recognized status, or a land base. Federally recognized status is very much a political tool, which tends to give the message to unrecognized tribes that they simply don't exist.

## ARTS

In keeping with a seeming Oregon paradigm, even the arts scene in the state is informal and participatory. Summer brings a bounty of music festivals, outdoor theater productions and art shows. Even normally solitary literary pursuits become group events, as Portland bookstores and coffeehouses vie with each other for number and prestige of author readings.

If you're wondering about the plethora of outdoor sculpture in Portland, it's due to the city's 1%-for-art program, established in 1980, which allocates 1.33% of funding for public buildings to the purchase and siting of public art.

## Music

The Oregon Symphony and the Portland Opera are both popular Portland institutions. One of few African American conductors of a major US orchestra, conductor James dePriest of the Oregon Symphony has led the 100-year-old institution into the 20th century by introducing more contemporary, avant-garde music into the repertoire.

Summer brings a number of noted classical-music festivals to the state. Chamber Music Northwest, a series of concerts by a superior ensemble of young musicians, play a large and varied program of chamber music in Portland during July and August. The Britt Festival in Jacksonville provides a series of informal concerts from June through Labor Day; these outdoor, evening concerts blend music and picnics. Eugene's Oregon Bach Festival is another noted concert series, held the last week in June and first week in July.

Portland has the state's most vital music club scene. Jazz, Celtic, punk, blues and country music can be found throughout the city in clubs that range from upscale to real dives.

The popular music scene really opens up during the summer. Throughout the state, weekend festivals bring all types of music to the concert stage. Sometimes it seems as if Portland's Waterfront Park is nothing more than a summertime concert stage with the Cinqo de Mayo celebration, June's Rose Festival, July's Blues Festival and the Brewer's Festival and The Bite in August. The Mt Hood Jazz Festival is one of the state's largest concert series, held in August in Gresham, a suburb of Portland.

## Theater & Film

Ashland's Oregon Shakespeare Festival is one of the state's crown jewels. During high season, performances are held on one outdoor and two indoor stages; while Shakespeare is the principal draw, contemporary drama and comedies are also produced. About 350,000 people a year attend performances in Ashland.

Portland Center Stage, formerly an affiliate of the Oregon Shakespeare Festival, also mounts productions at the Portland Center for the Performing Arts. This beautiful facility is also home to other dramatic companies, whose specialties range from musical comedy to Greek tragedy. Not all theater in Portland is so grand; a number of

OREGON

**Telephone Area Codes**
In November of 1995, Oregon added a new area code. The northwest region of the state, the Portland/Salem metro area and the extreme northern part of the coast retains the 503 area code. The rest of the state now has an area code of 541. For more information check the local telephone directory. ■

small troupes provide productions in more intimate settings.

In recent years, Oregon has become increasingly popular as a locale for films, due to its handsome landscapes and cheap labor. Portland's Old Town is especially popular for directors seeking turn-of-the-century authenticity. Films shot in Oregon include *Animal House, One Flew Over the Cuckoo's Nest, The Shining* and *Body of Evidence*.

Acclaimed director Gus van Sant, whose films include *Drugstore Cowboy, My Own Private Idaho* and *Even Cowgirls Get the Blues* lives in Portland. His films are shot largely in-state.

### Visual Arts

Oregon's center for painting and sculpture is Portland, which has a large number of galleries; the Portland Art Museum's collection includes Asian porcelains, a representative overview of European Art, and regional art shows.

The visual art scene in Portland is quite dynamic and sophisticated, considering the size of the city. A number of factors

account for this, including the existence of the museum art school, and some of the cheapest rents on the West Coast.

## INFORMATION
### Useful Phone Numbers

To check road conditions statewide, call 889-3999. To hear a local weather forecast, call 779-5990.

### Time

Most of Oregon is in the Pacific Time Zone. A small sliver of easternmost Oregon, containing Ontario, is in the Mountain Time Zone. The Pacific Time Zone is eight hours later than GMT/UTC, and three hours later than New York City, which is in Eastern Time.

Oregon observes the switch to daylight-saving time, which goes into effect from the first Sunday in April to the last Sunday in October.

### Taxes

Oregon has no sales tax or value added tax (VAT), only one of three states in the USA that can claim that distinction. However, accommodations in hotels, motels, lodges and B&Bs are subject to local bed taxes that can range from 4% to 7%; the price quoted or advertised by hoteliers for rooms may or may not include the tax. Ask to be certain.

### Gasoline

If you're driving, keep in mind that Oregon law prohibits you from pumping your own gasoline – all gas stations are full service, so just sit back and enjoy it.

# Portland

Oregon's largest city, Portland is at the junction of two great rivers; it is ringed by vast forests and dominated by ancient volcanoes. This vernal setting belies a cosmopolitan city with an easy-going, can-do spirit. Although nearly 1.5 million people live in the Portland metropolitan area, the city has the feeling of a friendly, smaller town.

One hundred miles from the Pacific Ocean, Portland is one of the West Coast's busiest ports. But nowadays, Portland is known less for its role on the front line of international trade, than for its 'lifestyle'. Perennially near the top of the list of the USA's 'most livable cities', Portland is known nationally for its progressive politics, its easy-going pace of life and its love of the outdoors and the environment. An hour's drive from the city center finds year-round skiing on a volcanic peak, rolling hills covered with vineyards and the rugged Pacific coast. But Portlanders don't live in their city just because of access to the countryside. Citizens are proud of their vibrant downtown, its beautiful parks and architecture and its worldly but unfussy comforts.

Settled initially by New England traders and Midwest farmers, Portland has always been practical, purposeful, and foresighted. It lacks the brash energy of Seattle or San Francisco, and their high prices. Its beautiful setting and friendly sophistication make Portland a great city to explore.

## HISTORY

Portland sits near the confluence of two of the West's mightiest rivers, the Columbia and the Willamette. Unsurprisingly, Portland's early growth was fueled by shipping and trade. The terminus of continental railroads, and port city to the Pacific Rim, Portland was ideally situated to export the agricultural riches of the western USA.

The settlement of Portland is inextrica-bly linked to nearby Fort Vancouver, the Hudson's Bay Company fur-trading post established in 1825 on the northern bank of the Columbia River. Retiring trappers moved south, up the Willamette River, to establish settlements. The first building in what would become Portland was erected in 1829 by Etienne Lucier, a former trapper who was looking to establish a farm along the Willamette River. Although Lucier abandoned his homestead a year later and moved further up the river to Champoeg, activity continued at the site of future Portland.

In 1844 two New Englanders filed a claim for 640 acres of land on the west bank of the Willamette. They built a store, platted streets, and decided to name the new settlement after one of their home-towns. A coin-toss resulted in Portland winning over Boston, and the new town was up and running.

Trade, not industry or natural-resource exploitation, was the engine that drove the growth of the city. The California Gold Rush of 1849 and the building of San Francisco demanded lumber, which was routed through the fledgling port city on the Willamette. At the same time, Oregon Trail settlers brought agriculture to the Willamette Valley and mining and ranching developed throughout the inland West. Each demanded a coastal city of trade, and Portland became that mercantile and shipping center for much of the Northwest.

Portland's primacy in the Northwest was solidified when the Northern Pacific Railroad arrived in 1883, linking Portland and the Pacific Northwest to the rest of the country. The first bridges were built across the Willamette in the late 1880s, and the city spread eastward. Portland's population increased five-fold between the years 1880 and 1900.

During the 20th century Portland has enjoyed steady growth. The influx of

workers to the ship-building factories during WW II was so great that an entire new city, called Vanport, was created in 1944 to house them. Unwisely built on a Columbia River flood plain, in 1948 a wall of water burst through a dike and destroyed Vanport, killing 18 people and leaving almost 20,000 homeless.

## ORIENTATION

Interstate 5 and I-84 intersect across the river from downtown Portland. Interstate 405 loops west off I-5 to provide a short-cut around the downtown core. Further to the east, I-205 cuts through Portland sub-

urbs of Clackamas and Gresham to Vancouver, WA. Because it avoids downtown traffic, I-205 provides a quick bypass through the metro area. West of downtown, Hwy 26 is the main arterial to the suburbs of Beaverton, Hillsboro and eventually to the northern Oregon coast.

In Portland, avenues are numbered and run north to south, whereas streets are named and run east to west. The north-flowing Willamette River and the east-west trending Burnside St quarter the city into Northwest, Southwest, Northeast and Southeast districts. Be attentive of address prefixes: for instance, NE Davis St and NW

Davis St are on opposite sides of the Willamette River; NW 6th Ave and SW 6th Ave are on opposite sides of Burnside.

If you're trying to find your way around Northwest Portland, there's an easy way to keep the streets straight. Named for early settlers, the street names proceed northward in alphabetical order. Thus, one block north of Burnside is Couch, followed by Davis, Everett, and so on.

## Neighborhoods
**Northwest Portland** The Northwest, as it's referred to by Portlanders, is the neighborhood bisected by NW 21st and 23rd Aves, north of Burnside. There's more street life here among the trendy boutiques, coffeehouses, brewpubs and galleries than anywhere else in the city; population and traffic density are both very high. The trendiness of the area has rubbed off on an old warehouse district just to the east, called the Pearl District. Between NW 14th and 10th Aves and NW Hoyt and Everett Sts, this area is now consigned to stylish galleries and urban loft apartments.

**Northeast Portland** Across the Willamette in Northeast Portland (also known as the Lloyd District), the neighborhood surrounding the nation's first full-blown shopping mall, the Lloyd Center, forms an adjunct to downtown. A major face-lift in recent years has converted this slightly faded institution (established in 1955) into one of the city's hottest shopping areas. Gentrification of surrounding streets, especially NE Broadway between 12th and 21st Aves, has brought an influx of good restaurants and specialty shops. Portland's largest cinema, the Rose Garden Arena (home of the NBA Trail Blazers), and the Oregon Convention Center are also here.

**Southeast Portland** Portland's funkiest, most diverse neighborhoods are in the inner Southeast; around here everything is 'alternative'. Along SE Hawthorne Blvd between 30th and 45th Aves, the Hawthorne District is full of bookstores, delis, antique stores, ethnic restaurants and coffeeshops where Reed College students, old hippies and the politically progressive hang out. Sellwood, an old working-class neighborhood, has converted itself into an antique-store ghetto. Sellwood streets along SE 13th Ave, between Tacoma and Bybee Sts, buzz with curio shoppers.

## Downtown
Constituting the Southwest quadrant of the city, and a piece of the northwest, downtown Portland is ringed by I-405 and the Willamette River. South of Burnside St is the modern high-rise center of the city; north of Burnside are Oldtown and Chinatown, remnants of Portland's 19th-century heyday.

Because Portland is a river town, important streets tend to be those that connect with bridges. Often called Bridge Town, the Portland metro area is graced by 12 bridges that cross the Willamette. Therefore, to get around downtown Portland, it pays to know what streets have bridges. Besides freeway bridges, remember that the Burnside Bridge connects the city's main east-west arterial; the Broadway Bridge is the main link between downtown and Northeast Portland, with access to both I-5 and I-84; the Morrison Bridge connects downtown to Southeast Portland also with on-ramps to I-84 and I-5 north.

Broadway is essentially downtown's main street (Broadway might have been known as 7th Ave, if settlers had consistently used numbers to designate avenues). Front Ave flanks Waterfront Park along the Willamette, and is the 'zero' avenue for numbering purposes. SW 5th and 6th Aves have been designated as a bus mall. Metropolitan Area Express (MAX), Portland's light-rail system, enters downtown on SW 1st Ave then loops through city-center on SW Morrison and Yamhill Sts. Within the downtown core ('Fareless Square'), all rides on public transport are free.

Almost all downtown streets are one way; traffic is restricted on SW 5th and 6th Aves which, as a bus mall, are primarily for bus access. Also, on the portions of Yamhill and Morrison Aves where there are

OREGON

OREGON

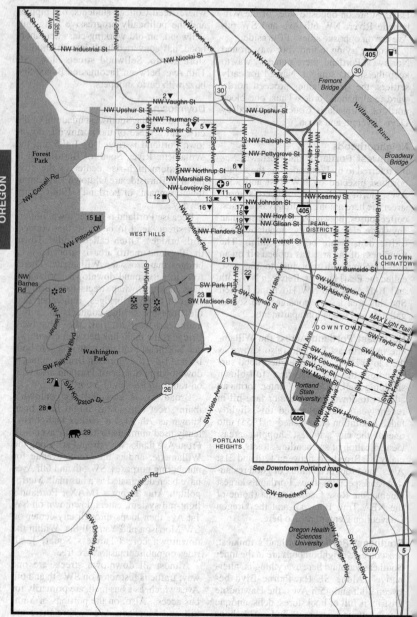

NW 35th Ave
NW 29th Ave
NW St Helens Rd
NW 14th Ave
NW Industrial St
NW Nicolai St
NW Vaughn St   2 ▼
NW Upshur St
NW Upshur St
NW Thurman St
3 ● NW 19th Ave   NW Savier St   4 ▼ 5 ▼
NW Raleigh St
NW Pettygrove St
NW Northrup St   6 ▼
NW Marshall St   ✚ 9   ■ 7
NW Lovejoy St   ▼ 11
12 ■   13 ▼   17 ▼   14 ▼
16 ▼   18 ▼
NW Johnson St
NW Hoyt St   19 ▼
NW Glisan St   20 ▼
NW Flanders St
NW Everett St
21 ▼
22 ▼
SW Park Pl
23 ■   SW Madison St
SW Salmon St
15 血

NW Front Ave
NW Veeon Ave
30 (405)
Fremont Bridge
Willamette River
Broadway Bridge
NW 19th Ave
NW 18th Ave
NW 14th Ave
NW 13th Ave
NW Kearney St
8 ●
(405)
PEARL DISTRICT
NW Broadway
NW 11th Ave
NW 10th Ave
OLD TOWN CHINATOWN
W Burnside St
SW Washington St
SW Alder St
MAX Light Rail
DOWNTOWN
SW Taylor St

Forest Park
NW Cornell Rd
NW Pittock Dr
WEST HILLS
NW Westover Rd
SW Kingston Dr
SW King Ave
SW 18th Ave

NW Barnes Rd
✿ 26
✿ 25   24 ✿
SW Fairview Blvd
27 ▲
28 ●
🐘 29
Washington Park
SW Kingston Dr
SW Flexar
SW Vista Ave
26
PORTLAND HEIGHTS

SW Patton Rd
SW Broadway Dr
30 ●
SW Bosch Rd
SW Patton Rd
99W
5
Oregon Health Sciences University
SW Terwilliger Blvd
SW Barbur Blvd

Portland State University
(405)
SW 11th Ave
SW Jefferson St
SW Columbia St
SW Clay St
SW Market St
SW Harrison St
SW Broadway
SW 6th Ave
SW 4th Ave
SW Front Ave
SW Main St

See Downtown Portland map

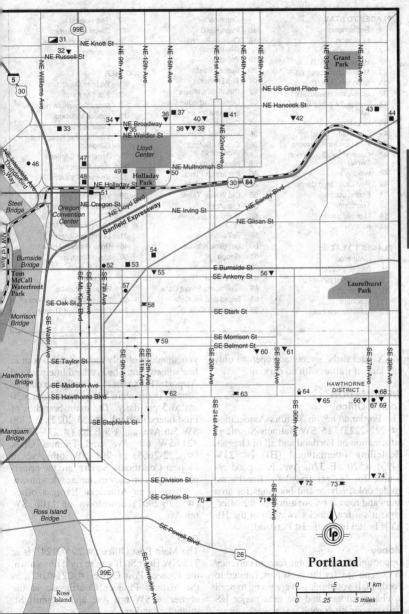

 OREGON

NE Knott St

NE Russell St

NE US Grant Place

NE Hancock St

Grant Park

NE Broadway

NE Weidler St

Lloyd Center

NE Multnomah St

Holladay Park

NE Holladay St

NE Oregon St

NE Lloyd Blvd

Oregon Convention Center

Banfield Expressway

NE Irving St

NE Sandy Blvd

NE Glisan St

Steel Bridge

Burnside Bridge

Tom McCall Waterfront Park

Morrison Bridge

Hawthorne Bridge

Marquam Bridge

Ross Island Bridge

E Burnside St

SE Ankeny St

SE Oak St

SE Stark St

Laurelhurst Park

SE Morrison St

SE Belmont St

SE Taylor St

SE Madison Ave

SE Hawthorne Blvd

SE Stephens St

HAWTHORNE DISTRICT

SE Division St

SE Clinton St

SE Powell Blvd

Ross Island

Portland

0       .5       1 km

0    .25    .5 miles

OREGON

| PLACES TO STAY | | | | | |
|---|---|---|---|---|---|
| 4 | Septembers | 14 | Delphina's | 70 | The Habitat |
| 6 | Wildwood | 16 | Papa Haydn | 72 | Santé Restaurant |
| 7 | Carriage Inn | 18 | Casa-U-Betcha | 73 | Third World Coffee |
| 12 | Heron Haus B&B | | (Northwest) | 74 | Indigine |
| 23 | MacMaster House B&B | 19 | Zefiros | | |
| 33 | Shilo Inn Lloyd Center | 20 | Basta's Pasta | **OTHER** | |
| 37 | Lion & the Rose B&B | 21 | The Ringside | 1 | Widmer Gasthaus |
| 41 | Portland's White House | 22 | Plainfield's Mayur | 3 | Fat Tire Farm |
| | B&B | 32 | Doris's Barbeque Cafe | 9 | Good Samaritan Hospital |
| 43 | Hojo Inn | 34 | Saigon Kitchen | 15 | Pittock Mansion |
| 44 | City Center Motel | 35 | Cadillac Cafe | 17 | Cinema 21 |
| 45 | Red Lion Inn/Coliseum | 36 | Ron Paul Charcuterie | 24 | International Rose Test |
| 47 | Comfort Inn Convention | 38 | Casa-U-Betcha | | Gardens |
| | Center | | (Northeast) | 25 | Japanese Gardens |
| 48 | Holiday Inn | 39 | Noodle Head | 26 | Hoyt Arboretum |
| 49 | Red Lion Lloyd Center | 40 | Paparazzi Pizza | 27 | Vietnam Veterans |
| 51 | Econo Lodge | 42 | Elizabeth's Cafe | | Memorial |
| 53 | Thriftlodge | 55 | Old Wives' Tales | 28 | World Forestry Center |
| 54 | Midtown Motel | 56 | Esparza's | 29 | Metro Washington Park |
| 64 | HI/AYH | 58 | Rimsky-Korsakoffee | | Zoo |
| | | | House | 30 | Metro Family YMCA |
| **PLACES TO EAT** | | 59 | Zell's | 31 | Dishman Center |
| 2 | L'Auberge | 60 | Bangkok Kitchen | 46 | Rose Garden Arena |
| 5 | Besaw's Cafe | 61 | Genoa | 50 | Lloyd Cinemas |
| 8 | BridgePort Brew Pub | 62 | Jarra's | 52 | East Avenue |
| 10 | Garbanzo's | 63 | Cafe Lena | 57 | La Luna |
| 11 | Misohapi | 65 | Hawthorne Street Cafe | 67 | Bagdad Theatre |
| 13 | Torrefazione Italia | 66 | Bread and Ink Cafe | 68 | Powell's Books for Cooks |
| | | 69 | Tabor Hill Cafe | 71 | Clinton Street Theate |

MAX tracks, the streets are open to only one lane of traffic, with no parking.

## INFORMATION
### Tourist Office
The Portland/Oregon Visitors Association (☎ 222-2223), 26 SW Salmon St, offers information on Portland and all of Oregon. Hostelling International (HI) (☎ 235-9493), 1520 SE 37th Ave, is a good resource for budget travelers. Brochures, guidebooks, advice and bookings for area tours and recreation are amongst the offerings; it's a few blocks away from the HI/AYH hostel in Southeast Portland.

### Money
Opportunities to exchange foreign currency in Oregon are, for the most part, limited to Portland. If you think you are going to need to change money and the next major US city on your itinerary is a few weeks away, you should probably make plans to wait in line somewhere. The Portland International Airport (PDX) has a foreign-exchange counter in the main lobby, open from 5:30 am to 5 pm daily. The main branches of First Interstate Bank (☎ 225-2022), at 1300 SW 5th Ave, and US Bank (☎ 275-7344), 321 SW 6th Ave, and Thomas Cook (☎ 222-2665) at 701 SW 6th Ave in Pioneer Courthouse Square, are the principal foreign-currency exchanges downtown.

There is an American Express office (☎ 226-2961) downtown at 1100 SW 6th Ave.

### Post
The Main Post Office (☎ 294-2124), is at 715 NW Hoyt St. If you're right downtown, the Pioneer Post Office (☎ 221-0282), in the historic Pioneer Courthouse at the corner of SW 6th Ave and Yamhill St, might be handier.

## Travel Agencies

Council Travel (☎ 228-1900, (800) 228-2854) at 715 SW Morrison St, specializes in student and discount travel. Journeys: A World Travel Company (☎ 226-7200), 1536 NW 23rd Ave, and Journeys at Powell's Travel Store (☎ 226-4849), 701 SW 6th Ave, both offer full-service ticketing, plus adventure and discount travel options.

## Bookstores

Portland is, by anyone's evaluation, one of the bookstore capitals of the USA. That people read so much here because it's always raining and dark is a frequently repeated canard. But no amount of flooding could really explain the success and quality of bookstores in Portland.

Megalithic and many-faced, Powell's City of Books is one of the nation's largest bookstores. The flagship store, known simply as the Burnside Store (☎ 228-4651, (800) 878-7323), 1005 W Burnside St, is a full city block of crowded bookshelves with over a million titles for sale. Powell's has become such a hangout that the Anne Hughes Coffee Shop, which is squeezed into a corner of the store, is as popular as most singles bars. Powell's City of Books is open from 9 am to 11 pm Monday to Saturday, until 9 pm on Sundays.

Not all Powell's Books stores are so big and imposing. Check out their specialty stores such as Powell's Technical Store (☎ 228-3906), only two blocks away at 33 NW Park St, Powell's Travel Store (☎ 228-1108), 701 SW 6th Ave, in Pioneer Courthouse Square, and Powell's Books for Cooks (☎ 235-3802), 3739 SE Hawthorne Blvd, which shares space with an Italian specialty food shop.

By no means do Portland's bookstore riches end with Powell's. Looking Glass Books (☎ 227-4760), 318 SW Taylor St, is a good general bookstore in downtown Portland. Nor'wester Bookshop (☎ 228-2747), 318 SW Washington St, is another small general store with a carefully selected inventory. Laughing Horse Books (☎ 236-2893), 3652 SE Division St, is Portland's best bookstore for readers on the political left. They also have a good selection of feminist and gay and lesbian titles. In Other Words (☎ 232-6003), 3437 SE Hawthorne Ave, offers new and used books by women writers, as well as video rentals.

Downtown used-book stores of note include Old Oregon Books (☎ 227-2742), 1128 SW Alder St, and Steve Holland's Books (☎ 224-4242), 527 SW 12th Ave. For a neighborhood full of used-book stores, try SE Hawthorne Blvd between 33rd and 38th Aves. Ask at any of these bookstores for a map of the neighborhood and its bookshops.

## Media

Portland's only daily newspaper is the *Oregonian*. There's both a morning and evening edition, though the latter is only available in downtown neighborhoods. The Friday *Oregonian* contains a weekly arts and entertainment section, called the *A&E*. *Willamette Week*, an alternative news-weekly, also contains full entertainment coverage; it's free and appears on Wednesdays. The principal gay/lesbian newspaper is a monthly called *Just Out*.

Oregon Public Radio is heard on 91.5 FM.

## Childcare

If you need a baby sitter while visiting Portland, contact NW Nannies (☎ 245-5288). They can provide childcare professionals to watch your child at your hotel. There are drop-in day care facilities at the Metro Family YMCA (☎ 294-3366), 2831 SW Barbur Blvd.

## Laundry

On the east side, go to the Washboard (☎ 236-4947), 2525 SE 20th Ave, where there are not only washers and dryers, but also an espresso bar and tanning salon.

## Medical Services

On the east side, go to Providence Medical Center (☎ 230-1111), 4805 NE Glisan St. On the west side, Good Samaritan Hospital and Health Center (☎ 229-7711), 1015 NW 22nd Ave, is the medical facility most

OREGON

convenient to downtown. Go to Good Samaritan Convenience Care Center (☎ 229-8090), at the same location, for minor illness and injuries; it's a lot cheaper and quicker than the emergency room, and is open from 9 am to 9 pm during the week, 10 am to 9 pm on weekends.

### Emergency

The Portland Police Station is at 1111 SW 2nd Ave.

### DOWNTOWN

Downtown Portland – busy, tree-filled and gregarious – is an urban success story. An activist city government began work in the 1970s to insure that Portland's business and nightlife did not flee the city center. The effort was largely successful, and downtown Portland is still vital and bustling. A cap on building height and a 1%-for-art program keep even the most modern areas human-sized and comfortable.

Any visitor to downtown should be armed with Powell's Walking Map of Downtown Portland. Free from any Powell's Bookstore and available from most hotels and information bureaus, the map charts a historical and architectural route through the city's center and provides hints for shoppers and travelers. Also available from information desks are more specialized map guides of local art galleries, public art and brewpubs.

If you don't have the walking tour map, the following sites are listed in an order that takes the visitor from the center of the city at Pioneer Courthouse Square, through a beautiful park flanked by historic civic buildings, down through the new commercial center and to the Willamette's waterfront park and marina. If you have time, an excursion into Oldtown and Chinatown is recommended for mavens of old architecture and colorful street life.

### Pioneer Courthouse Square

This red-brick plaza between SW Broadway and 6th Ave, and SW Morrison and Yamhill Sts, is usually regarded as the center of downtown Portland. A roaring fountain, a 'weather machine' sculpture and many levels of open-air seating bring people to the square to lounge, play music, eat lunch and gawk. Concerts, festivals, exhibits and rallies occur almost daily in summer, especially over the lunch hour.

On this block was one of Portland's grandest hotels; it fell into disrepair, and was torn down and replaced by a parking structure. When the city decided to build Pioneer Courthouse Square, downtown business interests blocked park funding. Grass-roots support for the square resulted in a program that encouraged citizens to buy and personalize the bricks that eventually built the square. As you walk across the square, read the names of the people whose contributions made the park possible.

Across 6th Ave is the **Pioneer Courthouse**. Built in 1875, this was the legal center of 19th-century Portland; the post office in its lobby is handy for city center visitors.

Most of downtown's principle shopping venues are within a two-block radius of Pioneer Courthouse Square.

### South Park Blocks

Many of Portland's most important museums and civic buildings are along the South Park Blocks, the 12-block-long greenway between SW Park and 9th Aves that runs through much of the downtown. Just as tempting to a traveler are the enormous old elms, beseeching flocks of pigeons and old, slumbering statues. This is a beautiful and leafy refuge from the bustle of downtown.

Facing Broadway, but backed up to the vernal South Park Blocks are the **Arlene Schnitzer Concert Hall** (☎ 228-1353 for concert information), home of the Oregon Symphony, and the **Portland Center for the Performing Arts**. The 'Schnitz,' as the symphony hall is known, is open only for performances, but the Center for Performing Arts is open during regular business hours. Stop by to check on performance schedules, and to admire the beautiful cherry-wood lobby. Both facilities face

## Portland's Public Art

The abundance of public art in Portland derives from city, county and state programs that require a certain percentage (usually 1%) of any major construction be set aside for public art. Pick up the brochure *Public Art Walking Tour*; it's $1 from area bookstores or information centers. Most public art is found along the 5th and 6th Ave Transit Mall, the South Park Blocks and near the Convention Center.

Many traditional commemorative statues are found in the South Park Blocks, though a number of more conceptual projects have slipped in since the park was refurbished in the 1980s. The South Park Blocks also flank the Portland Art Museum complex; note the amazing tromp l'oeil mural on the back of the Oregon Historical Center at Park Ave and Jefferson St.

The transit mall is lined with statues and fountains. Not to be missed is the enormous statue of the city's supposed protectress, Portlandia, which crouches above the entry of the Portland Building, at SE 5th Ave and Main St; on the building's second floor atrium is a display about Portland's public art and an information center. The mounted boulders, called Soaring Stones, outside Pioneer Place at Taylor St and 5th Ave, is known to locals as Stonehenge on a Stick.

Some of the most popular statues in the city are the bronze animals playing in the fountains surrounding the Pioneer Courthouse. The bronze female nude on 5th Ave near Washington St was made famous in the 1980's Expose Yourself To Art poster (featuring a former Portland mayor as a flasher).

As a river city, it's appropriate that Portland loves a fountain. The most notable is the Ira Keller Memorial Fountain at SW 4th Ave between Clay and Market Sts, in front of the Civic Auditorium, where a river's worth of water roars down a series of ledges. Salmon Springs Fountain, at the base of Salmon St, pulses and sprays according to an intricate, day-long schedule. Handsome Skidmore Fountain, located on SW 1st Ave under the Burnside Bridge, is one of Portland's oldest public art works, and was originally built as a watering trough for horses. ∎

onto SW Main St at Broadway; call 796-9295 for theater information.

The **Oregon Historical Society** (☎ 222-1741), 1200 SW Park St, maintains a museum, research library, press and bookstore in its complex along the South Park Blocks. Oregon's history is long and varied; at this oddly curated museum, it is not always represented very lucidly. The bookstore has a good collection of history books and regional travel guides. The complex is open from 10 am to 5 pm Tuesday to Saturday, and noon to 5 pm on Sunday. Admission is $4.50 for adults, $1.50 for children ages six to 16 and college students with ID, and $10 for families. Seniors enter free on Thursdays.

Across the park is the **Portland Art Museum** (☎ 226-2811), 1219 SW Park Ave. Its permanent exhibit of Northwest Native American carvings is especially good. The upper galleries contain a small but representative international collection.

Changing exhibits usually feature regional artists. The museum is open from 11 am to 5 pm Tuesday to Saturday, and 1 to 5 pm on Sunday. Admission is $5 for adults, $3.50 for seniors, and $2.50 children ages five to 16, except on the first Thursday of the month, when the museum is free from 4 to 9 pm. Pick up a schedule for the **Northwest Film Center**, which shows foreign and art films in a museum annex.

At the southern end of the Park Blocks is **Portland State University**. The park bustles with students between classes, and at lunch hour, when there's cheap and satisfying ethnic food sold from carts.

### Portland Building & Portlandia

Downtown Portland went through a building spurt during the 1980s that left the city with a vastly changed skyline and an international reputation for architectural innovation. No building has drawn more notoriety than the Portland Building at SW

OREGON

Union
Station
(Amtrak)

NW Kearney St
NW Johnson St
NW Irving St
405
NW Hoyt St
PEARL DISTRICT
NW Glisan St
NW Flanders St
NW Everett St
North
Park
Blocks
OLD TOWN & CHINATOWN
NW Davis St
NW Couch St
W Burnside St
SW Ankeny St
SW Ash St
SW Stark St
SW Morrison St
SW Washington St
SW Yamhill St
SW Taylor St
SW Alder St
Pioneer
Courthouse
Square
MAX Light Rail
Tom McCall
Waterfront
Park
South
Park
Blocks
SW Salmon St
SW Main St
SW Madison St
SW Jefferson St
Hawthorne
Bridge
SW Columbia St
SW Clay St
Portland
State
University
SW Market St
SW Mill St
SW Montgomery St
26
South
Park
Blocks
SW Harrison St
SW Hall St
SW College St
405
SW Jackson St
SW Montgomery St

**Downtown
Portland**

0        250        500 m
0        250        500 yards

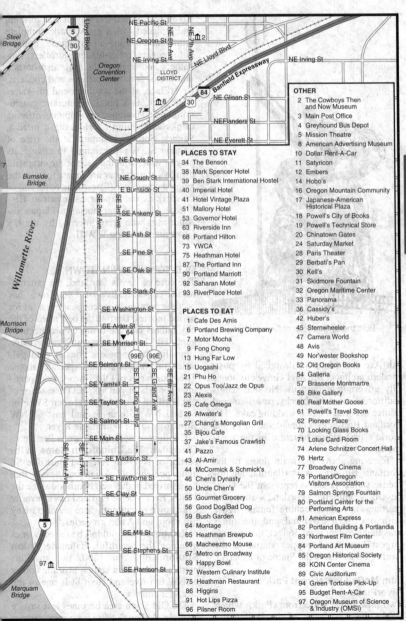

**OREGON**

**PLACES TO STAY**
34 The Benson
38 Mark Spencer Hotel
39 Ben Stark International Hostel
40 Imperial Hotel
41 Hotel Vintage Plaza
51 Mallory Hotel
53 Governor Hotel
63 Riverside Inn
68 Portland Hilton
73 YWCA
75 Heathman Hotel
87 The Portland Inn
90 Portland Marriott
92 Saharan Motel
93 RiverPlace Hotel

**PLACES TO EAT**
1 Cafe Des Amis
6 Portland Brewing Company
7 Motor Mocha
9 Fong Chong
13 Hung Far Low
15 Uogashi
21 Phu Ho
22 Opus Too/Jazz de Opus
23 Alexis
25 Cafe Omega
26 Atwater's
27 Chang's Mongolian Grill
35 Bijou Cafe
37 Jake's Famous Crawfish
41 Pazzo
43 Al-Amir
44 McCormick & Schmick's
46 Chen's Dynasty
50 Uncle Chen's
55 Gourmet Grocery
56 Good Dog/Bad Dog
59 Bush Garden
64 Montage
65 Heathman Brewpub
66 Macheezmo Mouse
67 Metro on Broadway
69 Happy Bowl
72 Western Culinary Institute
75 Heathman Restaurant
86 Higgins
91 Hot Lips Pizza
96 Pilsner Room

**OTHER**
2 The Cowboys Then and Now Museum
3 Main Post Office
4 Greyhound Bus Depot
5 Mission Theatre
8 American Advertising Museum
10 Dollar Rent-A-Car
11 Satyricon
12 Embers
14 Hobo's
16 Oregon Mountain Community
17 Japanese-American Historical Plaza
18 Powell's City of Books
19 Powell's Technical Store
20 Chinatown Gates
24 Saturday Market
28 Paris Theater
29 Berbati's Pan
30 Kell's
31 Skidmore Fountain
32 Oregon Maritime Center
33 Panorama
36 Cassidy's
42 Huber's
45 Sternwheeler
47 Camera World
48 Avis
49 Nor'wester Bookshop
52 Old Oregon Books
54 Galleria
57 Brasserie Montmartre
58 Bike Gallery
60 Real Mother Goose
61 Powell's Travel Store
62 Pioneer Place
70 Looking Glass Books
71 Lotus Card Room
74 Arlene Schnitzer Concert Hall
76 Hertz
77 Broadway Cinema
78 Portland/Oregon Visitors Association
79 Salmon Springs Fountain
80 Portland Center for the Performing Arts
81 American Express
82 Portland Building & Portlandia
83 Northwest Film Center
84 Portland Art Museum
85 Oregon Historical Society
88 KOIN Center Cinema
89 Civic Auditorium
94 Green Tortoise Pick-Up
95 Budget Rent-A-Car
97 Oregon Museum of Science & Industry (OMSI)

OREGON

Portlandia, Goddess of Commerce

5th Ave and Main St, designed by post-modern architect Michael Graves to house city government bureaus. No one seems indifferent about this blocky, pastel-colored edifice decorated like a wedding cake. The Portland Building is considered to be the world's first major structure in the post-modern style.

Towering above the main doors of the Portland Building is Portlandia, an immense statue meant to represent the Goddess of Commerce (Portland's supposed patroness). This crouching female figure with one hand extended and the other grasping a trident is, at 36 feet, the second-largest hammered copper statue in the world (the largest is the Statue of Liberty).

### Tom McCall Waterfront Park & RiverPlace

Two-mile-long Waterfront Park, which flanks the west bank of the Willamette River, was once a freeway. It was torn up, and replaced with a grassy park, complete with fountains and an esplanade. Popular with joggers, roller-bladers, strollers, sun-bathers and anglers, the park also hosts a number of summer festivals and concerts. RiverPlace, at the southern end of Water-front Park, is a hotel, restaurant, condo-minium and boutique development offering drinks and dining overlooking a marina. Salmon Springs Fountain, at the base of Salmon St, is programmed to change its play of water with the pace of the city; wild displays at rush hour are meant to calm the jangled commuter. Toward the north end of the park is the Japanese-American Historical Plaza, a memorial to Japanese-Americans who were interned by the US Government during WW II.

### OLD TOWN & CHINATOWN

The core of 1890s Portland, the tattered-on-the-edges reality of Old Town has become popular in recent years as a set for period movies. Despite the best plans of the city fathers and the district's architectural gems, Old Town resists gentrification. Missions for the homeless coexist with galleries, fine restaurants and specialty shops. The boundaries of Old Town vary depending upon whom you ask, but the essence of old Portland is captured between SW Pine St and NW Glisan St and east of NW Broadway to the Willamette River.

Contiguous with Old Town is Portland's Chinatown. The **Chinatown Gates**, at the corner of NW 4th Ave and Burnside St, announce the old Asian businesses that have thrived in this neighborhood since the 1880s. Everyone in Portland has a favorite Chinatown restaurant; there are also many gift shops and Asian groceries.

Rail travelers shouldn't be the only ones to enjoy the beautiful, Italianate **Union Station**. Built in 1890, the spacious marble-walled train station near the corner of NW 6th Ave and Hoyt St is one of the city's landmarks.

The Old Town area becomes less savory by night. Although there is no great danger, you may feel uncomfortable walking around alone. Taxiing in and out is probably a good idea.

## Saturday Market & Skidmore Fountain

A preserve of Victorian-era architecture, the district that surrounds the lovely Skidmore Fountain at SW 1st Ave and Ankeny St bustles on weekends when the Saturday Market (also open Sundays) sets up beneath the Burnside Bridge. Saturday Market is reputed to be the nation's largest outdoor craft fair. Street entertainers and ethnic food carts round out the carnival atmosphere. This seasonal market is in operation from the first weekend in March to Christmas Eve. The hours are from 10 am to 5 pm Saturdays, and 11 am to 4:30 pm Sundays.

Beside the fountain is **New Market Theatre**, built in 1871 as Portland's first theater for stage productions. Some of the city's oldest seafood restaurants share the neighborhood, as well as some of Portland's best art galleries.

## Oregon Maritime Center & Museum

Located at 113 SW Front Ave (between SW Ash and SW Ankeny Sts), this museum (☎ 224-7724) charts Portland's long history as a seaport and ship-building center. The museum is open Friday to Sunday from 11 am to 4 pm. May to October, it's open Wednesday to Sunday from 11 am to 4 pm. Admission is $2 for adults, $1.25 for seniors and students. Children under eight are free.

## WEST HILLS & WASHINGTON PARK

Behind downtown Portland are the West Hills, a ridge of ancient volcanic peaks that divide Portland from her westerly suburbs. Some of the city's most beautiful homes are ledged on the forested West Hills, overlooking downtown and distant Mt Hood. Here also is the enormous Washington Park complex that includes the city's zoo and rose gardens, with hiking access to larger wilderness parks and historic buildings. On a clear day, this is one of Portland's greatest glories.

To reach Washington Park and associated sites, take Tri-Met bus No 63 from downtown's SW Washington St. To reach the park by car, take the zoo exit off of Hwy 26, or follow signs for the Rose Gardens off W Burnside St at Tichner Drive.

## International Rose Test Gardens

Here is one of the reasons that Portland is called the Rose City. One of the nation's oldest rose gardens, and certainly one of the most stunningly situated, the rose gardens sprawl across 4.5 acres of manicured lawns, fountains and flower beds.

More than just a beautiful public park, the rose gardens are also the testing grounds for the American Rose Society and All-America Rose selections. Over 400 rose varieties are contained in the permanent gardens, including many old and rare varieties. From June to September, the scent and colors are almost overpowering.

## Japanese Gardens

Further uphill, past the tennis courts, this tranquil and intimate formal garden (☎ 223-4070) encompasses five acres of tumbling water, pools of koe, flowers, a tea house, a sand garden and views east onto Mt Hood. Admission to the Japanese Garden is $5 for adults, and $2.50 for seniors and students (including college students with valid ID). Children ages five and under are free. The garden is open from 10 am to 6 pm, April to May and the full month of September; hours are from 9 am to 8 pm, June to August; and from 10 am to 4 pm, October to March. Tours are available at 10:45 am and 2:30 pm, April to October.

## Metro Washington Park Zoo

In summer ride the Zoo Train from the rose gardens to Metro Washington Park Zoo (or follow Kingston Rd up the hill). The zoo (☎ 226-1561), 4001 SW Canyon Rd, is one of Portland's premier attractions. Exhibits focus on ecosystems and the interrelationships of animal life and the environment. Of special note are the zoo's Asian elephants; the Portland zoo main-

OREGON

tains one of the world's most successful elephant breeding programs. Inquire about summer concerts on the zoo's terraced lawns. To reach the zoo from downtown, follow Hwy 26 west one mile and take the zoo exit.

Admission to the zoo is $5.50 for adults, $4 for seniors 65 and over, and $3.50 for children ages three to 11 (children two and younger are free). Be aware that the zoo's free admission after 3 pm on the second Tuesday of every month has its downside: entry so late in the afternoon doesn't make for much more than an express tour of the park, especially during the fall-winter season. Zoo hours are from 9:30 am to 5 pm, April 3 to May 27; 9:30 am to 6 pm, May 28 to September 5; and 9:30 am to 4 pm, September 6 to April 2.

### World Forestry Center

Sharing the parking lot with the zoo is the World Forestry Center (☎ 228-1367), an educational facility that promotes understanding of the world's forests, their ecosystems and forestry industries. Opening hours are from 10 am to 5 pm daily; admission is $3 for adults, $2 for youth ages six to 18 and seniors 62 and up.

### Oregon Vietnam Veterans Living Memorial

Next to the zoo are these spiraling black granite slabs, inscribed with details of events and circumstances in both Vietnam and Oregon, conjuring up the memories of the tumultuous Vietnam War years.

### Hoyt Arboretum

Nine miles of trails wind through Hoyt Arboretum, a ridge-top tree garden above the zoo that features the world's largest collection of conifers, and many other labeled plants and trees. Pick up a map at the Tree House Visitor Center (☎ 228-8733), 4000 Fairview Blvd, open daily from 9 am to 3 pm. The park itself is open daily from 6 am to 10 pm.

### Forest Park

From the arboretum and Washington Park,

hiking trails join these more formal parks with Forest Park, which is part of a seven-sq-mile complex that comprises the largest urban wilderness area in any US city. Another handy entry to the park is at the western terminus of NW Upshur St. See the Activities section, below, for hiking information.

Wildlife watchers will want to visit the facilities of the **Portland Audubon Society** (☎ 292-6855), located in a gulch of Forest Park, 5151 NW Cornell Rd. Opening hours are from 10 am to 6 pm Monday to Saturday, and 10 am to 5 pm on Sundays. Below the excellent bookstore and information center is a 100-acre sanctuary in which to observe birds and other wildlife.

### Pittock Mansion

Also in the West Hills is Pittock Mansion (☎ 823-3624), 3229 NW Pittock Drive, built in 1914 by the then-editor of the *Oregonian* newspaper. Guided tours of this grand, 22-room house are available, but it is also worth a visit on a clear day simply for the spectacular views to the east. The house is open from noon to 4 pm daily; admission is $4 for adults, $3.50 for seniors 65 and over, and $1.50 for youth ages six to 18. Children under six are free.

### EAST SIDE
### Oregon Museum of Science & Industry (OMSI)

The OMSI (☎ 797-4000), 1945 SE Water Ave, has moved to its new location, across the Willamette from downtown. At its new home an Omnimax theater joins the museum's venerable exhibits about science and technology. Museum hours are from 9:30 am to 5:30 pm Saturday to Wednesday, and 9:30 am to 9 pm on Thursday and Friday. There's also a river-side cafe. Admission is adults/seniors $7/6; children ages three to 17, $4.50. There are separate entrance fees and hours for the theater and museum. Call OMSI's pre-recorded information line (above) to find out about the latest theater showings and special events.

### The Cowboys Then & Now Museum

This Portland museum (☎ 731-3333), 729 NE Oregon St, adjacent to a shopping center, commemorates the life and era of the Old West. The easiest way to find it is to take MAX to the 7th Ave station; it's one block to the north. It's open from 11 am to 5 pm Wednesday to Friday, and noon to 5 pm on weekends (closed Monday and Tuesday). Admission is free, although donations are gratefully accepted.

### American Advertising Museum

This museum (☎ 226-0000), at 524 NE Grand Ave, is apparently the country's only showcase devoted to the art of promotion. Its permanent exhibit charts the evolution of advertising over the past 100 years. Its hours are from 11 am to 5 pm Wednesday to Friday, and noon to 5 pm Saturday and Sunday. Regular admission is $3; seniors and children ages six to 12 pay only $1.50.

### Public Gardens & Parks

Portland's east side offers a rich variety of green space. Laurelhurst Park, near the corner of SE 39th Ave and Oak St, is a beautiful urban park, with a large duck pond, towering conifers, playgrounds and picnicking. Mt Tabor Park, near the corner of SE 69th Ave and Yamhill St, boasts of being the only city park in the country that's also an extinct volcano. Heavily forested, it's a great place to have a picnic, or to unleash pets and kids. Crystal Springs Lake, near lovely Reed College at SE 28th Ave and SE Woodstock St, is popular in early spring for the amazing display of flowering shrubs at its Rhododendron Garden. There are more than two thousand full-grown rhododendrons and azaleas here. The park winds past duck-filled ponds and streams. The Grotto (☎ 254-7371), NE 85th Ave at Sandy Blvd, is a religious retreat also known as the Sanctuary of Our Sorrowful Mother; it's open from 9 am to 5:30 pm daily. In addition to an outdoor shrine, the beautiful grounds of the Servite Monastery are maintained as a public sanctuary. Stream-side Leach Botanical Park (☎ 761-9503), 6704 SE 122nd Ave near Foster Rd, is a lovely five-acre estate now maintained by the city for its collection of rare plants. It's open to public scrutiny 9 am to 4 pm Tuesday through Saturday.

### HIKING

In Portland's West Hills, **Forest Park** offers hikers 30 miles of trails in one of the largest urban parks in the country. Several trails begin near the World Forestry Center: the **Wildwood Trail**, which winds for miles through deep forest, and the **40-Mile Loop**, a series of trails that link 35 state and city parks circling Portland. A map of the trail system is available from the City Parks Department (☎ 823-2223), on the 4th floor of the Portland Building, 1120 SW 5th Ave. Another trailhead begins at the western end of NW Upshur St.

Out past Lewis & Clark College in Southwest Portland is **Tryon Creek State Park** (☎ 653-3166), 11321 SW Terwilliger Blvd, with eight miles of trails. Stream-side wildlife include beavers and songbirds. In late March there are wondrous displays of trillium, a wild marsh lily.

### BIKING

Portland does its best to be bike-friendly. A map of metro-area bike routes is available from bike shops or Powell's Travel Store. Mountain bikers need go no further than the Leif Ericson Drive in Forest Park for an exhilarating backwoods workout. NW Upshur St (one block south of NW Vaughn St) is the best access to the trail for bikes.

For bicycle rentals, see the Getting Around section at the end of this chapter. You can repair bikes at the Bicycle Repair Collective (☎ 233-0564), 4438 SE Belmont St.

### SWIMMING

The following public indoor pools are open year round and are convenient to downtown: Dishman Center (☎ 823-3673), 77 NE Knott St; Buckman Pool (☎ 823-3668), 320 SE 16th Ave; and the Metropolitan Learning Center (☎ 823-3671), 2033 NW Glisan St. In summer, the outdoor pool at

OREGON

US Grant Park (☎ 823-3674), near the corner of NE 33rd Ave and US Grant St, is a great place for hot kids.

Public beaches and swimming along the Willamette and Columbia rivers are popular in summer. Sellwood Riverfront Park, on the east end of the Sellwood Bridge, is a good place for a picnic and a wade in the Willamette River (there's also an outdoor pool). Ten miles north of Portland, the beaches along the east side of Sauvie Island are also popular, and are reached from Hwy 30. Nude sunbathing becomes the norm the further north you go.

## GOLF

There are dozens of golf courses and driving ranges in the Portland Metro area; contact the chamber of commerce for a complete listing.

One of the city's best and most central is the Eastmoreland Golf Course (☎ 775-2900) 2425 SE Bybee Blvd. This 18-hole municipal course and driving range is nationally recognized. As it was founded in 1918, the grounds provide mature and beautiful landscaping. Another well-respected, city-owned course is Heron Lakes Golf Course (☎ 289-1818), 3500 N Victory Rd. At Heron Lakes, there are 27 holes, with fairways and traps to challenge the most complacent golfer.

## ORGANIZED TOURS

Walking tours of downtown Portland are usually offered each summer by some entrepreneurial citizen; contact the visitors center for information.

Gray Line Buses (☎ 285-9845) conduct guided bus tours of Portland during the summer; they also host tours to other northwest Oregon sites.

Explore Portland's maritime past and present on a riverboat or yacht cruise. The sternwheeler *Columbia Gorge* (☎ 223-3928), 1200 SW Front Ave, offers weekend tours of Portland's waterfront ($8.95 to $10.95); call for times and special seasonal cruises. Rose City Riverboat Cruises (☎ 234-6665), RiverPlace Marina, offers daily tours of Portland's riverfront

($10.50), and weekend tours of the Willamette River to the falls at Oregon City ($22).

## SPECIAL EVENTS

Portlanders have almost a pathological need to create festivals. At some point during the year, nearly every nationality and interest group claims a public park to celebrate their heritage with food, drink and music. Below are some of the many parties and gatherings that the city throws for itself. Contact the visitors center, for current information and a complete listings of events.

### Portland Rose Festival

The city's doyen of festivals and its oldest civic event is the Portland Rose Festival, held in early June. The beautiful floral display at the Rose Gardens is the nominal excuse for nearly two weeks of festivities, but the real focus of events are the parades (the Grand Floral is the second-largest floral parade in the nation), the riverfront carnival, immense naval ships docked right downtown, the crowning of the Rose Queen and the feeling of celebration in the air. Contact the Rose Festival (☎ 227-2681) for a schedule of events.

### Summer Celebrations

Portland's Gay Pride Parade & Celebration takes place in late June, and attracts almost 10,000 participants; contact Stonewall Northwest (☎ 223-1656) for more information.

In early July the Waterfront Blues Festival (☎ 282-0555) brings life to downtown's

The sternwheeler *Columbia Gorge*

riverside park. Later in the month, the region's beer-makers take over the waterfront festival grounds for the Oregon Brewers Festival. Stay late for live music. Call 241-7179 for details.

In early August, the Mt Hood Jazz Festival (☎ 666-3810) attracts nationally-recognized artists to Mt Hood Community College in Gresham, 12 miles east of Portland; call for details. A celebration of Portland's restaurants, called The Bite (☎ 248-0600) takes place in August on the Waterfront. Eat your fill and then rock out to local bands late into the night.

Over Labor Day in early September, downtown Portland is converted into ArtQuake (☎ 227-2787), the city's festival of fine and performing arts. Pioneer Courthouse Square becomes the sound stage for musical acts, while the rest of downtown is gridlocked with tents brimming with crafts and art.

## PLACES TO STAY

Lodging in Portland is a little idiosyncratic. Apart from the hostels, it's worth paying a little extra and staying in a reasonable hotel. Some dives really are dives.

There's often not a lot of price difference between a moderate hotel and its more luxurious neighbor, especially when special weekend rates kick in. If you plan to be in Portland on a weekend, call and ask about weekend packages at hotels that you wouldn't normally be able to afford.

The following have been selected with convenience to downtown as a guiding criterion. Outside of the central city, chain motels can be easily found clustered at freeway exits; on the east side, along 82nd Ave near the airport, is a strip of inexpensive motels.

## Camping

Portland is not very amenable to campers. If you are planning to visit downtown Portland, be prepared for a long commute from your campsite. For RV campsites in the Portland Metro area, check out *Fairview RV Park* (☎ 661-1047), 21401 NE Sandy Blvd, along the Columbia River near the

suburb of Gresham; it's 15 miles to downtown. Sites here are $21.50 per day. *Jantzen Beach RV Park* (☎ 289-7626), off I-5 exit No 308, a half mile west on Hayden Island Rd, is across the Columbia River from Vancouver, WA; it's eight miles to downtown. Hook-ups are $20 to $22.

Tent campers will certainly be more comfortable at attractive campgrounds in slightly more distant state parks. South of Portland about 25 miles, *Champoeg State Park* (☎ 678-1251) is a cradle of early Northwest history, and offers campsites in a beautiful riverside setting. Hiking, museums and bike trails complete the package; Champoeg is west of I-5 exit No 282. *Milo McIver State Park* (☎ 630-7150) stretches along the Clackamas River in a quiet sylvan setting. Exit I-205 at Hwy 224 and head east about 12 miles towards Estacada.

## Hostels

The *Portland International AYH Hostel* (☎ 236-3380), 3031 SE Hawthorne Blvd at 30th Ave, offers 47 beds to travelers in a great location in one of the city's most dynamic and youthful neighborhoods. Lodging is $12 for members, $15 for non-members. Take bus No 14 from downtown. Reservations are recommended in summer.

The downtown *YWCA* (☎ 223-6281), 1111 SW 10th Ave, offers women low-cost lodging, both dormitory and single rooms. Rates start from $7.63 for dormitory, BYOB-lodging (Bring Your Own sleeping Bag), and peak at $27.25 for sharing one of two rooms with a semi-private bath.

The *Ben Stark International Hostel* (☎ 274-1223), 1022 SW Stark St, is an old downtown hotel that has re-invented itself as a no-frills lodging. It's in the heart of the gay bar district, so be prepared for a slightly noisy but colorful stay. Singles/doubles cost $40/46.

## B&Bs

The stately old neighborhoods that ring downtown Portland contain a number of grand B&B inns. For a complete listing of area B&Bs, contact one of the following booking agencies: B&B Northwest (☎ 243-7616) or BJC B&B Reservations & Referral Service (☎ 281-9459). The visitors center also has up-to-date listings of B&Bs.

If you want to book your own B&B, then the following are among Portland's finest. On the east side, *Portland's White House*, (☎ 287-7131) 1914 NE 22nd Ave, offers six guest rooms, some with private baths, in a beautiful Greek Revival mansion. Rooms range from $96 to $112. The *Lion & the Rose* (☎ 287-9245, (800) 955-9247), 1810 NE 15th, is a fanciful, turreted Queen Anne mansion, and offers five guest rooms between $80 and $120. Both establishments are close to Lloyd Center.

On the west side, *Heron Haus* (☎ 274-1846), 2545 NW Westover Rd, is in a fabulous Tudor-style home in one of the city's most exclusive neighborhoods. Each of the six guest rooms has a private bath; prices range from $85 to $145. Within walking distance of the rose gardens is *MacMaster House* (☎ 223-7362), 1041 SW Vista Ave. There are six rooms, two with private bath; prices range from $70 to $100.

## Hotels

**Bottom End** Some older motor hotels offer a good value and clean rooms near the city center. *Saharan Motel* (☎ 226-7646), 1889 SW 4th Ave, is near Portland State University, just south of the city center. Singles/doubles are $32/36. *Midtown Motel* (☎ 234-0316), 1415 NE Sandy Blvd, $22/25, is across the Burnside Bridge from downtown. Even closer to downtown across the Willamette River is the *Thriftlodge* (☎ 234-8411), 949 E Burnside St, where rooms are $44/49.

Quieter, and in dynamic northwest Portland is the *Carriage Inn* (☎ 224-0543), 2025 NW Northrup St, singles/doubles are $42/45.

*Hojo Inn* (☎ 288-6891), 3939 NE Hancock St, with rooms for $40/42, and the *City Center Motel* (☎ 287-1107), 3800 NE Sandy Blvd, at $40/45, are a quick commute east of downtown off I-84's Hollywood exit.

**Middle** Right downtown, the face-lifted *Imperial Hotel* (☎ 228-7221), 400 SW Broadway, has single/double rooms at $65/70, and is convenient to downtown restaurants, shopping an entertainment. Likewise, the *Mallory Hotel* (☎ 223-6311), 729 SW 15th Ave, is only blocks away from the city center and offers free parking; rooms cost $65/70. Another good deal downtown is the *Mark Spencer Hotel* (☎ 224-3293), 409 SW 11th Ave, at $53/57. Ask for river-view rooms at the *Riverside Inn* (☎ 221-0711), 50 SW Morrison St, at the base of the Morrison Bridge. Single/double rooms are $75/85.

Another cluster of moderately priced hotels is found just across the Willamette River, between downtown and the Lloyd Center, within easy walking distance of the Convention Center. The *Red Lion Inn/Coliseum* (☎ 235-8311) is right on the Willamette River, 1225 N Thunderbird Way, singles/doubles are $72/77. *Shilo Inn Lloyd Center* (☎ 231-7665), 1506 NE 2nd Ave charges $60/70. The following hotels are right on the MAX lines, seconds away from the Convention Center: the *Comfort Inn Convention Center* (☎ 233-7933), 431 NE Multnomah St, at $59/62; the *Holiday Inn* (☎ 235-2100), 1021 NE Grand Ave, at $55/60; and the *Econo Lodge* (☎ 234-4391), (800) 424-4777), 518 NE Holladay, at $50/55.

Back downtown, but a bit pricier *The Portland Inn* (☎ 221-1611), 1414 SW 6th Ave, offers a pool and its own coffeeshop, with rooms for $70/75. The *Portland Marriott* (☎ 226-7600), 1401 SW Front St, at $79/85, and the *Portland Hilton* (☎ 226-1611), 921 SW 6th Ave, at $75/80, offer the facilities you'd expect from major international hotels.

**Top End** If it's time for a splurge, Portland offers a few classic old hotels with first-class service and amenities – and some of the best restaurants in the city. Prices for lodgings in these hotels are affected by room availability or the particular day of the week you stay, and many offer great weekend package deals.

The *Heathman Hotel* (☎ 241-4100), 1001 SW Broadway, is one of the city's finest. The Heathman's service is legendary: when Pavarotti stayed here, the Heathman prevailed on the city to stop daytime construction nearby so that the tenor could rest before his performance. Single/double rates are $105/115. *The Benson* (☎ 228-2000), 309 SW Broadway, with a lobby filled with chandeliers and lined with walnut, is another old showcase Portland hotel; it has undergone an update and makeover. Rooms range from $130 to $205. Topped by penthouse suites, the *Hotel Vintage Plaza* (☎ 228-1212), 422 SW Broadway, $120 to $210, and the art-deco *Governor Hotel* (☎ 224-3400), at the corner of SW 10th Ave and Alder St, $140 to $170, are examples of old neglected hotel buildings that have undergone complete renovation to emerge as beautiful, luxury accommodations, without losing their period charm.

New and right on the waterfront is the *RiverPlace Hotel* (☎ 228-3233), 1510 SW Harbor Way, $165/170. Ask for a room overlooking the marina. Across the Willamette River, near both Lloyd Center and the Convention Center, the *Red Lion Lloyd Center* (☎ 281-6111), 1000 NE Multnomah St, is the east side's nicest hotel. Rooms range from $115 to $145.

## PLACES TO EAT

Portland offers a wide variety of dining options, ranging from ethnic restaurants to classic American steak houses. The city's best food, whatever its origins, shares a concern for fresh, local ingredients and an often eclectic mingling of food traditions.

Light meals are often served at coffeehouses and brewpubs; see the Entertainment section, below, for listings.

### Downtown & Old Town

**Budget** *Bijou Cafe* (☎ 222-3187), 132 SW 3rd Ave, is Portland's favorite downtown place to eat breakfast. At lunch, they serve sandwiches and luncheon specials. *Macheezmo Mouse* (☎ 228-3491), 723 SW Salmon St and other metro locations, offers cheap and healthy Mexican food in a wildly decorated storefront. Most entrees are under $5.

Sausage lovers need go no further than *Good Dog/Bad Dog* (☎ 222-3410), 708 SW Alder St. Extremely meaty and spicy dogs of all descriptions make a quick and hearty meal for less than $5. Along SW Alder St, between 10th and 12th Aves, is a strip of cheap, quite good ethnic restaurants, ranging from Mexican, to Thai, to Indian. You will be hard-pressed to spend more than $8 a plate for dinner at any of these small, family-owned restaurants.

If you want a choice of quick foods and a look at local youth, go to *Metro on Broadway*, at the corner of SW Taylor St and Broadway, a small, hospitable food court. Late-night coffee and desserts are popular.

*Happy Bowl* (☎ 223-0809), 937 SW 5th Ave, offers cheap, tasty Asian food to go. Fill up on noodles for $3. One of Portland's best dining values is *Chang's Mongolian Grill* (☎ 243-1991), 1 SW 3rd Ave, where for one price ($5.95 at lunch, $8.50 at dinner) the customer selects a variety of fresh ingredients from an all-you-can-eat buffet, which is then seared on braziers.

If you have a picnic in mind, go to *Gourmet Grocery* (☎ 222-5495), 619 SW Park Ave, for good deli sandwiches and salads.

There are any number of pizzerias in Portland; arguably the best in downtown is *Hot Lips Pizza* (☎ 224-0311), 1909 SW 6th Ave, near Portland State University. Have pizza or focaccia by the slice, or order a custom pizza from such selections as goat cheese, prosciutto, apples, blue cheese, fresh herbs and sun-dried tomatoes; it offers free delivery downtown.

**Middle** *Bush Garden* (☎ 226-7181), 900 SW Morrison St, features a sushi bar and tatami table service. In Old Town, *Uogashi* (☎ 242-1848), 107 NW Couch St, features sushi and traditional Japanese specialties. Salmon sashimi goes for $10; vegetable tempura is $12.

*Uncle Chen's* (☎ 248-1199), 529 SW 3rd Ave, and *Chen's Dynasty* (☎ 248-9491),

622 SW Washington St, both offer very good and often innovative Chinese cuisine. Other Chinese restaurants line the blocks between Burnside and Everett Sts, and between NW 2nd and 4th Aves in Old Town/Chinatown. Explore on your own, or try *Fong Chong* (☎ 220-0235), 301 NW 4th Ave, for dim sum, *Phu Ho* (☎ 229-1888), 28 NW 4th Ave, for seafood, and *Hung Far Low* (☎ 223-8686), 112 NW 4th Ave, which is open all night and hums with night owls.

*Al-Amir* (☎ 274-0010), 223 SW Stark St, serves delicious Lebanese food in a delightful old building that was once the residence of Portland's Catholic Archbishop. A generous dinner portion of succulent lamb kabobs costs $12. *Alexis* (☎ 224-8577), 215 W Burnside St, is a fixture of Old Town, serving up well-prepared and generously portioned Greek food in a lively ambiance.

For a unique experience, go to the *Western Culinary Institute* (☎ 223-2245), 1316 SW 13th Ave, where chefs-in-training cook and serve meals for their willing, and sometimes understanding, customers. A five-course lunch goes for $7.95; reservations are required. *Higgins* (☎ 222-9070), 1239 SW Broadway, close to the Performing Arts Center, offers stylish ingredients and innovative preparations without high prices. Pork loin with a fig and ginger compote costs $13.

**Top End** Portland's most famous restaurant may not be its greatest, but *Jake's Famous Crawfish* (☎ 226-1419), 401 SW 12th Ave, captures more of the city's charm and esprit than fussier locales. Fresh seafood, steak, and a vibrant bar scene make this vintage landmark perennially popular. The same menu and atmosphere pervade Jake's sister restaurant, *McCormick & Schmick's* (☎ 224-7522), at the corner of SW 1st Ave and Oak St. Prices at these two bastions of traditional Portland cooking vary (there's usually a choice of nearly 25 fresh fish and seafood varieties), but $15 to $17 will buy a great meal and lots of atmosphere at either location. At McCormick &

Schmick's, there's an early-bird menu, available between 5 and 6:30 pm only, with daily fish specials in the $9 range.

*Opus Too* (☎ 222-6077), 33 NW 2nd Ave, is another seafood institution and one of Portland's best-loved restaurants, offering plenty of Old Portland atmosphere, live jazz and a wide selection of fresh fish; prices range from $15 to $20.

Don't always mistrust hotel restaurants. The *Heathman Restaurant* (☎ 241-4100), 1001 SW Broadway, serves the city's most refined and provocative dishes, and is probably the exemplar of oft-cited Pacific Northwest cuisine. Dishes like seared salmon with wasabi béarnaise sauce fetch $20. (The Heathman also serves a wonderful afternoon tea.) *Pazzo* (☎ 228-1515), 627 SW Washington St, in the Hotel Vintage Plaza offers downtown Portland's best Italian cooking. The designer pizzas are a real knockout at lunch ($7 to $9); dinner specials like cod cheeks and spring vegetable risotto cost around $17.

*Atwater's* (☎ 275-3600), 111 SW 5th Ave, offers fine dining 30 floors above the city in the Bankcorp Tower. Local rack of lamb, served with wild mushroom polenta, costs $24.

For the city's best Indian cuisine, you'll need to venture a bit out of downtown to *Plainfield's Mayur* (☎ 223-2995), 852 SW 21st Ave, housed in a refurbished grand Victorian home. For a full, multi-coursed Indian meal it's easy to spend $25 a head.

### Northwest Portland

One of the most-frenzied shopping areas of Portland by day, by evening the Northwest shifts gears and opens for dinner. Coffeehouses, brewpubs and wine bars are abundant and offer cheap snacks and refreshments. Be warned: Northwest Portland is often a nightmare for parking.

**Budget** For the neighborhood's best breakfast, head to *Besaw's Cafe* (☎ 228-2619), 2301 NW Savier St. Cleverly named *Misohapi* (☎ 226-4875), 914 NW 23rd Ave, offers good, inexpensive bento and Japanese light entrees. For a quick and easy neal, the Lebanese-style entrees at *Garzonzos* (☎ 227-4196), at the corner of NW 21st Ave and Lovejoy St, are a good value; a falafel sandwich is $4.

**Middle** For one of Northwest Portland's liveliest, spiciest experiences try the revisionist Mexican food at *Casa-U-Betcha* (☎ 222-4833), 612 NW 21st Ave. Traditional tortilla-based dinners are less than $9; more innovative dishes (wild boar and sausage stew) go for $12.

Though the architecture reveals the restaurant's former existence as a drive-in, *Basta's Pasta* (☎ 274-1572), 410 NW 21st St, serves up good, inexpensive pasta; the fettucine with fresh porcini mushrooms goes for $8. Basta's country-style bread is among the best in town. Busy and dependable *Delphina's* (☎ 211-1195), 2112 NW Kearney St, serves Italian entrees and pizza.

Though most come to *Papa Haydn* (☎ 228-7317), 701 NW 23rd Ave, for the incredible desserts, light meals and salads are very good and inexpensive.

**Top End** One of the city's best restaurants, trendy *Zefiros* (☎ 226-3394), 500 NW 21st Ave, features eclectic, Continental-influenced cuisine in a see/be-seen atmosphere.

You don't usually think of Australia when you think of Pacific Rim cuisine, but at *Septembers* (☎ 497-1097), 2330 NW Thurman St, amazing things happen when Aussies prepare Northwest Cuisine. Salmon poached in champagne and served with lobster roe and spinach cream is $17. Equally trendy and spendy is the dining room at *Wildwood Restaurant* (☎ 248-9663), 1221 NW 21st Ave, where noisy crowds of Northwest style-setters graze on ingredient-du-jour cuisine.

For French cuisine in a homey, country atmosphere, go to *Cafe des Amis* (☎ 295-6487), 1987 NW Kearney St. There's a bistro menu set at the $10 range, and pricier full dinners (such as filet mignon with garlic and port sauce) for $18 and thereabouts. *L'Auberge* (☎ 223-3302),

2601 NW Vaughn St, hearkens back to the French provinces for its inspiration. Its four-course feast, starring such favorites as filet mignon with onion marmalade, costs $36. You can also order a la carte dinners for about half the fun and money. On Sunday nights, you can sit in the quaint L'Auberge bar, watch old movies on TV, and mow through one of the best burgers this side of eternity.

For decades Portland's traditional choice for steak and prime rib has been *The Ringside* (☎ 223-1513), 2165 W Burnside St. The onion rings here are legendary, and the prime rib ($19.75) is about as good as red meat gets.

### Northeast Portland

Northeast Broadway near Lloyd Center is filling up with trendy eateries; stand at the corner of 15th Ave and Broadway and survey your choices.

**Budget** For breakfast and a no-fuss lunch, go to the *Cadillac Cafe* (☎ 287-4750), 914 NE Broadway. People in Portland argue over the best, inexpensive Vietnamese restaurant and *Saigon Kitchen* (☎ 281-3669), 835 NE Broadway, which also features Thai dishes, is always a top contender. Main dishes cost around $9. For value and spice, it's hard to beat *Noodle Head* (☎ 282-8424), 1708 NE Broadway, where nouvelle-cuisine-y Asian noodle dishes are served in heaping portions; you can easily fill up at dinner for $8. At *Paparazzi Pizza* (☎ 281-7701), 2015 NE Broadway, the emphasis is on real pizza – no pineapple or blue cheese here.

**Middle** *Casa-U-Betcha* (☎ 282-4554), 1700 NE Broadway, offers its cutting-edge Mexican food in wildly tiled surroundings. *Ron Paul Charcuterie* (☎ 284-5347), 1441 NE Broadway, offers light meals and desserts in a bistro-like atmosphere. By the time you assemble a meal out of various salads and entree specials, it's easy to spend $10 to $12. *Doris's Barbeque Cafe* (☎ 287-9249), 352 NE Russell St, offers Southern specialties and some of the city's

OREGON

best ribs: they're so messy that bibs are mandatory.

**Top End** Further up on Broadway, and higher up on the food chain, is *Elizabeth's Cafe* (☎ 281-8337), 3135 NE Broadway, where the cuisine is innovative and the atmosphere homey. Duck with walnuts, peas and blood-orange sauce goes for $16. There's outdoor seating during decent weather.

### Southeast Portland

**Budget** The funky, eclectic neighborhoods of Southeast Portland are where you would legitimately expect to find comfortable, cheap cafes, bakeries and coffeehouses. *Hawthorne Street Cafe* (☎ 232-4982), 3354 SE Hawthorne Blvd, in a refurbished old mansion, is popular for breakfast. It's very near the Hawthorne AYH hostel. Another neighborhood breakfast joint of choice is *Zell's* (☎ 239-0196), 1300 SE Morrison St.

One of the most popular scenes in this part of town is *Montage* (☎ 234-1324), 301 SE Morrison St. Open from 6 pm to 4 am, Montage is a creole nightspot with delicious, inexpensive dishes that you can assemble into a snack or a full meal, all while watching the arty creatures of the night. Vegetarian jambalaya goes for $7.

**Middle** *Tabor Hill Cafe* (☎ 230-1231), 3610 SE Hawthorne Blvd, and the *Bread & Ink Cafe* (☎ 239-4756), 3766 SE Hawthorne Blvd, are both fixtures, and popular for lunches and light dinners. Pasta, chicken and seafood dishes are the norm at both venues; prices for a full dinner range between $10 and $12. Known mostly for its desserts, *Papa Haydn* (☎ 232-9400), 5829 SE Milwaukie Ave, is also a great place for lunch or light dinners.

*Santé Restaurant* (☎ 233-4340), 3000 SE Division St, sets out to change the perception of health food. Set inside the organic grocery Nature's Northwest, Santé stresses healthy preparations of all-natural fruits and vegetables and free-range meats. It's not only good for you: the *Oregonian* once

named Santé the best restaurant in Portland. Jalepeno seafood stew goes for $11.

Authentic where others are trendy, the Tex-Mex food at *Esparza's* (☎ 234-7909), 2715 SE Ankeny St, has people lined up out the door. Home-smoked brisket ($9) is a specialty. Woman-owned *Old Wives Tales* (☎ 238-0470), 1300 E Burnside St, makes both vegetarians and children welcome.

In Portland, Thai food doesn't get much better than at the *Bangkok Kitchen* (☎ 236-7349), 2534 SE Belmont St. If Ethiopian food suits your palate, then *Jarra's* (☎ 230-8990), 1435 SE Hawthorne Blvd, is ready to serve you up searingly hot, authentically potent dishes.

**Top End** Nouveau-Indian cooking and Continental favorites mix and mingle at *Indigine* (☎ 238-1470), 3723 SE Division St. On Saturday nights, Indigine only serves its $26 Indian feast, an entire evening's worth of pungent scents and wondrous flavors. The meal includes seasonally selected raitas, breads, dals, chutneys and entrees. Reservations are usually mandatory for this popular Portland tradition. On Friday nights there's a three-course menu of both Continental and Indian food, entrees like rabbit in mustard sauce go for $19. From Tuesday to Thursday, the same menu is available a la carte.

Tiny and informal, *Westmoreland Bistro* (☎ 236-6457), 7015 SE Milwaukie Ave, offers noteworthy Continental-influenced food in a cafe that by day doubles as a wine shop. There's no menu, just the daily changing chalkboard; select your wine yourself, and add just $1 to its shelf price. Specials like sweetbreads with a port wine sauce go for $17.

Arguably Portland's best restaurant, *Genoa* (☎ 238-1464), 2832 SE Belmont St, is a prix-fixe bastion of *cucina Italiana*. If you want to splurge Italian style, then $45 for seven courses may not put you off.

### ENTERTAINMENT

The best guide to local entertainment is *Willamette Week (WW)*, a news weekly that comes out on Wednesdays, containing complete listings of all theater, music, clubs, cinema and events in the metro area. The Friday edition of *Oregonian* contains the *A&E*, an insert with arts information. Or call the 24-hour Events & Information Hotline (☎ 225-5555) for a synopsis of area happenings.

## Coffeehouses

Coffee is a phenomenon in the Pacific Northwest. Residents take coffee as seriously as others might wine or liquor. You will have no problem finding a good cup of coffee anywhere in the city. *Starbucks*, the Seattle-based coffee company, has branches everywhere. Locally owned *Coffee People* also has a number of venues, the most unique being the east-side's *Motor Mocha*, 535 NE Grand Ave, a drive-through espresso bar. At *Torrefazione Italia* (☎ 228-2528), 838 NW 23rd Ave, there's great Italian-style coffee as well as stylish surroundings.

However, for the coffeehouse experience, don't miss the following venues. Downtown, try *Cafe Omega*, 711 SW Ankeny St, an enclave of funky indolence. For that special pick-me-up, try their home-brewed beer. *Ann Hughes*, at Powell's City of Books (☎ 228-4651), 1005 W Burnside St, serves caffeine to book-shoppers; according to surveys, it's also one of the best singles scenes in the city.

In Southeast Portland, coffeehouses burgeon. *Cafe Lena* (☎ 238-7087), 2239 SE Hawthorne Blvd, features acoustic guitar and open-mike poetry; it's near the Hawthorne AYH hostel. Stacks of current periodicals available for reading in cozy, overstuffed living-room furniture make *Common Grounds Coffee House* (☎ 236-4835), 4321 SE Hawthorne Blvd, a comfortable place for introverts to become quietly politicized. Still within vicinity of the hostel is the eccentric *Rimsky-Korsakoffee House* (☎ 232-2640), 707 SE 12th Ave, next door to the Plaid Pantry (there's no sign, so act like a regular and barge right in). A tribute to Rimsky-Korsakov himself, this charming old house-turned-cafe frequently features live classical musicians. Also, be sure to check out the bathroom upstairs. Musicians of an alternative kind can be found on weekends at *Third World Coffee Co* (☎ 233-8968), 3588 SE Division St, the only coffeehouse in Portland serving coffee purchased directly from Third-World coffee farmers.

One of the most unique Portland coffeehouses is *The Habit* (☎ 235-5321), 2633 SE 21st St, an internet cafe. Computers with access to the internet are available for latte-swilling customers to log on, check e-mail, and surf the net. Choose to chat to other customers, or chat on-line. It costs $3 an hour to go on-line; all food purchases go towards the fee.

## Brewpubs

Perhaps it's due to all the water, but the Pacific Northwest has become a bastion of locally microbrewed beers. Small breweries have sprung up across the region, providing fantastic beers and ales to appreciative audiences. While most regular bars will offer at least one local brew, go to the brewery itself to get the real brewpub experience. Oregon law requires that food be served with alcohol, so most of the following brewpubs also feature snacks and light meals. Most brewpubs offer a taster's selection of the house brews. Don't be embarrassed to ask for suggestions; after a few drinks, people delight in their own opinions.

*BridgePort Brew Pub* (☎ 241-7179), 1313 NW Marshall St, is housed in an old, red-brick warehouse. Earthy and informal, there's outdoor seating on a former loading dock. Pizza by the slice and British-style brews make this pub very popular with the locals.

*Heathman Brewpub* (☎ 227-5700), 901 SW Salmon St, is a bit more upscale and convenient to downtown, combining a bakery, deli, salad bar and pizza oven with Widmer's German-style beers. Widmers has also opened its own brewpub called the *Widmer Gasthaus* (☎ 281-3333), 929 North Russell St, below the arches of the Fremont Bridge. It's worth the trip just to quaff the

OREGON

wonderful *weizen* (wheatbeer), but don't ignore the schnitzel at this bustling and friendly pub.

*The Pilsner Room* (☎ 220-1865), overlooking the Willamette River at RiverPlace esplanade, 0309 SW Montgomery St, manages to combine local brews (from the Hood River Brewery) with a singles bar atmosphere. *Portland Brewing Company* (☎ 222-7150), 1339 NW Flanders St, serves a dynamite Scottish ale, with live music on the weekends.

Ubiquitous *McMeniman's* brewpubs are found all over the city. They offer their own locally brewed ales, and a wide selection of ales, stouts and brews from other regional producers. Check the phone book for the McMeniman's nearest you. Also, McMeniman's has bought two historic movie houses and turned them into cinema-pubs. See the Bagdad and Mission theaters, below.

## Cinemas
*Lloyd Cinemas* (☎ 248-6938), on the corner of NE 15th Ave and Multnomah St, is the city's largest venue for new films. It's right off the MAX line's Lloyd Center stop. *Cinema 21* (☎ 223-4515), 616 NW 21st Ave, is Portland's art and foreign film theater. Even more unusual films make it to the *Northwest Film Center* (☎ 221-1156), 1219 SW Park St, part of the Oregon Art Institute. The *KOIN Center Cinema* (☎ 243-3515), 222 SW Columbia St, and the *Broadway Cinema* (☎ 248-6960), 1000 SW Broadway, are downtown's first-run movie complexes.

The *Mission Theatre* (☎ 223-4031), 1624 NW Glisan St, and the *Bagdad Theatre* (☎ 230-0895), 3702 SE Hawthorne Blvd, are both picturesque old movie theaters now owned by brewpubs. Order beer and snacks and watch a film. Call for current schedules.

The Rocky Horror Picture Show still runs at midnight on Saturdays at the *Clinton St Theatre* (☎ 238-8899) 2522 SE Clinton St. It comes complete with pre-show events and cabaret. Not a big crowd, but still a scream.

## Theater
Portland's showcase theatrical stages are at the *Portland Center for the Performing Arts* (☎ 796-9293), 1111 SW Broadway. Call for information on current shows; the recording gives phone numbers for ticket ordering. Portland Center Stage, a spin-off of Ashland's Oregon Shakespeare Festival troupe, and several other local theater groups perform here. Portland has a very active non-equity and student theater scene; check local papers for schedules.

The *Portland Repertory Theatre* (☎ 224-4491), 25 SW Salmon St, is a mainstream equity theater group. *Artist's Repertory Theatre* (☎ 242-9043), 1111 SW 10th Ave, specializes in revivals, dramas and ensemble pieces. *Echo Theatre/Do Jump Dance Theatre Co* (☎ 231-1232), 1515 SE 37th Ave, offers experimental dance and theater. *Firehouse Theatre* (☎ 289-5450), 5340 N Interstate Ave, puts on interracial and socially relevant productions, and *Portland Women's Theatre* (☎ 287-7707), 1728 NE 40th Ave, gives all-woman performances. Try *Tygres Heart Shakespeare Co* (☎ 222-9220), 710 SW Madison St, for Shakespearean and Elizabethan drama. *Triangle Productions* (☎ 246-8967) specializes in gay theater.

## Performing Arts
The oldest symphony orchestra west of St Louis, the *Oregon Symphony* has grown in stature in recent years with conductor James dePriest at its helm. Concerts are held in the beautiful, if not acoustically brilliant, Arlene Schnitzer Concert Hall (☎ 228-1353, (800) 228-7343), on the corner of Broadway and SW Main St; call for performance information.

The *Portland Opera*, (☎ 241-1802), which performs at the Civic Auditorium, 222 SW Clay St, is surprisingly good for a regional opera company. The company stages four operas a year. *Oregon Ballet Theatre* (☎ 222-5538), 1120 SW 10th Ave, is Portland's resident dance troupe, and stages a number of classical, as well as contemporary, dance programs each year.

Early summer brings the Chamber Music

Northwest series (☎ 223-3202), a nationally recognized season of chamber music concerts held at both Reed College campus and at Catlin-Gable School.

## Nightlife

Like Seattle, Portland is flush with live music and late-night clubs. For the most recent developments, check the Head Out section of *Willamette Week*. *Satyricon* (☎ 243-2380), 125 NW 6th Ave, serves up rough-and-ready punk and alternative rock in authentic grunge surroundings. Find more of Portland's club scene at the *Paris Theatre* (☎ 222-0566), 6 SW 3rd Ave, *LaLuna* (☎ 224-4400), 221 SE 9th Ave, where Monday night is Queer Night, and *Berbati's Pan* (☎ 226-2122), 19 SW Ankeny St. The *Lotus Card Room* (☎ 227-6185), 932 SW 3rd Ave, is ragged on the edges, but offers great local bands and hip-hop discos. If you just want to dance, try *Zorba's Dance Cafe* (☎ 294-0935), 1100 NW Glisan St, a smoke-free disco with a penchant for world-beat rhythms.

*Jubitz* (☎ 283-1111), 10310 N Vancouver Way, is a Portland institution: live, boot-stomping country music at an all-night truck stop. *Kell's* (☎ 227-4057), 112 SW 2nd Ave, offers Celtic music and Guinness on tap; there's also a bit of Ireland on Burnside at the *East Avenue* (☎ 236-6900), 727 E Burnside St. Catch the downtown jazz scene at *Brasserie Montmartre* (☎ 224-5552), 626 SW Park St, or at *Jazz de Opus* (☎ 222-6077), 33 NW 2nd Ave.

The hub of Portland's gay bar nightlife is found in the neighborhood flanking Stark St and SW 11th Ave. Find a wild and mixed gay/straight disco scene at the *Panorama* (☎ 221-7262), part of a three-bar complex at the corner of SW 10th Ave and Stark St; open till 4 am on the weekends. The 70s have never died at *Embers* (☎ 222-3082), 110 NW Broadway, a club with drag shows in the front and disco in the back. *Hobo's*, 120 NW 3rd Ave, offers a pleasant piano bar in a historic old storefront. The *City Nightclub* (☎ 223-2489), 13 NW 13th Ave, is an all-night, all-ages gay club with some of the best dance music in town.

For a quiet drink, go to *Cassidy's* (☎ 223-0054), 1331 SW Washington St, a bar right out of the 1890s, with a late-night influx of thespians. *Huber's* (☎ 228-5686), 411 SW 3rd Ave, is one of Portland's oldest bars, famous for its lethal Spanish coffees; expect lines late at night.

## Spectator Sports

The National Basketball Association's Portland Trail Blazers are an obsession in Portland. Not only are they *good* and frequently winners of the NBA Western Division Finals, but they can be maddeningly haphazard. The heart-in-your-mouth excitement that their capricious playing generates electrifies local sports fans, and makes home-court tickets nearly impossible to find.

Check the classified ads in the *Oregonian* for individual tickets from season ticket holders, or rely on scalpers near the Rose Garden Arena on N Williams Ave at Hassalo St. If you call far enough in advance, there are sometimes single tickets.

It's a little easier to get to see the Portland Winter Hawks (☎ 238-6366), Portland's Western Hockey League franchise. They also play at the Coliseum, but there are plans to move both the hockey and basketball venues to the Rose Garden Arena.

## THINGS TO BUY

Portland's main shopping district extends in a two-block radius from Pioneer Courthouse Square. Nordstrom, Meier & Frank and Sak's Fifth Avenue are all found here. Pioneer Place, a boutique mall, is found between SW Morrison and Yamhill Sts on 5th Ave.

### Art Galleries

Portland has a thriving gallery scene. For a full listing of downtown galleries, ask for the gallery walking-tour map at the visitors center, or check out the gallery listings in *Willamette Week* newspaper.

On the first Thursday of every month, the First Thursday Art Walk brings out Portland's art lovers. Galleries remain open to 8 pm, and many serve complimentary hors d'oeuvres. It's a great way to see both art and the arty set.

For a good representation of Northwest artists don't miss the following galleries: Elizabeth Leach Gallery (☎ 224-0521), 207 SW Pine St; Quintana Native American Art (☎ 223-1729), 139 NW 2nd Ave; Quartersaw Gallery (☎ 223-2264), 528 NW 12th; and Pulliam/Deffenbaugh/Nugent Gallery (☎ 228-6665), 522 NW 12th, the latter two at the heart of Pearl District's gallery row.

### Local Products
A good place to check out local crafts is Saturday Market, held on Saturdays and Sundays beneath the Burnside Bridge. You'll find higher quality and prices at Real Mother Goose (☎ 223-9510), 901 SW Yamhill St, a showcase of local artisans.

Made in Oregon stores offer locally made gifts and food products; they feature an excellent selection of Oregon wines as well. Locations near Saturday Market (☎ 273-8354), 10 NW 1st, and in the Galleria shopping center (☎ 241-3630), SW 10th Ave and Alder St, are convenient to downtown. There's also one in the airport's main terminal, perfect for last-minute gifts.

### Camping & Outdoor Gear
Downtown's best outdoor store is Oregon Mountain Community (☎ 227-1038), 60 NW Davis St; they also rent equipment, including skis. Warehouse-like REI (☎ 283-1300), 1798 Jantzen Beach Center, is located north on I-5, just shy of the Columbia River.

### Photographic Supplies
Downtown's most comprehensive camera and film supply store is Camera World (☎ 222-0008), 500 SW 5th Ave. For one-hour print development, check for the closest Flashback, or Sandy's Camera Shops. Both of these have several locations in central Portland.

### GETTING THERE & AWAY
### Air
Portland International Airport (PDX) is served by over a dozen airlines, with con-

nections to most major US cities. Commuter flights on Horizon Air (☎ (800) 547-9308) link Seattle and Portland every half hour during the day; in addition, there's frequent jet service linking San Francisco, Portland and Seattle on United Airlines (☎ (800) 241-6522), and on Alaska Airlines (☎ (800) 426-0333). There's a nonstop flight to Vancouver, BC, every two hours on Air BC (☎ (800) 663-0522). Bargain fares up and down the West Coast are available from Southwest Air (☎ (800) 435-9792), now offering regularly scheduled flights; some restrictions apply.

Regular flights from PDX on Horizon Air and United Express serve many smaller Oregon and Washington communities, such as Bend/Redmond, Pendleton, Eugene and Yakima.

Portland is the West Coast hub of Delta Airlines (☎ 242-1919, (800) 221-1212), with daily flights to Japan, Korea and Hong Kong.

Following are the addresses of major airlines with downtown offices:

Alaska Airlines
  530 SW Madison St (☎ 224-2547)
American Airlines
  1216 SW 6th Ave (☎ (800) 433-7300)
Delta Airlines
  1211 SW 5th Ave (☎ 242-1919)
Northwest Airlines
  910 SW 2nd Ave (☎ (800) 225-2525)
United Airlines
  502 SW Madison St (☎ (800) 241-6522)

### Bus
Greyhound buses (☎ 243-2323), 550 NW 6th Ave, connect Portland with cities along I-5, the major freeway that traverses the West Coast. There are nine buses a day to Seattle (less then $20 one way) and four to San Francisco. Greyhound serves Vancouver, BC via Seattle. Additionally, Greyhound serves outlying communities of Portland such as Bend and Newport.

Portland is the western terminus of buses traveling along I-84. Twice-daily service links Portland to both Chicago (through Spokane, WA and Montana) and Denver,

CO (through Boise, ID and Salt Lake City, UT).

For more colorful bus service, try Green Tortoise buses (☎ 225-0310). On Sundays and Thursdays, the bus leaves from 616 SW College, near Portland State University for Eugene and San Francisco. The converted buses are meant to be lounged around in: there are tables, mattresses, music and good conversation. The Green Tortoise to San Francisco takes a break in southern Oregon at an outdoor camp, where riders can sit around a campfire, take a sauna, or swim (in bathing suits or birthday suits) and eat a meal cooked by staff and volunteers. The one-way fare to or from San Francisco is $39. On Tuesday and Saturday, the bus leaves for Seattle ($15 one way). It is wise to make reservations a few weeks in advance, especially during the spring and summer.

### Train

Amtrak (☎ 241-4290, (800) 872-7245) at Union Station, NW 6th Ave at Hoyt St, offers service up and down the West Coast, with three trains daily to Seattle ($23 one way, $32 to $46 roundtrip), and two south to Eugene ($24 one way, $36 to $48 roundtrip) and on to California. San Francisco fares are $80 to $101 one way, $88 to $262 roundtrip. East/west trains travel the Columbia River Gorge on their way to and from Chicago (the *Empire Builder)* and Salt Lake City (the *Pioneer).*

### Car

Portland is at the junction of I-84 and I-5, part of the national freeway system. Travelers from the east on I-84 will pass through the magnificent Columbia River Gorge. Travelers arriving from the north or south on I-5 pass through verdant forests and farmland, within sight of the looming volcanic peaks of the Cascades. Highway 26 stretches from the Columbia River Gorge, through Portland, past Mt Hood, and on to Central Oregon.

Most major car-rental agencies have outlets both at the Portland International Airport (PDX) and downtown:

Avis
    PDX (☎ 249-4950, (800) 831-2847)
    330 SW Washington St, downtown (☎ 227-0220)
Budget
    PDX (☎ 249-6500, (800) 527-0700)
    2033 SW 4th Ave, downtown (☎ 249-6500)
Dollar Rent-A-Car
    PDX (☎ 249-4792, (800) 800-4000)
    132 NW Davis St, downtown (☎ 228-3540)
Hertz
    PDX (☎ 249-8216, (800) 654-3131)
    1009 SW 6th Ave, downtown (☎ 249-5727)

Frequently cheaper are local companies with older-model rentals. Close to Lloyd Center is Bee Rent-A-Car (☎ 233-7368), 84 NE Weidler St, and Practical Rent-A-Car (☎ 230-1103), 1315 NE Sandy Blvd.

### GETTING AROUND
### To/From the Airport

PDX is about 15 minutes east of downtown, along the Columbia River. Tri-Met's bus No 12 runs between PDX and downtown's 5th Ave bus mall (see below); allow 45 minutes for the journey. If you're taking bus No 12 from downtown to PDX, catch it outbound along 6th Ave. Buses depart about every 15 to 20 minutes.

The Airporter (☎ 249-1837), a private minibus company, runs between PDX and major downtown hotels; depending on the number of hotel stops, the $5 trip can take a half hour.

The taxi fare and tip to or from the airport and downtown will cost between $20 to $25.

If you're driving, the airport is east of Portland. From downtown, take I-84 east, follow signs to 1-205 north and get off at Exit No 24A.

### Bus & Light Rail

Portland's public transport company is called Tri-Met (☎ 238-7433). It operates the local commuter bus service as well as a light-rail train system called Metropolitan Area Express (MAX).

Within the downtown core, roughly bounded by I-405, the Willamette River and Hoyt St, all public transportation is free. Fareless Square, as this area is known,

OREGON

OREGON

was instigated in hopes of inducing down-town patrons to park their cars and use public transport. Outside this area there are three zones in the Tri-Met fare system; tickets for travel within zones 1 and 2, which covers most close destinations (including the zoo, the hostel and Lloyd Center), cost $1, all-zone passes are $1.30, seniors 50c. Your ticket is your transfer, good for two hours on all Tri-Met transport. Buy your ticket from the driver; no change is given.

Most downtown buses travel along 5th and 6th Aves, commonly called the 'bus mall'. Lined with outdoor art, these streets are largely off-limits to private vehicles.

The MAX is Portland's successful experiment in mass transit. Linking east Portland suburbs and the Lloyd Center/Convention Center area to downtown, these commuter trains have become a prototype of the city's public transit future. Work has commenced on light-rail lines to link downtown to Beaverton and western suburbs, and plans call for lines to run along the Willamette River between Lake Oswego and Vancouver, WA.

Tickets for MAX are figured according to the same zone map as Tri-Met buses. Bus and light-rail tickets are completely transferable (within the two-hour time constraints). However, tickets for MAX must be bought from ticket machines at MAX stations; there is no conductor or ticket-seller.

To purchase tickets in advance, or for more information, visit the Tri-Met Information Bureau (☎ 231-3198) at Pioneer Courthouse Square.

### Taxi
There are taxi stands near most major downtown hotels. Call the following for radio-dispatched cabs: Broadway Cab (☎ 227-1234), Radio Cab (☎ 227-1212) and New Rose City Cab (☎ 282-7707).

### Bicycle
Buy a *Getting There By Bike* map, available from bike shops and Powell's Travel Store, and see Portland over the handlebars. Rent a bike from Bike Gallery (☎ 222-3821), 821 SW 11th Ave or Fat Tire Farm (☎ 222-3276), 2714 NW Thurman St.

## AROUND PORTLAND
The Pacific Coast, the Columbia River Gorge and Mt Hood all make good day-trips from Portland. A popular loop tour combines a trip up the Gorge as far as Hood River, turning south on Hwy 35 to Mt Hood, and returning to Portland via Hwy 26.

### Sauvie Island
The largest island in the Columbia River, Sauvie Island is located only 10 miles north of Portland, but in ambiance, it seems much more distant. Here, vegetable gardens, berry fields and orchards stretch for miles. Shop for the Northwest's bounty at farmer's markets or pick your own produce from the orchards and fields. Much of the north end of the island is contained in the Sauvie Island Wildlife Area, a 20-sq-mile refuge for waterfowl. Ask at the refuge headquarters (two miles north on Sauvie Island Rd) for a map and bird-watching advice. During summer, the sandy beaches along the east side of the island are popular with picnickers and sunbathers. The island's flat, bucolic landscape is immensely popular with cyclists. Parking permits ($2, available at island businesses) are required if you plan to park at the beaches or wildlife refuge.

### Wine Country
Although grapes are grown in many parts of western Oregon, the focus of Oregon's wine trade is hilly Yamhill County, just south and west of Portland. Here, about 20 minutes from downtown, are prime plantings of pinot noir and chardonnay grapes, the famous Burgundy grape varieties which thrive in cool Oregon. Many vineyards are small, especially by California standards, but most are open daily for tasting and on-site sales. The area between Newberg and McMinnville is nominally the center of the wine country, easily reached from Portland on Hwy 99W.

## Mount St Helens (WA)

This Cascade volcano gained world-wide notoriety when it blew its top in 1980. Today, Mt St Helens National Volcanic Monument preserves 171 sq miles of volcano-wracked wilderness. From Portland, a trip to the new visitors center at Coldwater Ridge (off I-5 at Castle Rock, WA) takes just two hours, and affords a glimpse into the mouth of the crater.

**OREGON**

# Oregon Coast

Forest, mountain, beach, ocean and river all meet through a prism of mist and green translucence along the Oregon coast. Rocky headlands rise high above the ocean, dropping away to the pounding waves in cliffs hundreds of feet high. Spires and columns of rock march far out into the surging sea and arch up out of sandy beaches. The remains of ancient lava flows, many of these crags of basalt are now home to vast colonies of seabirds, sea lions and seals.

Rising just to the east of the shoreline is the Coast Range, a young mountain range deeply etched by great rivers and shrouded by a patchwork of deep forests and recent clear-cuts: these are the forests of the spotted owl controversy. Along the bays of mighty rivers like the Columbia, the Yaquina, the Rogue and the Umpqua, civilization grew first in Native American villages, whose members fished the bays, traded with inland tribes and hunted the mountain valleys.

The Oregon Dunes, among the largest ocean-fronting sand dunes in the world, drift along the edge of the coast for over 50 miles. From Charleston south to the California border, the beaches are increasingly flanked by high rocky cliffs and craggy tooths of rock, home to rookeries of puffins, penguin-like murres and wheeling gulls. Sea lions and seals bask on offshore rocks and whales arch out of the water to spout as they migrate to and from arctic waters.

For generations, families have returned to the same sleepy coastal town for long holidays. The last decade, however, has brought great changes to the Oregon coast. More than ever before, the coast is a destination for travelers from across the USA, with an estimated three million travelers visiting the 300-mile coastline annually; both the quality and quantity of facilities are growing quickly.

Thanks to a farsighted state government in the 1910s, the entire length of the Pacific coast in Oregon was set aside as public land. This has left most of the coast, especially in the central and southern regions, nearly untrammeled by development.

## HISTORY

Although Lewis and Clark visited the northern coast in 1805-6, and Astoria was founded as a fur trading fort in 1811, settlement didn't really start until the 1860s, after Native American tribes had been restricted to reservations. The southern Oregon coast was home to the Tutunis, or Coast Rogues, and the Coos, whose relations with the Whites escalated from bad to worse as increasing numbers of settlers and miners moved into their homelands.

Fishing, logging and agriculture formed the nucleus of the coast economy. Dairy farming was one of the first agricultural businesses to take hold along the northern coast. Gold was discovered in beach sand along the mouths of the large rivers to the south. However, the lodes were never very great, and the boom fizzled, but not before little settlements like Port Orford – in 1851 – took hold. The California Gold Rush and the boomtown of San Francisco demanded a ready supply of lumber and agricultural products, which the young coastal communities of southern Oregon were happy to ship out. The little port town of Bandon became a summer resort for wealthy San Franciscans who made the two-day journey by ship.

Transport remained the biggest stumbling block of economic development along the coast. While steamers and trains provided some transportation, the rugged coast was just too wild a place for a highway, given engineering technology and budgets of the day. Highway 101, which traverses the Pacific Coast north to south, wasn't completed through Oregon until the

**Conde McCullough**

The strikingly beautiful and massive bridges along Hwy 101 are the work of Conde McCullough, an engineer and lawyer who brought dramatic style to the utilitarian business of bridge building. McCullough worked for the Oregon State Highway Department from 1920 till 1946, spanning a period of unrivaled road and bridge construction.

Although McCullough designed bridges across the state, his most famous and remarkable bridges are along the Oregon coast. Until the 1930s, the coast was ill-served by highways, in part because the coast's many wide estuaries presented problems to contemporary bridge engineering, and partly because steel – the bridge-making ingredient of choice – didn't last very long on the stormy Pacific coast. In 1936, McCullough was given teams of WPA workers to span the final links of Hwy 101.

In order to arch over wide rivers and bays, McCullough turned to new engineering and design techniques. From France, he borrowed the Freyssinet method, which pioneered the use of prestressed concrete arches in bridge building. From the Arts & Crafts movement, he developed a sensitivity for harmony of structures and their natural surroundings. From the art deco movement, he borrowed a severe, neo-Gothic formality. The result was bridges that were able to span the wide gulfs of the Oregon coast in a high-flying, immediately identifiable style, bridges that have almost become metaphors for the coast itself.

McCullough's most famous bridges are across Coos Bay at North Bend, Alsea Bay at Waldport, Yaquina Bay at Newport, and across Cape Creek Bridge at Devil's Elbow State Park near Yachats. However, after seeing one McCullough bridge, you'll begin to recognize them at many other places across the state; the gasp-producing bridge that spans the Crooked River Gorge in central Oregon was also built by McCullough. ■

OREGON

1930s; some isolated sections weren't entirely finished until the 1960s.

In this century, logging has been by far the mainstay of the southern Oregon economy, as trees grow relatively quickly to enormous size in the coastal mountain range that flanks the Pacific. The port city of Coos Bay became the major shipping point for Port Orford Cedar, a versatile wood that once grew abundantly in southern Oregon (it's now quite rare, due to overcutting and disease). Coos Bay boomed during WW I and WW II, when the war machine demanded lumber. In the 1940s, Oregon became the largest timber producer in the USA; Coos Bay became the world's largest timber-shipping port.

The depletion of old-growth forests, federal protection of the forests that remain and the shipping of raw logs overseas for milling has spelled the end of the boom for many lumber-dependent workers and their families. Niche industries, such as lily bulb production, goat and cow dairy farms, wild mushroom hunting and tourism, seek to fill the gulf in local economies left by the decline in logging.

## FLORA & FAUNA
### Flora

The northern Oregon coast has dense forests of Western hemlock, Sitka spruce, red cedar and Douglas fir. These trees can grow to great age and enormous girth when conditions are right: old-growth trees (500 to 750 years old) frequently top 250 feet, and have a circumference of up to 20 feet. Southern Oregon forests were once dominated by the aromatic Port Orford Cedar, until overcutting and disease took over. Orange-barked madrones, myrtle trees and redwoods also appear in southern coastal forests.

Along the coastal headlands, thickets of salal, an evergreen shrub with waxy white flowers, battle the winds. Big leaf maples and red alder are found along streams and in clearings. The Pacific Yew tree, though less common, is in high demand; its needles and bark are used in the cancer medication taxol.

### Fauna

Tufted puffins, with orange and red bills, and murres nest on offshore islands and oceanside cliffs all preserved as the Oregon Islands National Wildlife Refuge. Black, long-necked cormorants are also frequent visitors to the coast, as are the five varieties of gulls.

The Oregon coast supports a population of about 1000 Steller's sea lions, a member of the seal family that can reach sizes of up to 12 feet in length and can weigh up to 1500 pounds. These enormous animals can be seen at Sea Lion Caves between Yachats and Florence, or through binoculars on many islands and sand spits along the central and southern coast. Smaller harbor seals are commonly seen along wharves in fishing towns.

## GETTING THERE & AWAY

The Oregon coast is not well served by public transport. However, it's not just the paucity of public buses (there are no trains, and only Astoria and Coos Bay have scheduled air service) that makes travel difficult: it's almost impossible to find out what service there is. Only Astoria, Newport and

Coos Bay have staffed bus stations that answer queries. Other towns simply have stops in grocery store parking lots and at gas stations.

### Air

Horizon Air (☎ (800) 547-9308) provides eight flights daily from Portland to the Astoria Airport on the northern coast, and eight flights daily to Coos Bay's North Bend Airport on the southern coast. The usual one-way fare to Astoria ranges from $39 to $82, depending on how early you book; to North Bend is $156; however, there are discounts on some early morning and weekend flights.

### Bus

Bus travelers will find that bus service is sketchy to nonexistent along the northern Oregon coast. In particular, there is currently no public transport between Cannon Beach and Lincoln City along Hwy 101. Raz Transportation (☎ 738-5121 in Seaside, 325-5641 in Astoria) operates a local

---

### The Great Outdoors

While wandering along the pounding surf, beachcombing and gazing out to sea are principal diversions of the coast, there are a lot of activities as well.

**Biking** The Oregon Coast Bike Route follows busy Hwy 101 along the Oregon coast between Astoria and Brookings. There are some side trips along less-congested roads. Most cyclists travel north to south, in the direction of the wind, then take public transportation back to their original destination. Be warned that the cardboard carton in which buses and airlines require you to pack your bicycle are hard to find toward the end of the tourist season. For a free brochure about the route, contact the Dept of Transportation in Salem (☎ 986-4000); a good book describing the route and other biking routes along the coast is *Bicycling the Pacific Coast* by Tom Kirkendall (The Mountaineers, Seattle, 1991).

**Charter Fishing** Vastly reduced numbers of salmon have changed the charter fishing industry. Charter boats still leave from most ports, but bottom fish (like flounder and ray), tuna, shark, halibut, rockfish and red snapper are now the common catches. Call the state Fish & Wildlife Department (☎ 229-5403) for information on the season, or contact a charter operation for local details and restrictions.

Most charters will offer several options that range in price from $35 to $55 a trip. An Oregon fishing license is required, which is generally available from most charter operations.

**Whale Watching** The high capes and headlands of the Oregon coast are good vantage points to watch for gray whales. There are both spring and fall migrations; the spring

intercity bus service, providing two buses a day between Portland, Astoria and Seaside. In Portland, catch the buses at the downtown bus depot.

Sunset Transit (☎ 325-0563) provides two buses daily between Astoria, Seaside and Cannon Beach. Fares are $2.50 one way, $4 roundtrip.

Greyhound buses traveling between Portland and San Francisco, via Hwy 18, make stops in Lincoln City, Newport and Yachats several times daily in each direction. Tickets are purchased either upon boarding, or upon arrival at the next bus depot. Call the bus depot in Newport (☎ 265-2253) for the latest schedule information.

Valley Retriever buses connect the Greyhound lines running along the coast and the Willamette Valley. Buses make three trips to Corvallis ($10). The first bus of the day continues on to Bend ($36). The Newport bus depot is the contact point for both companies.

Lincoln County's Central Coast Connec-

tions (☎ 265-4900) offers weekday transport between Newport and Lincoln City, and Newport and Yachats. Fares cost 50c to $2; there is no weekend service.

# Northern Oregon Coast

Oregon's northern coast begins at the Columbia River and stretches south to Florence. Oregon's most famous beach resorts – Seaside, Cannon Beach and Lincoln City – are here on long strips of sandy beach. Affable Newport, known since the 1860s for its oysters, is now known for its aquarium, the largest in the Northwest. Astoria is the oldest US settlement west of the Mississippi.

Increasingly, the coast between Newport and Seaside is the domain of tourism. Proximity to Portland and the Willamette Valley means that most coastal towns are now

**OREGON**

migration – peaking in March – brings the whales closer to the shore. Favorite whale-watching spots include Cape Sebastian, Cape Blanco, Cape Perpetua, Neahkahnie Mountain and Cape Arago. On weekends at most of these sites, volunteers from local wildlife groups will answer questions and help locate whales. Although whales can occasionally be seen with the naked eye, it's a good idea to have a good pair of binoculars.

Many charter fishing boats also offer whale watching trips. Excursions last about two hours; prices range from $12 to $18.

**Clamming & Crabbing** Most Oregon beaches are open for gathering shellfish. A state fishing license is not needed, though you must abide by the bag limits stated in the most recent Fish & Wildlife guidelines (available from most public offices on the coast). Otherwise all you need is a shovel and a bucket. Mussels are found in abundant numbers along intertidal rocks. Clams require a bit of excavation along riverbeds and sandy beaches. Razor clams quickly burrow into the sand and demand a fair amount of spading to unearth. Be sure that the shellfish is free of red tide. (See information on red tide in the Facts for the Visitor chapter.)

Dungeness crab live in quiet bays along the coast and are easily caught. Rowing out into the bay and waiting for the crab rings to fill is a relaxing way to snare a fine meal. Many marinas will rent a boat and crab rings, and will clean and boil the crabs for around $35 for a two-hour rental.

**Surfing** Surfers appear all along the beach, but the best waves are in coves along headlands and capes. Popular spots are near Otter Cove, Sunset Beach and Smugglers Cove. Surf gear can be rented in larger cities along the coast. A board, wetsuit and booties rent for about $35 a day. ∎

WASHINGTON

Hammond
Warrenton
Astoria  *Columbia River*
Fort Clatsop
National Monument
Olney
To Portland
30
202
26

PACIFIC
OCEAN

Seaside
Saddle Mountain
3283 ft
Saddle
Mountain
State Park

Cannon
Beach
Sugarloaf Mtn
2858 ft
Onion Peak
3064 ft
26
Oswald West
State Park
Manzanita
Nehalem
Bay
53
Tillamook
National
Forest
To Portland

101
Garibaldi
Tillamook
Bay
6

Tillamook

Siuslaw
National
Forest
Three Capes
Scenic Route
101

Pacific
City
22
To McMinnville
Sheridan
18
Willamina
22
Lincoln
City
*Salmon River*

Depoe
Bay
229
223

Yaquina Head
Natural Area
Newport
Yaquina
Bay
Toledo
*Yaquina River*
Siuslaw  Marys
National  Peak
Forest  4097 ft
20
To Corvallis
Table Mtn
2804 ft
Waldport
Alsea
Bay
34

Yachats
Cape
Perpetua

**Northern
Oregon Coast**

0    15    30 km
0    10    20 miles

101
Mapleton
36
126
To Eugene
Florence
Oregon Dunes
National
Recreation Area
*Siuslaw River*
To Reedsport

dominated by weekenders. Some coastal restaurants don't even bother opening until the weekend; prices double at upscale lodgings on Friday night. Galleries and boutiques now grace buildings that once served the needs of sailors and loggers. It's easy to feel appalled – and then a little guilty – that all this development was built for the tourist.

Highway 101 stretches the length of the northern Oregon coast, and crosses to Washington State on the five-mile-long Astoria Bridge. Highway 30 follows the Columbia River from Portland to Astoria; Portland is also linked to the coast by Hwy 26 to Cannon Beach and Seaside, by Hwy 6 to Tillamook, and by Hwy 18 to Lincoln City. The other main artery from the Willamette Valley to the coast is Hwy 20, which links Corvallis and Newport. Traffic along the coast can be very heavy in summer. Heavy traffic is also the norm along the arteries that feed Portland crowds to their weekend homes on the coast.

## ASTORIA

Astoria (population 9945) sits at the mouth of the five-mile-wide Columbia River. The 4.1-mile-long **Astoria Bridge** on Hwy 101 is the world's longest continuous-truss bridge, crossing the Columbia River to Washington State. The city contains a great deal of history and scruffy charm.

Lewis and Clark and the Corps of Discovery tolerated the winter of 1805-6 at a crude fort along an inlet of Youngs Bay, just south of present-day Astoria. When they returned to St Louis they told all who would listen about the great wealth in pelts in the Pacific Northwest, and within months the first fur-trapping expeditions began to thread their way into the West. John Jacob Astor and his Pacific Fur Trading Company established a small fur-trading fort in the spring of 1811 at the mouth of the Columbia, making this the first US settlement in the West.

Trade and fishing made Astoria a very powerful and wealthy city in the late 19th century. A salmon cannery opened here in 1866, the first of many businesses that would capitalize on the immense runs of salmon in the Columbia River. Other industries, such as sawmills, flour mills, shipping and deep-sea fishing, took hold, and by the turn of the century, Astoria was Oregon's second-largest city. The city's reputation for affluence and gentility was rivaled only by its reputation for bawdy excess in the bar and brothel district near the harbor.

Magnificent Victorian homes built on the cliffs overlook downtown and the Columbia River. While the local economy has bottomed out over the last 20 years, and the once booming harbor has largely gone derelict, Astoria is beginning to revitalize. Low rents and a sense of history attract a number of artists, writers and restaurateurs.

## Orientation
The main downtown district is perched on a relatively narrow slip of land between the river and the steep slopes of the residential area. Highway 101 enters the city from the south along Youngs Bay Bridge, almost instantly to corkscrew up and cross the towering Astoria Bridge.

Streets in the residential area behind downtown contain many lovely homes, but the streets can be *very* steep; some streets are closed to trailers and RVs. It's a good idea to park and walk if you plan to explore these areas.

## Information
The Astoria Visitors Center (☎ 325-6311) is at 111 W Marine Drive, Astoria, OR 97103; the post office (☎ 325-6311) is at 748 Commercial St.

Godfather's Books & Espresso Bar (☎ 325-8143), 1108 Commercial St, is a nice bookstore, with a selection of books on local travel and history. *North Coast Times Eagle*, a monthly journal of 'art and opinion' has quite a lot to say about coastal issues and also gives a good idea of what's going on in the galleries. Coast Community Radio is heard at 91.9 FM.

Clean Services Coin Laundry (☎ 325-2027), 823 W Marine Drive, offers both self-service and drop-off laundry facilities. The Astoria-area hospital is the Columbia

Memorial Hospital (☎ 325-4321), 2111 Exchange St.

## Historic Astoria Homes
Astoria contains some of the most lovingly restored and precipitously poised homes outside of San Francisco. During the 1880s, sea captains, and other captains of industry, built magnificent homes overlooking the Columbia River. Many fell into disrepair after WW II (some distinguished houses still need attention), though the last decade's renewed interest in historic homes has brought these beauties back to life.

The Flavel House (see Other Museums, below) is the only historic home regularly open for touring; however, many others are now operated as B&Bs. Most historic homes have an informational plaque outside, giving basic information about the structure.

A quick walk through the blocks around 8th to 17th Sts and Grand to Exchange Sts will lead you to Grace Episcopal Church – Astoria's oldest (1885), the Heritage Museum, the Foard House – a magnificently ornate Queen Anne home built in 1892, now wildly painted and carefully restored, and the Rosebriar Hotel, built in 1902, and for many years a convent.

If you'd like a guided tour of this district, contact Historical Tours of Astoria (☎ 325-3005) at 612 Florence Ave. A walking tour map and brochure about historic homes is available from the Heritage Museum (see Other Museums, below) for $3.

## Columbia River Maritime Museum
The 150-year-old seafaring heritage is well interpreted and displayed at the Columbia River Maritime Museum (☎ 325-2323), 1792 Marine Drive, a modern, 25,000-sq-foot facility.

In the main hall of the museum there are a number of small boats and a periscope from a US Navy submarine from which to watch river traffic on the Columbia. The galleries explore Astoria's maritime past, including the salmon-packing industry, local lighthouses, the evolution of boat design, delicate ivory scrimshaw work and

OREGON

OREGON

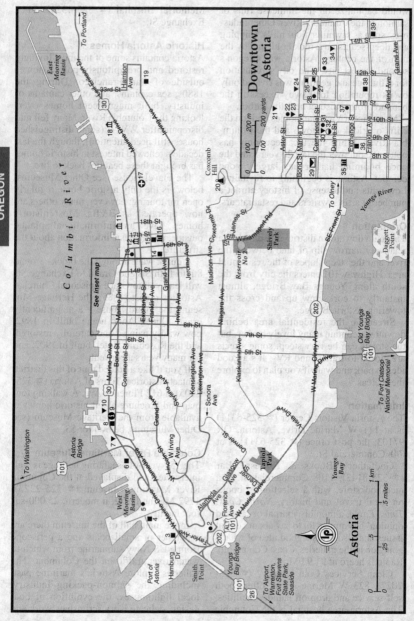

| PLACES TO STAY | | 23 | Ricciardi Gallery & Espresso | 12 | Heritage Museum |
|---|---|---|---|---|---|
| 3 | Bayshore Motor Inn | 24 | Columbian Cafe-Fresca Deli | 13 | Hertz |
| 4 | Red Lion Inn | | | 16 | Foard House |
| 6 | Dunes Motel of Astoria | 25 | Astoria Coffee Company | 17 | Columbia Memorial Hospital |
| 8 | Lamplighter Motel | 26 | Flying Barney's Coffeehouse | | |
| 14 | Grandview B&B | | | 18 | Upper Town Fire Fighters Museum |
| 15 | Columbia River Inn | 27 | Danish Maid Bakery & Coffee Shop | | |
| 19 | Astoria Inn B&B | | | 20 | Astoria Column |
| 36 | Clementine's B&B | 30 | Peri's | 22 | Persona Vintage Clothing |
| 38 | Franklin Station B&B | 34 | Community Store | 28 | Godfather's Books & Espresso Bar, Finnware |
| 39 | Rosebriar Hotel | | | | |
| | | **OTHER** | | 29 | Post Office |
| **PLACES TO EAT** | | 1 | Clean Services Coin Laundry | 31 | Art Reigns |
| | | | | 32 | Bus Depot |
| 7 | Cafe Uniontown | 2 | Historic Tours of Astoria | 33 | Liberty Theater |
| 8 | Pig 'n Pancake | 5 | Tiki Charters | 35 | Flavel House |
| 10 | Josephson's Smoke House | 9 | Visitors Center | 37 | Elk's Club |
| 21 | Pier 11 Feed Store Restaurant & Lounge | 11 | Columbia River Maritime Museum | | |

a creepy display on harpoons. Also part of the museum is the Columbia Lightship No 604, a floating lighthouse that was moored for years outside the mouth of the Columbia; the boat is open to visitors. The small bookshop and gift store is quite good and offers a number of titles specific to Astoria and its seafaring history.

The museum is open daily from 9:30 am to 5 pm. Admission is $5 for adults, $4 for seniors and $2 for students; children under six are free.

### Other Museums

Housed in the former City Hall building, the **Heritage Museum**, 1618 Exchange St, contains a commemoration of Astoria's fishing past, as well as an exhibit dedicated to the various ethnic communities that came together to form the city; take note of the Tong shrine. Another room is dedicated to the Clatsop Indians and the early days of exploration. Check upstairs to see if there are any art shows.

Captain George Flavel was one of Astoria's leading citizens during the 1870s and 1880s. He built this highly ornamented mansion, **Flavel House**, 441 8th St, with great views over the harbor (especially from the three-story corner tower) in order to keep an eye on his own fleet of Flavel

ships which he guided across the Columbia River bar.

The house has been restored throughout and has been repainted to its original colors. The grounds are also being returned to Victorian-era landscaping.

The **Upper Town Fire Fighters Museum**, 2986 Marine Drive, is a fire hall-turned-museum housing a collection of vintage fire-fighting equipment. The museum also displays photos of Astoria's big fire in 1922.

Hours for the museums are daily from 10 am to 5 pm, May to September, and from 11 am to 4 pm, October to April. Admission is $5 for adults, $2.50 for children, which gets you into all three museums. Contact the Clatsop County Historical Society Museums (☎ 325-2203) for more details.

### Astoria Column

Built in 1926, this 125-foot tower rises high on Coxcomb Hill. The exterior of the column was painted with figures and scenes of the westward sweep of US exploration and settlement, though both the paintings and the sentiments behind them are now pretty faded. A series of 166 spiraling steps leads to the top of the column, from which there are good views over

**OREGON**

Astoria, the Clatsop Spit and Youngs Bay. From downtown follow 14th St south (uphill) to Jerome Ave. Turn east one block and continue up 15th St to the park entrance on Coxcomb Drive.

### Fort Clatsop National Memorial
Reconstructed Fort Clatsop (☎ 861-2471), just eight miles south of Astoria off Hwy 101, is well worth a stop, especially for families with children, or anyone with an interest in the history of the West.

The Corps of Discovery stayed here in the winter of 1805-6. The expedition named their small fortification Fort Clatsop, after the local Native American tribe that had befriended them. Life was pretty rudimentary: food, salt and high spirits were in short supply, especially as the camp was infested with vermin and the winter was excessively wet (even for Astoria).

The site is now administered by the NPS. The modest log structure is built according to sketches left by Lewis and Clark. During the summer, costumed docents demonstrate the various pastimes and tasks of the corps, including candle making and leather tanning. They also give demonstrations of frontier skills like flintlock marksmanship and cedar canoe building.

The visitors center, about 100 yards from the fort, contains a very good interpretation of the events and personalities that came together at Fort Clatsop, including artifacts from the Clatsops, diary selections from the corps and a number of slide and video presentations.

Fort Clatsop is open everyday except Christmas. The visitors center is open from 8 am to 5 pm (to 6 pm June 10 to Labor Day). Admission is $2 for adults or a maximum of $4 for the whole family. Children and seniors.

### Charter Fishing
The Columbia's convergence with the Pacific is a noted fishing area. Tiki Charters (☎ 325-7818), 352 Industry St, offers charter trips for bottom fish and sturgeon and salmon fishing when the seasons open. Tiki also offers river cruises. A 1½-hour

tour of the Astoria waterfront costs $15, while an eight-hour cruise of the Columbia River estuary costs $60. All trips depart from the West Mooring Basin, just west of Astoria Bridge. In nearby Warrenton, contact Warrenton Deep Sea Inc (☎ 861-1233), 95 NE Harbor Place, for sturgeon and bottom-fish trips.

For season information, licenses and tackle, contact Tackle Time Bait Shop (☎ 861-3693), 530 E Harbor St.

### Special Events
The Clatsop County Fair is held the first weekend of August at the fairgrounds, 421 20th St. Events include an equestrian and livestock show, crafts fair, food booths, musical entertainment and a beef barbecue.

Astoria's biggest celebration is the Scandinavian Festival (☎ 325-6311), held the third weekend of June to honor the area's Swedish, Finnish and Norwegian heritage. The festival includes ethnic food booths, dance contests, the crowning of Miss Scandinavia and a parade through downtown. Events take place at the high school, 1001 W Marine Drive.

### Places to Stay
**Camping** The most pleasant campgrounds in the area are out on the Clatsop Spit near Warrenton, just southwest of Astoria. *Kampers West Kampground* (☎ 861-1814), 1140 NW Warrenton Drive, has tent sites for $14 and RV hook-ups for $15. *KOA Astoria Warrenton Seaside* (☎ 861-2606), 1100 NW Ridge Rd, is in Hammond. A tent site is $19 per night, hook-ups are $21, and cabins start at $31.

**Hostels** The closest hostel is the *Fort Columbia Hostel* (☎ (206) 777-8755) across the Astoria Bridge in Chinook, WA. (See Chinook in the Southwest Washington chapter for more information.)

**B&Bs** If you've been considering a night in a B&B, Astoria is a good place to do it, as there are some gorgeous homes here.

*Astoria Inn B&B* (☎ 325-8153), 3391

Irving Ave, is an 1890s farmhouse in the eastern limits of town. Rooms range from $70 to $85. *Clementine's B&B* (☎ 325-2005), 847 Exchange St, is an 1888 Italianate mansion with five guest rooms and prices from $45 to $90.

*Franklin St Station B&B* (☎ 325-4314, (800) 448-1098), 1140 Franklin Ave, offers six rooms, each with private bath, some with river views; decks hang off the hill overlooking the town; rooms range from $63 to $115. *Columbia River Inn B&B* (☎ 325-5044, (800) 847-2475), 1681 Franklin Ave, is an ornate 1870 home decorated with period furnishings; there's a garden in the back; the five guest rooms each have a private bath and range from $70 to $80.

*Grandview B&B* (☎ 325-5555), 1574 Grand Ave, sits on a double lot, with stunning views of the river; the three two-bedroom suites range from $39 to $92. *Rosebriar Hotel* (☎ 325-7427), 636 14th St, originally built as a lodging in 1902, which later became a convent. This lovely B&B sits high above the street, with wide porches, a brick patio and nicely landscaped grounds; rooms range from $40 to $109.

**Hotels** Most hotels are right along Hwy 30 and can be noisy. Hotels with rates ranging from $45 to $75 include *Lamplighter* (☎ 325-4051), 131 W Marine Drive; *Dunes Motel of Astoria* (☎ 325-7111, (800) 441-3319), 288 W Marine Drive; and the *Bayshore Motor Inn* (☎ 325-2205), 555 Hamburg Ave.

The *Crest Motel* (☎ 325-3141, (800) 421-3141), 5366 Leif Ericson Drive, is on the eastern edge of Astoria, on a small, wooded and grassy hill overlooking the river; rates are $45/52.

Rooms at the *Red Lion Inn* (☎ 325-7373, (800) 547-8010), 400 Industry St, all have balconies and views over the river and marina; prices range from $59 to $84. The *Shilo Inn* (☎ 861-2181, (800) 222-2244), 1609 E Harbor Drive, across the Youngs Bay Bridge in Warrenton, has a pool and fitness center and offers suite-style rooms

with microwaves and refrigerators; rooms range from $85 to $115.

**Places to Eat**

The cozily old-fashioned *Danish Maid Bakery & Coffee Shop* (☎ 325-3657), 1132 Commercial St, is right out of the 1950s and is a good spot for a sweet roll and a cup of coffee. If you require a full breakfast, go to the *Pig 'n Pancake* (☎ 325-3144) 146 W Bond St; breakfasts don't get much more basic or bountiful than this.

The *Community Store* (☎ 325-0027), 1389 Duane St, is a really good natural-foods store and organic grocery; it's also one of the hippie gathering places of Astoria.

For fresh-cut sandwiches and homemade soup, go to *Peri's* (☎ 325-5560), 915 Commercial St. The views are better than the food at *Pier 11 Feed Store Restaurant & Lounge* (☎ 325-0279), 77 11th Ave, at 10th and 11th Sts, right on the water in an old cargo warehouse. It's notable as one of the few places open for Sunday lunch.

*Cafe Uniontown* (☎ 325-8708), 218 W Marine Drive, was established in 1934 in the old fish-processing district and was frequented by Scandinavian fishermen and longshoremen. The restaurant is now a favorite of local gastronomes. Full dinners range from $11 to $17.

*Columbian Cafe-Fresca Deli* (☎ 325-2233), 1114 Marine Drive, offers a selection of fish each night, chosen daily from local fishing boats, then served with fresh local vegetables. Prices range from $10 to $15. Don't let the down-on-its-luck facade of this family-owned cafe put you off: the food is great.

**Entertainment**

**Coffeehouses** The *Astoria Coffee Company* (☎ 325-7173), 1154 Commercial St, is the place to get your caffeine jolt. At *Flying Barney's Coffeehouse*, 1161 Marine Drive, rock bands, poets and folk singers grace the small stage; the work of local artists appears on the walls. This is as alternative as Astoria gets, and it's usually pretty fun. *Ricciardi Gallery & Espresso*

OREGON

(☎ 325-5450), 108 10th St, offers coffee and an art gallery, and is a great place to unwind and chat in an informal studio atmosphere.

**Theater & Cinema** *Shanghaied in Astoria*, a spoofy comedy/musical about the bad old days of Astoria is put on by the Astor Street Opry Company Theatre (☎ 325-6104), and is performed at the *Elk's Club*, 453 11th St. Tickets range from $5 to $12. It's actually kind of fun.

The old *Liberty Theater* (☎ 325-4191), 1203 Commercial St, shows first-run movies.

**Live Music** For a bit of nightlife, head to the bar at *Cafe Uniontown* (☎ 325-8708), 218 W Marine Drive, where there's live acoustic music Thursday, Friday and Saturday nights.

**Things to Buy**
The last of many canneries and smokehouses that once thrived here, Josephson's Smoke House (☎ 325-2190), 106 Marine Drive, produces a wide range of smoked fish and shellfish. Gift packs and clam chowder are also available.

Finnware (☎ 325-5720), 1116 Commercial St, has gifts from Scandinavia such as crystal, jewelry, sweaters and handicrafts.

Astoria has been attracting artists for a number of years and, now that storefront rent in the downtown area is cheap, suddenly Astoria is filled with quite a number of interesting galleries and antique stores. A complete list of local galleries appears in the *Daily Astorian Vacation Guide*, available from the visitors center; or start looking at Art Reigns (☎ 325-6030), 965 Commercial St, a local cooperative gallery, or at Ricciardi Gallery (☎ 325-5450), 108 10th St. Another shop of interest is Persona Vintage Clothing (☎ 325-3837), 100 10th St, a great second-hand clothing store with fashions from days gone by.

**Getting There & Around**
The Astoria Airport is on Flightline Drive, off Hwy 101 near Fort Clatsop, west of Astoria. Horizon Air (☎ 861-0254) provides flights to/from Portland.

The Astoria bus depot (☎ 325-5641) is at 364 9th St; the fare on Raz Transportation between Portland and Astoria is $15. Astoria Transit System (☎ 325-0563) buses provide service to Warrenton (as close to Fort Stevens as public transport gets) and to Seaside, and Sunset Transit (☎ 325-0563) has service with Seaside and Cannon Beach.

Pacific Transit (☎ (206) 642-9418) out of Long Beach, WA, offers bus service across the Astoria Bridge to communities on the Long Beach Peninsula.

There's a Hertz rental car agency (☎ 325-7700) at 1492 Duane St. Call Roadrunner Transportation (☎ 325-3131) for a cab.

## FORT STEVENS STATE PARK
Located on the Clatsop Spit, the long neck of sand that flows along the Columbia River out to its final debouchment into the Pacific Ocean, Fort Stevens State Park (☎ 861-1671) commemorates the historic military and strategic garrisons here and offers near-endless beach access and camping facilities. A number of roads wind through the six-sq-mile park; stop at the campground office or the museum for a map. There is a $3 day-use fee from mid-May to the end of September. To reach the park from Astoria, cross the Youngs Bay Bridge on Hwy 101 and turn toward Warrenton and Hammond on Fort Stevens Hwy. It's 10 miles west of Astoria.

### Fort Stevens Military Museum Area
The Military Museum (☎ 861-2000) explains the history and lore of the fort; the displays capture especially well the mood of the nation and the Astoria area during WW II. There's a free trail guide available from the museum that points out the areas of historic interest, including the reconstructed Civil War earthworks, complete with moat. Hardly anything except concrete foundations remain of the extensive barracks, command stations, hospital and other military buildings but by far the most interesting remnants are the concrete bat-

teries – grim, warren-like garrisons dug into sand dunes.

The museum's hours are slowly cut back as winter approaches. Summer hours are from 10 am to 6 pm daily, June to September; winter hours are 10 am to 4 pm Wednesday to Sunday, November to April. Call for other times. Admission is by donation.

## Peter Iredale Shipwreck

Crossing the Columbia bar was a very dangerous enterprise and over 2000 ships have sunk or wrecked while attempting to enter the Columbia River, earning the area the name 'Graveyard of the Pacific'. On the sands of Fort Stevens is the rotting hull of one such ship, the *Peter Iredale*.

In 1906, the British four-masted freight ship sailed from Australia to Astoria to pick up a load of wheat. As the ship approached the Columbia bar, it encountered a dense fog, and the crew lost their bearings. A strong wind kicked up and the ship ran aground on the Clatsop Spit. No lives were lost in the accident, but the ship was so battered it was declared a total loss.

To reach the wreck, follow signs for the Fort Stevens Campground area; drive past the campground entrance about one mile, to the beach access. The ship is just there, like the skeleton of a whale on the beach.

## Organized Tours & Re-enactments

Between Memorial Day and Labor Day, several tours are offered by volunteers; the schedule changes often so call for tour times (☎ 861-1671); all tours leave from the Military Museum.

A guided walking tour explains the functions and history of Battery Mishler, an underground garrison built in 1900; tickets are $2 adult, $1 children. Tour the 37-acre fort grounds in a 2.5-ton army truck; tickets are $2.50 for adults, $2 for children.

Over Labor Day Weekend, there are re-enactments of Civil War battles using period weapons.

## Places to Stay

With 400 campsites, *Fort Stevens State Park* (☎ 861-1671) is the largest camp-

---

### Mines & Submarines

Fort Stevens was established at the height of the Civil War in 1863 by orders of President Abraham Lincoln. US military leaders feared a widening of the conflict to the western states and territories that were officially Unionist. Fort Stevens, however, did not see action during the Civil War.

The Columbia River's increasing strategic importance as a trade and transportation route led to a substantial upgrading of Fort Steven's armaments in the early 1900s. At the height of WW II, 2500 soldiers were stationed here. Guns were ready for assault from the Japanese Navy and much of the Columbia's mouth was planted with mines.

On the night of June 21, 1942, a Japanese submarine approached the mouth of the Columbia, following local fishing vessels up the channel in order to elude mines. The submarine fired 17 shells around Fort Stevens but did no damage, and no firepower was returned, as the submarine was out of range of the fort's guns. Fort Stevens is the only military installation in the continental USA to be fired on by a foreign power since the War of 1812.

After WW II, the fort was demilitarized, and the facility was used by the Coast Guard and the military reserves. In 1976, the fort was acquired by the state and turned into a state park. ■

---

ground in the state parks system. Facilities include showers, hiking and biking trails and wheelchair-accessible restrooms. Near the campground is a small fresh-water lake with a boat launch and swimming area; access to ocean beaches is less than a mile away. Fees are $16 for tent campers and $18 for full hook-ups.

Just outside the boundaries of the state park is the lovely *Officer's Inn B&B* (☎ 861-0084), 540 Russell Place, with eight guest rooms, each with a private bath, ranging from $56 to $71. This 9000-sq-foot building is truly spectacular; officers had it pretty nice in 1906. From the B&B, it's an easy walk to the Military Museum and tours.

OREGON

## Getting There & Around

The determined could probably take a bus from Astoria to Warrenton and then call a cab. Keep in mind, however, that you'll have to cover a lot of ground on foot in order to see the whole park. See Astoria for transit information.

Bicycles are a popular way of getting around the park, and the park's network of trails features a two-mile bike path along the beach. Maps are available at entrance booths or the Military Museum.

## SEASIDE

Subtlety is not among the allures of Seaside, one of the largest of Oregon's oceanfront resort towns (population 5480). On summer weekends, the town's central precinct – dominated by bumper car tracks, fish & chips shops, video-game arcades and gift stores – is completely thronged with tourists. Bicycles, so-called 'fun-cycles' and 'surreys' largely have the run of Seaside's boardwalk, called 'the prom'. Pedestrians simply serve as the obstacles along the course. The miles of sandy beach are actually quite pleasant, largely because most visitors are off buying things.

Summer holidays in Seaside are a family tradition. At its best, Seaside seems old-fashioned and venerable, but it can also seem garish and crowded. Generally, kids will like it here; adults may want to seek out more calming surroundings. Quiet Gearhart (population 1045) across the Necanicum River is an alternative.

## Orientation & Information

Seaside is 76 miles northwest of Portland on Hwy 26.

The old town center is a few blocks from the beach along Holladay Drive. Broadway, the main tourist strip, intersects Holladay Drive and leads out to the beach and the Turnaround, where a statue of Lewis and Clark overlooks the Pacific. (Although a plaque claims that this was the end of the expedition's journey, the claim smacks of boosterism: the party went as far south as Cannon Beach. What they did do here was make salt from saltwater.) The prom is a

two-mile-long cement boardwalk stretching along the beach. To reach Gearhart from Seaside take Hwy 101 (its called Roosevelt Drive in town) north and cross the Necanicum River. In half a mile, turn west on Pacific Way (it's the first blinking light).

The Seaside Visitors Bureau (☎ 738-6391, (800) 444-6740) is at 7 North Roosevelt Drive, Seaside, OR 97138.

## Biking

Seaside Surrey Rentals (☎ 738-0242), 151 Ave A, is one of many companies in Seaside that rents bicycles, tandems or 'fun-cycles', the hopped-up tricycles that speed along the surf and menace pedestrians on sidewalks.

## Golf

Gearhart Golf Links (☎ 738-5248), just north of Gearhart on N Marion St, was established in 1892, making it the second-oldest in western North America The 18-hole course is built in the British 'links' fashion. A newer course in Gearhart is The Highlands (☎ 738-0959), off Del Rey Beach Rd. This nine-hole course was originally designed as an 18-hole field until the second nine holes were discovered to be prime habitat for an endangered butterfly. The Seaside Golf Course (☎ 738-5261), 451 Ave U, in Seaside, is a nine-hole course that's popular with tourists and novice players.

## Surfing

To rent surfing gear and to get advice on where to hit the waves, go to Cleanline Surf Company (☎ 738-7888), at 710 1st St. They also rent in-line skates and boogie boards.

## Special Events

Avoid Seaside when it's convulsed with one of its festivals. Rooms are impossible to find; you'll look for hours just for a place to park. The Miss Oregon Contest is held here every July, usually the weekend after the Fourth of July. The Hood to Coast Relay Marathon, a team endurance race that begins on Mt Hood and follows Hwy

26 all the way to Seaside, not only jams the main road between Portland and Seaside with runners on a busy summer weekend, it also packs out Seaside, where a huge beach party is thrown for the runners. The relay is usually held the third weekend in August. The Seaside Beach Volleyball Tournament is held on the beach the weekend before Labor Day. Call the visitors center for more information.

## Places to Stay
Here's one of those places where room prices fluctuate wildly. The rates below are meant as a median price. If you plan to be in Seaside on a summer weekend, reserve a room well in advance, especially if you want rooms with a view or rooms close to the beachfront.

**Camping** Most campgrounds at Seaside are near Hwy 101. *Circle Creek Campground* (☎ 738-6070), one mile south of town, offers both tent and RV sites in a grassy meadow alongside a river. Tent sites are $14 a night, $18 for full hook-ups. There are showers and a laundry. *Bud's Campground & Grocery* (☎ 738-6855), 4410 Hwy 101, is across from the turnoff for Gearhart and offers showers, laundry, a store and gas station. Tent sites are $12 per night, full hook-ups $17. For less noisy campsites, go north to *Fort Stevens State Park*, or drive inland to *Saddle Mountain State Park*.

**B&Bs** The *Gilbert House B&B* (☎ 738-9770), 341 Beach Drive, is a large, classic beach house just one block from the beach and downtown; the 10 guest rooms all have private baths; rooms range from $70 to $90. *Beachwood B&B* (☎ 738-9585), 671 Beach Drive, is a lovely, 1900 Cape Cod-style home on a double lot with a beautifully landscaped yard complete with hammock; the three guest rooms each have a private bath; one comes with a fireplace and Jacuzzi.

**Hotels – bottom end** The *Mariner Motel* (☎ 738-3690), 429 S Holladay Drive, is an older motel near the old downtown center; it's a 10-minute walk from the beach; singles/doubles begin at $45/50. The *Coast River Inn* (☎ 738-8474), 800 S Holladay Drive, is five blocks from the beach and offers kitchenettes; it's well maintained and rooms range from $49 to $65. Only a block from the beach, the *City Center Motel* (☎ 738-6377), 250 1st Ave, is an aging motel. It's nothing fancy, but it has location; rooms are $57/62 (add $10 if it's the weekend).

**Hotels – middle** The *Tides Condominiums* (☎ 738-6317), 2316 Beach Drive, near the frenzy of downtown, is one of the best deals in Seaside. Oceanview studio rooms can start as low as $56, though prices between $70 and $80 are more common.

*Sundowner Motor Inn* (☎ 738-8301), 125 Oceanway, one block off the beach, has rooms for $64 to $70. Some of the least expensive oceanview rooms in central Seaside are at the *Inn On the Prom* (☎ 738-5241), 361 S Prom, with rooms beginning at $65. The *Huntley Inn* (☎ 738-9581), 441 2nd Ave, is five blocks from the beach, near the convention center. Rooms range between $60 and $77.

**Hotels – top end** The *Edgewater Inn* (☎ 738-4142), 341 S Prom, offers two different lodging options close to the beach. Brand-new rooms fronting the Pacific begin at $120 while rooms in an older wing begin at $69. At the six-floor *Seaside Beach Club* (☎ 738-7113), 561 S Prom, condo-style rooms ranging from $84 to $150 overlook the beach.

The attractive *Hi-Tide Motel* (☎ 738-8414), 30 Ave G, is right on the beach with lots of views and amenities. Rooms range from $85 to $110. *Inn at the Shore* (☎ 738-3113), 40 Ave U, has spacious suites with fireplaces, balconies and great views; rooms range from $79 to $219. The *Shilo Inn* (738-9571, (800) 222-2244), 30 N Prom, sits right at the Turnaround, the equivalent of ground zero in Seaside, and offers a great restaurant, room service, an indoor pool, fireplaces, a spa, exercise facilities and meeting rooms. It's one of the nicest lodgings on the northern coast. Rooms range from $104 to $194.

**Resorts** The *Gearhart-by-the-Sea Resort* (☎ 738-8331), 1157 N Marion Ave, offers condominium rooms overlooking the ocean and easy access to a great restaurant and to Gearhart Golf Links. One-bedroom apartments start at $117, two-bedroom units start at $130.

**Vacation Home Rentals** Pacific Northwest Properties (☎ 738-2600, (800) 203-1681), at 1905 'B' Spruce St rents private homes.

### Places to Eat

The old-fashioned *Harrison Bakery* (☎ 738-5331), 608 Broadway, offers coffee and baked goods. Eggs Benedict is the specialty at *Blue Dolphin* (☎ 738-4231), 504 Broadway. At *Little New Yorker on Broadway* (☎ 738-5992), 604 Broadway, start the day with a bagel, or try the panuzzi, the house specialty (it's a beef sausage sandwich), for $4.25. The whole-grain bread here is the best in Seaside.

*Alternatives* (☎ 738-5286), 846 Ave C, has natural foods, organic groceries and a juice bar. The *Wine Haus Deli* (☎ 738-0201), 21 N Columbia St, offers sandwiches, soups and a great wine selection.

At *Pudgy's* (☎ 738-8330), 227 Broadway, there's a good selection of fresh fish and steak dishes in the $13 range; the atmosphere is quiet and pleasant. For Mexican food, go to *Miguel's Fine Mexican & Seafood* (☎ 738-0171), 412 Broadway, where a chili relleno dinner costs $8. *Vista Sea Cafe* (☎ 738-8108), 150 Broadway, is a lively new restaurant with sandwiches, gourmet pizzas and microbrewed beers.

At *Shilo Inn Restaurant* (☎ 738-8481), 30 N Prom, innovation and tradition link up to produce some wonderful, if pricey, cuisine. Lobster and scallops au gratin goes

for $23; free-range veal rib-eye served with port wine demi-glace and grilled lentil cakes is $22. There's also an extensive regional wine list.

The *Pacific Way Bakery & Cafe* (☎ 738-0245), 601 Pacific Way in Gearhart, is in a charming old storefront with a cozy back garden. Omelets, waffles and fresh baked breads have people lined up out the door.

The best beachfront restaurant along this part of the coast is undoubtedly the *Oceanside Restaurant* (☎ 738-7789), also in Gearhart at 1200 N Marion Drive. Part of Gearhart-by-the-Sea Resort, the restaurant offers a wide selection of meat, seafood and pasta dishes. Specialties like rack of lamb or angel hair pasta with shrimp and crab go for around $15, and there are also daily salmon specials like poached salmon with orange and rosemary hollandaise.

### Things to Buy

Riverhouse Metaphysical General Store (☎ 788-8370) 2010 S Holladay Drive, probably isn't what you expect to find at an Oregon beach town. Primarily a store that sells historic and ethnic beads, the Riverhouse also sells herbs, crystals and books. The bead collection here is one of the largest in the Pacific Northwest – it includes beads from ancient Egypt and Rome, as well as trading beads from the native Clatsops. (The store also serves as a kind of headquarters for pagan events and groups along the northern coast.)

### Getting There & Around

The bus fare on Raz Transportation (☎ 738-5121), 201 S Holladay Drive, between Portland and Seaside is $13. Sunset Transit (☎ 325-0563) provides service with Astoria and Cannon Beach, and Astoria Transit System (☎ 325-0563) buses provide local service around Seaside. See Getting There & Away at the beginning of this chapter for more information on bus travel.

Holladay Car Rental (☎ 738-6596), is at 601 S Roosevelt Drive. Roadrunner Transportation (☎ 738-3131) is Seaside's cab company.

## SADDLE MOUNTAIN STATE PARK

Thirteen miles east of Seaside on Hwy 26, this woodsy state park centers around Saddle Mountain (3283 feet), the highest peak in northwest Oregon.

The barren monolith of stone that juts up out of the dense forest was formed underwater when molten rock rose up through soft sedimentary deposits and hit sea water. The magma cooled rapidly, creating the curious formations, called pillow basalt, that hikers encounter on the top of the mountain. Later, as North America rammed into the old Pacific seafloor, the formation containing Saddle Mountain was hoisted high above sea level, and erosion eventually wore away the softer sedimentary rock, leaving this gray volcanic plug exposed.

During the last ice age, Saddle Mountain remained unglaciered, and became a refuge for alpine plants. Today, these plants still survive on the flanks of the mountain.

A **hiking** trail leads from the campground area up through wildflower meadows to the top of Saddle Mountain. Views from the top are pretty spectacular, but the trail is steep and grueling. Once on top, the trail is quite exposed as it crosses the mountain's rocky face; storms can blow in quickly from the ocean, so be prepared for changeable weather. If you want to hike to the botanical area, follow the trail up about a mile. From the campground, it's about three miles to the top of Saddle Mountain. Saddle Mountain State Park (738-9373) offers 10 campsites for $9 each for tent campers only. There are flush toilets and drinking water.

To reach Saddle Mountain State Park, follow Hwy 26 to Necanicum Junction, 13 miles east of Seaside. Half a mile toward Portland, a sign indicates the seven-mile paved road that winds through clearcuts and young forests on its way to the park.

## CANNON BEACH

Miles of sandy beaches, broken by immense basalt promontories and rocky tide pools, front Cannon Beach (population 1270). Directly behind, the Coast Range rises in steep parapets.

Cannon Beach is without a doubt one of the most popular beach towns of northern Oregon, and at the right time, it can be very charming. Unlike Seaside's Coney Island-like atmosphere, Cannon Beach is artsy and a little smug. It wasn't until the 1970s that Cannon Beach became a real focus for vacationers, a fact that partially explains why it isn't marred by unsightly developments. The city is so accustomed to upscale visitors that the city council has, in a case that has gone to the Oregon Court of Appeals, successfully blocked the building of a federally funded low-cost housing development (many of the day workers are currently shipped in on special buses from Hillsboro, near Portland). Apparently, Cannon Beach is meant to be reserved for the wealthy.

Some of the coast's premier hotels and restaurants are here, as well as interesting shops and galleries. The small downtown area is especially delightful. The area around Hemlock St is filled with little alleys winding around a maze of boutiques and cafes. In summer the streets are ablaze with flowers. If you like the plantings, go to Holland's Flowers (☎ 436-2574), 255 N Hemlock St, in the courtyard, where gardeners can acquaint themselves with the coastal plants.

Prices of accommodations shoot through the roof in summer. And without long-standing reservations, you can forget about getting into the trendy restaurant that may well have been the reason for a spontaneous trip to Cannon Beach in the first place. Just getting around the streets can be problematic. On a sunny Saturday, you'll spend the better part of an hour just finding a place to park. Thankfully, most people that visit Cannon Beach come to poke around the shops, leaving lots of space down by the lovely beaches.

### Orientation & Information

Cannon Beach, 78 miles northwest of Portland, is on a short loop road off Hwy 101, nine miles south of Seaside.

The Cannon Beach Chamber of Commerce & Information Center (☎ 436-2623),

OREGON

2nd St, Cannon Beach, OR 97110, has a lodging map, which gives prices of all accommodations in the area. The *Cannon Beach Magazine*, a list of local businesses and activities, is also helpful.

### Beaches

The beaches at Cannon Beach are some of the most beautiful in Oregon, with **Haystack Rock** and other outcroppings rising out of the surf. Tide pools around the base of Haystack Rock are great for observing intertidal creatures as well as for watching seabirds. There's easy access to the beach at the end of Harrison St downtown, or at the end of Gower St a mile south.

A third beach access is at Tolovana Beach Wayside, about three miles south of Cannon Beach along Hemlock Ave. Other beach points are accessible at Hug Point State Park, five miles south on Hwy 101.

You can rent bikes and tandems at Mike's Bike Shop (☎ 436-1266), 248 N Spruce St. If you want a fun-cycle, however, you can rent one from Manzanita Fun Merchants (☎ 436-1880), 1140 S Hemlock St.

### Galleries

White Bird Gallery (☎ 436-2681), 251 N Hemlock St, did a lot to establish the town's reputation as a serious artists' community. In this warren-like building, two or three artists are featured at one time. The gallery also has interesting pottery and crafts.

Another noted gallery is North by Northwest (☎ 436-0741), 239 N Hemlock St, which specializes in glass art and ceramics. Valley Bronze (☎ 436-2118), 186 N Hemlock St, is a showroom for the noted foundry in Joseph, where Western bronze sculptures are cast.

### Ecola State Park

Just to the north of Cannon Beach is Ecola State Park, with picnic areas, short walks to dramatic beach vistas and longer hikes to a remote headland overlooking a lighthouse island.

A group from the Lewis and Clark Expedition, including Sacajawea, journeyed to the Cannon Beach area in the winter of 1806, when the Clatsops told them of a beached whale on the Pacific shore south of Fort Clatsop. The corps were motivated in part by curiosity and by hunger: Clark wanted whale blubber from which he hoped to render nutritious oil for cooking.

After an arduous two-day journey, the group climbed up over this headland, later called Tillamook Head, and down to today's Cannon Beach. The word 'ecola' means whale in the Clatsops' language. Unfortunately for the expedition, a party of Tillamook Indians had preceded them to the whale, and nothing was left but a 105-foot-long skeleton. Clark traded for 300 pounds of blubber and a few gallons of oil before the group mounted Tillamook Head again and returned to Fort Clatsop. This trip to Cannon Beach marks the farthest reach of the expedition's westward journey.

From the parking lot a short, paved trail leads along a brush-lined path to views of Cannon Beach's seven-mile long sandy shore, sharply punctuated with stone monoliths, all hunkered beneath the Coast Range, which edges close to the coast. This is one of the most photographed vistas in the state.

Beneath the headland are picnic tables; trails lead from the paved path both down to the beach and to Indian Beach, a mile and a half north of the viewpoint. At Indian Beach, rocky cliffs hedge round a secluded sandy cove, a favorite with surfers and anyone else wanting to escape the hordes at Cannon Beach. In summer, there is a road from the main Ecola State Park parking lot to the Indian Beach Picnic Area.

Longer hiking trails lead to **Tillamook Head**, looming 1200 feet above the crashing Pacific. This trail, which is the same as the one traversed by the Corps of Discovery, affords tremendous vistas of a series of offshore islands, which are now protected as wildlife refuges. **Tillamook Lighthouse**, sits out to sea on a 100-foot-high seastack. Now inactive, the lighthouse is used as a columbarium, or resting place for cremation ashes. The seven-mile trail ends at the end of Sunset Blvd in Seaside.

In summer, a $3 day-use fee per vehicle is collected.

## Haystack Program in the Arts & Sciences

Portland State University (PSU) sponsors a six-week series of seminars each summer at Cannon Beach. Most of the courses offered are either writers' workshops or seminars devoted to music or the visual arts; however, in recent years classes that explore the ecology of the Oregon coast have been added. The quality of the classes is usually quite high; nationally recognized artists and writers serve as faculty.

The seminars may be taken for college credit through PSU. Courses vary in length from a weekend to a five-day week and cost between $145 and $350. Although PSU does not provide housing, they do have a list of both public and private lodgings available to students. Contact Portland State University, Extended Studies (☎ 725-8500, (800) 547-8887, ext 8500), PO Box 751, Portland, OR 97207.

## Sandcastle Day

Cannon Beach's largest festival – indeed one of the most famous on the entire coast – is Sandcastle Day, held on a Saturday in June (the date changes due to the tides; call the visitors center (☎ 436-2623) for exact dates). It's great fun, and the resulting sculptures are usually very impressive. Teams compete for the most original and well-executed sand sculpture, many of which go far beyond standard castles. Each team is limited to eight members and has a 21-sq-foot patch of sand as raw material; four hours is the time limit for construction.

Be warned that Cannon Beach is usually booked up on this weekend, so call well in advance. Parking and general mobility in the town is also much worse than usual.

## Places to Stay

Cannon Beach is not a cheap place to stay. The older motels that anywhere else would be rundown and cheap are instead quaint and expensive here. As elsewhere along the northern coast, mid-week, off-season, rates are lower. Some of the mid-range accommodations also have non-view rooms at a much cheaper rate.

**Camping** The *RV Resort at Cannon Beach* (☎ 436-2231, (800) 847-2231), Hwy 101 and Elk Creek Rd, has an indoor pool and laundry facilities; sites range between $20 and $29; there are no tent facilities. *Sea Ranch RV Park* (☎ 436-2815) across from the entrance to Ecola State Park, has full hook-ups for $16, and tent sites for $12.

**B&Bs** The *Tern Inn* (☎ 436-1528), 3663 S Hemlock St, offers two guest rooms with private baths; rooms have fireplaces and ocean views; prices range from $85 to $105.

One of the newest and certainly one of the nicest lodgings at Cannon Beach is the *Stephanie Inn* (☎ 436-2221, (800) 633-3466), 2740 Pacific St, an exclusively adult resort motel operated as a very upscale B&B. Gabled and turreted in a kind of Queen Anne-revival style, this 'country inn' sparkles with leaded glass and chandeliers. Rooms have terraces and fireplaces; breakfast and an afternoon wine gathering are included in the price. Mountainview rooms start at $109, oceanview rooms at $189.

**Hotels – bottom end** The older *McBee Motel* (☎ 436-2569), 888 S Hemlock St, is kind of charming; some rooms have kitchens and fireplaces; rates are between $30 and $95. *Hidden Villa* (☎ 436-2237), 188 E Van Buren St, a few blocks from the beach, charges from $35 to $75.

**Hotels – middle** The old brick *Cannon Beach Hotel & Restaurant* (☎ 436-1392), 1116 S Hemlock St, was once a boarding house for loggers. Rates are between $49 and $119. Rates are good at *Major Motel* (☎ 436-2241), 2863 Pacific St, considering that many rooms face the ocean. Basic rooms start at $49, rooms with kitchenettes start at $59, and rooms with views begin at $79.

*Blue Gull Inn Motel* (☎ 436-2714, (800)

507-2714), 487 S Hemlock St, has cabins, studios and houses, most a block away from the beach. Prices range from $60 to $105. Likewise, the *Sand Trap Inn* (☎ 436-0247), 539 S Hemlock St, controls a number of houses and cabins, ranging from $45 to $95. *Quiet Cannon Lodgings* (☎ 436-2415), 732 N Spruce St, rents a number of homey cabins close to the beach at the north end of Cannon Beach, off bustling Hemlock St. Rooms range from $65 to $85.

Close to downtown, *The Waves Oceanfront Motel* (☎ 436-2205), 188 W 2nd St, offers rooms in several nearby homes in addition to the motel. Rates are between $75 and $169; many rooms have kitchens, some have fireplaces. *Webb's Scenic Surf* (☎ 436-2706), on N Larch St between 2nd and 3rd Sts, also close to downtown, offers oceanfront rooms with kitchens from $49 to $126.

The *Tolovana Inn* (☎ 436-2211, (800) 333-8890), 3400 S Hemlock St, near Tolovana Beach State Wayside, is a large complex of privately owned condos that are rented out when the owners aren't there. The accommodations in the back usually have reasonable prices, considering that all rooms have kitchens and access to an indoor pool and recreation room; there's also great beach access. Prices range from $59 to $199.

**Hotels – top end** All offer the usual luxuries of fireplaces, kitchens, pools, etc. *Best Western Surfsand Resort* (☎ 436-2274, (800) 547-6100), at Oceanfront and Gower Sts, has rooms ranging from $124 to $155. *Hallmark Resort* (☎ 436-1566, (800) 345-5676), 1400 S Hemlock St, fronts onto Haystack Rock and offers an indoor swimming pool, a weight and exercise room, guest laundry, fireplaces and kitchenettes, and pets are allowed; rates range from $99 to $159. *Haystack Resort Inn* (☎ 436-1577, (800) 499-2220), 3339 S Hemlock St, offers oceanview rooms with fireplaces and kitchens; there's also an indoor pool and pets are allowed; rates are $89 to $149.

**Vacation Home Rentals** Steve Martin Management Co (☎ 436-1197) at PO Box 219, Cannon Beach, OR 97110, rents private homes.

## Places to Eat

Bear in mind that Cannon Beach is a weekender's kind of place. While hotels may be cheaper on weekdays, almost all of Cannon Beach's better places to eat are closed Monday and Tuesday.

**Breakfast** Start the day with coffee and muffins at the *Espresso Bean* (☎ 436-0522), 1355 S Hemlock St, or downtown at the *Coffee Cabana* (☎ 436-0851), 219 N Hemlock St. *Cannon Beach Bakery* (☎ 436-2592), 144 N Hemlock St, offers a full line of baked goods, including good cinnamon rolls.

*Midtown Cafe* (☎ 436-1016), 1235 S Hemlock St, has pastries fresh from the oven, as well as omelets and frittatas, all made from organic ingredients. The Midtown is also one of the few places along the coast where you can find bagels and lox. Another great breakfast place is the *Lazy Susan Cafe* (☎ 436-2816), 126 N Hemlock St, where fluffy omelets and waffles lead the menu.

**Lunch** *Heather's* (☎ 436-9356), 271 N Hemlock St, in the thick of the maze-like courtyards downtown serves sandwiches and light snacks. *Ecola Seafood Market & Deli* (☎ 436-9130), 123 S Hemlock St, offers fresh fish for sale, as well as good fish & chips and crab. At *Pizza a Fetta* (☎ 436-0333), 231 N Hemlock St, in the courtyards, pizza is served by the slice. For burgers and local microbrews go to *Bill's Tavern* (☎ 436-2202), 188 N Hemlock St; there's seating in the back garden in good weather. *Doogers* (☎ 436-2225), 1371 S Hemlock St, has good food and is one of the few establishments that's open on Mondays and Tuesdays.

**Dinner** *Pullucci's Italian Restaurant* (☎ 436-1279), 988 S Hemlock St, serves well-prepared pasta dishes that don't cost a bundle. *J P's Restaurant* (☎ 436-1392), 1116 S Hemlock St, in the Cannon Beach Hotel, serves a good selection of dishes at fair prices in a bistro atmosphere.

For fine dining, two restaurants stand out. *The Bistro Restaurant & Bar* (☎ 436-2661) is a tiny establishment in the courtyard that serves very good seafood dishes prepared from locally caught fish like halibut with raspberry beurre blanc and seafood stew, rich with the scent of clams and saffron. The Bistro also has chicken and beef dishes. Dinners are in the $11 to $20 range.

*Cafe de la Mer* (☎ 436-1179), 1287 S Hemlock St, is one of the best loved restaurants on the Oregon coast and serves some splendid seafood dishes. Quality doesn't come cheap; dinners are mostly in the $20 to $25 range.

### Entertainment
The community *Coaster Theatre* (☎ 436-1242), 108 N Hemlock St, puts on drama and musical comedies, chamber music concerts and events associated with the Haystack Program in the Arts.

### Getting There & Around
Cannon Beach, for all its popularity, is not well serviced by public transportation. There are two buses a day from Seaside on Sunset Transit (☎ 325-0563); they pick up across from the information center on 2nd St, and at the *RV Resort at Cannon Beach*, at Hwy 101 and Elk Creek Rd. You can also flag them down along the route.

A wheelchair-accessible shuttle runs the length of Cannon Beach, from Les Shirley Park in the north to Maher and Hemlock Sts in the south. The bus runs every half hour from 10 am to 6 pm; a donation is requested.

### OSWALD WEST STATE PARK
Nine miles south of Cannon Beach on Hwy 101, this beautiful preserve of beach, mountain, rocky headland and coastal rain forest is named after Governor Oswald West, who championed the state's milestone beach-access bill, putting all ocean-

front land into public ownership. A tent-only campsite, a lovely beach popular with surfers and miles of hiking trails in lush old-growth forests make this state park a real treasure.

**Short Sands Beach** is an isolated little beach where dense forests press down to the edge of the beach, and two creeks run together in the tide line. Two major headlands, Neahkahnie Mountain and Cape Falcon, reach far out into the Pacific, protecting a small bay, called **Smugglers Cove**. Fishing and leisure boats frequently anchor offshore, and the rocky prominences along Cape Falcon are good places to watch for seabirds. Smugglers Cove is one of the north coast's most popular places to surf.

To reach the beach requires about a quarter-mile hike. Be sure to follow the new signs pointing to the beach trail; the trail from the old picnic area has largely washed away.

### Hiking
Two excellent hikes begin from the campground. The easiest leads two miles out to **Cape Falcon**, a sheer headland rising 750 feet out of the Pacific. Expansive views from here stretch past Neahkahnie Mountain to distant Cape Lookout far to the south. The trail passes through a magical old-growth coastal rain forest, with ancient Sitka spruce and fir trees towering high above. When the trail passes through a clearing, all manner of plant life springs forward, including vibrant ferns, salmonberries and dense stands of salal. At the viewpoint, stands of salal are so thick and high that you'll need to blindly trust that the trail leads out of the maze.

For a more strenuous hike, a four-mile path leads from the campground to the top of **Neahkahnie Mountain**, the 1661-foot coastal mountain that rises between Cape Falcon and Manzanita. The trail crosses a small stream, and after passing through forests, opens out onto a wide meadow, edged by sheer cliffs that drop away to the raging Pacific. After crossing Hwy 101, the trail climbs to the summit, where views are amazing; on a clear day, you can see 50 miles out to sea.

## Camping

The Oswald West campground is one of the few in the state parks system devoted to tent camping: a short quarter-mile hike on a paved trail is required to reach the 36 campsites. The campsites are available from March to mid-autumn. They are $13 a night. Wheelbarrows are provided to get your gear from the roadside parking lot to your tent space. The campsites are in dense mature forest; flush toilets and drinking water are available. While this is undeniably a lovely place to camp, Oswald West is popular with young campers, particularly surfers, and can get rowdy. Ecola State Park (☎ 463-2844) handles reservations.

## NEHALEM BAY

The Nehalem River rises high in the Coast Range, and courses through some of the Coast Range's wildest country. This bright, rushing river slows down considerably as it approaches the Pacific, creating both a

---

### The Mystery of Neahkahnie Mountain

According to stories told by Nehalem Bay's Tillamook and Clatsop tribes, long ago a Spanish ship landed at the base of Neah-kahnie Mountain. The crew disembarked, dug a deep hole in the side of the mountain and lowered a chest into the cavity. Crew members placed heavy bags inside the chest, sealed the chest and then the captain of the ship shot a Black sailor, whose body was thrown on top of the chest before it was buried. The Native Americans who had witnessed the scene abandoned the site, fearing the spirits of the murdered man.

This tale might have simply been considered Native American folklore, if it weren't for a series of uncanny incidents.

By the time explorers reached the Nehalem Bay area, the tribes along northern Oregon had gathered a great deal of beeswax along the shore. Beeswax, used in candlemaking, was a common article of trade aboard 17th-century Pacific-going Spanish vessels. Old shipping records document that a number of Spanish ships bearing beeswax were lost in the northern Pacific.

Large amounts of beeswax have been discovered along the northern coast of Oregon, especially along the Nehalem Spit. Some of the large chunks of beeswax found on the coast were carved with cryptic letters and patterns; one piece was engraved with the date 1679, others with crosses and designs. In total, about 10 tons of beeswax have been uncovered along the Oregon coast.

Then, around 1890, a farmer found a curiously carved rock in a meadow on the south-ern face of the mountain. Etched in the rock were Christian crosses; the letters D, E and W; arrows; and a series of dots. Later, other rocks were discovered nearby that repeated the letters and designs. The immediate assumption was that the stones contained infor-mation that would, if properly decoded, lead to the buried treasure.

Early in the century, there was a lot of digging in the side of the mountain, and many people claim to have solved the mystery of the buried treasure. However, no one has come forward with the treasure, nor has anyone produced a theory that adequately accounts for all the elements of the story.

The state parks department now tries to limit wildcat excavation on the mountain. The curiously carved rocks, usually called the Neahkahnie Stones, are on display at the Tillamook Pioneer Museum, as are several pieces of etched beeswax. ■

wide estuarial valley that is prized by farmers, and narrow Nehalem Bay, protected from the lashings of the Pacific by a seven-mile-long sand spit.

A developing fishing industry in the bay led to the establishment of the towns Wheeler and Nehalem in the 1870s. Along with Manzanita – on the ocean side of the spit – these communities nestle in one of the coast's most spectacular settings. Jagged peaks reach heights of 3000 feet, while just north of Manzanita, magical Neahkahnie Mountain rises above the Pacific, dropping away in 700-foot-high cliffs to the pounding waves. Wide, white-sand beaches stretch seven miles from Neahkahnie Mountain to the end of the Nehalem Spit.

Given the beauty of the area, these communities are relatively ignored, lacking the near-carnival atmosphere of the more famous beach destinations like Cannon Beach and Lincoln City. Manzanita (population 590), with a lovely sandy beach and dramatic rocky cliffs and good restaurants downtown, is the center of tourism. There is beach access along the entire length of Ocean Rd, west of downtown. Right on the river, historic and colorful Nehalem (population 235) and Wheeler (population 335) are becoming centers for antique boutiques and recreation.

### Wineries
One the oldest wineries in Oregon and one of the few on the coast, Nehalem Bay Winery (☎ 368-5300), 34965 Hwy 53, north of Wheeler, originally made fruit wines like cranberry and loganberry wines, but now also makes pinot noirs and reislings. The winery is one of the stops on the Fun Run Express Train (see Garibaldi, below) and is open from 10 am to 5 pm daily.

### Fishing & Crabbing
Wheeler and Nehalem used to have charter fishing, but the declining number of salmon has all but ruined that business. The bay, however, is exceptional for crabbing. Contact Wheeler Marina (☎ 368-5780),

278 Marine Drive, Wheeler, to rent a boat and crab rings. Two miles south of Wheeler, there's Brighton Marina (☎ 368-5745), with more boat rentals; if you don't have any luck, you can buy fish from the marina's fish shop.

The Nehalem River is famous for its steelhead and trout fishing. Contact SMS Guide Service (☎ 368-7409) if you'd like a guide.

### Other Activities
The quiet waters of Nehalem Bay are good for contemplative paddling; the estuaries are also rich in bird life. Rent a **kayak** from Annie's Kayaks (☎ 368-6005), along Wheeler's Main St. Manzanita Surf & Sail (☎ 368-7873), 150 Laneda Ave, rents surf and boogie boards and windsurfing gear.

On weekends, a trailer full of horses appears at the end of Nehalem Beach Rd. Show up there and join a **horseback riding** group, or contact Sundown Beach Rides (☎ 368-7170), 320 Laneda Ave, for mounts at other times.

Plain-old bicycles are available for rent from Manzanita Fun Merchants (☎ 368-6606), 186 Laneda Ave, Manzanita.

### Places to Stay
**Camping** *Nehalem Bay State Park* (☎ 368-5154), on the extensive dunes of the Nehalem Spit has nearly 300 campsites, with showers, horse paths and stables, wheelchair-accessible bathrooms, firewood and a boat ramp. Fees range around $17. The turnoff for the park is between Manzanita and Nehalem on Hwy 101. *Paradise Cove Resort & Marina* (☎ 368-6333, (800) 345-3029), half a mile south of Wheeler on Hwy 101 is an RV campground with tremendous views over the Nehalem Bay with rugged mountains rearing up immediately behind.

**B&Bs** The *Arbors at Manzanita* (☎ 368-7566), 78 Idaho Ave, Manzanita, offers two oceanview rooms with private baths for $90 to $100. *View of the West Country Inn* (☎ 368-5766), 294 Hall St, Wheeler, is an

OREGON

old inn high above town, with rooms from $65 to $80.

**Hotels** In Manzanita, *Sunset Surf Motel* (☎ 368-5224), 248 Ocean Rd, has some ocean views and an outdoor pool. Prices vary widely depending on whether you're staying in the old or new building, so expect to pay anywhere between $55 and $109 for your most basic room. *Manzanita Beach Fireside Inn* (☎ 368-1001, (800) 368-1001), 114 Laneda St, is only a block from the beach and near restaurants and shops. Basic rooms start at $55; there is a $15 to $20 discount on weeknights.

*Inn at Manzanita* (☎ 368-6754), 67 Laneda Ave, has Manzanita's most sought-after lodgings between the beach and downtown. Rooms have hot tubs and fireplaces, and range from $95 to $140.

*Wheeler Fishing Lodge* (☎ 368-5858), 580 Marine Drive, off Hwy 101, is an old motel once dedicated to anglers. The small rooms have been renovated, and the motel courtyard leads to a marina with great views of Nehalem Bay and the Coast Range. Basic rooms start at $50 to $60, and spa rooms range from $70 to $105.

**Places to Eat**
In Manzanita, *Coffee Etcetera* (☎ 368-6030), 507 Laneda Ave, has good coffee and home-baked pastries. For more of a coffeehouse atmosphere, go to *Manzanita News and Espresso* (☎ 368-7450), 500 Laneda Ave. For a full breakfast, Wheeler's *Treasure Cafe* (☎ 368-7740), 92 Rorvik St, serves breakfast from 6 am till 'noon-ish'. You can sit outside at picnic tables, take in the view and savor oyster hash for $7.

*Cassandra's* (☎ 368-5593), 411 Laneda Ave, Manzanita, has the area's best pizza. Manzanita also offers some of the northern coast's best, and most expensive, dining. *Jarboe's* (☎ 368-5113), 137 Laneda Ave, is housed in an old, very small cottage; the menu changes daily. Meals are available a la carte, with most main dishes in the $15 range, or on a prix-fixe menu, at $25. Entrees feature local fresh fish and seafood, often mesquite-grilled. Call for reserva-

tions; there are only eight tables at Jarboe's and the restaurant is only open Thursday to Monday evenings.

The other restaurant of note in Manzanita is *Blue Sky Cafe* (☎ 368-5712), 154 Laneda Ave, a less formal and less precious dining experience than Jarboe's. The menu features pan-Pacific touches, such as soy-tamarind salmon and sushi served with goat cheese. Entrees range from $15 to $18; the regional wine list is extensive.

## GARIBALDI

Garibaldi (population 915) began its life as a lumber town. Today, this scrappy little village wrestles a living from deep-sea fishing. Seated at the northern edge of Tillamook Bay on the Miami River, Garibaldi is the premier charter fishing town on the northern coast, and there is beach access throughout the town, which is essentially just one block wide and three miles long. While it won't win any awards for quaintness, this hard-working community is a nice antidote to the enforced cuteness of many of Oregon's coastal towns. Stop and walk around the harbor area and watch salmon, crab, halibut and shrimp come off fishing boats; or rent a boat and some crab rings and go get yourself a crab dinner.

The chamber of commerce (☎ 332-0301) at 202 Garibaldi Ave, Garibaldi, OR 97118, can provide a full list of charter fishing companies.

Garibaldi is 10 miles north of Tillamook and 18 miles south of Manzanita.

## Fun Run Express Train
In 1911, Southern Pacific constructed a rail line from Hillsboro to Tillamook, which wound down the Nehalem Valley through Rockaway Beach and Garibaldi. Regular rail service has long since terminated, but today, on summer weekends, the Fun Run Express (☎ 355-8667) cruises the Southern Pacific rails on a 28-mile run between Garibaldi and the Nehalem Bay Winery with stops at Rockaway Beach and Wheeler. Conductors wander through the cars, relat-

ing the history of the rail lines and the region. There is a restroom and light concession service on the train.

Trains depart from Garibaldi's Lumberman Park twice a day, at 10 am and 2 pm, on weekends from May to the end of October. Passengers can board the train at any of the stops. A roundtrip journey takes 3½ hours, with a half-hour break at the winery. The fare is $10 adult and $5 children 12 and under; there's a family fare of $30.

### Charter Fishing & Whale Watching
Fishing is excellent off Garibaldi, whether in Tillamook Bay or the Pacific. Charter boats fish for whatever is in season or available at the time, including salmon, cod, red snapper or rockfish. Most charter fishing boats also run whale-watching trips during the spring migration. Troller Deep Sea Fishing (☎ 332-3666, (800) 546-3666), 304 Mooring Basin Rd, and Siamez Charters (☎ 842-2200) both specialize in deep-sea fishing. At Garibaldi Marina (☎ 322-3312), 302 Mooring Basin Rd, you can rent boats, crab rings, tackle, and whatever else you need to outfit your own fishing trip.

### Places to Stay & Eat
Don't expect fancy accommodations in Garibaldi; the facilities here are designed for a clientele with deep-sea fishing on their minds. You can't beat the prices, however.

Garibaldi's lumbering past is still alive at the *Old Mill Marina Resort* (☎ 322-0324), at 3rd St and American Ave, a large and pleasant campground on the grounds of a turn-of-the-century lumber mill. There are lots of grassy expanses in the campground, plus a marina, a swimming pool and a separate tent area. Rates are $12 for tent sites and $18 for hook-ups. *Old Mill Restaurant*, in the complex, serves fried seafood and standard American food three times daily.

The *Harbor View Inn* (☎ 322-3251), Mooring Basin Rd, is right on the docks; rooms range from $32 to $54. At *Tilla-Bay Motel* (☎ 322-3405), 805 Garibaldi Ave,

between 8th St and Hwy 101, rooms range from $31 to $39.

Closer to the traffic on Hwy 101, *Pelican's Perch Guest Suites* (☎ 322-3633), 112 E Cypress Lane has homey rooms from $65 to $75.

At *Miller's Seafood Market & Cafe* (☎ 322-0355), 1007 Garibaldi Ave, you'll find some of the freshest fish & chips on the Oregon Coast. *Bozzio's* (☎ 322-3601) is more of a dinner house, with steak and seafood as the specialties. Crab legs are $13, razor clams are $11, and steak begins at $9.

### TILLAMOOK
The Tillamook Indians who controlled the land around Tillamook Bay were renowned hunters. They lived in framed, woven-reed houses in villages and the aristocracy practiced head-flattening and decorative tattooing. They refused to enter the Indian Wars of the 1850s and were essentially disbanded by White settlement in the area, never to be granted a reservation.

Today, the first thing that you'll notice when you arrive in Tillamook (population 4145) is the smell: it's fairly obvious that *a lot* of cows live in the area. Five coastal rivers flow from the mountains into flat Tillamook Bay, making it perfect for raising dairy cattle. Cheese making and other dairy-related industries are the focus of the local economy. The Tillamook Cheese Factory ships out 40 million pounds of cheese – mostly cheddar – each year.

Tillamook's other attraction is a massive WW II-era hangar for reconnaissance dirigibles that's now an aviation museum.

Tillamook is one of the few working towns left on the coast. Coffeeshops haven't yet evolved into espresso bars, and the local feed store – not the metaphysical bookstore – is where the locals converge.

### Orientation & Information
The only way to get to Tillamook is by car. Going south Hwy 101 follows the Nestucca River through pastureland and heavily lumbered mountains. Alternatively, the slower

OREGON

### The Bayocean Folly

The four-mile-long Bayocean Sandspit that reaches across the mouth of Tillamook Bay was the site of one of the Oregon coast's most ambitious, and ultimately foolish, resort developments. In 1906, a land developer from Kansas City decided that the narrow spit would be turned into a vast entertainment, recreation and housing complex called Bayocean. A grand hotel, natatorium, docks, rail access and four miles of paved streets were completed by 1912.

However, winter storms began to eat away at the spit; by 1932, the natatorium collapsed into the sea, and in 1952 a storm so lashed the area that the Bayocean Spit was breached in three places, leaving its tip an island. Erosion continued to work away at the spit, and the last house of the Bayocean resort community tumbled into the sea in 1960. ■

but prettier 30-mile Three Capes Scenic Route follows the coast.

The visitors center (☎ 842-7525) is in the parking lot of the Tillamook Cheese Factory at 3705 N Hwy 101, Tillamook, OR 97141. The post office, bookstores, laundry, etc, are all within 1st and 3rd Sts.

### Cheese Factories

Cheese production began in Tillamook in the 1890s, when an English cheesemaker brought his cheddaring techniques to the fledgling dairies along Tillamook Bay.

Two cheese factories in Tillamook are open for tours. The Tillamook Cheese Factory (☎ 842-4481), about two miles north of town at 4175 N Hwy 101, is the largest and most famous, visited by over 750,000 people a year. There are self-guided tours, videos explaining the cheese-making process, and samples of cheese and ice cream available. In the large sales and deli area, many regional foods, wines and gifts are for sale. There's also a small cafe for light meals. Opening hours are from 8 am to 8 pm daily; admission is free.

At the Blue Heron French Cheese Company (☎ 842-8281), 2001 Blue Heron Drive off N Hwy 101, cheesemakers serve samples and sell locally produced Brie and Camembert along with other European-style cheeses. There is a wine-tasting bar in this converted barn that offers four wine samples for $1; you get to choose from a selection of 12 to 15 regional wines.

### Tillamook Pioneer Museum

Housed in the old courthouse, this county museum (☎ 842-4553) at 2106 2nd St, is worth a stop. There's a natural science display of shorebirds and waterfowl, or more exactly, a paean to the art of taxidermy. Other items of note include a display of artifacts and photographs of the Tillamook tribe; carved beeswax from a 17th-century Spanish ship that wrecked somewhere in the Pacific; and the Neahkahnie Stones, whose curiously carved surfaces were meant to point to a legendary buried treasure near Manzanita.

The bookstore has a good selection of regional history and travel. The museum is open from 8:30 am to 5 pm, Monday to Friday, and noon to 5 pm on the weekend. Entry is $2 adult, $1 for seniors and students.

### Tillamook Naval Air Museum

Tillamook Naval Air Station, opened in 1943, is one of 10 air bases built by the US Navy during WW II for a fleet of blimps that patrolled the northern Pacific looking for enemy warships. The one remaining hangar is open to the public as the Tillamook Naval Air Museum (☎ 842-1130), about three miles south of Tillamook off Hwy 101.

The enormous wooden building covers seven acres. Only half the hangar is currently used by the museum, but there's enough room for two dirigibles, a hot-air balloon and a large collection of old fighter planes including a Spitfire, a Messerschmidt and an Avenger – the same type of aircraft George Bush was shot down in.

Opening hours are from 9 am to dark daily from May to September and from 9 am to 5 pm daily the rest of the year.

Admission is $5 for adults, $2.50 for children ages six to 12.

**Air tours** over Tillamook Bay and the Three Capes are available from the airfield adjacent to the museum. Contact Tillamook Air Tours at 842-1942.

## Munson Creek Falls

The highest waterfall in the Coast Range, Munson Creek Falls drops 266 feet down a succession of mossy, stair-stepped ledges. The easy half-mile hike to the falls passes through a dense forest. To reach the trailhead, drive seven miles south of Tillamook on Hwy 101 to a gravel road with signs indicating Munson Creek County Park. The trailhead is 1.6 miles east.

## Golf

Given the proximity to the Tillamook Cheese Factory, it is not surprising to learn that the 18-hole Alderbrook Golf Course (☎ 842-6413), 7300 Alderbrook Rd, was both a dairy and a golf course from the late 1930s to 1967.

## Special Events

The Dairy Parade & Festival (☎ 842-7525), is held the last weekend of June – the Dairy Month. Celebrations include a parade, street dance and the crowning of the Dairy Queen. The Tillamook County Fair (☎ 842-2272) is held Thursday to Saturday the second week in August. Events include horseracing, livestock, home and garden shows, a carnival and musical performances. Both festivals are held at the county fairgrounds, 4603 3rd St.

## Places to Stay

**Camping** *Pleasant Valley RV Park* (☎ 842-4779) just six miles south of Tillamook on Hwy 101 has tent sites for $14, and RV sites for $16.50 to $19.50. Garibaldi and the Three Capes Scenic Route also have great campgrounds (see those sections for details).

**Hotels** The *Mar-Clair Inn* (☎ 842-7571), 11 Main Ave, is right downtown along the Trask River. Rooms range from $52 to $80.

The *El Ray Sands Motel* (☎ 842-7511, (800) 257-1185), 815 Main Ave, is on the south end of Tillamook; $47 to $70.

*Western Royal Inn* (☎ 842-8844, (800) 624-2912), 1125 N Main Ave is an older, well-kept motel on the Hwy 101 strip; $40 to $109. *Shilo Inn* (☎ 842-7971, (800) 222-2244), 2515 N Hwy 101, is one of the newest accommodations in Tillamook, with rooms from $59 to $99.

## Places to Eat

*M J's Bakery & Coffee House* (☎ 842-6200), 212 Main St, is a clean and pleasant bakery with fresh baked goods and traditional breakfasts. *Muddy Waters Coffee & Tea Co* (☎ 842-1400), 1904 3rd St, is a small espresso shop with a good selection of newspapers. It's a good place to unwind from driving harrowing Hwy 101.

Some of the best food is served in Mexican restaurants. *Casa Medello* (☎ 842-5768), out on the Hwy 101 strip, offers good deals in well-prepared Mexican food. *La Mexicana Restaurant* (☎ 842-2101), 2203 3rd St, has an extensive menu including prawns mole for $9, lobster a la Mernier for $16, and oysters sautéed in hot sauce for $8. There are also standard Mexican dishes for under $8.

*McClaskey's* (☎ 842-5674), 2102 1st St at Pacific Ave, offers sandwiches and soups for lunch; a house specialty, the oyster burger, goes for $7. For dinner, steak, pasta and fresh seafood are in the $10 range.

## THREE CAPES SCENIC ROUTE

This highway is an alternative route to Hwy 101, between Tillamook and the Pacific City junction. The 30-mile route passes through three state parks with some of the coast's most stunning headlands and some charming towns that are among the few beach towns not bisected by busy Hwy 101.

The pace of traffic is slow. Unless you plan on stopping at the state parks, you may want to stay on Hwy 101. If you tire of the winding road, two side roads – at Netarts and Sand Lake – will return you to Hwy 101.

OREGON

OREGON

### Cape Meares State Park

Ten miles west of Tillamook, this 233-acre park is a welcome relief from the relentless clearcutting that edges much of the Three Capes Drive. Of interest is the **Cape Meares Lighthouse**, built in 1890. During the summer, a small gift shop is open at its base and the curious can hike up to the top of the building. Also, the **Octopus Tree** is a massive Sitka spruce whose low-slung branches reach far out from the base of the tree before spreading upward. Native American legends hold that the tree was shaped to cradle funeral canoes.

There are hiking trails to both sites from the parking lot.

### Oceanside

Once an unheralded beach resort, Oceanside has been 'discovered'. Now a massive condominium resort clings to the headland above the town. Rising immediately out to sea are the towering 400-foot-high Three Arch Rocks, preserved as a seabird refuge; seals and sea lions also take their place on the flanks of these dramatic protrusions.

**Places to Stay & Eat** The nicest place to stay in Oceanside is *House on the Hill Motel* (☎ 842-6030), on Maxwell Point on the bluff above Oceanside; rooms are $65 to $110.

Widely noted for its good food, *Roseanna's Cafe* (☎ 842-7351), 1490 NW Pacific St, has a casual maritime atmosphere. The service, however, is excruciatingly slow. People from the city often note that people on the coast live at a slower pace, but after waiting 20 minutes for your table to be cleared and set, it's hard not to jump in and help out. Bring your patience, if not a snack, for you may need it.

### Netarts

Netarts offers few facilities for the traveler, and the locals prefer it that way. The area is known for its excellent clamming and fishing. Rent a boat at Bay Shore RV Park & Marina (☎ 842-7774), about a mile south

of Netarts on Three Capes Drive and try your luck at crabbing. Or take a boat across the narrow bay and sunbathe on the spit with the sea lions.

Five miles south, Pearl Point Oyster Farm (☎ 842-6371), a small family operation, produces some of the best oysters in Oregon: check out the remarkable *yamomotos*. Show up at an opportune moment, and the owners may give away a free kitten for every dozen oysters you buy!

There is camping at *Bayshore RV Park & Marina* (☎ 842-7774), a mile south of Netarts on Three Capes Drive; sites start at $17.50. The *Terimore Motel* (☎ 842-4623), 5105 Crab Ave, sits high on a cliff; rates range from $40 to $80.

### Cape Lookout State Park

This 2000-acre state park (☎ 842-4981) includes the entire length of sandy Netarts Spit, as well as Cape Lookout, jutting out nearly a mile from the mainland, like a finger pointing out to sea. The cliffs along the south side of the cape rise 800 feet from the Pacific's pounding waves. The rock exposed at Cape Lookout, as at the other capes along this route, is formed of Columbia Basin basalts, the lava flows that traveled here 15 million years ago from a spot near present-day Idaho.

**Hiking** The most popular hiking trail in the park is to the end of Cape Lookout. The trail begins either at the campground, where it climbs 2.5 miles up to a ridge-top parking lot; or, you can drive to here and hike 2.5 miles to the cape's cliff edge, with views of Cape Kiwanda to the south.

Informal hiking trails lead out onto Netarts Spit, a grassy dune that stretches nearly four miles across Netarts Bay. Clamming is popular at low tides along the wide sandy beach.

**Camping** Cape Lookout (☎ 842-4981) campground, has nearly 250 campsites at the park, 197 intended for tents. Facilities include showers, evening ranger programs in the summer, meeting rooms and wheelchair-accessible toilets. Sites can be reserved during the summer; contact the state parks department for forms. Fees for camping begin at $15 a night for tents, and go to $18 for full hook-ups.

## Cape Kiwanda

The third in this route's trilogy of capes is Cape Kiwanda, a sandstone bluff that rises just north of the little town of Pacific City. To reach Cape Kiwanda requires a hike up the spine of the dunes that drape around the cape. The top of the dunes is a popular place to hang-glide.

Just over the dune is the Pacific and miles and miles of sandy beach. The beaches south along the Nestucca Spit are part of **Bob Straub State Park**, which provides restrooms, a parking lot and easy beach access.

Pacific City is noted for two things: its Haystack Rock and the dory fleet. Watching dory crews struggle from the beach, into the surf and out to sea is usually quite amusing.

**Places to Stay & Eat** *Cape Kiwanda RV Park* (☎ 965-6230), 33005 Kiwanda Rd, has 130 RV sites with hook-ups and a separate tent-camping area. *Inn at Pacific City* (☎ 965-6366), 35215 Brooten Rd, is a nice, newly built lodging with moderately priced rooms at $39 to $49. *Three Capes Motel* (☎ 965-6464), 35280 Brooten Rd, has rooms ranging from $37 to $60.

There are a number of burger and fish & chips restaurants in Pacific City. Instead, *Grateful Bread Bakery* (☎ 965-7337), 34805 Brooten Rd, serves breakfast and lunch – sandwiches, soups and pizzas – either indoors, or, in good weather, on the deck. The French loaf is excellent. Go to *White Moon Cow Cafe* (☎ 965-5101), 35490 Brooten Rd, for espresso and pastries.

Cozy and unpretentious, *The Riverhouse* (☎ 965-6722), 34450 Brooten Rd, on the Nestucca River, is one of the favorite restaurants along this stretch of the coast. Dinners range between $11 and $19.

## LINCOLN CITY & AROUND

A seven-mile-long series of commercial strips, motels, snack bars and gift shops that fronts onto a fairly wide if lackluster stretch of sandy beach, Lincoln City (population 6090) is also the principal trade center for a large area of the coast, so lumber yards, supermarkets and car dealerships also crowd along Hwy 101. Lincoln City is also known for its complex of outlet stores, off East Devil's Lake Rd at Hwy 101, where dozens of national chain stores dump their seconds and last year's models at reduced prices.

Mention Lincoln City at a Portland party, and people will crescendo over each other to tell their favorite 'Lincoln City is so tacky that . . . ' story. Lincoln City has become the beach town you love to hate. Understandably, the local business community smarts under such criticism. When a well-known guidebook called Lincoln City an example of 'tourism in its worst conceivable form', the Lincoln City governing council passed a resolution banning the sale of the book in the town (never mind that there really isn't a bookstore in town). The brouhaha made front-page news across the state.

The truth is that Lincoln City *isn't* a very attractive town, and it sprawls uncontrollably across too much of the Oregon coast. The good news is that rooms are plentiful and inexpensive, and if you like lying on the beach, there's a lot of it here.

## Orientation

Lincoln City is divided into quadrants by the D River and Hwy 101. Highway 18 from the Willamette Valley joins Hwy 101 in town.

To the north is one of the coast's major capes, Cascade Head and to the south, Gleneden Beach, the site of Salishan Lodge, the Oregon coast's most upscale retirement and golfing resort.

## Information

The visitors center (☎ 994-3070, (800) 452-2151) is at 801 SW Hwy 101, Lincoln City, OR 97367.

The post office (☎ 994-2148) is at 1501 SE Devil's Lake Rd. The daily newspaper is the Lincoln City *News Times*. North Lincoln Hospital (☎ 994-3661), is at 3043 NE 28th.

## Beaches

Lincoln City's seven-mile stretch of wide sandy beaches endears the town to holiday-makers, particularly family groups. The main public access points are at the D River State Wayside, in the center of town where the river meets the Pacific; at the north end of Lincoln City, at Road's End State Wayside off Logan Rd; and along Siletz Bay south of town at the end of SW 51st St at Taft City Park.

## Cascade Head & Harts Cove

A favorite hiking destination, Cascade Head was slated to become a resort development in the 1960s, but the Nature Conservancy bought up the land, and worked with the USFS to have the area declared a Scenic Research Area.

There are two trails to the vista, both off Hwy 101. For the first, follow Hwy 101 north one mile from the junction with Hwy 18, turn west on Three Rocks Rd, and follow signs for the trailhead, 2.7 miles away. To find the second trail, turn west off Hwy 101 four miles north of the Hwy 18 junction onto USFS Rd 1861, called Cascade Head Rd. The trailhead is 3.3 miles along this road.

One mile further down USFS Rd 1861 is the trailhead to the 2.6-mile hike to Harts Cove, a remote meadow along a bay lined with cliffs; the area is frequented by sea lions.

## Sitka Center for Art & Ecology

A series of summer workshops on nature, art and Native American culture are held at this private educational facility at Cascade Head Ranch along Three Rocks Rd. For information on the courses, contact the Sitka Center (☎ 994-5485) at PO Box 65, Otis, OR 97368.

## Neskowin

The small town of Neskowin has scarce facilities but that's the way the citizens want it. There is camping at *Neskowin Creek Resort* (☎ 392-3082), 50500 Hwy 101; full hook-ups are $20, tent sites $12. For hotels, look for the small resorts just off the beach, including *Pacific Sands* (☎ 392-3101), 48250 Breakers Blvd, where suites are around $120, and *The Chelan* (☎ 392-3270), 48750 Breakers Blvd, with suites for two people at $70; there's a $10 charge for each extra guest.

*Hawk Creek Cafe* (☎ 392-3838), 4505 Salem Ave, serves up great breakfasts. For dinner there are pizzas, burgers and a few seafood specials. Dinner prices range from $8 to $14.

## Salishan Lodge

Superlatives are often used to describe Oregon's only four-star resort, the pricey *Salishan Lodge* (☎ 764-2371), Hwy 101 at Gleneden Beach, south of Lincoln City. This rambling 1000-acre resort has a first-rate golf course, ringed by a number of retirement homes and condominiums. Rooms in the condos range from $109 to $239.

*The Dining Room*, is credited with preparing the best menu in the state. Dinners, however, usually total about $50 to $60 a person, before exploring the extensive wine list. The restaurant offers tours of the wine cellar containing over 20,000 bottles. The food can be excellent, and the service slightly ostentatious. Meals in the *Sun Room*, the casual dining room, are much more reasonable; sandwiches at lunch hover at the $8 mark.

## Activities

For bike rentals, go to David's Bicycle Rental (☎ 996-6001), 960 SE Hwy 101. Canoeing on Devil's Lake, east of town, and on Siletz Bay, is popular for recreation and for **wildlife viewing**. Blue Heron Landing (☎ 994-4708), 4006 W Devil's Lake Rd, rents both canoes and motor boats.

**Surfing** is an increasingly popular pastime along the coast. Rent equipment at Oregon Surf Shop (☎ 996-3957), 4933 SW

Hwy 101, or at Safari Town Surf Shop (☎ 996-6335), 3026 NE Hwy 101.

## Kite Festivals

The self-proclaimed 'Kite Capital of the World', Lincoln City hosts three annual Kite Festivals. Enormous kites – some over 100 feet in length – take off to twist and dive in the ocean breezes. It's a colorful event by day and by night, when kites are illuminated.

The spring festival is usually held the second weekend in May; the fall festival is usually held the last weekend of September. Both festivals are held at the D River State Wayside in the center of Lincoln City. Call the visitors center for more details.

## Places to Stay

Lincoln City offers some of the coast's most reasonably priced lodging, especially if you're willing to listen to the roar of traffic rather than the sea. And in Lincoln City, you're rarely more than a five-minute walk from the beach no matter where you stay.

**Camping** *Devil's Lake State Park* (☎ 994-2002), at NE 6th Drive and Hwy 101, is a five-minute walk to the action on the D River beach and downtown Lincoln City. There are showers and flush toilets; there's also swimming and boating in freshwater Devil's Lake. Camping fees are $16 for tents, $18.25 for full hook-ups. The *Lincoln City KOA Kampground* (☎ 994-2961), 5298 NE Park Lane, is near the northern edge of Devil's Lake, but isn't so convenient to the beaches. Facilities include showers, laundry, flush toilets, public phone, a gas station and a playground. Tent sites are $15, full hook-ups cost $20, and cabins cost $27.

**B&Bs** The *Brey House B&B* (☎ 994-7123), 3725 NW Keel Ave, offers four rooms with private baths; some rooms have decks and fireplaces. Three of the rooms have ocean views and are $85 a night. The single room without an ocean vista is $65 a night. The *Palmer House* (☎ 994-7932), 646 NW Inlet

Ave, has three guest rooms with ocean views.

**Hotels – bottom end** One of the best deals in town is the *Captain Cook Inn* (☎ 994-2522), 2626 NE Hwy 101. Rooms are well maintained; rates are $35 to $45. Just down the street is *Budget Inn* (☎ 994-5281), 1713 NW 21st St; all rooms have queen-sized beds and some have balconies and wheelchair-accessible units. Single/double rooms are $33/38. At the *City Center Motel* (☎ 994-2612), 1014 NE Hwy 101, the rooms are a bit more functional, for $28/32.

**Hotels – middle** The following establishments share the bluff view with the upscale Inn at Spanish Head. At the *Ester Lee* (☎ 996-3606), 3803 SW Hwy 101, there's both a new and an old wing; The old units have fireplaces, kitchens and patios. Rooms range from $50 to $75. Next door at the *Edgecliff Motel* (☎ 996-2055), 3733 SW Hwy 101, where rooms cost $45 to $65. For both of these motels, there is a steep, two-block, beach access road.

Down on the beach along a quiet street are two relatively ignored motels. At the *Westshore Oceanfront Motel* (☎ 996-2001), 3127 SW Anchor Ave, rooms range from $40 to $60 and have no phones. Rooms at *Sandcastle Beachfront Motel* (☎ 996-3612), 3417 SW Anchor Ave, range from $50 to $80 (nonsmoking rooms also available).

Other inexpensive hotels are near Siletz Bay, where the beaches are probably less thronged than those in the center of town. At the *Rodeway Inn on the Bay* (☎ 996-3996), 861 SW 51st St, rooms begin at $45. *Dock of the Bay* (☎ 996-3549, (800) 362-5229), 1116 SW 51st St, with rooms ranging from $50 to $149, has a swimming pool, hot tubs and a sauna.

There are also pretty good deals in the mid-section of Lincoln City, along the edge of bluffs. Most are older hotels that are well-maintained and perfectly nice. *Pelican Shores* (☎ 994-2134), 2645 Inlet Ave, fronts right onto the beach; there's both an indoor and an outdoor pool; rooms range from $52 to $89. Uphill at the *Nordic Motel* (☎ 994-8145), 2133 NW Inlet Ave, there's a pool and spa facilities. Rooms range from $52 to $89.

**Hotels – top end** The *Inn at Spanish Head* (☎ 996-2161), 4009 SW Hwy 101, is Lincoln City's most noted hotel. The main access is on the bluffs, but the rooms descend in stairsteps along the face of the bluff to the level of the beach; how they got permission to build on the beach is a good question. Amenities include a pool, saunas and hot tubs, exercise facilities and a guest laundry; rooms have patios or balconies. Rooms range from $97 to $169. The restaurant is quite good.

At the north end of Lincoln City is *Shilo Inn Oceanfront Resort* (☎ 994-3655), 1501 NW 40th St, a sprawling, new development. A total of 146 beachfront rooms range from $88 to $99. Right at city center is *Best Western Lincoln Sands* (☎ 994-4227, (800) 528-1234), 535 NW Inlet Ave. Rooms start at $95, breakfast included.

**Vacation Home Rentals** To rent a private home contact Oregon Coast Vacation Rentals (☎ 994-5674), 1734 NW Harbor Ave, Lincoln City, OR 97367.

## Places to Eat
**Breakfast** *Audreys* (☎ 994-6210), 1725 SW Hwy 101, has the best breakfasts in Lincoln City with dishes like Mexican Eggs Benedict and crab-shrimp omelet for $7.50, and the wonderful biscuits and gravy for $2.95. *L'il Sambo's* (☎ 994-3626), 3262 NE Hwy 101, serves traditional and good breakfasts; the rest of the day Sambo's offers all-you-can-eat specials. It's not fancy, but it's one of the real deals in Lincoln City.

**Lunch & Dinner** *Cafe Roma* (☎ 994-6616), 1437 NW Hwy 101, serves pastries, sandwiches and espresso drinks, and sells new and used books. This is also about as close to an alternative hangout as you'll find in Lincoln City.

*Yen-Ha Coast* (☎ 994-7557), 4649 SW

Hwy 101, is a new Asian seafood restaurant. Head to *Red's BBQ* (☎ 994-2626), 220 SE Hwy 101, for a meal of beef brisket, or barbecued chicken or ham. *Kyllo's Ethnic* (☎ 994-3179), 1110 NW 1st Court, overlooks the D River and the Pacific. While the food is pretty good, this echo chamber of a restaurant errs on the side of minimalism, except for the exuberance of the staff, who have been trained to be overly prompt and aggressively pleasant. The menu focuses on zesty seafood dishes like grilled halibut with a black bean salsa ($13).

*Chameleon Cafe* (☎ 994-8422), 2145 NW Hwy 101, has meat-free dishes plus a number of pasta dishes and sandwiches. *Galucci's Pizza* (☎ 994-3411), 2845 NW Hwy 101, serves the best pizza in Lincoln City and has an extensive salad bar.

*Otis Cafe* (☎ 994-2813), three miles northeast of Lincoln City on Hwy 18, is an unpretentious little diner in the woods that serves up great home-baked bread and pies; the German hash browns with melted cheese and the ample burgers are popular. On weekends anticipate a wait.

The *Bay House* (☎ 996-3222), 5911 SW Hwy 101, about two miles south, is an elegant restaurant overlooking Siletz Bay. The menu is seasonal but always features standards like local seafood and fish, rack of lamb and duck. Orange and rosemary-marinated grilled salmon goes for $19.

## Entertainment
**Brewpubs** The *Lighthouse Brew Pub* (☎ 994-7238), 4157 N Hwy 101, is in a shopping mall just north of Lincoln City. The brewpub is an offshoot of the McMeniman's chain out of Portland, and serves light meals.

## Getting There & Around
See Getting There & Away at the start of this chapter for information on air and bus travel. Greyhound and Central Coast Connections buses both stop in Lincoln City. The depot for Greyhound is at SE 14th St and Hwy 101; Central Coast Connections buses to Newport set off from Otis Junction

(slightly north of Lincoln City) at 7 am, noon and 4:15 pm.

Call Lincoln Cab Company (☎ 996-2003) if you've become too frustrated trying to figure out the bus system.

## DEPOE BAY

This small fishing community is 11 miles south of Lincoln City. South of the town, Hwy 101 climbs up to Cape Foulweather, 500 feet above the Pacific.

The tiny six-acre boat basin was formed when the pounding waves battered a narrow channel through the basalt cliffs. The 50-foot-wide passage out to the ocean can be a challenge. Today, whale-watching trips and charter fishing are popular, as is watching the boats maneuver through the passage. Parts of the film *One Flew Over the Cuckoo's Nest* were filmed here. Both the chamber of commerce and a post office are along Hwy 101.

### Charter Fishing & Whale Watching

This is one of the coast's busiest charter fishing harbors, offering good ocean fishing, and whale watching during the spring whale migration. Contact the following for prices and information: Dockside Charter (☎ 765-2545), or Tradewinds Sportfishing (☎ 765-2345). Fishing trips begin at $45. Whale-watching trips are usually under $10 for an hour-long excursion.

### Places to Stay & Eat

At *Holiday RV Park*, (☎ 765-2302), north on Hwy 101, sites range between $13 to $17; facilities include a swimming pool and laundry.

The nicest place to stay in Depoe Bay is the *Channel House Inn* (☎ 765-2140), 35 Ellingson St, an old inn right on the mouth of the harbor with 11 rooms, decorated according to a nautical theme. Rooms range from $55 to $200. *Holiday Surf Lodge* (☎ 765-2133), just north of the bridge on Hwy 101, offers an indoor swimming pool, spa facilities and ocean views from all rooms, for $39 to $80.

The *Sea Hag* (☎ 765-2734) 58 E Hwy 101, has fried fish and seafood, a salad bar

and good clam chowder. The area's best dining is at the *Whale Cove Inn* (☎ 765-2255), two miles south on Hwy 101, with great shoreline views and seafood dishes. Try smoked scallops or salmon at the *Siletz Tribal Smokehouse* (☎ 765-2286), 272 SE Hwy 101, a business owned by the tribe that also sells gift items from the Siletz Reservation.

### Getting There & Around

Three northbound and three southbound Greyhound buses pass through Depoe Bay daily. The southbound buses stop at Depoe Bay Fire Hall on Hwy 101, northbound buses stop at the Whistle Stop Market, Hwy 101 and Schoolhouse Rd, and at Liberty Market, 466 NE Hwy 101.

Central Coast Connections buses passes through six times daily. See Getting There & Away at the start of this chapter for further information.

## NEWPORT

Oregon's second-largest commercial port, Newport (population 8675) was first explored by fishing crews in the 1860s, who found high-quality oyster beds at the upper end of Yaquina Bay. In 1866 a road was built from Corvallis to the coast and Newport's first hotel, the Ocean House, was built (on the site of the present Coast Guard Station). During the 1870s, steamboats brought holidaymakers up from San Francisco.

Summer cottages and hotels began to appear on the north side of the sheltered harbor, along Nye Creek. Newport continues to expand north along the headland and Hwy 101 as tourism dominates the local economy. Old downtown Newport, centered on Bay Blvd, is still a very lively seafront, complete with seafood markets, the smells of a working port and the bark of seals. The gray and rather ramshackle buildings along the water's edge are fish-processing plants. On the other side of Bay Blvd are chandlers, 24-hour restaurants, art galleries and brewpubs. About halfway down Bay Blvd there's a wax museum, a so-called undersea garden on a floating barge and a Ripley's Believe It or Not! museum.

A better use of time may be a boat excursion around Yaquina Bay, or a trip out into the Pacific to view whales, or even popping into a bayfront restaurant for a beer and a bowl of clam chowder.

### Information

There's a visitors center (☎ 265-8801, (800) 262-7844) at 555 SW Coast Hwy, Newport, OR 97365. The post office (☎ 265-5542) is at 310 SW 2nd St. Canyon Way Books (☎ 265-8615), 1216 SW Canyon Way, is one of the coast's best

bookstores; pick up a book-on-tape for the road.

Eileen's Coin Laundry (☎ 265-5474), 1078 N Coast Hwy, has drop-off and self-service facilities. Pacific Communities Hospital (☎ 265-2244) is at 930 SW Abbey.

### Oregon Coast Aquarium

Opened in 1992, the Oregon Coast Aquarium (☎ 867-3474, 867-3123), 2820 SE Ferry Slip Rd, has become one of the biggest attractions in Oregon. Room-sized exhibits are grouped by ecosystem with interactive displays to explain the dynamics

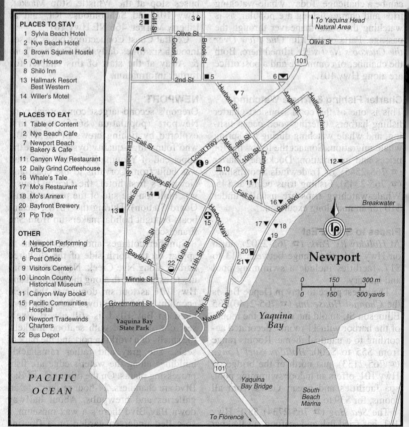

**PLACES TO STAY**
1  Sylvia Beach Hotel
2  Nye Beach Hotel
3  Brown Squirrel Hostel
5  Oar House
8  Shilo Inn
13 Hallmark Resort
   Best Western
14 Willer's Motel

**PLACES TO EAT**
1  Table of Content
2  Nye Beach Cafe
7  Newport Beach
   Bakery & Cafe
11 Canyon Way Restaurant
12 Daily Grind Coffeehouse
16 Whale's Tale
17 Mo's Restaurant
18 Mo's Annex
20 Bayfront Brewery
21 Pip Tide

**OTHER**
4  Newport Performing
   Arts Center
6  Post Office
9  Visitors Center
10 Lincoln County
   Historical Museum
11 Canyon Way Books
15 Pacific Communities
   Hospital
19 Newport Tradewinds
   Charters
22 Bus Depot

To Yaquina Head
Natural Area

**Newport**

Yaquina Bay
State Park

Yaquina
Bay

PACIFIC
OCEAN

Yaquina
Bay Bridge

South
Beach
Marina

To Florence

0   150   300 m
0   150   300 yards

of the various forms of life found there. At a supervised 'petting area', visitors can touch the denizens of a tide pool and ask marine specialists questions. Especially arresting are the luminous jellyfish in cylindrical floor-to-ceiling aquariums.

Outside, trails lead around natural-looking enclosures for seals, sea lions and sea otters; the seabird aviary includes puffins and murres. A great favorite with kids is the giant octopus that lives in a glass-walled sea grotto. Other trails lead from the aquarium along Yaquina Bay estuarial wetlands.

The aquarium is open daily from 9 am to 6 pm, May 15 to October 14, and daily 10 am to 4:40 pm the rest of the year. Admission is $7 for adults, $5 for seniors and students 12 to 18 years of age, and $3 for children ages four to 11. There's a cafe and a gift shop with books on the premises. To reach the aquarium, cross onto the south end of the Yaquina Bay Bridge, turn east onto SE 32nd St, and follow the signs a half mile.

## Mark O Hatfield Marine Science Center

This older science center (☎ 867-0100), 2030 Marine Science Drive, run by Oregon State University, has some aspects in common with the new aquarium (a glowering octopus and a hands-on tide pool), but exhibits here also focus on the deterioration of the marine environment and the impact of political policies on our oceans. Hours are the same as the Oregon Coast Aquarium, above; admission is free.

## Yaquina Bay State Park

The Yaquina Bay Lighthouse was originally meant to be the partner of a lighthouse on Cape Foulweather 10 miles north. However, the engineers couldn't get the building materials up the steep headland. Apparently two lighthouses for Newport was one too many, and in 1874 the Yaquina Bay Lighthouse was extinguished, and the building left derelict – or so it seemed. Visit the lighthouse to hear the ghost story of a young woman's mysterious disappearance;

there's even a short film. The lighthouse is open as a museum (☎ 867-7451) from noon to 4 pm daily; you can tour the living quarters and climb the steps to the lookout; admission is by donation.

The state park occupies a green and brushy bluff above the point where Yaquina Bay and the Pacific meet, immediately west of the Yaquina Bay Bridge's north embankment. Picnic tables and grassy meadows make this a good place to bring a lunch.

## Lincoln County Historical Museum & Burrows House

What sets this small community museum (☎ 265-7509), 545 SW 9th St, apart from the others is an excellent collection of Siletz artifacts, including beaded robes, headdresses, baskets and tools, donated by a woman who ran a trading post on the nearby Siletz reservation.

Behind the museum is the Burrows House, an old boarding house that preserves household goods, furnishings and kitchen tools from the turn of the century.

Both museums are open Tuesday to Sunday, from 10 am to 5 pm, June to September; and from 11 am to 4 pm, the rest of the year. Admission is free, though donations are encouraged.

## Beaches

There's beach access down a trail from Yaquina Bay State Park and at several points along Elizabeth St. Nye Beach, at the west end of 3rd St, was one of the first of Newport's beach developments; there's still access along Coast St. At Agate Beach State Wayside, three miles north of the Yaquina Bay Bridge, there's ample parking and restrooms, as well as beach access. The city's beaches are also off Hwy 101.

## Yaquina Head Natural Area

This 100-acre preserve is three miles north of Newport on an exposed headland. The coast's tallest, still-functioning, lighthouse here is open to visitors. The real treat though, is the extensive tide pool area below the bluffs. The BLM, which administers the site, is planning the development of a wheelchair-accessible marine garden along the tide pools.

## Charter Fishing & Whale Watching

With its deep and sheltered harbor, Newport is a noted base for charter fishing trips out into the Pacific. Contact the following for information on fishing trips, or for whale-watching trips during the migration season: South Beach Charters (☎ 867-7200), at South Beach Marina; Newport Tradewinds (☎ 265-2101), 653 SW Bay Blvd; and Newport Sportfishing (☎ 265-7558), 1000 SE Bay Blvd.

To rent a boat and crab rings, contact Embarcadero Dock (☎ 265-5435), 1000 SE Bay Blvd.

## Golf

Play the fun nine-hole Agate Beach Golf Course (☎ 265-7331), 4100 NE Golf Course Drive, or travel a few miles east toward Toledo to play nine holes on the heart-shaped green at Olalla Valley Golf & Restaurant (☎ 336-2121), 1022 Olalla Rd, Toledo.

## Special Events

One of the coast's premier events, the Newport Wine & Seafood Festival (☎ 265-8801) takes place at South Beach Marina in late February, when people hereabouts usually can use something to cheer them up. Besides wine and seafood tasting, there's also a crafts fair. This festival is popular; make sure to reserve rooms in advance.

The Nesika Illahe Powwow (☎ 444-2532), held the second weekend of August, celebrates the restored federal recognition of the Siletz tribe. Dancing, crafts and food fill the little town of Siletz, 14 miles northeast of Newport. Admission is free.

## Places to Stay

**Camping** *South Beach State Park* (☎ 867-4715), two miles south of Newport on Hwy 101, has 254 campsites with showers, flush toilets and a playground. Access to the beach is good; there are a number of hiking

trails within the park. Make reservations for the summer months. Sites cost $17.

Seven miles north is *Beverly Beach State Park* (☎ 265-9278), with over 300 campsites and a $17 camping fee. There's easy access to the beach, showers, wheelchair-accessible restrooms, summer programs and firewood.

---

### The Confederated Siletz Tribes

The Native Americans that lived around the Siletz, the Yaquina and the Alsea rivers hunted seals and sea lions, netted salmon and gathered shellfish. Their cultural and religious life centered around the invocation of animal spirits through shamans; these rituals assured them of bountiful hunting and fishing.

In 1855, they were restricted to the Coast Reservation, a 2160-sq-mile block of land including all territory west of the Coast Range between Tillamook and Reedsport. Two years later, many of the Takelma and the Latgawa Indians who had been sent to the Grand Ronde Reservation walked to the Coast Reservation, near Siletz. The tribes became known as the Confederated Siletz Tribes.

In 1865, the US Government removed a 25-mile-wide parcel of land around Yaquina Bay in order to make way for the oyster harvesting and tourism.

By the 1950s, less than 8.5 sq miles of the original reservation remained in Siletz hands. Under President Dwight Eisenhower the Siletz and 43 other groups of western Oregon lost their tribal status in 1954. With no reservation lands, no government assistance for education or community facilities, and no further official recognition of the tribe's cultural or ethnic status, the cohesion of the tribe frayed.

In 1973, a group of Siletz petitioned the government to reinstate legal recognition of the tribe, and in 1977 President Jimmy Carter signed a law restoring the Siletz as a federally acknowledged tribe. The law did not reinstate any land to the tribe, although some forested BLM land has subsequently been transferred to the tribe's ownership. ■

**Hostels** One of only two hostels on the Oregon Coast, the *Brown Squirrel Hostel* (☎ 265-3729), 44 SW Brook St, is in a former church. Dorm-style beds cost $12; kitchen and laundry facilities are available. It's open year round.

**B&Bs** The *Oar House* (☎ 265-9571), 520 SW 2nd St, is a grand old home built in 1900, with four guest rooms, each with private bath, ranging from $90 to $120. For a less-formal stay, the *Sea Cliff B&B* (☎ 265-6664), 749 NW 3rd St, offers three guest rooms with shared bath in a rambling old building that also houses an artsy coffeehouse. The rooms go for $75.

**Hotels – bottom end** Hotels in Newport are divided into those that face the Pacific, and those that face Hwy 101. There's obviously quite a difference in price.

There are plenty of older, well-kept motels along Hwy 101 north of Newport, most of which allow pets and have kitchens in the rooms. The truth-in-advertising honor goes to *Penny Saver Motel* (☎ 265-6631), 710 N Coast Hwy. There are scads of rooms not all of which face right onto the highway; rates are $38/42 a single/double. Another good deal is *Newport Motor Inn* (☎ 265-8516), 1311 N Coast Hwy, with nonsmoking rooms; rates are $39/42. At *Willer's Motel* (☎ 265-2241), 754 SW Coast Hwy, rooms are $36 to $75.

**Hotels – middle** Near Nye Beach are a couple of beachfront motels with moderate prices. The *Viking Motel* (☎ 265-2477), 729 NW Coast St, has cottages above the beach (prices start at $55); and rooms in oceanfront condominiums (prices start at $85). A private stairway leads down to the beach. Just behind the Viking is the *Waves Motel* (☎ 265-4661), 820 NW Coast St, with rooms at $48/55.

Newport's most charming lodging options are in two converted old hotels facing the ocean. The *Sylvia Beach Hotel* (☎ 265-5428), 267 NW Cliff St, is a hotel for book lovers with each room decorated in the style of a famous author. The 3rd-floor library that towers over the Pacific would be a waste of ocean view if the guests weren't all bibliophiles. The Sylvia Beach is very popular, so reservations are a must. All rooms have private baths; prices begin at $63 and go to $130, with breakfast included.

A few yards away, the *Nye Beach Hotel* (☎ 265-3334), 219 NW Cliff St, is also a restored 1910s hotel with spacious and comfortable rooms ranging from $40 to $85. Some include fireplaces, balconies and hot tubs. A cafe on the main floor is open for three meals a day.

**Hotels – top end** Each of the following offer many options, including fireplaces and hot tubs. Prices are for the basic room package.

The grandest is the *Embarcadero Resort* (☎ 265-8521, (800) 547-4779), behind the marina in Yaquina Bay at 1000 SE Bay Blvd. Rooms are in condo-like suites; prices range from $85 to $162. Out on the headland is the enormous *Shilo Inn* (☎ 265-7701, (800) 222-2244), 536 SW Elizabeth St. This lodging complex offers almost 200 rooms with ocean views, numerous restaurants and convention facilities. Rooms begin at $79/85 a single/double. The *Hallmark Resort Best Western* (☎ 265-8853, (800) 982-8668), 744 SW Elizabeth St, also sits above the beachfront; rooms begin at $80/85.

**Resorts** Nine miles north of Newport is the *Inn at Otter Crest* (☎ 765-2111, (800) 452-2101), a destination resort with 100 suites overlooking the ocean, a swimming pool, tennis courts, spa and exercise facilities and an on-premises restaurant and lounge. The location, just under the headland at Cape Foulweather, is outstanding, with miles of beach and tide pools just outside your door. Rooms begin at $79 to $99, depending on the view.

**Vacation Home Rentals** Contact Yaquina Bay Property Management (☎ 265-3537), 1164 SW Coast Hwy, Suite C, Newport, OR 97365.

OREGON

**OREGON**

## Places to Eat
Like most beach towns, there's no end of family-style eateries offering fast food. What's unusual is that Newport also offers a number of good, and sometimes innovative, restaurants that make the most of the harbor's fresh fish and seafood.

**Breakfast** *Nye Beach Cafe* (☎ 265-3334), 219 NW Cliff St, in the hotel, offers good omelets and great views. In good weather, there's seating on the veranda above the beach. A standby for early morning fishing crews and late-night revelers is the 24-hour *Pip Tide* (☎ 265-7797), 836 SW Bay Blvd. For coffee and pastries, go to the *Daily Grind Coffeehouse* (☎ 265-6263), 156 SW Bay Blvd or *Newport Beach Bakery & Cafe* (☎ 265-7231), 715A SW Hurbert St, for cinnamon rolls, croissants and breads right from the oven.

**Lunch & Dinner** For burgers, go to *Big Guy's Diner* (☎ 265-5114), 1801 N Coast Hwy. *Mo's Restaurant* (☎ 265-2979), 622 SW Bay Blvd, is a kind of tradition. Mo's seafood restaurants were started decades ago by Mohava Niemi, a local Siletz whose clam chowder and fried fish became the standard of coastal fare. The first Mo's is still here among the crusty bayfront chandlers and bars. Directly across the street, on the edge of the wharf, is *Mo's Annex* (☎ 265-7512), 657 SW Bay Blvd. Both offer buckets of steamed clams, baskets of fried fish and bowls of creamy clam chowder.

The *Whale's Tale* (☎ 265-8660), 452 SW Bay Blvd, is yet another Newport tradition, considered a kind of shrine to 1960s' hippie restaurants. You can't beat its location on the waterfront or its cozily exaggerated maritime motif; this is Newport's most convivial restaurant for favorite seafood dishes. A dinner of Yaquina Bay oysters goes for $13; for the real seafood enthusiast, there's the Captain's Plate with five kinds of fresh fish for $17.

Upscale *Canyon Way Restaurant* (☎ 265-8319), 1216 SW Canyon Way is in an old storefront complex with a bookstore, gift shop and deli. Although innovative fresh seafood preparations make up much of the menu, there are also good steak, prime rib and delicious barbecued lamb ribs ($14). From 5 to 6 pm, the restaurant offers an early menu, with most entrees around $9. Throughout the evening, the light entree menu offers dishes for around $10. For the real experience choose from the a la carte menu, where daily seafood specials like scallops in pernod cream with leeks goes for $19. Save room, if possible, for the wondrous desserts.

At Sylvia Beach Hotel's dining room, the *Table of Content* (☎ 265-5428), 267 NW Cliff St, dinners for non-guests are by reservation only; the prix-fixe menu is $17.50 a person.

## Entertainment
The *Bayfront Brewery* (☎ 265-3188), 748 SW Bay Blvd, is the brewpub for local Rogue Ales, and offers sandwiches and other light entrees in the $6 range.

*Newport Cinemas* (☎ 265-2111) is at 5837 N Coast Hwy. The *Newport Performing Arts Center* (☎ 265-2787), 777 W Olive St, is Newport's venue for touring regional and national entertainment.

## Getting There & Around
Newport is one of the only coastal towns with a bona fide bus depot (☎ 265-2253), 956 SW 10th St. Greyhound buses pass through; fares to Portland are $16.75. Valley Retriever buses to Corvallis and Bend also depart from here, and Central Coast Connections buses link Newport to other towns along the coast. See Getting There & Away at the start of this chapter for further information.

Call Yaquina Cab Company (☎ 265-9552) to hire a cab.

## WALDPORT
Waldport (population 1665), at the mouth of the Alsea River, revels in its 'relative obscurity'. There is inexpensive lodging and a relative dearth of attractions. Here are long stretches of sandy beach, with a number of day-use state park access points.

Seal Rock, where a massive hump of rock protects a beach and tide pools, is a good place for young children to explore the coast.

Highway 34, following the Alsea River from the Willamette Valley, is one of the most scenic routes between the valley and the coast.

The Waldport Visitors Center (☎ 563-6086) is at 620 NW Spring St, Waldport, OR 97394. The Waldport Ranger Station for the Siuslaw National Forest (☎ 563-3211) is at 1049 SW Pacific Coast Hwy. The post office (☎ 563-3011) is at the corner of Hemlock and Johns Sts.

## Alsea Bay Bridge Historical Interpretive Center

Travel along Oregon's rugged coast was not always simple, as this interesting museum of transport (☎ 563-2002) makes evident. The facility traces the history of transportation routes along the coast, beginning with trails used by Native Americans, and moving on to the sea, rail and finally, road routes now in use.

The center is at the southern end of the Alsea Bay Bridge and is open daily from 9 am to 4 pm Memorial Day to Labor Day, and from 9 am to 4 pm Wednesday to Sunday the rest of the year; admission is free.

## Fishing

A number of friendly fishing outfitters and moorages flank the lower reaches of the river and bay, providing rental boats, tackle and refreshments for anglers. Contact Oakland's Fish Camp (☎ 563-5865), by milestone 4 on Hwy 34, for a sample of rates and services. The Alsea Bay is also one of the very best **crabbing** areas in the state; to rent a boat and crab rings, contact Dock of the Bay Marina (☎ 563-2003), along the Old Town Wharf. The upper river is widely noted for its fall steelhead fishing; for a professional outfitting service, call Gene O's Guide Service (☎ 563-3171) or write PO Box 43, Waldport, OR 97394.

## Places to Stay

At *Beachside State Park* (☎ 563-3023), four miles south of Waldport on Hwy 101, there are over 80 sites for $15 to $18, showers and wheelchair-accessible restrooms. Just down the road is *Tillicum Beach*, a USFS campground with 60 campsites at $10, flush toilets and drinking water.

Most hotels here have kitchenettes and let in the pets. At the *Waldport Motel* (☎ 563-3035), 170 SW Arrow St, rooms range from $30 to $45. There are ocean views at *Alsea Manor Motel* (☎ 563-3249), 190 SW Arrow St; rooms are $49 to $55.

Charming *Cape Cod Cottages* (☎ 563-2106), 4150 SW Hwy 101, has small whitewashed cabins with ocean views. All units have kitchens and fireplaces, and range in price from $60 to $75.

## Places to Eat

Family-style restaurants with fish & chips and sandwiches pretty much begin and end the selection here. However, for espresso and muffins, head to *Bumps & Grinds Coffeehouse* (☎ 563-5769), 225 Waldport St. The *Seafood Grotto* (☎ 563-5104), at Spring Court and Hwy 101, is as good a place as any for steak, fish and seafood.

*Kozy Kove Kafe* (☎ 528-3251), nine miles east of Waldport on Hwy 34 in Tidewater is on a kind of log barge and claims to be the coast's only floating restaurant. It's charming in a whimsical way, with nice views over the river and attendant bird life. The food is pretty good, too: steak and prime rib ($14), honey-fried chicken ($11), seafood entrees like scallops with garlic and mushrooms ($16) and even a selection of Mexican food.

## Getting There & Around

Greyhound and Central Coast Connections buses pass through Waldport. See Getting There & Away at the start of this chapter for more information. Bus stops are at the Waldport Ranger Station, 1049 SW Pacific Coast Hwy, and the Waldport Senior Center, 265 Elsie Highway.

**OREGON**

## YACHATS & AROUND

The Alsea word 'Yachats' (pronounced Ya-HOTS), means 'at the foot of the mountain'. It's an apt description of this wonderful little community at the base of massive Cape Perpetua. Yachats (population 580) is homey and welcoming, yet rugged and wind-whipped, preserving the illusion that this is a village that the tourist industry hasn't yet discovered.

Beginning at Cape Perpetua and continuing south about 20 miles is some of Oregon's most spectacular shoreline. This entire area was once a series of volcanic intrusions, which resisted the pummeling of the Pacific long enough to rise as oceanside peaks and promontories. Tiny beaches lined by cliffs seem almost serendipitous; acres of tide pools appear and disappear according to the fancy of the tides and are home to starfish, sea anemones and sea lions. Picturesque lighthouses rise above the surf. It's a beautiful area; if it weren't so far from centers of population, it would certainly be more highly developed than it is.

Seven miles south of Yachats is a small community sometimes called Searose Beach or Tenmile Creek, with a number of B&Bs and a motel above the beach.

The Yachats Chamber of Commerce (☎ 547-3530) is at 441 Hwy 101, Yachats, OR 97498.

### Beaches

Beaches around here are small, private affairs that have to share space with expanses of tide pools and rocky spires. The closest beach to Yachats is to the north, often called **Smelt Sands Beach** for the run of smelts, a sardine-sized fish, that ground themselves here during spawning season. At the mouth of Yachats River is Yachats State Park, with a wheelchair-accessible trail along the surf.

South of Yachats, **Strawberry Hill Wayside** and **Neptune State Park** offer enjoyable prowling among intertidal rocks and sandy inlets. Sea lions are common along this part of the beach.

One of the most enchanting of all beaches in Oregon is the little sandy cove at

**Devil's Elbow State Park,** about 10 miles south of Yachats, with the Heceta Head Lighthouse keeping guard, a dense forest bounding the beach and a Conde McCullough bridge arching across placid Cape Creek.

### Cape Perpetua

Cape Perpetua, two miles south of Yachats, was first sited and named by England's Captain James Cook in 1778. This remnant of a volcano is one of the highest points on the Oregon coast. Views from the cape are incredible, taking in coastal promontories from Cape Foulweather to Cape Arago. The USFS has designated the 2700-acre area as a Federal Scenic Area and offers a visitors center, camping, hikes and trails to ancient shell middens, tide pools and unique natural formations.

From Hwy 101, turn on USFS Rd 55, and follow the signs to Cape Perpetua Viewpoint.

The Cape Perpetua Visitors Center provides good background material on the human and natural history of Cape Perpetua with displays on the culture of the Alsea tribe who journeyed here to feast on the abundant shellfish near the tide pools. Middens, or centuries-old mounds of shells, attest to their banqueting.

Other exhibits discuss the ecology of the seashore (focusing on intertidal life) and the natural life of the dense spruce, cedar and hemlock forests. From the viewing platforms, watch for migrating whales. A small gift shop provides one of the best selections of books in the area on local travel and natural history. Slide and video shows about Cape Perpetua are screened according to demand.

The visitors center (☎ 547-3289) is open from 9 am to 6 pm daily May to September, and from 10 am to 4 pm Saturday and Sunday the rest of the year.

**The Devil's Churn** Deep fractures in the old volcano allow waves to erode narrow channels into the headland, creating the compelling Devil's Churn. Waves race up a deep but very narrow channel between basalt ledges, then shoot up the 30-foot inlet only to explode against the narrowing sides of the channel.

Trails from the visitors center, or from the Devil's Churn parking lot one mile north, follow steep stairs that are frequently slick and muddy. Only the sure of foot should go all the way to the bottom, and even then, care is demanded near the edge of the channel. Children must be supervised.

From the base of the Devil's Churn trail, turn south to explore acres of tide pools.

**Hiking** Most of the sites at Cape Perpetua require a short stroll, but there are longer day hikes along the ocean and into forested wilderness areas.

The most popular hike is the 1.3-mile climb from the visitors center up to the lookout on Cape Perpetua. This area was first developed by the CCC during the 1930s; the rock shelter at the top of the cape was used as a lookout for enemy vessels during WW II.

An easier trail down to the tide pools is the **Captain Cook Trail**. This paved 1.2-mile-roundtrip trail leaves from the visitors center and passes through dense stands of salal before reaching ancient shell middens. Watch for the spouting horn, a geyser-like blast of water that shoots out of a sea cave.

The **Giant Spruce Trail** leads up Cape Creek from the visitors center to the so-called Giant Spruce, a 500-year-old tree with a nine-foot circumference. The seven-mile **Cook's Ridge-Gwynn Creek Loop Trail** leads back into the deep forests along Gwynn Creek. Follow the Oregon Coast Trail south from the visitors center, and turn up Gwynn Creek. The trail returns along the ridge between Gwynn and Cape creeks.

### Heceta Head Lighthouse

At **Devil's Elbow State Park,** 14 miles south of Yachats, turn west to the beachside parking lot. On a bluff to the north is **Heceta House,** an 1893 lighthouse keeper's house, now used as a facility of Lane County Community College. From the parking lot a trail leads to this lovely white-washed structure (occasionally the house is open, and visitors can prowl through its heavily remodeled rooms), and on to the Heceta Head Lighthouse, built in 1894. The cape and the buildings were named for Bruno Heceta (pronounced he-SEE-ta), a Spanish navigator who explored the area in 1775.

The lighthouse is still functioning and is not open to the public, but the trail continues to the end of the cape. The lighthouse is one of the most photographed features in Oregon, particularly from the viewpoint on Hwy 101 a mile south of the park.

### Sea Lion Caves

This enormous sea grotto (☎ 547-3111), 91560 Hwy 101, filled with smelly, shrieking sea lions is a highlight of the central Oregon coast. A 208-foot elevator deposits you in a small natural shaft that opens onto the larger grotto. From this observation point 50 feet above the cave, you can watch almost 200 Steller's sea lions clammering onto rocks, jockeying for position at the top of ledges and letting loose with mighty roars.

The wildlife viewing area has a negative reputation, perhaps due to overly aggressive promotion. Certainly, during high season a carnival atmosphere takes over and the lines for the elevator make it seem like an unpalatable peep show. Visit early in the day, or off-season, to enjoy one of the world's largest known sea caves.

The Sea Lion Caves is a privately owned

and operated site; go to the gift shop before heading to the elevator. Opening hours are from 9 am to 7 pm May to September and 9 am to 4 pm October to April. Admission is $5 for adults, $3 for children ages six to 15.

## Places to Stay

**Camping** At the *Cape Perpetua Campground*, administered by the Siuslaw National Forest, there are 37 campsites for $10.

Seven miles south of Yachats is the *Sea Perch Campground* (☎ 547-3505), with 75 sites near Tenmile Creek. Facilities include showers, flush toilets and hook-ups, plus a small grocery store; oceanview sites are $20; others $18. At *Carl G Washburne State Park*, 13 miles south, there are nearly 70 campsites, with showers and flush toilets; rates are $15 to $18. Although the campground is on the wrong side of the road from the ocean, trails lead to beaches, and to a four-mile hiking trail system within the park.

**B&Bs** The following B&Bs are seven miles south of Yachats, in the little community that slumbers at the mouth of Tenmile Creek. All have oceanview rooms and access to a small beach. The most eye-catching is the *Ziggurat B&B* (☎ 547-3925), 95330 Hwy 101, which is more like some fanciful temple (hence the name) than a private home. The three rooms are filled with commissioned furniture and art. Prices range from $85 to $110. *Sea Quest B&B* (☎ 547-3782), 95354 Hwy 101, has five guest rooms each with private baths and entrances, spas and decks. Rooms range from $95 to $250.

**Hotels** At the northern end of Yachats, the *Dublin House* (☎ 547-3200), at 7th St and Hwy 101, offers an indoor swimming pool, kitchens and oceanview rooms; the hotel can also arrange fly-fishing trips and lessons. Rooms range from $49 to $125. The *Fireside Motel* (☎ 547-3636), 1881 N Hwy 101, has rooms with wood-burning stoves; pets are OK; rooms range from $58 to $80.

The *Adobe Resort Inn* (☎ 547-3141, (800) 522-3623), 1555 Hwy 101, includes a restaurant and lounge on its premises. Most rooms have ocean views, and some have fireplaces and balconies. There's also an exercise room, hot tub and sauna. Rooms range from $60 to $150.

*Shamrock Lodgettes* (☎ 547-3312), 105 S Hwy 101, seems to sit in a large park by the ocean. There's lodging either in a modern motel unit, or the older cabins. Some rooms have kitchens, the modern units have ocean views. Rates range from $67 to $95.

There are more options in out-of-the-way pockets south of Cape Perpetua. One of the real deals along this part of the coast is *The See Vue* (☎ 547-3227), 95590 Hwy 101, in Tenmile Creek. The rooms are theme decorated: there's the Sante Fe Room, the Northwest Room, the Princess & the Pea Room and so on. All have ocean views, there are some kitchens and fireplaces, and dogs are allowed. Rooms range from $40 to $60.

Even more remote is the *Oregon House* (☎ 547-3329), 94288 S Hwy 101, set on a cliff nine miles south of Yachats. A private estate built in the 1930s and 1950s, the various buildings – the gardener's cottage, the orchid greenhouse, the main lodge and an art studio – have been renovated and converted into one-of-a-kind accommodations. Most units have ocean views and kitchens, some have fireplaces, and all have private baths; several of the units have two bedrooms and can sleep from four to six guests. No pets are allowed, and some units have restrictions on children. For those who like their seclusion and who value a break from chain motel rooms, this is a favorite. Rates fall between $40 and $105.

**Vacation Home Rentals** Contact Yachats Village Rentals (☎ 547-3501) at 128 Beach Ave, Yachats, OR 97498.

## Places to Eat

The choices are limited, but limited to some of the best and most pleasant places along the entire coast. *New Morning*

*Coffeehouse* (☎ 547-3848), at 4th St and Hwy 101, will get you into the laid-back pace of beach life. Espresso, pastries and conversation are the pastimes here. For breads and even more pastries, go to *On The Rise Bakery* (☎ 547-3440), 281 Hwy 101, a homespun affair with good scones and slices of pizza.

At *Yachats Crab & Chowder House*, (☎ 547-4132) 131 Hwy 101, fresh seafood and light entrees are served up; you can get a full dinner of crab chowder and a salad for less than $6.

For many, dinner at *La Serre* (☎ 547-3420), at 2nd and Beach Sts, is a highlight of a trip to Yachats. The waiters dress in rather silly pioneer outfits but the food is as good as any on the coast. The cioppino is great ($15), as is the steak.

### Getting There & Away

Greyhound buses pass through Yachats on their way up and down the coast. Call the depot in Newport for the latest bus stop information. Central Coast Connections buses bound for Newport depart from Clark's IGA grocery store, on the corner of W 2nd St and Hwy 101, weekdays only at 7 am, 1 and 4 pm. See Getting There & Away at the beginning of this chapter for more information.

# Southern Oregon Coast

While the northern Oregon coast surely boasts beautiful locations, the southern coast is a near continuous succession of dramatic seascapes. Far from any major population center and serviced by few and slow roads, none of the towns along the southern coast are experiencing the kind of boom evident at Cannon Beach or Lincoln City to the north. Don't go looking for exquisite sauces for your mesquite-grilled calamari or a four-star resort. Chowder and modest older motels are more the norm in this part of the state.

Much of the coastline here is nearly pristine and in many places approaches the condition of wilderness. Find a favorite sandy beach at the end of a hiking trail, and chances are that you'll have it to yourself on all but the busiest summer weekends.

## FLORENCE

For years, Florence (population 5475) was one of the beach towns you loved to hate: strip commercial development stretched along the highway for miles, the whine of dune buggies navigating sandy bluffs filled the air, and the extensive, if characterless, sandy beaches were thronged with idle family groups. In the last few years, however, the center of life in Florence has shifted away from the malls along Hwy 101 to the Old Town along the Siuslaw River, with good restaurants, coffeehouses and interesting shops. Fishing boats come and go from the harbor, bearing their burden of freshly caught salmon, flounder or shrimp and seals bark

for handouts from spectators along the wharf.

Florence is at the northern end of the Oregon Dunes National Recreation Area, and a lot of the increasing sophistication of the amenities in Florence has to do with the growing appreciation of the dunes as something other than sandy hills to be dominated by dunes buggies and dirt bikes. Let's face it: bird watchers and dune hikers demand a different ambiance than do crazed teenagers on all-terrain vehicles.

The estuary along the Siuslaw River was home to the Siuslaw, a small tribe related to the Umpqua and Coos further south. The Siuslaw lived in underground shelters roofed with wooden frames. For their diet, they both fished in the river and hunted the dense forests for game. Generally peaceable, the Siuslaw were removed from their homelands in 1859 and marched northward to the Alsea Reservation near Yachats. When that reservation closed in 1875, most of the Siuslaw were bereft of land and drifted back to the Florence area. The Siuslaw were among the coastal

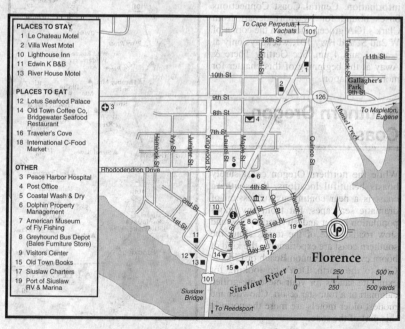

**PLACES TO STAY**
1  Le Chateau Motel
2  Villa West Motel
10  Lighthouse Inn
11  Edwin K B&B
13  River House Motel

**PLACES TO EAT**
12  Lotus Seafood Palace
14  Old Town Coffee Co,
    Bridgewater Seafood
    Restaurant
16  Traveler's Cove
18  International C-Food
    Market

**OTHER**
3  Peace Harbor Hospital
4  Post Office
5  Coastal Wash & Dry
6  Dolphin Property
   Management
7  American Museum
   of Fly Fishing
8  Greyhound Bus Depot
   (Bales Furniture Store)
9  Visitors Center
15  Old Town Books
17  Siuslaw Charters
19  Port of Siuslaw
    RV & Marina

**Florence**

To Cape Perpetua, Yachats

To Mapleton, Eugene

Gallagher's Park

Rhododendron Drive

Siuslaw Bridge

To Reedsport

Siuslaw River

0   250   500 m
0   250   500 yards

tribes that unsuccessfully sued the federal government in 1917 for remuneration for the loss of their reservation lands.

## Orientation

Highway 126 heads east from here toward Eugene, 63 miles distant. South of Florence is the Oregon Dunes National Recreation Area. North of town, the coast again becomes wild and rocky.

Roughly speaking, Old Town is under the Siuslaw Bridge and can be reached by turning down Maple St from Hwy 101.

The best access to ocean beaches is off South Jetty Rd, about a mile south of the Siuslaw Bridge. From the South Jetty Rd north to the mouth of the Siuslaw, the beach is closed in summer to vehicles. Another beach access is at Heceta Beach, about three miles north of Florence. Turn west on Heceta Beach Rd.

## Information

The Florence Chamber of Commerce (☎ 997-3128) is at 270 Hwy 101, Florence, OR 97439, just north of the bridge.

The post office (☎ 997-2533) is at 770 Maple St. Old Town Books (☎ 997-6205), 1340 Bay St, is a small bookstore that offers a little bit of everything, even gifts and coffee.

The Coastal Wash & Dry (☎ 997-8717) is at 1339 Rhododendron St. Peace Harbor Hospital (☎ 997-3128) is at 400 9th St.

## Siuslaw Pioneer Museum

This regional museum (☎ 997-7884), 85294 S Hwy 101, contains the usual mementos of lumbering and items from old kitchens, but also has a good selection of Siuslaw artifacts. The museum documents the story of the US Government's initial land-grab and subsequent shabby judicial treatment of the Siuslaw, which has left the tribe with no land claim. Opening hours are from 10 am to 4 pm, Tuesday to Sunday, with a $1 donation asked of adults.

## American Museum of Fly Fishing

At this Old Town museum (☎ 997-6102), 280 Nopal St, a large private collection of hand-tied flies are displayed in frames. Some flies date back to the 1800s, and the 15,000 flies in the collection represent the work of fly-tiers from more than 20 countries. There's also a number of fishing-related sculptures and paintings. The museum is open daily from 10 am to 5 pm, May 15 to September 30; other times by appointment. Admission is $2.50.

## Darlingtonia Botanical Wayside

At this small park five miles north of Florence on Hwy 101, boardwalks lead out into dense wetlands to a patch of *Darlingtonia californica*, the unusual flesh-eating plant also called pitcher plant or cobra-lily. Placards explain the life cycle of these oddities. Apparently, their meat-eating ways evolved because the soils available to them are generally very low in nutrients. The process of luring insects in and digesting them is quite slow and unspectacular; however, it's pretty interesting to visit the Darlingtonia bog to see these rare plants in their native habitat.

## Fishing

Siuslaw Charters (☎ 997-8961), on the harbor, offers **charter fishing** trips, as well as seasonal trips for whale watching.

The Siuslaw River has a major salmon and steelhead run in the fall. Additionally, there's good cutthroat and rainbow trout fishing. There are a number of fishing access points east of town toward Mapleton. For a fishing guide on the Siuslaw River, contact Gary Wolgamott (☎ 268-4911).

## Golf

Sixty-foot high dunes surround the 18-hole Ocean Dunes Golf Links (☎ 997-3232), 3345 Munsel Lake Rd, threatening golfers with the world's worst sand trap.

## Horseback Riding

Rent a horse for beach riding at C&M Stables (☎ 997-7540), 90241 N Hwy 101.

OREGON

## Rhododendron Festival

Held the third weekend of May, the Rhododendron Festival (☎ 997-3128) has been celebrated for over 80 years to honor the ubiquitous shrubs that erupt into bloom in May. A floral parade, flower show, the Rhodie Run, a crafts fair and a slug race are some of the events.

Woodsman Native Nursery (☎ 997-2252), 4385 N Hwy 101, offers lots of local bloomers and climbers for sale; even if you're not in the market, it's a really pleasant stop.

## Places to Stay

**Camping** The most pleasant campgrounds in the Florence area are north of town where streams are trapped by the dunes and form fresh water lakes. *Alder Dune*, seven miles north on Hwy 101, and *Sutton*, six miles north, are both USFS campgrounds with flush toilets and access to lakes and the beach. Sites at both campgrounds cost $10. Happily, there is no dune buggy access at this part of the dunes.

For RVers who want to camp right on the Pacific, go to *Heceta Beach RV Park* (☎ 997-7664), on Heceta Beach Rd, which has showers and a laundry; all sites are $15. There are both tent and RV sites right on Florence harbor in Old Town at *Port of Siuslaw RV & Marina* (☎ 997-3040), at 1st and Harbor Sts. There are showers, a boat launch and easy access to shops and restaurants; sites are $12.

**B&Bs** The *Edwin K B&B* (☎ 997-8360), 1155 Bay St, is an attractive arts & crafts home down along the Siuslaw River near Old Town. The four nicely furnished units each have private baths; one room has a balcony and its own waterfall! Rooms range from $75 to $105.

**Hotels** The best deals are along Hwy 101, where there's a plenitude of older motels. *Villa West Motel* (☎ 997-3457), 901 Hwy 101, is well maintained, and takes pets; singles/doubles are $38/42. *Le Chateau Motel* (☎ 997-3481), 1084 Hwy 101, offers a pool, hot tub and guest laundry; rooms

are $48/51. Stay closer to Old Town, right under Siuslaw Bridge at the *River House Motel* (☎ 997-3933), 1202 Bay St, with hot tubs and views of the river; it's $78 for riverview rooms, $64 for views of the parking lot. Equally close to Old Town, but along Hwy 101, is the *Lighthouse Inn* (☎ 997-3221), 155 Hwy 101; rates are $58/63.

For views over the old harbor area, cross the Siuslaw Bridge and climb the hill to *Best Western Pier Point Inn* (☎ 997-7191), 85625 Hwy 101, an upscale motel with balconies facing onto the river and spa facilities; rooms range between $69 and $89. Florence's beachfront resort is *Driftwood Shores* (☎ 997-8263, (800) 422-5091 in Oregon, (800) 824-8774 out of state), 88416 First Ave, which offers condo-style suites, all with ocean views. Most rooms have kitchens and fireplaces, and there's an indoor pool; rooms begin at $106.

**Vacation Home Rentals** To rent a private home for extended stays in Florence, contact Dolphin Property Management (☎ 997-7368), 396 Hwy 101, Florence, OR 97439.

## Places to Eat

Start the day at *Old Town Coffee Co* (☎ 997-7300), 1269 Bay St, where there's espresso and pastries. For an incredible omelet, head out to *Blue Hen Cafe* (☎ 997-3907), 1675 Hwy 101.

Along the harbor in Old Town are quite a number of good cafes and fish markets that will serve up inexpensive fish & chips and clam chowder. *Traveler's Cove* (☎ 997-6845), 1362 Bay St, is part international folk art shop and part cafe, with a back deck (overlooking the water) where sandwiches and light lunches are served; try the hot crab and toast for $7.

Great views and a lively market atmosphere make *International C-Food Market* (☎ 997-9646), 1498 Bay St, a popular spot for lunch or dinner.

*Bridgewater Seafood Restaurant* (☎ 997-9405), 1297 Bay St, is one of Florence's better restaurants, housed in an old hotel dining room near the waterfront. Fresh seafood is the specialty; there's a seafood buffet for $13. Under the bridge and facing the Siuslaw River is *Lotus Seafood Palace* (☎ 997-7168), 1150 Bay St, where the local seafood bounty is prepared Chinese-style. The *Windward Inn* (☎ 997-8243), 3757 N Hwy 101, is home to the south coast's best fine dining. Steak, fresh seafood and pasta dishes are standard features, with bread and pastries baked fresh daily at the restaurant's bakery. Average dinners run about $15.

### Getting There & Away

The intercity buses stop at Bales Furniture Store (☎ 997-1123), 175 Nopal St. Two Greyhound buses a day come down from Portland via Lincoln City on the way to San Francisco along Hwy 101. The one-way fare from Portland is $21. There are two buses a day from Eugene; a ticket from there to Florence is $12.75.

### OREGON DUNES NATIONAL RECREATIONAL AREA

The Oregon Dunes stretch for 50 miles between Florence and Coos Bay, forming the largest expanse of coastal sand dunes in the USA. The National Recreation Area was created in 1972, and takes in 50 sq miles. Adjacent to the area are Honeyman and Tugman state parks.

The dunes front the Pacific Ocean but undulate east as much as three miles to meet coastal forests, with a succession of curious ecosystems and formations be-

tween. Streams running down from the Coast Range form lakes surrounded by Sahara-like banks of sand. A number of hiking trails, bridle paths and boating and swimming areas have been established throughout this unique place, and the entire region is noted for its abundant wildlife, especially birds.

That's the good news. Ownership of the areas adjacent to the Oregon Dunes is mixed: some of the land is controlled by the state park system, and a lot of it is privately owned. Many of the lakes are flanked by resort homes and are churned by motor boats. And, however democratic it may seem, the National Recreation Area is open to 'mixed use', meaning that about half of the area is dominated by off-road vehicles (ORVs) or all-terrain vehicles (ATVs) which means dune buggies and dirt bikes tearing up and down the dunes and the tell-tale smell and demonic whine of two-stroke engines in the air.

The USFS has decided to cut back on the areas open to vehicular use, in order to increase hiking access and wildlife territory. Be sure to get a map of the area in order to determine where the restrictions are in place. The lower half of the dunes, south of Reedsport, sees the most ORV traffic, and the upper half has the most hiking trails.

### Information

The headquarters for Oregon Dunes National Recreation Area (☎ 271-3611) is

OREGON

---

**Mountains of Sand**

The wild and rocky coasts of southern Oregon are the western flanks of the Klamath geologic province, once an island that stood offshore from the West Coast. The coast along this section of Oregon is so steep and rocky, and the continental shelf so narrow, that there is little place for beaches or sand deposits. However, the major rivers of the area – the Chetco, the Smith, the Rogue and the Coquille – are constantly flushing sand into the ocean. The waves battering the headlands are also constantly reducing the coastline to sand. Since there is no place for it to accumulate along the coast, this bounty of sand shifts northward along ocean currents. Between Cape Arago and the volcanic seaside mountains south of Cape Perpetua – a 50-mile-long area – no cliffs or rock formations resist the flows of sand, and it washes ashore and forms into massive dunes. The Oregon Dunes, now protected by the government, contain some of the largest oceanfront dunes in the world. Some are 500 feet high and form banks sometimes three miles deep. ■

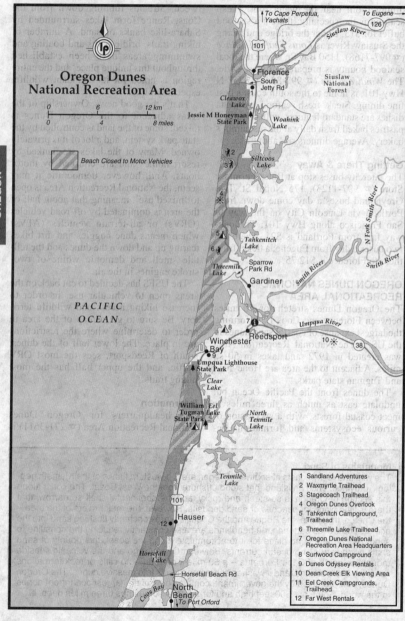

# Oregon Dunes National Recreation Area

0    6    12 km
0    4    8 miles

Beach Closed to Motor Vehicles

PACIFIC OCEAN

To Cape Perpetua, Yachats

To Eugene

Siuslaw River

101

126

Florence

South Jetty Rd

Siuslaw National Forest

Cleawox Lake

Jessie M Honeyman State Park

Woahink Lake

Siltcoos Lake

Tahkenitch Lake

Sparrow Park Rd

Threemile Lake

Gardiner

N Fork Smith River

Smith River

Smith River

Umpqua River

Reedsport

38

Winchester Bay

Umpqua Lighthouse State Park

Clear Lake

Eel Lake

North Tenmile Lake

William Tugman State Park

Tenmile Lake

101

Hauser

Horsfall Lake

Horsfall Beach Rd

North Bend

Coos Bay

To Port Orford

1   Sandland Adventures
2   Waxmyrtle Trailhead
3   Stagecoach Trailhead
4   Oregon Dunes Overlook
5   Tahkenitch Campground, Trailhead
6   Threemile Lake Trailhead
7   Oregon Dunes National Recreation Area Headquarters
8   Surfwood Campground
9   Dunes Odyssey Rentals
10  Dean Creek Elk Viewing Area
11  Eel Creek Campgrounds, Trailhead
12  Far West Rentals

OREGON

at 855 Highway Ave, Reedsport, OR 97467. In addition to hiking information and maps, there's a 20-minute film that explains the formation of the dunes and the different ecosystems found here. The hours are from 8 am to 4:30 pm Monday to Friday.

The designation of ORV and non-ORV areas is set up to limit ORV use, but hikers have access rights to all Oregon Dunes areas. However, hikers exploring areas open to ORVs should remain keen to the direction of ORV traffic, since the pleats and folds of the dunes often make it difficult to see or be seen. Climbing the crest of a high dune is an especially bad place to be when some kid comes flying over the top on a motor-cross bike. Although the foredune areas make for easy walking, they are often key access routes for ORVs. Red (sometimes orange) flags waving above the dunes indicate oncoming ORVs. If one is moving fast in your direction, get out of the way!

## Hiking

Short hikes from roadside trailheads lead through the dunes, lakes and scrub forests out to the beach. Once on the beach, long hikes along the shore can lead to other trails. Be sure to pick up a trail map and the brochure *Hiking Trails in the Oregon Dunes National Recreation Area* from the headquarters.

From the **Stagecoach Trailhead**, three easy, short trails lead along a river and wet-lands, affording good wildlife viewing. One of these, the **Waxmyrtle Trail**, winds along the Siltcoos River, where herons, deer and waterfowl can be seen. Part of this trail passes an area protected for nesting snowy plovers, a threatened species of shorebird that has only six known nesting sites in Oregon. In 1.5 miles, hikers reach the beach. The other trails from the Stage-coach Trailhead lead to a freshwater lagoon or up to a forested vista point. To reach this trailhead, turn at the sign for Siltcoos Dunes and Beach Access Rd, 7.5 miles south of Florence on Hwy 101. There are a number of campgrounds here.

Another trailhead is found at the **Oregon Dunes Overlook**, 10 miles south of Florence. This wheelchair accessible vista also serves as a trailhead for a mile-long hike to the beach.

For a longer loop trail through dunes, forest and marsh, take trails west from Tahkenitch Campground Trailhead, five miles north of Reedsport on Hwy 101. The **Tahkenitch Dunes Trail** leads to the beach in less than two miles. Walk south along the beach until directional posts point to the **Threemile Lake Trail**, which passes a freshwater lake and goes through deep forests before reaching the campground. The entire loop trail is roughly six miles long.

To see some of the biggest dunes in the area, take hikes from the Eel Creek Camp-grounds trailhead, eight miles south of Reedsport. The 2.5-mile **Umpqua Dunes Trail** leads out from the campground into a wilderness of massive sand peaks before reaching the beach. This trail involves some dune climbing, and probably isn't for the casual hiker. The trail can be unpleasant in windy weather.

## Swimming & Canoeing

In Jessie M Honeyman State Park (☎ 997-3641) there are two lakes. **Cleawox Lake** is the smaller of the two, and although motorized boats are allowed here, most speed boats prefer **Woahink Lake**, which is deeper and doesn't fill with weeds. Canoes and pedal boats are available for rent at the park concession along Cleawox Lake.

Both lakes have designated swimming areas. Cleawox Lake is especially popular with children as the west bank of the lake is a high sand dune, and skittering down the sand into the water is a common activity.

Likewise, in William Tugman State Park, there's boating and swimming in **Eel Lake**. Although motorized boats are allowed, a 10-mph speed limit keeps the water-skiers away.

## Off-Road Vehicles

About 30% of the visitors to the Oregon Dunes come to race around on ORVs, which include dune buggies, all-terrain vehicles, motorcycles, souped up pick-ups

OREGON

and jeeps. Some restrictions apply: drivers of ORVs must have a driver's license, or else be supervised by an adult who has one; vehicles (except motorcycles) must have roll bars and seat belts; and vehicles have to sport a red flag at least nine feet high in order to increase their visibility. Oregon's regular speeding and drinking-while-driving laws apply to ORV operators.

There are any number of concessions in the Oregon Dunes area that rent ORVs; most also offer dune tours on large ORVs. Near Florence, Sandland Adventures (☎ 997-8087), 85366 S Hwy 101 S, about a mile south of the Siuslaw Bridge, rents a full line of ORVs and offers dune buggy tours. Near Reedsport, go to Dunes Odyssey Rentals (☎ 271-4011), 75303 Hwy 101, Winchester Bay. Down south by North Bend, try Far West Rentals (☎ 756-2322), 2580 Broadway, in the little community of Hauser.

One-hour rental of an ORV usually ranges between $30 and $35; prices go down for subsequent hours rented. There's a hefty deposit, which can be left as a check or credit card imprint. Tours of the sand dunes are generally $15 for a half-hour jaunt and $25 for an hour's outing.

### Places to Stay

**Camping** *Jessie M Honeyman State Park* (☎ 997-3641), three miles south of Florence on Hwy 101, is one of the most popular state parks in the Oregon system, for good reason. There are nearly 400 campsites, swimming and boating in Cleawox and Woahink lakes and lots of hiking and recreation in the dunes. Facilities include showers, flush toilets, a camp shop, boat and bike rentals and ranger-led tours and activities. If you're planning on camping here in midsummer, reservations are a good idea. Campsites range from $15 to $18.

*William Tugman State Park* is along Eel Lake, eight miles south of Reedsport, and offers 115 sites with hook-ups. There's swimming and boating in the lake, showers, a wheelchair-accessible fishing pier and a playground. Camping fees are $15.

Campgrounds associated with the National Recreation Area are generally a little less crowded and offer fewer amenities. There are four separate campgrounds off Siltcoos Dunes and Beach Access Rd, 7.5 miles south of Florence, all with flush toilets and water, but no hook-ups.

In the southern section of the Oregon Dunes, the *North, Mid* and *South Eel Creek Campgrounds*, all have drinking water and flush toilets. These campgrounds are just a mile from lake recreation at Tugman State Park. Sites cost $10.

If you're looking for adventure, you can camp informally anywhere in the National Recreation Area.

## REEDSPORT

Three miles from where the mighty Umpqua River joins the Pacific Ocean, Reedsport (population 4870) is the historic port that ushered out the immense bounty of logs cut in the wide Umpqua River drainage.

Reedsport wasn't established until the early years of this century, when the forests along the Umpqua River began to fall. Because the town was founded on a flood plain, many of the buildings were built on stilts. Sidewalks and businesses in the harbor area were several feet above grade in dry weather, which led to problems for inebriated sailors and lumberjacks. Gradually, the business district was filled in with soil from the surrounding hills, but that didn't help much: in 1961, another enormous flood swept through downtown, destroying many buildings.

Winchester Bay, out by the bar on the Umpqua River, has long been a stopping point for fishing boats; in the last 30 years it has become the state's largest sport-fishing port.

With today's limits on logging, and uncertain seasons for charter sport fishing, plain seaside communities like these have been at odds to find a tourist draw to suit the realities of the 1990s. For travelers, these towns offer inexpensive lodging and access to the Oregon Dunes National Recreation Area.

## The Kuitsh Indians

The Kuitsh Indians, often referred to as the Lower Umpquas, lived along the estuarial plains at the mouth of the Umpqua River. The Kuitsh were linguistically related to the Coos Indians further south and shared much of their culture and lifestyle.

Contact between the Kuitsh and traders was initially friendly. However, relations quickly worsened when Iroquois scouts, in the employ of White trappers, ambushed and killed 14 Kuitsh. When Jedediah Smith, a trapper, chanced into the Umpqua bay in 1821, his party was attacked by the Kuitsh, leaving 13 dead.

Smallpox and fever brought in by traders weakened the Kuitshs' resistance to the influx of settlers to the region in the 1850s. They were incarcerated on the Alsea Reservation in 1859. But the reservation was dissolved in 1875, leaving them landless. ■

## Information

Contact the Lower Umpqua Chamber of Commerce (☎ 271-3495, (800) 247-2155) at PO Box 11, Reedsport OR, 97467, or visit the office at the junction of Hwys 101 and 38.

Just across the street from the Chamber of Commerce are the offices for the Oregon Dunes National Recreation Area (☎ 271-3611), at 855 Highway Ave.

The post office (☎ 271-2521) is at 301 Fir Ave. The local hospital is Lower Umpqua Hospital (☎ 271-2171), 600 Ranch Rd.

## Umpqua Discovery Center Museum

This recently opened facility (☎ 271-4816), 409 Riverfront Way, was built for two quite distinct purposes: first, to interpret the natural and human history of the Umpqua River valley, including the culture of the Umpqua Indians and the early steamboat era; second, to focus on exploration of Antarctica. The centerpiece of this exhibit is the laboratory ship *Hero*, sitting in Reedsport harbor just as it was after its most recent scientific expedition to Antarctic waters. The ship is available for tours. There are separate admissions to each part of the center at $3 for adults and $1.50 for students. To tour the *Hero* and to visit the

Umpqua River section, there's a single admission of $5 for adults and $2.50 for children. Opening hours are from 10 am to 6 pm Sunday to Friday, and 10 am to 9 pm on Saturday. From October to March, hours are from 10 am to 6 pm, Wednesday to Sunday.

## Beaches

Ziolkouski Beach in Winchester Bay is a peaceful, although somewhat windswept, expanse of sand bordering the Oregon Dunes. The first parking area provides access to the jetty, while the last parking area is extremely popular for its ATV staging area, dune access trail and pit toilets. The least popular second parking lot caters to the indecisive, who choose which way to walk once they get there. The gate to this 'day-use only' area is locked at 9 pm.

A lesser-known and less-developed beach access road can be found three miles north of Reedsport. Continue north on Hwy 101 about a mile past the stinky International Paper mill, and turn left onto Sparrow Park Rd. This gravel road continues another three miles before ending at the beach. After a short hike towards the river, there is great **clam digging** here, not to mention a large sea lion hangout. Vehicles should be parked with respect to the incoming tide.

Seastacks are a distinctive feature of the Oregon coast.

**OREGON**

## Umpqua Lighthouse State Park

Umpqua Lighthouse was built in 1894, replacing the original that toppled off a nearby sandy headland during a winter storm in 1861. The lighthouse is still in operation and isn't open to visitors. Directly opposite the lighthouse is a whale-watching platform, with displays that explain various whale species and their habits. Also at the lighthouse, in an old barracks, is a small free museum with memorabilia from the early days of the Coast Guard.

The other draw in the park is **Lake Marie**, a small freshwater lake with swimming, non-motorized boating and picnicking. From the parking area, there's also a hiking trail around the lake and access to the Oregon Dunes, which gets pretty heavy ORV usage.

## Dean Creek Elk Viewing Area

East of Reedsport on Hwy 38, in a grassy meadow alongside the road, live a herd of about 100 Roosevelt elk. The elk, one of the largest members of the deer family in North America, live in the refuge, along with herons, nutria, black-tailed deer and Canadian geese. The elk are almost always in sight from the road; however, it's probably safest to turn in to one of the two viewing areas (which feature interpretive information), so as not to get run over by logging trucks.

## Fishing

While salmon fishing is subject to quickly imposed and confusing regulations and limitations, there's still dependable deep-sea fishing for bottom fish, halibut, shark and other brawny specimens. **Charter boats** leave from Winchester Bay at Gee & Gee Charters (☎ 271-3152), 465 Beach Blvd.

Some of the best fishing on the Umpqua is from jetties and wharves right in Reedsport and Winchester Bay. For advice, licenses and tackle, go to the Reedsport Outdoor Store (☎ 271-2311), 2049 Winchester Ave.

## Jet Boat Tours

Jet boats leave the Reedsport harbor and journey upriver as far as Mill Creek; another tour explores the harbor and the mouth of the Umpqua. Both trips leave daily, at 10 am and 1 pm, from Umpqua Jet Adventures (☎ 271-5694), 423 Riverfront Way, in the newly developed Waterfront area. The fare is $15; call for times and availability. Off-season, the jet boats leave only as reservations justify, so call ahead.

## Golf

Forest Hills Country Club (☎ 271-2626), 1 Country Club Drive, is a nine-hole course, buried within a quiet residential area.

## Places to Stay

**Camping** Perhaps due to the charter fishing industry, RV campgrounds abound around Reedsport and Winchester Bay. Some of these face onto the docks area, and are too exposed for tent campers. Find quieter and more sheltered campsites south of Winchester Bay. At *Umpqua Lighthouse State Park*, one mile south of Winchester Bay, there are campsites near freshwater Lake Marie, with easy beach and boat-launch access. There are showers and drinking water; rates are $15 to $17 a night. Contact the State Parks Department to reserve a site in advance.

Between Reedsport and Winchester Bay is the *Surfwood Campground* (☎ 271-4020), 75381 Hwy 101, with both tent and RV sites. Showers and a swimming pool are among the facilities; sites cost $12 to $14 a night.

**Hotels** Most hotels in Reedsport are right on Hwy 101, tend to be clean and simple, offer kitchenettes and take pets. The *Salty Seagull* (☎ 271-3729), 1804 Hwy 101, is a great deal with two-room units for $40/42 a single/double. The *Tropicana Motel* (☎ 271-3671), 1593 Hwy 101, has a pool; rates are $40/42. The *Douglas County Inn* (☎ 271-3686), 1894 Winchester Ave, takes pets and offers kitchenettes for $44/47. The *Best Western Salbasgeon Inn* (☎ 271-4831, (800) 528-1234), 1400 Hwy 101, is Reedsport's best motel, with an indoor pool, spa and hot tub and meeting rooms for $69/74.

Off busy Hwy 101, *Winchester Bay Friendship Inn* (☎ 271-4871, (800) 424-4777), 390 Broadway, Winchester Bay, is a large motel with views over Umpqua harbor. Rooms begin at $58; spa rooms are also available. Seven miles east of Reedsport, the *Salbasgeon Inn of the Umpqua* (☎ 271-2025), 45209 Hwy 38, has rooms right on the Umpqua River. The inn was once popular as an angler's resort, but now is more of a romantic hideaway; rooms begin at $63. (The name 'Salbasgeon' is the invention of a local hotelier, who merged the words 'salmon', 'bass' and 'sturgeon' to reflect the fishing possibilities of the area.)

### Places to Eat
Unsurprisingly, for a charter fishing community, big breakfasts and fresh fish are the specialties of Reedsport and Winchester Bay. The longtime local favorite for family dining is the *Windjammer Restaurant* (☎ 271-5415), 1281 Highway Ave, Reedsport, which is open for three meals a day. Check out *Don's Diner* (☎ 271-2032), 2115 Winchester Ave, for good burgers; finish up with Umpqua Dairy ice cream.

For the Reedsport approach to fine dining, go to *Unger's Landing* (☎ 271-3328), 151 Rainbow Plaza. This restaurant on a boat docked near the Umpqua Discover Center offers a seafood combination sautée with shrimp, salmon, scallops and halibut for $15; a New York steak is $12. For Italian food, go to *Red Shoes Cafe* (☎ 271-3650), 454 Fir Ave, where the chef makes his own sausages; a spaghetti dinner goes for $6.25.

The *Seafood Grotto* (☎ 271-4250), 115 8th St, in Winchester Bay, offers fresh seafood and standard American meals in a old-fashioned maritime atmosphere.

### Getting There & Away
Porter Enterprises operates a local bus service to Reedsport via Florence or Eugene. The 22nd St Market, across from the high school at the corner of Hwy 101

and 22nd St, serves as the stop; call Greyhound for information. Buses pick up from Reedsport for Newport, with connections to Corvallis, but service is infrequent.

## COOS BAY & NORTH BEND
The largest natural harbor between San Francisco and Seattle, Coos Bay (population 15,150) has long been a major shipping and manufacturing center, driving the engines of commerce and industry of most of southern Oregon. The port facilities here are thronged with foreign vessels waiting to take on board immense mountain-high stacks of timber. Smokestacks and warehouses line the bay and the smell of freshly cut wood fills the air.

Coos Bay had its beginnings in the 1870s as a ship-building center called Marshfield, but it wasn't until WW I created a vast market for local cedar trees – used to construct airplanes – that the area really boomed. For many years, Coos Bay was the largest timber-shipping port in the world.

The bloom went off the rose in the late 1980s, as the coastal forests were cleaned of easily harvested timber and remaining forests fell under the protection of federal laws. Lumber mills closed, due to the lack of suitable timber and also due to the fact that large forest-product conglomerates found it cheaper to mill remaining timber either in other countries or offshore, using foreign labor. Recent commercial fishing restrictions, due to salmon scarcity, have also dealt an economic blow to Coos Bay.

### Orientation
The city of Coos Bay, along with its twin, North Bend (population 9760), combine to make up the largest urban area on the Oregon coast. Coos Bay has the larger downtown area, roughly flanked by Johnson and Park Aves, 6th St and the bay. West of the city, the Cape Arago Hwy leads nine miles to Charleston, a fishing village on an inlet at the end of the Coos Bay, and then on to a clutch of beautiful state parks.

North Bend is at the end of the peninsula that juts into the bay, and begins north of

**OREGON**

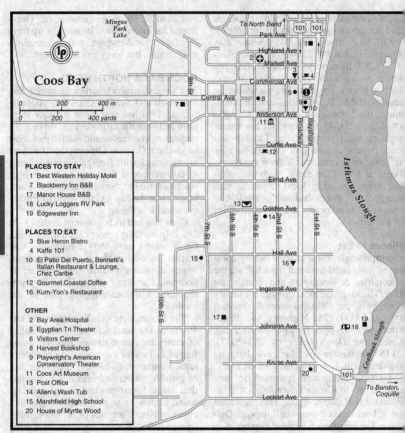

**Coos Bay**

0    200    400 m
0    200    400 yards

**PLACES TO STAY**
1  Best Western Holiday Motel
7  Blackberry Inn B&B
17  Manor House B&B
18  Lucky Loggers RV Park
19  Edgewater Inn

**PLACES TO EAT**
3  Blue Heron Bistro
4  Kaffe 101
10  El Patio Del Puerto, Bennetti's
    Italian Restaurant & Lounge,
    Chez Caribe
12  Gourmet Coastal Coffee
16  Kum-Yon's Restaurant

**OTHER**
2  Bay Area Hospital
5  Egyptian Tri Theater
6  Visitors Center
8  Harvest Bookshop
9  Playwright's American
    Conservatory Theater
11  Coos Art Museum
13  Post Office
14  Allen's Wash Tub
15  Marshfield High School
20  House of Myrtle Wood

Thompson Rd, with its western border along Fir St. From North Bend, Hwy 101 sails across the Coos Bay on high-flying McCullough Bridge into the southern edges of the Oregon Dunes National Recreational Area.

### Information

Contact the Bay Area Chamber of Commerce (☎ 269-0215, (800) 824-8486), 50 E Central Ave, Coos Bay, OR 97420. The post office (☎ 267-4514) is at 4th St and Golden Ave. Harvest Bookshoppe (☎ 267-5824), 307 Central Ave, is buried in Coos Bay's city center pedestrian mall.

Allen's Wash Tub (☎ 267-2814), 255 Golden Ave, is open 24 hours a day and offers a drop-off service. The Bay Area Hospital (☎ 269-8111) is at 1775 Thompson Rd.

### Coos County Historical Museum

This museum (☎ 756-6320), in Simpson Park at 1220 Sherman Ave, North Bend, offers artifacts and photos from the area's history. The collection of Coos beadwork and basketry is good, as are the mementos from the days when Coos Bay was a world-class shipping center. Also note the myrtle wood coins, which were issued as legal tender during the Depression. It's open from 10 am to 4 pm, Tuesday to Saturday; admission is $1 for adults, 50c for children ages five to 12.

The bay of the Coos River was the traditional home of the Hanis Coos, one of the tribes moved to the Alsea Reservation in the late 1850s. However, when that reservation was dissolved, the remaining Hanis Coos drifted back to the Coos Bay area without any land holdings. Attempts to receive compensation for the taking of their reservation lands, or to gain acknowledgment as a tribe from the government, has met with failure. The Hanis Coos, Siuslaw and the Lower Umpqua tribes are currently confederated and number about 500 members.

### Coos Art Museum

The Coos Art Museum (☎ 267-3901), 235 Anderson Ave, is the only civic art gallery on the Oregon coast. It hosts touring shows and exhibits and has a permanent collection of prints by modern artists. The museum is open from 11 am to 4 pm, Tuesday to Sunday.

### Activities

Rent **scuba** gear at Sunset Sports (☎ 756-3483) in the Pony Village Mall on Virginia Ave in North Bend.

Access to the 18-hole Kentuck Golf Course (☎ 756-4464), 680 Golf Course Rd, North Bend, is via East Bay Drive at the north end of the McCullough Bridge. The North Bend Swimming Pool (☎ 756-4915), 1500 Pacific Ave, is the bay area's only indoor **swimming** pool, just off the Cape Arago Hwy behind Pony Village Mall.

### Special Events

The Oregon Coast Music Festival (☎ 267-0938), is one of southern Oregon's largest festivals, with three weeks of musical acts in July between Bandon and Florence, although the concerts center in Marshfield High School Auditorium at Hall Ave and 7th St in Coos Bay.

The Blackberry Arts Festival is held in downtown Coos Bay the fourth Saturday in August. Booths selling blackberry food items are the most apparent reason for this

late summer shindig, but local arts & crafts people are also on hand.

### Places to Stay

**Camping** There are oceanside campgrounds near Charleston, only 11 miles west, or else north in the Oregon Dunes National Recreational Area. See either section for more information. For an urban setting, go to *Lucky Loggers RV Park* (☎ 267-6003, (800) 267-6426), 250 E Johnson Ave; sites begin at $15.

**B&Bs** The *Blackberry Inn B&B* (☎ 267-6951), 843 Central Ave, close to downtown Coos Bay, is a 1903 home with four guest rooms for $55. The *Manor House B&B* (☎ 269-1224), 955 S 5th Ave, is an imposing home built in 1911. There are five guest rooms, decorated according to theme. Only one room has a private bath. Rooms range from $55 to $60.

**Hotels** One of the cheapest places to stay is *City Center Motel* (☎ 756-5118), 750 Connecticut Ave, North Bend; singles/doubles are $38/40. There's quite a view of the bridge at *Bay Bridge Motel* (☎ 756-3151) 33 Hwy 101, on the other side of the bay from North Bend. For a view, rooms begin at $51; in the back, you'll pay $41 for a double room.

In Coos Bay, most hotels overlook the busy harbor or sit by busy Hwy 101, or often both. *Bayshore Motel* (☎ 267-4138), 1685 N Bayshore Drive, offers cut-rate rooms with queen-size beds; rates are $37/40. A bit more upscale, the *Best Western Holiday Motel* (☎ 269-5111), 411 N Bayshore Drive, has an indoor pool, weight room and spa and guest laundry; rooms are $68/71. The *Edgewater Inn* (☎ 267-0423, (800) 635-0852), 275 E Johnson Ave, offers an indoor pool, decks overlooking the harbor, and kitchenettes; it costs $74 for harborview rooms, $69 without. Business travelers prefer *Red Lion Inn* (☎ 267-4141), 1313 N Bayshore Drive, which offers views over the harbor, courtesy vans to the airport and an outdoor

OREGON

pool; rates are $77/82. The restaurant here is pretty good, too.

## Places to Eat
While Coos Bay may not have Oregon's best food, you won't need to look very hard for reasonably priced, easy-to-devour meals.

*Kaffe 101* (☎ 267-4894), 134 S Broadway, offers espresso drinks and muffins. Likewise, at *Gourmet Coastal Coffee* (☎ 267-5004), 273 Curtis Ave, there are bagels and pastries to go with cafe lattes. *Chez Caribe* (☎ 267-2589), 274 S Broadway, serves soups and salads in a 'Euro-tropical' setting, in addition to standard coffeeshop fare. En route to Cape Arago, the *Cranberry Sweets Coffee Shop* (☎ 888-6072), 1005 Newmark Ave, serves breakfast to early-rising beachcombers; lunch and cranberry candies are also available.

At *Blue Heron Bistro* (☎ 267-3933), 100 W Commercial Ave, the menu goes continental with pasta dishes and fresh fish for lunch and dinner; scampi and fettuccine in a cheese and garlic sauce goes for $12.50.

Table-side flambé dishes are a specialty at *Red Lion Inn Restaurant & Lounge* (☎ 267-4141), 1313 N Bayshore Drive. Sante Fe filet mignon and chili-stuffed sole are standard features at *El Patio Del Puerto* (☎ 269-7754), 252 S Broadway. *Benetti's Italian Restaurant & Lounge* (☎ 267-6066), 260 S Broadway, remains a consistent favorite with locals. The *Hilltop House Restaurant & Lounge* (☎ 756-4160), just north of the McCullough Bridge at 166 North Bay Drive, makes for a pleasant escape from the downtown bay area. Steak and seafood make the menu for fine dining.

*Kum-Yon's Restaurant* (☎ 269-2662), 835 S Broadway, features familiar Chinese and Japanese favorites along with a distinguished Korean menu.

## Entertainment
**Cinemas** The *Egyptian Tri* (☎ 267-3456), 229 S Broadway, shows first-run films. There aren't many of these old-style movie houses around anymore, and it's worth a trip simply to admire the theater's Egyptian

motif. If the movie is lousy, it may be more entertaining to sit in the lap of the giant concrete-molded, gold-painted mummy.

In contrast, the *Pony 4 Theaters* (☎ 756-3447) adjacent to the Pony Village Mall on Virginia Ave, is a boringly modern theater.

**Theater** The Coos Bay Area has a surprising number of local theater groups. Contact *Playwright's American Conservatory Theater* (☎ 269-2501), 226 S Broadway, Coos Bay, *Little Theater on the Bay* (☎ 756-4336), 2100 Sherman Ave, North Bend, and *Dolphin Players* (☎ 269-0215), to find out what's on the boards.

## Things to Buy
**Myrtle Wood** Across southern Oregon, wherever tourists have been known to tread, there are myrtle wood gift shops. While you may or may not want to buy milled bowls, Christmas tree ornaments, golf clubs and ornamental clocks made out of this rare wood, do go into one of the gift shops to find out what the fuss is about. At House of Myrtle Wood (☎ 267-7804), 1125 S 1st St, you'll find a large gift shop filled with carved wood products, as well as kiosks selling other Oregon products like fudge and jelly. Take the free factory tour (offered on the hour when there's demand) to find out all you need to know about myrtle wood production.

**Chocolate** Although the south coast is more renowned for its cranberry confections than for its chocolate, the International Restaurant & Deli (known locally as the German Deli) (☎ 756-0621), 1802 Virginia Ave, near the Pony Village Mall in North Bend, sells chocolate bars molded into a bas-relief of Leonardo da Vinci's *The Last Supper*. Available in milk, white or dark chocolate, these inexpensive bars are made especially for the Easter season. The deli also sells candy crosses.

## Getting There & Around
Buses from Portland and Lincoln City come to Coos Bay along the coast; tickets

can be as low as $19 one way. There are two buses between Eugene and Coos Bay; the fare is $23 one way. The depot (756-4900) is at 2007 Union Ave, North Bend.

Call Yellow Cab (☎ 267-3111) for a ride.

## CHARLESTON

West of Coos Bay on Cape Arago Hwy, Charleston is the state's busiest commercial fishing port and one of Oregon's premier sport fishing harbors. There's a kind of maritime hustle and bustle to the town that makes it a nice stopover on the way to the trio of splendid state parks on the headlands fronting Coos Bay.

South of Charleston is the Seven Devils Rd. This winding road serves both as a short cut between Charleston and Bandon and as access to a number of popular beaches south of Cape Arago like Whisky Run and Agate.

The Charleston Information Center (☎ 888-2311), PO Box 5735, Charleston, OR 97420, is at the corner of Cape Arago Hwy and Boat Basin Drive.

### Sunset Bay State Park

This beautiful park (☎ 888-4902) takes in a small, protected bay walled by extremely dramatic cliffs. It is popular with swimmers, divers and surfers, as well as hikers and vista-lovers. The year-round campground here is one of the most popular on the coast.

These grounds were once part of the Simpson estate (see Shore Acres State Park below) and boasted a popular cliffside hotel in the 1910s. Cape Arago Lighthouse sits right offshore on a rocky crag, linked to shore by a footbridge (no public entry). Waves over 75 feet in height regularly overwhelm the headlands here, spraying unsuspecting tourists.

To reach Sunset Bay State Park from Charleston, take Cape Arago Hwy three miles west of Charleston. A three-mile, cliff-edged hiking trail continues south from Sunset Bay and links the three state parks.

### Shore Acres State Park

Louis Simpson, an important shipping and lumber magnate, was exploring for new stands of lumber in 1905, when he discovered this wildly eroded headland and decided that the location would make a good site for a country home. After buying up the 320 acres, he built a three-story mansion here, complete with formal gardens and tennis courts. He called his estate Shore Acres.

The original home burned in 1921, and by the time Simpson rebuilt the house, his fortune, and the lumber industry, were in decline. By the 1930s, Simpson found it too expensive to maintain the house and grounds. The land passed to the State Parks Department in 1942. The house was eventually bulldozed, and the gardens neglected.

In 1971, the State Parks Department began reconstructing the formal gardens, including the sunken water garden and rose garden, using photographs and interviewing Simpson family members and friends to keep the restoration as historically accurate as possible.

A trail leads out from the gardens to the cliffs. Here, in a glass-protected vista point (near where the original mansion stood), the wild surf hammers against the headlands. In good weather, the trail continues on to the beach.

At the entrance to the gardens is the old garden house, which serves as a free museum of the old estate. There are picnic facilities; a $3 day-use fee helps support the gardens. The park (☎ 888-3732) is one mile south from Sunset Bay Park along the Cape Arago Hwy, or along the hiking trail.

### Cape Arago State Park

Another wild vista point above a pounding sea is Cape Arago State Park, at the termination of Cape Arago Hwy. The North Cove section of the park is closed to humans in the spring to protect the young sea lion pups that come onshore. This is a good place to look for migrating whales in spring. Trails lead down to the beach where there are great tide pools off the rocks at South Cove.

Picnic tables are scattered along the green and grassy headland near the parking area. The three-mile hiking trail takes off north from here and leads back to Shore Acres and then to Sunset Bay.

## South Slough National Estuarine Reserve

Charleston sits on a body of water evocatively called South Slough, which, south of the town, widens from a tidal river basin into a vast, muddy estuary. South Slough National Estuarine Reserve, five miles south of Charleston on Seven Devils Rd, was the nation's first estuary preserve. The interpretive center (☎ 888-5558), PO Box 5417, Charleston, OR 97420, provides a good multimedia introduction to the rich abundance of life that inhabits these estuaries, and offers guided walks with naturalists; call beforehand, as the schedule changes, or you can take your own tour by hiking along several interpretive trails. Wildlife viewing is great here, especially for shorebirds. Canoeists can explore the life of the estuary by coordinating with the tides; ask at the interpretive center for tide information.

The interpretive center is open from 8:30 am to 4:30 pm daily during summer and the same hours Monday to Friday the rest of the year; admission is free. The trails remain open dawn to dusk. If you'd like to canoe around the estuary, Coos Bay U-Haul (☎ 269-1333), 763 S Broadway, Coos Bay, rents canoes for $15 per day.

## Charter Fishing & Whale Watching

Charleston remains an important fishing center, and several charter companies offer sport fishing packages. Contact Betty Kay Charters (☎ 888-9021, (800) 752-6303), on the Charleston Boat Basin, or Bob's Sport Fishing (☎ 888-4241), 7788 Albacore Ave, for more information. Betty Kay also offers whale-watching trips during the spring migratory season.

## Places to Stay & Eat

*Sunset Bay State Park*, (☎ 888-4902), three miles southwest of Charleston on Cape Arago Hwy, has tent sites for $15, electrical hook-ups for $16, and full hook-ups for $17. Showers, drinking water and a playground are available. Contact the State Parks Department for reservations during the summer. *Bastendorff Beach County Park* (☎ 888-5353), just west of Charleston on Cape Arago Hwy, has convenient campsites near a stretch of beach and offers showers, fire pits and playgrounds.

The *Talavar Inn & Retreat* (☎ 888-5280), 4367 Cape Arago Hwy, is a rustic home built in 1945 across the bay from Charleston. There are two guest rooms, one with private bath and balcony. Prices range between $65 and $85.

A popular place with anglers, *Captain John's Motel* (☎ 888-4041), 8061 Kingfisher Drive, has a great location right on the boat basin. Rooms, some with kitchenettes, start at $48.

The *Portside Restaurant* (☎ 888-5544), Charleston Boat Basin, serves an extensive menu including fresh fish, beef, lobster, salmon, razor clams and a fine bouillabaisse. Full dinners range from $12 to $15.

## BANDON

The little town of Bandon (population 2390) is one of the real jewels on the Oregon coast. Bandon-by-the-Sea, as its promoters have renamed it in recent years, sits at the bay of the Coquille River. South of town are miles of sandy beaches, rhythmically broken by outcroppings of towering rock, home to a large number of chattering seabirds. Ledges of stone rise out of the surf to provide shelter for seals, sea lions and myriad forms of life in tide pools.

Jetties reach out into the bay to protect the old port area, still active with fishing boats and Coast Guard vessels. For the traveler, the center of Bandon is Old Town, which houses most of the town's cafes, gift shops and taverns. One of the Oregon coast's only hostels, a good bookstore and loads of galleries and artists' studios lend

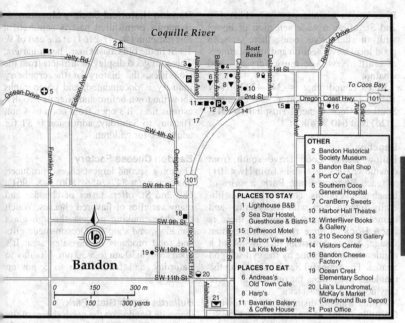

OREGON

**OTHER**
2 Bandon Historical Society Museum
3 Bandon Bait Shop
4 Port O' Call
5 Southern Coos General Hospital
7 CranBerry Sweets
10 Harbor Hall Theatre
12 WinterRiver Books & Gallery
13 210 Second St Gallery
14 Visitors Center
16 Bandon Cheese Factory
19 Ocean Crest Elementary School
20 Lila's Laundromat, McKay's Market (Greyhound Bus Depot)
21 Post Office

**PLACES TO STAY**
1 Lighthouse B&B
9 Sea Star Hostel, Guesthouse & Bistro
15 Driftwood Motel
17 Harbor View Motel
18 La Kris Motel

**PLACES TO EAT**
6 Andreas's Old Town Cafe
8 Harp's
11 Bavarian Bakery & Coffee House

Bandon a focus and vigor lacking in most other coastal communities; even the logging and farming locals seem proud to think that their little town has developed into an 'artists' colony'. Bandon also has the reputation of being a center of alternative spirituality.

As in most coastal towns, fishing, logging and lumber mills propel the local economy. Bandon suffered a setback in 1914 when the old downtown burned. The town quickly rebuilt, focusing its energies on tourism. But, in September 1936 a smoldering forest fire burned almost every building in Bandon within a few hours, leaving 12 dead. Only today's Old Town survived the blaze.

Today, Bandon's most noteworthy industry is cranberry farming. In fall, watch for fields filled with low-growing, bright-red berries: these bogs yield a considerable percentage of the US cranberry harvest. One local company makes much-touted cranberry candies, and the tart fruit turns up frequently in local breads and desserts. Bandon's largest annual event, the autumn Cranberry Festival, brings together cooks, craftspeople and gardeners to honor the berry.

## Orientation

The main commercial district of Bandon is called Old Town, a five-block nucleus of restaurants and shops along 1st and 2nd Sts at the Bandon Harbor. Many of the famous Bandon beaches are found just south of town along Beach Loop Drive. North of town, dunes, rather than rocky cliffs, dominate the coast. From Bandon, it's 21 miles north to Coos Bay on Hwy 101 and 27 miles south to Port Orford. Highway 42S leads inland from Bandon to the town of Coquille.

## Information

The Bandon Visitors Center (☎ 347-9616) is at 2nd St and Chicago Ave. The post office (☎ 347-3406) is at 105 12th St. Winter-

River Books & Gallery (☎ 347-4111), 170 2nd St, offers a wide selection of books with an alternative focus; there's also a good local travel section and an assortment of crafts, New Age music, crystals and whatnot.

Lila's Laundromat (☎ 347-4222), Hwy 101 at 11th St, also offers dry cleaning. Southern Coos General Hospital (☎ 347-2426) is at 640 W 4th St.

### Beaches
Follow Beach Loop Drive south from downtown (or follow signs from Hwy 101) to reach **Bandon State Park**, a series of beach access points. The beach here is liberally interspersed with rocky crags and monoliths. The most famous of these is **Face Rock**, a huge rock with a human visage. Native American legends tell of a maiden turned to stone by the evil sea god Seatka. The vengeful Seatka also flung the maiden's pet kittens far out to sea, where they now rise as seastacks.

Within walking distance of downtown is **Coquille Point**, at the end of SW 11th St, where steps lead down the bluff to the rocky beach. The offshore crags are protected as wildlife preserves.

### Bandon Historical Society Museum
Bandon's event-filled past is captured in this museum (☎ 347-2164) at the end of W 1st St in the old Coast Guard headquarters. There's a good display of artifacts from the Coquilles, the history of the cranberry industry is documented, and photographs show the town before and after its two disastrous fires. It's open from noon to 4 pm, Tuesday to Saturday; admission is $1 for adult, 50c for children.

### Bandon Cheese Factory
Oregon's second-largest cheese producer, this factory (☎ 347-2456, (800) 548-8961), 680 2nd St, offers tastes of cheddar and many varieties of flavored cheeses. Watch the cheesemaking process through glass windows, and shop for Oregon-made gifts and food products in the sales area. It's open from 8:30 am to 5:30 pm, Monday to Saturday, and from 9 am to 5 pm on Sunday.

### Bullards Beach State Park
Opposite Bandon on the north shores of the Coquille River, this state park (☎ 347-2209) offers beach access to the dune country north of Bandon. Hiking and

---

### Native American Rivalries
Near present-day Bandon, the Miluk Coos, a branch of the Coos Indians from further north, were dominant, while inland along the Coquille River, the forests were controlled by the Coquille Indians, culturally and linguistically part of the Rogue Indian nation to the south. Relations between these two tribes were largely hostile; each regularly raided the other for slaves.

In 1851, the Miluk Coos were sent to Yachats, to live on the Alsea Reservation along the coast with other Coos Indians, and the Coquilles, along with many of the other southern Oregon tribes were freighted north on steamships to the Grande Ronde Reservation on the Yamhill River in 1856.

This century each of the tribes sued the federal government to settle land claims. The Coos lost their claim, but the Coquilles, along with other Rogue tribes, received a sum of more than $3 million in compensation. A number of the Miluk Coos were able to prove some Coquille ancestry and successfully petitioned to receive part of the Coquilles' settlement. However, this move caused great disharmony within the remaining body of the Miluk Coos, as it weakened that group's claim for federal acknowledgment as a tribe.

Today, the Coquille Indian Tribe contains both Miluk Coos and Coquilles and was acknowledged as an official tribe in 1989. Neither tribe has any reservation lands, though the Coquilles own a small parcel of land where a sacred rock once stood (the rock was blown up for riprap for the Bandon harbor jetties). The Coquilles plan to build a ceremonial longhouse and museum on their holding. ■

Bandon lighthouse

biking trails wind through the woods or to the beach, and there's also an equestrian camp and bridle paths. The **Coquille River Lighthouse**, built in 1896, hasn't functioned as such since 1939, but it has been restored as a fairly basic museum commemorating boat travel. Informal tours can be arranged by request; ask at the Bullards Beach State Park office. There are flush toilets, picnic areas and a popular campground here.

### Fishing
The Bandon area offers good fishing both on the Coquille River and the Pacific Ocean. Steelhead, red snapper, rainbow trout and ling cod are good in the Coquille, as is Chinook salmon, but the season can be pretty crowded for the quantity of fish remaining in the river. Crabs are numerous in the bay as well. For fishing information, licenses, crab rings and tackle, go to the Bandon Bait Shop (☎ 347-3905), along the harbor.

Port O' Call (☎ 347-2875), 155 1st St, offers **charter fishing** for bottom fish and halibut, as well as salmon fishing within the waters of the bay.

### Whale Watching
The bluffs south of Bandon are popular places to spot migrating whales in winter and spring. A good place to watch in the morning is Coquille Point, off the end of SW 11th St.

### Golf
Nine-hole Bandon Face Rock Golf Course (☎ 347-3818), 3225 Beach Loop Rd, allows players to pit themselves against the tempests of the Pacific on this pretty, beach-facing course.

### Special Events
On Memorial Day weekend, Bandon kicks off its festival season with the Bandon Sandcastle Contest and the Storm Watchers Wine & Seafood Festival (☎ 347-9616). Teams compete to build the most imaginative structures along the beachfront, while regional wine producers match their vintages with fresh seafood. Other activities include the annual blessing of the fleet. The festival is held at The Barn in City Park, at 11th St and Jackson Ave.

The Coquilles' Native American Salmon Bake & Powwow (☎ 267-4587), held the last weekend of June in the Old Town area, features salmon traditionally baked in a fire pit, corn on the cob and fry bread. Drumming, dancing and a crafts fair round out the event.

Bandon's largest civic event is the Cranberry Festival (☎ 347-2277), usually held the first weekend in October. There's a parade, the crowning of the Cranberry Queen, a craft show, music, a beef barbecue and the food fair, where cranberries find their way into dozens of dishes prepared by local cooks.

### Places to Stay
**Camping** Two miles north of Bandon on Hwy 101, *Bullards Beach State Park* (☎ 347-2209) offers almost 200 campsites with easy access to ocean beaches. A thin forest shelters these campsites from the worst of the wind, which can be quite fierce around here. Facilities include flush toilets, showers, an equestrian area and an RV dumping area. Tent sites are $16, full hookups are $17.

**Hostels** The *Sea Star HI Hostel* (☎ 347-9632), 375 2nd St, is the only HI/AYH hostel on the Oregon coast. At this very pleasant inn, there are dorms for $12 to

OREGON

$15, or private rooms for couples and families, from $45 to $75 a night. The facility includes common areas, a kitchen and a laundry room. Adjoining the hostel is a good natural-foods restaurant.

**B&Bs** The *Lighthouse B&B* (☎ 347-9316), 650 Jetty Rd, has great views of the lighthouse from the four guest rooms with private baths. Some rooms have fireplaces; rates range between $80 and $100. The *Sea Star Guesthouse* (☎ 347-9632), 370 1st St, is part of the same complex as the hostel, but with better views and more privacy. Two units have kitchenettes; all include breakfast in the *Sea Star Bistro*; rooms start at $60.

**Hotels** Bandon hotels are divided into those in town and those along the Beach Loop Rd south of town, which afford more or less direct beach access and ocean views.

Out along the loop road, one of the best deals is *Bandon Beach Motel* (☎ 347-4430), 1110 SW 11th St, where singles/doubles start at $50/55. *Table Rock Motel* (☎ 347-2700), 840 Beach Loop Rd, has two family cottages for rent; rooms start at $48. *Windermere Motel* (☎ 347-3710), 3250 Beach Loop Rd, offers older but refurbished chalet-like cottages on the beach south of Bandon for $74.

On the main highway, try the following older motels. *La Kris Motel* (☎ 347-3610), at Hwy 101 and 9th St, is well-maintained, pets are OK and rooms are $43/47. *The Driftwood Motel* (☎ 347-9022), 460 Hwy 101, is an older motel right downtown; singles/doubles are $52/58.

On the bluff above Old Town is the *Harbor View Motel* (☎ 347-4417, (800) 526-0209), 355 2nd St, a newer facility affording great views of the bay and ocean. Complimentary breakfast, a spa and wheelchair-accessible rooms are among the draws; rates are $75/80.

**Resorts** At *The Inn at Face Rock* (☎ 347-9441, 638-3092), 3225 Beach Loop Rd, you have the Pacific Ocean on one side, and

a golf course on the other. The condo-style suites have great ocean views and fireplaces starting at $84. There's also a lounge and restaurant in the main lodge.

**Vacation Home Rentals** To rent a home in Bandon, contact Coastal Vacation Rentals (☎ 347-3009, (800) 336-5693), PO Box 702, Bandon, OR 97411.

### Places to Eat

The *Bavarian Bakery & Coffee House* (☎ 347-9812), 170 2nd St, has great pastries and espresso drinks. At the *Sea Star Bistro* (☎ 347-9632), 370 1st St, there's strong coffee and imposing omelets to begin the day, with Mediterranean-style (mostly meat-free) food dominating lunch ($5 to $8) and dinner service ($12 to $15, served Thursday to Saturday only). The pasta and baked goods are all homemade. The woodsy dining room is filled with youthful travelers from the hostel upstairs, and the service is fairly informal and unexpecting.

*Andrea's Old Town Cafe* (☎ 347-3022), 160 Baltimore Ave, is a bright and airy storefront overgrown with house plants and comfortable booths. The real treat here is the lamb raised on Andrea's farm. The dinner menu changes daily, with most entrees (like Russian braised lamb shanks) for $10 to $15. Cheesecake is another specialty. Andrea's is open for breakfast and lunch daily; evening service is daily in the summer, but only on Fridays and Saturdays in the dead of winter.

Another Old Town favorite is *Harps* (☎ 347-9057), 130 Chicago Ave, a small bistro whose menu reflects fresh local ingredients and careful preparations like the cream of shrimp soup with shallots and tarragon, or the famed halibut with spicy pistachio sauce ($16). Pasta dishes and steak range between $10 and $15. It's open for dinner only.

*Bandon Boatworks* (☎ 347-2111), at the end of South Jetty Rd, has wonderful views of the Coquille Lighthouse and the Pacific Ocean. Dishes on the extensive menu are prepared carefully, though without advenure. On Sundays, Boatworks serves a Mexican menu.

## Entertainment

The local performing arts center, *Harbor Hall Theater* (☎ 347-4404), 325 2nd St, plays host to regional and national artists, bands and theatrical touring companies.

*Bandon Playhouse* (☎ 347-9881) is an ambitious community theater that stages musicals, classic drama and contemporary plays at the auditorium of Ocean Crest Elementary School at 9th St and Allegany Ave.

## Things to Buy

CranBerry Sweets (☎ 347-9475), at 1st St and Chicago Ave, makes cranberry-based candies. At their factory outlet, there are free samples, plus a video showing the cranberry harvest. Other homemade candies, cranberry products and food gifts are available.

Old Town Bandon also offers a startlingly wide selection of craft shops, art galleries and artists' studios. The largest selection of art is found at the 210 Second St Gallery (☎ 347-4133).

## Getting There & Away

Greyhound buses stop and pick up at McKay's Market, Hwy 101 at 10th St. A one-way fare from Eugene is $17.

## PORT ORFORD

Sleepy Port Orford (population 1025) is so far from most centers of population that it hasn't yet been developed as a tourist trap, but it's not for lack of beauty; Port Orford is magically situated on a grassy headland overlooking a natural harbor. In fact, Port Orford is one of Oregon's only true ocean harbors (others are situated along the mouths of rivers), and has a long history as a fishing and lumber port. Port Orford cedar is an especially important export.

During WW II the southern Oregon coast was repeatedly hit by the Japanese with incendiary balloons aiming to ignite the forests of the Pacific coast, which they believed were important to the building of US military ships and airplanes.

Port Orford is on Hwy 101, 27 miles south of Bandon, and 20 miles north of Gold Beach. Just north of town is Cape Blanco, one of the westernmost points of the continental USA. South of the town rises Humbug Mountain, one of the highest seaside peaks along the coast.

If a beautiful ocean view, a great beach and a few friendly businesses are all you require, you may fall under the spell of Port Orford. For information, stop at the Battle Rock Information Center (☎ 332-8055), or write PO Box 637, Port Orford, OR 97465.

### Battle Rock

In the 1850s, Port Orford was the scene of some of the state's bloodiest encounters between Native Americans and the Whites trying to establish a settlement. Tututnis, or Coastal Rogues, were especially resistant to White incursions and had a fearsome reputation with early fur traders and miners.

In June 1851, a group of men took up positions on a natural promontory (now known as Battle Rock), surrounded by water on three sides and connected to land only at low tide. When a group of Tututnis approached the rock, the White men opened fire at point-blank range with a small cannon, killing 13. Later, the setters killed several Tututni chiefs and went on to establish Port Orford without further conflict.

In early spring 1856, after gold had been discovered along the southern Oregon coast, the Tututnis attacked Port Orford, killing 26 settlers, and then continued their campaign all along the coast, burning most settlements between Port Orford and California. But, by mid-spring most Tututnis were driven away from the coast by US Army troops and moved inland to join the Takilmas and other southern Oregon tribes who were also fighting the army and miners in conflicts that came to be called the Rogue River War.

In total, almost 1500 Native Americans were incarcerated and shipped out of Port Orford in just one year.

## Humbug Mountain State Park

At Humbug Mountain State Park (☎ 332-6774), six miles south of Port Orford on Hwy 101, mountains edge down to the ocean and heavily wooded Humbug Mountain rises 1748 feet from the surf. A three-mile trail leads from the campground (or from the trailhead parking lot just to the south) through beautiful virgin forests – the groves of now-rare Port Orford cedar here are the largest remaining along the Oregon coast – to the top of the mountain for a great view of Cape Sebastian and the dramatic Pacific Ocean.

When White settlers first came to the area, the Tututnis lived in a large village along the beach just north of Humbug Mountain. Facilities at the park include wheelchair-accessible flush toilets and a large campground.

## Cape Blanco State Park

First sighted in 1603 by Spanish explorer Martin d'Anguilar, Cape Blanco's thin neck of land juts far out into the Pacific withstanding the lashing winds and fierce winter storms – more than 100 inches of rain fall here a year, and the wind frequently passes the 100-mph mark. These conditions, and the treacherous, rocky coastline hereabouts, make Cape Blanco a real danger to ships. The state park is four miles north of town and five miles west on an access road.

The current **Cape Blanco Lighthouse** was built in 1870 and is the highest and oldest operational lighthouse in the state. You can take a tour (limited to five people) between 10 am to 5 pm Thursday to Monday. The tour schedule runs on demand and admission is by donation.

A mile east of the lighthouse is **Hughes House** (☎ 247-6676), 91814 Cape Blanco Rd, a two-story Victorian home built in 1898 by Patrick Hughes, an Irish dairy rancher and sometime gold miner. Tours are available from 10 am to 5 pm, Thursday to Monday (beginning at noon on Sunday). Admission is by donation.

Both sites operate seasonally in coordination with the campground, and are gen-erally closed from early October to the end of April.

## Places to Stay & Eat

Six miles south of Port Orford on Hwy 101, *Humbug State Park* (☎ 332-6774), offers a great campground that's right on the beach yet protected by the coastal forest. There are over 100 campsites; $15 for a standard site, $17 for hook-ups. Showers and flush toilets are available. At *Cape Blanco State Park* (☎ 332-6774), there are 58 campsites on a rocky headland with great views of the lighthouse. There are flush toilets, showers, a boat ramp and an RV dump station; all sites have electrical hook-ups and are $17.

The *Home by the Sea B&B* (☎ 332-2855), 444 Jackson St, is a newer home with four guest rooms. Views are wonderful, rooms are $70 and $75. The *Castaway-by-the-Sea Motel* (☎ 332-4502), 545 W 5th St, has oceanview rooms above the harbor, some with fireplaces at $53/58 for a single/double. The *Shoreline Motel* (☎ 332-2903), 206 6th St, is an easy walk to the beach and to shops; rooms are $41/46. The *Sea Crest Motel* (☎ 332-3040), 1 S Hwy 101, offers oceanview rooms for $48/53.

The *Truculent Oyster* (☎ 332-9461), 236 Hwy 101, is a friendly bar and restaurant and a fun place to eat fresh seafood. Selections change seasonally, with prices ranging between $9 and $14 at dinner. The *Whale Cove* (☎ 332-7575), 190 Hwy 101, is a family-style restaurant serving breakfast all day, and pretty good burgers.

## Getting There & Away

Greyhound stops at the Circle K (☎ 332-3181), 914 N Oregon St; two buses a day go north and south along the coast.

## GOLD BEACH

While Gold Beach (population 1640) faces out onto the Pacific, its soul looks inland to the Rogue River, which meets the ocean here. The recreation-minded resort facilities in the area make Gold Beach a favorite with well-heeled travelers who like a little bit of the outdoors with their leisure.

Gold Beach is named for the oceanfront

mines that yielded gold in the 1850s. Apparently, the Rogue River brings gold dust downstream when in flood; over the centuries, gold accumulated into bands in the dark sand dunes along the river's mouth. The little settlement here didn't amount to much until the early years of this century when the salmon-rich waters of the Rogue caught the fancy of gentleman anglers like Jack London and Zane Grey and captured the entrepreneurial zeal of Thomas Hume, who established a salmon cannery here.

If you're not an angler, Gold Beach's main allure is jet boats that zip up the Rogue River to remote upstream outposts and beauty spots in the Rogue River Wilderness Area. Most of these trips include a stop for lunch at rustic lodges in the little community of Agness.

Leading inland from Gold Beach is USFS Rd 33, also called Agness Rd, which follows the Rogue upriver to Agness and Illahe (in town, the road is called Jerry's Flat Rd). This road, wrapped in old-growth forests, is paved as far as Illahe and is an alternative for Rogue River explorers who can't abide jet boats. For off-road enthusiasts, USFS Rd 33 continues on to Powers and down the South Fork Coquille River to Myrtle Point.

Despite its centrality for recreation on the Rogue, the joylessly utilitarian town of Gold Beach doesn't offer the charm or esprit evident in many other coastal towns.

The Gold Beach Chamber of Commerce (☎ 247-7526) and the Siskiyou National Forest offices (☎ 247-6651) are at 1225 S Ellensburg Ave, Gold Beach OR 97444. The post office (☎ 247-7610) is on Moore St.

From Gold Beach it's 44 miles south to the California border and 78 miles north to Coos Bay.

### Curry County Museum
This small museum (☎ 247-6113), 920 S Ellensburg Ave, preserves Native American and early settlement history. Of particular interest are the displays relating to the beachfront gold rush in the late 1880s. The

museum is open from noon to 4 pm, Tuesday to Sunday, from June to October; noon to 4 pm, Saturdays only, the rest of the year. Donations are accepted.

### Cape Sebastian State Park
Seven miles south of Gold Beach, this small park is mostly a vista point on a rocky cliff-hung headland, but what a vista! On clear days, the seascapes stretch for miles, from California to Cape Blanco. A short trail leads from the parking lot out to the cliff's edge. Hardy hikers can continue down a steep trail to the beach at the base of the cape.

### Hiking
The 40-mile **Rogue River Trail** ends (or begins) at Illahe. Day hikers who want to explore the Rogue River canyon can hike 4.5 miles one way up to Flora Dell Creek, where a waterfall drops into the Rogue. For information on long-distance hikes along the Rogue River Trail, see the Wild Rogue Wilderness Area in the Southern Oregon chapter.

### Jet Boat Tours
The Rogue River is one of Oregon's wildest and most remote rivers, with access largely limited to hikers and white-water rafters. However, you can explore the lower reaches of the Rogue on jet boat tours, which use hydrofoils that can skim over the surface of shallow streams and river rapids. Jet boats were originally used to deliver mail to far-reaching outposts. The tours travel to the rugged and barren canyon whose walls tower 1500 feet above the river in the Rogue River Wilderness Area. Wildlife viewing is good, with deer, elk, otters, beavers, eagles and osprey seemingly unaffected by the deafening growls of the jet boat engines.

Two companies offer similar trips: a six-hour excursion to the little resort community of Agness, 30 miles inland; or a slightly longer run that goes past Agness to shoot white-water rapids. Both these trips include a layover for lunch in one of three lodges at Agness. A longer eight-hour trip

OREGON

features lighter and smaller jet boats that are able to climb shallow rapids up to Blossom Bar Rapids. This trip includes a lunch break at *Paradise Bar Lodge*, 50 miles up the river.

Contact either Jerry's Rogue Jets (☎ 247-4571, (800) 451-3645), or Rogue River Mail Boats (☎ 247-7033, (800) 458-3511).

Despite what all the brochures say, the times and frequency of trips are variable, so call ahead and reserve a space. Costs range from $27.50 for the trips between Gold Beach and Agness to $65 for the trip between Gold Beach and Paradise Bar; lunches are not included.

### Places to Stay

**Camping** Closest to Gold Beach, and on the Rogue River's south bank, is *Indian Creek Recreation Park* (☎ 247-7704), 94680 Jerry's Flat Rd. There's a separate tenting area, showers and a shop for provisions. Sites are $12 for tents, $20 for full hook-ups. *Four Seasons RV Resort* (☎ 247-4503), 96526 N Bank Rogue Rd, is right on the river; tents are $15, RV hook-ups $18. Fishing is the thing here, with a boat ramp, guide service and tackle shop on the grounds.

If tent campers want to avoid the comforts of RV campgrounds, head up USFS Rd 33 toward Agness for nine miles to *Lobster Creek Campground*, a USFS campground on the banks of the Rogue River; sites are $3. Further up USFS Rd 33 there's a nice riverside facility at Illahe called *Illahe Campground*. More formal RV sites are available at *Agness RV Park* (☎ 247-2813), 04215 Agness Rd. Sites are $12 for tents and $15 for electric hook-ups.

**B&Bs** The *Inn at Nesika Beach* (☎ 247-6434), 33026 Nesika Rd, is a Victorian-style inn with four guest rooms, private baths and ocean views; three have fireplaces. Rates range from $85 to $115.

**Hotels** For a town its size, Gold Beach has a surprising number of hotels. Most are modest but nice, though there are also

several resorts and lodges to cater to anglers and such.

The *City Center Motel* (☎ 247-6675), 150 Harlow St, is a clean, older motel with singles/doubles at $44/47. The *Drift In Motel* (☎ 247-4547), 715 N Ellensburg Ave, is on the river near the bridge; rates are $45/50. At the *Inn at Gold Beach* (☎ 247-6606), 1435 S Ellensburg Ave, the rooms have views and cost $60/68.

**Lodges** Take USFS Rd 33 to reach the three rustic lodges at Agness that serve the needs of groups of anglers, jet boat passengers and the occasional stray traveler. *Lucas Lodge* (☎ 247-7443), 03904 Cougar Lane, offers rooms in the 1910s-era lodge ($35) or in cabins ($45 to $60). At the *Singing Springs Resort* (☎ 247-6162), on USFS Rd 33, rooms are in cabins ($45 or $60) or in the motel ($40/$45 for singles/ doubles). The newest of the lodges is the *Cougar Lane Resort* (☎ 247-7233), 04219 Agness Rd, which offers rooms ($35 to $45) in motel-like units. Each of the above lodges offers buffet-style lunch and dinner.

*Tu Tu Tun Lodge* (☎ 247-6664), 96550 N Bank Rogue River Rd, seven miles east of Gold Beach, is a rustic hideaway on the north banks of the Rogue River. Large rooms with decks, a pool and access to boats and fishing off the dock make this one of the southern Oregon coast's few destination resorts. Prices start at $120. The dining room is private and is rumored to serve wonderful meals to lodge guests.

**Resorts** Overlooking the ocean from downtown, the *Gold Beach Resort & Condominiums* (☎ 247-7066), 1330 S Ellensburg Ave, is a new resort offering condo-style rooms starting at $90 with access to an indoor pool and spa; some rooms have fireplaces. *Jot's Resort* (☎ 247-6676, (800) 367-5687), 94360 Wedderburn Loop, just north of the bridge, is one of the original resorts on this part of the coast. It has nearly 150 guest rooms and condo suites overlooking the harbor, two pools and a marina with boat rentals and fishing guide service; rooms start at $90.

**Vacation Home Rentals** Contact South Coast Properties & Management (☎ 247-5555), at 135 S Campbell St, Gold Beach, OR 97444.

## Places to Eat

There's nothing very memorable about the restaurant selection in Gold Beach. Chowder and fish & chips seem to be the basic menu selections whether you eat high or low. You might as well go for views and atmosphere.

The *Nor'Wester Seafood Restaurant* (☎ 247-2333), Port of Gold Beach, serves grilled salmon, halibut or whatever's in season, as well as good steaks. Full dinners are in the $15 range. *Rod & Reel* (☎ 247-6823), 94321 W River Rd, part of Jot's Resort, offers a large variety of seafood and beef dishes; a shrimp-stuffed fillet of sole is $15. The Rod & Reel is also a good place for an old-fashioned breakfast.

## Getting There & Away

The Greyhound station (☎ 247-7710) is at 310 Colvin St. Two buses run each way daily; the fare between Gold Beach and Florence is $17.50 and to Brookings it's $5.50.

## BROOKINGS

Just six miles north of the California-Oregon border on Hwy 101, on the bay of the Chetco River, Brookings (population 4900) is a bustling town with lots of traffic crossing the state line to avoid sales taxes. The harbor is one of Oregon's busiest, with both commercial and sport fishing lending a bustle to the bayfront.

Logging has long held the economy here, but, as elsewhere along the coast, recent restrictions have largely halted further clear-cutting. Many loggers, savvy in the ways of the forest, have turned their hands to wild mushroom collecting for a living. Chanterelles, black trumpets, morels and porcinis are among the forest's bounty.

Brookings leads the nation in Easter lily-bulb production. In July, fields south of town are filled with bright color and heavy scent. Roads lead inland from Brookings up the Chetco River to the western edge of Kalmiopsis Wilderness Area, the state's largest and one of its most remote. Oregon's only redwood forests are also found up the Chetco River; some groves are preserves in Loeb State Park, also known for its myrtle trees.

Oregonians throughout the rest of the state refer to Brookings as being 'in the banana belt' of the state. During the winter, temperatures hover around 60°F, which is indeed balmy compared to the stormy climes in the north.

Brookings was the site of one of only two mainland US air attacks during WW II. A seaplane launched from a Japanese submarine in early September 1942 succeeded in bombing Mt Emily, behind the city. The main goal of the attack was to burn the forests, but they failed to ignite. There were no casualties. To see the bomb site, a source of peculiar fascination to the locals, follow South Side Chetco River Rd, and look for signs to 'Bomb Site' (or ask at the visitors center for a map).

### Orientation

To get from inland southern Oregon to Brookings requires a trip down Hwy 199, called the Redwood Hwy, from Grants Pass to Crescent City, California, and then north 15 miles. From Grants Pass to Brookings along this route is 105 miles. From Brookings, the next town north on Hwy 101 is Gold Beach, 39 miles away along the spectacular cliff-lined coast.

What is referred to as Brookings is in fact two towns, Brookings proper, north of the Chetco River, and Harbor on the south shore, where the boat basin is. In the following addresses, note that the innocent-sounding Chetco Ave is actually Hwy 101.

### Information

The Brookings-Harbor Chamber of Commerce (☎ 469-3181, (800) 535-9469), is at 16330 Lower Harbor Rd, Brookings, OR 97415. The Chetco Ranger Station (☎ 469-2196) is at 555 5th St.

The post office (☎ 469-2318) is at 711 Spruce St. You can wash your dirty clothes at Old Wash House Laundromat (☎ 469-

OREGON

3975), in the Brookings Harbor Shopping Center at the corner of Shopping Center Ave and Grootendorst Lane.

### Beaches
There are beaches all along the Brookings seafront north of the mouth of the Chetco River. One nice in-town beach access is at the end of Wharf St, where **Mill Beach** and Agnew Park offer sandy beaches and views of promontories off Chetco Point.

There are miles of beaches, rocky cliffs and outcroppings and shoreline hiking trails at **Harris Beach State Park** (☎ 469-2021), just north of Brookings off Hwy 101. From the picnic area, there are views of Goat Island, Oregon's largest offshore island and a bird sanctuary. Harris Beach State Park also offers campsites.

### Chetco Valley Historical Society Museum
This community museum (☎ 469-6651), 15461 Museum Rd, is housed in an 1857 stagecoach station – Brookings' oldest building. The museum's items of special interest include an odd iron cast of a woman's face whose resemblance to Queen Elizabeth I is speculative, and a cedar canoe used by Native coastal fishers. Adjacent to the museum is the world's largest cypress tree, with a trunk girth of 27 feet.

The museum is open Wednesday to Sunday, from noon to 5 pm, the end of May to Labor Day. From March to the end of May, and from Labor Day Weekend to the last day of October, the museum is open from noon to 4 pm, Thursday to Sunday. From November to March it's closed. Admission is $1 for adults, 50c for children under 12.

### Azalea State Park
At this 26-acre park, hundreds of wild azaleas (some over 200 years old) hold forth in fragrant bloom in late May and early June. The rest of the year, Azalea Park is a pleasant place for a picnic or a stroll. The park is east of downtown near the corner of Pacific Ave and Park Rd.

The annual **Azalea Festival** (☎ 469-3181) on Memorial Day Weekend (last weekend in May), focuses on Azalea State Park. The festivities include a floral parade, crafts fair and food booths.

### Alfred A Loeb State Park
This state park was established to protect two of Oregon's rarest and most cherished trees: the redwood and the myrtle. There's fishing and swimming in the Chetco River, and the park offers one of the most pleasant public campgrounds on the southern coast.

Two hiking trails lead through the dense forest from the trailhead at Loeb State Park's picnic area. Three-quarter-mile **Riverview Nature Trail** follows the river through old-growth myrtle, ending at the highway. The trail then continues as the 1.25-mile **Redwood Nature Trail**, which climbs up the hillsides above the river to loop through a grove of ancient redwoods. One tree with a girth of 33 feet is reckoned to be over 800 years old. A brochure available at the trailhead identifies plant varieties along both trails.

Loeb State Park is 10 miles east of Brookings along North Bank Chetco River Rd.

### Samuel H Boardman State Park
This 11-mile-long oceanfront state park begins four miles north of Brookings and contains some of Oregon's most beautiful coastline. Cliffs drop hundreds of feet into the surf and steep hiking trails lead down to tiny, beautiful beaches huddled at the base of a rocky canyon. Marching far out to sea are tiny island chains, home to shorebirds and braying sea lions. There's no development along this stretch of the beach; this is how wild and ominous the Oregon coast must have seemed to both Native and White settlers.

Highway 101 winds through Boardman State Park, often creeping along cliffs high above the raging Pacific. The grading and spans necessary for building a road along these cliffs was so difficult and expensive that several portions cost more than a million dollars a mile to construct in the 1930s.

There are a number of turnouts, picnic areas and view points along the road. At most, hiking trails lead from the parking lots to either a secluded beach or a more dramatic panorama.

**Lone Ranch Picnic Area**, the southernmost turnout, is a secluded beach with swimming and tide pool exploring in a sandy cove studded with seastacks. Just one mile to the north is **Cape Ferrelo**. A short path leads out to the tip of the cape; from here, spring whale watching is popular. At **Whalehead Cove**, a patchy but paved road drops steeply down to a fine little beach, sheltered on all sides by rocky headlands. This is a great place for picnicking or sunbathing. **Indian Sands Beach** is so named because for hundreds of years Native Americans harvested shellfish here, leaving high mounds of shells along the foredunes. From the turnout on Hwy 101, a steep trail leads down to the ocean, where the beach is flanked by sandstone cliffs colored light red by iron deposits.

After Hwy 101 crosses the Thomas Creek Bridge, Oregon's highest at 345 feet, take the turn for **Natural Bridge Viewpoint**, where a short trail leads to views of rock arches just off the coast. The arches are the remains of sea caves that have been collapsed by the pounding of waves. Likewise, at **Arch Rock Point**, the volcanic headlands have been eroded to leave the arch of a lava tube. Follow the paths down to Whiskey Creek, where there are great tidal pools.

There are picnic tables and toilets at most of the above sites, but there are no campgrounds in the park.

### Hiking

For many hikers Boardman State Park is notable as the southern entry point of the **Oregon Coast Trail**, a long-distance trail that traverses the entire length of Oregon's Pacific coast. While not all sections are currently complete (hikers have to walk along Hwy 101 for short stretches), in Boardman Park two complete stretches of the trail offer good hikes.

The southern access to the Oregon Coast Trail begins at the Cape Ferrelo parking lot, and leads north along headland cliffs, tide pools, rocky escarpments and beaches until joining Hwy 101 seven miles later at the Thomas Creek Bridge. The second, two-mile section of the Oregon Coast Trail begins at the Natural Bridge Viewpoint and ends at Miner Creek. The trail passes through some precipitous parts along the cliffs – parents should watch children carefully through open, grassy headlands and deep rainforests. Watch along the rocky seastacks for coastal fauna such as puffins, gulls, murres, cormorants and curious seals and sea lions.

Hikers with a high-clearance vehicle can take a long drive to a short hike in Kalmiopsis Wilderness Area. Oregon's largest wilderness area, the Kalmiopsis is a range of mountains noted for its rare botanical specimens. (See the Kalmiopsis Wilderness in the Southern Oregon chapter.)

Drive up North Bank Chetco River Rd and then onto USFS Rd 1909 for about 13 miles to the Vulcan Lake Trailhead. The trail into this remote rock cairn lake is 1.4 miles.

A number of long-distance trails also lead out from the Vulcan Lake Trailhead. For more information about the Kalmiopsis Wilderness Area, contact the Chetco Ranger Station in Brookings (above) or the Siskiyou National Forest Headquarters (☎ 479-5301).

### Fishing

The Chetco River is famous for its winter steelhead and fall Chinook salmon runs. Some of the best fishing areas are on the North Bank Chetco River Rd above Loeb State Park. For guided fishing trips, contact Gary Klein's Salmon & Steelhead Guide Service (☎ 469-6627), 613 Hassett St.

**Charter fishing** boats are numerous in Brookings. With the current ban on salmon fishing, most ocean sport-fishing trips focus on bottom fish like flounder, rock fish and halibut. For information on charter fishing, contact Star Charters (☎ 469-5151), 16011 Lower Harbor Rd, or Sporthaven Marina Rivers West (☎ 469-3301),

16372 Lower Harbor Rd, which also offers fishing trips on the Chetco River.

## Places to Stay

**Camping** Brookings is blessed with two fine state park campgrounds in close proximity. At *Loeb State Park*, 10 miles east of Brookings on North Bank Chetco River Rd, there are 53 campsites with full hookups in a fragrant grove of rare myrtle trees; all campsites are $14 a night. *Harris Beach State Park*, two miles north of Brookings on Hwy 101, offers over 130 campsites, including a separate tent-camping area right on the ocean. Showers, flush toilets and a coin laundry are among the amenities here; campsites range from $14 to $17. The contact number for both state parks is 469-2021.

For RV campers who want to be closer to Brookings, there's *Beachfront RV Park* (☎ 469-5867, (800) 441-0856), 16035 Boat Basin Rd, with 173 sites right on busy Brookings harbor. Fees range from $12 to $14.

**B&Bs** The *Holmes Sea Cove B&B* (☎ 469-3025), 17350 Holmes Drive, is a modern seafront home with great views over the Pacific. Each of the three rooms has private baths and entrances; rates range from $80 to $95. The *South Coast Inn B&B* (☎ 469-5557, (800) 525-9273), 516 Redwood St, is an arts & crafts-style home with four guest rooms with private baths, a hot tub and sauna and ocean views; rooms range from $69 to $89.

**Hotels** The *Chetco Inn* (☎ 469-5347), 417 Fern St, one block off busy Hwy 101, is a renovated 1910s hotel. Rooms with old claw-foot tubs begin at $38; remodeled rooms with showers and ocean views run up to $50. *Pacific Sunset Motel* (☎ 469-2141), 1144 Chetco Ave, has singles/doubles for $48/52. The *Spindrift Motor Inn* (☎ 469-5345), 1215 Chetco Ave, is on the ocean side of Hwy 101, with good views, a little less noise than others on the strip and rooms for $44/49. The *Westward Motel*

(☎ 469-7471), 1026 Chetco Ave, is a well-maintained older motel with kitchenettes and nonsmoking rooms; rates are $42/46.

*Best Western Beachfront Inn* (☎ 469-7779, (800) 468-4081), 16008 Boat Basin Rd, faces right onto the ocean with its back to the active boat harbor. It is Brookings' finest lodging, with a swimming pool and some suites, private decks and kitchenettes; rooms begin at $89.

## Vacation Home Rentals

For short-term home rentals, contact Practical & Professional Property Management (☎ 469-6456), 611 Spruce, Brookings, OR 97415.

## Places to Eat

*Rubios* (☎ 469-4919), 1136 Chetco Ave, is an unprepossessing little restaurant that turns out formidable Mexican food. Favorites include chili rellenos and the fresh seafood sautées; the salsa is locally noted and is for sale both at the restaurant and around town. Dinners range from $7 to $11.

*Mama's Italian Restaurant* (☎ 469-7611), 703 Chetco Ave, serves pretty good old-fashioned pasta and pizza; dinner ranges from $8 to $14. Mama's is also a good place for traditional breakfasts.

*Wharfside Restaurant* (☎ 469-7316), 16362 Lower Harbor Rd, doesn't look like much from the outside, but the fish come right off the boats and it's where the locals go for fish & chips. You'll have trouble spending more than $10 here for dinner. *O'Holleran's Restaurant & Lounge* (☎ 469-9907), 1210 Chetco Ave, is the place to go for good steak ($15) and traditional seafood dishes ($14 and up).

Brookings' most upmarket restaurant, *Caffe Fredde*, and the adjacent and less expensive *Basil's Bar & Grill* (☎ 469-3733), 1025 Chetco Ave, serve fresh fish and regional meat with the sort of nouveau Italian sauces that are mandatory in Portland and Seattle but rare along the coast. Caffe Fredde, at the rear of the restaurant complex, serves dishes like grilled salmon with artichokes and chicken with pears ($15 to $18). There's a good, if pricey, wine list. Basil's Bar & Grill, a bistro in the front portion of the restaurant, serves pasta and chicken dishes under $10.

## Getting There & Away

**Bus** Brookings is served by two Greyhound buses a day, which run between Portland and San Francisco along Hwy 101. The fare between Portland and Brookings is $32.

**Train** For those continuing south to California, Amtrak (☎ (800) 872-7245) offers shuttle-bus service to their station 383 miles away at Martinez, CA (slightly north of Berkeley), where connections can be made to destinations on either the *San Joaquin, Capitol* or *Coast Starlight* lines. Two buses daily make the 10-hour trip on Greenbelt Stages (☎ (800) 861-6122) and depart from the San Joaquin/Capitol Throughway Stop at Brookings' Sentry

Market, at Hwy 101 and 5th St. Tickets cost $52 one way or $62 roundtrip, and are by advance purchase only. Call Amtrak or Greenbelt Stages for information on local ticketing agents.

**Bicycle** For cyclists who choose to ride with the wind and cycle south, Brookings marks the end of the Oregon Coast Bike Route. From here many opt to take a bus back to their original point of departure, in which case bicycles must be packed in special cardboard boxes. Escape Hatch Sports & Cycles (☎ 469-2914), 656 Chetco Ave, gives away bicycle boxes as they are available. Boxes tend to be in scarce supply toward the end of the summer.

## Getting Around

Coast Rent-A-Car (☎ 469-5321), is at 530 Chetco Ave. Brookings Del-Cur Yellow Cab Co (☎ 469-4800) provides local taxi service.

# Columbia River Gorge & Mt Hood

The Columbia River's enormous canyon carved through the Cascade Mountains is one of the Pacific Northwest's most dramatic and scenic destinations. The river, over a mile wide, winds through a 3000-foot-deep gorge flanked by volcanic peaks and austere bands of basalt. Waterfalls tumble from the mountain's edge and fall hundreds of feet to the river. Clinging to the cliff walls are deep green forests, filled with ferns and moss.

Immediately south of the Columbia River Gorge rises 11,235-foot Mt Hood, Oregon's highest peak. Mt Hood is an all-season, outdoor playground for all of northern Oregon. Besides skiing at the five ski areas, the mountain is popular with hikers, mountain climbers and those who come to marvel at the extravagant WPA-era Timberline Lodge.

The Columbia River divides Washington and Oregon, and both states share the wonders of the Gorge. Rather than arbitrarily divide the following sites according to state boundaries, Gorge sites and activities for both Oregon and Washington are included in this chapter. Pay attention to phone area codes (this part of Washington is 509; all of Oregon is 503). Also, there's no reciprocity between the two states regarding fishing or hunting licenses.

## The Gorge

This awe-inspiring chasm has long served as more than a scenic wonder. As the only sea-level passage through the Cascade and Sierra mountains between California and the Canadian border, the Columbia River Gorge has been a transportation corridor for centuries.

Five hundred years ago, nowhere in the Northwest boasted such a cosmopolitan mix of peoples as the area around The Dalles. During the great fall and spring migrations of salmon, the shores were lined with many Native American tribes trading, fishing, performing ceremonies, gambling and socializing. The migratory hunting and gathering tribes of the Columbia plateau converged with the river and ocean-going tribes of the coast; they swapped stories in a pidgin language derived from Chinookan and Sahaptian, later incorporating words from English, French and Russian.

Over many generations, into the rocky bluffs and outcroppings along this busy area thousands of pictographs and petroglyphs were drawn, for ceremonial, informational and decorative purposes.

Lewis and Clark floated down the Gorge in the autumn of 1805, and later, the overland route of the Oregon Trail terminated at The Dalles. Here pioneers were forced to negotiate the rapids at the Cascade Locks or choose to attempt the Barlow Trail over Mt Hood, a dangerous end to a wearying 2000-mile journey.

As the West opened up, there was a great demand for better transportation through the Gorge. The Northern Pacific's transcontinental rail line – only the second in North America – pushed through the Gorge in 1883, and orchards of apple, cherry and pear began to develop along Gorge-side valleys, now that the railroad provided a market for agriculture.

The Columbia River Hwy of the 1910s, a marvel of modern engineering and a beautiful scenic route, opened the Gorge to automobile traffic. A series of dams transformed the Columbia River into a major waterway and hydroelectric source. Beginning with Bonneville Dam in 1938, the Columbia became a series of slackwater reservoirs enabling boats to range far inland.

The Gorge was declared a National Scenic Area in 1986, a move that regulates further development of the area.

A freeway now zips through the Gorge, but it takes only a little effort to get out of the fast lane and partake of the spectacular recreational opportunities available. Hikes to waterfalls and wildflower habitats, back-country camping, as well as swimming, fishing, sailing and – notably – windsurfing on the Columbia River make the Gorge a favorite outdoor getaway for many Northwest residents and visitors.

## ORIENTATION & INFORMATION

Two highways pass through the Gorge, one each on the north and south banks of the Columbia River. Heavily traveled, river-level I-84 traverses the Oregon side, and is by far the quickest route through the Gorge; it also offers access to the most popular sites and activities. Washington's Hwy 14 follows the north bank of the river; while much slower, it does offer spectacular vistas.

Remains of the historic Columbia River Hwy (Hwy 30) exist in two sections, between Troutdale and Warrendale, and between Mosier and The Dalles. This narrow, winding and spectacular road links together waterfalls, vista points and forest trailheads.

Hood River and The Dalles are the major commercial centers in the Gorge, and provide ample lodging and dining opportunities. Washington-side towns are smaller and less tourist-oriented. Campers will find a number of state parks on both sides of the river, though on summer weekends campsites can be scarce, especially if the winds suit the purposes of windsurfers.

It's 63 miles between Portland and Hood River; 21 miles further east is The Dalles.

A number of good books and maps describe hikes and other recreation in the Gorge. For a good introduction to Gorge activities, look at *The Columbia River Gorge: A Complete Guide* by Philip Jones (Seattle, The Mountaineers, 1992). Another good resource for hikers and explorers in the western Gorge is the *Trails of the Columbia Gorge* map, published by the USFS. A good resource for Gorge hikers and photographers wishing to see more is *A Waterfall Lover's Guide to the Pacific Northwest* (Seattle, The Mountaineers, 1989), which gives directions to a total of 49 falls along the Gorge.

## GETTING THERE & AWAY

The closest airport to the Gorge is Portland's PDX. Five Greyhound buses a day travel along the Oregon side of the Colum-

### Ice Age Floods

During the most recent ice age, which lasted until 15,000 years ago, 2500-foot-high glaciers filled the valleys that drained western Montana. An enormous lake covering 3000 sq miles – called Glacial Lake Missoula – formed behind the ice dam. However, when the water level of the lake grew high enough, it floated the plug of ice, and the entire lake of glacial meltwater and icebergs rushed through the Columbia Basin in a flood of catastrophic dimensions.

At full flood, swiftly flowing waters lashed 1000 feet above the present site of The Dalles. The intense currents of the flood scoured out the constrictive Columbia watercourse and cut away the canyon walls. The waterfalls along the Gorge were formed when the floods flushed away the stream paths that entered the Columbia River, leaving streams instead to tumble over towering cliffs.

As astonishing as the magnitude of these floods, is the fact that over the course of about 2000 years they recurred at least 40 times. The ice dam would re-form after each flood, and would fill with meltwater until the dam lifted with the pressure of the water. Each time that the flood coursed through the Gorge, the chasm was cut deeper and the canyon walls scoured cleaner.

About 700 years ago, an enormous landslide fell into the Gorge, briefly damming the Columbia River and forming the mighty rapids that were later called the Cascades. The Native American myth of the 'Bridge of the Gods' – a rock arch that once spanned the Columbia – apparently derived from this jumble of rock strewn across the river. ∎

OREGON

bia River, on I-84. See individual towns for information.

Amtrak serves both sides of the Gorge. The *Pioneer* runs every other day between Portland and Salt Lake City, stopping at Hood River and The Dalles. The *Empire Builder* follows the north side of the Columbia, and stops at Bingen and Wishram; it runs four times a week.

## HISTORIC COLUMBIA RIVER HIGHWAY

The western section of the old Columbia River Hwy, which links together some of the most spectacular sights in the Gorge,

runs between Troutdale and Warrendale. It can be a very slow road in high season; think twice before taking a trailer or large RV on Hwy 30. It's a precarious route built for Model Ts, not mobile homes. Despite admonitions, the narrow, shoulderless Columbia River Hwy is frequently jammed with huge RVs in summer.

Even if there's not much traffic, you'll be tempted to stop and picnic in wildflower meadows, and to hike in to more remote waterfalls.

Two turn-of-the-century Oregon business and civic leaders, Sam Hill and Simon Lancaster, are credited with the idea for

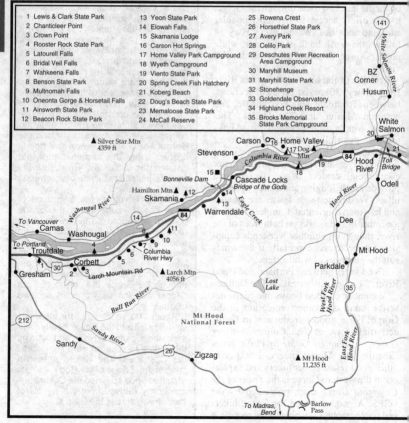

| 1 | Lewis & Clark State Park | 13 | Yeon State Park | 25 | Rowena Crest |
|---|---|---|---|---|---|
| 2 | Chanticleer Point | 14 | Elowah Falls | 26 | Horsethief State Park |
| 3 | Crown Point | 15 | Skamania Lodge | 27 | Avery Park |
| 4 | Rooster Rock State Park | 16 | Carson Hot Springs | 28 | Celilo Park |
| 5 | Latourell Falls | 17 | Home Valley Park Campground | 29 | Deschutes River Recreation Area Campground |
| 6 | Bridal Veil Falls | 18 | Wyeth Campground | 30 | Maryhill Museum |
| 7 | Wahkeena Falls | 19 | Viento State Park | 31 | Maryhill State Park |
| 8 | Benson State Park | 20 | Spring Creek Fish Hatchery | 32 | Stonehenge |
| 9 | Multnomah Falls | 21 | Koberg Beach | 33 | Goldendale Observatory |
| 10 | Oneonta Gorge & Horsetail Falls | 22 | Doug's Beach State Park | 34 | Highland Creek Resort |
| 11 | Ainsworth State Park | 23 | Memaloose State Park | 35 | Brooks Memorial State Park Campground |
| 12 | Beacon Rock State Park | 24 | McCall Reserve | | |

an automobile route through the Gorge. Together they journeyed to Italy, Switzerland and Germany to view European mountain roads. They were particularly impressed with routes along the Rhine River, and with Axenstrasse Tunnel in Switzerland with its windows, hewn out of rock, affording views onto Lake Lucerne.

With strong backing from Portland businessmen, Hill and Lancaster convinced the Oregon government to finance the Columbia River Hwy, which would be the first road linking The Dalles to Portland through the Gorge. To these idealists, the highway was not meant to be an intrusion on the wilderness; instead, the road was designed to be a part of the landscape. Italian stonemasons crafted the retaining walls and arches out of native stone, and local basalt was used to build public buildings along the highway. The fidelity to simple materials and designs from nature exemplify a particularly Northwestern version of the Craftsman movement, which reached an apotheosis in structures like Timberline Lodge on Mt Hood.

The road between Troutdale and Hood River opened in 1915; the section between Hood River and The Dalles was finished in 1922. The opening of the road – the first

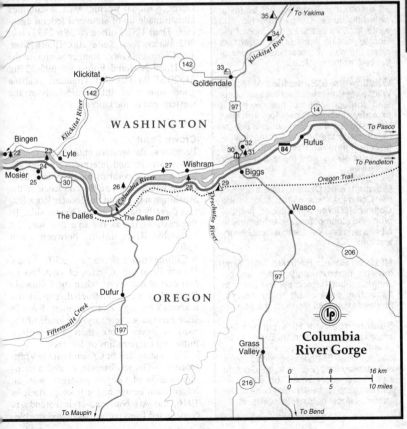

OREGON

large-scale paved road in the Northwest – was greeted with excitement across the USA.

## Orientation

There are several options for getting onto Hwy 30 from Portland. If you follow the signs along I-84 and take exits No 16B or 18, then you'll pass through snaggles of suburban traffic before you reach the highway. If you get lost, remember that Stark St becomes Hwy 30.

For easier and more pleasant access, take exit No 20 for Oxbow State Park, on the east side of the Sandy River, and follow the river until signs point the way up to the Columbia River Hwy. Exit No 22 at Corbett also joins Hwy 30 just shy of the first vista points. To reach this section of Hwy 30 from the east, take exit No 35 at Ainsworth State Park.

## Information

Most of the following sites are waterfalls and viewpoints contained in the Columbia Gorge National Scenic Area, a complex bureau made up of state and federal agencies. Their USFS office (☎ 386-2333) is at 902 Wasco Ave, Suite 200, Hood River. The Columbia Gorge Ranger Station of the Mt Hood National Forest (☎ 695-2276), 31520 SE Woodard Rd, Troutdale, is also a good source of information about the western end of the Gorge.

## Crown Point

Famous as the western entry to the Gorge, this viewpoint and interpretive center sits atop a craggy point of basalt. Views from the park look down on Beacon Rock on the Washington side, and on Rooster Rock 800 feet directly below on the Oregon side. To the east, as far as the eye can see, the Columbia River unfurls between green cliffs.

Coiling down from the cliffs below Crown Point are a series of switchbacks and curves that were, when the Columbia River Hwy was constructed, considered marvels of design and execution. Even in such precipitous territory, the grade of the road is never more than 5%, with a minimum curve radius of 100 feet.

The centerpiece of Crown Point is **Vista House**, a Gorge observatory and a commemoration of Oregon pioneers, with an information center and gift shop. Built in 1916, the Art Nouveau-style rotunda is constructed from native basalt and marble.

---

### OUTDOORS IN THE GORGE

**Hiking the Waterfalls** After winding down the cliffs from Crown Point, Hwy 30 enters the Gorge's most bountiful waterfalls area. Gorge Trail No 400 winds for 35 miles along the face of the Gorge, passing many of the major falls along the way. You can hike portions of the trail, or the whole thing.

**Wildflowers & Butterflies** At McCall Wildflower Preserve near Rowena, paths lead through cliff-top meadows that explode with blossoms in April and May. Yellow-flowered balsomroot and cobalt-blue lupines are among the many wildflowers found at this beautiful vista point. It's also a great place to watch for butterflies.

**Sternwheeler Cruise** Take a tour of the Columbia's Cascade Locks in the *Columbia Gorge*, an historic paddle-propelled steamboat. Take in the beautiful scenery, and learn about local history and lore.

**Mt Hood Scenic Railroad Tour** Wind through blossom and fruit-laden orchards on this historic rail line beneath the snowy peak of Mt Hood; bring a bottle of local wine along for the ride.

**Stonehenge** Sam Hill's curious full-scale replica of the ancient British monument is a good place to spend an equinox or an Earth Day; pretend you're in a faraway land. Zip up to the Goldendale Observatory when the sun sets, and stargaze for free through one of the nation's largest public telescopes. ■

## Larch Mountain

At 4100 feet, Larch Mountain is one of the highest peaks rising out of the Gorge; from its flanks flow Multnomah and Oneonta creeks.

A paved USFS road winds up the side of the mountain to a picnic area and trailhead. From here, a short trail leads to **Sherrard Point**, a rocky promontory over the Gorge with views across dense forests onto five volcanic peaks. On a clear day, the vistas are spectacular; it's one of the few places where the sheer magnitude of the Gorge and the Cascade Range can be seen.

To reach Larch Mountain, leave the Columbia River Hwy between Chanticleer Point and Crown Point at a Y-junction: follow signs for 'Larch Mountain Rd', which trends south from the main highway. It's a slow 14 miles from the junction to the picnic area. Take the trail on the far right side of the parking lot (not the steps); it's a quarter mile to the viewpoint. This road is closed during the winter.

## Latourell Falls

The first major waterfall you encounter coming east on Hwy 30, Latourell Falls drops 249 feet into a rocky pool. A 10-minute hike leads to the base of the falls and back along Latourell Creek to a picnic area in Talbot State Park. It's about two miles roundtrip to Upper Latourell Falls, a 100-foot-high chute. Both trails begin at the bridge over Latourell Creek.

According to Native American legend, Latourell Falls represents the spirit of the Coyote God's wife, who was transformed into this beautiful waterfall to prevent her from ever leaving her husband.

## Bridal Veil Falls

It's a one-mile roundtrip hike in to Bridal Veil Falls, a substantial, two-tiered cascade that first plunges 100 feet in one direction, and immediately turns a right angle to drop another 60 feet. The moderately steep trail to the falls also passes the spectral remains of an old mill and lumber flumes.

Also at Bridal Veil State Park is a wheelchair-accessible interpretive nature trail.

Paths lead onto a meadow where spring wildflowers abound; in April look for the blue-flowering camas, a onion-like bulb that was a staple of the Native American diet. The trail also leads to cliff-edge viewpoints over the Columbia.

## Wahkeena Falls

Indians named this 242-foot waterfall Wahkeena, meaning 'the most beautiful'. While modern taste may favor more spectacular chutes, Wahkeena Falls also serves as a trailhead for some of the most popular hiking trails in the Gorge. One justly popular trail, the **Perdition Trail No 421**, climbs up the side of the falls, then mounts the canyon wall to join the Larch Mountain Trail No 441. Follow this trail down Multnomah Creek to the top of the awe-producing falls of the same name; from here the trail descends to Multnomah Falls Lodge. The trail is a bit more than three miles long.

This trail was closed by the Gorge forest fire of 1991, and slopes burned free of undergrowth are now highly susceptible to erosion. Although it was repaired, landslides sometimes spill across the trail during heavy rains. You may want to call the Columbia Gorge Ranger Station to make sure the trail is open if you're counting on hiking the Perdition Trail.

## Multnomah Falls

At 642 feet, Multnomah Falls is the second-highest non-seasonal waterfall in the USA, and one of the most spectacular sites in the Northwest. The falls drop twice: once over 560 feet from a notch in an amphitheater of vertical rock, and then another 70 feet over a ledge of basalt. A short trail leads to an arch bridge directly over the second falls.

Native American legends tell of a maiden princess who leapt to her death from these cliffs in order to save her people from pestilence. The Great Spirit created the Multnomah Falls in her memory; her face appears in the shifting rainbows of mist floating from the upper falls.

Multnomah Falls was one of the major sites

along the old Columbia River Hwy. Multnomah Falls Lodge, constructed in 1925, was built as a restaurant and stop-over for travelers. Today it offers good food in the lovely, rustic 2nd-story restaurant, and snacks and gift items on the main floor.

Continue past the viewing bridge up a steep trail (Larch Mountain Trail No 441) to the top of the falls. The Larch Mountain Trail continues up Multnomah Creek, leading – arduously – to the top of Larch Mountain, the highest peak along the Gorge; or hikers can make a loop by catching the Perdition Trail to Wahkeena Falls.

The waters of Multnomah Creek form a popular small swimming lake with many shaded picnic spots, in **Benson State Park**, which is accessible from I-84.

**Note** Drivers on I-84 should note that the exits for Multnomah Falls are from the freeway's left-hand lanes. More importantly, the on-ramps back onto the freeway also join the left lanes, normally the freeway's fast lanes. This means that slow-moving vehicles are forced to merge into heavy, fast-moving traffic. Exercise caution.

### Oneonta Gorge & Horsetail Falls
These two closely spaced sites are easily accessible from Hwy 30; however, a highly recommended hike leads behind these curiosities to a more remote falls and views onto a deep, stream-filled fissure.

**Oneonta Gorge** is a narrow chasm cut into a thick basalt flow by Oneonta Creek. Walls over a hundred feet high arch over the stream. This peculiar ecosystem, preserved as Oneonta Gorge Botanical Area, is home to a number of rare, cliff-dwelling plants which thrive in this moist, shadowy chasm. There's no room along the sheer walls of Oneonta Gorge for a trail. However, for those unperturbed by the thought of wet sneakers, the shallow stream can be waded for about a quarter mile to **Oneonta Falls**, where Oneonta Creek drops 75 feet into its gorge.

Only a few hundred feet east of Oneonta Gorge is **Horsetail Falls**, which drops out of a notch in the rock to fall 176 feet. While the waterfall is easily seen from the turnout along Hwy 30, hikers should consider the three-mile **Horsetail-Oneonta Loop Trail**. Starting at Horsetail Falls, the trail quickly climbs up the side of the gorge wall and along the edge of a lava flow. The trail continues behind **Ponytail Falls** (also called Upper Horsetail Falls) which pours out of a tiny crack into a mossy cirque. The trail then drops onto Oneonta Creek, with great views over its narrow gorge and waterfalls. The trail returns to Hwy 30 about a quarter mile west of the Horsetail Falls trailhead.

### Elowah Falls
One of the most stunning Gorge waterfalls, 289-foot Elowah Falls is much less visited than its brethren along the Columbia River because it's not easily linked to the scenic Columbia River Hwy, and you need to hike nearly a mile to see it.

Like Multnomah Falls, Elowah Falls plunges into an enormous rock-walled bowl. Mosses, ferns and wildflowers thrive in the mists and breezes. From a short wooden bridge across McCord Creek, hikers too will be cooled by the falls' wafting mists.

To reach Elowah Falls requires just enough diligence to guarantee the falls relative obscurity. If you are already on Hwy 30, then at Ainsworth State Park, where all signs invite the driver to rejoin I-84, instead continue east on Frontage Rd toward Dodson. If you're traveling on I-84, take the Ainsworth State Park exit No 35, and follow the eastbound Frontage Rd. From this point, continue 2.5 miles until, at signs for Yeon State Park, you see a parking area on the right side of the road. It's a two-mile roundtrip hike to Elowah Falls, with some steep switchbacks. From the same trailhead, the **McCord Creek Falls Trail** leads to the top of the Elowah Falls, with views into the falls' enormous rock bowl, and then to **McCord Falls** higher up on the same stream. The roundtrip to McCord Creek Falls is 2.5 miles.

### Places to Stay
**Camping** Campers are in luck with *Ainsworth State Park* (☎ 731-3411), three

miles east of Multnomah Falls. Besides campsites ($15 for full hook-ups) and picnic areas in a pretty wooded grove, Ainsworth Park provides easy access to trails leading to Horsetail and Elowah falls.

**Hotels** None of the above sites is more than 35 miles from Portland, or 25 miles from Hood River, both of which offer lots of lodging and eating options. The *Bridal Veil Lodge* (☎ 695-2333), in Bridal Veil State Park, is the only hostelry along this stretch of the Gorge. There are two rooms available at this 1920s-era lodge ($65 a night, by reservation only), which is in a mossy, well-shaded dell near the waterfall.

**Places to Eat**
At the beginning of the scenic highway, along the Sandy River is *Tad's Chicken N Dumplins* (☎ 666-5337). Open for dinner only, the food is agreeably old-fashioned; Tad's is famous for its fried chicken. Having drinks on the deck over the Sandy River is also popular.

The best place to eat in the area is *Multnomah Falls Lodge* (☎ 695-2376). The stone-vaulted dining room, a preserve of rustic, Craftsman-era architecture, is reason enough to frequent this historic lodge. Lunch sandwiches go for $6 to $9, while at dinner there's chicken stuffed with smoked salmon and served with rosemary sauce for $15, prime rib for $18.

## CASCADE LOCKS
An early Gorge transport center and summer home to the sternwheeler *Columbia Gorge*, Cascade Locks (population 970) derives its name from the navigational locks that cut through these series of treacherous rapids. Although plans to cut the locks around the Cascades were authorized in 1874 by the US Congress, construction wasn't completed until 1896, long after the railroads had come to dominate trade and transportation through the Gorge. The finished canal was 90 feet wide and 3000 feet long.

Steamboat traffic through the Gorge continued throughout the early years of this century, but ended when Bonneville Lake flooded the old rapids in 1938. The town boomed throughout the 1930s, when the area was home to thousands of construction workers drawn to the WPA project's promise of employment.

The Bridge of the Gods, a steel cantilever bridge spanning the Columbia River at Cascade Locks, was built in 1926, thus replacing the legendary one.

The Native Americans who lived along the Gorge believed that once a bridge of rock, called the Bridge of the Gods, spanned the Columbia River. It was tended by Loo-Wit, a venerable but very old and homely woman. The spirit of Mt Adams, called Klickitat, and the spirit of Mt Hood, called Wy'east, fell to feuding, as they both loved the female spirit of Squaw Mountain (a lesser Cascade peak). The two volcanic peaks exploded in anger, hurling rock and fire. Finally so many rocks were thrown between the two peaks that the Bridge of the Gods collapsed. Loo-Wit, the bridge guardian, fell with the bridge. However, the Great Spirit felt sorry for her, and granted her wish to be made young and beautiful once more. She moved west from the warring peaks where she came to rest as Mt St Helens.

## Orientation & Information
Cascade Locks is 44 miles east of Portland on I-84, exit No 44. Stevenson, WA is three miles east of the Bridge of the Gods. There's a 75c toll to cross the bridge. From Cascade Locks it's 19 miles to Hood River. The main street in town is Wa-Na-Pa St.

The Cascade Locks Visitor Center (☎ 374-8619, (800) 374-8619), PO Box 355, Cascade Locks, OR 97014, is in the Marine Park complex, about a half-mile down Wa-Na-Pa St from exit No 44.

## Cascade Locks Historical Museum
The museum (☎ 374-8535), in the Marine Park complex on Wa-Na-Pa St, is in an old lockmaster's residence, built in 1905. Besides a good display of Native American artifacts, the museum commemorates the early transportation history of the Gorge. Also on exhibit is a fishwheel, a waterwheel-like machine designed to harvest vast amounts of migrating salmon. Fishwheels proved so successful in trap-

ping fish in the early years of this century that they were outlawed in order to protect salmon from extinction. Outside the museum is the old steam locomotive the *Oregon Pony*, the first train to run along the Oregon Portage Railroad in 1862.

### Columbia Gorge Sternwheeler

Embarking from the eastern end of the old lock system within Marine Park is the diesel-powered *Columbia Gorge* (☎ 374-8427). Cruises are offered along the Columbia River from the third weekend in June to the last week in September. There are three cruises daily, at 10 am, 12:30 and 3 pm; no reservations are necessary. Besides providing an unusual vantage point from which to see Bonneville Dam and the beautiful scenery of the Gorge, the cruise offers historical commentary on the Oregon Trail, Native American lore and the Lewis and Clark expedition; call to inquire about special musical or brunch cruises.

There is an on-board snack bar, with both indoor and outdoor seating. Tickets are $9.95 for adults, $5 for children ages four to 12, and children under four are free.

### Places to Stay

**Camping** Campers can stay alongside the old lock canal at *Cascade Locks Marine Park* (☎ 374-8619), on Wa-Na-Pa St or at the *Cascade Locks KOA* (☎ 374-8668), on the east end of town.

East of Cascade Locks are more forest parks with campgrounds. Take I-84 exit No 51 to reach *Wyeth Campground*, a USFS campground just off the freeway. At exit No 56, *Viento State Park* offers camping in a pleasantly wooded area; from the picnic area near the river, windsurfers frequently set sail.

**Hotels** *Scandian Motor Lodge* (☎ 374-8417), at Wa-Na-Pa and Oneonta Sts in Cascade Locks, is the town's best lodging option, with single/double rooms at $43/48. Cross the Bridge of the Gods to Stevenson, WA (see below) for other options.

### Places to Eat

Basic food predominates in Cascade Locks. Try the *Cascades Inn Restaurant* (☎ 374-8340) in the Columbia Gorge Center, on the corner of Wa-Na-Pa and Oneonta Sts, for family dining. The *Char Burger* (☎ 374-8340), 714 SW Wa-Na-Pa St, serves good burgers and onion rings; sometimes in the parking lot local Native Americans sell smoked salmon. After a long, thirsty hike, go to *Salmon Row Pub* (☎ 374-8511), at the corner of Wa-Na-Pa and Regulator Sts. It's a pleasant pub offering pizza and sandwiches and microbrewed beers.

## AROUND CASCADE LOCKS
### Bonneville Dam

Bonneville Dam was one of the largest and most ambitious of the Depression-era New Deal projects. Completed in 1937, it was the first major dam on the Columbia River.

The building of the dam brought Oregon thousands of jobs on construction crews, and the cheap electricity that it produced promised future industrial employment. President F D Roosevelt officiated at the dam's opening in 1938, attended by cheering throngs of thousands.

The two hydroelectric powerhouses together produce over a million kilowatts of power, and back up the Columbia River for 15 miles.

The Bradford Island Visitor Center is accessed from the Oregon side by crossing one of the two powerhouse dams. Fish ladders, which allow migrating fish to negotiate around the dams, circle around the visitors center. In season, salmon and steelhead trout leap up the ladder, and a fish-counter is on duty, tabulating the numbers of migrating fish; both can be seen from a glass-walled underwater viewing area.

On the main floor of the visitors center are displays of local Native American culture and the history of the dam; there is also a slide and video theater.

From the Washington side of the dam, follow signs to the Visitor Orientation Building near the second powerhouse. From here there's access to self-guided tours of the hydroelectric generation facilities and to views over another fish ladder.

All facilities at Bonneville Dam (☎ 374-8820) are free; it's open from 9 am to 5 pm daily. From May to October, the dam is open to 8 pm.

## Bonneville Fish Hatchery

At this fish hatchery (☎ 374-8393) – Oregon's oldest – are reared many of the salmon that are returned to the Columbia River, helping to augment natural salmon runs. Here too is the nation's only hatchery for white sturgeon. At viewing ponds, visitors can watch and feed enormous mature trout and sturgeon.

The hatchery is directly west of the dam, and is accessed from the same road and keeps the same hours.

## Eagle Creek Recreation Area

Hikes up a spectacular side canyon of the Gorge are the highlight of this popular recreational area. The **Eagle Creek Trail No 440**, constructed in 1915, was a kind of engineering feat. Volunteers blasted ledges for trails along vertical cliffs, spanned a deep chasm with a suspension bridge, and burrowed a 120-foot tunnel behind a waterfall. If you have time for only one day hike in the Gorge, this should be it.

The classic day hike into Eagle Creek leads up along the face of a cliff to a viewpoint over Metlano Falls. Part of the trail then drops back to a streamside near Punchbowl Falls, a good spot to break for lunch or to splash in pools of cool water. Casual day hikers can return at this point; the hike is an easy 4.5-mile roundtrip stroll.

More ambitious hikers can continue along to High Bridge, a suspension bridge spanning a deep crevice, and Tunnel Falls, so named because of the 120-foot tunnel blasted into the rock behind the falls. Work your way through the tunnel for great views up and down Eagle Creek's canyon. The roundtrip hike from the trailhead to High Bridge is 6.5 miles; to Tunnel Falls and back, a strenuous 12 miles.

Be warned that the Eagle Creek Trail is very popular. Try to avoid summer weekends when the trail throngs with hikers. Some sections of the trail inch along vertical cliffs, with cable handrails drilled into the cliff-side for safety. This isn't a good trail for unsupervised children or unleashed pets.

Just east of the Eagle Creek trailhead is the *Eagle Creek Campground*, with WPA-era stone shelters. Backpackers will be more interested in campsites further up Eagle Creek. Just past High Bridge is *Tenas Campground*; nearer to Tunnel Falls is *Blue Grouse Campground*.

To reach the trailhead from eastbound I-84, take exit No 41. Westbound travelers need to take the Bonneville Dam exit No 40, and double back one mile.

## STEVENSON (WA)

The little town of Stevenson (population 1100) was just a slumbering mill town along the Columbia River with nice riverside parks until the views from the hills above the village caught the fancy of Oregon-based resort developers. Stevenson still maintains its small town feel, though the quality of the restaurants and coffee (espresso has arrived) has improved. For travelers who aren't prone to luxury hotels or first-class museums, Stevenson's riverfront parks, with swimming, windsurfing, picnicking and playgrounds will also be a draw.

## Orientation & Information

Stevenson is 38 miles east of Vancouver, WA on Hwy 14, and three miles from the Bridge of the Gods, with access to Oregon and I-84.

Contact the Skamania County Chamber of Commerce (☎ (509) 427-8911) at PO Box 1037, Stevenson, WA 98648. For local hiking and recreational information in the Gifford Pinchot National Forest, contact the Wind River Ranger Station (☎ (509) 427-5645) eight miles north of Carson, WA.

## Columbia Gorge Interpretive Center

Established by the Skamania County Historical Society and Washington state, the

OREGON

interpretive center (☎ (509) 427-8211), below Skamania Lodge on 2nd Ave near Rock Creek Cove, is the first museum in the Gorge to attempt to weave together the many threads – Native American, early explorer, pioneer settlers, logging, fishing, shipping, power generation, recreation – that form the complex history of this area. The center's new, 15,000-sq-foot facility opened in early 1995 at a cost of $10 million.

The center is open from 9 am to 5 pm daily. Admission is adults/seniors $5/4; children ages six to 12 are $3.

**Places to Stay**

Campers will want to stay at *Home Valley Park*, a lovely park right on the river with a swimming beach, picnic area and camp-sites ($7). The park is near the community of Home Valley, on Hwy 14 four miles east of Stevenson.

At *Sojourner Inn* (☎ (509) 427-7070), Berge Rd, Home Valley, there are five rooms and four baths; evening meals are by reservation. The *Econo Lodge* (☎ (509) 424-5628, (800) 424-7777), just east of Stevenson on Hwy 14, is a good, cheap motel, with single/double rooms at $50/60.

The *Skamania Lodge* (☎ (800) 221-7117), 1131 SW Skamania Lodge Way, is the main draw of the entire Gorge when it comes to resort accommodations. Opened in 1993 by the same company that developed the Snoqualmie Falls Lodge in Washington (known worldwide by *Twin Peaks* fans), and Portland's ornate gem, the Governor Hotel, the Skamania Lodge is easily the most comfortable and beautiful lodging in the Gorge. The facilities include swimming pools, exercise rooms, horseback riding, tennis courts, an 18-hole golf course and windsurfing lessons. Rooms start at $95 and go up to $185 a night for suites with views of the river.

**Places to Eat**

Windsurfers and the spillover from the Skamania Lodge have created a market for lively, tasty, informal food in Stevenson. At *Gretchen's Deli* (☎ (509) 427-7667), 220 SW 2nd Ave, there's espresso, pastries and homemade desserts. The *Big River Grill* (☎ (509) 427-4888), 192 SW 2nd Ave, is a comfortable little cafe with nice salads and light entrees. A grilled salmon salad is $7.50; a steak dinner is only $11. At *El Rio* (☎ (509) 427-4479), right across the street from the Big River Grill, the motto is 'Big Strong Mexican Food'; combination plates start at $3.95; shrimp fajitas go for $7.50.

For fine dining overlooking the Gorge, go to *Skamania Lodge* (see Places to Stay, above). The emphasis here is on high-quality local ingredients prepared with determined eclecticism. Fresh Chinook salmon is roasted on an alder plank ($19), a local Native American method, while rack of lamb is served with a red curry sauce ($20).

**AROUND STEVENSON**
**Carson Hot Springs**

Feeling stiff and sore after days of traveling? Then this old-fashioned restorative spa (☎ (509) 427-8292) might be just what you need. After soaking in 126°F mineral water, you're swaddled in towels to bake a while, then unrolled and massaged vigorously. The whole experience is redolent of the past – including the tiled bathing chambers and wordlessly efficient masseurs. In addition to the hot-springs therapy, there's a golf course right up the hill; RV and tent sites are available, as well as rooms and food in the venerable St Martins Hotel (see below). The hot springs are busy – winter with skiers, summer with hikers – so it pays to call ahead and make a reservation for treatment. The hot-springs complex is about half a mile north of Hwy 14, just east of Carson (three miles east of Stevenson, WA) on the Wind River.

Soakers can stay at the historic *St Martins Hotel* (☎ 427-8292) which features therapeutic soaks in the mineral hot springs and sessions with massage therapists. Rooms start at $35. Cabins are also available for $38, and the Hot Tub Suite costs $100. Campers get a pretty good deal with tent spaces at $4.50, and RVs at $10 to $12.50.

## Dog Mountain

Hikes up this imposing 2900-foot sentinel over the Gorge are popular, especially in May, when wildflowers are abundant along the trail. The grade is frequently steep, and the elevation gain is almost 3000 feet, so this isn't a casual stroll. But once on top, the views up and down the Columbia River, and onto the nearby Cascade volcanoes, are spectacular. Allow six hours roundtrip.

To reach the trailhead for Dog Mountain Trail No 147, drive nine miles east of Stevenson, near Hwy 14 milepost 54.

## Beacon Rock State Park

One of the Gorge's most conspicuous landmarks, 848-foot Beacon Rock rises like an enormous thumb from the north bank of the Columbia River. The state park (☎ (509) 427-8265), on Hwy 14 three miles east of Skamania, WA, or seven miles west of the Bridge of the Gods, is one of the most pleasant on the north side of the Columbia River, and offers hiking, mountain bike trails, picnicking, camping and river access.

In myth, the rock was the final resting place of the Native American princess Wahatpolitan and her young son. She sought refuge on the rock when her father became angry about her marriage to an unsuitable warrior. Mother and son died atop the rock, and legends say that in the howling of the winds, you can hear the mother's grief.

There's **hiking** for just about everyone in Beacon Rock State Park. Most famous is the ascent up the face of Beacon Rock itself. Following a route first laid out by the Biddle family, a three-quarter-mile trail with 53 switchbacks clambers up the south face of the rock. The views from the top are amazing.

For a short, easy-going hike, there's a nature trail through a wetlands meadow to tiny Riddell Lake. For a more strenuous hike to the top of the Gorge, consider a climb up **Hamilton Mountain**. At 2445 feet, Hamilton Mountain is the most westerly of the peaks that rise out of the Gorge. If you're not up to the five-hour roundtrip

hike to the top, then consider hiking a mile up the trail to Hardy and Rodney falls. To reach the trailhead, park in the picnic area lot; a branch of the trail also leads out from the campground.

Beacon Rock offers one of the few **rock climbing** opportunities in the Gorge, as the rock comprising this sheer volcanic plug is much more stable than other cliffs in the area. The majority of climbs are on the south face of Beacon Rock, where 60 routes have been documented. The routes are for experienced climbers only.

Old logging and fire roads wind through the park's 4500 acres. These mostly deserted roads are available for **mountain biking**, and offer access to the upper reaches of Hardy Creek, as well as to the back side of Hamilton Mountain. Horseback riders also use the roads, so be courteous. Access to the road system begins at a locked gate about half a mile up the Group Camp road.

Beacon Rock State Park offers camping with no hook-ups. The 33 sites are across

---

### An Oregon State Park . . . in Washington?

Reckoned to be the second largest monolith in the world (the largest is the Rock of Gibraltar), Beacon Rock was very nearly an Oregon state park, even though it is in Washington.

Early this century, the Army Corps of Engineers decided that they needed riprap for a jetty in the Columbia River, and they made plans to blow up Beacon Rock in order to access its cache of rock. The owners of the Beacon Rock at the time, the Biddle family, offered to donate the property to the state of Washington in order to preserve the landmark as a state park. However, the governor refused the offer. Not to be thwarted, the Biddle family then offered the land to the state of Oregon, to be turned into an Oregon state park in Washington. Finally, the Washington governor was embarrassed into accepting the gift, and a Washington state park was formed. ■

the road from Beacon Rock and the Columbia River, but are in a forested area near a small stream. Overnight fees are $10.

## HOOD RIVER & AROUND

Situated at the mouth of a broad valley along the Columbia River, Hood River (population 4725) is the Gorge's most dynamic city. It's the center for recreation on the Columbia River, along the Gorge and for nearby Mt Hood. A combination of strong river currents, prevailing westerly winds and a vast body of water make the Columbia River around Hood River the center of windsurfing mania. When the conditions are right – and they are frequently so in the Gorge – thousands of windsurfers (or sailors as they prefer to be called) will be zipping across the wide Columbia River at any given moment.

Because of this, Hood River is one of the most international and youth-oriented towns in the Northwest: stroll along the steep streets in the old part of town, and hear bronzed athletes speaking French, Japanese or German. A sense of fun and youthfulness pervades the town, which, combined with access to good food and nightlife, make this a great base from which to explore the Gorge.

South of town, the river of the same name drains a wide valley filled with orchards. During the spring, nearly the entire region is filled with the scent and color of pink and white blossoms. Later on, fruit stands spring up along roadsides, selling apples, pears, cherries, berries and vegetables. Watch for wineries: wine grapes are the most recent crop to find a home in this fabulously fruitful valley. Highway 35, which traverses the valley, leads up the south and east flanks of Mt Hood, only 25 miles south.

### Orientation

Hood River is 63 miles east of Portland on I-84 and 19 miles west of The Dalles. On Hwy 35, it's 45 miles between Hood River and Government Camp on Mt Hood.

The old part of Hood River faces onto the Columbia River, along steeply terraced streets cut into the walls of the Gorge. The I-84 exit No 63 puts you onto 2nd St, which crosses the rail lines to intersect with Oak St, the town's old main street. This attractive area is filled with boutiques devoted to recreation, coffeehouses and upbeat street life.

### Information

The Hood River County Chamber of Commerce (☎ 386-2000, (800) 366-3530), is in the Port Marina Park, Hood River, OR 97031. Besides the usual volunteers and brochure racks, there's a large raised relief map/display of the surrounding area that helps make sense of local geography.

The headquarters for the Columbia River Gorge National Scenic Area (☎ 386-2333) are in the Wacoma Center, 902 Wasco Ave.

The Hood River post office (☎ 386-2600) is at 4th St and Cascade Ave. Waucoma Bookstore (☎ 386-5353), 212 Oak St, is a good bookstore with a strong regional travel section. It also sells local USGS and Green Trail maps. The local paper is the *Hood River News*. Oregon Public Radio is heard on 94.3 FM.

You can wash those dirty clothes at the Westside Laundry (☎ 386-5029), 1911 W Cascade Ave. Hood River Memorial Hospital (☎ 386-3911) is at the corner of 13th and May Sts.

### Hood River County Historical Museum

This regional museum (☎ 386-6722), in Port Marina Park along the Columbia River, retells the history of the Hood River area. Native American artifacts, pioneer quilts and early logging equipment are some of the displays at this generally well-thought-out museum. It is open from 10 am to 4 pm, Wednesday to Saturday, April to October; admission is free.

### Mt Hood Scenic Railroad

This rail line (☎ 386-3556), built in 1906, once transported fruit, berries and lumber from the upper Hood River Valley to the main railhead in Hood River. The line was reborn in the 1980s when train enthusiasts brought vintage diesel-electric engines and rolling stock back to the line. The train now operates between late April's Blossom Festival and autumn's Harvest Fest as a scenic excursion through the valley, beneath the snowy peak of Mt Hood and past fragrant orchards.

Trains depart from the depot at 110 Railroad Ave, just under the viaduct between I-84 exit No 63 (2nd St) and downtown Hood River. Two four-hour excursions are offered daily, at 10 am and 3 pm. The train stops for about an hour in Parkdale, an old farm and orchard town with antique stores and a couple of cafes. Call ahead for reservations as the train is frequently sold out.

### Wineries

A number of wineries have opened in the Hood River area in recent years. Hood River Vineyards (☎ 386-3772), 4693 Westwood Drive, and Three Rivers Winery (☎ 386-5453), 275 Country Club Rd, offer wine-tasting; both are found off Country Club Rd, west of Hood River.

Distillers are also springing up around Hood River. At the Eve Atkins Distilling Company (☎ 354-2550), Marichelle brand *eau de vie* (brandy) is made from local fruits. The tasting room at 4420 Summit Drive, out toward Odell off Hwy 35, is open from 11 am to 5 pm, from Monday to Saturday.

### Lost Lake

The postcard photo of Mt Hood from 240-acre Lost Lake – the white mountain peak rising from a deep-blue lake amid a thick green forest – is probably the most famous image of Oregon's most famous volcano. This side-trip onto the northern flanks of Mt Hood is a popular place to visit when the Gorge gets hot.

To reach Lost Lake, take Hwy 281 south from Hood River to Dee. Signs will point to Lost Lake Rd; the lake is 25 miles south of Hood River.

### Windsurfing

If you've never windsurfed, Hood River is ready to teach you, outfit you with sail and

board and dress you in seemingly mandatory fluorescent gear. For lessons, visit any number of outfitters in Hood River.

Rhonda Smith Windsurfing Center (☎ 386-9463) is in the Port Marina Park; Front Street Sailboards (☎ 386-4044) is at 207 Front St; Mistral Hi-Wind Center (☎ 386-6086) is at 505 Cascade Ave; and Hood River Windsurfing (☎ 386-5787) is at 101 Oak St. They all rent and sell equipment and gear; a full rig for a day costs about $40; lessons run $50 to $60, including equipment.

The area's biggest windsurfing event is the **Gorge Blowout** (☎ 667-7778), held the first weekend in July. This 20-mile downwind sailboard race from Stevenson, WA to Hood River also includes course racing along the waterfront, and a beach party at Port Marina Park.

If your degree of interest in windsurfing only extends to watching, then a couple of Hood River locations are good. The Port Marina Park, a marina and jetty area on the Columbia River, is the town's major departure point for the sailors. Take I-84 exit No 64.

Another popular windsurfing area is directly across from Hood River on the Washington side, at wide spots along Hwy 14 near the Spring Creek Fish Hatchery (this area is known as Swell City to avid sailors) and Doug's Beach State Park, a bit further east.

For sportswear, head to B Jammin (☎ 386-6660), Kerrit's Activewear (☎ 386-

OREGON

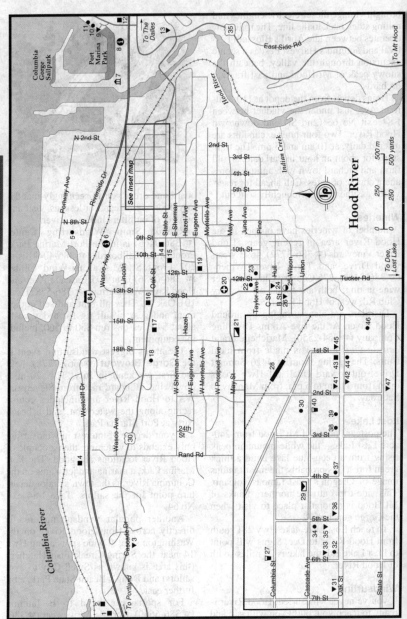

Hood River

To The Dalles

East Side Rd

To Mt Hood

Columbia Gorge Sailpark

Port Marina Park

Columbia River

To Portland

Hood River

Indian Creek

To Dee, Lost Lake

Tucker Rd

N 2nd St
N 8th St
Portway Ave
Riverside Dr
Wasco Ave
Lincoln
Westcliff Dr
Wasco Ave
24th St
Rand Rd
Cascade Dr

See inset map

State St
E Sherman
Hazel Ave
Eugene Ave
Montello Ave
May Ave
June Ave
Pine
9th St
10th St
12th St
13th St
Oak St
15th St
Hazel
18th St
W Sherman Ave
W Eugene Ave
W Montello Ave
W Prospect Ave
May St

2nd St
3rd St
4th St
5th St
10th St
12th St
Taylor Ave
C St
B St
Hull
Wilson
Union

1st St
2nd St
3rd St
4th St
5th St
6th St
7th St
Columbia St
Cascade Ave
Oak St
State St

500 m
500 yards
250
250
0
0

**OREGON**

1145) and Windwear (☎ 386-6209), all on Oak St.

### Fishing

The Hood River is noted for a good steelhead trout run throughout the year, with an especially good summer run. Fishing is best in the lower three miles, near town. The river is also fine for rainbow trout.

Steelhead and sturgeon are taken from the Columbia River near Hood River, while bass thrive in the small roadside ponds beside the river. Fishing for salmon in the Columbia River is now restricted; visit the Gorge Fly Shop (☎ 386-6977), 416 Oak St, for up-to-date information, tackle and licenses.

### Other Activities

To rent skis and snowboards before heading off for Mt Hood, go to Boardsports (☎ 386-5363), 202 Cascade Ave; they also have in-line skates. Wind Rider Bikes (☎ 386-4172), 202 Cascade, and Fat Tire Farm (☎ 387-2277), Port Marina Park, rent mountain bikes.

The nine-hole Hood River Golf & Country Club (☎ 386-3009), on Country Club Rd west of Hood River, has beautiful mountain views, rentals, a club house and wineries nearby. The city pool is on the corner of May St at 17th Ave. Swim in the Columbia River at Koberg Beach, two miles east of Hood River off I-84 exit No 67 (westbound only).

### Special Events

The Hood River Valley springs to life with the Blossom Festival (☎ 386-2000), held the third weekend of April. Tours through the orchards, fragrant and colorful with bloom, are the main event. Complete the weekend with visits to an antique fair, musical events and special food and craft booths in Hood River and smaller orchard communities.

The Hood River County Fair (☎ 354-2865) is held the last weekend of July; it features a carnival and agricultural competitions. The fair is held at the county fairgrounds, south of Hood River at Odell.

The Hood River Apple Jam (☎ 387-7529), the third Saturday of August, is an outdoor music festival held at the Port Marina Park, with food and family entertainment.

The annual Columbia River Cross Channel Swim (☎ 386-2000) is held on

Labor Day. More than three hundred swimmers brave the cold water and strong currents of the Columbia to cross from Hood River to Bingen.

The Hood River Harvest Fest (☎ 386-2000), held the second weekend of October, celebrates the agricultural bounty of the valley with local crafts, food and musical entertainment at the Hood River Expo Center along the riverfront.

## Places to Stay

**Camping** The closest public campgrounds are at *Viento State Park*, eight miles west of Hood River, where there are 63 campsites along the river; $11 fee. *Memaloose State Park* is accessible from west-bound I-84 only. It's about 11 miles east of Hood River, and offers over a hundred campsites; $11 fee (no reservations). Call 374-8811 for information on either park. A lot of windsurfers opt to camp out at these local state parks, which means that many of them are packed and kind of rowdy on weekends.

**B&Bs** The Dutch Colonial *Hackett House B&B* (☎ 386-1014), 922 State St, was built in 1903, and offers four guest rooms with shared bath; room rates range from $40 to $60. The *Inn at the Gorge* (☎ 386-4429), 1113 Eugene St, is an attractive 1908 home with wide porches; the three rooms have private baths and separate guest entrances. Rates range from $62 to $78. The *State Street Inn* (☎ 386-1899), 1005 State St, is a 1930s home with rooms ranging from $45 to $75.

Hood River's most exclusive B&B is *Lakecliff Estate B&B* (☎ 386-7000), 3020 Westcliff Drive. Designed by Albert Doyle, the architect responsible for the Multnomah Falls Lodge, this historic, 1908 summer home sits on three wooded acres on the cliffs above the Columbia River. There are four guest rooms, with rates from $80 to $90.

**Hotels** It can be extremely hard to find rooms in Hood River during summer (especially if the wind is blowing advanta-

geously), so plan well ahead. If Hood River is all booked up, try The Dalles, 21 miles east, where there are usually plenty of rooms.

It's a bit homely, and on a busy street, but *Prater's Motel* (☎ 386-3566), 1306 Oak St, is just about the only reasonable place to stay in Hood River. There are only seven rooms, with single/doubles at $45/50, so call ahead. For a bit more money, stay at the *Vagabond Lodge* (☎ 386-2992), 4070 Westcliff Drive. You'll love the neighborhood, and the rooms at the back have great views over the river. Rates range from $60 to $90. Closer to the city center, there are condo-like rooms at *Love's Riverview Lodge* (☎ 386-8719), 1505 Oak St; singles/doubles are $60/65.

The *Best Western Hood River Inn* (☎ 386-2200, (800) 828-7873), 1108 E Marina Way, is right on the river, and offers a swimming pool, restaurant and meeting rooms. Rooms with a river view run $90/95; it's $10 less to look out onto the parking lot. The *Hood River Hotel* (☎ 386-1900), 102 Oak St, is a 1913 hotel that's been tastefully refurbished; rooms range from $65 to $145; basic riverview rooms are $95.

If you are looking for a classy and romantic place to stay in Hood River, there's really only one choice: *The Columbia Gorge Hotel* (☎ 386-5566, (800) 345-1921), 4000 Westcliff Drive. Built in 1921 by Simon Benson, one of the early backers of the Columbia River Hwy, this beautiful, Spanish-influenced hotel sits in a five-acre garden directly above 207-foot Wah Gwin Gwin Falls. The hotel is listed in the National Register of Historic Places; rooms range from $150 to $190.

**Lodges** *Lost Creek Lodge* (☎ 386-6366), PO Box 90, Hood River, OR 97031, is right on Lost Lake, and rents canoes and small boats (no motorized boats allowed), and the fishing is good for trout. The lodge rents small, basic cabins ($60) and campsites ($12); there's a small store but no restaurant.

## Places to Eat

**Budget** If you are hungry for a full breakfast, go to *Bette's Place* (☎ 386-1880), 416 Oak St. Let 'eggs Benedict' ($4.95) be your mantra. At *The Coffee Spot* (☎ 386-1772), 12 Oak St, grab a pastry for breakfast, or get one of their deli salads to go. Plan a picnic at *Pastabilities* (☎ 386-1903), 106 Oak St, where Italian deli dishes are available to go. Hood River's favorite pizza is found at *Andrew's Pizza & Bakery* (☎ 386-1448), 107 Oak St. Pizza is available whole or by the slice ($2); there's also a full range of other baked goods. *Wy'east Naturals* (☎ 386-6181), 110 5th St, is the local organic and natural-foods store; there's also a deli with take-out items.

*Purple Rocks Art Bar & Cafe* (☎ 386-6061), 606 Oak St, offers vegetarian breakfasts and other light meals, but the funked-out indolence of this cafe makes it a good place to catch up with a newspaper or write letters. Sometimes there's acoustic entertainment in the evenings.

**Middle** *Big City Chicks* (☎ 387-3811), 1303 13th St, offers healthy food from all sorts of cultures, all for very inexpensive prices. Moroccan apricot chicken with vegetable couscous is a real hit for $6.95; raspberry salmon with wild mushrooms for $8.95 is also sure to please.

*The Gorge Cafe* (☎ 386-8700), Port Marina Park, is right on the waterfront and offers light meals and sandwiches; it's open summer only. *Grace Su's China Gorge* (☎ 386-5333), 2680 Old Columbia River Drive, offers spicy Sichuan-style food. *Sixth Street Bistro & Loft* (☎ 386-5737), on the corner of 6th St and Cascade Ave, has good burgers, pasta dishes ($8 to $10) and full dinners (chicken marsala for $12), as well as local microbrews. There's outdoor seating in a garden area. *The Mesquitery* (☎ 386-2002), 1219 12th St, is Hood River's best barbecue joint, with just-right spicy sauces. Prices are in the $8 range for ribs or chicken.

There's equal parts food and tomfoolery at *Horsefeathers* (☎ 386-4411), 115 State St. Burgers ($7), Thai food, pasta ($10 to

$12) and steak for $15 are served in ample portions. There's plenty of beer to wash it all down, and with great views over the Gorge, this is an engagingly collegiate-style hangout.

**Top End** As the name indicates, at *Pasquale's Ristorante* (☎ 386-1900), 102 Oak St, Italian cuisine is the specialty. The charming dining room is in the historic Hood River Hotel. Pasta dishes go for $10 to $12; lamb chops with green peppercorn sauce, $15. *Riverside Inn* (☎ 386-2200) in the Best Western Hood River Inn, offers great views and innovative cooking. Favorites are the Northwest bouillabaisse ($15) and spicy salmon ($17).

The only views at the *Stonehedge Inn* (☎ 386-3940), 3405 Cascade St, are of antiques. This well-loved restaurant is located in a graciously dilapidated old home in a wooded grove. There's a light entree menu, with a la carte dishes going for around $10, or full dinner such as veal chantrelle ($17.50) or duck a l'orange ($16.50).

Double the prices and your expectations at *Columbia River Court* in the Columbia Gorge Hotel (☎ 386-5566), 4000 Westcliff Drive, one of Oregon's best restaurants. The most famous meal served in this beautiful river-view dining room is the 'Farm Breakfast' brunch, served both Saturday and Sunday. The five-course extravaganza will leave you wondering what farmer could have conceived of such bounty (or at $23 a head, what farmer could afford it). Reservations are a must. Dinner offers local salmon, lamb and game prepared a la Northwest; there's also a five-course menu for $38.

## Entertainment

At any given moment, there are hundreds of twenty-something athletes in Hood River. After a day on the slopes or on the river, it's time to head out for nightlife. Catch a movie at *Trail Twin Theater* (☎ 386-1666), on Tucker Rd, or go for a drink at one of Hood River's rowdier spots. At the *River City Saloon* (☎ 386-4005),

OREGON

on the corner of 2nd and Cascade Sts, there's live music and dancing three to four nights a week. Right on the river, and with live music on the weekends, is the *Gorge Cafe* (☎ 386-8700), Port Marina Park. If you like it loud and rowdy, then across the bridge in Bingen, WA, the *Northshore Bar & Grill* (☎ 493-4440), 216 W Steuben St, is the place, with live music on weekends.

*Full Sail Brewpub* (☎ 386-2281), 506 Columbia St, Hood River's own brewery, has developed a loyal following across the Northwest with such offerings as its rich golden ale. The hours are odd: open daily noon to 8 pm only.

### Getting There & Away

Greyhound (☎ 386-1212), 1205 B St, offers five buses a day from Hood River to Portland and points east. Fares are $10.50 one way to/from Portland.

Amtrak's *Pioneer* arrives in Hood River three times a week in either direction. On Sunday, Tuesday and Thursday the westbound train arrives at 12:48 pm. On Monday, Wednesday and Saturday the eastbound train arrives at 12:55 pm. The one-way fare from Portland is $14. The depot is under 2nd St, off the east end of Cascade St.

For car rentals in Hood River, contact Rent-A-Wreck (☎ 386-8776), 1040 12th St, or Knoll Motor Co (☎ 386-3011), 1111 12th St. Call Hood River Taxi (☎ 386-2255) for a cab.

### THE DALLES

As an important transport hub on the Oregon Trail, The Dalles (population 11,370) played a preeminent role in the history of White settlement in Oregon. French-Canadian trappers used the area as the head of navigation for transporting furs to Fort Vancouver. They named the rocky bench of land below the river rapids *Les Dalles*, meaning flagstones, apparently referring to the shards of rock strewn everywhere.

The first White settlement at this transport spot was a Methodist mission, established in 1838 by Daniel Lee to minister to the native peoples. Within three years a Catholic mission was established here as well, and the representatives of the two faiths spent more time bickering with each other than saving souls. In 1854 the town of The Dalles was platted, and a town charter granted in 1857.

The discovery of gold and the establishment of open-range agriculture in eastern Oregon made The Dalles an important trade town and transport point. For a time the flow of gold into The Dalles was so great that the Federal Government operated a mint in the town.

Then as now, the Gorge was the principal corridor between eastern and western Oregon, and almost all freight bound in either direction passed through The Dalles. Steamboats docked at the riverfront; stagecoaches rattled off to far-flung desert communities. The streets were crowded with miners, ranchers and traders.

The completion of first the railroad and then barge lines through Columbia River reservoirs served to increase freight transport through The Dalles. Today, The Dalles continues its legacy as a thriving transport hub. The area is also the nation's largest producer of sweet cherries, and orchard workers from Latin America lend the community a distinct Hispanic character. The recreational boom of the last decade has smarted up the shopping and eating options a bit, but The Dalles remains largely hard working and practical.

### Orientation

The Dalles is 84 miles from Portland along I-84. Highway 197 cuts south from The Dalles to Bend, 131 miles south. The Dalles Bridge crosses the Columbia River to link up with Hwy 14 in Washington.

The Dalles is built on a series of steep terraces, with rocky outcroppings jutting up unexpectedly in the middle of streets and people's backyards. Ask for a walking tour map at the visitors center; it's worth the walk to see the fins and ledges of rock incorporated into streets and gardens.

The main business district lies along 2nd and 3rd Sts, each one-ways. Above this

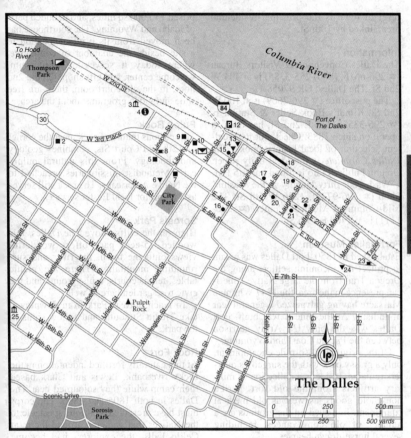

**The Dalles**

OREGON

level of town is the principal residential area, linked by 10th St.

## Information
The Dalles Convention & Visitors Bureau (☎ 296-6616, (800) 255-3385) is at 404 W 2nd St, The Dalles, OR 97058.

The post office (☎ 296-2609) is at 100 W 2nd St. Klindt's Book Seller & Stationers (☎ 296-3355), 315 E 2nd St, has been in operation since 1883. Check out its excellent selection of local history books. *The Dalles Chronicle* is the local daily paper. Oregon Public Radio is found on 91.5 FM.

Wash your dirty laundry at the Washin' Shop (☎ 296-9722), 1256 W 6th St. The Mid-Columbia Medical Center (☎ 296-1111) is at 1700 E 19th St.

## Fort Dalles Museum
Established in 1850, Fort Dalles was meant to protect the incoming settlers along the Oregon Trail from the large Native American presence in the area, the 1847 Whitman Massacre having galvanized a general fear of Indians. At the time it was built, Fort Dalles was the only US Army garrison between the Pacific Coast and Wyoming.

Of the original 10-sq-mile encampment, only a grassy park with the surgeon's quarters remains. Inside is a collection of military artifacts from the old fort, period household goods, as well as old medical equipment. In a shed on the grounds are a number of old conveyances, including several horse-drawn hearses.

The museum (☎ 296-4547) is at the corner of 15th and Garrison Sts, and is open from 10:30 am to 5 pm Monday to Friday, and 10 am to 5 pm Saturday and Sunday, March to October. In winter it's open from noon to 4 pm, Wednesday to Friday, and 10 am to 4 pm Saturday and Sunday. Admission is $2 for adults, children/students are free.

## Original Wasco County Courthouse
When this courthouse (☎ 296-4798), 406 W 2nd St, was built in 1859, it served as county seat for the largest county in US history. At the time, Wasco County comprised 130,000 sq miles, and included parts of Idaho and Wyoming. The courthouse has been moved from its original location to a site beside the chamber of commerce, where today it serves as a museum, welcome center, and gift shop. On the 2nd floor, in the old courtroom, there are free slide and video programs about the area.

## Pulpit Rock
This curious thumb of rock, near the corner of 12th and Court Sts, combines geology and theology. From this natural pulpit, early Methodist missionaries preached to the Native Americans. The rock still serves as a pulpit for local Easter services.

## Sorosis Park
High on the cliffs above The Dalles, this wooded 15-acre park offers wonderful views onto the town, the river and surrounding mountains. There are picnic tables, tennis courts, a playground and the civic rose garden here as well.

To reach Sorosis Park from downtown, take Trevitt St south, and follow signs to the park.

## Rock Fort
At this naturally fortified indentation in the rocky riverbank, Lewis and Clark based their camp while they sojourned near The Dalles in both 1805 and 1806. The corps must have presented a curious spectacle to the Natives that gathered around them; at Celilo Falls, the explorers had become infested with fleas. Lewis wrote in his journal:

[The fleas] are very troublesom and dificuelt to get rid of, perticularly as the men have not a Change of Clothes to put on, they strip off their Clothes and kill the flees, dureing which time they remain nakid.

To reach Fort Rock from downtown, follow Hwy 30 west (it becomes W 6th St). Turn right on Webber St, and drive toward the river into an industrial area. Turn right on 1st St and continue half a mile to a sign pointing to a parking area. There's not much interpretive information at Fort

Rock, but kids and Lewis-and-Clark buffs will enjoy the site.

### The Dalles Dam & Lock

The Dalles Dam, built in 1957, produces enough electricity to power a city the size of Seattle. Access to this power came at a price, however. The dam's reservoir, Lake Celilo, flooded the culturally rich area around Celilo Falls, for thousands of years a meeting place and fishery for Native Americans.

The falls had hampered commercial navigation on the Columbia River since the days of the fur traders, and all the old transportation routes, as well as the troublesome falls themselves, were inundated when The Dalles Dam impounded the river, creating 24-mile-long Lake Celilo.

Tours of the facilities are offered from two points. In Seufert Park, east on the frontage road from I-84 exit No 87, is The Dalles Dam Visitor Center (☎ 296-9778). This small museum and information center contains the usual homage to hydroelectricity, along with exhibits on local history. From here, a small train (no charge) leaves every half hour to visit the dam itself. The visitors center and tour-train operate daily from 9 am to 5 pm, June to Labor Day weekend.

To forgo the train ride, take I-84 exit No 88 directly to the dam. The self-guided tour of the turbines and powerhouse is open year round from 9 am to 5 pm, Monday to Friday.

### Horsethief State Park

At this Washington state park (☎ (509) 767-1159), just across from The Dalles, are preserved some of the most famous remaining pictographs along the Columbia River. *Tsagaglalal*, or 'She Who Watches', is probably the most widely known image: an owl-like female presence presiding over what was once a thriving Native American crossroads.

The pictograph area, once open to the public, can now be visited only on a guided tour, due to recent malicious vandalism. The park is open from April to October,

and free tours are offered Friday and Saturday only, at 10 am. Reservations are recommended, as tours are limited to 30 people.

The central aspect of the park is Horsethief Lake, a small inlet of Lake Celilo. Rising from the eastern edge of the lake are the imposing basalt walls of Horsethief Butte, popular with beginning rock climbers. There's no parking area for Horsethief Butte, but at milepost 86 on Hwy 14 there's a trailhead to the cliffs.

Green, well-watered Horsethief Park also offers fishing and swimming in the lake, as well as camping and picnicking.

### Windsurfing

Hood River may wear the crown when it comes to the windsurfing lifestyle, but the wind blows at The Dalles too. Along Lake Celilo, behind The Dalles Dam, a number of parks offer access to wide expanses of wind-whipped water. A favorite entry point on the Oregon side is Celilo Park, nine miles east of The Dalles. Avery Park, four miles upriver from Horsethief State Park, offers good access to the river from the Washington side.

For lessons and equipment in The Dalles area, contact Gorge Windsurfing (☎ 298-8796), 420 E 1st St.

### Fishing

While the locals fish for sturgeon, walleye and panfish in the Columbia River above The Dalles Dam, for many the real angling scene is the Deschutes River, which joins the Columbia just upriver from The Dalles. For information, tackle and guide service, go to Young's Sporting Goods (☎ 296-2544), 515 E 2nd St. For guided fishing trips on the John Day, Columbia or Deschutes rivers, contact Glenn Summers (☎ 296-5949), PO Box 436, The Dalles, OR 97058.

### Other Activities

Rent a bicycle at Life Cycles (☎ 296-9588), 418 E 2nd St. Skis, snowboards and in-line skates are available at Stone's Ski & Sports (☎ 298-5886), 500 E 2nd St. Walker

.Memorial Pool (☎ 298-2020), 602 W 2nd St, is in Thompson Park, just west of downtown.

Aquatic Adventures Scuba Center (☎ 298-8115), 215 Court St, offers diving lessons and certification. If you're an experienced diver, you can rent tanks here to go diving in the Columbia River dams.

### Special Events
The Dalles' biggest summer event is Fort Dalles Day (☎ 296-6616, (800) 255-3385) held the second weekend of July. There's a parade and chili cook-off, but the big event is the PRCA Rodeo. Call for details and rodeo tickets.

### Places to Stay
**Camping** The closest public campground to The Dalles is in Washington, across The Dalles Bridge at *Horsethief State Park* (☎ (509) 767-1159), two miles east on Hwy 14 from the junction with Hwy 197.

On the Oregon side, *Memaloose State Park*, 11 miles west of The Dalles on I-84 (westbound access only), offers riverside camping at a spot overlooking a Native American burial island. Fourteen miles east of The Dalles, there's a nice campground at *Deschutes State Park* (☎ 739-2322).

For a basic RV park close to The Dalles, go to *Lone Pine RV Park* (☎ 296-9133), 335 E Hwy 197, which is just north of I-84 exit No 87.

**B&Bs** *Captain Gray's Guest House* (☎ 298-8222), 210 W 4th St, is a well-preserved Queen Anne confection; rooms range from $50 to $65. *The Williams House B&B* (☎ 296-2889), 608 W 6th St, is one of the most elaborate homes in a town full of historic buildings. This 1899 Queen Anne mansion with wraparound porches is in a garden setting, with a small creek running alongside. There are two guest rooms and a full suite; rates are $55 to $75.

**Hotels** The Dalles has a large number of affordable hotels. The *Shamrock Motel* (☎ 296-5464), 118 W 4th St, is right downtown, single/double rooms are $30/34.

*Oregon Motor Motel* (☎ 296-9111), 200 W 2nd St, also downtown, offers a pool; rooms are $46/52. The nicest lodging downtown is the *Best Western Tapadera Inn* (☎ 296-9107), 112 W 2nd St, with a pool, room service and restaurant; singles/doubles are $58/63.

If you want a view, go to the *Inn at the Dalles* (☎ 296-1167), 3550 SE Frontage Rd. Above the eastern edge of town, the hotel has an outdoor pool; pets are OK, and it has some kitchenettes; rooms cost $32/35.

On the river, near The Dalles Bridge, are two large motel complexes. At the *Shilo Inn* (☎ 298-5502), 3223 NE Frontage Rd, there is a spa, outdoor pool, meeting rooms and guest laundry; pets are OK; rooms are $60/65. The *Lone Pine Motel* (☎ 298-2800, (800) 955-9626), 351 Lone Pine Drive, has an indoor pool; rooms are $60/$65.

On the west end of town is another hotel strip. The *Quality Inn* (☎ 298-5161), 2114 W 6th St, offers a pool, hot tub, guest laundry and some kitchenettes; singles/doubles are $65/69. *Days Inn* (☎ 296-1191), 2500 W 6th St, offers kitchenettes and indoor pool for $58/60.

### Places to Eat
Espresso and cinnamon rolls from a drive-through window makes *Holsteins Coffee Co* (☎ 298-2326), at the corner of E 3rd and Taylor Sts, the place to stop when you're in a hurry (there's pleasant seating inside, too). For a more sedate start to your day, go to *La Crema* (296-6969), 221 W 4th St, where espresso drinks are served in an old home in a shaded neighborhood.

For a picnic, stock up on deli items and sandwiches from *Kingfish Seafood & Wine Shop* (☎ 296-1501), 213 Court St; they also serve fresh fish & chips. For authentic Mexican food, try the selection at *Guadalajara* (☎ 296-4996), 728 E 3rd St. A tamale and a taco for lunch is $4.

*Baldwin Saloon* (☎ 296-5666), 205 Court St, has in its 120-year history been a bar, brothel, saddlery and warehouse. Now it's back to its original purpose, serving up good food and strong drinks. Fresh oysters are a specialty (pan-fried for dinner at $12), though it's hard to beat the burgers ($6) and tasty barbecued ribs ($9).

*Wasco House* (☎ 296-5158), 515 Liberty St, is another historic building (built in 1865) put to good use. Grilled fresh salmon and halibut are $14; filet mignon and baby-back ribs at the same price are the house favorites; there's a lounge upstairs. At an entirely different level of sophistication, *Ole's Supper Club* (☎ 296-6708), 2620 W 2nd St, is totally unprepossessing on the exterior, but this is where the locals come when they want a really good steak or prime rib dinner ($15). The wine selection is probably the best in town.

### Getting There & Away
Greyhound and Amtrak share a depot (☎ 296-2421) at 201 1st St.

There are five Greyhound buses a day between The Dalles and Portland. Two buses a day link The Dalles to Spokane and Montana. One-way fare to Portland is about $13.

Amtrak's westbound *Pioneer* arrives in The Dalles at 10:59 am on Sunday, Tuesday and Thursday. The eastbound service gets to The Dalles at 1:23 pm on Monday, Wednesday and Saturday. Fare one way to Portland is $16.

For car rentals in The Dalles, contact Brace Bros Rent-a-Car (☎ 296-3761), 1119 W 2nd St. Call West Way Taxi (☎ 296-5621).

### AROUND THE DALLES
### Rowena Crest
The Columbia River Hwy reached Hood River in 1915; it took seven years for the highway to reach The Dalles. One of the engineering challenges involved in con-structing this second part of the Gorge highway was dealing with the Rowena Crest, a plateau hundreds of feet above the Columbia River. With characteristic aplomb, the road builders corkscrewed the highway down the cliff face to the river's edge.

The views along this section of old Hwy 30 are spectacular: between Hood River and The Dalles, the heavy vegetation of the western Gorge diminishes, and suddenly the barren, basaltic architecture of the Gorge becomes apparent. The black walls of rock rear back from the river's edge, notched here and there with deeply incised canyons.

On top of Rowena Crest is a roadside viewpoint, and access to hundreds of acres of meadowlands now preserved as a wild-flower sanctuary. Established by the Nature Conservancy, the **Governor Tom McCall Reserve** on Rowena Plateau is one of the best places to see native plants, to watch raptors hovering on updrafts and to enjoy great views. From the viewpoint parking area, cross the road and a stile, and follow trails through grassy meadows. In April and May, the wildflower display is amaz-ing, with balsamroot, wild parsley, pentse-mons and wild lilies leading out. On spring weekends, volunteers often lead informal wildflower-identification hikes. Be very careful of poison oak.

To reach this section of the historic Columbia River Hwy from The Dalles, follow W 6th St westward out of town until it becomes Hwy 30 or take I-84 exit No 69 at Mosier, and travel east on Hwy 30.

### DESCHUTES RIVER RECREATION AREA
The mighty Deschutes River, Oregon's second-largest, rises far to the south in the Three Sisters Wilderness Area. By the time it reaches the Columbia River, it has cut a massive canyon through much of Central Oregon. At this state park, the Deschutes and the Columbia rivers meet.

For recreationalists, it's a busy place. The fishing is great, and rafting parties take out after their four-day ride down the Deschutes from Sherar's Bridge, while anglers put in to fish Lake Celilo. Hiking trails explore the east side of the river's desert canyon: the park is a good place to watch for raptors and migrating songbirds, and to view seasonal wildflowers. In spring, especially, when western Oregon is dank and wet, this is a great place to find sage-scented warmth and sun.

## Hiking

From the south end of the park, there are trails for both hikers and mountain bikers. The Atiyeh River Trail follows the Deschutes closely, through old homesteads, springs and groves of willow and locust trees. The Upper River Loop follows a path along the side of the canyon, through sagebrush and rocky outcroppings. After about a mile on this trail, another steeper trail, the Ferry Springs Trail, divides off and leads to a rock-strewn spring high on the canyon's wall, with good views over the river and desert hills. All three of these trails meet up at the end of the park, making for different combinations of loop trails.

The mountain biking trail leads off from near the park entrance. This path was once the railbed for the Deschutes Railroad Company, which attempted but failed to build a line to Bend early this century.

On all hikes, watch for snakes.

## Fishing

Trails follow the Deschutes for 12 miles from its mouth on the Columbia River, allowing anglers to hike into remote fishing holes (no motorized vehicles are allowed between the park and Mack's Canyon Campground, 25 miles south). Summer steelhead fishing is very good along this stretch.

At the mouth of the river, where it meets Lake Celilo, there's good fishing for walleye, steelhead and sturgeon.

## Camping

There are 34 campsites (☎ 739-2322) along the river, some under the shade of cottonwood trees. This can be a popular spot during summer weekends; $9 is the overnight fee (no hook-ups available).

## MARYHILL MUSEUM

Eccentric Sam Hill is responsible for some of the most famous building projects in the Gorge, not the least of which is the Maryhill Museum (☎ (509) 773-3733) 35 Maryhill Museum Drive. Known for its quirky collections, the museum is the perfect focus for a day-trip up the Gorge from Portland, or a great stop for anyone needing a break from I-84 heat and traffic. The museum also offers classes, lectures and concerts. Call ahead for information.

As the story of Maryhill is odd, so is the

### What in the Sam Hill . . . ?

Sam Hill was an impertinent young lawyer in Minneapolis in the 1880s whose reputation was made in part by his success in bringing legal suits against the Great Northern Railroad. Great Northern mogul James Hill (no relation at the time) decided to co-opt the young attorney. James Hill brought Sam into the company, and soon into his family: Sam wooed and married James' daughter Mary.

With the Great Northern's financial security behind him, Sam Hill turned toward a life of good works. His great contribution to the Northwest was the Columbia River Hwy, the region's first paved road and a wonder of engineering and scenic value. Hill worked closely with Oregon businessmen and state officials to promote the road, which began construction in 1913.

At the same time that the highway was being built, Hill began construction of a vast country home at the top of an 800-foot cliff along the Columbia River. Ever an idealist, Hill hoped that the estate would be home to him and his wife (who refused to live in this god-forsaken country), and the center of a utopian Quaker farm community.

The Maryhill Castle, as it was then called, was constructed to resemble a French country chateau, and encompasses 20,000 sq feet. However, Hill's plans began to fall apart when his wife returned to her beloved Philadelphia, and the imported Belgian Quakers found the desiccated cliff-sides unsuitable for agriculture. Hill's enthusiasm for the project flagged, and the building was not completed until 1926, when Hill's friend, Queen Marie of Romania came to the USA to dedicate Maryhill as a museum. However, the museum did not open to the public until 1940. ∎

collection of artifacts it houses. Queen Marie of Romania, feeling a fondness for the museum, donated a great many unusual items, including the dress she wore to the coronation of Czar Nicholas II and several pieces of enormous furniture she supposedly made herself.

Downstairs is a very good collection of Native American baskets, carvings, tools and other cultural items. Also, there is another curiosity: one of the world's largest collections of chess sets.

One of Hill's jet-set friends was Loie Fuller, an American dancer with ties to artistic circles in Paris. After WW I, she helped Hill obtain a collection of French drawings and sculpture by a then-unheralded artist named Auguste Rodin. A cast of his *The Thinker* now greets visitors on the 3rd floor.

A more recent addition to the curiosities is a collection of French fashion mannequins. In 1945 some of the top houses of the Parisian fashion trade, seeking to revitalize the industry, sewed haute-couture clothing for a traveling display. Artists of the time, including Jean Cocteau, painted backdrops for the mannequins, and special music was composed to accompany the viewing. The show toured Britain and the USA and orders for fashions came pouring into Paris. The mannequins, the clothing and the painted screens languished in San Francisco until arts maven Alma de Bretteville Spreckels, another long-time friend of Sam Hill, arranged for them to be donated to Maryhill.

Almost neglected in all these odd displays is a small, but quite fine collection of late-19th and early-20th-century landscape and portrait paintings. Also, in a basement display area are changing exhibits of works by regional artists.

Maryhill Museum is 10 miles south of Goldendale, WA on Hwy 97, and 22 miles east from The Dalles, along I-84; cross the Hwy 97 bridge and look up: you can't miss it. The museum is open from 9 am to 5 pm daily, March to November. Admission for adults/children is $4/2.

The area around Maryhill is locally acclaimed for the quality of its fruit, especially peaches and apricots. A number of fruit stands spring up along Hwy 14 in July.

## Stonehenge

Never one for small gestures, Sam Hill built a full-scale replica of Salisbury Plain's Stonehenge a few miles from Maryhill on the cliffs above the Columbia River. Dedicated as a memorial to Klickitat County's WW I dead, his Stonehenge is built of poured concrete, and was constructed to represent Stonehenge as it was when it stood intact (not knocked over and cluttered like its English cousin).

Hill planned that his Stonehenge would line up for celestial events like equinoxes and such, but there's a difference of opinion between adherents as to whether the key stone is in the right place. You can imagine that this is a popular place for odd, usually harmless rites and ceremonies.

To reach Sam Hill's Stonehenge from Maryhill, continue east on Hwy 14 past the Hwy 97 junction. One mile later, follow signs to the right for Stonehenge. You can't miss it.

## Places to Stay & Eat

The place to camp is *Maryhill State Park* (☎ (509) 773-5007). At the base of the Hwy 97 bridge on the Washington side, this large, riverside campground offers swimming, boating and windsurfing access, as well as covered picnic shelters. There are 50 campsites with showers and hot water.

Across the Columbia River from Maryhill is the little town of Biggs. This is a busy crossroads for trucks and travelers along both Hwy 97 and I-84, so there are a number of non-descript motels. The best bet is the *Best Western Riviera Inn* (☎ 739-2501); it's got a pool, which is a real plus in this hot canyon. Single/double rooms are $55/60.

There's a small cafeteria in the basement at Maryhill Museum. The lines can be long, and food runs out. At such times, drive across the Columbia River to Biggs and eat at the *Biggs Cafe* (☎ 739-2395). Formerly a drive-in with car hops, the old service area is still covered with a protective metal roof, which provides much-needed shade in summer.

## GOLDENDALE (WA)

Up over the escarpment of the Gorge, on a fertile plateau beneath forested hills and distant Mt Adams, lies Goldendale (population 3375), a small agricultural community that serves as one of Washington's gateways to the Gorge. Settled in 1872, by the turn of the century there was sufficient wealth in Goldendale to build an impressive collection of late Victorian homes. One of the old homes is now open as a museum; for fans of turn-of-the-century design, this ought to be a certain stop.

Nearby is Goldendale Observatory, maintained by the state parks department as a free public observatory.

### Orientation & Information

Goldendale is east of The Dalles and about 10 miles north of the Columbia River on Hwy 97. Drivers towing large loads need to be aware that the climb up out of the Gorge on Hwy 97 is very protracted: the steep uphill pull is nearly eight miles long. Vehicles prone to overheating will surely do so, especially on sweltering summer days.

You can write the Goldendale Chamber of Commerce (☎ 773-3400), PO Box 524, Goldendale, WA 98620. During the summer, there's an informational kiosk near the entrance to Maryhill State Park.

### Goldendale Observatory State Park

Located on an old volcanic cone just north of town, this observatory (☎ (509) 773-3141), 1602 Observatory Drive, houses a 24.5-inch reflecting telescope built by the volunteer labor of four Vancouver, WA-area retirees. These four men donated the telescope to the state with the condition that it be made available to the public for the study and better understanding of astronomy. The telescope is one of the largest available to the public in the USA.

The best time to go is in the evening when there are programs, which include a number of videos, slide presentations and talks. Depending on what's going on astronomically, there are also views through the telescope to planets, galaxies, stars and comets. Admission is free.

The observatory is open from 2 to 5 pm, and 8 pm to midnight, Wednesday to Sunday, May to September. October to April it's open from 2 to 5 pm and 7 to 9 pm. Call ahead to confirm times and ask about special programs.

### Presby House Museum

Winthrop Presby came to Goldendale in 1888, and eventually became an attorney and state senator. He built his 20-room mansion in 1902. In the 1970s the Klickitat County Historical Society took possession of this splendid Queen Anne home, and turned it into a community museum.

Thankfully, much of the old structure is still intact, and rooms have been outfitted sparely – for a museum – preserving the feel of a turn-of-the-century home. Note especially the beautiful fireplaces and fine leaded glass.

The Presby House Museum is open from 9 am to 5 pm daily from May to October. Admission is $2 for adults and $1 for students; children under 12 are free.

### Places to Stay

Campers in the Goldendale area will want to stay at either *Maryhill State Park* down on the Columbia River (see below), or, if it's too hot in the Gorge, go to *Brooks Memorial State Park* (☎ (509) 773-4611), 13 miles north of Goldendale on Hwy 97. This cool and wooded park is near the Klickitat River; hiking trails explore the pine forests and beaver dams along the stream. There are 45 campsites, some with hook-ups. In the day-use area are picnic tables and playing fields.

The *Ponderosa Motel* (☎ (509) 773-5842), 775 E Broadway Ave, is a well-kept motor hotel off the main highway not far from downtown Goldendale. Single/double rooms are $45/48. The newest and nicest place to stay in town is the *Far Vue Inn* (☎ 773-5881), at the Simcoe St exit from Hwy 97; rooms are $48/52.

At the confluence of three streams in the forests, eight miles north of Goldendale along Hwy 97, stands *Highland Creek Resort* (☎ (509) 773-4026), a rural retreat with a central lodge and chalet cabins with hot tubs. The beauty of the setting appeals to anglers, or to anyone wishing for a quiet place to escape. Some small rooms are available for $46, but larger cabins with hot tubs range from $105 to $135.

### Places to Eat
For a coffee jolt or sandwiches for lunch, go to *Goldendale Espresso* (☎ (509) 773-7070), 104 E Main St. For a good breakfast, served all day, and steak for dinner, go to the *Homestead* (☎ (509) 773-5559), at the Simcoe St exit off Hwy 97. The *Roadhouse 97*, (☎ (509) 773-3553), three miles north on Hwy 97, is a diner that does a good job with standard fare. For food verging on cuisine, go to *Highland Creek Resort*, eight miles north of Goldendale on Hwy 97. In this beautiful dining room, plan on spending about $25 for such dishes as pork tenderloin with forest mushrooms or seasonal game specialties.

# Mt Hood

The state's highest peak at 11,235 feet, Mt Hood looms above all of northern and central Oregon. As a child you drew mountains like this: a snow-capped triangle of rock that incises the skyline, solitary and commanding. Mt Hood, rising above the deep forests, is as close as there is to a single, iconic image of Oregon, a metaphor for the state.

It's also a wildly popular destination for sightseers and recreationalists. On its flanks is Timberline Lodge, the mountain retreat of your fantasies. There are five major ski resorts, cross-country skiing is as easy as renting skis and gliding away from the shop toward the mountain, and in summer hikers traverse the flanks of the mountains to find hidden lakes and wildflower meadows.

Mt Hood rises on the shoulders of the Western Cascades, a long ridge of older volcanoes stretching between Mt Rainier and Mt Shasta. These volcanoes erupted between 40 and 20 million years ago, so long ago that their peaks have long since eroded. Although Mt Hood began to erupt toward the end of the last ice age, it's clear that there have been many more recent eruptions. The peak's near-perfect conical shape is evidence that new lava flows have repaired whatever damage Pleistocene-era glaciers – which retreated about 10,000 years ago – had done. Geologists reckon that Mt Hood's last major eruption was about 1000 years ago, although Native American lore and early settlers both report small eruptions in the last 200 years.

Mt Hood was known to local Native Americans as Wy'east, who in myth was a brash young warrior fond of fiery outbursts and cantankerous behavior, like hurling fire and rock into the air. In 1792, English Captain William Broughton, under the command of Captain George Vancouver, sailed up the Columbia River as far as Crown Point, and first sighted Mt Hood. He named the peak after a famed British admiral, Lord Samuel Hood.

### ORIENTATION
Mt Hood remains accessible year round on Hwy 26 from Portland, and from Hood River on Hwy 35. Together with the Columbia River Hwy, these routes comprise the Mt Hood Loop, one of the most popular scenic road excursions in the USA. Government Camp is at the pass over Mt Hood, and – such as it is – constitutes the center of business on the mountain. From Portland, it's 56 miles to Government Camp; from Hood River, it's 44 miles. Highway 26 continues on to Madras and Bend. From Madras to Government Camp is 40 miles.

Most facilities for travelers are on the western side of Mt Hood, and serve Portlanders as they zip back and forth to the mountain. At the little villages of Sandy, Welches, Zigzag, Wemme and Rhododendron, all on Hwy 26, are a number of

OREGON

restaurants and motels that cater to passers-through.

## INFORMATION

The Mt Hood Area Chamber of Commerce (☎ 622-4822) and the USFS tourist information office, are at the Mt Hood Information Center (☎ 622-4822), 65000 E Hwy 26, 15 miles east of Sandy. Just up the road in Welches is the Mt Hood Recreation Association (☎ 622-3017), 68260 E Welches Rd, a clearing-house for information about recreation on Mt Hood.

Maps, special use permits and other related information can be obtained from the Zigzag Ranger Station (☎ 622-3191, 666-0704 in Portland), which serves the Mt Hood National Forest. This USFS office is at the Mt Hood Information Center (see above) and is open from 7:45 am to 4:30 pm every day except holidays.

The most convenient post office on Mt Hood is at Government Camp (☎ 272-3238), 88331 E Government Camp Loop. Hoodland Family Medical Clinic (☎ 622-3126), 24461 Welches Rd, in Welches, is the nearest medical facility. Hours are 8:30 am to 5 pm Monday to Friday.

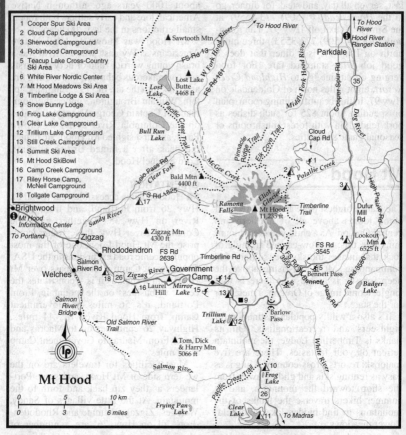

1   Cooper Spur Ski Area
2   Cloud Cap Campground
3   Sherwood Campground
4   Robinhood Campground
5   Teacup Lake Cross-Country Ski Area
6   White River Nordic Center
7   Mt Hood Meadows Ski Area
8   Timberline Lodge & Ski Area
9   Snow Bunny Lodge
10  Frog Lake Campground
11  Clear Lake Campground
12  Trillium Lake Campground
13  Still Creek Campground
14  Summit Ski Area
15  Mt Hood SkiBowl
16  Camp Creek Campground
17  Riley Horse Camp, McNeil Campground
18  Tollgate Campground

**Mt Hood**

0        5        10 km
0     3      6 miles

**The Barlow Pass**
Some of the first explorations of the area around Mt Hood were carried out by trailblazers seeking an alternative route for Oregon Trail pioneers. The original emigrant trail brought travelers overland to The Dalles, from which point began a treacherous journey on raft through the Columbia River Gorge. Samuel Barlow decided to find an all-land route to the Willamette Valley, and in 1845 began to scout the passes over Mt Hood for a suitable trail. The route he blazed left The Dalles, passed Dufur, crossed the White River near Tygh Valley and then climbed on to Barlow Pass near Government Camp. To this point, the pioneers who followed Barlow's trail (no philanthropist, Barlow was charging a hefty toll for travelers to take what became known as the Barlow Rd) agreed that this route was better than the white-water raft trip down the Columbia River. However, the near-vertical descent of Laurel Hill, just west of Government Camp, changed many minds. The road here was so steep that wheels had to be taken off wagons and the wagon bodies lowered down the hill on winches strapped to trees. The toll charged for this inconvenience was $5 per team, and $1 for every man, woman and head of cattle.

The Barlow Rd remained the principal route to Mt Hood through 1919, when the state government obtained the route and proceeded to construct a new paved road to join with the Columbia River Hwy. ■

OREGON

## Weather & Road Reports

The pass at Mt Hood receives a lot of snow, and in all but the best of winter weather, travelers should check on road conditions before starting up the mountain. For state-wide road conditions, dial the 24-hour information line (☎ 976-7277, 889-3999). State law requires traction devices to be carried in vehicles during most of the winter, and trailers are often banned.

During the winter, ski conditions are often included in local TV and radio weather reports. However, for the most up-to-date conditions it's best to call the ski areas directly to hear prerecorded information: Mt Hood Meadows & Hood River Meadows (☎ 227-7669), Timberline (☎ 222-2211), Mt Hood SkiBowl (☎ 222-2695) and Summit Ski Area (☎ 272-0256).

In winter, if you park a vehicle at most places on Mt Hood, you'll need to buy a Winter Sno-park permit; $1.50 daily, $2.50 three-day or $9 for a season pass. They are available at most sports rental stores along Hwy 26, and from most businesses in Government Camp and at Timberline Lodge.

## TIMBERLINE LODGE

One of the unquestioned masterpieces of the WPA-era building boom, Timberline Lodge (☎ 272-3311, 231-7979 in Portland) is the culmination of a kind of rustic Craftsman design that came to be known as Cascadian, the influence of which is still being felt in contemporary building.

The building of Timberline Lodge in 1936 and 1937 was the largest of the federal make-work projects directed by the WPA in Oregon, employing up to 500 workers to construct the four-story, 43,700-sq-foot log and stone lodge. For many employed on the project, Timberline was more than just a job, it was an expression of a cultural ideal. As stated in a 1937 publication that accompanied the dedication:

In Mt Hood's Timberline Lodge the mystic strength that lives in the hills has been captured in wood and stone, and in the hands of laborer and craftsman, has been presented as man's effort at approximating an ideal in which society, through concern for the individual, surpasses the standard it has unconsciously set for itself.

There is hardly an element of the building that was not hand-crafted, from the selection of stones in the massive lobby fireplaces to the hand-loomed coverlets on the beds. In an effort to impede as little as possible on the natural beauty of the area, architects not only quarried local stone and utilized local timber, they also designed the six-sided central tower to echo the faceted peak of Mt Hood; the steeply slanted wings leading away from the common rooms are meant both to shed the heavy snowfalls and to resemble mountain ridges. Even the exterior paint was specially mixed to match the color of mountain frost.

The interior of the lodge is where the careful workmanship is most evident. The central fireplace rises 92 feet through three floors of open lobby; all the furniture in the hotel was made by hand in WPA carpentry halls, and murals and paintings of stocky, stylized workers, in the best Socialist-Realist tradition, adorn the walls.

The Rachael Griffin Historic Exhibition Center, on the main floor, displays some of the history of the lodge in tools, drawings, weavings and photographs. In the Coyote Den room, nearby, a free 30-minute video discusses the building of the lodge. The USFS offers 30 to 45-minute free interpretive tours of the lodge during the day.

Of course, Timberline Lodge is not a museum, it is a hotel, ski resort and restaurant. Don't feel so reverential about this magnificent old building that you don't at least enjoy a hot chocolate on the mezzanine, or strap on some skis and get out onto the mountain. And don't forget about Timberline Lodge's quirkier side: the horror movies *The Shining* and *Hear No Evil* were both filmed here – pass by room 217 ('redrum redrum') for a quick chill.

## SKIING
### Downhill

Throughout Oregon, paper bags from grocery stores are often laden with discount coupons to ski areas during the winter months. The G I Joe's chain of sporting goods stores also offers advance discounts and package deals.

Mt Hood Meadows (☎ 337-2222), 76 miles from Portland and 36 from Hood River, is the largest ski area on Mt Hood, and is generally considered to have the best conditions, as it is on the sunnier, drier side of Mt Hood. It also has Mt Hood's most challenging slopes, with 20% of its runs rated 'advanced'. The vertical drop is 2777 feet, and there are 77 runs; lift tickets range between $28 and $36. Snowboarders have a separate area. Facilities include two day lodges, five places to eat and three bars; rentals and lessons are available.

Timberline Lodge (☎ 231-7979) is famed for its magnificent ski lodge and its year-round skiing (it has the longest ski season in North America, with lifts running till Labor Day). Ski teams from all over the world flock here for summer training, and take advantage of the 2660-foot vertical drop and 30 runs. The ski area is also noted for its good intermediate skiing. A lift ticket ranges from $16 early week to $28 weekends. There's a separate snowboarding area. Timberline Lodge is five miles north of Hwy 26 from Government Camp.

Mt Hood SkiBowl (☎ 272-3206), off Hwy 26 just west of Government Camp, is America's largest night-ski area, and the closest ski area to Portland. The course has a vertical drop of 1500 feet with 33 runs (210 acres of the ski area are under lights). Lift tickets range from $11 to $20.

Summit Ski Area (☎ 272-0256, 294-2104 in Portland) is a family and beginners-oriented ski area with gentle terrain. There's a mere 320-foot drop, and lift tickets range between $10 and $15. This is a good place for lessons in both alpine and cross-country, and there's also a separate sledding area. Summit Ski Area is right in Government Camp, at the east end of the loop road.

Cooper Spur Ski Area (☎ 352-7803), is on the east slopes of Mt Hood, on Cooper

Spur Rd, off Hwy 35, 26 miles south of Hood River. This ski area caters to beginning skiers and to families; it also offers, at $10, the cheapest lift tickets on Mt Hood. There's a 500-foot drop and seven runs.

## Cross-Country

All Mt Hood downhill ski areas except for Cooper Spur also offer groomed cross-country ski trails. Just down the road from Mt Hood Meadows is Hood River Meadows (☎ 337-2222, ext 262), known also as the Nordic Center. Mt Hood Meadows operates this area as a private cross-country ski club with about nine miles of groomed trails. Ski rentals and instruction are available; trail-use fees are $10 for a full day, $7 for a half day. Hood River Meadows is open from 9 am to 4 pm Wednesday to Sunday, and everyday during holidays.

Tea Cup Lake, with 18.6 miles of groomed trails, is operated by the Oregon Nordic Club; a donation is asked for use of the trails. It's on Hwy 35, opposite Hood River Meadows. A few miles from the Hwy 26 junction, the White River Nordic Center on Hwy 35 is another popular public ski area with 14.3 miles of groomed trails.

The adventurous can break out of the day-trip rut and ski to Elk Meadows. Superb views of Mt Hood's east face await, and a wooden shelter accommodates overnight skiers. Contact the Hood River Ranger District (☎ 352-6002, 666-0701 in Portland) for more information. Trail access begins from the Clark Creek Sno-park on Hwy 35, 6.5 miles east of the Hwy 26 junction.

A list of other trails in the area is available from any Mt Hood National Forest office; trails lead off from all snow-park locations.

## Sledding

At Snow Bunny Lodge, 1.5 miles east of Government Camp on Hwy 26, are three supervised innertubing and saucer sled areas. This is great fun for kids and families. However, you can't bring your own equipment; you have to rent.

## Rentals

It's probably easiest to rent downhill skis at ski areas, although a number of rental shops also supply both alpine ski packages and cross-country equipment. In Government Camp, rent cross country skis at the Race Base (☎ 272-3519), 88220 E Government Camp Loop, or from Winter Fox Shop (☎ 272-3380), in the Huckleberry Inn at 88611 Government Camp Loop. If you're driving up from Portland, you can also stop in Sandy to rent ski equipment at Otto's Cross-Country Ski Shop (☎ 668-5947), 38716 Pioneer Blvd, or at Winter Fox Shop (☎ 668-6500), 38454 Pioneer Ave. It usually costs between $12 and $15 a day to rent cross-country skis, boots and poles.

## HIKING

Ask anyone for advice on their own favorite hiking trail, and you'll get a lot of different, opinionated answers. The USFS has an excellent free pamphlet called *Day Hikes Around Mt Hood* that lists 30 hikes that range greatly in difficulty and popularity. Hikers should also have the 1:100,000 series map of Mt Hood from Geo-Graphics or the Mt Hood National Forest map, both available from most outdoor stores and from ranger stations.

Following are a few deservedly popular day hikes on trails that are easy to moderate in grade: on a sunny weekend these trails won't provide an experience of wilderness solitude, but they are well-loved for good reasons.

## Ramona Falls

There is a lower and an upper trailhead to beautiful Ramona Falls, which tumbles 120 feet down a face of mossy, columnar basalt. To reach the trail, turn north at Zigzag onto Lolo Pass Rd for five miles; turn right on USFS Rd 1825 for three miles. The first trailhead is here; however, a very rocky road leads to an upper trailhead, 1.4 miles distant. From the lower trailhead, the falls is a 7.5-mile roundtrip hike.

OREGON

## Mirror Lake

Another very popular trail climbs up to Mirror Lake, which serves as a reflecting pond for the mass of Mt Hood rearing up in the near distance. Follow Hwy 26 west 1.5 miles from Government Camp. The trailhead begins at the gravel carpark between mileposts 51 and 52. This easy four-mile roundtrip hike through thick forest gains only 700 feet, and is perfect for casual hikers.

## Salmon River Trail

The Salmon River Trail follows the Salmon River through lush old-growth forests; the grade is very gentle and the trail parallels a USFS road much of the way, so it's easy to arrange a shuttle. To find the trailhead, at Zigzag turn south on Salmon River Rd and drive three miles to a sign for the Old Salmon River Trail. Most day hikers continue on the trail to the Salmon River Bridge for a 2.6-mile hike. The trail continues along the Salmon River for those who want a longer hike.

## Laurel Hill Trail

Hike a piece of history on Laurel Hill Trail. This trail follows a section of the Barlow Trail that was roundly cursed by the Oregon Trail pioneers who were forced to winch their wagons down the precipitous slopes. Thanks to the CCC, who constructed the present trail in the 1930s, modern hikers have it somewhat easier than the pioneers. The trail also follows a portion of the original Mt Hood Loop, constructed in 1921 as the first paved road over Mt Hood. The upper trailhead is near milepost 52, 2.5 miles west of Government Camp on Hwy 26, just off of USFS Rd 552. The lower trailhead is just off Hwy 26 on USFS Rd 2639, called the Kiwanis Camp Rd. The trail is 3.7 miles long, all up or downhill, depending on which trailhead you choose.

## Timberline Trail

The most noted long-distance trail on Mt Hood is the Timberline Trail, which circumscribes the mountain at the timberline level. The entire hike around the mountain takes three to five days of backpacking, and is advisable only after the snow melts, in mid-July, until snowfall, usually in mid-October. Portions of the trail make good day hikes, especially from two car-accessible trailheads.

A popular day hike along the Timberline Trail leads from the back of the Timberline Lodge to **Zigzag Canyon Overlook**. This 4.5-mile roundtrip hike leads through wildflower meadows to a vista across a 700-foot-deep canyon cut in the flank of Mt Hood by glacial streams. This easy hike has an elevation change of only 500 feet, and is perfect for moderately keen walkers.

A more remote departure point on the Timberline Trail is from **Cloud Cap Trailhead** on the eastern side of Mt Hood. To reach the trailhead, turn on Cooper Spur Rd from Hwy 35, following signs for the so-named ski area; and from there, continue another 11 miles up a fairly good graveled road toward Cloud Cap and Tilly Jane campgrounds. The road ends at Cloud Cap, a historic lodge turned mountain-rescue station.

From the trailhead, hikers have two choices. One trail follows the Timberline Trail west towards **Elk Cove**, winding through forests and meadows with great views over the Gorge and the Cascade peaks in Washington. There is no loop trail, so simply hike to a convenient ending point and retrace your steps.

Or, follow the Timberline Trail towards 'Gnarl Ridge', up barren rock fields for 1.2 miles. At this point, views open up over **Eliot Glacier** and onto the summit of Mt Hood. Follow **Cooper Spur Trail** uphill for a couple of hundred yards to a CCC-built stone shelter for even more expansive views to the north and east. To complete the loop, return to the Timberline Trail, and continue straight downhill on the trail to Tilly Jane Campground, one mile away. From there, it's an easy half-mile hike back to the Cloud Cap Campground and trailhead.

## Lookout Mountain

For a charming and easy hike that affords views onto Mt Hood, consider a hike up Lookout Mountain, on the high escarpments east of Mt Hood. To reach the trailhead, turn off Hwy 35 onto the USFS Rd 44 (Dufur Mill Rd), for four miles; turn south onto USFS Rd 4410 (High Prairie Rd) uphill for five miles. From this trailhead, the path to Lookout Mountain passes through lovely wildflower meadows and marshes, all the more enchanting for being so close to the top of a mountain. From the trailhead, it's an easy 1.2-mile stroll to the 6525-foot summit of Lookout Mountain, where you seem to gaze at Mt Hood eye to eye across a deep valley.

## CLIMBING

The world's second most climbed peak over 10,000 feet, after Japan's Mt Fuji, Mt Hood is accessible, relatively easy to climb, and many Oregonians feel that their lives cannot be complete without climbing it at least once. Debate still rages as to whether the first known ascent was made in 1845 or 1857. In 1867 the first women made the climb in full-length skirts, and photographs of Victorian ladies roped together on the slopes adorn the walls of the Mazama Lodge. About 10,000 people climb Mt Hood every year. It's been climbed both by a woman wearing high heels, and by a man without any legs!

This is not to say Mt Hood doesn't require technical climbing skills; every year there are always a few who manage to get killed making the ascent. Climbing is best between May and mid-July, and a typical climb from Timberline Lodge on the south side takes 10 to 12 hours. Experienced climbers who wish to organize their own climb can obtain information from the Mt Hood Recreation Association (☎ 622-3017), 68260 E Welches Rd, Welches.

### Climbing Instruction & Trips

The program director at Art of Adventure (☎ (800) 972-4270), brings her expertise from over 15 years of leading excursions for Outward Bound. Art of Adventure offers day-long climbing instruction and climbs every weekend between mid-May and July. There are also occasional climbs on weekdays. Cost is $75 each for the class and the climb.

Northwest School of Survival (☎ 668-8264), has an eight-hour climbing program for beginners. Successful completion of the program entitles students to then sign up for a trip to the summit, which may or may not be consecutive with their class. There are 15 to 20 climbs between early April and early August, and it's best to book at least two months in advance. Climbers must rent or buy their own gear, and make their own arrangements for transportation and accommodations. The cost is $88 for instruction, and $95 for the climb.

The Mazamas (☎ 227-2345), 909 NW 19th Ave, Portland, a climbing and mountaineering club founded in the late 1800s, has some climbs for beginners. Membership isn't necessary, although you should realize that this is a club, not a guide service. There are usually about 12 to 15 climbs each summer. Trip leaders volunteer; not all take beginners. Climbs for non-members cost $14, and climbers are expected to come prepared with their own gear and knowledge of how to use it. The Mazamas' multi-session climbing school in January includes a trip to the summit, and is the best deal at $125.

### Equipment Rental

In the Portland area, climbing equipment can be rented from REI at one of two locations: (☎ 283-1300), 1798 Jantzen Beach Center, or (☎ 624-8600), 7410 Bridgeport Rd in Tigard. Their $20 climbing package includes plastic boots, crampons and an ice ax. Helmets cost an extra $5.50. The same list of equipment at Oregon Mountain Community (☎ 227-1038), 60 NW Davis St, also in Portland, rents for about $20 to $24 (helmet included).

## FISHING

There's good lake fishing for families at popular and heavily stocked Trillium Lake near Government Camp. Clear Lake offers

OREGON

good rainbow and brook trout fishing, and Lost Lake has a marina and good trout fishing.

For stream fishing, the best opportunities are on the Salmon River, a southerly tributary of the Sandy River. The summer steelhead run here is the real excitement. The Salmon River is accessed from the community of Brightwood on Hwy 26, by good USFS roads and trails leading to isolated pools and rapids in deep old-growth forest. On the east side of Mt Hood, Hwy 35 follows the East Fork Hood River, which can be good fishing for rainbow trout.

The Fly Fishing Shop (☎ 622-4607), at the Hoodland Park Plaza in Welches, specializes in guided fly fishing adventures both on the upper Sandy River and in other areas of the state. Walk-in trips start at $60, float trips at $200 (for two people); fishing licenses are available here as well.

## OTHER ACTIVITIES
Three Nines Golf Course, a 27-hole course, is in Welches at The Resort at the Mountain (☎ 622-3101), 68010 E Fairway Ave.

The Race Base (☎ 272-3519), at 88220 E Government Camp Loop, rents mountain bikes at $5.50 an hour or $16 for half days.

During the summer, Mt Hood SkiBowl (☎ 272-3206) is transformed into a race course for weekend warriors. Bike rentals cost $7 to $27 (helmet and trail pass included with rental), and a chairlift up the mountain costs $2 to $3 per trip, or $12 for a full day pass. Trail passes alone cost $3. This special area is open from 11 am to 6 pm Saturday and Sunday only.

For all manner of outdoor adventures, contact The Wild Side (☎ 354-3112). Captain Tad Burke leads fishing, mountain biking, hiking, cross country skiing and combination trips. Scenic driving and photographic tours are also available.

## PLACES TO STAY
### Camping
Camping on Mt Hood makes a convenient get-away from Portland, so competition for sites can be fierce. Reservations for some campgrounds can be made by calling the Mt Hood National Forest's reservation system (☎ (800) 280-2267) between 5 am and 6 pm. Get an early start – it may take awhile to get through. Reservations can also be made by mail, 10 to 14 days in advance; obtain a reservation form from the nearest ranger district office. There is a $7.50 charge on top of the daily camping fee for making a reservation.

Fees for camping at the following sites range between $10 and $12; each of the following campgrounds offer drinking water and vault toilets, but no hook-ups.

**West Side** On the west side of Mt Hood, a number of USFS campgrounds are convenient to Hwy 26. At the base of Mt Hood is *Tollgate Campground*, one mile east of Rhododendron, a CCC-constructed campground with 15 campsites. *Camp Creek Campground*, three miles east of Rhododendron, offers 24 campsites, some of them streamside.

*Riley Horse Camp* caters to equestrians, but it's a great place for anyone to stay if you don't mind the lingering odor of horse manure. There's nearby access to several trails on Zigzag Mountain, including Ramona Falls. From Hwy 26 at Zigzag go north on Lolo Pass Rd for four miles, turn east on USFS Rd 1825, and then make a right onto USFS Rd 380. Sites cost $9. Camping is free at *McNeil Campground*, right next door, although there's no potable water.

Up on Mt Hood, the popular *Still Creek Campground*, is just half a mile east of

Government Camp, and offers 27 campsites. From here, all the recreation on Mt Hood is in your backyard. Even more popular is *Trillium Campground*, on the shores of beautiful Trillium Lake. Fifty-five campsites with running water, a fishing pier and a boat ramp, are located in a post-card setting with Mt Hood rising above a placid lake.

**East Side** East of Mt Hood, Hwy 35 cuts off and heads toward Hood River, while Hwy 26 continues to Madras. On Hwy 35, the *Robin Hood Campground* is 12 miles north of Government Camp on the East Fork of Hood River. *Sherwood Campground* is four miles further north along the river.

Eight miles southeast of Government Camp on Hwy 26, the *Frog Lake Campground* offers 33 campsites along the shores of a tiny lake; at *Clear Lake Campground*, 10 miles south of Government Camp on Hwy 26, there are 28 campsites and good fishing.

**RV Campgrounds** *Mt Hood RV Village* (☎ 622-4011, 253-9445 in Portland, (800) 255-3069), 65000 E Hwy 26 near Brightwood, is a huge resort complex with over 420 sites, the only RV campground on Mt Hood with hook-ups. Facilities include showers, flush toilets, indoor swimming pool, playground, electronic game arcade and laundry. Rates are $18 a night for full hook-ups.

**Hostels**
*Silcox Hut* (☎ (800) 547-1406, 231-5400 in Portland) is a rustic, European-style alpine hut on Timberline's ski slopes, a mile above the lodge. Recently reopened after standing empty for over 20 years, Silcox Hut sleeps 24 in dormitory-style accommodations. Check in at Timberline Lodge, and then hike or take a snowcat to the hut. For $50 you get lodging in a bunkroom, roundtrip snowcat transportation, dinner and breakfast. Lodgers should bring their own sleeping bag. Call the Timberline Sales Office (☎ 295-1827) for reservations.

**B&Bs**
In Welches, the *Old Welches Inn B&B* (☎ 622-3754), 26401 E Welches Rd, makes use of the original Welches Hotel, built in 1890. Rooms in the main lodge range from $65 to $75 a night; a separate one-bedroom cottage is $100.

**Hotels**
The very green *Shamrock Deluxe Motel* (☎ 622-4911, 622-4003), 12 miles east of Sandy at 59550 E Hwy 26, is one of the best deals in the area, with basic room packages starting at $29, and a room with fireplace, kitchen and cable TV going for $59. *Snowline Motel* (☎ 622-3137), 73260 SE Hwy 26, in Rhododendron, offers basic motel rooms at $40/50; some units have fireplaces.

With one exception, lodging in Government Camp is pretty expensive; and is often hard to find with short notice. The *Huckleberry Inn* (☎ 272-3325), 88611 E Government Camp Loop, offers several lodging options, from dormitory-style rooms ($16), to deluxe rooms that sleep up to 10 people ($90).

The newest and most attractive lodging is *Mt Hood Inn* (☎ 272-3205, (800) 443-7777), 87450 E Government Camp Loop, with suites and spa facilities. Rooms start at $90. *Thunderhead Lodge Condominiums* (☎ 272-3368), 87451 E Government Camp Loop, offers an outdoor heated swimming pool, and full kitchens. Rooms range from $80 to $180.

On the east side of Mt Hood is the handsome *Inn at Cooper Spur* (☎ 352-6692), 10755 Cooper Spur Rd, south of the community of Mt Hood. Rooms are available in two-bedroom cabins or in rooms in the lodge. Single/double rooms start at $62/72, and cabins cost $118 to $128. Facilities include hot tubs and tennis courts. Inn at Cooper Spur is 19 miles north of Government Camp on Hwy 35, and 25 miles north of Hood River.

**Resorts**
The *Timberline Lodge* (☎ 272-3311, 231-7979 in Portland), Timberline, OR 97028,

OREGON

five miles north of Government Camp, offers so many options in the way of accommodation packages with ski facilities, instruction and meals, that it's best to call or write to obtain their latest price leaflet. Basic room rates run $60 for a room with two bunk beds to $160 for a large room with a fireplace. Different package deals are available throughout the year, including a 'stay the night and ski free' deal, in which a complimentary lift ticket is thrown in on certain nights. See Timberline Lodge, earlier in this chapter, for more information.

*The Resort at the Mountain* (☎ 622-3101), 68010 E Fairway Ave, in Welches, is a large resort that focuses on its 27-hole golf course by summer, and ski and winter recreation packages in winter. Facilities include a swimming pool, tennis courts and two restaurants. Rooms begin at $87 for a studio; fireplace rooms begin at $155 and suites at $180.

## PLACES TO EAT

Highway 26 up to Mt Hood from Portland offers a number of restaurants known mostly for their hearty breakfasts and afternoon cocktail bars, both favorites with the skiing crowd. There's espresso and pastries at *Don Guido's* (☎ 622-5141), on Hwy 26 in Rhododendron. At the *Barlow Trail Inn* (☎ 622-3122), also in Rhododendron, breakfast is served all day, and is a favorite before hitting the slopes. *Alpine Hut Restaurant & Lounge* (☎ 622-4618), 73665 E Hwy 26, serves breakfast, lunch and dinner, and is well established as a skiers' pit stop. At Welches, stop at *Michael's Bread & Breakfast* (☎ 622-5333), one block south of Hwy 26 on E Welches Rd, for fresh-baked cinnamon rolls, cookies and bread.

Food in Government Camp is pretty basic. The *Huckleberry Inn* (☎ 272-3325), 88611 Government Camp Loop, is a 24-hour family restaurant featuring home-style cooking and a steakhouse in the evenings; huckleberry pies are a specialty. *Mt Hood Brewing Company & Brew Pub* (☎ 272-3724), 87304 E Government Camp Loop,

is Mt Hood's only brewery, and a very pleasant place it is. Their English-style beers go well with the very tasty 'gourmet' pizzas served here: the goat's cheese and pesto pizza is $9. A number of sandwiches and other light meals are also available.

Five miles north at Timberline Lodge (☎ 272-3311), there are five different restaurants. In the day lodge, *Wy'east Kitchen* has snacks for skiers; the *Country Store* serves espresso drinks, desserts and pastries. In the old lodge, the *Blue Ox Deli* is graced by a tiled mosaic of the legendary Paul Bunyan and his ox Babe, and serves soups, sandwiches and light meals. At the *Ram's Head Bar* light snacks are available along with drinks. Continental-style food is served in the beautiful log-beamed *Cascade Dining Room*. Prices range from $15 to $23 for entrees like bouillabaisse and nightly salmon specials.

If you're on the slopes, it's worth remembering that *Silcox Hut*, a mile above Timberline Lodge, serves food and beverages to passers-by between 11 am and 3 pm.

## GETTING THERE & AWAY

### Bus

Although Greyhound offers bus services to Mt Hood, the timing of the buses isn't really convenient for recreationalists. There's only one bus a day, and that leaves Portland late in the afternoon; the return bus comes down the mountain just after noon. The fare is $15 one way.

**Ski Buses** During the peak season which is from mid-December onwards, there are two buses daily to Mt Hood Meadows (☎ 287-5438), one coming from Beaverton, and the other from Salem. You will find various pick-up points in the Portland area; it's best to call to determine the one nearest you. The cost is \$49 for combination roundtrip transportation and lift ticket.

Timberline Lodge (☎ 231-7979) operates buses from the Portland area to the lodge from December to March. Departure points are the G I Joe's stores in Gresham, 700 NW Eastman Parkway, Beaverton, 3485 SW Cedar Hills Blvd, and Portland, 3900 SE 82nd Ave. A combination roundtrip transportation and lift ticket can be purchased at any G I Joe's store through their Ticketmaster (☎ 224-4440) outlets.

# Willamette Valley

Between Portland and Eugene stretches the Willamette Valley, the incredibly fertile agricultural basin that was the destination of the Oregon Trail pioneers. A hundred and fifty years after the migration, the Willamette Valley is still the center of Oregon with three quarters of the state's population living here. While the upper valley near Portland is filling with suburbs, much of the rest of the valley is still quiet and rural, with slumbering old villages tucked into green landscapes and vineyard-covered countryside.

The historic sites in the northern valley and the Yamhill County vineyards are in easy reach of Portland for day-trips, though B&B inns may entice travelers for country weekends. In the mid-valley is Salem, the state capital, bustling with politicians and issues, and center to a sprawling network of suburbs. Corvallis and Eugene, in the southern valley, are dominated by the state's two universities. Both are dynamic and engaging small cities with good, inexpensive food and lodging.

Most travelers zoom up and down the Willamette Valley on I-5. It's a pity, because side roads lead through beautiful farmland to sites as varied as vineyards, monasteries, historic settlements and charming old towns whose pedigree extends back to the 1840s. Because the valley is largely flat and criss-crossed with slow-moving roads, the Willamette is a great place to explore on bicycle.

## HISTORY

The Willamette Valley was home to a large number of Native Americans before the arrival of settlers. The Chinook and Calapooian tribes were the most numerous until their numbers were decimated by diseases like small pox inadvertently introduced by White settlers. By the time the Calapooians were gathered onto Grande Ronde Reservation, they only numbered 42 members

and were gradually amalgamated into the tribal mix on the reservation; there are no Calapooian speakers today.

The first White settlement in the valley was in an area called French Prairie, in the triangle between St Louis, St Paul and Champoeg, where French-Canadian trappers, retiring from the Hudson's Bay Company, established a small farming community in the 1820s. As US pioneers began to arrive and vie for land, the area soon became the scene of British/US rivalries.

Under a treaty signed in 1818, Oregon was part of an area held in joint occupancy by Britain and the USA. At a historic meeting in Champoeg in May of 1843, a report was read which proposed the establishment of a US-style self-government. It was defeated, as most of the settlers were loyal to the Hudson's Bay Company, and many of the French-Canadians withdrew from the meeting in disgust at the US settlers' audacity.

The remaining settlers regrouped. Joe Meek, the legendary trapper and mountain man, brought the issue to a head by exclaiming, 'Who's for a divide? All in favor of the report and an organization follow me.' He drew a line in the sand, and the 'divide' commenced: those for the USA stood on one side; those favoring the British status quo stood on the other. When the active participants were counted, 50 men stood on each side of the divide. Two French-Canadians, Etienne Lucier and FX Matthieu, after a heated conversation, decided to join the US side of the divide. The jubilant winners formed a committee to organize a program of government. Thereafter, the British claim to lands in the Pacific Northwest was increasingly insecure. Had the vote gone differently, Oregon and Washington might now be part of Canada.

By 1855, over 50,000 people made the

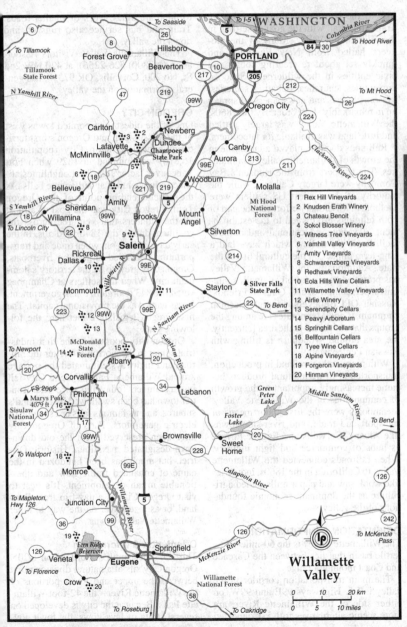

1 Rex Hill Vineyards
2 Knudsen Erath Winery
3 Chateau Benoit
4 Sokol Blosser Winery
5 Witness Tree Vineyards
6 Yamhill Valley Vineyards
7 Amity Vineyards
8 Schwarzenberg Vineyards
9 Redhawk Vineyards
10 Eola Hills Wine Cellars
11 Willamette Valley Vineyards
12 Airlie Winery
13 Serendipity Cellars
14 Peavy Arboretum
15 Springhill Cellars
16 Bellfountain Cellars
17 Tyee Wine Cellars
18 Alpine Vineyards
19 Forgeron Vineyards
20 Hinman Vineyards

Willamette Valley

0    10    20 km
0    5    10 miles

trek to the Northwest along the Oregon Trail, almost all with the goal of settling in the Willamette Valley. Many of the pioneers hailed from New England, and quickly set about re-creating social and civic entities in the wilderness. Schools, universities, churches, debating societies, Masonic lodges and newspapers all sprang up in remarkably short order. By the 1860s, the Willamette Valley was largely settled and little land was available for latecomers.

Religious doctrine played a large role in the growth of Willamette Valley communities. The trappers from the Hudson's Bay Company were largely Catholic, while the majority of the earliest US settlers were Methodist. Missionary efforts on the part of both religious groups led to the establishment of various educational and cultural facilities in the valley, which have had a long-term impact on the cultural life of the state. Additionally, the Willamette Valley has provided haven for other small, sometimes persecuted sects. Quaker Friends, Russian Old Believers, utopian German communists and Mennonites are among the groups that emigrated to the area (currently, the area around Woodburn is filling with Russian Pentecostals).

With more and more land in production, transportation of agricultural products became increasingly important to the growth of communities in the Willamette Valley. Steamboats were the first major means of transport and trade; and river-side towns like Albany, Corvallis and Eugene thrived as hubs of commerce and light industry. When railroads connected the Willamette Valley to California in the 1860s, industries like wool, saw and paper mills joined agriculture as the dominant economic foundations of the valley.

## ORIENTATION & INFORMATION

The Willamette Valley is the 60-mile-wide, fertile basin that lies between the Cascade and Coast mountain ranges.

The main transportation corridor in the valley is I-5. Highways 99E and 99W, on either side of the Willamette River, are more scenic alternatives to I-5. Connected

to them are a lace work of smaller roads. Train and bus service also runs up and down the valley.

The Willamette Valley Visitors Association (☎ (800) 526-2256), at 420 NW 2nd St, No 200, Corvallis, OR 97330, has general information on the valley.

## OREGON CITY

One of the oldest incorporated towns west of the Mississippi, and Oregon's first territorial capital, Oregon City (population 16,810) was founded in 1829 when Fort Vancouver factor John McLoughlin established a lumber mill at Willamette Falls. As the official ending-point of the Oregon Trail, Oregon City was the goal of almost all the pioneers that ventured across the continent during the 1840s and 50s. In the early days of Oregon, when trade and transportation depended largely on riverboats, Oregon City grew to be the territory's dominant city. When the settlers at Champoeg voted in 1843 to organize self-government, it was named as the provisional capital. The first Oregon legislature met here the following year.

Oregon City boomed as the first industrial center in the Northwest. After the railroad and highways eliminated the portage around Willamette Falls, Oregon City fell into a slumber. Today, this once-vital frontier town has been swallowed by Portland's suburbs, and its famous falls is a snaggle of electric generators. Parts of Oregon City have been preserved, with the old downtown designated a National Historic District, but much has been bulldozed in the name of enhanced traffic flow and questionable urban development. It's best to visit Oregon City as a day-trip from Portland, or as a stopover on the way to other Willamette Valley towns.

### Orientation & Information

Thirteen miles south of Portland on I-205, Oregon City sits at a natural division point between the upper and lower portions of the Willamette River – the 42-foot Willamette Falls. Because the city is developed on several strata of lava flows, the town gov-

**The Father of Oregon**

Most of the early pioneers who crossed the Oregon Trail arrived in Oregon without any provisions left from their long journey. The thriving British fur-trading post at Fort Vancouver, on the north bank of the Columbia, was self-sufficient as far as grain and livestock production was concerned, and Hudson's Bay Company factor John McLoughlin was generous with the US settlers for credit on food and seed stock. This was in direct contradiction with Hudson's Bay Company policy, and in 1845 McLoughlin was relieved of his duties as chief factor. He chose to move to his land holdings in Oregon City, where he planned to retire amongst the settlers he had generously aided.

However, distrust of the former British agent and general narrow-mindedness led the US citizens to treat their former benefactor poorly. Although many of the settlers still owed McLoughlin money for goods and services they had received at Fort Vancouver, the provisional government took away McLoughlin's land holdings in Oregon City after he moved there. McLoughlin, now often referred to as the Father of Oregon, eventually became a US citizen; however, his land claim was not returned to his heirs until five years after his death in 1857. ∎

OREGON

ernment has built a municipal elevator between Railroad and 7th Sts that gives free rides between the upper residential areas and the river level commercial district.

The Oregon City Chamber of Commerce (☎ 656-1619), is at 500 Abernethy Rd, Oregon City, OR 97045. The post office (☎ 656-0821) is at 606 15th St.

### McLoughlin House

When John McLoughlin moved to Oregon City in 1845, he built this home for his family. Now a museum (☎ 656-5146), 713 Center St, the house originally stood in downtown. In 1909 it was slated for demolition, and concerned citizens raised money to move the house up onto the bluff where it now stands.

At the time the house was built, most settlers lived in shanties and log cabins, and this two-story clapboard home with three bedrooms was often referred to as McLoughlin's Mansion. Over the years, McLoughlin had accumulated considerable wealth, and his solid, simple good taste is evident throughout. The house is maintained as it would have been when the

McLoughlins lived here. The museum is definitely worth a side trip if you are interested in period furnishings or life in early Oregon.

Immediately next door is the **Barclay House**, built in 1849 by Dr Forbes Barclay, one of McLoughlin's closest friends. It now serves as a gift shop and ticket office for the McLoughlin House museum. Between the two houses, in an ivy-covered plot, are the graves of McLoughlin and his wife Marguerite.

The McLoughlin House is open from 10 am to 4 pm, Tuesday to Saturday, and 1 to 4 pm on Sunday. It's closed Mondays, holidays and the month of January. Admission is adults/seniors $3/2.50, children ages six to 17, $1.50, and children under six are free. You can ask for a tour, or explore on your own.

### Clackamas County History Museum

Only one floor of this imposing modern structure is open to the public, and much of the display space is taken up with a paean to hydroelectricity. There's a good exhibit on Native American basketry, though, and the photos of what Willamette Falls once looked like are interesting. The museum (☎ 655-5574), 211 Tumwater Drive, is open from 10 am to 4 pm, Tuesday to Friday, and 1 to 4 pm, Saturday and Sunday; admission is adults/seniors $3/2, children under 12, $1.50. Admission price includes a tour through the **Stevens-Crawford House** (☎ 655-2866), 603 6th St, a 1907 home owned by a pioneer Oregon family. The house now preserves everyday items from the homes of early settlers.

### End of the Oregon Trail Interpretive Center

This brand new facility (☎ 657-9336), at Washington and Abernethy Rds, is at the literal end of the Oregon Trail. This museum and interpretive center commemorates the struggle of the Oregon pioneers on their overland journey, the challenges they faced when they arrived in Oregon and the plight of the Native Americans they displaced. It's open daily from 10 am to 5 pm; admission is $2 for adults, $1.50 for seniors and $1 for students under 18.

### Willamette Falls

The Willamette Falls was a center of fishing and trade for many Indians of the northern Willamette Valley. When the salmon migrated up the Willamette River, the falls was a very active place, as many journeyed to the area to net and harpoon fish, which were dried for later use.

Today, see the city's most prominent natural landmark from Willamette Falls Vista, along Hwy 99W, immediately west of downtown. The water just below the falls is still popular with salmon anglers; it's also spectacular in spring when thousands of migrating lamprey eels climb up the rocks.

The impoundment on top of the falls was built to divert water to mills and hydroelectric generators, which now utterly dominate the river and the waterfall.

### Special Events

The Oregon Trail Pageant (☎ 657-0988) is held the last three weeks of July and the first week of August at 7:15 pm at Clacka-

mas Community College, 19600 S Molalla Ave. On weekends, actors, dancers and musicians gather to perform *Oregon Fever*. This outdoor show incorporates a two-act play about pioneers on the Oregon Trail, accompanied by fiddlers and dancers performing period tunes, and story-telling and talks on pioneer history. There are no shows on Sunday or Monday. Tickets are $9 for adults and $5 for children five to 15 years of age.

### Places to Stay & Eat

For those who want to spend the night, there are several B&Bs and relatively inexpensive motels. Directly across from the McLoughlin House is the *Hydrangea B&B* (☎ 650-4421), 716 Center St, a 1908 home with two guest rooms for $60. Also near the museum is *Jagger House B&B* (☎ 657-7820), 512 6th St, an 1880 home with three guest rooms ranging from $65 to $75.

Down near the Willamette, the *Inn of the Oregon Trail* (☎ 656-2089), 416 S McLoughlin Ave, is an ornate 1867 farmhouse with a nicely landscaped garden. Rooms at this B&B range from $48 to $85. On the main floor is Fellows Restaurant, open for lunch only.

The *Lewis Motel* (☎ 656-7052), 18710 S Hwy 99E, is a well-maintained, older hotel south of town with single/double rooms for $32/35. For something a bit more central to freeway exits, try the *Val-U Inn Motel* (☎ 655-7141, (800) 443-7777), 1900 Clackamette Drive; rooms are $56/60.

Oregon City is hardly the culinary capital of Oregon. For coffee and lunchtime sandwiches go to *Back to the Grind* (☎ 655-1130), 710 Washington St, a pleasant cafe near the museum area. Otherwise, there's fast food out by the freeway exits.

### Getting There & Away

Portland's Tri-Met bus system (☎ 238-7433) offers service to Oregon City. Bus No 79 leaves Portland every half hour throughout the day; pick up/drop off in Oregon City is at the Oregon City Transit Center on 11th St between McLoughlin and Main Sts. The one-way fare is $1.30.

## AROUND OREGON CITY
### Champoeg State Park
One of the very first settlements in Oregon, Champoeg (apparently derived from the French *champ* for field) was situated on a flood plain along a bend in the Willamette River. After the historic 1843 vote, the town continued to grow as the era of riverboat travel brought increasing trade to the Willamette Valley. The French-Canadians who established the town, mill and fur warehouses at Champoeg didn't anticipate the fury of the Willamette River. In December 1861 an enormous flood swept through the Willamette drainage. By the time the flood waters reached Champoeg, 27 feet of water rushed over the flood plain on which the town was built. After the flood had subsided, only three buildings of the old town remained.

Champoeg was never rebuilt. In 1901, the area was designated a state park. Today, the sites of many long-gone buildings are noted with plaques. With 107 acres of old-growth woodland and grassy meadow, campsites and nature trails, beautiful Champoeg State Park is deservedly well loved.

Ten miles of hiking and biking trails wind through the park. The hiking-only trail hugs the banks of the Willamette River, while the paved biking trail curves through the woods. Both offer excellent access to old-growth hardwood forests.

**Orientation & Information** Champoeg State Park is 25 miles south of Portland, off I-5 exit No 278. It's 19 miles southeast of Oregon City. There's a $3 day-use fee per vehicle.

Near the entrance to the park, the Champoeg Visitors Center (☎ 678-1251), 8239 Champoeg Rd NE, serves as an interpretive center. Besides explaining events that led up to the famous vote at Champoeg with displays and films, the center also provides information about the Calapooians and the flood patterns of the Willamette River. The visitors center and gift shop are open daily from 9 am to 5 pm.

**Pioneer Mothers Memorial Cabin Museum** Closer to the Willamette, near the location of the old village of Champoeg, the local Daughters of the American Revolution have built a reconstruction of a pioneer-era log cabin. The cabin/museum (☎ 633-2237) is filled with artifacts that were brought across the Oregon Trail, and other articles of frontier life. It's open from noon to 5 pm, Wednesday to Sunday; closed December and January.

**Places to Stay** Campsites at Champoeg State Park are much sought after due to the park's verdant setting and proximity to Portland. There are 46 sites with hook-ups; an additional 30 non-hook-up sites accommodate overflow. Shower facilities are also available. Call the visitors center for more information (no reservations, though).

### Aurora
Established in 1856 by Dr William Keil and his followers, the remains of this utopian colony of a small German Protestant sect are a reminder of the many and varied motives of people who came across the Oregon Trail to settle. Nowadays, Aurora (population 620) is famous for its many antique stores. If you have an eye for collectibles and antiques, then you could easily while away several hours here.

To reach Aurora from the south, take I-5 exit No 278 and go east for three miles. For a more scenic route Hwy 99E also runs through Aurora; it's 13 miles southwest of Oregon City.

**Old Aurora Colony Museum** This five-building museum complex (☎ 678-5754), at 2nd and Liberty Sts, tells the story of the utopian community in artifacts and exhibits. Included in the museum is a number of the old musical instruments, historic quilts, old tools and conveyances, a log cabin and a pioneer garden. Guided tours are offered three times a day in summer, at 11 am, 1 and 3 pm. Entry is $2.50 adults, $1 children under 12. The museum is open from 10 am to 4:30 pm, Tuesday to Saturday and 1 to 4:30 pm on Sunday, May to September.

OREGON

## The Aurora Colony

Dr William Keil, born in Prussia in 1811 (where he trained as a tailor before emigrating to the USA in 1831), had many near-fanatical interests, including the search for mystical cures for diseases (his title of 'Doctor' was self-conferred), Protestant communal religion, botany, magnetism and the theater. After developing his religious following in Pittsburgh, PA, and Bethel, MO, he decided to relocate the colony to the West Coast. In 1855 Keil and his followers migrated over the Oregon Trail. A wagon containing the embalmed body of Keil's son Willie led the wagon train. Keil had promised the young boy that he would lead the westward migration, but the 19-year-old died of fever before the journey commenced. Keil embalmed the body with home-distilled alcohol, and set his casket at the front of the convey. The migrants had no trouble with Native American hostility along the route, apparently due to the quality of the food and alcohol that the commune members doled out – or perhaps because the Indians were wary of the bizarre funeral procession.

The Aurora Colony, as the commune was called, was for many years very prosperous and successful. At its peak, the colony owned 15,000 acres of land. The town of Aurora contained a number of shops, flour mills, a tannery, bakery, a school and a hotel, as well as homes laid out exactly on a streetless grid (only two houses per block, and only footpaths leading between homes).

The only radical social belief in his fundamentalist brand of Christianity was the communal sharing of property. The members of the colony were admonished to live somewhat apart from non-communists, but the community relied on selling their products to the general public for income. Furniture, food stuffs, leather goods and cloth from Aurora artisans found a ready market in the Willamette Valley (Aurora sausages were especially prized). The large Aurora Colony Hotel was on the stage line between Portland and California, and was a great favorite with travelers because of the food and drink served there. Another somewhat quirky feature of the commune was the emphasis placed on music. Adherents were encouraged to sing and play instruments; the colony's brass band was a popular institution at public gatherings both in Aurora and around the state.

However, Aurora Colony was unable to operate closely with regular Oregon society and yet maintain the kinds of ideals and adherence that demand isolation. Particularly nettlesome to the commune members was Keil's reluctance to allow young followers to marry and start families. After Keil's death in 1877, the colony dissolved into the larger rural culture of the Willamette Valley. ∎

The rest of the year it's open from 1 to 4:30 pm, Thursday to Sunday.

## YAMHILL COUNTY WINE COUNTRY

The valleys between the rolling oak-forested hills of Yamhill County have been prime agricultural real estate since the days of the Oregon Trail pioneers. But the valley waited until 1965, passing through various agricultural stages, for the event that may have revealed the region's true calling: the planting of wine grapes near Dundee.

In 30 years, the wine industry in Oregon has grown from the crazy notion of a few zealous students of enology to a multimillion dollar industry. The wine country is convenient to Portland: an hour's drive leads to dozens of vineyards in a landscape of rolling hills, oak forests and lazy streams. The beauty and tranquility of the valley, as well as a number of high-quality B&Bs and restaurants, make this a favorite weekend destination.

## Orientation

Yamhill County is just southwest of the Portland metro area. Highways 99W and 18 are the main roads through the wine country; watch for the blue roadside signs pointing to wineries. Newberg is 15 miles south of Portland on Hwy 99W. McMinnville, on Hwy 18, is another 25 miles south.

## Information

The Yamhill County Wineries Association (☎ 434-5814) can brief you on the wines and vineyards of the area. Their free map of Yamhill County wineries is an excellent resource, with a brief discussion of individual wineries and of local restaurants and lodgings.

Contact the Newberg Area Chamber of Commerce (☎ 538-2014), 115 N Washington St, Newberg, OR 97132, or the McMinnville Chamber of Commerce (☎ 472-6196) at 417 N Adams St, McMinnville, OR 97128, for information.

For medical emergencies, contact the McMinnville Community Hospital (☎ 472-6131), 603 S Baker St.

## Getting There & Away

Two buses a day link Newberg and McMinnville to Portland and the Oregon Coast. In Newberg, catch the bus (☎ 538-5517) at 211 E 1st St. In McMinnville, the bus stops at the Baker Street Market (☎ 434-9472), 523 S Baker St. A one-way fare from Portland to McMinnville is $6.25.

## Wineries

There are presently over 30 established wineries in Yamhill County, with many more starting up each year. So unless you have a lot of time on your hands – and a designated driver – you will need to pick and choose to make up your own touring itinerary.

The following wineries you won't want to miss because of their quality wine or appealing location, or both. However, by all means do stop at other wineries: you'll get a friendly welcome from proud winemakers no matter where you visit. If you have time for only one stop, it ought to be at the **Oregon Wine Tasting Room** (☎ 843-3787), eight miles south of McMinnville on Hwy 18 at Bellevue, where at least 30 Oregon wines are available for tasting and hundreds are for sale; it's open from 11 am to 5:30 pm daily.

**Sokol Blosser Winery** (☎ 864-2282, (800) 582-6668), 5000 Sokol Blosser Lane, Dundee, has some of the very best wines in the state and a small gift shop; it's open from 11 am to 5 pm daily. **Knudsen Erath** (☎ 538-3318), also in Dundee on Worden Hill Rd, is a topnotch winery with a great pinot noir; it's open from 10:30 am to 5:30 pm daily May 15 to October 15 and from 11 am to 5 pm the rest of the year.

Loved by tourists for its 'vineyard lifestyle', **Rex Hill Vineyards** (☎ 538-0666), at 30835 N Hwy 99W, Newberg, is an upscale winery with a tasting room; it's open from 11 am to 5 pm daily April to December; during February and March, it's open Friday, Saturday and Sunday. **Yamhill Valley Vineyards** (☎ 843-3100), 16250 SW Oldsville Rd, McMinnville, is open from 11 am to 5 pm daily June to November and Saturday and Sunday only from March to May. Try the pinot gris.

**Witness Tree Vineyards** (☎ 585-7874), 7111 Spring Valley Rd NW, Salem, is just south of Lafayette on Hwy 221. The facilities stay open from noon to 5 pm on weekends and holidays (except Thanksgiving), March to Christmas Eve. Low-key and informal, **Amity Vineyards** (☎ 835-2362) is at 18150 Amity Vineyards Rd SE, Amity. Try their hearty wines from noon to 5 pm daily, May to December, weekends only February to April. **Chateau Benoit** (☎ 864-2991), 6580 NE Mineral Springs Rd, Carlton, offers a good sauvignon blanc, great views and lovely tasting room. The hours are 10 am to 5 pm daily.

OREGON

**The Wine Country**
The state's first grape vine was planted by the Jesuits at St Paul in the 1830s, but it took 150 years for savvy viticulturists to realize Oregon's winemaking potential. Oregon's mild climate, and long but not terribly hot summers, allow some of the world's most noble but fussy grapes to thrive here.

Chardonnay and Pinot Noir grapes – the grapes of France's Burgundy region – flourish here. Oregon's chardonnays are generally light-textured and lemony white wines in the French style, lacking the thick oakiness of Californian and Australian chardonnays. Also much praised are Oregon pinot noir wines, delicate red wines that develop a refined fruitiness from mellow Oregon summers.

Pinot Gris, another European grape suited to a cool climate, also produce white wines of distinction. Riesling grapes are amongst the most widely planted grapes in the area, reflecting the sweeter wine tastes of the 1970s, when many of the vineyards were planted. In Oregon, these grapes produce a pleasantly fruity, off-dry wine. Less successful are wines made from Cabernet Sauvignon and Merlot grape varieties, which normally need more sun and heat to ripen their complex flavors than northern Oregon usually affords.

Most vineyards are family-owned and operated. Nearly all vineyards welcome visitors to their tasting rooms, which are sometimes grand edifices, but just as often homey affairs tucked into the corner of fermentation rooms. Oregon's so-called 'wine country,' is convenient to Portland: an hour's drive into Yamhill County leads to dozens of vineyards in a landscape of rolling hills, oak forests, and lazy streams. For those who would like to spend more time in the countryside, break off from the main highways and follow the blue signs to vineyards and wineries around Newberg, Dundee, Lafayette, Carlton and McMinnville. ■

**Organized Tours** A number of tour companies in Portland offer personalized tours of the vineyards. Oregon Vineyard Tours (☎ 786-0732) 2926 SW Periander St, specializes in wine-country tours. Try also Ecotours (☎ 245-1428), 1906 SW Iowa St, and Van Go Tours (☎ 292-2085), SW Barnes Rd.

**Newberg**
Newberg (population 13,735) is a fast-growing commercial hub at the edge of Portland suburbs and the beginnings of the wine country. Founded originally as a Quaker settlement, little of the town's original quiet ways remain; instead, strip malls and shopping centers now lend the town its allure. The slightly make-believe world of wine-making has yet to transform Newberg from a scruffy milltown to the cultural center it would like to be. Dundee, officially two miles west on Hwy 99W, is pretty much just an adjunct to Newberg's sprawl.

George Fox College, founded in 1885 as a Quaker institute of higher education, is a private college with an enrollment of 1200 students. Herbert Hoover, the 31st president of the USA, spent his youth in Newberg.

In addition to wine grapes, the locale is famous for its plums and nut production. Local produce is often available from roadside stands and markets.

**Hoover-Minthorn House** This restored 1881 home (☎ 538-6629), 115 S River St, is the boyhood home of Herbert Hoover. His uncle, Dr Henry Minthorn, helped to raise young Hoover between 1884 and 1889, and the family home – the oldest remaining in Newberg – is now a museum of period furnishings and early Oregon history. It's open from 1 to 4 pm daily, March to November, and 1 to 4 pm Saturday and Sunday the rest of the year; admission is $1.50 adults, $1 children and seniors.

**Places to Stay** Probably the cheapest place to stay in the wine country, the *Town & Country Motel* (☎ 538-2800) is a no-frills hotel on the east side of town; single/double rooms are $44/48. The *Shilo Inn* (☎ 537-0303), 501 Sitka Ave, is Newberg's upscale lodging choice with rooms ranging from $59 to $79, and offers a pool, hot tub and guest laundry; pets are allowed.

*Partridge Farm B&B* (☎ 538-2050), 4300 E Portland Rd, offers four guest rooms in a Victorian farmhouse, with rates ranging from $60 to $90. Outside are landscaped gardens and pastures filled with llamas and game birds. *Springbrook Hazelnut Farm* (☎ 538-4606), 30295 N Hwy 99W, is a 70-acre estate with rooms in either an old carriage house or in the guest wing of the large historic farmhouse. Guests have access to the swimming pool and tennis court. Rooms range from $74 to $125.

**Places to Eat** Start the day with espresso and fresh pastries at the *Coffee Cottage* (☎ 5385126), 808 E Hancock St. At *The Noodle* (☎ 537-0507), 2320 Portland Rd, just about every form of pasta is served; prices range from $7 to $11 for a full dinner.

The best places to eat in the area are in Dundee, just down the road from Newberg. The *Red Hills Cafe* (☎ 538-8224), 976 Hwy 99W, is a real find. Unassuming and informal, the restaurant serves a changing menu featuring local products. Prices for dishes like pork tenderloin stuffed with prunes and fennel, or beef with wild mushrooms average around $15. *Tina's* (☎ 538-8880), 760 Hwy 99W, considers itself a 'French country' restaurant featuring local lamb, rabbit, vegetables and seafood. Dishes like roast duck with green olives go for $17. Both these restaurants offer vegetarian entrees and have extensive wine lists featuring local vintages.

**McMinnville**

In many ways, McMinnville (population 19,175) is a gratuitous suburb without the accompanying city to justify the sprawl. However, there's no denying that McMinnville is the center of the local wine industry. Like Newberg, though, McMinnville awaits the gentrifying effects of the lucrative, upmarket wine trade. The *Spruce Goose*, built by Howard Hughes out of Oregon lumber and reckoned to be the world's largest airplane, is housed here, grounded at a CIA-linked airbase, but is currently not available for tours. That, along with a couple of good restaurants, pleasant hotels and plenty of B&Bs, pretty much encapsulates the attraction of the town.

**Activities** A favorite weekend tour for cyclists is to ride the backroads of the wine country; pick up maps at the Newberg or McMinnville visitors center. However, as neither Newberg nor McMinnville offer rental bicycles, you'll need to bring your own **bicycle** or rent one in Portland.

Get a bird's eye view of the wine country from Vista Balloon Adventures (☎ 625-7385), 575 SE Mansfield St, Sherwood. From April to November, **hot-air balloons** lift off from Newberg and drift across the vineyards of Yamhill County. The flight, which includes a champagne breakfast, lifts off at dawn seven days a week, and costs $350 per couple, or $600 for a group of four. Advance reservations are required.

**Special Events** Held at Linfield College in McMinnville the last weekend of July, the International Pinot Noir Celebration (☎ 472-8964) is one of the largest wine fairs in the Northwest, and increasingly an important testing ground for pinot noir wines from all over the world. The festival continues for three days, with tastings, discussions and winery tours included in the event. Registration for the entire event is $350 a person; however, on the final Sunday of the celebration, there's a public tasting with tickets set at $35. Write to the International Pinot Noir Celebration, Box 1310, McMinnville, OR 97128, for registration details

**Places to Stay** Inexpensive and perfectly satisfactory, the *Safari Motor Inn* (☎ 472-5187), 345 N Hwy 99W, offers a spa and exercise facility, with single/double rooms at $42/47. At the *Paragon Motel* (☎ 472-9493), 2065 Hwy 99W, there's a pool, and pets are OK; rooms are $40/80. McMinnville's nicest lodging is the *Best Western Vineyard Inn* (☎ 472-4900), 2035 S Hwy 99W, with an indoor pool, spa, guest laundry and mini suites. Rooms begin at $62.

The chamber of commerce has a complete listing of B&Bs. Here are three of the nicest. Downtown, *Steiger Haus B&B* (☎ 472-0821), 360 Wilson St, is a new home offering five bedrooms with private baths; rates range from $65 to $90. Out in the country, *Mattey House* (☎ 434-5058), 10221 NE Mattey Lane, is nestled in a vineyard. The 1869 farmhouse has four rooms ranging from $65 to $75. *Youngberg Hill Farm Inn* (☎ 472-2727), 10660 Youngberg Hill Rd, is a working farm. This immense home sits on a 700-acre estate filled with sheep, deer and grape vines. Rooms are $75 to $100.

**Places to Eat** Get wired for a day out in the wine country at *Cornerstone Coffee* (☎ 472-4471), 403 E 3rd St; it's McMinnville's locally owned coffee roaster.

For dinner, there's only one place to go. *Nick's Italian Cafe* (☎ 434-4471), 521 E 3rd St, is justifiably renowned as one of the best restaurants in the state. Nick's doesn't come by its reputation by being upscale. In fact, this old diner hasn't changed much in decor since the 1930s. But the food is the thing; the five-course set menu at $29 a person (call ahead for vegetarian meals) includes an appetizer, bowl of incredible minestrone, salad, pasta course and entree. Add to this a really comprehensive wine menu filled with local wines, and you're looking at a great gastronomic evening. Nick's isn't a secret, and seating is limited, so call ahead for reservations. On evenings other than Saturday, you can order a la carte.

The only question in McMinnville is where to eat lunch. *Sir Hinklemans* (☎ 472-1309), 729 E 3rd St, offers sandwiches, salads and pasta in a 1907 home, with seating on the patio in good weather; they're also open for dinner if you can't get into Nick's (or can't face five courses of Italian food). Best bet is to fix a picnic and head for the vineyards.

Six miles south of McMinnville, at the crossroads called Bellevue, is a trio of businesses under a single roof. *Augustine's* (☎ 843-3225) above the Oregon Wine Tasting Room and Lawrence Gallery, is an excellent restaurant, featuring local meat and produce and an extensive local wine list. Shrimp and scallop Florentine goes for $15; leg of lamb with mushroom polenta is $17.

**Things to Buy** Most wineries have pre-boxed bottles for sale, which make good gifts for wine-drinking friends. If you're buying wine for yourself, wineries will also arrange the shipping for case lots of wine. Many wineries also feature a small gift shop with other food-related items from Oregon.

At Bellevue, six miles south of McMinnville on Hwy 18, is Lawrence Gallery (☎ 843-3633), part of a wine-tasting room and restaurant complex. This famed gallery features local and regional artists and craftspeople. Paintings of the wine country and art glass seem to be the dominant products, although there's also jewelry and photography; check out the outdoor sculpture garden.

Lafayette, between Dundee and McMinnville on Hwy 99W, has turned its 1910, three-story school into Oregon's largest antique market. At the Schoolhouse Antique Mall (☎ 864-2720), 748 3rd Ave, over a hundred different dealers share space, dividing up the school's eight original classrooms into wild collections of old collectibles, furniture and whatnot.

**SALEM**

The Oregon state capital, Salem (population 111,375) is a sprawling and slightly soulless city filled with gray marble buildings and bureaucrats: it's the sort of place that residents brag about being a good place to raise a family.

For the traveler, there are relics to visit,

like the oldest university west of the Rocky Mountains, and the box-like state capitol. A couple of mammoth private estates from the 1880s are preserved as public parks, gardens and museums. Downtown is pleasant enough; its unquestioned earnestness makes the city center seem like a museum of the 1950s.

Established in 1840, Salem was the second mission founded by the Methodist missionary Jason Lee in the middle Willamette Valley. As the Methodist's efforts at converting the Calapooians hadn't been very successful at the first mission (they killed off the entire tribe with smallpox), in Salem the missionaries decided to establish an institution for schooling the children of the White settlers. The Oregon Institute held its first class in 1842; by 1853 the school had been charted as Willamette University.

In 1851 the legislature voted to move the capital from Oregon City to Salem. However, when the disgruntled members of the legislature convened in Salem in 1853, they found only half a dozen families living there, with very little in the way of accommodations or facilities. They voted to move the capital to Corvallis, which they did in 1855. Legislators were even less charmed with Corvallis than with Salem, and the capital moved back and remained in Salem thereafter.

## Orientation & Information
Salem is a very confusing place to drive, with roads coming into the city at many angles, and with a numbering system that defies easy understanding. Most of the city lies on the east side of the Willamette River. State St, which winds through the city, divides the city into north and south halves. Therefore, an address with a SE tag is south of State St, and east of the Willamette. Highways 22, 213, 219, 99E and I-5 all access the city.

**Tourist Offices** Salem Convention & Visitors Association (☎ 581-4325, (800) 874-7012) is at 1313 Mill St SE, Salem, OR 97310. The Oregon State Tourism Division

(☎ 373-1270, (800) 547-7842) is at 775 Summer St, Salem, OR 97310.

**Post** The main post office (☎ 370-4700) is at 1050 25 St SE; however, the Pringle Park office (☎ 370-4774), 410 Mill St, is more convenient to downtown visitors.

**Bookstores** Salem's best independent bookstore is Jackson's Books (☎ 399-8694), at 320 Liberty St SE (also known as Pacific Hwy).

**Media** The Salem *Statesman Journal* is the city's daily paper. Oregon Public Radio is heard on 91.5 FM.

**Laundry** The State St Laundromat (☎ 371-6130), 2515 State St, offers drop-off service as well as dry cleaning.

**Medical Services** Salem Memorial Hospital (☎ 370-5200), is at 665 Winter St SE.

## Oregon State Capitol
The state's first capital building was burned by incendiaries in 1856, and a domed neo-Greek edifice was built to replace it. However, that capital building burned in 1935, and the current capitol was completed in 1939. Designed by Francis Keally, the capitol (☎ 378-4423), at Court and Capitol Sts, is very much a product of the 1930s. Bauhaus and art-deco influences are apparent, especially in the strident bas-relief in the front statuary and the hat-box-like cupola. The building is faced with gray Vermont marble, and the interior is lined with brown travertine from Montana. The legislative chambers are paneled with Oregon oak and walnut.

The most notable features of the Oregon capitol are four WPA-era murals lining the interior of the rotunda, each depicting a turning point in Oregon history. An earthquake in March 1993 severely cracked the interior of the rotunda, including the murals. The area is currently closed to visitors, but the murals can be seen from a viewing point. Surmounting the dome is the gleaming Oregon Pioneer, a 23-foot-

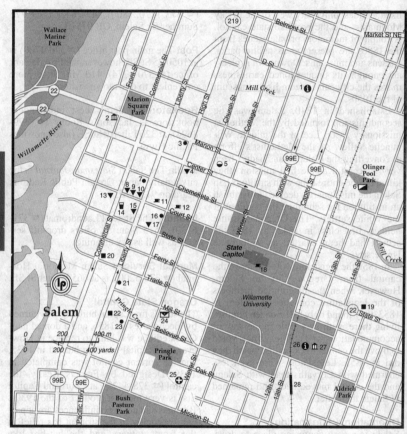

high gilded statue depicting a stylized early male settler. The capitol grounds are landscaped with native trees and plants of Oregon.

The building is open to the public on weekdays from 8 am to 5 pm, Saturday from 9 am to 4 pm, and Sunday from noon to 4 pm. From Memorial Day to Labor Day tours are offered free of charge, and run more or less hourly. Call ahead to check the schedule, or to arrange a tour during other times of the year. There's a gift shop on the main floor with Oregon products, gifts and tour information.

## Willamette University

Just south of the capitol, Willamette University (☎ 370-6231), 900 State St, is apparently the oldest collegiate institution in North America west of the Missouri. The oldest remaining building on the campus is Waller Hall, built between 1864 and 1867. Willamette University, currently with 2500 students, is well-respected for its liberal arts undergraduate program and for its law school.

## Bush Pasture Park

One of Oregon's leading citizens of the late

| PLACES TO STAY | | 13 | Night Deposit | 5 | Greyhound Bus Depot |
|---|---|---|---|---|---|
| 19 | Salem Grand Motel | 14 | Willamette Brew Pub | 6 | Olinger Pool |
| 20 | Execulodge | 15 | Dahlia at the Reed | 7 | Anderson's Sporting |
| 22 | City Center Motel | 17 | Jonathon's Oyster Bar | | Goods |
| | | 18 | Oasis Cafe | 16 | Cherriots Bus Office |
| PLACES TO EAT | | | | 21 | Jackson's Books |
| 4 | Arbor Cafe | OTHER | | 23 | Salem Cinema |
| 8 | Great Harvest Bakery | 1 | Oregon State Tourism | 24 | Post Office |
| 9 | Dairy Lunch Cafe | | Division | 25 | Salem Memorial Hospital |
| 10 | Indian Palace | 2 | Gilbert House Children's | 26 | Tourist Office |
| 11 | Governor's Cup | | Museum | 27 | Mission Mill Village |
| 12 | The Beanery | 3 | Salem Center Movieland | 28 | Amtrak Station |

**OREGON**

19th century was Asahel Bush, who established a newspaper in Oregon City in 1851, but moved his presses to Salem in 1853 along with the state capital. Bush was a true firebrand, advocating the rights of workers and farmers against the merchant classes and calling the Republican politicians 'lickspittles and toadies of official whiggery.'

He began to build his Salem mansion in 1877, by which time he was a highly successful banker. Surrounded by acres of gardens and a greenhouse, the Bush House was designed to be a self-sufficient farm. The estate and mansion are now preserved as the Bush Pasture Park (☎ 363-4714), 600 Mission St SE. The extensive grounds, now public gardens, include a large rose garden, picnic areas and hiking trails.

**Bush House**, the rambling Italianate mansion, is open as a museum and showplace of Victorian design. Note the marble fireplaces, 10 in all. Most of the wallpaper is original from the 1887 construction, and was made in France. The mansion is open from 2 to 5 pm Tuesday to Sunday, October to April and from noon to 5 pm the rest of the year. The house is open for tours only, which leave on the half hour; $2 for adults, students and seniors $1.50.

The reconstructed livery stable is the **Bush Barn Art Center** (☎ 581-2228), its main floor given over to the work of local artists and craftspeople; it's a good place to look for hand-crafted gifts and moderately priced art. The upstairs gallery displays touring art shows. It's open from 10 am to 5 pm Tuesday to Friday, and from 1 to 5 pm Saturday and Sunday.

**Deepwood Estate**
Adjacent to the Bush Estate, this Queen Anne mansion (☎ 363-1825), 1116 Mission St SE, was built in 1894 on six acres of grounds. Topped by turrets and bejeweled with decorative moldings, the house manages to be fanciful and imposing at the same time. Especially beautiful are the stained-glass windows. The estate grounds contain a nature trail and a formal English tea garden complete with gazebo. It's open for tours daily, May to September, from noon to 4:30 pm, except Saturday when the grounds are reserved for weddings. During the winter the estate is open from 1 to 4 pm on Sunday, Monday, Wednesday and Friday. Admission is $2 adults, $1.50 seniors and students; there's free access to the grounds during daylight hours, except on holidays.

**Gilbert House Children's Museum**
Built to honor Salem native A J Gilbert, who invented the Erector Set, this hands-on children's center (☎ 371-3631), 116 Marion St NE, is half a technology and science museum, and half a playroom. There's a wide selection of things to do here, from the Wet & Wild Room, where there's bubble-making and a mock hydroelectric dam, to the Mask Room, where kids can fashion their own masks, to a puppet theater, where children can put on shows.

The museum is open from 10 am to 5 pm, Tuesday to Saturday, and Sunday, Monday and holidays, noon to 4 pm. Admission is $4 per person; seniors ages 60 and older, or anyone visiting during economy hours (3 to 5 pm) pay only $3.

### Mission Mill Village

This five-acre museum complex (☎ 585-7012), 1313 Mill St SE, houses the visitors center, a regional museum, a number of restored pioneer homes and a massive, water-powered wool mill preserved as a museum.

A clutch of old pioneer buildings face onto a grassy plaza. They include **Jason Lee Home & Parsonage** built in 1841. Also collected here is an old church and the J D Boon home built in 1847. Each of these buildings is maintained pretty much as it was in the 1840s.

The **Thomas Kay Woolen Mill** was built in 1889, and was powered by the Mill Creek, which still runs through the grounds and still turns water wheels in the power house. Guided tours of the mill follow the process of washing, carding, dying and weaving the wool. Tours of the above two sites depart on the hour; tickets are adult/senior/students $5/4.50/2. Note: the tour of the mill and the tour of the pioneer homes are each one hour long, and are held consecutively, the ticket good for both.

The **Marion Museum of History** (☎ 364-2128), 260 12th St SE, has a good exhibit on the local Calapooian culture and society, as well as pioneer artifacts. One display tells the story of Salem's long-gone Chinatown, and another examines the history of the region's hop industry. It's open from 9:30 am to 4:30 pm, Tuesday to Saturday. Admission is $1, or 50c for seniors and students.

### Activities

You can rent cross-country and downhill skis, as well as snowboards, at Anderson's Sporting Goods (☎ 364-4400), 241 Liberty St NE, before heading off to Santiam Pass, 85 miles east on Hwy 20. Rent rafts, kayaks and canoes from Santiam Outfitters (☎ 585-2628), 1595 Cottage St NE.

Olinger Pool (☎ 588-6332), 1310 A St NE, right by Mill Creek, is the city's indoor pool. For the outdoors, go to Walker Pool (☎ 588-6334) near the junior high school at 1075 8th St NW. Salem Golf Club (☎ 363-6652), 2025 Golf Course Rd S, is semi-private, and Salem's oldest. Call ahead to find out public playing hours.

### Special Events

The biggest party of the year in Salem is the Oregon State Fair (☎ 378-3247) held the 12 days prior to Labor Day. There's lots going on: livestock shows, wine judging and tasting, amusement rides, flower shows, a petting zoo, concerts and horse races are among the activities offered. Take 17th St north to access the fairgrounds and Expo Center; admission is $6 for adults, $1 for students.

Over two hundred artists from around the country bring their work to the Salem Art Fair & Festival (☎ 581-2228), the state's largest juried art show. The free art fair is held the third weekend of July, at the Bush Pasture Park and Bush Barn Art Center. For the weekend, the estate grounds are turned into a kaleidoscope of art demonstrations, performance art, children's activities, craft goods and food carts.

### Places to Stay

**Camping** The closest campground to Salem is the *KOA Salem* (☎ 581-6736, (800) 826-9605), 3700 Hagers Grove Rd SE, with 202 campsites, showers, market and a separate tenting area. Fees range from $13.50 for tents to $18 for full hook-ups.

**B&Bs** The *State House B&B* (☎ 588-1340), 2146 State St, offers six guest rooms, two in a back cottage, ranging from $45 to $65. There's also a penthouse room in the main house.

**Hotels** To stay close to the capitol, try the *Salem Grand Motel* (☎ 581-2466), 1555 State St, with single/double rooms for

$29/38 and an indoor pool. *City Center Motel* (☎ 364-0121, (800) 289-0121), 510 Liberty St SE, right downtown, has rooms for $38/40; pets are welcome, and there is guest laundry. The *Execulodge* (☎ 363-4123, (800) 452-7879), 200 Commercial St SE, is also right downtown; rooms are $60/65. There's an outdoor pool and meeting rooms.

There is a large concentration of hotels at I-5's Market St exit No 256. *Best Western New Kings Inn* (☎ 581-1559), 3658 Market St NE, offers rooms at $53/57, an indoor pool, spa facilities, play area and restaurant. The *Super 8* (☎ 370-8888, (800) 800-8000), 1288 Hawthorne Ave NE, allows pets and there's an outdoor pool; rates are $48/52. The *Quality Inn* (☎ 370-7888), 3301 Market St NE, has full-restaurant and small convention facilities. There's an indoor pool, guest laundry and suites; rooms range from $70 to $115.

## Places to Eat

**Budget** Straight out of the 1930s, *Dairy Lunch Cafe* (☎ 363-6433), 347 Court St, is the place to go for an old-fashioned breakfast, or for a lunch featuring fresh cheeses. At *Great Harvest Bakery* (☎ 363-4697), 339 Court St NE, you can get a cup of coffee and fresh-baked muffins and breads. *Off Center Cafe* (☎ 363-9245), 1741 Center St NE, offers sandwiches and healthy, often vegetarian meals. The diner in the basement of the capital building, *Oasis Cafe* (☎ 371-6483), at Court and Capitol Sts, is operated by the same owners, and offers unexpectedly tasty food. At *Heliotrope Natural Foods* (☎ 362-5487), 2060 Market St NE, there are vitamins, health foods, organic produce and deli items. The buffet at the *Indian Palace* (☎ 371-4808), 377 Court St NE, offers a good lunch value at $5.95 for all you can eat; they also offer tandoori-baked meats.

**Middle** If you're in the area on Sunday, then the brunch at *Eola Winery* (☎ 623-2405), 501 S Pacific Hwy (99W), in Rickreall, 11 miles west of Salem on Hwy 22, is an amazing feast. This $12.95, all-you-can-

eat brunch offers omelets, Belgian waffles, fruit, desserts and wondrous fried potatoes, accompanied by local wines and champagne. The food is miles better than the tired fare offered at most brunches. Brunch is served from 10 am to 2 pm on Sundays only. For a bit of upscale dining, go to the *Arbor Cafe* (☎ 588-2353), 380 High St NE, where there's quiche, pasta and salads.

**Top End** At the *Night Deposit* (☎ 585-5588), 195 Commercial St NE, the menu is a pan-Pacific blending of grilled steak ($15), seafood, raspberry pistachio chicken ($14) and Asian preparations; after dinner, head into the lounge, which has the air of a coy singles bar. *Jonathon's Oyster Bar* (☎ 362-7219), 445 State St, is a popular watering hole; fill up on jambalaya for $12 or local oysters at 75c followed by a bottle from their good selection of wines. *Dahlia at the Reed* (☎ 363-5414), 189 Liberty St NE, is in Salem's old opera house, which has gone through a questionable refurbishing. The Dahlia offers one of Salem's most enterprising, eclectic menus. Hazelnut sole goes for $12, while beef medallions Madagascar is $15.

## Entertainment

**Coffeehouses** A real hangout is *Allann Bros Beanery* (☎ 399-7220), 545 Court St NE. In summer, tables spill into the street; young staffers buzz with political intrigue, speculation and caffeine. Just down the street is the *Governor's Cup* (☎ 581-9675), 471 Court St NE, with a slightly more hushed coffeehouse scene.

**Brewpubs** The *Willamette Brew Pub* (☎ 363-8779), 120 Commercial St NE, brews a number of English-style ales, though the specialty here is the marionberry ale, brewed with just a whisper of Salem's trademark berry. In the back of the pub are a number of pool tables; out front there's live music on weekends and informal dining.

**Cinema** *Salem Cinema* (☎ 378-7676), 445 High St SE, is as close to an arts cinema as

Salem gets. Foreign and offbeat films are usually featured. The theaters at *Salem Center Movieland* (☎ 588-3456), at Marion and High Sts, are central and offer first-run films.

**Theater** *Pentacle Theatre* (☎ 364-7200), 324 52nd Ave NW, is Salem's semi-professional theater company. Their 10-play season is a highlight of the city's cultural life.

**Live Music** *LB Day Amphitheatre* (☎ 378-3247), in the state fairgrounds near Lana Ave and Silverton Rd, is the local concert facility for touring music groups. Call to see what's up-coming.

Hear the local groups on the weekends at *The Down Under* (☎ 364-2914), 3170 Commercial St SE, or at *Westside Station* (☎ 363-8012) 610 Edgewater St NW.

### Getting There & Away
**Air** Horizon Airlines (☎ (800) 547-9308) operates flights between Portland and Salem Airport (☎ 588-6314). The airport is just east of I-5 exit No 253 on Hwy 22. The Hut Airport Shuttle (☎ 363-8059) provides service to/from town.

**Bus** There are eight Greyhound buses a day between Portland and Salem; one-way fare is $7.50. There's one bus a day between Salem and Bend, and five a day between Salem and Newport ($21 one way). The depot (☎ 362-2428) is at 450 Church St NE.

**Train** Amtrak offers one train a day both north and south out of Salem, running between Seattle and Sacramento. The station (☎ 588-1551) is at 13th and Oak Sts.

**Car** For a rental, contact Budget (☎ 362-0041), 3065 Ryan Drive; Enterprise Rent-A-Car (☎ 364-1991), 808 SE 12th St; or Key Car Rental (☎ 378-0849), 1095 Commercial SE.

### Getting Around
Cherriots (☎ 588-2877) buses serve the Salem metropolitan area. Standard fare is 75c, though buses are free in the downtown area. Maps, free permits and instructions for carrying bikes on buses can be obtained by stopping at the main office, 183 High St NE. There is no bus service on Sunday.

Call Salem Yellow Cab Co (☎ 362-2411) for a lift.

## AROUND SALEM
### Iris Gardens
Willamette Valley's most beautiful crops are undoubtedly grown by the many flower and bulb nurseries in the area. Two iris farms near Salem are among the largest in the world, and are open to visitors in the spring.

**Cooley's Gardens** (☎ 873-5463), 11553 Silverton Rd NE, Silverton, opens its nursery free to the public in mid May and early June when iris blossoms cover the 250-acre farm. To reach Cooley's Gardens, take Hwy 213 from Salem toward Silverton; the farm is two miles west of Silverton, or 11 miles east of Salem. **Schreiner's Iris Gardens** (☎ 393-3232), about two miles north of Salem at 3625 Quinaby Rd, Salem, opens 10 acres of its grounds for free iris-viewing from mid-May through the first week of July. Both these nurseries are open daily from 8 am to dusk during the viewing season.

### Mount Angel
The little town of Mount Angel (population 2930) with its ersatz Bavarian-style storefronts and its lovely Benedictine Abbey, is like an Old-World holdover in the Oregon countryside. Visit during Octoberfest for maximum effect. Another interesting sideline, the town's old Catholic church, built in 1910, with mural-covered walls, was badly damaged in the 1993 Willamette Valley earthquake, which was centered near here.

Contact the Mount Angel Chamber of Commerce (☎ 845-9440), 5 N Garfield St, for information.

**Mount Angel Abbey** Founded in 1882, this Benedictine monastery (☎ 845-3030), off College St, sits on a 300-foot butte in the middle of the Willamette Valley. The lovely setting alone justifies a side trip to the abbey. Cascade volcanic peaks rise above the mottled cropland and paths wind through old forests, past red-brick buildings and manicured lawns. Tours of the abbey are available by prior arrangement, or you can pick up a walking tour map at the gift shop. Besides the church buildings, there's an interesting collection of ancient manuscripts on display in the library. Lodging is available at the abbey for those seeking a spiritual retreat.

**Mount Angel Octoberfest** One of the state's largest harvest festivals is held in Mount Angel. It was the founding Swiss Catholic settlers that helped launch the hop-growing industry in the Willamette Valley. What better place to celebrate beer, sausage and sauerkraut?

The Octoberfest has grown substantially in the years since Oregon has developed a viable wine and microbrewery industry to legitimize the festival's Old World pretensions. Lots of German food stands, brass bands and dancers, craft displays and beer and wine make this a fun day-trip. A bus from the downtown takes visitors up the hill to the abbey for free tours of the grounds and facilities.

When you go, watch out for traffic: thousands of people turn up for Octoberfest, slowing traffic on local narrow roads to a standstill. Try to avoid the weekend, or at least go early to find a parking spot.

Mt Angel Octoberfest is held Thursday to Sunday on the third weekend of September. No admission charged. Mt Angel is 18 miles northeast of Salem on Hwy 214.

**Wineries**
Some of Oregon's finest wines are grown across the Willamette River from Salem in the Eola Hills. Just as to the north, there are many wineries throughout this area to explore. **Redhawk Vineyard** (☎ 362-1596), 2995 Michigan City NW, Salem, is noted for its great pinot noir. The tasting room is open on weekends from noon to 5 pm, May to September.

**Eola Hills Wine Cellars** (☎ 623-2405), 501 S Pacific Hwy (99W), Rickreall, has one of the least-glamorous tasting rooms, but some of the best wines in the state, especially a marvelous chardonnay. It's open from noon to 5 pm daily.

**Schwarzenberg Vineyards** (☎ 623-6420), 11975 Smithfield Rd, Dallas, offers a nice, lemony chardonnay in a beautiful setting; it's open from 11 am to 5 pm Tuesday to Sunday.

On an imposing hill top on the east side of the river, **Willamette Valley Vineyards** (☎ 588-9463), 8800 Enchanted Way, Turner, is Oregon's only publicly traded winery. Visit from 11 am to 6 pm daily.

**Silver Falls State Park**
Oregon's largest, 8700-acre Silver Falls State Park (☎ 873-8681), 26 miles east of Salem on Hwy 214, is an easy day-trip from Portland, Salem and Eugene. After a rainy spring morning, when the sun comes out, it's hard to resist the temptation to drive to Silver Falls State Park to see the falls in torrent, and walk amongst wildflowers in moist and shady forests.

In the 19th century, the tremendous volume of falling water surrounded by virgin forest caught the attention of logging interests, and a saw mill was built near South Falls. The area was lumbered, and by the time the NPS surveyed the area in the 1920s and 30s, the judgment was that Silver Falls had simply been too altered by humans to qualify as a national park. The land was subsequently handed over to Oregon, which designated the area as a state park in the 1940s. Thankfully, the forest has largely healed, and this magnificent park is a busy place year around.

There's a $3 fee per vehicle, per day for use of the park. If you plan only to hike the loop trail, you can avoid paying the fee by commencing your hike at the North Falls trailhead. There's no fee to use that parking lot; there aren't any facilities either.

**Hiking & Biking** The most famous hike in the park is the **Trail of Ten Falls Loop**, a seven-mile, roundtrip trail that joins all of the major falls in the park. The trail isn't particularly difficult, though the spray from the waterfalls can make parts of the trail slippery and muddy.

The principal point of access to the trail system is off Hwy 214, either at South Falls, near the picnic and camping areas on the South Fork Silver Creek, or at North Falls, near the northern boundary of the park on the North Fork Silver Creek.

What makes the waterfalls in the park so magical is the fact that you can walk behind several of them. North Falls plunges 136 feet over a lava flow, and South Falls drops 177 feet. The spray from the falling water has over the millennia eroded away the softer subsoils beneath the lava flows, creating hollow caverns behind the rocky edge of the waterfall.

Between falls, the trail passes through thick forests filled with a variety of ferns, moss and wildflowers. Watch for mule deer and beaver, and grand displays of butterflies.

Mountain bikers have their own four-mile trail along the canyon walls. Begin the trail at the South Falls day use area.

**Picnicking** The vast day use area near South Falls is a deservedly popular place, almost too much so on summer weekends. Silver Creek is impounded here to form a small lake, a favorite with young waders and swimmers. Mature trees tower overhead, and picnic tables are scattered throughout the forest. The WPA built a number of stone shelters and the South Falls Nature Lodge during the Depression, which are now on the National Register of Historic Places.

**Places to Stay** The main campground (☎ 873-8681) is just upstream from the South Falls day-use area. There are over a hundred campsites, half of which are reserved for tent campers. Showers, wheelchair-accessible rest rooms and a playground make this one of the most sought after campgrounds in the Willamette Valley. Note that no reservations are taken.

## ALBANY

Probably no town in Oregon presents such an ugly face to the freeway as Albany (population 34,125). As signs on I-5 announce the town, the freeway passes an enormous pulp mill surrounded by mountains of wood chips belching out clouds of foul, sulfurous-smelling air. Nearby is a chemical plant, infamous in the 1980s for its toxic-waste pools.

But if you are willing to avert your eyes and nose and turn into downtown Albany, the intrusions of the 20th-century industrial landscape fall away. Once a thriving river port and rail center, the affluence and pride of Albany is easily seen in its civic and residential architecture. Many grand homes still line the streets of the old town center; even modest homes were constructed with panache and flourish. The old downtown area was bypassed when modern highways were built through the Willamette Valley, leaving the old residential and commercial districts largely intact.

If your penchant is for antiques, then Albany is your town; so many businesses downtown are antique stores that the entire district seems like one antique mall.

### Orientation

Albany is 22 miles south of Salem on I-5 and is connected to Corvallis, 13 miles southwest, by Hwy 20. The city center is about two miles west of the freeway exits. About 350 homes and buildings in downtown Albany are registered as National Historic Sites, making it one of the most concentrated havens of historic architecture in the Northwest. On a nice day, a walk through the old homes district is a pleasant way to spend an hour or two.

The visitors center offers maps and resources for self-guided tours of the historic residential and commercial districts, as well as maps of the area's many covered bridges. Ask for their free map of 10 covered bridges. A suggested 2½-hour auto tour from Albany leads to five of them.

## Information

The Albany Visitors Association (☎ 928-0911, (800) 526-2256), is at 300 2nd Ave SW, PO Box 965, Albany, OR 97321. An information kiosk at 8th Ave and Ellsworth St explains the history of Albany and charts walking tours.

The post office (☎ 967-7927) is at 525 2nd Ave SW. The Rainbow's End Book Company (☎ 926-3867), 250 Broadalbin St SW, is a very good general bookstore with an outstanding selection of regional guides and histories. The Albany *Democrat-Herald* is one of the state's oldest papers,

and public radio can be heard on 103.1 FM or 550 AM.

Dirty clothes go to the Cleanery (☎ 928-2405), 2504 Santiam Rd SE, and Albany's General Hospital (☎ 926-2244) is at 1046 6th Ave SW.

## Historic Districts

The citizens of Albany have taken great care in the restoration of these old buildings. In general, period-house colors, landscaping and ornamentation has been reproduced with an eye toward historic authenticity.

**OREGON**

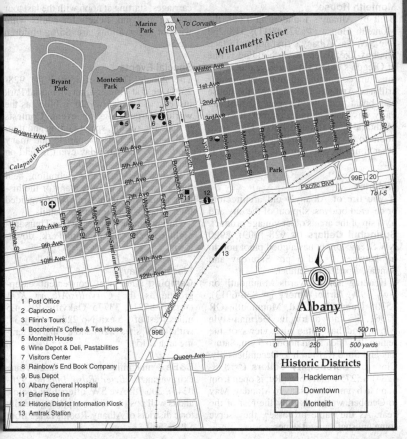

1 Post Office
2 Capriccio
3 Flinn's Tours
4 Boccherini's Coffee & Tea House
5 Monteith House
6 Wine Depot & Deli, Pastabilities
7 Visitors Center
8 Rainbow's End Book Company
9 Bus Depot
10 Albany General Hospital
11 Brier Rose Inn
12 Historic District Information Kiosk
13 Amtrak Station

**Albany**

**Historic Districts**
Hackleman
Downtown
Monteith

The **Downtown District** is the old commercial and industrial area. The **Monteith District**, southwest of downtown, was developed by the town's founders – Walter and Thomas Montieth in 1848. These Scottish brothers, along with other prosperous merchants, comprised the 'Republican' side of town. Democratic settler Abram Hackleman laid out an adjoining neighborhood in 1853 for the working-class settlers. Rivalries between the **Hackleman District**, just east of downtown, and the Monteith District continued throughout the 19th century.

### Monteith House

Built by Albany's founders in 1849, the Monteith House (☎ 928-0911), 518 2nd Ave SW, was Albany's first home. In fact, this box-like, federal-style building is one of Oregon's oldest structures, and is now a museum containing displays of pioneer artifacts. Among other features, the house can boast that the Oregon Republican Party was founded under its roof. It's open Memorial Day through Labor Day, from noon to 4 pm, Wednesday to Sunday, other times by appointment; admission is free.

### Wineries

If you tire of Albany's old architecture or covered bridges, slip out of the city and try a sip of the area's other vintage product. **Springhill Cellars** (☎ 928-1009), 2920 NW Scenic Drive, has a good pinot noir to try between 1 and 5 pm Saturday and Sunday, April to December.

Heading north towards Monmouth on Hwy 99W, **Airlie Winery** (☎ 838-6013), 15305 Dunn Forest Rd, Monmouth, OR 97361, is known for its German-style wines, and has some nice views of the region. It's open from noon to 5 pm, Saturday and Sunday, March to December only. Close by, **Serendipity Cellars** (☎ 838-4284), 15275 Dunn Forest Rd, is open from noon to 6 pm, Wednesday to Monday, May to October, weekends only the rest of the year. As the name professes, they serve some unusual varietal wines.

### Activities

**Swimming** There's an outdoor pool at Swanson Center (☎ 967-4323), 705 Railroad St SE.

**Golf** The Golf Club of Oregon (☎ 928-8338), 905 NW Spring Hill Drive, is an 18-hole course across the Willamette River.

### Organized Tours

Tours of the historic districts can be arranged by contacting Flinn's Tours (☎ 928-5008), 222 1st Ave W. On Sundays in July and August, Flinn's offers hourly tours of the historic districts in horse-drawn carriages, starting at noon with the last tour leaving at 4 pm; tickets for adults with/without reservations are $5/6; children are $4.

### Special Events

The Albany Timber Carnival (☎ 928-2391), held at Timber-Linn Memorial Park just east of I-5 on Hwy 20, is billed as the world's largest logging event. Contests include log-rolling, speed-cutting and tree-scaling. There's also a parade and many food carts. The three-day event is held on the Fourth of July weekend.

During the Victorian Celebration, held the last weekend in July, many of the historic homes in Albany are open for guided tours. The visitors center has details.

During summer, there are free Thursday-night concerts at Monteith Park, downtown.

### Places to Stay

**Camping** The most convenient campground is the *Corvallis/Albany KOA* (☎ 967-8521), 33775 Oakville Rd, 4.5 miles west of I-5 exit No 228 on Hwy 34, with 92 RV sites ($20) and a separate tenting area ($15).

**B&Bs** A magnificent, 1880s Queen Anne extravaganza, *Brier Rose Inn* (☎ 926-0345), 206 7th Ave SW, offers four rooms, and is well positioned for exploring the historic districts of Albany. Rooms range from $49 to $69.

**Hotels** Along old Hwy 99E (Pacific Blvd) are a number of older, inexpensive hotels. The *Star Dust Motel* (☎ 926-4233), 2735 Pacific Blvd SE, is just across from a park. Some rooms have kitchenettes, and pets are allowed; single/double rates are $50/55. The *Comfort Inn* (☎ 928-0921), 251 Airport Rd SE, offers a covered swimming pool and spa facilities; rooms are $59/64.

The *Best Western Pony Soldier Motor Inn* (☎ 928-6322, (800) 634-7669), 315 Airport Rd SE, has a pool, meeting rooms and guest laundry; rates are $62/68.

**Places to Eat**
A good place to fuel up in the morning is *Boccherini's Coffee & Tea House* (☎ 926-5703), 208 1st Ave SW. They also have sandwiches and salads at lunchtime. In the Two Rivers Market the *Wine Depot & Deli* (☎ 967-9499), 300 2nd Ave SW, prepares deli sandwiches and salads. In the same lobby *Pastabilities* serves up a wide range of pasta dishes. Lunch or dinner at either location is in the $6 range.

One of Albany's best loved and most noted restaurants is *Novak's Hungarian Paprikas* (☎ 967-9488), 2835 Santiam Rd SE. Specializing in central European dishes, Novak's is known for its good sausages, sweet and sour cabbage and great desserts. For lunch, you'll spend around $6; at dinner there's both a light menu ($7 range), and full Hungarian-style dinners from $8 to $14.

For Italian cuisine in a historic storefront, head to *Capriccio* (☎ 924-9932), 442 1st Ave SW. Dishes like gnocchi with pesto go for $11.50, stuffed chicken with rosemary for $12.50.

**Getting There & Away**
Five Greyhound buses run between Portland, Albany and Eugene. There is also a once-daily service both to Klamath Falls and to Bend. The bus depot (☎ 926-2711), is at 108 4th Ave SE.

Amtrak's *Coast Starlight* running between Seattle and Sacramento stops once daily in Albany, the northbound train at 1:20 pm, the southbound at 3:32 pm. The station (☎ 928-0885) is at 110 10th Ave SW.

To rent a vehicle, contact Oregon Automotive Rental Services (☎ 926-7617), 181 34th Ave SW.

**Getting Around**
Albany Transit System (☎ 967-4301), 250 Broadalbin St SW, in City Hall, operates city buses for 50c on weekdays. The city of Albany also operates the Linn-Benton Loop System (☎ 967-4318) that runs buses weekdays between Albany and Corvallis for 85c. Buses make stops at Oregon State University in Corvallis and Linn-Benton Community College, six miles south of Albany on Hwy 99. The bus also stops outside of Albany's City Hall at Broadway and 2nd St. Bicycles are welcome on the loop free of charge, no permit needed; ask the driver for assistance.

For a cab call Timber Town Taxi (☎ 926-5588).

**CORVALLIS**
Home to Oregon State University (OSU), Corvallis (population 45,470) is a pleasant town at the base of the Coast Range, coursed by the Willamette River and surrounded by miles of farms, orchards and vineyards. The shops and vintage storefronts in the old, tree-lined downtown are busy, filled with bakeries, bookstores and cafes. If this sounds kind of idyllic, well, it kind of *is* idyllic in Corvallis: publications have rated the small city as one of the most livable 'micropolitan' cities, based on safety, environment, housing and education.

It's certainly hard to imagine a more prototypic university town. Over half of the city's population studies or works at the university, and another substantial percentage works at the Hewlitt Packard plant north of town. What's left of the citizenry is seemingly busy making espressos, selling bikes and keeping all the lawns and trees tended.

For the traveler, Corvallis is an easy

OREGON

**PLACES TO STAY**
1   Harrison House B&B
16  Econo Lodge
20  Madison Inn B&B
23  Towne House Motor Inn

**PLACES TO EAT**
2   Tam Tip Thai Cuisine
3   Bombs Away Cafe
5   Young's Kitchen
6   Java Rama
7   Clodfelters
12  Michael's Landing
13  McMenimans
24  Valley Restaurant
29  New Morning Bakery
32  Old World Deli
33  The Beanery

**OTHER**
4   Gilfillin Auditorium
8   Nearly Normals
9   Memorial Union
10  Linn-Benton Loop Bus Stop
11  Gill Coliseum, Homer Museum
14  Visitors Center
15  Linn-Benton Loop Bus Stop
17  Book Bin
18  Greyhound Bus Depot
19  Corvallis Arts Center
21  Corvallis Transit Office
22  Hertz Rent-A-Car
25  Squirrel Tavern
26  Peak Sports
27  Anderson's Sporting Goods
28  Peacock Tavern
30  Grass Roots Books
31  Post Office

To Peavy Arboretum,
McDonald State Forest

Washington Park

Willamette River

To Airport

Pioneer Park

Avery Park

Central Park

Oregon State University

Corvallis

Parker Stadium

Oak Creek

place to spend a day drinking coffee, browsing in bookstores, watching students and waiting for dinner in one of many diverse restaurants. It's also a good base from which to explore this part of Oregon: as implied in its name, Corvallis is at the 'heart of the valley.'

### Orientation & Information
Corvallis is at the junction of Hwys 20, 34 and 99W, along the west banks of the Willamette River. It's 43 miles between Corvallis and Eugene on Hwy 99W; it's 13 miles from Corvallis to Albany.

**Tourist Office** The Corvallis Convention & Visitors Bureau (☎ 757-1544, (800) 334-8118), at 420 NW 2nd St, has the details on the city and the annual festivities.

**Post** The post office (☎ 758-14121) is at 311 SW 2nd St.

**Bookstores** The Oregon State University Bookstore (☎ 737-4323), is at 2301 SW Jefferson Way, in Memorial Union. For a good selection of alternative books, magazines and music, go to Grass Roots Books (☎ 754-7668), 227 SW 2nd St. The Book Bin (☎ 752-0040), 351 NW Jackson Ave, is the town's best used-book store.

**Media** Oregon Public Broadcasting has one of its studios in Corvallis. Listen to it on 103.1 FM or 550 AM. The OSU student newspaper, the *Barometer*, is published every weekday during the university term, and weekly during summer session.

**Laundry** Suds & Suds (☎ 758-5200), 935 NW Kings Blvd, markets itself to OSU's Greek system by boasting to be Corvallis' only laundromat-cum-tavern. More serious laundry is done at Campbell's Cleaners (☎ 752-3794), 1120 NW 9th St, open from 7 am to 11 pm daily.

**Medical Services** Good Samaritan Hospital (☎ 757-5111) is at 3600 NW Samaritan Drive to the north of town.

### Oregon State University
Just west of downtown, the green and leafy campus, filled with red-brick buildings, was founded in 1852 as Corvallis College, but didn't take off until 1868, when the college received the federal government's land grant to establish an agricultural college. Today, OSU offers a broad range of degrees in the arts and sciences, specializing in computer and technical fields, engineering, pharmacy, as well as agricultural sciences and veterinarian medicine. The university usually suffers in comparison to University of Oregon in Eugene, but beyond typical liberal arts egocentrism, it's hard to see why. Contact the OSU Administrative Services (☎ 737-0123) if you're interested in more details.

The campus, conforming to a vague quad and courtyard design, is bounded on the north by Monroe Ave, which is home to a number of student-oriented businesses. Washington Way flanks the campus on the south; the university merges with downtown around 11th St. Jefferson Way winds up into the campus past parking lots and speed bumps. The campus itself is 500 acres, although the university controls nearly 62 sq miles of forest, cropland and grazing land for agricultural research.

The most notable building on campus is the **Memorial Union**, the student-union building. Flights of marble stairs lead past a flag-draped vestibule to a beautiful commons room which has 18-foot ceilings and is filled with overstuffed furniture and lined with books. The university bookstore is here, along with a number of coffee shops and cafes open to students and visitors.

**Horner Museum** (☎ 754-2951), in the basement of Gill Coliseum, is the university's museum of natural history, and includes a collection of Oregon minerals (including fluorescent specimens), and a good collection of Native American artifacts. The 13,000-year-old sagebrush sandals found near Fort Rock in central Oregon – the oldest human remains ever found in the state – are on display here. The museum may be closing due to budget cutbacks, so call first.

OREGON

### Wineries

Never to forget that, above all else, this is wine country, there are two cellars that offer tasting. **Bellfountain Cellars** (☎ 929-3162), 25041 Llewellyn Rd, is open from 11 am to 6 pm, Friday to Sunday, April to November. Take Hwy 99W five miles south and turn west on Llewellyn Rd. **Tyee Wine Cellars** (☎ 753-8754), seven miles south off Hwy 99W at 26335 Greenberry Rd, is open from noon to 5 pm on weekends, May to October (and Thanksgiving weekend).

### Activities

Rent cross-country and downhill ski equipment at Anderson's Sporting Goods (☎ 757-1666), 137 SW 3rd St, and bikes from Peak Sports (☎ 754-6444), 129 NW 2nd St.

White Water Warehouse (☎ 758-3150), 625 NW Starker Ave, offers raft and kayak rentals and also runs **white-water trips** to the Rogue, Santiam, Deschutes and Umpqua rivers.

The university-owned Trysting Tree Golf Club (☎ 752-3332), 34028 Electric Rd, is one of the state's toughest. This 18-hole course offers 25 sand traps and a number of physics-defying greens, and is purposely free of large trees in order to let the capricious weather have its way with your ball.

### Special Events

Held the last weekend of June, the Corvallis Folklife Festival is one of Oregon's largest folk-music festivals. There are also food booths, workshops on folklore and arts & crafts. The festival is held in Starker Park, across from the Corvallis Country Club on Country Club Drive.

Held on the second weekend of July in Central Park at Monroe Ave and 7th St, Da Vinci Days is a celebration of the arts, sciences and technology, seeking to bridge the gap between high art and big science. Interactive displays include exhibits of computer-generated art, animation, virtual reality machines and other cutting-edge technical facilities. There's also music, food and wine booths and children's events.

The area's largest event, the Fall Festival, is held the last weekend of September in Central Park. The focus of the festival is local arts & crafts, with a juried art show featuring the work of nearly 150 artists, with loads of booths selling arts & crafts. Local wineries, breweries and restaurants are also on hand to sell their wares, and live music fills the streets (there's a street dance on the Saturday night).

### Places to Stay

**Camping** Just south of town, *Willamette Park* (☎ 757-6918) is a large grassy field that serves as a campground. There are also nature trails through the woods and access to the river for boating and angling. To reach the park, turn east on Goodnight Ave, one mile south of downtown; overnight fees are $7. The *Corvallis/Albany KOA* (☎ 967-8521), just a few miles east at 33775 Oakville Rd, offers full services for RVs.

**B&Bs** The popular *Madison Inn B&B* (☎ 757-1274), 660 SW Madison Ave, is in the old homes district between downtown and the university. Eight guest rooms ranging from $60 to $120 are available in this 1901 inn. On the other side of the campus, the *Harrison House* (☎ 752-6248), 2310 NW Harrison Blvd, offers four rooms in a Dutch Colonial residence, from $45 to $65.

**Hotels** Sitting right on the Willamette River just north of downtown, the *Econo Lodge* (☎ 752-9601), 101 NW Van Buren Ave, offers suites and non-smoking rooms, and lets in pets; single/double rooms start at $35/38. At the *Towne House Motor Inn* (☎ 753-4496), 350 SW 4th St, between the university and downtown, rooms are $38/49; there are non-smoking rooms and some kitchenettes; pets are OK. *Travel Inn* (☎ 752-5917), 1562 SW 3rd St, is also close and offers an outdoor pool, kitchenettes and a play area; prices are $35/42.

Up a few notches in price and distance, the *Best Western Grand Manor Inn* (☎ 758-

8571), 925 NW Garfield Ave, has a pool and spa facilities; rooms cost $67/73.

## Places to Eat

**Budget to Middle** The *New Morning Bakery* (☎ 754-0181), 219 SW 2nd St, is a good place for coffee and fresh baked rolls and muffins; light lunch and dinners are served as well. For good take-out sandwiches and picnic-makings go to the *Old World Deli* (☎ 752-8549), 341 SW 2nd St. Sandwiches, soup and salads are the order of the day at the *Valley Restaurant* (☎ 752-0933), 136 SW 3rd St, a bustling little cafe that's a favorite with the locals. *Nearly Normals* (☎ 753-0791), 109 NW 15th, is a mostly vegetarian cafe with sandwiches, soups, burritos and other ethnic fare.

On Monroe Ave, up near the university, there's a bunch of inexpensive and lively restaurants with some really good food; at each of the following, you can get in and out for less than $6 if you try. *Tarn Tip Thai Cuisine* (☎ 757-8906), 2535 NW Monroe Ave, offers the best Thai cooking in town. Undoubtedly the best and most amusing Mexican restaurant in Corvallis is *Bombs Away Cafe* (☎ 757-8380), 2527 NW Monroe Ave. The food is innovative and really tasty; there's a good selection of local beers. *Young's Kitchen* (☎ 757-1626), 2051 NW Monroe Ave, features both Japanese and Korean dishes.

**Top End** For fine dining, *Gables Restaurant* (☎ 752-3364), 1121 NW 9th St, leads the list. At this converted old home, prime rib, steak and chicken are served, but the chef gets more adventurous with the specials. Grilled ahi tuna with peach salsa goes for $16. Housed in Corvallis's old train depot, *Michael's Landing* (☎ 754-6141), 603 NW 2nd St, has the air of a steakhouse. It's right on the river, with drinks on the patio. Prime rib is the specialty here (starting at $13), and there's also pasta and seafood.

## Entertainment

OSU offers a broad spectrum of entertainment, lectures and readings, films and theater. Call the recorded weekly calendar (☎ 737-6445) for a listing of events.

**Coffeehouses** Up near the university, *Java Rama* (☎ 758-5639) 2047 NW Monroe Ave, is a real student hangout with live music on weekends, and a backyard patio during the summer. Closer to downtown (in a refurbished old storefront), *Allann Bros Beanery* (☎ 735-7442), 500 SW 2nd St, is a quieter place for a cup of coffee. Watch for events on the weekends.

**Brewpubs** Portland-based *McMenimans* (☎ 758-6044), 420 NW 3rd St, has one of its few out-of-town locations in Corvallis. As usual, these pubs pour their own excellent brews, and a large selection of ales and stouts from other local brewers. Up next to the university, *Clodfelters* (☎ 758-4452), 1501 NW Monroe Ave, is a calmer place for a drink, with a selection of regional microbrews and local wines.

**Cinemas** OSU's International Film Series (☎ 737-2450) offers art and foreign films in *Gilfillan Auditorium* near the corner of Orchard Ave and 26th St. For first-run releases, try *Ninth St Cinema World* (☎ 758-7469), 1750 NW 9th.

**Live Music** The principle venue for live music in Corvallis is the *Peacock Tavern* (☎ 754-8522), 125 SW 2nd St, where blues and rock are the usual fare. Upstairs, at the *Top of the Cock* (☎ 757-3560), the music is a little twangier, with country rock the current obsession. Across the street, there's an older crowd at *Squirrels Tavern* (☎ 753-8057), 100 SW 2nd St, where jazz and acoustic music is featured on weekends.

**Spectator Sports** OSU's Beavers are frequent contenders in both college football and basketball. The football team plays at Parker Stadium, at 26th St and Stadium Ave; the basketball team plays at Gill Coliseum, 26th St and Washington Ave. Call 737-4455 for information on upcoming games and tickets.

OREGON

### Getting There & Away
**Air** A small local carrier called Pacific Air (☎ 754-6744) offers six flights a day between Corvallis Municipal Airport and Portland International Airport. The airport is three miles south of town on Hwy 99W. One-way fares begin at $39.

**Bus** Five Greyhound buses a day link Portland, Corvallis and Eugene. The one-way fare between Corvallis and Eugene is $5; between Portland and Corvallis is $11. The bus depot (☎ 757-1797) is at 153 NW 4th St.

**Car** Hertz Rent-A-Car (☎ 752-2134) is at 300 SW 4th St. Further out of town, U-Save Auto Rental (☎ 758-3350) is at 4820 Philomath Blvd.

### Getting Around
Corvallis Transit (☎ 757-6998), 501 Madison Ave, operates city buses on weekdays; the one-way fare is 50c. A convenient route map is printed in the phone book. Corvallis is also served by Linn-Benton Loop buses, which run between Corvallis and Albany. Pick up the bus at the university, at the corner of 15th St and Jefferson Ave.

Call A-1 Taxi (☎ 754-1111) to hire a cab.

## AROUND CORVALLIS
### Peavy Arboretum & McDonald State Forest
Both these areas are administered by OSU. At the former, two interpretive walks wind through 40 acres of forest. From the arboretum, trails continue into McDonald Forest, a research forest with eight miles of hiking and mountain bike trails. Take Hwy 99W north for eight miles, then turn west at the signs to get to the forests.

### Mary's Peak
Mary's Peak, at 4097 feet, is the highest peak in the Coast Range. Just 16 miles from Corvallis in the Siuslaw National Forest, Mary's Peak is a favorite with student hikers, especially when clear weather allows views across the Willamette Valley to the glaciered Central Oregon Cascades.

To reach the hiking trail to the peak, follow Hwy 20 to Philomath, six miles west. Continue on Hwy 20 for 1.5 miles past the junction with Hwy 34, and turn onto USFS Rd 2005, called the Woods Creek Rd. Follow this good graveled road for 7.5 miles, until reaching the trailhead. The 4.2-mile hike climbs quickly through a dense hemlock forest before finally breaking out into the Mary's Peak Scenic Botanical Area, full of ferns, salal, firs and wildflowers.

An alternative route for the less ambitious (or for those picking up hikers on the top), involves driving most of the way up Mary's Peak from the other side. Take Hwy 34 10 miles west of Philomath to USFS Rd 3010, called Mary's Peak Rd. This winding road loops around the mountain, arriving at a parking area and primitive campground less than a mile from the top.

On a clear day, the views are amazing; however, don't be surprised if haze and smoke from the Willamette Valley limits the expanse during mid-summer.

## EUGENE
In many ways, Eugene (population 118,370) is the prototypic Oregon town, drawing its energy from equal measures of pragmatism and idealism. At the southern end of the wide Willamette Valley, the city maintains its solid, working-class base in the timber industry; yet the state's largest college campus and some of its most unconventional citizens also call Eugene home.

Established in 1846 by Californian settler Eugene Skinner, Eugene developed as a railroad hub and trading center for wheat, fruit, dairy and ever-present timber products. During the 1960s, Eugene became a synonym for the back-to-the-earth social movement. The city was rightly famous for its alternative communes, leftist politics and drug culture: in short, its 'hippie lifestyle.' Unrest built over US involvement in the Vietnam War, and the university became a hotbed of civil disobedience and counterculture.

In some ways, life in Eugene seems to be a denial that the '60s have passed. Many of the city's successful businesses are owned by former 'radicals.' Although more prosaic than during the heydays of the '60s, activism is still *de rigueur* in Eugene. Environmental issues especially motivate students, placing them again at odds with the community whose long-time economic base was in the forest products industry.

Parks flank the Willamette River much of the length of Eugene, and some of the state's most beautiful public gardens grace its hillsides.

Travelers will find sophisticated yet inexpensive dining, lively shopping districts and a youthful, relaxing and fun-seeking atmosphere that almost succeeds in making Eugene seem good for you. The Revolution may have failed, but at least the food is better.

## Orientation

Eugene is cradled in hills at the southern end of the wide Willamette Valley where two major tributaries, the Coast Fork and the McKenzie River, join the Willamette River. Directly east of Eugene is the city's blue-collar suburb of Springfield (population 45,765).

The I-5 runs north-south through Eugene, and I-105/Hwy 126 cuts through east-west, depositing the traveler on 6th Ave, just south of the market district. Willamette St divides Eugene's numbered avenues into east and west.

The University of Oregon has extensive wooded grounds, roughly girded by Franklin Blvd and 18th Ave, and Alder and Agate Sts; the University exit (No 192) off I-5 feeds onto Franklin Blvd, which becomes Broadway through downtown, and Hwys 90 and 126 to the east.

## Information

**Tourist Office** The Eugene Convention & Visitors Bureau (☎ 484-5307, (800) 452-3670 inside Oregon, (800) 547-5445 out-

side Oregon) is at 305 W 7th Ave, Eugene, OR 97401.

The Willamette National Forest office (☎ 465-6521) is at 211 E 7th Ave. The BLM District Office (☎ 683-6600), is at 2890 Chad Drive.

**Money** Change money at the US Bank (☎ 836-4001), 811 Willamette Ave.

**Post** The main post office (☎ 341-3611) is at 520 Willamette St.

**Bookstores** The University of Oregon Bookstore (☎ 346-4331) is at the corner of E 13th Ave and Kincaid St. Eugene's premier used-book store is Smith Family Bookstore, with two locations: near the university (☎ 345-1651) at 768 E 13th Ave, and downtown (☎ 343-4717) at 525 Willamette St. The Book Mark (☎ 484-0512), 856 Olive St, has Eugene's best selection of maps, as well as books on outdoor activities. Marketplace Books (☎ 343-5614), 296 E 5th Ave (in the 5th Street Public Market), has a good selection of new books, including a good travel and recreation section. Mother Kali's Books (☎ 343-4864), 2001 Franklin Blvd, is a good feminist bookstore.

**Media** The daily newspaper is the Eugene *Register-Guard*. The Friday paper contains an arts & events section. *Eugene Weekly* is the city's alternative newsweekly, with hip-biased arts coverage. The *Daily Emerald* is the university newspaper. The biweekly *Comic News*, is a local product that brings together political cartoons from around the world.

**Laundry** Club Wash (☎ 342-1727), 595 E 13th Ave, is open 24 hours.

**Medical Services** If you need medical attention, go to Sacred Heart General Hospital (☎ 686-7300), 1255 Hilyard St between 11th and 13th Sts.

## Fifth St Public Market

At E 5th Ave between Pearl and High Sts, this is the anchor of a small but lively shop-

OREGON

OREGON

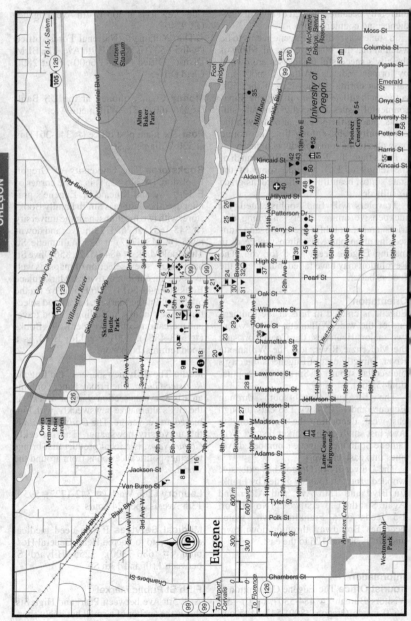

To I-5, Salem

105    126

Centennial Blvd

Autzen
Stadium

Alton
Baker
Park

Foot
Bridge

Mill Race

Franklin Blvd

Bus
99
126

To I-5, McKenzie
Bridge, Bend,
Roseburg

Moss St

Columbia St

53    Agate St

Emerald
St

University of
Oregon

54    Onyx St

University St

56

Pioneer
Cemetery

Potter St

55    Harris St

52

51    Kincaid St

50

48

49

42

43

41

40

13th Ave E

Kincaid St

Alder St

Hilyard St

26

25

Patterson Dr

11th Ave E

47

46

45

Ferry St

Mill St

34

33

39

44

High St

12th Ave E

Pearl St

14th Ave E

15th Ave E

16th Ave E

16th Ave E

17th Ave E

19th Ave E

Coburg Rd

Country Club Rd

126

Willamette River

105

126

Skinner Butte Loop

Skinner
Butte
Park

3rd Ave E

4th Ave E

5th Ave E

6

7

5

4

3

2

12

1

11

10

13

14

15

6th Ave E

7th Ave E

8th Ave E

21

22

23

24

30

31

32

36

38

37

29

99

Broadway

Oak St

Willamette St

Olive St

Charnelton St

Lincoln St

Lawrence St

Washington St

Jefferson St

Madison St

Monroe St

Adams St

Amazon Creek

10th Ave E

Jefferson St

Lane County
Fairgrounds

Owen
Memorial
Rose
Garden

126

2nd Ave W

3rd Ave W

9

17

18

20

28

27

2nd Ave W

4th Ave W

5th Ave W

6th Ave W

7th Ave W

8th Ave W

10th Ave W

Broadway

11th Ave W

12th Ave W

13th Ave W

14th Ave W

15th Ave W

16th Ave W

17th Ave W

18th Ave W

Jackson St

8

16

Van Buren St

Railroad Blvd

Blair Blvd

1st Ave W

2nd Ave W

3rd Ave W

Chambers St

Eugene

600 m

600 yards

300

300

0

0

To Airport,
Corvallis

To Florence

99

99

126

Tyler St

Polk St

Taylor St

Chambers St

Amazon Creek

Westmoreland
Park

| PLACES TO STAY | | | | |
|---|---|---|---|---|
| 8 | Red Carpet Motel | 23 | West Brothers Barbeque, Eugene City Brewery | 19 | Holt Center, Hilton Hotel, Convention Center |
| 9 | Courtesy Inn | 24 | Full City Coffee | 20 | WOW Hall |
| 16 | Executive House Motel | 30 | Zenon Cafe | 21 | Saturday Market |
| 17 | Downtown Motel | 31 | Ambrosia | 22 | Good Times |
| 25 | Manor Motel | 36 | The Kiva | 29 | The Eugene Mall |
| 26 | 66 Motel | 39 | High St Pub | 32 | Bus Depot |
| 27 | Atherton Place B&B | 41 | China Blue, Fall Creek Bakery | 35 | U of O Playing Fields |
| 28 | The Oval Door B&B | | | 38 | Berg's Ski Shop |
| 33 | Campus Inn | 42 | Rennie's Landing | 40 | Sacred Heart General Hospital |
| 34 | Eugene Motor Lodge | 48 | Excelsior Cafe | | |
| 37 | Timbers Motel | 49 | Glenwood Inn | 43 | U of O Bookstore |
| 55 | Duckworth B&B | | | 44 | Lane County Historical Museum |
| 56 | Campus Cottage B&B Inn | **OTHER** | | | |
| | | 3 | Amtrak Station | 45 | The Bijou |
| **PLACES TO EAT** | | 4 | Euphoria Chocolates | 46 | New Max's Tavern |
| 1 | Hilda's | 11 | Down To Earth | 47 | Club Wash |
| 2 | Oregon Electric Station | 12 | Post Office | 50 | Smith Family Bookstore |
| 5 | Steelhead Brewing Co | 13 | Smith Family Bookstore | 51 | U of O Museum of Art |
| 6 | La Chantrelle Restaurant | 14 | 5th St Public Market | 52 | Deady Hall |
| 7 | Jo Federigo's Bar & Cafe | 15 | Pedal Power Bicycles | 53 | U of O Museum of Natural History |
| 10 | The Beanery | 18 | Visitors Bureau | 54 | MacArthur Court |

ping and cafe district. The 'Market,' once an old mill, is in fact a boutique mall; besides the lures of shopping, there's a good bakery and a number of inexpensive and ethnic places to eat in the building's central atrium. In neighboring blocks there's a good antique store, a brewpub and chocolatier.

### Eugene Mall
In the thorough-going fit of urban renewal, most of Eugene's old downtown core was torn down, the buildings replaced with 1960s-era structures, and much of the area turned into a pedestrian mall. The project has been less than successful.

The mall, in the blocks between 8th to 10th Aves and Charnelton to Oak Sts, is now filled with small specialty shops and cafes. You'll certainly have no trouble finding great food. After closing off all vehicular traffic in a 12-block area during the 1960s, the city has been slowly opening the streets back up to cars, trying to lure people back to the city center.

### Eugene Saturday Market
The outdoor market in the park near E 8th Ave and Oak St brings in a grand mix of Eugene characters: buskers, vegetable hawkers, tie-dye artisans, mimes, ethnic food stands and craftspeople. It's great fun, and a good introduction to Eugene's peculiar vitality. Saturday Market is open every Saturday from 10 am to 5 pm, except from Christmas to April 1.

### University of Oregon
Established in 1872, although classes didn't begin until 1876, the University of Oregon (☎ 346-3014) is the state's foremost institution of higher learning, with a focus in the arts, sciences and law. The forest-like campus sits just south and east of downtown; the streets flanking the university – especially 13th Ave – are strewn with student-oriented bars, bookstores and coffeehouses. Tours of the campus are offered twice daily during the summer break.

The campus is filled with historic, ivy-covered buildings. The oldest is **Deady Hall**, which for the first 10 years of the university, *was* the university.

The university's **Museum of Art** (☎ 346-3027), 1430 Johnson St, is renowned for its extensive collection of

Asian and regional contemporary art. The **Museum of Natural History** (☎ 346-3024), 1680 E 15th Ave, is housed in a replica of a Native American longhouse. Its collection is the state's best display of fossils, Native American artifacts and geologic curiosities. Both are open Wednesday to Sunday from noon to 5 pm, with free admission.

**Pioneer Cemetery** was once in a field but is now surrounded by the campus. Reading tombstones at one of Eugene's oldest cemeteries gives a vivid insight into life and death in the early settlement. Note especially the graves of Civil War veterans.

### Lane County Historical Museum
This local museum (☎ 687-4239), sits in the county fairgrounds at 740 W 13th Ave. A collection of historic artifacts document the growth of communities in the area. A popular exhibit details the experiences of Oregon Trail pioneers who made their way across the continent to settle in Lane County. Old logging tools and technology are also prominent in the collection. The museum is open Wednesday to Friday from 10 am to 4 pm, and Saturday noon to 4 pm; admission is adults/seniors $2/1, 75c for children ages three to 17.

### Skinner Butte
Directly north of downtown is Skinner Butte. A hike to the top provides a good orientation and a little exercise (there's also a road to the top; follow the signs from Skinner Butte Loop). On the narrow strip of land between the wooded butte and the Willamette River, Eugene Skinner established the first business in Eugene. The grassy waterfront is now a park, popular with joggers and picnickers. There is also rock climbing along the landmark's western face. A number of beautiful Victorian homes ring the butte.

### Alton Baker Park
Extending for five miles along the Willamette River, this is a series of parks, bike and jogging paths and picnic areas. Paths lead

through oak groves; watch for songbirds and waterfowl.

From downtown, the easiest access to the park network is on the north side of Skinner Butte (follow High St north). Follow the paths hugging the river's edge beneath the Hwy 126 bridge to the **Owen Memorial Rose Garden**. This lovely park features carefully trained climbing roses, as well as ornamental trees. Dominating all is an old cherry tree planted in the 1860s. From the university area, cross the footbridge to the park on the northern banks of the river.

### Hendricks Park Rhododendron Garden
In May, this garden puts on a spectacular floral display. On a hill above the city, the garden is part of a larger park featuring native trees and shrubs. Over 5000 varieties of rhododendron and azalea erupt into bloom in the spring, along with dogwood and daffodils. During the rest of the year, the park is a quiet, vernal retreat with lovely views, worthy of a picnic. To reach Hendricks Park, turn south off Franklin Blvd onto Agate St, and then turn east onto Heights Blvd.

### Mount Pisgah Arboretum
This 120-acre plant sanctuary features trails that wind through a number of Northwest plant habitats, including a marsh, conifer forest and wildflower meadows. At the gate to the arboretum there are brochures that help identify plant and animal species. To reach the arboretum, take I-5 south to the 30th Ave exit, and turn east, following the signs. It's seven miles outside of Eugene.

### Wineries
Nestled in the hills at the southern end of the Willamette Valley are a number of good wineries. Take a picnic to **Hinman Vineyards** (☎ 345-1945), 27012 Briggs Hill Rd, to enjoy their nice facility and grounds; they're open from noon to 5 pm daily. To get there from Eugene, go west on W 11th

St, left on Bailey Hill Rd, right on Spencer Creek Rd, and left on Briggs Hill Rd.

Go north on Hwy 99W about 20 miles to get to **Alpine Vineyards** (☎ 424-5851), 25904 Green Peak Rd, in Monroe. Known for a nice light chardonnay, you can visit them from noon to 5 pm daily, June 15 to September 15, weekends only the rest of the year. It's closed Christmas to January 31.

Noted for their red wines, **Forgeron Vineyards** (☎ 935-1117), 89697 Sheffler Rd, Elmira, is open from noon to 5 pm daily, June to September, and weekends only October to May, but is closed January. Elmira is west of Veneta along Hwy 126.

### Biking

Rent a mountain bike or a tandem from Pedal Power Bicycles (☎ 687-1775), 545 High St, then take off for the park.

### Skiing

To rent cross-country or downhill skis, go to Berg's Ski Shop (☎ 683-1300), 367 W 13th Ave. The closest skiing is either near Willamette Pass, south of Eugene on Hwy 58, or up the McKenzie River on Hwy 126 to Santiam Pass.

### Swimming

There's an outdoor pool at Amazon Park, near Hilyard St and E 26th Ave, and a year-round indoor pool at Sheldon Pool (☎ 687-5314), 2445 Willakenzie Rd. At Armitage State Park, north of Eugene on Coburg Rd, there's swimming in the McKenzie River when the weather allows.

### Golf

There are a number of golf courses in the Eugene area. Try Oakway Golf Course (☎ 484-1927), 2000 Cal Young Rd, for a beautiful 18-hole course with lots of mature trees. The nine-hole Laurelwood Golf Course (☎ 687-5321), 2700 Columbia St, is just south of the university.

### Special Events

There's no doubt about it: Eugene knows how to throw a party.

**Oregon Bach Festival** While the music of Bach, especially the concertos and cantatas, takes center stage at the Hult Center for the Performing Arts (see Entertainment), the festival has recently branched out to include concerts of contemporary music and jazz. Held for two weeks in late June and early July, the festival features about 25 separate concerts. Ticket prices begin at $7. Contact the Bach Festival Office (☎ 867-5000), University of Oregon Music School, 18th Ave, for ticket information.

**Oregon Country Faire** Two weeks after the Bach Festival (the weekend after the Fourth of July) and just about as far as you can get from highbrow pretensions, the Oregon Country Faire is a riotous three-day celebration of Eugene's folksy, hippie past and present. Booths are crammed with health food, tie-dyed garments, candles, herbs and crafts. Wandering minstrels, jugglers and mimes entertain. On the festival's many stages watch a variety of vaudeville acts, musicians and theater groups. Mostly gone are the old days when clothing was optional and drugs passed freely in the crowd. But it's still full of infectious high spirits and a kind of otherworldly goodwill.

The fair is held 15 miles west of Eugene on Hwy 126, near Veneta. If you are driving to the fair, note that parking anywhere close can be difficult. Avoid the parking nightmare and take the Country Faire Express bus service, which offers free bus transportation between Lane County Fairgrounds in Eugene, at West 13th Ave and Monroe St, and the fair in Veneta.

Contact the festival headquarters (☎ 343-4298) at PO Box 2972, Eugene, OR 97402.

**Lane County Fair** This agricultural fair is held the third week of August at the Lane County Fairgrounds (☎ 687-4294). Events include livestock shows, live music, a carnival and fruit and vegetable displays.

**Eugene Celebration** On the last weekend of September, this celebration takes over downtown Eugene. Concerts, juried fine art

OREGON

shows and author events are some of the event's elements, but by far the most vital part of the event is the street fair. In time-tested Eugene fashion, food vendors mix with political activists, organic farmers with jewelry makers and all with students fresh from summer break. The visitors center has the details.

## Places to Stay

**Camping** While most campsites in the area are primarily for RV campers, they all have tenting areas. *KOA Kamping World* (☎ 343-4832), a quarter-mile west of I-5 exit No 199, is six miles north of Eugene, and charges about $15 a night. Nine miles south of Eugene at Creswell (exit No 182) is the *KOA Sherwood Forest* (☎ 895-4110), 298 E Oregon Ave; sites are about $12 a night. West of Eugene, along Fern Ridge Reservoir, is the *Fern Ridge Shores Campground* (☎ 935-2335). Follow Hwy 126 seven miles west of Eugene, and turn north on Ellmaker Rd. Lakeside sites go for $15.

**B&Bs** For general information, *B&B Innkeepers* (☎ 345-7799) is a clearing house for Eugene area B&Bs; they can also help with listings throughout the state. In the meantime, *Atherton Place B&B* (☎ 683-2674), 690 W Broadway, offers three rooms, ranging from $50 to $70, in a 1928 Dutch Colonial. *The Oval Door* (☎ 683-3160), 988 Lawrence St, is a newer home in an old neighborhood, with four guest rooms ranging from $65 to $83.

The *Campus Cottage B&B Inn* (☎ 342-5346), 1136 E 19th Ave, next to the University of Oregon campus, has four rooms, three with private baths, for $87 to $117. The *Duckworth B&B* (☎ 686-2451), 987 E 19th Ave, is an English-style home from 1926, with three rooms for $75 to $85, one with private bath; there's also a player piano.

**Hotels – downtown** If you're planning to spend some time in Eugene, call ahead for a room in one of several older hotels on the edge of the downtown area; it's an easy stroll to shopping, restaurants and parks. The *Courtesy Inn* (☎ 345-3391), 345 W 6th Ave, with single/double rooms at $35/40, and the *Downtown Motel* (☎ 345-8739), 361 W 7th Ave, $38/43, are both attractive hotels convenient to downtown businesses. Continue west on 6th Ave for a strip of inexpensive motels, like the *Red Carpet* (☎ 345-0579), 1055 W 6th Ave, and the *Executive House* (☎ 683-4000), 1040 W 6th Ave, with rooms for around $35/38.

Immediately south of downtown is *Timbers Motel* (☎ 343-3345), 1015 Pearl St. The sparsely decorated rooms make up in convenience for what they lack in style; the cheapest rooms are in the basement, for about $15 cheaper than regular rates of $34/37.

The *Eugene Hilton* (☎ 342-2000), 66 E 6th Ave, is right in the center of downtown, and is part of the convention center complex. It's also just next door to the artsy goings-on at the Hult Center. Be prepared to pay for the convenience; rooms start at $65 and go up to $150.

**Hotels – university area** Right along Broadway, which turns into Franklin Blvd (Hwys 99 and 126), you'll find a strip of inexpensive motels and restaurants, all handy to the university and riverside parks. Unless there's a special event going on, you can count on finding a room. If you want to call ahead, try one of the following: *Manor Motel* (☎ 345-2331) at 599 E Broadway, has single/double rooms for $26/30, and a pool. The *66 Motel* (☎ 342-5041), 755 E Broadway, rates the rooms at $28/32, pets are OK. *Eugene Motor Lodge* (☎ 344-5233), 476 E Broadway, has single/double rooms for $34/40, some with kitchenettes; there's a pool, and they allow pets. The *Campus Inn* (☎ 343-3376), 390 E Broadway, $44/55, also thinks pets are OK.

## Places to Eat

You're not going to have any trouble finding something good to eat in Eugene. The quality and variety of food here surpasses much of what gets flogged as cuisine in cities like Seattle and Portland.

And what's better, even the best restaurants will offer items to fit on a student's budget.

**Downtown** Start out the day at *Full City Coffee* (☎ 344-0475), 842 Pearl St, for espresso drinks and pastries.

For the budget traveler, there are food carts with ethnic food on the pedestrian mall. In the atrium of the Fifth Street Market building (on 5th Ave between Pearl and High Sts), there's a great bakery and a number of small ethnic restaurants to choose from. Try *Mekala's* (☎ 342-4872), 296 E 5th Ave, for good Thai food. If you've been looking for a good health-food store, head to *The Kiva* (☎ 342-8666), 125 W 11th Ave, which offers organic produce, bulk foods and deli items.

A short distance north from downtown is the city's spiciest restaurant, *Hilda's* (☎ 343-4322), 400 Blair Blvd, featuring Central and South American cuisine. If you're on a budget, the *tapas* are a good value. At the *West Brother's Barbeque* (☎ 345-8489), 844 Olive St, home-brewed ales are teamed with superior barbecued ribs ($11.95) from the 'usual' menu; on the 'unusual' menu find vegetarian and eclectic ethnic specials.

Intimate *La Chantrelle* (☎ 484-4065), 207 E 5th Ave, prepares French classics and submits robust local standards like game to continental treatments. For steak and seafood, go to the *Oregon Electric Station* (☎ 485-4444), 27 E 5th Ave. The restaurant is housed in an old railroad station, with wood and brass fixtures everywhere. In the waiting room, settle into an easy chair for a pre-dinner drink.

Two of Eugene's best restaurants face each other across East Broadway at the edge of the pedestrian mall. *Ambrosia* (☎ 342-4141), 174 E Broadway, features regional Italian cuisine and wood-fired specialty pizzas in a wonderfully preserved turn-of-the-century bar. *Zenon Cafe* (☎ 343-3005), 898 Pearl St, is undoubtedly one of the best restaurants in Oregon. Its extensive international menu, ranging from beef vindaloo to grilled quail to a great Caesar salad, makes imaginative use of local meats, mushrooms, fish and vegetables. Vegetarian dishes have their own section of the menu; desserts are equally compelling; even the bread is excellent. A number of 'small plates' are available as appetizers or light meals. Entree and salad total about $20.

**University Area** *Fall Creek Bakery* (☎ 484-1662), 881 E 13th Ave, has coffee and pastries to get you going. For a full breakfast, with bleary-eyed students, try the *Glenwood Inn* (☎ 687-0355), 1340 Alder St.

University-area haunts provide inexpensive food. Besides the brewpubs in the area, check out *China Blue*, 879 E 13th Ave, for northern Chinese food, and *Rennie's Landing* (☎ 687-0600), 1214 Kincaid St, for burgers and beer.

The *Excelsior Cafe* (☎ 342-6963), 754 E 13th Ave, in a beautiful old home, is one of Eugene's finest restaurants. The menu changes seasonally, and ranges from pasta dishes to leg of lamb. Prices are modest considering the quality (fresh salmon with sun-dried tomato aïoli is $13.95); the menu also offers 'light suppers' for around $7.

**Entertainment**

The University of Oregon is host to a large number of touring and local performing-arts groups. There are also a number of public lectures, films and activities. Call the Cultural Forum (☎ 346-4373) or pick up a copy of the *Daily Emerald* for information about campus activities.

The Hult Center for the Performing Arts, (☎ 687-5000) at 6th Ave and Willamette St, adjacent to the convention center and the Hilton, is the main civic performance space; the Eugene Opera, Symphony and Ballet each perform here, as well as numerous festival acts and touring groups.

**Coffeehouses** *Java Joes* (☎ 484-9504), 2692 Willamette St, offers music on weekend evenings. *The Allann Bros Beanery* (☎ 342-3378), 152 W 5th Ave, offering desserts and light meals, has folk and live jazz music.

OREGON

**Brewpubs** Eugene has three brewpubs; most bars and taverns serve locally brewed beers. Kitty-corner to the Fifth Street Market, the *Steelhead Brewing Co* (☎ 485-4444), 199 E 5th Ave, serves German-style beers and light meals in an airy old store-front; you can usually find an empty table and enough quiet to talk. *Eugene City Brewery* (☎ 345-8489), 844 Olive St, connected to West Brother's Barbeque, is a more student-oriented brewpub. Strong, dark ales are good here, well matched to the fiery entrees on the restaurant side of the business. *High Street Pub* (☎ 345-4905), 1243 High St, near the campus, is a popular meeting place that is half pub, half coffeeshop.

**Cinemas** *The Bijou* (☎ 686-2458), 492 E 13th Ave, is Eugene's art and foreign movie house. At *Movies 12* (☎ 741-1231), 2850 Gateway St, in the Gateway Mall in Springfield, a dozen first-run movies are playing at any given time.

**Live Music** *WOW Hall* (☎ 687-2746), at 8th Ave and Lincoln St, is an old union hall, and is the main venue for touring bands; call for a listing of upcoming events. At *Good Times* (☎ 484-7181), 375 E 7th Ave, there's a lively bar scene with standard, straight-forward rock music and dancing. Clubs like *New Max's Tavern* (☎ 342-6365), 550 E 13th Ave, offer more alternative music. For jazz, go to *Jo Federigo's Bar & Cafe* (☎ 343-8488), 259 E 5th Ave. Check the *Eugene Weekly* or the *Daily Emerald* for other venues and current listings.

**Spectator Sports** The Eugene Emeralds are a Class A baseball team who play during the summer at Civic Stadium (☎ 342-5367). The University of Oregon Ducks are the much loved, though not always very successful, sports teams of the university. The basketball team plays at MacArthur Court, at the university; the football team plays at Autzen Stadium, just east of downtown. Call 346-4461 for a current schedule of University of Oregon sports events.

**Things to Buy**
There's nothing more symbolic of Eugene than the business called Down to Earth (☎ 342-6820), 532 Olive St. This shop, full of garden and farm supplies, kitchen gear and food-preservation equipment, contains everything you need to establish a modern, wholly organic homestead. Add to it a cafe and a plant nursery, and you've got a great place to play out your farming fantasies. Where else could you buy a bagel, a vegetable juicer and a self-composting toilet?

Euphoria Chocolates (☎ 343-9223), 199 E 5th Ave, are locally famed candy makers; try the truffles.

If the shops in downtown's Market District and the Eugene Mall don't have what you need, the 140 stores in Valley River Mall, just north of city center off Delta Hwy, surely will.

**Getting There & Away**
**Air** Four airlines serve the Eugene's Hahlon Sweet Airport (☎ 687-5544), 20 miles northwest of town on Hwy 99. Horizon Air (☎ (800) 547-9308); Alaska (☎ 800-426-0333); United Airlines (☎ (800) 241-6522); and American Airlines (☎ (800) 433-7300) each link Eugene to Portland and other West Coast cities.

There is no public transportation between Eugene and the airport.

**Bus** Ten Greyhound buses a day link Portland and San Francisco to Eugene; a one-way fare to Portland is $13. Porter Stage Lines links Eugene to Bend with twice-daily mini-van service; the fare is $17 one-way. The bus depot (☎ 344-6265) is at 987 Pearl St.

The Green Tortoise (☎ 937-3603) also passes through Eugene on their twice-weekly run up and down the West Coast. The one-way fare to Portland is $10, to San Francisco $39. Make sure to call for reservations and pick-up times.

**Train** Amtrak offers once-daily service both north to Portland and south to Sacramento on the *Coast Starlight*. The southbound train leaves at 4:52 pm, the northbound train departs at 12:05 pm. Fare between Eugene and Portland is $24 one way, between Eugene and San Francisco the fare is $104. The Amtrak depot (☎ 687-1383) is at E 4th Ave and Willamette St.

**Car** Avis (☎ 688-9053), Budget (☎ 688-1229) and National Car Rental (☎ 688-8161) each have an office at the Eugene airport. Enterprise (☎ 344-2020), 810 W 6th, and A-Way Rent-A-Car (☎ 683-0847), 110 W 6th St, each have offices near downtown Eugene.

### Getting Around

Although not large, downtown Eugene can be an infuriating place to drive around. An extensive one-way grid was imposed on the city during the city's urban-renewal heyday; little subsequent growth has justified the tangled mess that it created.

Bike riders should rejoice. Not only are they generally free of the maddening one-way street system; many Eugene streets make room for bike lanes.

The Lane Transit District (☎ 687-5555) operates the local bus company. Fares are 75c; for maps and information go to their office at 10th Ave and Willamette St.

Call Emerald Taxi (☎ 686-2010) for a cab.

# McKenzie River Valley

The single term 'McKenzie' identifies a river, a mountain pass, a historic and spectacular highway, and one of Oregon's most unique and wondrous natural areas. Great fishing, easy hikes and rafting trips make this one of the state's premier recreation areas.

The McKenzie River is one of Oregon's most beautiful and mysterious rivers. A creature of the area's relatively recent volcanic history, the river plays hide and seek with the lava flows that cross its path. Over the course of millennia, waves of molten rock rolled down the flanks of the Cascades, damming the McKenzie to form the lakes and the marvelous waterfalls that characterize its upper reaches. In other areas, however, the river chooses to seep through the porous lava, only to reappear as bubbling springs further downstream. A National Recreation Trail opens the richly forested upper reaches of the McKenzie River to hikers.

One of the state's most astonishing drives follows a tributary of the McKenzie River through a heavily glaciated valley, up a hair-raising escarpment to McKenzie Pass, where the central Oregon volcanic peaks loom across barren lava flows – some only hundreds of years old.

While the McKenzie River area is an easy day-trip from either Eugene or the Bend area, USFS campgrounds and charming cabin accommodations at McKenzie Bridge will tempt the traveler to make the McKenzie River the focus of a longer visit.

The region is named for Donald McKenzie, an early fur trapper with J J Astor's Pacific Fur Company. McKenzie explored the upper Willamette Valley in 1812, in the process noting the river that would come to bear his name. After gold was discovered in central Oregon in the 1860s, Willamette Valley residents hacked a trail over barren lava flows near the present McKenzie Pass. Astonishing as it seems today – now, the McKenzie Pass Hwy is hardly a thoroughfare – sufficient traffic once frequented the trail to justify a toll station.

### ORIENTATION

The little community of McKenzie Bridge offers accommodations and food, and is usually considered the gateway to McKenzie area recreation. McKenzie Bridge is 50 miles east of Eugene on Hwy 126. Five miles east of McKenzie Bridge, Hwy 242 (the Old McKenzie Hwy) splits off and heads toward McKenzie Pass on its way to Sisters, 34 miles distant (the pass is usually

OREGON

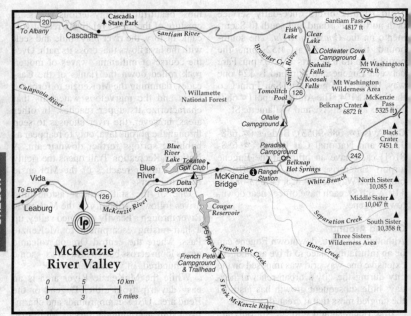

**McKenzie River Valley**

closed November to June). Highway 126, which follows the McKenzie River valley north, joins Hwy 20 and crosses the Cascades at Santiam Pass (which remains open year round).

## INFORMATION

For information on the McKenzie River area, contact the McKenzie River Chamber of Commerce (☎ 896-3330) at PO Box 1117, Leaburg, OR 97489.

For information on recreation in the area contact the McKenzie River Ranger Station (822-3381), 57600 Hwy 126, McKenzie Bridge. The ranger station has good information on mountain biking and hiking trails. They also issue overnight permits for camping in the Three Sisters Wilderness.

The closest post office (☎ 822-3305) is at 51748 Cascade St, in Blue River.

## GETTING THERE & AWAY

The Eugene bus system, Lane Transit District (☎ 687-5555), provides service to

McKenzie Bridge via bus No 91. On weekdays there are two early-morning buses, one afternoon and one late-afternoon bus departing from Eugene's downtown bus mall for McKenzie Bridge. On Saturdays there is one morning and one late-afternoon bus. Trips to McKenzie Bridge take slightly over an hour. In McKenzie Bridge the bus can be met at the bridge or the ranger station. The fare is 80c.

## McKENZIE BRIDGE & HIGHWAY 126

Little more than a general store and a few cabins, the little crossroads of McKenzie Bridge offers the traveler food, drink and lodging in a stunning physical setting. Between the junction of Hwys 242 and 20, Hwy 126 follows the main branch of the McKenzie River north through a steep valley to the river's source. The McKenzie River National Recreational Trail skirts the river between McKenzie Bridge and the trailhead, two miles north of Clear Lake.

## Hiking

One of Oregon's showcase Wild & Scenic rivers, the McKenzie River is graced with the 26.5-mile **McKenzie River National Recreation Trail**, which follows the here-again, gone-again cascading river from its inception to the hamlet of McKenzie Bridge. Access points appear at several points along Hwy 126, so hikers can select whatever portion of the trail suits their schedule or fancy.

Starting at the trailhead near **Fish Lake,** there are nice day hikes downstream to **Clear Lake**. Here the trail divides. To the east, the trail passes the large spring of an underground river, several groves of old-growth forest, an extensive lava flow, to arrive at Coldwater Cove Campground. To the west, the path follows the lake past Clear Water Resort, where food, boat rentals and lodging are available.

For day hikers, access to another easy series of trails begins at the **Sahalie Falls**, where a footbridge crosses the upper falls viewpoint to join the McKenzie River Trail for a two-mile stroll to Carmen Reservoir past **Koosah Falls**. On the highway side of the river is the more developed and shorter **Waterfall Trail**, which links Sahalie with Koosah falls. Parts of this trail is wheel-chair accessible.

For nearly four miles, the McKenzie disappears between Carmen Reservoir and Tamolitch Pool. Long-distance hikers are treated to a lush growth of cedar and fir trees along the dry river bed.

Day hikes can also reach stunning **Tamolitch Pool** from the south. Turn off Hwy 126 at **Trail Bridge Reservoir**, but follow the gravel road to the right, past the maintenance buildings to the McKenzie River trailhead. The two-mile trail passes through a mossy lava flow before coming upon the mighty McKenzie River surging up in a cliff-lined bowl of rock ('Tamolitch' means 'bucket' in Chinookan). Eerily calm and emerald, Tamolitch Pool is an unforgettably magical site.

Although lower portions of the McKenzie River Trail are open to mountain bikes, the trail is narrow and steep (certainly across the most recent lava flows), and offers bikers a fairly joyless challenge.

## Fishing

The McKenzie River is one of the most storied fishing streams in Oregon. The favorite quarry of anglers is the redside trout, a variant of the rainbow whose sides are flecked with orange spots. The best fishing water is west of Blue River, where, as the river slows down, there are more pools and deeper water. Access to the river along this stretch is fairly restricted, however, as it passes through private land. Various state and county parks provide the most dependable access. Fishing for summer steelhead is also good along this stretch.

A summer release of hatchery rainbows between Belknap Hot Springs and McKenzie Bridge means that fishing is good throughout the Willamette National Forest lands, where frequent campgrounds and streamside trails allow easy access.

A number of restrictions apply to fishing at various places along the McKenzie River, so check with local tackle shops or the Fish & Wildlife office in Springfield (☎ 726-3515) for current regulations. In general, no rainbow or redside longer than 14 inches may be kept, in order to maintain natural propagation.

A number of outfitters in the Eugene area offer guided fishing trips on the McKenzie River. Contact Prince River Outfitters (☎ 896-3941) in Vida, for a information on year-round fishing trips on drift boats. Other outfitters include Bob Spencer's McKenzie River Guide Service (☎ 741-4882), in Springfield.

## Rafting

White-water trips are popular on the McKenzie River. The following outfitters offer half and full-day excursions. McKenzie River Adventures (☎ 549-1325, 822-3806) in Sisters, offers a half-day run with lunch. Jim Berl (☎ 822-6003), 56324 McKenzie Hwy, in McKenzie Bridge, offers both rafting and fishing packages. McKenzie Pontoon Trips (☎ 741-1905), in

OREGON

Springfield, shoots the river in pontoon rafts.

Half-day trips are generally in the $30 range; full-day excursions range between $50 and $65.

## Golf

You wouldn't expect to find a first-class golf course out in the woods along the McKenzie River, but Tokatee Golf Club (☎ 822-3220, (800) 452-6376 in Oregon), three miles west of McKenzie Bridge on Hwy 126, is reckoned to be one of the toughest golf courses in Oregon, and is ranked by *Golf Digest* as one of the top 25 public courses in the nation. The holes wind along foothills, through forests and past streams and lakes, and the capricious valley winds are as much a part of the challenge as the topography.

## Places to Stay

**Camping** Between Blue River and the junction of Hwy 20, USFS campsites appear regularly along the McKenzie River. About three miles east of McKenzie Bridge, the *Paradise Campground* offers 64 campsites in a beautiful riverside grove, with drinking water and flush toilets. *Delta Campground,* three miles east of Blue River, offers 39 campsites with drinking water and flush toilets; there's also a short nature trail through the woods that identifies trees and plants and discusses forest ecology.

Camp on the quiet side of Clear Lake at *Coldwater Cove Campground,* 18 miles north of McKenzie Bridge on Hwy 126. A mile downriver is *Ice Cap Campground* on the shores of Carmen Reservoir, where there's good trout fishing. Ice Cap is also close to hiking trails leading to spectacular waterfalls. *Ollalie Campground,* 11 miles north of McKenzie Bridge on Hwy 126, offers water and flush toilets. Fees at USFS campgrounds are $7 per night.

**Hotels** *Sleepy Hollow Motel* (☎ 822-3805), 54791 McKenzie Hwy, presents a standard motor inn, with motel rooms at singles/

doubles $33/39. The Sleepy Hollow is just next to Tokatee Golf Club.

**Lodges** Most lodging in the mountain community of McKenzie Bridge is in free-standing cabins, most of which are charmingly furnished and completely modernized. Overlooking the McKenzie River, the historic *Log Cabin Inn* (☎ 822-3432), 56483 McKenzie Hwy, is a handsome old lodge built in 1906. Its old-fashioned woodsy charm is accentuated by the good food served in its wood-paneled restaurant. Nine cabins line the river behind the lodge, each with a porch and fireplace; rates begin at $50.

*The Horse Creek Lodge* (☎ 822-3243), 56228 Delta Drive, offers lodging for groups in the four-bedroom Delta House ($240), or in individual cabins (starting at $50). *The Country Place* (☎ 822-6008), 56245 Delta Drive, offers three cabins on the river, ranging from $61 to $73 a night, each with full kitchens and living areas; a four-bedroom house is also available.

Just off Hwy 126 on Belknap Springs Rd is the *Belknap Lodge & Hot Springs* (☎ 822-3512). Rooms are available in the lodge itself ($75) or in cabins ($35). Campsites are also available. Non-guests can relax in the mineral pool for $3. The lodge was up for sale at press time, so call ahead to make sure it's still open.

**Resorts** Four miles south of the junction of Hwys 20 and 126 is *Clear Lake Resort,* McKenzie River Hwy, (no phone), which offers rustic cabins on the shores of 200-foot deep Clear Lake. It's a lovely spot except for the gasoline generators. A basic cabin (sans bathroom) starts at $18. Rowboat rentals and a cafe are pluses.

## Places to Eat

About three miles west of McKenzie Bridge is the *Rustic Skillet* (☎ 822-3400), a family restaurant offering three meals a day; they maintain an understandable pride in their homemade pies. The dining room at the *Log Cabin Inn* (☎ 822-3432), is charming and old fashioned. Steaks and prime rib

## McKenzie Pass

McKenzie Pass was first traversed by White settlers in 1862, when Felix Scott and a party of 250 men, on their way to the Central Oregon gold fields, blazed a trail up to and across the area that is now known as McKenzie Pass. By 1872, John Craig scouted a slightly different trail across the lava fields, and opened a toll road from McKenzie Bridge to Sisters ($2 per wagon, $1 per horseman, and only 5c per sheep). Craig worked to secure a US mail delivery route for the McKenzie Pass trail, linking Eugene and Prineville. He started across the pass with Christmas mail from McKenzie Bridge in December, 1877, but never appeared at Camp Polk (near Sisters). His frozen body was found early the next year. Near the pass, a historical monument commemorates his death. ■

lead the menu, though there are unusual and intriguing dishes involving venison and buffalo as well as local trout; dinners range between $12 and $15; it's open for lunch and dinner.

### McKenzie Highway

Highway 242 up Lost Creek Valley to the lava fields of 5325-foot high McKenzie Pass offers stunning views of the Cascade Range, intriguing hikes, and access to one of the largest and most recent lava flows in the continental USA. Even with such scenic competition, you're likely also to remember the highway itself: one local observer mused that the road was 'seemingly engineered by a madman.' From the pass area, Hwy 242 suddenly drops 4000 feet down the glaciated face of Lost Creek Valley, along a series of astonishingly narrow hairpin curves. If you plan to travel Hwy 242, make sure your brakes are in good shape; trailer travel is not suggested.

### Three Sisters Wilderness Area

This 580-sq-mile wilderness area spans the Cascade Range, with access both from the Bend Area on the east, and from the McKenzie River area on the west.

The focal points of the wilderness area are the glaciered Three Sisters, three recent volcanic peaks topping 10,000 feet in height. The wilderness takes in widely varying types of environments, though most of the wilderness accessible from the west side is dense, old-growth forest coursed with strong rivers and streams. It's also a haven for wildlife: Oregon's small population of wolverines live here, as do cougars and black bears. The area is traversed by the Pacific Crest Trail, which is easily accessed at McKenzie Pass.

Other trails lead up stream valleys to lakes and views onto the peaks, and are accessed by *USFS Rd 19*, also known as the Aufderheide National Scenic Byway. One popular trailhead on this route is at the French Pete Campground, where a trail leads up French Pete Creek to Wolverine Meadows through old-growth forests.

For more information, contact the McKenzie River Ranger Station (☎ 822-3381), 57600 Hwy 126. The best map of the area is the Three Sisters Wilderness Map published by Geo-Graphics, available at most local outdoor stores or by writing to 18860 SW Alderwood Drive, Beaverton OR 97006; or call 591-7635.

### Dee Wright Observatory

Perched on a swell of frozen rock, this fortress of lava built by the CCC surveys a desolate volcanic landscape. Its arched windows frame 11 volcanic peaks. Built in the 1930s, the observatory was named for a USFS trail guide. At its base begins the half-mile **Lava River Trail**, an interpretive trail explaining the volcanic formations.

### Hiking

The **Upper & Lower Proxy Falls** tumble over glacier-carved walls to disappear into lava flows. An easy half-mile hike leads to these delicate but popular falls. The easily overlooked trail begins directly east of milepost 64.

Have a close-up view of a lava dam from **Linton Lake Trail**. The easy 1.2-mile trail begins across from Alder Springs Camp-

OREGON

ground, and leads to lava-dammed Linton Lake. In the distance, Linton Falls roars over the valley edge (no trail leads to the falls) and tumbles to the lake.

The subterranean waters of Lost Valley collect and surge to the surface in the lower valley. Directly east of milepost 59, turn north into a large clearing. Walk 100 yards along an informal trail to a lovely spot where the creek surfaces at **Lost Valley Spring**.

The Pacific Crest Trail crosses McKenzie Pass near the west edge of the Dee Wright Observatory parking lot. It's three miles across lava flows to **Little Belknap** and **Belknap Craters**. Follow a good trail north along an easy grade, but be aware that there's no water or shelter along the trail; on a hot day, the hike can be oppressive.

A popular half-day hike leaves from Scott Lake Campground, six miles west of the pass. The trail winds past several small lakes (which act as reflecting ponds for the Three Sisters peaks), and on to **Hand Lake**; there and back make this an easy three-mile stroll.

Five miles west of McKenzie Pass is the beginning of the **Obsidian Trail**, at Frog Camp Campground; it's one of the most popular and gentle entrances into the Three Sisters Wilderness. Day hikers might consider a 2.5-mile hike through thick forest to reach a 50-foot high lava flow. From the top is a sudden and exhilarating view directly onto the Three Sisters. The trail continues past Obsidian Cliffs to join the Pacific Crest Trail in another 1.5 miles.

### Places to Stay

Facilities are fairly basic at nearby campgrounds. *Scott Lake Campground* offers a pretty lakeside site for tenters, but no running water. A mile east of McKenzie Pass is *Lava Camp Lake Campground*, with similarly informal amenities.

Down in Lost Creek Valley, *Limberlost Campground* is just five miles east of McKenzie Bridge, on Hwy 242. The campground sits in a nice wooded location, near the springs of Lost Creek.

# Upper Willamette River & Highway 58

Southeast from Eugene, the Willamette River leaves its wide valley and becomes a rushing, mountain river. That is, when it isn't impounded by dams. The reservoirs at Dexter and Lowell dam the mainstem of the Willamette River, and above Oakridge, the Middle Fork of the Willamette is also dammed. Only the North Fork of the Willamette runs unimpeded from its headwaters at Waldo Lake. (A National Forest Scenic Byway follows USFS Rd 19 along the North Fork; forests here are extremely thick, and are home to such rare species as the spotted owl and wolverine; the road eventually emerges north near McKenzie Bridge.)

Traffic is heavy along steeply pitched Hwy 58; you'll be glad for the opportunity to turn off the road and take in the sight of something besides a hurtling log truck. The scenery along most of the route consists of dense Douglas fir forests and the now usual handmaiden of these groves, clear-cuts. At the crest of the Cascades, near Willamette Pass, are a number of beautiful lakes and Oregon's second highest waterfall; a popular hot springs bubbles up just beside the road at another point.

The only town along Hwy 58 is Oakridge (population 3145), a logging town with basic services for travelers.

### ORIENTATION & INFORMATION

Highway 58 follows the Willamette River from near Eugene to tie into Hwy 97 south of Bend. The entire route is 85 miles long; Oakridge is 35 miles from Eugene, Willamette Pass is 52 miles from Eugene.

The Oakridge-Westfir Chamber of Commerce (☎ 782-4146) can be reached at PO Box 217, Oakridge, OR 97463.

For information about the Willamette National Forest and the local wilderness areas, contact the Oakridge Ranger Station (☎ 782-2291), 46375 Hwy 58, Oakridge.

## McCREDIE SPRINGS

These undeveloped riverside hot springs are a popular and convenient stopover for savvy travelers along Hwy 58, who let the steaming waters soak away the rigors of driving one of the state's busiest routes. Don't expect seclusion here, or demure modesty. The largest pool isn't called the Party Pool for nothing; McCredie Hot Springs are popular with U of O students from Eugene, especially on weekends.

McCredie Hot Springs are 45 miles east of Eugene on Hwy 58; look for a large unpaved parking area just past the turn off for the Blue Pool Campground. Informal trails lead to Salt Creek and the hot springs, 100 yards distant.

## SALT CREEK FALLS

This roaring giant of a falls is, at 286 feet, Oregon's second highest; easy access from Hwy 58 makes it a must-see. All-ability trails lead out to the top of the falls, where you can crane your neck over the edge to

see the trails of mist strike the mossy rocks far below. Standing just feet from the edge of a major waterfall is an uncanny, rather disquieting experience. Another trail leads to more distant viewpoints and eventually to the base of the falls. A picnic area and flush toilets are also available.

## WALDO LAKE

The headwaters of the mighty Willamette River, Waldo Lake is also one of the purest bodies of water in the world: at an elevation of 5414 feet on the very crest of the Cascades, Waldo Lake has no stream inlets, and the only water that enters the lake is snowmelt and rainfall. Few mosses or algae are able to exist in this pure water, resulting in the amazing transparency of the lake; studies indicate that objects 115 feet below the surface of the lake are visible.

Other superlatives attend Waldo Lake: it is Oregon's second largest natural lake at nearly 10 sq miles, and the state's second deepest lake at 420 feet. Obviously, such a

OREGON

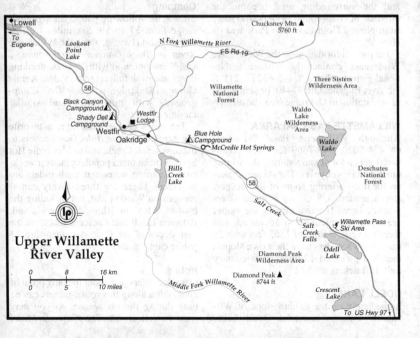

body of water is delicate, and boating and fishing restrictions apply. No motorized boats are allowed; afternoon winds make the lake popular for sailing.

The west and north side of the lake are contained in the **Waldo Lake Wilderness,** a 148-sq-mile area filled with tiny glacial lakes and meadows. Waldo Lake Wilderness is contiguous with the Three Sisters Wilderness to the north.

Three USFS campgrounds flank the eastern half of the lake and hiking trails lead off into the wilderness. The 20-mile **Waldo Lake Trail** circles the lake; a less ambitious hike leads from North Waldo Campground to the outlet of the Willamette River, a 3.4 mile one-way hike that edges the lake and sandy swimming beaches. Make a loop trail by returning via Rigdon Lakes, which lie at the base of a volcanic butte.

Because of the lake's elevation, trails aren't free of snow until June, and are closed in October. In the interim, the lake and the surrounding area become the province of cross-country skiers who leave from plowed Gold Lake Sno-Park area on Hwy 58.

For more information on the Waldo Lake Wilderness, contact the Willamette National Forest office (☎ 465-6521), 211 E 7th Ave, Eugene, OR 97440; or stop at the ranger station in Oakridge (see above).

### WILLAMETTE PASS SKI AREA

Although Willamette Pass Ski Area (☎ 484-5030, 345-7669 for snow conditions) gets a lot of snow during the winter, much of it is pretty wet. The ski area makes up for it by offering some of the steepest slopes around: US Olympic speed skiers practice here. The majority of the slopes are rated intermediate to advanced, and there's a vertical drop of 1563 feet with 29 runs. Snowboarders have their own slopes; there's a groomed 12-mile, cross-country trail. Lift tickets are $22.

### ODELL LAKE

Immediately on the eastern slope of Willamette Pass is beautiful Odell Lake, resting in a steep glacial basin. Odell Lake is but one of many lakes in the area; a rustic lodge and campgrounds ring nearby Crescent Lake, and more remote Summit Lake is preferred by purists.

Odell, Crescent and Summit lakes flank the **Diamond Peak Wilderness Area,** a 126-sq-mile preserve of lakes, craggy mountains and deep forests. Hiking trails lead into this relatively unexplored wilderness from lakeside campgrounds. A popular hike from the Odell Lake Lodge leads 3.8 miles to **Fawn Lake,** below two rugged peaks. From the Trapper Creek Campground, energetic hikers should consider the 4.3-mile one-way hike to **Yoran Lake** to reach a great view of 8744-foot Diamond Peak. The Pacific Crest Trail winds through the high country in the wilderness; pick up the trail at Willamette Pass and wind through old forests to Midnight Lake, an easy 3.3-mile one-way hike.

### PLACES TO STAY
#### Camping

Sites at the following public campgrounds range from $7 to $9. Six miles west of Oakridge on Hwy 58, along the Willamette River is *Black Canyon Campground*, a USFS campground with 72 sites; drinking water and vault toilets are provided. A mile closer to Oakridge is *Shady Dell Campground*, with nine sites and similar facilities.

Ten miles east of Oakridge, a favorite campground is *Blue Hole*. Good access to fishing on Salt Creek, and to McCredie Hot Springs make this a popular place on weekends. Running water and vault toilets are provided. There are three lovely campgrounds on Waldo Lake, not including the boat-in sites on Rhododendron Island. Between Odell and Crescent lakes, on the east slopes of the Cascades, there are 11 public campgrounds.

#### Hotels

Oakridge offers just about the only point of civilization along this route; motels can be busy during the ski season, so you may want to call ahead. The *Cascade Motel*

(☎ 782-2602), 47487 Hwy 58, and the *Ridgeview Motel* (☎ 782-3430), 47465 Hwy 58, are $30/$34. The *Best Western Oakridge Inn* (☎ 782-2212), 47445 Hwy 58, is Oakridge's most pleasant lodging, and offers rooms at $52/58.

### B&Bs

A stone's throw from Oregon's longest covered bridge, the *Westfir Lodge* (☎ 782-3103), 47365 1st St, Westfir, was formerly the executive offices of a logging company. However, the Craftsman-style building was converted into a spacious B&B in the early 1990s. Four guest rooms share two bathrooms in this handsome, rambling building, and an English-style flower garden makes the side patio a charming place to relax. Rates are $55 a night.

### Lodges

*Odell Lake Lodge* (☎ 443-2540), six miles east of Willamette Pass, offers a variety of lodging options. Rooms in the lodge range from $36 to $48; all have private baths. There are also 13 cabins scattered along the lakefront, each with bathrooms, fully equipped kitchens and wood-burning stoves. Four-person cabins range from $65 to $80; six and eight-person cabins range between $80 and $135. One cabin sleeps 16

for $195. The lodge is busy during ski season, so early reservations are a must. The mailing address of the lodge is PO Box 72, Crescent Lake, OR 97425.

The lodge also offers a full range of rental equipment, from cross-country skis, mountain bikes, canoes and motor boats to snow shoes.

### PLACES TO EAT

Home-cooking is the hallmark at the *Sportsman Cafe* (☎ 782-2051), 48127 Hwy 58, open 24 hours a day, with standards like chicken fried steak ($9) and sandwiches to please logger and traveler alike. Sort of a logging-museum-cum-restaurant *Timber Jim's Pizza* (☎ 782-4310), 47527 Hwy 58, is a popular place to stop on the way back from the ski slopes. Pizza and pasta are the favorites here; there's also a salad bar. Tables are hewn from immense logs, and old photos of forests-we-have-known adorn the log walls. For espresso and fresh bakery products, go to *Miss McGillicuty's* (☎ 782-2033), 47772 Hwy 58.

The dining room at the *Odell Lake Lodge* (433-2540) offers home-style cooking, with steaks, fried chicken and mashed potatoes fetching $10 to $12. The dining room is pleasant and wood-paneled; the food is tasty, especially after a long hike.

OREGON

# Southern Oregon

Some of Oregon's most magical sites are contained within the valleys of the Rogue and Umpqua rivers and the Klamath Basin, including Crater Lake National Park. Magic of another sort takes place at Ashland, home of the Oregon Shakespeare Festival.

The Rogue River, known for its challenging white-water rafting, rises from the flanks of Crater Lake before plunging oceanward in a spectacular mountain-lined gorge, and the brooding and quixotic North Fork of the Umpqua River draws in anglers from around the world to match wits with steelhead trout, the monarch of Oregon rivers.

The Siskiyou Mountains expose some of Oregon's oldest and most puzzling geology, rich in vivid peridotite and serpentinite rock that originally formed as ocean bedrock. Here, the thick fir forests of the north are replaced by orange-barked madrona, scrub oak and brushy manzanita. Cougars are more common in the south than anywhere else in Oregon, and another rare species is occasionally sighted: the Sasquatch, or Big Foot.

The communities of southern Oregon differ sharply in their genesis from the communities along the Willamette River. The Oregon Trail pioneers who settled the Willamette Valley were usually well-off New Englanders, whereas the settlers of southern Oregon were largely displaced southerners and Confederate soldiers migrating westward at the vanguard of gold rushes.

This mountainous region remained much more socially conservative than the rest of Oregon, and developed a highly autonomous sensibility, but the traditional insularity was broken in the 1960s when young people moved here, setting up farms and communes as part of the 'back to the land' movement.

Southern Oregon's social conservatism

and homogeneity are today both challenged and triumphant. The Oregon Citizen's Alliance (OCA), an arch-conservative religious movement, is a phenomenon of southern Oregon. However, the OCA is currently finding a statewide audience even as southern Oregon fills up with educated professionals, displaced Californians, actors and wine-growers.

## GETTING THERE & AWAY
### Air
The Medford/Jackson County Airport is north of Medford, off Table Rock Rd. Flights link Medford to Portland and San Francisco; United (☎ (800) 241-6522) and Horizon (☎ (800) 547-9308) are the primary carriers.

Cascade Airport Shuttle (☎ 488-1998) services Ashland; it costs $8 per person with a $16 minimum. Reservations are required.

The major car-rental companies, Hertz (☎ 773-4293), Avis (☎ 773-3003) and Budget (☎ 773-7023), are represented at the airport.

### Weather & Road Reports
Siskiyou Pass on I-5 between Oregon and California is known for its treacherous winter driving conditions. Call the state road report (☎ 976-7277) if there's any question about road conditions.

## ASHLAND
Home to the internationally renowned Oregon Shakespeare Festival (OSF), Ashland (population 17,320) is the cultural center of southern Oregon, and one of the most pleasant towns in the state.

Theater, B&Bs and food dominate life here: 350,000 people a year come to Ashland to attend the productions at the OSF's three venues, which include a large outdoor theater dedicated to Elizabethan drama. The restaurant scene is almost as lively as

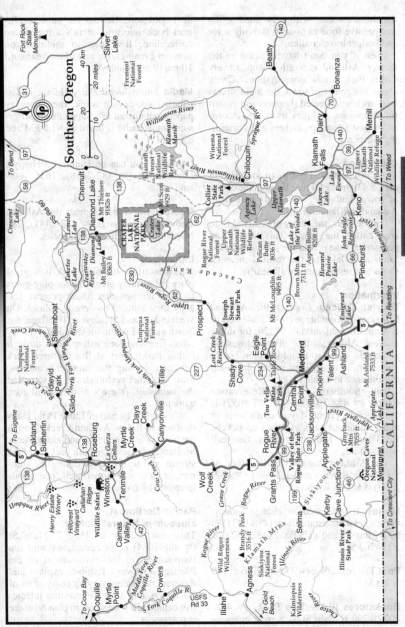

the theater scene, with very good, often inexpensive food to nourish starving actor and budget traveler alike.

Even if you don't have a ticket to the theater, Ashland is worth a stop. Lovely Lithia Park winds along Ashland Creek above the center of town, the main streets buzz with well-heeled shoppers and youthful bohemians, and park trails meander for miles past swans, picnickers and declaiming thespians.

## Orientation

There is a north and south exit for Ashland off I-5. Highway 99 runs through the center of town, and Hwy 66 winds east from Ashland to Klamath Falls.

For travelers, the center of Ashland is an area called the Plaza. This streamside pedestrian zone is near the junction of East Main and Oak Sts; the festival theaters, shops and restaurants are all nearby.

## Information

**Tourist Offices** Contact the Ashland Chamber of Commerce (☎ 482-3486), 110 E Main St, Ashland, OR 97520, for information. Although this office closes on weekends, there is an information booth, open from 10 am to 7 pm, on the plaza near the entrance to Lithia Park.

The Southern Oregon Reservation Center (☎ 488-1011, (800) 547-8052) is the place to phone if you don't want to make numerous calls to round up tickets, B&B lodging and other extras. One call will do it all.

The Ashland Ranger District office of the Rogue River National Forest (☎ 482-3333) is at 645 Washington St.

**Money** If you need to change money, there's a 1st Interstate Bank (488-0431) at 67 E Main St, and a US Bank (482-1522) at 30 N 2nd St.

**Post** The post office (☎ 482-3986) is at 120 N 1st St.

**Bookstores** Bloomsbury Books (☎ 488-0029), 290 E Main St, is a great independent bookstore. Besides the large, intelligent book selection, there's a mezzanine coffeeshop. It's open to midnight on summer evenings, the rest of the year until 10 pm (9 pm Sundays).

**Media** The *Ashland Daily Tidings* is distributed six days a week; the Thursday paper contains an arts supplement. Jefferson Public Radio is heard on 91.5 FM and 89.1 FM.

**Laundry** You can do laundry at Henry's Laundromat (☎ 482-2658), 1656 Ashland St.

**Medical Services** Contact the Ashland Community Hospital (☎ 482-2441), 280 Maple St, for medical emergencies.

## Lithia Park

This beautiful, 100-acre park is a great place for a shady picnic, or for play-goers to plow through that Shakespearean tragedy they avoided reading in college. On Wednesdays and Sundays at 10:30 am, the Northwest Museum of Natural History offers free hour-long nature walks through Lithia Park; meet at the northern park entrance. During the summer, concerts, films and other performances are staged at the bandshell; there's also a small rose garden.

Although not a part of Lithia Park, paths continue to follow Ashland Creek through the back side of the Plaza and along Water St. Bars and cafes have built decks over the stream, and on Tuesdays during the summer, crafters and farmers sell their goods from booths and tents.

## Pacific Northwest Museum of Natural History

This new facility at 1500 E Main St (☎ 488-1084) is an educational and fun introduction to the environment of the Pacific Northwest. Exhibits explain and illustrate the widely varying ecosystems of the region, and a very interesting interactive exhibit allows visitors to plan resource management.

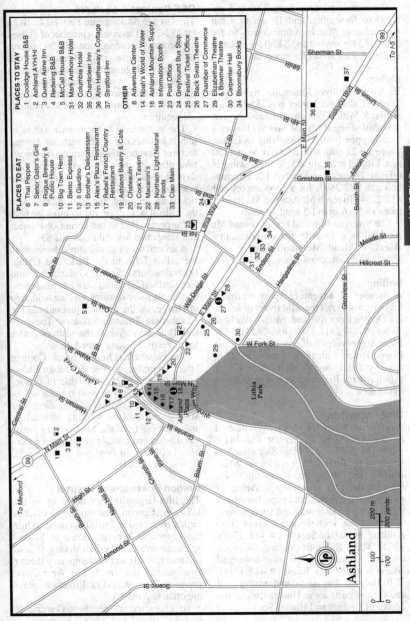

**PLACES TO STAY**

1 Coolidge House B&B
2 Ashland AYH/HI
3 Queen Anne Inn
4 Redwing B&B
5 McCall House B&B
31 Mark Anthony Hotel
32 Columbia Hotel
35 Chanticleer Inn
36 Ann Hathaway's Cottage
37 Stratford Inn

**PLACES TO EAT**

6 Thai Pepper
7 Senor Gator's Grill
9 Rogue Brewery & Public House
10 Big Town Hero
11 Bento Express
12 Il Giardino
13 Brother's Delicatessen
15 Alex's Plaza Restaurant
17 Rebel's French Country Restaurant
19 Ashland Bakery & Cafe
20 Chateaulin
21 Cook's Tavern
22 Macaroni's
28 Northern Light Natural Foods
33 Ciao Main

**OTHER**

8 Adventure Center
14 Noah's World of Water
16 Ashland Mountain Supply
18 Information Booth
23 Post Office
24 Greyhound Bus Stop
25 Festival Ticket Office
26 Chamber of Commerce
27 Black Swan Theatre
29 Elizabethan Theatre & Bowmer Theatre
30 Carpenter Hall
34 Bloomsbury Books

Ashland

The museum is open from 9 am to 5 pm April to November, and 10 am to 4 pm November to March. Admission is $6 for adults, $5 for seniors and $4.50 for children under 15. Call ahead for group rates.

### Skiing

High in the Siskiyou Mountains, right on the Oregon/California border is 7235-foot Mt Ashland. With 325 inches of snow a year, downhill skiing at Mt Ashland Ski Resort is usually open from Thanksgiving to Easter. There are 22 runs, with a total drop of 1150 feet. Lift tickets begin at $16. Night skiing is offered Thursday to Sunday. For information call 482-2897; for a snow report call 482-2754. To reach Mt Ashland Ski Resort, take exit No 6 from I-5 south of town.

The Siskiyou National Forest around Mt Ashland is a favorite for cross-country skiers. Ashland Mountain Supply (see above) also rents cross-country skis.

### Rafting

A number of adventure sport outfitters make it easy to raft the wild rivers of southern Oregon from Ashland. Noah's World of Water (☎ 488 2811, (800) 858-2811), 53 N Main St, provides half-day trips down the Rogue River, with three departures daily from Ashland. Noah's also offers longer trips down the Rogue River and other rivers in the area.

### Other Activities

A raft of adventure travel options is offered by the Adventure Center (☎ 488-2819, (800) 444-2819), 40 N Main St, a clearinghouse of local recreation outfitters. While white-water rafting dominates the offerings, see them for adventures as various as mountain-bike rentals and trips, horseback riding, hot air ballooning and spelunking.

Or you can rent mountain bikes from Ashland Mountain Supply (☎ 488-2749), 31 N Main St, and explore the back country. Ashland's public, nine-hole **golf** course is called Oak Knoll (☎ 482-4311), 3070 Hwy 66. The public **swimming** pool and tennis courts are in Hunter Park, at the corner of Holmes and Hunter Sts.

### OSF Courses & Lectures

The Oregon Shakespeare Festival Institute (☎ 482-2111) sponsors a number of classes and lectures in conjunction with its productions. The courses range from two-week seminars for high school drama students, to symposiums for school and community theater directors, to ticket/lecture packages for five or nine plays. Advance reservations are required.

The institute also sponsors a series of public lectures during the summer. Formal lectures on scholarly and dramatic subjects take place on most Fridays and Wednesdays at noon, and are delivered by visiting academics, actors and directors. Advance tickets are required, and are available from the festival box office; the lectures are held at Carpenter Hall at the corner of Pioneer and Hargadine Sts. Admission is $3.

A second series of noontime discussions are called Talks in the Park, and feature festival actors, directors, designers and technical staff. The talks are informal question-and-answer sessions, and are held, free of charge, on the grounds just outside the Elizabethan Theatre, Sundays, Tuesdays and Thursdays. Ask at the visitors center for a 'Festival Noons' schedule.

The Southern Oregon State College offers a number of course through Elderhostel (☎ 552-6378), available to seniors ages 55 and older. The most popular week-long session is called 'From Script to Stage', and involves working with actors and directors from the Shakespeare Festival. To register, contact the national Elderhostel office at 80 Boylston St, Suite 400, Boston, MA 02116.

### Oregon Shakespeare Festival

The fifth-largest theater company in the USA, the Oregon Shakespeare Festival is highly respected and wildly popular. While the repertoire here is rooted in Shakespearean and Elizabethan drama, it also features revivals and contemporary theater from around the world. The West Coast premiers of West End or Broadway plays are often in Ashland.

To characterize the theater scene in

### The Festival's Beginnings

The Methodist Church is responsible for an important fixture of life in Ashland. The young town was included in the church's community adult-education program called the Chautauqua Series, an annual event that brought lectures, concerts and theater to far-flung communities. Ashland's Chautauqua Hall was built early in the century, and was a dilapidated wooden shell in the 1930s. A professor of drama at the local college, named Angus Bowmer, noted the resemblance of the roofless structure to drawings of Shakespeare's Globe Theatre. He convinced the people of Ashland to sponsor two performances of Shakespeare's plays (and a boxing match – the Bard would have approved) as part of the town's 1935 Fourth of July celebration. The plays proved a great success, and the Oregon Shakespeare Festival was off and running. ∎

Ashland as a 'festival' is a quaint reference to the troupe's early days as a summertime event. Nowadays, the official festival productions begin in February and end in October. There are three festival theaters. The Elizabethan Theatre, which seats 1200, is an outdoor stage; it can get chilly under the stars, so dress prudently. Open from June to October only, productions here are almost exclusively Shakespearean or period tragedies. The Angus Bowmer Theatre seats 600 and is the stage for both Shakespearean and contemporary drama and comedy. The Black Swan, a small theater with 150 seats, is the playhouse for more experimental and intimate works.

The festival theaters are near the intersection of Main and Pioneer Sts, at the base of Lithia Park.

**Tickets** Getting tickets for the festival productions can be a challenge. The summer run is sold out months in advance, so the only chance to get tickets at the last minute is to wait in line at 6 pm at the ticket office

(☎ 482-4331), 15 S Pioneer St, in the theater courtyard, when unclaimed tickets go on sale, or to wait around for scalpers. If you're up for it, there are $8 standing room tickets for the outdoor performances. Ticket prices range from $22.50 to $28.50; kids get 25% off. There are no Monday performances. June 8 to September 5, the box office is open from 9:30 am to 8:30 pm; in spring and fall it closes at 8 pm.

**Theater Tours** The Festival also offers backstage tours of the theaters. Like seemingly everything else, these $8 tours ($6 children ages five to 17) are immensely popular, and require advance reservations. Tours begin at 10 am in front of the Black Swan Theatre; call the ticket office for availability and reservations.

If you fail to get a ticket for a performance or for the tour, you can pay $2 to visit the Exhibit Center (just behind the ticket office) to view costumes and relics of OSF history. Admission to the exhibit center is included in the Backstage Tour.

### Other Special Events

Ashland's biggest festival outside of the summer theater season is the wintertime Festival of Light. Beginning the day after Thanksgiving and continuing through New Year's Day, the festival includes candlelight tours of historic homes, special theater performances and displays of art and holiday lights. Contact the visitors center for more information.

The opening of the Elizabethan Theatre is the impetus for the Feast of Will. This momentous event, usually held the third Friday of June, is celebrated with food booths in Lithia Park, a parade and fireworks.

Not sanctioned by the chamber of commerce, but tons of fun, is Halloween in Ashland. Just imagine what all those actors get up to.

### Places to Stay

On any given summer evening, thousands of people converge on Ashland to see the plays. Don't expect to pull into town and easily find a room. Reservations are absolutely necessary, especially at B&Bs (some won't even take walk-ins).

The easy way around the hassle of finding a room is to contact one of the reservation services and let them do the work. Call Southern Oregon Reservation Center (☎ 488-1011, (800) 547-8052) for room reservations, as well as ticket, ski and recreation packages. The Ashland B&B Clearinghouse (☎ 488-0338) can help you find a room in a B&B, and can offer suggestions for other lodging options.

The following prices are for the high season; rates can drop by half in the off-season.

**Camping** The KOA Glenyan (☎ 482-4138), 5310 Hwy 66, is primarily a shady RV campground with some tent sites, four miles out of Ashland near Emigrant Lake. Like everything else in Ashland, prices are stiff ($19), facilities pleasant and reservations suggested. Emigrant Lake Recreation Area is a county park and campground alongside the lake. It's a bit more rustic, and about half the price. If you're camping out of season, then the Jackson Hot Springs Resort (☎ 482-3776), just two miles north of Ashland on Hwy 99, might be the place for you. Besides grassy campsites, the resort offers naturally heated swimming pools and mineral baths. Rates are $12 a night, and it's $5 to use the hot pools.

**Hostels** The Ashland AYH Hostel (☎ 482-9217), 150 N Main St, is a great hostel in a great location. Located in one of the town's B&B neighborhoods, the hostel is only blocks from downtown, theaters and nightlife; rates are $11 for members, $13 for non-members.

**B&Bs** For many people, staying in Ashland is inseparable from staying in so-called 'English-style' at a B&B inn. At last count, Ashland had about sixty B&Bs, which often share only initials with their more humble British cousins. Most are magnificent old Victorian homes with two to three luxury bedroom suites. Expect to

pay top dollar to stay at these small, exclusive inns, but if sleeping in an antique-filled room followed by a fancy breakfast appeals to you, here's your chance. It's an Ashland tradition.

Use one of the reservation services to shop the options. If you want to make your own reservations, check on the following, as they are convenient to the theaters. The Queen Anne Inn (☎ 482-0220), 125 N Main St, is an 1880 Victorian; rooms begin at $75. The Redwing B&B (☎ 482-1807), 115 N Main St, is an old Craftsman-style home; rooms are $95. The Coolidge House (☎ 482-4721), 137 N Main St, is a Victorian with an upper balcony overlooking the town; rooms start at $70. The McCall House (☎ 482-9296), 153 Oak St, is a mansard-roofed Victorian with eight guest rooms, starting at $90. Ann Hathaway's Cottage (☎ 488-1050), 586 E Main St, is a fancifully named old boarding house with six rooms at $85. The Chanticleer Inn (☎ 482-1919), 120 Gresham St, is another Craftsman-style home with six bedrooms; rooms range from $115 to $155. Most have private baths.

**Hotels** There's a number of middle-range ($50 to $60) hotels on Siskiyou Blvd (Hwy 99), most with swimming pools. Try the Ashland Motel (☎ 482-2561), 1145 Siskiyou Blvd, and neighboring Timbers Motel (☎ 482-4242), 1450 Ashland St, about a half mile from the theaters. The Palm Motel (☎ 482-2636), 1065 Siskiyou Blvd, rents out small houses in addition to motel rooms. The Stratford Inn (☎ 488-2151), 555 Siskiyou Blvd, is within walking distance of the theaters.

Two of Ashland's old, downtown hotels have been stylishly refurbished and updated. The Mark Antony (☎ 482-1721, (800) 926-8669), 212 E Main St, is the town's tallest building and a real architectural gem; it's listed on the Historic Register. Rooms begin at $63. The Columbia Hotel (☎ 482-3726), 262½ E Main St, is a modest-looking but charming establishment; rooms begin at $49 with shared bathroom, $74 with private bath.

Probably the most comfortable motel in Ashland is the *Ashland Hills Inn* (☎ 482-8310, (800) 547-4747), 2525 Ashland St, with spa facilities and a shuttle service to theaters; rooms are $60/65.

Save a little money and escape the theater crowds by staying in Phoenix, a small town seven miles north of Ashland. The clean and welcoming *Phoenix Motel* (☎ 535-1555), 510 N Main St, also has a pool; single/double rates are $30/34.

If these prices, or the absence of rooms, give you grief, then consider staying in Medford; it's only 10 miles away.

## Places to Eat

There's no difficulty in finding places to eat in Ashland. The three-block area around the festival stages must have more restaurants than anywhere else in the Pacific Northwest.

Ashland has the distinction of levying the only restaurant tax in the state. The 5% tax is added to prepared meals eaten in restaurants; 1% of the tax goes toward the purchase of green space in the city, and 4% goes toward the cost of a new sewage-treatment facility. There is no tax on unprepared food in grocery stores.

**Budget** Breakfasts are the order of the day at *Ashland Bakery & Cafe* (☎ 482-2117), 38 E Main St, and at the *Breadboard* (☎ 488-0295), 744 N Main St. Eat breakfast all day at *Brother's Delicatessen* (☎ 482-9671), 95 N Main St, a New York-style kosher deli.

Eat cheap at *Bento Express* (☎ 488-3582), 3 Granite St, and at *Big Town Hero* (☎ 488-1523), 75 N Main St, where meals are less than $4. Go a bit up-market next door on the deck at *Il Giardino* (☎ 488-0816), 5 Granite St, where pasta dishes start at $7.

**Middle** For fiery Asian cooking, go to the *Thai Pepper* (☎ 482-8058), 84 N Main St, where red pork curry costs $10, and tables overlook Ashland Creek. Next deck over is *Senor Gator's Cabo Grill & Liquor Stand* (☎ 482-4131), 92½ N Main St, with excel-

lent, affordable Mexican food; the shark tacos and lime chicken come recommended. *Rebel's French Country Restaurant* (☎ 482-0310), 29 N Main St, offers a best-of-the-locals wine list, and home-style French cooking. Quiche dinners, with salad and vegetables, start at $8.50. In the same price range is *Macaroni's* (☎ 488-3359), 58 E Main St, with pizza and Italian fast food.

For vegetarian and natural food dishes, go to *Northern Light Natural Foods* (☎ 482-9463), 120 E Main St, where the preparations are mostly Indian. At *Ciao Main* (☎ 482-8435), 272 E Main St, there are four-course, pre-theater Italian dinners for $15.

**Top End** For a splurge or special occasion, Ashland offers some of southern Oregon's best restaurants. Call ahead for reservations. The *Chateaulin* (☎ 482-2264), 50 E Main St, serves topflight French cuisine in an attractive wood-lined dining room; escalopes de veau go for $23. Browse next door in the restaurant's gourmet shop for fancy picnic fare. For steaks and seafood, go to *Omar's* (☎ 482-1281), 1380 Siskiyou Blvd. *Alex's Plaza Restaurant* (☎ 482-8818), 35 N Main St, turns American standards into cuisine; pork ribs go for $18. In summer there's seating above the creek. Just north of Ashland in Talent is *Chata's Restaurant* (☎ 535-2575). Pronounced HAH-ta, this venerable establishment is known for its eastern European specialties.

## Entertainment

**Brewpubs** Obviously, theater's the thing in Ashland, but after a day with the Bard, who can blame actor or spectator for being thirsty? Perhaps Oregon's best pint of ale is brewed by *Rogue Brewery & Public House* (☎ 488-5061), 31 Water St. The deck of this stream-side, smoke-free brewpub is snuggled under a highway ramp, but no matter; during the summer, there's live music. Try the Rogue Red Ale. Young theater-goers flock to *Cook's Tavern* (☎ 488-4626), 66 E Main St, for pool and drinks. The live music at the *Mark Antony*

OREGON

*Lounge* (☎ 482-1721), 212 E Main St, spills out onto streets on warm, summer evenings. For a quiet drink and snack, the back bar at the *Chateaulin* (☎ 482-2264), 50 E Main St, is popular with the after-theater crowd.

**Off 'Bardway' Theater** There's no question that the Shakespeare Festival is the big gun in town, but with all these actors and audience members flocking to the Ashland area, there's also a bevy of small, independent theater troupes and cabarets springing up. Contact the visitors center for details, or call the following for theater schedules and current locations: the *Lyric Theatre* (☎ 772-1555), the *Cygnet Theatre* for children's productions (☎ 488-2945), *Actors' Theatre* (☎ 482-9659) and the *Oregon Cabaret Theatre* (☎ 488-2902) for musical comedy.

### Getting There & Around

If you're looking to fly into the region, see Getting There & Away at the beginning of this chapter for information on the Medford/Jackson County Airport.

There are three Greyhound buses a day between Ashland and Portland; however, there is no bus station. Greyhound discharges and takes on passengers at the corner of 2nd St and Lithia Way. The nearest station is in Medford (see below). Green Tortoise (☎ (800) 227 4766) stops in Ashland on both north and southbound routes. Schedules are a bit tricky, so call for details and reservations.

For a cab, call Ashland Taxi (☎ 482-3065).

## MEDFORD & AROUND

What Medford (population 49,900) lacks in charm, it makes up for in location. Southern Oregon's largest city, Medford is at the center of the region's fruit and lumber industry, and is also central to southern Oregon's scenic and recreational glories. Ashland, Crater Lake, Oregon Caves National Monument and the Rogue River Valley are each convenient to the city and its inexpensive motels.

Medford's centrality is no accident. It began as Middleford when the Oregon & California Railroad Company came north from Sacramento in 1883. Existing towns in the valley, like Jacksonville and Central Point, refused to give the railroad a $25,000 payment to build a station, so the railroad established its own station, and platted a new town around it. Middleford became Medford, and the city was off and running.

Fruit trees, especially pears, are what made Medford famous. During the early years of this century thousands of acres of fruit trees were planted, the newly built railroad providing a national market. In April the valley is bathed in pink and white blossoms.

No one would claim that Medford is a tourist town, but its downtown offers a pleasant, streamside park and better food than the freeway stops.

### Orientation

Interstate 5 passes through the center of Medford; Hwy 62, often called the Crater Lake Hwy, heads northeast from Medford to Crater Lake National Park. Highway 99 is the main commercial strip in Medford; in town it divides into two one-way streets: Riverside Ave flows north and Central Ave flows south. Along these are most of Medford's cheaper motels and restaurants.

### Information

The Traveler's Information Center (☎ 776-4021) is south of town along Hwy 99 at 88 Stewart Rd. The Medford Visitors & Convention Bureau (☎ 779-4847) is at 304 S Central Ave. The Rogue River National Forest District Office (☎ 776-3600) is at 333 W 8th St.

The post office (☎ 776-1326) is at 333 W 8th St. The Medford daily newspaper is the *Medford Mail Tribune*. Jefferson Public Broadcasting is heard on 91.5 and 89.1 FM. BJ's Homestyle Laundromat (☎ 773-4803), 1712 W Main St, offers TV, snacks and games in addition to washers and dryers. For medical emergencies, contact Providence Hospital (☎ 773-6611) 1111 Crater Lake Ave.

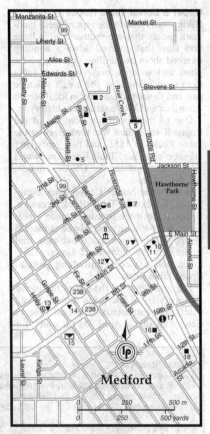

Medford

## Southern Oregon Museum & History Store

This regional museum (☎ 779-4847), 106 N Central Ave, tells the story of the valley's farming, logging, and mining past. The Southern Oregon Historical Society offices and research library are also here; the museum is noted for its large collection of period photographs. Admission is free.

## Harry & David's Country Store

Probably Medford's most famous fruiters are brothers Harry and David Holmes. During the early 1900s, their family orchard exported pears to grand European hotels. But when the 1930s' Depression years put an end to that market, the two brothers decided to start a fruit-by-mail venture. The result was the wildly successful Harry & David's fruit mail-order business, led by the Fruit-of-the-Month Club.

The 'outlet store' for the mail-order fruiters, this large produce-and-gift store (☎ 776-2277), immediately off exit No 27 on Circle Drive, is a great place to stock up on Oregon-made food products and fresh fruit. The prices and selection of fruit and vegetables are pretty good; you'll have no

trouble putting together a healthy, inexpensive picnic. There's also an espresso bar and candy shop.

Half a mile south of the Country Store is the **Jackson & Perkins Test & Display Gardens**, one of the nation's largest commercial rose growers, also owned by Harry & David's. Although the location – along a busy highway – isn't idyllic, the roses don't seem to mind. A few shadeless picnic tables are provided.

Free tours of the food and rose-packing operations are available; ask at the country store.

**Upper & Lower Table Rocks**

Hiking trails lead to the tops of these landmark mesas that are remnants of a large lava flow that coursed down a winding riverbed about two million years ago. Now plant and wildlife preserves, the Table Rocks are vestiges of the area's volcanic past and figure prominently in local Native American and White settlement history.

One of the first major conflicts of the Rogue River Indian War took place at the Table Rocks in 1851, and two years later the soon-abrogated Table Rock Treaty was signed here between the US Government and the Takilmas.

In 1979 the Nature Conservancy established the Lower Table Rock Preserve. Upper Table Rock was later made a preserve, and both are presently administered by the BLM, which has a two-mile trail leading to the summit of Lower Table Rock, and a steeper mile-long path to Upper Table Rock.

The grasslands on the top of the mesas are especially of interest to naturalists and wildflower enthusiasts. The best time to view plant life is April. Be on watch for turkey vultures and red-tailed hawks; rattlesnakes are also natives here. Vistas of the Rogue River valley, 800 feet below the cliff edge, are stunning.

To reach the Table Rocks from downtown Medford, follow Riverside Ave north past the junction with the Crater Lake Hwy, and take the next left on Table Rock Rd. The Table Rocks are about seven miles north of Medford. Just past Tou Velle State Park, the road forks and you will need to decide which Table Rock to climb.

The Medford BLM office (☎ 770-2200), 3040 Biddle Rd, has more information on the Table Rocks.

**Activities**

You can rent bikes from Cycle Analysis (☎ 776-6630), 410 E Main St, and cross-country skis at Rogue Ski Shop (☎ 772-8047), 309 E Jackson St.

Cedar Links Golf Course (☎ 773-4373), 3144 Cedar Links Drive, is an 18-hole course northeast of Medford toward White City.

Large, shady **Hawthorne Park** alongside Bear Creek is a pleasant place to

**Rogue River War**

The Rogue River Indians, technically the Takelmas, were given their popular name by French beaver trappers early in the 19th century. Termed *coquins*, or rogues, for their open hostility toward Whites, this fierce tribe truly earned its nickname once the expedition seeking an all-land route to the Willamette Valley opened up southern Oregon to settlers.

In 1846 a group of adventurous pioneers led by Jesse and Lindsay Applegate developed the South Road, or Scott-Applegate Trail, into Oregon. Although most settlers who chose this route continued over the mountains into the Willamette Valley, others liked the wide Rogue and Umpqua valleys and settled.

The Takelmas attacked immigrant parties, and refused to negotiate with the army to allow passage through their land. The discovery of gold near Jacksonville in 1852 – the first gold strike in southern Oregon – exacerbated tensions. Disenchanted gold panners from California streamed into the region. A series of conflicts developed between the Takelmas, the army and the settlers, with plenty of tit-for-tat butchery on each side. The Table Rock Treaty, signed in 1853, kept the peace until 1855 when miners raided a Takelma village and killed a large number of women and children. In retaliation the Takelmas attacked a mining camp and killed 16 people.

The so-called Rogue River War was on. The army pursued the Takelmas into wild canyons of the western Rogue Valley in late fall 1855, but the Takelmas eluded them. However, for the fleeing Indians, the remote canyons provided little winter shelter or food, and after several months of skirmishes, many of the Takelmas gave themselves up to the army. They were sent north to the Grand Ronde Reservation on the Yamhill River. ∎

unwind or escape the heat. Tennis courts, an outdoor swimming pool, picnic tables and a playground are some of the facilities. Follow Riverside Ave (Hwy 99) to the center of Medford, and turn east on 8th St. The park is just to the east of the I-5 freeway.

Follow directions to the Table Rocks to reach **Tou Velle State Park**, where there's swimming, fishing and picnicking at a shaded stretch of the Rogue River.

## Special Events

In April, when the orchards in the Rogue River valley are in bloom, it's time for the Pear Blossom Festival (☎ 773-9506). Held the second week in the month, the festival includes a crafts fair, parade, food events and a 20 K run.

The Jackson County Fair is held in Central Point, just north of Medford, during the last week of July. Livestock judging, a large midway and the home show comprise the basic components of this large agricultural exposition. The fair grounds are just east of I-5 exit No 32.

## Places to Stay

**Camping** Between Ashland and Medford, at I-5 exit No 24, there are two large RV parks (no tent camping). The *Holiday RV Park* (☎ 535-2183, (800) 452-7970) is on the west side of the freeway and the *Pear Tree RV Park* (☎ 535-4445, (800) 645-7332) is on the east. They both offer full facilities for just under $20.

Tent campers will want to continue past Medford to the little town of Rogue River. *Valley of the Rogue State Park* (☎ 582-1118) is set along the river, and offers showers, a laundry and group sites. The park is at 3792 N River Rd; follow signs from I-5 exit No 45A. Fees begin at $15.

**B&Bs** *Under the Greenwood Tree* (☎ 776-0000), 3045 Bellinger Lane, is a beautiful, old home on a 10-acre orchard southwest of town. The house was built in 1862, and has four guest rooms with private baths. The breakfasts are especially good; after-

noon tea is served to guests at 4:30 pm. Rooms are $125 a night.

**Hotels** Highway 99 (Riverside and Central Aves) is lined with lots of perfectly good and inexpensive motels.

The following are south of downtown, close to I-5 exit No 27: the *Sierra Inn* (☎ 773-7727), 345 S Central Ave, *Harvey's Motel* (☎ 779-6561), 510 S Central Ave, and the *Sis-Q* (☎ 773-8411), 722 S Riverside. North of downtown is another strip of motels: the *Knights Inn* (☎ 773-3676), 500 N Riverside Ave, the *Tiki Lodge* (☎ 773-4579), 509 N Riverside Ave, and the *Cedar Lodge* (☎ 773-7361), 518 N Riverside Ave. All offer rooms in the $30 to $40 range.

If you're looking for something upscale in Medford, then the *Red Lion Motor Inn* (☎ 779-5811), 200 N Riverside Ave, is a good choice. It offers a swimming pool and suite-style rooms beginning at $70.

## Places to Eat

There are plenty of fast-food operations clustered around the freeway exits, but downtown offers more options and character. For breakfast pastries or baguette sandwiches, head to *Boulangerie Rue de Main* (☎ 772-5532), at the corner of W Main and Holly Sts. They also serve espresso drinks. *CK Tiffens* (☎ 779-0480), 226 E Main St, offers home-baked breads and meals that stress natural ingredients, often with an ethnic slant. Vegetarian dishes are available. Lunch specials, like eggplant couscous, are under $5.

Mexican laborers are the muscle behind the region's farm economy; they also provide some of the area's best food. *La Burrita* (☎ 770-2848), 603 N Riverside Ave, is famous for its chimichangas and enormous servings for very little money. For good Mexican food in a more attractive setting, go to *Mexico Lindo* (☎ 734-2175), 945 S Riverside Ave; set back in a courtyard beneath trees, the restaurant looks like a storybook hacienda.

Grab a sandwich from *Deli Down* (☎ 772-4520), 406 E Main St, and head to Hawthorne Park. The *Grub Street Grill*

(☎ 773-4805), 35 N Central Ave St, is Medford's brewpub, and serves sandwiches for under $5.

The *Hungry Woodsman* (☎ 772-2050), 2001 N Pacific Hwy, is a Medford tradition with Bunyanesque servings and decor, and an all-American kind of menu, with steak, chicken and seafood dinners starting at

$11. Downtown, *Digger O'Dells* (☎ 779-6100), 333 E Main St, is another steakhouse/saloon that wears its past on the walls.

Forego steaks for cuisine in *Streams* (☎ 776-9090), 1841 Barnett Rd, specializing in Oregon-grown products prepared with zesty sauces and herbs. Fish and pasta

## The States of Jefferson, Shasta & Jackson

The southern counties of Oregon and the northern counties of California, isolated from the major power centers of their respective states, have long been home to strong secessionist movements. While legislation to create a 'State of Shasta' was introduced twice in the California legislature during the early 1850s, the most serious attempt at secession occurred in 1854 when a public meeting was held in Jacksonville to gauge support for a separate 'Jackson Territory.' Response was very positive, and the group planned a convention the next year to be attended by delegates representing all southern Oregon and Northern Californian counties. At the convention, held in January in Jacksonville, H G Ferris of Siskiyou County was elected president of the new state, and individual secession resolutions were drafted to be presented to legislatures in Oregon and California. The outbreak of the Rogue River War, between the Oregon settlers and Rogue River natives forced the breakup of the convention, and the initiative lost steam for a few years. Plans for a new state, this time called Siskiyou, emerged again in 1857 and 1909.

The most memorable secessionist movement occurred in 1941, when residents aimed to attract nationwide attention to Oregon's and California's neglect of this rural area. A state judge in Crescent City spearheaded the action, and the insurrection began at Gold Beach. The State of Jefferson officially seceded from California and Oregon on Thursday, November 27, and it was planned that the territory would secede every Thursday thereafter. In Yreka, residents set up roadblocks on Hwy 99 to interrogate travelers crossing the new state line. These border patrols circulated copies of the state's declaration of independence. A newly appointed governor was officially inaugurated at the Yreka Courthouse on December 3. The occasion was celebrated by a torchlight parade, and border patrol stations passed out windshield stickers to motorists which read, 'I have visited Jefferson, the 49th State'.

The hoopla in the State of Jefferson captured national attention. Stanton Delaplane of the *San Francisco Chronicle* even received the 1941 Pulitzer Prize for regional reporting of the secessionist movement. Unfortunately for the State of Jefferson, the nation soon had more pressing news to attend to: the bombing of Pearl Harbor. Once again, the State of Jefferson took a back seat to more serious considerations.

Motivations behind the region's secession have varied. The most common argument has been that the Jefferson territory was of uniform character, unique and distinct from either Oregon or California. Furthermore, the area is remote from the states' centers of population and power. The people of Jefferson felt that their under-represented interests could only be protected by the creation of a separate state.

It's also wise to remember that many of the original settlers in this mining region were Confederate soldiers displaced by the Civil War, and they knew a thing or two about secession. During the Civil War, Jefferson territory was host to a number of secret Confederate organizations. 'Knights of the Golden Circle' and 'Friends of the Union', met openly in Jacksonville, and were joined by disgruntled proponents of the 'State of Jackson'. Secession was a strong possibility throughout the war, and a frequent topic of discussion at such meetings; this time the new nation was to be known as the 'Pacific Republic'. When a Confederate plot to capture Alcatraz and Fort Point in California was uncovered, the ringleaders were discovered to be Pacific Republic proponents. ∎

dominate the menu; linguini with smoked trout, walnuts and pesto goes for $10.

### Getting There & Away

See Getting There & Away at the start of the chapter for information on the Medford/Jackson County Airport.

The Greyhound Bus Station (☎ 779-2103) is at 212 Bartlett St. Six buses link Medford daily with Portland and San Francisco; a one-way fare between Medford and Portland is $32.

Rogue River Transit (☎ 779-2877) is the local bus company that links communities in this part of the Rogue River valley. The main transfer point in the system is in downtown Medford at the corner of Front and 8th Sts. For the traveler, the buses that run between Medford and Ashland (on the half hour, $1.25 fare), and Medford and Jacksonville (on the hour, $1 fare) are probably most useful. There is no Sunday service.

For a cab, call Metro Taxi (☎ 773-6665).

## JACKSONVILLE

The oldest settlement in southern Oregon, Jacksonville is a well-preserved and beautifully renovated community little changed since the 1880s.

A gold-prospecting town situated on the main stage route between California and the Willamette Valley, Jacksonville was a trade center from the start. It was important enough to be named the seat of Jackson County, but lost that title in the 1920s when the railroad built Medford nearby, luring away local commerce.

For the next 40 years, the town slumbered, unvital but unaltered. By the 1960s, renewed interest in the region's history, and early attempts to preserve the town's architectural heritage were rewarded when the US Government named the entire downtown area a National Historic Landmark District, one of only eight such designations in the country. Over one hundred individual buildings are listed on the Historic Register.

In addition to its reputation as an open-air museum, Jacksonville is also home to the Britt Festival, a summer-long musical celebration that presents a wide assortment of internationally known musicians.

### Orientation & Information

Jacksonville is six miles east of Medford on Hwy 238. The center of the old downtown is at the corner of California and Oregon Sts. From there the town spreads out in a four-block radius.

The Jacksonville Chamber of Commerce (☎ 899-8118) at 185 N Oregon St, has further information.

### Jacksonville Museum of Southern Oregon History

The former county courthouse has been converted into Southern Oregon's showcase museum (☎ 773-6536), 206 N 5th St, and is a good place to start a tour of the town. The two-story, Italianate courthouse was built in 1883, and remained the Jackson County seat until it was moved to Medford in 1927.

The museum contains a tribute to photographer Peter Britt, who was the first to take pictures of Crater Lake. There are also displays on local history. The old county jail, adjacent, is now a children's museum. Ask at the museum for a walking tour map of Jacksonville history. The museum is open daily from 10 am to 5 pm; admission is $2.

### Britt Gardens

Peter Britt's mansion once sat in these lovely gardens at S 1st and W Pine Sts. Though the house burned in 1960, the grounds remain as a public park. Note the redwood tree, planted by Britt to commemorate the birth of his son Emil.

### Jeremiah Nunan House

This ornate Victorian home (☎ 899-1890), 635 N Oregon St, was built in 1892 by Jeremiah Nunan, a local merchant. The house was bought from a catalog, and shipped here unassembled from Tennessee, hence its sobriquet 'the Catalog House'. The home is furnished with period antiques. It's open for tours daily except Tuesday, from

OREGON

late May to late September. Tours leave on the hour and half hour, from 10:30 am to 5 pm.

## Beekman House

This restored home at 470 E California St was built in 1873 by Cornelius Beekman, who founded Oregon's second bank (still standing at the corner of California and 3rd Sts). Tours are conducted by actors in period dress from noon to 5 pm, Memorial Day to Labor Day weekend; admission is $2.

## Organized Tours

Hour-long narrated tours on motorized trolley cars (from San Francisco) leave from the corner of California and 3rd Sts on the hour from 10 am to 4 pm. Call 535-5617 for more information.

Or view Jacksonville from a horse-drawn surrey. Jackson Carriage Service (☎ 476-1426) tours also depart from California and 3rd Sts.

## Peter Britt Music Festival

These summertime, outdoor concerts are justly renowned throughout the Pacific Northwest as a showcase for a wide variety of musical performers and entertainment. Held mid-June to Labor Day weekend in the Britt Pavilion at the corner of 1st and Fir Sts, there is limited reserved seating; patrons are instead encouraged to bring picnics and spread out on the grassy hillside. The picnic aspect of the festival is not to be overlooked. Most restaurants in the vicinity are happy to prepare a hamper with a couple of hour's notice. The festival was originally dedicated to classical music, but it now encompasses a bit of everything, from standard jazz to taiko drummers, from folk singers to country crooners. In recent years, performers have included the likes of Art Garfunkel, Ricky Skaggs and Taj Mahal.

Tickets for the Britt Festival go quickly. Contact the festival office (☎ 773-6077, (800) 882-7488) at PO Box 1124, Medford, OR 97501, for information and reservations.

## Places to Stay

**Camping** There's a lovely Jackson County campground on the Applegate River, just over the hill from Jacksonville. Follow Hwy 238 west from Jacksonville about eight miles to the little community of Ruch. *Cantrall-Buckley Campground* is just beyond the town, on the banks of the river.

**B&Bs** Unsurprisingly, most lodgings in Jacksonville stress their authentic furnishings, and are rather expensive. Contact the Jacksonville B&B Association, PO Box 787, Jacksonville, OR 97530, for a complete listing of area B&Bs. The following establishments are representative. *Colonial House B&B* (☎ 770-2783), 1845 Old Stage Rd, is a 1916 Georgian mansion sitting on a five-acre holding. The two suites have private baths; prices start at $95. The *Old Stage Inn* (☎ 899-1776), 883 Old Stage Rd, is an 1857 farmhouse with four bedroom units, two with private baths; rooms begin at $90. The *McCully House* (☎ 899-1942), 240 E California St, is one of Jacksonville's earliest homes, built for the town's first doctor. Upstairs are three guest rooms with private baths; downstairs is an intimate restaurant and lounge; rooms are $85.

**Hotels** The *Jacksonville Inn* (☎ 899-1900), 175 E California St, is a refurbished hotel built in 1863, filled with antiques and modern comforts. There are only eight rooms, so reservations are suggested; breakfast is included. The inn's dining room is one of the best in southern Oregon. Rooms begin at $80.

Less expensive is the *Stage Lodge* (☎ 899-3953), 830 N 5th St. Single/double rooms are $67/69.

## Places to Eat

Resist the ubiquitous fudge and frozen yogurt shops and eat in the historic dining rooms. (Call ahead to order picnic hampers for the festival.) The *Jacksonville Inn Dinner House* (☎ 899-1900), 175 E California St, is in the lobby of the hotel, and is one of the state's best restaurants. A full seven-course dinner with a stuffed hazelnut chicken main dish is $20. *Bella Union Restaurant* (☎ 899-1770), 170 W California St, offers a wide range of prices and preparations, from sandwiches to pasta to full dinners in the $13 range. Try the antique-filled dining room at *McCully House Inn* (☎ 899-1942), 240 E California St, for classy and inventive dishes featuring local ingredients.

### Getting There & Away

Medford's Rogue River Transit service offers one bus an hour from Medford to Jacksonville. The bus leaves on the hour from Medford at the corner of Front and 8th Sts; the Jacksonville stop is in front of the Southern Oregon Museum at 206 N 5th St.

### GRANTS PASS

From the freeway, Grants Pass (population 18,120) looks like just another down-on-its-luck mill town, and a homely one at that. Upon closer inspection, however, Grants Pass reveals itself to be a pleasant

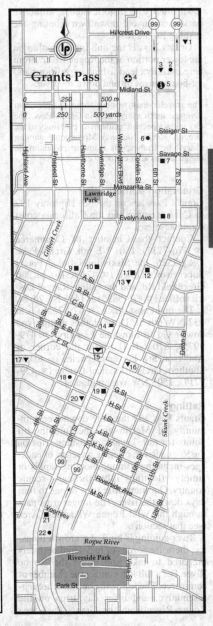

**PLACES TO STAY**

| | |
|---|---|
| 7 | Uptown Motel |
| 8 | Victorian Hotel |
| 9 | Clemens House B&B |
| 10 | Martha's B&B Inn |
| 11 | Wilson House Inn |
| 12 | Redwood Motel |
| 19 | Knight's Inn Motel |
| 21 | Riverside Inn |

**PLACES TO EAT**

| | |
|---|---|
| 1 | Matsukaze |
| 3 | Pongsri's |
| 13 | Yankee Pot Roast |
| 14 | Java House |
| 16 | Granny's Kitchen |
| 17 | The Brewery |
| 20 | Sunshine Natural Foods |

**OTHER**

| | |
|---|---|
| 2 | Budget Rent-A-Car |
| 4 | Southern Oregon Medical Center |
| 5 | Chamber of Commerce |
| 6 | Full Cycle |
| 15 | Post Office |
| 18 | Baker Sports |
| 22 | Hellgate Jet Boat Excursions |

OREGON

town filled with historic homes, attractive parks and an old downtown fronting the rushing Rogue River.

Grants Pass is the hub for recreation on the lower portion of the Rogue River. From here outfitters lead fishing expeditions and jet-boat cruises up and down the river.

The traveler may wonder about the prevalent caveman motif everywhere in Grants Pass. The city takes a peculiar pride in its proximity to the Oregon Caves National Monument, naming everything from sports teams to philanthropic organizations after cartoony cave-dwellers.

### Orientation & Information

Grant's Pass lies on the I-5. Highway 199 to Cave Junction and the California coast originates here.

Contact the Chamber of Commerce (☎ 476-7717), 1501 NE 6th, Grants Pass, OR 97526, the Siskiyou National Forest Supervisor's Office (☎ 471-6516), at 200 Greenfield Rd, and the Galice Ranger District office (☎ 476-3830) at 1465 NE 7th St.

The main post office (☎ 479-7526) is at 132 NW 6th St. Dirty clothes getting you down? Go to Sunshine Laundry (☎ 479-9975), 870 NE D St (at the corner of Anderson St). For emergencies go to the Southern Oregon Medical Center (☎ 479-9717), 1505 NW Washington St.

### Rafting

Grants Pass and the little downriver community of Merlin are the jumping-off points for raft, kayak and fishing trips on the Rogue River, offering a variety of packages including fishing, shooting rapids or simply floating idly through scenic country. Outfitters offer trips of one to four days down the river. The longer trips pass through the Wild Rogue Wilderness Area (see that section).

River guiding is kind of a growth industry; there are dozens of registered outfitters prepared to take you down the Rogue River. For a full list, contact the chamber of commerce. The following outfitters are representative, and offer day trips on the Rogue River from the Grants Pass area

(most also offer trips in the Wild Rogue Wilderness Area, and rentals as well).

**Orange Torpedo Trips**
PO Box 1111V, Grants Pass, OR 97526, for white-water raft and kayak trips (☎ 479-5061).

**Rogue Wilderness, Inc**
PO Box 1647, Grants Pass, OR 97526 for day trips and raft rentals (☎ 479-9554, 800 336-1647).

**Otter River Trips**
12163 Galice Rd, Merlin, OR 97532, for fishing or raft trips (☎ 476-8590).

**Sundance Expeditions**
14894 Galice Rd, Merlin, OR 97532, for kayaking classes and guided tours (☎ 479-8508).

**River Trips Unlimited**
4140 Dry Creek Rd, Medford, OR 97504, for scenic or fishing excursions (☎ 779-3798).

**Rogue/Siskiyou River Adventures**
PO Box 4295 Medford, OR 97501 (☎ 779-3708).

### Jet Boat Tours

Guided jet boat tours leave from downtown and explore the downstream Rogue River canyon. A number of tour options are available, including lunch trips and dinner excursions. The guides are usually knowledgeable about local history, lore and wildlife.

Prices vary, most starting at $20; be sure to call ahead. Tours are offered from May to September. Boats leave from a dock between the downtown bridges. Contact

Hellgate Jet Boat Excursions (☎ 479-7204, (800) 648-4874), 953 SE 7th St, for reservations and information.

Jet boat tours also leave from the small town of Rogue River, between Medford and Grants Pass, and explore a section of the river upstream from Savage Rapids Dam. Contact Jet Boat River Excursions (☎ 582-0800), PO Box 658, Rogue River, OR 97537. The business is just off I-5 exit No 48; watch for signs.

### Fishing
A number of Grants Pass-area outfitters provide fly-fishing instruction and guide service. Contact the chamber of commerce for a complete list of outfitters, or get in touch with the following for representative prices and services: Briggs Rogue River Guide Service (☎ 476-2941, (800) 845-5091), 2750 Cloverlawn Drive, Grants Pass, OR 97527, or Geoff's Guide Service, (☎ 474 0602) 2578 Midway St, Grants Pass, OR 97527.

### Other Activities
Bicycle rentals are available from Bill's Bikekraft (☎ 479-3912), 1515 Redwood Ave (near the fairgrounds), and Full Cycle (☎ 471-0535), 1330 NW 6th. Rent cross-country skis from Baker Sports (☎ 476-0388), 226 SW G St.

The Grants Pass Golf Club (☎ 476-0849), 230 Espey Rd, is an 18-hole course with nice views over the Rogue valley. Call ahead to find out daily hours for public play.

### Special Events
The Josephine County Fair (☎ 479-3215) is held the third weekend of August in Grants Pass at 1451 Fairgrounds Rd.

The Jedediah Smith Mountain Man Rendezvous brings hatchet throwing and musket firing to Grants Pass. The festival goes on for six days, starting the Tuesday before Labor Day and lasting through the weekend. This he-man festival ends with a buffalo barbecue and is held at Sportsmans Park, five miles north of Grants Pass, off I-5 exit No 61.

Looking even further back into the past, the Renaissance Arts Festival takes place the second weekend of July in Riverside Park. Jugglers, actors and acrobats mingle with regional arts and crafts people in a kind of high-spirited costume contest.

### Places to Stay
**Camping** The Grants Pass area is rich in camping options. A number of RV-oriented campgrounds are clustered along the Rogue River near town. One of the best is *Riverpark RV Resort* (☎ 479-0046, 800-677-8857), 2956 Rogue River Hwy (Hwy 99), at a pretty spot along the river; tent sites go for $11, RV sites for $16.

Josephine County maintains a number of attractive county parks. Most convenient to Grants Pass is *Whitehorse Park*, six miles west of town on Upper River Rd. *Indian Mary Park* is further afield, about eight miles west of Merlin, but it's right on the river, with hiking, fishing and swimming. Contact the Josephine County Parks Department (☎ 474-5285), 101 NW A St, Grants Pass, OR 97526, to make reservations.

**B&Bs** Grants Pass has a number of very nice historic B&B inns. The *Clemens House* (☎ 476-5564), 612 NW 3rd St, is a 1905 Craftsman-style home with three bedrooms; rooms begin at $65. *Riverbanks Inn* (☎ 479-1118), 8401 Riverbanks Rd, sits on five acres of riverfront, with five rooms and two cottages. Rooms range between $75 and $150. The *Wilson House Inn* (☎ 479-4754), 746 NW 6th St, is a 1908 neo-Georgian home with four guest rooms at $85. *Martha's B&B Inn* (☎ 476-4330), 764 NW 4th St, is an old Victorian farmhouse with a wraparound porch; rooms begin at $55. All have private baths.

For more B&Bs, contact the Oregon B&B Directory, 230 Red Spur Drive, Grants Pass, OR 97527.

**Hotels** There are a number of older, inexpensive ($30 to $45) hotel/motels along Sixth St: *Redwood Motel* (☎ 476-0878), 815 NE 6th St, *Uptown Motel* (☎ 479-2952), 1253 NE 6th St, the *Victorian Motel*

(☎ 476-4260), 1001 NE 6th St, and the *Knight's Inn Motel* (☎ 479-5595), 104 SE 7th St.

The *Riverside Inn* (☎ 476-6873, 800 334-4567), 971 SE 6th St, is the largest and best-located lodging in Grants Pass. Right downtown, with rooms and decks that front the Rogue River, this is also the departure point for jet boat tours. Rooms range from $60 to $175.

Opened in 1873 and in continuous operation ever since, the *Wolf Creek Tavern* (☎ 866-2474) is a stage coach-era hostelry that has survived as a charming small hotel and restaurant. Located 20 miles north of Grants Pass on the old California/Oregon stage line (and, incidentally, the I-5 which follows much of the old stage route), the inn has housed celebrities such as Jack London, Clark Gable and Mary Pickford. There are eight guest rooms, beginning at $50. The restaurant offers lunch and dinner; dinner prices for hearty meals based on steak and local trout range from $9 to $15.

**Resorts** Anglers and rafters may want to consider staying at a Rogue River lodge, where float trips to fishing holes can be part of the housing package. The *Galice Resort* (☎ 476-3818), 1174 Galice Rd Merlin, OR 97532, offers rentals and guided trips, as well as lodging and food. Lodging in cabins begins at $45; rooms in the lodge begin at $75. The upscale *Morrison Lodge* (☎ 476-3825), 8500 Galice Rd, Merlin, OR 97532, likewise rents and guides. Lodging in deluxe cabins includes a four-course dinner and a breakfast, and runs $80 per person.

### Places to Eat
For home-baked pastries and old-fashioned breakfasts, go to *Granny's Kitchen* (☎ 476-7185), 117 NE F St. *Della's* (☎ 476-8513), 1802 NW 6th St, is another breakfast favorite, open 24 hours. For espresso and scones, go to *Java House* (☎ 421-1922), 412 NW 6th St. Stock up on healthy foodstuffs and organic deli sandwiches and

salads at *Sunshine Natural Foods* (☎ 474-5044), 128 SW H St.

As elsewhere in the agricultural valleys of southern Oregon, Mexican food is both inexpensive and authentic. Try *Mexx's* (☎ 474-6399) at 820 NE E St. *Pongsri's* (☎ 479-1345), 1571 NE 6th St, is southern Oregon's best Thai restaurant, and a good place for vegetarian food in an otherwise meat-prone town. *Matsukaze* (☎ 479-2961), 1675 NE 7th St, at the corner of Hillcrest, features Japanese favorites. For hearty meat and potatoes, and waiters in period get-ups, go to *Yankee Pot Roast* (☎ 476-0551), 720 NW 6th St.

You'd expect a place called *The Brewery* (☎ 479-9850), 509 SW G St, to be a brewpub. Instead, this restaurant/bar is housed in an old, red-brick brewery that used to make beer in the rowdy days of old Grants Pass. Dinner choices range from pasta to steak and salmon, and prices range from $12 to $15. At the *Hamilton House* (☎ 479-3938), 344 NE Terry Lane, there's fine dining in a historic old home.

### Getting There & Around
For transportation between Grants Pass and Medford Airport, contact Airport Transit Service (☎ 479-3217). The fare is $8; call ahead for reservations.

There are five Greyhound buses a day between Portland and Grants Pass. Contact the station (☎ 476-4513), 460 NE Agness Ave, for more information.

For rental vehicles, contact Budget Rent-A-Car (☎ 471-6311), 1590 NE 7th St. Or call a cab at Grants Pass Cab (☎ 476-6444).

### WILD ROGUE WILDERNESS AREA
After the confluence of Grave Creek, the Rogue River enters a canyonland of deep forest, wild, choppy mountains and river chasms. Much of this 40-mile stretch of river is contained in the Wild Rogue Wilderness Area, a rugged, 56-sq-mile preserve of plants, wildlife and untamed river.

It is this section of the Rogue that has made it one of the most legendary whitewater rivers in the USA. Definitely not for amateurs, this trip takes at least three days;

abundant class IV rapids and waterfalls make this a rafting trip to plan very carefully; hiring a guide service is a good idea for all but the most experienced.

Often neglected, the **Rogue River Trail** is a 40-mile hiking trail that links the edges of the wilderness, from Grave Creek to Illahe. In summer, the trail can be very hot, black bears have learned to raid camps for food and portions of the path are so precipitous that pack horses are not allowed. This is a trail for the hearty and adventurous. Day hikers can sample this rugged landscape by hiking along the Rogue River from the Grave Creek launch site to Whiskey Creek, a seven-mile roundtrip past waterfalls and rapids.

### Orientation & Information
To reach the Wild Rogue Wilderness Area, take the Merlin exit from I-5. The Merlin Galice Rd runs through Merlin and Galice, and on to the head of the Rogue River Trail.

If you plan to float the Rogue independent of outfitters, you will need a permit from the USFS. From almost 100,000 applications, 10,000 permits are issued after a lottery process. For raft permits and more information contact the Rand Visitors Center (☎ 479-3735), 14335 Galice Rd, Merlin, OR 97532.

### Rafting
The following outfitters provide guided white-water trips down the wild portion of the Rogue River. You do not need a permit if you accompany an outfitter registered with the USFS; contact the agency at the above address for the most current listing of licensed outfitters.

A three-day trip down the Rogue River costs upwards of $500.
The following are long-established outfitters:

River Trips Unlimited
   4140 Dry Creek Rd, Medford, OR 97504
   (☎ 779-3798)
Rogue/Siskiyou River Adventures
   PO Box 4295 Medford, OR 97501 (☎ 779-3708)

Rogue Wilderness Inc
   PO Box 1647, Grants Pass, OR 97526
   (☎ 479-9554, (800) 336-1647)
Sundance Expeditions
   14894 Galice Rd, Merlin, OR 97532 (☎ 479-8508)

### Places to Stay & Eat
Although much of this region is roadless and has now been designated a wilderness area, several old-fashioned lodges still operate along the river. Facilities are usually rustic, a central lodge with bedroom cabins scattered amongst the trees. Plan well ahead, and make sure to call for reservations; lodging averages $65 a night (this includes the next day's packed lunch). The lodges, starting upstream and going downstream, are the *Black Bar Lodge* (☎ 479-6507); the *Mariel Lodge* (☎ 479-4923), the *Paradise Lodge* (☎ 247-6504), and the *Half Moon Lodge* (☎ 247-6968).

Primitive campgrounds exist along the Rogue River Trail; call the Rand Visitors Center for information.

# Illinois River Valley

Rising in the Siskiyou Mountains and draining a wide, forested valley before plunging into a wilderness gorge on its way to meet the Rogue River, the Illinois River valley remains one of Oregon's most remote and neglected corners. While the Oregon Caves National Monument ought to keep the Illinois River valley in the forefront of tourism, the isolation of the area suits various kinds of back-to-the-earth idealists. Amongst the ghostly remnants of gold-mining towns like Kerby, utopian communes nestle against the fortress-like settlements of survivalists.

Remoteness also suits the wilderness areas. The Kalmiopsis Wilderness Area, coursed by the Illinois River, is a preserve of rare plants and rugged mountains. The Illinois River, whose roilsome waters are colored an uncanny green from the outcrops of serpentinite through which it flows, is one of the west's most challenging

OREGON

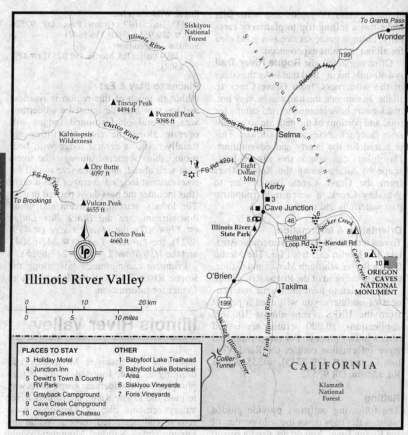

**Illinois River Valley**

| PLACES TO STAY | OTHER |
|---|---|
| 3  Holiday Motel | 1  Babyfoot Lake Trailhead |
| 4  Junction Inn | 2  Babyfoot Lake Botanical |
| 5  Dewitt's Town & Country | Area |
| RV Park | 6  Siskiyou Vineyards |
| 8  Grayback Campground | 7  Foris Vineyards |
| 9  Cave Creek Campground | |
| 10  Oregon Caves Chateau | |

white-water rivers. Only the most experienced kayakers should attempt to navigate the river.

## ORIENTATION & INFORMATION
Cave Junction is 32 miles south of Grants Pass along Hwy 199, which is frequently referred to as the Redwood Hwy. The Oregon Caves National Monument is 20 miles east of Cave Junction on Hwy 46. The final eight miles of the road are quite steep and narrow. Leave trailers or any other towed vehicle at designated areas.

The Illinois Valley Visitor Information Center (☎ 592-2631) is at 201 Caves Hwy,

Cave Junction, OR 97523. The Siskiyou National Forest's Illinois Valley Ranger Station (☎ 592-2166), 26568 Redwood Hwy, has information about outdoor recreation.

## CAVE JUNCTION
The little community of Cave Junction (population 1165) exists to serve the needs of tourists bound for the Oregon Caves; it's also the main trade town for the farming communities of the Upper Illinois River.

*DeWitt's Town & Country RV Park* (☎ 592-2656), one mile south of Cave Junction on Hwy 199, is a pleasant campground along the Illinois River; rates begin at $12. The *Junction Inn* (☎ 592-3106), 406 S Redwood Hwy, is the largest and most comfortable lodging in Cave Junction; single/double rooms are $45/50. *Holiday Motel* (☎ 592-3003), 24810 Redwood Hwy, between Cave Junction and Kerby, is also a good choice; rates are $44/48.

There are a number of fast-food restaurants along the highway, so there's no problem finding something quick to eat. The *Pizza Deli* (☎ 592-3556), 249 N Redwood Hwy, is the unlikely name of Cave Junction's brewpub. The beers are German-style, while the food ranges from sandwiches to pizzas.

### KERBY

Three miles north of Cave Junction, Kerby was founded as Kerbyville in 1858, when it was the center of gold prospecting in the area. Today what's left of the town is preserved as an open-air museum. The Kerbyville Museum (☎ 592-2076) contains remnants of the area's mining and logging history, as well as arrowheads and old pianos. For a small fee, concessionaires will teach the curious how to pan gold from nearby streams.

### OREGON CAVES NATIONAL MONUMENT

These caverns are a popular family destination. In addition to the caves themselves, the monument features hiking trails and accommodations in a beautiful old lodge, the Oregon Caves Chateau.

The Oregon Caves began as limestone deposits laid down in a shallow sea about 200 million years ago. Movements of the continental crust eventually hoisted the limestone up into the Siskiyou Mountains, molten rock forced its way up into rock faults, baking the rock that it came in contact with, forming marble. Continued movement of the Siskiyou Mountains exposed the marble formations and water began to carve tunnels and caves in the soft rock.

The cave (there is actually only one cave) contains about three miles of cham-

---

**The Discovery of the Oregon Caves**

In 1874 an early pioneer in these parts, Elijah Davidson, was out hunting when his dog came upon the trail of a bear. Bruno, the dog, followed the spoor into a crack in the side of a steep mountain slope, and disappeared. A howl of distress prompted the young hunter to follow his hound inside the cave entrance. Davidson was quickly lost in the dark labyrinth, and only escaped by following the cold stream back to the cave entrance (Bruno made it out alive as well).

Thus was discovered Oregon Caves. In following years, locals explored the cave, and its fame as a tourist attraction grew during the early 20th century. The cave was made a national monument in 1909 in order to protect and regulate the site. ■

---

bers, the largest of which is about 240 feet long. A fast moving stream, called the River Styx, runs the length of the cave.

In addition to the underground tours, the monument grounds contain a number of hiking trails. The Cliff Nature Trail is a three-quarter-mile loop trail with signs identifying plants and geology of the Siskiyou Mountains. For a longer hike, take the Big Tree Trail, a three-mile loop trail through old-growth forest. The highlight of the hike is a huge Douglas fir that's reckoned to be at least 1200 years old.

A pair of wineries lie off Hwy 46: **Foris Vineyards** (☎ 592-3752), 654 Kendall Rd, and **Siskiyou Vineyards** (☎ 592-3727), 6220 Oregon Caves Hwy. Both provide wine-tastings from 11 am to 5 pm year round (Siskiyou Vineyards has shorter winter hours), and offer attractive picnic grounds.

### Organized Tours

Tours of Oregon Caves run year round and leave from the chateau at least once an hour and last about 75 minutes. Tour groups are limited to 16 people, and tickets cost $5.75 for adults and $3.50 for children ages six to 11, who must be of a minimum height of 42 inches to enter. Call the chateau (☎ 592-3400) for tour information.

The tour passes through a half mile of

passages, with a total vertical climb of 218 feet. Make sure to bring warm clothing, as the cave preserves a year-round temperature of 41°F, and be prepared to get a little wet. If you visit the cave in the rainy season, you will get a vivid sense of how erosion carves through rock, and how the slow drip and flow of water build formations. Some of the small, almost insignificant formations, like cave popcorn, pearls and moonmilk, are as interesting as the classic pipe organs, columns and stalactites.

## Oregon Caves Chateau

Even if spelunking is not your interest, consider a side trip to the caves to see this won-

derful log lodge. Built in 1934, the chateau is a six-story hotel and dining room straddling the River Styx as it issues forth from the cave. The common rooms, with a huge central fireplace and windows overlooking the forest and a plunging ravine, look as if they are from another, perhaps mythic, era.

The chateau (☎ 592-4300) is open for lodging and dining from Memorial Day to the last weekend of September. Food is available year round downstairs in a snack bar. Rates begin at $60.

## Places to Stay

There are a number of USFS campgrounds just outside the monument, before Hwy 46 begins to climb the mountainside. Closest to the monument is *Cave Creek Campground*. However, at *Grayback Campground* you can reserve a site by calling (800) 283-2267.

## KALMIOPSIS WILDERNESS AREA

One of the largest and most unique wilderness areas in the state, the Kalmiopsis is famous for its rare plant life and curious geology. This segment of the Klamath geologic province was formed when the North American continent collided with the Pacific Ocean floor about 200 million years ago. Offshore sedimentary beds buckled up and formed mountain-high ridges that didn't initially adhere to North America. So, as the continent inched westward, the proto-Siskiyous pivoted and rolled along the continental edge.

At one point, between 50 to 100 million years ago, a 60-mile gulf opened between the Siskiyou formation and the continent. The vegetation continued to evolve, and when the Siskiyous eventually docked against the North American continent and were fused to it by volcanic intrusions, the plant life in the Siskiyous was quite different from the mainland.

Today the mountains of the Kalmiopsis Wilderness Area are still home to unusual and unique plant species. The pink-flowered *Kalmiopsis leachiana* and the rare Port Orford cedar are found almost nowhere else on earth. The *Darlingtonia* (also

---

### Loners & Idealists

There's something about the mountains and valleys of the Illinois River drainage that attracts loners and idealists. Gold prospectors were the first Whites to settle in the region, but the thousands of hopefuls who flooded in deserted just as quickly when the gold ran out early this century.

Today, the Illinois River valley is known for two seemingly opposing social phenomena. In the 1960s, 'back-to-the-earth' utopians founded Takilma, a then-notorious 'hippie' commune. The community still exists, although today it attracts less public indignation. Only the weathered sign stating 'Nuclear Free Zone' on the outskirts of the community gives an indication that Takilma is anything more than an outpost of rural poverty. The other recent immigrants to the Illinois River are enclaves of backwood survivalists, whose compounds are meant to provide safety from outside intervention of Big Brother's many manifestations.

In some sort of fusion of these two social movements, the most recent development in the Illinois River valley is the rise of marijuana farming. The right climactic conditions, inaccessible tracts of public forest, and underpopulation make this corner of Oregon one of the most noted marijuana growing areas in the western USA. ∎

called the pitcher plant) doesn't look to the impoverished soil for nutrition. This carnivorous plant instead traps and digests insects in its long throat.

If you have the time and don't mind getting off the main road, one easy hike leads into this curious region, through dense forests and meadows – a designated botanical area – to Babyfoot Lake. This short hike is a good place for viewing the unique plant life of the Kalmiopsis. The deep-green Babyfoot Lake is surrounded by a thick growth of Brewer's weeping spruce, Port Orford cedars and madrona trees. Watch for pitcher plants in the meadows.

There is a primitive campground at Babyfoot Lake.

For information, contact the Siskiyou National Forest Headquarters (☎ 479-5301), 200 NE Greenfield Rd, Grants Pass, OR 97526.

### Getting There & Away
Five miles north of Cave Junction, turn west off Hwy 199 onto Eight Dollar Mountain Rd (USFS Rd 4201), and follow signs for Babyfoot Lake Trailhead. It's a winding 20-mile drive to the trailhead. In addition to the entrance listed above, the wilderness area is also accessible from Brookings on the Oregon Coast on USFS Rd 1909 to the Chetco River.

# Umpqua Valley

The Native American word Umpqua means 'thunder water', an apt description of this mighty river, renowned for its beauty and recreational opportunities. The North Fork of the Umpqua River is especially treasured for summer steelhead fishing. Highway 138, which follows the North Fork through deep forests and past waterfalls and lakes to Crater Lake National Park, is one of the most scenic drives in the state.

Roseburg, the hub of the Umpqua valley, is known mostly for its logging, but nowadays, the locals are as apt to be discussing the harvest of pinot noir grapes as Douglas

firs. Roseburg is an inexpensive base of operations for trips to the Oregon coast as well as to the peaks of the Cascades.

The North Fork of the Umpqua River was the homeland of the Southern Molala tribe, closely related to the Klamath Indians who lived along the lakes of south central Oregon. The South Fork of the Umpqua was the homeland of the Upper Umpqua tribe, related to the Rogue Indians.

They resisted early trading relations with White trappers and traders. In the 1840s, as White pioneers began to settle the river valleys, the Molalas and Umpquas were forced further into the mountains. Their plight worsened after the Applegate Trail brought emigrants into southern Oregon, and the California Gold Rush drew fortune hunters across their lands. In 1855 both tribes signed a treaty removing them from the Umpqua Valley and consigning them to the Grande Ronde Reservation on the Yamhill River.

One band of the Upper Umpquas under Chief Napesa refused to leave their lands, and eventually took to the forests; despite many attempts to round them up, they eluded capture and lived in seclusion. These refugees became known as the Cow Creek tribe; their descendants now live in the Canyonville area.

### ORIENTATION & INFORMATION
The Umpqua River rises in Maidu Lake, high in the Cascades, and drains over 5500 sq miles of the Cascade and Coast mountains before debouching into the Pacific at Reedsport. Highways 38 and 138 parallel the mainstem Umpqua River and the North Fork along most of its length; Hwy 227 and USFS roads follow the South Fork from Canyonville.

Interstate 5 shoots through the Umpqua valley north to south; just about the only town of consequence in the entire drainage is Roseburg.

### ROSEBURG
Roseburg (population 17,910) has a real lived-in, worked-in feel. It has been hard-

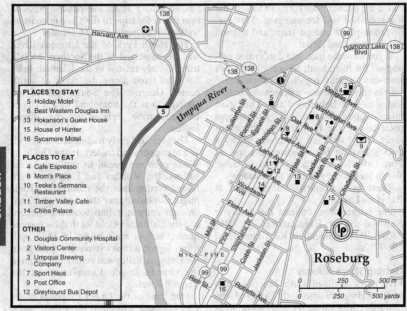

**PLACES TO STAY**
5  Holiday Motel
6  Best Western Douglas Inn
13  Hokanson's Guest House
   House of Hunter
16  Sycamore Motel

**PLACES TO EAT**
4  Cafe Espresso
8  Mom's Place
10  Teske's Germania
   Restaurant
11  Timber Valley Cafe
14  China Palace

**OTHER**
1  Douglas Community Hospital
2  Visitors Center
3  Umpqua Brewing
   Company
7  Sport Haus
9  Post Office
12  Greyhound Bus Depot

Roseburg

hit by changes in the logging industry, and there's a general down-on-its-luck feeling in the air. Nonetheless, enormous lumber mills ring the town, and entire forests lie supine at the mill south of town.

Roseburg was born when town-founder Aaron Rose arrived at the South Fork in 1851 and built a tavern to service passing pioneers. The Oregon & California Railroad arrived from Portland in 1872 and discontinued construction for over a decade due to lack of funds, leaving Roseburg its southern terminus. Rail workers congregated here, and an entire neighborhood, called the Mill-Pine Neighborhood, grew up along the rail lines to house them

Large-scale logging didn't start until WW II, but when it did, Roseburg – Oregon's single greatest source of virgin trees – quickly became one of the greatest lumber mill towns in the world.

For today's visitor, Roseburg offers abundant motel rooms, and a good regional and natural history museum. The hills south of Roseburg shelter vineyards as well as a drive-through zoo.

### Orientation
Roseburg lies in a bowl-like valley, near where the South and North forks of the Umpqua River meet. The old downtown area is located on the eastern side of the South Fork Umpqua River, while I-5 and new businesses are on the western side. Pine and Stephens Sts are the main thoroughfares through the downtown area; Harvard St leads west from the freeway to parks and the new commercial district.

### Information
For information, contact the City of Roseburg Visitors & Convention Bureau (☎ 672-9731) at 410 SE Spruce St, PO Box 1262, Roseburg, OR 97470. The headquarters for the Umpqua National Forest (☎ 672-6601) is at 2900 Stewart Parkway. The Roseburg Fish and Wildlife Dept (☎ 440-3353) is at 4192 N Umpqua Hwy.

The post office (☎ 673-5326) is at 519 SE Kane St. You can do laundry at Clothes Hamper Laundromat (☎ 672-0240), 2428 W Harvard Ave. For medical emergencies, go to Douglas Community Hospital (☎ 673-6641), 738 W Harvard Ave.

## Douglas County Museum of History & Natural History

The Douglas County Museum (☎ 440-4507, (800) 452-0991), just east of exit No 123, near the fairgrounds, is definitely worth the stop. Part of the museum serves as an interpretive center of local Cow Creek Indian culture and history. There are also photographs and relics of the region's early White settlers. The museum is open Tuesday to Saturday from 10 am to 4 pm, and Sundays noon to 4 pm; a $2 donation is requested.

## Mill-Pine Historic Neighborhood

These 15 blocks of houses near the railroad tracks were constructed specially for rail workers and their families between 1884 and 1900 when the Oregon & California Railroad line stopped in Roseburg for 10 years due to lack of funding to continue south. The neighborhood was placed on the National Register of Historic Places in 1985.

To reach the Mill-Pine district from downtown Roseburg, turn south on Stephens St, and turn west on Woodward Ave. Most of the historic homes are along Mill and Pine Sts between Rice and Woodward Aves. The visitors center passes out a guide to the historic homes.

## Activities

While most anglers head up the North Fork Umpqua River to fish the waters around Steamboat, there's also good **fishing** where the North and South Forks converge. To reach this area, travel seven miles west on Garden Valley Rd, and follow signs to River Forks Park.

Before setting out on a self-guided **rafting** trip, check with the Umpqua National Forest (see Orientation & Information, above) for guidelines. Rent a raft

from North Umpqua Equipment Rental (☎ 673-5391) at 14168 N Umpqua Hwy. Guided river trips are available from North Umpqua Outfitters (☎ 673-4599), PO Box 1574, Roseburg, OR 97470.

Rent bicycles and car racks from J & L's Bicycle Center (☎ 672-8139), 1217 NE Walnut St. Cross-country ski rentals are available from the Sport Haus (☎ 672-3018), 506 SE Jackson. The area around Diamond Lake, 90 miles west on Hwy 138, is a favorite for cross-country skiing.

The Roseburg area's public **golf** course is The Knolls (☎ 459-4422), 1919 Recreation Lane, 16 miles north in Sutherlin. The club offers 18 holes, a club house and full rental facilities.

## Special Events

Roseburg goes Western at the Umpqua Valley Rodeo, held the second weekend of June at the Douglas County Fairgrounds. Information and tickets are available from the visitors center. The Summer Arts Festival, (☎ 672-2532) which brings together the works of over 100 regional artists, is held at the Umpqua Valley Arts Center on last weekend of June.

The Douglas County Fair (☎ 440-4505), complete with carnival, entertainment, livestock and garden shows, is held the second week in August at the fairgrounds just east of I-5 exit No 123.

## Places to Stay

**Camping** The county operates *Fairgrounds RV Park* (☎ 440-4505) at 2100 Frear St, at the fairgrounds off I-5 exit No 123 near the South Fork. Sites cost $10 to $12.

*Amacher County Park* (☎ 672-4901) at Winchester, five miles north of Roseburg at exit No 123, is right on the North Fork Umpqua River, but it's also right underneath the freeway bridge. Tent sites are $9, RV sites are $12.

There's more rural camping at *Whistler's Bend County Park* (☎ 673-4863), 2828 Whistler's Rd, a beautiful wooded spot on a horseshoe bend of the North Fork Umpqua River. In addition to camping ($7), there

OREGON

are picnic facilities and fishing access. Go 12 miles west of Roseburg on Hwy 138, and west three more miles on Whistler's Rd.

Fishing also features at *Twin River Vacation Park* (☎ 673-3811), 433 River Forks Park Rd, where the North and South Fork Umpqua rivers come together. Tent sites are $12, full RV hook-up sites are $18.

**B&Bs** *Hokanson's Guest House* (☎ 672-2632), 848 SE Jackson St, right downtown, was built in 1882 and is listed in the National Register of Historic Places; rates are $65 and $75. Just above downtown is the *House of Hunter* (☎ 672-2335), 813 SE Kane St, in a nice neighborhood of beautiful old homes. There are five guest rooms, ranging in cost from $50 to $105.

**Hotels** The best lodging deals in Roseburg are along old Hwy 99, now Stephens St. On the north end of town are *Budget 16* (☎ 673-5556), 1067 NE Stephens St, and the *Rose City Motel* (☎ 673-8209), 1142 Stephens St. To the south are the *Sycamore Motel* (☎ 672-3354), 1627 SE Stephens St, and the *Holiday Motel* (☎ 672-4457), 444 SE Oak Ave. Prices are in the $25 to $45 range.

The nicest motels are two Best Westerns. Downtown is the *Best Western Douglas Inn* (☎ 673-6625), 511 SE Stephens; rooms are $50/55. Out at freeway exit No 125 is the *Best Western Garden Villa Motel* (☎ 672-1601, (800) 547-3446 in Oregon, (800) 528-1234 outside Oregon), 760 NW Garden Way, for $58/68. Both have pool, exercise room and hot tub, and accept pets.

**Places to Eat**
Breakfast is an important meal in Roseburg. *Mom's Place* (☎ 672-8459), 634 SE Cass Ave, opens at 3 am for the mill workers; meals are large and tasty. Another spot for a traditional logging-town breakfast or lunch is the *Timber Valley Cafe* (☎ 673-8369), 807 SE Stephens St. For espresso and croissants, go to *Cafe Espresso* (☎ 672-1859), 368 SE Jackson.

The best purveyor of prime rib and steak

in Roseburg is *Brutke's Wagon Wheel* (☎ 672-7555), 227 NW Garden Valley Blvd. If you're looking for more variety, try Roseburg's ethnic restaurants: *Teske's Germania Restaurant* (☎ 672-5401), 647 SE Main St, for German food, *Los Dos Amigos* (☎ 673-1351), 537 SE Jackson St, for Mexican, and *China Palace* (☎ 672-8899), 968 NE Stephens St, for Sichuan and Hunan preparations.

The *Umpqua Brewing Company* (☎ 672-0452), 328 SE Jackson St, brews English-style beers and ales, and serves them in a restored and pleasant old bar. The brewpub also offers pizza and burgers.

### Getting There & Away
Greyhound runs four buses a day along I-5; the one-way fare between Roseburg and Eugene is $11. The depot (☎ 673-3348) is at 835 SE Stephens St.

## AROUND ROSEBURG
### Umpqua Valley Wineries
The Umpqua valley is home to some of Oregon's oldest wineries. Most are in the rolling hills west of Roseburg, and specialize in pungent pinot noirs and German-style reislings and gewurztraminers.

For a full listing of Umpqua valley wineries, contact the visitors center; the following are representative and easy to find: **Henry Estate Winery** (☎ 459-5120), 687 Hubbard Creek Rd, **Hillcrest Vineyard** (☎ 673-3709, (800) 736-3709), 240 Vineyard Lane, **Callahan Ridge** (☎ 673-7901), 340 Busenbark Lane, and **La Garza Cellars** (☎ 679-9654), 491 Winery Lane. La Garza also offers a deli and restaurant.

### Wildlife Safari
Located 10 miles southwest of Roseburg near Winston is a 600-acre Wildlife Safari, one of the largest drive-through zoos in the USA. A three-mile loop takes vehicles through a series of enclosures featuring (successively) animals from Africa, Asia and North America. Lions, elephants, giraffes, hippos – they're all here, lolling around the Oregon countryside.

To find Wildlife Safari, take I-5 exit No

119, drive four miles to Lookingglass Rd and follow the signs. It's open from 8:30 am to dusk during summer; the rest of the year from 9 am to 5 pm on weekdays, to 6 pm on weekends. Admission is $9.95 for adults, $8.50 for seniors and $6.75 for children ages four to 12. There's also a $1 vehicle charge.

## Oakland

Tiny Oakland (population 855), 20 miles north of Roseburg, was originally a stopover on the Portland-Sacramento stage line in the 1850s, and it's one of the best-preserved frontier towns in Oregon. Several of Oakland's original businesses still operate in the old storefronts; others have become antique and craft stores. This is a good place get off the freeway and stop for a break. The Oakland Chamber of Commerce (☎ 459-4531), is at 117 3rd St.

The weekend after Labor Day Oakland sponsors the Umpqua Valley Wine, Arts & Jazz Festival. For more information, call 672-2648.

*Tolley's 'Beckley House' B&B* (☎ 459-9320), 338 SE 2nd St, is an 1890s Queen Anne home with two guest suites for $65 to $85. *Tolley's* (☎ 459-3796) 115 Locust St, is also a beautifully preserved restaurant. It's the sort of place where couples from Roseburg come for a romantic evening. Dishes like roast duck with raspberry sauce and prawns Dijon are around $18.

## NORTH FORK UMPQUA RIVER

The North Fork of the Umpqua River alternates between dark pools of quiet, swirling waters and surging cascades that send the river frothing over steep escarpments. Deep forests crowd down to the river's boulder-strewn edge; enormous volcanic crags rise above the trees and twist down to flank the river.

Highway 138 follows the North Fork of the Umpqua River from Roseburg to Crater Lake. The North Fork is also known as one of the state's premier fishing streams.

Call the Umpqua National Forest's North Umpqua Ranger Station at 496-3532. During the summer months, a National Forest Information Center (☎ 793-3310) is open at Diamond Lake.

### Waterfalls

The North Fork of the Umpqua River contains one of Oregon's greatest concentrations of waterfalls, with short hikes leading to most of them.

Steamboat Creek is prime spawning grounds for salmon and steelhead (fishing is prohibited the length of the stream). At **Little Falls** and **Steamboat Falls** the fish struggle up this fast-moving stream, offering a glimpse into the life-cycle of anadromous (ocean-going) fish. Turn at Steamboat onto USFS Rd 38. Little Falls is just one mile upstream; travel six miles along USFS Rd 38 to Steamboat Falls Campground, where a short trail leads to the viewing area.

**Toketee Falls** drops 120 feet in two stages, first into a mist-filled bowl flanked by columns of basalt, and then a final 80-foot plunge into a deep gorge. The waterfall viewpoint is at the end of an easy half-mile stroll through deep forests; to find the trailhead, turn at Toketee Junction onto USFS Rd 34, and take an immediate left to a parking area.

Awe-provoking **Watson Falls** is, at 272 feet, one of the highest waterfalls in Oregon. To reach the falls, turn onto USFS Rd 37, which is two miles east of Toketee Junction. Park at the picnic area, and follow the half-mile trail. It climbs steeply through mossy old-growth forest to end at a footbridge with great views onto the falls.

To reach **Lemolo Falls** requires a bit more of a hike and some off-road driving, but seeing this wild 100-foot waterfall is worth it. Turn off Hwy 138 at USFS Rd 2610 (Lemolo Lake Rd) and continue 4.3 miles to the lake, where you'll need to choose between two trails. The first proceeds left onto USFS Rd 3401, the Thorn Prairie Rd, for a quarter mile and then right onto USFS Rd 800 for two miles to reach the trailhead. The trail is a steep one-mile descent to the base of the falls. Or continue on USFS Rd 2610 over the reservoir's spillway and turn left on USFS Rd 600. Continue half a mile to the point where the North Umpqua Trail crosses the road. Follow this trail 1.5 miles downstream to the falls.

## Diamond Lake

Glaciers from the last ice age gouged out the basin of 3200-acre Diamond Lake, a beautiful deep-blue lake directly north of Crater Lake. It's an extremely popular lake for anglers and boaters, and winter brings lots of cross-country skiers.

The headquarters for recreation is the attractive **Diamond Lake Lodge** (☎ 793-3333, (800) 733-7593), Diamond Lake Resort, Diamond Lake, OR 97731. Located right on the lake, the lodge offers rooms, cabins, camping, restaurants, and rentals of cross-country skis, mountain bikes, boats, ice skates and even horses. Guided snowcat and cross-country ski tours to Crater Lake are also available.

Another winter skiing opportunity offered at the lodge is snowcat skiing. Snowcats take a limited number of downhill skiers to the top of 8363-foot Mt Bailey; the trails down the mountain are some of the steepest in the Northwest. Only 12 skiers a day can go; the $160-a-day price tag includes lunch at a shelter at the top of the mountain.

To reach Diamond Lake, take the North Umpqua Hwy (Hwy 138) east from Roseburg for 80 miles.

## Hiking

The principal trail is the 77-mile **North Umpqua Trail**, which follows the river from near Idleyld Park to Lemolo Lake. One good access point is the **Wright Creek Trailhead**, on the south side of the North Fork Umpqua River, just after the bridge on USFS Rd 4711. Follow the trail 5.5 miles upstream through old-growth forest to Mott Bridge, near Steamboat.

Several shorter hikes lead to natural curiosities and Native American sites. From Susan Creek Campground, 33 miles east of Roseburg on Hwy 138, the two-mile roundtrip **Indian Mounds Trail** passes Susan Creek Falls before climbing up to a

vision-quest site. Another short hike, the 1.5-mile **Fall Creek Falls National Recreation Trail** begins at a footbridge four miles east of Susan Creek Campground, and leads up a narrow fissure in columnar basalt formations to Jobs Garden, a natural shade garden of ferns and mosses, and on to Fall Creek Falls, a double-tiered cascade.

Another hiking trail leads to the popular **Umpqua Hot Springs**, a series of natural hot springs that flow down a bare hillside to join the North Fork. Turn at Toketee Junction onto USFS Rd 34 and turn right on Thorn Prairie Rd (USFS Rd 3401). For a 1.8-mile hike, stop just short of the bridge over the river, and follow the North Umpqua Trail upriver to the hot springs. If you're in a hurry to get to the hot springs, continue driving on Thorn Prairie Rd for another 1.5 miles; from the car park, hike the last quarter mile.

Rising to the east of Diamond Lake is **Mt Thielsen**, one of the most distinctive of the Cascade peaks. At 9182 feet, Mt Thielsen is not the highest peak in the region, but it is undoubtedly the thinnest. Glaciers ate away the conical slopes of the 100,000-year-old volcano, leaving only a narrow plug of basalt to rise like a spire. Referred to as the Lightening Rod of the Cascades, it is so often struck that the rocks at the summit have been recrystalized into fulgurites by electrical fusion. The final 80-foot finger of rock is just as precipitous as it looks, and requires technical climbing skills. The Mt Thielsen Trailhead is found one mile north of the junction of Hwys 138 and 62.

## Fishing

The North Fork of the Umpqua River is one of the best loved fishing streams in Oregon, but special regulations limit the season and fishing methods along much of the river; for up-to-date information, contact the Fish & Wildlife office in Roseburg.

The summer steelhead run on the river is one of the reasons for the fame of the North Fork; fly-fishing-only restrictions are in place between Rock Creek and Soda

Springs. Spring Chinook, coho salmon, rainbow trout and German brown trout are also found.

One of the reasons for the North Fork's popularity is not just the relative abundance of fish, but also the river itself. This is classic fly-fishing water, especially in the area around Steamboat, where a great inn and fly shop caters to the needs of anglers.

### Places to Stay & Eat

**Camping** Between Idleyld Park and Diamond Lake there are dozens of campgrounds, many right on the river; for a full list of public campgrounds, stop at Umpqua National Forest office (☎ 672-6601), 2900 Stewart Parkway. Fees for the following BLM and USFS sites average $8 a night unless otherwise noted; none offer hook-ups for RVs.

At the lower end of the North Fork Umpqua River are *Susan Creek Campground*, 33 miles east of Roseburg and *Bogus Creek Campground*, 18 miles east of Glide.

Near Steamboat, *Canton Creek Campground* sits on the banks of Steamboat Creek a quarter of a mile up USFS Rd 38 from Steamboat. Six miles further along is *Steamboat Falls Campground*, near the famous falls and fish ladder.

In the middle section of the river, the nicest campground is *Horseshoe Bend*, 30 miles east of Glide. The North Fork Umpqua River flows on three sides of this forested campground, making it popular for angling and rafting. *Boulder Flat*, six miles further east, is a primitive campground with good fly-fishing access and great views onto lava formations along the river.

In the upper reaches of the river, campgrounds tend to cluster around lakes. There are five public campgrounds around Lemolo Lake and three around Diamond Lake.

**Hotels** *Dogwood Motel* (☎ 496-3404), five miles east of Idleyld Park, is a favorite with anglers. Some rooms have kitchens; rates begin at $45 a night.

**Lodges** *Lemolo Lake Resort* (☎ 793-3300), HOC-60 Box 79B, Idleyld Park, OR 97447, is located on Lemolo Lake, 75 miles east of Roseburg, with magical views across the lake to the precipitous face of Mt Thielsen. Facilities include indifferently maintained A-frame cabins ($45), RV campsites, a boat ramp, a small store and cafe.

*Diamond Lake Resort* (☎ 793-3333, (800) 733-7593) offers standard motel rooms ($54), two-bedroom cabins with kitchens ($85 to $95), and one small house for six ($135). Light meals are available all day in the *Diamond Lake Cafe*; for fine dining go to the *Mt Thielsen Dining Room*. Both restaurants are in the main lodge.

**Resorts** The *Steamboat Inn* (☎ 496-3495), 42705 Hwy 138, is an unlikely institution. Located 38 miles east of Roseburg on the banks of the North Fork Umpqua River, this upscale fishing lodge offers first-class accommodations and food in the middle of the wilderness. Stay in rustic streamside cottages ($85 to $125 a night) or in suites beside the lodge ($195). The famed lodge restaurant is open for breakfast and lunch, but the real treat is the nightly Fisherman's Dinner served family-style to overnight guests (and nonguests with reservations). The fixed menu changes nightly; it's $30 per person. From November to March, it's open weekends only.

# Upper Rogue River Valley

From Medford, Hwy 62 (Crater Lake Hwy) heads north and east following the Rogue River to its headwaters. Past Shady Cove, the valley walls close in and the silvery river quickens. Dense forests robe the steep mountainsides, with sheer volcanic formations thrusting through the blanket of green.

The Rogue River is noted for some of

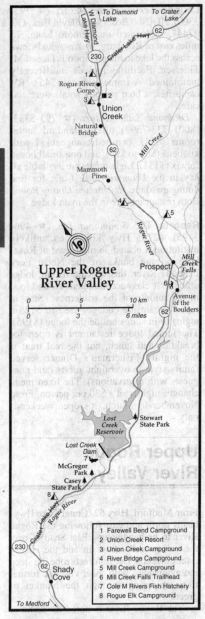

## Upper Rogue River Valley

| | 5 | | 10 km |
|---|---|---|---|
| 0 | 3 | | 6 miles |

1 Farewell Bend Campground
2 Union Creek Resort
3 Union Creek Campground
4 River Bridge Campground
5 Mill Creek Campground
6 Mill Creek Falls Trailhead
7 Cole M Rivers Fish Hatchery
8 Rogue Elk Campground

OREGON

the best steelhead and trout fishing in the state, and modern-day adventurers put the river to a new use as well. In summer, the Rogue River between Lost Creek Reservoir and Shady Cove is clotted with rafts and kayaks; on peak summer weekends, three or four boats float by each minute. Above Lost Creek Lake, the river abandons any semblance of gentleness, and channels a gorge through thick lava flows. Tributary streams tumble hundreds of feet over sheer walls to join the frenzied Rogue.

Coming upriver from Medford about 25 miles on Hwy 62, **McGregor Park** is a good place for a picnic or a stretch right by the base of Lost Creek Dam. If you brought your own raft, then this is the place to put it in the Rogue River. There's also an interpretive center focusing on the history, wildlife and geology of the Rogue River.

Next door is one of the largest fish hatcheries in the West, the **Cole M Rivers Fish Hatchery** which produces a preponderance of the salmon, trout and steelhead fry that restocks rivers throughout the region.

Above Lost Creek Reservoir, the terrain becomes rougher, and the Rogue River rages through deep canyons. The **Mill Creek Falls** trailhead is about one mile west of Prospect; a short stroll leads to the brink of a chasm where Mill Creek plunges 173 feet to join the river. After another hundred feet further and tiny Barr Creek also tumbles off the cliff. Another short trail leads to the **Avenue of the Boulders**, where the river drops through a series of rocky cataracts.

Further north, take a short hike through groves of ancient trees in the old-growth forest of **Mammoth Pines**, midway between Prospect and Union Creek.

About one mile east of Union Creek Resort, the Rogue River goes underground for 200 feet, where it borrows a lava tube for its channel. A short trail with explanatory signs leads to this **Natural Bridge**, across the surging river and to the points where it pours into and then issues from a jumble of rock.

Just a little further upriver is the **Rogue River gorge**, cutting a sheer-walled cleft into lava flows where a number of tributary creeks come together. While the word 'gorge' is a bit misleading, especially if you've been to the Columbia River recently, the quarter-mile trail along this narrow, turbulent section of the Rogue River is magical. At one point the trail drops down into the chasm, where the spray and mist sustain a shadowy moss garden.

The upper reaches of the river are in the Rogue River National Forest. Contact the Forest Supervisor's office (☎ 776-3600), at 333 W 8th St, Medford, OR 97501. In Prospect, stop at the Ranger Station (☎ 560-3623) along Hwy 62.

## HIKING

For long distance hikes, the **Upper Rogue River Trail** follows the river for 47 miles between Prospect and Crater Lake National Park. Trails on both the east and west sides of the river between the Natural Bridge and the Rogue River gorge are great for day hikers. Consult the Rogue River National Forest map or ask at ranger stations for other hiking options.

## FISHING

Fishing is legendary on the Rogue River: Zane Gray, Herbert Hoover, Jack London and Teddy Roosevelt were early champions of the river.

In the stretch of river above Tou Velle State Park to Lost Creek Dam, salmon and steelhead fishing is especially good. Between Shady Cove and the dam the road hugs the river, and there are frequent parks and easy access to the riverbank. Many outfitters offer fishing trips on the Rogue River. The Rogue River Guides Association, PO Box 792, Medford, OR 97501, is a group representing river outfitters; contact them for a listing of fishing and floating options.

## RAFTING

The Rogue River is known for its raft trips. Though the real action is far downriver, most people find the gentle bumps and grinds of the section between Lost Creek Dam and Shady Cove are adventure enough.

The slightly scrappy-looking town of Shady Cove is a convenient center for both guided raft trips and for raft rentals. Among the options are: Raft Rite Rentals (☎ 878-4005), 21103 Hwy 62, Rapid Pleasure Raft Rental, (☎ 878-2500) 21411 Hwy 62, and Rogue Rafting Company (☎ 878-2585), 7725 Rogue River Drive. All offer free shuttles to the launching site.

## PLACES TO STAY
### Camping

There are a number of campgrounds near Shady Cove. For RV campers, one of the best is *Fly Casters RV Park* (☎ 878-2749), 211655 Hwy 62, with riverside sites for $20. *Rogue Elk Park*, halfway between Shady Cove and Lost Creek Lake is a county park with showers, raft-launching areas and good fishing.

On Lost Creek Lake, about eight miles from both Prospect and Shady Cove, the nicest place to camp is *Joseph Stewart State Park* (☎ 560-3334), with several hundred campsites alongside the reservoir. Showers, boat launches and bicycles paths are some of the offerings. Tent sites begin at $10.

There are a number of USFS campgrounds further up on the Rogue River. Contact the Forest Supervisor's office (☎ 776-3600) for details. *Mill Creek Campground* and *River Bridge Campground* are both close to food and drink at Prospect. *Union Creek* and *Farewell Bend* are close to Union Creek.

### Hotels

In Shady Cove the *Royal Coachman* (☎ 878-2481), 21906 Hwy 62, with singles/doubles at $32/36, and the *Maple Leaf Motel* (☎ 878-2169), 20717 Hwy 62, $31/36, are perfunctory riverside motels with some kitchenettes.

The Rogue River's real treasure is the *Prospect Hotel* (☎ 560-3664), 391 Mill Creek Rd, a grand, old hotel built in 1889. The setting is beautiful, amid deep forests with the distant roar of the Rogue River.

The hotel has a wraparound porch with a porch swing, and a notably good dining room. Although the rooms are charming, they are authentically small; no children or dogs are allowed; smoking is also prohibited. Behind the hotel are a few modern motel units where these vices are allowed; prices of rooms range between $45 to $85.

At Union Creek, there is an old 1930s lodge, called the *Union Creek Resort* (☎ 560-3565). Rooms are available in the old lodge and in free-standing cabins, beginning at $38.

## PLACES TO EAT

In Shady Cove, eat at *Mac's Diner* (☎ 878-6227), 22225 Hwy 62, for sandwiches and light meals. Just upriver from Shady Cove is the *Rogue River Lodge* (☎ 878-2555), 24904 Hwy 62, a more upscale bar and supper club right on the river. The best restaurant in the area is *Bel Di's* (☎ 878-2010), 21900 Hwy 62, where you can sit at a table laid with linen and crystal and look over the Rogue River. The menu mixes continental preparations and local ingredients; entrees start around $15.

The century-old dining room at the *Prospect Hotel* has been lovingly maintained, with brass, oak and chandeliers from another era. The food's quite good too, with trout, steak and seafood dinners starting at $12. The Sunday brunch here is popular, and continues to 2 pm.

In Union Creek, the place to eat is *Beckie's Cafe* (☎ 560-3563), with logger-style breakfasts and hearty food throughout the day. On a hot day, Beckie's ice-cream parlor next door to the cafe is a mandatory stop.

# Crater Lake National Park

The deepest lake in the USA, and Oregon's only national park, Crater Lake is a stunning landmark to the violent geologic forces that have formed the Northwest.

Known mostly as a beauty spot – yes, you too will exclaim when you first glimpse this perfectly symmetrical, uncannily blue body of water – Crater Lake also offers hiking and cross-country skiing trails, a boat ride to a rugged island and scenic drives around the lip of the crater.

About 500,000 people visit the 286-sq-mile park annually. But after spending a considerable amount of time getting to the park, few people do more than take a few photos from the vista points, and then hurry on. It's true Crater Lake is no Yellowstone or Yosemite, but exploring the park's side roads will lead to interesting areas and recreational oppurtunities, and the historic Crater Lake Lodge, built between 1909 and 1915, has recently been reopened after six years of extensive renovation.

## ORIENTATION

Crater Lake National Park can be reached from Medford or from Klamath Falls on Hwy 62. From Medford, it's 72 miles to Crater Lake; from Klamath Falls, it's 73 miles. Crater Lake is also reached from Roseburg along Hwy 138, a distance of 87 miles. If you are driving south along Hwy 97, it's 90 miles from Bend to the park.

## INFORMATION

The south entrance to the park is open year around; the north entrance is not usually open until June and remains open until snow closes it, usually in October. Rim Rd opens and closes about the same time. There is a $5 fee per vehicle to visit the park. Food concessions, an information center and a gift shop make up Rim Village, on the southern edge of the caldera.

For information on Crater Lake National Park, contact the park headquarters (☎ 594-2211), PO Box 7, Crater Lake, OR 97604. The park offices are just south of Rim village.

## RIM DRIVE

A 33-mile loop road winds around the rim of Crater Lake, giving access to assorted viewpoints, trailheads and side roads. The paved one-way-only route begins on the northwest edge of Crater Lake and follows the lip of the crater clockwise until the road ducks behind **Cloudcap**, a point rising 2000 feet above the lake. A paved side road leads to the crest of Cloudcap, affording some of the best views of the lake and distant peaks like Mt Shasta and Mt McLoughlin. A few miles later, another side road off the rim drive leads 10 miles southeast to **The Pinnacles**, where water erosion has carved extensive pumice and ash formations into 100-foot spires and minarets called hoodoos. Rim Rd continues in a full loop all the way around the lake.

## CLEETWOOD COVE TRAIL

The mile-long Cleetwood Cove Trail is the only access to the lake itself and is very popular, since the end of the trail also serves as the departure point for the **Crater Lake Boat Tour**. About 500 people a day struggle down the 700-foot descent to the water, making this foot path more of an expressway than an escape.

Boats leave from the dock on the hour between 10 am and 4 pm, and conduct two-hour cruises around Crater Lake's 25-mile perimeter; park rangers provide geologic and historic information. The boat stops at

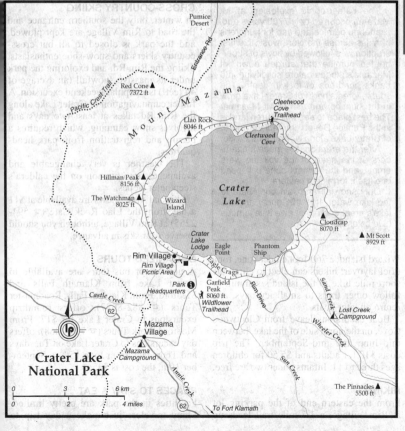

**Crater Lake National Park**

0    3    6 km
0    2    4 miles

OREGON

## Rhiolite Explosions

The ancient mountain whose remains now form Crater Lake was Mt Mazama. It was a roughly 12,000-foot volcanic peak, heavily glaciered, that had been inactive for many thousands of years until for some reason, the volcano came to life again. Rhiolite, a kind of molten rock that, unlike basalt, contains a high concentration of water, created a very violent eruption. Geologists know that the lava that caused the eruption at Mt Mazama was rhiolite because it came to the surface as pumice, a type of rock infused with so many air chambers (due to the expanding water in the lava) that it floats on water.

The catastrophic explosion at Mt Mazama occurred only 7700 years ago, scattering pumice and ash for hundreds of miles across the Northwest; this first eruption was followed by flows of super-heated pumice that surged down Mt Mazama's slopes before solidifying into banks hundreds of feet in depth. The sparse forests north of Crater Lake grow in the pumice and ash of Mt Mazama. The best place to see this barren land is in the Pumice Desert, immediately north of Crater Lake along North Entrance Rd.

After the eruption, the magma chambers at the heart of the volcano were empty, and the summit cone collapsed into itself, forming a caldera.

Only snowfall and rain contribute to the lake water. It is this purity and the lake's great depth that give it its famous blue color. ∎

**Garfield Peak** to an expansive view over the lake; in July the slopes are covered with wild flowers. Even better vistas are seen from the eastern edge of the Rim Rd, where **Mt Scott** – the highest peak on the perimeter of Crater Lake – rises 8929 feet. The trailhead to Mt Scott is across the road from the Cloudcap viewpoint road.

A less ambitious climb to a Crater Lake viewpoint follows a one-mile trail from the northwest stretch of Rim Rd to **The Watchman**, an old lookout tower. From the park headquarters, another short one-mile nature trail leads through the **Castle Crest** wildflower gardens.

## CROSS-COUNTRY SKIING

In winter, only the southern entrance and the road to Rim Village are kept plowed, and the park is closed to all but cross-country skiers and snow-shoe enthusiasts. Skiing the Rim Rd, and exploring the park under its massive snowfall (an average of 44 feet!) is a popular weekend excursion. A full circumnavigation of Crater Lake along the Rim Rd takes at least two days and involves snow camping, which requires a permit and registration from park headquarters.

The weather is very changeable and avalanches are common on the caldera's steep outer slopes.

Skis and snow shows are available at $11 a day from the Llao Rock Cafe (☎ 594-2255) at Rim Village, although you should reserve your skis in advance.

## ORGANIZED TOURS

A number of bus tours are available to Crater Lake from Klamath Falls and Medford. From Klamath Falls, Roadmaster Tours (☎ 882-8687), offers roundtrip excursions to Crater Lake for $17. From Medford, York Tours (☎ 779-1068), offers day excursions to Crater Lake on Tuesdays and Thursdays from June 15th to September 10th; the cost is $35.

Wizard Island, a 760-foot cinder cone, for a brief layover; hikers can elect to climb the short mile hike to the island's summit, or follow other trails to small icy bays, and return on later boats.

Boat excursions leave from Cleetwood Cove, on the north side of the lake, between mid-June and mid-September. The trip costs $10 for adults and $5.50 for children ages three to 11. Infants under two are free.

## HIKING

From the eastern end of the parking lot at Rim Village, a 1.7-mile trail leads up

## PLACES TO STAY & EAT

Facilities in the park are pretty limited. Many travelers just make a day trip to

Phantom Ship, Crater Lake

Crater Lake from Medford, Roseburg, Bend or Klamath Falls. However, if you want to stay in the vicinity, and campsites and lodging in the park are booked up, then try the small community of Fort Klamath, just 15 miles southeast of Crater Lake on Hwy 62. Keep in mind that everything closes up at the end of October, when the snow takes over, and opens again around April. The season varies, so it's best to call ahead if you're on the fringe of those months.

## Crater Lake

*Mazama Campground*, near the park's south entrance, offers minimal facilities on a first-come, first-serve basis. There are 12 more sites in a much more remote area at the *Lost Creek Campground*, on the road to The Pinnacles. There is an $11 fee.

In the park you can choose between *Mazama Village Motor Motel* (☎ 830-8700), at $78 a night in high season, and the grand old *Crater Lake Lodge* (☎ 594-2511). Rooms at the lodge are $99 for a single and $109 for a double, with two-bed suites topping out at $169. See below for more information on the lodge. There's family dining at the *Watchman Restaurant*, cafeteria meals at the *Llao Rock Cafe*, and snacks at the *Mountain Fountain* snack bar, all in Rim Village.

## Fort Klamath

*Crater Lake Campground* (☎ 381-2275), PO Box 485, on Hwy 62, is a full-service campground with showers, tepees, cabins and laundry facilities. Tent sites cost $12, RV sites are $16.

*Fort Klamath Lodge* (☎ 381-2234), offers both motel rooms ($30/35) and RV sites ($12). The *Crater Lake Resort* (☎ 381-2349), PO Box 457, Hwy 62, offers lodging in one and two-bedroom cabins ($35 to $45), and also offers RV sites ($14).

Drive to the junction of Hwys 97 and 62, 14 miles south, to the *Rapids Cafe* (783-

### The New Crater Lake Lodge

When the NPS began construction of the old Crater Lake Lodge in 1909, they had in mind a grand, timber and stone lodge in the rustic Cascadian style, featuring huge fireplaces, tree trunks as columns and rafters, and a sense of being part of the landscape. However, after the frame of the building was completed, federal funding dried up; the lodge was completed hastily in a slap-dash manner, and opened to the public.

Eighty years later, time, the park's formidable weather, and innumerable earthquakes had taken their toll. The foundations were crumbling, the roof was giving in, and walls were sagging. In 1988, the lodge closed due to safety concerns, and plans were announced to raze the building, as engineers judged that it was no longer structurally sound enough to justify a remodel. After a strong public outcry, Congress came up with the money to preserve the lodge by essentially rebuilding the entire structure. A new foundation, roof frame and steel and concrete structure replaced the old, while maintaining the historic appearance and much of the layout. Many elements of the old lodge were recycled by disassembling old fixtures, cleaning them and then replacing them in the new structure.

Some things did change. The lodge's original 150 cramped guest rooms were reduced to 71, each more sizable and with private bathrooms. The food in the lodge restaurant – which has one of the most astonishing views in the world – has been updated to represent the dishes of Northwest cuisine. Still, there are no telephones or TVs in the room: this is supposed to be a get-away, after all.■

2263), for home-cooking and notably good pies.

# Klamath Falls & Basin

Klamath Falls (population 18,085) is one of the state's most economically challenged cities. The end of logging-as-we-knew-it has left K Falls, as most people refer to the town, with one of the worst unemployment rates in the state.

Recently, Klamath Falls has done its best to promote itself as a retirement destination, and has been particularly successful in luring military retirees to the area. With some of the best bird watching in the west, great fishing in the beautiful Williamson and Klamath rivers, and easy access to all-season recreation in the Cascades, in the local national forests and on Oregon's largest lake, the Upper Klamath, Klamath Falls has a lot to offer.

Klamath Falls is also known throughout the state as one of the most conservative communities in Oregon. Evangelical Christian churches seem to flourish here, and keep close watch on the social and political fabric of the community; Klamath Falls was the birthplace of the Oregon Citizens Alliance.

## ORIENTATION
The old downtown area is at Main St and Klamath Ave, although most of the recent commercial growth has occurred south of town, along S 6th St and Hwy 39.

Klamath Falls is 79 miles from Medford on Hwy 79, and 63 miles from Ashland on Hwy 66. Klamath Falls is often used as a jumping-off point to visit Crater Lake, which is 73 miles to the north on Hwys 97 and 62.

## INFORMATION
The Klamath County Chamber of Commerce (☎ 884-5193), is at 507 Main St, Klamath Falls, OR 97601. There's also a visitors center at the Klamath County Museum (☎ 884-0666, (800) 445-6728), 1451 Main St. For information on recreation on public lands contact the Klamath Ranger Station (☎ 883-6824), 1936 California Ave.

The post office (☎ 884-9226) is at 317 S 7th St. The *Herald & News* comes out daily except Saturday. Jefferson Public Radio can be found on KSKF 90.0 FM. Oregon Institute of Technology's KTEC at 89.5 FM is an alternative public radio station. Robert's Wash & Dry (☎ 882-5417), is at 5911 Peck Drive, and the local hospital is the Merle West Medical Center (☎ 882-6311) at 2865 Daggett St.

## FAVELL MUSEUM OF WESTERN ART & INDIAN ARTIFACTS
Undoubtedly the best collection of Native American artifacts in Oregon, this impressive museum (☎ 882-9996), 125 W Main St, provides a fascinating interpretation of Western American culture. The collection is the life work – or obsession – of Gene Favell, a Lakeview native. Opened in 1972, the Favell Museum houses an eclectic smorgasbord of Native American tools, weapons, basketry and beadwork. The museum is open 9:30 pm to 5:50 pm Monday to Saturday. Admission is $5 for adults and $4 for students and seniors.

## KLAMATH COUNTY MUSEUM
Housed in the old art-deco National Guard Armory, this community museum (☎ 883-4208), 1451 Main St, features displays on the natural history of the Klamath lakes area, as well as exhibits that discuss the local Native American culture and the events of the Modoc War. The museum is open Monday to Saturday from 9 am to 5:30 pm during the summer, and 8 am to 4:30 pm during the winter; a $1 donation per adult is asked.

## BALDWIN HOTEL MUSEUM
Built in 1904, the Baldwin Hotel (☎ 883-4207), 31 Main St, first served as a hardware store before being turned into a showcase hotel in 1911. In its day, presi-

**Klamath Falls**

PLACES TO STAY
1  Boarding House Inn B&B
3  Maverick Motel
13  Klamath Manor B&B
14  Molatore's Motor Inn
   & Restaurant
16  Travelodge

PLACES TO EAT
6  Saddle Rock Cafe
9  Old Town Pizza
11  Hobo Junction
18  Taqueria Masfina

OTHER
2  Klamath County Museum
4  Amtrak Station
5  Bus Depot
7  Chamber of Commerce
8  Ross Ragland Theatre
10  All Season Sports
12  Post Office
15  Baldwin Hotel Museum
17  Favell Museum of Western Art

OREGON

dents Teddy Roosevelt, Taft and Wilson stayed here. The hotel has retained its glory, with many of its original fixtures and furnishings intact. Two tours are offered for $2 and $4. The museum is open Tuesday to Saturday from 10 am to 4 pm, June to September.

## KLAMATH BASIN WILDLIFE REFUGES

Six wildlife refuges totaling more than 284 sq miles string along the old basin of ice-age Modoc Lake, stretching from Upper Klamath Lake in Oregon to Tule Lake in California. The refuges support over 400 species of wildlife. These lakes are important stopovers on the Pacific flyway – 45,000 ducks and 26,000 Canadian geese are hatched here annually. Concentrations of up to two million birds are possible in spring and fall peak seasons. The basin is also prime winter territory for bald eagles.

For more information about the Klamath Basin National Wildlife Refuges (☎ (916) 667-2231), contact the headquarters at Route 1 Box 74, Tulelake, CA 96134, or the Oregon Dept of Fish & Wildlife (☎ 883-5732), 1400 Miller Island Rd W, Klamath Falls, OR 97603.

There are no organized tours to the

The USA's national bird, the bald eagle has a wing span of up to eight feet;
the head and tail feathers turn white only in adulthood.

refuges, but all are open to visitors. Check with local officials for seasonal closings due to nesting or other circumstances. Following is basic information about the principal Klamath Basin refuges in Oregon.

The **Upper Klamath Refuge** is on the northwestern shore of shallow, marshy Upper Klamath Lake. Tule rushes fill the lake, lending shelter to colonies of cormorants, egrets, herons, cranes, pelicans and many varieties of ducks and geese. Access to the preserve is by canoe only, which can be rented at Rocky Point Resort (see Lodges, below). To reach the refuge, follow Hwy 140 north from Klamath Falls to Harriman Lodge, and follow the signs to the Rocky Point Resort and the refuge.

The **Bear Valley Refuge**, west of Worden, is known mostly as a wintering area for bald eagles; 500 to 1000 gather here between December and February. To

reach the refuge, follow Hwy 97 south to Worden, and turn west on the Keno-Worden Rd.

The **Lower Klamath Refuge** probably offers the best year-round viewing and the easiest access of the Klamath refuges. Established in 1908 as the nation's first wildlife refuge, this 83-sq-mile preserve begins in Oregon and stretches south into California. This mix of open water, shallow marsh, cropland and grassy upland is home to many species of wildlife; for a quick overview of the area, take the self-guided loop drive, five miles east of the western entrance to the refuge on Hwy 161, also called State Line Rd.

## ACTIVITIES

Rent cross-country skis at All Season Sports (☎ 884-3863), 714 Main St.

The Upper Klamath River provides some

of the best **white-water rafting** in Oregon. Cascade River Runners (☎ 883-6340), PO Box 86, Klamath Falls, OR 97601, operates between April and October and offers one and two-day trips down the river with enough thrills (several class IV rapids) for even jaded rafters. Day trips cost $99 for adults, $89 for youths 14 to 18 years of age. The two-day trips involve a night of camping; the $230 adult and $205 youth price includes all meals and necessary equipment.

Trophy-sized rainbow trout are taken from the Williamson River north of Upper Klamath Lake, though dependable access is a problem. The best access is in Winema National Forest lands, or from Collier State Park, north of Chiloquin. For licenses, information and fish stories, contact Williamson River Anglers (☎ 783-2677), at the junction of Hwys 62 and 97, near Chiloquin.

## SPECIAL EVENTS

Every February, the Klamath Basin Eagle Conference is held at the Oregon Institute of Technology and is open to the public. This meeting of conservationists, ecologists and bird-watchers includes lectures, workshops, and field trips, plus a wildlife art show and film festival. Call the Oregon Department of Fish & Game (☎ 883-5732) or the chamber of commerce for information.

**OREGON**

### The Klamath & Modoc Indians

The Klamath lakes were the traditional homelands of the Klamath and Modoc tribes; although the tribes were related linguistically and lived close geographically, they were fierce rivals, and were among the last of Oregon's Native Americans to have contact with White settlers and explorers. Relations were initially friendly, but the development of the the Applegate, or Southern Oregon Trail, that crossed Modoc land infuriated the Modocs. After a Modoc raid left 18 White settlers dead near Tule Lake, pioneer vigilante groups and the Modocs began a series of fierce clashes. The US Army intervened in 1863 and built Fort Klamath to protect settlers from Indian hostilities.

By 1864 the Modocs and the Klamaths were forced to sign a treaty consigning them to the same reservation, north of Upper Klamath Lake. A group of Modocs under the leadership of Chief Keintpoos, better known as Captain Jack, left the reservation in 1865 and returned to the Tule Lake area, where White farmers were beginning to settle. By the 1870s, the remaining Modocs on the reservation removed to the far eastern edge of the tribal land in order to protect themselves from the hostility of the Klamaths.

Captain Jack demanded a separate Modoc reservation, but was refused. He and his people began to raid emigrant wagon trains for livestock and food. The army moved in on the Modocs stronghold in 1872, but a group of 170 Modoc warriors successfully withstood army troops numbering in the thousands.

In April of 1873, government officials approached the Modoc stonghold under a flag of truce; the Modocs opened fire, killing a general and the federal Superintendent of Indian Affairs, Rev E Thomas. The Oregon Indian superindendent, A B Meacham, was shot five times, knifed and left for dead. A young Modoc princess, Winema, hurried to the Meacham's rescue, and acted as interpreter and intermediary between the army and the Modocs.

Captain Jack and his chiefs were captured in June of 1873; the Modoc chief and three of his men were hanged at Fort Klamath, and other leaders sent to Alcatraz Prison for life sentences. The remainder of Captain Jack's followers were sent to Oklahoma for resettlement.

The Klamath Reservation had totaled 1560 sq miles in 1864, but by 1986 had been whittled away by the government and Klamath landowners to nothing. Many Klamaths, Modocs and some Northern Paiutes today live near the town of Chiloquin, 30 miles north of Klamath Falls. For more information about the Klamath tribes and local events, call 783-2219 or (800) 524-9787. ■

The Klamath Memorial Rodeo & Indian Dancing Festival (☎ 883-3905, 882-2284) is held at the Klamath County Fairgrounds, 3531 S 6th St, over Memorial Day weekend. The Klamath County Fair & Jefferson State Rodeo (☎ 883-3796), is held the first weekend of August at the fairgrounds.

Tribal Treaty Days, Powwow & Rodeo (☎ 783-2218), held at the Chiloquin Rodeo Grounds, offers an all-Indian Rodeo, marathon run, parade and salmon barbecue to celebrate the Klamath Indians' return to federally recognized tribal status in 1986.

## PLACES TO STAY
### Camping
At KOA's *Kampgrounds of Klamath Falls* (☎ 884-4644), 3435 Shasta Way, full hookups run around $20 and tent sites are $14. *Oregon 8 RV Park* (☎ 882-0482), is three miles north of Klamath Falls 5225 N Hwy 97, and sites are $12.

Directly west of Klamath Falls rise the Cascade Mountains, where there's cooler and shadier camping. *Lake of the Woods Resort* (☎ 949-8300), 950 Harriman Route on Lake of the Woods, has tent sites ($8), RV sites ($12) and cabins for four ($40 to $65); there's also a room for four in the lodge for $32. The lodge is open year round, though they close Mondays and Tuesdays except in summer. Boat, cross-country ski, snowmobile and ice-skate rentals are available.

### B&Bs
The *Klamath Manor B&B* (☎ 883-5459, (800) 956-5459), 219 Pine St, is a nicely decorated and restored turn-of-the-century home convenient to downtown. Prices range from $45 to $65. *The Boarding House Inn B&B* (☎ 883-8584, (800) 272-1256), 1800 Esplanade Ave, was once a lodging for rail workers in the early 1900s. All four guest rooms have private baths and full kitchens. Rates range between $45 to $65.

*Thompson's B&B by the Lake* (☎ 882-7938), 1420 Wild Plum Court, offers views over Upper Klamath Lake and the Cas-

cades. There are four guest rooms, two with private baths; all have private entrances. Rooms begin at $65.

### Hotels
A few miles north of Klamath Falls are a couple of good deals in lodging: *High Chaparral Motel* (☎ 882-4675), 5440 Hwy 97 N, and the *Oregon 8 Motel* (☎ 883-3431), three miles north of Klamath Falls at 5225 Hwy 97 N, are in the $30 to $35 range.

In town, rooms at the *Maverick Motel* (☎ 882-6688), 1220 Main St, the *Travelodge* (☎ 882-4494), 11 Main St, and *Molatore's Motor Inn* (☎ 882-4666), 100 Main St, are $35 to $50.

The *Cimarron Motel* (☎ 882-4601), 3060 S 6th St, the *Best Western Klamath Inn* (☎ 882-1200), 4061 S 6th St, and the *Red Lion Inn* (☎ 882-8864), 3612 S 6th St, are pricier at $40 to $70. All hotels listed have pools.

### Lodges
*Rocky Point Resort* (☎ 356-2287), 28121 Rocky Point Rd, is on the northwest end of the Upper Klamath Lake, near the wildlife refuge. From Hwy 140, turn at Harriman Lodge and follow the signs. Tent sites are $12, RV sites run $14 to $16, motel rooms start at $45 and cabins in the woods next to the lake start at $59. There's a full-service marina and tackle shop, restaurant and cocktail lounge. It's open May to December only.

## PLACES TO EAT
For espresso, bagels and pastries, go to *Renaldo's Cafe Espresso* (☎ 884-3846), in Campus Square Plaza, north of the city center on Kit Carson Way.

*Hobo Junction* (☎ 882-8013), 636 Main St, has sandwiches and light meals. *Old Town Pizza* (☎ 884-8858), 722 Main St, serves Klamath Falls' best pizza. *Taqueria Masfina* (☎ 884-5648), 1002 E Main St, is one of many good Mexican restaurants in the area and is open for traditional Mexican breakfasts.

*Molatore's Restaurant* (☎ 884-6298),

100 Main St, part of the large motel complex, is open for three meals a day. *Saddle Rock Cafe* (☎ 884-1444), 1012 Main St, was one of Klamath Falls' first fine restaurants, with pasta and carefully seasoned sauces and rotisserie chicken. At lunch, the salads are a welcome relief after traveling through Red Meat Country. *Chez Nous* (☎ 883-8719), 3927 S 6th St, sounds like a French restaurant, but most people go there for the steak and seafood. *Fiorella's* (☎ 882-1878), 6139 Simmers Ave, offers 11 different pastas, including gnocchi ($11.50), and four veal preparations (veal piccata is $16), as well as chicken and filet mignon.

## ENTERTAINMENT

The art-deco *Ross Ragland Theater* (☎ 884-5483), 218 N 7th St, serves as the stage for the community symphony and chorus, as well as country & western celebrities and Broadway troupes. *Pelican Cinemas* (☎ 884-5000), 2626 Biehn St, offers six screens worth of first-run movies.

## GETTING THERE & AWAY

### Air

Klamath Falls International Airport (☎ 883-5372) is off Hwy 140 south of town. Horizon Airlines (☎ 884-3331) offers six flights a day to/from Portland; the cheapest one-way fare between the cities is $118. United Express offers four flights a day between San Francisco and Klamath Falls; a one-way fare is around $85. Reno Air flies between San Jose and Klamath Falls three times a day; fares begin at $83.

### Bus

Greyhound (☎ 882-4616) offers bus service to Bend, Portland, Medford and Eugene from their bus station at 1200 Klamath Ave. One-way fare from Klamath Falls to Portland is $33; to Medford, $17.

### Train

Amtrak's *Coast Starlight* passes through twice daily. A one-way fare between San Francisco and Klamath Falls is $88 to $166, depending on advance booking; between Portland and Klamath Falls, ticket prices range between $72 and $128. The depot (☎ 884-2822) is at S Spring St and Oak St.

### Car

Hertz Rent-A-Car (☎ 882-0220) is at 6815 Rand Way, and Avis (☎ 882-7273), 6817 Rand Way, are both near the airport.

# Central Oregon

For many people, central Oregon *is* recreation. Fishing, white-water rafting, rock climbing, skiing, hiking and wildlife viewing begin the list of outdoor activities that make Oregon's fair-weather region a favorite destination. The Deschutes and the Metolius rivers are famous throughout the USA for trout fishing, and the thousands of acres of golf courses are considered by many the region's real treasure.

It's impossible to ignore the geography of central Oregon. The power of volcanoes and the resolve of erosion have each indelibly marked the landscape with spectacular formations. Ten million years of prodigious volcanic activity in northeastern Oregon covered the land in successions of massive lava flows, creating a magma base that is reckoned to be, in some places, up to a half mile deep. The rivers and streams of central Oregon managed to carve extraordinary canyons through the deep lava beds, the Deschutes and Crooked rivers in particular incising amazing gorges into the tortured volcanic landscape.

The Deschutes River, which descends from the Cascades to the Columbia River, cutting from south to north through central Oregon, is the region's main river and home to brown and rainbow trout (locally known as 'red-sides' for their coppery flanks). Steelhead trout make their dramatic seasonal runs up it; watch them hurl themselves up the torrent at Sherar's Falls.

Central Oregon's dry, sunny climate and high elevation – between 3000 and 4000 feet in elevation – give rise to an ecosystem called the High Desert, characterized by ponderosa pines, sagebrush and scrub juniper. An array of animals find a home in this transitional landscape. Raptors, including golden eagles and red-tailed hawks are commonly seen hunting the open forests. Mule deer are pervasive throughout the region, and coyotes have adapted hastily to the inexorable suburbanization of central

Oregon and are as happy to eat domestic cats as more traditional rodent fare.

Once the domain of the Wasco Indians, the Oregon Trail and later the promise of gold brought settlers to the area; the native tribes were relegated to the Warm Springs Reservation in 1855. Cycles of drought finished off all but the most persistent of the early homesteaders, until the 1940s when the US Government built irrigation dams along the Deschutes. With a little water the fertile volcanic soil blossomed with traditional farm crops like alfalfa.

This part of the state has long been the provenance of cattle ranchers and irrigation farmers, but the region's beautiful setting and exceptional recreational opportunities have begun to lure a new breed of settler. Businesses began to relocate to central Oregon as 'lifestyle' considerations came to figure into corporate decisions. Retirees moved here to escape the clouds and gloom of coastal climates. As a result, real-estate developers have subdivided much of this high-savanna land into semi-rural suburbs and resort communities.

## GETTING THERE & AWAY
### Air
Redmond boasts the region's only airport served by commercial airlines. The Redmond/Bend Airport is just southeast of Redmond on Hwy 97, 18 miles north of Bend. United Express (☎ (800) 241-6522) and Horizon Air (☎ (800) 547-9308) fly into the airport from Portland, Eugene, Seattle and San Francisco. The one-way airfare to/from Portland is about $70.

CAC Transportation's (☎ 382-1687, (800) 955-8267) Redmond Airport Shuttle links Bend to the airport; the shuttle is available by reservation only; fares to Bend begin at $15.

Rental-car agencies found at the Redmond/Bend Airport include Budget (☎ 923-0699), Hertz (☎ 923-1411, (800)

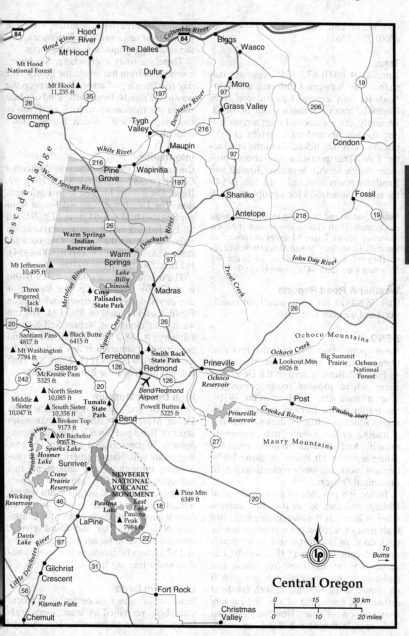

OREGON

**Central Oregon**

0     15     30 km

0   10   20 miles

To
Burns

654-3131) and National (☎ 548-8166, (800) 227-7368).

## Train

Amtrak (☎ (800) 872-7245) operates one train a day between California and Portland. Its only central Oregon stop is in Chemult, about 65 miles south of Bend. Presently, the northbound train arrives at 9 am; the southbound train arrives at 7:55 pm. You can buy tickets from the conductor. CAC Transportation (see above) provides shuttle service between Chemult and Bend; by reservation only, the fare is $45 for an individual, $55 for a couple.

**Note** If you do end up having to spend the night in Chemult, *Digit Point Campground* is on the shores of Miller Lake, 12 miles northwest of Chemult. Or try the *Chemult Motel* (☎ 365-2228) on Hwy 97. For home cooking, go to the *Big Mountain Cafe* (365-4475) along Hwy 97.

## Weather & Road Reports

Call 389-4815 for up-to-date road conditions and weather forecasts.

## BEND

Bend (population 24,715), the focus of Oregon's fastest growing area, started out as Farewell Bend, a ford in the Deschutes River where pioneer roads converged. Later a ranch site, and then, in the 1910s, the trailhead for intense logging of the region's vast pine forests, the town was just a trading center, albeit in a stunningly beautiful location, until the development of skiing areas on Mt Bachelor in the 1960s brought more and more recreationalists to the central Oregon.

Today, it's possible to have ambivalent feelings and hard to get over first impressions of Bend. Is it a swaggering little city with tons of wholesome recreation out its back door, or is it just a real-estate developer's dream come true? Highway 97 traverses one of the most relentless and god-awful commercial strips you'll encounter in the Northwest, with fast-food restaurants, real-estate offices and car lots stretching on for miles. However, a second look reveals downtown Bend, an older,

prosperous area with beautiful riverside parks, great restaurants, coffeehouses, reasonable lodging and browseable shops.

There's activity everywhere. Ski bums, cowboys in from the ranch, the gentry on a day-trip from a golf resort, kayakers on the way to the rapids: Bend is the kind of place where it's mandatory to look as if you're enjoying yourself, which happily isn't difficult.

## Information

Contact the Central Oregon Welcome Center (☎ 382-3221), 63085 N Hwy 97, Bend, OR 97701, for free tourist information. The Deschutes National Forest Ranger Station (☎ 388-5664) is at 1230 NE 3rd St. For lodging reservations and recreation referrals, contact the Central Oregon Recreation Association (☎ (800) 800-8334), PO Box 230, Bend, OR 97709.

The downtown post office (☎ 389-0408) is at 47 NW Oregon Ave. The *Bulletin* is the city's daily newspaper, and Oregon Public Radio is heard on 91.3 FM. You can wash your clothes at Nelson Self-Service Laundry (☎ 388-2140), 407 SE 3rd St, and seek medical attention at St Charles Medical Center (☎ 382-4321), 2500 NE Neff Rd, just north of Pilot Butte State Park.

## High Desert Museum

One of Oregon's best museums, the High Desert Museum (☎ 382-4754), six miles south of Bend on Hwy 97, charts the development of central and eastern Oregon. Beginning with Native Americans and proceeding through White settlement, this indoor/outdoor facility provides insights not only into history, but also into nature, wildlife, art and rural society. It's open from 9 am to 5 pm daily expect for Christmas, New Year's Day and Thanksgiving; admission is $5.50 for adults, $5 for seniors and $2.75 for children ages five to 12; children under four are free.

## Downtown Bend

Bend's old commercial center has in recent years been revivified by smart shops, galleries and fine restaurants. It's easy to spend several hours drinking coffee, nosing through bookstores and looking at antiques.

Public parks stretch along the Deschutes River throughout town. **Drake Park** and a calm stretch of the river called **Mirror Pond** lie just behind downtown, and are beautiful spots for a picnic. Paths link Drake Park to Columbia Park upstream and Pioneer Park downstream.

**The Deschutes County Historical Center**, a community museum, is in Bend's 1914 grade school, on Idaho Ave between Wall and Bond Sts. The museum houses artifacts of the area's Native American and pioneer history. It's open from 1 to 4:30 pm, Wednesday to Saturday.

### Hiking

If you want to stretch you legs but don't have time to head out into the wilderness, go to Shevlin Park, five miles west of Bend on Newport Ave. This 700-acre county park offers forest hikes and picnic facilities along Tumalo Creek.

For a bird's-eye view of Bend, climb Pilot Butte, on the eastern fringes of town. Part of a small state park, the butte is the

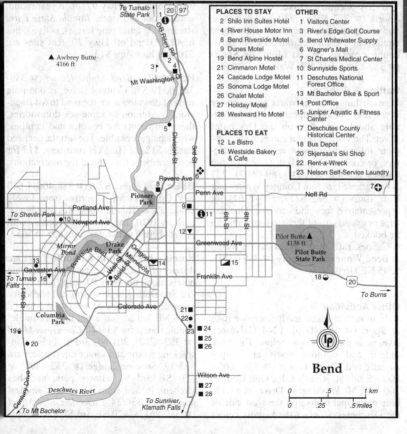

**PLACES TO STAY**
2 Shilo Inn Suites Hotel
4 River House Motor Inn
8 Bend Riverside Motel
9 Dunes Motel
19 Bend Alpine Hostel
21 Cimmaron Motel
24 Cascade Lodge Motel
25 Sonoma Lodge Motel
26 Chalet Motel
27 Holiday Motel
28 Westward Ho Motel

**PLACES TO EAT**
12 Le Bistro
16 Westside Bakery & Cafe

**OTHER**
1 Visitors Center
3 River's Edge Golf Course
5 Bend Whitewater Supply
6 Wagner's Mall
7 St Charles Medical Center
10 Sunnyside Sports
11 Deschutes National Forest Office
13 Mt Bachelor Bike & Sport
14 Post Office
15 Juniper Aquatic & Fitness Center
17 Deschutes County Historical Center
18 Bus Depot
20 Skjersaa's Ski Shop
22 Rent-a-Wreck
23 Nelson Self-Service Laundry

**Bend**

OREGON

cone of an ancient volcano. If you don't feel like walking up, ride your mountain bike (there's also a paved road to the top for cars).

Tri Mountain Sports (☎ 382-8330), 815 NW Wall St, rents hiking gear, and Columbia Outfitters (☎ 389-8993), 939 NW Bond St, is a good place to buy sweaters, coats and other brand-name outdoor clothing.

### Skiing
Don't feel left out. Rent some skis and get outdoors like everyone else. Ski rentals are available at Mt Bachelor (see below), but if you want to rent them beforehand, try Skjersaa's Ski Shop (☎ 382-2154), 130 SW Century Drive, or Sunnyside Sports (☎ 382-8018), 930 Newport Ave; downhill, cross-country, and snowboard equipment is available from both. For cross-country rentals, try Tri Mountain Sports (☎ 382-8330), 815 NW Wall St.

### Rafting & Fishing
Hire a fishing or white-water guide service if you feel unknowledgeable or uncomfortable about recreation on the Deschutes River. The visitors center can provide complete information about registered outfitters, or contact either High Desert Drifter Guides & Outfitters (☎ 389-0607), 721 NW Ogden St, or Sun Country Whitewater Raft Tours (☎ 382-6277, 593-2161) for representative fees and services. One-day trips or excursions of three to four days can be booked.

Canoes, rafts, and kayaks can be rented at Bend Whitewater Supply (☎ 389-7191), 2245 NE Division St.

### Other Activities
Rent mountain bikes at Mt Bachelor Bike & Sport (☎ 382-4000), 1244 Galveston Ave, or at the ski shops, below. There are indoor and outdoor pools at Juniper Aquatic and Fitness Center (☎ 389-7665), 800 NE 6th St. River's Edge Golf Course, 200 NW Mt Washington Drive, is an 18-hole municipal course on the west side of the Deschutes. Contact the visitors center

for a complete listing of the golf resorts in the area.

### Places to Stay
For a centralized lodging and recreation-reservation service, contact the Central Oregon Recreation Association (☎ 382-8334, (800) 800 8334), PO Box 230, Bend, OR 97709.

**Camping** There are dozens of USFS campgrounds in the Deschutes National Forest; contact the Bend Ranger Station (☎ 388-5664), 1230 NE 3rd St, for complete information. Close to Bend and a little more civilized is the *Bend KOA* (☎ 382-7728), 63615 N Hwy 97, open year round, with a pool and store. *Tumalo State Park*, stream-side amid pine forests, is five miles north of Bend off Hwy 20; tent sites are $10, full hook-ups $13.

**Hostels** *The Bend Alpine Hostel* (☎ 389-3813), 19 SW Century Drive, is one mile west of downtown, on the road to Mt Bachelor. In addition to same-sex dormitories, there are rooms for couples and families; wheelchair accessible. The simple, per head rate, is $12 for HI/AYH members, $15 for non-members. Call ahead for reservations.

**B&Bs** *Lara House B&B* (☎ 388-4064), 640 NW Congress St, is across from lovely Drake Park. This Historic-Register home, built in 1910, has five guest rooms (with private baths) with rates from $55 to $65.

**Hotels – bottom end & middle** There are dozens of inexpensive, perfectly adequate hotels along the Hwy 97 strip (here called 3rd St). During high season call ahead for reservations. *Dunes Motel* (☎ 382-6811), 1515 NE 3rd St, has a hot tub and single/double rooms for $38/41. *Cimmaron Motel* (☎ 382-8282), 201 NE 3rd St, offers non-smoking rooms and senior rates; prices are $35/39. *Sonoma Lodge* (☎ 382-4891) at 450 SE 3rd St, allows pets, and has kitchens in non-smoking rooms; singles/doubles are $30/34. *Cascade Lodge Motel* (☎ 382-2612), 420 SE 3rd St, has an outdoor pool and non-smoking rooms for $32/35. *Chalet Motel* (☎ 382-6124) at 510 SE 3rd St, allows pets and has non-smoking rooms; singles/doubles are $30/34. *Holiday Motel* (☎ 382-4620), 880 SE 3rd St, also with non-smoking rooms, offers continental breakfast; rates are $32/36. *Westward Ho Motel* (☎ 382-2111), 904 SE 3rd St, has a pool and lets the pets stay; rates are $35/39. *Chaparral Motel* (☎ 389-1448) 1300 SE Hwy 97, has laundry and kitchen facilities for $30/34. And finally, *Super 8* (☎ 388-6888), 1275 SE Hwy 97, offers laundry and an indoor pool at $49/55.

**Hotels – top end** The *RiverHouse Motor Inn* (☎ 389-3111), 3075 N Hwy 97, sits at a beautiful location with views onto the 18-hole golf course and the Deschutes River. There are full health spa facilities, and two pools. Single/double rooms begin at $58/64, and go to $99 for more deluxe rooms with views. *Bend Riverside Motel* (☎ 389-2363), 1565 Hill St, offers condominium-style accommodations ($69), riverside cabins ($75), as well as regular rooms ($49). It's in a pleasant location near the river and Pioneer Park and has an indoor pool.

Bend's newest accommodation is the turreted *Shilo Inn Suites Hotel* (☎ 389-9600), 3105 O B Riley Rd, on the north end of Bend along the Deschutes River. Facilities include an indoor pool, sauna and fitness center. Basic single/double rooms begin at $81/91.

Ten miles north of Bend is the *Deschutes River Ranch* (☎ 382-7240), 20210 Swalley Rd, Bend, OR 97701, a resort and guest ranch with fishing, horseback riding and tennis courts on a 410-acre working ranch. Lodging is in completely furnished, three-bedroom homes; rates start at $125. Take Hwy 20 to Redmond-Bend Hwy near Tumalo State Park and turn on Tumalo-Deschutes Hwy; turn right on Swalley Rd.

**Places to Eat**

Most of the restaurants listed below are within a two-block radius in the small city center. Wall and Bond Sts run parallel to each other, with Franklin, Minnesota and Oregon Aves crossing them. Highway 97 also has a high density of restaurants, particularly fast-food chains.

Outside of Portland, Bend probably offers the best selection of gourmet food stuffs and wine in the state. If the rigors of traveling have you longing for good cheese or a healthy snack, try one of the following. *La Strada* (☎ 388-0222), 114 NW Minnesota Ave, offers fresh pasta, cheeses and other Italian specialty items. *Chelsea Lane* (☎ 385-5648), 135 NW Minnesota Ave, has a great wine selection, some deli items and fancy tobacco products. For healthier options, try *Nature's General Store* (☎ 382-6732), 1950 NW 3rd St (in Wagner's Mall). Here you'll find organic produce, a juice bar, diet supplements and a deli.

**Budget** *Westside Bakery & Cafe* (☎ 382-3426), 1005 NW Galveston Ave, is across the Deschutes River from downtown. Breakfast or lunch is the main attraction, but you can also load up on sweet rolls and pastries before hitting the slopes. For a traditional and abundant breakfast, go to *Arvard's Cafe & Lounge* (☎ 389-0990), 928 NW Bond St. It's the sort of old-fashioned eatery where you can enjoy your early morning hash browns up front, while others in the back begin the first drink of the day.

*Cafe Santé* (☎ 383-3530), 718 NW Franklin Ave, is a classy vegetarian restaurant open for breakfast and lunch; vegetarian lasagna goes for $5.75. For pizza, go to *Stuft Pizza* (☎ 382-4022), 125 NW Oregon Ave; it's cheap, it's tasty, it's smoke-free, and on Saturday nights there's stand-up comedy.

*Baja Norte* (☎ 385-0611), 801 Wall St, is a lively Mexican grill and a tasty and inexpensive place to see and be seen. Fill up on seafood tacos for less than $5. Be sure to take in the amazing tortilla-making machine in the waiting area; outdoor seating is available.

*Deschutes Brewery & Public House* (☎ 382-9242), 1044 NW Bond St, serves up Bend's microbrewed bitter, ale and porter in a gregarious pub atmosphere. The food is equally festive. *Cafe Paradiso* (☎ 385-5931), 945 NW Bond St, is a great place to hang out. Settle into the easy chairs and couches, and enjoy pastries and live evening entertainment. For coffee on the run, go to *Coffee & Co* (☎ 389-6464), 835 NW Wall St.

**Middle** *Yoko's Japanese Restaurant* (☎ 382-2999), 1028 NW Bond St, features Bend's only sushi bar. A dinner portion of vegetable tempura cost $9. *Giuseppe's Ristorante* (☎ 389-8899), 932 NW Bond St, serves old-fashioned Italian entrees such as chicken parmesan for $13. *Pasha's* (☎ 382-5859), 61 NW Oregon Ave, offers superlative Lebanese cuisine. For $13.50 snack out on *masa*, a selection of spreadable and dippable delicacies from the appetizer menu.

*Pescatore* (☎ 389-6276), 119 NW Minnesota Ave, blends fresh seafood and Italian traditions. Between 5 and 6:30 pm there's an early-dinner menu, with most dishes under $10. Full dinners, like a seafood cioppino, start at $14.

*McKenzie's Restaurant & Bar* (☎ 388-3891),1033 NW Bond St, is a non-smoking restaurant in a historic storefront. Steak, pasta and seafood dominate the menu, though there's also a number of game specialties, like antelope steak for $15.

**Top End** *Pine Tavern Restaurant* (☎ 382-5581), 967 NW Brooks St, is probably Bend's best-loved restaurant. Steak, trout and lamb don't get much better than this; prices are in the $15 range. *Le Bistro* (☎ 389-7274), 1203 NE 3rd St, serves upscale French food in a renovated church. Their trademark seafood Wellington goes for $18. It's open for dinner only.

Menu eclecticism is the order of the day at starkly decorated *Rosette* (☎ 383-2780), 150 NW Oregon Ave. Asian and Continental cooking traditions meld here. Salmon with pink peppercorn sauce goes for $17.

### Getting There & Around

For information on air and train travel, see Getting There & Away at the beginning of this chapter.

Greyhound provides two buses a day between Portland and Bend via Madras and Redmond; one bus links Eugene and Bend via Sisters. There's one bus a day along Hwy 97 between Bend, Klammath Falls and points in California. The bus depot (☎ 382-2151) is at 2045 E Hwy 20.

Contact Rent A Wreck (☎ 385-7711, (800) 562-0242), 315 SE 3rd St or Cheap Wheels (☎ 389-8893, (800) 392-5440), 63360 N Hwy 97, for rental vehicles. Call Owl Taxi (☎ 382-3311) for a cab.

## NEWBERRY NATIONAL VOLCANIC MONUMENT

While much of central Oregon is dominated by high mountains, the area south of Bend is dramatically influenced by a mountain that's largely absent. Newberry Crater was once one of the largest and most active volcanoes in North America, and its impact is seen in much of central Oregon.

The Newberry volcano began erupting about 500,000 years ago, and successive flows gradually built a steep-sided mountain almost a mile above the surrounding plateau. Lava flows were incredibly voluminous, and flowed along the Deschutes drainage to reach as far north as Madras. As with Crater Lake, the summit of the volcano collapsed after a large eruption, creating a caldera. Recent immense obsidian flows partially served to divide the caldera into East and Paulina lakes.

Native Americans frequented Newberry Crater in order to collect obsidian, from which they fashioned arrowheads. Such obsidian was a valuable item of trade, and Oregon obsidian has been found in archeological sites throughout the West.

Newberry Crater was discovered by explorer and trapper Peter Skein Ogden in 1826. Paulina Peak and Lake were named for Chief Paulina of the Snake Indians, who led a bloody war against settlers during the 1860s. He and his band retreated to Newberry Crater to avoid pursuit.

During the 1980s, energy companies became interested in the geothermal potential underlying Newberry Crater. By tapping into the old volcano, these companies proposed to generate 1500 megawatts of energy annually. In response, a group of recreationalists, environmentalists and politicians pushed through legislation to preserve the 78-sq-mile area as a national monument, which was signed into law in 1990.

## Information
The Lava Lands Visitor Center (☎ 593-2421), 58201 S Hwy 97, about 11 miles south of Bend, provides information and exhibits on the geology, wildlife and archeology of the Newberry National Volcanic Monument. A short trail leads to a lava flow. The ranger at the center has information on off-road exploration and remote destinations. Ask about campgrounds and road conditions at the information desk/bookshop.

## Lava Butte
A perfect cone rising 500 feet above the surrounding lava flows, Lava Butte is a cindery vent on the flanks of Newberry Crater. A road spirals up the side of the butte to an observation deck, with spectacular views of the Cascades and nearby volcanic formations; between Memorial Day and Labor Day shuttle buses runs from the visitors center to the butte summit every half hour from 9 am to 5 pm.

Follow signs from the visitors center to **Benham Falls** on the Deschutes River. More a series of rapids than a waterfall, Benham Falls was formed when lava from Lava Butte flowed down and blocked the river. Watch for otters during the half-mile hike.

## Lava River Cave
Lava tubes are formed when the surface of a lava flow solidifies, allowing the still-molten rock below it to flow out. The resulting cave, which often follows the course of a buried streambed, is clean and dry compared to caves caused by water

erosion. Lava River Cave, one of many in the monument but the only one that's developed for visitors, is the longest lava tube in Oregon. Bring a flashlight and explore the cave on your own or rent a lantern at the gate, about one mile south of the visitors center.

## Lava Cast Forest
About 6000 years ago, a wall of molten lava 20 feet deep flowed down from Newberry Crater and engulfed a forest of mature trees. The trees incinerated, but not before cooling and solidifying the lava. The resulting casts or molds of the forest are seen on a mile-long interpretive trail. The Lava Cast Forest is nine miles east of Hwy 97 on Lava Cast Forest Rd.

## Newberry Crater
An enormous volcanic caldera in which nestles two lakes famous for great fishing, Newberry Crater is a favorite spot for camping and exploring truly remarkable volcanic geology. Looming above everything is 8000-foot Paulina Peak, a remnant of the much higher mountain that collapsed during the eruption that formed the present five-mile wide crater.

Once one large lake, **Paulina** and **East lakes** are now separated by a lava flow and a pumice cone. The larger of the two bodies of water, Paulina Lake is over 250 feet deep; a seven-mile trail circles the lake. Ice Age glaciers carved a niche in the side of the crater, allowing Paulina Creek to drain the lake via a 100-foot-high waterfall. With no visible inflow or outflow, East Lake seems hermetic. However, snow melt and springs feed the lake, and it drains through subterranean passages into Paulina Lake.

While the area's newly conferred status as a national monument is sure to increase the flow of tourists to Paulina and East Lakes, anglers have known about these fishing holes for years. Reckoned to offer some of the best fishing in Oregon, these lakes weren't even stocked with fish until a turn-of-the-century sportsman carted some rainbow trout up into the crater and planted them in East Lake. Due to the lakes' great depths and the constant flow of fresh mineral spring water, fish thrive here.

A short trail halfway between the two lakes leads to the **Big Obsidian Flow**. An enormous flow of obsidian – formed when silica-rich lava cools quickly into translucent, glass-like formations – careens down the south flank of Newberry Crater. Take care about contact with flakes of obsidian, and be mindful of your shoes: walking on broken obsidian is exactly like walking on shards of glass.

The **Newberry Crater Rim Loop trail** encircles Paulina Lake and is a good place for hiking and mountain biking, with a number of campgrounds within reach.

From Hwy 97 take Paulina East Lake Rd to Newberry Crater.

### Places to Stay & Eat

LaPine, stretched along the highway like an attenuated truck stop, is the closest town to Newberry Crater. It's at the southern end of the Cascade Lakes Hwy, and the junction of Hwy 31, which leads east to Oregon's Great Basin country.

Campgrounds in *Newberry Crater* usually aren't open until late May, and remain open to October. A total of eight campgrounds crowd around East and Paulina lakes, so there's no shortage of campsites. Contact the Lava Lands Visitor Center for more information. *LaPine State Recreation Area*, on the banks of the Deschutes River north of LaPine (four miles from Hwy 97) has campgrounds and access to fishing on the Deschutes River. The recreation area provides a short hike to the Big Tree, Oregon's largest ponderosa pine.

*Paulina Lake Lodge* (☎ 536-2240), PO Box 7, LaPine, OR 97739, is a small fishing resort with cabins, a restaurant, general store and boat rentals. It's open year round and is popular with cross-country skiers and snowmobilers. *East Lake Fishing Resort* (☎ 536-2230), PO Box 95, LaPine, OR 97739, is also an unassuming lodge for anglers, with cabins, a restaurant open for lunch and breakfast only, and a store that supplies the wherewithal for a fishing trip. The *Master Host Motor Inn* (☎ 536-

1737), 52560 Hwy 97, is a couple miles north of LaPine, and offers non-smoking rooms and takes pets; singles/doubles are $38/42. The *West View Motel* (☎ 536-2115), 51371 Hwy 97 in LaPine, is a well-kept older unit; $34/38.

For family-style food, go to the *Harvest Hut* (☎ 536-1493), 51453 Hwy 97, or the *LaPine Inn* (☎ 536-2029), 51490 Hwy 97.

## MT BACHELOR

At 9065 feet, Mt Bachelor is scarcely the highest mountain in the Cascade Range. But its position grants it another title: that of the best skiing mountain in the region. Located slightly east of the main line of Cascade peaks (22 miles southwest of Bend), the colder, continental air of central Oregon meets up with the warm, wet Pacific air of western Oregon. The result is tons of fine, dry snow, with ample sunshine.

For more information about Mt Bachelor contact Mt Bachelor Resort (☎ 382-2442, (800) 829-2442), PO Box 1031, Bend, OR 97709.

### Skiing

Mt Bachelor is almost perfectly conical in shape, except for a small, distinct crater at its top. Nine lifts ease waiting in lines and take skiers directly to the peak of the mountain. Fifty-four runs trace routes to the base of the mountain, with a total vertical drop of 3100 feet. With almost 300 inches of snow a year, the season begins in November and can last until June.

Ski and snowboard rentals are available at Mt Bachelor Ski and Sport Center (☎ 382-2442) at the base of the lifts, or from ski shops in Bend (see Bend, above). A one-day lift ticket is $33, or you can purchase a 10-day pass for $305. The Sport Center offers day-care, multiple food options, lessons and shopping.

Mt Bachelor also offers 34 miles of groomed cross-country trails, though the $9 day-pass may prompt skiers to check out the many cross-country trails at adjacent Dutchman Flat, on public land. To reach the Dutchman Flat area go past the turnoff for Mt Bachelor on Hwy 46; almost immediately there is a large parking area. This is as far as the snow plows maintain the highway during winter. From here on, you'll need skis or snowmobiles. If you park at the Dutchman Flats snow park (or at any of the other snow parks along Hwy 46), you'll need a Sno-Park permit, which costs $2.50 from area businesses.

To check on ski conditions, call 382-7888.

## Hiking & Biking

During the summer the summit lift ($9 adult, $4.50 children ages seven to 12) takes hikers and mountain bikers to the top of the peak, and you may choose to ride the lift back down. Trails are open from 10 am to 4 pm. You can rent mountain bikes at Sunrise Lodge.

## Places to Stay & Eat

The least expensive lodging in the area is in Bend, although, on weekends during the winter season, rooms are a premium. Between Bend and Mt Bachelor there's a clutch of upscale lodgings, many in the 'resort' mold popular to this area. They all run shuttle buses to Mt Bachelor. *Mt Bachelor Village* (☎ 389-5900, (800) 547-5204), 19717 Mt Bachelor Drive, offers condo-style accommodations, with an outdoor pool, tennis courts and hiking trails. Unit (they're not rooms, but 'units') prices start at $80 a night.

Closer to the mountain is *Best Western Entrada Lodge* (☎ 382-4080, (800) 528-1234), 19221 Century Drive, a large, comfortable motel without the pretensions of a 'life-style' resort. There's a pool and hot tubs. Single/double rooms are $45/50; pets are OK.

The largest resort and the closest accommodations to Mt Bachelor, is the *Inn of the Seventh Mountain* (☎ 382-8711, (800) 542-6810), 18575 S Century Drive. In addition to accommodations in condominium lodges (beginning at $56), there are dozens of recreational activities offered to guests: swimming pools with a water slide, tennis courts, an 18-hole golf course, ice-skating

rink, horse-back riding and bike paths, to name a few. There are also three restaurants to choose from.

*Sunriver Lodge* (☎ 593-1221, (800) 547-3922), PO Box 3609, Sunriver, OR 97707, just downhill from Mt Bachelor, has had a lot to do with establishing central Oregon's reputation as an enclave of upscale outdoor recreation. Rooms, condominiums and some private homes are available for rent at prices ranging from $105 to $350 a night. While not cheap, if the cost of a large house is divided among a number of people, with access to the extensive recreational facilities included, then it's not an unreasonable splurge. The Sunriver resort amenities include two 18-hole golf courses, tennis courts, riding stables, 25 miles of paved bike paths and five restaurants.

## Getting There & Away

A shuttle bus runs three times a day between Mt Bachelor and the ski area's corporate offices (☎ 383-2442), 335 SW Century Drive, Bend.

## THE CASCADE LAKES

Long ago, lava from the nearby volcanoes choked this broad basin beneath the rim of the Cascade Range. Lava flows dammed streams, forming lakes; in other areas, streams flowed underground through porous lava-fields to well up as lake-sized springs. Still other lakes formed in the mouths of small, extinct craters.

Highway 46 is a designated National Forest Scenic Byway. Usually called the Cascade Lakes Hwy, or the Century Drive (the loop road is roughly 100 miles long), it leaves Bend to travel west and south between high mountain peaks and to link together alpine lakes. Bicyclists speed along the road in summer, while snowmobilers take possession during the long winter months. Beyond Mt Bachelor, the road is closed from November to mid-May.

Tiny **Todd Lake** offers views of Broken Top, and relative seclusion, as getting there requires a quarter-mile hike. **Sparks Lake**, in a grassy meadow, is in the process of transforming itself from a body of water to

OREGON

a reedy marsh. It's a good place for bird-watching. **Hosmer Lake** is stocked with catch-and-release Atlantic salmon, making it popular with jaded anglers. It's less commercial than nearby lakes and has beautiful views of Mt Bachelor. At **Little Lava Lake** the waters from the subterranean seepings of lakes further up the basin finally pool and send forth a stream – the beginnings of the mighty Deschutes River.

The Deschutes is dammed at **Crane Prairie Reservoir**. The forest wasn't cleared before it was flooded, resulting in a lake of ugly dead snags. But an eyesore for some is habitat for others; ospreys make use of the dead trees for nesting and fish the shallow lake water. Once considered a threatened species, ospreys have thrived here, with over 100 nesting pairs of osprey now returning annually to this protected wildlife preserve. Park at the Osprey Observation Point just east of the highway to watch these birds dive-bomb fish from their craggy perches.

The **Twin Lakes** were formed when molten rock came in contact with groundwater. The resulting explosion created deep, perfectly symmetrical craters, which later filled with water. Both North and South Twin Lakes are noted for their good fishing.

The Bend & Fort Rock Ranger District Office (☎ 388-5664) can answer questions and send brochures.

### Places to Stay & Eat

There are public campgrounds at each of the lakes along the route. The resorts listed below usually provide hook-ups for RVs.

A number of the Cascade Lakes have woodsy rustic cabin 'resorts' on their shores, which are usually homey, family-oriented facilities with a pleasant, live-in atmosphere. They also offer meals, boat rentals and groceries, making them popular with anglers, boaters and wildlife watchers. Among those available are: *Elk Lake Resort* (☎ YP7-3954) PO Box 789, Bend, 97709, open year round; *Cultus Lake Resort* (☎ YP7-3903) PO Box 262, Bend, 97709; and *Twin Lakes Resort* (☎ 385-

2188) PO Box 3550, Bend, 97709. The odd-looking phone numbers for some are radio phones; ask the operator for mobile service when dialing.

### THREE SISTERS WILDERNESS

Hiking trails depart from the Cascade Lakes Hwy (Hwy 46) into the 580-sq-mile Three Sisters Wilderness. This preserve is dominated by four volcanic peaks and is popular for hikes to remote lakes surrounded by wildflower meadows.

One of the most popular hikes in the area is to Green Lake Basin, high on a plateau between 9173-foot Broken Top and 10,358-foot South Sister. These celadon-green lakes are the centerpiece of a tremendous wildflower display in July and August, at which time the area throngs with crowds. Try to avoid the weekends. There are two trailheads to the Green Lakes. If you don't mind a rough road, turn north from Hwy 46 at Todd Lake, and continue three miles to Crater Creek Ditch. Turn left and continue to the trailhead. It's about 4.5 miles to the lakes.

If you don't have an off-road vehicle, then park at the Green Lakes trailhead along Hwy 46 above Sparks Lake and hike north. The almost 4.4-mile trail is fairly steep but passes some great waterfalls.

Ambitious hikers might consider climbing South Sister. It's Oregon's third-highest peak, but the southern approach doesn't demand any technical equipment. The steep 5.6-mile trail begins near Devils Lake (near Sparks Lake just off the Cascade Lakes Hwy), and is passable only in late summer.

Three Sisters Wilderness contains 111 lakes; an easy hike into an area densely packed with small lakes begins at the Six Lake Trailhead, a half mile south of Elk Lake on Hwy 46. You'll hit the first lake after about a mile of hiking; to reach a basin full of lakes (and in summer, mosquitoes), continue another four miles.

For maps and more information, contact the Deschutes National Forest (☎ 388-2715), 211 NE Revere St, Bend, 97701.

## SISTERS

Located near a large meadow with stunning views of snowy Cascade peaks, Sisters (population 760) straddles the line where the mountain pine forests mingle with the desert sage and juniper.

Surely just about the most congested small town in Oregon, Sisters is a victim of its own success. Once a stage-coach stop and trade town for loggers and ranchers, Sisters was revitalized as a town when the city fathers decided to 'Westernize' the main shopping area. The false-fronts and hitching posts worked: Sisters is now packed full of people shopping the galleries and gift shops housed in oh-so-Western storefronts.

Sisters gives proof of its *real* Western character during the second weekend of June, when the **Sisters Rodeo** comes to town; it's reckoned to be one of the best in the state. The rodeo grounds are about four miles south of town on Hwy 20. For tickets call (800) 827-7522.

Even the agricultural land surrounding Sisters has taken on a curious, unreal quality. The purebred horses may not seem out of place, but the llamas definitely do (Sisters is the nation's largest llama-breeding area). And if you thought you passed a reindeer ranch on the way from Redmond, you were right.

Despite the town's commercial bent, there's no getting around the beauty of the Sisters area and the appeal of its clear, dry climate.

### Orientation & Information

Highway 20 forms Sisters' principal and quite congested main street, though it's generally referred to as Cascade St. One block south is Hood St, and one block north is Main St. Cross streets are Ash, Elm, Fir and Spruce Sts, from west to east respectively.

Contact the Sisters Area Chamber of Commerce (☎ 549-0251), PO Box 476, Sisters, OR 97759, and the local Forest Service office (☎ 549-2111) for information. The post office (☎ 549-3561) is at 160 Fir St.

### Places to Stay

**Camping** Campers are welcome in the city park, at the southern end of Sisters. There's a USFS campground about five miles west of town at *Indian Ford*. The *Sisters KOA* (☎ 549-3021) is about four miles south of Sisters on Hwy 20. There's a separate tent area, a heated swimming pool and other modern amenities; rates begin at $15.

The savvy tent camper will continue on to the Metolius River (see below), with its abundance of campsites in a beautiful valley filled with old-growth ponderosa pines.

**Hotels** The nicest place to stay in Sisters is the *Best Western Ponderosa Lodge* (☎ 549-1234), 505 Hwy 20 W, a spacious two-story motel built in a park-like meadow (complete with gamboling llamas) just north of the town; single/double rooms are $66/70.

*Sister's Motor Lodge* (☎ 549-2551), 600 W Cascade St, with single/doubles for $36/42, is a comfortable older motel from before resort era.

**Resorts** *Black Butte Ranch* (☎ 595-6211), PO Box 8000, Black Butte Ranch, OR, 97759, is the crown jewel of central Oregon resorts. Located eight miles north of Sisters on Hwy 20, the development fringes a vast meadow and lake, with Mt Washington and the Three Sisters towering over all.

Lodging is either in condominium lodges, or in one of the large private homes available for rent. Prices begin at $50 for a very plain room, and move up quickly. With golf courses, pools, horseback riding and tennis, Black Butte delivers all the amenities you'd expect from this class of resort, but its greatest asset is that it seems integrated into, and not imposed onto, the landscape. And what a landscape. If you're looking for a central Oregon splurge, this is it.

### Places to Eat

*The Sisters Bakery* (☎ 549-0361), 120 E Cascade St, is the place for fresh pastries and coffee. If you just need coffee to refuel,

OREGON

try the *Sister's Coffee Company* (☎ 549-0527), 342 W Hood St.

Locals swear by *Papandrea's Pizza* (☎ 549-6081), 325 E Hood St, a thick-crusted pie designed for hearty central Oregon appetites. The *Depot Deli* (☎ 549-2572), 351 W Cascade St, serves soup and sandwiches. If you'd like food for a picnic, try the *Ranch House Delicatessen & Wine Shop* (☎ 549-8911), 310 E Hood St. *The Gallery Restaurant* (☎ 549-2631), 230 W Cascade St, offers standard American cuisine in a room decorated with the owner's rifle collection.

*The Hotel Sister's Restaurant* (☎ 549-7427), 105 W Cascade St, is housed in a refurbished hotel, though no rooms are rented. Burgers, Mexican food and steak are the best bets here. Their self-mythologized Bronco Billy barbecued chicken and ribs average $14.

By night, there's live music in the hotel's old-fashioned bar. At its most infectious, the music can be a jam session of local musicians, emboldened by a couple of drinks.

### Things to Buy
It's a sign of economic prosperity that Sisters now has its own Christmas shop. Sisters was *invented* for shoppers, so it seems foolish not to take advantage of what it does well.

Galleries and gift shops epitomize Sisters, and some of them are quite good. Christmas Mountain Magic (☎ 549-1155), 516 W Cascade St, sells ornaments and trimmings year round. Three Sisters Folk Art Gallery (☎ 549-9556), 138 W Hood St, has an interesting selection of Oregon and Northwest crafts. Soda Creek Gallery (☎ 549-0600), 178 S Elm St, is a major Western art gallery with both blue-chip and regional artists. Ponderosa Woodworks (☎ 549-8153) 160 E Hood St, is a showroom for handmade pine furniture.

For both ski and bicycle sales and rentals, go to friendly Eurosports (☎ 549-2471), 115 W Hood St. For hiking gear, try Mountain Supply (☎ 549-3251), 148 W Hood St.

### Getting There & Away
Greyhound passes through Sisters twice daily. Buses stop at the corner of Elm St and Hwy 20; there's no station here, so call the Bend station (☎ 382-2151) for information.

### HOODOO SKI AREA
Hoodoo, Box 20, Hwy 20, Sisters, OR 97759, is Oregon's oldest downhill ski area, located 25 miles west of Sisters at the crest of the Cascades at Santiam Pass. A total of 22 runs drop from a summit elevation of 5700 feet.

Snow conditions here are often better than at other Cascade divide ski areas, due to the north-facing slopes. Call 822-3799, (800) 949-5438 for snow conditions. There's night skiing Thursday to Saturday. Facilities include two day lodges and complete rental and instruction packages. Lift tickets are $20 a day. Hoodoo also offers groomed cross-country ski trails starting at many of the Sno Parks along Santiam Pass.

### THE METOLIUS RIVER
As if by enchantment, the Metolius River bursts out of a ferny cleft in Black Butte, a fully formed river at birth. As it flows north through its beautiful pine-filled valley, the Metolius passes beneath rugged Mt Jefferson, Oregon's second-highest peak.

It's astonishing that such a magical valley has not been turned into an expensive, golf-course-ridden resort; instead, the valley remains the province of campers, as the USFS maintains a dozen campgrounds along the river.

The spring-fed river maintains a constant temperature, a fact much appreciated by local trout. Fly-fishing on the Metolius is world renowned, and special restrictions are in place to keep it that way. Consult fishing regulations before casting your line.

### Orientation & Information
To reach the following destinations along the Metolius River, turn off Hwy 20, 10 miles north of Sisters, and follow USFS Rd 14.

The Metolius Recreation Association (☎ 595-6117) can be contacted at PO Box 64, Camp Sherman, OR 97730.

## Camp Sherman

This sleepy little settlement, about five miles north of Hwy 20 on USFS Rd 14, seems from another era, with its general store and streamside cabins beneath towering pines. Primarily a supply venue and post office for campers and anglers, Camp Sherman offers a few rustic accommodations and a spiffy new restaurant.

## Metolius Springs

A short path leads through a forest of ponderosa pines to these remarkable springs, where the Metolius flows out of a hillside. From the viewing area above the springs, there's a wonderful view of the already-wide river winding through a grassy meadow, with Mt Jefferson directly above.

Oddly, there is no sign for the Metolius springs as you come in from Hwy 20. To find the Head of the Metolius, turn east at the sign for 'Campgrounds' which appears about two miles after joining USFS Rd 14. The springs are about a mile down this road.

## Wizard Falls Fish Hatchery

You may or may not find visiting fish hatcheries compulsively fascinating, but you'll find few in such beautiful surroundings. Enormous old pines tower above the tanks; lawns stretch between log out-buildings, all with the Metolius River splashing beside. The buildings date to President Franklin Roosevelt's WPA program that created jobs for unemployed Americans during the Great Depression. All in all, it seems more like a park than a fish production area.

Signs describe the various fish produced at the hatchery; be sure and check out the tank with rare and unusual fish.

To reach the fish hatchery, continue on USFS Rd 14 past Camp Sherman for five miles.

## Hiking

Trails lead from the Metolius Valley up into the **Mt Jefferson Wilderness Area.** While many hikes into these alpine areas are more than day-trips, a few shorter hikes access the area's high country. From the USFS's Jack Lake Campground, a 4.5-mile roundtrip hike climbs up to Canyon Creek Meadows, where summer produces a vibrant wildflower display and great views onto rugged **Three Fingered Jack,** a peak on the Cascade summit. To reach the trailhead from Sisters, drive 13 miles west on Hwy 20. Just south of Suttle Lake, turn north on the 'Jack Lake Rd,' or USFS Rd 12. It's about eight miles to the trailhead.

From the same access road, a shorter hike leads to a high mountain lake. As above, turn onto USFS Rd 12, and after one mile leave the main road and take a west-turning fork (USFS Rd 1210) toward **Round Lake.** From the Round Lake Campground, a two-mile trail leads past tiny Long Lake to **Square Lake,** nestled in thick forest.

For less strenuous hikes, follow the hiking trails on either side of the Metolius River between Wizard Falls Fish Hatchery and Pioneer Ford campground. It's about a 2.5-mile hike with lots of opportunity to see raptors and streamside mammals like mink.

## Places to Stay

**Camping** With over a dozen campgrounds facing the Metolius River and more in the forests near Mt Jefferson, there should be no problem finding campsites except on busy holiday weekends. The further downriver you go from Camp Sherman, the better the chances are for relative solitude. The *Pioneer Ford* campground, about nine miles north of Camp Sherman, is a good choice. Tent campers take note: two campgrounds, *Pine Rest* and *Riverside* (both above Camp Sherman), are reserved for tenters only. Campgrounds in the area charge $7 a night. Contact the Deschutes National Forest office (☎ 549-2111) in Sisters for complete camping information.

OREGON

**Lodges** Camp Sherman offers a few rustic accommodations, largely designed with fly-fishers in mind. Be sure to call ahead; serious anglers often have rooms booked well in advance. *Metolius River Lodge* (☎ 595-6290), PO Box 110, Camp Sherman, OR 97730, offers a number of lodging options in free-standing cabins overlooking the river, starting at $61. A bit more upscale is the *Metolius River Resort* (☎ 595-6281), PO Box 1210, Camp Sherman, OR 97730, with lodging in three-bedroom condominium units. Prices begin at $130 a night.

### Places to Eat
*Kokanee Cafe* (☎ 595-6420) is open for three meals a day, and even it if weren't the only restaurant in Camp Sherman, this would be a hard act to beat. Located near the Metolius River, this attractive log-cabin restaurant manages to be happily busy yet secluded. Dinner choices range from burgers to seafood fettuccine for $12; go Western and have a buffalo steak for $18.

## REDMOND
In the trio of towns that make up central Oregon's resort triangle, Redmond (population 8365) is the most neglected. On a treeless plain between the Cascade and Ochoco mountains, it lacks the refinement and make-believe of more full-blown resort towns, and doesn't offer much in the way of charm. But things are changing. Redmond now has a resort community nearby, and a few boutiques and espresso shops are bravely colonizing the old downtown. While most high-flyers prefer Bend or Sisters, at least in Redmond there's still a chance that travelers might see real ranchers or farmers.

Redmond was established in 1905, when government programs brought first irrigation canals, and then settlers, to the high desert. However, here as elsewhere in trendy central Oregon, agriculture is giving way to golf courses and real-estate developments.

The Deschutes County Fair & Rodeo (☎ 548-2711), filled with the scents and sounds of an old country fair, is held the first weekend of August at the fairgrounds at the junction of Hwys 97 and 126.

### Orientation & Information
Redmond lies at the junction of two major routes. Highway 126 acts as a short cut to roads linking eastern Oregon to Eugene and Salem, while Hwy 97 joins I-84 to California. It's a busy town with a lot of traffic flowing through it, as befits a town that calls itself the Hub of central Oregon.

Contact the Redmond Chamber of Commerce (☎ 923-6442) at 106 SW 7th St, Redmond, OR 97756, for visitor information. The post office (☎ 548-2622) is at 507 SW 8th St, and the Central Oregon District Hospital (☎ 548-8131) is at 1253 N Canal Blvd.

### The Fantastic Museum
A good-natured collection of memorabilia and outright junk, this museum (☎ 923-0000), one mile south of Redmond on Hwy 97, also has more than its share of real oddities, like an early sedan of President John

---

**Crooked River Dinner Train**
The Prineville Municipal Railroad is the only city-owned railway in the country; Prineville citizens raised the money to build the line in 1919 in order to link the town to the mainline rail lines at Redmond.

Today you can ride this historic line through canyon and ranchland and get a fine dinner, by taking the Crooked River Dinner Train (☎ 388-1966), 115 NW Oregon St, Suite 24, Bend. The journey begins two miles north of Redmond (off Hwy 97 at O'Neil Hwy), and takes about 2½ hours. The $69 ticket includes a four-course meal with three choices of entrees and entertainment by a theater group. There are seasonal excursion trains with other themes, like wine tasting and holiday events. The train departs at 6:30 pm on Friday and Saturdays only; on Sunday, there is a brunch run; it's open year round. Reservations are required. ■

F Kennedy and the contents of Elizabeth Taylor's *Cleopatra* dressing room. It's open daily from 10 am to 5 pm; adults $5, children $2.

## Places to Stay

**B&Bs** *Dolliver House B & B* (☎ 548-1606), 652 S 6th St, is right downtown. That's the good news; it's also between two busy streets, which is the bad news. The Dolliver offers six rooms with rates starting at $40.

**Hotels** For an inexpensive stay in downtown Redmond, go to the *City Center Motel* (☎ 548-3447), 350 NW 6th St; single/double rates are $21/27. The *Redmond Inn* (☎ 548-1091, (800) 833-3259), 1545 S Hwy 97, has an outdoor pool; singles/doubles are $44/50.

For a step up in comfort and a step back in time, there's the *Nendel's New Redmond Hotel* (☎ 923-7378), 521 S 6th St, a renovated historic hotel downtown. The rooms are well appointed; there's a spa and exercise room. Single/doubles are $48/55. On the south edge of town is the new *Rama Inn* (☎ 548-8080, (800) 821-0543), 2630 SW 17th Place, with a pool, conference facilities and exercise room for $60/66.

**Resorts** The Redmond-area resort is called *Eagle Crest* (☎ 923-2453, (800) 682-4786), 1522 Cline Falls Rd, about six miles southwest of Redmond off Hwy 126. As elsewhere in central Oregon, the emphasis is on health and recreation, with 18-hole golf, tennis, swimming, horseback riding, weight room and so on. Lodging is in either the lodge hotel where rooms begin at $60, or in condos which sleep up to eight people, starting at $119.

## Places to Eat

The *Paradise Grille* (☎ 548-0844), 404 SW 6th St, serves up reasonably priced mesquite-grilled meats, and Sante Fe-inspired dishes like tequila prawns. *Sully's of Redmond* (☎ 548-5483), in Nendel's New Redmond Hotel at 521 SW 6th St, is Redmond's other restaurant of note. Classic Italian cooking shares the kitchen with steak; dinners range from $10 to $16.

Six miles north of Redmond in Terrebonne is *La Siesta* (☎ 548-4848), 8320 N Hwy 97, one of those little restaurants in an out-of-the-way place that somehow manages to command an enormous reputation. Here it's home-style Mexican food that brings people in from miles around.

## Getting There & Around

For information on air and train travel to central Oregon, see Getting There & Away at the beginning of this chapter. Greyhound buses link Redmond to Portland and Bend. The depot (☎ 923-1923) is at 2456 S Hwy 97. There are also several rental car agencies at the airport. Call City Cab at 548-0919.

## SMITH ROCK STATE PARK

A world-renowned venue for rock climbers, Smith Rock is an amazingly jagged and precipitous series of cliffs, carved by the misleadingly passive-looking Crooked River. The formation is related to the colorful tuff deposits of the John Day Fossil Beds. Ancient volcanoes spewed out vast amounts of hot ash, which settled into thousand-foot-deep drifts and, as the ash cooled, fused into stone.

Today, Smith Rock's rust-colored palisades and 800-foot-high cliffs loom over the pools of the Crooked River. Good weather brings out scores of climbers to scale Smith Rock. If you're not a climber, then the seven miles of hiking trails in the state park might be of interest. Or bring a picnic and binoculars and watch the climbers hanging off the rock face.

Rough campsites are offered. During climbing season, a cafe springs up (great huckleberry ice cream), as well as a shop that peddles gear to climbers and offers climbing lessons; contact Juniper Junction/Smith Rock Climbing School (☎ 548-0749). To visit Smith Rock State Park, drive six miles north of Redmond on Hwy 97, turn east at Terrebonne onto Smith Rock Rd, continue for another three miles.

### Skein Ogden Scenic Wayside

While driving along the prairie-like lava plateau on Hwy 97 north of Redmond, there is no indication you're in the neighborhood of a river, much less one at the bottom of an 400-foot-deep chasm. Crossing the bridge that vaults the Crooked River Canyon is guaranteed to elicit a gasp. Stop at the small park area and have a longer look over the edge and at the two bridges.

Building the Crooked River Rail Bridge was no mean feat in 1911; workers scaled rope ladders from the canyon floor to the bridge girders, and, as elsewhere in central Oregon's highly competitive early railroad history, there was sabotage and mischief from rival rail crews. The highway bridge was designed by Conde McCullough, famed architect of Oregon coast bridges. The bridge became infamous in 1960 when a woman threw her two children to their deaths from the bridge. She became the first woman to be sentenced to death in Oregon, though she was later pardoned by then-governor, Mark Hatfield. The canyon is nine miles north of Redmond.

### PRINEVILLE

The old ranch town of Prineville (population 5626) backs up to the gently sloping Ochoco Mountains and sits in about the only wide spot in the otherwise precipitous Crooked River Valley. The town's first structure was a saloon built in 1868, establishing a tone for the early history of the settlement, a time of commerce from lumber and ranching. Vicious range wars between partisans of cattle and sheep ranching divided the young community in the 1900s, when cattlemen slaughtered upwards of 10,000 head of sheep and several sheepherders. More peaceable now, Prineville continues to be a ranch supply center.

### Orientation & Information

Prineville is at the junction of Hwys 26 and 126; Hwy 26 is the town's main street, and is called 3rd St in local addresses.

The Prineville Chamber of Commerce (☎ 447-6304) is at 390 N Fairview St. For information on hiking and camping, contact the Prineville Ranger District (☎ 447-9641), 2321 E 3rd St. The Ochoco National Forest Headquarters (☎ 447-6247), 3000 E 3rd St, and the State Forestry Department (☎ 447-5658), 220710 Ochoco Hwy, are also in Prineville.

The Prineville post office (☎ 447-5652) is at 155 N Court St, and the local laundry is Ochoco Plaza Coin Laundry (☎ 447-2120), 1595 E 3rd St.

### AR Bowman Museum

This museum (☎ 447-3715), 246 N Main St, is full of mementos and artifacts from the region's pioneer and early ranching days. It's open from noon to 5 pm Wednesday to Saturday, March to December, also Sundays, 31 May to Labor Day.

### Ochoco Creek Park

This shady, stream-side municipal park is a good place to picnic or to unleash hot or weary travelers. There's a swimming pool, tennis courts and a playground. The park is one block north of 3rd St at Fairview St.

### Prineville Reservoir

This long, narrow lake backs up through an arid juniper and sage savanna, a vivid band of green water in an otherwise desert landscape. Formed when Bowman Dam impounded the Crooked River, Prineville Reservoir is famous for bass fishing. It's also a favorite for boating, swimming and just plain summertime cooling off. In late summer, the green water is due to algae blossoms, not sparkling fresh water. At the state park, there are campsites and picnic areas as well as a boat launch.

To reach Prineville Reservoir, turn south from Hwy 26 onto Juniper Canyon Rd. It's 17 miles to the state park. Or, for great views of the river's rim-rocked valley, take scenic Hwy 27 to Bowman Dam; it turns to gravel after the dam and eventually meets Hwy 20 between Bend and Burns.

### Places to Stay

**Camping** While the best camping is in the Ochoco Mountains (see below), closer to

Prineville campers can stay at *Ochoco Lake State Park* along Hwy 26 just east of town, or a $4 fee. There's also camping at *Prineville Reservoir State Park*, 17 miles south of town.

**Hotels** Kids will like staying at the *Rustler's Roost* (☎ 447-4185), 960 W 3rd St, as the 2nd-floor balconies give the place a Wild-West atmosphere. Single/double rooms are $44/49. Right downtown, the *Ochoco Inn & Motel* (☎ 447-6231), 123 3rd St, is a modern motel with good prices and a restaurant adjacent; single/doubles are $27/33.

*Carolina Motel* (☎ 447-4152), 1050 E 3rd St, is an attractive, older motel out on the road to Mitchell; rates are $26/30. For more comfort and a pool, try the *Best Western of Prineville* (☎ 447-8080), 1475 E 3rd St, on the eastern outskirts of Prineville, near the Ochoco Plaza shopping mall; rooms start at $48.

### Places to Eat

*Gee's* (☎ 447-6115), 987 W 2nd St, offers good Sichuan and Mandarin Chinese food; Kung-pao beef goes for $9. *Cinnabar Restaurant* (☎ 447-3880) 123 E 3rd St, is the place for steak and American-style food. Even for a New York steak, it's hard to spend more than $10 here.

There's now espresso in Prineville. Near the corner of W 3rd and Locust Sts, on the west end of town, *Dancer's Coffee* maintains a coffee cart.

### Getting There & Away

Greyhound (☎ 447-3646), 152 W 4th St, offers Prineville one-bus-a-day service between The Dalles and Bend. The People Mover offers Monday, Wednesday, Friday service between Bend, Prineville and John Day.

### THE OCHOCO MOUNTAINS

After the immense lava flows of eastern Oregon began to spill down the Columbia Basin about 17 million years ago, only the highest elevations of central Oregon remained above the tremendous floods of lava, including the ridges of the Ochocos.

A series of meadows and streams ringed by gentle peaks, the Ochocos are now a beautiful, if undramatic, range of mountains undulating across much of Oregon's vast central province. The region is known mostly for its population of deer and elk. Majestic stands of mature ponderosa pine and juniper, spring wildflower meadows and wilderness areas offer the visitor a serene and largely unvisited outdoor destination. The region's gentle topography and many USFS roads make it great for mountain bikers (except during hunting season).

### Mill Creek Wilderness

Of the three wilderness areas in the Ochocos, Mill Creek, north of Ochoco Creek, is the most accessible. Hikes through old-growth pine forests and curious volcanic formations make for satisfying day outings.

To reach the Mill Creek Wilderness, follow Hwy 26 east from Prineville for nine miles, and turn north on USFS Rd 33 for nine miles. Wildcat Campground is just off the road.

From the Wildcat Campground trailhead, a gentle trail winds along the East Fork of Mill Creek through a lovely pine forest. For a long day-hike, continue along the trail to **Twin Pillars**, two spire-like volcanic crags.

An even more impressive rock tower is **Stein's Pillar**, reached by a short hike from USFS Rd 3350. This 400-foot-high thumb of rock is popular with experienced climbers; it wasn't successfully scaled until 1950.

### Big Summit Prairie

Another little-visited destination in the heart of the Ochocos is reached by well-maintained and scenic USFS roads. East of Prineville, roads climb up to a high central plateau. Surrounded by old forest, this large meadow encompasses about 35 sq miles of rolling pasture land. During late spring, the wildflowers are marvelous. Although much of Big Summit Prairie is privately owned and used as grazing land, roads ring the meadow.

**OREGON**

Take Hwy 26 12 miles east of Prineville, turn onto Ochoco Creek Rd, then at the Ochoco Campground turn onto USFS Rd 42.

### Places to Stay

The USFS maintains a number of campgrounds in the Ochoco Mountains. Convenient to hikers in the Mill Creek Wilderness is the *Wildcat Campground*, right along Mill Creek at the base of the wilderness area, for a $4 fee.

More utilitarian for travelers along the highway is *Ochoco Divide Campground*, 30 miles east of Prineville on Hwy 26 at the summit of Ochoco Pass, at $3. Near Big Summit Prairie is *Ochoco Campground*, about six miles east of Hwy 26 on USFS Rd 22.

## MADRAS

The seat of Jefferson County and a major agricultural trade town, Madras (population 3820) is at the junction of Hwys 26 and 97. On a broad and arid upland the town is surrounded by fields of curious crops, such as garlic and mint. In fact, the Madras area is one of the principal producers of mint in the USA. Along the eastern and southern skyline are craggy volcanic buttes, and to the west, the towering Cascades.

For the traveler, Madras is hardly a major destination in itself, but the town is a useful jumping-off point for recreation on Lake Billy Chinook, 10 miles west, and for visits to nearby Warm Springs Reservation.

### Information

Contact the chamber of commerce (☎ 475-2350), 197 SE 5th St, PO Box 770 Madras, OR 97411. The post office (☎ 475-3157) is at 230 6th St.

### Jefferson County Museum

This small museum (☎ 475-3808), 502 D St, on the top floor of the old courthouse, features a collection of frontier-era wedding dresses, and an old-time optometrist's office. Check out the old jail to the back of the building. It's open from 2 to 5 pm, June

to Labor Day. Admission is free, but donations are welcome.

### Places to Stay

For campers, the first choice should be *Cove Palisades State Park* (☎ 546-3412) at Lake Billy Chinook. Otherwise, the *KOA Madras* (☎ 546-3046), nine miles south of Madras on Hwy 97, is the other choice in the immediate area.

Both the *Juniper Motel* (☎ 475-6186) 414 N Hwy 26, singles/doubles $28/32 and *Hoffy's Motel* (☎ 475-4633), 600 N Hwy 26, $38/42, are at the north end of town, and are well kept and reasonably priced. Right downtown is the *Leisure Inn* (☎ 475-6141), 12 SW 4th St, a motor inn with a pool; pets are welcome. Rooms are $35/39. On the south end of town is *Sonny's Motel* (☎ 475-7217), 1539 SW Hwy 97. There's a pool, non-smoking rooms, a restaurant, and dogs are welcome; singles/doubles are $42/45.

### Places to Eat

*Mexico City* (☎ 475-6078), 215 4th St, is Madras's best Mexican restaurant. For Mexican baked goods and a selection of great food to go, try *Pepi's Mexican Bakery* (☎ 475-3286), 221 5th St.

The *Original Burger Works* (☎ 475-3390), 84 SW 4th St, serves large, tasty burgers and sandwiches. Try *Grandma Huffy's* (☎ 475-7369), 600 N Hwy 26, for standard American fare.

### Getting There & Away

The Greyhound bus depot (☎ 475-4469), 839 SW Hwy 97, is serviced by the Bend-Portland line; there is one bus a day in each direction.

## AROUND MADRAS
### Crooked River National Grassland

Administered by the USFS, this preserve of grass and scrub forest offers an interesting introduction to the high desert ecosystem which covers much of this part of Oregon.

From a trailhead nine miles south of Madras on Hwy 26 the **Rim Rock Springs Trail** winds through juniper savanna to a small marsh. The 1.5-mile route overlooks volcanic buttes and scrambles up lichen-covered formations. The springs are home to raptors and pronghorn and mule deer, and are a stopover for migrating birds.

The Crooked River National Grassland (☎ 447-9640), at 2321 E 3rd St, has more information about the grassland.

### Priday Agate Beds

North of Madras 11 miles along Hwy 97 is Richardson's Recreational Ranch, (☎ 475-2680), Gateway Rte, Box 440, Madras, OR 97741, which now owns and operates the famous rock-hounding area known as the Priday Agate Beds. In addition to plume agates, amateur geologists can dig for thundereggs, the agate and crystal-filled geode that's the Oregon state rock. Admission is free, but you must pay 45c per pound of stones you want to take out with you.

Although the Richardsons loan out picks, it's a good idea to bring your own shovels, hammers, and chisels. There's a gift shop with cut and polished rocks at the ranch, as well as a shower for dusty rock hounds. Free camping is available for customers; there are no hook-ups.

### Lake Billy Chinook

West of Madras the irrigated fields come to an abrupt end. Here, the three prodigious rivers of central Oregon – the Deschutes, Crooked and Metolius – join at Lake Billy Chinook. This large and spectacular canyon reservoir is a major playground for local residents. Its swallow-your-gum precipitousness and popular **Cove Palisades State Park**, with a marina, campground, boat launches and picnic areas, make the lake a great stopover for the traveler as well.

From Madras, follow signs to Cove Palisades State Park. The road (here called Jordan Rd) drops to lake level and climbs through first the Crooked and then the Deschutes river canyons. Separating these two gorges is a flat-topped, razor-thin isthmus called the Island, with cliffs towering 450 feet above the lake water.

The marina (with boat rentals), a cafe and the boat launch are at the base of the Crooked River canyon; most other tourist facilities are on the Island. Nearly 100 campsites are available here (fees start at $10), as well as a swimming beach and hiking trails. Be sure and stop at the **Crooked River Petroglyph**, an elaborately carved boulder near the gulch on the Island. The boulder was moved to this location when the dam was built; the flooding waters covered many similar stone carvings by early Native Americans. From the park office, a nature trail winds to viewpoints and picnic areas along the Deschutes canyon.

Jordan Rd continues to the Metolius branch of the lake; however, much of the lower portions of its canyon are privately owned and accessible only by boat. Fifteen miles from the state park the road passes into USFS land, and there are two lakeside campgrounds. (Alternatively, after nine miles head south at the Sisters junction and follow a good gravel road to Hwy 20 near Sisters.)

Lake Billy Chinook and Cove Palisades Park (☎ 546-3412) are both very popular; during summer weekends, the water is thick with jet boats, speed boats and waterskiers. Avoid weekends or high season if you value quiet or solitude. Also, the west shore of the reservoir (accessible only by boat) belongs to the **Warm Springs Reservation**; it's forbidden to trespass, or even to land a boat, on reservation land.

### LOWER DESCHUTES VALLEY

North of Madras, the rushing Deschutes River digs its deep and awe-inspiring canyon through the lava flows of the Columbia River. Rising above the arid, rim-rocked gorge to the west is Mount Hood, solitary and white. This is the most remote and magical portion of the Deschutes Canyon, long the homeland of Chinook Indians. Scented by sage and juniper, here the Deschutes seems mystical and other-worldly.

Fishing and rafting are popular pastimes on this section of the powerful Deschutes.

OREGON

The river also passes the Warm Springs Reservation, whose residents have developed an excellent cultural museum of traditional Native American society and history, and a golf and hot-springs resort.

## Warm Springs Reservation

Home to three groups, the Wasco, the Tenino, and the Northern Paiute (the Confederated Tribes), Warm Springs Reservation is a beautiful homeland that stretches from the peaks of the Cascades in the west to the banks of the Deschutes River to the east.

The Wasco, whose culture combined fishing elements of coastal tribes with the hunting and gathering heritage of plateau Indians, are native to this region. The Teninos, originally from the northern bank of the Columbia River, share with the Wasco their reliance on the Columbia salmon runs for sustenance and cultural focus. In 1855 a treaty between the Teninos, the Wascos and the US Government was signed, confining the tribes to a reservation of 725 sq miles to the west of the Deschutes River and east of the Cascades.

After the Bannock/Paiute War of 1878 in southeastern Oregon, a part of the Northern Paiute Indian Federation was moved to the reservation. The Paiutes are a desert group from eastern Oregon; their removal from that area was largely part of a strategy to divide the tribe into small, indefensible units.

The **Pi Ume Sha Treaty Days Celebration** is held on the third weekend of June at Warm Springs. Competitive dancing, horse races and a rodeo make this one of the reservation's biggest powwows.

---

### The Railroad Race

As the area east of the Cascades became better explored, it quickly filled up with farmers and ranchers. The Homestead Acts especially lured in thousands of hopeful, but largely inexperienced, settlers. However, for these agricultural producers, there was no ready market for their goods: with only the most rudimentary overland trails for freight roads, and the wild, impassable Deschutes River as the only waterway, there was no transportation corridor into or out of Central Oregon.

Two railroad companies – the Oregon Trunk Line and the Deschutes Railroad Company – sized up the opportunities, and began in 1909 to build lines up opposite sides of the Deschutes Canyon. Competition flared between the two crews as they hewed a railbed out of the rock walls. Railroad owners spurred workers into longer and harder shifts, each seeking to be the first to arrive in the fast-growing agricultural basin of central Oregon. Sabotage and bloody fights erupted; gunfire frequently disrupted the laying of track.

Finally, the Deschutes Railroad Line, on the east side of the canyon, called it quits, after spending millions of dollars to prepare the railbed. The Oregon Trunk Line, affiliated with Great Northern Railroad's James J Hill, completed its line to Bend in 1911. The grain, cattle and logs of central Oregon suddenly had a market.

The west-side line still operates (by Burlington Northern); the east-side grade of the Deschutes Railroad is used for roads and hiking paths. ∎

**Information** Contact the Confederated Tribes of the Warm Springs Reservation (☎ 553-1161), 1233 Veteran St, PO Box C, Warm Springs, OR 97761, for information about the residents and events on the reservation.

**Warm Springs Museum** Opened in 1993, the Warm Springs Museum (☎ 553-3331), just west of the town of Warm Springs, is a wonderful evocation of traditional Native American life and culture, comprised of artifacts, audio-visual presentations, educational displays, exhibits of cultural art, and recreations of villages.

There's a gift shop and a fine art gallery in the facility. It's open from 10 am to 5 pm daily. Admission is $5 for adults, $4.50 for seniors and $2.50 for children under 12. There's also a family rate of $15.

**Kah-Nee-Ta Resort** In the early 1970s the Confederated Tribes built this hot-springs spa. It's popular with families and sun-starved Portlanders, and is a great stopover for travelers. Facilities include an 18-hole golf course, horseback riding, tennis, fishing, and, of course, swimming in pools fed by hot springs. There are two restaurants, with Native American specialties (like game hen baked in clay).

Lodging options include rooms in a handsome lodge overlooking the Warm Springs River beginning at $90; or down near the hot springs themselves, the condo-like cottages rent for $169 a night. There's also lodging in traditional tepees for $50. Kah-Nee-Ta Resort (☎ 553-1112, (800) 831-0100) is 11 miles north of the town of Warms Springs on well-marked reservation roads.

**Lower Deschutes Canyon**
Downstream from the little town of Maupin (population 470), the Deschutes River burrows an ever-deeper gorge before joining the Columbia River. This 70-mile stretch of the Deschutes is extremely popular for its white-water rafting and fishing. If you don't mind rough graveled roads, or getting some dust in your car, follow fishing access roads along the river to explore this dramatic canyon.

Maupin, nestled along a bend in the Deschutes, is nominally the hub of the lower Deschutes River. River recreation, with boat rentals, fly-fishing lessons, organized float trips and rudimentary food and lodging options are available in town.

Just west of the Deschutes River at the little community of Tygh Valley, eight miles north of Maupin on Hwy 197, the **All-Indian Rodeo** (☎ 255-3385), a wild evocation of Native America and the Old West, is held on the second weekend of May.

**Orientation & Information**
From Maupin, river-access roads diverge from Hwy 197 and wind up and downriver. Below Sherar's Bridge the roads are gravel and very washboarded; the road ends at Mack's Canyon, 17 miles below Sherar's Bridge. From there the river is accessible only by raft until it reaches the Columbia River, 25 miles later.

Contact the Greater Maupin Chamber of Commerce (☎ 395-2599), PO Box 220 Maupin, OR 97037, for information on the area.

**Tygh Valley State Wayside**
A series of waterfalls on the White River and a ghostly 1930's electric power station make this little park an oddly compelling place to stop for a hike or picnic. The first spectacular waterfall is seen from the manicured park grounds; scramble down the rough path to the river's edge to find that the river drops over two other rock ledges in quick succession.

Tygh Valley State Wayside is about four miles east of the little town of Tygh Valley on Hwy 216.

**Sherar's Bridge**
In 1979 the Warm Springs Reservation bought 888 acres around Sherar's Bridge

OREGON

on the Deschutes River. Here, the mighty river, rushing down its deep desert canyon, cuts into a flow of lava, and rages through a gorge only 20 feet across. This extraordinarily turbulent series of rapids, called **Sherar's Falls**, is a traditional fish netting location for Warm Springs Indians. The surrounding area is now de facto reservation; non-tribe members can fish from the rock cliffs, but only tribe members are allowed to use the netting platforms.

Plan to visit the Sherar's Bridge area during the heavy runs of salmon from March to October, when you can watch Native Americans dip nets on long poles into the furious waters.

Highway 216 winds down the steep Deschutes canyon to cross over this wild stretch of the river. The most spectacular approach is from the east, as the highway corkscrews down an escarpment before reaching the river.

### Fishing

Fly-fishing on the Deschutes River is renowned throughout the USA. The challenge of the river, the abundance of fish, and the beautiful remoteness of the desert canyon combine to make this an angler's paradise.

To preserve the Deschutes fishery, certain restrictions are enforced. Angling from a boat of any sort is prohibited. Native steelhead trout must be released unharmed when caught. Native fish can be recognized by the unclipped adipose fin (the back, top fin); hatchery fish have notched adipose fins. No live bait or barbed hooks are allowed on this stretch of the river.

The Deschutes River's great reputation as a sport-fishing river is due to the presence of three types of fish: rainbow and steelhead trout and Chinook salmon. Steelhead and Chinook are both anadromous, or sea-going, spending their lives in the Pacific Ocean and returning to the streams of their birth to spawn.

Fishing for Chinook and steelhead is best below Sherar's Falls, while trout fishing is best above. Call the Fish & Wildlife Bureau (☎ 475-2183) for information.

The Fly Shop (☎ 395-2565), 7 N Hwy 197, in Maupin, is a great place to buy tackle, specialized flies and to find out what the fish are thinking.

Mike McLucas (☎ 395-2611) is the grand old man of the Deschutes River; what he doesn't know about the secret lairs and habits of Deschutes steelhead isn't worth spit.

### Rafting

The Deschutes River near Maupin provides one of the Northwest's great white-water trips with a number of class IV rapids.

The unnavigable Sherar's Falls is an obstacle in the river between Maupin and the Columbia River. The Maupin-Sherar's trip can be done in a day; if you're headed for the Columbia River be prepared to camp overnight. All floaters on the Deschutes River are required to carry a boater pass, available from area businesses.

For raft rentals, river gear, shuttle service and guided trips, contact Deschutes U-Boat (☎ 395-2503), PO Box 144, Maupin, OR 97037. The storefront is near the Oasis Cafe along south Hwy 197.

The following companies have guided trips down the Deschutes: Ewing Whitewater (☎ (800) 538-7238), PO Box 427, Maupin, OR 97037, Deschutes River Navigation (☎ 475-3174), PO Box K, Madras, OR 97741, and Deschutes Whitewater Service (☎ 395-2232), on the north side of the Deschutes Bridge on Hwy 197. Contact the chamber of commerce for a full listing of local outfitters.

### Places to Stay

**Camping** There are a great number of informal campgrounds along the Deschutes River. Call the Deschutes National Forest Ranger Station (☎ 388-5664) for more information.

For more amenities, go to the *Maupin City Park*, just north of the Hwy 197 bridge. Below Sherar's Bridge, there are a number of BLM campgrounds with minimal facilities. The nicest are at *Beavertail*, eight miles south of Sherar's Bridge, and at *Mack's Canyon*, where, after 17 miles, the bouncy eastside Deschutes River road terminates.

**Hotels** Most lodging in Maupin is designed for the recreationalist. There's nothing sophisticated, cheap or even memorable about most. The *Oasis* (☎ 395-2611), just south of the Hwy 197 bridge, offers the best deal in Maupin lodging. The tiny-looking, free-standing cabins are quite well equipped and are a marvel of efficient design; prices start at $44. *CJ Lodge*

(☎ 395-2404), 304 Bakeoven Rd, is an old motel transformed into a sort of B&B; rooms begin at $40.

**Places to Eat**
The *Oasis Cafe* (☎ 395-2611), south on Hwy 197, is the best of Maupin's marginal restaurant offerings. Breakfasts are fried up with the angler in mind; at night, a comfy kind of home-cooking pervades the tiny cafe. You'll have a hard time spending more than $10 a person for a decent steak and a slice of homemade pie.

OREGON

# Northeastern Oregon

The old Oregon Trail traversed this corner of Oregon, making early pioneers the first to glimpse the high mountains, imposing canyons and lava plateaus. Today, this part of the state offers the traveler a full-strength dose of history and remarkable scenery.

Rambunctious old cow towns like Baker City and Pendleton are centers of historic ranch lands, and relive their early days with wild rodeos and a nationally recognized pioneer museum. The Wallowa Mountains rise, seemingly spontaneously, from wide agricultural valleys. Often referred to as the Oregon Alps, the Wallowas contain 19 of Oregon's 25 highest peaks. High mountain lakes and wilderness hikes make this range a favorite recreational destination.

Oregon's wild volcanic genesis began here. The most amazing of the prodigious lava flows was the Grande Ronde eruption, which occurred about 17 million years ago. The molten basalt flowed from a crack in the earth that was sometimes over 100 miles long. The lava was so fluid that it flowed as far as the Pacific Ocean before cooling, a distance of 460 miles.

East of the Wallowas, along the Oregon/Idaho border, the earth suddenly gives way: the Hells Canyon of the Snake River, the deepest gorge in North America, cuts a chasm more than a mile deep. This is astonishingly wild and remote country, scarcely accessible except by boat or on foot. Backroad explorers can inch along cliff-edged roads and climb to high viewpoints in order to glimpse this spectacular wilderness canyon.

## HISTORY
The Northeast corner is home to several Native American groups, the Cayuse, Umatilla, Wallawalla and Nez Perce tribes. Lewis and Clark's Corps of Discovery engaged in friendly trading with them in 1805-6, and were especially impressed with the civility of the Nez Perce.

Tantalized by the persistent legend of the Blue Bucket mine – a kind of lost El Dorado somewhere in the Blue Mountains – fortune hunters began to focus on eastern Oregon. As they encroached on the Wallowa Mountains, the ancestral homeland of the Nez Perce, relations quickly deteriorated between the Native Americans and Whites. A series of tit-for-tat murders began the Nez Perce War in 1877. Chief Joseph and 800 Nez Perce fled Oregon, hoping to reach Canada and freedom from Army retribution. Instead, they were defeated in Montana, just shy of the Canadian border, and sent to reservations in Oklahoma.

The Union Pacific Railroad opened a transcontinental rail line linking Omaha with Portland in 1884, via Baker City and La Grande, and, with the Indians incarcerated on reservations, the region quickly filled with farmers and ranchers.

## ORIENTATION
Northeastern Oregon is cut diagonally by I-84, which links Boise and Salt Lake City to Portland, and basically follows the route of the old Oregon Trail throughout the region. On the freeway, it's 208 miles from Portland to Pendleton, and 221 miles from Pendleton to Boise.

Highway 395 cuts south from Washington's Tri-Cities to Pendleton, and continues southward to John Day and Burns. The other major road in the area is Hwy 82, which links La Grande to the Wallowa Mountain resort towns of Enterprise and Joseph. From here, smaller roads explore the remote and precipitous canyons of the Snake and the Grande Ronde rivers.

## GETTING THERE & AWAY
### Air
Pendleton is northeastern Oregon's air hub, receiving regularly scheduled flights from

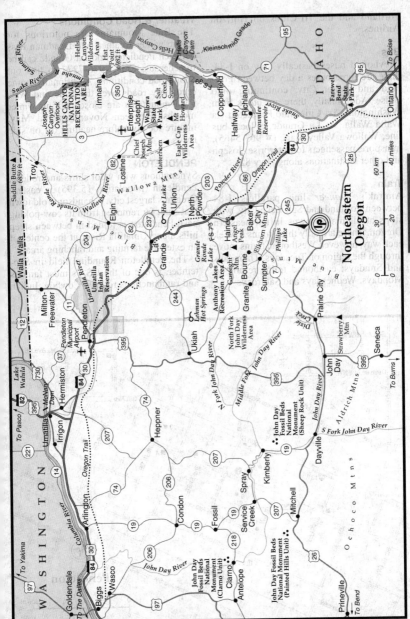

OREGON

Portland and the Tri-Cities on Horizon Airlines.

### Bus

Greyhound buses basically stay on I-84; there are three buses a day between Portland and Baker City, continuing onto Boise. Additionally, there are buses from Washington's Tri-Cities into Pendleton via Walla Walla. At La Grande, a local bus line, Wallowa Valley Stage (☎ 963-5465), transports passengers to Enterprise, Joseph and other destinations along Hwy 82.

### Train

Amtrak's *Pioneer* line parallels I-84 between Portland and Salt Lake City, with stops at all major towns in northeastern Oregon. There are only three trains a week each way, however. Westbound trains move through the region on Tuesdays, Thursdays and Sundays; eastbound trains return on Mondays, Wednesdays and Saturdays.

### Weather & Road Conditions

The Blue Mountains are notorious for severe winter weather, and Deadman Pass between Pendleton and La Grande can be treacherous. Call 1-976-7277 to find out about road conditions. Additionally, some secondary roads over the Blue and Wallowa mountains are closed during winter months. Between November and May, inquire locally before heading off on side roads.

## PENDLETON

Synonymous with wool shirts and rodeos, Pendleton (population 15,395) is eastern Oregon's largest city. A handsome old town that's not far removed from its cow-poking past, Pendleton is folded in between steep hills along Umatilla River at the center of an extensive farming and ranching area.

The Pendleton Roundup, held in September, is one of the USA's most famous and rambunctious rodeos. Cowboy, Indian

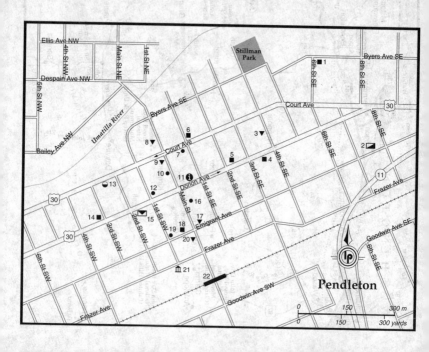

and tourist mingle in a hell's-a-poppin' four-day tribute to the Old West.

Beautiful, old residential areas filled with Queen Anne homes flank the downtown, where red-brick storefronts straddle the Prohibition-era underground commercial district that in the 1910s was the center for socially undesirable trades.

Food and lodging in Pendleton are cheap, and, like the hospitality, they're served up Western-style. It's a good place to stop for lunch, or to stock up on ranch supplies.

## Orientation

Pendleton is at the western edge of the arching Blue Mountains; extensive lava plateaus covered with wheat fields spread out to the west. Interstate 84 passes through the city; additionally, Hwy 395, linking Spokane, WA, and Burns, passes through Pendleton, as does Hwy 11 to Walla Walla, WA. Pendleton is 208 miles from Portland; it's 221 miles to Boise, ID.

| PLACES TO STAY | |
|---|---|
| 1 | Swift Station Inn |
| 4 | Travelers Inn |
| 5 | Let 'Er Buck Motel |
| 6 | Tapadera Inn |
| 14 | Longhorn Motel |
| 18 | Working Girls B&B |

| PLACES TO EAT | |
|---|---|
| 3 | Raphael's Restaurant |
| 8 | Cimmiyotti's |
| 9 | Rainbow Bar & Grill |
| 17 | El Charrito |
| 20 | Great Pacific Wine & Coffee Co |

| OTHER | |
|---|---|
| 2 | Taylor Park |
| 7 | Hamley's Saddlery |
| 10 | Blue Mtn Sports |
| 11 | Visitors Center |
| 12 | Armchair Books |
| 13 | Greyhound Bus Depot |
| 15 | Post Office |
| 16 | Pedaler's Place |
| 19 | Pendleton Underground Tours |
| 21 | Umatilla County Historical Museum |
| 22 | Amtrak Station |

The Umatilla River cuts through town, with most of the commercial development on the south side. Highway 30 becomes Court (one way westbound) and Dorion (one way eastbound) Aves in town. The intersection of Court and Dorion Aves with Main St is the center of downtown.

## Information

The Pendleton Chamber of Commerce (☎ 276-7411) is at 25 SE Dorion Ave, Pendleton, OR 97801. Headquarters for the Umatilla National Forest (☎ 276-3811) are on the other side of I-84 at 2517 SW Hailey Ave.

The post office (☎ 278-0203) is at 104 SW Dorion Ave. Regional books and general good reading are available from Armchair Books (☎ 276-7323), 39 SW Dorion Ave. Pendleton's daily newspaper is the *Eastern Oregonian*. Oregon Public Radio is heard on 90.9 FM.

Do something about those dirty clothes at the Laundry Room (☎ 276-7782), 121 SW 18th St, and go to Saint Anthony Hospital (☎ 276-5121), 1601 SE Court Ave, for health needs.

## Pendleton Woolen Mills

The Pendleton Woolen Mills (☎ 276-6911), 1307 SE Court Ave, was founded in Pendleton in 1909 by members of a family that had been weaving wool in Oregon since 1863. Built principally to scour local wool, it also produced blankets to sell on the nearby Umatilla Reservation. Today, its woolen products are known world-wide, and are produced nationally at 14 different locations. The red-brick mill is a Pendleton landmark.

The factory's salesroom is open Monday to Friday, from 8 am to 4:45 pm, and Saturday from 8 am to 2 pm from May to September. From October to April, the Saturday hours change to 9 am to 1 pm.

Free, short tours of the factory, showing the old weaving process, are given year round, Monday to Friday at 9 and 11 am and 1:30 and 3 pm. Tour groups are limited to 15, so call ahead.

## Hamley's Saddlery

If you've never been in a real saddlery, stop by Hamley's (☎ 276-2321), 30 SE Court Ave, which is world-famous for its hand-made saddles. Ask nicely and they'll show you the saddle-making process. Upstairs is a maze-like gallery of Western art.

## Umatilla County Historical Museum

This museum (☎ 276-0012), 108 SW Frazer Ave, is housed in Pendleton's hand-some old railroad station. Displays include an Oregon Trail commemoration, local Native American artifacts and memorabilia of the region's sheep industry and wool mills. The museum is open from 10 am to 4 pm Tuesday to Saturday; admission is by donation.

## Activities

Blue Mountain Sports (☎ 276-2269), 221 S Main St, rents downhill and cross-country skis, and other outdoor gear. Rent mountain bikes at Pedaler's Place (☎ 276-3337), 318 S Main St.

At the corner of SE Dorion Ave and 7th St is Taylor Park, where picnic tables, a playground, and a swimming pool await travelers. The 18-hole Pendleton Country Club (☎ 278-1739), south on Hwy 395, is open to non-members.

## Organized Tours

At the turn of the century, beneath Pendleton's old storefronts boomed a network of businesses and establishments. Literally driven underground by prohibition and social tensions, saloons, Chinese laundries, card rooms and other businesses found cozy tunnels in which to operate. Pendleton Underground Tours (☎ 276-0730), 37 SW Emigrant Ave, tours the town's old, subterranean business district. Also offered is the 'Cozy Rooms Bordello Tour' which visits an 1890s brothel. Each tour costs $5 per person and lasts 45 minutes. Call ahead for reservations and tour times.

## Pendleton Roundup

Promoters call it the USA's best rodeo. The Pendleton Roundup, established in 1909, is certainly one of the West's biggest parties. Held the second full week of September, Wednesday to Saturday, the Roundup is an all-out, Dionysian celebration of horse and cowboy. The rodeo is the main event, but the whole town swells with activity from cowboy breakfasts, Native American beauty pageants, dances and art shows. The Happy Canyon Pageant, the Confederated Tribe's biggest powwow, is held in conjunction with the Roundup on the rodeo grounds.

The rodeo grounds are on Court Ave (Hwy 30) west of downtown. Lodging is scarce at Roundup time, so plan well in advance. For ticket information and a schedule of events, contact Pendleton Roundup (☎ (800) 457-6336), 1205 SW Court Ave.

## Places to Stay

**Camping** Tent campers will want to stay at *Emigrant Springs State Park*, 26 miles east on I-84, a historic Oregon Trail site; rates are $10 for tents, $14 for full hook-ups. Quieter but even more distant is *Umatilla Forks*, a USFS campground, 32 miles east

Jacksonville (BM)

The old ranch town of Paisley (BM)

Cape Falcon and Smuggler's Cove (BM)

Mt Thielsen over Lamalo Lake (BM)

Leslie Gulch and Owyhee River (BM)

Rock columns near Ione (BM)

Seastacks along the Oregon coast (KS)

of Pendleton on Hwy 30. Take the road to Mission, continue to Gibbon and follow the river to the national forest boundary. RV campers should try *Brooke RV & MH Court* (☎ 276-5353), 5 NE 8th St ($16), or *Stotlar's Mobile Home Court* (☎ 276-0734), 15 SE 11th St ($15); both are on the Umatilla River.

**B&Bs** The *Swift Station Inn* (☎ 276-3739), 602 SE Byers Ave, offers four rooms in a historic home, starting at $80. *Working Girls B&B* (☎ 276-4767), 21 SW Emigrant Ave, offers rooms in an old downtown hotel with a shady past. The five guest rooms are decorated with period furnishings, and range from $55 to $65.

**Hotels** Downtown there is *Travelers Inn* (☎ 276-6231), 310 SE Dorion Ave, with a hot tub and pool. Single/double rooms cost $44/47. Less expensive is the *Let 'Er Buck* (☎ 276-3293), 205 SE Dorion Ave, where singles/doubles are $23/31. The *Tapadera Inn* (☎ 276-3231), 105 SE Court Ave, has its own bar and restaurant; rooms are $33/38. *The Longhorn* (☎ 276-7531), 411 SW Dorion Ave, is central and welcomes pets; rooms run $27/32.

Out by freeway exit No 210 there is the usual assortment of lodging choices. *Motel 6* (☎ 276-3160), 325 SE Nye Ave, is a good deal at $30/36. More upscale is the *Red Lion Inn Pendleton* (☎ 276-6111), 304 SE Nye Ave, where rooms begin at $69.

### Places to Eat
For lighter fare and espresso, try the *Great Pacific Wine & Coffee Company* (☎ 276-1350), 402 S Main St; they can also provide the makings for a good picnic with wine and deli products.

There's good Mexican food at *El Charrito* (☎ 276-2038), 322 S Main St. Check out the *Rainbow Bar & Grill* (☎ 276-4120) 209 S Main St, for late-night burgers and beer, and for its cool neon.

Another local favorite is *Cimmiyotti's* (☎ 278-2468), 137 S Main St, featuring steak and Italian food in a bar/dining room that recalls an Old West speakeasy.

*Raphael's Restaurant & Lounge* (☎ 276-8500), 233 SE 4th St, began as the diner at the Pendleton Airport. The food was so good that the locals would make the trip to the airport just to eat dinner. Success brought chef/owners Raphael and Robert Hoffman downtown to a beautifully refurbished old home, where their food is more popular than ever. Fresh seafood and smoked prime rib ($14) are favorites; try the venison marsala for $18.50. Reservations are recommended.

### Getting There & Around
**Air** Horizon Air (☎ 276-9777, (800) 547-9308) connects Pendleton's Municipal Airport to Portland with five flights daily; two flights daily link Pendleton with Washington's Tri-Cities. The airport is about five miles west of town on Hwy 30.

**Bus** Three Greyhound buses pass daily between Pendleton and Portland, and from Pendleton to Boise and points east. There's also service to Walla Walla and Washington's Tri-Cities. The depot (☎ 276-1551) is at 320 SW Court Ave.

**Train** The Amtrak station (☎ 276-1827) is at 17 SW Frazer Ave. See Getting There & Away at the beginning of this chapter for information on train lines.

**Car & Taxi** Hertz Rent-A-Car (☎ 276-3783) does its business at the airport. For a local weather forecast and road reports, call 276-0103. Contact Elite Taxis at 276-8294.

## MILTON-FREEWATER
This agricultural community (population 5630) lies in a beautiful fertile valley at the western base of the Blue Mountains. The region is one of the nation's largest producers of peas, onions, asparagus, fruit and wheat, and exudes a prosperous and wholesome feeling.

Milton was founded in 1872 by W S Frazier as a center for the up-and-coming farming community in the northern Walla Walla River valley. The hard-working

OREGON

**5200 Tons of Nerve Gas**
As you cross the Columbia plateau south of Hermiston along I-84, through rural farm communities and extensive tracts of irrigated land, keep your eyes peeled for the Umatilla Army Depot, where the US Military stockpiles chemical and conventional weapons. Built in the early years of WW II as a weapons repository, the 30-sq-mile Umatilla Depot currently stores about 12% of the nation's chemical weapons, including 5200 tons of nerve gas.

In 1994 the army announced plans to close the depot. All conventional weapons have been removed from the site, leaving only the chemical weapons, which the army proposes to destroy by incineration. ■

families who settled here decided to prohibit the sale of alcohol in their town. As the community grew, more and more citizens were dissatisfied living in a 'dry' town, and in 1889 moved across the railroad tracks to found Freewater, where freer spirits prevailed. The twin cities finally merged in 1951.

Frazier's 1868 farm home is now **Frazier Farmstead Museum** (☎ 938-4636), 1403 Chestnut St, containing household goods, furniture and old farm implements. The six-acre grounds are a preserve of 19th-century fruit trees and shrubs; there's also a large garden of heirloom roses. The museum is open from 11 am to 4 pm Thursday to Saturday, and from 1 to 4 pm on Sundays, April to December. Admission is by donation.

Milton-Freewater is 10 miles from Walla Walla, WA, and 27 miles from Pendleton on Hwy 11. The Milton-Freewater Chamber of Commerce, (938-5563, (800) 228-6736), is at 505 Ward St, Milton-Freewater, OR 97862.

### Places to Stay & Eat
Campers should head up the Walla Walla River to *Harris County Park* (☎ 938-5330), 10 miles southeast of Milton-Freewater on Walla Walla River Rd. There's camping

and fishing right on the river. Campsites with hook-ups are $15, tents are $10. In town, there's the *Morgan Inn* (☎ 938-5547) 104 N Columbia (Hwy 11), with kitchenettes and non-smoking single/double rooms for $35/38.

Go to the *Oasis* (☎ 938-4776), on Lamb St (also called the old Walla Walla Hwy), an authentic old roadhouse straight out of the 1920s, and *Wee Bit o' Heather* (☎ 938-5486), on Hwy 11 North, for authentic Western food.

The nearby town of Weston's old, red-brick commercial center is listed in the National Register of Historic Places. Make a detour to this lovely Old West town and have lunch at the *Longbranch Cafe & Saloon* (☎ 566-3478), 201 E Main St, a well-preserved old watering hole with a lively cafe alongside.

### Getting There & Away
Greyhound buses between Walla Walla and Pendleton stop at Milton-Freewater. Contact the depot in Pendleton for schedules.

### LA GRANDE
Located at the head of a vast valley ringed by snowy peaks, La Grande (population 11,890) is a college town (Eastern Oregon State College is the only four-year institution east of the Cascades) and trade center for the area's farms and ranches.

Early French traders, upon seeing the broad, seemingly circular valley, declared it to be the Grande Ronde, or big circle. Indeed, from the historical marker on Hwy 30 above town, it seems as if the valley forms a giant ring between mountain peaks.

The Oregon Trail crossed the valley; at La Grande the pioneers rested and prepared to traverse the Blue Mountains. Some immigrants understood the agricultural potential of the wide, well-watered valley and settled. La Grande was established in 1864; a tavern on the south bank of the Grande Ronde River was the catalyst for the town's early growth. Today, a wealth of inexpensive eating and lodging options, and plenty of recreational opportunities in the sur-

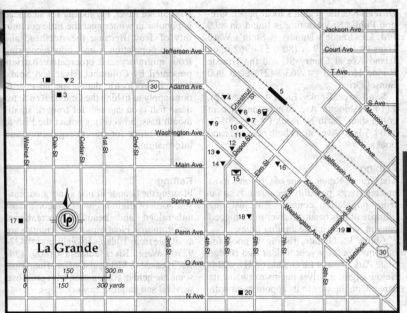

La Grande

| 0 | 150 | 300 m |
| 0 | 150 | 300 yards |

rounding mountains and canyons, make La Grande a great place to spend a night or two.

## Orientation

Located on the Grande Ronde River, a confluent of the Snake River, La Grande is at the juncture of I-84 and Hwy 82, the road to the Wallowa Mountains.

The town is 44 miles from Baker City, 52 miles from Pendleton and 259 miles from Portland.

## Information

Contact the La Grande/Union County Chamber of Commerce (☎ 963-8588, (800) 848-9969) at 2111 Adams Ave, La Grande OR, 97850. The La Grande Ranger Station of the Wallowa-Whitman USFS (☎ 963-7186), is at 3502 Hwy 30. Current fishing regulations and information about wildlife preserves can be obtained from the Fish & Wildlife Office (☎ 963-2138), 107 20th St.

The post office (☎ 963-2041) is at 1202 Washington Ave. The La Grande *Daily*

### PLACES TO STAY

1   Greenwell Motel
3   Stardust Motel
17  Stange Manor B&B
19  Royal Motor Inn
20  Pitcher Inn B&B

### PLACES TO EAT

2   Farmhouse Restaurant
4   Steele's
6   Sydney's
7   One Smart Cookie
8   Benchwarmer's Pub
9   Nature's Pantry
12  Mamacita's
14  Ten Depot St Restaurant
16  Cousin Vinnie's Italian Cafe
18  Centennial House

### OTHER

5   Amtrak Station
10  Earth N' Book
11  Anson Ski Shop
13  Sunflower Books Etc
15  Post Office

*Observer* is the region's local paper. Oregon Public Broadcasting is found on 89.9 FM. La Grande's laundry is Stein's Wash Haus (☎ 963-9629 or (800) 574-9629), on Island Ave at Cherry St, and the Grande Ronde Hospital (☎ 963-8421) is at 900 Sunset Drive.

Sunflower Books Etc (☎ 963-5242), 1114 Washington Ave, features an adjacent coffeeshop. Earth N' Book (☎ 963-8057), 1104 Adams Ave, offers both new and used books.

### Fishing

The Grande Ronde is one of Oregon's most unsung rivers, probably because it is so far from population centers. But just one glimpse of this beautiful river in its rugged canyon will stir innate angling urges.

Above La Grande, fishing is good for rainbow trout; try your luck at Red Bridge State Park, west of La Grande on Hwy 244. Below Elgin, the river begins to furrow its canyon, on the way to its appointment with wild Snake River. Fly fishing for steelhead is popular in winter near the little community of Troy. Because the steelhead and salmon population is only now recovering from migratory and procreative barriers presented by Columbia River and Snake River hydroelectric dams, special restrictions apply to fishing the Grande Ronde for these fish (you can fish for trout or smallmouth bass, however). Contact the Fish & Wildlife office for current regulations and information.

### Rafting

Floating the Grande Ronde's enormous canyon north of Elgin is one of Oregon's most unheralded and beautiful recreational opportunities. Float trips and raft rentals are available from Tilden's River Tours (☎ 437-9270). Wapiti River Guides (☎ (800) 488-9872) based in Idaho, also offers float trips; some are held in conjunction with primitive survival and nature-lore workshops.

## Skiing

Spout Springs Resort (☎ 556-2164), between Weston and Elgin on Hwy 204, is northeastern Oregon's low-key ski area. The vertical drop is only 550 feet, and the summit of the runs is at 5500 feet. However, it's the quality and quantity of the snow that make skiing here interesting; and with lift tickets at only $16, it's a good place to take a family or group.

For downhill skiers, there are 11 runs and two double chairlifts and one T-bar. There are also 13 miles of groomed cross-country ski trails. Rent downhill and cross-country skis from Anson Ski Shop (☎ 963-3660), 112 Depot St.

## Places to Stay

**Camping** Convenient but right beside the freeway is *Hilgard Junction State Park*, eight miles west of La Grande at I-84 exit No 252; sites are $10. *Catherine Creek State Park* (☎ 963-0430) is eight miles southeast of Union on Hwy 203; rates are $7 weekdays, $8 weekends. Both offer primitive sites, no hook-ups.

RV campers can go to the *Sundowner Mobile Park* (☎ 963-2648), 1806 26th St, where some space is saved for travelers. *The Broken Arrow Lodge* (see below) offers a few spaces to RVers near the motel.

**B&Bs** A 1920s Georgian mansion once owned by a lumber baron, the *Stange Manor Inn* (☎ 963-2400), 1612 Walnut St, offers five guest rooms, each with private bath, starting at $65. The *Pitcher Inn* (☎ 963-9152), 608 N Ave, offers four guest rooms furnished with antiques in a 1925 home; rooms start at $55. At the nearby town of Union, the *Queen Anne Inn* (☎ 562-5566), 782 North 5th St, is in one of eastern Oregon's oldest Victorian homes; rates start at $45.

**Hotels** La Grande has an abundance of inexpensive accommodations along the old 'main drag' Hwy 30, which is called Adams Ave in town. Take I-84 exit No 259 for the *Stardust Motel* (☎ 963-4166), 402 Adams Ave, where single/double rooms are $28/30, and the *Greenwell Motel* (☎ 963-4134), 305 Adams Ave, where rooms are $25/30; both allow pets.

Downtown, stay at the comfortable *Royal Motor Inn* (☎ 963-4154), 1510 Adams Ave; rates are $36/40. Further east along old Hwy 30 are other older, well-kept motels. The *Orchard Motel* (☎ 963-6160), 2206 Adams Ave, takes pets and offers no-smoking rooms and kitchenettes for $28/30; the *Moon Motel* (☎ 963-2724), 2116 Adams Ave, is $26/30, and the *Broken Arrow Lodge* (☎ 963-7116), 2215 Adams Ave, has rooms for $26/28.

If you want to stay out near the freeway ramps, you may do so at exit No 261. Awaiting you are the *Super 8* (☎ 963-8080), 2407 East R Ave, with a pool, spa and single/doubles for $48/50. At the *Best Western Pony Soldier* (☎ 963-7195, (800) 528-1234), 2612 Island Ave, with a pool, hot tub and conference rooms; rooms are $58/60.

## Places to Eat

La Grande offers a surprisingly diverse and affordable selection of dining options. For espresso and freshly baked muffins, go to *One Smart Cookie* (☎ 963-3172), 1119 Adams Ave. For a traditional breakfast, go to *Sydney's* (☎ 963-6500), 1115 Adams Ave.

*Cousin Vinnie's Italian Cafe* (☎ 963-2353), 1302 Adams Ave, serves Italian food in a bistro atmosphere; their pizzas are delivered free in town. For sandwiches and lighter fare, go to *Steele's* (☎ 963-9692), 1011 Adams Ave, or to *Benchwarmers Pub* (☎ 963-9597), 210 Depot St, a sports bar where they pour microbrewed ales and serve hamburgers. For a vegetarian deli and other natural foods, go to *Nature's Pantry* (☎ 963-7955), 1907 4th St. Across the street from the Stardust and Greenwell motels is handy *Farmhouse Restaurant* (☎ 963-9318), 401 Adams Ave.

*Mamacita's* (☎ 963-6223), 110 Depot St, provides a good, bustling value in Mexican food; most full dinners are in the $6 range. *Ten Depot Street* (☎ 963-8766), at, of course, 10 Depot St, offers full-blown steak

OREGON

and fresh seafood meals in an old Mason's lodge; local loin of lamb with herbs goes for $18. *Centennial House* (☎ 963-6089), 1606 6th St, offers fine dining in an old home built in 1890. Their prix fixe lunch, at $4.95, is one of La Grande's best deals. At dinner, pasta goes for $9 and steak and lamb are a bit more.

### Getting There & Around

The Greyhound bus depot (☎ 963-5165) is at 2108 Cove Ave; buses pass through four times daily. The Wallowa Valley Stage Line (the Greyhound depot has information) offers once daily service to Joseph and Enterprise; the fare is under $10 for the two-hour trip. See Getting There & Away at the beginning of this chapter for more information.

Amtrak (☎ (800) 872-7245), at Depot and Jefferson Sts, offers three trains weekly between Portland and Salt Lake City.

Rental cars are available from Tamarack Ford (☎ 963-2161), 2906 Island Ave (toward Island City). Call Designated Driver Cab Co (☎ 963-6960) for a lift.

### AROUND LA GRANDE
### Grande Ronde River

The upper reaches of the Grande Ronde River, one of Oregon's most dramatic and beautiful rivers, can be explored by taking Hwy 244 eight miles west of La Grande from I-84 exit No 252.

At the site of today's Hilgard State Park, just off the freeway exit, Oregon Trail pioneers gathered their strength before climbing up over the Blue Mountains. Information kiosks explain how the pioneers winched their wagons down the steep slopes of the Grande Ronde valley.

Highway 244 follows the river through a lovely, narrow valley, filled with meadows and farmland, ponderosa pines and aspen trees. At Red Bridge State Park, eight miles west on Hwy 244, there's a beautiful picnic area right on the river, with good access for anglers.

The highway continues up the valley, then climbs up to a low pass. Cross-country skiing is popular here in the winter. Skiers,

and other explorers, like to end their day with a soak at Lehman Hot Springs (☎ 427-3015), 40 miles from La Grande. Highway 244 then continues to Ukiah, a little mountain community (note the aptly named Antlers Saloon), at the junction with Hwy 395. Ukiah is 56 miles from La Grande.

### Hot Lake & Union

Some of eastern Oregon's first settlements were in the Grande Ronde valley, southeast of La Grande. This lovely rural area combines old Victorian farm homes with spooky hot springs.

At Hot Lake, nine miles south of La Grande on Hwy 203, 2.5 gallons per minute of super-heated water reach the surface at nearly the boiling point, and pour into a large pond. The Nez Perce, Cayuse, Umatilla and the Wallawalla groups considered the extensive geothermals (reportedly the world's largest hot spring) a sacred area, and treated the entire valley, which was known as the 'Valley of Peace', as a cease-fire zone.

From Hot Lake, continue on Hwy 203 to Union, the first settlement in the area, established in 1862. Union has a number of well-maintained Victorian buildings, as well as the **Union County Museum** (☎ 562-6003), 311 S Main Ave. Continue

---

**The Haunted Sanatorium**

As early as 1864, White settlers recognized Hot Lake's economic viability and proceeded to build a series of lakeside health resorts at the edge of the eight-acre lake. The grandest of all was built in 1906, a huge sanatorium/hotel with hundreds of rooms. In the 1930s, a fire destroyed the grand ballroom and library, leaving just the brick hospital/hotel intact.

The Hot Lake Resort closed in the 1980s, and is widely considered to be haunted. Listen closely, late on a winter's day, with plumes of sulfurous vapor dancing across the lake, to hear the screams. Attempts in recent years to revive Hot Lake as a resort have met with failure. ∎

on to Cove on Hwy 237, which, when first settled, was at the edge of a shallow lake. Return via Island City to La Grande.

## Blue Mountain Interpretive Center

Hiking paths and interpretive displays flank a portion of the Oregon Trail, still quite visible after 150 years, at this new park. The Blue Mountains were an incredible concern to the pioneers. Not only were the grades quite steep, the crossing of the Blues came at the end of the journey, usually in early September, and early snow storms could make the journey miserable if not impossible.

Along the footpaths, interpretive panels and costumed docents document the challenges, dangers and choices that faced the Oregon Trail travelers. The displays and short hikes inject a dose of reality to glamorized notions of pioneer life; a kind of foreboding begins to fill the forest.

The center is 13 miles west of La Grande off I-84 exit No 248. From the exit, follow well-marked gravel roads about three miles toward the little community of Kamela. The center is open year round, during daylight hours only.

## BAKER CITY

Baker City (population 9300), situated at the head of a wide valley beneath the snow-capped Elkhorn Mountains, is Oregon's richest geological region, with 75% of the state's mineral wealth, and one of eastern Oregon's oldest commercial centers. Nearly all phases of Oregon's development have been played out in Baker City's rich history.

Once the largest and most boisterous city between Salt Lake City and Portland, Baker City was a colorful, two-fisted party town during the latter years of the 1800s, with miners, cowboys, sheepherders, shopkeepers and loggers keeping each other company in the city's many saloons, brothels and gaming halls. Still an authentic Western town, Baker City's wide streets and gracious architecture recall both the swagger and courtliness of a not-too distant past.

With its abundant facilities, Baker City is a good gateway to Hell's Canyon, the Wallowa Mountains and other eastern Oregon destinations.

## Orientation

Located at the point where the Powder River leaves the Blue Mountains and enters its wide agricultural valley, Baker City is on I-84, at the junction with Hwy 7 to John Day, and of Hwy 86 to Hells Canyon. Baker City is 44 miles from La Grande on I-84.

## Information

The Baker County Visitors & Convention Bureau (☎ 523-3356, (800) 523-1235) is at 490 Campbell St, Baker City, OR 97814. The headquarters for the Wallowa-Whitman National Forest (☎ 523-6391) and the regional BLM office (☎ 523-6391) are at 1550 Dewey Ave. The Wallowa-Whitman National Forest Ranger District office (☎ 523-4476) is at 3165 10th St.

The post office (☎ 523-4237) is at 1550 Dewey Ave. Betty's Books (☎ 523-7551), 1813 Main St, is the local independent bookstore, with a selection of regional history and touring books. The Baker City daily newspaper is called the *Baker City Herald* and Oregon Public Radio is heard on 91.5 FM.

The Baker City Laundry (☎ 523-9817) is at 815 Campbell St. Baker City's medical center is St Elizabeth Hospital (☎ 523-6461), 3325 Pocahontas Rd.

## Downtown

The old downtown retains much of its turn-of-the-century architecture and charm, and quite a bit of the city center is listed in the National Register of Historic Places.

Several blocks of downtown, near Valley Ave and 1st St, are built of locally quarried basalt. **Hotel Baker**, still the tallest building in Oregon east of the Cascades, was built in 1929 (this nine-story landmark is now converted to apartments). Oregon's largest display of gold in its mineral state is found in the bank lobby at 2000 Main St, and includes a nugget weighing over 80

OREGON

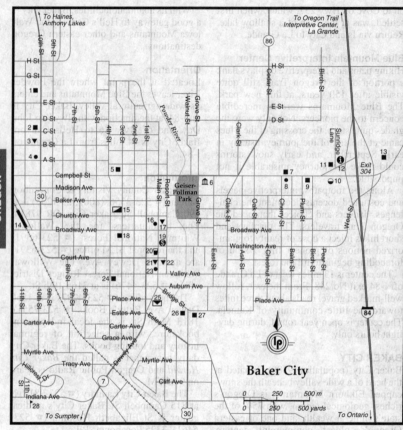

**Baker City**

PLACES TO STAY
1   Western Motel
2   Trail Motel
5   Grant House B&B
7   Quality Inn
9   Eldorado Inn
11  Best Western Sunridge Inn
13  Super 8 Inn
18  Royal Motor Inn
24  A Demain B&B
26  Friendship Inn
27  Oregon Trail Motel

PLACES TO EAT
3   Inland Cafe
17  Brass Parrot
20  Main Event
21  Blue & White Cafe
22  Front St Cafe
27  Oregon Trail Restaurant

OTHER
4   Ellison Motors
6   Oregon Trail Regional Museum
8   Baker City Laundry

10  Greyhound Bus Depot
12  Visitors Center
14  Amtrak Station
15  YMCA Gym
16  Blue Mtn Sports
19  US Bank
23  Betty's Books
25  Post Office, Forest Service HQ, BLM (Federal Offices)
28  Baker Golf Course

ounces. It's open to the public during regular banking hours.

A brochure describing a walking tour of buildings on the Historic Register in the city center is available from the visitors center or the Oregon Trail Regional Museum.

## Oregon Trail Regional Museum

Housed in a showcase natatorium built in 1920, this museum of local history contains a number of interesting exhibits. The large space that once contained the pool (which was fed by hot water springs) now contains furniture, vehicles and machinery from Baker City's frontier days. An extensive mineral collection, including a display of florescent rocks, will be of interest to more than avid rock collectors. The museum (☎ 523-7636) is at 2490 Grove St, at Campbell St, and is open daily from 10 am to 4 pm May to October. An entrance donation is requested.

Across Grove St from the museum is **Geiser-Pollman Park** alongside the Powder River. There are picnic tables and a playground.

## National Historic Oregon Trail Interpretive Center

A major historic and educational facility, the Oregon Trail Interpretive Center (☎ 523-1843) is the nation's foremost memorial to the pioneers who crossed the West along the Oregon Trail. Built on windswept Flagstaff Hill, four miles east of Baker City along Hwy 86, it overlooks well-preserved wagon ruts from the 1840s and 50s. The center opened in 1992 and is a must-see for anyone with an interest in the history of the West.

It was from this pass that emigrants along the Oregon Trail first saw the fertile and inviting uplands of Oregon, reminding the dispirited travelers of Oregon's promise. After traveling across deserts and canyon lands for weeks, the pioneers emerged from the aptly named Burnt Water Valley and onto Flagstaff Hill, where the Powder River Valley blossomed beneath the forested Blue Mountains.

The 23,000-sq-foot center contains a maze of interactive displays, artifacts, films and exhibits that stress the day-to-day realities, choices and predicaments of the pioneers as they struggled across the West. A trail system explores an old mining claim, the arid sagebrush ecosystem and the ruts of the original Oregon Trail.

The center is open from 9 am to 6 pm, May to September, and 9 am to 4 pm, October to April. Admission is free. Take

OREGON

I-84 to exit No 302 (onto Hwy 86) just north of Baker City.

## Eastern Oregon Museum
This museum (☎ 856-3568), at 610 3rd St in Haines, 10 miles northwest of Baker City on Hwy 30, is Haines' local museum of frontier memorabilia. Housed in the old high school gymnasium, the museum basically preserves everything collectible from the Haines community, including old china, tools and clothing. It's an appealing collection of stuff, some of which is finally getting old.

The museum is open from 9 am to 5 pm daily, April to October.

## Activities
Baker City is a jumping-off point for downhill and **cross-country skiing** at Anthony Lakes Mountain Resort (☎ 963-4599, 856-3277) in the Blue Mountains. Rent cross-country skis at Blue Mountain Sports (☎ 523-5702), 2101 Main St.

The YMCA pool (☎ 523-3189) is at 2020 Church Ave. The Baker Golf Club (☎ 523-2358), 2801 Indiana Ave, is a nine-hole course with views over the mountains and valleys. A highlight is the clubhouse, built in 1936 by the WPA.

## Miner's Jubilee
Baker City's Miner's Jubilee, is held the third weekend in July. Events include a porcupine race (animal rights activists need not attend), gold-panning competitions, a street dance and food booths. Contact the visitors center for more details.

## Places to Stay
**Camping** The *Mountain View Holiday Trav-L-Park & Mobile Manor* (☎ 523-4824, (800) 323-8899), 2845 Hughes Lane, accommodates both tent and RV campers; there's a heated pool. Take exit No 304 off I-84, follow Campbell St and head right 10th St for one mile. *Oregon Trails West RV Park* (☎ 523-3236) just off exit No 302, has a separate tenting area.

**B&Bs** *A Demain B&B* (☎ 523-2509), 1790 4th St, is a splendid old Victorian home, with rooms starting at $55. At the *Grant House B&B* (☎ 523-6685), 2525 3rd St, rooms are $40 to $45. If you're staying alone, you receive a slight discount.

**Hotels** At exit No 304 there is a cluster of chain motels. At the *Super 8* (☎ 523-8282), 250 Campbell St, single/double rooms cost $39/53. The *Eldorado Inn* (☎ 523-6494), 695 Campbell St, has rooms for $36/39. At the *Quality Inn* (☎ 523-2242), 810 Campbell St, rooms range between $37 and $55, and between $50 and $65 at *Best Western Sunridge Inn* (☎ 523-6444), 1 Sunridge Lane. Close by is all manner of fast food.

Stay closer to old downtown at the *Royal Motor Inn* (☎ 532-6324), 2205 Broadway Ave, and spend $33/36 for lodging. Also near downtown is the *Oregon Trail Motel & Restaurant* (☎ 523-5844), 211 Bridge St, where rooms are $32/38, and the *Friendship Inn* (☎ 523-6571), 134 Bridge St, which has rooms for $25/33.

Along the old Hwy 30 (10th St) are a number of comfortable, equally inexpensive lodgings. At the *Trail Motel* (☎ 523-4646), 2815 10th St, rooms go for $26/30. *The Western Motel* (☎ 523-3700), 3055 10th St, offers lodging for $27/34.

## Places to Eat
Although there is the usual clumping of fast-food restaurants at the freeway exits, drive downtown to find more interesting options. *Front Street Cafe* (☎ 523-7536), 1840 Main St, is the place for breakfast (try their many fried-potato options), lunch, light dinner and good coffee. *Blue & White Cafe* (☎ 523-6792), 1825 Main St, is a classic diner. More upscale is the *Brass Parrot* (☎ 523-4266), 2190 Main St, featuring Mexican specialties and steak in the $10 to $12 range. For microbrews and hamburgers in a sports bar atmosphere, stop at *The Main Event* (☎ 523-6988), 1929 Main St. If you're staying on 10th St, go to the *Inland Cafe* (☎ 523-9041), 2715 10th St, for home-style cooking popular with the locals.

For steak, drive 10 miles north on Hwy 30 to Haines, where the *Haines Steak House* (☎ 856-3639) has the reputation of serving Oregon's best steak as well as having a great chuck wagon salad bar. It's open for dinner only.

### Getting There & Around
The Greyhound depot (☎ 523-5011), 515 Campbell St, is served by four buses a day each way along its Portland-Boise route. Amtrak (☎ (800) 872-7245) offers three passenger trains a week between Portland and Salt Lake City. The station is at 2803 Broadway Ave.

Contact Ellison Motors (☎ 523-4488), 2615 10th, for short-term car rentals. For local road conditions call ☎ 523-6417. Call Baker City Cab (☎ 523-6070) for a taxi.

### THE BLUE MOUNTAINS
Rising to the west from ranch land near Baker City, the Blue Mountains were responsible for the magnificently rich gold strikes that established towns like Sumpter, Granite and Baker City itself. These and other boom towns that have passed out of existence thrived here in the 1860s (ask at the Baker City visitors center for a brochure on the area's old mining towns). Now more famous for their excellent skiing and stands of pine forests, the Blue Mountains offer back roads to ghost towns, high mountain lakes, river canyons and hiking trails. The Elkhorn Drive, a National Forest Scenic Byway, circles the gold-rich Elkhorn Range.

### Orientation & Information
Highway 7 connects I-84 with Hwy 26 to the south, traversing the Blue Mountains. From Sumpter, USFS Rd 24 leads to Granite, and USFS Rd 73 goes to Anthony Lakes.

The Wallowa-Whitman National Forest Headquarters (☎ 523-6391) at 1550 Dewey Ave, Baker City, OR 97814, has information on the scenic byway and the Blue Mountains.

### Elkhorn Drive Scenic Byway
Designated by the USFS, this 106-mile loop drive between Baker City and Granite (along Hwys 7 and 30, and USFS Rd 73) leads to many of the area's historic and recreational sites in the Elkhorn Range, and to a multitude of pleasant public campsites along Phillips Lake. The eastern Oregon Gold Rush began in these mountains, when prospectors discovered colors at Griffin Creek south of Baker City in 1861.

By the way, those patches of dead pines between Granite and Gunsight Pass along USFS Rd 73 aren't all due to clear-cutting and forest fires. The byway passes through regions heavily afflicted with mountain pine beetles.

### The Blue Gold Mountains
The Blue Mountains were Pacific reefs and islands before the North American continent collided with them about 200 million years ago, wedging them up to mountain heights. Between 160 and 120 million years ago, molten intrusions shot through the new mountains, forming batholiths, or sub-surface lakes of lava that hardened into igneous rock.

This unerupted lava was mostly made up of granite, but it also contained a number of other minerals. As the molten rock cooled, the various component minerals hardened differentially, as each have distinct melting points. Liquid gold, having a very low melting point, squeezed into veins as surrounding rock began to solidify.

The discovery in the 1860s of gold nuggets in streams in the Blue Mountains led to the unearthing of significant gold veins, or lodes, at several locations in the region. The richest lodes have been found in an arc between John Day, Baker City and Ukiah.

Ghost-town enthusiasts will find the Blue Mountains dotted with ruined mining camps. Easily reached from Sumpter is Bourne, seven miles up Cracker Creek; gold mines are still producing in the area. Granite, 15 miles up Hwy 24, is a ghost-town in aspect; however, its population is actually growing – it recently reached 10 residents. ∎

OREGON

## Phillips Lake

Formed by the dammed Powder River, Phillips Lake offers good summer trout fishing; ice-fishing is also very popular in the winter. Public campgrounds ring the lake, making it a good stopover for families. The largest, *Union Creek* is just off Hwy 7. On the south side of the lake are two smaller, less-developed campgrounds.

## Sumpter

A relic of the early gold and lumber boom days, Sumpter (population 125), 28 miles west of Baker City, now makes a living as a 'ghost town.' In 1862 five Confederate soldiers discovered gold in the area, but it wasn't until the Sumpter Valley Railroad reached the townsite in 1896 that it really began to boom. The town quickly grew to include 4000 residents, an opera house, three newspapers and a hospital.

The arrival of the railroad allowed the development of 'hard rock' mining, which entailed underground mining of veins and processing of the ore by stamp mills. Much of the city burned in a 1917 fire. Between the wars, the area was dredged for gold, leaving the valley's rocky soil in orderly piles. Today, Sumpter preserves its few remaining original buildings as tourist shops and antique stores. An abandoned, evil-looking gold dredge sits beside the town; there's talk of making it and the dredge ponds into a state park.

The narrow-gauge **Sumpter Valley Railroad** was the economic lifeline of this area from the 1890s to the 1930s. Linking Prairie City on the John Day River to Baker City, the line served the mining, logging and livestock interests in the Blue Mountains. A portion of the wood-fired steam service remains open during summer weekends, linking Sumpter and Phillips Lake. Excursions leave Sumpter Depot at 10 am, noon, 2 and 4 pm, Memorial Day to the last weekend of September. Passage is $4 adult, $3 child.

## Anthony Lakes Recreation Area

Right below the impressive crags of Gunsight Mountain and Angel Peak is a lake basin offering campgrounds, fishing and hikes to alpine meadows. In summer, it's a popular get-away for families. In winter, downhill and cross-country skiers take over, as these remote mountains offer Oregon's best powder skiing.

Take USFS Rd 73, which climbs 19 miles to the Anthony Lakes area from the small town of North Powder (population 460, elevation 3256 feet) on I-84; it's open year round only as far as the ski area. In summer, the road continues over Elkhorn Summit Pass (at 7392 feet, the highest paved road in Oregon) to join the Elkhorn Drive byway.

### Hiking

Along the shores of Grande Ronde, Mud and Anthony lakes are USFS campgrounds, which make the lakes popular for trout fishing and hiking. Trails lead out from Anthony Lake to several other small lakes. For a short hike, follow the **Elkhorn Crest Trail** east from the lake, and hike up to Black Lake, immediately below impressive Gunsight Mountain. A steeper climb leads up Parker Creek to tiny Hoffer Lakes.

### Skiing

The Elkhorn Mountains' height and location virtually guarantees tons of powdery snow each winter. Anthony Lakes Mountain Resort (☎ 963-4599) has the highest base elevation in Oregon (7100 feet) and 21 runs. The resort offers rentals, a day lodge with a restaurant and lounge and ski instruction. Lift tickets begin at $20.

Cross-country skiing is also popular. The lodge maintains six miles of groomed trails, and nearby are miles of snowy USFS roads to explore.

### Places to Stay & Eat

Besides the basic campgrounds at Anthony Lakes ($5), the closest lodgings are in North Powder. The *Powder River Motel* (☎ 898-2829) 850 2nd St, offers single/double rooms at $32/34.

In Sumpter, brand-new and comfortable, the log-built *Depot Inn Motel* (☎ 894-2522) shows that there's still some life left;

single/double rooms are $40/45. Other lodging options are available in Baker City or La Grande.

Three meals a day are served at the Anthony Lakes Resort lodge during the ski season. There's basic food at the *North Powder Cafe* (☎ 898-2332), 1011 2nd St, down the hill in North Powder. The *Elkhorn Saloon* (☎ 894-2244) in Sumpter serves pizzas and burgers in a bar/restaurant combination; it's closed Mondays.

# The Wallowa Mountains

A spectacular mountain range tucked into Oregon's far northeastern corner, the Wallowas are one of the state's premier scenic and recreational destinations. Rising precipitously from park-like farm and ranch land, the Wallowas loom to 10,000 feet, with 17 individual peaks over 9000 feet. Ice-age glaciers carved sharp crags and deep canyons into the Wallowas. The moraines of one such glacier now impounds Wallowa Lake. Eastern Oregon's highest peak – the 9832-foot Matterhorn – and only remaining glacier are found in the Wallowas.

Much of the high country is part of Eagle Cap Wilderness, a 715-sq-mile natural area studded with high mountain meadows and lakes. It is no coincidence that the Wallowas are known as the 'Alps of Oregon'.

## THE NORTHERN WALLOWAS
Pressed up against the Wallowas' north face, which rises up 4000 feet above the valley, two little-changed Old West burgs, Enterprise and Joseph, slumber in one of the Northwest's most dramatic settings. Beauty, isolation and small-town rents draw artists to the area, in particular to Joseph, which now has a national reputation as a center for Western and wildlife art.

Directly behind Joseph is Wallowa Lake, a glacial lake flanked by towering peaks.

The lake is large enough to support an incredibly popular state park and deep enough for Wally, the Wallowa Lake Monster, sightings of which are the stuff of Native American legend and recent scientific debate.

The USFS has designated the Wallowa Mountain Loop Rd, which links Joseph and Halfway, and the Imnaha River Rd, as scenic byways. The road to Hat Point, with views into Hells Canyon, is the area's most famous and most intimidating. Back roads such as these abound; mountain bikers, cross-country skiers, anglers and other lovers of nature and dramatic landscape will cherish this part of northeast Oregon.

Because of the overwhelming beauty and scenic variety, visitors should not be surprised to find that trails, campgrounds and fishing holes get crowded in high season. In particular, the lovely state park at Wallowa Lake can be oppressively over-utilized during summer weekends.

## ENTERPRISE
Wallowa county seat, and trade center for the area's vast farming and ranching operations, Enterprise (population 1940) both looks and feels the part of a handsome, red-blooded Western town. Much of the original downtown, built in the 1890s, is still here and functions as the mercantile center.

Enterprise is a friendly kind of town that makes you want to spend a day or two, and you probably should: it's a perfect center for exploring the sights of northeastern Oregon.

### Orientation & Information
Enterprise is 65 miles from La Grande on Hwy 82; from here it's only six miles to Joseph on Hwy 82 and 12 miles to Wallowa Lake.

The Wallowa County Chamber of Commerce (☎ 426-4622), 107 SW First St, Enterprise OR 97282, is open Monday to Friday, from 10 am to 3 pm. The Wallowa-Whitman National Forest office and the Hell's Canyon National Recreational Area office share space (☎ 426-4978) at 88401 Hwy 82, Enterprise, OR 97282.

OREGON

The post office (☎ 426-3555) is at 201 W North St. Wallowa Memorial Hospital (☎ 426-3111), 401 E First St, serves the entire Wallowa Valley. The Bookloft (☎ 426-3351), 107 E Main St, is one of eastern Oregon's best bookstores, complete with a friendly coffee bar, regional guides and the latest bestsellers.

## Activities
Rent cross-country skis at Wallowa Outdoors (☎ 426-3493) 110 S River St, and bikes from Cycle Life Bike Shop (☎ 426-6134), 212 W North St; ask here for advice on local mountain-bike trails.

## Hells Canyon Mule Days
Hells Canyon Mule Days (☎ 426-6191) is Enterprise's unlikely tribute to our equine friend, with a downtown mule parade and a full, mule-only rodeo, held the weekend after Labor Day.

## Places to Stay
**Hotels** The *Ponderosa Motel* (☎ 426-3186), 102 SE Greenwood St, takes pets and offers non-smoking rooms; single/doubles are $42/44. The *Wilderness Inn* (☎ 426-4535), 301 W North St, offers the same, but with a sauna; rates are $44/46. The *Melody Ranch Motel* (☎ 426-4986), 402 W North St, offers lodging in the motel or in free-standing cabins for $38/42.

## Places to Eat
*Cloud 9 Bakery* (☎ 426-3790), 105 SE 1st St, offers espresso, fresh baked goods and fresh-cut sandwiches. For natural foods, a deli and a juice bar, stop by the *Common Good Marketplace* (☎ 426-4125), 100 Main St.

*Toma's Restaurant* (☎ 426-4873), 309 S River St, offers burgers and steak, with prices ranging from $8 to $15. *Mountaineer Cafe* (☎ 426-6564), 307 W North St, serves lighter meals in the $5 to $7 range, in a renovated home. *Cafe Olé* (☎ 426-4888), 107 SW 1st St, is the place for Mexican food.

## Getting There & Away
Catch the Wallowa Valley Stage Line (☎ 963-5465) at the Mountain Mart Station, 302 W North St. There's one bus a day between La Grande and Enterprise; the fare is under $9; call for times.

## JOSEPH
Like Enterprise, Joseph (population 1095) is little changed physically from its 1880s boom days – until you look closely. About half the old storefronts are now world-renowned art galleries. Valley Bronze, one of the largest and most respected foundries in the nation, relocated to Joseph in the 1970s, bringing an intense artistic focus to this old frontier town. Today, not only the foundry, but artists, gallery owners and mavens of bronze sculpture flock to Joseph. Combine this with the Wallowa recreational elite, and it means that this is small-town Oregon in appearance only.

All that good taste means that the amenities in Joseph are a cut above what you'd expect in a similar-sized town elsewhere in Oregon, but remain inexpensive.

## Orientation & Information
It's six miles from Joseph to both Enterprise and Wallowa Lake State Park. Highway 350 leaves from Joseph for Imnaha (28 miles) where the Hat Point road climbs up to Hells Canyon vistas. Seasonal USFS Rd 39, part of the Wallowa Mountain Loop Byway, divides off Hwy 350 seven miles east of Joseph, to wind over the east flank of the Wallowas to Hwy 86 near Halfway, 65 miles to the south.

The Joseph Chamber of Commerce (☎ 432-1015) is at 102 E First St, Joseph, OR 97846. The post office (☎ 432-3231) is at 101 N Main St.

## Galleries
If Western art is your thing, then you'll find plenty to occupy a day in Joseph. Surely no other town in Oregon can boast more galleries than bars, but Joseph is no ordinary Western town.

The town is most noted for its cast bronze sculpture, due to the existence of the **Valley Bronze Foundry**, which now employs 65 people, and is noted throughout the world for its ability to cast large statuary. Tours of the Valley Bronze Foundry are offered daily, and can be scheduled at the Valley Bronze Showroom (☎ 432-7551), 18 S Main St.

Other Western Art galleries line Main St. The **Manuel Museum** (☎ 432-7235) Main and East Sts, is the studio of bronze artist David Manuel; there's also a sculpture garden. The **Wildhorse Gallery** (☎ 432-4242), 508 N Main St, offers more bronzes and Western-themed original art and prints.

The **Wallowa Lake Gallery** (☎ 432-9555), 19 S Main St, features wildlife art and blue-chip Western prints.

## Wallowa County Museum

This community museum (☎ 426-6095), at the corner of 2nd and Main Sts, housed in an old 1888 bank, contains artifacts and mementos from the region's history. Especially interesting is the display on Nez Perce history; this old bank's robbery in 1896 is another item of particular fascination to the locals.

## Special Events

Chief Joseph Days, held the last weekend of July, features four rodeos, Native American dancing, and a 10 K run, among other activities. Plan ahead if you are going to need lodging during Chief Joseph Days; it gets pretty tight in both Joseph and Enterprise, and at Wallowa Lake. Contact the chamber of commerce for more information.

Taking its epithet as the 'Switzerland of America' seriously, Joseph hosts an Alpenfest (☎ 432-4704) in late September. Alpenfest features folk music and dancers, German food and local crafts. Be there for the yodeling contest.

Twice weekly, local actors re-enact the daring 1896 Joseph bank robbery along Main St, and on weekends stage period melodramas at the Manuel Museum.

## Places to Stay

**Camping** In season, the real action is a few miles south at Wallowa Lake, but campers who want to avoid the bustle of the state park should try *Hurricane Creek Campground* seven miles south of Joseph on USFS Rd 8205, also called Hurricane Creek Rd; it's free.

**Hotels** The *Indian Lodge Motel* (☎ 432-2651), at the corner of Main and 3rd Sts, is clean and comfortable; singles/doubles cost $43/50. *Chandler's Bed, Bread & Trail Inn* (☎ 432-9765), 700 S Main St, is cozy, with the sort of hearty breakfast you'll want before struggling up the Wallowas. Rooms start at $60.

## Places to Eat

*Cactus Jack's* (☎ 432-6220), 100 N Main St, housed in a historic storefront, is a bar on one side and restaurant on the other. The food's tasty, and don't hesitate to opt for the specials (Wednesday offers all-you-can-eat beef ribs). *The Country Kitchen* (☎ 432-1195), 500 N Main St, offers commendable country-style cooking three meals a day.

## Getting There & Away

Wallowa Valley Stage Line (☎ 963-5465) has bus service between La Grande and Joseph; the fare is under $10 for the two-hour trip.

## WALLOWA LAKE

Wallowa Lake is an excellent example of a morainal lake, formed when successive glaciers plowed down out of the Wallowas. As these glaciers flowed out of high mountain valleys, they pushed a bulwark of displaced rock. These morains eventually stopped the progress of the glacier, which melted, creating a lake basin. Today, the morainal walls of Wallowa Lake rise 900 feet above the plateau at nearby Joseph. Rising precipitously on three sides of the lake are Wallowa peaks; Chief Joseph Mountain rises vertically a mile above the lake.

Old Chief Joseph, father of Chief Joseph,

OREGON

### Chief Joseph & the Nez Perce

The Wallowa Mountains are at the center of the Nez Perce traditional homeland, which once encompassed adjacent areas of Washington and Idaho. Early treaties effectively divided the Nez Perce into a band that lived in the Wallowa Valley, and another that lived along the Clearwater River in Idaho. In a move that demonstrated US diplomatic scheming as well as inter-tribal rivalries, in 1863 the Idaho Nez Perce signed a treaty that turned the Oregon reservation lands over to White settlement, while maintaining the Idaho homelands. The Oregon Nez Perce, under Chief Joseph, refused to recognize the treaty and remained in the Wallowas.

The battle of Little Bighorn in Montana fanned distrust of Indians everywhere, just as conflicts between settlers and Chief Joseph's Nez Perce left several White men dead. Judging that flight to Canada was a wiser choice that waiting for punishment at the hands of the army, Chief Joseph and 800 Nez Perce fled eastward. They crossed Idaho and Montana, alternately eluding and fighting the army (most notably at the battle of the Big Hole in western Montana) before being apprehended within miles of the Canadian border. The Wallowa Nez Perce were initially removed to Indian Territory, now Oklahoma, before being allowed to return to the Colville Reservation in Washington. The Idaho Nez Perce remain on the Lapwai Reservation in Idaho. ■

is buried at a beautiful site at the north end of the lake.

Now a small resort community, Wallowa Lake has a sizable huddle of motels, B&Bs, guest lodges and restaurants. Write to the Wallowa Lake Tourist Committee, PO Box 853, Joseph, OR 97846, for information.

### Wallowa Lake State Park

Reckoned to be one of the most beautiful state parks in the western USA, Wallowa Lake State Park (☎ 432-4185) is the center of activities at the south end of Wallowa Lake. A swimming beach, boat launches and rentals and most modern facilities are offered.

### Mount Howard Gondola

The gondola (☎ 432-5331) leaves from Wallowa Lake and climbs 3200 feet to the top of 8200-foot Mt Howard; the tramway is the both the steepest and longest in North America. The ride is thrilling enough, but the real rewards are the alpine hikes around Mt Howard's summit, with views onto Hells Canyon, the Wallowas and Idaho's Seven Devils. The tramway operates from 10 am to 4 pm daily June to Labor Day, weekends only in May and September; tickets are $12 for adults, $10 for seniors and $6 for children.

### Eagle Cap Wilderness Area

This is, at 715 sq miles, Oregon's largest wilderness area. Glacier-ripped valleys, high mountain lakes and marble peaks are some of the rewards that long-distance hikers find on overnight treks; there are few hiking destinations that readily suit the schedules of day hikers.

A number of trailheads lead into Eagle Cap Wilderness from the south end of Wallowa Lake. One of the most popular hikes from here is the six-mile one-way hike to **Aneroid Lake,** where the remains of a cabin settlement adds to the alpine lake's mystique. Other day hikes from Wallowa Lake simply require hiking up trails until lunch, and then returning. From the upper Lostine Valley or from USFS Rd 39's Sheep Creek Summit there is easier day-hike access to the Eagle Cap's high country. The Wallowa-Whitman National Forest office (☎ 426-3519) in Enterprise has more information.

Another option is **horse** or **llama pack trips**. Eagle Cap Wilderness Pack Station, (☎ 432-4145), 59761 Wallowa Lake Hwy, offers a variety of horseback options. For llama excursions contact Hurricane Creek Llama Treks (☎ 432-4455).

### Jazz at the Lake

The Jazz at the Lake festival (☎ 962-3593), the middle weekend of July, features regional acts in a picnic setting.

### Places to Stay

*Wallowa Lake State Park* (☎ 432-8855) offers multitudes of camping sites complete with flush toilets and showers. Set in a grove of ponderosa pines and cottonwoods, sites can fill up on weekends in good weather. Wallowa Lake is one of 13 state parks that allow reservations, which are a good idea during the summer. Campsites without/with hook-ups are $15/17 nightly; it's open April to October.

**B&Bs** Somewhat set apart from the amusement-park aspect of Wallowa Lake is *Tamarack Pines Inn B&B* (☎ 432-2920), 60073 Wallowa Lake Hwy. Accommodations for two people cost $63 to $75, depending upon whether you stay in Tammy, Heidi, Michele or Lynn's room.

**Hotels** *Historic Wallowa Lake Lodge* (☎ 432-9821), Rte 1 Box 320, is a fine-looking old hotel on the shores of the lake, with a beautiful fireplace-dominated lobby, but tiny rooms. Also available are lakeside cabins. Lodging ranges from $50 to $115. *Matterhorn Swiss Village* (☎ 432-4071), 59950 Wallowa Lake Hwy, offers chalet-like cabins starting at $45. Rates increase during the summer, during which time lodgers may be expected to stay a minimum of five nights. *Eagle Cap Chalets* (☎ 432-4704), 59879 Wallowa Lake Hwy, offers accommodations ranging from cabins and condos to a honeymoon suite;

room rates run from $46 to $75. *Flying Arrow Resort* (☎ 432-2951), 59782 Wallowa Lake Hwy, features cabins and a pool. Like the Matterhorn, rates are seasonal, and lodgers may be required to stay a minimum number of nights. Double-occupancy cabins start at $60.

### Places to Eat

Most food options at Wallowa Lake would be more properly designated as concessions than dining, with the following exceptions. The dining room at the *Wallowa Lake Lodge* (☎ 432-9821), 60060 Wallowa Lake Hwy, retains the charm of another era, and the food aspires to cuisine with steak, salmon and chicken leading the menu. Most dishes are in the $12 range. For very good German and Hungarian specialties, go to *Vali's Alpine Deli & Restaurant* (☎ 432-5691), 59811 Wallowa Lake Hwy. There's only one meal (in the $10 range) on the menu per day: what the chef cooks up is what you get. Call ahead to find out what's cooking, and for reservations: this is a very popular restaurant.

### WALLOWA MOUNTAIN LOOP RD

From Joseph, paved USFS Rd 39 climbs up onto Sheep Creek Summit, east of the Wallowas' main peaks. Here, mountain bikers and skiers, each in their own season, share dominion. The road then winds along the middle reaches of the lovely Imnaha River, and pushes over another ridge to arrive at Hwy 86, midway between Halfway and Copperfield, on the southern side of the Wallowas.

While landscapes along the road are pleasing enough, the real benefit of USFS Rd 39 is that it links the northern and southern halves of the Wallowas, travel between which would otherwise require hundreds of miles of driving.

From Ollokot Campground, USFS Rd 3960 follows the Imnaha River west up to trailheads into the Eagle Cap Wilderness. Follow this road to find a number of remote riverside campgrounds.

This loop also gives access to the only paved viewpoint onto Hells Canyon. At

OREGON

Hells Canyon Overlook, about two miles off USFS Rd 39 on USFS Rd 3965, a vista point looks into the canyon (no glimpses of the river, however), with interpretive displays, picnic tables and toilets.

USFS Rd 39 is closed in winter due to snow. Call ahead to the USFS office (☎ 426-4978) in Enterprise in early spring or late fall to find out if the road is open. It's 65 miles between Joseph and Halfway along this route. There are no gas stations on these routes, and no services. Plan your trip accordingly.

## GRANDE RONDE CANYON COUNTRY

While the eye is drawn naturally upwards to the Wallowas, around here mountains are only half the story. Rivers rushing to meet the Snake River in its mile-deep Hells Canyon are themselves obliged to carve massive canyons. The following day-trip from Enterprise or Joseph explores remote and beautiful river canyons. This drive may be a good alternative for those for whom the terror-producing drive up single-lane roads to Hat Point above Hells Canyon is simply too heart-stopping.

North of Enterprise, Hwy 3 (which becomes WA Hwy 129) heads off toward Lewiston, ID across high plateaus striped with forests and meadows. At the Joseph Canyon Overlook, there's a vista over Joseph Creek. The land drops away 2000 feet in a dizzying series of ledges, revealing successive flows of lava. It's as if someone had mined inverted ziggurats from the earth.

Barely across the Washington state line the road plunges down into the massive 3000-foot-deep Grande Ronde Canyon. The magnitude of this gash in the earth imparts a real sense of insignificance: nothing leading up to this chasm from either side prepares the traveler for the immensity of the scene. Cross the Grande Ronde and climb up switchback after switchback to the north side of the gorge. Fields Spring State Park & Campground, on the northern rim of the canyon, offers picnicking and short hiking trails to more canyon vistas from Puffer Butte.

For a loop trip, return to the Grande Ronde bridge and turn west (near the roadhouse at Boggan's Oasis) toward Troy. A good graveled road follows the Grande Ronde River back into Oregon beneath towering, forested cliffs. Troy lies at a curve in the river, literally in the middle of nowhere, a tiny community dominated by a small fishing lodge. The log-built *Shilo Inn Lodge* (☎ 828-7741), welcomes anglers and campers with good food, drinks, and lodging in a captivatingly remote setting. Gravel roads from Troy give access to trails leading into the canyons of the Wenaha-Tucannon Wilderness Area.

Roads lead back to Hwy 3 via Flora, or south to the town of Wallowa via Maxville. Both routes include steep climbs on good gravel roads.

## THE SOUTHERN WALLOWAS

Ringing the Wallowa Mountains to the south is the Powder River valley. Just as beautiful and just as handy to mountain recreation, the little towns of Richland and Halfway are much less hyped and overrun than their counterparts to the north. Additionally, Hwy 86, which follows the Powder River from near Baker City, leads to Oregon's only riverside access to Hells Canyon.

### Orientation & Information

Richland is 40 miles from Baker City; it's an additional 30 miles to Copperfield on Hwy 86, on the Snake River. Hells Canyon boat trips begin below the Hells Canyon Dam; roads to the boat landing cross onto and follow the Idaho side of the Snake River 28 miles before crossing over the dam's spillway back into Oregon.

The Hells Canyon Chamber of Commerce (☎ 742-5772), 160 S Main St, Halfway, OR 97834, has information on the southern Wallowa region.

### Richland

Richland (population 170) is an idyllic little town surrounded by old dairy farms at the base of the Wallowas. It's also near water recreation at Hewitt Park on the Snake River's Brownlee Reservoir.

For travelers without the time or the nerve to explore the Snake River's more spectacular northern gorge, a compelling enough view of the river is gained by following a secondary road from Richland toward Huntington (follow 1st St). A quick climb up good roads affords a view onto the Snake and the canyon it's beginning to cut.

**Hewitt Park** (☎ 893-6147) is on the Powder River, which here is backed up by the Snake's Brownlee Reservoir. It's a pleasant park that offers camping ($8), swimming and fishing. Hewitt Park is two miles east of Richland off Hwy 86.

**Places to Stay & Eat** *Eagle Valley RV Park* (☎ 893-6161), a quarter-mile east on Hwy 86, is an alternative to Hewitt Park for campers. The clean and new *Hitching Post Motel* (☎ 893-6176), on Main St, is Richland's only lodging; it's two hours from the jet boats at Hells Canyon Dam; single/doubles are $38/40.

The *Longbranch Restaurant & Saloon* (☎ 893-6169) serves good food, which is offered in bounty, with delicious fried bread. The *Shorthorn Heifer Restaurant & Bar* (☎ 893-6122), at the corner of 2nd and Main Sts, is the place for ample breakfasts designed for hard-working ranch hands.

### Halfway

Halfway (population 320) is as close to a tourist town as there is in the southern Wallowas, though don't come looking for galleries or boutiques; Halfway is the center of a pleasant little farm community. The beautiful green valley is filled with old barns and hayfields; as in the northern Wallowas, the meadows suddenly turn perpendicular and rise to mountain peaks.

Halfway does offer a pleasant restaurant and two well-loved B&Bs. Follow USFS Rd 413 eight miles up to ghostly Cornucopia (delightful names seem endemic to the Wallowas) for access to recreation in the Eagle Cap Wilderness Area.

The Pine Ranger Station (☎ 742-7511) is one mile south of Halfway at Pine. Address

queries to General Delivery, Halfway, OR 97834.

**Baker County Fair** Halfway comes alive for this annual fair, complete with rodeo, stock show and carnival. The fair is held the first weekend of September at the fairgrounds, a mile east on Hwy 86, and then south on Fairgrounds Rd.

**Places to Stay & Eat** The *Halfway Motel* (☎ 742-5722), 170 S Main St, offers lodgings in two different buildings, a traditional motel and a complex of trailer houses. Rooms range between $35 to $45. There's a lot more charm at the *Birch Leaf Farm B&B* (☎ 742-2990), a rural Victorian farmhouse turned country inn; rooms begin at $65. Take USFS Rd 413 north; at Jimtown Store take the east fork in the road. The *Clear Creek Farm B&B* (☎ 742-2238), four miles north of Halfway on E Pine Rd, offers seclusion, a pond for swimming and rooms for $55.

The favorite spot for dining is *Amador's* (☎ 742-2025), 166 N Main St, tucked into an abandoned church and is appropriately alcohol free. The menu is small but well chosen; entrees like chicken tarragon go for $11. Forego the restrained atmosphere for standard offerings at the *Stockman's Cafe & Lounge* (☎ 742-2301) on Main St.

# Hells Canyon

The Snake River has been flowing through Hells Canyon for only about 13 million years. In fact, because the Snake River has cut so much rock from the Wallowa and Seven Devils ranges, the mountains and valleys in the region are rising. Such action makes the land mass much lighter than it once was. Consequently, the land buoys upward, which forces the Snake to dig its canyon ever deeper. Today, the mighty Snake River hurtles down its narrow, 6500-foot-deep Hells Canyon, losing 1300 feet of elevation between Farewell Bend and Lewiston, ID – a distance of just 70 miles.

On the plateaus edging Hells Canyon, wildflower displays peak in June, when Indian paintbrush, lupines and yellow balsamroot enliven the cliff edges. Ponderosa pines and brushy juniper grow in protected swales. Up here, there's about 25 inches of rainfall a year. However, 5500 feet down in the canyon, only 10 inches fall. Prickly pear cactus and short-seasoned grasses eke out an existence on the thin soils along the canyon floors.

Nez Perce legend had it that Coyote, the trickster figure of Native American lore, dug Hells Canyon with a stick to protect the tribe from the Seven Devils. The strategy would seem to have worked, for the Seven Devils Mountains remain firmly rooted on the Idaho side of the Snake River.

Cliff-dwelling bighorn sheep and mountain goats live along the canyon walls. Elk and mule deer are common, and black bears and mountain lions also haunt side valleys. Along the river's edge are found blue herons, various ducks and geese, and – on grassy embankments – sage grouse. Floating on updrafts are hawks, and bald and golden eagles. Rattlesnakes are also common.

For such a forlorn and severe landscape, there's a long and rich human history in Hells Canyon. Prehistoric Indians lived along the Snake River throughout the canyon, as evinced by abundant pictographs, petroglyphs and pit-dwellings. The Nez Perce and Shoshone battled for dominance along this stretch of the Snake, with the Nez Perce defeating their rivals at Battle Creek.

Relics of the mining era, from the 1860s to 1920s, are found throughout the canyon, and tumbled-down shacks remain from the unlikely settlement attempts of turn-of-the-century homesteaders.

The Hells Canyon National Wilderness (☎ 426-4978) can be contacted at PO Box 490, Enterprise, OR 97828. There's also an information center at the Hells Canyon Dam (☎ 785-3395).

## HELLS CANYON WILDERNESS AREA

This wilderness area is part of the larger Hells Canyon Recreation Area, and takes in portions of three national forests and two states. Containing 297 sq miles in Oregon and Idaho, this roadless wilderness flanks the river from above Hells Canyon Dam to Dug Bar, near the mouth of the Imnaha River. Here is where Hells Canyon cuts a trench in the earth nearly 8000 feet deep, making it the deepest canyon in North America and the deepest river gorge in the world.

Most of the terrain is made up of precipitous rock wall, and steep, slot-like side valleys. Also included in the wilderness is Idaho's rugged Seven Devils Mountains, a ring of monumental peaks surrounding a remote lake basin (see Riggins, ID).

The little campground community of Copperfield is a crossroads of activity for recreation on the Snake. Highway 71 from Cambridge, ID, drops into the Snake River valley here, forming this small oasis of

---

### Massacre at Hells Canyon

One of Oregon's worst massacres happened in Hells Canyon. Throughout the West, immigrant Chinese sought work and fortune in restless gold camps, frequently reworking spent mine tailings for the traces of gold that they might still hold. In 1887, a group of Chinese were working a sandbar just south of the mouth of the Imnaha. A group of lawless cowboys – there were many in the Hells Canyon area at the time – had just crossed the Snake River from Idaho, and came across the Chinese encampment. They robbed the miners of their gold and, in the process, shot and killed all the Chinese in the camp. For their trouble, the killers made off with less than $5000 in gold dust.

The estimate of Chinese killed in the execution/robbery ranges between 10 and 34. The six men were eventually indicted and tried in Enterprise in 1887, but were acquitted by their jury. ■

OREGON

accessibility in Hells Canyon. Just about anyone who fishes, boats or hikes in Hells Canyon comes through here.

The real action is below Hells Canyon Dam, 28 miles north (downriver) from Copperfield. The canyon gets more and more precipitous, until only towering rock walls channel the river's surging current. The dam briefly pools the Snake in a slack-water reservoir, before releasing the river to boil down the mile-deep canyon. Between here and Lewiston, ID, 70 miles away, the Snake drops 1300 feet in elevation, creating wild scenery and fear-producing river rapids which attract sang-froid jet boat tourists, wild-eyed rafting enthusiasts, and hearty long-distance hikers.

## HAT POINT

Not surprisingly, Hells Canyon is a difficult place to visit. South of the Wallowas there is river access from below Copperfield. But the classic view of the river is from high above the canyon, on the Oregon side, from a lookout tower near Hat Point.

The view from the top is not the only part of this trip that will take your breath away. The road upward from Imnaha, especially the first five miles, will test the nerves of any driver or passenger. There are other, less-terrifying views over this tortuous landscape, but no other affords views onto the Snake River.

To reach Hat Point, follow Hwy 350 to the little community of Imnaha. From here, a steep but very narrow graveled road climbs up the Imnaha River canyon. If you are not accustomed to driving on challenging mountain roads, or have experienced anything close to vertigo, this road will be a very unpleasant experience. There are no guardrails along the first five miles of this single-lane road, and very few turnouts. Recent road work has improved the quality of the road bed, but not its pitch or its width. Don't even think about taking a trailer up.

Once you gain the ridge top, however, the road travels gingerly through forest and meadows to Hat Point to end at a fire tower; scramble to the top and peek down onto the Snake River, a roilsome thread of water a mile below.

The panorama from this viewpoint is almost beyond expressing: from meadows covered in wildflowers, an enormous gash in the earth splits open and drops down near-vertical cliffs. On each side of the canyon, mountains reach toward 10,000 feet. Across the canyon are the Seven Devils, a cluster of rugged peaks in Idaho. Behind are the towering, glacier-bit pinnacles of the Wallowas. There's a real sense of primordiality here, of vastness and omniscience.

It's 23 miles from Imnaha to Hat Point along USFS Rd 4240; allow at least two hours each way for the journey. The road is closed during winter; it's generally open from late May till snowfall. Call the Hells Canyon National Recreation office in Enterprise (☎ 426-4978) if you have questions about road conditions or passability.

## Hiking & Camping

From the Hat Point viewpoint, a hiking trail edges off the side of the canyon; it's a steep four miles to another vista from the top of the river cliffs. From this viewpoint, it's another four miles down to the river itself.

At the cliff-top viewpoint, long-distance hikers can join the High Trail, which angles along the canyon walls north to Dug Bar. All these trails will mightily test your endurance if you're not in good shape.

There are a few primitive campsites at Hat Point. The closest facilities are in Joseph.

## Imnaha River Valley

The Imnaha River digs a parallel canyon just to the west of Hells Canyon that would be of great interest – if it weren't for the grandeur of its neighbor. But the Imnaha valley offers good roads, fishing access and beautiful pastoral scenery in addition to the region's mandatory vertical cliff faces.

The Imnaha River Rd (USFS Rd 3955) follows this lovely narrow valley between the tiny hamlet of Imnaha and the junction of USFS Rd 39. The lower valley (the northern end) is very dramatic, as the river

OREGON

cuts more and more deeply through stair-stepped lava formations. The upper valley (going south) is bucolic, with meadows and old farmhouses flanking the rushing river.

North of Imnaha gravel roads continue for 20 miles to Imnaha Bridge; from there to the Snake River confluence the road is suitable only for off-road vehicles.

From Imnaha Bridge, several **hiking** trails begin. The Imnaha River Trail follows the trenching, furiously churning Imnaha River to its confluence with the Snake. The Nee-Me-Poo Trail, which follows the path of Chief Joseph and the Nez Perce through three states, begins just north of the bridge, and in 3.5 miles climbs to a view point over the Snake.

There are public fishing access points along the length of the river. The USFS maintains two convenient and handsome campgrounds at the southern end of the canyon. Ollokot and Blackhorse campgrounds are right on the river; near the junction of USFS Rd 39.

## HIKING
There are long-distance, riverside trails on both the Oregon and Idaho shores of the Snake River, but reaching them is a challenge. The rugged cliffs along the Hell's Canyon Dam are too steep for hiking trails, although a short, mile-long trail from the jet boat launch area does pick its way down the Oregon side before ending precipitously. For longer hikes, you will need to start from trailheads along the ridges, and hike down to the river. Hat Point is a good place to drop onto the Oregon Snake River Trail, on the river's western edge. On the Idaho side, there's road access to the river at Pittsburgh Landing, near White Bird, ID. From here, hikers can walk back up into the wilderness area along the Idaho Snake River Trail. It's a good idea to talk to rangers before setting out, as this is extremely remote and challenging wilderness.

## RAFTING & JET BOAT TOURS
By far the easiest way to see Hells Canyon is on a jet boat tour. These turbine-powered, flat-bottomed boats are able to maneuver shallow water and rapids, making them ideal to skim along the torrents of the Snake River, even though they are also very noisy and annoying if you aren't among the passengers.

From the landing just below Hells Canyon Dam, Hells Canyon Adventures, Inc (☎ 785-3352, (800) 422-3568) offers jet boat tours daily from Memorial Day weekend to the end of September. They offer several different tour options: two-hour afternoon excursions, starting at 2 pm and costing $25; the 10 am three-hour excursion (which includes lunch) for $30 a person, and an all-day, $50 tour leaving at 9 am which runs all the principal rapids of the canyon, and includes lunch and a stop at the Kirkwood Ranch Museum. For all tours, children under 12 are half price. Hells Canyon Excursion offer other tours, including float trips and fishing charters. Reservations are required.

Another local outfitter specializes in fishing and white-water raft trips. Canyon Outfitters (☎ 742-4110), offers three or four-day rafting and fishing trips from April to October. Included in the excursion price ($645 or $795) is a night's lodging and breakfast in Halfway, and all meals for the trip. At the end of the trip, jet boats pick up floaters and anglers and return them to Hells Canyon Dam, eliminating the need for lengthy shuttle trips on dodgy roads.

Both outfitters are licensed by the USFS; if you plan to raft the Snake River on your own, you'll need a permit from the Hells Canyon Wilderness office in Enterprise. This is not a river for novices.

## PLACES TO STAY & EAT
Just below Oxbow Dam, where Pine Creek joins the Snake River at the beginning of Hells Canyon, is the vibrantly green and hospitable *Copperfield Campground* (☎ 785-3323) which provides tenting ($1) and RV sites ($3) along the river; there are showers and toilets, and also a playground and picnic area. The *Hells Canyon Inn* (☎ 785-3393), also in Copperfield, provides light meals.

Five miles downriver on the road to Hells

Canyon Dam is *Hells Canyon Campground*. It's right on the river and less crowded than Copperfield. Kleinschmidt Grade, a five-mile long, steep and narrow gravel road climbs up a precipitous grade to Cuprum, ID from the campground. Take note that while some road maps show the grade leaving from Copperfield it actually begins at Hells Canyon Campground.

If you want a roof you'll have to venture back to Halfway, Richland or Cambridge, ID.

# John Day Country

Oregon rivers take erosion seriously. And none more so than the John Day River, a canyon-cutter almost from its inception. This river gives its name to the enormous swath of land it drains in the center of Oregon, and also to the John Day Fossil Beds, three national monuments where erosion has exposed spectacular formations rich in the remains of prehistoric life.

This rough and underpopulated region is one of the least visited parts of the state, and undeservedly so. The colorful fossil-bed parks, the dramatic canyons, and the rushing river itself make the John Day area a worthwhile side trip.

The reason that you visit this part of

---

**Who was John Day?**
Named for an early frontiersman, John Day is so common a label in this part of the state as to be all-purpose; a river, two towns, a dam, a series of parks were all named for a man who never visited the area. As a trapper for the Pacific Fur Company, John Day was floating down the Columbia River with a companion when the small party was ambushed, robbed and stripped by hostile Cayuse Indians at the mouth of the Mau Hau River. The two survived the ordeal and returned to safety in Astoria. Thereafter, the river was named for the ill-starred John Day. ∎

---

Oregon is that its beauty is almost unnervingly awesome – and that it is utterly remote. The town of John Day, at the eastern edge of the region, provides the most complete tourist amenities. Outside of John Day, most small towns usually have a single motel. Don't expect luxury; in fact, if there was any part of a trip through Oregon where you would consider a night or two of camping, this might be it. Roll out the sleeping bags, watch the stars and listen to the howls of coyotes.

## ORIENTATION
The town of John Day is at the eastern edge of the river basin that bears the same name; however, many of the sights associated with the John Day River are found further west, between Dayville and Service Creek. The Sheep Rock Unit, the closest, is 41 miles east on Hwy 26 and Hwy 19; the most distant, the Clarno Unit, is over 120 miles west. Information on the area is available in John Day.

## RAFTING
From Clarno Bridge to Cottonwood Bridge, a distance of 70 miles, the John Day River cuts a deep canyon through basaltic lava flows on its way to the Columbia River. No roads reach the canyon here; along the river are the remains of homesteads, Native American petroglyphs and pristine wildlife habitat.

This lower portion of the John Day River is popular with river rafters, as the scenery is awe-inspiring and the river provides only a few steep chutes. Besides, it's the only way to get there. There are several outfitters that offer guided trips down the John Day River; most float trips through this roadless area take four days. For representative prices contact the CJ Lodge (☎ 395-2404) in Maupin.

If you feel adventurous and have the experience, you can rent a raft and plan your own trip; some rapids are class III to IV, so it's not for novices. John Day River Outfitters (☎ 575-2386) in John Day, is one area rental shop. If you plan a trip down the John Day, be sure to contact the BLM office (☎ 447-4115), PO Box 550, Prineville, OR 97754, for maps of rapids and further information; they can also provide you with more names of outfitters.

### GETTING THERE & AWAY

It's not easy to get to John Day on public transport, and once you get to the town, you can't get much further. You'll need a vehicle or bicycle to visit any of the areas of interest. There are no car rentals in the area, so plan ahead.

The People Mover (☎ 575-2370) offers once-daily bus service between Prineville and Prairie City, with stops in John Day and Mitchell.

### JOHN DAY

The town of John Day (population 1900) strings along a narrow passage of the John Day River valley, at the confluence of gold-rich Canyon Creek. For a community with a long history and a rich heritage drawing on mining, ranching and logging, John Day is an oddly colorless and hermetic place to visit. There's little left from the glory days, and what has replaced it is grimly utilitarian. The pervasive Christian sloganeering in shop windows doesn't add to the cheer, but rather the contrary.

#### Orientation & Information

John Day is 264 miles east of Portland on Hwy 26 and 94 miles southwest of Baker City. It's the only town of consequence in this part of Oregon. Luckily there are decent amenities for travelers.

The Grant County Chamber of Commerce (☎ 575-0547) is at 281 W Main St, John Day, OR 97845. The administrative headquarters of the John Day Fossil Beds (☎ 575-0721) are also in John Day, at 410 W Main St. The supervisor's office of the Malheur National Forest (☎ 575-1731) is at 139 NE Dayton St. The Long Creek & Bear Valley Ranger Station (☎ 575-2110) is at 528 E Main St.

The post office (☎ 575-1897) is at 151 W Canyon Blvd, and the Blue Mountain Hospital (☎ 575-1311), is at 170 Ford Rd.

### Kam Wah Chung & Co Museum

This tiny stone building (☎ 575-0028), built in 1866, served as an apothecary for Ing Hay, a Chinese herbalist and doctor. During the 1880s, the structure served as community center, temple, pharmacy, general store and opium den for the population of Chinese that came to John Day to rework mine tailings. Ing Hay's reputation as a healer was wide-spread; many White miners availed themselves of his lore.

The museum gives a unique look into the day-to-day life of the Chinese in the mining West, and commemorates an otherwise ignored facet of frontier history. Have a look into the old bunkroom-cum-opium den and note the beams blackened from opium smoke.

The museum is just off Hwy 26 at the city park, and is open from 9 am to noon and 1 to 5 pm, Monday to Thursday, closed Friday, and from 1 to 5 pm Saturday and Sunday, May to October only. Admission is $2.

### Grant County Historical Museum

This community museum (☎ 575-0721) features relics of a Gold Rush town, including a mineral display, assay equipment and an 1865 miner's cabin (once owned by frontier poet Joaquin Miller); there's also a number of old pianos and organs. The museum is on Hwy 395 in Canyon City and is open from 9:30 am to 4:30 pm, Monday to Saturday, 1 to 5 pm Sunday, June to September. Admission is $2 for adults, $1 for teens and seniors, and 50c for children ages six to 12.

### Places to Stay

**Camping** The best place to camp is at *Clyde Holliday State Park* (☎ 575-2773), a streamside park six miles west of town. There are showers and flush toilets; fees start at $8. The *J Bar L* (☎ 575-1123), 15 miles south of John Day on Hwy 395, was formerly a hot springs and guest ranch; it now has RV and tent sites.

**Hotels** Hundreds of miles from anywhere, the town has a captive audience, and lodgings tend to be eagerly sought and rather expensive. On any given night, all rooms in John Day may be rented. Call ahead for reservations. For a relatively inexpensive motel, try the *Budget 8 Motel* (☎ 575-2155), 711 W Main St; single/double rooms are $32/37. The *Sunset Inn* (☎ 575-1462) 390 W Main St, is a modern unit with a pool and restaurant in the complex for $38/40. The *Dreamers Lodge*, (☎ 575-0526), 144 N Canyon Blvd, is a pleasant and popular motel with kitchenettes; rates are $40/44. For a little more room, try the suite-type rooms at the *Best Western Inn* (☎ 575-1700), 315 W Main St; singles/doubles go for $48/52.

**Guest Ranches** Put on your cowboy boots and stay at the *Ponderosa Cattle Company Guest Ranch* (☎ 542-2403, (800) 331-1012), 32 miles south of John Day on Hwy 395. This 187-sq-mile ranch in the Sylvies Valley dates back to the 1860s, though the guest-ranch lodge and eight cabins are only a few years old. Activities include fishing, horseback riding, wildlife viewing and working alongside the hired hands. During high season (here, it's called 'cowboy season') – between May and October – a four-day minimum stay is required; room, board and unlimited riding for four days is $700; a week-long package costs $1250. Contact the ranch at HC 30 Box 190, Seneca, OR 97873.

### Places to Eat

For breakfast or light meals, go to the *Mother Lode Restaurant* (☎ 575-2714), 241 W Main St; it's where the locals start their day. Steak is the specialty at the *Grubsteak Mining Co* (☎ 575-1970), 149 E Main; $12 buys you a rib steak dinner.

The *Apricot Tree* (☎ 575-1408) is one mile west of town on Hwy 26, in a converted Victorian home; it's the area's only fine-dining establishment, with dishes like beef stroganoff or chicken Kiev for $15. The lodge restaurant at *Ponderosa Cattle Company Guest Ranch* (☎ 542-2403, (800) 331-1012), is open to non-guests for evening meals; reservations are requested.

### Getting There & Away

The *People Mover* bus (☎ 575-2370) between Prineville and Prairie City stops daily in John Day. Catch the bus at 409 NW Bridge St.

## PRAIRIE CITY

This small, attractive town (population 1145) was born of the Gold Rush. On nearby Dixie Creek, prospectors found gold in 1862. A mining camp was built on the steep slopes of the gold-rich drainage, but after heavy rains, the original buildings began to slide down the hillside. Prairie City, whose name is only accurately descriptive when compared to the original, gradually listing settlement, was established nearer to the valley floor, and became the trading town for the upper valley.

Prairie City was the western terminus of the Sumpter Valley Railroad, a narrow gauge line completed in 1910 that carried goods and passengers to and from Baker City. The line served to create a market for the lumber from the pine forests of the western Blue Mountains. The line remained operational until 1946.

Forest products remain big business here, as witnessed by the large lumber mill just west of town.

### Information

The Malheur National Forest Ranger Station (☎ 820-3311), PO Box 156, Prairie City, OR 97896, has recreational information. The Grant County Chamber of Commerce in John Day can answer questions about Prairie City.

### DeWitt Museum

A monument to Prairie City's varied past, the museum (☎ 820-3598) just across the John Day River on Bridge St in Depot Park, is housed in the turn-of-the-century train depot, which also contains the station master's apartment. Exhibits on the Sumpter Valley Railroad fill the waiting rooms, while household goods recreate life upstairs in the private quarters. It's an affable mix of this and that and makes a good detour for a picnic or saunter. It's open from 10 am to 3 pm, Thursday to Saturday, May to October; admission is $2.

### Places to Stay & Eat

The city maintains a nice, shady campground right on the John Day River at Depot Park, next door to the museum. Fees range from $9 to $13. For more secluded campsites, head south to the Strawberry Mountains (see below).

Oddly, Prairie City is bereft of a decent motel. If you don't want to camp, try out a local ranch B&B called *B&B by the River* (☎ 820-4470). About 2.5 miles east of Prairie City, right on the John Day River, fishing, hunting and hiking are recreational options. As this is a working ranch, you can join the ranch hands, or simply enjoy the home-grown eggs and meat. Rooms are $50 a night.

Head to *The Bakery* (☎ 820-3674), 234 NW Front St, for muffins and espresso. The *Little Diner* (☎ 820-4353), 142 NW Front St, is like many things in Prairie City – self-explanatory. *Ferdinand's* (☎ 820-9359), 128 Front St, pours Portland microbrews and serves pizza in the evenings. This old storefront used to be a meat market; note the carved stone bull's head above the door. For a steak dinner, go to *Branding Iron* (☎ 820-9792) on the corner of Front and Johnson Sts.

### AROUND PRAIRIE CITY
#### Strawberry Mountain Wilderness Area

This 107-sq-mile wilderness contains a range of 15-million-year-old volcanoes. After smothering nearby valleys in thick basalt flows, the peaks of the Strawberry Mountains were incised by glaciers during the ice ages, leaving them razor-edged. Eventually, retreating glaciers created lake basins beneath these craggy ridges.

Named for the wild strawberries that thrive on the mountain slopes, the Strawberry Range is covered with ponderosa and lodgepole pines. On the southern slopes of the wilderness, there are isolated stands of mature forest. In the wildflower meadows at Wildcat Basin, look for Indian paint-

brush and wild iris. Bighorn sheep, reintroduced here after they were hunted out by early miners, are often seen along the ridges at Sheep Rock. Black bears and mountain lions have also made a comeback in the wilderness.

The Strawberry Mountains contain deceptively high country for eastern Oregon: much of the wilderness is above 6,000 feet, and the highest peak – Strawberry Mountain – rises to 9038 feet.

**Hiking** A popular, 2.5-mile roundtrip dayhike winds up a steep valley to **Strawberry Lake**, nestled beneath 9000-foot-high peaks. If there's time to go a mile further, continue past the lake to **Strawberry Falls**. To reach the trailhead, turn south at Canyon City, and follow signs; it's 11 miles to the trailhead.

Circle around to the south side of the wilderness area on Hwy 14 and paved USFS Rds 65 and 16, past old ponderosa pines and wide meadows, to find more trails. Hike into **High Lake Basin**, 2.6 miles roundtrip, from a trailhead high up the mountainside. From USFS Rd 16, turn on USFS Rd 1640 toward Indian Springs Campground. The trailhead is 11 miles up a steep graveled road.

**Places to Stay** Strawberry Mountain Wilderness Area has a number of good campgrounds. The most convenient for travelers will be *McNaughton Springs*, eight miles south of Prairie City on the Strawberry Lake Road, or *Trout Farm*, in a lovely streamside spot on USFS Rd 14 south of Prairie City.

### Middle & North Forks

North of John Day and Prairie City are the valleys of the Middle and North Forks of the John Day River, which rise in the west slopes of the Blue Mountains. These steep valleys shared the early mining history of the region, with boomtowns like Galena and Susanville, along the Middle Fork, now left to ghostly inhabitants. Explore these old mining town from USFS Rds 18 and 58, north from Prairie City (follow signs for Susanville), or turn onto USFS Rd 20 at Austin to follow the Middle Fork all the way to Hwy 395.

In 1984 the mighty canyon of the North Fork John Day River's upper reaches was designated as a wilderness area. The centerpiece of the 190-sq-mile **North Fork John Day Wilderness Area** is the 25-mile North Fork John Day National Recreation Trail which follows the river, beginning at North Fork John Day Campground near Granite and ending at Big Creek Campground along USFS Rd 52.

Other attractions of the wilderness include tableaus of steep canyons leaning over a swift, narrow river; go snooping around in old miners' cabins and watch for wildlife, which is plentiful here. Elk are especially abundant – over 50,000 head live in the area.

For information contact the North Fork John Day Ranger District (☎ 427-3231) in Ukiah.

## JOHN DAY FOSSIL BEDS NATIONAL MONUMENT

Interesting geology and spectacular scenery don't always occur together. But in the John Day fossil country, the two form an amazing team. At Picture Gorge, the John Day River rips through an immense lava flow and begins digging its trench to the Columbia River. The countryside becomes drier, with sagebrush replacing pine forests. Along the canyon walls, bluffs of startling color appear, eroded into bizarre spires and crenelations.

### Orientation & Information

The national monument includes 22 sq miles at three different sites, the Sheep Rock, Clarno and Painted Hills units. Each site has hiking trails and interpretive displays. Sheep Rock has the only staffed visitors center. To visit all the units in one day requires quite a bit of driving, as over 100 miles separate the fossil beds.

The John Day Fossil Beds National Monument Headquarters (☎ 575-0721) are located at 420 W Main St, John Day. There is also a visitors center at the Sheep Rock Unit.

### Sheep Rock Unit

The Sheep Rock Unit on the John Day River consists of two different fossil beds, a river canyon and the Cant Ranch House Visitors Center (☎ 987-2333). This handsome 1917 ranch house is part fossil display, part pioneer museum and part paleontology laboratory.

Some of the monument's important

---

**A Plant & Animal Pompeii**

Within the soft rocks and crumbly soils of John Day country reposes one of the greatest collections of fossils in the world. Discovered in the 1860s by clergyman and geologist Thomas Condon, these fossil beds were laid down between 40 and 25 million years ago, when this area was a coastal plain with a tropical climate. Roaming the forests were saber-toothed tigers, pint-sized horses, bear-dogs and other early mammals.

Then, the climate and geology of the region began to change. A period of extensive volcanism of an almost unbelievable scale commenced, producing clouds of ash and mudflows that buried entire ecosystems in a matter of hours, like a plant and animal Pompeii, trapping unfortunate Eocene and Miocene-era denizens. The cycle recurred over millennia: life would return to the area, and again be buried beneath the residue of distant eruptions. Finally, the soft, easily eroded ash and mud that formed these beds – thousands of feet deep in some areas – was covered with several layers of molten ash and lava, which formed a resistant coating over the old mudflows. Only the Ochoco, Blue and Wallowa mountains bobbed above the lava.

Sealed beneath layers of rock were the old marsh and meadow lands – now known as the John Day Fossil Beds National Monument – awaiting the mightily erosive John Day River to unlock their story. Fossils of over a hundred different animal species have been found in the monument. ■

## Bhagwan Shree Rajneesh

Out here, in a barren desert canyon, occurred one of Oregon's most interesting and peculiar episodes.

The religion of Bhagwan Shree Rajneesh has most commonly been described as a mix of Eastern religion and pop psychology. Taoism, Hinduism, Tranticism, Buddhism, Zen, Sufism and even Christian theologies have contributed to the Bhagwan's practices and preachings. Since the beginning of his career as a religious figure in his native India in the early 1970s, Rajneesh's following has been comprised mostly of disillusioned Westerners. Middle-aged divorced women and doctors, lawyers and movie producers were especially drawn to the guru's worldwide ashrams. Followers referred to themselves by the Hindu title *sannyasin*. Upon initiation, these devotees renounced the rest of the world for a new Sanskrit name and a string of wooden beads with a picture of the Bhagwan on it called a *mela*. They dressed only in clothes the color of the sunset (red, orange, purple).

Rajneeshis attracted national media attention in the early 1980s when Bhagwan Shree Rajneesh transformed a ranch near Antelope into a multi-million dollar commune called Rajneeshpuram. Fleeing tax evasion, the Indian guru purchased the 64,000-acre Big Muddy Ranch (one of Oregon's largest) for $6 million, and beat it out of Pune, India, with the intention of building an isolationist 'oasis in the desert' – a self-sufficient city with its own fertile valley created by a private lake and dam. Since these plans violated state land use laws and threatened the water rights of long-time residents, Rajneesh's first move was to take over nearby Antelope, a town with property already zoned for city use. Residents of Antelope watched in disbelief as the Bhagwan flooded the town with followers, and renamed the Antelope Cafe (the town's only general store-cum-cafe) Zorba the Buddha. The predominantly Rajneeshie population then voted the local city council out of office and changed the town's name to Rajneesh, leaving the new council to legalize nudity in the public park, approve a hike in the water rates, and make plans to raise local taxes. Property left behind by fleeing locals was promptly snatched up by the Rajneeshis.

The commune at Rajneeshpuram itself became unpopular as stories of the Bhagwan's posh lifestyle and the rampant hedonism of his followers circulated in journalistic accounts. The complex included $35 million of modular homes, and the state's largest greenhouse and reservoir. Complete transportation facilities were provided to the commune via Buddhafield Transport Co, which even catered to air travelers by operating an airport and Air Rajneesh airline. The 'work is worship' 12-hour-workday philosophy was misinterpreted as justification for running a slave labor camp. Endless murmurs of drug use, sexual orgies and a blossoming arsenal of private weapons and arms created a leery public, as did reports of a scheme to increase Rajneesh votership and political power by busing in homeless people from San Francisco to register to vote as

---

fossil findings are on display here, including parts of a saber-toothed tiger and a three-toed horse. Exhibits explain the complex series of geologic events that conspired to form the John Day Formation. In the laboratory, you can watch as paleontologists and students clean more recent finds. Part of the large ranch house, built by a Scottish ranch family early this century, is preserved to display period furnishings and everyday items. There's a ranger on duty to answer questions; the shaded grounds of the visitors center are a good place for a picnic beside the river. The visitors center is open from 9 am to 5 pm daily, and is 10 miles northwest of Dayville. Take Hwy 19 north from Hwy 26.

In the immediate vicinity of the visitors center are a number of startling-looking formations. **Sheep Rock** rises immediately behind the center. This steep-sided mesa rises up hundreds of feet to a small cap of rock.

**Picture Gorge** Between the Old West town of Dayville (population 145), on Hwy

a resident of Rajneeshpuram. At the height of it all, Rajneesh's commander-in-chief Ma Anad Sheela announced to the public that she would 'paint the bulldozers with blood,' before she would witness the collapse of the Bhagwan's empire. (The Bhagwan was apparently under a vow of silence shortly before his appearance in the USA, so it was really Ma Anad Sheela who was running the show. Serving as his commanding officer, it was Sheela who in fact arranged for the purchase of the ranch, oversaw its operation, and served as the Bhagwan's spokesperson.)

Fishy-looking marriages between US citizens and foreigners turned heads at the INS, while the IRS raised its eyebrows at the fleet of 90 Rolls Royces given as 'gifts' to the Bhagwan. Mud-slinging between leaders of the commune forced the Bhagwan to give the FBI a formal invitation to investigate criminal activity at Rajneeshpuram, eventually resulting in its closure.

When in September of 1985 Ma Anad Sheela suddenly left the commune, Rajneesh broke his vow of silence to declare her a fascist dictator. He poured forth a long chain of crimes she had committed while in her leadership of the commune: the murder attempt she had plotted on the life of his personal physician; her involvement in a mass salmonella poisoning of The Dalles residents (individual Rajneeshis went from salad bar to

salad bar in all of the city's restaurants, tainting them with salmonella they carried with them in glass vials – more than 750 people got sick); her plot to murder Oregon's attorney general, Dave Frohnmeyer, and another attorney; and her mass spying and eavesdropping through a sophisticated wiretapping and bugging system. It wasn't long before Sheela was apprehended in West Germany and indicted for eavesdropping and attempted murder. The Bhagwan, guilty of immigration violations, was apprehended in flight at an airport in North Carolina in October. Having pleaded guilty, he was deported to India in November, and members at the commune dispersed soon thereafter. The Bhagwan returned to Pune, where, after taking the new name of Osho, he died in 1990. The ashram at Pune survived his death and currently functions as the worldwide headquarters for Osho's disenfranchised flock. ■

26 and Sheep Rock, the John Day River incises its way through 1500 feet of lava flow to begin its vocation as a canyon-cutter. The transition is especially startling from the east approach: the heretofore placid-seeming river passes through a meadow-like valley before turning abruptly northward, slicing through the hillside. The gorge, wide enough only for the river and the road, is named for the pictographs drawn there by early Indians. Look for the pictographs near milestone 125, on the west side of the road; ponder the mentality of those who see fit to spray paint over these dim drawings which are hundreds of years old.

**Blue Basin** From this trailhead, two miles north of the visitors center of Hwy 19, several hikes lead out into the John Day fossil formations. The **Island in Time Trail** is a well-maintained mile-long path that climbs up a narrow waterway to a badlands-basin of highly eroded, uncannily green sediments. Along the trail are displays that reveal fossils protruding from the soil. The trail dead-ends at a natural box canyon: high around are barren, castellated walls rich in 25-million-year-old life forms.

For a longer hike, the **Overlook Trail** climbs up the side of the formation to the rim of Blue Basin. The views onto the fossil beds and the layer-cake topography of the John Day valley are worth struggling up the three-mile-loop trail.

At **Cathedral Rock**, a mile north on Hwy 19, erosion has stripped away a hillside to reveal the highly colored, banded sediments of the John Day Formation beneath a thick cap of basalt. No plant life grows in this poor and quickly eroded soil, which gives the outcropping the look of a fanciful, greatly deteriorated building.

**Foree Picnic Area** At this day-use area, a couple of miles further north on Hwy 19, trails lead off into more fossil-rich formations. The **Foree Loop Trail** winds half a mile around a green mud-stone badlands; the **Flood of Fire Trail** winds up to a ridge-top viewpoint over the John Day River.

**Places to Stay & Eat** Just north of the fossil beds on Hwy 19 is *Asher's RV Park* (☎ 934-2712), a barren plot suitable only for hardened RVers; rates are $8 for hookups, $6 for tents. Tent campers will want to continue up to Kimberly, and turn east onto Hwy 402, where there are two shady, riverside BLM campgrounds, *Lone Pine* and *Big Bend*, right on the North Fork John Day River. Bring your fishing pole, as it's hard to resist the river.

In Dayville, the *Fish House B&B* (☎ 987-2124) on Main St, offers five rooms – two in a freestanding cottage – and a small RV or tenting area. Rooms range from $35 to $50; camping fees are $5 and $10 a night. Nearby is the *Dayville Diggins Cafe* (☎ 987-2132).

At *Lands Inn B&B* (☎ 934-2333), you get the choice of staying in a cottage or in a comfortably equipped tepee; rates are $55 and $30, respectively. Lands Inn is five miles east of Hwy 19, just north of the Blue Basin trailheads.

Some of the most beautiful sunsets you'll ever see can be viewed from Spray, 30 miles northwest of the visitors center on Hwy 19. That's reason enough to stay at *Asher's Motel* (☎ 468-3569), where single/double rooms go for $30/32. Spray's local eatery is the *Rim Rock Cafe* (☎ 468-2861).

### Painted Hills Unit

This formation near the town of Mitchell (population 160), consists of low-slung, banded hills of highly differentiated colors. Red, yellow and ochre-hued ash from a series of volcanic eruptions drifted into beds hundreds of feet deep about 30 million years ago. Because there is no cap rock to protect them from erosion, the Painted Hills have slumped into soft mounds, rather like evil-colored, melting ice cream.

The Painted Hills are easily dismissed as a cliché: as one of central Oregon's most visited natural sites, people troop in, line up at the viewpoints, and take requisite photos. Follow one of the following hiking trails to get away from the crowds and the overly familiar, postcard vistas.

The easy **Fossil Leaf Trail** winds over the top of one of the banded hills, with interpretive signs pointing out plant life and geologic history. The **Caroll Rim Trail** winds to the top of a high bluff, for great views over the Painted Hills. For a longer hike out into a badlands plant and wildlife preserve, take the three-mile **High Desert Trail** loop.

At the unit headquarters (☎ 462-3961), there are picnic tables above a sheep-filled meadow. The Painted Hills are three miles west of Mitchell on Hwy 26, then six miles north on a good gravel road.

**Places to Stay & Eat** The closest campgrounds are in the Ochoco National Forest. *Ochoco Pass Campground* is 15 miles west of Mitchell on Hwy 26. Mitchell is a one-street town squeezed into a steep ravine. The *Sky Hook Motel* (☎ 462-3569) above the town, is Mitchell's sole lodging option, with rooms starting at $35.

Mitchell does a bit better when it comes to cafes: there are two to choose from, the *Blueberry Muffin Cafe* (☎ 462-3434) and the *Sidewalk Cafe* (☎ 462-3459).

## Clarno Unit

The Clarno Unit is the most remote of the fossil beds, and requires some patient driving along winding, though paved, roads. The formation is at the base of the John Day River's canyon, which is about as rugged and wild-looking country as you'll see in Oregon. From the divide on Hwy 218 between Clarno and Antelope, the view over the canyon opening up below is guaranteed to elicit a gasp of astonishment.

The oldest of the three fossil bed monuments, the 40-million-year-old Clarno Unit exposes mud flows that washed over an Eocene-era forest. The Clarno Formation eroded into distinctive, sheer-white cliffs topped with spires and turrets of stone. A series of short interpretive trails pass through boulder-sized fossils containing logs, seeds and other remains of an ancient forest.

**Places to Stay & Eat** The closest facilities to Clarno are in Fossil (population 465), a charming little town with plank sidewalks and old stone storefronts, 18 miles east on Hwy 218.

Five miles east of Fossil on Hwy 19 is *Bear Hollow County Park*, a pleasant, shady campground along a stream. Five miles further, Hwy 218 climbs over a pass and begins dropping into the John Day River canyon. Here, campers and picnickers should stop at *Shelton Wayside*, a state park with campsites ($7) and hiking trails.

The *Fossil Hotel* (☎ 763-4075), 105 First St, has single/double rooms for $30/32. The hotel also offers RV pads. When in Fossil, eat at *Chica's Country Cafe* (☎ 763-4328), for good ranch-style cooking and large helpings. Across the street at the *Shamrock* (☎ 763-4896), steak, chicken and a salad bar are the order of the day.

It seems unlikely, but a couple of notable B&Bs are found out in this isolated countryside. *McRae Ranch B&B* (☎ 736-2287 or 489-3345) is a 100-year-old ranch house sitting on 18 sq miles right on the John Day River at Clarno, just minutes from the fossil beds. The B&B offers three rooms, with a choice of continental or full ranch breakfast ($5 extra); rooms range from $35 to $45.

Up the hill from Antelope, on Hwy 97, is working ghost town of Shaniko. The *Shaniko Hotel* (☎ 489-3441) was an imposing landmark when it was built in 1909; it's now noteworthy as a comfortable, completely refurbished B&B. Rates range from $55 to $85; there's a restaurant on the main floor of the hotel.

OREGON

# Southeastern Oregon

This vast, underpopulated region of desert, mountain, canyon and marsh contains some of Oregon's most unusual and unvisited scenery. Towering fault-block peaks rise above powder-white dry lake beds; lava flats cleave to reveal a tiny thread of river, burrowed hundreds of feet below the prairie surface; clouds of migratory birds bank to land in a wetland refuge.

Historically, southeastern Oregon was the home to huge open-range cattle and sheep outfits; today, almost two thirds of this region is still managed by the BLM as rangeland. Some of the names that appear on maps are not towns, but ranch headquarters, boots and hats are part of the dress code and pickup trucks are the conveyance of choice.

Given the arid climate, southeast Oregon is also home to a surprisingly varied and plentiful wildlife population. Malheur Wildlife Refuge is one of the nation's major nesting and migratory stopovers along the Pacific Flyway. Watch for glimpses of speeding pronghorns, listen for coyotes and keep a sharp eye peeled for bighorn sheep along high, rocky escarpments.

There aren't many paved roads through this lonesome piece of land, and the flat, straight highways that do cross this region encourage speeding. Don't look for luxurious accommodations in this obscure corner. In fact, except in Burns and Ontario, lodging is hard to come by. Distances are great out here, and you can't depend on little towns for much except a gas station. Plan your trip to end up near a town if you need a place to stay. But the traveler who's willing to turn off the main roads will find

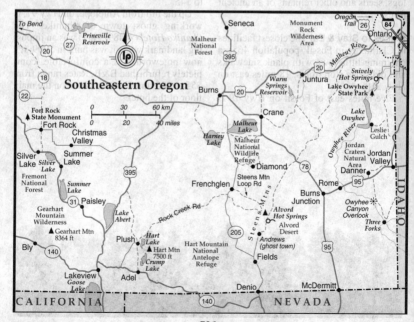

The Sawtooth Mountains reflected in Redtooth Lake (BM)

Autumn in the Caribou National Forest (BM)

River rafting, Salmon River (RF)

Lake Pend Oreille (BM)

Wheat fields near Orofino (BM)

Silver City, near Caldwell (BM)

Lower Mesa Falls (BM)

Cataldo Mission, the oldest building in Idaho (BM)

Soda Springs Geyser (BM)

this one of Oregon's most spectacular and uncrowded destinations.

## GEOGRAPHY

This corner of Oregon represents the continent's northernmost extension of the Great Basin. Basin and range formations developed in the last 10 million years when a series of roughly parallel faults shattered bedrock beneath thick pre-existing lava deposits. One side of the fault was hoisted upwards, while the side facing it slumped downwards. Some of the rising fault blocks rose to the height of mountains. Meanwhile, lakes formed in the basins below the rising escarpments. During ice ages, the lakes were very large, isolating the fault

---

### The Bannock Indian War

The Oregon Trail crossed the Snake River near present-day Nyssa. As pioneers began to settle the valleys of this corner of Oregon, and after the discovery of gold in the Owyhee Mountains of Idaho, the Whites came into conflict with the Native Americans.

Cattle drives began arriving from Texas in the late 1860s, but for the land to be used for cattle, it had to be cleared of Native Americans. Heavy-handed policies, corruption by US Government Indian agents and incarceration on inadequate reservations led to an uprising of the Paiute, Bannock and Snake tribes in 1878, known as the Bannock Indian War. Members of these tribes left their reservations, effectively declaring war against many of the settlers who had divided up their traditional hunting grounds and homelands into ranches and mining claims. The Indians attempted to revitalize old tribal alliances and to mobilize braves across the west (they hoped to lure Sitting Bull, the victor of Little Bighorn, down from Canada to join them) in order to throw out settlers. The Native American groups were pursued by the army, and did battle at Camp Curry west of Burns, and at Willow Creek, but factional and tribal infighting ultimately undid their efforts to force the Whites from their old homelands. ■

---

blocks as long, ridge-like islands. Because the climate has turned much drier in recent centuries, few of the remaining lakes have external drainage, and are consequently highly alkaline. Other of the old lakes are playas, or dry lake beds.

Unlike the basin and range area, where scant rainfall finds no outlet, the neighboring and equally arid Owyhee region is deeply incised with canyons. The Owyhee River collects its deep-dug tributaries at Three Forks, and flows northward, flanked by lava cliffs 1000 feet high.

Northern Lake County is a continuation of the high volcanic plains of central Oregon, which were formed by floods of molten basalt. The region owes its most remarkable volcanic landmarks to enormous explosions caused when hot lava shot up through shallow ice-age lake water and mud flats. The resulting explosions caused such uncanny phenomena as Fort Rock.

## GETTING THERE & AWAY

Public transport only shoots by on the periphery of this fairly remote country. Amtrak and Greyhound provide service to Ontario, along the Idaho border. There are two buses a day between Klamath Falls and Lakeview and one bus a day between Bend, Burns and Ontario. You'll need an automobile to get to almost all sites of interest in southeast Oregon.

## BURNS

Named by a wistful early settler for the Scottish poet Robert Burns, this town (population 2880) was established in 1883 as the watering hole and social center for incoming settlers and roving cowhands. As the only settlement of any size for hundreds of miles, by the late 1880s it boasted five saloons and three newspapers, and served as the capital of a vast cattle empire. With the arrival of the railroad in 1924, the timber resources of the Blue Mountains north of Burns attracted developers.

Today, this isolated town is the county seat and center of trade for the enormous agricultural district of Harney County. Burns, and immediate neighbor Hines, are useful jumping-off points for expeditions into even more remote environs.

## Orientation & Information
Highway 20 links Burns to Bend, and Hwy 395 heads north to John Day.

The Harney County Chamber of Commerce (☎ 573-2636) is at 18 West D St, Burns, OR 97720. The Burns District BLM office (☎ 573-5241) is at 12533 Hwy 20 W, Hines. For information on the surrounding national forests, contact the Malheur National Forest Ranger Station (☎ 573-7292) in Burns, and the Ochoco National Forest Ranger Station (☎ 573-7292) in Hines. The post office (573-2931) is at 100 S Broadway.

## Harney County Historical Museum
This museum (☎ 573-2636), 18 West D St, is known throughout Oregon for its collection of pioneer-era photographs. It also contains relics of the region's Native American and pioneer settler heritage in a building that once housed a brewery. From May to October, the museum is open from 9 am to noon, and 1 to 5 pm Monday to Friday, and 9 am to noon on Saturday.

## Crystal Crane Hot Springs
This out-of-the-way hot springs spa (☎ 493-2312), is 25 miles east of Burns on Hwy 78. It might be just what you need if you've been bumping around the back roads of southeastern Oregon. The springs flow into a large swimming pool, and also small private bath houses. Massages are available by appointment; a few guest cabins and facilities for campers are also available.

## Special Events
The High Desert Fiddlers Contest (☎ 573-1323) in late June, brings together regional talent for a dance and jamboree. The Harney County Fair, held the weekend after Labor Day, also includes a rodeo. The fairgrounds are south of Burns on Egan St.

## Places to Stay
**Camping** The closest public campground to Burns is *Idlewild Campground*, 17 miles north along Hwy 395, in the Malheur National Forest. RVers should stop at *Village RV & Mobile Park* (☎ 573-7640), a quarter mile north of Burns on Hwy 20; rates begin at $10. *The Sands* (☎ 573-7010) is an RV-only campground two miles west of Burns on Hwy 20; sites begin at $8.

**Hotels** The *Silver Spur Motel* (☎ 573-2077), 789 N Broadway Ave, is comfortable and close to downtown; single/double rooms are $32/34. The *Orbit Motel* (☎ 573-2034), a half mile north of Burns, has a heated pool and rooms for $30/34. The *Royal Inn* (☎ 573-5295), 999 Oregon Ave, offers a sauna, hot tub and pool for $40/45. *Best Western Ponderosa Motel* (☎ 573-2047), 577 W Monroe St, features a heated pool and cable TV, for $42/44.

## Places to Eat
Stop at the *Steens Mountain Cafe* (☎ 573-7226), 195 N Alder St, for sandwiches, big breakfasts and pizza. The *Powerhouse*

---

### Cattle Country
Harney Basin and the Blitzen River valley in particular were two of the first and greatest venues in the days of eastern Oregon's cattle barons. Certainly the most notorious of these was Pete French, who in the 1880s owned the 156-sq-mile P Ranch that stretched from Harney Lake to Frenchglen. At once patrician and unscrupulous, French resisted the rising tide of settlers who came to homestead this part of the state. His patrician sense of land ownership extended beyond his own land title, and he evicted settlers who dared to claim land in areas where he considered he had grazing privileges. In 1897, French was shot by Ed Oliver, a settler with whom French feuded over land ownership. His death, and the acquittal of Oliver, effectively ended the rootin'-tootin' days of the open range in Oregon. ∎

(☎ 573-9060), 305 E Monroe St, in an old power station, offers steak and cocktails; $12 will buy a rib steak and a trip to the salad bar. *The Elkhorn Cafe* (☎ 573-3201), 475 N Broadway Ave, normally offers good home-style Western cooking; but when the Thai-born cook is at the grill, ask for the Thai menu. The *Pine Room Cafe* (☎ 573-6631), 543 W Monroe St, offers some of the high desert's best food, with homemade baked goods and hand-cut steak. A specialty of the house is chicken livers in brandy sauce ($10); fresh salmon goes for $15. It's open evenings only.

## MALHEUR NATIONAL WILDLIFE REFUGE

Covering 289 sq miles of lake, wetland and prairie, the Malheur National Wildlife Refuge is one of the West's most important breeding and resting areas for birds traveling along the Pacific Flyway. It is also home to high-desert mammals such as pronghorn, mule deer and coyote, and to upland game birds such as sage grouse and quail. You don't need to be a life-long birder to enjoy exploring the refuge. The abundance of wildlife, a museum of 200 mounted birds, plus nearby Diamond Craters volcanic area, make this a great family detour.

In 1908 President Theodore Roosevelt created the refuge in response to the annihilation of species of birds used to make hats. Pete French's P Ranch, comprising much of the lower drainage of the Blitzen River, was added to the refuge in 1936.

Generally speaking, there are two parts to the preserve. Malheur and Harney lakes, the principal bodies of water on the preserve, were once one large, ice-age body of water. However, now only Malheur Lake regularly receives fresh water inflow from the Sylvies and Blitzen rivers. While very shallow (it has a maximum depth of six feet), Malheur Lake remains fresh. Harney Lake only receives water from occasional Malheur Lake overflow, and when it holds water, that water is very alkaline.

While these large, shallow bodies of water are clearly a draw to waterfowl, the best wildlife viewing is found south along the Blitzen River, where wide, grassy marshes and ponds provide shelter to an abundance of animal life. Between refuge headquarters and Frenchglen are 35 miles of intersecting gravel roads and paths, all offering great wildlife-viewing opportunities.

Between Burns and the refuge, Hwy 205 crosses an odd geologic formation. Rising sharply more than 300 feet from the flat desert surface is a tongue of rock only a quarter of a mile across but several miles in length. Called Wright's Point, this landmark was formed when lava flows filled an ancient streambed; the thick basalt has resisted erosion, and remains after less hardy formations have worn away.

### Orientation & Information

At the Malheur National Wildlife Refuge headquarters, 32 miles south of Burns along Hwy 205, there are interpretive exhibits and information about exploring the area. Also available is a map guide to the refuge that shows the road system, and highlights 'hot spots' where wildlife viewing is most rewarding.

Contact the Malheur National Wildlife Refuge (☎ 493-2612) for more information.

### Wildlife & Bird Watching

Over 200 species of birds have been sighted at Malheur National Wildlife Refuge. The apex of the viewing season begins in spring. Waterfowl migration peaks in March, shorebirds arrive in April, and songbirds wing in during May. During summer, waterfowl broods skim across the ponds and lakes. By fall, the refuge is a staging ground for southward bird migrations.

The **George M Benson Memorial Museum**, in the refuge headquarters, contains 200 mounted specimens of animals found in the area. Ignore the strong smell of formaldehyde and learn about the wildlife that lives in the refuge.

Other animals live in the valley and in the rough breaks above the Blitzen River.

Campers will hear the howl of coyotes and the hoot of owls; bald eagles and other large raptors patrol the environs.

## Diamond Craters

Adjacent to the wildlife refuge, 55 miles south of Burns along Hwy 205, is the Diamond Craters Outstanding Natural Area. A series of volcanic craters, cinder cones and other lava formations, Diamond Craters were formed about 2500 years ago. Pick up an interpretive brochure from the BLM office in Burns to learn more about volcanics, and to find a map of the area's rather confusing road system.

## The Round Barn

Twenty miles north of Diamond off Happy Valley Rd, is Pete French's Round Barn, the 100-foot-wide structure used to buck out broncos in the glory days of the open range. Built in the 1880s, the barn has been donated to the Oregon Historical Society and can be visited informally.

## Places to Stay & Eat

**Hostels** The real deal in southeastern Oregon lodging is the *Malheur Field Station* (☎ 493-2629), near the refuge headquarters. The field station is a 'Nature Hostel' open year round to individuals or groups visiting the wildlife refuge. In addition to reasonably priced meals in the dining hall, cooking facilities are available in some housing units. Accommodations are heated, and laundry facilities are provided. During peak seasons, classes and lectures are offered. Bring your own bedding and towel. Lodging starts at $11 a night; meals at $5.

**Hotels** Burns has the most rooms to offer travelers. However, those more interested in Western heritage will want to stay at small, historic hotels. In the tiny community of Diamond, just about the only surviving business is the *Diamond Hotel* (☎ 493-1898). This refurbished vintage hotel offers five rooms to guests starting at $45 for a double, and a good meal (guests only) that's all the more toothsome for the

real Western ambiance. Take the Diamond Grain Camp Rd east from Hwy 205.

Further south, the *Frenchglen Hotel* (☎ 493-2825) is a charming old hotel and state monument, pretty much unaltered in appearance since it was built in the 1910s. Make sure to call ahead, because the hotel is popular with people looking for real Western ambiance and hospitality. Dinners are family-style, and served promptly and abundantly at 6:30 pm; reservations are required. There are eight small, plain guest rooms, starting at $40.

**Guest Ranches** The *McCoy Creek Inn* (☎ 493-2131), in Diamond, is a real treasure in this lonely country. This guest ranch in a steep canyon offers lodging in a self-contained bunkhouse unit, or in the ranch house, starting at $55 a night. The real pleasure here, especially after watching birds all day or bumping up the back of the Steens Mountain, is the food.

## ONTARIO

Oregon's most easterly population center, Ontario (population 9555) and its surrounding communities are often considered an extension of Idaho's fertile Snake River valley. Ontario even shares the Mountain Time Zone with neighboring Idaho. Agriculture remains the backbone of the local economy. The Malheur, Payette and Owyhee rivers join the Snake's wide valley here, with irrigated farms producing varied crops; the region is the nation's largest producer of peppermint.

During WW II, interned Japanese Americans from western Oregon were moved to the Ontario area, where they were forced to work in the fields. After the end of the war, several Japanese families remained, and became land-owning farmers. Today, eastern Oregon's only Buddhist temple is in Ontario, and the Japanese American citizens celebrate their ancestry during the midsummer Obon Festival.

## Orientation & Information

Interstate 84, and Hwys 20, 26 and 95 intersect near Ontario, putting the city at the hub of eastern Oregon's principal thoroughfares. The Snake River forms Ontario's eastern boundary and the Oregon/Idaho state line. Downtown streets are divided by Oregon St and by Idaho Ave into NE, NW, SE and SW quadrants. Avenues run east-west, while streets run north-south.

The Ontario Visitors & Convention Bureau (☎ 889-8012) is at 88 SW 3rd Ave, Ontario, OR 97914. The Vale Chamber of Commerce (473-3800) is at 275 N Main St, Vale, OR 97918. Contact the Nyssa Chamber of Commerce (☎ 372-3091) at 212 S Main St, Nyssa, OR 97913.

The central post office (☎ 889-8382) is at 88 SW 2nd Ave. The *Ontario Argus Observer* is the local newspaper. Oregon Public Broadcasting is heard on 104.5 FM. Holy Rosary Hospital (☎ 889-5331) is at 351 SW 9th Ave.

### Special Events

Thunderegg Days during the first week of June brings together dozens of rock dealers and collectors at the school grounds in Nyssa, on Hwy 201 at Good Ave. 'Thunderegg' is the local name for geodes, which are baseball-sized spheres of agate formed in volcanic tuff.

Local cowboys come in off the range for Vale's Fourth of July Rodeo. It's one of eastern Oregon's largest and most authentic celebrations of the Old West. The rodeo grounds are south of town on Longfellow St.

Ontario's Obon Festival, a celebration of the area's Japanese American residents, takes place in mid-July. Japanese food, dancing and tours of the temple, 286 SE 4th St, are among the activities.

The Malheur County Fair takes place in Ontario in early August. In addition to three nights of rodeo, there's the Lamb Fest. The county fairgrounds are at 795 NW 9th Ave.

### Places to Stay

**Camping** There are three campgrounds 25

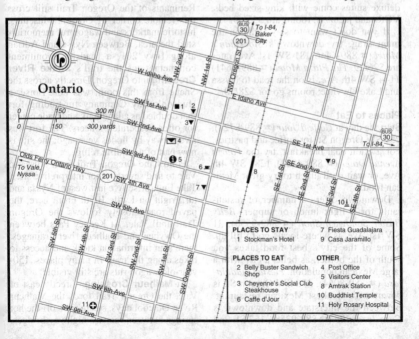

**PLACES TO STAY**
1 Stockman's Hotel

**PLACES TO EAT**
2 Belly Buster Sandwich Shop
3 Cheyenne's Social Club Steakhouse
6 Caffe d'Jour

7 Fiesta Guadalajara
9 Casa Jaramillo

**OTHER**
4 Post Office
5 Visitors Center
8 Amtrak Station
10 Buddhist Temple
11 Holy Rosary Hospital

miles north of Ontario on I-84 at historic Farewell Bend. At *Farewell Bend State Park*, rates are $13 for tents, $15 for hookups. In Nyssa, campers can find room at the *Kiwanis Park* near the school (Hwy 201 at Good Ave). In Ontario, RV campers can stay at *Curtis' Neat Retreat*, on the Idaho side of the line (see Payette, ID). In Vale, the *Prospector Travel Trailer Park* (☎ 473-3879) has sites for RVs and tent campers; fees begin at $14. It's a quarter-mile north of the junction of Hwys 20 and 26.

**Hotels** Most of Ontario's hotels are clustered around I-84 exits. The following lodgings are near exit No 376, and indicate the variety you'll find there. *The Holiday Motel* (☎ 889-9188), 615 E Idaho Ave, offers a swimming pool and non-smoking single/double rooms at $21/25. At the *Super 8* (☎ 889-8282), 266 Goodfellow St, rooms start at $50. A little more comfortable is the *Colonial Inn Best Western* (☎ 889-2600), 251 Goodfellow St, where deluxe suites come with king-sized beds, VCRs and jacuzzis; rooms are $55/60.

If you don't want to stay right on the main drag, try downtown's *Stockman's Motel* (☎ 889-4446), 81 SW 1st Ave; rates are $26/29. *The Plaza Motel* (☎ 889-9641) 1144 SW 4th Ave, is on the road to Nyssa and Lake Owyhee; rooms go for $28/30.

### Places to Eat

Start the day at *Caffe d'Jour* (☎ 889-8727), 257 SW Oregon St, for coffee and pastries. For a traditional breakfast, try the *Fourth Avenue Diner* (☎ 889-4052), 1281 SW 4th Ave, or wait until lunch to try great Mexican food.

Downtown offers a number of restaurants for a light lunch or supper. *Belly Buster Sandwich Shop* (☎ 889-9550), 31 SW 1st Ave, is where locals go to fill up. Some of the city's best food takes you south of the border, as befits a city with a large Mexican population. *Fiesta Guadalajara* (☎ 889-8064), 336 SW Oregon St, is downtown's liveliest Mexican restaurant. Between the interstate and downtown is *Casa Jaramillo* (☎ 889-9258), 157 SE 2nd

Ave, for 25 years an Ontario institution. A dinner of carne asada (roasted meat in a kind of green chili stew) costs $9.

For fine dining in Ontario, try *Cheyenne's Social Club Steakhouse* (☎ 889-3777), 111 SW 1st Ave, where the specialty is steak and seafood. A filet mignon goes for $15.

### Getting There & Away

Greyhound Bus (☎ 889-5112), 510 NW Oregon St, offers two coaches east and west daily through Ontario, linking Portland, Boise, ID and Salt Lake City, UT.

Amtrak's *Pioneer*, linking the same cities, has a west and eastbound train every other day. The Amtrak station is at Oregon St and SW 3rd Ave.

For car rental, inquire at Action Chrysler-Nissan (☎ 889-8989), 180 East Lane.

## AROUND ONTARIO

### Old Oregon Trail

Remnants of the Oregon Trail still cross this remote corner of Oregon. Museums, historic markers and wagon rut memorials stud the area. Between Nyssa and Adrian along Hwy 201, a roadside monument commemorates the trail's **Snake River Crossing** into Oregon. Directly across the Snake from this point was Fort Boise, a Hudson's Bay Company fur-trading fort that doubled as a landmark and trade center for often desperate pioneers. The fort was swept away by floods years ago; the site is now part of a wildlife refuge.

Follow the Oregon Trail from Nyssa to Vale to find several other interpretive sites. Take Enterprise Ave just west of Nyssa and turn right on Lyttle Blvd. From here, the paved road closely follows the Oregon Trail until Vale. At Keeney Pass between the Owyhee and Malheur river drainages, there's an information kiosk and access to hikes along the trail. In many places, 150-year-old wagon ruts are still visible.

At **Malheur Crossing**, directly east of Vale, the Oregon Trail fords the Malheur River. On cool days, steam rises off the hot springs between the two highway bridges, which served as a laundry and bathing area for Oregon Trail travelers.

North of Hwy 26, east of Vale rises **Malheur Butte**. This lone, mesa-like landmark is the remains of a volcanic plug; from its summit, the Paiutes watched the progress of the Oregon Trail pioneers.

## Farewell Bend
At this point, travelers along the old Oregon Trail left the valley of the Snake River, which they had more or less followed since central Idaho, and climbed up into the desert uplands of eastern Oregon.

Before undertaking the strenuous journey through desert landscapes to the imposing Blue Mountains, Oregon Trail travelers usually rested at Farewell Bend, grazing livestock, gathering wood and otherwise preparing themselves for the arduous trip ahead. Today Farewell Bend State Park, which is 25 miles north of Ontario on I-84, commemorates this placid pioneer wayside with a picnic and play area, boat launch and large campground.

For a side trip, leave the freeway at the state park and follow a good graveled road north 60 miles to Richland, south of the Wallowa Mountains. The road never leaves the side of the Snake as it trenches deeper and deeper into the volcanic plateau. This is rugged land, and an enchanting detour into the Snake River canyon country for travelers who don't plan to spend time in Hells Canyon.

## OWYHEE RIVER
Cutting a slash across the unyielding desert, the Owyhee River furrows deep beneath the desert surface on its way to the Snake River, draining a vast region extending into Idaho and Nevada.

Part of the Owyhee's allure to modern-day explorers lies in its extreme remoteness. Over 250 miles in length, the upper Owyhee River is crossed only once by a road of any sort. Furthermore, the river cuts an astonishingly deep and narrow canyon with sides so steep that it is frequently impossible to follow the river even on foot. Nor is it always possible to explore the river by boat, as there are several impassable rapids between Rome and Three Forks.

## Leslie Gulch-Succor Creek Byway
While easy access to the river is beguilingly limited and difficult, the average traveler can explore a sample of this wildly eroded country by traveling along the BLM-designated Leslie Gulch-Succor Creek National Back Country Byway, which ends (or begins) at a junction with Hwy 95, 18 miles north of Jordan Valley. This 52-mile off-the-beaten-path gravel route passes landscapes of surpassing grandeur, as well as prime wildlife viewing areas.

Follow the road south from near Adrian, through miles of sagebrush, thin grass and rolling hills until it drops steeply down onto Succor Creek. Here, 100-foot-high vertical walls of volcanic tuff grudgingly divide to allow the stream and road to wind through a landscape reminiscent of biblical Petra. Succor Creek State Park sits at a narrow end of the canyon; with facilities for campers and picnickers (no water); take time to hunt for thundereggs, Oregon's state rock.

The eroded landscape is even more spectacular at Leslie Gulch, a 16-mile side road from the byway that drops over into the Owyhee River Canyon. This steep, though

**OREGON**

---

### Hawaiian Namesakes
Although homeland to the Paiute and Snake Indians, this corner of Oregon is instead named for another, altogether unlikely, native people. In 1819, the Hudson's Bay Company brought in two Hawaiian islanders as beaver trappers. They were killed by local Indians along the river, which now bears a name derived from the islands of their birth. *Owyhee* is one early phonetic spelling of *Hawaii*. ∎

usually passable gravel road careens down a narrow creek channel incised through vividly colored volcanic rock and eroded into amazing pinnacle and turreted formations. The narrow ribbon of Owyhee Reservoir awaits at the base of the canyon, as well as rough campsites (bring water). Bighorn sheep haunt these rock cliffs; watch for them as they come down to drink at the creekside.

## Owyhee Dam & Reservoir

At 417 feet in height, Owyhee Dam was once the highest dam in the world. Built in a spectacular desert canyon, this dam backs up the Owyhee River into Lake Owyhee, stretching 50 miles to the south. At Lake Owyhee State Park, on the east lakeside, there's a campground and picnic area; fishing and watersports are both popular activities for local residents.

It's worth the drive to the reservoir and state park just to glimpse the Owyhee's dramatic canyon. Even here, where the gorge is less precipitous than at more remote sites upstream, sharp escarpments of colorful volcanic rock drop off hundreds of feet to the reservoir below.

## Jordan Craters

A sort of lava theme park, these formations have erupted since White settlement of North America. Craters, blow-holes and lava tubes are amongst the volcanic outcroppings. The lava flow dammed Cow Creek to form Cow Lakes, where there's informal camping and fishing. The BLM now protects Jordan Craters as a natural area to preserve the ecosystem. Watch out for snakes.

To reach 28-sq-mile Jordan Crater Natural Area, travel nine miles north along Hwy 95 from Jordan Valley; turn west and drive 26 miles along a gravel road to reach the volcanic site.

## Rome

Here, along Hwy 95, is the only bridge to cross the Owyhee River. Both the river and the landscape are misleadingly placid at this old-time ford. A gravel road south of

---

### The Grave of Jean-Baptiste Charbonneau

One of the early West's most colorful characters is buried at the old Inskip Ranch, near Danner. Jean-Baptiste Charbonneau was the son of Toussaint Charbonneau and Sacajawea, who accompanied Lewis and Clark's Corps of Discovery on their journey across the western USA between 1805 and 1806. In all those pictures of Sacajawea, young Pomp, as he was known to the corps, is the one in the papoose. Having been the youngest member of the expedition was just the beginning of his incredible life. Captain Clark was so taken with the young half-French, half-Indian infant, that he sent the child to private schools in St Louis at his own expense. At Fort Union in Montana, the adolescent Charbonneau met German nobleman-cum-scientist Prince Paul von Wurtemberg, who was impressed by the well-educated boy. He took Charbonneau back to Germany with him, where Charbonneau spent the next six years as a courtier. During this time, he learned five languages fluently and traveled across the Continent and to Africa with the prince. Charbonneau eventually returned to the western USA. He served as a guide through the Montana wilderness, trapped furs, served as alcalde at a California mission and prospected for gold in the 1850s California Gold Rush. In 1866, he hankered to return to Montana, where gold fever had broken out. He got no farther north than Danner, then a stage stop, where he died of pneumonia at the age of 61.

To visit the gravesite, follow signs to Danner and look for the ruins of an old ranch. ■

---

Rome leads to rough country where the Owyhee River leaves its gorge. After a few miles, park the vehicle and hike over to the canyon for a view of the Owyhee far below. Three miles north of Rome, along a county road, are the outcroppings for which Rome was named. The fancifully named 'Pillars of Rome' are highly eroded cliffs of volcanic tuff several hundred feet high.

There's a tiny cafe (☎ 586-2294) in Rome that rents RV sites.

## Three Forks

At Three Forks, the main body of the Owyhee River meets two tributaries, the North and Middle forks. At this meeting place of canyons, burrowed deep beneath the level plateau surface, is a small, enchanting oasis of cottonwoods and prairie grasses. Two miles of steep switchbacks (high-clearance vehicles only) lead down the canyon wall to this site, where an early homestead and a primitive campground await. Here, the gorges cut by the rivers are hundreds of feet deep, but only 20 to 30 feet across. It's a magical point, unvisited and unworldly.

To reach Three Forks, turn south on the good gravel road one mile east of the Danner junction on Hwy 95. After 17 miles, Owyhee Canyon Overlook provides a glimpse of the river channeling its narrow gorge hundreds of feet beneath the prairie surface; another 18 miles brings you to Three Forks. Alternatively, seven miles east of Jordan Valley, a county road turns south and leads 35 miles to Three Forks. Both roads are well marked.

At the river's confluence is a nice swimming hole, and informal hikes are possible along the canyon floor. There are river-side hot springs after a two-mile scramble up the main branch of the Owyhee. Ranch trails can serve as mountain-bike paths. Make sure to close gates after you. Rafters can brave the Owyhee River only in spring run-off; it's generally recognized as one of Oregon's most treacherous streams, especially the stretch between Three Forks and Rome.

## Rafting

The Owyhee River is one of the West's most challenging white-water rivers, particularly the upper stretch below Three Forks, which contains a number of class IV rapids. Downstream from Rome the river is less turbulent, but the scenery – highly eroded desert cliffs – is still topnotch. The Owyhee River contains enough water to be safely rafted only in the early spring, usually March through May. There basically aren't any businesses of any sort out here, let alone a raft rental shop, so if you plan to shoot the river on your own, you need to bring gear in from elsewhere.

Wapiti River Trips (☎ (208) 628-3523, (800) 488-9872) Box 1125, Riggins, ID 83459, is one of the few outfitters that offers trips on the river. In addition, Wapiti offers some Owyhee River trips with instruction on survival skills and nature lore.

## JORDAN VALLEY

The closest thing to a town in this enormous desert area is Jordan Valley. Only five miles from the Idaho border, Jordan Valley (population 414) shares much of that state's early gold-mining history. The first large-scale cattle drive arrived here in 1869, establishing JV (as Jordan Valley is frequently abbreviated) as the center of a huge stock-raising country.

Basque shepherds also flooded into this area in the 1890s, leaving an ongoing influence on Jordan Valley, as a glance at the phone book evinces. The Frontone, a stone ball court used to play a traditional Basque game called *pelota*, still stands in Jordan Valley.

Unfortunately, little else remains of the glory days of the town. Truck stops now give the town its identity.

### Places to Stay & Eat

Jordan Valley's two motels are found right along Hwy 95. Quaint in name only, the *Basque Station Motel* (☎ 586-2244), with single/doubles for $36/40, and the *Sahara Motel* (☎ 586-2810), at $32/34, are, like much of the rest of the town, off-shoots of successful gas stations.

An old Basque hostelry has been converted into the *Old Basque Inn* (☎ 586-2298). The standard steak-dominated menu also features a few Basque dishes (roast lamb for $15), and on Saturday night there's a seafood buffet. It's open for three meals a day. *JV Restaurant* along Hwy 95 is where the truckers stop.

OREGON

### THE ALVORD DESERT

Once a single, huge 400-foot-deep lake, the Alvord Basin is now a series of playas, or dry lake beds. Alternating with irrigated alfalfa fields, sagebrush prairies and old ranches are startlingly white alkali beds, the residue of centuries of lake evaporation. And above everything looms the Steens Mountains.

During wet years, the Steens send forth torrents of spring runoff, and the lower basins fill with water. The prairies explode with grass. The basin justifies its historic reputation as an important livestock grazing range. But since the late 1980s, a severe drought has gripped the area. Years of relentless sun have forced ranch families to reconsider the traditional Western lifestyle established by four previous generations of ranchers.

The 75-mile gravel road between Fields and Hwy 78 is well-maintained and open all year.

### Alvord Hot Springs

Directly below the summit of the Steens, a few miles north of the near-ghost town of Andrews and about a hundred yards off the Fields-Denio Rd, the hot springs shelter is hard to miss. Some travelers have reported unhappy altercations with locals about use of the hot springs; others claim to have used the facility with no problem. At the minimum, be respectful of other users and the site.

### Places to Stay & Eat

In the isolated community of Fields, the *Field General Store, Motel & Cafe* (☎ 495-2275) offers hotel rooms, gas, groceries, a post office and a cafe. Further south, Denio straddles the Oregon/Nevada border. Once an Oregon town, the post office crossed the street into Nevada in 1950. Officially now in Nevada, Denio's *Highway 140 Junction Motel & Restaurant* (☎ (702) 941-0371) offers the usual border town casino scene. Rooms range from $40 to $45.

Burns Junction is a welcome sight to anyone needing gasoline, or a basic bite to eat. However, the word 'junction' could not possibly connote anything more basic than the facilities found here in this remorseless stretch of desert. Even though there is a motel, only car repairs or bad planning can justify spending a night.

### STEENS MOUNTAIN

The highest peak in southeastern Oregon, Steens Mountain is part of a massive, 30-mile-long fault block range. Easily one of the most spectacular sights in Oregon, the range was formed about 15 million years ago when the Steens side of the fault rose nearly 10,000 feet.

On the west slope of the range, ice-age glaciers bulldozed massive U-shaped valleys into the flanks of the mountain; to the east, the Steens drop off dizzyingly to the Alvord Desert, 5000 feet below. Although surrounded by desert, the Steens tower high enough above alkali basins to maintain delicate alpine meadows and lakes.

Climbing up the back side of the Steens, the traveler passes through a quick succession of eco-zones. Beginning in stark sagebrush desert, the mountain rises hastily through a band of junipers, into aspen forests, and finally into fragile, rocky tundra. Wild mustangs range along the southern reaches, elk, mule deer and pronghorn graze along the western flanks, and bighorn sheep cling to the eastern precipices. The rocky faces are also home to many raptors, including golden eagles. Wildhorse Lake contains the rare Lahontan trout, found only in fresh-water lakes in the Great Basin. The Steens' high alpine meadows produce a riot of wildflower color in mid summer, including many rare and sensitive varieties.

Although homesteaders attempted to settle the more hospitable valleys of the Steens, this landscape had traditionally been home to Basque sheepherders and enormous flocks of sheep. Changes in public land grazing laws in the 1930s ended sheep production on the Steens. The area is now managed for recreational uses and wildlife habitat, as well as limited livestock grazing.

## Steens Mountain Loop Road

Beginning in the charming hamlet of Frenchglen, this graded, though occasionally fear-provoking, road negotiates the 4500-foot climb up the back side of the Steens onto the mountain's crest, and back down along the side of a glacier-ripped gorge, providing access to the BLM's 304-sq-mile **Steens Mountain Recreation Area**. The first four miles of the road pass through the Malheur Wildlife Refuge, and by the old P Ranch buildings, once owned by cattle baron Pete French. Climbing steadily, the road passes through juniper-clad uplands, by meadows and shallow lakes, and onto a wide, tundra-like plateau that looks like an incinerated Scottish Highlands, before the land begins to fall away in deep canyons.

**Kiger Gorge**, running north from the main body of the Steens, drops 1200 feet from the rim near the car park; look at the top of the canyon's eastern facade and see a notch carved in the rock wall by a side glacier.

The road climbs up onto the crest of the range, and continues along a narrow spit of land between the eastern flank of the range and a second glacier-carved valley, the **Little Blitzen**. Side roads branch off to various overlooks: the most tempting is the road to **Wildhorse Lake** and to **Steens Peak**. Leading to the range's highest point, it's a steep, narrow road, not for most cars. Park and walk if you have doubts; it's about one mile roundtrip.

The road then drops sharply down the side of **Big Indian Gorge**, around corners that will make you long for guard rails. After crossing the Blitzen River, the road crosses sage and juniper savannas before reaching Hwy 205, 10 miles south of Frenchglen.

The Steens Mountain Byway is also promoted as a mountain bike trail, but before two-wheelers get too carried away, remember that much of this trail is above 8000 feet; if you're not used to the altitude, even a gentle sashay around the parking lot will take your breath away. In the Steens, it's not always clear whether it's the views, vertigo or the altitude that leaves you breathless.

## Places to Stay

Only four miles from Frenchglen along the Steens Mountain Loop Rd is *Page Springs Campground*, a pretty site along the Blitzen River. Further up the mountain are two more isolated campsites: *Fish Lake*, 18 miles from Frenchglen, popular with trout anglers; and *Jackman Park*, 21 miles from Frenchglen. Both offer drinking water and pit toilets.

## Getting There & Away

A good, all-weather gravel road, the Fields-Denio Rd, crosses the Alvord Desert directly below the base of the Steens, linking Fields and Hwy 78.

The Steens are accessible by a fair-weather, 66-mile loop road; at 8000 feet, it's Oregon's highest. Maintained by the BLM, the road has been designated as a Back Country Byway. Most family cars will make the trip without incident, but be prepared for some bumpy roads, especially on the southern end of the loop. The road is open as weather allows, between June and November.

The blacktailed jackrabbit can be found throughout the northwestern USA; it has ears more than six inches long.

OREGON

# Lake County

Cowboys, shifting deserts, fault-block mountains and alkaline lakes only begin to characterize this enormous county. Covering almost 8500 sq miles, but with less than one person to each of those miles, this is big, lonesome country.

For a county named for water, there's remarkably little of it here. When you pull into Christmas Valley or Silver Lake, don't be disappointed if you don't see any water. The locals haven't seen any for years either: the lakes in question are playas.

Highway 31 cuts through this lonely country, passing from a landscape characterized by its volcanic past to one dominated by enormous fault-block mountains. It's quite a distance between outposts, so keep a supply of water and the gas tank filled. Lakeview is the seat of the county and the best bet for lodging; to the west lies Hart Mountain and the Warner Lakes. The region to north of Lakeview along Hwy 31 is chock full of geological curiosities.

Stands of sagebrush cover much of the desert-like plains, while to the west the Fremont National Forest offers recreation in cool, ponderosa pine forests.

## HART MOUNTAIN & WARNER LAKES

Hart Mountain and the Poker Jim Ridge form a near vertical escarpment 3600 feet above Warner Lakes. These remote and seldom-visited wildlife areas contain mag-

### Order of the Antelope

There are few odder fraternal organizations than the Order of the Antelope, an exclusive all-male society that until recently met annually at the Hart Mountain National Antelope Refuge. The Order was established in 1932 to lobby the federal government for the establishment of the refuge; the original members were local businessmen and politicians from Lake County who camped each summer at the reserve's so-called 'Blue Sky Hotel', a hot-springs campground, and had a guys-only weekend. The refuge was created in 1936, and Order has been celebrating ever since, as the weekend get-away devolved into a no-holds-barred party.

The Order's membership is limited to the sons, sons-in-law and grandsons of the original members, plus invited male guests, who have traditionally included Oregon governors, US senators, congressmen and even a US Supreme Court Judge. Whatever high-minded ideals may have motivated the first members, recent gatherings of the Order have been marked by extreme drunkenness, public lewdness and gambling.

The Order's party was considered simply a men-only, whiskey-driven gathering of 500 men until an *Oregonian* newspaper reporter infiltrated the annual blow-out in 1991 and reported back on contests involving massive amounts of drink, genitalia exposure, profanity and reams of pornographic material and beer cans strewn about the camp. The butchered rear ends of cows and deer decorated trees and signposts. To make the situation even more seamy was the fact that the party was held on public wilderness land under a special-use permit from the federal Fish & Wildlife Department. (Although the department had tried for years to revoke the permit, Oregon's senators and congressmen could be depended on to use their clout to reinstate it.)

After the *Oregonian* article, other stories about the Order began to materialize, including incidents where members had menaced tourists who had unknowingly showed up to visit the refuge during the party. The outcry against the Order's event was swift. As the gathering took place on federal land, women and minorities could no longer be excluded, and strict controls over environmental degradation would be enforced. Politicians who used to provide cover for the Order began to back away. The Order's special-use permit was permanently revoked in 1992, and the group has had to look elsewhere for a place to party. ∎

nificent scenery, stellar plant and wildlife viewing and unforgettable expanses of open space and magnitude. Both are near the tiny community of Plush, 43 miles northeast of Lakeview.

Off-road explorers will want to continue east through the Hart Mountain Antelope Refuge, and on to Frenchglen. Rock Creek Rd, designated a BLM Scenic Byway, passes through expansive prairies covered with sagebrush and thin grass, and eventually connects with Hwy 205. It's a slow, frequently rough road; allow several hours to travel the 50 miles between Plush and Frenchglen. Make sure you have plenty of fuel before embarking on this route.

### Hart Mountain Antelope Refuge

Created in 1936 as a refuge for pronghorn antelope, the Hart Mountain National Antelope Refuge is home to roughly 1700 pronghorn on the 430 sq miles of sagebrush desert and steep mountain ravines. With so much room to roam, it's possible to visit the refuge and not see antelope: keep an eye open for a cloud of dust, which the antelope kick up as they zip from place to place. Bighorn sheep were re-introduced to Hart Mountain in the 1970s, and have established a foundation herd. Coyotes, jack rabbits and kangaroo rats are also common denizens of this desert plateau.

Over 330 species of wildlife have been recorded in the refuge, making this a prime viewing area for desert and prairie animals including various raptors, burrowing owls, snakes and of course antelope.

From Plush, the road to the refuge crosses the Warner Lake basin, before it begins to climb up a steep crevice in the face of the Hart Mountain fault block. Three thousand feet later, the road emerges onto the prairie-like expanses of the antelope refuge. From here, there are magically expansive views: Hart Mountain, 8065 feet in elevation, drops off precipitously to Hart Lake, while to the north, Poker Jim Ridge plunges off onto a series of dried lake beds. It's easy to explore this amazing rim of rock on foot – in fact, it's hard to resist.

The US Department of Fish & Wildlife

office (☎ 947-3315) in Lakeview has details on the refuge. The office is on the 3rd floor of the post office building, at G and Center Sts in Lakeview.

At the refuge field headquarters, 25 miles east of Plush on the Frenchglen road, pick up a brochure and information about recent wildlife sightings. The facility is often unstaffed, but this is the only place on the refuge with water and a toilet. Make the most of it.

### Petroglyph Lake

Make a detour to this small watering hole flanked by a rocky cliff. Here, early Indians scratched symbols and animal likenesses. Follow the path to the cliff's end for the best display. This area is rich in petroglyphs and pictographs, remains from the region's long native inhabitancy. Ask at refuge headquarters for other sites.

### Warner Valley Lakes

Not an official wildlife refuge (the official name for the area is the Warner Wetlands Area of Critical Environmental Concern) this lake basin is a de facto preserve for migrating waterfowl and desert wildlife. Bulrushes and cottonwoods grow at lakes' edge, while the dry lake beds support alkali grass, greasewood and sagebrush.

Nesting white pelicans are so numerous at Pelican Lake that the lake's been named for them. Seasonally abundant waterfowl in the lakes include Canadian geese, pied-billed grebes, snowy egrets, whistling swans and all manner of ducks (a checklist of bird species is available from the BLM office or from the antelope refuge). These shallow lakes are also the only habitat in the world for the Warner sucker, a bottom-feeding fish.

The entire Warner Valley was one enormous, 500-sq-mile lake at the end of the most recent ice age. Now, only three lakes – Pelican, Crump and Hart – hold water on a more than seasonal basis, and in drought periods these three can get pretty muddy. However, during wet springs, run-off can fill much of the basin (the lakes drain to the north), offering migrating waterfowl a resting and refueling stopover, and mule deer a watering hole.

The land abutting this series of marshy lakes and playas is about half-public, half-private land, but the public roads give good access to most viewing areas.

Contact the Lakeview BLM office (☎ 947-2177), 1000 9th St, Lakeview.

### Places to Stay & Eat

The little community of Plush has very basic facilities. The *Hart Mountain Store* (☎ 947-2491) is a small store/cafe that also sells gasoline. Campers are welcome in the town's park.

*Hot Springs Campground*, in the refuge, offers informal campsites along a lovely wooded creek, about four miles south of the refuge headquarters on a graveled road; no fee. A plus is the open-air bathhouse which traps a hot spring, just the thing after a dusty day of hiking. Informal hiking trails lead up the side of Hart Mountain and its west-facing cliffs. Gentler trails from the campground lead up aspen-shaded creeksides.

Lakeview, 43 miles to the southwest of Plush, offers all services.

### LAKEVIEW

There's no longer any lake in view at Lakeview (population 2580). Lakeview is the highest city in Oregon at an elevation of 4800 feet, and is the seat of Lake County. Established in 1876, the town was frequently the scene of raucous and bloody disputes over land, especially when cattle and sheep interests clashed. Almost all the original town burned in 1900, and was rebuilt with red brick. Lakeview is still a major trading center for farmers and ranchers, and is the largest town for hundreds of miles.

Goose Lake used to be much closer to town. Locked in a steep bowl flanked on the east by the rims of Warner Mountains, the 150-sq-mile lake once flowed into the headwaters of the Pit River in northern California. The increasingly arid climate, as well as diversion of stream water into

irrigation, have worked to diminish the size of the lake, which is receding into California (35% of Goose Lake is in Oregon, with the rest across the border).

### Orientation & Information

Lakeview is 96 miles east of Klamath Falls on Hwy 140, and 142 miles south of LaPine on Hwy 31. It's 139 miles between Burns and Lakeview on Hwy 395. It takes a kind of devotion, or else *extreme* carelessness, to end up out here.

The Lake County Chamber of Commerce, (☎ 947-6040), is at 513 Center St, Lakeview, OR 97630. The Lakeview Ranger District of the Fremont National Forest (☎ 947-3334), is at 524 North G St. The BLM office (☎ 947-2177) is at 1000 9th St. The US Department of Fish & Wildlife office (☎ 947-3315) is on the 3rd floor of the post office building.

The post office (☎ 947-2280) is at 18 South G St. Lake District Hospital (☎ 947-2114) is at 700 South J St. Diane's Corner (☎ 947-3886), at 1103 N 4th St is the place to do laundry.

### Lake County Museum

Lakeview's newest museum (☎ 947-2220), 118 South E St, preserves the Western heritage of this old lumber and cow town. It also boasts some excellent artifacts of its earlier inhabitants such as bark sandals, dolls and pioneer potato mashers. The museum is open from noon to 4 pm, Thursday to Saturday, May to October. A $2 donation is requested.

### Schminck Memorial Museum

Next door to the county museum, at 128 South E St, this museum (☎ 947-3134) maintains the home of one of the town's earliest and most successful residents. After spending years of amassing family heirlooms and collecting everything imaginable, Dalph and Lula Schminck finally succumbed to pressure from friends and neighbors to see their stuff. In 1936 they formally transformed their bungalow into a museum. Family history is displayed side by side with collections of barbed wire and other oddities. It's open from 1 to 5 pm, Tuesday to Saturday. Admission is $1.

## Hiking

Old-growth ponderosa pine forests, cliffside hikes and solitude are the attractions at **Gearhart Mountain Wilderness**, northwest of Lakeview in the Fremont National Forest. Erosion has rounded the landscape of these meadowy mountains, except for the resistant volcanic plugs that rise to steep summits. Gearhart Mountain Trail transects the wilderness area, passing through meadows to reach the summit of Gearhart Peak. To the north, the trail passes tiny Blue Lake.

To reach Gearhart Mountain from Lakeview, drive west on Hwy 140 and turn north at the little community of Quartz Mountain onto USFS Rd 3660. The trailhead is at Lookout Rock, near the Corral Creek Campground, 11 miles from the highway.

## Skiing

Seven miles east on Hwy 140, Warner Canyon Ski Area (☎ 947-5001) has 14 runs and about three and a half miles of cross-country trails. Though there's only a 730-foot vertical drop, the inexpensive lift tickets – $14 a day – should get skiers' attention. There are no ski rentals at the ski area, so you'll need to rent skis in Lakeview, or bring your own.

## Hang-Gliding

Towering, treeless fault-block rims and prevailing westerly winds make Lakeview one of Oregon's centers for hang-gliding. Favorite departure spots are **Black Cap Peak**, which rises over the town of Lakeview, and the southern end of **Abert Rim**, 20 miles north of Lakeview. Despite the sport's popularity here, hang-gliding rentals and lessons are not available from any businesses in the area.

## Places to Stay

**Camping** *Junipers Reservoir RV Resort* (☎ 947-2050), 11 miles west on Hwy 140,

has a ranch setting; tents are also welcome; rates are $14/17. The campground is an official Oregon Wildlife Viewing Area, with deer, bald eagles and coyotes seen often. *Goose Lake State Park* is 14 miles south of Lakeview, right on the California border; facilities include a swimming beach, showers and electrical hook-ups; rates are $13. *Willow Creek Campground* is a USFS campground, eight miles east on Hwy 140, then six miles south on USFS Rd 3915. *Chandler Wayside*, 15 miles north on Hwy 395, is convenient to travelers heading north from Lakeview.

*Hunter's RV Park Inc* (☎ 947-4968), two miles north on Hwy 395, is a fragment of what used to be a motel and RV complex with a geyser. Hunter's also sports a grocery store, gas station, laundry and restaurant with good pizza. Rooms are available for $32/36 at the adjacent *Geyser Inn* (☎ 947-4800).

**Hotels** *AA Motel* (☎ 947-2201), 411 North F St, offers kitchen units, cable TV, a restaurant next door and single/double rooms for $30/35. *Lakeview Lodge* (☎ 947-2181), 301 North G St, has senior rates. Expect to pay about $34/38. *Rim Rock Motel* (☎ 947-2185), 727 South F St, welcomes pets and offers kitchenettes. Rooms here start at $30/34. *Skyline Motor Lodge* (☎ 947-2194), 414 North G St, has a pool and hot tub; rooms are $44/52.

**Resorts** *Aspen Ridge Resort* (☎ 884-8685), PO Box 2, Bly, OR 97622, is a new guest ranch 45 miles west of Lakeview, and is probably the nicest place to stay in this corner of Oregon. Rooms range from $65 to $85. The 7000-sq-foot lodge has a good restaurant (open to the public) and there are also self-catering cabins available. As the resort is part of a large working ranch, there's lots of room for recreation: wildlife viewing, horseback riding, mountain biking and fishing are some of the options. The resort is 18 miles southeast of Bly. Turn off Hwy 140 about a mile east of Bly, and continue on USFS Rd 3790 (Fishhole Creek Rd).

## Places to Eat

Lakeview is the kind of hard-working town where you can expect big, meat-filled meals. *Eagle's Nest Food & Spirits* (☎ 947-4824), at 117 North E St, features fresh prime rib as their specialty. *Plush West* (☎ 947-2353), 9 North F St, offers good steak, lamb and seafood in a steakhouse atmosphere. For breakfast and more casual dining, *Mom's Corner Cafe* (☎ 947-5044), 930 South F St, is good and respectable, just like mom. *Java Stop* (☎ 947-4422), 25 North E St serves up coffee, espresso muffins and the like.

## Getting There & Away

There are two Greyhound buses a day between Klamath Falls and Lakeview; passage is $16.50 each way. The bus station (☎ 947-2255) is at 619 Center St.

## LAKE ABERT

Lake Abert, nearly 62 sq miles in size, is one of the last remnants of vast lakes that covered this landscape during the last ice age (look for benchmarks of the old shore-lines on hillsides). With only one active fresh-water source, and no outlet, it is Oregon's largest salt lake. The lake's mineral content is so high that it's dangerous to swim here. Brine shrimp abound, however, and migratory birds make Lake Abert a lunch stop.

From the east shores of Lake Abert rises Abert Rim, the highest fault escarpment in the USA. Formed when geologic forces boosted up the rim while the lake dropped, the uneroded face of Abert Rim rises 2000 feet above the lake. The south face of the rim is a popular hang-gliding spot for residents around Lakeview.

## PAISLEY

Paisley (population 345), where the Chewaucan River leaves its mountain valley and flows into marshland, is an attractive old ranch town with the feel of the Old West. Paisley was once headquarters for some of the largest open-range ranches in Oregon; ZX Ranch, which controls over a million acres of land, still operates in the area.

Roads lead westward into the Fremont National Forest, an over-looked but pleasant range of mountains filled with ponderosa pines and quiet streams.

## Paisley Ranger Station Compound

The Paisley Ranger Station of the Fremont National Forest was built in the 1930s by the CCC. The grounds and buildings are still in daily use, and typify the period's rustic architectural style. Within the compound visit the Paisley Ranger District (☎ 943-3114), 303 Hwy 31. Here they have a self-guiding brochure and recreational information for the area.

## Paisley Mosquito Festival

During the last weekend of July, the town celebrates the Mosquito Festival (☎ 943-3303) with a parade, buffalo meat barbecue, street dance and the crowning of Miss Quito.

## Places to Stay & Eat

*Summer Lake Lodge* (☎ 943-3993) offers food and single/double rooms at $25/30, including breakfast. The *Summer Lake B&B* (☎ 943-3983) is south of town. Rooms here are $35/45, with condo units available for $60. Breakfast is an extra $5.

Seven miles west from Paisley, in the Fremont National Forest, is a lovely campsite at *Marster Spring*. To get there turn west at Paisley's only traffic light. Back in town, the *Miles Motel* (☎ 943-3148), has completely adequate rooms beginning at $23.

The *Pioneer Saloon & Restaurant* is, on one side, a great, old bar filled with the drawls of ranchers thinking out loud. On the other side, the bar staff serves good, homemade Mexican food. Try the *Homestead Restaurant* (☎ 943-3187), for family dining.

## SUMMER LAKE

Towering above both the town and the sometime body of water called Summer

## Sagebrush

The otherwise arid landscape of central and eastern Oregon is dominated by a botanical abundance of the dusty gray sagebrush *(Artemesia tridentata)*. Although it shares a common name with culinary sage, the strong-smelling, pitchy sagebrush of the desert isn't welcome at the table: tales abound of frontier cooks who mistakenly added sagebrush leaves to poultry stuffing, with sad results.

Sagebrush was generally treated with scorn by the American settler of the high desert, as it occupied land that ought be producing wheat. Others saw gold in the brushy, gray shrubs. During the homesteading era, highly optimistic boosters of the high desert claimed that sagebrush could be harvested and used for a base for perfume and for paper production. The distilled pitch of sagebrush was also touted as containing valuable amounts of tar, wood alcohol and acetic acid; the branches were thought a good source of charcoal. At least one factory plant opened east of Bend in 1910 to extract the untapped riches of the sagebrush that spread for hundreds of miles across the desert.

Native Americans had been at least as inventive in use of sagebrush. For the Indian peoples of this region, the shaggy, stringy bark of the plant was used in making rope, sandals and kindling.

More recently, sagebrush has been touted as a natural alternative to flea-powders and collars used on household pets, due to its strong scent. Actually, the odor of sage is a natural defense mechanism to ensure the plant's survival. The decay of fallen leaves releases a toxic compound that actually limits the growth of would-be competitor species. Although naturopathic pet owners may believe they are sparing themselves and their pets from the effects of harmful pesticides, they may not know that crushed leaves in kitty's eco-collar also possess volatile chemicals that may cause a mild allergenic effect. ■

Lake is Winter Ridge, a 7100-foot-high fault block. This little community witnessed one of Oregon's worst human disasters. On Christmas Day, 1894 most of the town's 200 inhabitants were celebrating the holiday at the town hall when fire broke out, killing 43 and seriously injuring 31 others.

Today, Summer Lake, 68 miles north of Lakeview on Hwy 31, is home to an unpleasant rest stop, and a lodge with food and rooms; at nearby Summer Lake Wildlife Area, there's good bird watching.

### Summer Lake Hot Springs

This spa (☎ 943-3931), 20 miles south of Summer Lake, offers therapeutic mineral waters. Besides the swimming pool, there are camp sites on a bluff overlooking the receding waters of Summer Lake.

### NORTH LAKE COUNTY

This region is chock full of geological curiosities. The following sites are easily reached by most family automobiles and are near to main thoroughfares; others – equally interesting – require four-wheel drive or a greater commitment of off-road travel time.

Ask locally for directions to oddities like Big Hole, The Devil's Garden, Fossil Lake and the Lost Forest. Christmas Valley-Wagontire Rd joins Fort Rock and Christmas Valley to Hwy 395, linking many of the odd volcanic and desert features of the area.

The Silver Lake Ranger District (☎ 576-2107), on Hwy 31 at the west end of Silver Lake, has recreational and travel information. The Lakeview Chamber of Commerce, or the BLM office in Lakeview (☎ 947-2177), 1000 9th St S, Lakeview, OR 97630, has brochures on the volcanic formations.

### Hole in the Ground

This enormous blast hole was left when super-heated steam and lava came in contact with a muddy, shallow sea bottom about 15,000 years ago. The resulting explosion created a perfectly circular crater a mile across and 300 feet deep. The rocks that ring the crater were thrown there by the force of the explosion (the crater was once credited to the impact of a meteorite). To reach Hole in the Ground, drive six miles north of the Fort Rock junction on Hwy 31; the crater is another six miles along a graveled road.

## Fort Rock

A similar series of underwater blasts created Fort Rock, 35 miles southeast of LaPine on Hwy 31. This entire area was a huge ice-age lake stretching for hundreds of miles across central Oregon. Rising molten rock came into contact with mud and lake water, creating a series of massive explosions. As the ash and rock were thrown into the air, they came to rest in a ring. The tuff ring grew in height until the walls of the formation were hundreds of feet in height. Wave action from the lake eventually breached the southern wall, giving access to this otherwise impregnable formation.

Today, Fort Rock is half a mile across and rises 325 feet from a dry, perfectly flat lake bed. From a distance, the formation looks remarkably like a fortress or a sports stadium.

Early Indians lived in caves in and around Fort Rock. It is here that, in 1938, archeologists found sagebrush-fiber sandals and other tools, dating from 13,000 years ago. The site is one of the earliest known human habitations in North America.

Fort Rock State Monument is two miles north of the town of Fort Rock. The park facility offers a picnic area and bathrooms. There are a number of informal trails around and over the formation. The vertical faces are popular with novice rock climbers.

In the nearby town of Fort Rock, the Homestead Village Museum commemorates the community's homestead heritage with an assemblage of old buildings and relics.

Archeologists have discovered remains of an early native culture dating from 9000 to 13,000 years ago in caves near Fort Rock in Lake County. Sandals, tools, weapons and ceremonial items point to a relatively complex culture. Pictographs in the area also depict images of men harpooning fish – an odd sight in today's desert landscape. The ancestors of the Paiute tribe gradually moved into the area; their hunting and gathering culture suited the increasingly arid climate.

## Crack in the Ground

Like its volcanic cousins, Crack in the Ground is self-descriptive. Formed about 1000 years ago when thick, cooling lava flows faulted and began to sink, this crack in the earth surface is two miles long, an average of seven to 10 feet across, and up to 70 feet deep. From the parking lot there are trails leading to the bottom of the crack; depending on your stamina and curiosity it is possible to scramble along the bottom for quite a distance.

Turn north on the gravel road that begins one mile east of the town of Christmas Valley. The next eight miles are dusty; the last mile, after you climb up on the lava flow, is quite rough. Careful driving is necessary; vehicles without high clearance will require a show of deft driving.

## Places to Stay

Camping is informal, as most of the land is publicly owned. Though it's prohibited, people often camp inside the rim of Fort Rock. There's running water at the state park parking lot. For something more legal, turn south one mile west of Silver Lake and drive 10 miles to *Silver Creek Marsh Campground* in the Fremont National Forest.

This is big, lonesome country, with long distances between towns. Before you push on 100 miles to the next town, you may want to call ahead to find out if there are motel rooms available.

The *Desert Inn Motel* (☎ 576-2262) in Christmas Valley is clean and dependable. Single/double rooms start at $20/24. *Lakeside Terrace Motel & Restaurant* (☎ 576-2309), Christmas Valley, sits beside the golf course, and pretends to be somewhere besides a desert; rooms run $23/30. *Silver Lake Motel* (☎ 576-2131), in Silver Lake, is unassuming but adequate, and rooms cost $21/27.

**Places to Eat**

*Bill's Desert Cafe & Bar* (☎ 576-2221), is Silver Lake's lone eatery. Bypass it at your risk. *Christmas Valley Lodge* (☎ 576-2333), is that town's steak house; next to the golf course, it serves drinks to thirsty putters.

OREGON

# Idaho

IDAHO

# Facts about Idaho

IDAHO

For many people, Idaho is synonymous with wilderness. Over nine million acres of the state is federally protected as roadless wilderness areas, and more than double that acreage is administered by the USFS. Idaho has more runnable white water for rafting than any other state; names like the River Of No Return and Hells Canyon bring a smile to the faces of white-water enthusiasts around the world. Wildlife otherwise very rare in the USA – woodland caribou, forest wolves and wolverines – are still found here. To paraphrase the slogan advanced by the state tourism bureau, Idaho is what the rest of the USA used to be.

However, to conceive of Idaho as an untouched piece of raw nature is to overlook a great deal. The entire southern half of the state is an arid desert, now turned into a major agricultural area by diverting almost the entire flow of the Snake River into irrigation projects. Idaho's most famous product is of course the potato, but hundreds of other crops, from mint to melons to marigolds, grow in the Snake River Basin under mile after mile of rotating sprinklers.

Even the vast forests and wilderness areas of northern and central Idaho are not the overlooked outback they once were. The woods ring with the sounds of hikers, mountain bikers, skiers, white-water rafters and hunters, and a dozen small towns throughout the state are booming as centers for outdoor recreation. The Idaho wilderness may be protected from further mining and logging, but the incredible boom in adventure and eco-tourism – and the state's aggressive marketing of its natural beauty – threaten the wilderness ethos just as surely.

It's almost a cliché to note that Idaho is a state of extremes. The most obvious and stark contrast is between the wooded and mountainous north and the agri-business-dominated irrigated desert of the south. However, the contradictions inherent in Idaho don't end with the landscape. Many

**OFFICIAL IDAHO**
**Admitted to statehood:** July 30, 1890
**Population:** 1,006,749
**Area:** 83,574 sq miles, 14th largest in USA
**Capital:** Boise
**Nickname:** Gem State
**Bird:** mountain bluebird
**Flower:** syringa
**Gemstone:** star garnet
**Tree:** white pine

other Western states also encompass more than one state's worth of geography, and yet seem to have a social cohesion and sense of purpose largely absent here. People can seem suspicious of outsiders and indifferent to issues beyond their community. From the insular Mormon farm towns of southeastern Idaho, to the youthful and trend-seeking crowds on the streets of Boise, to the Aryan Nation headquarters in the Panhandle, there seems to be little that ties these communities together.

Travelers will find a profusion of recreational opportunities here, with plenty of outfitters, resorts and guides to get you outdoors and up a hill, down the slopes or through the rapids. The scenery is diverse, and often spectacular, and the price – this is by far the least expensive part of the Northwest – is right.

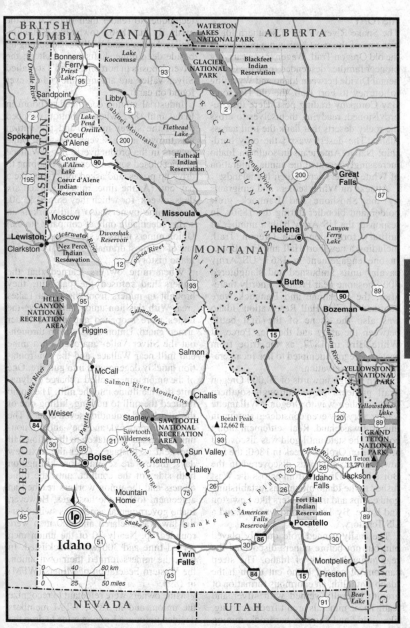

## HISTORY

The Snake River valley of southern Idaho was one of the most harrowing portions of the old Oregon Trail. Wagon trains carrying pioneer families descended from the Continental Divide between Idaho and Wyoming to journey to Fort Hall, the old Hudson's Bay Company trading post. Here they re-provisioned, readying themselves to cross the rocky deserts that flank the trail across Idaho. The desert wasn't the only hardship: Native Americans in southern Idaho increasingly resented the annual migration of White settlers across their homelands.

Attacks on White settlers and emigrants by the Shoshone and Bannock grew bolder and bloodier during the 1850s. In response, the US Army built a number of military forts along the Oregon Trail, including a new Fort Hall and Fort Boise. In one engagement in 1863, US Army cavalry units ambushed and slaughtered 400 Shoshone near Preston. Shortly thereafter, the Shoshone and Bannock were confined to Fort Hall Reservation. Idaho was also the scene of the first battle between the army and the Nez Perce, at White Bird in 1877, as the tribe from eastern Oregon attempted to flee incarceration on its reservation.

Even though upwards of 50,000 Oregon Trail pioneers passed through southern Idaho on their way to Oregon's Willamette Valley, very few even considered staying in this arid wasteland. Real settlement didn't come to the state until gold was discovered at Pierce on Orofino Creek in 1860; the following year, gold was discovered in the Boise basin. Drifters from across the West rushed to the Idaho mountains, establishing gold camps and trade centers like Lewiston and Boise. By 1863, Idaho was declared a US Territory.

The easily panned gold quickly played out, but not before miners discovered the real mineral wealth of Idaho. The steep canyons of central Idaho cut through the Idaho Batholith, an enormous formation of granite liberally veined with silver and lead. These minerals aren't free-occurring, like gold, and require hardrock mining techniques to render their riches from the earth. By the 1880s, towns like Ketchum, Hailey, Kellogg and Wallace had sprung up beside deep mine shafts and smelters; the silver deposits in northern Idaho's so-called Silver Valley are amongst the richest ever found on earth.

Industrial mining continued to boom in Idaho until 1892, when the bottom dropped out of the silver market and the nation was thrown into a severe recession. Mine owners in the productive Kellogg-Wallace district closed some silver mines, hoping to drive up prices, and asked miners to take a pay cut. (At the time, miners worked six days a week, for which they earned $3.50; some mine owners also paid workers in scrip redeemable only at company stores.) Union miners refused, setting the stage for one of the most dramatic series of events in Idaho history.

When mine owners learned that the miners had refused the pay cut, they brought in miners from the Great Lakes area. With this non-union labor force, the mines were reopened and placed under armed guard. Union miners from throughout the Silver Valley marched on a mine and mill near Wallace, and the confrontation quickly degenerated into gun fire. One of the union miners rolled a charge of dynamite down a flume into the mill. The bomb reduced the mill to nothing, killing one of the guards and wounding seven others. The guards surrendered, and they and the non-union workers were taken to the union hall and held as hostages. Over the next few days, there were several more killings on both sides of the conflict, until the mine owners and the union workers reached an agreement to free the hostages, However, Idaho governmental action was swift. Martial law was declared and 400 men were rounded up. Nearly 20 of the union men served time and 300 were blacklisted. In turn, the miners formed their own union, the Western Federation of Miners (WFM) in 1893.

Mine owners were reluctant to recognize the union, and in 1899, WFM members decided to force a Kellogg mine to drop the blacklist and hire union workers. The mine owner refused to comply with union demands, and 1000 workers gathered and blew up the mill. Although no one was injured, reaction was severe. Governor Frank Steunenberg ordered the area placed under martial law, and federal troops arrested practically the entire male population of the Coeur d'Alene Valley, finally incarcerating 1100 men in outdoor enclosure (some men remained here over a year, spending the winter without shelter). The state was determined to stamp out unionism, and forbade mine owners from hiring union workers. Martial law remained in effect for 11 months.

Five years later, the organized labor movement was again in the national headlines when then-retired Governor Steunenberg was assassinated outside his home in Caldwell. Police quickly apprehended a drifter named Harry Orchards. A Pinkerton detective elicited a confession from Orchards, who claimed he was a hit man hired by the leaders of the WFM. The union leaders were arrested and tried for murder. A celebrity trial ensued, with Clarence Darrow as counsel for the defense. In the end, the union leaders were acquitted. Orchards was sentenced to hang, but instead served life in the old Idaho State Penitentiary.

In the 20th Century, many federal projects have brought big science and military spending to the state, but not all change came courtesy of the government. In 1936, a group of investors associated with the Union Pacific Railroad developed a European ski resort near the old smelter town of Ketchum. Called Sun Valley, the resort was soon the playground of Hollywood and the wealthy elite. In many ways, Sun Valley presaged the boom of recreation and the resort lifestyle so prevalent in today's Idaho.

Even though public and private spending has worked to alter the landscape and economy of Idaho, creating such cosmopolitan getaways as Sun Valley, much of the state remains very rural and conservative. In recent years, northern Idaho especially has become notorious for its enclaves of neo-Nazis and White supremacists; the area around Hayden Lake and Rathdrum Prairie are especially infamous. The Bureau of Alcohol, Tobacco & Firearms' stand-off with Randy Weaver, a heavily armed tax-protester, in 1992 lead to the death of Weaver's wife and son, and has gone on to become one of the rallying cries of the modern Militia Movement. One-time Libertarian Party presidential candidate 'Bo' Gritz has founded a 'Christian Patriots' community in central Idaho. In Idaho, you don't have to go very far back in the woods to find extreme animosity toward the federal government, minority groups, the New World Order or gun control.

**The Desert Blooms**

Although Mormon farmers had worked up from Utah into the southeast corner of Idaho as early as 1860 – founding Franklin, Idaho's first White settlement – agricultural development of the vast Snake River basin waited for the Carey Act. This 1894 bill offered to donate tracts of federally owned arid land to developers of irrigation projects. The act was immensely popular in Idaho; with as large a river as the Snake coursing through thousands of square miles of deep, fertile but dry volcanic soil, all that was lacking were the dams to hold and divert the water. A total of 65 separate irrigation projects totaling over 938 sq miles sprang up across southern Idaho as a result of the Carey Act.

In 1900, the Twin Falls area was the first major irrigation project in Idaho. Vegetable and fruit farms developed closer to the Oregon border, at Caldwell, Nampa and Payette, while closer to the Rockies, from Blackfoot to Ashton, the potato was the crop of choice. Idaho remains the largest producer of potatoes in the nation; 70% of the crop is processed for the fast food industry! ■

## GEOGRAPHY

There are essentially two different geographic areas to Idaho. The Rocky Mountains dominate the Panhandle area – the narrow arm squeezed between Washington and Montana – and the deep mountain canyons of central Idaho. As the mountains rise higher, approaching the central spine of the Continental Divide, just across the border in Montana more rainfall is wrung out of the prevailing easterly airflows, supporting both deep forests and mighty rivers.

In the Panhandle, the landscape is also dominated by enormous lakes and low-slung, heavily-forested mountain ridges, remnants of ice-age glaciation. Farms, lumber mills and resort communities – notably Coeur d'Alene and Sandpoint – populate this hospitable province.

Much of central Idaho is comprised of the highly contorted Salmon and Clearwater river drainages. These rivers both drain directly into the Snake River in its famed Hells Canyon, the deepest gorge in North America. Consequently, both the Salmon and Clearwater cut notable canyons as they rush to their rendezvous. This deeply incised country is some of the most remote land in the continental USA, and much of it is preserved as wilderness. Few roads pass through this rugged area; Hwy 95 didn't link northern and southern Idaho until 1938; Hwy 12 passing east-west wasn't completed until 1962.

Nearly all of the broad southern base of Idaho is part of the arid Snake River basin. Although the Snake River rises in Yellowstone National Park, and forms a reflecting pool for the Grand Tetons in that national park, the majority of the river's traverse of Idaho is across a relentless lava plateau. Most of the land paralleling the interstate and the river through the bottom third of the state is flat and dusty, while to the south rise mirage-like fault block mountains thinly clad with vegetation.

Outside the range of irrigation sprinklers, the land is still lonesome and inhospitable. But all you have to do is add water to the rich soil of the basin to produce extravagant bounty; the proliferation of Snake River irrigation dams has enabled this desert plateau to bloom with a thousand different crops. The main centers of Idaho population are here also, in large farm trade towns like Twin Falls, Pocatello and Idaho Falls. The state capital of Boise sits on the northern verge of the basin, with easy access to the foothills of the Rockies.

## CLIMATE

As in other things, the climate of Idaho is capable of great extremes. Rain and snowfall is greatest in the deep forests of the Panhandle, where upwards of 60 inches of precipitation are possible. However, in the summer, when the lakeside resorts throng with visitors, the weather is usually clear and balmy, with highs in the 90°s. In winter, storms surge down out of Canada, blanketing the area with snow and low temperatures; travel can be difficult across mountain passes, and many facilities remain closed from October through May. Lows temperatures below 0° are not unusual.

The mountains and canyons of central Idaho experience much the same cold, winter weather as the north, but summer temperatures are notably warmer. In the steep canyons of the Snake and Salmon rivers, summer days can be airless and oppressively hot. Lewiston in August can be a sweltering experience, with daily highs headed for 100°s. Evenings tend to cool off sufficiently to warrant a jacket, however.

In the great desert sweep of the Snake River basin in southern Idaho, winters tend to be milder than in the north. Winter low temperatures hover in the teens, but even in winter most days are sunny. Summer weather can be oppressively hot, especially when combined with the humidity from the irrigation projects. Temperatures can exceed 100° for days at a time in July and August; even evening temperatures rarely drop below 80° during these hot spells. Early summer is a pleasant time to travel across southern Idaho, when 80° days predominate, and the native vegetation hasn't yet baked in the summer heat. Rainfall is scant in southern Idaho. In the valley bottom, rainfall can be as low as eight inches annually; Boise, set against the foothills, receives 12 inches of precipitation a year.

## POPULATION & PEOPLE

Idaho is home to just over a million people, the vast majority of whom live in the southern part of the state. Boise alone is home to more than a quarter of the population. Idaho remains much more rural than other Pacific Northwest states, with 43% of the population living on farms or in rural districts.

At 94%, the Idaho population is overwhelmingly White. According to the 1990 census, people reporting to be of Hispanic origin make up 5% of the population, though the actual percentage in southern Idaho during the agricultural season is much higher. Many road and business signs are in Spanish here, and Latin American foods are everywhere in markets, grocery stores, and road-side stands. Native Americans comprise the second-largest ethnic group in Idaho, but still only make up about 1% of the population. There are six reservations in Idaho, the largest being the Nez Perce near Lewiston, and Fort Hall, home to the Shoshone and Bannock tribes near Pocatello.

Mormonism is one of the largest organized religions in the state. Communities in the southeast corner of the state especially are dominated by spires of Latter Day Saint temples.

## ARTS

Idaho isn't anywhere close to the cutting edge of the artistic world, but if you're fond of Western or wildlife art, then Boise has a number of galleries that are worth exploring. Some galleries and markets near the Nez Perce Reservation feature the work of local native artists, including bead and leatherwork, and carvings.

### Literature

Two of Idaho's greatest claims in literature are Ezra Pound, the poet, who was born in Hailey in 1885, and Ernest Hemingway, who made his home in Ketchum before committing suicide there in 1961. Pound only lived in Idaho for two years, however, and he achieved his greatest fame in Paris and his greatest notoriety in St Elizabeth's prison hospital after WW II. Hemingway frequently visited Idaho, obsessed as he was by hunting and fishing. He didn't actually move to Idaho until 1960; a touching memorial to the Nobel Prize-winning novelist stands in a grove of cottonwood trees above Ketchum. Though hardly of the same rank in terms of literary reputation, Edgar Rice Burroughs, the creator of Tarzan, spent his formative years in Idaho working on ranches.

Another noted writer of the previous generation is Vardis Fisher, a novelist and essayist who chronicled Idaho during the 1930s and '40s and is now best known for penning the state guide to Idaho for the WPA.

### Performing Arts

As in most things, Boise is the center for the state's musical scene. In terms of classical music, Boise has a full array of musical institutions, including an opera, symphony and ballet. Boise has a few live music venues, but nothing like the scene found in coastal Northwest cities.

Live music in much of Idaho means live country-&-western music on the weekends at the local honky-tonk. Summer brings music festivals to Sandpoint and Boise, and the National Fiddlers contest to Weiser.

### Theater & Film

There are a number of theater troupes in Boise, including one equity group. Dinner and mystery theater are more the norm.

Idaho makes an appearance now and then in films. Bill Forsyth's *Housekeeping* was shot near Bonners Ferry, even though the film is meant to take place in British Columbia. A few scenes of Gus Van Sant's *My Own Private Idaho* were shot in state, and Robert Redford's cinema-verité *Downhill Racer* takes place partially in Sun Valley.

IDAHO

## INFORMATION
### Telephone
The area code for all of Idaho is 208.

### Time
The Idaho Panhandle is in the Pacific Time Zone, which is eight hours behind GMT/ UTC, and three hours behind New York City. All the rest is in the Mountain Time Zone, one hour ahead of Pacific Time.

### Taxes
Idaho sales tax is 5%. There is also an additional 6% bed tax in effect statewide.

# Southern Idaho

Southern Idaho is dominated by the Snake River and the broad desert basin through which it flows. Formerly a mostly lifeless tract of lava flows, sagebrush and scorpions, the region now blooms with hundreds of irrigated crops and is one of the most important food-producing areas in the entire USA.

The wide southern base of Idaho contains by far the majority of the state's population and is the center of Idaho's economy. Idaho's capital and largest city, Boise, is here. Known for its exuberant and youthful lifestyle, Boise is a worthy destination for travelers who enjoy a hip, easy-going city that's hell-bent on outdoor recreation. Other communities along the Snake River are mostly devoted to the needs of area farmers and ranchers, but welcome travelers with inexpensive rooms and a wary courtesy. In the Sawtooth Range, Ketchum and Sun Valley are synonymous with celebrity, great skiing and the affluent fantasy world of the New West.

Traveling across southern Idaho can be a long and grueling affair, especially in the summer, when temperatures regularly reach into the 100°s and the pervasive irrigation projects boost the humidity percentage toward the same number. Distances are great, and even freeway driving won't get you where you want to be in a hurry. Caldwell to Rexburg is over 300 miles; during the journey there's scarcely a hill to be seen, and mile after mile of irrigated field and desert pasture eventually make for poor company.

Make the most of it by pulling off the freeway to explore the green, spring-filled Hagerman Valley and the pleasant downtowns of Twin Falls and Idaho Falls. The eastern edge of the region bumps up against the Rocky Mountains, with easy access to two of the greatest of the US national parks – Yellowstone and Grand Teton.

## HISTORY

The desert basin of the Snake River is home to two related, indigenous tribes, the Shoshone and the Bannock. These people have lived in southern Idaho at least since the end of the last ice age, when this was a much more hospitable and lake-filled area. The fortunes of both tribes were immensely boosted when they became the first of the Northwest tribes to get horses, procured from Spanish colonies from the south.

With the horses' mobility, the Shoshone-Bannocks quickly became one of the dominant Indian groups in the West, ranging across the Rockies onto the Great Plains to hunt buffalo and onto the Columbia plateau to trade and plunder. The Shoshone-Bannock developed a reputation among other native tribes for fierce, warlike aggression.

The first White explorers in southern Idaho were fur trappers; during the primacy of the Hudson's Bay Company, British interests held sway across southern Idaho to the crest of the Continental Divide in Wyoming. The Oregon Trail entered Idaho near Montpelier, in the southeast corner of the state, and wound north to the Snake River. Early pioneers traveled to the HBC's Fort Hall, near modern-day Blackfoot, to trade for food and goods before embarking on the long trail across Idaho.

By the 1860s, relations between the Shoshone-Bannock tribe and the Whites had frayed considerably. Crossing southern Idaho became one of the most dangerous portions of the Oregon Trail, with the natives ambushing wagon trains with increasing frequency and violence. The US Army moved in and built a number of forts along the trail, and they inflicted a bloody and devastating defeat on the Shoshone in 1863, at the Battle of Bear River, near Preston.

The modern history of southern Idaho is

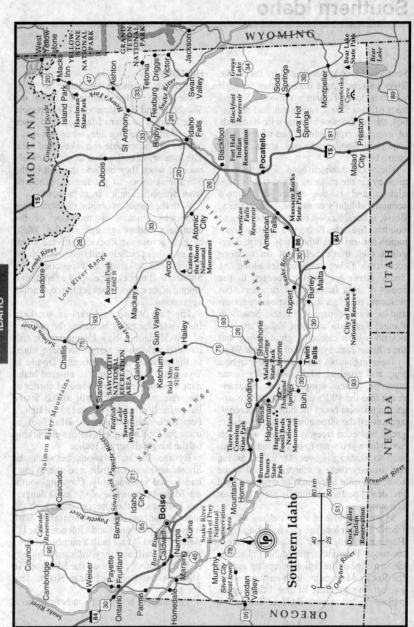

Southern Idaho

largely the story of irrigation. Under the provisions of the Carey Act of 1894, the federal government agreed to deed approximately one million acres of publicly held desert land to a state or individuals if the land was irrigated and opened for farming. Idaho farmers and developers rose to the challenge and dammed the Snake and other southern Idaho rivers at every conceivable location. By 1930, over 600,000 acres of desert land had been reclaimed for agriculture. Agribusiness is by far the largest segment of the Idaho economy, and the state produces one-third of the nation's potatoes and most of its peas, onions and processed vegetables.

In 1949, the Idaho National Energy Laboratory, an experimental nuclear energy facility, was established near Arco. The world's first nuclear reactor was developed here, and in 1956 Arco became the first city in the world to operate on nuclear energy. The site has been named a National Historic Landmark; research into nuclear science and radioactive waste disposal continues here.

### GEOGRAPHY & GEOLOGY

Between the arch of the Rocky Mountains and the beginnings of North America's Great Basin lies a trough of land about 200 miles across that in geologically recent times filled to brimming with extensive lava flows. Beginning about two million years ago and lasting until about two thousand years ago, unremarkable-looking shield volcanoes on the northern edge of the basin cracked open to ooze immense amounts of molten basalt, filling the valley with deposits up to 5000 feet deep.

It's across this desolate plateau that the mighty Snake River cuts its path, rising from a lake in Yellowstone Park and cutting across the base of the Grand Tetons before venturing into the desert. This is a resolutely flat landscape, and the topographical variations of the Snake River plain across southern Idaho are too minor to relieve the monotony. East of Burley, the Snake River stays on the surface of the lava formations, but by Twin Falls, the river has

begun to cut a massive desert canyon nearly 400 feet deep.

Along the southern fringe of the Snake River basin rise fault-block mountains, including the Owyhee, which drain into Oregon, and the Wasatch, whose rivers contribute to the Great Salt Lake.

### GETTING THERE & AWAY

The main roads through southern Idaho are I-84, which links Oregon to Boise, Twin Falls and Salt Lake City, UT, and I-15, which runs north from Salt Lake City to Pocatello, Idaho Falls and on into Montana. Other major roads include Hwy 20, which links Idaho Falls to Yellowstone National Park, and Hwy 95, which connects I-84 along Idaho's western border to Lewiston in central Idaho.

Boise Municipal Airport is the primary airport for the region, with connections to most US cities. Twin Falls, Pocatello and Idaho Falls also have regional airports, with connections to West Coast cities, Salt Lake City and Denver, CO. There's limited commercial air service to Sun Valley.

Buses generally stick to the freeway system, connecting Salt Lake City to the West Coast via communities along the Snake River. One bus a day follows the interstate highways connecting Boise to Pocatello and Butte, MT. Buses also connect Boise to Lewiston and to Reno, NV.

Amtrak's *Pioneer* line crosses Idaho, with four stops weekly each way. Pocatello, Shoshone (for Twin Falls) and Boise are the assigned stops.

# Southwestern Idaho

### BOISE

Boise (population 130,000) is a high-spirited and thoroughly enjoyable city that manages to meld the vestiges of the cowboy Old West with the sophistication of the urban Pacific Northwest. A large part of Boise's vibrancy derives from the fact that it's the state capital, it's Idaho's largest city

IDAHO

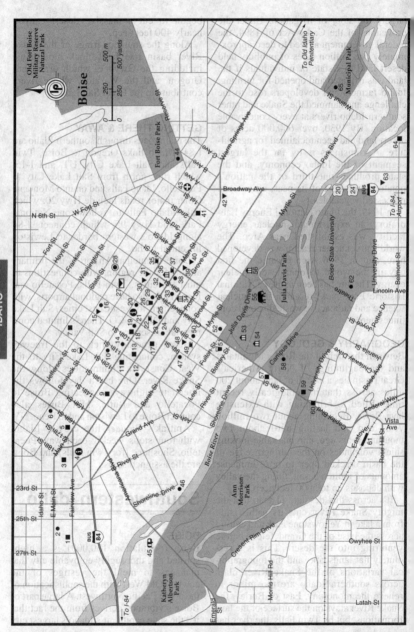

**IDAHO**

and it's home to a major university, a triple crown that no other city in the Northwest can claim. Add to it the aura of a recreational resort, and you begin to arrive at its special youthful élan.

Boise is a small city, relatively speaking, and easy to get around in. Although the locals will blandly talk about this or that downtown district, outsiders will find Boise easy to maneuver in and a lot of fun to explore. There's none of the scruffy, urban stress of Portland or Seattle, and no undercurrent of crime or hostility. But there's plenty of street life: cafes and restaurants remain open late

into the night, and on hot summer evenings crowds from nightspots spill out onto the sidewalks.

Boise is at the edge of the vast Snake River Plain, backed up to the foothills of the Sawtooth Range. The name 'Boise' derives from the French word for 'wooded', and the city does its best to live up to its billing. City parks are numerous and well watered, providing a welcoming shimmer of green to locals and travelers alike. The Boise Greenway follows the Boise River through the length of town; this recreational frontage links many of the city's established parks and civic institutions.

The city was born of a gold rush, and much of its late-19th-century architectural core remains.

Boise is one of the fastest-growing cities in the nation. Young people have flocked here for the excellent and accessible outdoor recreation: there is more outdoors and more tanned, muscular bodies here than almost anywhere in the Northwest. Mountain biking and white-water rafting are so well-loved as to be near-mandatory pursuits; in winter, skiers take off for nearby ski resorts.

## History

The town of Boise grew up alongside Fort Boise, which the army established in 1863 to protect Oregon Trail pioneers from native reprisals. However, the growth of the town was more closely tied to the Idaho gold rush.

Gold was first discovered in central Idaho in 1860, establishing Lewiston as the state's first town and territorial capital. However, fertile gold placers were found in 1862 near Idaho City in the Boise basin, and many people headed south, lured by tales of rich prospecting. By the time the second legislature met in Lewiston in 1864, the area around Boise had drained off most of central and northern Idaho's population, and the delegates voted to move the capital to Boise. Partisans of Lewiston put the state seal under armed guard to prevent the seat of government from moving, and it wasn't until the following year that federal troops succeeded in seizing the seal and the territorial records and moving them to Boise.

Boise grew fitfully throughout the rest of the 19th century, but like the rest of southern Idaho it received a boost when federal irrigation projects brought canals and reservoirs to the desert plateau along the Snake River. More recently, Boise has been very successful at attracting major businesses to headquarter here. Morrison Knudsen Co, the engineering-construction giant, Boise Cascade, the forest-products leader; Ore-Ida Foods; Albertson's, the supermarket chain; JR Simplot, the agricultural chemical manufacturer; and Hewlett Packard each are headquartered or maintain a large corporate presence in the city.

## Orientation

Boise is located along the Boise River, just north of I-84. The east access route from I-84 follows Broadway Ave and enters downtown along Front St; the west access follows Fairview Ave and enters downtown along Main St.

The main business and shopping district is between State and Grove Sts, and between 9th and 4th Sts. The main north-south street is Capitol Blvd, which runs from the state capitol building across the Boise River, past Boise State University and to the base of the hill dominated by the towering Morrison Knudsen Depot.

Many restaurants and nightspots are found in so-called Old Boise, which is more or less centered at 6th and Main Sts. Another downtown center of activity is The Grove, at 8th and Grove Sts, where a large fountain, public plaza and the Boise Convention Center provide a natural gathering place. The 8th St Market Place, a gentrified warehouse district, is a landmark but somewhat sleepy shopping area just south of downtown.

Streets in the older section of Boise (north of the river) are a puzzle of different grids, and when the arbitrarily arranged blocks of streets meet, rather bizarre and confusing intersections are the rule. In general, numbered streets run north-south, and named streets run east-west.

Boise has an extensive park system, and many of the parks are linked by the paved Boise Greenway, a 19-mile hiking and biking path along the Boise River. The long string of parks and public green spaces includes Julia Davis Park, Warm Springs Golf Course, the Boise State University campus and Discovery State Park, outside of Boise. The Pioneer Walk near Ann Morrison Park connects the Greenway with Front St, downtown. The grounds of Old Fort Boise are also a park, with hiking trails winding through its 466 acres.

## Information

**Tourist Offices** The Boise Convention & Visitors Bureau (☎ 344-7777), 168 N 9th St, is open weekdays from 8:30 am to 5 pm. There are also tourist information centers downtown at 850 W Front St, at the convention center and in the capitol building at 8th and Bannock Sts. The AAA office (☎ 342-9391) is at 3040 Elder St, off I-84 exit No 53, opposite the airport.

Boise has two USFS offices. The Forest Supervisor office for the Boise National Forest (☎ 364-4100) is downtown at 1750 Front St. On Boise's eastern outskirts is a district ranger station (☎ 343-2527), 5493 Warm Springs Ave. Get information about state parks from the Idaho State Parks headquarters (☎ 327-7444), 7800 Fairview Ave.

For information on road conditions in southwest Idaho, call 376-8028. For conditions statewide, call 336-6600.

**Post** There's a post office downtown (☎ 343-5647) at 8th and Bannock Sts, near the capitol building.

**Bookstores** The Book Shop (☎ 342-2659), 906 Main St, specializes in travel books, maps and books on Idaho. For magazines and out-of-town newspapers head to Coffee-News (☎ 344-7661), 801 W Main St. Roads Less Traveled (☎ 384-5075), 1700 Vista Ave, is an independent bookstore selling new and used books, specializing in small-press titles. There's a good selection of books on Idaho history and travel at the Idaho Historical Museum (☎ 334-2120), 610 Julia Davis Drive.

**Media** Pick up a copy of the *Idaho Statesman* for mainstream daily news. Boise also has scads of mostly free, local alternative papers, the most prominent being the *Boise Weekly*, which has useful entertainment listings and reviews. Another good place to look for nightlife listings and community features is *The Arbiter*, Boise State University's official (but still irreverent) student newsweekly. Get gay, lesbian and bisexual news in *Diversity*, or Idaho-flavored feminist essays in *Women's Times*. Current political issues are parodied monthly in the *Idaho Comic News*. Public radio is heard on KBSU at 90.3 FM and on KBSX at 91.5 FM.

**Laundry** Downtown, the Sixteenth Street Coin-Op Laundry (☎ 345-3958), 215 N 16th St, is open long hours and has large washers for dirty sleeping bags.

**Medical Services** Saint Alphonsus Regional Medical Center (☎ 378-2121), 1055 N Curtis Rd, is off I-84. St Luke's Regional Medical Center (☎ 386-2269), 190 E Bannock St, is closer to downtown.

## Walking Tour

Most of the following downtown Boise sites are laid out with a walking tour in mind. The tour begins at the state capitol building, proceeds through old Boise and cuts through Julia Davis Park, where several museums and the city zoo are located. The tour then crosses the Boise River to the Boise State campus and returns to the downtown area past the Basque Museum to The Grove, the city's central plaza. Another option for a quick overview of the city is the **Boise Tour Train** (see Organized Tours below).

## Idaho State Capitol Building

Construction of the Idaho capitol began in 1905 and was completed in 1920. Modeled after the domed Capitol in Washington, DC, the Idaho state capitol was built of convict-quarried sandstone from nearby Table Mountain. However, the rather dowdy-looking exterior belies the handsome interior, faced with four different colors of marble and embellished with mahogany woodwork.

The 1st floor of this 201,000-sq-foot building contains a number of epic sculptures and a display of rare Idaho gemstones. Step into the rotunda and gaze upward into the dome, which rises nearly 200 feet to end in a patch of sky-blue emblazoned with 43 stars (Idaho was the 43rd state admitted to the union). The legislative chambers are on the 3rd floor, and

IDAHO

Idaho State Capitol (BM)

**IDAHO**

the viewing galleries are on the 4th floor. Idaho's capitol is the only geothermally heated statehouse in the nation; water from hot springs five blocks away is pumped into the building's radiators. Tour the grounds of the capitol to see a number of trees planted by various presidents and the commemorative statues, which include one of Governor Frank Steunenberg, who was assassinated in 1905.

The capitol is at Capitol Blvd and Jefferson St. It's open to the public for self-guided tours from 8 am to 6 pm Monday to Friday, and from 9 am to 5 pm on Saturday. Free guided tours are available only when the legislature is in session (usually from January to March). For more information, call 334-2470.

### Old Boise
From the capitol, proceed down Capitol Blvd to Main St. From this corner east along Main St to about 3rd St is a district of fine old buildings – many renovated into shops and restaurants – that recalls Boise's turn-of-the-century opulence. Don't miss the **Egyptian Theatre** from 1927, a way-over-the-top early theater and vaudeville hall that is decorated in full King Tut shtick. At 6th Ave and Main St is the **Bicycle History Museum** (☎ 345-5335), a privately owned collection of antique bicycles, posters, prints and memorabilia from the mid 19th century to the present. A study of the future of nonreplenishable natural resources led Paul Niquette to simulate life for five years in a hypothetical 'Post-Petroleum Age', which sparked his bicycle collection. Highlights include the largest bicycle in the world, the 64-inch Columbia Expert, eccentric rear-steered and sail-powered models and a 16th-century sketch of a chain-driven safety bicycle by a pupil of Leonardo da Vinci. It's open from 10 am to 6 pm Monday to Friday, and from 10 am to 5 pm Saturday. Admission is free.

### Julia Davis Park
This lovely park fronts onto the Boise River and contains many of Boise's important museums and cultural institutions, as well as the civic **rose garden**.

The premier museum in the state is the **Idaho Historical Museum** (☎ 334-2120), 610 N Julia Davis Drive, which provides an excellent overview of the state's rich historic heritage. Displays follow a general timeline of Idaho history and include good coverage of the region's Native Americans, the Oregon Trail pioneers and the mining frontier. Exhibits include a re-created saloon, blacksmith's forge, pioneer kitchen and a Chinese apothecary shop. The museum is open from 9 am to 5 pm Monday to Saturday, and from 1 to 5 pm Sunday; admission is free. Immediately next door to the museum is the **Pioneer Village**, a collection of old pioneer buildings, most dating from the mid to late 19th century.

Also in the park is the **Boise Art Museum** (☎ 345-8330), 670 S Julia Davis Drive, which features permanent and traveling exhibits of visual arts, including a good collection focusing on American Realism. It's open from 10 am to 5 pm

Tuesday to Friday, and from noon to 5 pm Saturday and Sunday. The museum is free from 10 am to 9 pm on the first Thursday of every month. Regular admission is $3/2 for adults/seniors and students; children (up to age 18) are $1.

In the middle of the park is **Zoo Boise** (☎ 384-4230). The zoo boasts the largest display of birds of prey in the Northwest, including bald and golden eagles and indigenous hawks. Also on display are Idaho big game animals like moose, elk and bighorn sheep. In addition to traditional exotic zoo favorites from Africa, there's also a children's petting zoo. The zoo is open daily from 10 am to 5 pm. Admission is $3 for adults and $1.50 for seniors; children ages four to 11 are $1.25. Zoo admission is half price on Thursday.

The **Discovery Center of Idaho** (☎ 343-9895), 121 Myrtle St, is a museum of experiential, hands-on science that is popular with children. Check out the cool magnetic sand. It's open from 9 am to 5 pm Tuesday to Friday, from 10 am to 5 pm Saturday, and from noon to 5 pm Sunday. Admission is $4 for adults and $3 for seniors; children (up to age 18) are $2.50.

### Boise State University
Across a footbridge from Julia Davis Park is Boise State University (BSU), Idaho's largest with an enrollment of over 14,000 students. The university was founded in 1932 and was made a part of the state university system in 1974. Consequently, there's little historic or notable architecture on the 110-acre campus, but the setting – along the Boise River Greenway – and the quad-like symmetry of the red-brick buildings make for a pleasant stroll.

### Basque Museum & Cultural Center
Across the Boise River from BSU along Capitol Blvd are two sites that commemorate the Basque pioneers and residents of Idaho. The Basque Museum & Cultural Center (☎ 343-2671), 611 Grove St, tells the story of these Pyrenean people who settled in Idaho from the late 19th century onward; southwest Idaho contains one of the largest Basque settlements outside of Europe. Besides the museum, the cultural center features language classes, a reading room and a gift shop. Next door, at 607 Grove St, is the **Cyrus Jacobs-Uberuaga House**, built in 1864 as a boarding house for Basque immigrants. The boarding house (Boise's first brick building) is now part of the museum. Both sites are open from 10 am to 4 pm Tuesday to Friday, and from 11 am to 3 pm Saturday; admission is by donation.

### The Grove
At Grove and 8th Sts is Boise's unofficial city center, The Grove, a brick-lined plaza containing a large fountain, sculptures and a pedestrian area. Summer concerts, sunbathing, hackey-sacking and general lolling about is the order of business here most of the year. Boise Center, the local convention facility, also faces onto The Grove, as do a number of cafes. Don't come here looking for shade, however. The Grove is named for the street it interrupts, not for an abundance of trees.

### Old Idaho Penitentiary
Idaho's first penitentiary was built in 1870 and was used for incarceration until 1974, when a new facility was built and the original grounds were turned into a museum (☎ 334-2844), 2445 Penitentiary Rd. Placed on the National Register of Historic Places in 1974, this old prison is creepy, fascinating and very well-curated, as it teaches a lot about changing cultural notions of punishment and criminality, showing how prison architecture and facilities changed to reflect this.

Begin a tour of the prison by watching the 15-minute film that describes the different phases of the prison's construction and the various Wild West desperadoes who were jailed here. A brochure leads you on a self-guided tour through the prison yards. Open for viewing are most of the remaining buildings, including various cell blocks, the solitary confinement cells, the Death Row building and the gallows. The small rose garden in the prison yard was formerly

**IDAHO**

used for executions. Outside the walls is the Women's Ward, where Idaho's female inmates were housed (a total of 215 women served time here).

A few of the prison buildings contain exhibits. One unique display explores the topic of prison tattoos. Interpretive exhibits of Idaho's transportation history are also on display in the old shirt-making factory.

The Old Idaho Penitentiary is open daily from 10 am to 6 pm during the summer, including state holidays; during the rest of the year, it's open daily from noon to 5 pm and closed major holidays. Guided tours are offered once daily at 1 pm. Admission is $3 for adults and $2 for seniors and children.

Just outside the penitentiary is the **Idaho Botanical Garden** (☎ 343-8649), 2355 Penitentiary Rd, with nine theme gardens, including a Basque, Heirloom Rose and Butterfly Garden; the Meditation Garden seems an odd place, backed up against the prison walls! The grounds are open from 9 am to 5 pm Tuesday to Thursday, and from noon to 8 pm Friday to Sunday, April 15 to October 15. Admission is $2 for adults and $1 for seniors and children.

## Morrison Knudsen Nature Center

The high point of this park, wetlands area and natural history exhibit (☎ 334-2225), 600 S Walnut St (behind the Idaho Department of Fish and Game office), is the underwater viewing windows that allow a peek into life in a simulated mountain stream. Watch trout gobble tadpoles and insect larva. Outdoor paths lead along the stream to a wetland pond and a habitat demonstration area. The museum and underwater viewing area are closed Mondays, and hours are seasonal. Admission is $2.50 for adults and $1.50 for seniors and students; children ages six to 12 are 50c. The stream area is open daily from sunrise to sunset and is free of charge.

## Morrison Knudsen Depot

The grand Union Pacific Railroad Station, a whitewashed, red-tiled affair that looks more like an old Spanish mission than a train station, stands on a hill above Boise.

The station, built in 1925, was mothballed when Union Pacific ceased passenger rail service in 1971. Twenty years later, Morrison Knudsen bought the building and restored it into a museum and cultural center (☎ 386-7500), 2603 Eastover Terrace. Exhibits in the Great Hall (the vestibule of the old station) include railroad memorabilia, a telling of the region's rail history and an interpretation of Morrison Knudsen's contribution to the rail industry. It's open from 10 am to 4 pm Monday to Friday. Admission is $3 for adults and $2 for seniors and students; children ages six to 18 are $1.

Amtrak trains stop at the station; however, today's passengers are only allowed into a tiny, unhistoric corner of this grand edifice.

## Organized Tours

The Boise Tour Train (☎ 342-4796) departs from Julia Davis Park (near the Historical Society) to tour Boise in open-air train cars. Tours operate daily during the summer, Wednesday to Sunday during September, and weekends only in October and May; call for departure times. Admission is $6 for adults and $5.50 for seniors; children ages three to 12 are $3.50.

Destination Idaho (☎ 343-9366), 500 W Idaho St, Suite 215, will design custom tours of the Boise area, including guided outdoor activities and ski trips.

## Rafting & Floating

A number of river outfitters lead float trips from Boise to more distant rivers. The closest river with challenging white-water is the Payette River, which flows south from Payette Lake past Cascade.

Headwaters River Company (☎ 793-2348, (800) 876-7238), PO Box 1, Banks, ID 83602, operates white-water rafting trips down the Payette River from Banks, 42 miles north of Boise on Hwy 55. Easygoing, introductory half-day shoots start at $30 for adults; full-day trips (lunch included) start at $66. Headwaters also offers multiple-day trips and kayak lessons. Idaho Whitewater Unlimited (☎ 888-3008),

1042 E Ustick St, Meridian, ID 83642, and Cascade Raft Company (☎ 462-3292, (800) 292-7238), PO Box 6, Garden Valley, ID 83622, both offer float trips down all forks of the Payette River.

Coeur d'Alene-based ROW (River Odysseys West/Remote Odysseys Worldwide) (☎ 756-0841, (800) 451-6034), PO Box 579, Coeur d'Alene, ID 83816, has one of the largest menus available, with multiple-day trips on several rivers throughout Idaho in oar rafts, paddle rafts and inflatable kayaks. They also lead international trips to Ecuador, Turkey, France and Nepal! Boise is the meeting point for many trips, including three to six-day trips on the Snake River through Hells Canyon ($610 to $1080) and four to seven-day trips on the Owyhee River fork of your choice ($845 to $1250). Snake River float/horseback trips and Snake/Salmon or Snake/Lochsa River combinations can be arranged upon request.

Wilderness River Trips at MacKay Bar (☎ (800) 635-5336), 3190 Airport Way, Boise, ID 83705, has float trips through the Middle and Main Forks of the Salmon River, and they offer float trips through the Birds of Prey section of the Snake River.

If you're interested in renting a raft to make your own run down the river, contact the Wheels R Fun shop (listed above) or Idaho River Sports Sales & Rentals (☎ 336-4844), 1521 N 13th St.

## Swimming
Go to the Natatorium and Hydrotube (☎ 345-9270), in Municipal Park at 1811 Warms Springs Ave, where the waters come from some of the region's many hot springs. Wild Waters (☎ 322-1844), just off I-84 exit No 50, is an entire complex that combines a waterslide, swimming pool and a number of cooling water-related activities.

## Golf
You shouldn't have any problem finding a place to golf in Boise. The closest 18 holes to downtown are at the Warm Springs Golf Club (☎ 343-5661), 2495 Warm Springs

Ave, right on the Boise River and Greenway. Quail Hollow (☎ 344-7807), 4520 N 36th St, lies on northernmost borders of Boise, as does Plantation Golf Course (☎ 853-4440), 6515 W State St, across the river from the fairgrounds. Public courses on the southern side of Boise include Indian Lake Golf Course (☎ 362-5771), 4700 S Umatilla Ave near the airport; take the exit off I-84 at Cole Rd and travel south. You can continue west on I-84 and take the Cloverdale Rd exit south for the new Boise Ranch Golf Course (☎ 362-6501), 6501 S Cloverdale Rd.

## Other Activities
The main focus for recreation in Boise is the Greenway, the 19-mile **hiking**, **biking** and jogging trail that links many of the city's parks.

Wheels R Fun (☎ 343-8228), at Shoreline Drive and S 13th St, rents rollerblades, bikes, rafts and innertubes from its convenient location near the Greenway. It's $18 for eight hours of rollerblade or bike rental (all safety equipment included). Those put off by the $36 raft rental should get an innertube instead for $4. It's open daily in the summer, only weekends during spring and fall, and closed in the winter.

Idaho Mountain Touring (☎ 336-3854), 915 W Jefferson St, rents bikes and camping equipment. A full-day mountain bike rental costs $23, which includes a helmet and lock.

If you want to head out into the mountains, consider taking a llama along. High Llama Wilderness Tours (☎ 323-0868), 2500 Mill Way, use llamas as pack animals on fishing, hiking and photography trips.

## Special Events
On the first Thursday of every month, art galleries downtown stay open extended hours into the evening, using the occasion to open new exhibits on the First Thursday Art Tour (☎ 336-2631). The Boise Art Museum is also open late and admission is free on this day.

Open-air concerts abound in Boise during the summer. Alive After Five

(☎ 336-2631), held every Wednesday evening (5 to 7 pm) from the first Wednesday in May till the last Wednesday in September, features free live music at The Grove in downtown Boise. Every Wednesday evening in July there's a free rock concert at the Julia Davis Park Bandstand.

Boise's biggest summer festival is the Boise River Festival, which takes over several city parks and features parades, fireworks, free concerts, theater and sporting events. This family-oriented event is held the last Thursday to Sunday in June. Contact the visitors bureau at 344-7777 for more information.

Boise celebrates its Basque heritage with the San Inazio Basque Festival (☎ 343-2671), the last weekend of July. Besides folk dancing, music and food booths, the festival also brings in special guests from Boise's sister cities in the Pyrenees.

The Western Idaho Fair (☎ 376-3247), held in late August at the fairgrounds on Chinden Blvd, is a celebration of the state's agricultural bounty, with a carnival, a rodeo and various farm products, livestock, and garden competitions.

The City Arts Celebration (☎ 336-4936) fills the month of September with special performances, films and exhibits; Joan Baez was here in 1994. One part of the festival is Art in the Park (☎ 345-8330), a large arts-&-crafts festival held in Julia Davis Park.

### Places to Stay

**Camping** KOA Boise (☎ 345-7673), just off I-84 exit No 57, is a full-service campground with a swimming pool, laundry and playground. Standard sites for tents are $17.50; hook-ups are $22. On the River RV Park (☎ 375-7432), 6000 Glenwood St, offers swimming and fishing in the Boise River. Campsites range between $10 and $17.50. To reach the campground, take I-84 exit No 46 and continue north for four miles. Turn east (toward Boise) on Hwy 20/26 for nearly four miles, and turn north onto Glenwood St. There's RV-only camping at the attractive Americana Kampground (☎ 344-5733), 3600 Americana Terrace, right on the Greenway; rates range between $12 and $17.

**B&Bs** The Idaho Heritage Inn B&B (☎ 342-8066), 109 W Idaho St, is a large, old Boise home near downtown and the capitol. Six guestrooms are available, and prices range from $55 to $95; bicycles are available for guests. The Robin's Nest B&B (☎ 336-9551), 2389 W Boise Ave, is a 19th-century Victorian home with rooms from $65 to $95.

**Hotels – bottom end & middle** It's not hard to find a moderately priced motel or hotel in Boise. With so many to choose from, try to stay close to downtown or near where your business takes you, and enjoy walking the busy evening streets.

Just outside of downtown are a number of inexpensive older motels. For $25 to $50, you can get a room at the Cabana Inn (☎ 343-6000), 1600 Main St, or the Capri Motel National 9 Inn (☎ 344-8617), 2600 Fairview Ave, which takes pets and has a sauna and restaurant. The Sands Motel (☎ 343-2533), 1111 W State St, offers basic single/double rooms for $25/28.

Another motel strip lies next to BSU along Capitol Blvd. The Boisean Motel (☎ 343-3645, (800) 365-3645), 1300 S Capitol Blvd, has an outdoor pool and kitchenettes, and rooms range between $30 to $75. The University Inn (☎ 345-7170, (800) 345-7170), 2360 University Drive, has a restaurant and an outdoor pool. Pets are allowed, and rooms are $42 to $64. Near the east end of the campus, Boise River Inn (☎ 344-9988), 1140 Colorado Ave, has an outdoor pool, free continental breakfast and rooms with kitchenettes for $50/55.

You don't need to pay more to stay near the heart of downtown. The Boise Centre Travelodge (☎ 342-9351, (800) 255-3050), 1314 Grove St, has an outdoor pool and rooms for $34 to $55. The Best Western Safari Motor Inn (☎ 344-6556, (800) 541-6556), 1070 Grove St, is one of the sweeter deals in Boise with an outdoor pool, free continental breakfast, sauna and jacuzzi and rooms for $41 to $72. Both places allow pets.

The grande dame of Boise lodging is undoubtedly the *Idanha Hotel* (☎ 342-3611), 928 Main St, a lovely Queen Anne-style hotel built in 1901. The Idanha has been renovated enough to make it comfortable for modern travelers without losing its venerability and charm. It offers free continental breakfast and has a good restaurant; ask for one of the turret rooms. Rates range from $45 to $62.

**Hotels – top end** Though the following are generally newer and offer more amenities, you'll find that the prices aren't necessarily much higher than other places. The *Boise Park Suite Hotel* (☎ 342-1044, (800) 342-1044), 424 E Park Center Blvd, is popular with business travelers and offers free continental breakfast, fitness center and pool; rooms range from $59 to $115. The *Statehouse Inn* (☎ 342-4622, (800) 243-4622), 981 Grove St, is convenient to downtown, has a spa and allows pets; rooms run $59 to $110. Just across the river from downtown is the *Ramada Inn* (☎ 344-7971, (800) 727-5010), 1025 S Capitol Blvd near BSU. There's a pool, hot tub and restaurant; rates are $42 to $150.

The *Owyhee Plaza Hotel* (☎ 343-4611, (800) 821-7500 in Idaho, (800) 233-4611 out of state), 1109 Main St, is an original old Boise hotel that has been completely renovated, with the lodging now contained in a new addition. There's an outdoor pool, a good restaurant and a free airport shuttle; rooms are $53 to $95. The *Red Lion Hotel/Downtowner* (☎ 344-7691, (800) 547-8010), 1800 Fairview Ave, isn't as close to city center as the name purports, but it's popular with business travelers and the well-heeled. There's a restaurant, an outdoor pool and a fitness center, and pets are allowed; rates run $59 to $119. The *Red Lion Hotel/Riverside* (☎ 343-1871, (800) 547-8010), 2900 Chinden Blvd, is right on the river and Greenway, and it functions as a small convention hotel. There's an outdoor pool, restaurant and fitness center; rooms are $69 to $295.

## Places to Eat
**Budget & Middle** Just when you thought you'd never see lox and bagels this side of Manhattan, there's *Rocky Mountain Bagel Bakery* (☎ 338-9907), 407 W Main St, just another reminder that we have the recent trend of immigrants, and not the Oregon Trail pioneers, to thank for Boise's boom in good restaurants. The *Brick Oven Beanery* (☎ 342-3456), 8th and Main Sts, is right on The Grove and offers a lot of outdoor seating. The food here is inexpensive, hearty and quite good, ranging from salads to burgers and pot pies; most dishes are under $5. For inexpensive ethnic food, go to *Wok King* (☎ 345-1779), 2146 Broadway Ave, for very good traditional Chinese food. For Thai food, go to *Bangkok House* (☎ 336-0018), 624 W Idaho St. Dinner at either of these runs between $5 and $8.

If you're looking for a good health-food store to stock up on organic groceries, try the *Boise Co-op* (☎ 342-6652), 1674 Hill Rd, Idaho's largest natural foods store. The *Earth Food Cafe & Juice Bar* (☎ 342-7169), 2907 W State St, offers healthy, international vegetarian cuisine.

*Cafe Ole Restaurant & Cantina* (☎ 344-3222), 404 S 8th St in the 8th St Market Place, serves good Mexican food in a very pleasant if somewhat kitschy dining room. Still, the sound of fountains and the cool of the basement shade is welcome after the searing heat of Boise. Specialties like seafood rellenos are $9; most traditional dishes are in the $7 to $8 range. The margaritas here are locally noted. Also near the 8th St Market Place is *Pizza Chef Gourmet Pizza* (☎ 389-1040), 370 S 8th St, where a slice of pizza and a salad is $4.50.

For some reason, Italian food has taken off in Boise. A good and inexpensive place to fill up is *Noodles* (☎ 342-9300), 6th and Main Sts, which has a good selection of Italian food centering on pasta, salads and

IDAHO

pizza. It's a good place to take a family or a group that can't make up its mind. If it's just pizza you want, go to *Louie's* (☎ 344-5200), 620 W Idaho St, for Boise's favorite pie. *Amore's* (☎ 343-6435), 921 W Jefferson St, offers outstanding, light Italian food – much of it vegetarian – with a trattoria atmosphere; there's also lots of outdoor seating. Chicken lasagna is $11.

Go to *Aladdin's Egyptian Restaurant* (☎ 368-0880), 111 Broadway Ave, for good Mediterranean cuisine. There's belly dancing on Friday nights.

**Top End** Boise has its share of high-flight restaurants that serve very good food, from both the traditional and trendy ends of the cuisine spectrum. However, even the top of the menus here will seem moderate in cost compared to West Coast standards.

For a traditional Italian meal served in a cozy setting in the lower level of a historic building, go to *Renaissance* (☎ 344-6776), 5th and Main Sts. Old favorites like chicken and veal picatta get treated well here, as do entree pasta dishes like pesto al pasta ($12). The seafood choices change daily and range from $14 to $16. Also old fashioned, but in a different way, is the *Gamekeeper Restaurant* (☎ 343-4611), 1109 Main St in the Owyhee Plaza Hotel. At this bastion of traditional American dining, tableside flambé and carving feats are executed by the waitstaff in a stately old dining room redolent of the 1920s. Remember steak Diane ($23), crepe Suzette, cherries jubilee, duck a l'orange? Well, they're still here and just as delicious as when our parents loved to eat them.

Somewhat of a local celebrity, the chef at eponymous *Peter Schott's* (☎ 336-9100), 10th and Main Sts in the lovely Idanha Hotel, offers a very eclectic menu that ranges from dishes originating in Schott's native Austria (Wiener schnitzel at $13) to the cutting edge of West Coast cooking. For fresh seafood, go to *Milford's* (☎ 342-8382), S 405 8th St, where there's a good selection of fresh oysters from the Pacific's best bays and a wide variety of fish. Dinner

prices hover around $15; fresh Oregon sole in a parmesan crust is $16.

### Entertainment
**Coffeehouses** *Koffee Klatch* (☎ 345-0452), 409 S 8th St, is a central meeting place for caffeine-lovers, with live music, light food service and a friendly crowd. *Coffee-News* (☎ 344-7661), 801 W Main St, rings a change on the coffeehouse format by adding espresso to a huge selection of magazines and newspapers; half a block off The Grove, it's a late-night hangout for the self-styled intelligentsia. *Moxie Java* (☎ 343-9033), 570 W Main St, is another central-Boise gathering place, with lots of outside seating along trendy Main St. *Flying M Espresso & Fine Crafts* (☎ 345-4320), 500 W Idaho St, is a coffeehouse somewhere between artsy and homey. Pastries, coffee drinks and light lunch entrees are served on old, mismatched, thrift-store dinette sets; there's music in the evenings and folk art for sale.

**Brewpubs** Just a few blocks from downtown is Boise's best brewery. The *Table-Rock Brewpub & Grill* (☎ 342-0944), 705 Fulton St, offers a wide selection of German-styled beers and ales and a wide-ranging and well-executed food menu. *Harrison Hollow Brew House* (☎ 343-6820), 2455 Bogus Basin Rd, is on the way to the local ski resort and is a favorite for *aprés ski* snacking and quaffing.

**Cinemas** Sit in the lap of the mummy and then see first-run releases at the *Egyptian Theatre* (☎ 342-1441), 700 W Main St, a wildly evocative showcase from the glory days of movie houses. Also downtown is the *8th St Market Place Theatre* (☎ 342-0229), 8th and Broad Sts. For art and foreign films, head to *The Flicks* (☎ 342-4222), 646 Fulton St.

**Theater** The *Idaho Shakespeare Festival* (☎ 336-9221) runs mid-June to early September, with performances held outdoors at 400 Park Center Blvd in Park Center Park.

The *Boise Little Theatre* (☎ 342-5104), 100 E Fort St, the *Stage Coach Theatre* (☎ 342-2000), 2000 Kootenai St, and *Knock 'Em Dead Dinner Theatre* (☎ 385-0021), 807 W Idaho St, are each regional theatrical companies of note.

**Performing Arts** For one-call-does-it-all information on arts and entertainment in Boise, call the ArtsLine (☎ 376-2787). Tickets for many of the performing arts and concerts in Boise are available from Select-A-Seat (☎ 385-3535).

Most of the following companies perform at either the *Morrison Center for the Performing Arts* (☎ 385-1609), 1910 Campus Drive, or at the *BSU Special Events Center* (☎ 345-3531), 1800 University Drive, both on the BSU campus. Boise's professional dance troupe is the Ballet Idaho (☎ 385-1110). Boise Master Chorale (☎ 344-7901) offers concerts in October, December, March and May. Boise Opera (☎ 345-3531) brings grand opera to the Gem State. The Boise Philharmonic (☎ 344-7849) provides musical accompaniment to most of the above, and it performs its own series of concerts.

The *Oinkari Basque Dances* (☎ 336-8219) is an internationally acclaimed Basque dance troupe. They perform at various festivals and cultural events throughout the year; call for a schedule of upcoming performances.

**Nightlife** One of the really happening places for drinks is the *Piper Pub & Grill* (☎ 343-244), 8th and Main Sts, on a balcony above this busy downtown corner.

Boise's busiest gay bar is *The Emerald Club* (☎ 342-5446), 415 S 9th St. Don't let the address fool you: the entrance is around the corner on Borah St. A happy mix of gay, lesbian and straight people meet here to dance to old-fashioned disco hits. Up the street at *The Oly* (☎ 342-1371), 1108 W Front St, is an unassuming little hole-in-the-wall gay bar with a back garden and the feeling of a local's hangout.

**Live Music** Free outdoor music and summer entertainment happens at The Grove, the city's public gathering spot at 8th and Grove Sts.

Rock and garage bands perform both upstairs and downstairs at *Tom Grainey's* (☎ 345-2505), 107 S 6th St. For Boise's punk and grunge scene, go to *Neurolux* (☎ 343-0886), 111 N 11th St. Thursday night is Neuro-Lush night (also known as 'Throw-up Thursday'), when beers are just a buck. Check out the cool mirrored neon-pink pool room. The *Blues Bouquet* (☎ 345-6605), 1010 Main St, is the place for the blues, and *Pengilly's* (☎ 345-6344), 513 Main St, Boise's oldest bar, is acoustic on Monday but rocks out the rest of the week.

**Spectator Sports** BSU collegiate sports is the closest Boise gets to professional athletics. Football and basketball are especially popular; call 385-1515 for schedule info and 385-1285 for tickets. Boise State Broncos teams all play at BSU and the Bronco Stadium, Morrison Center and the Pavilion. Call 385-3438 for information on women's basketball, volleyball, gymnastics, wrestling and track & field.

**Things to Buy**
The 8th St Market Place, at 8th and Broad Sts, is a newly restored warehouse turned public market area. Produce, seafood, wine, cheese, crafts, clothing and gift shops are among the many venues here. For Idaho souvenirs, head to Taters (☎ 338-1062), 249 S 8th St, just outside the convention center. There are more potato-themed gifts here than you thought possible.

**Getting There & Away**
**Air** Boise Municipal Airport (☎ 383-3110), 3501 Airport Way, is the principal airport for all of Idaho and is served by most major US carriers, including Delta (☎ (800) 221-1212), United (☎ (800) 241-6522), Northwest (☎ (800) 225-2525) and Horizon (☎ (800) 547-9308). Southwest Air (☎ (800) 435-9792) has inexpensive

flights to Boise from several cities in the West; tickets between Portland or Seattle and Boise can be as little as $30. Empire Air (☎ (800) 392-9233) links Boise with Lewiston and Coeur d'Alene.

**Bus** The Greyhound bus station (☎ 343-3681) is at 1212 W Bannock St. The principal service links Boise with other cities along the I-84 corridor, from Salt Lake City to Portland; to cities along the I-86 and I-15 corridor (to Pocatello and north to Butte); and to cities north and south along Hwy 95 between Spokane and Reno.

**Train** Amtrak's *Pioneer* line links Boise directly with Seattle, Portland, Denver and Chicago, with trains four days a week. Boise is the last major stop in Idaho for westbound trains, which depart in the wee hours of the morning and stop at Ontario, Baker City, Pendleton and Portland before arriving in Seattle the same day. Late-night eastbound trains hit Twin Falls (via Shoshone) and Pocatello before continuing onto Denver, Omaha and Chicago. The train station (☎ 336-5992) is at 1701 Eastover Terrace in the Morrison Knudsen Depot.

**Car** Major car rental chains at the airport (mostly on Airport Way) include: Avis (☎ 383-3350), Hertz (383-3100), Budget (☎ 383-3090) and National (☎ 383-3210). There are also discount agencies like Dollar (☎ 345-9727), Thrifty (342-7726) and Payless (342-7780). While not at the airport, Alamo (☎ 336-1904), 2770 S Orchard St, is nearby. Call Agency (☎ 323-0535), 6555 Overland Rd, or Enterprise (☎ 375-0555) for vehicle delivery to your motel.

Downtown agencies are limited to National (383-1110), 2820 W Main St, and Practical (☎ 344-3732), 2565 W Main St.

### Getting Around
**Bus** Boise Urban Stages buses (☎ 336-1010) are called the BUS, and catching one from the transit mall (Main and Idaho Sts between 9th St and Capitol Blvd) can be confusing. Look for numbered bus shelters, which don't correspond to the numbers of the buses that stop there and are sometimes reassigned to different buses on Saturdays. Not all routes run on Saturday, and there's no service on Sunday. Get schedule information at the BUS office, 300 S Ave A, or from businesses around town. Adult fare is 75c. Ask the driver for a free transfer if you anticipate a bus change; otherwise you'll have to pay the fare twice.

The BUS runs a bus to and from the airport. Catch bus No 4 from shelter No 1 at the corner of Idaho St and Capitol Blvd.

**Taxi** Boise has plenty of cab companies. For starters, try Kwik-Yellow-Orange (☎ 345-5555), which also dispatches Twilight Taxi, Checker Cab and others, or Blue Line Taxi (☎ 384-1111).

## AROUND BOISE
### World Center for Birds of Prey
This interpretive center (☎ 362-8687), 5666 W Flying Hawk Lane, was founded as a rehabilitation facility for injured birds of prey, but its popularity has shifted the

Peregrine falcon

center's focus to include more and more educational displays. Exhibits are geared to dispelling myths about raptors and teaching about the complex environmental requirements for healthy populations of birds of prey. Tours are given of the nursery (some rare birds like the peregrine falcon are incubated here) and the rehab center, and there are outdoor flight displays starring trained falcons. Also on display is an adult harpy eagle, one of the world's largest raptors.

To reach the center, take I-84 exit No 50 and head six miles south on S Cole Rd (the route is well signed). It's open from 9 am to 5 pm Tuesday to Sunday for most of the year, and from 10 am to 4 pm November to February. Admission is $4 for adults and $3 for seniors; children ages four to 16 are $2.

### Snake River Birds of Prey National Conservation Area

Just beyond the World Center for Birds of Prey begins a 755-sq-mile refuge for raptors, established in 1993 and administered by the BLM. The refuge encompasses the densest nesting concentration of birds of prey in North America, and it includes breeding grounds to over 800 pair of falcons, eagles, hawks and owls during the spring. The refuge stretches for 80 miles along an arid, cliff-lined section of the Snake River, flanked by a desert area abounding with ground squirrels and jackrabbits (prime raptor fixin's).

The refuge begins 15 miles south of Boise, off I-84 exit No 44, just beyond Kuna, where there's a visitors information center. Pick up a free visitors guide, which includes a map and suggested driving tour of the refuge. The 56-mile loop auto tour from Kuna takes three to four hours.

Other forms of recreation are allowed on the refuge. A 10-mile hiking trail follows the north side of the river between Swan Falls Dam and Celebration Point. This same stretch is popular as a raft trip, with just enough white water to make the trip exciting. Wilderness River Trips (see Activities in Boise above) at MacKay Bar offers float trips through the area, as does

Whitewater River Shop Tours (☎ 922-5285), 252 N Meridian Rd in Kuna. Snake River Canyon Jet Boat Tours (☎ 922-5285) has trips through this scenic area, though these aren't wildlife tours.

The only developed campground is at Cove Recreation Site on the CJ Strike Reservoir (no hook-ups). Other sites are primitive.

For more information, contact the BLM Boise District Office (☎ 384-3300), 3948 Development Ave, Boise, ID 83705.

### Bogus Basin Ski Resort

This convenient ski area (☎ 332-5100) is just 16 miles north of Boise on Bogus Basin Rd. Both downhill and cross-country (17 miles of nordic trails) skiing are available as well as a public race course, nightskiing, sleigh rides, child care, instruction and rentals at Black Diamond Sports Rental Shop.

There are two skiing areas in the resort: the Bogus Creek Area has restaurants, lifts up Deer Point (7070 feet) and offers most services at the Bogus Creek Lodge. Continue to the Pioneer Area for lifts up Shafer Butte (7590 feet) and lodging at the Pioneer Inn (also with restaurants) and Pioneer Inn Condominiums (☎ 332-5224, (800) 367-4397 for both lodgings); rooms range between $84 and $97 and are discounted to around $68 midweek. It's open from 10 am to 10 pm weekdays and from 9 am to 10 pm weekends. The lift tickets cost $26, but after 4 pm they're $16. For a snow report call 342-2100. From downtown Boise, take Hays St north to Harrison Blvd north, which leads directly onto Bogus Basin Rd.

### NAMPA

West of Boise, the agricultural heartland of Idaho continues along the heavily irrigated Snake River valley. Between Nampa (population 28,500) and the Oregon border is Idaho's principal region for the production of onions, mint and sugar beets. Wine grapes are also grown, and five wineries operate in the area. A lot of commercial vegetable seed is produced here as well, including seed for radishes, lettuce, onions, sweet corn and carrots.

Most people zoom through this portion of Idaho, but Nampa, a quintessential farm town, tempts the traveler with the most reasons to exit the freeway. The downtown area has been dressed up with young trees and flower boxes, and a number of the old storefronts have been converted into antique shops. By far the most imposing building in Nampa is the Baroque-styled train depot from 1903, which now houses the county museum.

The biggest event of the year here is the Snake River Stampede, one of the state's largest rodeos, held the third weekend of July.

### Orientation & Information
The main strip through Nampa is Hwy 30, which intersects with 1st and 2nd Sts, the main streets in the old downtown area. Nampa is 20 miles west of Boise on I-84.

The Nampa Chamber of Commerce (☎ 466-4641) is at 1305 3rd St S. The post office (☎ 466-8938) is at 123 11th St S.

### Places to Stay
Right off I-84 at exit No 36 is *Mason Creek RV Park* (☎ 465-7199), 807 Franklin Blvd, with sites from $10 to $16.50.

*Alpine Villa Motel* (466-7819), 124 3rd St S, offers some kitchenettes and has rooms from $30. *Desert Inn* (☎ 467-1161), 115 9th St S, has an outdoor pool, pets are OK, and rooms are between $34 to $48. Shilo Inn operates two motels in Nampa. The *Shilo Inn Nampa Blvd* (☎ 466-8993), 617 Nampa Blvd, has rooms from $51 to $60, and the *Shilo Inn Nampa Suites* (☎ 465-3250), 1401 Shilo Drive, has suites from $68. Each offers a pool, spa facilities and hot tubs.

### Places to Eat
You have a choice of great places for breakfast. *Say You Say Me* (466-2728), 820 Caldwell Blvd, produces what surely must be one of the world's largest omelets – made with eight eggs! Fried potato dishes are another favorite. *The Little Kitchen* (☎ 467-

9677), 1224 1st St S, is another excellent place for morning meals – or whenever, as it offers breakfast anytime.

*Red Sage Grill & Pub* (☎ 466-9233), 512 12th St, offers ribs, burgers and salads. *Ranch House Steakhouse & Saloon* (☎ 466-7020), 1809 Karcher Rd, is an old-fashioned supper club serving steak; there's dancing on the weekends. *Maria's Hacienda* (☎ 467-3064), 102 11th St N, and *El Rinconcito* (☎ 446-6963), 824 1st St S, are two of the best local Mexican restaurants.

### Getting There & Away
The bus depot (☎ 467-5122), 315 12th St S, serves both the east-west Greyhound line and Trailways buses that run between Boise and Winnemucca, NV, along Hwy 95.

### CALDWELL & AROUND
Another major farming center, Caldwell (population 18,595) has lost its old town center to the Hwy 30 strip, here called Cleveland Blvd. Caldwell is home to the oldest four-year institute of higher learning in the state. Founded as the College of Idaho in 1891, the facility produced many of the early leaders of Idaho. The college is now called Albertson's College. South of Caldwell, around Lowell Lake, are a number of wineries. Idaho's largest and probably most famous is the **St Chapelle Winery** (☎ 459-7222) on Hwy 55 just north of Marsing. In addition to the usual tasting and sales room is the 'Jazz at the Winery' concert series held from mid-June to early August on Sunday afternoons.

Caldwell is one of the gateways into remote southwestern Idaho, a sparsely populated desert plateau that is home to large cattle ranches, old gold camps and US Air Force bombing ranges. The arid peaks of the Owyhee Mountains give rise to the canyon-cutting rivers of the same name that gather spectacularly to drain southeastern Oregon.

Backroads enthusiasts might be tempted to visit **Silver City**, one of the most authentic and atmospheric mining camps in the

Northwest. Established in the 1860s, Silver City was for a while one of Idaho's major towns, with the usual mining-camp mix of bar, brothel, brewery and bank. The spooky old hotel's dining room and bar is still open for business, though the roads leading in (17 miles from Jordan Valley, OR or 23 miles from Hwy 78) are very rough and for high-clearance vehicles only.

Highway 78 follows the route of the south cut-off of the Oregon Trail, which followed the south bank of the Snake River. About 10 miles south of Marsing is **Givens Hot Springs**. These were a welcome stop for the pioneers, who blocked the hot water flows for bathing and laundry.

For tourist information, contact the Caldwell Chamber of Commerce (☎ 459-7493) at 300 Frontage Rd. The post office (☎ 459-7489) is at 821 Arthur St. Greyhound buses (☎ 459-2816) stop at 1017 Arthur St.

### Places to Stay & Eat

There are campsites ($5 to $8.50) at *Givens Hot Springs* (☎ 495-2000, (800) 874-6046), now a commercial enterprise that offers the mineral waters in a swimming pool or small private soak rooms. There are easy-to-find motels out at the freeway exit, but try the *Sundowner Motel* (☎ 459-1585), 1002 Arthur St, for cheaper rooms closer to downtown. Single/doubles are $32/42.

The Hwy 30 strip between Nampa and Caldwell is lined with fast-food and impromptu food booths selling homemade Mexican food to the local agricultural workers. For some of the best Texas-style barbecue around, go to *The Armadillo* (☎ 459-1226), 4808 E Cleveland Blvd, where ribs, steak and smoked prime rib are offered at reasonable prices. In downtown Caldwell, head upstairs to *Acapulco Mexican Restaurant* (☎ 463-0007), 708 Main St, a pleasant place to eat local Mexican food; it's where the Caldwell business set goes for lunch.

A good excuse to turn off the freeway and take the slow road along Hwy 78 is that two very good restaurants share this unlikely corner of Idaho. The *Sandbar* (☎ 896-4124), 18 1st St E, one block east of

Marsing on Hwy 78 from the junction with Hwy 95, is a lounge and supper club sitting beside the Snake River, and although the menu doesn't aim toward innovation, the steak, fresh seafood and weekend prime rib are excellent. Ten miles west of Murphy is the *Blue Canoe* (☎ 495-2269), another popular steak and seafood dinner house with a flair for Cajun spices. Both of these popular restaurants are open for lunch and dinner; a steak dinner runs between $12 to $15 at either place.

## PAYETTE & FRUITLAND

Payette (population 5780) and Fruitland (population 2559) sit across the Payette River from each other, and both look across the Snake River at Ontario, OR. There's nothing particularly special for the traveler about any of these hardworking farm towns, except to realize that most of the country's frozen or processed potatoes, and a sizable potion of the nation's onion crop, come from around here.

Who knows why, but when it came time to divvy up the tourism responsibilities between these three towns, most of the motels, restaurants and public transportation went to Ontario, while the campgrounds went to Payette and Fruitland. For tourist information, contact the Payette Chamber of Commerce (☎ 642-2362), 700 Center Ave, Payette, ID 83661.

### Places to Stay & Eat

*Lazy River RV Park* (☎ 642-9667), 11575 N River Rd, is four miles north on Hwy 95 and offers 12 spaces. Facilities include showers, laundry and a dump station; sites are $10. Across the bridge in Fruitland is *Curtis' Neat Retreat* (☎ 452-4324), 2701 Alder St, with hook-ups for $17. If you want to stay in Idaho, the only motel on this side of the Snake River is *Montclair Motel* (642-2693), 625 S Main St. Single/double rooms with kitchenettes are $25/37; pets are permitted.

## WEISER

At Weiser (population 4607), the Snake River valley begins to constrict, readying to

**IDAHO**

plunge down into Hells Canyon. Weiser is a transitional city between the flat Snake River valley and the foothills of the Rockies. Surrounded by irrigated orchards, Weiser is one of the most architecturally significant small towns in Idaho, containing a large number of handsome private homes and civic buildings.

Weiser is also the site of the historic Intermountain Institute, a school built for the college preparation of Idaho's rural youth. The school was founded on the outskirts of Weiser in 1899, with a Christian, slightly utopian bent. Male and female students were educated together, and they helped fund the school by working in school dairies, broom factories and bakeries. Discrimination by race or religion was banned. The institute went under during the Depression, and the buildings went through a long series of uses before being developed as the local museum and the festival grounds for the Weiser Fiddlers Festival.

For tourist information, stop by the Weiser Chamber of Commerce (☎ 549-0452) at 8 E Idaho St, Weiser, ID 83672. The post office is at W 1st and W Main Sts.

### National Old Time Fiddlers Contest
Weiser is known across the country as the scene of one of the nation's foremost fiddle festivals. Held the third week of June, the event attracts upwards of 400 folk musicians of all ages from across the USA and Canada. The highlight of the event is the crowning of the National Grand Champion Fiddler. In conjunction with the festival is a crafts fair, food concessions, parade, rodeo and cowboy-poet gathering. For more information, contact the chamber of commerce.

### Places to Stay & Eat
*Indian Hot Springs* (☎ 549-0070), 914 Hot Springs Rd, is six miles northwest of Weiser and offers 11 sites. Tents are $8, full hook-ups $12. Facilities include a mineral-water swimming pool (open to noncampers), hot tub, showers and a dump station. *Gateway RV Park* (☎ 549-2539),

229 E 7th St, along Hwy 95 at Weiser River Bridge, offers 25 spaces; hook-ups are $12. Laundry and shower facilities are available. *Monroe Creek Campground* (☎ 549-2026, 549-3540), 822 Hwy 95, 1.5 miles north of town, has $9 tent sites and $12 hook-ups. Facilities include a spa/hot tub, showers, laundry, dump station and a small store.

In Weiser, the *State Street Motel* (☎ 549-1390), 1279 State St, has singles/doubles for $30/35; pets are welcome. *Colonial Motel* (☎ 549-0150), 251 E Main St, offers kitchen units; rooms run $30 to $38. *Indianhead Motel & RV Park* (☎ 549-0331), 747 Hwy 95, offers 15 spaces and eight units; shower and laundry facilities are available. Hook-ups are $14; motel rooms go for $30 to $50.

For a meal, there's good value at *The Beehive* (☎ 549-3544), 611 Hwy 95, where the lunch buffet is just $4.95, and the supper buffet is a dollar more. The Beehive is open 24 hours, six days a week (closed Sunday).

# Sawtooth Range

## SUN VALLEY & KETCHUM
Idaho's most famous and popular resort area, Sun Valley and Ketchum (population 2960) are squeezed into a narrow valley beneath steep, lightly forested mountains. This geological quirk is wedded to a piece of meteorological serendipity that ensures that tons of very dry powdery snow dumps on the surrounding mountains. The result is world-class skiing in the very heart of the Rocky Mountains.

While Ketchum began its life in the 1880s as a mining and smelting center, Sun Valley sprang to life in 1936 as the creation of Averell Harriman, then chairman of the board of the Union Pacific Railroad. Harriman and the railroad were interested in creating a destination ski resort in the West. Taking European ski resorts as a model, Harriman hired an Austrian count to tour the western USA looking for a suitable site to build the resort. The count chose the

Ketchum area, and the railroad spent $1.5 million on the 220-room lodge and resort facility.

Sun Valley almost immediately became a playground for the rich and famous; it's worth touring around the lobby of Sun Valley Lodge just to see all the photos of the glitterati on skis: Lucille Ball, the Kennedys, Gary Cooper, Mary Pickford, Darrel Zanick, Arnold Schwartzenegger and many, many others. Ernest Hemingway eventually made his home in Ketchum; he also committed suicide here in 1961.

Today, Sun Valley and Ketchum are more popular and trendy than ever. The area has succeeded in becoming a year-round destination resort. And increasingly, the wealthy are moving to the area to live year round: one of the first comments that first-time visitors usually make as they drive into Ketchum is 'Wow! Look at the size of that house!' Somewhere along the line, Sun Valley has gone from being a sports resort to a lifestyle resort. Sun Valley isn't just a place to ski, it's a place to decorate your house, try on fancy clothes and buy art. People come to Sun Valley to engage in fantasies. The rich and influential get themselves up in gear and clothing that wouldn't be appropriate anywhere else on earth. Yet the buffalo skin coats, enormous turquoise-banded cowboy hats and buckskin skirts of the rich and trendy are perfectly in keeping with life here, the make-believe world of an idealized Wild West.

## Orientation

Ketchum sits in the Big Wood River Valley, just below Galena Pass on Hwy 75. There are several discrete areas to this resort community. Ketchum is the main commercial district, with tons of restaurants, hotels and boutiques. One mile to the northeast is the resort of Sun Valley, with its imposing lodge, condominiums, home tracts and golf course. Just south of Sun Valley, past Dollar Mountain, is a new resort community called Elkhorn. Communities have also grown up at the base of Bald Mountain, particularly around the ski-lift sites at River Run and Warm Springs. Brand new housing developments stretch up and down the valley.

## Information

The Sun Valley-Ketchum Chamber of Commerce (☎ 726-4533, (800) 634-3347) can be reached at Box 2420, Sun Valley, ID 83353, or visit the center at the corner of 4th and Main Sts. Be sure and ask for a vacation planner, which has a complete list of recreational outfitters, lodging and other businesses. For information about hiking, biking or camping, contact the Ketchum Ranger Station (☎ 622-5371), just north of Ketchum on Hwy 75.

The Main Street Bookcafe (☎ 726-3700), at the corner of 2nd and Main Sts in Ketchum, has a good selection of books and magazines as well as a coffee bar with desserts and snacks.

Wash those dirty clothes at the Tub Laundromat (☎ 726-9161), 320 E Sun Valley Rd, Ketchum.

## Skiing

**Downhill** Sun Valley offers some of the best and most popular ski runs in the USA. There are two mountains to choose from. The most famous and challenging skiing is on Bald Mountain, just west of Ketchum. From a summit height of 9150 feet, 64 runs descend 3400 feet; almost two-thirds of the runs are rated for advanced skiers. There are 13 lifts, which leave from River Run Plaza, south of Ketchum off 3rd St, and from Warm Springs Lodge, northwest of Ketchum on Warm Springs Rd. Call 622-2231 if you have ski-related questions about Sun Valley's facilities, as it can be hard to get past the reservation personnel that staff all the toll-free numbers. A second ski area, Dollar Mountain, is close to the resort at Sun Valley, and it was the original ski area during the 1930s. Dollar Mountain's 13 runs are less challenging than Bald Mountain's, and they are a favorite for beginners and family skiing. Snowboarding is allowed on both mountains. Instruction, rentals and all manner of amenities are available at the lodges

IDAHO

(including two on-slope restaurants and a log lodge on 8600-foot Seattle Ridge).

Lift tickets aren't inexpensive, starting at $49 for a one-day adult pass. The three to seven-day packages (ranging from $95 to $200) make the per-day fee a bit more reasonable. Another savings for families is that children under 17 ski free – one kid per parent – as long as the family is staying in a participating lodging. Lodging/ski packages are also available from the resort. Dollar Mountain has its own rates and information line (☎ 622-2231). For information about special rates on theme weekends and package deals, or general information about skiing at the resorts, call Sun Valley's central reservation number (☎ (800) 634-3347). Call (800) 635-4150 for the latest snow report.

**Cross-Country** Not everyone comes to Sun Valley for the slopes. Nordic skiing is also very popular. The Sun Valley Nordic Center (☎ 622-2251) is part of the Sun Valley Resort complex, and it offers a complete rental and instruction center and access to 25 miles of groomed trails. There's also a groomed trail system, instruction and rentals at Elkhorn Resort (☎ 622-4511).

Head out into the backcountry for more of a wilderness experience. USFS land begins just to the north of Ketchum, and any snowed-under logging road is fair game. Continue onto Galena Summit, the divide along Hwy 75 between the Salmon and Big Wood rivers, where there's heavy snow and plenty of impromptu ski trails. Also near the pass is Galena Lodge (☎ 726-4010), 24 miles north of Ketchum, a cross-country ski center with rentals, lessons and access to an extensive trail system.

**Fishing**
The Big and Little Wood rivers and Silver Creek – all convenient to Ketchum and the resorts – are each very popular fishing rivers for native trout. Consequently, there are quite a few restrictions. Silver Creek is strictly catch-and-release and is limited to fly fishing. There are also catch-and-release

sections of the two Wood rivers as well, so it's a good idea to contact a local outfitter for a river map and a list of restrictions.

For a guided fishing trip, contact a local outfitter. Sun Valley Outfitters (☎ 622-3400), 651 Sun Valley Rd, Ketchum, offers fly fishing as well as rafting trips. Silver Creek Outfitters (☎ 726-5282), 507 N Main St, Ketchum, guides fly fishing trips and sells the sportswear to get you there.

**Rafting & Floating**
For half and full-day white-water trips down the Salmon River, contact Two-M River Outfitters (☎ 726-8844), PO Box 163, Sun Valley, ID 83353, or White Otter Outdoor Adventures (☎ 726-4331), 211 Sun Valley Rd. In addition, both offer daytime calm-water floats and dinner floats. Adventurers can choose from oar boats, paddle rafts and inflatable kayaks, though there may be age restrictions. In addition, White Otter also offers trips on other rivers, including trips to the Murtaugh section of the Snake River, boat rentals, day hikes and mountain bike tours. Expect to pay a minimum of $40 for a half-day trip, $60 for a full-day.

**Horseback Riding**
Galena Stage Stop Corrals (☎ 726-1735, 774-3591), north of Ketchum on Hwy 75, has short 1½ hour rides, half-day rides and full-day rides with prices ranging from $20 to $60 during the summer. Call for reservations. There are also stables at the resort.

**Sleigh Rides**
Sleigh rides have been part of the Sun Valley Resort package from the early days. Trips leave from the resort and journey to a log cabin in the woods, where lunch or dinner is served. Call the resort for more information.

**Other Activities**
While skiing is obviously the raison d'etre of Sun Valley and Ketchum, there's a vast selection of other outdoor recreation available both winter and summer. Get a listing of outfitters and guides from the chamber

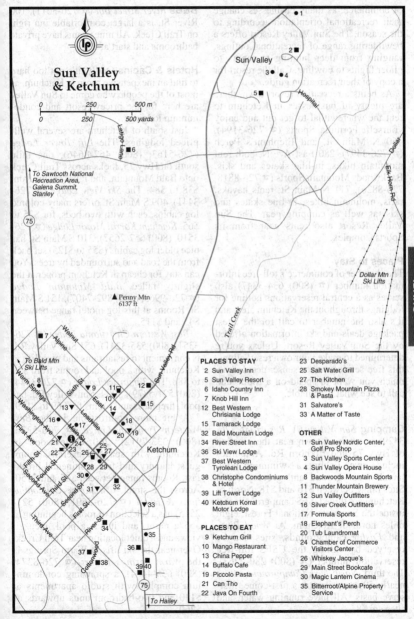

**Sun Valley & Ketchum**

0      250      500 m
0      250      500 yards

To Sawtooth National
Recreation Area,
Galena Summit,
Stanley

▲ Penny Mtn
6137 ft

▲ Dollar Mtn
Ski Lifts

To Bald Mtn
Ski Lifts

Sun Valley

Hospital

Elk Horn Rd

Dollar

Trail Creek

Sun Valley Rd

Lehnjo Lane

Walnut
Alpine

Warm Springs
Washington Ave
First Ave
Sixth St
East
Leadville
Main St
Fifth St
Fourth St
Second Ave
Third St
Third Ave
River St
Cottonwood

Second Ave
First Ave

Ketchum

To Hailey

IDAHO

**PLACES TO STAY**
2  Sun Valley Inn
5  Sun Valley Resort
6  Idaho Country Inn
7  Knob Hill Inn
12  Best Western
    Chrisiania Lodge
15  Tamarack Lodge
32  Bald Mountain Lodge
34  River Street Inn
36  Ski View Lodge
37  Best Western
    Tyrolean Lodge
38  Christophe Condominiums
    & Hotel
39  Lift Tower Lodge
40  Ketchum Korral
    Motor Lodge

**PLACES TO EAT**
9  Ketchum Grill
10  Mango Restaurant
13  China Pepper
14  Buffalo Cafe
19  Piccolo Pasta
21  Can Tho
22  Java On Fourth

23  Desparado's
25  Salt Water Grill
27  The Kitchen
28  Smokey Mountain Pizza
    & Pasta
31  Salvatore's
33  A Matter of Taste

**OTHER**
1  Sun Valley Nordic Center,
   Golf Pro Shop
3  Sun Valley Sports Center
4  Sun Valley Opera House
8  Backwoods Mountain Sports
11  Thunder Mountain Brewery
12  Sun Valley Outfitters
16  Silver Creek Outfitters
17  Formula Sports
18  Elephant's Perch
20  Tub Laundromat
24  Chamber of Commerce
    Visitors Center
26  Whiskey Jacque's
29  Main Street Bookcafe
30  Magic Lantern Cinema
35  Bitterroot/Alpine Property
    Service

of commerce, as many businesses change their recreational orientation according to the season. The Sun Valley Resort offers a bewildering range of recreational outings, ranging from deer hunting to tennis to glider flights to bowling. Call the resort for a copy of their recreation guide.

As befits a recreation resort town, there are plenty of businesses in Ketchum to rent the wherewithal to get out and enjoy yourself. Formula Sports (☎ 726-3194), 460 N Main St, and Elephant's Perch (☎ 726-3497), 280 East Ave N, both rent mountain bikes, in-line skates and skis. Backwoods Mountain Sports (☎ 726-8818, 726-8826), 711 N Main St, rents kayaks, rafts, mountain bikes, in-line skates and skis, as well as camping gear. The Sun Valley Resort also rents gear from its Sports Complex.

## Places to Stay

The chamber of commerce's toll-free information number (☎ (800) 634-3347) also serves as a central reservations hotline for lodgings throughout the Ketchum area, and it's also the number to call for the latest package deals and ski information offered by the Sun Valley Resort. Unless you're determined to make your own reservations, this free service makes sense: decide how much you want to spend on a room, and call to see what's available.

**Camping** *Sun Valley RV Resort* (☎ 726-3429) is south of town near the junction of Hwy 75 and Elkhorn Rd. Amenities include river fishing, a swimming pool, laundry, playground and grocery store. Sites range between $16 and $18. North of Ketchum are three USFS campgrounds just inside the Sawtooth National Forest, eight miles north of Ketchum. At *Wood River* and *Easley* campgrounds, sites can be reserved by calling the USFS toll-free reservation number (☎ (800) 280-2267). The third, *North Fork Campground*, offers nearly 50 campsites on a first-come, first-serve basis. All have running water, and sites are $8.

**B&Bs** *River Street Inn* (☎ 726-3611), 100 River St, is a large, comfortable inn right on Trail Creek. All nine rooms have private bathrooms and start at $120.

**Hotels & Cabins** Oddly, it's not too hard to find an inexpensive room in Ketchum, as most of the people who come to Sun Valley are here for the pricey resort and condominium lodgings.

Just south of Ketchum are several well-priced lodgings. The *Lift Tower Lodge* (726-5163, (800) 462-8646), one mile south on Hwy 75, looks across Trail Creek onto Bald Mountain, and it has rooms from $38 to $84. The *Ski View Lodge* (☎ 726-3441), 409 S Main St, offers many-colored log cabins, each with two beds, for $35 to $65. *Ketchum Korral Motor Lodge* (☎ 726-3510, (800) 657-2657), 310 S Main St, has nice older log cabins ($55 to $125) set back from the road and surrounded by trees. You can stay for cheap in Ketchum proper at the slightly faded *Bald Mountain Lodge* (☎ 726-9963, (800) 892-7407), 151 S Main St. Rooms at this log motel range between $45 and $115.

*Best Western Christiania Lodge* (☎ 726-3351, (800) 535-3241), 651 Sun Valley Rd, is convenient to restaurants and nightlife in Ketchum, with a pool and rooms from $59 to $88. The *Tamarack Lodge* (☎ 726-3344, (800) 521-5379), 500 E Sun Valley Rd, has pool, fireplaces and rooms for $69 to $139.

A bit more comfortable is the *Best Western Tyrolean Lodge* (☎ 726-5336, (800) 333-7912), 260 Cottonwood in Ketchum, with spa and exercise room, guest laundry and free continental breakfast. Rooms range between $65 and $150. Across the street, *Christophe Condominiums & Hotel* (☎ 726-5601, (800) 521-2515) has a selection of rooms beginning at $55 a night, and it has a pool, jacuzzi, views and a quiet location near Trail Creek. Over near the ski lifts at Warm Springs is the *Warm Springs Resort* (☎ 726-8274, (800) 635-4404), a sprawling condominium complex with studio apartments at $110 and two-bedroom units upwards of $260.

Ketchum also offers some of the most luxurious accommodations in Idaho; get out your credit card and revel in comfort at one of these small, exclusive hotels. The *Knob Hill Inn* (☎ 726-8010, (800) 526-8010), 960 N Main St, sits on a rise above Ketchum and Sun Valley, with sumptuous rooms, a pool, spa, sauna and two restaurants. Rooms range between $150 and $300, and breakfast is included. The *Idaho Country Inn* (☎ 726-1019), 134 Latigo Lane, is another small luxury hotel, with 10 spacious rooms, great views and hot tubs. Rooms start at $125.

**Resorts** The doyen of all Ketchum-area lodgings is undoubtedly the *Sun Valley Resort* (☎ 622-4111, (800) 786-8259), Sun Valley Rd, Sun Valley. The grand old lodge (made of cement, even though it doesn't look like it) is still very impressive, with 200-odd rooms, a princely lobby and a fashionable lounge that fronts onto an ice rink. Within the massive resort complex, called Sun Valley Village, are a total of six restaurants, a movie theater, any number of shops, sport rental operations, a golf course and a wide selection of lodging options.

In the lodge itself, rooms range between $125 and $285 a night. At *Sun Valley Inn*, a motel-like adjunct to the resort, rooms start at $100 and peak at $190 for a family suite. Condominiums flank the old lodge, with studio apartments renting for $100 a night, and four-bedroom units bringing $280. There are also five luxury cabins that rent for $500 to $700 a night. Each of the above accommodations are available in various ski-lift packages as well, with four to seven-night packages available. Check the resort's vacation guide for a summary of the head-spinning details.

*Radisson's Sun Valley Resort at Elkhorn* (☎ 622-4511, (800) 333-3333) in Elkhorn, a mile south of Sun Valley on Elkhorn Rd, is the other major destination resort in the Ketchum area. Located right at the lifts for Dollar Mountain, Elkhorn (as the resort is called locally) has a golf course, sports facilities, a number of restaurants and rooms in

the lodge or condo units. Studios start at $108; four-bedroom suites start at $250.

**Vacation Home Rentals** Stay in a private home or condominium (there are some fabulous residences in the area) and see how the other half lives. Contact Bitterroot/Alpine Property Service (☎ 726-5394, (800) 635-4408), 500 S Main St, or *High Country Property Rentals* (☎ 726-1256, (800) 726-7076) for rentals in all price ranges.

**Places to Eat**
If you like to eat, then Ketchum is as close to paradise as it gets in Idaho. In a town with a year-round population of about 2900, there are over 80 restaurants listed in the Yellow Pages. You'll find no end of good restaurants here, and with a couple exceptions, most offer good values for on-the-cheap travelers.

Start the day at *Java on Fourth* (726-2882), 191 4th St, Ketchum, an espresso bar that's also open late at night for great-looking homemade desserts. *Buffalo Cafe* (☎ 726-9795), 320 East Ave N, starts off with omelets and serves buffalo burgers ($6) for lunch. Another favorite breakfast place is functionally named *The Kitchen* (☎ 726-3856), 200 Main St; an omelet with hashbrowns is $6.

For a good pizza, head to *Smokey Mountain Pizza & Pasta* (☎ 622-5625), 200 Sun Valley Rd, which is popular with families. Sit on the outdoor deck and wolf down inexpensive Mexican food at *Desperado's* (☎ 726-3068), 4th St and Washington Ave. For something a bit lighter, go to *Can Tho* (☎ 726-6207), 460 N Washington Ave, the local Vietnamese restaurant.

You don't need to dress up or spend much money to eat out in style in Ketchum. For moderately priced Italian food, try *Piccolo Pasta* (☎ 726-9251), 220 East Ave N, which offers a three-course meal for $13. There's good value and a friendly welcome in a converted old home now known as the *Ketchum Grill* (☎ 726-4460, 726-7434), 520 East Ave, where braised lamb shanks and polenta go for $12; vegetarian choices make up half the menu. *Mango Restaurant* (☎ 726-8911), 571 E 4th St, offers an eclectic menu that veers from pasta to tortillas and touches on other ethnic cuisines in between. You'll spend $17 for grilled quail and braised endive. At *A Matter of Taste* (☎ 726-8468), 200 S Main St, the emphasis is on bistro dining, with continental classics reworked with an Idaho twist: pheasant ravioli is $17.

For superior Asian food, be sure to go to *China Pepper* (☎ 726-0959), 511 Leadville; try the chili prawns with coriander ($17). At the *Salt Water Grill* (☎ 726-5083), 280 N Main St, there are steak, sushi and seafood; trout *mernieure* is $14. The best Italian restaurant in the area is *Salvatore's* (☎ 726-3111), 111 Washington Ave N, with pasta dishes in the $13 range and traditional veal dishes for $20.

If you're looking for special-occasion fine dining, then go to Sun Valley Resort's *Lodge Dining Room* (☎ 622-2150), the most exclusive restaurant in the Ketchum area. The traditional French cuisine doesn't come cheap in this beautiful dining room – figure on $25 for entrees – but the evening is complete with live musical entertainment and liveried waitstaff. Try the popular Sunday brunch for $16. For a little less elegance and a little less money, try *The Ram* (☎ 622-2225) at the resort, where steaks or roast duck go for $15.

## Entertainment
**Brewpubs** *Thunder Mountain Brewery* (☎ 726-1832), 591 E 4th St, is a lively place to quaff a pint and talk about snow conditions.

**Cinema** In Ketchum, the *Magic Lantern Cinema* (☎ 726-4274), 207 Washington Ave N, shows first-run films. In Sun Valley, the *Opera House* (☎ 622-2244) shows films and has occasional musical events.

**Live Music** Ketchum isn't exactly Las Vegas, but there's a steady stream of musicians passing through Sun Valley and environs. Most bars and lounges will have music on weekends; one good place to

catch up on music and the local scene is *Whiskey Jaques* (☎ 726-3200), 206 N Main St. In summer, the Jazz on the Green series takes over the Elkhorn Plaza every Thursday evening. Call the resort at 622-4511 for information.

Free classical music concerts are offered on the Sun Valley Esplanade during August, performed by the Sun Valley Summer Symphony; call 622-5607 for details. Another, rather unlikely place to catch acoustic music is the *Main Street Bookcafe* (see Information, above).

**Ice Skating** One of the most popular summer events is the Sun Valley Ice Show (☎ 622-2231), held at the rink just behind the lodge. World-class skaters – the likes of Katarina Witt and Brian Boitano are regulars – skate here every Saturday evening. The $25 ticket price also wins you a place at the outdoor buffet table.

## Getting There & Away
**Air** The closest airport is in Hailey, 12 miles south on Hwy 75. Otherwise, Twin Falls or Boise are the closest air hubs, and from there, it's best to rent a car.

**Bus** Sun Valley Stages (☎ 383-3085 ) dispatches buses from Twin Falls and Boise to the ski resorts *during the ski season only*. Call for a schedule.

## Getting Around
**Bus** Ketchum Area Rapid Transit (KART) buses (☎ 726-7140) are free and serve the Ketchum-Sun Valley resort area with direct service to the slopes from selected resorts and lodges. Call for stops and schedule information.

**Car** Avis (☎ 788-2382) and Budget (☎ 788-3660) operate out of the Hailey airport. U-Save Auto Rental (☎ 622-9312) and Practical Rent-A-Car (☎ 788-3224), 512 N Main St, each have offices in Ketchum.

**Taxi** Call A-1 Taxicab (☎ 726-9351) for a lift.

## STANLEY

The old ranching community of Stanley, at the headwaters of the Salmon River, sits in one of the most drop-dead beautiful sites in the USA. The incredibly rugged and aptly-named Sawtooth Mountains form a sudden wall of pink granite behind miles and miles of lush spring-fed meadows. At the base of the peaks – there are 40 higher than 10,000 feet – a multitude of small lakes collect snow melt. These stunning reflecting pools are ringed with campgrounds, small family resorts and fishing lodges.

It's a magical, exquisite area, and land developers and resort ranchers have taken notice. While there's nothing as organized as Sun Valley here, the resort mentality is firmly entrenched. Celebrity ranchers are more common than sheepherders, quite a switch from even two decades ago.

For the traveler, the Stanley area offers loads of hiking in the beautiful Sawtooth Wilderness Area, as well as camping and genteel recreation along high mountain lakes; the Salmon River is noted for its fine fishing. In winter, cross-country skiing is very popular here, as is organized snowmobile touring.

Sawtooth Wilderness & National Recreation Area

## Orientation & Information
For information on the area, contact the Stanley-Sawtooth Chamber of Commerce (☎ 774-3411, (800) 848-7950 for travel packet orders only). The visitors center shares a space with the community center on Hwy 21. For information on hiking and camping in the Sawtooth Wilderness, stop at the Stanley Ranger Station (☎ 774-3681), three miles south of town on Hwy 75.

## Sawtooth National Recreation Area
Part of the 400-sq-mile Sawtooth National Recreation Area, the 340-sq-mile Sawtooth Wilderness Area is Idaho's most popular roadless area due to its great beauty and its relative ease of access. Both areas are administered by the USFS (☎ 774-3681).

The wilderness area is on the west side of the national recreation area, and it spans both the east and west slopes of the Sawtooth Range. The most heavily used portion of the wilderness is on the east slope, as Hwy 75 and numerous USFS roads give easy access to trailheads; hiking from lakeside campgrounds into the wilderness area is especially popular. From the west, the only convenient access is from Grandjean, on the South Fork of the Payette River.

## Stanley Museum
Located in an old USFS ranger station, this museum (☎ 774-3517), about a half mile north of town on Hwy 75, tells the story of the old pioneer and ranching days of the Salmon Valley. It's open from late May to Labor Day; admission is by donation.

## Hiking
The wilderness is well networked with hiking trails, which makes planning several-day, trans-wilderess hikes relatively simple. Day hikes to alpine lakes are also easy. From the eastern access along Hwy 75, major trails into the Sawtooth Wilderness leave from Pettit and Yellow Belly lakes; these two lakes can be linked by a several-day loop trip via Toxaway Lake. Trails flank Redfish Lake Creek and climb up a narrow canyon to connect with the long-distance **Idaho State Centennial Trail**, the major north-south trail that accesses the more remote high country of the western Sawtooths. For superb views on a day hike, travel up Iron Creek Rd and hike to Sawtooth Lake, a mirror for 10,190-foot Mt Regan. You can also pick up the Centennial Trail from Grandjean.

## Fishing
Sockeye salmon once returned to Redfish Lake all the way from the Pacific Ocean. However, since 1989 no fish have returned, which means that this fish is now probably extinct in Idaho. Fishing is seasonally good for trout in Redfish, Stanley and Alturas Lakes. Go to McCoy's Gift & Tackle Shop (☎ 774-3377), one mile off Hwy 21 on the corner of Niece Ave and Ace of Diamonds Rd, and find out where the fish are striking.

## Rafting
One of Idaho's most noted and popular white-water trips is the Middle Fork of the Salmon River; the trip leaves from below Dagger Falls, which is off USFS Rd 198 (Bear Valley Rd), 17 miles north of Stanley on Hwy 21. If you choose to float the river on your own, you'll need a permit from the USFS, available from the Middle Fork Ranger District, PO Box 750, Challis, ID 83226. Otherwise, most of the outfitters in the state offer five to six-day float trips down a hundred miles of this designated Wild & Scenic river. For a sample of the trips available, contact Middle Fork River Expeditions (☎ 774-3659, (800) 801-5146), PO Box 199, Stanley, ID 83278, or Middle Fork Rapid Transit (☎ 774-3440, (800) 342-9728), 160 2nd St W, Twin Falls, ID 83301.

If you're interested in rafting the 'River of No Return', you have probably already noticed that it's a long way from the put-in site to the end of the shoot at Riggins. Fortunately, there's River Rat Express (☎ 774-2265) in Stanley, which offers convenient bus and car transportation service (summer only) for rafters here and on other rivers.

If you don't have the time for an extended raft trip, contact Triangle C Ranch Whitewater Expeditions (☎ 774-2266), PO Box 69, Stanley, ID 83278. They offer half and full-day trips down the mainstem Salmon River.

### Horseback Riding
Redfish Corrals (☎ 774-3311), at Mystic Saddle Ranch near Redfish Lake, offers 1½ hour, half-day and full-day horseback rides into the Sawtooth Wilderness Area during the summer. Contact the ranch itself (☎ 774-3591) for summer trips into the Sawtooths, including single or multiple-day hiking, fishing and pack trips. Bow or rifle hunting trips for elk or mule deer are offered in the fall. Write to Jeff & Deb Bitton, Mystic Saddle Ranch, Stanley, ID 83278.

### Sports Rentals
Sawtooth Rentals (☎ 774-3409, 734-4060), 13 River Rd, has snowmobiles and equipment for rent during the winter, with guided trips and instruction available. The rest of the year the business rents float-trip equipment, ATVs, jet skis and mountain bikes.

### Places to Stay
**Camping** Head three miles south of town on Hwy 75 and five miles west on Redfish Rd to reach the sizeable *Glacier View Campground* (open June to Labor Day) or *Redfish Outlet Campground* (open June 15 to September 20). Both of these USFS campgrounds offer quick access to swimming, boating, canoeing, fishing and hiking in the Redfish Lake recreation area, and they are convenient to boat rentals and groceries. The scenic *Salmon River Campground*, only five miles east of Stanley on Hwy 75, is great for impromptu fishing on the Salmon River. It's open June 15 to September 15. The campgrounds listed have hand-pumped water and some flush toilets,

and none have hook-ups. Sites range from $8 to $12.

**Hotels & Cabins** In keeping with the fashionable New West look prevalent in Stanley, all the following except one are log cabin-style lodgings. The exception is the *Redwood Motel* (☎ 774-3531), in Lower Stanley (on Hwy 75, one mile north of Hwy 21), a well-maintained older motel with rooms from $34 to $45. It's open late May to October. *Danner's Log Cabin Motel* (☎ 774-3539), Hwy 21 at Wall St, has lodgings in rustic cabins, some with kitchens, for $40 to $70. *Creek Side Lodge* (☎ 774-2213, (800) 523-0733) is right on Valley Creek and offers private decks and good views of the Sawtooths. All rooms come with kitchenettes and range between $70 to $100. The *Triangle C Ranch* (☎ 774-2266), north on Hwy 21, offers eight nice log cabins starting at $55. The *Sawtooth Hotel* (☎ 774-9947), at the west end of Ace of Diamonds Rd, operates as a B&B, and they furnish fishing guides; rooms are $27 to $75.

The *Mountain Village Lodge* (☎ 774-3661, (800) 843-5475), at the junction of Hwys 75 and 21, is a large, attractive log motel with 60 rooms, a restaurant, lounge and conference space. The lodge also offers seasonal car rental and airport transportation. Also nice is *McGowan's Salmon River Cabins* (☎ 774-2290, (800) 447-8141), in Lower Stanley (on Hwy 75, one mile north of Hwy 21). Each of these roomy log cabins overlooks the river and comes with a kitchenette and a rack of horns above the door; they run $75 to $100.

### Places to Eat
Food is pretty basic in Stanley, and it's pretty much limited to *Mountain Village Restaurant & Saloon* (☎ 774-3661, 774-3680) at the Mountain Village Lodge, which focuses on homestyle ranch cooking and offers three meals a day.

### HAILEY
Hailey is notable for a couple of things.

Just 12 miles south of Ketchum, Hailey boasts the airport for the Sun Valley area. Hailey was also the birthplace of poet Ezra Pound in 1902, back when this area was noted for its lead and silver mines. It's not too much to hang a shingle on, but because of the resort mentality so prevalent in this part of Idaho, simply being close to Ketchum comprises a degree of enchantment. Proximity is also good for budget travelers, who can commute between the slopes at Bald Mountain and the less expensive motel rooms in Hailey.

For tourist information on the area, contact the Hailey Chamber of Commerce (☎ 788-2700), PO Box 100, Hailey, ID 83333. The local bookstore is Different Drummer Books & Coffee (☎ 788-4403), 120 N Main St.

### Places to Stay & Eat
If you're looking for cheap, head to the old *Hailey Hotel Bar & Grill* (☎ 788-3140), 201 S Main St, which rents seven basic rooms for $30 to $35. The humble *Hitchrack Motel & Grocery Store* (☎ 788-2409), 619 S Main St in Bellevue, just south of Hailey, is also inexpensive, with rooms starting at $40. The *Airport Inn* (☎ 788-2277), 820 4th Ave S, is near the south of town next to the airport. Rooms at this modern motor inn range between $46 and $58.

For a shot of espresso before hitting the slopes, go to *Java on Main* (☎ 788-2444), 310 N Main St. Old-fashioned breakfasts are the specialty at *Sun Rise Cafe* (☎ 788-8793), 106 N Main St. The most enjoyable place to eat in Hailey is the brewpub at *Sun Valley Brewing Co* (☎ 788-5777), 201 N Main St, which offers burgers and snacks in addition to its noted ales.

### Getting There & Away
The Freidman Memorial Field is the only airport near Ketchum with regularly scheduled flights. Horizon (☎ (800) 547-9308) flies in from Seattle, Portland, Spokane and Boise; roundtrip flights from the West Coast can be as low as $138. SkyWest (☎ (800) 453-9417) flies in from Salt Lake City.

# Snake River Plain

## MOUNTAIN HOME & AROUND
From Boise, I-84 crosses one of the most flat and tedious pieces of the Snake River plateau. Unrelieved even by irrigation, here the native sage and shortgrass desert is preserved.

Mountain Home (population 8900) is somewhat deceptively, or perhaps wishfully, named, as it lies in the middle of this barren plain. Mountain Home is nine miles east of Mountain Home Air Force Base, and it's the trade center for far-flung ranches that extend from here down to the Nevada border along Hwy 51. Mountain Home also has the distinction of having Idaho's highest mean temperature; summer highs hover in the 100° range.

For more information about the area, contact the Mountain Home Chamber of Commerce (☎ 587-4334), PO Box 3, Mountain Home, ID 83647. The Greyhound bus stops at Hiler's Conoco at the corner of 5th N & 2nd E Sts.

### Bruneau Dunes State Park
During the ice-age Bonneville Flood, a meander in the Snake River swirled sand-laden soil through a river bend now contained in Bruneau Dune State Park (☎ 366-7919). The river receded, leaving a high-sided rocky bowl full of sand. Prevailing winds have swirled the sand deposits – and others like them – into enormous dunes, which form the centerpiece of the park.

The central dune is usually over 450 feet high, and it overlooks a small lake (the lake is historically recent, the result of an artificially high water table due to region's ubiquitous irrigation). Both are very popular with children and youthful adventurers, who like to scamper up the dunes and roll back down to land in the water. By midsummer, the lake is filled with algae and is pretty icky. Yet children and hardened anglers persist in making the most of this desert lake.

Be sure and stop at the visitors center, which gives a good lesson in the natural history of the Idaho desert and the peculiar dunes found here. There are also campgrounds beside the lake; be aware that this is a very hot place in midsummer. A $2-per-vehicle charge is levied at the park. Bruneau Dunes State Park is 20 miles south of Mountain Home on Hwy 51.

## Three Island Crossing State Park

At this historic river crossing, now a state park (☎ 366-2394), the main branch of the Oregon Trail crossed the Snake River. This site was chosen by the first trailblazers because three islands divide the wide river into smaller, more easily fordable segments. From here, the pioneers who chose to ford the river continued along the more hospitable northern flank of the Snake River, while those unable or unwilling to ford the river here were consigned to the Southern Cut-Off, a barren and dangerous trail through blistering desert.

The visitors center offers a good overview of the history and hardships of the Oregon Trail and preserves a number of original artifacts found here and at other points along the trail. The crossing here was the object of quite a bit of dread to the emigrants, as a sampling of pioneer diaries in the visitors center makes clear. Floating all one's belongings in a Conestoga wagon across the Snake River – even if it is divided into thirds – was a dangerous enterprise. A Conestoga wagon is on display near the visitors center, and it's hard to believe that people would attempt to cross the Snake – let alone the continent – in such a contraption. A portion of the Oregon Trail winds off through the park to disappear in the sagebrush; it's easy to see the remnants of the trail descending the steep hill across the Snake River from the park, where the crossing began.

There's a lovely picnic area in the park, overlooking the three islands, as well as a pleasant campground. Visitors pay $2 per vehicle. Three Island Crossing is 26 miles southeast of Mountain Home on I-84.

## Places to Stay

**Camping** *Mountain Home KOA* (☎ 587-5111), 220 E 10th N, offers laundry facilities, showers, LP gas, a dump station and a convenience store. Standard sites are $13; hook-ups are $17. The state parks at both *Bruneau Dunes* and *Three Island Crossing* have nice campgrounds, with flush toilets and showers; sites are $9.

**B&Bs** *Rose Stone Inn* (☎ 587-8866, (800) 717-7673) has five guest rooms with rates from $35 to $65, and pets are welcome.

**Hotels** Each of the following offers a swimming pool, which you'll surely appreciate after a long day traveling in the summer heat; all take pets. The *Towne Center Motel* (☎ 587-3373), 410 N 2nd St E, has singles/doubles at $24/32. *Motel Thunderbird* (☎ 587-7927), 910 Sunset Strip & Hwy 30 W, offers rooms with kitchenettes for $23/30. *Hi Lander Motel and Steak House* (☎ 587-3311), 615 S 3rd St W, has rooms for $29/37 and offers workout facilities, kitchens and a restaurant. *Best Western Foothills Motor Inn* (☎ 587-8477), 1080 Hwy 20, with a spa/hot tub, free continental breakfast and a restaurant, is a good deal at $32/40.

## Places to Eat

Start the day at *Stoney's Desert Inn* (☎ 587-9931), 1500 Sunset Strip, or end it there, as it's open 24 hours. If you're looking for sandwiches and salads for picnics, go to the *German Deli* (☎ 587-2925), 190 E 2nd St N, for authentic German cold cuts and potato salad. Another local favorite is the *Top Hat Southern BBQ* (☎ 587-9223), 145 N 2nd St E, for Tex-Mex grills. *Chapala Restaurant* (☎ 587-6925), 650 N 2nd St E, is the best local Mexican restaurant.

## HAGERMAN VALLEY

One of the most scenic areas in southern Idaho is the Hagerman Valley, a stretch of the Snake River canyon containing the famed Thousand Springs. Scores of underground river channels cascade from cliffside springs into a green and fertile valley. Here, too, is a prehistoric fossil bed that's now preserved as a national monument, and the Malad River Gorge, a cleft in the basalt plateau filled with spring-fed waterfalls.

Most of these sites are accessed by Hwy 30. This short route between Twin Falls and Bliss is much more scenic and enjoyable than the dull and relentless freeway it parallels. Campgrounds and hot springs are also abundant along this stretch of road, making it a good place for a stopover.

To reach the Hagerman Valley, either follow Hwy 30 west from Twin Falls toward Buhl or take I-84 exit No 141 at Bliss and drive south toward Hagerman. The 48-mile byway is also called Thousand Springs Scenic Route.

## Hagerman Fossil Beds National Monument

High on a bluff above the Snake River is a famed fossil bed known as the 'horse quarry' for the hundreds of skeletons of prehistoric horses found here in the 1930s. Recently named a national monument (☎ 837-4793), the fossil beds were created between two and three million years ago when this desert canyon was a grassland dotted with lakes and marshes. The primary fossil findings have been *Equus simplicidens*, a cloven-hoofed horse (the Idaho state fossil, incidentally) and ancient camels, although the remains of over 90 different species have been found here.

National monument status was conferred in 1988, and development of the site has been slow. A temporary visitors center finally opened, and it has a number of informative displays regarding the fossil beds and the prehistoric natural history of the area. There's also a theater with a slide and video presentation. The visitors center is in Hagerman, directly across from the high school, at the corner of Reed St and Hwy 30.

You can view the fossil beds from a boardwalk overlook and exhibit area by driving south of Hagerman three miles and crossing the Hwy 30 bridge over the Snake River. Turn west onto an unmarked paved

road that follows the river on the south bank. Continue on this road for about 12 miles until signs appear giving directions to the monument site (the park service has intentionally made this area rather difficult to find until the site is better developed, due to fear of vandalism). Gathering fossils is not allowed, and direct access to the fossil beds is prohibited.

On Saturdays during the months of August and September, the park rangers conduct special natural history programs, two of which include a guided tour of the fossil beds. Call ahead to receive a schedule of summer events.

## Thousand Springs

From the mountain slopes of the Rocky Mountains far to the north drain innumerable streams and rivers. When these water sources reach the lava-clogged Snake River Plain, they plunge underneath the valley's porous surface and flow through subterranean aquifers as underground rivers. The Snake River's canyon cuts a 400-foot-deep trench through various levels of these lava flows, exposing the aquifers, which plunge down the canyon walls as springs.

Geologists believe that the aptly named Thousand Springs constitute part of the Lost River, which drains a large mountain valley north of Arco only to disappear beneath the lava flows of the Craters of the Moon National Monument. Highway 30 accesses the stretch of the Snake River where cascades of water gush out of the northern canyon walls, forming a lush green valley and a notably scenic area.

Elsewhere, an area like this would at least be preserved as a state park. However, this is Idaho, and no one wastes a source of water, no matter how scenic. Much of the water is diverted directly into fish hatcheries and trout farms (90 percent of the nation's farm-raised trout come from here), and the rest is channeled into irrigation.

A couple of sections of the Thousands Springs have been preserved. The Nature Conservancy owns three miles of springs along the Snake River, and they open their property to visitors from Memorial Day to

Labor Day, on Friday through Monday afternoons. Trails lead down to the river and to the springs, and volunteers are available to answer questions. Once a year, the conservancy leads a canoe trip down the Snake River past the springs area. For more information, call 536-6797. To reach the Nature Conservancy property, turn off I-84 exit No 155 at Wendell, and follow signs toward Hagerman (away from Wendell). After three miles, turn south at the sign for Buhl. Follow this road for 2.5 miles and turn west at a road called 3200 South. In two miles the road comes to a T-junction; take the left turning to Thousand Spring Grade.

Another preserved area of the Thousand Springs is the Niagara Springs unit of the Malad Gorge State Park (see below). Here, a huge spring drains from the cliffs at 250 cubic feet per second to fill Crystal Springs Lake. Facilities include a picnic area and restrooms, and the lake is noted for its good fishing (there's a wheelchair-accessible fishing dock). To reach the park, leave I-84 at exit No 157 and follow Rex Leland Hwy south nine miles. The last mile, down the 350-foot-high canyon wall, is steep and narrow, and it isn't recommended for trailers or motor homes.

From the south, both the above sites can be accessed from Hwy 30 via Clearlakes Rd at Buhl.

**Boat Tours** For a boat tour of the Thousand Springs area, contact 1000 Springs Tours (☎ 837-9006), Hwy 30 at Hagerman St in Hagerman. They have three launch sites, at Hagerman, from Sliger's Thousand Springs Resort and from Twin Falls. Tours are scheduled according to reservation demand, so you'll need to call ahead and find out what's planned for when you visit. Tours and costs vary, ranging from an hour tour from Twin Falls, for $15 for adults and $12 for children, to a trip from Hagerman to Riley Falls for $25 for adults and $17 for children.

### Malad Gorge State Park
Another geological curiosity along this stretch of the Hagerman Valley is this dramatic gorge cut by the Malad River. After cutting across the lava plateau the river drops 60 feet into an extremely narrow, 250-foot-deep gorge to cut its way to its appointment with the Snake, two miles later. From the parking area, a path leads to a swinging foot bridge that crosses the chasm and to about a mile's worth of trails on the northern edge of the gorge.

The best viewing area of the Malad's falls, called the Punch Bowl, is from just beside I-84; from here, you can also see a number of springs gushing out of the canyon walls. Facilities at the park (☎ 837-4505) include a picnic area and restrooms. To reach the park, take I-84 exit No 147 and follow signs one mile to the park.

### Rafting
The Hagerman Valley is a popular family rafting trip, noted not so much for its white-knuckle excitement as for the opportunity to explore the wildlife and geology of the Snake River canyon. Trips leave from below Lower Salmon Falls Dam and float to near Bliss. Hagerman Valley Outfitters (☎ 837-6100), PO Box 245, Hagerman, ID 83332, offers daily half-day trips for $40, and a dinner float is an extra $10. High Adventure River Tours (☎ 733-0123), PO Box 222, Twin Falls, ID 83303, offers full-day trips starting at $50.

### Places to Stay
**Camping** There are a great many campgrounds along this portion of the Snake River, some featuring hot springs. *Rock Lodge & Campground* (☎ 837-4822), one mile north of Hagerman on Hwy 30, offers campsites ($8 to $13) as well as cabins ($55). *Sligar's Thousand Springs Resort* (☎ 837-4987), five miles south of Hagerman on Hwy 30, offers sites along the Snake River, with a swimming pool. Tent sites are $7; hook-ups are $14. *Banbury Hot Springs* (☎ 543-4098), ten miles north of Buhl on Hwy 30, then two miles east (follow the signs), has campsites and access to swimming and soaking in naturally heated pools. Facilities include a laundry; sites are $6 to $11.50.

IDAHO

**Hostel** Convenient to visiting the Hagerman Valley is the *Gooding Hotel B&B and AYH Hostel* (☎ 934-4374) at Gooding, north of the valley at the junction of Hwys 26 and 46. Beds in the hostel's dorm rooms are $9/12 for members/nonmembers, and rooms in the B&B are $35 to $50.

**Hotels** There's not too much to say about the *Siesta Motel* (☎ 543-6427), 629 S Broadway Ave in Buhl, but it is cheap, with rooms starting at $24. Also in Buhl is the *Oregon Trail Motel* (☎ 543-8814), 510 Broadway Ave S, a well-kept older motel. A jump up in class is the *Hagerman Valley Inn* (☎ 873-6196) in Hagerman, with single/double rooms at $37/40.

### Places to Eat
There are a number of uninspiring eateries along Hwy 30, but a couple stand out. *Frog's Lilypad* (☎ 837-6227), on the east end of Hagerman on Hwy 30, is a very popular, very cute restaurant for breakfast and lunch; burgers are the primary fare here. At *The Riverbank* (☎ 837-6462), 191 N State St, fresh Snake River catfish, hush puppies and other self-described Ozark dishes are served along with fish and steaks.

### TWIN FALLS
Twin Falls (population 27,750) is one of the many southern Idaho towns that blossomed along with the crops after the massive Snake River irrigation projects went in at the turn of the century. Twin Falls is a pleasant if sprawling farm and ranch trade center, and it's convenient for exploring the Hagerman Valley and the hinterlands south in the Sawtooth National Forest.

North of town are two remarkable waterfalls on the Snake River. Shoshone Falls is 53 feet higher and once carried more water than Niagara Falls; the namesake Twin Falls reunite two water courses of the ancestral Snake River. However, all these sites have been neutered as a result of Idaho's dam-building craze.

The Snake River cuts a mighty canyon

through this part of Idaho, and there's no better place to view it from than Perrine Bridge on Hwy 93 as it cuts south from I-84 to Twin Falls. Just east of here is where the stunt man Evel Knievel attempted to jump the canyon in 1974 aboard a rocket-powered motorcycle.

### Orientation
Twin Falls is six miles south of I-84 along Hwy 93, on the south side of the Snake River. Highway 93 becomes Blue Lakes Blvd in the city, while southern Idaho's other main arterial, Hwy 30, becomes Addison Ave. What's odd and confusing is that Twin Falls' old and appealing downtown is nowhere near these two modern business strips and is easy to completely overlook. To find downtown, go to the junction of Blue Lake Blvd and Addison Ave and turn onto Shoshone St, which intersects with Main St at the heart of downtown, seven blocks later.

### Information
Twin Falls Chamber of Commerce (☎ 733-3974, (800) 255-8946) is at 858 Blue Lakes Blvd N, Twins Falls, ID 83301. The Buzz Langdon Visitors Center (☎ 734-9531) is in the car park for the Snake River Canyon viewing area at Perrine Bridge. The headquarters of the Sawtooth National Forest (☎ 737-3200) is at 2647 Kimberly Rd E.

The post office (☎ 733-4380) is at 253 2nd Ave W. The Twin Falls *Times-News* is the daily newspaper. For local arts coverage and a look at local issues, pick up a copy of *The Monthly*.

BJ's Washtub (☎ 734-3109), in Centennial Sq at 671 Blue Lakes Blvd, offers drop-off service and will even deliver clean clothes. For health emergencies, go to Magic Valley Regional Medical Center (☎ 737-2000), 650 Addison Ave W.

### Herrett Museum
This museum (☎ 733-9554 for the college switchboard), off N College Rd on the College of Southern Idaho campus, preserves an impressive private collection of Northwest and Central American native

artifacts. The collection, which contains nearly 10,000 artifacts, was put together in the 1950s and '60s by a local couple whose primary interest was pre-Columbian art from Central and South America, augmented by a cross section of tools and weapons from the Snake River plateau. The collection was bequeathed to the college, which built the present museum and recently added a gallery of contemporary art and a planetarium to the complex. The hours are from 9:30 am to 8 pm Tuesday, from 9:30 am to 4:30 pm Wednesday through Friday, and from 1 to 4:30 pm Saturday. Admission to the museum is free.

### Twin Falls Historical Museum

This community museum (☎ 734-5547), 144 Taylor St, tells the story of the irrigation boom that built Twin Falls, and it's a good place to become acquainted with the agricultural history that still forms the backbone of this heavily rural area. Exhibits include old farm equipment, photographs and a completely furnished pioneer cabin. It's open from noon to 5 pm Monday through Friday, May 1 through mid-September.

### Shoshone Falls

Once considered one of the natural wonders of Idaho, this 212-foot-high falls is still impressive, but more for what must have been than for what it is currently. Between the power dam built right at the top of the falls and the massive amounts of water removed from the river by upstream irrigation projects, there's often only a trickle of water left to stream over the cliffs. Early in the spring the falls are fullest, as no one has gotten around to irrigating yet.

What is undeniably pleasant is the public park and picnic area at the falls, beneath the bare canyon walls. At any given time, more water is being pumped onto the verdant lawns and grounds here than is tumbling over the falls.

To reach the falls, take Falls Rd east off Blue Lakes Blvd and drive four miles to 3300 East Rd, a well-signed road turning to

the north. There's a $2 admission fee to the falls and park area.

Just upriver are Twin Falls, or rather, what's left of them. So successfully has the Idaho Power Company converted the falls to hydropower that there's hardly any water left even to coat the rock face.

### Rafting & Floating

Twin Falls is the center for rafting on the Bruneau and Snake rivers. Besides the popular Hagerman Valley trips, guided white-water trips are available above Twin Falls on the so-called Murtaugh section of the Snake River. Contact High Adventure River Tours (☎ 733-0123), PO Box 222, Twin Falls, ID 83303, for information; a long day trip complete with lunch costs $100. If you want to rent your own gear, go to River Rat White Water Toyz (☎ 733-3136), 238 Blue Lake Blvd.

### Golf

Surely one of the most dramatically situated courses anywhere, the Canyon Springs Golf Club (☎ 734-7609) is a nine-hole course at the base of the Snake River canyon just north of Twin Falls. Watch for the turn off of Blue Lake Blvd just across from Magic Valley Mall. Directly across the river beneath the north canyon wall is another golf course, this one private. Twin Falls Municipal (733-3326) is the 18-hole public course; it's off Addison Ave on Grandview Drive, east of town.

### Other Activities

If you want to go **swimming**, the municipal pool (☎ 734-2336) is at 756 Locust St N. The deserts of Idaho may not seem like the natural place for **scuba diving**, but two local shops offer diving lessons and rentals for use in Snake River reservoirs. Contact Scuba Adventure & Travel (☎ 733-8822), 147 Main Ave E, or Deep Magic Scuba (☎ 733-8203), 236 Main Ave N, for more information.

If you need to stock up on any sporting or recreational gear before heading out, go to Blue Lake Sporting Goods (☎ 733-6446), 1236 Blue Lake Blvd.

IDAHO

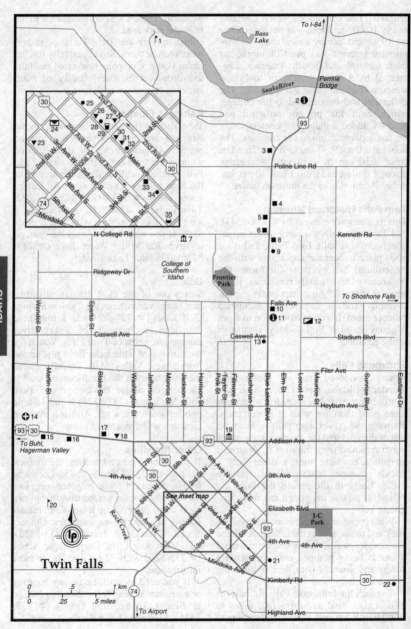

| PLACES TO STAY | | OTHER | |
|---|---|---|---|
| 3 | Comfort Inn | 1 | Canyon Springs Golf Club |
| 4 | Motel 6 | 2 | Buzz Langdon Visitors Center |
| 5 | Ameritel Inn | 7 | Herrett Museum |
| 6 | Best Western Canyon Springs Inn | 9 | Blue Lake Sporting Goods |
| 8 | Super 8 Motel | 11 | Chamber of Commerce |
| 10 | Weston Inn | 12 | Twin Falls Municipal Pool |
| 15 | Holiday Motel | 13 | BJ's Washtub |
| 16 | Monterey Motor Inn | 14 | Magic Valley Regional Medical Center |
| 17 | Best Western Apollo Motor Inn | 19 | Twin Falls Historical Museum |
| 33 | Econo Lodge | 20 | Twin Falls Municipal Golf Course |
| | | 21 | River Rat White Water Toyz |
| PLACES TO EAT | | 22 | Twin Cinema |
| 18 | Rock Creek Inn | 24 | Post Office |
| 23 | Buffalo Cafe | 25 | Deep Magic Scuba |
| 26 | Mama Inez | 28 | Mall Cinema |
| 27 | A'Roma Italian Cuisine | 29 | Dunken's Draught House |
| 30 | Uptown Bistro | 32 | Scuba Adventure & Travel |
| 31 | Metropolitan Bakery & Cafe | 34 | Petersen's Western Wear |
| | | 35 | Greyhound Bus Depot |

**IDAHO**

## Places to Stay

**Camping** *Anderson Campground* (825-5336), a half mile east on the frontage road from I-84 exit No 183, offers 120 spaces; standard sites cost $11, and full hook-ups are $18. It has a swimming pool, laundry facilities, showers, LP gas and a store. The *Twin Falls-Jerome KOA Kampground* (☎ 324-4169), one mile north of I-84 exit No 173, has a pool, laundry, miniature golf and a load of other activities. Basic sites are $15.50; hook-ups are $20.

However, it's worth the half-hour commute to Twin Falls to stay in one of the pleasant campgrounds in the verdent Thousand Springs area (see Hagerman Valley above).

**Hotels** Lodging in Twin Falls is found basically along the city's two long commercial strips. Convenient to travelers coming in from I-84 is the development along Blue Lakes Blvd, also known as Hwy 93. The first three motels listed offer a swimming pool, spa and continental breakfast. *Comfort Inn* (734-7494), 1893 Canyon Springs Rd, just off Hwy 93, is the first motel you come to upon entering Twin

Falls, and singles/doubles are $42/48. *Ameritel Inn* (736-8000, (800) 822-8946), 1377 Blue Lakes Blvd, also offers wheelchair access, workout facilities and kitchens. Rooms begin at $49/54. The *Weston Inn* (733-6095), 906 Blue Lakes Blvd N, has rooms for $36/41.

*Motel 6* (734-3993), 1472 Blue Lakes Blvd N, has a swimming pool and rooms for $30/36. *Best Western Canyon Springs Inn* (734-5000, (800) 727-5003), 1357 Blue Lakes Blvd, is wheelchair accessible and has a spa; rates are $47/52. The *Super 8 Motel* (734-5801), 1260 Blue Lakes Blvd, has free continental breakfast and rooms for $40/46.

West of town along Hwy 30 is another motel strip with slightly older motor inns. The *Holiday Motel* (733-4330), 615 Addison Ave W, has rooms for $30/37. The *Monterey Motor Inn* (733-5151), 433 Addison Ave W, has a swimming pool, spa and free continental breakfast; rates begin at $27/33. *Best Western Apollo Motor Inn* (733-2010), 296 Addison Ave W, has a swimming pool and rooms for $39/44.

To stay downtown, about the only option is the slightly faded but acceptable *Econo*

*Lodge* (☎ 733-8770), 320 Main Ave S, with rooms starting at $33.

## Places to Eat
You'll have absolutely no trouble finding perfectly acceptable food along the Hwy 93 strip leading into Twin Falls. However, take the trouble to find your way to the old downtown area, where a number of locally owned restaurants serve up some very good food in friendly surroundings.

Join local ranchers at the *Buffalo Cafe* (☎ 734-0271), 218 4th Ave W, the place to go for a big, traditional breakfast; the house specialty is a dish called 'buffalo chips', or fried potatoes smothered with tasty gravy. Home to Twin Falls' slightly alternative side, *Metropolitan Bakery & Cafe* (☎ 734-4457), 125 Main Ave E, is a great bakery and espresso bar specializing in delicious pastries the likes of which you probably can't find outside of Europe. On Thursday evenings, there's live acoustic music.

The *Uptown Bistro* (☎ 733-0900), 117 Main Ave E, is one of Twin Falls' favorite restaurants. During the week, sandwiches and light fare (pasta, salads) are under $9; on Friday and Saturday nights, the bistro turns to fine dining, with classic continental dishes making an appearance. Beef Wellington is $18; intriguing chicken Vera (which the menu describes as 'named after a ghost I once worked with') is $15. *Mama Inez* restaurants featuring Southwestern dishes are found in a number of southern Idaho towns. Mama's restaurant in Twin Falls (☎ 734-0733), 164 Main Ave N, is especially pleasant, with unusual dishes like crab tacos and six different egg creations.

*A'Roma Italian Cuisine* (☎ 733-0617), 147 Shoshone St N, has mandatory checkered tablecloths and inexpensive pasta and salads for lunch during the week; on Friday and Saturday evenings only A'Roma is open for dinner, with traditional Italian and Twin Falls Italian dishes (tenderloin finger steaks with spaghetti for $16) leading the menu. The city's best steak house is the *Rock Creek Inn* (☎ 734-

4151), 200 Addison Ave W, with prime rib dinners for $15.

## Entertainment
**Brewpubs** *Dunken's Draught House* (☎ 733-8114), 102 Main Ave N, offers 21 draft beers, including some cask-conditioned ales. The old bar is light, airy and a very pleasant place to escape the heat of a summer afternoon.

**Cinemas** *Mall Cinema* (☎ 733-5570) is at 146 Main Ave N and *Twin Cinema* (☎ 734-2400) is at Kimberly Rd and Eastland Drive.

## Things to Buy
Petersen's Western Wear (☎ 733-1719), 336 Main Ave S, is a large, well-stocked Western clothing shop. If you're hankering after a pair of boots or a pearl-snap shirt, this is the place.

## Getting There & Away
**Air** The Twin Falls-Sun Valley Regional Airport is served by Horizon Airlines (☎ 734-9440, (800) 547-9308), United (☎ (800) 241-6522) and SkyWest Airlines (☎ 734-6232, (800) 453-9417).

**Bus** The Greyhound depot (☎ 733-3002) is at 461 2nd Ave S. Two Greyhound buses a day travel east and west on I-84 between Portland, Boise, and Salt Lake City; one bus a day travels from Twin Falls to Pocatello and Butte, MT. Sun Valley Stages (☎ 383-3085), with winter service to Ketchum, operates from 119 S Park Ave W.

**Train** The Amtrak connection for this part of Idaho is 30 miles north of Twin Falls at Shoshone; the unstaffed depot is at 304 Rail St. There are four trains a week each way on the *Pioneer Line*, which runs from Chicago to Salt Lake City, Portland and Seattle. For information, call Amtrak at (800) 872-7245.

**Car** Avis (☎ 733-5527, (800) 831-2847), National (☎ 733-3646, (800) 227-7368) and Budget (☎ 734-4067, (800) 527-0700) are at the airport. Hertz (☎ 733-2668, (800) 654-3131) has an office at 210 Shoshone St W. If you're looking for something cheaper, try Used-A-Car Rental (☎ 733-6637, (800) 481-6637).

## Getting Around

The local public transport service is called Trans (☎ 736-2133, (800) 531-2133). Trans operates buses on weekdays only, and besides the city routes, it offers commuter bus service to Buhl, Gooding (the closest hostel), Kimberly and Burley.

For a cab, call 733-9101.

## BURLEY

Near the junction of Interstates 84 and 86, and almost exactly midway across Idaho, Burley (population 10,000) is probably not the kind of place you dreamed of spending a night in Idaho, but because of its absolute centrality, chances are you'll end up pulling off the freeway and having to do so anyway. Burley doesn't offer much to divert the traveler, but there are plenty of motel rooms here and a couple good cafes.

A branch of the Oregon Trail cuts just to the south of Burley. The City of Rocks, a curious rock formation that from a distance resembles a spired city, was a famous pioneer landmark; it's now a state park.

## Orientation & Information

Burley is 40 miles from Twin Falls, and 77 miles west of Pocatello. Nine miles east of Burley, I-84 cuts to the southeast toward Salt Lake City, 170 miles distant. Four miles north of Burley is Rupert, another farm town.

The street that links Burley to the freeway is called Overlook Ave; Hwy 30 cuts through downtown as Main St.

For information about the area, contact the Mini Cassia Chamber of Commerce (☎ 436-4793), 324 Scott Ave, Rupert, ID 83318. The Greyhound bus depot (☎ 678-0477) is at 1214 Oakley Ave, Burley.

## Places to Stay

**Camping** The *Snake River Campground* (☎ 654-2133) is eight miles east of Burley

at Declo. Take I-84 exit No 216 and follow it to the intersection with Hwy 25. The campground is right beside the river and offers a laundry, grocery store, swimming pool and playground. Sites are $12 for tents, $17 for hook-ups.

**Hotels** Right at the freeway exit is *Budget Motel* (☎ 678-2200), 900 N Overland Ave, a vast and perfectly pleasant motel with rooms from $35 to $51. Right next door is the *Best Western Burley Inn* (☎ 678-9532), 900 Overland Ave, with a swimming pool; rooms are $49 to $71. The *Grenwell Motel* is an attractive older motel that takes pets, offers some kitchen units and has rooms for $28 to $52.

## Places to Eat

For old-fashioned family dining, Burley offers two gems. *Connor's Cafe* (☎ 678-9367), just north of the Burley/I-84 interchange at the Philips 66 station, is kind of the archetype of truck stop cafes. The food isn't fussy but it's full of flavor, there's no bottom to your coffee cup, and the staff is friendly. Nothing on the menu tops $10, and make sure to leave room for pie.

In town, *Price's Cafe* (☎ 678-5149), 2444 Overland Ave, is another good cafe. It has a daily, 36-foot-long 'smorgasbord' buffet table with an all-you-can-eat lunch for $5; dinner is $6. *Tio Joe's* (☎ 678-9844), 262 Overland Ave, is the best of the local Mexican restaurants.

## CITY OF ROCKS NATIONAL RESERVE

Administered jointly by the NPS and Idaho State Parks, this 22-sq-mile site (☎ 824-5563) contains a jumble of ancient granite – some of the oldest exposed rock in North America – that wind, rain and weather have eroded into a thousand fantastic shapes. Since the days of the Oregon Trail, passersby have engaged in fits of imagination, seeing visions of cities, castles and dozens of symbolic shapes. The Elephant Head, the Squaw Papoose, the Kaiser's Helmut and the King's Throne are just a few of the scores of fancifully named

IDAHO

formations in the park. The Twin Sisters, two spires of rock, are over 62 stories high.

The California Cut-Off, a branch of the Oregon Trail that veered down into northern California, passed through the City of Rocks, and impressions of the formations figured vividly in pioneer diaries. On Register Rock, the names and initials of Oregon Trail travelers are still visible, written with axle grease on a rock face.

Rock climbing has become a very popular activity at the park, with 500 designated routes on a variety of rocks. Campgrounds at the park are primitive ($8), though there is running water.

To reach City of Rocks from Burley, take Hwy 27 south for 17 miles to Oakley, and follow the signs on a paved then gravel road to the park, 19 miles later. The park can also be reached from I-84 exit No 245; turn west toward Malta, and then follow signs to Elba and Almo, a total of 30 miles. The park begins two miles west of Almo.

## MASSACRE ROCKS STATE PARK

Interstate 86 between Burley and Pocatello is another of those long, relentless stretches of freeway that occur with frequency through southern Idaho. The landscape is perfectly flat and grimly arid; you'll find yourself looking forward to plots of irrigation and manicured rest areas.

The Oregon Trail pioneers also dreaded passing through this area. This part of the trail traversed the homelands of the Shoshone and Bannock tribes, and the emigrants watched in fear for war parties; this was one of the most dangerous portions of the Oregon Trail. Nowadays, Massacre Rocks State Park is a very pleasant place with lovely private campsites; a rock engraved with pioneer names is also nearby. A small visitors center (☎ 548-2672, 548-2472) tells the story of Massacre Rocks and of the Native and pioneer histories that converge at this spot. Two nature trails lead into a sagebrush savanna.

Register Rock, a lump of basalt inscribed with the names of passing emigrants, is just south of the state park; the oldest name on the rock dates from 1849. Now elaborately protected with Plexiglas shields and a roofed structure, the autographs of the pioneers are barely visible. This is a nice place for a picnic, though. There is a fee of $2 per vehicle.

### Places to Stay & Eat

There are 51 campsites at the park, each set back in a landscape of juniper and sage, most overlooking the Snake River. Facilities include showers and flush toilets, and all sites have full hook-ups ($11).

The closest traditional lodgings are at American Falls (population 3700), a charmless little town beside a hydroelectric reservoir 10 miles north on I-86. Early developers in Idaho seemingly couldn't resist building dams on waterfalls, so don't go looking for the falls in American Falls: the 50-foot cascade was obliterated by dams in 1925. And don't go looking for the

---

### Killings at Massacre Rocks

The killings that elicited the name of Massacre Rocks actually occurred several miles east of the state park. In 1862, well after the initial emigration of White settlers across the Oregon Trail, the natives along the Snake River were increasingly hostile to the wagon trains that crossed their plateau. Three separate emigrant groups, in a total of 52 wagons, were progressing west from Fort Hall when the lead wagon train was attacked. In this and following battles 10 men and women were killed; they were brought back to the Massacre Rocks area to be buried.

Revisionist history (along with a solid dose of Hollywood horse dramas) has placed the killings at a gatelike passage between two upright pillars near the southern end of the park. However likely an ambush site the passage might seem, the killings took place far from there. ■

old town center either: it was flooded by reservoirs, and a new town was built higher on the riverbanks in 1927. If you need to stay here, the best bet is the *Hillview Motel* (☎ 226-5151) at I-86 exit No 40. Rooms start at $28.

Odd as it sounds, one of the best places to eat around here is *Melody Lanes* (☎ 226-2815), 152 Harrison St. Yes, it's a bowling alley cafe, serving abundant breakfasts and good luncheon sandwiches. If this doesn't appeal to you, check out the fast food at the freeway on-ramps.

## POCATELLO

Pocatello (population 60,000) is Idaho's second-largest city and one of its most historic. Established as a rail junction in 1884, when the north-south rails between the gold fields in Montana and Salt Lake City were joined with the east-west rails of the Union Pacific, Pocatello thrived as the center of a vast agricultural area, the center of Idaho's noted potato fields.

However, present-day Pocatello is not immediately appealing. The handsome but decrepit old downtown remains in a pre-gentrified state, and the rest of the city sprawls along suburban streets.

Pocatello is home to Idaho State University (☎ 236-3662), which has 11,100 students. The university has an emphasis in the sciences and technological fields.

### Orientation

What's commonly known as Pocatello actually includes Chubbuck, a town just to the north. Both these communities were carved out of the Fort Hall Indian Reservation by railroad moguls during the 1880s.

Downtown Pocatello is south of the rail tracks on Main St and Arthur Ave. However, modern businesses have changed their orientation to serve the new transportation corridor, Interstates 15 and 86, which join here. The main strip in town is now Yellowstone Ave, which connects to I-86 from exit No 61, and South 4th and 5th Aves, which provide access to Idaho State University and eventually downtown along I-15 from exit No 67.

### Information

Greater Pocatello Chamber of Commerce (☎ 233-1525) can be contacted at 2695 S 5th Ave, Pocatello, ID 83205. The Pocatello Ranger District (☎ 236-7500), in the Federal Building at 250 S 4th Ave, Suite 187, oversees the Caribou National Forest. To find out about road conditions, call 233-6724.

The post office (☎ 234-0777) is at 205 S Main St. To do laundry, head to the Sunshine Laundry Center (☎ 237-9960), 1442 Yellowstone Ave. For a medical emergency, go to Pocatello Regional Medical Center (☎ 234-0777), 777 Hospital Way.

### Bannock County Historical Museum

This regional museum (☎ 233-0434), 105 S Garfield Ave, in a former Carnegie library, contains a series of displays mostly of interest to railroad buffs, although there's the usual collection of Native American weapons and tools. During the summer it's open daily from 10 am to 6 pm; the rest of the year from 10 am to 2 pm Tuesday to Saturday. Admission is $1 for adults and 50c for children.

### Fort Hall Replica

Pocatello's main tourist attraction is the re-created Hudson's Bay Company's Fort Hall (☎ 234-1795) in Ross Park, near the corner of 5th Ave S and Barton Rd. Although Fort Hall – one of the most noted landmarks and stopovers on the Oregon Trail – was built in 1834 about 15 miles north of here, the replica of Fort Hall was built in Pocatello in 1963. Within the encampment are displays focusing on the various eras of the fort's history, including a Native American tepee. It's open during the summer from 9 am to 7 pm daily; from April through Memorial Day from 10 am to 2 pm Tuesday to Saturday; and from Labor Day to the end of September from 10 am to 2 pm daily. Regular admission is $1 for adults, 50c for children ages 13 to 18, and 25c for children ages 6 to 12.

### Idaho Museum of Natural History

Near the corner of S 5th Ave and E Dillon

IDAHO

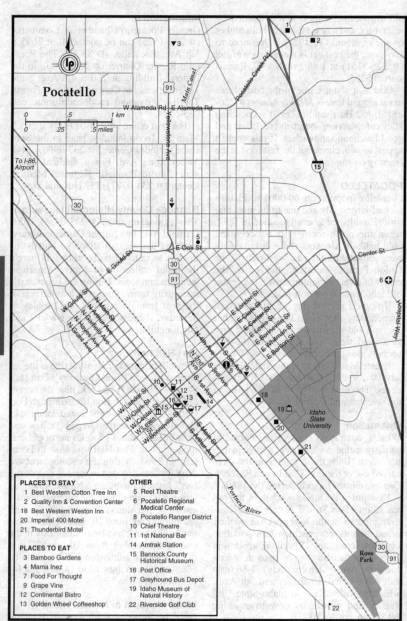

# Pocatello

**PLACES TO STAY**
1 Best Western Cotton Tree Inn
2 Quality Inn & Convention Center
18 Best Western Weston Inn
20 Imperial 400 Motel
21 Thunderbird Motel

**PLACES TO EAT**
3 Bamboo Gardens
4 Mama Inez
7 Food For Thought
9 Grape Vine
12 Continental Bistro
13 Golden Wheel Coffeeshop

**OTHER**
5 Reel Theatre
6 Pocatello Regional Medical Center
8 Pocatello Ranger District
10 Chief Theatre
11 1st National Bar
14 Amtrak Station
15 Bannock County Historical Museum
16 Post Office
17 Greyhound Bus Depot
19 Idaho Museum of Natural History
22 Riverside Golf Club

IDAHO

St on the Idaho State University campus, this museum (☎ 236-3317) is largely a paean to prehistoric reptiles. Kids will love the six life-size moveable dinosaurs. It's open from 9 am to 5 pm, Monday to Saturday. Admission is free.

### Activities
Ross Park has a **swimming** pool (☎ 234-9977) as well as most other outdoor sports facilities.

Pocatello has two excellent 18-hole **golf** courses, the Highland Golf Course Club (☎ 237-9922), 201 Van Elm Lane, and Riverside Golf Club (☎ 232-9515), southeast of Pocatello on I-15 between Portneuf and Inkom.

### Places to Stay
**Camping** *Pocatello KOA Campground* (☎ 233-4587), 9815 W Pocatello Creek Rd, is off I-15 exit No 71. Sites are $17 to $22, and facilities include a laundry and playground.

**Hotels** Almost all the lodgings in Pocatello are out along the interstate highways. Convenient to I-86 exit No 61 is *Days Inn* (☎ 237-0020), 133 W Burnside Ave, with rooms from $44 to $55 and a swimming pool. Also with a pool and with rooms from $21 to $39 are the *Motel 6* (☎ 237-7880), 291 W Burnside Ave, and *Nendel's Inn* (☎ 237-3100), 4333 Yellowstone Ave.

Somewhat swankier lodgings are near I-15 exit No 71. The *Best Western Cotton Tree Inn* (☎ 237-7650), 1415 Bench Rd, has rooms for $55 to $150, and the *Quality Inn & Convention Center* (☎ 233-2200), 1555 Pocatello Creek Rd, has rooms for $42 to $69.

The best deals in Pocatello are along old Hwy 30, now 5th Ave, near the university. The *Best Western Weston Inn* (☎ 233-5530), 745 S 5th Ave, has a pool and rooms for $35 to $70. You can't beat the prices at the *Imperial 400 Motel* (☎ 233-5120), 1055 S 5th Ave, just across from the campus, with rooms between $23 and $60, or at the *Thunderbird Motel* (☎ 232-6330), 1415 S 5th Ave, whose rates run from $22 to $36.

What's more, both have a swimming pool, and pets are welcome.

### Places to Eat
The place to go for start-me-up morning espresso and pastries is the *Grape Vine* (☎ 232-5218), 466 S 5th Ave. *Food for Thought* (☎ 233-7267), 504 E Center, is a convenient, slightly collegiate place for soups, salads, sandwiches and dessert. The *Bamboo Gardens* (☎ 238-2331), 1200 Yellowstone Ave, is Pocatello's best choice for Hunan and Sichuan cooking, while *Mama Inez* (☎ 234-7674), 350 Yellowstone Ave, turns out great Tex-Mex food from the chain's original restaurant.

The *Golden Wheel Coffeeshop* (☎ 234-1754), 230 W Bonneville, is an excellent restaurant in an unlikely location. This faded old hotel dining room hasn't been updated since the mid-50s, but the food here is remarkably good and inventive. Try the breast of duck with a chipotle/plum wine sauce served over linguini ($11) or a wine-braised loin of pork with a compote of pears and hefeweizen ale ($13). Don't turn away when you see the dining room, and don't get discouraged with the aimless service; the food is worth it.

The other restaurant of note in Pocatello is the *Continental Bistro* (☎ 233-4433), 140 S Main St, in a handsome old bar and storefront. The menu is broad and up-to-date, and it encourages a meal of smaller dishes. A grilled steak and gorgonzola cheese salad ($7) can easily make a meal; an entree of veal medallions with wild mushrooms is $17. There are daily seafood and steak specials, the wine list is impressive, and regional microbrews are served in the bar.

### Entertainment
The *Chief Theatre*, 215 N Main St, is Pocatello's performing arts center. Call 232-4433 for current events. For cheap movies, go to *Reel Theatre* (☎ 233-2300), 310 E Oak St.

On Friday and Saturday nights, local bands tune up at *1st National Bar* (☎ 233-1516), 232 W Center St.

**IDAHO**

## Getting There & Around
**Air** Pocatello Municipal Airport, four miles west of town off I-86 exit No 56, is served by Horizon (☎ (800) 547-9308), SkyWest (☎ (800) 453-9417) and United Express (☎ (800) 241-6522).

**Bus** There's one Greyhound bus a day along I-86 north to Butte, MT and east to Burley. There's also one bus south to Salt Lake City. The depot (☎ 232-5365) is at 215 W Bonneville.

**Train** Amtrak's *Pioneer* makes four stops weekly at Pocatello on its run between Seattle and Chicago. The station (☎ 234-2150) is at 300 S Harrison.

**Car** Hertz (☎ 233-2970, (800) 654-3131) and Avis (☎ 232-3244, (800) 831-2847) have agencies at the Pocatello Airport. U-Save Car Rental (☎ 237-9010, (800) 426-5299) is at 1407 Yellowstone Ave.

**Taxi** For a cab, call 232-1115.

## BLACKFOOT
Idaho is the potato source for the nation, raising one-third of the nation's crop, and the spud capital of Idaho is Blackfoot (population 11,000). Irrigated potato fields stretch off in all directions; pull off the road and admire all the rail cars filled with tubers. For tourist information, contact the Blackfoot Chamber of Commerce (☎ 785-0510), PO Box 801, Blackfoot, ID 83221.

Between Pocatello and Blackfoot is the main body of the Fort Hall Reservation, shared by the Shoshone and Bannock tribes. About half of the reservation's original 525,000 acres are still owned by the tribes.

### Idaho's World Potato Exposition
If you need a break from freeway driving, pull off to visit this good-natured and educational visitors center (☎ 785-2517) devoted to the humble potato; it also promises 'a free tater to every out-a-stater' (you have a choice of baked or uncooked). Housed in an old rail depot, this museum

and information center offers videos and a walk-through exhibit of potato history and horticulture. It's open daily from 9 am to 5 pm; admission is $2.

### Special Events
The Fort Hall Reservation's biggest event is the Shoshone-Bannock Indian Festival, which is held the second week of August on the reservation. For information, call 785-2080.

### Places to Stay & Eat
*Alder Inn B&B* (☎ 785-6968), 384 Alder St, offers four rooms at $50. The *Riverside Inn* (☎ 785-5000), 1229 Parkway Ave, has a swimming pool and allows pets; rooms range from $40 to $65.

For breakfast and family dining, go to *Homestead Family Restaurant* (☎ 785-0700), 1355 Parkway Drive. The dinner club of choice in Blackfoot is the *Colonial Inn* (☎ 785-1390), 659 S Ash St.

## IDAHO FALLS
Dominated by the spire of its Mormon temple, Idaho Falls (population 50,000) is a prototypic Idaho farm and ranch center, with well-heeled farmers lending the city its veneer of sophistication. For the traveler, what's near Idaho Falls is probably more important than what's in the city: from here, Yellowstone and Grand Teton national parks are within a day's drive; Montana is just a couple of hours north; and to the east is the Craters of the Moon National Monument.

Idaho Falls began its life in the 1860s as a crossroads; the Snake River had chewed a channel no more than 60 feet across into the underlying lava flow here, which brought first a ferry then a bridge to the fledgling community (then called Eagle Rock). The transportation hub soon attracted other businesses, and then the railroad, and the town was up and running.

Oddly, there is no falls at Idaho Falls. Local business interests thought that the city would attract more settlers if the community were named something other than Eagle Rock, and a group of investors from

## Fort Hall

Fort Hall was established between Pocatello and Blackfeet in 1834 by Boston fur entrepreneur Nathaniel Wyeth, and it was one of the first US settlements in the Northwest. Wyeth's trading post was meant to provide competition to the British Hudson's Bay Company fort on the Boise River; however, the HBC didn't waste much time undercutting Wyeth's prices, and the Yankee was force to sell out to the HBC in 1836.

Under the British, Fort Hall became a major trading center with the local Native Americans and a fortuitous stopover for thousands of Oregon Trail pioneers headed for the Willamette Valley. The emigrant trains stopped here after crossing the Continental Divide at South Pass to replenish their supplies before striking off across the deserts along the Snake River. The HBC closed Fort Hall in 1856 due to increasingly hostile relations with the Shoshone and Bannocks; nothing remains at the site of the old fort. ∎

Chicago decided on the moniker 'Idaho Falls'. However, in 1911 a diversion weir for a hydroelectric project created a 20-foot 'falls' near downtown, thereby bringing nature and the Snake River into compliance with the fancy of local boosters.

### Orientation

Just north of Idaho Falls, Hwy 20 splits off to head to Yellowstone National Park, while I-84 continues north toward Butte, MT. The shortest route to Grand Teton National Park is east along Hwy 26.

As in other Idaho cities, downtown Idaho Falls has been neglected in favor of commercial strips leading out to suburbs. However, the center of the city contains some charming architecture, and a few business still struggle on. To reach downtown, take I-15 exit No 118 and follow Broadway St across the Snake River to Hwy 26, which becomes Yellowstone Ave. City center is wedged between the river and Yellowstone Ave.

Through Idaho Falls, both banks of the Snake River have been converted to a greenway. These riverside hiking and biking trails link together a number of larger parks and make for a nice stroll.

### Information

For information on this part of the state, including the gateways to Yellowstone and Grand Teton, contact the Eastern Idaho Visitor Information Center (☎ 523-1010, (800) 634-3246) at 505 Lindsay Blvd, Idaho Falls, ID 83628. The ranger station (☎ 523-1412) at 3659 E Ririe Hwy serves the Palisades District of the Targhee National Forest. To check on mountain passes and road conditions, call 745-7278.

The post office (☎ 523-3650) is at 605 4th. For medical help, go to Eastern Idaho Regional Medical Center (☎ 529-6111), 3100 Channing Way. Wash those dirty clothes at Broadway Wash-N-Dry (☎ 529-5385), 1711 Broadway St.

### Bonneville County Historical Museum

This community museum (☎ 522-1400), 200 N Eastern Ave, in the handsome old Carnegie Library, preserves the history of the old settlement of Eagle Rock – including a re-created main street business district – as well as Native American artifacts. Another display explains the historic development of nuclear energy at the nearby Idaho National Engineering Laboratories. It's open daily from 10 am to 5 pm Monday through Friday, and from 1 to 5 pm on Saturday. Admission is $1 for adults and 25c for children.

### Places to Stay

**Camping** The *Idaho Falls KOA* (☎ 523-3362), 1440 Lindsay Blvd, offers a swimming pool, laundry, playground and a number of recreational options. Standard sites are $16.50; hook-ups are $21.50.

**Hotels** Most lodgings face onto Idaho Falls' riverside greenway, many with a view of the diversion dam they call the falls and of the stark white spire of the Mormon temple. All of the following have swimming pools and spa facilities. *Holiday Inn*

*West Bank*, (☎ 523-8000, (800) 432-1005), 475 River Parkway, is right on the greenway; rooms range between \$55 and \$95. *Best Western Stardust* (☎ 522-2910), 700 Lindsay Blvd, faces the falls and has rooms from \$45 to \$85. *Shilo Inn* (☎ 523-0088), 780 Lindsay Blvd, doubles as a convention center; rooms are \$69 to \$105. *Quality Inn* (☎ 523-6260), 850 Lindsay Blvd, has rooms for \$40 to \$60.

You'll have to get off the greenway to find Idaho Falls' few inexpensive lodgings. The *Evergreen Gables Motel* (☎ 522-5410), 3130 S Yellowstone Ave, is a good deal, with rooms from \$19 to \$35; there are cooking units, and pets are OK. The *Towne Lodge* (☎ 523-2960), 255 E St, is another older motel with clean and comfortable rooms; rates run from \$30 to \$40.

### Places to Eat

Somewhat oddly, in the middle of Mormon Idaho is one of the most beautiful coffeeshops anywhere. The *High Desert Rose Coffee Roasters* (☎ 528-5464), 504 Shoup Ave, is in the main gallery of an ornate old department store, and it has been beautifully renovated into an espresso bar and cafe that serves light meals. If you're weary of the freeway, pull in and relax with a latte and marvel at the architecture. For fresh baked goods, head to *Wheat Blossom Bakery* (☎ 528-6146), 445 A St.

If Idaho meat and potatoes have you hankering for something ethnic, try *Saigon Restaurant* (☎ 529-8799), 3390 S Yellowstone Hwy. At *Lost Arts Brew & Breadworks* (☎ 528-9288), 298 D St, the yeastly arts meet up. This brewpub and bakery offers microbrews and freshly baked bread, sandwiches and light snacks.

A night out on the town in Idaho Falls means *Jake's Steak & Fish House* (☎ 524-5240), which offers an eclectic menu of Western favorites. A bit more salt-of-the-earth is the *Loft Restaurant* (☎ 523-1977), 3 N 3800 E, an old-fashioned steakhouse and cocktail lounge in a log cabin.

### Getting There & Away

**Air** Fanning Field Airport is west of the city just off I-15 exit No 119. The airport is served by Horizon Airlines (☎ (800) 547-9308), United (☎ (800) 241-6522) and SkyWest Airlines (☎ (800) 453-9417).

**Bus** Greyhound buses stop at the depot (☎ 522-0912) at 2874 N Holmes St on their way between Pocatello and Butte along I-15.

### Getting Around

**Bus** Idaho Fall's ambitious regional bus service is called the CART (☎ 522-2278), which serves a wide-ranging district from its offices at 850 Denver St. In addition to local destinations, buses run north to Rexburg, northwest to Salmon and east to Driggs.

**Car** Avis (522-4225) and Hertz (☎ 529-3101) are each available at the airport; Rent-A-Wreck (☎ 529-8411) is located at 720 W Broadway.

**Taxi** Call East Way Taxi (☎ 525-8344) for a cab.

### AROUND IDAHO FALLS
### Craters of the Moon
### National Monument

Throughout southern Idaho, the north slope of the Snake River Basin is a vast, uneroded lava flow, scarcely approached by roads and almost completely uninhabited. A portion of this flow is contained in Craters of the Moon National Monument (☎ 527-3257), an 83-sq-mile showcase of volcanism. The volcanic activity that formed the Craters of the Moon ceased only 2000 years ago, and the various craters, lava caves and cinder cones look so fresh and barren that they seem to have erupted only last week.

Stop at the visitors center for a free map of the roads and trails through the park, and check out the displays and videos explaining the volcanic history of the area. The most popular route through the park is the seven-mile loop road to the Big Craters area. At a number of stops, short hikes lead onto the edge of craters and out to lava caves (which are undeveloped, so bring your own flashlights if you plan to explore). If you plan to do much hiking, remember that barren black basalt absorbs heat, and by midmorning on a sunny day temperatures on the flows can be well over 100°. Volcanic rock is also very sharp, so wear strong shoes or boots and mind small children.

There's a small campground near the visitors center, with running water and flush toilets ($10). This is a pretty bleak place to camp, however. Craters of the Moon National Monument is 85 miles east of Idaho Falls on Hwy 20.

## Idaho National Engineering Laboratory

Talk about bleak in this part of Idaho and you could be talking about the Idaho National Engineering Laboratory (INEL), which, along with Hanford in Washington State, is one of the US Government's primary atomic energy and technology test sites. Located 20 miles east of Arco and 46 miles west of Idaho Falls in a stretch of unrelievedly grim desert, this facility was established in 1949 in the heyday of excitement about the potential peacetime use of a split atom. The first electrical generation using nuclear fission took place here in 1951, and four years later, Arco became the first community in the world to be powered by atomic energy.

---

### The Inventor of Television

Philo Farnsworth was born in Rigby in 1906, and early on he showed a remarkable talent for science and physics. At the ripe age of 19, Farnsworth had formulated the technical theory behind the cathode ray tube, which was able to transmit images received electronically. In 1934, a London-based company hired Farnsworth to design the prototype of the modern TV set. Farnsworth went on to license his product with Philco, RCA and later NBC, helping usher in the age of TV. ∎

---

The world's first nuclear power plant, known as EBR-1, is a National Historic Landmark. This breeder reactor now serves as a visitors center (☎ 526-2331) for the enormous 890-sq-mile nuclear reservation and tells the story of the development of nuclear energy in the Idaho desert. Guided tours of the facility are offered.

Although the nuclear power facilities have long since been mothballed, the reservation is still the site of major nuclear research and development projects, many in conjunction with the Pentagon. Another major project at the laboratory is figuring out what to do about spent nuclear fuel from power plants and atomic submarines. Lockheed, the aircraft manufacturing giant, currently manages the reservation for the Department of Energy and employs 6700 people.

To reach the INEL, take Hwy 20 east of Idaho Falls. The visitors center and EBR-1 reactor are open daily from 8 am to 4 pm from Memorial Day to Labor Day; there is no entrance fee. Guided tours of other INEL facilities can be arranged by calling 526-0050.

## Jefferson County Historical Society Museum

This community museum (☎ 745-8423), 110 N State St in Rigby, 14 miles north of Idaho Falls on Hwy 20, would be another unremarkable collection of local memorabilia if it weren't for the fact that one of the Rigby locals was Philo Farnsworth, the inventor of the TV.

The museum maintains a collection of early TV sets and charts the history of the broadcast image. It's open from 1 to 5 pm on Tuesday and Thursday to Saturday; it's open Wednesday from 1 to 8 pm. Admission is by donation.

## REXBURG & AROUND

Rexburg (population 12,800) is noted for Ricks College, founded in 1888 as one of the first Mormon academies in Idaho, and for the seed-eye potato industry, which is centered hereabouts. Rexburg is also one of the communities that was inundated by the

Teton Flood in 1976, when the Teton Dam burst. The main floors of Rexburg's magnificent Mormon temple were flooded, and the temple is now a museum of the Rexburg area and of the flood.

For more information on the area, contact the Rexburg Chamber of Commerce (☎ 356-5700), 134 E Main St, Suite 1, Rexburg, ID 83440. For information on the Targhee National Forest, head to St Anthony, about seven miles north of Rexburg, where the USFS has an office (☎ 624-3151), 420 N Bridge St. The Rexburg post office (☎ 356-5031) is at 140 S Center St. The CART (☎ 356-9033) bus from Idaho Falls stops at 74 W Main St.

### Teton Flood Museum

It's worth visiting this museum (☎ 356-9101), 51 N Center St, just to see the beautiful twin-steepled Mormon temple that houses it. The temple was built in 1911 from locally quarried basalt, and it was bought by the city as a museum and meeting house after the temple sustained considerable damage in the 1976 Teton Flood.

In June of that year, the Teton Dam, constructed on the Teton River about 20 miles east of Rexburg, was full of spring runoff when the earth-filled dam gave out, releasing 80 billion gallons of water into the river. The flood lashed through Rexburg, Blackfoot and Idaho Falls before being absorbed into the backwaters of American Falls Dam. Six people died in the flood as well as 18,000 head of livestock; 25,000 people were driven from their homes.

The flood is the main focus of the museum, with exhibits recounting the various stages of inundation and destruction. This being Idaho, there's also a display on the local potato industry as well as historic artifacts from early settlers. It's open from 10 am to 5 pm Monday to Saturday. Admission is by donation.

### Folk Dance Festival

Rexburg is a happening place from the last weekend of July to the first week in August when Ricks College hosts the Idaho International Folk Dance Festival. The festival attracts dance troupes from around the world. For more information, call 356-5700.

### Places to Stay & Eat

In St Anthony, *Riverbend RV Park* (☎ 624-3213) is a full-service RV park on Henry's Fork of the Snake River. Head west on Hwy 20 Business to 2660 E Hwy 20, and then travel north to Fun Farm Rd. Sites start at $11.

There are a couple of inexpensive places to stay in Rexburg. The *Calaway Motel* (☎ 356-3217), 361 S 2nd St W, has rooms starting at $22. At *Rex's Motel* (☎ 356-5477), 357 W 4th St S, rooms go for $20 to $35. For a little more comfort, the *Rexburg Days Inn* (☎ 356-9222), 271 S 2nd St W, is right in town and has a pool; rooms are $38 to $70. On the edge of town is the *Best Western Cottontree Inn* (☎ 356-4646), 450 W 4th St S, the area's nicest lodging, with a swimming pool, restaurant and hot tubs; rates range from $44 to $100.

A popular restaurant for inexpensive family dining is *Me & Stan's* (☎ 356-7300), at the corner of W Main St and S 2nd St W. *La Fiesta* (☎ 359-1984), 136 W Main St, is the local Mexican restaurant.

# Northeastern Corner

North of Ashton, Hwy 20 climbs steadily out of the potato-rich plains and into heavy lodgepole pine forests. The walls of a vast volcanic caldera rise above the trees, and in the distance rise the mountains of Yellowstone National Park. Similarly, east of Rexburg the hills get steeper, the streams pick up their pace and the drab ochre of the desert is gradually overcome by green. As you turn a corner near Tetonia, suddenly the sky is filled with three massive peaks – the Grand Tetons have begun.

Idaho shares a sliver of Yellowstone National Park with Wyoming, and Grand Teton National Park is nearly as close. If you're visiting eastern Idaho, you should definitely consider visiting either or both of these popular and beautiful parks. Following each of the park listings below are the towns that most closely serve them.

## YELLOWSTONE NATIONAL PARK

On the eastern edge of Idaho is a small slice of Yellowstone National Park, the nation's oldest, largest and perhaps most popular national park. It's well known for its hot mineral springs and geysers, for its pristine mountain lakes and rivers and for its abundant wildlife. Once you reach the high, 6300-foot plateau drained by the beautiful Henry's Fork River, there's a palpable sense of being at the top of the continent, at the beginning of rivers. The air is clear and rich with the scent of pitch and filled with the sounds of rushing water.

Highway 20 is one of the main access roads, and it enters the park via West Yellowstone, MT. This is the busiest of all the park entrances, handling half of the estimated 2.5 million people who come to visit each year. This road can become dismally choked with RVs and campers, especially during high season, so if you want to experience the kind of reverie described above, you're best advised to turn off the highway and explore a few of the sideroads in this lovely area. Take your time getting to Yellowstone; the crowds will still be waiting for you.

Entrance to Yellowstone costs $10 a vehicle, or $4 for people on foot, bicycle, motorcycle or bus. The entry ticket is good for both Yellowstone and Grand Teton parks, and it lasts for seven days. The park remains open year round; however, roads are open to vehicles generally between late May and early November. In winter, the park is open to cross-country skiers and snowmobile tours. For more information about the park, contact Yellowstone National Park (☎ (307) 344-7381), WY 82190.

## ISLAND PARK & MACKS INN

The entrance roads to major national parks are usually clogged with cheesy motels, dubious restaurants, gimmicky tourist traps and cheap souvenir shops. Highway 20 leading into Yellowstone certainly is no exception. The main venue for these products and services is Island Park, an attenuated string of business one street deep, charmlessly scattered along the highway. Macks Inn is a privately owned 'resort' that fills up an otherwise lovely spot along the Henry's Fork just north of Island Park.

For better or worse, you'll probably end up staying or eating at one of these locations, since even in the off season, these are slow roads, and facilities are few and far between.

### Orientation & Information

It's 49 miles between Rexburg and Island Park on Hwy 20, and another 29 miles to the Yellowstone Park entrance at West Yellowstone, MT. For information about the Island Park area, contact the Island Park Chamber of Commerce (☎ 558-7448), PO Box 83, Island Park, ID 83429. The Island Park Ranger Station (☎ 558-7301) is located between Macks Inn and Island Park and can be contacted at PO Box 20, Island Park, ID 83429.

### Big Springs

The Henry's Fork of the Snake River is one of loveliest rivers in Idaho, hurrying purposefully through the meadows and open forests below Yellowstone Park. The river rises magically out of a cleft in a wooded slope, where a series of springs deliver the Henry's Fork from sources deep within the volcanic mountain.

To visit Big Springs – and you should – turn east just shy of Macks Inn, and follow USFS Rd 59 for five miles to the parking area. A trail leads to the springs, while another nature trail follows the newborn river for a mile. The campground at Big Springs is one of the best places to stay in the area.

### Upper Mesa Falls

After the Henry's Fork leaves the volcanic caldera from which it springs, it begins to drop in a series of steep falls as it rushes to

IDAHO

meet the Snake River. The most impressive of these falls is Upper Mesa Falls, on Hwy 47, which parallels busy Hwy 20 between Ashton and a junction seven miles south of Island Park.

The falls is 114 feet high, and wheelchair-accessible paths lead to overlooks that seem dangerously close to the water's edge. Photographers will be challenged to capture the rainbow caught in the spray of the falls.

Two miles farther downstream is Lower Mesa Falls. Although it is a mighty enough torrent, dropping 65 feet in a series of constricted cascades, the viewing area is high above the falls.

### Harriman State Park

In 1902, after the establishment of Yellowstone National Park, investors in the Union Pacific Railroad bought a 4500-acre ranch on the banks of the Henry's Fork with the intention of developing the land as a hunting and fishing resort. Railroad Ranch, as the holding was known, didn't evolve into a typical dude ranch. It instead operated as a working ranch and getaway for the wealthy shareholders of Union Pacific, including Solomon Guggenheim, Charles Jones and Edward Harriman. Elaborate outbuildings were built, including a mammoth horse barn, a number of elegant cabins and bunkhouses for the ranch hands.

The ranch was deeded to the state of Idaho as Harriman State Park (☎ 558-7368) in 1961 by the children of Edward Harriman; this gift actually spurred the establishment of the state park division. The old ranch buildings are now open for viewing, and 16,000 acres of land around the ranch have been designated as the Harriman Wildlife Refuge. The park is also popular with anglers, who itch to tangle with the legendary Henry's Fork rainbow trout.

### Outfitters

L&D Fly Fishing at the Three Rivers Ranch (☎ 652-3750), Box 856, Warm River, Ashton, ID 83420, offers fishing, trail rides, backpacking and float trips

down the Henry's Fork, the South Fork of the Snake and the Teton Rivers. For a fishing trip, contact Henry's Fork Anglers (558-7525) in Island Park.

### Places to Stay & Eat

There are a number of commercial campgrounds along this stretch of highway, but some of the USFS campgrounds are really lovely and are worth the short drive. *Big Springs* is at the beginnings of the Henry's Fork River, five miles east of Macks Inn. *Box Canyon Campground* is just south of Island Park. *Upper Coffee Pot* is just south of Macks Inn. Each of these campgrounds has running water but pit toilets; camping fees are $8. For more information, contact the ranger station in Island Park.

*Henry's Fork Landing Cafe & Motel* (☎ 558-9201), in Island Park, offers boat rentals and float trips as well as a cafe and motel rooms. One of the nicer places to stay in Island Park is *Pond's Lodge* (☎ 258-7221), with rooms in an attractive log lodge or in free-standing cabins; lodgings range from $40 to $160.

*Macks Inn Resort* (☎ 558-7272), at Macks Inn, is a one-stop lodging, dining and recreational headquarters. In addition to RV campsites ($15), they have a motel and lodge with rooms ranging from $27 to $105. Other facilities include a grocery store, laundry, showers and guided raft trips.

There aren't any hidden secrets to dining around Island Park. The only notable eating experience is *The Chalet* (558-9953), which has great hashbrowns, homemade pies and ceaseless banter between the three generations of family that run the place.

### GRAND TETON NATIONAL PARK

The usual postcard shot of the Grand Tetons is taken from the Wyoming side of the range, but the mountains are equally beautiful from the 'backside' in Idaho. And this, the stunning scenery, is the primary attraction of Grand Teton National Park, which is just across the Wyoming border. Six glacier-carved crags top 12,000 feet, and the eastern face of the peaks drops into a fault-block basin – the famous Jackson Hole – filled with mountain lakes and streams (including the nascent Snake River). All these gorgeous mountains also make for great skiing and climbing.

Highway 22 from Victor is plowed year round over Teton Pass to Jackson. Other roads around the park are also kept clear. Backcountry hiking trails can be snowed under as late as July, so plan your trip accordingly. Entry to the park is $10 per vehicle, or $4 per person on foot, bicycle or motorcycle. The same ticket gets you into Yellowstone National Park, and it's good for a week. For information on the park, contact Grand Teton National Park at (307) 733-2880.

Several of the small Idaho ranching towns just across the border from Jackson Hole and Grand Teton National Park are undergoing great changes as the glitzy, boutique-inspired New West culture takes hold. While celebrity ranches haven't taken over the valleys near Tetonia, Driggs and Victor quite yet, the shift is clear: espresso shops, art galleries and designer jeans are as easy to find as stock whips and veterinary supplies.

## DRIGGS

Even five years ago, Driggs (population 2900) was a sleepy cow town in a fertile mountain valley. It's now a kind of boomtown of the New West, boasting a dozen new restaurants, art galleries and several trendy recreation-oriented businesses. Condos are rising in pastures like mushrooms, and a mall is going in. Flashy mountain bikes share the streets with beat-up pick-up trucks.

You don't need to wonder why, if you look east. The Grand Tetons are *right there*, looming over the town. There's a limited amount of real estate with these views and with this access, and the character of the town is changing fast.

### Orientation & Information

Highway 33 runs from Rexburg 39 miles

straight toward Wyoming before turning south and running parallel to the border. Tetonia is eight miles north of Driggs, and Victor is nine miles south, both on Hwy 33. The only access to the upscale ski resort at Grand Targhee, WY, is through Driggs; the resort is 12 miles east on a secondary road. From Victor, Jackson, WY, is 23 miles east.

For information on the area, contact Teton Valley Chamber of Commerce (☎ 354-2500), 50 N Main St, Driggs, ID 83422. The Teton Basin Ranger District office (☎ 354-2431) is in Driggs at 525 S Main St.

Teton Valley Hospital (☎ 354-2383) is at 283 N 1st St E. Laundry & Lunch (☎ 354-2718) offers more than just clean clothes at 190 N Main St.

### Grand Targhee Ski Area

Grand Traghee Ski Area (☎ (800) 827-4433) has become known and revered for the incredible depth of its powder snow (over 500 inches of snow dumps here each winter!), its high mountain location (the lifts take skiers to elevations over 10,000 feet) and the casual but professional service and amenities. There are two ski areas at Grand Targhee. At the top of three lifts are 1500 acres of runs, with a total vertical drop of 2200 feet in over three miles. Grand Targhee has also been a leader in the development of snow-cat skiing, wherein large snow machines haul skiers to the top of otherwise inaccessible and ungroomed slopes for a real wilderness ski experience. Ski tickets at the traditional ski area are $35 for adults, while snow-catting will cost upwards of $160 a day. Snowboards are welcome on all slopes.

Grand Targhee offers a full range of rentals and instruction, as well as accommodations in three different housing units. The ski area also operates a nordic ski center. To reach Grand Targhee from Driggs, drive east toward Alta, WY, on USFS Rd 009. The ski area is 12 miles from Driggs, eight miles across the Wyoming border.

## Activities

There is no lack of recreation in the Tetons, and the first place you should head is Yostmark Mountain Equipment (☎ 354-2828), 12 E Little Ave. This well-stocked outfitter offers kayaks, mountain bikes, skis and camping gear for rent as well as a full-line of sports equipment, clothing and gear for sale. The staff is also very friendly and able to give advice on hikes, and so on.

**Fishing** is great in the Teton River, which drains this beautiful valley. Pick up a license and fishing tips from Basin Travel Stop (☎ 354-2787), 111 N Main St.

The Grand Tetons are reckoned to be one of the premier **rock-climbing** destinations in the USA. For rock-climbing gear and information, go to Mountaineering Outfitters (☎ 354-2222), 62 N Main St.

## Places to Stay

**Camping** *Larsen's Mobile Home Park* (☎ 345-2205), 73 S Main St, has RV hookups for $10. The *Teton Valley Campground* (☎ 787-2647) is in Victor one mile south of town on Hwy 31. Facilities include a swimming pool, laundry and grocery store. Standard sites are $18; hook-ups are $23.

Ten miles east of Driggs, *Teton Canyon Campground* is a USFS campground that's really in Wyoming, on the way to Grand Targhee. Take USFS Rd 009 east, toward Alta, to the end, veering right at the fork onto USFS Rd 025. *Pine Creek Campground* is another USFS campground five miles southwest of Victor on Hwy 31. Head six miles south of Victor on Hwy 33 to *Trail Creek Campground*. Sites at these campgrounds are each $7 a night; call the USFS office in Driggs for more information.

**B&Bs** *Teton Creek B&B* (☎ 354-2584), 41 S Baseline Rd, offers four rooms with mountain views for $45 to $65.

**Hotels** The following motels are in Driggs. The *Pines Motel & Guest Haus* (☎ 354-2774), 105 S Main St, has rooms starting at $30. The *Super 8* (☎ 354-8888), 133 S Hwy 33, has single/double rooms at $40/45. *Intermountain Lodge* (☎ 354-

8153), 34 Ski Hill Rd, one mile east of Driggs, offers lodging in two-bed log cabins with kitchens and full baths for $59. *Best Western Teton West* (☎ 354-2962), 476 N Main St, has an indoor pool and rooms from $50 to $80.

Up in Tetonia, the *Teton Mountain View Inn* (☎ 456-2741, (800) 625-2232) is the place to stay, with rooms for $40 to $80. In Victor, the *Timberline Motel* (☎ 787-2772), at the junction of Hwys 31 and 33, is a nice log motel with rooms from $30 to $50.

## Places to Eat

*Table Mountain Natural Foods & Cafe* (☎ 354-8663), 285 N Main St, serves espresso and healthy food throughout the day. The *Breakfast Shoppe* (☎ 354-8294), 65 N Main St, is also open for lunch. *Teton Bakery & Restaurant* (☎ 354-2732), 68 N Main St, is a great bakery with luscious pastries, french bread and submarine sandwiches.

*O'Rourke's Fine Food & Beer* (☎ 354-8115), 42 E Little Ave, is a bar and cafe that mostly serves sandwiches in the $5 range. Across the street at *Mike's Eats* (☎ 354-2797), 10 N Main St, Mike serves breakfast, pizza and barbecue burgers in a handsome old storefront.

For homestyle food in Tetonia, go to *Trails End Cafe* (☎ 456-2202), 110 N Main St. Down in Victory, the *Knotty Pine Supper Club* (☎ 787-2866), 58 S Main St, is a great place for a steak; there's live music on the weekends.

## Getting There & Away

The CART bus (☎ 522-2278) from Idaho Falls stops at 47 S Main St in Driggs.

## SWAN VALLEY

North of Idaho Falls, the Snake River abruptly turns east and then south to flow through a steep-sided valley in the Caribou Mountains. Vegetation is sketchy at first, and then trees become denser, until near the Wyoming border the forests of the Rocky Mountains take hold.

As you travel through southern Idaho, you become accustomed to thinking of the

Snake as a desert river, nearly sucked dry by the irrigation needs of Idaho agribusiness. But here, in what is called the Swan Valley, the Snake is a mountain river, full of vigor, glinting rapids and trout. Of course, this is Idaho, so the river has to be dammed at least once, and it is, by Palisades Dam.

Fishing is the main recreation in these parts, and there's plenty of river and lake access along Hwy 26, which runs the length of the valley. Most of the amenities here are designed with anglers in mind. Don't be surprised if your cafe doubles as a bait shop.

### Orientation & Information
The little community of Swan Valley is nominally the center of this lovely rural valley, but don't expect much more than country stores and basic lodgings in the area. From Swan Valley, it's 50 miles east to Jackson, WY. For more information about the region, contact the Swan Valley Chamber of Commerce (☎ 483-3972), PO Box 19, Swan Valley, ID 83449.

### Fishing
The Snake River below Palisades Dam is a noted fly fishing stream for big cutthroat and brown trout, and a number of outfitters offer guided fly fishing trips on the river. Mountain Stream Outfitters (☎ 483-3332), 3378 Hwy 26, leads fishing trips; fishing trips (and raft trips) are also offered out of South Fork Lodge (see below).

### Places to Stay & Eat
There are a number of USFS campgrounds along the river, including *Big Elk Creek* and *Palisades*, both east of Irwin on Hwy 26. The *South Fork Lodge* (☎ 483-2112), four miles west of Swan Valley on Hwy 26, has both campsites ($13) and lodge rooms (from $75 to $110). The restaurant at the lodge is the best place to eat in the valley. The *Sandy Mite Fly Shop & Cafe* (483-2609), in Swan Valley, solves two of your problems at once.

# Southeastern Idaho

This remote corner of Idaho was one of the busiest during frontier times: Hudson's Bay Company trappers explored the river valleys looking for furs, Oregon Trail pioneers traversed the mountain passes to reach the Snake River, and Mormon settlers moved north from Utah to establish farms and communities.

Hardly a hotbed of activity now, southeastern Idaho's prime attraction is the appealing patchwork of farms and ranches along the river valleys and the rugged and arid mountains that shoulder up the horizon in this underpopulated province. For a glimpse of rural western America, a drive through southeastern Idaho is as good as it gets. Idaho has designated two routes through the area as scenic and historic byways; each is marked on the state highway map and can be linked by visiting the following sites. There is no public transport through this area.

### SODA SPRINGS & AROUND
Soda Springs (population 4050) was a stop along the old Oregon Trail, and pioneers were apparently amused by the geysers and effervescent spring water found in the area. Although apocryphal stories relate that travelers added sugar to the water to make frontier soda pop, a small taste of the spring water will convince otherwise.

A number of open pit mines operate in the area, as evinced by the enormous phosphorus processing plant north of town. Operated by Monsanto, the plant has poured slag into the same area since 1953; currently slag is dumped at a rate of five times an hour, 24 hours a day. The contorted pile looks a lot like a lava flow, especially when the slag is still molten. On the plant's east side there's been an attempt to reclaim the slaglands by planting grass.

### Information
The Soda Springs Chamber of Commerce (☎ 547-4470) can be reached at PO Box

IDAHO

697, Soda Springs, ID 83276. The Soda Springs Ranger District office (☎ 547-4356), 421 W 2nd St S, serves the Caribou National Forest. The post office (☎ 547-3794) is at 220 S Main St.

### Geyser Park
In 1937, the city was drilling a well, hoping to hit a hot springs for the local swimming pool, when it hit a pocket of water infused with carbon dioxide. The well created a geyser that sprayed water 150 feet into the air. However, as the newly made geyser was only a block off Main Street, the mineral water spray soon began to discolor the city's buildings. The situation was resolved by creating a park and capping off the geyser with a timer. Currently, the geyser is scheduled to erupt on the half hour. The park is one block west of downtown Soda Springs; you can't miss it.

### Hooper Springs
Many of the soda springs for which the area is named are currently inundated by Alexander Reservoir, west of town. An example of what attracted the Oregon Trail emigrants to the area can still be seen north of town at Hooper Springs Park, where a bubbling soda water springs churns to the surface. Go ahead and taste the water – it's available both from the pool or from a fountain – but don't expect it to taste like the bottled water you're accustomed to.

The park is also a pleasant place for a picnic, and there are views onto the phosphorus slag heap just across the way. Hooper Springs is two miles north of Soda Springs on Hwy 34.

### Formation Springs & Cave
Ancient cold springs feed these wetlands and crystal clear pools at the base of the Aspen Mountains, which are protected as a Nature Conservancy preserve. The water that bubbles to the surface here is believed to have been in the earth for 13,000 years! The water contains high concentrations of travertine, which have shaped and molded some peculiar geologic formations, the star

of which is the thousand-foot-long Formation Cave. The ponds are also popular nesting areas for waterfowl. To visit Formation Springs, follow Hwy 34 four miles north to Trail Canyon Rd and turn east for 1.5 miles.

### Places to Stay & Eat
*Dike Lake Campground* (☎ 236-6880) is a BLM campground 11 miles north on Hwy 34, on the southeast end of Blackfoot Reservoir. *Eight Mile Campground* is a USFS campground 13 miles south of town on USFS Rd 425. Pick up Eightmile Rd either by traveling south on 3rd St E or by heading a few miles east on Hwy 30. Turn onto USFS Rd 425 (Eightmile Canyon Rd). Although there are no camping fees, both campgrounds have drinking water.

Lodging and food are simple but pleasant in Soda Springs. All the following are located on Hwy 30. The *Caribou Lodge & Motel* (☎ 547-3377), 110 W 2nd St S, has rooms from $26 to $44. At the *Lakeview Motel* (☎ 547-4351), 341 W 2nd St S, rooms go for $22 to $40. *J-R Inn* (☎ 547-3366), 179 W 2nd St S, is probably the nicest place to stay in Soda Springs with rooms between $28 to $42. The *Trail Motel & Restaurant* (☎ 547-3909), 213 E 2nd St S, with rooms at $20 to $45, also has a few RV spaces at $9.

For good family dining go to *Ender's Cafe* (☎ 547-4980) at 76 S Main St.

### MONTPELIER
Montpelier (population 6000) is right on the path of the old Oregon Trail (Hwy 30 follows the route between Montpelier and Soda Springs), though the town was established in 1864 by Mormon pioneer farmers. By far the most exciting event in the town's history occurred in 1896, when Butch Cassidy and his gang robbed the bank.

South of Montpelier is Bear Lake, a dwindling, shallow and almost land-locked lake divided by the Idaho/Utah state line. Bear River, which once fed Bear Lake, now totally bypasses the lake as it tumbles down out of Wyoming to head north toward Soda

## Battle of Bear River

North of Preston occurred one of the bloodiest recorded battles in Idaho history. Known as the Battle of Bear River, the 1863 engagement pitted US Army troops under the command of Colonel Patrick Connor against a village of Shoshone Indians. On a freezing day in January, Connor lead 300 men against an encampment of about 500 Indians. The Shoshone miscalculated the resolve and ferocity of the army battalions and allowed the troops to breach the swollen Bear River. The infantry and the cavalry units moved in on the village, torching all the tepees and indiscriminately killing men, women and children. Contemporary reports claim that up to 350 to 400 Shoshone died in the village; only 22 US soldiers died. ■

Springs. The lake is kept from becoming saline by a piece of ingenuity on the part of local farmers. A canal links Bear River to the lake, where the water is stored until downriver farms need the water. Another canal then feeds the water back into the river.

### Orientation & Information

Montpelier is in the Bear Lake valley, a flat basin between barren mountain ranges. East from Montpelier, Hwy 30 continues to follow the Oregon Trail into Wyoming. Highway 89 continues south to Bear Lake via Paris, an early Mormon settlement boasting a historic Mormon temple.

For information on the area, contact the Bear Lake Convention & Visitors Bureau (☎ 945-2072, (800) 448-2327) at PO Box 26, Fish Haven, ID 83287. The national forest ranger station (☎ 847-0375) is at 432 Clay St.

### Bear Lake State Park

Bear Lake is a startlingly green, fault-block lake 20 miles south of Montpelier. The lake and state park (☎ 945-2790) are both immensely popular with locals, though they are little known to the outside world. There are two sections to the state park, the North and East Beach units, both affording boat ramps for motor boats and broad expanses of white sandy beaches. Although camping is allowed, there are no established campgrounds.

On the marshy north end of Bear Lake is the **Bear Lake National Wildlife Refuge,**

primarily a waterfowl preserve. The refuge is of interest to bird watchers, as it contains a nesting colony of white-faced ibis; whooping cranes have also been known to visit.

### Minnetonka Cave

This limestone cave 12 miles west of St Charles winds 1800 feet into the mountainside, past a profusion of fanciful shapes and colorful formations. One-hour tours of the cave are offered by the USFS between June 15 and Labor Day. For more information, call the Montpelier ranger station (☎ 847-0375).

### Places to Stay & Eat

*Montpelier KOA* (☎ 847-0863), two miles east on Hwy 89, offers a swimming pool and sites from $13 to $17. Near Minnetonka Cave is *St Charles Canyon*, a USFS campground with drinking water ($8).

For cheap, you can't beat the *Michelle Motel* (☎ 847-1772), 401 Boise St, with single/doubles at $20/23. Equally inexpensive is the *Budget Motel* (☎ 847-1273), 240 N 4th St, with rooms between $20 and $40. The nicest place to stay is *Best Western Crest Motel* (☎ 847-1782), 243 N 4th St, with rooms between $40 and $75.

Unfussy cooking is the norm in Montpelier. *7M Country Cafe* (☎ 847-0208), 24312 Hwy 89, offers basic homecooking. The *Ranch Hand Cafe* (☎ 847-1180), at 23200 Hwy 30, is a truck stop with good family dining; the towering reader board above the restaurant announces the day's

IDAHO

specials and the chef's most recent cream-pie extravaganza.

## PRESTON

Preston (population 3850) is part of the earliest settled portion of Idaho. Mormon farmers pushed up the Cache Valley from Logan, UT in 1860 and founded Franklin, seven miles south of Preston.

Preston is in the Bear River Valley just eight miles north of the Idaho/Utah border. For tourist information, contact the Preston Chamber of Commerce (☎ 852-2703), 32 West Oneida St, Preston, ID 83263.

The post office (☎ 852-0263) is at 55 E Oneida St.

### Places to Stay & Eat

Preston's sole accommodation is the pleasant *Plaza Motel* (☎ 852-2020), 427 S Hwy 91, with rooms between $31 and $42.

*Shipley's Country Kitchen* (☎ 852-0332), 101 N State St, is the place to go for a tasty breakfast or lunch. For steaks and the usual Western supperclub fare, the *Main Street Grill* (☎ 852-1447), 96 S State St, is notably enjoyable and worth a splurge. Full dinners run between $12 to $15.

# Central Idaho

Central Idaho is the enormous mountainous midsection of Idaho, a contorted piece of real estate cleaved by the Clearwater, Salmon and Payette rivers. The turbulent Snake River cuts just to the west, incising a mile-deep gorge along the border between Oregon and Idaho. This remains the largest section of wilderness in the continental USA, with much of the land accessible only by hiking, floating, horseback riding or driving for scores of miles along marginally passable roads. This isn't a countryside that easily yields up its wonders to the casual visitor.

To see or experience much of this vast and wild country requires a bit of planning and initiative. Luckily, there are innumerable outfitters and recreational guide services out there who will ease your entry into the wilderness. There's hardly a community in central Idaho that doesn't offer at least one guide service, and most guides provide a full array of recreational options. In all probability, the same outfitter can take you rafting, hunting, fishing, mountain biking, cross-country skiing, horseback riding – if you can do it outdoors, you'll find someone willing to sell you the service. In the following listings, guide services are described mostly with an eye to white-water rafting and float trips (which, next to hunting, is the major outdoor sport); however, if your interests are different or multiple, most outfitters will be glad to accommodate you.

## HISTORY

Petroglyphs along the canyon walls of the mighty rivers that drain central Idaho indicate a long human habitation of the area; however, the rough and unyielding terrain, combined with the harsh climate, didn't make this a very inviting homeland for the historic tribes of Native Americans. Most natives were content to pass through the

canyons on their way to and from more hospitable regions.

The Nez Perce, the mightiest of the Plateau tribes of the inland Northwest, made their homes on the grasslands and meadows on the western slopes of the Rockies. When Lewis and Clark passed through the Clearwater and Snake River valleys in 1805-6, the Nez Perce welcomed them and traded for horses and food. The respect was mutual: Lewis and Clark noted that the Nez Perce were the most honorable and civilized of all the Native American tribes that the corps had encountered.

Central Idaho's deeply eroded river valleys cut through the mineral-rich Idaho Batholith, famous for its silver and copper deposits, which made this a busy area during the late-19th-century heyday of gold and mineral mining. Ghost towns and mining adits are about all that are left from the mining past. The homesteading boom at the beginning of the century brought hopeful settlers to the valley floors, and a few big ranches remain (often with 'dudes' rather than cattle as the main income generator). In the last decade, a recreation and vacation-home boom has brought major changes to many small Idaho towns. Places like Riggins or Salmon, once known as lumber or agricultural centers, are now filled with mountain bike and raft shops, and a new generation of ranchers scrambles to entice outsiders to fish, float or hunt on their property – a far cry from the isolationist ethic of yesteryear.

## ORIENTATION & INFORMATION

Most of central Idaho is served by a only few north-south roads. The main arterial through this part of the state is Hwy 95, and between Boise and McCall, Hwy 55. Hundreds of miles to the east, Hwy 93 begins in Missoula, MT and goes south through

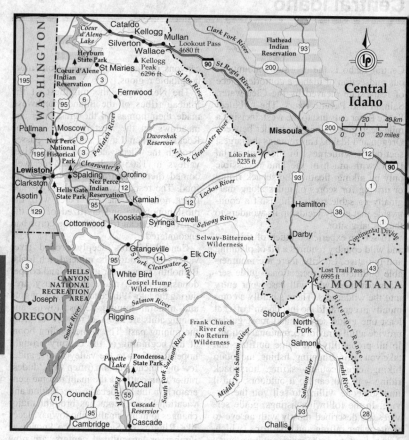

Idaho, following the Upper Salmon River until Challis and continuing to Twin Falls. Trying to cut east-west through this part of Idaho is a very long and time-consuming process. Only Hwy 12, along the region's northern edge, makes its slow way across the state.

As the few roads throughout the patchwork of wilderness areas that comprises central Idaho are heavily traveled and very meandering and irregular, allow ample time to get where you're headed; you'll need it.

## GETTING THERE & AWAY
### Air
Lewiston is the only town in the region with regularly scheduled air service, though a number of charter services provide flights between destinations of your choice. Pioneer Air Service (☎ 634-5445, 634-7127), based out of McCall, will pick you up or deliver you to Boise or Lewiston for about $200 per flight. The central Idaho backcountry is filled with remote airstrips, and a number of pilots will fly you and your gear into the wilds and let you hike,

bike or float back out. For information on backcountry flights, ask at local chambers of commerce, or call Mountain Bird Inc (☎ (800) 448-3413) in Salmon or Challis for information.

## Bus

Central Idaho is served by Northwestern Trailways (☎ (800) 366-3830). Two buses a day link Spokane to Moscow and Lewiston; one bus a day continues south to Grangeville, Riggins, McCall and Boise.

Floaters may want to avail themselves of River Rate Express (☎ 774-2265, 733-8003), a bus shuttle service that drops off and picks up white-water rafters in central Idaho.

## LEWISTON & CLARKSTON

The twin cities of Lewiston, ID (population 30,000), and Clarkston, WA (population 7000), sprawl across the flood plains where the mighty Snake and Clearwater rivers meet. These bustling towns are centers of a vast agricultural area whose products include peas, lentils, wheat and livestock. Lewiston is often referred to as the 'Inland Port', as the Columbia and Snake river dam and lock system have created hundreds of miles of slackwater reservoirs that allow barges to travel all the way from Lewiston to Portland, OR. The enormous Potlatch Lumber Mill on the Clearwater River is one of the largest timber-product facilities in the state; the factory's sour, sulfurous odor is immediately noted by visitors, but to locals, it smells like jobs.

These hardworking towns are overlooked by bare, massive canyon walls, seared to a brown-gold by midsummer. This desert-like aridity belies the great confluence of waters here, and it's this rendezvous of rivers that has propelled Lewiston and Clarkston to become the recreational center for all of north-central Idaho. Just upriver on the Snake River is the white water and wilderness of Hells Canyon, reached by a number of Lewiston-based jet-boat tours. Up the Clearwater River is storied fly fishing as well as hiking and biking in vast national forests. Down-river on the Snake River, just across the Washington border, the quiet lake produced by Lower Granite Dam is a favorite for boating, watersports and fishing, especially for massive ancient sturgeon.

These friendly river cities are relatively new to the pretensions and subtleties of tourism, and amenities here are basic and inexpensive. As a center for outdoor recreation and exploration, however, Lewiston and Clarkston are pleasant and authentically Idaho.

## History

The towns' namesakes, Lewis and Clark, passed through here on both legs of their early 1800s expedition, though there was not settlement in the area until 1860, at the beginning of the Idaho gold rush. The confluence of the Snake and Clearwater rivers was the head of steamboat navigation from Portland, and the area boomed as a transport and trade center. At the time, the land at the confluence was part of the Nez Perce Reservation, and the Indian Agent would not allow permanent settlement; thus, for two years Lewiston was a tent settlement with a population of 2000.

In 1863, Lewiston – the first incorporated town in Idaho – was named territorial capital; however, partisans of Boise stole the state seal in 1865 and decamped to the south, leaving Lewiston to file suit to regain the capital, to no avail.

Lewiston and Clarkston continued to grow as trade and transport hubs, especially as federal irrigation projects brought orchards to flower along the protected and temperate canyon bottoms. However, the biggest advance for the area came in 1955, when the Army Corps of Engineers began to build the four Snake River dams that, in 1975, brought slackwater to the port of Lewiston. Lewiston is the USA's most inland port: vessels drawing less then 14 feet and weighing less than 12,000 tons can journey all the way from the mouth of the Columbia River to the grain-loading docks at Lewiston, 470 miles from the Pacific Ocean.

IDAHO

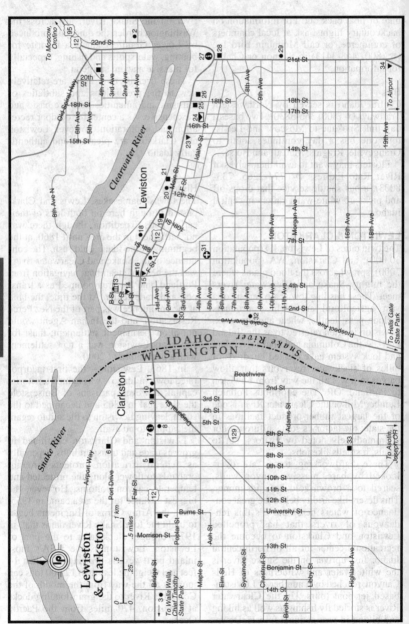

| PLACES TO STAY | |
|---|---|
| 1 | Hillary Motel |
| 4 | Best Western Rivertree Inn |
| 5 | Hacienda Lodge |
| 6 | Quality Inn |
| 9 | Motel 6 |
| 19 | Travel Motor Inn |
| 21 | Tapadera Inn |
| 25 | Pony Soldier Motor Inn |
| 26 | Sacajawea Motor Inn |
| 28 | Ramada Inn |
| 33 | Highland House |

| PLACES TO EAT | |
|---|---|
| 10 | Tomato Bros |
| 14 | Jonathan's Restaurant |
| 15 | Cabo San Lucas |
| 23 | Country Cookery |
| 34 | Zany's |

| OTHER | |
|---|---|
| 2 | Cee-Mee-Nee-Kum |
| 3 | Beamer's Hells Canyon Tours |
| 7 | Clarkston Chamber of Commerce |
| 8 | Darling Fuel & Laundromat |
| 11 | Jay's Gone Fishin' |
| 12 | Lewis & Clark Interpretive Center |
| 13 | Luna House Museum |
| 16 | Copa Cabeana |
| 17 | Kling's Stationers |
| 18 | Pedals-N-Spokes |
| 20 | Scenic River Charters |
| 22 | Clearwater Landing |
| 24 | Lewiston Post Office |
| 27 | Lewiston Chamber of Commerce |
| 29 | Follet's Mountain Sports |
| 30 | Snake River Adventures |
| 31 | St Joseph Regional Medical Center |
| 32 | Cougar Country Lodge |

## Orientation

Lewiston and Clarkston face each other across the Snake River; the Clearwater River meets the Snake at a right angle immediately north of Lewiston, and their combined flows head due west. The effect is that of a huge T with towns tucked under its arms.

Two bridges link Clarkston and Lewiston, with the Hwy 12 bridge linking the two towns' business districts. A third bridge crosses the Clearwater just east of downtown Lewiston and joins with Hwy 95. North on Hwy 95, the road climbs 2000 feet up a very long and steep canyon wall called Lewiston Hill.

South of Clarkston in Washington, past the enormous outcropping of basalt called Swallows Crest, is the small community of Asotin, along the banks of the Snake.

The old downtown of Clarkston is located along 5th and 6th Sts, although many businesses have relocated out to Bridge St (Hwy 12). Similarly, in Lewiston the old downtown is located along Main St, below an imposing bluff of rock. While downtown is gentrifying just as fast as the times allow, many businesses are now located out along 21st St, which leads to suburban communities. In Lewiston, pay attention to street addresses; numbered streets run north-south, numbered avenues run east-west.

## Information

**Tourist Offices** The Lewiston Chamber of Commerce (☎ 743-3531) is located at 2207 E Main St, Lewiston, ID 833501. The Clarkston Chamber of Commerce (☎ (509) 758-7712, (800) 933-2128) is at 502 Bridge St, Clarkston, WA 99403. Don't forget that Clarkston phone numbers take Washington's 509 area code; Lewiston's area code remains 208.

The USFS headquarters for the Hells Canyon National Recreation Area (☎ (509) 758-0616) is at 2535 Riverside Drive in Clarkston. For river permit reservations and information call (509) 758-1957. There's also an Idaho Department of Fish & Game office (☎ 743-6502) at 1540 Warner Ave.

**Post** Lewiston's post office (☎ 743-3551) is at 1613 Idaho St; in Clarkston, drop mail off at 949 6th St.

**Bookstores** Kling's Stationers (☎ 743-8501), 704 Main St, offers a selection of local tour guides and a large choice of regional maps.

**Media** The daily paper is the *Lewiston Morning Tribune*.

**Laundry** Have it all at Darling Fuel & Laundromat (☎ (509) 758-6927), 5th and Bridge Sts, Clarkston, which offers not only complete laundry service, but a car wash, convenience store, bottled gas and RV disposal facilities.

**Medical Services** St Joseph Regional Medical Center (☎ 799-5700) is at 415 6th St.

### Lewiston Levee Parkway

If you're from another part of the world, it's easy to underestimate the attraction of greenways and parks in arid areas like Idaho. Lewiston's Levee Parkway runs along the Clearwater and Snake rivers for a total of 21 miles (though the most heavily used portion is the five miles from the Clearwater Bridge down to Hells Gate State Park) and is a source of great pride and enjoyment to residents. On a nice day, the riverside trail is thronged with walkers, bikers, bird watchers and anglers, for whom access to the river and to greenery is a comfort and luxury.

Two interpretive displays are found along the parkway. **Clearwater Landing** is just behind the Port of Lewiston, and its displays explain the history of navigation on the Snake River system. At the point of confluence of the Clearwater and the Snake is the **Lewis & Clark Interpretive Center**, a visitors center that explains the early exploration of the valley, focusing on the Corps of Discovery expedition and the native groups who lived in the valley.

In front of the interpretive center is the **Tsceminicum Sculpture** (pronounced *si-min'-i-kum*), which means 'meeting of the waters' in Nez Perce. While the main figure in the sculpture is a native Earth Mother from whose hands the rivers flow, no less than 79 animals, representing characters in Indian legends, grace both sides of a wall that is in fact an extension of the central Earth Mother figure's wild mane. Try to find the mosquito without looking at the interpretive brochure. To reach the Lewis & Clark center, follow D St or Levee

Bypass toward the rivers' confluence, and watch for signs for the parking area.

### Luna House Museum

The Luna House Museum (☎ 743-2535), at 3rd and C Sts, is operated by the Nez Perce County Historical Society and is named after the Luna House Hotel, which used to occupy the site. Displays include pioneer and Nez Perce Indian artifacts. It's open from 9 am to 5 pm, Tuesday to Saturday; admission is free.

### Asotin County Museum

Across the Snake River in Washington, this museum (☎ (509) 243-4659) is south of Clarkston in the town of Asotin, at 3rd and Filmore Sts. The main museum building is a 1922, concrete-block building that served as a funeral home for 50 years. Outside, the grounds are littered with the Asotin County Historical Society's healthy accumulation of historic buildings, including a one-room school, a log cabin, a pioneer home and a blacksmith shop. Old carriages and one of the largest known collections of branding irons are housed in the old pole barn. It's open from 1 to 5 pm, Tuesday to Saturday; admission is free.

### Hells Gate State Park

This popular state park (☎ 799-5015), four miles south of downtown Lewiston on Snake River Ave, is the antidote to the often scorching hot days at the bottom of the Snake River canyon. The 960-acre park offers a swimming beach, full-service marina, campground, picnic area and ample room to relax along the Snake River. Hells Gate offers a series of short hiking trails, and it's the southern access point for the Levee Parkway trail. **Horseback riding** is another popular pastime; five miles of bridal paths wind through the park and up to an overlook. During the summer, horses are available for rent from the corral between the marina and the campgrounds; call Hells Gates Stables (☎ 743-3142) for information.

The **Williams Memorial Visitors**

**Center**, at the center of the park, is worth a visit. Colorful and well-designed displays explain the geology and history of the Snake River system and touch on the plant and wildlife of central Idaho. There's a staff ranger on duty to answer questions.

The marina at the park is the departure point for most jet boat tours up the Snake River; many charter fishing trips leave from here as well. The park has a day-use fee of $2 per vehicle.

### Old Spiral Highway

The canyon wall to the north of Lewiston was a longtime impediment to transport and commerce with the grain-rich Palouse Hills. Finally, in 1914, with improved engineering and technology, a road was devised that snaked up Lewiston Hill, slowly climbing 2000 feet in 9.5 miles – with 64 switchbacks – to reach the plateau. Nowadays, a stretch of freeway zips up the hill, but those looking for great views across the Snake and Clearwater rivers should take the old highway, now known as the Old Spiral Highway. Catch the Old Spiral Highway north of Lewiston, at the second intersection past the bridge off Hwy 12/95.

### Buffalo Eddy Pictographs

Twelve miles south of Asotin, WA, on Snake River Rd, is a jumble of rocks that constricts the Snake River into a fast-moving channel. On the rocks are number of well-preserved petroglyphs of warriors brandishing weapons; it's easy to imagine that these images once warned of a prehistoric territorial boundary.

There's no sign for the petroglyphs, but they're easy to find. From Asotin, continue on 1st St until it becomes graveled Snake River Rd. The road winds through an increasingly sheer canyon until it passes through a narrow crevice between two rock faces. Pull off the road and explore the rocks near the river for the petroglyphs.

If you want to have more of a look at the Hells Canyon country, but don't fancy a jet-boat excursion, continue on Snake River Rd, which follows the river to the mouth of the Grande Ronde River. The

canyon walls get higher and higher, and increasingly striated by basalt lava flows; the landscape is stark and otherworldly. The road eventually joins Hwy 3 in Oregon, a fairly bumpy 31 miles from Buffalo Eddy.

### Chief Timothy State Park

Located eight miles west of Clarkston on Hwy 12 in Washington, this state park and interpretive center (☎ (509) 758-9580) serves a recreational and an educational function. The park is mostly located on a landscaped island in Lower Granite Lake on the Snake River, with over 11,000 feet of freshwater shoreline to draw swimmers, picnickers and sunbathers to the swimming beaches. Campers are invited to use the boat ramps and moorage docks, making this a popular place for water-skiing weekends.

The island was once a hill that overlooked a short-lived pioneer community called Silcott, and before that, the valley here was the site of the first farm of Nez Perce Chief Timothy, who at the urging of US Government Indian Agents decided to pursue an agrarian life. The completion of the Lower Granite Dam transformed this location into an island in 1975.

The **Alpowai Interpretive Center**, just before the short bridge to the island, is located on the site of a Nez Perce Indian village from the turn of the 19th century. The center tells the story of the geologic and human history of the area and includes an audiovisual program. It's open from 1 to 5 pm Wednesday through Sunday, Memorial Day weekend to Labor Day, other times by appointment; admission is free.

### Fishing

Find live bait, tackle and fishing licenses for both Washington and Idaho at Jay's Gone Fishin' (☎ (509) 758-8070), 118 Bridge St in Clarkston. Remember that most jet-boat companies do a side business in fishing excursions. Two jet-boat outfitters that focus more on fishing and less on blasting through the canyon at full speed are Scenic River Charters (☎ 746-6808, 746-6443), 1209 Main St in Lewiston, and

Mainstream Outdoor Adventures (☎ 983-2261, 743-0512, (800) 800-8382), PO Box 1751, Lewiston, ID 83501.

### Rafting & Floating

Purists who scorn noisy jet boats can ride the Snake River in a dory, a small, wooden craft resembling a drift boat. Contact Northwest Dories (☎ (800) 877-3679), PO Box 216, Altaville, CA 95221 (or locally at 743-4201, 1127-B Airway Ave, Lewiston, ID 83501), for information on multiple-day Snake River tours ($650 to $950). Next best is Beamer's (see Jet Boats above) four-night 'Boat 'n Float' tour ($700), which shoots the rapids in a rubber raft, zooming over the slow parts in a jet boat.

Lewiston also happens to be the meeting place for three to five-day guided rafting trips down the 'River of No Return' portion of the Salmon River offered by River Odysseys West (☎ 765-0841, (800) 451-6034), PO Box 579, Coeur d'Alene, ID 83816. The put-in site for this particular stretch of the Salmon River is far from Lewiston. Cost is $510 to $840. See the main listing under Boise.

### Jet Boat Tours

Although the Hells Canyon of the Snake River begins 50 miles south of Lewiston, the city is the center for upstream jet boat tours of the deepest canyon in North America. Operators offer a wide variety of single-day ($65 to $250) and multiple-day trips and dinner cruises ($40 to $50), and most offer fishing expeditions on the side. Trips depart from either the Hells Gate State Park marina in Lewiston or the Swallows Crest Park boat launch in Clarkston.

Expect a day trip to cover anywhere from 90 to over 200 miles. Lunch and beverages are provided, though you'll want to bring a small cooler of your own on some of the longer summertime trips. Buffalo Eddy Pictographs, the Kirkland Historical Ranch, swimming holes and mountain goat herds are typical destinations. Beamer's Hells Canyon Tours (☎ (509) 758-4800; Clarkston (208) 743-4800; Lewiston (800) 522-6966), 1451 Bridge St in Clarkston, is famous for its overnight mail trip to outlying ranches ($215); they have day trips from $80. Snake Dancer Excursions (☎ 743-0890,

Brown trout are popular fishing quarry in Idaho.

(800) 234-1941), 614 Lapwai Rd, Lewiston, and River Quest Excursions (☎ 746-8060, (800) 589-1129), both have day trips from $85. For half-day trips ($50) contact High Roller Excursions (☎ 746-5740, (800) 456-2779), 3523 8th St, Lewiston; full-day trips cost $75 to $120.

The only two companies going all the way to Hells Canyon Dam are based in Lewiston: Snake River Adventures (☎ 746-6276, (800) 262-8876), 227 Snake River Ave ($150), and Cougar Country Lodge (☎ 746-3546, (800) 727-6190), 805 Snake River Ave ($250); shorter day trips start at $65 and $85, respectively.

### Other Activities

If you'd like to **golf**, great views await at the desertlike Bryden Canyon Public Golf Course (☎ 746-0863), 445 O'Conner Rd, near the airport, where you'll play among sagebrush and stunted pines. There's **cross-country skiing** in the winter at Field Springs State Park, 30 miles south of Clarkston. Follett's Mountain Sports (☎ 743-4200), 1019 21st St, Lewistion, rents skis and other recreational equipment. **Bikes** can be rented from Pedals-N-Spokes (☎ 743-6567), 829 D St.

### Lewiston Roundup

The area's biggest whoop-up is the Lewiston Roundup (☎ 746-6324), one of the oldest and best rodeos in the state. As it's held the weekend before the Pendleton Roundup, on the first or second weekend in September, it gets the same big-name rodeo competitors. It's quite a party, and the whole community turns out for the street dances, parades, carnival, Nez Perce dancing and other events. The Lewiston Roundup Grounds are at 7000 Tammany Creek Rd, south of Lewiston.

### Places to Stay

**Camping** Campers should head to *Hells Gate State Park* (☎ 799-5015), four miles south of Lewiston on Snake River Ave. Standard sites cost $9, hook-ups $12. Reservations are accepted for an additional

$6. On an island in the Snake River is *Chief Timothy State Park* (☎ (509) 758-9580), eight miles west of Clarkston on Hwy 12 in Washington. Tent/RV sites cost is $10/14. Facilities at both parks include showers, a boat basin and a swimming beach.

**B&Bs** *Highland House* (☎ (509) 758-3126), 707 Highland Ave in Clarkston, is an 1890s Victorian home done up English-style. The five guest rooms (three with private facilities) cost from $35 to $80. The contemporary *Cliff House B&B* (☎ (509) 758-1267), 2000 Westlake Dr, eight miles west of Clarkston, hangs over the Snake River just above Chief Timothy State Park. Rooms cost $60 to $75; two-day minimums on weekends and holidays.

**Hotels** All of Clarkston's motels are right along the Hwy 12 strip. *Hacienda Lodge* (☎ (509) 758-5583), 812 Bridge St, is a nice, older motel, with single/double rooms for $32/38; pets are OK. *Motel 6* (☎ (509) 758-1631), 222 Bridge St, has a pool, and rooms are $36/42. *Quality Inn* (☎ (509) 758-9500), 700 Port Drive, also has a pool, and children under 18 are free with parents; rates are $63/69. *Best Western Rivertree Inn* (☎ (509) 758-9551, (800) 528-1234), 1257 Bridge St, has a pool, exercise room and sauna, and some kitchenettes; rates are $53/58.

In Lewiston, there are three in the $40/50 range: the *Travel Motor Inn* (☎ 743-4501), 1021 Main St, is closest to the old town; *Tapadera Inn* (☎ 746-3311), 1325 Main St, takes pets and has a free continental breakfast; and *Sacajawea Motor Inn* (☎ 746-1393, (800) 333-1393), 1824 Main St, is a large complex with all the usual extras. *Pony Soldier Motor Inn* (☎ 743-9526), 1716 Main St, goes after the business trade with large rooms ($57/65), pool and in-room modem. The *Ramada Inn* (☎ 799-1000, (800) 232-6730), 621 21st St, has views over the strip and the Clearwater River for $80/90.

If you want cheap, head across the Clearwater River from Lewiston where the

*Hillary Motel* (☎ 743-8514, 746-9353), 2030 North-South Hwy, has rooms ranging from $24 to $40.

## Places to Eat
If you're staying along motel row in Lewiston, then the *Country Cookery* (☎ 743-4552), 1516 Main St, will be right down the street and is a good place for breakfast. For burgers in a '50's theme restaurant, go to *Zany's* (☎ 746-8131), 21st St at 19th Ave. At *Tomato Bros* (☎ (509) 758-7902), 200 Bridge St in Clarkston, the wood-fired pizzas are quite good, as are the salads and pasta.

Even though it's named *Cabo San Lucas* (☎ 746-5681), 504 Main St, this isn't a Mexican restaurant. Instead, you'll find imaginative dishes from all over, like whiskeyed chicken and seafood fettucine ($12). More traditional fine dining is found at *Jonathan's* (☎ 746-3438), 301 D St, in the lower floor of an old town storefront. For dinner with a view, head to *Three Mile Inn* (☎ (509) 243-4158), about three miles south of Asotin on Snake River Rd in Washington. The dining room overlooks the rugged canyon and the river; the menu offers steak, seafood and pasta from $10 to $17.

## Entertainment
**Coffeehouses** *Copa Cabeana* (☎ 746-7766), 513 Main St, is a pleasant espresso shop/exhibition space in the old town area; with acoustic music on the weekends, this is about as alternative as Lewiston gets.

## Things to Buy
North Lewiston has a number of shops that sell local Nez Perce-made jewelry and artifacts. Cee-Mee-Nee-Kum (☎ 743-3989), 2317 1st Ave N, has Nez Perce beadwork, seed and cut beads. Marsh's Trading Post (☎ 743-5778), 1105 36th St N, has Native American-made goods, beads and some antiques. Although the Nez Perce Express II (☎ 748-6225), 7411 North-South Hwy, looks like a convenience store, it also sells jewelry.

## Getting There & Around
**Air** Horizon Airlines (☎ 743-9293, (800) 547-9308) provides service from the Lewiston-Nez Perce Regional Airport (☎ 746-7962) to Spokane, Seattle, Boise, Pullman and Portland. Empire Airlines (☎ 746-8866, (800) 392-9233) has flights to Boise and Coeur d'Alene. The airport is located south of Lewiston, off of 17th St (which turns into 5th St).

**Bus** Northwest Trailways (☎ 746-8108, (800) 366-3830) operates two buses a day to Spokane ($20), and one bus a day to Boise ($33). The depot is at 3120 North-South Hwy, at the Super 8 Motel.

**Car** Hertz (☎ 746-0411), Budget (☎ 746-0488) and National Car Rental (☎ 743-0176) are all at the Lewiston-Nez Perce Regional Airport. Rent-A-Wreck (☎ 746-9585) is at 102 Thain Rd.

**Taxi** Call Black & White Cab Co (☎ 743-4596) in Lewiston, or Clarkston Cab Co (☎ (509) 758-2185) in Clarkston, for a taxi.

## MOSCOW
Moscow, at the eastern edge of the wheat and lentil fields of the Palouse Hills, is home to the University of Idaho. It's very much a university town; the full-time population of 18,500 is boosted during the school year by 11,000 students. There's much more of an alternative bent here than in Pullman, WA – Moscow's academic sister city just seven miles away – with good coffee, a good bookstore and several movie theaters.

## Orientation
While the rolling agricultural landscape of the Palouse Hills is to the west of town, to the east is the Clearwater National Forest and the beginnings of the Rocky Mountains. Moscow is 33 miles north of Lewiston and about 80 miles south of Spokane, WA, and Coeur d'Alene. Boise is a long 283 miles to the south.

## Information

Pick up visitors information at the chamber of commerce (☎ 882-3581), 411 S Main St, just behind the Farmers Market. For information about the nearby Clearwater National Forest, stop by the USFS office (☎ 882-2301) at 1221 S Main St.

The main post office is at 220 E 5th St, and there's another station at the university. Bookpeople of Moscow (☎ 882-7957), 512 S Main St, is totally packed with books and is a great place to browse and, inevitably, to buy. The University of Idaho bookstore (☎ 885-6469) is on Deakin St across from the student union. Tune in to Northwest Public Radio at 91.7 FM.

Homestyle Laundry (☎ 882-1241) is in the Palouse Empire Mall, just west of downtown on the way to Pullman. Moscow's Gritman Medical Center (☎ 882-4511), 715 S Washington, has 24-hour emergency services.

## University of Idaho

More notable for the color it imparts to the town than for any particular feature of the campus, the university (☎ 885-6424) around 6th and Rayburn Sts has something of a reputation as a party school. Academically, natural resource fields are strong at this land-grant university. Stop by the student union building to hang out, read the bulletin boards and check the pulse of the campus.

Perhaps the university's finest feature for the casual visitor is the Shattuck Arboretum, along Nez Perce Drive, a shady place to wander or rest. It's behind the administration building.

## Latah County Historical Society

The historical society (☎ 882-1004) has exhibits displayed in parts of the high-Victorian McConnell Mansion at 110 S Adams St, and they have a good library, with a special emphasis on genealogy, a few blocks away at 327 E 2nd St. The mansion museum is open from 1 to 4 pm, Tuesday to Saturday; the library is open from 9 am to noon and 1 to 5 pm, Tuesday to Friday. There's a shop in the McConnell Mansion with a selection of regional history books and a walking tour brochure of historic Moscow homes.

## Appaloosa Museum & Heritage Center

Appaloosa Museum (☎ 882-5578), 5070 Hwy 8 W, nearly straddling the state line on the Moscow-Pullman Hwy, is worth at least a quick stop. The museum focuses on the history of the horse breed developed by Nez Perce and Palouse Indians, making for an interesting twist on Native American history. The Appaloosa Horse Club, which sponsors **trail rides** and other events, also has their headquarters here (same phone). The museum is open from 8 am to 5 pm, Monday to Friday, and from 9 am to 3 pm on Saturday, June to August; admission is by donation.

## Camas Winery

Stop by the downtown Camas Winery (☎ 882-0214) for a sip of Hog Heaven Red (a sherry-grape blend), Palouse Gold (a muscat-riesling blend) or a dry chardonnay. The winery and tasting room are housed in a great old brick building at 110 S Main St; it's open from noon to 6 pm, Tuesday to Saturday.

## Activities

The University of Idaho's 18-hole **golf** course (☎ 885-6171), 1215 Nez Perce Drive, has the reputation of being rather tough, with lots of hills. If you want to **swim**, the University of Idaho's indoor pool (☎ 885-6180, 885-6381) is open to the public when it's not being used for classes (call for schedule). During the summer, cool off in Gormley Park's outdoor pool.

## Special Events

From May to October, the Farmers Market (☎ 882-5553) is open Saturday mornings to bring the Palouse garden bounty to shoppers. The market is at Friendship Square (Jackson St between 4th and 5th Sts).

The Lionel Hampton Chevron Jazz Festival (☎ 885-6765) brings big-name jazz performers to the University of Idaho to

IDAHO

play alongside university students in late February or early March.

## Places to Stay
**B&Bs** *The Cottage* (☎ 882-0778), 318 N Hayes St, is an old bunkhouse-turned-B&B. It's an appealingly private retreat close to downtown, and rooms go for $85 a night. *Beau's Butte B&B* (☎ 882-4061), 702 Public Ave, is just north of downtown. Rooms go for $50 to $55 ($5 extra gets a private bath), and there's an indoor hot tub available to guests.

Five miles north of town, *Peacock Hill B&B* (☎ 882-1423), 1245 Joyce Rd, looks down onto Moscow and the Palouse; it has three rooms running from $55 to $95. Horseback riding and cross-country skiing are offered here.

**Hotels** There are three inexpensive motels in the $30/35 range for singles/doubles: *Hillcrest Motel* (☎ 882-7579), 706 N Main St, doesn't have a pool and doesn't allow pets, but it's a perfectly reasonable place to stay. Another pretty basic place in the heart of downtown is *Royal Motor Inn* (☎ 882-2581), 120 W 6th St; pets are an extra $2. Or try the *Motel 6* (☎ 882-5511), 101 Baker St, just off W Pullman Rd. Rooms at the *Super 8 Motel* (☎ 883-1503), 175 Peterson St, a mile from downtown, go for $33/41.

For a few dollars more, the *Mark IV Motor Inn* (☎ 882-7557, (800) 833-4240), 414 N Main St, offers airport transportation, an indoor pool and a hot tub; singles/doubles are $41/43, and pets are OK.

*Best Western University Inn* (☎ 882-0550, (800) 528-1234), 1516 W Pullman Rd, is near Moscow's big shopping mall. Rooms start at $66/75, and there's an indoor pool.

## Places to Eat
*The Beanery* (☎ 882-7646), 602 S Main St, is a comfortable place to sprawl with the morning paper, a muffin and some coffee. Besides coffee and baked goods, this is a good soup and sandwich spot.

Another hip hangout is *Cafe Spudnik* (☎ 882-9257), 215 S Main St. Start the day

at the Beanery, then head to Cafe Spudnik for dinner. (Don't try to be fashionably late, though; the Spudnik closes up fairly early, around 8:30 pm.)

Between the Beanery and Spudnik, Main St is peppered with restaurants. The *Main St Deli* (☎ 882-0743) and *West 4th Bar & Grill* (same phone) are notable for the atmosphere lent by their setting in the old Moscow Hotel, 313 S Main St.

If you want to check out the Palouse's bounty, buy lentils at the *Moscow Food Co-Op*, (☎ 882-8537), 310 W 3rd St. This excellent co-op has a deli that serves a variety of vegetarian sandwiches and a bakery that turns out good bagels.

*MJ Barleyhoppers* (☎ 883-4253), 507 S Main St, is a popular brewpub. Just out of downtown *The Treaty Grounds Brew Pub* (☎ 882-3807), 2124 W Pullman Rd, also helps quench students' thirst for good beer and conviviality.

## Entertainment
Catch a movie at one of downtown Moscow's three theaters: the *Micro Moviehouse* (☎ 882-2499), 230 W 3rd Ave, the *Kenworthy* (☎ 882-4924), 508 S Main St, and just a hop away, the *Nuart* (☎ 882-9340), 516 S Main St.

## Getting There & Away
**Air** Moscow shares the Pullman-Moscow Airport, (☎ 334-4555), just over the state line off Hwy 270 in Pullman, WA. Horizon Air (☎ (800) 547-9308) flies in from several northwest cities.

**Bus** Northwestern Trailways (☎ 882-5521, (800) 366-3830) runs buses between Spokane and Moscow. The Moscow bus station is at 120 W 6th St.

**Car** Auto rentals are available at the Pullman-Moscow Airport through Budget (☎ (509) 332-3511, (800) 527-0700), Hertz (☎ 332-4485, (800) 654-3131) or Sears (☎ 332-5230, (800) 527-0770).

## Getting Around
Moscow/Latah Public Transit buses (☎ 882-

8313) run weekdays from 8 am to 4:30 pm, but not along any set route. Call at least 24 hours in advance to schedule a ride. Priority service is given to seniors and people with mobility problems. Link Transportation (☎ 882-1223, (800) 359-4541) is a private shuttle company with service around the Moscow-Pullman area. Call them if you need a ride to or from the airport.

If you need a cab, call Richard's Taxi (☎ 882-1881).

# Clearwater River Valley

Beneath barren, narrow canyon walls, Hwy 12 winds east from Lewiston along the rushing Clearwater River. Gradually, the pace of the river quickens, and the cliffs, at first soft with vegetation, begin to bristle with fir and pine forests as they lengthen into mountain peaks: the Rockies have begun.

Along this narrow, often very winding road are pull-outs for anglers, white-water rafters and hikers who frequent this beautiful river valley. One rule of thumb: the farther east you drive, the more stunning the landscape and the wilder the river gets. Facilities for travelers are few and far between, though the little logging towns are doing their best to revamp as tourist and recreation centers.

Most of the land south of the river between Lewiston and Kooskia is part of the 137-sq-mile Nez Perce Reservation, established in 1855 but later downsized in 1877. For information about the reservation and Nez Perce events, contact the Nez Perce Tribe of Idaho, (☎ 843-2253), PO Box 305, Lapwai, ID 83540.

## ORIENTATION & INFORMATION
Highway 12 links Lewiston to Missoula, MT along one of the most scenic mountain roads in the Northwest. Highway 12 is *very* winding and can be a slow drive during the summer when traffic piles up behind log

trucks and RVs. If you're in a hurry to get across Idaho, try another route. The pass over the Continental Divide at Lolo Pass into Montana (elevation 5235 feet) can be especially snowy and dangerous in winter; for road conditions, call 746-3005. There is no public transportation along this portion of Hwy 12.

## NEZ PERCE NATIONAL HISTORICAL PARK
A unit of the national park system, this amorphous collection of far-flung sites is described somewhat apologetically in the official brochure as 'as much an idea as it is actual physical property'. Considering that its noble goal is to honor the Nez Perce tribe's important legend and battle sites, as well as to note historic locations important to White exploration and missionary work, the park ought to be a lot more interesting than it is. The park's 24 sites are spread around four different counties, and it would take 400 miles of driving to link them all. Few of them are worth making a long detour for, as some sites are comprised of little more than a distant rock outcropping, a place where Lewis & Clark camped or a plowed field where an old fort once stood.

The one site that definitely warrants a stop is the visitors center at the **Spalding Site** (☎ 843-2261), eleven miles east of Lewiston in Spalding. Besides an excellent small museum devoted to the Nez Perce, there's a good film about the tribe and a book and gift shop. Just down the hill is the site of the Spalding Mission, established by Henry and Eliza Spalding in 1836. The Spaldings were part of the same missionary team as the ill-starred Narcissa and Marcus Whitman, who were killed near Walla Walla, WA in 1847.

A couple of other sites near the headquarters give a sense of what the rest of the park is like. Out on Hwy 12, both within five miles of the headquarter's road, are **Coyote's Fishnet** and **Ant and Yellowjacket**, both barely visible rock outcroppings imbued with legends for the Nez Perce. The **Spalding Home**, five miles south of the headquarters on Hwy 95,

IDAHO

requires even more imagination: it's currently a wheatfield.

Pick up a brochure and map of the park from the headquarters, and decide what route to take to visit a few more sites. Unless you are a devotee of this sort of thing, you will probably find there are more interesting things to do in Idaho.

## OROFINO

The largest of the towns along the Clearwater, Orofino (population 3800) is at the point where the landscape begins to change from high desert canyons to the Rocky Mountains. As the town's name makes clear (it means 'fine gold' in Italian), Orofino was born of the gold rush: the state's first strike was made in 1860 in the mountains east of here, near Pierce. More recently, the town has served as a logging center for operations in the Clearwater National Forest.

Orofino can be a busy place in summer, due to massive Dworshak Reservoir, seven miles west of town. The reservoir is a haven for power-boat-oriented watersports, fishing and weekend RV camping.

Contact the City of Orofino Chamber of Commerce (☎ 476-4335), PO Box 2221, Orofino, ID 83544, for tourist information. For hiking and recreation information in the Clearwater National Forest, contact the visitors information center at the USFS Supervisor's Office (☎ 476-4541), 12730 Hwy 12. They also have maps of recreation sites on the Dworshak Reservoir.

### Dworshak Dam & Reservoir

This 1973 dam on the North Fork Clearwater River possesses a number of superlatives: it's the largest straight-axis concrete dam in the USA, the largest dam ever constructed by the Army Corps of Engineers and the third-tallest dam in the nation. The 53-mile-long reservoir impounded by the dam is also incredibly popular in summer for recreational boaters, with water-skiing the sport of choice; paddlers take refuge in the 'nonmotorized' section of upper Elk Creek. The banks of the reservoir also offer two nice campgrounds (busy on summer

weekends), picnic areas, boat launches and swimming beaches, which now operate under the aegis of newly created **Dworshak State Park** (☎ 476-5994).

The visitor center (☎ 476-1255) is on the west side of the dam, and free guided tours of the dam are available during summer months; call for schedules. The **Dworshak National Fish Hatchery** (☎ 476-4591), below the dam at the confluence of the Clearwater River, is the largest producer of steelhead trout and spring Chinook in the world. This massive facility is open from 7:30 am to 4:30 pm daily for self-guided tours.

Dworshak Dam is seven miles west from downtown Orofino on Ahsahka Rd; the state park and recreation areas are 17 miles farther.

### Outfitters

Clearwater Outfitters (☎ 476-5971), 4088-A Canyon Creek Rd, Orofino, ID 83544, offers a number of recreational activities on the Clearwater River, including float trips and steelhead fishing; powerboat excursions on Dworshak Reservoir are also available. Other activities offered include photographic trips and trail rides. For guided fishing trips, stop in at the Clearwater Drifters and The Guide Shop (☎ 476-3531), 140th St and Hwy 12, which specializes in steelhead fishing on the Clearwater River.

### Places to Stay & Eat

Campers should head to *Dworshak State Park* (☎ 476-5994), where at Freeman Creek Campground there are 105 campsites (waterfront sites reserved for tenters!), showers, bathrooms and a swimming beach for $9 a night. Also along the reservoir is the Corps of Engineers-operated *Dent Acres Recreation Area* (no phone) with similar facilities to the state park; primitive campsites ring the reservoir, a number accessible only by boat.

The *Helgeson Place Hotel* (☎ 476-5729) is a remodeled old hotel right downtown at Michigan and Johnson Aves; rooms are $32 to $40. Also downtown but off the busy main streets is the *White Pine Motel* (☎ 476-7093), 222 Brown St, an attractive newer motel with rooms from $31 to $48.

Food is pretty basic in Orofino. The best bet is the *Clearwater Bakery & Cafe* (476-3025), 214 Johnson Ave, serving breakfast and lunch Monday to Saturday. Otherwise, the *Ponderosa Restaurant* (☎ 476-4818), 220 Michigan Ave, offers the sort of hearty steaks, chops, and potatoes that keep loggers going.

## KAMIAH

Kamiah (population 1400) is a pleasant town on a wide curve of the Clearwater River and a major center of Nez Perce population and culture. The one-street downtown looks old-fashioned and historic, and the townsfolk are friendly. In fact, the locals have been welcoming strangers here for centuries: Lewis and Clark camped here with the Nez Perce for four weeks in 1806, at aptly named Long Camp (one of the sites of the Nez Perce National Historical Park).

More recently, the Militia Movement has come to stay. One-time Libertarian Party presidential candidate 'Bo' Gritz has established 'Almost Heaven', an antigovernment community of so-called 'Christian Patriots', near Kamiah.

For more information about the area, contact the Kamiah Chamber of Commerce (☎ 935-2290), 513 Main St.

### The Heart of the Monster

The small stone outcropping beside Hwy 12 is a sacred Nez Perce site, central to the tribe's ancient creation myth, and a site in the Nez Perce Historical Park. Supposedly, the mound is the heart of the monster that died in the process of giving rise to the region's native peoples. From the carpark, about two miles east of Kamiah, a short walk leads to an overview of the rock, where recordings relate the myth in both English and Nez Perce.

### Places to Stay & Eat

For campers, the enormous *Lewis-Clark Resort & RV Park* (☎ 935-2556), two miles east of Kamiah on Hwy 12, is the place to go for a full-service RV campground with hook-ups ($10) and even a few log cabins ($39). Right in town on Hwy 12 is the *Kamiah Inn Motel* (☎ 935-0040), a well-kept older motel with singles/doubles for $29/32. The *Clearwater 12 Motel* (☎ 935-2171, (800) 935-2671), also on Hwy 12, is new and modern, accepts pets for a fee and has some kitchenettes; rooms run $35/45.

In rural areas, the best restaurants are often truck stops. *Jilinda's* is the restaurant at Bill's Conoco, five miles east of Kamiah, and it's where the locals go for better-than-usual family fare and a good salad bar.

### KOOSKIA

At Kooskia (population 724), the Clearwater River divides into its Middle and South Forks, and travelers will have to decide whether to cut south on Hwy 13 or continue on Hwy 12 toward Montana.

IDAHO

### Nez Perce Creation Myth

According to myth, Meadowlark told Coyote that a monster was devouring all the other creatures. Coyote put five knives and some fire-making tools in his pack, swung it over his back, and set off to confront the monster. After exchanging challenges with each other, the monster inhaled Coyote, and Coyote tumbled inside the belly of the monster, where all the other animals were waiting. Coyote found the monster's heart, lit a fire, and began to carve off portions. Finally, he cut the heart free, and the monster died, allowing the captured animals to escape. Coyote butchered the monster and scattered all the parts of its body to the winds; the bits were transformed into various Indian tribes. Fox reminded Coyote that he had neglected to leave a portion of the body to create a tribe for the valleys of the Clearwater and Snake Rivers. Coyote washed his hands, and with the monster's blood created the Nu-me poo, 'The People', or the Nez Perce. ∎

Kooskia is an old, rather plain-looking town, but it's a good place to stock up on supplies or to get information if you plan to head off into the woods. The Lochsa Ranger Station (☎ 926-4274), just across the Clearwater Bridge off Lowry St, has information about recreation, camping and sights in the hundreds of miles of wilderness between here and the Continental Divide.

### Outfitters

The following outfitters each offer float trips along the Clearwater and Selway rivers, which are good rafting trips for families. Whitewater Adventures (☎ 733-4548), 1953 San LaRue, PO Box 184, Twin Falls, ID 83303-0184, offers fishing and float trips on the Selway River. Coolwater Ranch Outfitters (☎ 926-4707), HCR 75, PO Box 97, Kooskia, ID 83539, also offers guided fishing and hunting trips, trail rides, backpacking and snowmobile excursions.

### Places to Stay & Eat

Follow Hwy 12 east into national forest lands to find an abundance of public campgrounds. The *Mount Stuart Inn* (☎ 926-0166), 006 S Main St, is new, with single/double rooms for $25/31. The *Rivers Cafe* (☎ 926-4450), 018 N Main St, is an appealing, backwoodsy restaurant downtown serving homestyle meals.

### LOCHSA RIVER

The winding 99-mile stretch of Hwy 12 between Kooskia and Lolo Pass, first along the Middle Fork Clearwater River and then the Lochsa River, was only completed in 1962 due to the formidable river canyons and rugged terrain through which it coils. Beyond the tiny settlements at Lowell and Syringa, incursions of humanity are few, making this area a prime outdoor recreation area.

White-water rafting and kayaking are very popular on the surging Lochsa River. Highway 12 is the only east-west road through central Idaho, and it gives access to the northern section of the 2095-sq-mile

Selway-Bitterroot Wilderness. Hanging footbridges lead across the Lochsa River to remote, long-distance wilderness destinations. Less ambitious hikes lead to hot spring pools in the midst of green forested meadows.

In summer, winding Hwy 12 is heavily traveled – be content to watch the beautiful scenery since it's dangerous and ultimately futile to try and overtake every slow-moving car or truck. Although there are gas stations at Lowell and Syringa, and then seven miles into Montana at Lolo Hot Springs, these close up early in the evening, so fuel up while you can. There is also a hospital in Syringa (☎ 983-1700) at W Main and N B St.

### Hot Springs

The upper stretch of the Lochsa River is fed by a number of hot-springs streams. Easy hikes from Hwy 12 lead to two popular, undeveloped soaking pools. To find **Weir Hot Springs**, drive just east of milepost 142 to the bridge over Weir Creek. Follow a trail on the west side of the stream half a mile to find the pool. **Jerry Johnson Hot Springs** are very popular and not a place for the bashful or prudish. These extensive hot springs pool in three different areas, so it's possible to get a real party going. The USFS has been trying to save the hot springs from their own popularity by limiting camping at the springs before the area gets completely trashed. To find Jerry Johnson Hot Springs, continue east past milepost 152 to the parking area for the Warm Springs Pack Bridge across the Lochsa River. Cross the bridge, and the hot springs are easily found at the end of a mile-long hike.

### Rafting

The Lochsa River is a fast-moving river that drops quickly through a narrow river canyon. The streambed is chock-a-block with house-sized boulders and innumerable chutes. During most times in early summer, travelers can pull off Hwy 12 and watch a steady flow of rafters and kayakers shoot the rapids.

If you'd like to get out on the river yourself, you'll need to have your own gear, as most rental outfits won't rent equipment for use on the Lochsa. There are a number of class III and IV rapids, so this isn't a stream for novices. You will probably find plenty of other people around at put-in locations to ask for advice. For a guided raft trip, contact Holiday River Expeditions (☎ 983-2299), 126 W Main St in Grangeville. A day trip begins at $90. River Odysseys West (☎ 765-0841, (800) 451-6034), PO Box 579, Coeur d'Alene, ID 83816, also has day trips from $82 to $103, plus two and three-day trips from $215 to $395. Day trips down the Selway River cost $73.

Wilderness Trails at Three Rivers Resort & Campground (☎ 926-4430), HC 75, Box 61, Kooskia, ID 83539, offers trail rides at their guest ranch near Lowell as well as float trips down the Lochsa, Selway and Clearwater rivers.

### Places to Stay & Eat
There are quite a number of USFS campgrounds along the Selway River and along the Lochsa River on Hwy 12. The best of the lot is *Wilderness Gateway*, 25 miles east of Lowell, with water, flush toilets and easy access to hiking in the wilderness area. Traditional lodging is pretty much limited to two places. The *Three Rivers Resort* (☎ 926-4430) at Lowell, 23 miles east of Kooskia on Hwy 12, is a pleasant riverside hodgepodge of RV spots ($16), riverview cabins ($69 to $93) and motel rooms ($39). The rustic *Lochsa Lodge* (☎ 942-3405), just 12 miles shy of the Montana border, has unplumbed cabins ($28), motel rooms ($38) and a three-bed log cabin ($65).

The two resorts have cafes, but a favorite stop for frequent travelers are the two cafes in the tiny settlement of Syringa, seven miles west of Lowell. The *Syringa Cafe* (☎ 926-0057) and the *Middlefork Cafe* (☎ 926-0169) are both known for good, homecooked meals, followed by near-obligatory slices of huckleberry pie.

# Salmon River & Hells Canyon

Cutting through the heart of Idaho's national wilderness areas is the Salmon River – as it turns west across the center of the state, its wild, boiling white water and barren precipitous canyon have earned it the sobriquet the 'River of No Return'. Even Native Americans found the territory inhospitable, and Lewis and Clark – no milquetoasts themselves – were forced to reconsider a trip down the river. Today, 75 miles of the Salmon, from Shoup in east Idaho to 27 miles east of Riggins, is accessible only on foot or by raft and is protected as a federal wild and scenic river.

Another of the Northwest's most remote and wild areas is Hells Canyon National Recreation Area on the Snake River. From Idaho, there is only one maintained road leading to the river itself, at Pittsburgh Landing, but there are several roads near Riggins that lead to dramatic views of this great gorge, which is the deepest in North America. From here, the hearty can hike their way around the mountains and down into the canyon. Both the Snake and Salmon rivers are popular for white-water rafting, and you'll find most outfitters based out of Riggins. If you want to know more about visiting and hiking Hells Canyon, see the Hells Canyon section in the Northeast Oregon chapter.

### GRANGEVILLE
Highway 95 climbs up out of the valley at Craigmont to cross Camas Prairie, a broad volcanic plateau cut on each side by deep canyons. Surrounded by wheat farms and cattle ranches, Grangeville (population 3666) is an old agricultural trade town that is changing to accommodate tourism as it becomes one of the main jumping-off points for Central Idaho's three enormous wilderness areas, the Gospel Hump, Selway-Bitterroot, and Frank Church River of No Return. While the town itself doesn't

IDAHO

offer much more than adequate facilities, it's where you can get to from here that makes the town noteworthy.

## Orientation

Grangeville is on Hwy 95, 64 miles south of Lewiston. East of Grangeville, Hwys 13 and 14 lead to the tiny community of Elk City, 63 winding miles later. One of the most remote towns in Idaho, Elk City is the division point for yet more obscure roads that dead-end at distant trailheads for hiking and horseback excursions into the surrounding wilderness areas.

## Information

For tourist information, contact the Grangeville Chamber of Commerce (☎ 983-0460), 201 E Main St, Grangeville, ID 83850. The Nez Perce National Forest office (☎ 983-1950), just east of Grangeville on Hwy 13 at 319 E Main St, is the place to go for information on the vast tracts of public land and wilderness areas to the east.

## St Gertrude Museum

A satisfying side trip from the small town of Cottonwood, 14 miles north of Grangeville on Hwy 95, leads to a Benedictine nunnery and an eclectic museum of early Idaho history.

The Priory of St Gertrude was established in 1920, and the Romanesque-style stone chapel and convent was completed in 1925, with the nuns providing much of the labor. The chapel, with its twin 90-foot towers, is open to visitors.

Next door, St Gertrude's Museum (☎ 962-3224) began as a collection of relics gathered by one of the Sisters in the convent, an expert in Idaho pioneer history. Highlights include personal belongings of Buckskin Bill, a mountain trapper, and of Polly Bemis, a Chinese slave girl, Nez Perce artifacts and cultural items of the Montagnard (Mountain) people of Vietnam. The hours are imprecise: if the museum isn't open during the daytime, head to the Priory and the curators will open it; or, call to make an appointment

(☎ 962-7123, 962-3224). Admission is by donation; follow signs from Hwy 95 in downtown Cottonwood to reach the monastery.

## White Bird Battlefield

Just south of Grangeville, Hwy 95 climbs to the edge of the Salmon River canyon and then shoots down a steep ravine to meet the river near the town of White Bird. The modern highway is a fairly impressive piece of roadbuilding. However, history buffs should slow down and take the old road built in 1915, itself an engineering feat in its day. This old highway has been designated the **White Bird Battlefield Auto Tour**, as the first real battle of the so-called Nez Perce War was fought on this steep escarpment in 1877. This very slow and winding road is 16 miles long; battle sites are keyed to a tour brochure available from the information post at the beginning of the route.

## Pittsburgh Landing

Although the Hells Canyon gorge at Pittsburgh Landing is nowhere near as rugged and impenetrable as the areas above and below, the 1½-hour, 17-mile journey over rough, though perfectly passable, gravel roads provides a good glimpse of the area's geology and landscape. The relatively gentle, sandy terrain around Pittsburgh Landing was a longtime Nez Perce camp, and it was popular during the short and unlikely 1910s homesteading boom in Hells Canyon, when 21 homesteads clung to life along this stretch of desert canyon. Now Pittsburgh Landing offers a campground (with piped water; sites are $6), and it's a popular lunch stop for jet boat tours and rafters. There is also a trailhead here for an easy, if long, 30-mile hike along the river to Hells Canyon Dam.

To reach the Pittsburgh Landing road, leave Hwy 95 at White Bird and turn west on USFS Rd 493, the Deer Creek Rd.

## Rafting

Holiday River & Bike Expeditions (☎ 983-1518, (800) 628-2565), PO Box 86,

## The Battle at White Bird

The Oregon Nez Perce had traditionally lived peaceably with White settlers around the Wallowa Mountains, even though the land was not protected as reservation land. However, Indian/White relations deteriorated across the West in the aftermath of the Battle of the Little Bighorn in 1876. The US Army ordered the Oregon bands of Nez Perce to comply with a treaty they had not signed, which moved them from their homelands to a parcel of land in Idaho (the current Nez Perce Reservation). Eventually, the remaining Nez Perce chiefs reluctantly agreed to move onto the reservation, and they gathered their people and camped at Tolo Lake near Grangeville.

However, several young braves impetuously decided to settle scores with some White settlers along the Salmon River (one of the settlers had killed in cold blood the elderly father of two of the braves). On June 13, three braves left the camp and killed three settlers along the Salmon River. The next day, a larger party of Nez Perce left camp and raided further settlements, killing 15 more Whites. The chiefs realized that moving onto the reservation was no longer an option, as the army would exact a terrible justice on tribe members. Instead, they decided to flee to freedom in Canada. The entire encampment – over 800 people and 2500 horses – moved off the Grangeville plateau and dropped into the White Bird Canyon to prepare for their journey.

An army force of about 100 men, under the command of Captain David Perry, rode south from Fort Lapwai to apprehend the Nez Perce and prevent further bloodshed.

On June 17, the army command inched down the steep ravine toward the Nez Perce camp. A contingent of warriors rode out to parley under a white flag, but trigger-happy soldiers fired upon the delegation. Battle was initiated, and the Nez Perce and army troops clashed at several points along the steep hillside. In a decisive battle that lasted only about an hour, 34 of the army troops were killed, with no casualties on the Nez Perce side.

However, even in victory, the chiefs realized that they had no choice but continue their flight. They withdrew across the Salmon River and began their ultimately failed journey to Canada. ∎

**IDAHO**

Grangeville, ID 83530, offers two and four-day guided raft trips on the Lochsa and Salmon rivers ($300 to $465). You're expected to provide your own tent and sleeping bag, though sleeping kits can be rented from the company. Rafts, bikes and intertubes are usually available for rent. Longer five and six-day trips down the Salmon and Snake rivers meet in Boise (see listing under Boise).

### Places to Stay & Eat

*Monty's Motel* (☎ 983-2500), 700 W Main St, is clean and new, with a pool, and pets are welcome; rooms range from $30 to $45. The *Crossroads Motel* (☎ 938-1420), 622 W Main St, has rooms from $35 to $60.

Grangeville offers a number of mom-and-pop cafes, but one place stands out. *Oscar's Restaurant* (☎ 983-2106), 101 E Main St, tries its best to be upmarket (they

have an espresso machine), but this pleasant old restaurant is notable for its steak: the menu offers a selection of 12 different cuts! Don't panic if you've passed your quota on red meat: they also serve Mexican food, sandwiches, chicken and seafood.

### Getting There & Away

Get bus information and tickets from Blake's Service (☎ 983-0721), a Sinclair gas station on Hwy 95 N. The Northwest Trailways Spokane-Boise bus from Lewiston passes through Grangeville on Hwy 95 and continues south to Riggins and McCall.

### RIGGINS

Between White Bird and Riggins, Hwy 95 follows the Salmon River through its narrow canyon. Sometimes the valley walls fall back to allow a farm or ranch to set up business; often the rock cliffs close in to constrict the rushing water.

This area is just about the only easily accessible portion of the Salmon River. Riggins (population 500), at a dramatic, cliff-lined curve in the river, is the center for guided white-water rafting on the mainstem and Middle Fork Salmon rivers and for trips down the Hells Canyon of the Snake River. Near Riggins is also access to Hells Canyon National Recreation Area, with camping, hiking and dramatic views of the gorge and the surrounding mountains.

## Orientation & Information

Riggins is a long, one-street kind of town. Street numbers are scarce, and the following businesses are on Hwy 95, which doubles as the main street in town.

For a complete list of Riggins outfitters, contact Salmon River-Riggins Area Chamber of Commerce (☎ 628-3778), PO Box 289, Riggins, ID 83549. In summer, there's an informational kiosk (☎ 628-3340) in a gravel lot at the center of town.

Get good maps and other information on Hells Canyon from the Hells Canyon National Recreation Area office (☎ 628-3916), PO Box 832, Riggins, ID 83549.

## Hells Canyon National Recreation Area

A number of roads lead west from Riggins to climb up onto the 7000-foot ridge that separates the Snake and Salmon rivers. From here, hiking trails lead to the **Seven Devils Mountains**, a remote area of barren rugged peaks and lake basins on the edge of the Snake River canyon, and down into Hells Canyon itself. Even if you don't have time for these long-distance hikes, travelers with a little time to spare can drive up slow roads to the canyon's rim just for the dramatic views.

The most popular drive, easily accessed by most vehicles, is the Windy Saddle Rd. From Riggins, drive about a quarter mile south on Hwy 95 and take USFS Rd 517, just past the Hells Canyon NRA headquarters. The gravel road climbs steadily for 17 miles, arriving at the rim and Seven Devils

Lake & Campground after about an hour's drive. From here, trails lead off into the Seven Devils Lake basin, along the rim, and down into the canyon. The road continues two miles north to **Heaven's Gate Lookout**: at 8430 feet, it's one of the highest viewpoints in the Hells Canyon area, with breathtaking views into the canyon, onto the Wallowa Mountains in Oregon and back onto the Seven Devils.

A second viewpoint is gained by following USFS Rd 241 west from Hwy 95, a quarter mile north of Riggins, to **Iron Phone Junction**. The road is rather steep and rough, climbing to the rim in 15 miles (1½ hours), where there are excellent views into Hells Canyon and onto Oregon. High-clearance vehicles can make a 17-mile loop trip along the rim by following other USFS roads before descending again on USFS Rd 241, or by continuing along the rim on USFS Rd 420 for 25 miles to the Pittsburgh Landing Rd (see Grangeville, above).

All these roads are fair-weather roads only – they are sometimes still closed by snow well into June. If you have any doubt about road conditions, stop at the ranger station in Riggins for information. For more information about Hells Canyon National Recreation Area, see the Hells Canyon section of the Northeast Oregon chapter.

## Rafting

Riggins is ground zero for white-water rafting in Central Idaho. In general, there are four kinds of trips offered by most outfitters. Day and part-day trips float the lower Salmon River in the vicinity of Riggins. Longer trips, from three to six days, float the Middle Fork of the Salmon River, the mainstem Salmon River from Shoup, and the Snake River through Hells Canyon. If you're planning one of the longer trips, be sure to shop around and ask questions: there's sometimes quite a difference in price between outfitters, and depending on how much you want to rough it, you may opt to spend the extra money.

You'll definitely need reservations for any of the longer trips, which have limited space and book up well in advance during the height of the season. Day trips will usually have space for rafters without reservations.

The following offer several-day or part-day floating options; call for information on longer excursions. Epley's Whitewater Adventures (☎ 628-3533, (800) 233-1813), PO Box 987, McCall, ID 83638, has half/full-day trips from $30/55. Discovery River Expeditions (☎ 628-3319, (800) 755-8894) has half/full-day trips for $35/60.

Day trips down the Salmon River from Riggins through River Odysseys West (☎ 765-0841, (800) 451-6034), PO Box 579, Coeur d'Alene, ID 83816, cost $73; two-day trips cost $250.

Folklore wilderness trips led by a modern-day mountain man are offered through Wapiti River Guides (☎ 628-3523, (800) 488-9872), PO Box 1125, Riggins, ID 83459. These trips, which float the Lower Salmon River in dories, rafts and kayaks, are fun and earthy. They start at $40 to $65 for a half or full-day trip and go up to $750 for five days.

Salmon River Experience (☎ 882-2385, (800) 892-9223), 812 Truman St, Moscow, ID 83843, offers one and two-day raft trips from Riggins ($50 to $170) down the Salmon River and multiple-day trips down the Salmon and Snake rivers; there are also mountain biking/raft combination trips.

Meadow Creek Outfitters/Osprey Adventures (☎ 839-2424), on McKenzie Creek Rd, 22 miles north of Riggins, offers day float trips for $60 and multiple-day rafting and horsepacking trips from $150 to $390.

Experienced do-it-yourselfers will want to contact Northwest Voyagers (☎ 628-3021, (800) 727-9977), Salmon River Rt 1, Lucile, ID 83542-0373, to rent rafts, kayaks, mountain bikes and equipment. (Note that advance permits are necessary to float wilderness rivers without guides.) Guided single and multi-day trips down the Salmon and Snake rivers by these folks cost $70 to $950. They also offer four-day rafting/

mountain biking or rafting/horsepacking trips ($750).

Exodus (☎ (800) 992-3484) specializes in combination raft/jet boat excursions, which run in length from half a day to six days. Combination multi-day trips through River Adventures (☎ 628-3952, (800) 524-9710), PO Box 518, Riggins, ID 83549, involve rafting, jet boating and even horsepacking through the Salmon and Snake river valleys ($300 to $750). They also offer mild-mannered sightseers a plain, day-long jet-boat trip ($85) through either Hells Canyon or the Salmon's 'River of No Return'.

### Other Activities
Aside from river trips, most of the above companies also outfit for **fishing** and horsepacking expeditions. Exodus (☎ (800) 992-3484) guides anglers to steelhead, trout, bass and sturgeon in the Salmon River. Wapiti River Guides (☎ 628-3523, (800) 488-9872) also has steelhead fishing ($250 per day). Contact River Adventures (☎ 628-3952, (800) 524-9710) for sturgeon and steelhead fishing on the Snake River. Northwest Voyageurs (☎ 628-3021, (800) 727-9977) offers a five-day steelhead trip for $1200.

Meadow Creek Outfitters Guest Ranch (☎ 839-2424), McKenzie Creek Rd (22 miles north of Riggins off Hwy 95), offers a half/full day of **horseback riding** for about $40/60.

### Places to Stay
**Camping** *Sleepy Hollow RV Park* (☎ 628-3402), on the south end of town on the other side of the Salmon River bridge, has hook-ups from $12. The small *Riverside RV Park* (☎ 628-3390, 628-3698) promises grassy sites on the river for $6 to $12.

**Hotels** All of the following motels are located right along Hwy 95. One of the nicer places in town is the *River View Motel* (☎ 628-3041), with rooms ($35 to $55) overlooking the river. The *Riggins Motel* (☎ 628-3001) is a well-maintained older motel with lots of shady trees and rooms

from $28 to $80. *Salmon River Motel*
(☎ 628-3231), 1203 S Hwy 95, has rooms
from $33 to $74.

Combine lodging and rafting and stay at
*Whitewater Adventure Lodge* (☎ 628-3830,
(800) 574-1224), eight miles south of
Riggins on Hwy 95. In addition to offering
rooms for $25 to $60, the lodge outfits for
rafting trips.

Nine miles up Salmon River Rd is the
*The Lodge at Riggins Hot Springs* (☎ 628-
3785), PO Box 1247, Riggins, ID 83549.
Rooms are available in the main lodge
building or in a triplex cabin. The high-
season lodging rates of $225 to $300
include three meals a day and access to the
hot springs swimming pools.

### Places to Eat
*Glenna's Deli* (☎ 628-3997), behind the
Riggins Visitor Information Center, offers
sandwiches, salad, soup and pastries, and
they will pack picnic lunches for raft trips.
The *Cattlemen's Restaurant* (☎ 628-3708)
is where to go for breakfast and for family-
style dining the rest of the day.

### Getting There & Away
There's a highway stop for the Northwest
Trailways Spokane-Boise bus at city hall, a
brick building on Hwy 95. There's no ticket
agent here, so you'll have to call Trailways
(☎ (800) 366-3830) for schedule and
fare information. Catch it southbound to
McCall and northbound to Grangeville,
Lewiston and Moscow.

# Payette River Valley

### McCALL
The lakeside resort community of McCall
(population 2488) is a pleasant, friendly
place that – unlike many other resort towns
in Idaho – tries to keep the hype and glitz
on medium. Certainly, there are the mandatory watersports, great winter skiing, good
restaurants and nice lodging, but the pace
of life here is calm and conducive to relaxing. In summer, most of the color comes

from the myriad flower boxes along the
streets and in front of businesses instead of
from lycra-spandex body suits.

McCall sits beside Payette Lake, and the
Payette River begins its journey to the
Snake River by flowing through the town.
Along the lakefront is a marina, with the
outdoor decks of bars and restaurants
backed up to the lake and views of distant
mountains. Unfortunately, this is about as
close as casual visitors might get to the
lake, as there's limited public access,
except at Ponderosa State Park to the north
of town.

If you do visit Lake Payette, however,
watch out. The lake is rumored to have a
monster living in it, a la Loch Ness. If you
see it, its name is Sharlie.

### Orientation
Highway 55 enters town from the northwest as Lake St, turns south at the heart of
downtown and leaves McCall as 3rd St.
The shopping and dining focus of the town
is fairly diffused along the three miles that
Hwy 55 follows the lake.

### Information
The McCall Area Chamber of Commerce
(☎ 634-7631) is at 116 3rd St, 83638. Head
to the Payette USFS ranger district office
(☎ 634-1453, 634-0400), 202 W Lake St,
for information on recreation in the Payette
National Forest.

Blue Grouse Books (☎ 634-2434) in
McCall Drug, at 2nd and Lenore Sts, is a
good source for local travel and history
books. For a laundry emergency, head to
McCall Laundry Center (☎ 634-2858) on
3rd St at the south end of town, near the
airport. And for a medical emergency, go to
McCall Memorial Hospital (☎ 634-2221),
1000 State St.

### Ponderosa State Park
There are two sections to this lakeside state
park (☎ 634-2164). The main unit is on a
peninsula, slightly northeast of McCall
near the end of Davis Ave. Locals flock
here in the winter to build ice sculptures
and to cross-country ski. Boating, fishing

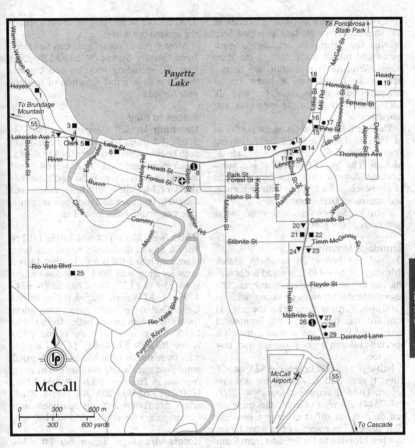

**IDAHO**

McCall

Payette Lake

Payette River

McCall Airport

To Ponderosa
State Park

To Brundage
Mountain

To Cascade

0    300    600 m
0    300    600 yards

| PLACES TO STAY | PLACES TO EAT | OTHER |
|---|---|---|
| 1   The Chateau | 2   Lardo's Restaurant | 7   McCall Memorial Hospital |
| 3   Shore Lodge | &  Saloon | 8   Payette National Forest |
| 5   Riverside Motel & | 3   The Narrows |      Ranger Station |
|      Condominiums |      Restaurant | 11  Blue Grouse Books |
| 6   Brundage Bungalows | 4   Lake Street Cafe | 13  McCall Vacations |
| 9   1920 House B&B | 10  Yacht Club Restaurant | 16  Sports Marina |
| 14  Hotel McCall | 12  Moxie Java | 17  Gravity Sports |
| 18  Mill Park Condominiums | 15  Mountain Java | 26  Chamber of Commerce |
| 19  Aspen Timeshare | 20  Huckleberry Restaurant | 28  Bill's Gas & Grocery |
|      Condominiums | 23  Maria's |      (Bus Stop) |
| 21  Woodsman Motel | 24  The Mill Steak | 29  McCall Laundry Center |
| 22  Scandia Inn Motel |      & Spirits | |
| 25  Northwest Passage B&B | 27  Pancake House | |

and swimming are popular pastimes in the summer. A single-lane graveled loop crowns the peninsula, leading to great views and hiking trails through the deep forest. Wildlife is also abundant here – deer make themselves at home in the campground while beavers, fox and elk keep their distance in the meadows and marshes.

The North Beach Unit is on the north end of Payette Lake, reached by following Warren Wagon Rd from the west side of McCall. The North Beach Unit is a summertime, day-use-only area. Noted for its sandy beach, it's a favorite with swimmers and non-motorized boaters.

There's a $2-per-vehicle day-use fee at both units of the park.

### Brundage Mountain

One of the better ski areas in Idaho, Brundage (☎ 634-7462) is noted for churning out Olympic ski-team members. The resort offers 1300 acres of skiing, with an 1800-foot vertical drop. The longest ski runs are over two miles long. Equipment rentals and lessons are available; there's a special children's ski program and day care, too.

Full-day adult lift tickets are $23, or $18 after 1 pm. Call 634-5650 for a snow report. Guided snow cat tours (☎ (800) 888-7544) are also offered; the snow-cat can drop skiers off at otherwise inaccessible slopes. The resort is open from 10 am to 4 pm Monday to Friday, and from 9 am to 4 pm on weekends and holidays. The season generally runs from mid-November to mid-April.

Brundage is located eight miles north of McCall off Hwy 55.

### Activities

The Payette River is noted for its **whitewater rafting**. Contact the local outfitters at Canyons Incorporated (☎ 634-4303), PO Box 823, McCall, ID 83638, for information on floating or **fishing** the Payette and the Salmon rivers. They also offer **boating** and kayaking trips on Payette Lake, or rent a boat from Sports Marina (☎ 634-8361),

1300 E Lake St, and join the crowds speeding around the water.

Most types of sports gear can be rented from Gravity Sports (☎ 634-8530), 503 Pine St, including bicycles and canoes; they also have a full selection of outdoor gear for sale.

### Places to Stay

**Camping** *McCall Campground* (☎ 634-5165), 1.5 miles south on Hwy 55, offers both hook-ups and tent sites for $13 to $15. *Ponderosa State Park* (☎ 234-2164), near the end of Davis Ave on the northeast outskirts of McCall, offers flush toilets and showers. Tent sites and hook-ups are available year round from $9 and up.

**B&Bs** *Hotel McCall* (☎ 634-8105), 1101 N 3rd St, an old downtown motel, has been renovated into a B&B inn. The hotel has a great location near the lake. Rooms range from $59 to $123. *The Chateau* (☎ 634-4196), 1300 Warren Wagon Rd, is an old Cape Cod-style home with four guest rooms (two with private baths) from $70 to $115. Close to downtown is the *1920 House B&B* (☎ 634-4661), 143 E Lake St, with three rooms from $65 to $70. Nestled amid pine trees a few minutes out of town *Northwest Passage B&B* (☎ 634-5349, (800) 597-6658), 201 Rio Vista Blvd, offers five rooms and one apartment in a contemporary home from $65 to $160.

**Hotels** *Brundage Bungalows* (☎ 634-8573), 308 W Lake St, are refurbished cabins set back among trees; they come with kitchenettes and VCRs and begin at $55. The *Riverside Motel & Condominiums* (☎ 634-5610, (800) 326-5610), 400 W Lake St, is one of the most attractive motels in town, set on the banks of the Payette River and decorated during summer months with an abundance of flower boxes; there are also condos. Motel rooms run from $40 to $54, some with kitchenettes; studio condos are from $74, two bedrooms from $85. The *Scandia Inn Motel* (☎ 634-7394), 400 N 3rd St ($40 to $59), and the *Woodsman Motel* (☎ 634-7671), 402 N 3rd

St ($29 to $54), a log lodge-like motel, face each other across the highway and are convenient to a number of good restaurants. Just west of McCall is the *Village Inn Motel* (☎ 634-2344), 1005 W Lake St, which has clean, snug rooms with radiator heat and some kitchenettes; singles/doubles begin at $39/49.

**Resorts** The most elegant lodging in McCall is the *Shore Lodge* (☎ 634-2244, (800) 657-6464), 501 W Lake St, with rooms overlooking the lake and a beautiful log and stone foyer and dining room. The facility offers two restaurants, complete recreational facilities, a hot tub and sauna. Streetside rooms start at $73, lakeside suites at $144.

The lakeside *Mill Park Condominiums* (☎ 634-4151, (800) 888-7544), 1410 Mill Rd, is not far from Ponderosa State Park; accommodations range between $95 and $160. *Aspen Timeshare Condominiums* (☎ 634-2136), 1607 N Davis Ave, entices visitors with athletic club membership and proximity to the golf course. Stay for $75 to $125 per night.

**Vacation Home Rentals** McCall Vacations (☎ 634-7056), 317 E Lake St, offers a large selection of furnished condominiums and cabins, all with kitchens, from $70 to $150 per night.

### Places to Eat
Remember, this is a resort town, so resort prices apply. That's the bad news. The good news is that, by and large, the food is better here than many places in the state.

Start the day at *Mountain Java* (☎ 632-8268), 501 Pine St, or *Moxie Java* (☎ 632-3607), 312 E Lake St, with espresso and pastries. For something more hearty, head to *The Pancake House* (☎ 634-5849), 201 3rd St. Also a favorite for a traditional breakfast is *The Huckleberry* (☎ 634-8477), 402 3rd St, which also offers inexpensive meals throughout the day.

Try the *Lake Street Cafe* (☎ 634-8551), 406 W Lake St, for homestyle family dining.

*Lardo's Restaurant & Saloon* (☎ 634-8191) 600 Lake St, offers pasta, steak and hamburgers ($8 to $12); the bar is the traditional choice of sportsmen. *Yacht Club Restaurant* (☎ 634-4396), 203 E Lake St, has a huge menu with American and Italian food, served in a waterfront-view dining room. Most pasta dishes are under $10; chicken Marsala is $15. *Maria's* (☎ 634-7436), N Hwy 55 at Timm St, is one of McCall's favorite restaurants, and it serves authentic Mexican food from Acapulco. Full dinners at this cantina start at less than $8 a meal.

*The Mill Steak & Spirits* (☎ 634-7683), Hwy 55 at Stibnite St (across from Maria's), is McCall's premier steakhouse, with prices to match. A New York steak at this log supper club runs $20. The finest dining room in McCall is at *The Narrows* (☎ 643-2244) in the Shore Lodge, 501 West Lake St. Tables set with linen and crystal overlook Payette Lake. The menu is limited to five daily selections heavy on Northwest cuisine; loin of elk with forest mushrooms goes for $18.

### Getting There & Away
Bill's Gas & Grocery (☎ 634-2340), 147 3rd St (Hwy 55), is where the Northwest Trailways bus stops, with connections to Boise ($15) and points north to Spokane. A ticket to Lewiston costs $21.

## CAMBRIDGE
Cambridge (population 328) is an unassuming little town at the crossroads for traffic heading to and from Hells Canyon on Hwy 71 and between the mountain towns of central Idaho and the farm country along the Snake River plain. If you're traveling north on Hwy 95, Cambridge makes a more comfortable – and cheaper – place to spend the night than often-sweltering Payette or Weiser.

From Cambridge, Hwy 71 drops over into the Hells Canyon, where jet-boat tours leave from below Hells Canyon Dam; see the Hells Canyon chapter in Northeast Oregon for more information.

IDAHO

**Outfitters**

If you're spending time in the Cambridge area, contact Hughes River Expeditions (☎ 257-3477), PO Box 217, Cambridge, ID 83610, for information on a number of river trips, including floats on the Bruneau, Owyhee, Middle and Lower Fork Salmon rivers, and the Hells Canyon of the Snake River. Fishing, hunting and trail-riding trips are also offered.

**Places to Stay & Eat**

*Hunters Inn* (☎ 257-3325), on Superior St, is many things, including a motel, B&B, bistro and espresso shop. Motel rooms range between $20 and $35; rooms in the historic B&B (also called the Cambridge House) are $45. At *Frontier Motel & RV Park* (☎ 257-3851), 240 S Superior St, hook-ups are $14 and motel rooms start at $27.

Breakfast is the meal that people in the country are most likely to go out to eat, and at *Kay's Cafe* (☎ 257-3561), on Superior St, breakfast is served all day. Steak and homemade pies are also excellent here.

# Upper Salmon River Valley

The Salmon River manages to flow in every direction but up as it unwinds out of the tightly knotted mountains of central Idaho. After leaving the broad basin at the foot of the Sawtooth Mountains near Stanley, the Salmon follows a long easterly and then northerly path until pivoting to thunder to the west down the wild river canyon that gave the river its common nom de guerre, the River of No Return.

This rural part of the Salmon River valley only hints at the wilderness gorge through which it later flows. Large cattle ranches and irrigated meadows flank the river, and the steep mountains that rise on each side are mostly barren and treeless. Idaho's highest peaks pierce the sky to the south of the Salmon River valley, and to the

east are the incised ridges of the Bitterroot Mountains, which carry the Continental Divide and the Idaho/Montana border. Only the upper reaches of these peaks trap much moisture, leaving the slopes and valleys arid.

## GETTING THERE & AWAY

The only public transport in this area is The CART (☎ 522-2278), Idaho Falls' public transport system, which offers two buses a week from its offices at 850 Denver St to Challis and Salmon. One-way fare from Idaho Falls to Salmon is $22.

## CHALLIS

Challis (population 1200) is the trade town for a widespread ranching and mining community. During the 1960s, a large open-pit molybdenum mine opened southwest of town; other mines in the area tap tungsten, copper and cobalt. Challis is also the crossroads of Hwys 93 and 75. South of Challis on Hwy 93, the desolate Lost River valley unrolls beneath the mighty Lost River Range, which contains Borah Peak, the state's highest at 12,662 feet.

This arid valley was the scene of the one of the worst earthquakes in recent US history. In October, 1983, a tremor measuring 7.3 on the Richter scale dropped the valley floor nine feet and raised the peak six inches. Two children were killed in the quake.

Challis is a small town, and the following businesses are all found along the main highway; there are no street addresses. For more information about the area, contact the Challis Chamber of Commerce (☎ 879-2771), PO Box 1130 Challis, ID 83226.

### Places to Stay & Eat

For campers, the *Challis Hot Springs* (☎ 879-4442), 4.5 miles west on Hwy 93, offers camping spaces for $11.50 to $15 and access to hot springs swimming pools. Otherwise, there are a number of informal BLM campsites along the river between Challis and Salmon.

It's a long way between stops out here, and Challis has more than its share of modern, attractive motels; most of the following also have restaurants alongside. The log *Village Inn Motel & Restaurant* (☎ 879-2239) on Hwy 93 offers kitchenettes and rooms from $30 to $50. The *Challis Motor Lodge & Lounge* (☎ 879-2251) has rooms for $26 to $42. The *Northgate Inn* (☎ 879-2490) overlooks the bluffs on the Salmon River and has rooms from $32 to $46.

## SALMON & AROUND

Salmon (population 3200) was just another ranch and lumber town in a wide and fertile valley until proximity to the River of No Return and the current obsession with white-water rafting spurred new life. Today, Salmon is hardly a resort town, but the newest and healthiest-looking businesses here cater to the throngs who come to raft, fish or otherwise seek recreation.

Although float trips are available on just about every stretch of the upper Salmon, the real action begins 21 miles north of town near North Fork. Here, Hwy 93 continues north to cross Lost Trail Pass, while a paved, then gravel, road follows the Salmon as it turns west and heads into its deep canyon. From put-in spots along the river is where the five to six-day float trips through the River of No Return begin.

Lewis and Clark passed through the area in 1805. They ignored advice from the friendly Shoshone, crossed the Continental Divide at Lemhi Pass and dropped onto the Salmon River. The expedition intended to float down the Salmon to the Columbia and then to the Pacific. However, the corps quickly found that the Salmon was indeed an impassable river, as the Shoshone had promised. The expedition was forced to climb back over the Continental Divide into Montana and to find its way down the Bitterroot Valley to Lolo Pass and the more hospitable Clearwater River valley.

For information about Salmon, contact the Salmon Valley Chamber of Commerce (☎ 756-2100), 200 Main St, Salmon, ID 83467. For information on rafting the Salmon River without a guide service, contact the North Fork Ranger District (☎ 865-2383), North Fork, ID 83466.

Permits are distributed by lottery once a year in the spring, so you'll need to plan well ahead.

### Rafting

The main objective of outfitters in the Salmon and North Fork area is boating the mainstem Salmon River. These trips take at least five days and will include stays at downriver lodges or campgrounds. Note that many of the outfitters listed under Riggins (above) and elsewhere offer float trips down the Salmon, while many of the outfitters based out of Salmon offer jet-boat or short excursions on the Salmon.

Idaho Adventure River Trips (☎ 756-2986) offer both day trips and longer excursions on the Salmon. Other local river outfitters include Warren River Expeditions (☎ 756-6387), PO Box 1375, or Wilderness River Outfitters & Trail Expeditions (☎ 756-3959), PO Box 871, both in Salmon, ID 83467. In addition to the classic white-water trip, both outfitters offer fishing trips. Wilderness River Outfitters also offers backpacking and llama-packing trips into the Salmon River country, as well technical mountaineering training, cross-country skiing and float trips on the desert rivers, the Owyhee and Bruneau.

If you don't have most of a week to spend drifting the Salmon, you may be more interested in a motorized trip down the river. Both the Arctic Creek Lodge (☎ 865-2372), PO Box 116, North Fork, and Salmon River Tours Co (☎ 865-2375), PO Box 7, North Fork, ID 83466, offer fishing and power and jet boating along the entire Salmon River.

### Places to Stay & Eat

There are a number of campgrounds around Salmon. One of the most convenient is *Salmon Meadows Campground* (☎ 756-2640), two blocks north on St Charles St, off Main St, with sites for $12 to $15.

In town, the *Suncrest Motel* (☎ 756-2294), 705 S Challis St, is pleasant and clean; pets are OK. The newest and most inviting motel in Salmon is *Stagecoach Inn Motel* (☎ 756-4251), 201 Hwy 93 N, with rooms from $41 to $61. Farther from town and along the river is *Wagons West Motel* (☎ 756-4281), 503 Hwy 93 N, with rooms from $31 to $54.

Stay closer to the action on the river at the *North Fork Store & Cafe* (☎ 865-2412) in North Fork. This all-encompassing business offers a campground with sites from $8 to $12.50, rooms in the motel from $32 to $42, the promised store and cafe, and jet-boat and raft trips. If you're looking for a guest ranch, then consider *Indian Creek Ranch* (☎ 394-2126), HC64, Box 105, North Fork, ID 83466, 11 miles west of North Fork on the Shoup road. The ranch offers fishing, hunting, trail rides,

backpacking and snowmobiling on a working ranch. Eighteen miles south of Salmon on Hwy 93, *Twin Peaks Ranch* (☎ 894-2290, (800) 659-4899) offers an array of wilderness adventures, including backcountry trail rides, white-water raft trips, fishing and shooting at a beautifully maintained dude ranch. Such comforts and attention don't come cheap: cabin accommodations range from $960 to $1285 weekly, which includes all meals.

Food is pretty basic in Salmon. Try breakfast or lunch at the *Smokehouse Cafe* (☎ 756-4334). Another Main St eatery worth checking out is the *Salmon River Coffee Shop* (☎ 756-3521), with basic but well-prepared chops, steak, chicken, salad bar and burgers.

# Idaho Panhandle

Northern Idaho connotes mainly two things to most Northwesterners. First, this thin sliver of Idaho wedged between Canada, Washington and Montana is known for its dense forests, deep, glacier-dug lakes and mighty rivers. This largely unpopulated land is where many local residents head for family fishing and boating vacations. But the panhandle's remoteness has also made it attractive to various right-wing survival-

ist and White supremacist groups, such as the Aryan Nation, who have infiltrated the Pacific Northwest in general and northern Idaho in particular. While only a small minority of people are associated with these movements, media coverage has tended to emphasize them unduly.

The average traveler is more likely to confront a moose or a bear than a civilian militia unit in this beautiful, lake-gemmed

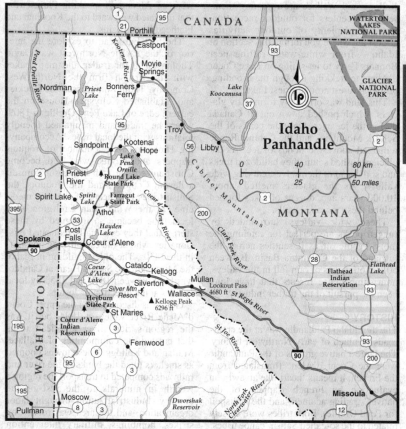

**Fire of the Century**
Northern Idaho was the scene of one of the worst forest fires of the century. In 1910, over three million acres – about one-sixth of the state's woodlands – burned during a drought-filled summer. The devastation was enormous: nine billion board feet of timber was destroyed, devastating wildlife habitat in some of the deepest forests in the state. Many a Northern Idaho frontier community went up in flames; about one-third of Wallace was destroyed, and scores of people, mostly firefighters, died. ∎

area. There are 60 lakes within 60 miles of Coeur d'Alene, including Priest, Pend Oreille and Coeur d'Alene, which serve as playgrounds for nearby Spokane, WA. Meanwhile, the old mining towns of Kellogg and Wallace are recasting themselves as centers for outdoor recreation. You'll find plenty of outdoor activities almost anywhere you turn in this section of Idaho – from white-water rafting near Bonners Ferry to jet-skiing on Lake Coeur d'Alene to trekking through the brooding, primeval forest around Priest Lake.

This land was originally formed by glaciers, which pushed down out of Canada during the ice ages. Only the peaks of the Selkirk Mountains and the Cabinet Range remained above the floods of ice. As the glaciers pushed south, they bulldozed rocks and soil ahead of themselves, carving wide valleys. As the glaciers melted, about 10,000 years ago, dozens of lakes formed behind these morainal walls.

These wide valleys surrounded by rugged peaks are perfect for catching the moist Pacific air as it scuttles across the lowland of the Columbia Basin. Between 50 and 60 inches of rain fall in the valleys, nourishing dense forests that have long been the pursuit of the timber industry.

## HISTORY
The thin Idaho Panhandle was at the crossroads of much of early Northwest history. The largest native groups of the Panhandle were the Coeur d'Alene (translated from the French, it means 'heart like an awl', an evaluation by French trappers of the natives' trading acumen) and the Kalispell (or Pend Oreille). Both tribes were closely related to the so-called Salish 'canoe tribes'

of the Pacific coast. On the enormous lakes of northern Idaho and nearby Montana, these peoples subsisted on fishing and hunting, a life remarkably similar to that of coastal tribes. A third tribe, the Kutenai, were an Algonquin-speaking Plains tribe that migrated westward to the Kootenai and Flathead River basins.

The first European to explore the interior of the Pacific Northwest was David Thompson, a fur trader and map maker with the British firm the North West Company. Thompson crossed the Rockies and established Kullyspell House on the eastern edge of Lake Pend Oreille in 1809, where he traded and maintained friendly relations with the local tribes. Accompanying Thompson were a number of Iroquois trappers and scouts, who had become Christianized. Through Thompson, himself a devout Catholic, and the Iroquois, the Salish tribes first heard of the 'big medicine' of the White man's religion. One local tribe became so intrigued by these stories that they eventually requested missionaries, who began establishing missions in the 1840s. The oldest building in Idaho, the Mission of the Sacred Heart at Cataldo, was built between 1848 and 1853 by local Indians at the direction of Jesuits.

Gold was discovered on the upper Coeur d'Alene River valley in 1884, but it was the region's rich silver and lead veins that created the communities of Wallace, Mullan and Kellogg. These towns boomed as smelters lined the banks of the river and railroads competed to transport the region's wealth in minerals to the rest of the country. Industrialization brought labor organization, and the area was rocked by strikes, bombings, military intervention and social unrest through the 1920s. Silver mines are still producing around the Wallace area; over $5 billion in metals have been mined here abouts, making this one of the world's richest mining regions. However, decades of silver and lead smelting in the area – now referred to as the Silver Valley – has denuded the mountain slopes of trees: those that weren't killed by the smelting fumes were cut by the mining companies to use as supports in mine shafts.

## GETTING THERE & AWAY
### Air
Empire Airlines (☎ (800) 392-9233) hubs out of Coeur d'Alene, with links to Boise and Lewiston. Spokane International Airport is only 33 miles west in Washington and has connecting flights to most major cities in the west.

### Bus
Several daily Greyhound buses (☎ (800) 231-2222) link the towns along the I-90 corridor from Spokane to Missoula.

## COEUR D'ALENE
Coeur d'Alene sits at the head of the beautiful, deep blue lake of the same name, which snakes through a glacier-dug channel between low, green-laden mountains. With such a beautiful location, it's no wonder that the town has made the most of its recreational attributes; Coeur d'Alene has been a tourist destination since the 1910s.

Coeur d'Alene began as a civilian community alongside the army's Fort Sherman, which was founded in 1878 by Civil War General William Sherman to keep local Indians in line. The town boomed after Mullan Rd brought gold diggers in to prospect the upper reaches of the South Fork Coeur d'Alene River. Steamboats were the principal means of transport and freight haulage in the area until the 1920s.

Today, Coeur d'Alene is the most popular of the many lakefront resort areas in northern Idaho, and it offers fishing, water sports, steamboat rides, jet-skiing –

basically, if you can do it in the water, you can do it here. Coeur d'Alene can get really packed in the summer, when water-skiers and jet-skiers pretty much rule the water. Coeur d'Alene is an ideal place for family vacations – don't expect any jet-setters to show up unannounced. Even the much-vaunted, lakeside resort hotel seems designed not so much to impress the sophisticated world traveler as to cater to Idaho residents looking to splurge.

### Orientation
Interstate 90 runs east-west along the northern edge of the lake, linking Coeur d'Alene to Missoula, MT (163 miles), and Spokane, WA (33 miles). Highway 95 is the main north-south route: from Coeur d'Alene, Sandpoint is 44 miles north and Lewiston is 121 miles south. The Coeur d'Alene Indian Reservation wraps around the south end of the lake.

There are essentially two commercial districts in the town. The newest is the commercial strip along Hwy 95 at the junction of I-90, where chain hotels, fast food emporia and shopping malls await. The old downtown district has also been recently regentrified; the old storefronts and motels along Sherman Ave have been smarted up and offer boutique restaurants and shopping for vacationers. The most prominent building on both the shore and skyline is the Coeur d'Alene Resort, known to most people simply as the Resort.

### Information
**Tourist Offices** The Greater Coeur d'Alene Convention & Visitors Bureau (☎ 664-0587, (800) 232-4968 in Idaho) is at 202 Sherman Ave. The Coeur d'Alene Area Chamber of Commerce (☎ 664-3194) is at 1621 N 3rd St, Coeur d'Alene, ID 83814.

There's a USFS office (☎ 765-7223) at 1201 Ironwood Drive, which has information on the Idaho Panhandle National Forest.

**Post** The post office (☎ 664-8126) is at 111 N 7th St; the zip code is 83814.

IDAHO

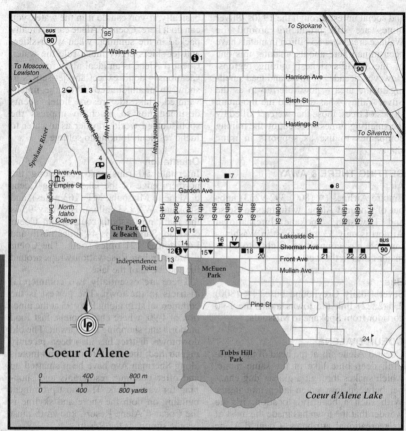

Coeur d'Alene

**PLACES TO STAY**

3   Pines Resort Motel
4   Robin RV Park & Campground
7   Gregory's McFarland House B&B
13   Coeur d'Alene Resort
18   Flamingo Motel
20   Blackwell House
21   State Motel
22   Star Motel
23   Sandman Motel

**PLACES TO EAT**

11   3rd St Cantina
14   Tito Macaroni's
15   Crickets Oyster Bar

16   Coffee Roastery
19   Rustler's Roost

**OTHER**

1   Chamber of Commerce
2   Greyhound Bus Stop
5   Fort Sherman Museum
6   YMCA Pool
8   Northwest Summer Playhouse
9   Museum of North Idaho
10   TW Fishers
12   Visitors Center
17   Post Office
24   Coeur d'Alene Resort
     Golf Course

**Media** The *Coeur d'Alene Press* is the town's daily paper. For public radio, tune to FM 91.9, for Spokane's KPBX.

**Medical Services** For medical emergencies, go to Kootenai Medical Center (☎ 667-6441), 2003 Lincoln Way.

## Museum of North Idaho & Fort Sherman Museum

The Museum of North Idaho (☎ 664-3448), 115 Northwest Blvd, charts local history from the indigenous Coeur d'Alenes through the logging and steamboat years up to the establishment of the Farragut Naval Training Station during WW II. The museum also operates the Fort Sherman Museum, which is near the corner of Empire St and College Drive on the grounds of North Idaho College. There's not much left of old Fort Sherman except the log powder house, but the museum preserves artifacts and historic photos of the army fort. On the grounds are vintage logging and forest-industry equipment and memorabilia, including a 1924 smoke-chaser's cabin. Both facilities are open from 11 am to 5 pm Tuesday to Saturday, April through October, and on Sundays in July and August. Admission is $1.50 for adults, 50c for children ages six to 16, or $4 for a family, and it covers both museums.

## City Park & Beach

The recreational and leisure heart of Coeur d'Alene is this popular, lakeside beach at the edge of the downtown area. During the summer, it's a crush of people swimming, sailing, jet-skiing, windsurfing and otherwise enjoying the sun and lake. A number of concessions and rental companies operate from the park, from Independence Point city dock, and from the nearby Coeur d'Alene Resort marina. There are the usual canoes, kayaks, paddleboats and more – all available for rent from North Shore Rentals (☎ 664-1175).

For the slightly more adventurous, there's **parasailing**. Lake Coeur d'Alene

Parasail (☎ 756-5367), at the Independence Point city dock, takes people about 500 feet above the lake for a quick spin and a lovely view. Or, take to the air in more traditional fashion on a **sea plane ride**. Brooks Sea Plane (☎ 664-2842), at the Independence Point sea plane terminal, offers aerial tours of lakes Coeur d'Alene and Pend Oreille. Twenty minute flights are $40 for adults and $20 for children; longer excursions are available as well.

## Silverwood Theme Park

This may not be why you came to Idaho, but Silverwood (☎ 683-3400), 15 miles north of Coeur d'Alene on Hwy 95, offers the kind of carnival and theme park atmosphere that is sure to get the attention of any kids in your entourage. In addition to a full battery of amusement rides, there's a rather idealized recreation of a mining camp, complete with sing-alongs, silent films and live stage shows. An authentic steam train transports passengers around the 500-acre site and is menaced by desperadoes in the backwoods. There's even an air show, and the daring can take rides on a vintage biplane (Silverwood was once a private airport). One price pays for all rides and activities (except for food at the restaurant and concessions). Entrance is $17.99 for everyone ages eight to 64; it's $8.99 for ages three to seven and for those 65 and older. The park is open daily from mid-June to Labor Day, and weekends only from the weekend before Memorial Day through the second weekend of June and for the month after Labor Day.

## Emerald Creek Public Garnet Mines

One of the world's only public garnet-digging areas is south of Lake Coeur d'Alene, five miles south of Fernwood, off Hwy 3 on USFS Rd 447. The site is administered by the USFS and is open to the public from Memorial Day to Labor Day. Garnet delving requires a $5 permit per person, and you need to bring your own

IDAHO

IDAHO

---

**Gettin' Hitched**

No kidding – Coeur d'Alene is the wedding capital of the Northwest. No blood test, witnesses or waiting are necessary. There are a number of wedding chapels in town; some B&Bs and the Resort host so many ceremonies that they have a clergy person on staff. You *will* need to be 18, or have a parent's permission, and licenses run $28 to $33. ∎

---

shovel, bucket and (ideally) a screen; be prepared to get muddy. For more information, contact the St Maries Ranger District (☎ 245-2531) at PO Box 407, St Maries, ID 83861.

### Lake Cruises

For decades, the only way to get around Coeur d'Alene Lake was by boat, and at the height of the Idaho gold rush, paddle wheel steamboats plied the waters between the railroad terminus at Coeur d'Alene and the docks near Cataldo. That era is relived with tour boat cruises by Lake Coeur d'Alene Cruises (☎ 765-4000), whose offices are at the Adventure Center in the Resort. A number of different cruises are available on different days – ranging from brunch and dinner cruises to journeys to St Maries on the St Joe River – so it's a good idea to call and find out what the sailing schedule is for any particular day. The most popular trip is the 90-minute cruise along the northern end of the lake; this cruise is offered at least once daily from early May through the second week of October. Tickets are $10.75 for adults and $9.75 for seniors; children ages three to 10 are $6.75. Cruises leave from the marina at the Resort.

Another, more personalized option for exploring Coeur d'Alene Lake is a sailboat cruise on *Crest of Eden I* (☎ 661-0403, (509) 924-8425). For a one-day minimum payment of $180, up to six people can arrange a personalized tour of the lake, which can also include meals catered by the crew. Special dinner cruises are avail-

able in good weather for $129 for two. Call ahead to schedule a sailing.

### Rafting

River Odysseys West (ROW) (☎ 765-0841, (800) 451-6034), offers a number of day-long river trips on local rivers like the St Joe and the Clark Fork. Day trips, which include lunch, cost between $73 on weekdays and $86 on weekends. ROW also offers guided, multiple-day excursions on the more challenging Salmon, Snake and Lochsa rivers.

### Golf

Coeur d'Alene is unique for having the world's first and only floating green, run by the Coeur d'Alene Resort (☎ 667-4653). Play 18 holes and spend the afternoon sinking fish. The Coeur d'Alene Public Golf Course (☎ 765-0218), 2201 Fairway Drive, is an 18-hole public course with relatively low green fees.

### Other Activities

If Lake Coeur d'Alene doesn't suit your fancy, you can **swim** in the YMCA pool (☎ 667-3415) at 606 River Ave. Or, head to Wild Waters (☎ 667-6491), 2119 Government Way, an enormous **water slide** complex. It's right along I-90 at exit No 12, and your kids aren't going to let you drive by without stopping. There's also a traditional swimming pool and a picnic area. From downtown Coeur d'Alene, there is a convenient, two-mile **hike**. The Tubbs Hill Trail leaves from the Coeur d'Alene Resort's northernmost parking lot and crosses McEuen Park before climbing through forests in Tubbs Hill Park to a viewpoint over the lake; the trail then loops back.

### Organized Tours

A 1½-hour city tour (☎ 664-4215, 667-7314) on a **double-decker bus** departs twice daily from the Iron Horse Restaurant parking lot at 407 Sherman Ave, Memorial Day weekend to Labor Day. The fare is $5 for adults and $3 for children ages 12 and under.

## Art on the Green

Art on the Green is a three-day arts-&-crafts gathering that melds music, theater, visual arts and food. The festival takes over the lakefront area of North Idaho College and is usually held the first weekend of August. For more information contact the visitors center.

## Places to Stay

**Camping** *Wolf Lodge Campground* (☎ 664-2812) is east of Coeur d'Alene off I-90 exit No 22 at 12425 E I-90. This attractive campground sports a swimming hole on the river and has grassy sites for RV and tent campers near the lake ($12 to $16). It's open April through November. There are more grassy sites closer to town at the year-round *Robin RV Park & Campground* (☎ 664-2306), 703 Lincoln Way ($15.50 to $17.50). *Coeur d'Alene RV Resort* (☎ 534-4654), 429 33rd, west of Coeur d'Alene in Post Falls at I-90 exit No 7, is pretty posh for a campground, with full amenities plus an indoor pool, whirlpool, putting green, playground, recreation director and cable TV. Full hook-ups and tents start at $24.

**B&Bs** *Blackwell House* (☎ 664-0656), 820 Sherman Ave, is a 1904 mansion with eight guest rooms (some with shared bath) with rates ranging from $75 to $119. *Gregory's McFarland House B&B* (☎ 667-1232), 601 Foster Ave, is an old foursquare home with a wraparound porch; it's decorated with English antiques, lace and chintz. All five bedrooms have a private bath and go for $65 to $120. For complete information about local B&Bs, call the Coeur d'Alene Bed & Breakfast Association at 664-6999.

**Hotels** There's a clutch of chain motels out at I-90 exit No 12. If you're planning to spend any time in Coeur d'Alene, avoid the commercial strip and head downtown. Each of the following is an older, well-maintained terrace-style motel, and each is convenient to beaches, recreation and shopping. Otherwise, they differ little except in

price. The *Flamingo Motel* (☎ 664-2159, (800) 955-2159), 718 Sherman Ave, has a great location near downtown, and with single/double rooms at $60/65, it's a good value. Farther up the street, the *State Motel* (☎ 664-8239), 1314 Sherman Ave, offers rooms at $50/55. Unlike the following, the Flamingo and the State accept pets.

Closer to the freeway ramps are the *Star Motel* (☎ 664-5053), 1516 Sherman Ave, which offers a swimming pool and rooms at $55/58, and the *Sandman Motel* (☎ 664-9119), 1620 Sherman Ave, with some cooking units and rates around $45/55. A bit west of downtown along the Spokane River is the slightly upscale *Pines Resort Motel* (☎ 664-8244), 1422 Northwest Boulevard, with a pool, spa facilities and suites. Rates range from $65 to $149.

**Resorts** The 338-room *Coeur d'Alene Resort* (☎ 765-4000, (800) 688-5253), at Front Ave and 2nd St, has done more to put Coeur d'Alene on the tourism map than anything since the glaciers left. With three lounges, two restaurants (one with an 18-foot salad bar) and a recreation center complete with a private bowling alley and racquetball court, the resort is designed to please. The lakefront setting, overlooking a marina and a 3.3-mile-long floating boardwalk, is certainly lovely enough, and you'll basically find everything you associate with four-star resorts. A recent addition to the resort is its 18-hole golf course, with its signature floating green located on an offshore island. In winter, ski packages are available in conjunction with Kellogg's Silver Mountain.

There's a wide range of lodging options at the resort, depending on views, hot tubs and the like. The least expensive rooms begin at $99; suites range up to $245.

**Vacation Home Rentals** Rent a private home for your vacation from Coeur d'Alene Property Management (☎ 765-0777), 1900 Northwest Blvd, or from Resort Property Management (☎ 765-6035), 1801 Lincoln Way, Suite No 4.

IDAHO

## Places to Eat

As befits a resort town, there are plenty of restaurants in Coeur d'Alene, though food of much distinction is oddly lacking. Thankfully, so are high prices: a full dinner at most of the following is in the $10 to $12 range.

The *Coffee Roastery* (☎ 664-0452), 511 Sherman Ave, is downtown's best espresso bar, with morning pastries and evening desserts. The *3rd Street Cantina* (☎ 664-0693), 201 3rd St, serves Mexican food in the old train station. *Rustler's Roost* (☎ 664-5513), 819 Sherman Ave, offers breakfast all day and 'North Idaho-style barbecue'. *Tito Macaroni's* (☎ 667-2782), 210 Sherman Ave, is a pleasant pasta house. For a steak and Pacific coast bivalves head to *Crickets Oyster Bar* (☎ 765-1990), 424 Sherman Ave.

For fine dining go to *Beverly's* (☎ 765-4000), on the seventh floor of the Coeur d'Alene Resort. You can't beat the view, and the menu (with seafood, steak and Continental-influenced cuisine) is also impressive. Expect to spend around $20 for fresh seafood specials.

## Entertainment

**Brewpubs** *TW Fishers* (☎ 664-2739), 204 2nd St, offers pub grub in addition to a fine selection of ales. Tours of the brewery are available daily between 1:30 and 5:30 pm; call ahead to schedule.

**Cinemas** First-run films are shown at *Coeur d'Alene Cinemas* (☎ 667-3559), 3555 Government Way, and *Showboat III Tri-Cinemas* (☎ 772-5695), N 5725 Pioneer Drive.

**Theater** If you want to catch a little theater, Carrousel Players (☎ 667-0254) offers revivals of Broadway musicals during their summer season. Productions are held at the *North Idaho College Auditorium*. The *Northwest Summer Playhouse* (☎ 667-1323) is an equity theater group that mounts three shows each season, one of which is presented at the outdoor amphitheater at Kellogg's Silver Mountain

Ski Resort. Other shows are staged in the theater at 1320 E Garden Ave.

## Getting There & Away

**Air** Empire Airlines (☎ (800) 392-9233) has its hub at Coeur d'Alene, with links to Boise and Lewiston.

**Bus** Three Greyhound buses a day stop in Coeur d'Alene on the route between Spokane, WA and Missoula, MT. The station (☎ 664-3343) is at 1527 Northwest Blvd.

## Getting Around

North Idaho Community Express (NICE) (☎ 664-9769) operates the local bus system. There's one intercounty bus a day, which you can pick up at the Greyhound station, from Coeur d'Alene to Sandpoint; fare is $6 one way. Handy for locals and travelers alike is NICE's curb-to-curb service, where for $2.50 per person a driver will pick passengers up and take them anywhere within certain service areas.

Rental cars are available from Auto Rental of Coeur d'Alene (☎ 667-4905), 120 Anton Ave. If you need a cab, call Sunset Taxi (☎ 664-8000).

## WALLACE & THE SILVER VALLEY

The upper reaches of the South Fork Coeur d'Alene River contain some of the richest silver and lead veins in the world, and the valley has been the scene of intensive industrial mining from the 1880s to the present. While most of the old mining centers are now largely ghost towns, and the environmental damage caused by decades of mining is apparent throughout, there are a number of very good reasons to get off the freeway and explore this desolate-seeming area. Wallace (population 1400) possesses one of the best preserved turn-of-the-century town centers in the Northwest, a delight to anyone interested in historic architecture. This area also contains one of the most interesting treks in the country: decades ago railroads snaked their way down steep mountainsides and across narrow valleys to reach the Silver Valley mines, and today this engineering marvel, including the most expensive single sections of rail line ever laid, has been restored for use as a hiking and biking path.

## Orientation & Information

Wallace and Kellogg are nine miles apart along I-90. Missoula, MT is 121 miles east of Wallace, and Coeur d'Alene is 42 miles west of Kellogg. Both ends of Silver Valley are high mountain passes that are often socked in by storms, snow and ice. Just above Lake Coeur d'Alene on I-90 is Fourth of July Pass, which is deceptively low at 3070 feet. Lookout Pass, on I-90 at the Idaho/Montana border, can also be extremely icy in winter. For a winter road report, call 772-0531, or check with local authorities.

For tourist information, contact the Wallace Chamber of Commerce (☎ 753-7151), PO Box 1167 Wallace, ID 83873, or stop by the office at 509 Bank St.

For information on hiking, camping and mountain biking in the Panhandle National Forest, stop by the Wallace Ranger District office (☎ 752-1221), just west of Wallace in Silverton.

The Wallace post office (☎ 753-3435) is at 403 Cedar St.

## Historic Walking Tour & Museums

Wallace is one of the best preserved late-19th-century mining towns in the Northwest – the entire town is listed on the Historic Register. It's worth a stop just to look at the architecture and to get a sense of what life was like on the Idaho mining frontier a century ago. A good place to start a walking tour of town is at the **Wallace District Mining Museum** (☎ 753-7151), 509 Bank St, which also houses the visitors center. The museum chronicles both the history of the Wallace-area mines and the evolution of the mining techniques used to yield silver and lead ore from mile-deep shafts. The museum is open daily from 8:30 am to 6 pm (till 7 pm on weekdays), Memorial Day to Labor Day; the rest of the year it's open from 9 am to 5 pm weekdays and from 10 am to 5 pm on Saturdays.

Admission is $1 for adults and 50c for seniors and children.

Continue east to the corner of 6th and Bank Sts, where a collection of ornate commercial buildings still houses shops and businesses. Note especially the White & Bender building, with its pressed tin turrets. A block farther north on 6th St, at the corner of Cedar St, is the art-deco Civic Center Building, fronted with terra-cotta brick. A number of old hotels continue on the next block north, including the James, recently renovated and open as a restaurant and B&B.

The **Northern Pacific Depot Railroad Museum** (☎ 752-0111) sits at 6th and Pine Sts, beneath the freeway. Construction of I-90 through Wallace was halted for years while the fate of the old depot was debated: should it be torn down or moved to make way for the dual-lane carriageway? In the end, the depot was moved and turned into a museum of northern Idaho railroad history. The first floor of the handsome Queen Anne structure is constructed of Chinese bricks, while the third floor is topped by a Chateau-esque tower. The museum is open daily from 9 am to 7 pm Memorial Day to Labor Day, and from 10 am to 3 pm the rest of the year; admission is $2 for adults and $1.50 for seniors and students.

Return via Cedar St, past more storefronts and several grandiose structures housing the fraternal organizations of the day. The Eagles Building now houses the **Wallace District Arts Center** (☎ 753-8381), 515 Cedar St, a community arts organization with a performance space and a small gallery and gift shop dedicated to local artists. If you need another reason to stop in, there's a small espresso shop associated with the gallery.

Beyond 4th St, Cedar St becomes more residential, with a number of notable mansions built by successful merchants and captains of industry.

## Sierra Silver Mine Tour

A number of silver mines still operate in the Wallace area, but the only place you can go to see what happens underground is the

Sierra Silver Mine. Now depleted of silver, the mine is open for regularly scheduled tours. At the Sierra Silver Mine office (☎ 752-5151), 420 5th St in Wallace, climb on a trolley and ride to the mine entrance. The underground tour demonstrates the techniques and equipment of hard-rock silver mining. The mine is open for tours from 9 am to 4 pm from the second weekend in May through October; during June and July it's open from 9 am to 6 pm. Tours leave every 30 minutes. Admission for adults is $6.50, for seniors and children is $5.50; no children under four are allowed underground.

### Old Mission State Park

The Mission of the Sacred Heart, now a state park (☎ 682-3814), is the state's oldest building and one of the most interesting historical sites in Idaho, offering a glimpse into the meeting of Christianity and Native America (see aside). The state park, just off I-90 exit No 39 at Cataldo, also includes a visitors center with interpretive information and a picnic area; guided tours are available. There's also a self-guided, half-mile nature path that leads down to the river. The park is open from 8 am to 6 pm; admission is $2 per vehicle.

The park is the site of several annual events. On August 15, members of the Coeur d'Alene tribe make a pilgrimage to the mission to celebrate the Feast of the Assumption. After Mass, tribe members enact a pageant called 'The Coming of the Black Robes'.

### Silver Mountain Ski & Summer Resort

The Silver Mountain Ski Resort (☎ 783-1111) atop 6296-foot Kellogg Peak is doing its best to become a year-round destination. The centerpiece of both winter and summer activities is the gondola, which goes from the valley floor to Mountain Haus, Silver Mountain's lodge building and skiing base. The gondola is billed as the world's longest, carrying passengers 3.1 miles and gaining 3400 feet in altitude; the trip takes 19 minutes.

In winter the ski area offers your basic, quality Rocky Mountain ski experience, with lots of dry powder snow, 50 named runs and a 2200-foot vertical drop. Lift tickets are $31 a day; seniors and students are $24. Lessons and rentals are available.

There's almost more going on in the summer. The gondola remains in operation, carrying passengers up to the ski base, where a number of amusements and recreational opportunities await. A series of outdoor concerts and plays are performed in the band shell; the lodge restaurant remains open, as well as a barbecue concession. A number of hiking trails lead out to remote meadows and overlooks, and a network of mountain-bike trails leads back down to Kellogg. For the true top-of-the-mountain experience, continue on the ski lifts to the peak of Kellogg Mountain for panoramic views of three states and Canada.

Silver Mountain's summer program runs on weekends only from the Memorial Day weekend to June 15 and for the first two weekends of October; the lifts run daily from June 15 to the last weekend in September. Gondola prices are $9.95 for adults and $8 for seniors and students; children under six are free. To take the ski lift all the way to the peak is an additional $2/1 for adults/children. You can bring your own bike along on the gondola, or rent one from Loulou's at the Base Village.

To reach Silver Mountain, take I-90 exit No 49. Base Village is located at 610 Bunker Ave in Kellogg.

### Taft Tunnel Bike Trail

The Taft Tunnel Bike Trail is a rails-to-trails project that has converted 15 miles of Chicago, Milwaukee and St Paul Railroad track, tunnel and trestle into one of the most exhilarating recreation trails in the USA. The centerpiece of the trail is the Taft Tunnel, built in 1909. The 8771-foot tunnel was cut through solid rock from the Montana side of Lookout Pass through to Idaho. As the rail track descends in Idaho, it winds through another nine tunnels and over seven wooden trestles before reaching the valley floor.

## The First Idaho Mission

In the early 1800s, as the first European explorers and traders crossed the Rockies, Native American tribes in Montana and Idaho began hearing about Christianity for the first time. The Flatheads, a Salish tribe living in Montana, became so intrigued by stories of the 'Black Robes' and their religion that in the 1830s four delegations of Flatheads journeyed east to St Louis to ask for missionaries. In 1841, Father Pierre De Smet, a Jesuit, came west, establishing missions and then farms among the Salish tribes in western Montana and northern Idaho.

Father Smet traveled through the Silver Valley in 1842 and promised the Coeur d'Alene Indians their own mission and Black Robes. Missionaries joined the tribe shortly, and in 1848 they commenced building a mission on a bluff above the Coeur d'Alene River. In charge of construction was Father Anthony Ravalli, a remarkably talented, Italian-born Jesuit who was a physician, scientist, mechanic, artist, architect and sculptor – to say nothing of his calling as a priest.

Using only locally available products, Ravalli, another Brother and the enthusiastic Coeur d'Alenes set to work. The 3600-sq-foot church was built from a framework of mortised and tenoned beams, with dowels strung between. Straw and grass were woven through the dowels and then faced with river mud. The resulting walls were over a foot thick; no nails were used in any part of the structure. In fact, the only tools available to the Brothers and the Indians at the time were pulleys, pocket knives, an axe and ropes. To outfit the church, Ravalli turned his artistic training to local available goods: old tin cans became chandelier sconces, the rough pine altar was faux painted to resemble marble, and the walls were covered with newsprint, which was white-washed and then painted with floral designs.

The mission remained in operation until 1924. The church, and the parish house next door, were declared a state park in 1974 and restored. Both can be visited at Old Mission State Park near Cataldo. ■

For years, the abandoned tunnel and the old rail line were popular with in-the-know hikers and bikers, but an upsurge in activity in recent years forced the USFS, which controls access to the rail line, to close the Taft Tunnel and attempt to dissuade activity along the neglected trestles. The USFS felt it couldn't accept the increased liability as more people used the aging facilities.

However, due to lots of grassroots support and back-room political arm-twisting, the USFS has allocated the necessary funds to clear the tunnel and make the trestles safe for casual recreational use. The tunnel is planned to open as a hiking and biking trail in midsummer 1995.

To traverse the trail requires a head lamp for bikers and several strong flashlights for hikers; be prepared to get a little wet and chilly. Even though the grade never exceeds 1.7 percent, there are a lot of vertigo-inducing trestles along sheer cliffs and over steep rocky canyons. Whether you're on foot or on a bike, you'll have your heart in your mouth on several occasions.

To reach the beginning of the trail and Taft Tunnel, drive over Lookout Pass on I-90 and take exit No 5 for Taft Area. Turn south and follow Rainy Creek Rd for two miles, then take the road toward East Portal at the Y-junction. The parking area is immediately ahead, and just beyond is the gate to the tunnel. The trail follows the contours of Loop Creek until it meets the Moon Pass Rd, which leads in 20 miles to Wallace (via Placer Creek Rd).

For more information about the Taft Tunnel Trail, contact Taft Tunnel Preservation Society at PO Box 1222, Wallace, ID 83873; for a $1 donation, they will send a helpful map and letter. Information and rental mountain bikes are available from the Lookout Pass Ski Area (☎ 744-1392), on the Idaho/Montana border at I-90 exit No 0, and from Excelsior Bikes (☎ 786-3751), 10 W Portland Ave in Kellogg.

## Activities

In addition to the imposing ski resort at Silver Mountain, there's a small family-oriented **ski** run at Lookout Pass Ski Area (☎ 744-1301). Although there are no groomed trails, the pass is a popular place to cross-country ski, and they offer rentals. Just find a USFS road and head out.

If you want to **golf**, the Shoshone Country Club (☎ 784-0160), off I-90 exit No 54 between Wallace and Kellogg, offers 18 holes with nice mountain views.

## Places to Stay

**Camping** *Pinehurst KOA* (☎ 682-3612), off I-90 exit No 45, at 801 Division St, offers streamside campsites, with a heated pool, laundry and playground. Regular sites are $16, full hook-ups $20.

**Hostels** *Kellogg Inn* (☎ 783-4171), 834 W McKinley Ave in Kellogg, is the old HI/AYH hostel with a new name. Dormitory rooms are offered at $12 a night, and there's access to a full kitchen and recreation area.

**B&Bs** One of the first historic buildings restored in Wallace was *The Jameson* (☎ 556-1554), 304 6th St, a landmark hotel from 1900. Six refurbished rooms are now available a la B&B for $54. In Kellogg, another old hotel with a similarly colorful past is *The McKinley Inn* (☎ 786-7771, (800) 443-3505), 210 McKinley Ave. It's been comfortably renovated and offers eight guest rooms ranging from $45 to $75.

**Hotels** Some renovated old hotels become B&Bs, others just stay hotels. The *Brooks Hotel* (☎ 556-1571), 500 Cedar St in Wallace, was an old behemoth of a hotel until it was gutted and the room sizes doubled. Now, with rooms starting at $35 a night, this is one of the best lodging options in northern Idaho. For a standard terraced motel, head to the *Stardust Motel* (☎ 752-1213), 410 Pine St; singles/doubles are $44/49. The upscale *Best Western Wallace Inn* (☎ 752-1252), 100 Front St, offers a pool and spa, and rooms at $60/68.

## Places to Eat

There's not much to make a fuss over in these old mining towns, but an abundance of roadside cafes and drive-ins insure that no one will starve. In Wallace, check out the *Silveradough Bakery* (☎ 556-2281) for a cinnamon roll and coffee. *Bank Street Bistro* (☎ 556-2281), 612 Bank St, offers a range of dishes, including pasta, Mexican food and fresh baked breads, all for very moderate prices. The brass-and-wainscot-rich restaurant at *The Jameson* (☎ 556-1554), 304 6th St, is part of the refurbished old hotel; it's a good place to go for a burger at lunch or a steak at dinner. Dining at this landmark will set you back $10 to $15.

## Entertainment

Historic-Register towns always seem to have a summer theater group that specializes in melodrama, and Wallace is no exception. *Sixth St Melodrama* (☎ 752-8871), 212 6th St, offers campily diabolical theater from the first weekend of July through Labor Day weekend. Shows are mounted in the Lux Building, one of Wallace's oldest structures and formerly the site of one of the city's many brothels.

## Getting There & Away

Greyhound offers two buses a day to Wallace from other points on the I-90 corridor.

## SANDPOINT & LAKE PEND OREILLE

Sandpoint (population 5203) is a resort community and the largest town on Lake Pend Oreille. This beautiful, 90,000-acre lake nestled between forested hills is Idaho's largest, and it's the nation's second deepest next to Crater Lake in Oregon. In fact, the lake is so mammoth and deep that during WW II the US Navy developed a huge inland naval training base here that trained nearly 300,000 sailors for wartime duty. The navy still maintains a small submarine base on the lake that conducts experiments in underwater communications.

Nowadays, things are much more quiet,

IDAHO

and the bustling and attractive town of Sandpoint – with interesting shops, good restaurants and good weather – is one of the most pleasant places to visit in northern Idaho. The focus of life and recreation here is the lake, obviously, although winter brings abundant snows and energetic skiers to Schweitzer Mountain, just north of town.

A second resort area lies on the eastern shore of Lake Pend Oreille at Hope and East Hope. A profusion of campgrounds and marinas make this the preferred destination for campers and recreationalists. It's worth the drive to Hope on a summer's evening just to watch the sun set over the lake.

## Orientation

Sandpoint is 44 miles north of Coeur d'Alene and 64 miles south of the Canadian border, both on Hwy 95. Highways 2 and 200, both east-west arterials, also intersect at Sandpoint.

A one-way loop circles Sandpoint's downtown, running in a counterclockwise direction. First Ave follows the lakefront; Bridge St turns off 1st Ave and leads to City Beach, Sandpoint's principal recreational playground. There's public parking downtown on N 3rd Ave between Oak and Church Sts. A boutique shopping mall on an old bridge, called the Cedar St Bridge Public Market, extends the downtown shopping precinct over a small lagoon.

Other resort communities ring Lake Pend Oreille. Just east of Sandpoint on Hwy 200 is Ponderay, followed by Kootenai. Across from Sandpoint on the eastern edge of the lake are Hope and East Hope. At the extreme southern end of Lake Pend Oreille is Farragut State Park, formerly the naval training base.

## Information

The Sandpoint Chamber of Commerce (☎ 263-2161, (800) 800-2106) is on the north end of town at 100 Hwy 95 N, Sandpoint, ID 83864. There's a visitors center at the south end of town on Hwy 95 at the foot of the two-mile-long Hwy 95 bridge. The USFS office (☎ 263-5111), 1500 Hwy 2,

has information on the Idaho Panhandle National Forest.

The post office (☎ 263-2716) is at 210 N 4th Ave; the zip is 83864. And if you need to do laundry, head downtown to Nu-Way Wash-O-Mat (☎ 263-6332), 502 5th Ave. Bonner General Hospital (☎ 263-1441) is at 520 N 3rd Ave.

## City Beach Park

For most people who visit Sandpoint in the summer, the lake's the thing. Unless you're staying at a lakeside resort, you'll probably make your acquaintance with Lake Pend Oreille at City Beach, an easy stroll from downtown.

While most people head to City Beach for swimming and sunbathing, adjacent are a number of watercraft concessions and marinas. Directly across from the beach is a marina where sailboats, windsurfing equipment, paddleboats and canoes can be rented from Windbag Sailboat Rentals (☎ 263-7811). The marina is shared with Cutting Edge Waterski School (☎ 263-7811 summer, 263-3341 winter) and Aqua Sports (☎ 263-3194), which rents jet-skis.

During the summer the boat ramp at the beach is the departure point for a two-hour **boat tour**, which leaves at 2 pm daily. Tickets are purchased upon boarding and cost $9.50 for adults and $8.50 for seniors; children under 10 are $6.50. Lake Pend Oreille Cruises (☎ 263-4598) has more information.

## Farragut State Park

At the beginning of WW II, Eleanor Roosevelt was flying across the northern USA when she noted the expanse of Lake Pend Oreille glimmering in the Idaho forests. She knew that the navy and her husband, President F D Roosevelt, were looking for a large and remote inland lake to develop as a naval training camp. She reported back, and after a quick exploratory trip by the president, work commenced in 1942 on Farragut Naval Training Center, which for four years was the second-largest naval training base in the world.

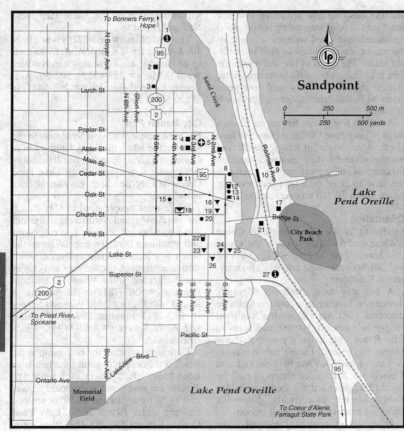

Sandpoint

IDAHO

The makeshift camp was decommissioned in 1946, and in 1964 it became Farragut State Park (☎ 683-2425). At 4000 acres, it is one of Idaho's largest and most popular parks. The $2 vehicle fee buys access to 16,000 feet of Lake Pend Oreille shoreline (there's a lifeguard at the swimming beach), to 20 miles of hiking trails and to a nine-mile designated mountain-bike path. The campgrounds here are a favorite for family vacations.

## Schweitzer Mountain Resort

Northern Idaho's most noted ski area is Schweitzer Mountain Resort (☎ 263-9555), (800) 831-8810), 11 miles north of Sandpoint off Hwys 2 and 95. Both downhill and cross-country skiers are accommodated, with night skiing offered Thursday through Saturday. From a top elevation of 6400 feet, 48 runs drop 2400 feet. Annual snowfall usually exceeds 300 inches. Full-day lift tickets (including night skiing) start at $32, with breaks for youth (seven to 17) and seniors (65 and over). The resort runs a midweek package deal for couples: overnight accommodation/lift tickets are $139. Restrictions apply, and you must make reservations. Overnight accommodations and condos are available, as are a number of options for dining, lessons and rentals. Kinder Kamp, a daycare program, allows adults to ski while kids are being entertained ($19 to $35). Lessons for kids start at $40.

In summer, the chairlift provides rides for both hikers and bikers who want to explore the high country. The condos remain open during summer as well.

## Activities

For **boating** and **watersports**, resorts all along Lake Pend Oreille have marinas offering moorage, rental and charter services. In addition to the marina at City Beach in Sandpoint, there's East Hope Marina (☎ 263-3083) and Holiday Shores Marina (☎ 264-5515), which are built practically on top of each other at 1165 Hwy 200 in East Hope.

The best **fishing** access is found along the eastern end of Lake Pend Oreille. Eagle Charters (☎ 264-5274), at the Holiday Shores Marina in Hope, and Diamond Charters (☎ 264-5283), which docks at the Pend Oreille Resort along Hwy 200 in Hope, are the area's main charter businesses.

A number of Sandpoint **sports rental** shops change to suit the season. At 5th Avenue Bike Board & Ski (☎ 263-5821), 512 Larch St, there's mountain-bike as well as ski-equipment rental. Likewise, the Alpine Boat & Ski Shop (☎ 263-5157), 213 Church St, does double duty as a ski shop and marina.

Hidden Lakes Country Club (☎ 263-1621), 8838 Lower Pack River Rd, east of Kootenai off Hwy 200, has an 18-hole **golf** course.

Western Pleasure Inc (☎ 263-9066), 4675 Upper Gold Creek Rd, about 4.5 miles outside of Kootenai off Gold Creek Rd, offers guided **horseback rides**.

## Special Events

Sandpoint's big summer event, which may be forced to move after 1997, is called the Festival at Sandpoint (☎ 265-4554), a music festival held the first two weeks in August. The series – which includes a wide variety of music ranging from country to jazz to classical and has attracted artists as different as Tony Bennett, Jan and Dean and Emmylou Harris – has grown so popular and so large that concerts take place in a number of venues in the Sandpoint area. In fact, it's become so big that many residents don't want it held in Sandpoint anymore, and a recent city council resolution would have it move after the 1997 season. Till then, the main stage is under the stars at Memorial Field; other events are held at Schweitzer Resort. The Panida Theatre (see the Entertainment section) sponsors theatrical events in conjunction with the festival.

The ski season brings the Winter Carnival, a celebration of rowdy snowy good times. Events include ice sculpture contests, live music concerts and a parade. Call the visitors center for more information.

IDAHO

### Places to Stay

**Camping** The woods are full of campgrounds. *Alpine Trailer Park* (☎ 263-4303), five miles south of Sandpoint at Hwy 95 and Sagle Rd, has RV hook-ups only starting at $10. Nearby is the *Sandpoint KOA* (☎ 263-4824), 100 Sagle Rd, with laundry, pool and recreation area. The multitude of sites range from $15 to $23.

West of Sandpoint along the Pend Oreille River is *Springy Point Recreation Area* (☎ 437-3133), a public campground that's a good place for tenters. There are flush toilets, showers and river swimming, all for $8; no hook-ups. To reach the campground, take Hwy 95 south across the bridge to Lakeshore Rd, the first road to the west. The campground is three miles farther.

Out on the eastern shores of Lake Pend Oreille are a number of really lovely campgrounds. In East Hope, *Samowen Campground* (☎ 263-5111) is a USFS campground on a lakeside peninsula that makes a thrifty alternative to the area's expensive resorts. Facilities include flush toilets but no hook-ups; sites are $9. Reservations through the national forest reservation service (☎ (800) 280-2267) are strongly recommended during high season. Samowen is two miles west of Hwy 200 on Spring Creek Rd. RVers may want a more civilized camping experience, and should head to *Beyond Hope Resort* (☎ 264-5251), three miles down Samowen Rd, off Hwy 200 E. Hook-ups start at $17.

*Round Lake State Park* (☎ 263-3489) on Dufort Rd, 10 miles south of Sandpoint on Hwy 95, is a developed campground with flush toilets and showers. Sites start at $9. It's open year round. In the summer the lake is a popular place for picnicking, swimming, fishing and hiking.

On the extreme southern end of Lake Pend Oreille is *Farragut State Park* (☎ 683-2425) with an abundance of campsites at two separate campgrounds. Snowberry Campground offers full hook-ups ($9) while Whitetail Campground offers tenting sites ($11). Facilities include flush toilets, showers and a swimming beach with a lifeguard. Farragut State Park is four miles east of Athol, which is 24 miles south of Sandpoint and 18 miles north of Coeur d'Alene on Hwy 95. Reservations are accepted and can be made by writing the park office at E 13400 Ranger Rd, Athol, ID 83801.

**B&Bs** *Page House B&B* (☎ 263-6585), 502 N 2nd Ave, downtown Sandpoint, is a historic home built in 1918 by Sandpoint's first mayor. There are three guest rooms, each with private bath, from $59 to $75. The *Angel of the Lake B&B* (☎ 263-0816), 410 Railroad Ave right on the lake and near downtown, is a beautiful home with four guest rooms for $60 to $75.

**Hotels** Try to stay close enough to downtown so you can walk to shops and to City Beach. Call ahead for reservations, as lodgings – especially on weekends – can be booked months in advance. *Best Spa Motel* (☎ 263-3532), 521 N 3rd Ave on the corner of Poplar St, offers hot tubs and large singles/doubles for $60/69. Next door is *K2 Motel* (☎ 263-3441), 501 N 3rd Ave, with rooms at $40/42. *Best Western Connie's Motor Inn* (☎ 263-9581), 323 Cedar St, is a large complex with a heated pool, spacious rooms and convention facilities; singles/doubles run $69/71.

For inexpensive access to the lake, you can't beat the *Lakeside Inn* (☎ 263-3717, (800) 543-8126), 106 Bridge St; it's only yards from the beach, and the prices aren't bad at $56/66. The Lakeside doesn't have the views of the *Edgewater Resort Motor Inn* (☎ 263-3194, (800) 635-2534), 56 Bridge St. This is the lodging of choice in Sandpoint as it's right on the marina and next to the beach. There's a spa, and golf and ski packages are available; it's $90/97 with substantial discounts off-season.

If you don't make reservations, you may end up staying a little farther from town. If so, the *Quality Inn* (☎ 263-2111), 807 N 5th Ave, is huge and chances are there will be a room ($44/52). The *Super 8 Motel* (☎ 263-9842), 3245 Hwy 95 N, is just north of Sandpoint in Ponderay; rooms are $36/42.

**Resorts** Along Lake Pend Oreille, the word 'resort' doesn't signify golf courses and spa facilities as much as marinas and access to the water. One of the nicest on the lake is *Pend Oreille Shores Resort* (☎ 264-5967), 1250 Hwy 200 in Hope, with condos and suites overlooking a busy marina. One-bedroom units start at $99; two bedrooms cost $159. The resort's Floating Restaurant is a favorite for a sunset meal or cocktail. For a completely different kind of view, there's *Green Gables Lodge* (☎ 263-9555, (800) 831-8810) at Schweitzer Mountain Resort. Of course, during the winter, skiing is the principal attraction, and rooms are expensive, with basic rooms starting at $119. However, the room rates drop almost by half during summer, when the lodge becomes the focus of mountain recreation, including mountain biking, llama treks, hiking and festival events.

**Vacation Home Rentals** Contact *Tamarack Knoll Enterprises* (also known as TKE Vacation Rentals) (☎ 263-5539), 395 Garfield Bay Rd, for information on lakefront cabins and condos and for lodging on cabin cruisers and other watercraft.

### Places to Eat
Sandpoint offers a relative profusion of good restaurants. *Java Adagio* at the Panida Theatre (☎ 263-4607), 300 N 1st Ave, is open early to serve espresso drinks, bakery goodies and light lunches. If the traveler's diet has you hankering for something healthy or organic, head for *Truby's Health Mart* (☎ 263-6513), 113 Main St.

Popular for breakfast and family dining, *Panhandler Pies* (☎ 263-2912), 120 S 1st Ave, offers homestyle cooking at very affordable prices. At the southern end of the Hwy 95 bridge is *Longhorn Barbecue Restaurant & Lounge* (☎ 263-5064), 1382 Hwy 95 S, with burgers, steak and ribs under $10. *The Hydra Restaurant* (☎ 263-7123), 115 Lake St, is light, airy and popular for its good values; it serves everything from sandwiches to chicken to steak.

Fine dining in Sandpoint means going

Continental. *Ivano's* (☎ 263-0211), 124 S 2nd Ave, is a good northern Italian restaurant with pasta dishes and veal and chicken specialties for $15. At *Bradley's* (☎ 265-0128), 202 N 2nd Ave, the emphasis is on country French cuisine, with everything from crepes to roast duck. *The Garden* (☎ 263-5187), 15 E Lake St, is near the lake and has outdoor seating in summer and a greenhouse dining room year round. The emphasis is on fresh seafood and old-fashioned European favorites like beef stroganoff ($14).

Dining in the Hope area focuses on views. *Tressle Creek Inn* (☎ 264-5942), 555 Hwy 200 E in Hope, is popular for pasta, steak and cocktails, and it has a charming setting over a small marina where a creek enters the lake. The renowned *Floating Restaurant* at the Pend Oreille Shores Resort (☎ 264-5967), 1250 Hwy 200, offers a stunning pageant of color over the lake when the sun sets; the steak and live lobster are good, too.

### Entertainment
**Cinemas** For first run films, go to Cinema 4 West (☎ 263-5811), 401 Oak St. Panida Theatre (☎ 263-9191), 300 N 1st Ave, doubles as a cinema for slightly out-of-the-mainstream films and as a performing arts stage.

**Nightlife** On weekend nights, a number of downtown bars offer live music and dancing. Two of the best are *Roxy's* (☎ 263-6696), 215 Pine St, and *Kamloops Bar & Grill* (☎ 263-6715), 302 N 1st Ave.

### Getting There & Around
**Bus** North Idaho Community Express (☎ 664-9769) operates one early-morning commuter bus to Coeur d'Alene a day. The bus stop is in the lot at Yokes Pac'n Save, 3295 Hwy 95 N.

**Train** Amtrak's *Empire Builder* line makes a late-night stop in Sandpoint four times a week. The train depot is behind the Cedar St Public Market on Railroad St. Call (800) 872-7245 for information.

IDAHO

**Car** Agency Rent A Car (☎ 263-4155) is at 315 S Ella Ave. Rentals are also available from retail dealerships such as Evergreen Ford Mercury Nissan (☎ 263-3127), 3215 Hwy 95 N.

**Taxi** If you want a taxi, Bonner Cab Co (☎ 263-7626) is the only ride in town.

## BONNERS FERRY

Bonners Ferry began as a ferry crossing on the Kootenai River during the Wild Horse Creek gold rush in Canada in the 1860s. Since its first boom, Bonners Ferry has gone through several other reincarnations, especially as a mill town. With lumbering on the skids, this dramatically situated town – in a deep canyon and straddling the large and turbulent Kootenai River – is now trying to make a living by tourism. There's plenty of recreation around here, especially fishing and rafting on the river, though it's the brooding, and sometimes unsettlingly dense, forests around here that most travelers will recall.

### Orientation

Bonners Ferry is 32 miles north of Sandpoint, and 32 miles south of the Canadian border crossing at Eastport, both on Hwy 95. Nine miles east of Bonners Ferry on Hwy 2 is the little community of Moyie Springs; it's 32 miles to Troy, MT.

The Kootenai River runs through the center of Bonners Ferry. The old downtown area is on the north side of the river, while newer development has spread to the south. There's also a cluster of businesses up on the plateau above the river canyon, near the junction of Hwys 95 and 2.

### Information

For more information on the area, contact the Bonners Ferry Chamber of Commerce (☎ 276-5922), 205 E Riverside, Bonners Ferry, ID 83805. For information about camping and recreation in local forests, contact the Bonners Ferry Ranger Station (☎ 267-5561), just south of Bonners Ferry on Hwy 95.

The local medical center is Boundary County Community Hospital (☎ 267-3141), 551 Kaniksu St.

The border crossing at Eastport (☎ 267-3966) on Hwy 95 is open 24 hours a day. The border crossing at Porthill (☎ 267-5309) on Hwy 1 is open daylight hours only.

### Moyie Bridge & Falls

One of the highest bridges in Idaho spans the Moyie River Canyon 11 miles east of Bonners Ferry on Hwy 2. The 1223-foot-long bridge sails 450 feet above the rushing river. To get a closer look at the river and its impressive double-drop falls, turn toward Moyie Springs at the west end of the bridge and follow the paved road south until a side road leads back underneath the bridge. This road proceeds to a number of overlooks onto this churning monster of a falls, which drops 140 feet in two chutes. In good Idaho tradition, the falls is dammed at the top for hydropower – imagine what this torrent would have been like if the water flow wasn't regulated.

### Rafting

The lower portion of the Moyie River is popular as a white-water river, as is the enormous and powerful Kootenai River. For information on raft trips, call Moyie River Outfitting Guide Service at 267-2108. They offer day-long white-water trips on the Moyie in the spring and rafting trips on the Kootenai through the summer. Either trip costs $55 per person.

### Places to Stay

**Camping** *Bonners Ferry Resort & KOA* (☎ 267-2422), two miles south of town on Hwy 95, offers both tent sites ($12), full hook-ups ($16) and cabins ($55); facilities include a heated pool, laundry and rec room. Located in a spectacular setting, where the Moyie and Kootenai rivers meet, the *Twin Rivers Resort* (☎ 267-5932), one mile east of Moyie Springs, offers a full-service RV park on 160 acres with access to fishing, hiking trails and river swimming. Campsites range from $10 for tents to $16 for full hook-ups.

**Hotels** *Kootenai Valley Motel* (☎ 267-7567), just south of Bonners Ferry on Hwy 95, is an attractive and well-kept old motel in a park-like grove of trees. Single/double rooms are $39/45. *Bonners Ferry Log Inn* (☎ 267-3986), two miles north of Bonners Ferry on Hwy 95, is a new and attractive log motel with nicely furnished rooms for $43/55. The local Best Western is the *Kootenai River Inn* (☎ 267-8511), across from downtown in the Kootenai River Plaza; it offers dramatic riverfront rooms starting at $50.

### Places to Eat

Grab an early morning espresso or a sandwich for lunch at *Deli Delite* (☎ 267-2241), 1106 S Main St. *Three Mile Junction Cafe* (☎ 267-3513), at the junction of Hwys 2 and 95, three miles north of Bonners Ferry, is worth a detour for great breakfasts and the daily sandwich-and-homemade-pie lunch special. The best Mexican food hereabouts is served at *Alberto's Mexican Restaurant* (☎ 267-7493), 222 E Riverside.

For the area's fine dining, go to *The Springs Restaurant* (☎ 267-8511) in the Kootenai River Inn. The Springs serves pasta, steak and fish in a river-edge dining room; full dinners run $12 to $15.

## PRIEST LAKE

If you're searching for isolation and wilderness, then Priest Lake might be what you're looking for: this area is remote even for Idaho. Traveling the lone road to Priest Lake, through dense forest and along the surging Priest River, it's easy to imagine that you're heading back into the forest primeval, which in many ways you are: from the shores of Priest Lake north, into the Canadian forests and on to the tundra at the Arctic Circle, wilderness spreads for hundreds of miles.

Priest Lake is another ice-age relic, gouged out of the basin between peaks of the Selkirk Mountains. The lake is actually two separate lakes, linked by a wide, 2.5-mile-long channel called the Thoroughfare; the combined length of the lakes is over 25 miles.

What sets Priest Lake apart from other northern Idaho lakes is development. There's not even a proper town along the lake's shores, let alone a convention hotel or high-class resort. The typical accommodation up here is a cozy, family-operated lodge with cabins and a small marina. If that doesn't sound enough like roughing it, there are dozens of campgrounds around the lake and, most beguilingly, a number of them on islands accessible only by boat.

The area around Priest Lake is some of the wildest in Idaho, and it's home to wildlife uncommon elsewhere in the Northwest. Traveling these dark, uncharted woods are herds of woodland caribou, grizzly bears, gray wolves, moose and wolverines. You'll be lucky to site these north-woods denizens, however, in part due to the density of the forests.

### Orientation

Twenty-two miles north of the little town of Priest River, Hwy 57 divides at the Coolin junction. A paved road, Hwy 57, continues 17 miles to Nordman, about half the way up the west side of the lake. Three miles east of Nordman is Reeder Bay, one of the most popular recreation sites on the lake. North from Nordman, a rough gravel road, maintained in summer only, continues over the Selkirks to Metaline Falls in Washington.

The moose is the largest species of deer in the world and is indigenous to Canada, the northeastern USA and the Rocky Mountains region.

The other fork off Hwy 57 leads to Coolin, where the road turns to gravel and winds up the east side of the lake to the Lionshead and Indian Creek units of Priest Lake State Park.

To refer to any of the little settlements along Priest Lake as a town is to exaggerate. Coolin and Nordman are the largest of these, and each offer a few shops, restaurants and lodgings. Most lodges will also offer a basic selection of groceries and camping goods and a restaurant. Otherwise, you're pretty much on your own.

### Information
For more information about the area, contact the Priest Lake Chamber of Commerce (☎ 443-3191), Steamboat Bay Rd No 121, Coolin, ID 83821. Contact the Priest Lake Ranger Station (☎ 443-2512), in Nordman, ID 83856, for information on camping, hiking and other outdoor recreation around Priest Lake.

### Places to Stay
**Camping** There are tons of campgrounds on Priest Lake. Priest Lake State Park (☎ 443-2200) has three units: Dickensheet Unit is near Coolin, on Priest River just below the lake; its primitive sites are popular with river rafters. Indian Creek Unit is 16 miles north of Coolin and is the most developed of the three units, offering both hook-ups and primitive sites right on the lakefront; there are showers and a small store. The Lionhead Unit is an additional eight miles north; there are no hook-ups, making this the preferred campground for tenters. Reservations for campsites can be made by writing Priest Lake State Park, Indian Creek Bay No 423, Coolin, ID 83821; sites are $6 to $8 a night.

Of the many USFS campgrounds near Priest Lake, the most popular is probably *Reeder Bay*, three miles east of Nordman and right on the lake, with drinking water, pit toilets, a boat slip and swimming beach; sites are $9.

The USFS also maintains two primitive campgrounds on Kalispell Island, and to reach them you'll need to either bring your own boat or rent one from the Priest Lake Marina (☎ 443-2405), off W Lake Shore Rd, about eight miles north of the Coolin junction on Hwy 57.

**Lodges** Each of the following are rustic lakeside resorts with a variety of lodging options, ranging from cabins to condos to lodge rooms. *Hill's Resort* (☎ 443-2551), on Luby Bay, has cabins, motel units, a marina and a restaurant and lounge. Room prices range from $80 to $225 a night. To reach the resort, follow Hwy 57 six miles north and take USFS Rd 1337 one mile east to the lake. *Elkins on Priest Lake* (☎ 443-2432), on Reeder Bay three miles east of Nordman, offers 28 cabins ($75 to $195) in the woods overlooking the lake, with a lodge restaurant and moorage for boats. The *Grandview Resort* (☎ 443-2433), also at Reeder Bay, offers lodge rooms, cabins and suites from $59 to $145; there's a swimming pool, restaurant and convenience store.

### Places to Eat
Most restaurants along Priest Lake are associated with lodges, and some offer good homestyle cooking. Otherwise, the selection is limited to a few restaurants at Coolin and Nordman. The *Blue Pelican* (☎ 443-2387), at Coolin, claims to be the area's font of fine dining, with steak and seafood in the $12 to $15 range. For breakfast, go to the *Tamrak Restaurant* (☎ 443-2987), at Lamb Creek, just north of the Coolin junction.

# Glossary

**adit** – A horizontal mine entrance.

**alkali** – Soluble mineral salts found in desert soils and lakes.

**anadromous** – A term used to describe fish that migrate up rivers from salt water to spawn in fresh water.

**basalt** – A hard, dense volcanic rock often having a glassy appearance.

**batholith** – A large mass of molten igneous rock (usually granite) that has intruded surrounding strata and cooled. One of the best examples of this is in Idaho.

**BLM** – Bureau of Land Management, an agency of the Department of the Interior which controls substantial portions of public lands in the West.

**boomtown** – A town that has experienced quick economic and population growth.

**brewpub** – A pub that brews and sells its own beer.

**caldera** – A very large crater that has resulted from a volcanic explosion or the collapse of a volcanic cone. Crater Lake in Oregon is an example of the latter.

**CCC** – Civilian Conservation Corps, a New Deal program established in 1933 to employ single unskilled young men, initially through the conservation of the wild lands of the USA. By 1940, most CCC jobs were oriented toward national defense work. Congress disbanded the CCC in 1942.

**clapboard** – A narrow board that is thicker on one edge; the boards are overlapped over a wooden building frame to form an outer wall.

**clear-cut** – A hated sight for environmentalists, this is an area where loggers have cut every tree, large and small, leaving nothing standing.

**coulee** – A deep ravine with sloping sides, which is usually dry during the summer.

**Craftsman** – A style of architecture developed during the Arts & Crafts Movement, which was a reaction to the perceived shoddiness of machine-made goods in the late-19th and early-20th centuries. This style of architecture and furniture design is typified by simple, functional designs hand-crafted in traditional mediums.

**FDR** – Franklin Delano Roosevelt, 32nd president of the USA (1933-1945). Roosevelt introduced the New Deal, a series of measures to increase employment and productivity during the Great Depression and WW II. Two New Deal programs were the CCC and the WPA.

**GMT** – Greenwich Mean Time

**grist mill** – A mill for grinding grain.

**grunge** – The ubiquitous 'Seattle' sound that became immensely popular in the early '90s with the rise of such bands as the Melvins, Soundgarden, Nirvana, Pearl Jam and a host of imitators. Grunge gear would include work boots, a flannel shirt and, for male devotees, a goatee.

**HI/AYH** – Hostelling International/American Youth Hostels – term given to hostels affiliated with Hostelling International, which is managed by IYHF (International Youth Hostel Federation).

**Hudson's Bay Company (HBC)** – An English trading company begun in 1670, which traded in all areas that had rivers draining into Hudson Bay. In the 18th century the HBC and its main rival, the Northwest Company, both set up forts and trading posts throughout the Northwest and what would become Canada. The two companies amalgamated in 1821.

**KOA** – Kampgrounds of America, a private RV-oriented organization that provides camping with substantial amenities throughout the USA.

**National Register of Historic Places** – *or* National Historic District – A listing of historic buildings, as determined by the NPS on nomination from property owners, local authorities and supporting evidence supplied by them, on the basis of significance in the development of a community.

**Northwest Passage** – The water route across North America from the Atlantic to the Pacific Ocean. Assuming that such a route must exist, which would aid trading, explorers from around the world searched for almost 300 years before Norwegian Roald Amundsen successfully navigated the route in 1906.

**NPS** – National Park Service, a division of the Department of the Interior which administers US national parks and monuments.

**NRA** – National Recreation Area, a term used to describe National Park Service units in areas of considerable scenic or ecological importance which have been modified by human activity, mostly major dam projects.

**ORV** – Off-road vehicle.

**pergola** – An arbor of columns supporting a trelliswork roof.

**petroglyph** – An ancient carving or inscription on a rock.

**pictograph** – A picture or symbol representing a word rather than a sound, usually drawn or painted on a rock.

**playa** – A dry desert lakebed.

**portage** – To carry a ship or boat over land to avoid an impassable stretch of river or from one body of water to another. Sometimes refers to the footpath or trail used for those purposes.

**REI** – Recreational Equipment Incorporated (known almost exclusively by its acronym). REI is one of the primary retailers of outdoor equipment in the USA.

**rift** – A thin fissure in a rock.

**riprap** – A pile of loose stones erected to form a foundation.

**rock hound** – A rock collector.

**RV** – Recreational vehicle, motorhome.

**salal** – A small, evergreen shrub (*Gaultheria shallon*) found in the Northwest; it has pink flowers and edible berries.

**scarp** – An escarpment; a steep slope resulting from erosion between two areas of differing elevation.

**seastack** – Hard volcanic coastal rock formations that were originally covered with softer sedimentary rock which has since eroded away.

**slag** – Glassy residue left as the result of the smelting of iron ore.

**USFS** – United States Forest Service, a division of the Department of Agriculture which implements policies on federal forest lands on the principles of 'multiple use', which includes timber cutting, watershed management, wildlife management and camping and recreation.

**USFWS** – United States Fish & Wildlife Service, an agency of the federal Department of the Interior with responsibility for fish and wildlife habitat and related matters.

**USGS** – United States Geological Survey, an agency of the federal Department of the Interior responsible for detailed topographic maps of the entire country. Widely available at outdoor-oriented businesses, USGS maps are particularly popular with hikers and backpackers.

**UTC** – Universal Time Coordinated.

**WPA** – Work Projects Administration, a New Deal program set up by President Franklin Roosevelt in 1935 to increase employment through a series of public works projects, including road and building construction, beautification of public structures (especially post offices), and a well respected series of state and regional guidebooks.

# Appendix I – State Abbreviations

The following is a list of the official US Postal Service state abbreviations that are used in mailing addresses and sometimes in general reference.

| | | | | | |
|---|---|---|---|---|---|
| **AK** | Alaska | **KY** | Kentucky | **NY** | New York |
| **AL** | Alabama | **LA** | Louisiana | **OH** | Ohio |
| **AR** | Arkansas | **MA** | Massachusetts | **OK** | Oklahoma |
| **AZ** | Arizona | **MD** | Maryland | **OR** | Oregon |
| **CA** | California | **ME** | Maine | **PA** | Pennsylvania |
| **CO** | Colorado | **MI** | Michigan | **RI** | Rhode Island |
| **CT** | Connecticut | **MN** | Minnesota | **SC** | South Carolina |
| **DC** | Washington, DC | **MO** | Missouri | **SD** | South Dakota |
| **DE** | Delaware | **MS** | Mississippi | **TN** | Tennessee |
| **FL** | Florida | **MT** | Montana | **TX** | Texas |
| **GA** | Georgia | **NC** | North Carolina | **UT** | Utah |
| **HI** | Hawaii | **ND** | North Dakota | **VA** | Virginia |
| **IA** | Iowa | **NE** | Nebraska | **VT** | Vermont |
| **ID** | Idaho | **NH** | New Hampshire | **WA** | Washington |
| **IL** | Illinois | **NJ** | New Jersey | **WI** | Wisconsin |
| **IN** | Indiana | **NM** | New Mexico | **WV** | West Virginia |
| **KS** | Kansas | **NV** | Nevada | **WY** | Wyoming |

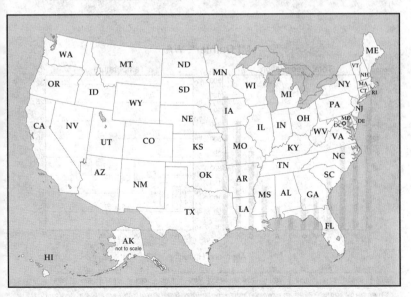

# Appendix II – Climate Charts

## Seattle, WA

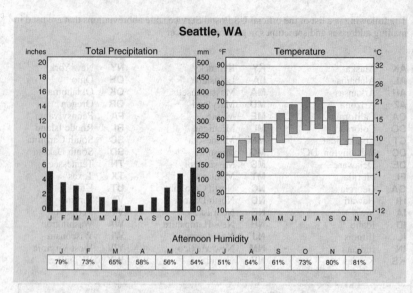

Total Precipitation | Temperature

| | J | F | M | A | M | J | J | A | S | O | N | D |
|---|---|---|---|---|---|---|---|---|---|---|---|---|
| Afternoon Humidity | 79% | 73% | 65% | 58% | 56% | 54% | 51% | 54% | 61% | 73% | 80% | 81% |

## Mt Rainier*, WA

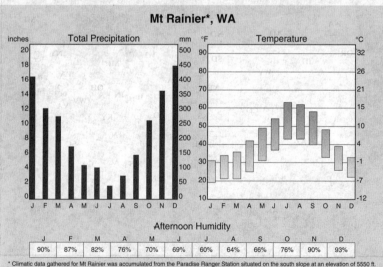

Total Precipitation | Temperature

| | J | F | M | A | M | J | J | A | S | O | N | D |
|---|---|---|---|---|---|---|---|---|---|---|---|---|
| Afternoon Humidity | 90% | 87% | 82% | 76% | 70% | 69% | 60% | 64% | 66% | 76% | 90% | 93% |

* Climatic data gathered for Mt Rainier was accumulated from the Paradise Ranger Station situated on the south slope at an elevation of 5550 ft.

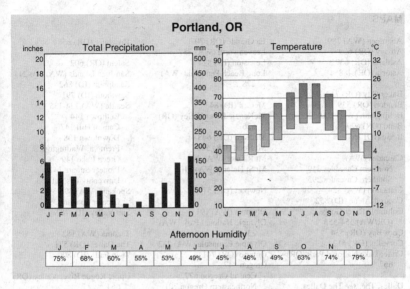

**Portland, OR**

Total Precipitation

Temperature

Afternoon Humidity

| J | F | M | A | M | J | J | A | S | O | N | D |
|---|---|---|---|---|---|---|---|---|---|---|---|
| 75% | 68% | 60% | 55% | 53% | 49% | 45% | 46% | 49% | 63% | 74% | 79% |

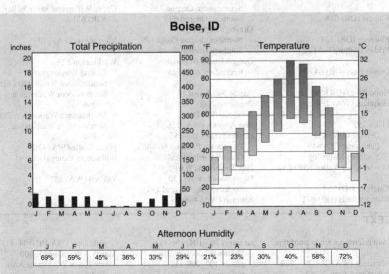

**Boise, ID**

Total Precipitation

Temperature

Afternoon Humidity

| J | F | M | A | M | J | J | A | S | O | N | D |
|---|---|---|---|---|---|---|---|---|---|---|---|
| 69% | 59% | 45% | 36% | 33% | 29% | 21% | 23% | 30% | 40% | 58% | 72% |

# Index

874

# LONELY PLANET PHRASEBOOKS

Building bridges,
Breaking barriers,
Beyond babble-on

Listen for the gems

Speak your own words

Ask your own
questions

Master of
your
own
image

- handy pocket-sized books
- easy to understand Pronunciation chapter
- clear and comprehensive Grammar chapter
- romanisation alongside script to allow ease of pronunciation
- script throughout so users can point to phrases
- extensive vocabulary sections, words and phrases for every situations
- full of cultural information and tips for the traveller

'...vital for a real DIY spirit and attitude in language learning' – Backpacker

'the phrasebooks have good cultural backgrounders and offer solid advice for challenging situations in remote locations' – San Francisco Examiner

'...they are unbeatable for their coverage of the world's more obscure languages' – The Geographical Magazine

Arabic (Egyptian)
Arabic (Moroccan)
Australia
 Australian English, Aboriginal and Torres Strait languages
Baltic States
 Estonian, Latvian, Lithuanian
Bengali
Burmese
Brazilian
Cantonese
Central Europe
 Czech, French, German, Hungarian, Italian and Slovak
Eastern Europe
 Bulgarian, Czech, Hungarian, Polish, Romanian and Slovak
Egyptian Arabic
Ethiopian (Amharic)
Fijian
French
German
Greek

Hindi/Urdu
Indonesian
Italian
Japanese
Korean
Lao
Latin American Spanish
Malay
Mandarin
Mediterranean Europe
 Albanian, Croatian, Greek, Italian, Macedonian, Maltese, Serbian, Slovene
Mongolian
Moroccan Arabic
Nepali
Papua New Guinea
Pilipino (Tagalog)
Quechua
Russian
Scandinavian Europe
 Danish, Finnish, Icelandic, Norwegian and Swedish

South-East Asia
 Burmese, Indonesian, Khmer, Lao, Malay, Tagalog (Pilipino), Thai and Vietnamese
Spanish
Sri Lanka
Swahili
Thai
Thai Hill Tribes
Tibetan
Turkish
Ukrainian
USA
 US English, Vernacular Talk, Native American languages and Hawaiian
Vietnamese
Western Europe
 Basque, Catalan, Dutch, French, German, Irish, Italian, Portuguese, Scottish Gaelic, Spanish (Castilian) and Welsh

# LONELY PLANET JOURNEYS

JOURNEYS is a unique collection of travel writing – published by the company that understands travel better than anyone else. It is a series for anyone who has ever experienced – or dreamed of – the magical moment when they encountered a strange culture or saw a place for the first time. They are tales to read while you're planning a trip, while you're on the road or while you're in an armchair, in front of a fire.

JOURNEYS books catch the spirit of a place, illuminate a culture, recount a crazy adventure, or introduce a fascinating way of life. They always entertain, and always enrich the experience of travel.

*'Idiosyncratic, entertainingly diverse and unexpected . . . from an international writership'*
– The Australian

*'Books which offer a closer look at the people and culture of a destination, and enrich travel experiences'*
– American Bookseller

## FULL CIRCLE
### A South American Journey
#### Luis Sepúlveda
##### Translated by Chris Andrews

*Full Circle* invites us to accompany Chilean writer Luis Sepúlveda on 'a journey without a fixed itinerary'. Whatever his subject – brutalities suffered under Pinochet's dictatorship, sleepy tropical towns visited in exile, or the landscapes of legendary Patagonia – Sepúlveda is an unflinchingly honest yet lyrical storyteller. Extravagant characters and extraordinary situations are memorably evoked: gauchos organising a tournament of lies, a scheming heiress on the lookout for a husband, a pilot with a corpse on board his plane . . . Part autobiography, part travel memoir, *Full Circle* brings us the distinctive voice of one of South America's most compelling writers.

Luis Sepúlveda was born in Chile in 1949. Imprisoned by the Pinochet dictatorship for his socialist beliefs, he was for many years a political exile. He has written novels, short stories, plays and essays. His work has attracted many awards and has been translated into numerous languages.

*'Detachment, humour and vibrant prose'* – El País

*'an absolute cracker'* – The Bookseller

This project has been assisted by the Commonwealth Government through the Australia Council, its arts funding and advisory body.

# LONELY PLANET TRAVEL ATLASES

Lonely Planet has long been famous for the number and quality of its guidebook maps. Now we've gone one step further and in conjunction with Steinhart Katzir Publishers produced a handy companion series: Lonely Planet travel atlases – maps of a country produced in book form.

Unlike other maps, which look good but lead travellers astray, our travel atlases have been researched on the road by Lonely Planet's experienced team of writers. All details are carefully checked to ensure the atlas corresponds with the equivalent Lonely Planet guidebook.

The handy atlas format means no holes, wrinkles, torn sections or constant folding and unfolding. These atlases can survive long periods on the road, unlike cumbersome fold-out maps. The comprehensive index ensures easy reference.

- full-colour throughout
- maps researched and checked by Lonely Planet authors
- place names correspond with Lonely Planet guidebooks
  – no confusing spelling differences
- legend and travelling information in English, French, German, Japanese and Spanish
- size: 230 x 160 mm

*Available now:*
Chile & Easter Island • Egypt • India & Bangladesh • Israel & the Palestinian Territories •Jordan, Syria & Lebanon • Kenya • Laos • Portugal • South Africa, Lesotho & Swaziland • Thailand • Turkey • Vietnam • Zimbabwe, Botswana & Namibia

---

# LONELY PLANET TV SERIES & VIDEOS

Lonely Planet travel guides have been brought to life on television screens around the world. Like our guides, the programmes are based on the joy of independent travel, and look honestly at some of the most exciting, picturesque and frustrating places in the world. Each show is presented by one of three travellers from Australia, England or the USA and combines an innovative mixture of video, Super-8 film, atmospheric soundscapes and original music.

Videos of each episode – containing additional footage not shown on television – are available from good book and video shops, but the availability of individual videos varies with regional screening schedules.

*Video destinations include:* Alaska • American Rockies • Australia – The South-East • Baja California & the Copper Canyon • Brazil • Central Asia • Chile & Easter Island • Corsica, Sicily & Sardinia – The Mediterranean Islands • East Africa (Tanzania & Zanzibar) • Ecuador & the Galapagos Islands • Greenland & Iceland • Indonesia • Israel & the Sinai Desert • Jamaica • Japan • La Ruta Maya • Morocco • New York • North India • Pacific Islands (Fiji, Solomon Islands & Vanuatu) • South India • South West China • Turkey • Vietnam • West Africa • Zimbabwe, Botswana & Namibia

*The Lonely Planet TV series is produced by:*
**Pilot Productions**
The Old Studio
18 Middle Row
London W10 5AT UK

**For video availability and ordering information contact your nearest Lonely Planet office.**

*Music from the TV series is available on CD & cassette.*

# The Mark Spencer Hotel

*Entitles the Bearer to a*

## Complimentary Continental Breakfast

*Please show this coupon to the Front Desk each Morning*

*Continental Breakfast served in the Lobby*

*6:30 am - 10:30 am*

# PLANET TALK

## Lonely Planet's FREE quarterly newsletter

We love hearing from you and think you'd like to hear from us.

***When***...is the right time to see reindeer in Finland?
***Where***...can you hear the best palm-wine music in Ghana?
***How***...do you get from Asunción to Areguá by steam train?
***What***...is the best way to see India?

***For the answer to these and many other questions read PLANET TALK.***

Every issue is packed with up-to-date travel news and advice including:

- a letter from Lonely Planet co-founders Tony and Maureen Wheeler
- go behind the scenes on the road with a Lonely Planet author
- feature article on an important and topical travel issue
- a selection of recent letters from travellers
- details on forthcoming Lonely Planet promotions
- complete list of Lonely Planet products

To join our mailing list contact any Lonely Planet office.

***Also available: Lonely Planet T-shirts. 100% heavyweight cotton.***

---

# LONELY PLANET ONLINE

### Get the latest travel information before you leave or while you're on the road

Whether you've just begun planning your next trip, or you're chasing down specific info on currency regulations or visa requirements, check out Lonely Planet Online for up-to-the-minute travel information.

As well as travel profiles of your favourite destinations (including maps and photos), you'll find current reports from our researchers and other travellers, updates on health and visas, travel advisories, and discussion of the ecological and political issues you need to be aware of as you travel.

There's also an online travellers' forum where you can share your experience of life on the road, meet travel companions and ask other travellers for their recommendations and advice. We also have plenty of links to other online sites useful to independent travellers.

And of course we have a complete and up-to-date list of all Lonely Planet travel products including guides, phrasebooks, atlases, Journeys and videos and a simple online ordering facility if you can't find the book you want elsewhere.

**www.lonelyplanet.com**
**or**
**AOL keyword: lp**

# LONELY PLANET PRODUCTS

Lonely Planet is known worldwide for publishing practical, reliable and no-nonsense travel information in our guides and on our web site. The Lonely Planet list covers just about every accessible part of the world. Currently there are eight series: *travel guides*, *shoestring guides*, *walking guides*, *city guides*, *phrasebooks*, *audio packs*, *travel atlases* and *Journeys* – a unique collection of travel writing.

## EUROPE

Amsterdam • Austria • Baltic States phrasebook • Britain • Central Europe on a shoestring • Central Europe phrasebook • Czech & Slovak Republics • Denmark • Dublin • Eastern Europe on a shoestring • Eastern Europe phrasebook • Estonia, Latvia & Lithuania • Finland • France • French phrasebook • German phrasebook • Greece • Greek phrasebook • Hungary • Iceland, Greenland & the Faroe Islands • Ireland • Italian phrasebook • Italy • Mediterranean Europe on a shoestring • Mediterranean Europe phrasebook • Paris • Poland • Portugal • Portugal travel atlas • Prague • Russia, Ukraine & Belarus • Russian phrasebook • Scandinavian & Baltic Europe on a shoestring • Scandinavian Europe phrasebook • Slovenia • Spain • Spanish phrasebook • St Petersburg • Switzerland • Trekking in Greece • Trekking in Spain • Ukrainian phrasebook • Vienna • Walking in Britain • Walking in Switzerland • Western Europe on a shoestring • Western Europe phrasebook

*Travel Literature:* The Olive Grove: Travels in Greece

## NORTH AMERICA

Alaska • Backpacking in Alaska • Baja California • California & Nevada • Canada • Florida • Hawaii • Honolulu • Los Angeles • Mexico • Miami • New England • New Orleans • New York City • New York, New Jersey & Pennsylvania • Pacific Northwest USA • Rocky Mountain States • San Francisco • Southwest USA • USA phrasebook • Washington, DC & the Capital Region

## CENTRAL AMERICA & THE CARIBBEAN

Bermuda • Central America on a shoestring • Costa Rica • Cuba • Eastern Caribbean • Guatemala, Belize & Yucatán: La Ruta Maya • Jamaica

## SOUTH AMERICA

Argentina, Uruguay & Paraguay • Bolivia • Brazil • Brazilian phrasebook • Buenos Aires • Chile & Easter Island • Chile & Easter Island travel atlas • Colombia • Ecuador & the Galápagos Islands • Latin American Spanish phrasebook • Peru • Quechua phrasebook • Rio de Janeiro • South America on a shoestring • Trekking in the Patagonian Andes • Venezuela

*Travel Literature:* Full Circle: A South American Journey

## ANTARCTICA

Antarctica

## ISLANDS OF THE INDIAN OCEAN

Madagascar & Comoros • Maldives • Mauritius, Réunion & Seychelles

## AFRICA

Africa - the South • Africa on a shoestring • Arabic (Moroccan) phrasebook • Cape Town • Central Africa • East Africa • Egypt • Egypt travel atlas • Ethiopian (Amharic) phrasebook • Kenya • Kenya travel atlas • Malawi, Mozambique & Zambia • Morocco • North Africa • South Africa, Lesotho & Swaziland • South Africa, Lesotho & Swaziland travel atlas • Swahili phrasebook • Trekking in East Africa • West Africa • Zimbabwe, Botswana & Namibia • Zimbabwe, Botswana & Namibia travel atlas

*Travel Literature:* The Rainbird: A Central African Journey • Songs to an African Sunset: A Zimbabwean Story

# MAIL ORDER

Lonely Planet products are distributed worldwide. They are also available by mail order from Lonely Planet, so if you have difficulty finding a title please write to us. North American and South American residents should write to Embarcadero West, 155 Filbert St, Suite 251, Oakland CA 94607, USA; European and African residents should write to 10 Barley Mow Passage, Chiswick, London W4 4PH; and residents of other countries to PO Box 617, Hawthorn, Victoria 3122, Australia.

## NORTH-EAST ASIA

Beijing • Cantonese phrasebook • China • Hong Kong • Hong Kong, Macau & Guangzhou • Japan • Japanese phrasebook • Japanese audio pack • Korea • Korean phrasebook • Mandarin phrasebook • Mongolia • Mongolian phrasebook • North-East Asia on a shoestring • Seoul • Taiwan • Tibet • Tibet phrasebook • Tokyo

*Travel Literature*: Lost Japan

## MIDDLE EAST & CENTRAL ASIA

Arab Gulf States • Arabic (Egyptian) phrasebook • Central Asia • Iran • Israel & the Palestinian Territories • Israel & the Palestinian Territories travel atlas • Istanbul • Jerusalem • Jordan & Syria • Jordan, Syria & Lebanon travel atlas • Middle East • Turkey • Turkish phrasebook • Turkey travel atlas • Yemen

*Travel Literature:* The Gates of Damascus • Kingdom of the Film Stars: Journey into Jordan

## ALSO AVAILABLE:

Travel with Children • Traveller's Tales

## INDIAN SUBCONTINENT

Bangladesh • Bengali phrasebook • Delhi • Hindi/Urdu phrasebook • India • India & Bangladesh travel atlas • Indian Himalaya • Karakoram Highway • Nepal • Nepali phrasebook • Pakistan • Rajasthan • Sri Lanka • Sri Lanka phrasebook • Trekking in the Indian Himalaya • Trekking in the Karakoram & Hindukush • Trekking in the Nepal Himalaya

*Travel Literature:* In Rajasthan • Shopping for Buddhas

## SOUTH-EAST ASIA

Bali & Lombok • Bangkok • Burmese phrasebook • Cambodia • Ho Chi Minh City • Indonesia • Indonesian phrasebook • Indonesian audio pack • Jakarta • Java • Laos • Lao phrasebook • Laos travel atlas • Malay phrasebook • Malaysia, Singapore & Brunei • Myanmar (Burma) • Philippines • Pilipino phrasebook • Singapore • South-East Asia on a shoestring • South-East Asia phrasebook • Thailand • Thailand travel atlas • Thai phrasebook • Thai audio pack • Thai Hill Tribes phrasebook • Vietnam • Vietnamese phrasebook • Vietnam travel atlas

## AUSTRALIA & THE PACIFIC

Australia • Australian phrasebook • Bushwalking in Australia • Bushwalking in Papua New Guinea • Fiji • Fijian phrasebook • Islands of Australia's Great Barrier Reef • Melbourne • Micronesia • New Caledonia • New South Wales & the ACT • New Zealand • Northern Territory • Outback Australia • Papua New Guinea • Papua New Guinea phrasebook • Queensland • Rarotonga & the Cook Islands • Samoa • Solomon Islands • South Australia • Sydney • Tahiti & French Polynesia • Tasmania • Tonga • Tramping in New Zealand • Vanuatu • Victoria • Western Australia

*Travel Literature:* Islands in the Clouds • Sean & David's Long Drive

# THE LONELY PLANET STORY

Lonely Planet published its first book in 1973 in response to the numerous 'How did you do it?' questions Maureen and Tony Wheeler were asked after driving, bussing, hitching, sailing and railing their way from England to Australia.

Written at a kitchen table and hand collated, trimmed and stapled, *Across Asia on the Cheap* became an instant local bestseller, inspiring thoughts of another book.

Eighteen months in South-East Asia resulted in their second guide, *South-East Asia on a shoestring*, which they put together in a backstreet Chinese hotel in Singapore in 1975. The 'yellow bible', as it quickly became known to backpackers around the world, soon became *the* guide to the region. It has sold well over half a million copies and is now in its 9th edition, still retaining its familiar yellow cover.

Today there are over 240 titles, including travel guides, walking guides, language kits & phrasebooks, travel atlases and travel literature. The company is the largest independent travel publisher in the world. Although Lonely Planet initially specialised in guides to Asia, today there are few corners of the globe that have not been covered.

The emphasis continues to be on travel for independent travellers. Tony and Maureen still travel for several months of each year and play an active part in the writing, updating and quality control of Lonely Planet's guides.

They have been joined by over 70 authors and 170 staff at our offices in Melbourne (Australia), Oakland (USA), London (UK) and Paris (France). Travellers themselves also make a valuable contribution to the guides through the feedback we receive in thousands of letters each year and on our web site.

The people at Lonely Planet strongly believe that travellers can make a positive contribution to the countries they visit, both through their appreciation of the countries' culture, wildlife and natural features, and through the money they spend. In addition, the company makes a direct contribution to the countries and regions it covers. Since 1986 a percentage of the income from each book has been donated to ventures such as famine relief in Africa; aid projects in India; agricultural projects in Central America; Greenpeace's efforts to halt French nuclear testing in the Pacific; and Amnesty International.

*'I hope we send people out with the right attitude about travel. You realise when you travel that there are so many different perspectives about the world, so we hope these books will make people more interested in what they see. Guidebooks can't really guide people. All you can do is point them in the right direction.'*

– Tony Wheeler

---

# LONELY PLANET PUBLICATIONS

**Australia**
PO Box 617, Hawthorn 3122, Victoria
tel: (03) 9819 1877  fax: (03) 9819 6459
e-mail: talk2us@lonelyplanet.com.au

**USA**
Embarcadero West, 155 Filbert St, Suite 251,
Oakland, CA 94607
tel: (510) 893 8555  TOLL FREE: 800 275-8555
fax: (510) 893 8563
e-mail: info@lonelyplanet.com

**UK**
10 Barley Mow Passage, Chiswick,
London W4 4PH
tel: (0181) 742 3161  fax: (0181) 742 2772
e-mail: lonelyplanetuk@compuserve.com

**France:**
71 bis rue du Cardinal Lemoine, 75005 Paris
tel: 1 44 32 06 20  fax: 1 46 34 72 55
e-mail: 100560.415@compuserve.com

**World Wide Web: http://www.lonelyplanet.com**
**or *AOL* keyword: lp**